Constitutional Law for a Changing America

9 edition

Constitutional Law for a Changing America

Institutional Powers and Constraints

9 edition

LEE EPSTEIN

Washington University in St. Louis

THOMAS G. WALKER

Emory University

Los Angeles | London | New Delhi
Singapore | Washington DC | Melbourne

FOR INFORMATION:

CQ Press

An Imprint of SAGE Publications, Inc.

2455 Teller Road

Thousand Oaks, California 91320

E-mail: order@sagepub.com

SAGE Publications Ltd.

1 Oliver's Yard

55 City Road

London EC1Y 1SP

United Kingdom

SAGE Publications India Pvt. Ltd.

B 1/I 1 Mohan Cooperative Industrial Area

Mathura Road, New Delhi 110 044

India

SAGE Publications Asia-Pacific Pte. Ltd.

3 Church Street

#10-04 Samsung Hub

Singapore 049483

Senior Acquisitions Editor: Michael Kerns

Editorial Assistant: Zachary Hoskins

Production Editor: Veronica Stapleton Hooper

Copy Editor: Alison Hope

Typesetter: C&M Digitals (P) Ltd.

Proofreader: Penelope Sippel

Indexer: Will Ragsdale

Cover Designer: Michael Dubowe

Marketing Manager: Amy Whitaker

eLearning Editor: Robert Higgins

Printed in the United States of America

Library of Congress Cataloging-in-Publication Data

Names: Epstein, Lee, 1958- author. | Walker, Thomas G., 1945- author.

Title: Constitutional law for a changing America. Institutional powers and constraints / Lee Epstein Washington University in St. Louis, Thomas G. Walker Emory University.

Other titles: Institutional powers and constraints

Description: Ninth edition. | Washington, DC : CQ Press, 2016. | Includes index.

Identifiers: LCCN 2015039013 | ISBN 978-1-4833-8405-4 (pbk. : alk. paper)

Subjects: LCSH: Constitutional law—United States. | LCGFT: Casebooks

Classification: LCC KF4550.E67 2016 | DDC 342.73—dc23 LC record available at http://lccn.loc.gov/2015039013

This book is printed on acid-free paper.

17 18 19 20 10 9 8 7 6 5 4 3 2

CONTENTS

CHRONOLOGICAL TABLE OF CASES

TABLES, FIGURES, AND BOXES

PREFACE

A QUARTER CENTURY has passed since *Constitutional Law for a Changing America: Institutional Powers and Constraints* made its debut in a discipline already supplied with many fine casebooks by law professors, historians, and social scientists. We believed then, as we do now, that there was a need for a fresh approach because, as political scientists who regularly teach courses on public law and as scholars concerned with the judicial process, we saw a growing disparity between what we taught and what our research taught us.

We had adopted books for our classes that focused primarily on Supreme Court decisions and how the Court applied the resulting legal precedents to subsequent disputes, but as scholars we understood that to know the law is to know only part of the story. A host of political factors—both internal and external—influence the Court's decisions and shape the development of constitutional law. Among the more significant forces at work are the ways lawyers and interest groups frame legal disputes, the ideological and behavioral propensities of the justices, the politics of judicial selection, public opinion, and the positions that elected officials take, to name just a few.

Because we thought no existing book adequately combined the lessons of the legal model with the influences of the political process, we wrote one. In most respects, our book follows tradition: readers will find that we include excerpts from the classic cases that best illustrate the development of constitutional law. But our focus is different, as is the appearance of this volume. We emphasize the arguments raised by lawyers and interest groups and the politics surrounding litigation. We incorporate tables and figures on Court trends and other materials that bring out the rich legal, social, historical, economic, and political contexts in which the Court reaches its decisions. As a result, students and instructors will find this work both similar to and different from casebooks they may have read before.

Integrating traditional teaching and research concerns was only one of our goals. Another was to animate the subject of public law. As instructors, we find our subject inherently interesting—to us, public law is exciting stuff. Many constitutional law books, however, could not be less inviting in design, presentation, or prose. That kind of book can only dampen enthusiasm. We have written a book that we hope mirrors the excitement we feel for our subject. We describe the events that led to the suits and include photographs of litigants and relevant exhibits from the cases. Moreover, because students and colleagues often ask us about the fate of particular litigants—for example, what happened to Fred Korematsu?—we attached "Aftermath" boxes to a select number of cases. In addition to providing a coda to the cases, the human element can lead to interesting discussions about the impact of decisions on the lives of Americans. We hope these materials demonstrate to students that Supreme Court cases involve real people engaged in real disputes, and are not merely legal names and citations.

Readers will also find material designed to enhance their understanding of the law, such as information on the Supreme Court's decision-making process, the structure of the federal judiciary, and briefing court cases. To broaden students' perspective on the U.S. legal system, we also have added boxes on the laws and legal practices of other countries. Students and instructors can use these to compare and contrast U.S. Supreme Court decisions on issues such as judicial review, privileges, and immunities for legislators, and the separation of powers system with policies developed in other countries. The use of foreign law sources in their opinions has sparked some disagreement among the justices. But the material we include here also has inspired lively debates in our classes, and we hope it will do the same in yours as well.

KEY REVISIONS

In preparing this ninth edition, we have strengthened the distinctive features of the earlier versions by making changes at two levels of the book—chapters and cases. We thoroughly updated individual chapters to include important opinions handed down through the 2014–2015 term. Since Chief Justice John G. Roberts took office in 2005, the Court has taken up many pressing issues of the day, including, of course, health care: we have included excerpts of *National Federation of Business v. Sebelius* (2012) in chapters 7 and 8, as we did in the last edition. For this edition, we have added four more Roberts Court cases. The first is *Zivotofsky v. Kerry* (2015), which seems to present a very small and narrow question about the place of birth on passports. In fact, though, it is a fascinating case pitting legislative versus executive power. *National Labor Relations Board v. Canning* (2014) asks the Court to address novel questions about the president's appointment power, and *Horne v. Department of Agriculture* (2015) raises equally interesting issues about the takings clause of the Fifth Amendment. Last but not least is *Hollingsworth v. Perry* (2013): the substantive question in this case was whether California could constitutionally ban same-sex marriage. The Court never got around to answering that question (though two years later it would go on to invalidate such bans), but it held that the defenders of the ban did not have standing. The debate between the justices in the majority and in dissent in *Perry*, though, is so interesting that we excerpt the case in chapter 2 ("The Judiciary").

But readers will find more than just updating. We tried to bring a fresh eye to each chapter, which mostly involved clarifying existing material. Our discussions of federalism (chapter 6) and the commerce clause (chapter 7) provide examples. In the last edition, we reworked some of this material to highlight new developments. Here we continue along the same path, moving even more of the commerce material to chapter 7 and adding more basic federalism material (including an excerpt of *Coyle v. Smith*) to chapter 6. We also reorganized the discussion of standing in chapter 2 to reflect a recent spate of suits (including *Perry*) induced by the government's unwillingness to defend its laws.

We have retained and enhanced those features pertaining to case presentation that have proved to be useful. We continue to provide key arguments made by the attorneys on both sides. Readers will also notice excerpts of both concurring and dissenting opinions; in fact, almost every case analyzed in the text now includes one or both. Although these opinions lack the force of precedent, they are useful in helping students to see alternative points of view.

We also provide URLs to the full text of the opinions and, where available, the URL to a Web site containing oral arguments in many landmark cases. We took this step because we recognize how rewarding it can be to read decisions in their entirety and to listen to oral arguments. Doing so, we believe, helps students to develop an important skill—differentiating between viable and less-viable arguments. Finally, we continue to retain the historical flavor of the decisions, reprinting verbatim the original language used in the *U.S. Reports* to introduce the justices' writings. Students will see that during most of its history the Court used the term "Mr." to refer to justices, as in "Mr. Justice Holmes delivered the opinion of the Court" or "Mr. Justice Harlan, dissenting." In 1980 the Court dropped the title. This point may seem minor, but we think it is evidence that the justices, like other Americans, updated their usage to reflect fundamental changes in American society—in this case, the emergence of women as a force in the legal profession and, shortly thereafter, on the Court itself.

STUDENT AND INSTRUCTOR RESOURCES

We continue to update and improve our Online Con Law Resource Center located at https://edge.sagepub .com/conlaw and hope instructors find this a valuable resource for assigning supplemental cases and useful study aids, as well as for accessing helpful instructor resources. Through the supplemental case archive professors and students can access excerpts of important decisions that we mention in the text but that space limitations and other considerations counsel against excerpting. Cases included in the online archive are indicated by boldface italic type in the text; see the Online Case Archive list at the end of the book for a complete list of those cases. In the archive these cases are introduced and excerpted in the same fashion as they are in the book. The archive now houses more than two hundred cases; we will continue to keep it current, adding important decisions as the Court hands them down.

The Online Resource Center also features some very handy study tools for students, including a set of interactive flash cards for each chapter that will help students review key terms and concepts, and links to a wealth of data and background material from CQ Press's reference sources, such as *Guide to the U.S. Supreme Court, The Supreme Court A to Z*, and our *Supreme Court Compendium* (which we coauthored with Harold J. Spaeth and Jeffrey A. Segal). Students can click to a bio of any justice, read a background piece on the origins of the Court, and view selected data tables on ideological means or on voting inter-agreements among justices by issue area. Also available are new hypothetical cases—sixteen for this volume—written by Stephen Daniels of the American Bar Foundation and Northwestern University, and James Bowers of St. John Fisher College. These rich, detailed hypotheticals, tied to specific chapters, are accompanied by both discussion and writing questions that will help spark conversation and serve as the basis for writing assignments.

We are grateful to Tim Johnson of the University of Minnesota for producing a great set of instructor's resources. In addition to a test bank that includes multiple-choice, short-answer, and hypothetical questions, he has created a set of discussion questions for each chapter. There are also case briefs for every case excerpted in the book and a full set of PowerPoint lecture slides. We would also like to thank Jeremy Buchman of Oregon State University, Rorie Spill Solberg of Oregon State University, and Liane Kosaki of the University of Wisconsin–Madison for their Moot Court Simulation in the Resource Center. Instructors can choose hypothetical cases and utilize their guidelines so students can play the roles of counsel or chief or associate justice. Rorie and Liane also blog for the Resource Center, tying current news events and developments to content in *Constitutional Law for a Changing America*.

Instructors can download all the tables, figures, and charts from our book (in PowerPoint or JPG formats) for use during lectures. To access all of these resources, be sure to click on "instructor resources" at clca.cqpress.com so you can register and start downloading.

ACKNOWLEDGMENTS

Although the first edition of this volume was published twenty-four years ago, it had been in the works for many more. During those developmental years, numerous people provided guidance, but none as much as Joanne Daniels, a former editor at CQ Press. It was Joanne who conceived the idea of a constitutional law book that would be accessible, sophisticated, and contemporary. And it was Joanne who brought that concept to our attention and helped us develop it into a book. We are forever in her debt.

Because this new edition charts the same course as the first eight, we remain grateful to all of those who had a hand in the previous editions. They include David Tarr and Jeanne Ferris at CQ Press, Jack Knight at Duke University, Joseph A. Kobylka of Southern Methodist University, Jeffrey A. Segal of the State University of New York at Stony Brook, and our many colleagues who reviewed and commented on our work: Judith A. Baer, Ralph Baker, Lawrence Baum, John Brigham, Gregory A. Caldeira, Bradley C. Canon, Robert A. Carp, James Cauthen, Phillip J. Cooper, Sue Davis, John Fliter, John Forren, John B. Gates, Edward V. Heck, Joshua Kaplan, Peter Kierst, David Korman, Cynthia Lebow, John A. Maltese, Wendy Martinek, Kevin McGuire, Wayne McIntosh, Susan Mezey, Richard J. Pacelle Jr., C. K. Rowland, Chris Shortell, Joseph Smith, Donald R. Songer, Harry P. Stumpf, and Artemus Ward. We are also indebted to the many scholars who took the time to send us suggestions, including (again) Greg Caldeira, as well as Akiba J. Covitz, Jolly Emrey, Alec C. Ewald, Leslie Goldstein, and Neil Snortland. Many thanks also go to Jeff Segal for his frank appraisal of the earlier volumes; to Segal (again), Rebecca Brown, David Cruz, Micheal Giles, Linda Greenhouse, Dennis Hutchinson, Adam Liptak, and Judges Frank H. Easterbrook and Richard A. Posner for their willingness to share their expertise in all matters of constitutional law; to Judith Baer and Leslie Goldstein for their help with the revision of the discrimination chapter in previous editions and their answers to innumerable e-mail messages; to Jack Knight for his comments on the drafts of several chapters; and to Harold J. Spaeth for his wonderful Supreme Court Database.

Most of all, we acknowledge the contributions of our editors at CQ Press—Brenda Carter, Charisse Kiino, and Sarah Calabi. Brenda saw *Constitutional Law for a Changing America* through the first five editions; Charisse came on board on the fifth and worked with us throughout the eighth. Both are just terrific, somehow knowing exactly when to steer us and when to steer clear. Sarah has become our latest editor and promises to continue the strong editorial leadership of her predecessors. We are equally indebted to Carolyn Goldinger, our copy editor on the first four editions and on the sixth edition. Her imprint, without exaggeration, remains everywhere. Over the years, she made our prose more accessible, questioned our interpretation of certain events and opinions—and was all too often right—and made our tables and figures understandable. There is not a better copy editor in this business. Period.

For this edition, we express our sincere thanks to our new copy editor, Alison Hope. Her attention to detail not only enhanced our prose but worked to improve the accuracy and relevance of what we wrote. Her efficiency and technical expertise are exemplary. We also express many thanks to Veronica Stapleton Hooper, our project editor; and to Raquel Christie for her wonderful assistance in acquiring photographs.

Finally, we acknowledge the support of our home institutions and of our colleagues and friends. We are forever grateful to our former professors for instilling in us their genuine interest in and curiosity about things judicial and legal, and to our parents for their unequivocal support.

Shortly before the fifth edition went to press, we learned that the *Constitutional Law for a Changing America* volumes had won the award for teaching and mentoring presented by the Law and Courts section of the American Political Science Association. Each and every one of the editors and scholars we thank above deserves credit for whatever success our books have enjoyed. Any errors of omission or commission, however, remain our sole responsibility. We encourage students and instructors alike to comment on the book and to inform us of any errors. Contact us at epstein@wust.edu or polstw@emory.edu.

Lee Epstein, St. Louis, Missouri
Thomas G. Walker, Atlanta, Georgia

SAGE edge for Students provides a personalized approach to help students accomplish their coursework goals in an easy-to-use learning environment. Go to **edge.sagepub.com/conlaw**.

ABOUT THE AUTHORS

Lee Epstein (PhD, Emory Univeristy) is the Ethan A. H. Shepley Distinguished University Professor at Washington University in St. Louis. She is a fellow of the American Academy of Arts and Sciences and the American Academy of Political and Social Science. She is author, coauthor, and/or editor of fifteen books, including *The Supreme Court Compendium: Data, Decisions, and Developments*, 6th Edition, with Jeffrey A. Segal, Harold J. Spaeth, and Thomas G. Walker; *Courts, Judges, and Politics,* 6th Edition, with Walter F. Murphy, C. Herman Pritchett, and Jack Knight; *The Choices Justices Make* with Jack Knight, which won the C. Herman Pritchett Award for the best book on law and courts; and *Advice and Consent: The Politics of Judicial Appointments* with Jeffrey A. Segal. Her most recent books are *The Behavior of Federal Judges* with William M. Landes and Richard A. Posner, and *An Introduction to Empirical Legal Research* with Andrew D. Martin.

Thomas G. Walker (PhD, Univeristy of Kentucky) is the Goodrich C. White Professor of Political Science at Emory University, where he has won several teaching awards for his courses on constitutional law and the judicial process. His book *A Court Divided,* written with Deborah J. Barrow, won the prestigious V. O. Key Award for the best book on Southern politics. He is the author of *Eligible for Execution* and coauthor of *The Supreme Court Compendium: Data, Decisions, and Developments,* 6th Edition, with Lee Epstein, Jeffrey A. Segal, and Harold J. Spaeth.

PART I

The U.S. Constitution

iStock/DanBrandenburg

An Introduction to the U.S. Constitution

1. UNDERSTANDING THE U.S. SUPREME COURT

An Introduction to the U.S. Constitution

ACCORDING TO President Franklin D. Roosevelt, "Like the Bible, it ought to be read again and again."[1] Senator Henry Clay said it "was made not merely for the generation that then existed, but for posterity—unlimited, undefined, endless, perpetual posterity."[2] Justice Hugo Black carried a copy with him virtually all the time. The object of all this admiration? The U.S. Constitution. To be sure, the Constitution has its flaws and its share of detractors, but most Americans take great pride in their charter. And why not? It is, after all, the world's oldest written constitution.

In what follows, we provide a brief introduction to the document—in particular, the circumstances under which it was written, the basic principles underlying it, and some controversies surrounding it. This material may not be new to you, but, as the balance of this book is devoted to Supreme Court interpretation of the Constitution, we think it is worth reviewing.

THE ROAD TO THE U.S. CONSTITUTION

While the fledgling United States was fighting for its independence from England, it was being run (and the war conducted) by the Continental Congress. Although this body had no formal authority, it met in session from 1774 through the end of the war in 1781,

establishing itself as a de facto government. But it may have been something more than that: About a year into the Revolutionary War, the Continental Congress took steps toward nationhood. On July 2, 1776, it passed a resolution declaring the "United Colonies free and independent states." Two days later, on July 4, it formalized this proclamation in the Declaration of Independence, in which the nation's founders used the term *United States of America* for the first time.[3] But even before the adoption of the Declaration of Independence, the Continental Congress had selected a group of delegates to make recommendations for the formation of a national government. Composed of representatives of each of the thirteen colonies, this committee labored for several months to produce a proposal for a national charter, the Articles of Confederation.[4] Congress passed the proposal and submitted it to the states for ratification in November 1777. Ratification was achieved in March 1781, when Maryland—a two-year holdout—gave its approval.

The Articles of Confederation, however, had little effect on the way the government operated; instead, the articles more or less institutionalized practices that had developed under the Continental Congress (1774–1781). Rather than provide for a compact between the people and the government, the 1781

---

1. Fireside chat, March 9, 1937.

2. Speech to the Senate, January 29, 1850.

3. The text of the Declaration of Independence is available at http://avalon.law.yale.edu/18th_century/declare.asp.

4. The full text of the Articles of Confederation is available at http://avalon.law.yale.edu/18th_century/artconf.asp.

charter institutionalized "a league of friendship" among the states, an agreement that rested on strong notions of state sovereignty. This is not to suggest that the charter failed to provide for a central government. As is apparent in figure I-1, which depicts the structure and powers of government under the Articles of Confederation, the articles created a national governing apparatus, however simple and weak. The plan created a one-house legislature, with members appointed as the state legislatures directed, but with

FIGURE I-1   The Structure and Powers of Government under the Articles of Confederation

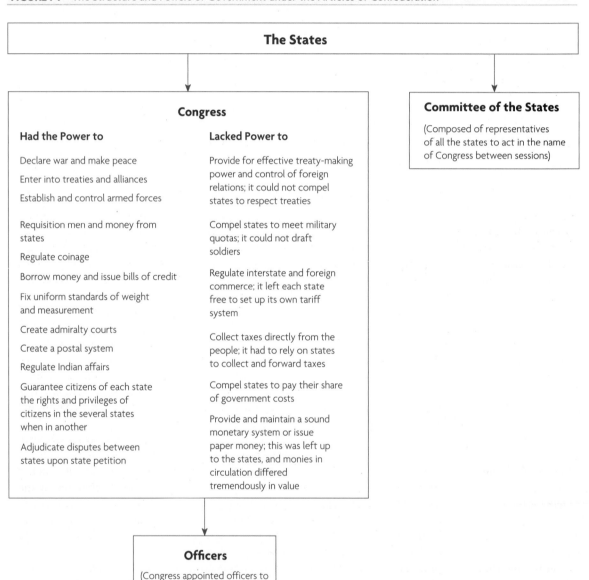

The States

Congress

Had the Power to	Lacked Power to
Declare war and make peace	Provide for effective treaty-making power and control of foreign relations; it could not compel states to respect treaties
Enter into treaties and alliances	
Establish and control armed forces	
Requisition men and money from states	Compel states to meet military quotas; it could not draft soldiers
Regulate coinage	
Borrow money and issue bills of credit	Regulate interstate and foreign commerce; it left each state free to set up its own tariff system
Fix uniform standards of weight and measurement	
Create admiralty courts	Collect taxes directly from the people; it had to rely on states to collect and forward taxes
Create a postal system	
Regulate Indian affairs	
Guarantee citizens of each state the rights and privileges of citizens in the several states when in another	Compel states to pay their share of government costs
	Provide and maintain a sound monetary system or issue paper money; this was left up to the states, and monies in circulation differed tremendously in value
Adjudicate disputes between states upon state petition	

Committee of the States

(Composed of representatives of all the states to act in the name of Congress between sessions)

Officers

(Congress appointed officers to do some of the executive work)

SOURCE: Adapted from Steffen W. Schmidt, Mark C. Shelley II, and Barbara A. Bardes, *American Government and Politics Today*, 14th ed. (Boston: Wadsworth, 2008), 42.

no formal federal executive or judiciary. And although the legislature had some power, most notably in the area of foreign affairs, it derived its authority from the states that had created it, and not from the people.

The condition of the United States under the Articles of Confederation was less than satisfactory. Analysts have pointed out several weaknesses of the articles, including the following:

- Because it allowed Congress only to requisition funds and not to tax, the federal government was virtually broke. From 1781 to 1783 the national legislature requested $10 million from the states and received only $1.5 million. Given the foreign debts the United States had accumulated during the Revolution, this problem was particularly troublesome.
- Because Congress lacked any concrete way to regulate foreign commerce, treaties between the United States and other countries were of limited value. Some European nations (e.g., England and Spain) took advantage by imposing restrictions on trade that made it difficult for America to export goods.
- Because the government lacked coercive power over the states, mutual cooperation among them quickly dissipated. The states engaged in trading practices that hurt one another economically. In short, they acted more like thirteen separate countries than a union or even a confederation.
- Because the exercise of most national authority required the approval of nine states and because the passage of amendments required unanimity, the articles stymied Congress. Indeed, given the divisions among the states at the time, the approval of nine states for any action of substance was rare, and the required unanimity for amendment was never obtained.

Nevertheless, the government accomplished some notable objectives during the years the Articles of Confederation were in effect. Most critical among these, it brought the Revolutionary War to a successful end and paved the way for the 1783 Treaty of Paris, which helped make the United States a presence on the international scene. The charter served another important purpose: it prevented the states from going their separate ways until a better system could be put into place.

In the mid-1780s, as the articles' shortcomings were becoming more and more apparent, several dissidents, including James Madison of Virginia and Alexander Hamilton of New York, held a series of meetings to arouse interest in revising the system of government. At a session in Annapolis in September 1786, they urged the states to send delegations to another meeting scheduled for the following May in Philadelphia. Their plea could not have come at a more opportune time. Just the month before, a former Revolutionary War captain, Daniel Shays, had led disgruntled farmers in an armed rebellion in Massachusetts. They were protesting the poor state of the economy, particularly as it affected farmers.

Shays's Rebellion was suppressed by state forces, but it was seen as yet another sign that the Articles of Confederation needed amending. In February 1787 Congress issued a call for a convention to reevaluate the current national system. It was clear, however, that Congress did not want to scrap the articles; in fact, it stated that the delegates were to meet "for the sole and express purpose of revising the Articles of Confederation."

Despite these words, the convention's fifty-five delegates quickly realized that they would be doing more than "revising" the articles: they would be framing a new charter. We can attribute this change in purpose, at least in part, to the Virginia delegation. When the Virginians arrived in Philadelphia on May 14, the day the convention was supposed to start, only they and the Pennsylvania delegation were there. Although lacking a quorum, the Virginia contingent used the eleven days that elapsed before the rest of the delegates arrived to craft a series of proposals that called for a wholly new government structure composed of a strong three-branch national government empowered to lead the nation.

Known as the Virginia Plan, these proposals were formally introduced to all the delegates on May 29, just four days after the convention began. And although it was the target of a counterproposal submitted by the New Jersey delegation, the Virginia Plan set the tone for the convention. It served as the basis for many of the ensuing debates and, as we shall see, for the Constitution itself (see table I-1).

The delegates had much to accomplish during the convention period. Arguments between large states and small states over the structure of the new government and its relationship to the states threatened to deadlock the meeting. Indeed, it is almost a miracle that the delegates were able to frame a new constitution, which they

TABLE I-1 The Virginia Plan, the New Jersey Plan, and the Constitution

ITEM	VIRGINIA PLAN	NEW JERSEY PLAN	CONSTITUTION
Legislature	Two houses	One house	Two houses
Legislative representation	Both houses based on population	Equal for each state	One house based on population; one house with two votes from each state
Legislative power	Veto authority over state legislation	Authority to levy taxes and regulate commerce	Authority to levy taxes and regulate commerce; authority to compel state compliance with national policies
Executive	Single; elected by legislature for a single term	Plural; removable by majority of state legislatures	Single; chosen by Electoral College; removable by national legislature
Courts	National judiciary elected by legislature	No provision	Supreme Court appointed by executive, confirmed by Senate

did in just four months. One can speculate that the founders succeeded in part because they were able to close their meetings to the public, a feat almost inconceivable today; a contemporary convention of the states would be a media circus. Moreover, it is hard to imagine that delegates from fifty states could agree even to frame a new charter, much less do it in four months.

The difficulties facing such an enterprise raise an important issue. A modern constitutional convention would be hard-pressed to reach consensus because the delegates would bring with them diverse interests and aims. But was that not the case in 1787? If, as has been recorded, the framers were such a fractious bunch, how could they have reached accord so rapidly? So, who were these men, and what did they want to do?

These questions have been the subject of lively debates among scholars. Many agree with historian Melvin I. Urofsky, who wrote of the Constitutional Convention, "Few gatherings in the history of this or any other country could boast such a concentration of talent." And, "despite [the framers'] average age of forty-two [they] had extensive experience in government and were fully conversant with political theories of the Enlightenment."[5] Indeed, they were an impressive group. Thirty-three had served in the Revolutionary War, forty-two had attended the Continental Congress, and two had signed the Declaration of Independence. Two would go on to serve as U.S. presidents, sixteen as governors, and two as chief justices of the United States.

Nevertheless, some commentators take issue with this rosy portrait of the framers. Because they were a relatively homogeneous lot—all white men, many of whom had been educated at the country's best schools—skeptics suggest that the document the framers produced was biased in various ways. In 1987 Justice Thurgood Marshall said that the Constitution was "defective from the start," that despite its first words, "We the People," it excluded "the majority of American citizens" because it left out blacks and women. He further alleged that the framers "could not have imagined, nor would they have accepted, that the document they were drafting would one day be construed by a Supreme Court to which had been appointed a woman and the descendant of an African slave."[6]

Along the same lines is the point of view expressed by historian Charles Beard in his controversial work *An Economic Interpretation of the Constitution of the United States,* which depicts the framers as self-serving. Beard says the Constitution was an "economic document" devised to protect the "property interests" of those who wrote it. Various scholars have refuted this view, and Beard's work, in particular, has been largely negated by other studies.[7] Still, by today's standards it is impossible to deny that the original Constitution discriminated on the basis of race and sex or that the framers wrote it in a way that benefited their class.

---

5. Melvin I. Urofsky and Paul Finkelman, *A March of Liberty,* 2nd ed. (New York: Oxford University Press, 2002), 94–95.

6. Quoted in *Washington Post,* May 7, 1987. See also Thurgood Marshall, "Reflections on the Bicentennial of the United States Constitution," *Harvard Law Review* 101 (1987): 1–5.

7. See, for example, Robert E. Brown's *Charles Beard and the Constitution* (Princeton, NJ: Princeton University Press, 1956). Brown concludes, "We would be doing a grave injustice to the political sagacity of the Founding Fathers if we assumed that property or personal gain was their only motive" (198).

Given these charges, how has the Constitution survived for so long, especially considering the U.S. population's increasing diversity? The answer lies in part with the Supreme Court, which generally has analyzed the document in light of its contemporary context. That is, some justices have viewed the Constitution as a living document and have sought to adapt it to their own times. In addition, the founders provided for an amending process to ensure the document's continuation. That we can alter the Constitution to fit changing needs and expectations is obviously important. For example, the original document held a slave to be three-fifths of a person for the purposes of representation, and a slave had no rights of citizenship at all. In the aftermath of the Civil War, the country recognized the outrageousness of such provisions and added three amendments to alter the status of blacks and provide for their full equality under law.

This is not to suggest that controversies surrounding the Constitution no longer exist. To the contrary, charges abound that the document has retained an elitist or otherwise biased flavor. Some argue that the amending process is too cumbersome, that it is too slanted toward the will of the majority. Others point to the Supreme Court as the culprit, asserting that its interpretation of the document—particularly at certain points in history—has reinforced the framers' biases.

Throughout this volume, you will have many opportunities to evaluate these claims. They will be especially evident in cases involving economic liberties—those that ask the Court, in some sense, to adjudicate claims between the privileged and the underdogs in society. For now, let us consider some of the basic features of that controversial document—the U.S. Constitution.

UNDERLYING PRINCIPLES OF THE CONSTITUTION

Table I-1 sets forth the basic proposals considered at the convention and how they got translated into the Constitution. What it does not show are the fundamental principles underlying, but not necessarily explicit in, the Constitution. Three are particularly important: the separation of powers/checks and balances doctrine, which governs relations among the branches of government; federalism, which governs relations between the states and the national government; and the principle of individual rights and liberties, which governs relations between the government and the people.

Separation of Powers/Checks and Balances

One of the fundamental weaknesses of the Articles of Confederation was their failure to establish a strong and authoritative federal government. The articles created a national legislature, but that body had few powers, and those it did have were kept in check by the states. The new U.S. Constitution overcame this deficiency by creating a national government with three branches—the legislature, the executive, and the judiciary—and by providing each with significant power and authority within its sphere. Moreover, the three newly devised institutions were constitutionally and politically independent of one another.

Articles I, II, and III of the Constitution spell out the specific powers assigned to each branch. Nevertheless, many questions have arisen over the scope of these powers as the three institutions use them. Consider a few examples:

- Article I provides Congress with various kinds of authority over the U.S. military—the authority to provide for and maintain a navy and to raise and support armies. But it does not specifically empower Congress to initiate and operate a draft. Does that omission mean that Congress may not do so?
- Article II provides the president with the power to "nominate, and by and with the Advice and Consent of the Senate, [to] appoint . . . Officers of the United States," but it does not specifically empower the president to fire such officers. May the president independently dismiss appointees, or is the "advice and consent" of the Senate also necessary for the executive to take those actions?
- Article III provides the federal courts with the authority to hear cases involving federal laws, but it does not specifically empower these courts to strike down such laws if they are incompatible with the Constitution. Does that mean federal courts lack the power of judicial review?

These examples illustrate just a handful of the questions involving institutional powers that the U.S. Supreme Court has addressed.

But institutional powers are only one side of the coin. We should also consider the other side—constraints on those powers. As depicted in figure I-2,

FIGURE I-2 The Separation of Powers/Checks and Balances System: Some Examples

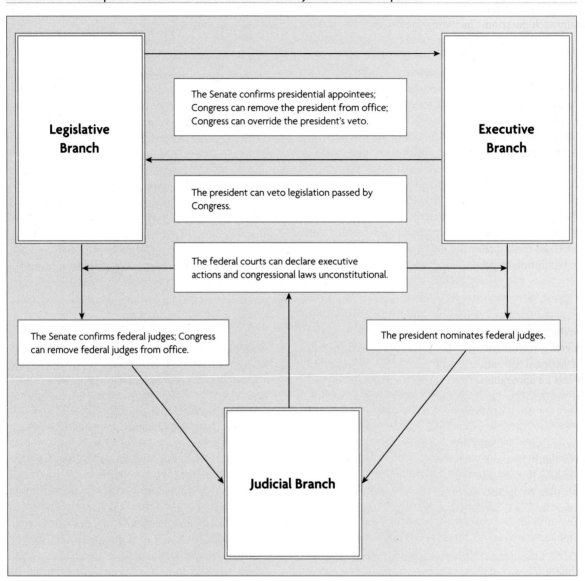

the framers not only endowed each branch with distinct power and authority over its own sphere but also provided explicit checks on the exercise of those powers such that each branch can impose limits on the primary functions of the others. In addition, the framers made the institutions responsible to different sets of constituencies. They took these steps—creating an intricate system of checks and balances—because they feared the concentration of powers in a single branch.

Although this system has been successful, it also has produced numerous constitutional questions, many of which become apparent when we have a politically divided government, such as a Democratic president and a Republican Congress, and when one party or the other is seeking to assert its authority. What is truly interesting about such cases is that they continue to appear at the Supreme Court's doorstep. Even though the Constitution is more than two hundred years old, the Court has yet to resolve all the "big" questions. During the past few decades the Court has addressed many such questions, including the following:

- May the president authorize the use of military commissions to try suspected terrorists?
- May Congress write into laws legislative veto provisions by which to nullify actions of the executive branch?
- May Congress pass legislation requiring the attorney general to appoint an independent counsel to investigate allegations of wrongdoing within the executive branch?

As you read the cases and narrative that follow, you will develop an understanding of how the Court has addressed these questions and many others relating to the separation of powers/checks and balances system.

Federalism

Another flaw in the Articles of Confederation was how the document envisioned the relationship between the federal government and the states. As already noted, the national legislature was not just weak—it was more or less an apparatus controlled by the states. They had set up the Articles of Confederation, and, therefore, they empowered Congress.

The U.S. Constitution overcame this liability in two ways. First, it created three branches of government, all with significant authority. Second, it set out a plan of operation for the exercise of state and federal power. This plan of operation, called *federalism*, works today under the following constitutional guidelines:

- The Constitution grants certain legislative, executive, and judicial powers to the national government. Those not granted to the national government are reserved to the states.
- The Constitution makes the national government supreme. The Constitution, all laws passed pursuant to it, and treaties are the supreme law of the land. American citizens, most of whom are also state citizens, and state officials owe their primary allegiance to the national government.
- The Constitution denies some powers to both national and state governments, some only to the national government, and still others only to the state governments.

By making the national government supreme in its spheres of authority, the Constitution corrected a defect in the Articles of Confederation. But in spite of the best efforts of the framers to spell out the nature of federal–state relations, the Constitution still left many questions unanswered. For example, the Constitution authorizes Congress to lay and collect taxes, but it is unclear whether the states also may exercise powers that are granted to the federal government. States are not expressly prohibited from collecting taxes. Therefore, may Congress and the states both operate taxing systems?

As you know, the answer to this question is yes, even though the Constitution does not explicitly say so. Instead, elected government bodies (through legislation) and courts (through interpretation) have defined the specifics of state–federal relations. The Supreme Court, in particular, by defining the boundaries of federal and state power, has helped shape the contours of American federalism.

Individual Rights and Liberties

For many of the framers, the most important purpose of the new Constitution was to safeguard individual rights and liberties. They created a limited government that would wield only those powers delegated to it and that could be checked by its own component parts— the states and the people. The majority of the founders felt it unnecessary to load the Constitution with specific individual rights, such as those later spelled out in the Bill of Rights. As Alexander Hamilton put it, "The Constitution is itself . . . a Bill of Rights." Under it, the government could exercise only those functions specifically bestowed on it; all other rights remained with the people. Hamilton and others felt that a list of rights might even be dangerous because it would inevitably leave some out.

For this reason and possibly others—some argue that the framers were too exhausted to continue—the Constitution was sent to the states without a list of rights. That omission became the source of major controversy and served as the vehicle by which states exacted a compromise over the Constitution's ratification.

By January 1788 four states had ratified the Constitution, but then the pace began to slow. A movement opposed to ratification was growing in size and marshaling arguments to deter state convention delegates. What these opponents, the so-called

Anti-Federalists, most feared was the Constitution's new balance of powers. They believed that strong state governments would provide the best defense against the accumulation of too much power by the national government and that the Constitution tipped the scales the other way. These fears were countered by the self-labeled Federalists, who favored ratification of the Constitution.

The Federalists' arguments and writings took many forms, but among the most important was a series of eighty-five articles published in New York newspapers under the pen name Publius. Written by John Jay, James Madison, and Alexander Hamilton, *The Federalist Papers*—as we shall see throughout this book—continue to provide great insight into the objectives and intent of the nation's founders.[8]

The debates between the Federalists and their opponents were often highly philosophical, with emphasis on the appropriate roles and powers of national institutions. Within the states, however, ratification drives were full of the stuff of ordinary politics—deal making. The Massachusetts ratifying convention provides a case in point. After three weeks of debate among delegates, Federalist leaders realized that they would achieve victory only if they could obtain Governor John Hancock's support. They called on Hancock at home and proposed that he endorse ratification on condition that a series of amendments be drawn up for consideration by Congress. The governor agreed as long as he would become president of the United States if Virginia failed to ratify or if George Washington refused to serve. Or he would accept the vice presidency. With the deal cut, Hancock went to the convention to propose a compromise—the ratification of the Constitution with amendments. The delegates went along with the plan, making Massachusetts the sixth state to ratify.[9]

This compromise—the call for a bill of rights—caught on, and Madison began to advocate it whenever close votes were likely. As it turned out, he and other Federalists needed to mention the point quite often: of the nine states ratifying after January 1788, seven recommended that the new Congress consider amendments. New York and Virginia probably would not have agreed to the Constitution without such an addition, and Virginia called for a second constitutional convention for this purpose. Other states began revising their own wish lists of specific rights they wanted included in the document.[10]

The Federalists realized that if they did not accede to state demands, either the Constitution would not be ratified or a new constitutional convention would be necessary. Because neither alternative was particularly attractive, it was agreed that the document would be amended as soon as the new government came into power. And with that promise came the ratification of the Constitution by the requisite number of states just a year after it was written. The ratification of the Bill of Rights, on December 15, 1791, quieted those who had voiced objections. But the guarantees these ten amendments provide continue to serve as fodder for debate and, most relevant here, for Supreme Court litigation. Many of these debates involve the construction of specific guarantees, such as free speech and free exercise of religion, under which individuals seek relief when governments allegedly infringe on their rights.

The debates also involve clashes between the authority of the government to protect the safety, health, morals, and general welfare of citizens and the right of individuals not to be deprived of their liberty without due process of law. These disputes arise from specific and often difficult questions. For example, may government force a business owner to pay employees a certain wage, or does that requirement infringe on the employer's liberty? May government force homeowners to vacate their houses if it needs the property to construct a road and is willing to pay the owners "fair market value" for their property, or does that interfere with a right contained in the Fifth Amendment? The answers to these questions and others like them reveal the contours of government power in relation to individual rights.

---

8. *The Federalist Papers* are available at http://thomas.loc.gov/home/histdox/fedpapers.html.

9. Joseph T. Keenan, *The Constitution of the United States* (Chicago: Dorsey Press, 1988), 32–33.

10. Alpheus T. Mason, ed., *The States Rights Debate*, 2nd ed. (New York: Oxford University Press, 1972), 92–93.

1

Understanding the U.S. Supreme Court

THIS BOOK is devoted to narrative and opinion excerpts showing how the U.S. Supreme Court has interpreted the Constitution.[1] As a student approaching constitutional law, perhaps for the first time, you may think it is odd that the subject requires more than 700 pages of text. After all, in length, the Constitution and the amendments to it could fit easily into many Court decisions. Moreover, the document itself—its language—seems so clear.

First impressions, however, can be deceiving. Even apparently clear constitutional phrases do not necessarily lend themselves to clear constitutional interpretation. For example, according to Article II, Section 2, the president "shall be Commander in Chief of the Army and Navy of the United States." Sounds simple enough, but could you, based on those words, answer the following questions, all of which have been posed to the Court?

- May the president, during times of war, order a blockade of ports in the United States?
- May Congress delegate to the president the power to order an arms embargo against nations at war?

- May the president, during times of war, order that alleged traitors or terrorists be tried by military tribunals rather than civilian courts?
- May the president, during times of international crisis, authorize the creation of military camps to intern potential traitors to prevent sabotage?

What these and other questions arising from the different guarantees contained in the Constitution illustrate is that a gap sometimes exists between the document's words and reality. Although the language seems explicit, its meanings can be elusive and difficult to interpret. Accordingly, the justices of the Supreme Court have developed various approaches to resolving disputes.

As figure 1-1 shows, however, a great deal happens before the justices actually decide cases. We begin our discussion with a brief overview of the steps depicted in the figure. Next, we consider explanations for the choices justices make at the final and most important stage, the resolution of disputes.

PROCESSING SUPREME COURT CASES

During the 2014–2015 term more than 7000 petitions arrived at the Supreme Court's doorstep, but the justices decided only 75 with signed opinions.[2] The disparity

---

1. This is not to say that the Supreme Court alone engages in constitutional interpretation. Many commentators have suggested that the president, Congress, and even the American people can also lay claim to playing a role in constitutional interpretation. See Walter F. Murphy's classic, "Who Shall Interpret the Constitution?," *Review of Politics* 48 (1986): 401–423. We discuss this idea in the introduction to Part II, and throughout the volume you will find examples of constitutional deliberation beyond the confines of the judiciary.

2. Data from the *Supreme Court Journal* for the October 2014 term, June 30, 2015. See www.supremecourt.gov/orders/journal/jnl14.pdf

between the number of parties who want the Court to resolve their disputes and the number of disputes the Court agrees to resolve raises some important questions: How do the justices decide which cases to hear? What happens to the cases they reject and to those the Court agrees to resolve? We address these and other questions by describing how the Court processes its cases.

Deciding to Decide: The Supreme Court's Caseload

As the figures for the 2014–2014 term indicate, the Court heard and decided less than 1 percent of the cases it received. This percentage is quite low, but it follows the general trend in Supreme Court decision making: the number of requests for review increased dramatically during the twentieth century, but the number of cases the Court formally decides each year did not increase. In 1930 the Court agreed to decide 159 of the 726 disputes it received. In 1990 the number of cases granted review fell to 141, but the sum total of petitions for review rose to 6,302—nearly nine times the number in 1930.[3]

But how do any of these cases get to the Supreme Court? How do the justices decide which will get a formal review and which will be rejected? What affects their choices? We consider these questions in turn below, for the answers are fundamental to an understanding of judicial decision making.

How Cases Get to the Court: Jurisdiction and the Routes of Appeal. Cases come to the Court in one of four ways: by a request for review under the Court's original jurisdiction or by three appellate routes— appeals, certification, and petitions for writs of certiorari *(see figure 1-1).* Chapter 2 explains more about the Court's original jurisdiction, as it is central to understanding the landmark case of *Marbury v. Madison* (1803). Here, it is sufficient to note that original cases are those that have not been heard by any other court. Article III of the Constitution authorizes such suits in cases involving ambassadors from foreign countries and those to which a state is a party. But because congressional legislation permits lower courts to exercise concurrent authority over most cases meeting Article III requirements, the Supreme Court does not

have exclusive jurisdiction over them. Consequently, the Court normally accepts, on its original jurisdiction, only those cases in which one state is suing another (usually over a disputed boundary) and sends the rest to the lower courts for initial rulings. That is why in recent years original jurisdiction cases have made up only a tiny fraction of the Court's overall docket—between one and five cases per term.

Most cases reach the Court under its appellate jurisdiction, meaning that a lower federal or state court has already rendered a decision and one of the parties is asking the Supreme Court to review that decision. As figure 1-2 shows, such cases typically come from one of the U.S. courts of appeals or state supreme courts. The U.S. Supreme Court, the nation's highest tribunal, is the court of last resort.

To invoke the Court's appellate jurisdiction, litigants can take one of three routes, depending on the nature of their dispute: appeal as a matter of right, certification, or certiorari. Cases falling into the first category (normally called "on appeal") involve issues that Congress has determined are so important that a ruling by the Supreme Court is necessary. Before 1988 these included cases in which a lower court declared a state or federal law unconstitutional or in which a state court upheld a state law challenged on the grounds that it violated the U.S. Constitution. Although the justices were supposed to decide such appeals, they often found a more expedient way to deal with them—by either failing to consider them or issuing summary decisions (shorthand rulings). At the Court's urging, in 1988 Congress virtually eliminated "mandatory" appeals. Today, the Court is legally obligated to hear only those few cases (typically involving the Voting Rights Act) appealed from special three-judge district courts. When the Court agrees to hear such cases, it issues an order noting its "probable jurisdiction."

A second, but rarely used, route to the Court is certification. Under the Court's appellate jurisdiction and by an act of Congress, lower appellate courts can file writs of certification, asking the justices to respond to questions aimed at clarifying federal law. Because only judges may use this route, very few cases come to the Court this way—fewer than a handful in the past six decades.[4] The justices are free to accept a question certified to them or dismiss it.

3. Data from Lee Epstein, Jeffrey A. Segal, Harold J. Spaeth, and Thomas G. Walker, *The Supreme Court Compendium: Data, Decisions, and Developments,* 6th ed. (Thousand Oaks, CA: CQ Press, 2015), Tables 2-5 and 2-6.

4. See Marcia Coyle, "Supreme Court Asked to Take Certified Question for Only Fifth Time in Six-Plus Decades," *National Law Journal,* August 3, 2009.

FIGURE 1-1   The Processing of Cases

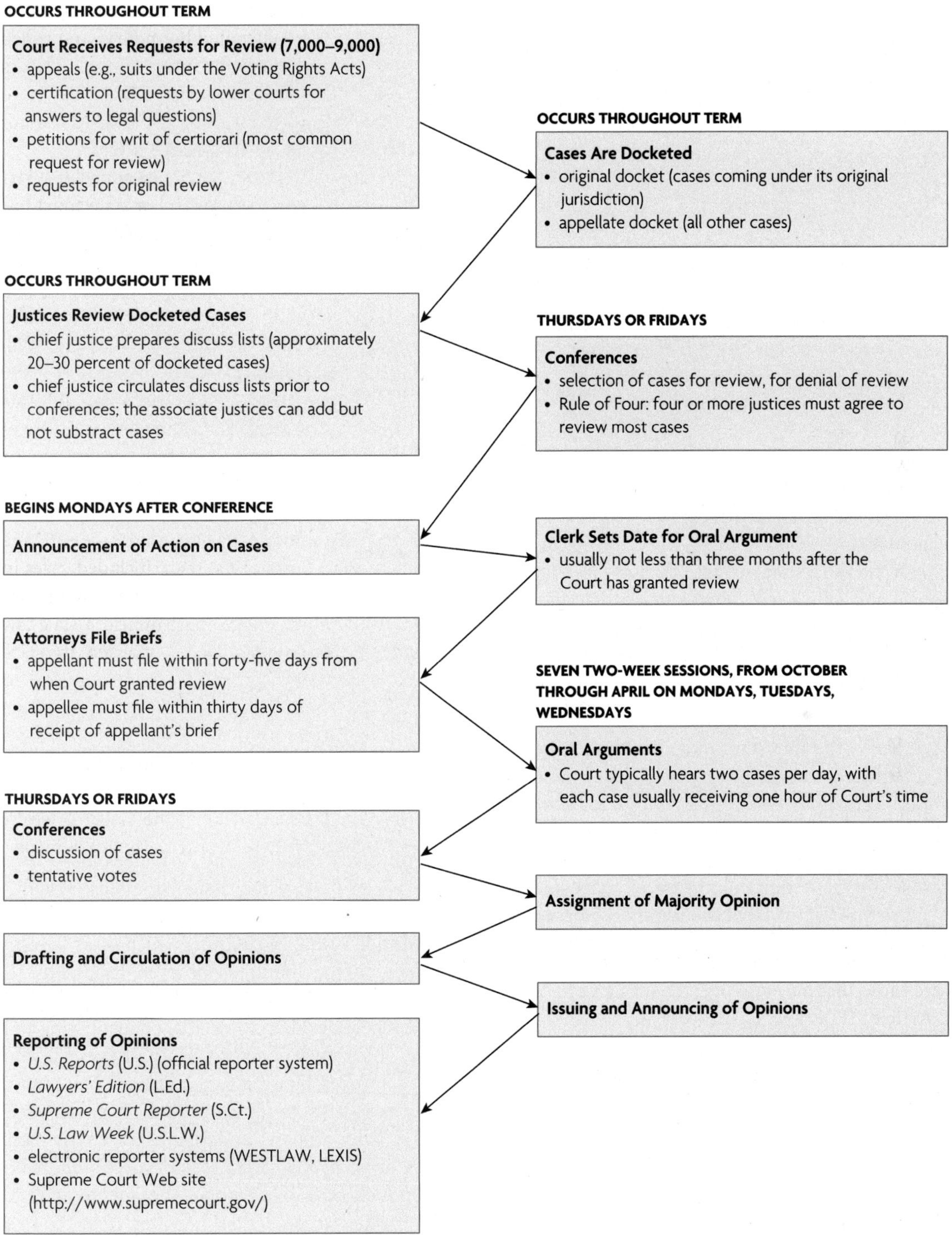

OCCURS THROUGHOUT TERM

Court Receives Requests for Review (7,000–9,000)
- appeals (e.g., suits under the Voting Rights Acts)
- certification (requests by lower courts for answers to legal questions)
- petitions for writ of certiorari (most common request for review)
- requests for original review

OCCURS THROUGHOUT TERM

Cases Are Docketed
- original docket (cases coming under its original jurisdiction)
- appellate docket (all other cases)

OCCURS THROUGHOUT TERM

Justices Review Docketed Cases
- chief justice prepares discuss lists (approximately 20–30 percent of docketed cases)
- chief justice circulates discuss lists prior to conferences; the associate justices can add but not substract cases

THURSDAYS OR FRIDAYS

Conferences
- selection of cases for review, for denial of review
- Rule of Four: four or more justices must agree to review most cases

BEGINS MONDAYS AFTER CONFERENCE

Announcement of Action on Cases

Clerk Sets Date for Oral Argument
- usually not less than three months after the Court has granted review

Attorneys File Briefs
- appellant must file within forty-five days from when Court granted review
- appellee must file within thirty days of receipt of appellant's brief

SEVEN TWO-WEEK SESSIONS, FROM OCTOBER THROUGH APRIL ON MONDAYS, TUESDAYS, WEDNESDAYS

Oral Arguments
- Court typically hears two cases per day, with each case usually receiving one hour of Court's time

THURSDAYS OR FRIDAYS

Conferences
- discussion of cases
- tentative votes

Assignment of Majority Opinion

Drafting and Circulation of Opinions

Issuing and Announcing of Opinions

Reporting of Opinions
- *U.S. Reports* (U.S.) (official reporter system)
- *Lawyers' Edition* (L.Ed.)
- *Supreme Court Reporter* (S.Ct.)
- *U.S. Law Week* (U.S.L.W.)
- electronic reporter systems (WESTLAW, LEXIS)
- Supreme Court Web site (http://www.supremecourt.gov/)

SOURCE: Compiled by the authors.

FIGURE 1-2   The American Court System

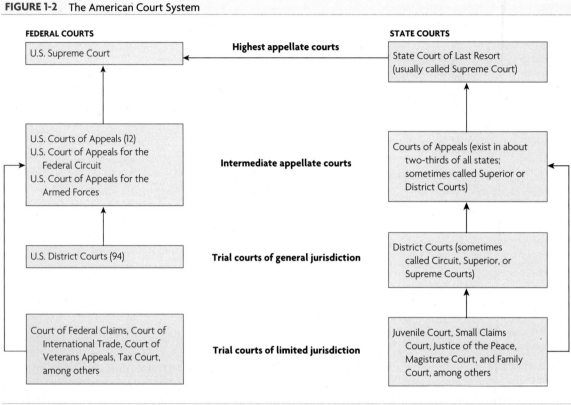

SOURCE: Compiled by the authors.

That leaves the third and most common appellate path, a request for a writ of certiorari (from the Latin meaning "to be informed"). In a petition for a writ of certiorari, the litigants desiring Supreme Court review ask the Court, to literally become "informed" about their cases by requesting that the lower court send up the record. Most of the eight thousand or so cases that arrive each year come as requests for certiorari. The Court, exercising its ability to choose the cases it will review, grants "cert" to less than 1 percent of the petitions. A grant of cert means that the justices have decided to give the case full review; a denial means that the decision of the lower court remains in force.

In sum, Article III of the U.S. Constitution enables the Supreme Court to decide cases that have not been heard by any other court, but the vast majority of disputes that reach the justices have already been resolved by another judicial body. The United States' approach is not the only way to design a legal system. For example, in a society that has created a single constitutional court, that tribunal

may have a judicial monopoly on interpreting matters of constitutional law; it may be the only forum in which citizens can bring constitutional claims *(see box 1-1).*

How the Court Decides: The Case Selection Process. Regardless of the specific design of a legal system, in many countries jurists must confront the task of "deciding to decide"—that is, choosing which cases to resolve from among the hundreds or even thousands they receive. The U.S. Supreme Court is no exception; it too has the job of deciding to decide, or identifying those cases to which it will grant cert. This task presents something of a mixed blessing to the justices. Selecting the seventy or so cases to review from the large number of petitions is an arduous undertaking that requires the justices or their law clerks to look over hundreds of thousands of pages of briefs and other memoranda. The ability to exercise discretion, however, frees the Court from one of the major constraints on judicial bodies: the lack of agenda control. The justices may not be able to

BOX 1-1   THE AMERICAN LEGAL SYSTEM IN GLOBAL PERSPECTIVE

THE AMERICAN legal system can be described as *dual, parallel,* and (for the most part) *three tiered.* It is dual because one federal system and fifty state systems coexist, each ruling on disputes falling under its particular purview. This duality does not mean, however, that state courts never hear cases involving claims made under the U.S. Constitution or that federal courts necessarily shun cases arising out of state law. In fact, the U.S. Supreme Court can review cases involving federal questions on which state supreme courts have ruled and can strike down state laws if they are incompatible with the U.S. Constitution. Similarly, many cases arising from state law and heard in state courts also contain federal issues that must be resolved.

Differences exist among the state court systems, but most today roughly parallel the federal system. Trial courts—the lowest rungs on the ladder—are the entry points into the system. In the middle of the ladder are appellate courts, those that upon request review the records of trial court proceedings. Finally, both systems have supreme courts, bodies that provide final answers to legal questions in their own domains.

Although a supreme court sits atop each ladder, the U.S. Supreme Court plays a unique role—it is the apex of both state and federal court systems. Because it can hear cases and ultimately overturn the rulings of federal and state court judges, it is presumably the authoritative legal body in the United States.

Some nations have created legal systems that, to greater or lesser extents, resemble the American system. For example, Japan, whose constitutional document was largely drafted by Americans, also has a three-tiered structure. Cases begin at the district (trial) court level, move to high courts (Japan's version of midlevel appellate courts), and, finally, move to the Supreme Court.[1] But other nations—first Austria, Germany, and Italy and later Belgium, Portugal, South Africa, Spain, and most of the countries of Eastern and Central Europe—have taken a much different approach. In these countries, the highest court is not a supreme court but a single constitutional court, which has a judicial monopoly on interpreting matters of constitutional law. Such a constitutional court is not a part of the "ordinary" court system; litigants do not typically petition the justices to review decisions of lower courts. Rather, when judges confront a law whose constitutionality they doubt, they are obliged to send the case directly to the constitutional court. This tribunal receives evidence on the constitutional issue, sometimes gathers evidence on its own, hears arguments, perhaps consults sources that counsel overlooked, and hands down a decision. But, unlike in the United States, the constitutional court does not decide the case because it has not heard a case—it has only addressed a question of constitutional interpretation. Although the court publishes an opinion justifying its ruling and explaining the controlling principles, the case still must be decided by regular tribunals. In some countries—for example, Germany, Italy, and Russia—public officials also may bring suits in the constitutional court challenging the legitimacy of legislative, executive, or judicial acts, and under some circumstances private citizens may initiate similar litigation. Where judicial action is challenged, the constitutional court in effect reviews a decision of another court, but the form of the action is very different from an appeal in the United States.

This type of court system is often called "centralized" because the power of judicial review—that is, the power to review government acts for their compatibility with the nation's constitution and to strike down those acts that are not compatible—rests in one constitutional court; other courts are typically barred from exercising judicial review, although they may refer constitutional questions to the constitutional tribunal. In contrast, the U.S. system is deemed "decentralized" because ordinary courts—not just supreme courts—can engage in judicial review. We shall return to this distinction in chapter 2 *(see box 2-1).*

---

1. Japan has summary courts with jurisdiction over minor civil and criminal cases. District courts (trial courts of general jurisdiction) can hear civil appeals from summary courts. For more details, see Herbert Jacob, ed., *Courts, Law, and Politics* (New Haven, CT: Yale University Press, 1996), chap. 6.

reach out and propose cases for review the way members of Congress can propose legislation, but the enormous number of petitions they receive ensures that they can resolve at least some issues important to them.

Many scholars and lawyers have tried to determine what makes a case "certworthy," that is, worthy of review by the Supreme Court. Before we look at some of their findings, let us consider the case selection process itself. The original pool of seven thousand to eight thousand petitions faces several checkpoints along the way *(see figure 1-1),* which significantly reduce the amount of time the Court, acting as a collegial body, spends deciding what to decide. The staff members in the office of the Supreme Court clerk act as the first gatekeepers. When a petition for certiorari arrives, the clerk's office examines it to make sure it is in proper form, that it conforms to the Court's precise rules. Briefs must be "prepared in a 6⅛-by-9¼-inch booklet, . . . typeset in a Century family 12-point type with 2-point or more leading between lines." Exceptions are made for litigants who cannot afford to pay the Court's fees. The rules governing these petitions, known as *in forma pauperis* briefs, are somewhat looser, allowing indigents to submit briefs on 8½-by-11-inch paper.[5]

The clerk's office gives each acceptable petition an identification number, called a "docket number," and forwards copies to the chambers of the individual justices. On the current (2015) Court, all the justices but Samuel Alito use the "certiorari pool system," in which clerks from the different chambers collaborate in reading and then writing memos on the petitions.[6] Upon receiving the preliminary or pool memos, the individual justices may ask their own clerks for their thoughts about the petitions. The justices then use the pool memos, along with their clerks' reports, as a basis for making a determinations about which cases they believe are worthy of a full hearing.

During this process, the chief justice serves as yet another checkpoint on petitions. Before the justices meet to make case selection decisions, the chief circulates a "discuss list" containing those cases he feels the Court should consider; any justice (in order of seniority) may add cases to this list but may not remove any. Less than a third of the cases that come to the Court make it to the list and are actually discussed by the justices in conference. The rest are automatically denied review, leaving the lower court decisions intact.[7]

This much we know. Because only the justices attend the Court's conferences, we cannot say precisely what transpires there. We can offer only a rough picture based on scholarly writings, the comments of justices, and our examination of the private papers of several retired justices. These sources tell us that the discussion of each petition begins with the chief justice presenting a short summary of the facts and, typically, stating his vote. The associate justices, who sit at a rectangular table, then comment on each petition, with the most senior justice speaking first and the newest member last. The associate justices may provide some indication of how they will vote on the merits of the case if it is accepted. As figure 1-3 shows, the justices record certiorari and merits votes in their docket books. But, given the large number of petitions, the justices apparently discuss few cases in detail.

By tradition, the Court adheres to the so-called Rule of Four: it grants certiorari to those cases receiving the affirmative vote of at least four justices. The Court identifies the cases accepted and rejected on a "certified orders list," which is released to the public. For a case granted certiorari or in which probable jurisdiction is noted, the clerk informs the participating attorneys, who then have specified time limits in which to turn in their written legal arguments (briefs), and the case is scheduled for oral argument.

Considerations Affecting Case Selection Decisions. This is how the Court considers petitions, but why do the justices make the decisions that they do? Scholars have developed several answers to this question. Two sets are worthy of our attention: legal considerations and political considerations.[8]

---

5. Rules 33 and 39 of the Rules of the Supreme Court of the United States. All Supreme Court rules are available at http://www.supremecourt.gov/ctrules/2013RulesoftheCourt.pdf.

6. Supreme Court justices are authorized to hire four law clerks each. Typically, these clerks are outstanding recent graduates of the nation's top law schools. Pool (or preliminary) memos, as well as other documents pertaining to the Court's case selection process, are available at http://epstein.wustl.edu/blackmun.php. See also Ryan C. Black and Christina L. Boyd, "The Role of Law Clerks in the U.S. Supreme Court's Agenda-Setting Process," *American Politics Research* 40 (2012): 147–173.

7. For information on the discuss list, see Ryan C. Black and Christina L. Boyd, "Selecting the Select Few: The Discuss List and the U.S. Supreme Court's Agenda-Setting Process," *Social Science Quarterly* 94 (2013): 1124–1144; and Gregory A. Caldeira and John R. Wright, "The Discuss List: Agenda Building in the Supreme Court," *Law and Society Review* 24 (1990): 807–836.

8. Some scholars have noted a third set: procedural considerations. These emanate from Article III, which—under the Court's interpretation—places constraints on the ability of federal tribunals to hear and decide cases. Chapter 2 considers these constraints, which

FIGURE 1-3   A Page from Justice Blackmun's Docket Books

	HOLD FOR	DEFER		CERT.			JURISDICTIONAL STATEMENT				MERITS		MOTION		
		RELIST	CVSG	G	D	G & R	N	POST	DIS	AFF	REV	AFF	G	D	
Rehnquist, Ch. J.					✓							✓			
White, J.				3								✓			
Blackmun, J.				✓							✓				
Stevens, J.				✓							✓				
O'Connor, J.				3								✓			
Scalia, J.					✓							✓			
Kennedy, J.				✓							✓				
Souter, J.				✓								✓			
Thomas, J.					✓							✓			

SOURCE: Dockets of Harry A. Blackmun, Manuscript Division, Library of Congress, Washington, DC.

NOTE: As the docket sheet shows, the justices have a number of options when they meet to vote on cert. They can grant (G) the petition or deny (D) it. They also can cast a "Join 3" (3) vote. Justices may have different interpretations of a Join 3, but, at the very least, it tells the others that the justice agrees to supply a vote in favor of cert if three other justices support granting review. In the MERITS column, REV = reverse the decision of the court below and AFF = affirm the decision of the court below.

Legal considerations are listed in Rule 10, which the Court has established to govern the certiorari decision-making process. Under Rule 10, the Court emphasizes "conflict," such as when a U.S. "court of appeals has entered a decision in conflict with the decision of another United States court of appeals on the same important matter," or when decisions of state courts of law resort collide with one another or with the federal courts.[9]

To what extent do the considerations in Rule 10 affect the Court? The answer is mixed. On one hand, the Court seems to follow the rule's dictates. The presence of actual conflict between or among federal courts, a major concern of Rule 10, substantially increases the likelihood of review; if actual conflict is present in a case, it has a 33 percent chance of gaining Court review, as compared with the usual 1 percent certiorari rate.[10] On the other hand, although the Court may use the existence of actual conflict as a

threshold consideration (cases that do not present conflict *may* be rejected), it does not accept all cases with conflict because there are too many.[11]

In short, Rule 10's stress on conflict in the lower courts may act as a constraint on the justices' behavior, but it does necessarily further our understanding of what occurs in cases meeting the criteria. That is why scholars have looked elsewhere—to *political* factors that may influence the Court's case selection process. Three such factors are particularly important. The first is the U.S. solicitor general (SG), the attorney who represents the U.S. government before the Supreme Court. Simply stated, when the office of the SG files a petition, the Court is very likely to grant certiorari. In fact, the Court accepts about 70 to 80 percent of the cases in which the federal government is the petitioning party.

Why is the SG so successful? One is that the Court is well aware of the SG's special role. A presidential appointee whose decisions often reflect the administration's philosophy, the SG also represents the interests of the United States. As the nation's highest court, the Supreme Court cannot ignore these interests. In addition, the justices rely on the SG to act as a filter; that is, they expect the SG to examine carefully the

include justiciability (the case must be appropriate for judicial resolution in that it presents a real "case" and "controversy") and standing (the appropriate person must bring the case). Unless these procedural criteria are met, the Court—at least theoretically—will deny review.

9. Rule 10 also stresses the Court's interest in "important" federal questions.

10. See Gregory A. Caldeira and John R. Wright, "Organized Interests and Agenda Setting in the U.S. Supreme Court," *American Political Science Review* 82 (1988): 1109–1127.

11. In fact, during any given term the Court rejects hundreds of cases in which real conflicts exist. See Lawrence Baum, *The Supreme Court,* 10th ed. (Washington, DC: CQ Press, 2009), 92–93.

cases to which the government is a party and bring only the most important to their attention. Furthermore, because solicitors general are involved in so much Supreme Court litigation, they acquire a great deal of knowledge about the Court that other litigants do not. They are "repeat players" who know the "rules of the game" and can use them to their advantage. For example, they know how to structure their petitions to attract the attention and interest of the justices. Finally, a recent study on the topic emphasizes less the SG's experience and more the professionalism of the SG and the lawyers working in his or her office. As the authors put it, they are "consummate legal professionals whose information justices can trust."[12]

The second political factor is the amicus curiae (friend of the court) brief. These briefs are usually filed by interest groups and other third parties after the Court makes its decision to hear a case, but they can also be filed at the certiorari stage *(see box 1-2)*. Research by political scientists shows that amicus briefs significantly enhance a case's chances of being heard, and multiple briefs have a greater effect.[13] Another interesting finding of these studies is that even when groups file *in opposition* to granting certiorari, they increase—rather than decrease—the probability that the Court will hear the case.

These findings suggest that the justices may not be strongly influenced by the arguments contained in amicus briefs (if they were, why would briefs in opposition to certiorari have the opposite effect?), but they seem to use them as cues. In other words, because amicus briefs filed at the certiorari stage are somewhat uncommon—less than 10 percent of all petitions are accompanied by amicus briefs—they do draw the justices' attention. If major organizations are sufficiently interested in an appeal to pay the cost of filing briefs in support of (or against) Court review, then the petition for certiorari is probably worth the justices' serious consideration.

In addition, we have strong reasons to suspect that a third political factor—the ideology of the justices—affects actions on certiorari petitions. Researchers tell us that the justices during the liberal period under

Chief Justice Earl Warren (1953–1969) were more likely to grant review to cases in which the lower court reached a conservative decision so that they could reverse, while those of the moderately conservative Court during the years of Chief Justice Warren Burger (1969–1985) took liberal results to reverse. It would be difficult to believe that the current justices are any less likely than their predecessors to vote on the basis of their ideology. Scholarly studies also suggest that justices engage in strategic voting behavior at the cert stage. In other words, justices are forward thinking; they consider the implications of their cert vote for the later merits stage, asking themselves, "If I vote to grant a particular petition, what are the odds of my position winning down the road?" As one justice explained his calculations, "I might think the Nebraska Supreme Court made a horrible decision, but I wouldn't want to take the case, for if we take the case and affirm it, then it would become precedent."[14]

The Role of Attorneys

Once the Supreme Court agrees to decide a case, the clerk of the Court informs the parties. The parties present their side of the dispute to the justices in written and oral arguments.

Written Arguments. Written arguments, called briefs, are the major vehicles for parties to Supreme Court cases to document their positions. Under the Court's rules, the appealing party (known as the appellant or petitioner) must submit its brief within forty-five days of the time the Court grants certiorari; the opposing party (known as the appellee or respondent) has thirty days after receipt of the appellant's brief to respond with arguments urging affirmance of the lower court ruling.

As is the case for cert petitions, the Court maintains specific rules covering the presentation and format of merits briefs. The briefs of both parties must be submitted in forty copies and not exceed 15,000 words. Rule 24 outlines the material that briefs must contain, such as a description of the questions presented for review, a list of the parties, and a statement describing the Court's authority to hear the case. Also worth noting: the Court's rules now mandate electronic submission of all

12. Ryan C. Black and Ryan J. Owens, *The Solicitor General and the United States Supreme Court: Executive Branch Influence and Judicial Decisions* (Cambridge: Cambridge University Press, 2012), 71.

13. Caldeira and Wright, "Organized Interests and Agenda Setting"; Ryan C. Black and Ryan J. Owens, "Agenda Setting in the Supreme Court: The Collision of Policy and Jurisprudence," *Journal of Politics* 71 (2009): 1062–1075.

14. Quoted in H. W. Perry Jr., *Deciding to Decide: Agenda Setting in the United States Supreme Court* (Cambridge, MA: Harvard University Press, 1991), 200.

BOX 1-2   THE AMICUS CURIAE BRIEF

The amicus curiae practice probably originates in Roman law. A judge would often appoint a *consilium* (officer of the court) to advise him on points where the judge was in doubt. That may be why the term *amicus curiae* translates from the Latin as "friend of the court." But today it is the rare amicus who is a friend of the court. Instead, contemporary briefs almost always are a friend of a party, supporting one side over the other at the certiorari and merits stages. Consider one of the briefs filed in **United States v. Windsor** (2013), the cover of which is reprinted here. In that case, the American Psychological Association and other organizations filed in support of Edith Windsor. They, along with Windsor, asked the Court

to invalidate the Defense of Marriage Act (DOMA), which defined *marriage* under federal law as a "legal union between one man and one woman." These groups were anything but neutral participants.

How does an organization become an amicus curiae participant in the Supreme Court of the United States? Under the Court's rules, groups wishing to file an amicus brief at the certiorari or merits stage must obtain the written consent of the parties to the litigation (the federal and state governments are exempt from this requirement). If the parties refuse to give their consent, the group can file a motion with the Court asking for its permission. The Court today almost always grants these motions.

No. 12-307

In The

Supreme Court of the United States

UNITED STATES OF AMERICA, PETITIONER

—v.—

EDITH SCHLAIN WINDSOR, IN HER CAPACITY AS EXECUTOR
OF THE ESTATE OF THEA CLARA SPYER, ET AL., *Respondents.*

On Writ of Certiorari to the United States
Court of Appeals for the Second Circuit

BRIEF OF THE AMERICAN PSYCHOLOGICAL ASSOCIATION, THE AMERICAN
ACADEMY OF PEDIATRICS, THE AMERICAN MEDICAL ASSOCIATION, THE AMERICAN
PSYCHIATRIC ASSOCIATION, THE AMERICAN PSYCHOANALYTIC ASSOCIATION,
THE CALIFORNIA MEDICAL ASSOCIATION, THE NATIONAL ASSOCIATION OF SOCIAL WORKERS
AND ITS NEW YORK CITY AND STATE CHAPTERS, AND THE NEW YORK STATE PSYCHOLOGICAL
ASSOCIATION AS AMICI CURIAE ON THE MERITS IN SUPPORT OF AFFIRMANCE

NATHALIE F. P. GILFOYLE
AMERICAN PSYCHOLOGICAL
ASSOCIATION
750 First Street, N.E.
Washington, DC 20002

WILLIAM F. SHEEHAN
Counsel of Record
ANDREW HUDSON
GOODWIN | PROCTER LLP
901 New York Avenue, N.W.
Washington, D.C. 20001
(202) 346-4000
wsheehan@goodwinprocter.com

PAUL M. SMITH
JENNER & BLOCK LLP
1099 New York Avenue, N.W.
Washington, DC 20001
Counsel for Amici Curiae

briefs (including amicus briefs) in addition to the normal hard copy submissions.

The clerk sends the briefs to the justices, who normally study them before oral argument. Written briefs are important because the justices may use them to formulate the questions they ask the lawyers representing the parties. The briefs also serve as a permanent record of the positions of the parties, available to the justices for consultation after oral argument when they decide the case outcome. A well-crafted brief can provide the justices with arguments, legal references, and suggested remedies that later may be incorporated into the opinion.

In addition to the briefs the parties submit to the suit, Court rules allow interested persons, organizations, and government units to participate as amici curiae on the merits—just as they are permitted to file such briefs at the review stage *(see box 1-2)*. Those wishing to submit amicus curiae briefs must obtain the written permission of the parties or the Court. Only the federal government and state governments are exempt from this requirement.

Oral Arguments. Attorneys also have the opportunity to present their cases orally before the justices. Each side has thirty minutes to convince the Court of the merits of its position and to field questions from the justices, though sometimes the Court makes small exceptions to this rule. In the 2011 term, it made a particularly big one, hearing six hours of oral argument, over three days, on the Patient Protection and Affordable Care Act, the health-care law passed in 2010. This was unprecedented in the modern era, but not in the Court's early years. In the past, because attorneys did not always prepare written briefs, the justices relied on oral arguments to learn about the cases and to help them marshal their arguments for the next stage. Orals were considered important public events, opportunities to see the most prominent attorneys of the day at work. Arguments often went on for days: *Gibbons v. Ogden* (1824), the landmark commerce clause case, was argued for five days, and *McCulloch v. Maryland* (1819), the litigation challenging the constitutionality of the national bank, took nine days to argue.

The justices are allowed to interrupt the attorneys at any time with comments and questions, as the following exchange between Justice Byron R. White and Sarah Weddington, the attorney representing Jane Roe in *Roe v. Wade* (1973), illustrates. White got the ball rolling when he asked Weddington to respond to an issue her brief had not addressed: whether abortions should be performed during all stages of pregnancy or should somehow be limited. The following discussion ensued:

WHITE: And the statute doesn't make any distinction based upon at what period of pregnancy the abortion is performed?

Weddington: No, Your Honor. There is no time limit or indication of time, whatsoever. So I think—

White: What is your constitutional position there?

Weddington: As to a time limit. . . . It is our position that the freedom involved is that of a woman to determine whether or not to continue a pregnancy. Obviously, I have a much more difficult time saying that the State has no interest in late pregnancy.

White: Why? Why is that?

Weddington: I think that's more the emotional response to a late pregnancy, rather than it is any constitutional—

White: Emotional response by whom?

Weddington: I guess by persons considering the issue outside the legal context, I think, as far as the State—

White: Well, do you or don't you say that the constitutional—

Weddington: I would say constitutional—

White: Right you insist on reaches up to the time of birth, or—

Weddington: The Constitution, as I read it . . . attaches protection to the person at the time of birth.

In the Court's early years, there was little doubt about the importance of such exchanges, and of oral arguments in general, because, as noted above, the justices did not always have the benefit of written briefs. Today, however, some scholars and even justices have questioned the effectiveness of oral arguments and their role in decision making. Chief Justice Earl Warren contended that they made little difference to the outcome. Once the justices have read the briefs and studied related cases, most have relatively firm views on how the case should be decided, and orals change few minds. Justice William J. Brennan Jr., however, contended that they are extremely important because they help justices to clarify core arguments.

Recent scholarly work seems to come down on Brennan's side. According to a study by Timothy Johnson and his colleagues, the justices are more likely to vote for the side with the better showing at orals. Along somewhat different lines, a study by Lee Epstein, William Landes, and Richard Posner shows that orals may be a good predictor of the Court's final votes: all else equal, the side that receives the greater number of questions tends to lose.[15] One possible explanation is that the justices use oral argument as a way to express their opinions and attempt to influence their colleagues, because formal deliberation (described below) is often limited and highly structured.

The debate will likely continue. Even if oral arguments turn out to have little effect on the justices' decisions, we should not forget the symbolic importance of the arguments: they are the only part of the Court's decision-making process that occurs in public and that you now have the opportunity to hear. Law professor Jerry Goldman has made the oral arguments of many cases available online at https://www.oyez.org. Throughout this book you will find references to this Web site, indicating that you can listen to the arguments in the case you are reading.

The Supreme Court Decides: Some Preliminaries

After the Court hears oral arguments, it meets in a private conference to discuss the case and to take a preliminary vote. Below, we describe the Court's conference procedures and the two stages that follow the conference: the assignment of the opinion of the Court and the opinion circulation period.

The Conference. Despite popular support for "government in the sunshine," the Supreme Court insists that its decisions take place in a private conference, with no one in attendance except the justices. Congress has agreed to this demand, exempting the federal courts from open government and freedom of information legislation. There are two basic reasons for the Court's insistence on the private conference. First, the Supreme Court—which, unlike Congress, lacks an electoral connection—is supposed to base its decisions on factors other than public opinion. Opening up deliberations to press scrutiny, for example, might encourage the justices to take notice of popular sentiment, which is not supposed to influence them. Or so the argument goes. Second, although the Court reaches tentative decisions on cases in conference, the opinions explaining the decisions remain to be written. This process can take many weeks or even months, and a decision is not final until the opinions are written, circulated, and approved. Because the Court's decisions can have a major impact on politics and the economy, any party having advance knowledge of case outcomes could use that information for unfair business and political advantage.

The system works so well that, with only a few exceptions, the justices have not experienced information leaks—at least not prior to the public announcement of a decision. After that, clerks and even justices have sometimes thrown their own sunshine on the Court's deliberations. *National Federation of Independent Business v. Sebelius* (2012) *(excerpted in chapters 7 and 8)*, involving the constitutionality of the health-care law passed in 2010, provides a recent example. Based on information from reliable sources, Jan Crawford of CBS News reported that Chief Justice Roberts initially voted to join the Court's four conservative justices to strike down the law but later changed his vote to join the four liberals to uphold it.[16]

So, while it can be difficult to know precisely what occurs in the deliberation of any particular case, from journalistic accounts and the papers of retired justices we can piece together the procedures and the general nature of the Court's discussions. We have learned the following: First, we know that the chief justice presides over the deliberations. The chief calls up the case for discussion and then presents his views about the issues and how the case should be decided. In order of seniority, the remaining justices state their views and vote. By Court practice, no justice speaks a second time until all other justices have had an opportunity to express their views.

The level and intensity of discussion, as the justices' notes from conference deliberations reveal, differ from case to case. In some, it appears that the justices had

15. Timothy R. Johnson, Paul J. Wahlbeck, and James F. Spriggs II, "The Influence of Oral Arguments on the U.S. Supreme Court," *American Political Science Review* 100 (2006): 99–113; Lee Epstein, William M. Landes, and Richard A. Posner, "Inferring the Winning Party in the Supreme Court from the Pattern of Questioning at Oral Argument," *Journal of Legal Studies* 39 (2010): 433–467.

16. Jan Crawford, "Roberts Switched Views to Uphold Health Care Law," CBS News, *Face the Nation,* July 1, 2012, http://www.cbsnews.com/8301-3460_162-57464549/roberts-switched-views-to-uphold-health-care-law/?tag=contentMain;contentBody.

very little to say. The chief presented his views, and the rest noted their agreement. In others, every Court member had something to add. Whether the discussion is subdued or lively, it is unclear to what extent conferences affect the final decisions. It would be unusual for a justice to enter the conference room without having reached a tentative position on the cases to be discussed; after all, he or she has read the briefs and listened to oral arguments. But the conference, in addition to oral arguments, provides an opportunity for the justices to size up the positions of their colleagues. This sort of information, as we shall see, may be important as the justices begin the process of crafting and circulating opinions.

Opinion Assignment and Circulation. The conference typically leads to a tentative outcome and vote. What happens at this point is critical because it determines who assigns the opinion of the Court—the Court's only authoritative policy statement, the only one that establishes precedent. Under Court norms, when the chief justice votes with the majority, he assigns the writing of the opinion. The chief may decide to write the opinion or assign it to one of the other justices who voted with the majority. When the chief justice votes with the minority, the assignment task falls to the most senior member of the Court who voted with the majority.

In making these assignments, the chief justice (or the senior associate in the majority) takes many factors into account.[17] First and perhaps foremost, the chief tries to equalize the distribution of the Court's workload. This makes sense: the Court will not run efficiently, given the burdensome nature of opinion writing, if some justices are given many more assignments than others. The chief may also take into account the justices' particular areas of expertise, recognizing that some justices are more knowledgeable about particular areas of the law than others. By encouraging specialization, the chief may also be trying to increase the quality of opinions and reduce the time required to write them.

Along similar lines, there has been a tendency among chief justices to self-assign especially important cases. Warren took this step in the famous case of *Brown v. Board of Education* (1954) and Roberts did the same in the health-care case. Some scholars and even some justices have suggested that this is a smart strategy, if only for symbolic reasons. As Justice Felix Frankfurter put it, "[T]here are occasions when an opinion should carry extra weight which pronouncement by the Chief Justice gives."[18] Finally, for cases decided by a one-vote margin (usually 5–4), chiefs have been known to assign the opinion to a moderate member of the majority rather than to an extreme member. The reasoning seems to be this: if the writer in a close case drafts an opinion with which other members of the majority are uncomfortable, the opinion may drive justices to the other side, causing the majority to become a minority. A chief justice may try to minimize this risk by asking justices squarely in the middle of the majority coalition to write.

Regardless of the factors the chief considers in making assignments, one thing is clear: the opinion writer is a critical player in the opinion circulation phase, which eventually leads to the final decision of the Court. The writer begins the process by circulating a draft of the opinion to the others.

Once the justices receive the first draft of the opinion, they have many options. First, they can join the opinion, meaning that they agree with it and want no changes. Second, they can ask the opinion writer to make changes, that is, *bargain* with the writer over the content and even the disposition—to reverse or affirm the lower court ruling—offered in the draft. The following memo sent from Brennan to White is exemplary: "I've mentioned to you that I favor your approach to this case and want if possible to join your opinion. If you find the following suggestions . . . acceptable, I can join you."[19]

Third, they can tell the opinion writer that they plan to circulate a dissenting or concurring opinion. A dissenting opinion means that the writer disagrees with the disposition the majority opinion reaches and with the rationale it invokes; a concurring opinion generally agrees with the disposition but not with the rationale. Finally, justices can tell the opinion writer that they await further writings, meaning that they want to study various dissents or concurrences before they decide what to do.

---

17. See, for example, Forrest Maltzman and Paul J. Wahlbeck, "May It Please the Chief? Opinion Assignments in the Rehnquist Court," *American Journal of Political Science* 40 (1996): 421–443; and Elliot E. Slotnick, "The Chief Justices and Self-Assignment of Majority Opinions," *Western Political Quarterly* 31 (1978): 219–225.

18. Felix Frankfurter, "The Administrative Side of Chief Justice Hughes," *Harvard Law Review* 63 (1949): 4.

19. Memorandum from Justice Brennan to Justice White, 12/9/76, re: 75-104, *United Jewish Organizations v. Carey.*

As justices circulate their opinions and revise them—the average majority opinion undergoes three to four revisions in response to colleagues' comments—many different opinions on the same case, at various stages of development, will be floating around the Court over the course of several months. Because this process is replicated for each case the Court decides with a formal written opinion, it is possible that scores of different opinions may be working their way from office to office at any point in time.

Eventually, the final version of the opinion is reached, and each justice expresses a position in writing or by signing an opinion of another justice. This is how the final vote is taken. When all of the justices have declared themselves, the only remaining step is for the Court to announce its decision and the vote to the public.

SUPREME COURT DECISION MAKING: LEGALISM

So far, we have examined the processes the justices follow to reach decisions on the disputes brought before them. We have answered basic questions about the institutional procedures the Court uses to carry out its responsibilities. The questions we have not addressed concern why the justices reach particular decisions and what forces play a role in determining their choices.

As you might imagine, the responses to these questions are many, but they can be categorized into two groups. One focuses on the role of law, broadly defined, and legal methods in determining how justices interpret the Constitution, emphasizing, among other things, the importance of its words, American history and tradition, and precedent (previously decided constitutional rulings). Judge Posner and his coauthors have referred to this as a legalistic theory of judicial decision making.[20] The other—what Posner et al. call a realistic theory of judging—also considers nonlegalistic factors, including the role of politics. "Politics" can take many forms, such as the particular ideological views of the justices, the mood of the public, and the political preferences of the executive and legislative branches.

Commentators sometimes define these two approaches as "should" versus "do." They say the justices

should interpret the Constitution in line with the language of the text of the document or in accord with precedent. They reason that justices are supposed to shed their personal biases, preferences, and partisan attachments when they take their seats on the bench. But, it is argued, justices *do not* shed these biases, preferences, and attachments; rather, their decisions often reflect their own political views or the views of those around them.

To the extent that approaches grounded in law originated to answer the question of how justices *should* decide pending disputes, we understand why the difference between the two groups is often described in terms of "should" versus "do." But, for several reasons, we ask you to consider whether the justices actually use the "should" approaches to reach decisions or whether they use them to camouflage their politics. One reason is that the justices often say they look to the founding period, the words of the Constitution, previously decided cases, and other legalistic approaches to resolve disputes because they consider these to be appropriate criteria for reaching decisions. Another is that some scholars express agreement with the justices, arguing that Court members cannot follow their own personal preferences, the whims of the public, or other non-legally relevant factors "if they are to have the continued respect of their colleagues, the wider [legal] community, citizens, and leaders." Rather, they "must be principled in their decision-making process."[21]

Whether they are principled in their decision making is for you to determine as you read the cases to come. For you to make this determination it is, of course, necessary to develop some familiarity with both legalism and realism. In the next section we turn to realism; here we begin with legalism, which, in constitutional law, centers on the methods of constitutional interpretation that the justices frequently say they employ. We consider some of the most important methods and describe the rationale for their use. These methods include originalism (whether original intent or original meaning), textualism, structural analysis, stare decisis analysis, pragmatism, and polls of other jurisdictions.[22]

---

20. Lee Epstein, William M. Landes, and Richard A. Posner, *The Behavior of Federal Judges: A Theoretical and Empirical Study of Rational Choice* (Cambridge, MA: Harvard University Press, 2013).

21. Ronald Kahn, "Institutional Norms and Supreme Court Decision Making: The Rehnquist Court on Privacy and Religion," in *Supreme Court Decision Making: New Institutionalist Approaches,* ed. Cornell W. Clayton and Howard Gillman (Chicago: University of Chicago Press, 1999), 176.

22. For overviews (and critiques) of these and other approaches, see Eugene Volokh, "Using the Second Amendment as a Teaching

Table 1-1 provides a brief summary of each, using the debate over congressional term limits as an example (in what follows, we supply more details). To understand this debate, you should know that several clauses in Article I of the Constitution contain requirements that all prospective members of Congress must meet: A senator must be at least thirty years old, and a representative must be twenty-five. Every member must be, when elected, an inhabitant of the state she or he is to represent. Finally, representatives must have been citizens of the United States for at least seven years, and senators must have been citizens for nine. In *Powell v. McCormack* (1969) the Court held that Congress could not add further qualifications. All duly elected persons must be seated unless they fail to meet the criteria set out in the qualifications clauses.

But may the states add qualifications? Legal briefs filed in the case, along with commentary about it, employed a range of methods of constitutional interpretation, as table 1-1 shows. Notice that no method seems entirely dispositive; rather, lawyers used those methods that supported their side. Ultimately, in *U.S. Term Limits, Inc. v. Thornton* (1995) *(excerpted in chapter 3)*, the Court held that the U.S. Constitution is the exclusive source of qualifications for members of Congress and the states may not add to the existing criteria (including term limits).

Originalism

Originalism comes in several different forms, and we discuss two below—original intent and original understanding (or meaning)—but the basic idea is that originalists like their Constitution "dead": that is, they attempt to interpret it in line with what it meant at the time of its drafting. One form of originalism emphasizes the intent of the Constitution's framers. The Supreme Court first invoked the term *intention of the framers* in 1796. In *Hylton v. United States* the Court said, "It was . . . obviously the intention of the framers of the Constitution, that Congress should possess full power over every species of taxable property, except exports. The term taxes is generical, and was made use of to vest in Congress plenary authority in all cases of

taxation."[23] In *Hustler Magazine v. Falwell* (1988) the Court used the same grounds to find that cartoon parodies, however obnoxious, constitute expression protected by the First Amendment.

No doubt, justices over the years have looked to the intent of the framers to reach conclusions about the disputes before them.[24] But why? What possible relevance could the framers' intentions have for today's controversies? Advocates of this approach offer several answers. First, they assert that the framers acted in a calculated manner—that is, they knew what they were doing, so why should we disregard their precepts? One adherent said, "Those who framed the Constitution chose their words carefully; they debated at great length the most minute points. The language they chose meant something. It is incumbent upon the Court to determine what that meaning was."[25]

Second, it is argued that if they scrutinize the intent of the framers, justices can deduce "constitutional truths," which they can apply to cases. Doing so, proponents say, produces neutral principles of law and eliminates value-laden decisions.[26] Consider speech advocating the violent overthrow of the government. Suppose the government enacted a law prohibiting such expression and arrested members of a radical political party for violating it. Justices could scrutinize this law in several ways. A liberal might conclude, solely because of his or her liberal values, that the First Amendment prohibits a ban on such expression. Conservative jurists might reach the opposite conclusion. Neither would be proper jurisprudence in the opinion of those who advocate an original intent approach, because both are value laden, and ideological preferences should not creep into the law. Rather, justices should examine the framers' intent as a way to keep the law value-free. Applying this approach to free speech, one adherent argues, leads to a clear, unbiased result:

Tool—Modalities of Constitutional Argument," http://www.law.ucla.edu/volokh/2amteach/interp.htm; Philip Bobbitt, *Constitutional Fate: Theory of the Constitution* (New York: Oxford University Press, 1982); and Lackland H. Bloom, *Methods of Constitutional Interpretation: How the Supreme Court Reads the Constitution* (New York: Oxford University Press, 2009).

23. Example cited by Boris I. Bittker in "The Bicentennial of the Jurisprudence of Original Intent: The Recent Past," *California Law Review* 77 (1989): 235.

24. Given the subject of this volume, we deal here exclusively with the intent of the framers of the U.S. Constitution and its amendments, but one also could apply this approach to statutory construction by considering the intent of those who drafted and enacted the laws in question.

25. Edwin Meese III, address before the American Bar Association, July 9, 1983, Washington, DC.

26. See, for example, Robert Bork, "Neutral Principles and Some First Amendment Problems," *Indiana Law Journal* 47 (1971): 1–35.

TABLE 1-1   Methods of Constitutional Interpretation as Applied to the Issue of State-Imposed Congressional Term Limits

METHOD	EXAMPLE
Originalism 1. **Intent.** Asks what the framers wanted to do.	"The framers would have been shocked by the notion of a state interfering with the ability of the people to choose whom they please to govern them." OR "The framers would have been shocked by the notion of the U.S. Supreme Court interfering with the decision of the people of a state to limit the terms of their representatives and senators."
2. **Original meaning.** Considers what a clause meant to (or how it was understood by) those who enacted it (or at the time of its enactment).	"It would have been more expedient for the framers simply to allow existing state law to define the qualifications for the elected, as they did with the qualifications for voters. But instead by establishing certain qualifications as necessary for office, the framers meant to exclude all others." OR "In the immediate post-ratification period, the qualifications clauses were understood to specify minimum, not exclusive, (dis)qualifications."
Textualism. Places emphasis on what the Constitution says.	"The qualifications clauses establish national, uniform qualifications for federal representatives and senators. Neither provision, on its face, grants either Congress or the states any authority to impose additional qualifications." OR "Nothing in the text of the qualifications clauses excludes states from adopting term limits as a method for rejecting candidates for federal legislative office."
Structural Analysis. Suggests that interpretation of particular clauses should be consistent with or follow from overarching structures or governing principles established in the Constitution—for example, the democratic process, federalism, and the separation of powers.	"That election to the national legislature should be open to all people of merit provides a critical foundation for democracy. Allowing individual states to craft their own qualifications for Congress would erode this structure." OR "Although the Constitution does set forth a few nationwide disqualifications for the office of presidential elector, in line with federalism principles, these disqualifications do not prohibit the states from adding any other eligibility requirements. Instead, Article II leaves the states free to establish qualifications for their delegates to the Electoral College."
Stare Decisis. Looks to what courts have written about the clause.	"In *Powell v. McCormack*, the Court said that qualifications fixed in Article I are exclusive and unalterable." OR "In *Powell*, the Court said that Congress may not alter the qualifications clauses; it did not limit the authority of the states to impose certain requirements. And, in fact, previous rulings suggest that the states enjoy this very power."
Pragmatism. Considers the effects of various interpretations, suggesting that courts should adopt the one that avoids bad consequences.	"Failure to interpret the qualifications clauses as fixed would encourage states to engage in bad practices, such as adding many more ballot requirements (e.g., barring lawyers from the ballot)." OR "Term limits, which could be eliminated if the qualifications clauses are interpreted as fixed, are an effective solution to the growing problem of long-term, entrenched incumbents—professional legislators who make remaining in office their life's work and thus deprive voters of genuine electoral choices."
Polling jurisdictions. Examines practices in the United States and even abroad.	"No state passed term limits provisions in the years following the adoption of the Constitution. Moreover, every Court that has considered the qualifications clauses has concluded that they are fixed." OR "In response to the unprecedented level of incumbent reelection, since 1990 more than 22 million votes have been cast in fifteen states in favor of term limits."

SOURCE: We adopt the framework for this table from Eugene Volokh, "Using the Second Amendment as a Teaching Tool—Modalities of Constitutional Argument," http://www.law.ucla.edu/volokh/2amteach/interp.htm. The details of the arguments come from the briefs and opinions in *U.S. Term Limits v. Thornton*.

Speech advocating violent overthrow is . . . not [protected] "political speech" . . . as that term must be defined by a Madisonian system of government. It is not political speech because it violates constitutional truths about processes and because it is not aimed at a new definition of political truth by a legislative majority.[27]

Finally, supporters of this mode of analysis argue that it fosters stability in law. They maintain that the law today is far too fluid, that it changes with the ideological whims of the justices, creating havoc for those who must interpret and implement Court decisions. Lower court judges, lawyers, and even ordinary citizens do not know if today's rights will still exist tomorrow. Following a jurisprudence of original intent eliminates such confusion because it provides a principle that justices can consistently follow.

The last justification applies with equal force to a second form of originalism: *original meaning or understanding*. Justice Scalia has explained the difference between this approach and intentionalism:

The theory of originalism treats a constitution like a statute, and gives it the meaning that its words were understood to bear at the time they were promulgated. You will sometimes hear it described as the theory of original intent. You will never hear me refer to original intent, because as I say I am first of all a textualist, and secondly an originalist. If you are a textualist, you don't care about the intent, and I don't care if the framers of the Constitution had some secret meaning in mind when they adopted its words. I take the words as they were promulgated to the people of the United States, and what is the fairly understood meaning of those words.[28]

By "textualist," Justice Scalia means that he looks at the words of whatever constitutional provision he is interpreting and interprets them in line with what they would have ordinarily meant to the people of the time in which they were written.[29] This is the "originalist" aspect of his method of interpreting the Constitution. So, while intentionalism focuses on the intent behind phrases, an understanding or meaning approach emphasizes "the

meaning a reasonable speaker of English would have attached to the words, phrases, sentences, etc. at the time the particular provision was adopted."[30]

Even so, as we suggested above, the merits of this approach are similar to those of intentionalism. By focusing on how the framers defined their own words and then applying their definitions to disputes over those constitutional provisions containing them, this approach seeks to generate value-free and ideology-free jurisprudence. Indeed, one of the most important developers of this approach, historian William W. Crosskey, specifically embraced it to counter "sophistries" such as the idea that the Constitution is a living document whose meaning should evolve over time.[31]

Chief Justice Rehnquist's opinion in *Nixon v. United States* (1993) *(excerpted in chapter 2)* provides a particularly good illustration of the value of this approach. Here, the Court considered a challenge to the procedures the Senate used to impeach a federal judge, Walter L. Nixon Jr. Rather than the entire Senate trying the case, a special twelve-member committee heard it and reported to the full body. Nixon argued that this procedure violated Article I of the Constitution, which states, "The Senate shall have the sole Power to try all Impeachments." But before addressing Nixon's claim, Rehnquist sought to determine whether courts had any business resolving such disputes. He used a meaning of the words approach to consider the word *try* in Article I:

Petitioner argues that the word "try" in the first sentence imposes by implication an additional requirement on the Senate in that the proceedings must be in the nature of a judicial trial. . . . There are several difficulties with this position which lead us ultimately to reject it. The word "try," both in 1787 and later, has considerably broader meanings than those to which petitioner would limit it. Older dictionaries define try as "[t]o examine" or "[t]o examine as a judge." See 2 S. Johnson, A Dictionary of the English Language (1785). In more modern usage the term has various meanings. For example, try can mean "to examine or investigate judicially," "to conduct the trial of," or "to put to the test by experiment, investigation. . . ." Webster's Third New International Dictionary (1971).

27. Ibid., 31.

28. Antonin Scalia, "A Theory of Constitutional Interpretation," remarks at the Catholic University of America, October 18, 1996, Washington, DC.

29. See Antonin Scalia, "Originalism: The Lesser Evil," *University of Cincinnati Law Review* 57 (1989): 849–865.

30. Randy E. Barnett, "The Original Meaning of the Commerce Clause," *University of Chicago Law Review* 68 (2001): 105.

31. W. W. Crosskey, *Politics and the Constitution in the History of the United States* (Chicago: University of Chicago Press, 1953), 1172–1173.

Nixon is far from the only example of originalism that you will encounter in the pages to come. Indeed, many Supreme Court opinions contemplate the original intent of the framers or the original meaning of the words, and at least one justice on the current Court—Clarence Thomas—regularly invokes forms of originalism to answer questions ranging from limits on campaign spending to the appropriate balance of power between the states and the federal government.

Such a jurisprudential course would have dismayed Thomas's predecessor, Thurgood Marshall, who did not believe that the Constitution's meaning was "forever 'fixed' at the Philadelphia Convention." And, in light of the 1787 Constitution's treatment of women and blacks, Marshall did not find "the wisdom, foresight, and sense of justice exhibited by the framers particularly profound." [32]

Marshall has not been the only critic of originalism (whatever the form); the approach has generated many other critics over the years. One reason for the controversy is that originalism became highly politicized in the 1980s. Those who advocated it, particularly Edwin Meese, an attorney general in President Ronald Reagan's administration, and defeated Supreme Court nominee Robert Bork, were widely viewed as conservatives who were using the doctrine to promote their own ideological ends.

Others joined Marshall, however, in raising several more-concrete objections to this jurisprudence. Justice Brennan in 1985 argued that if the justices employed only this approach, the Constitution would lose its applicability and be rendered useless:

We current Justices read the Constitution in the only way that we can: as Twentieth Century Americans. We look to the history of the time of the framing and to the intervening history of interpretation. But the ultimate question must be, what do the words of the text mean in our time? For the genius of the Constitution rests not in any static meaning it might have had in a world that is dead and gone, but in the adaptability of its great principles to cope with current problems and current needs. [33]

Some scholars have echoed the sentiment. C. Herman Pritchett noted that originalism can "make a nation the prisoner of its past, and reject any constitutional development save constitutional amendment." [34]

Another criticism often leveled at intentionalism is that the Constitution embodies not one intent, but many. Jeffrey A. Segal and Harold J. Spaeth pose some interesting questions: "Who were the Framers? All fifty-five of the delegates who showed up at one time or another in Philadelphia during the summer of 1787? Some came and went. . . . Some probably had not read [the Constitution]. Assuredly, they were not all of a single mind." [35] Then there is the question of what sources the justices should use to divine the original intentions of the framers. They could look at the records of the constitutional debates and at the founders' journals and papers, but some of the documents that pass for "records" of the Philadelphia convention are jumbled, and some are even forged. During the debates, the secretary became confused and thoroughly botched the minutes. James Madison, who took the most complete and probably the most reliable notes on what was said, edited them after the convention adjourned. Perhaps this is why in 1952 Justice Robert H. Jackson wrote,

Just what our forefathers did envision, or would have envisioned had they foreseen modern conditions, must be divined from materials almost as enigmatic as the dreams Joseph was called upon to interpret for Pharaoh. A century and a half of partisan debate and scholarly specification yields no net result but only supplies more or less apt quotations from respected sources on each side of any question. They largely cancel each other. [36]

Likewise, it may be just as difficult for justices to establish the original meaning of the words as it is for them to establish the original intent behind them. Attempting to understand what the framers meant by each word can be a far more daunting task in the run-of-the-mill case than it was for Rehnquist in *Nixon.*

---

32. Thurgood Marshall, "Reflections on the Bicentennial of the United States Constitution," *Harvard Law Review* 101 (1987): 1.

33. William J. Brennan Jr., address to the Text and Teaching Symposium, Georgetown University, October 12, 1985, Washington, DC.

34. C. Herman Pritchett, *Constitutional Law of the Federal System* (Englewood Cliffs, NJ: Prentice Hall, 1984), 37.

35. Jeffrey A. Segal and Harold J. Spaeth, *The Supreme Court and the Attitudinal Model Revisited* (New York: Cambridge University Press, 2002), 68. See also William Anderson, "The Intention of the Framers: A Note on Constitutional Interpretation," *American Political Science Review* 49 (1955): 340–352.

36. *Youngstown Sheet & Tube Co. v. Sawyer* (1952).

It might even require the development of a specialized dictionary, which could take years of research to compile and still not have any value—determinate or otherwise. Moreover, scholars argue, even if we could create a dictionary that would help shed light on the meanings of particular words, it would tell us little about the significance of such constitutional phrases as "due process of law" and "cruel and unusual punishment."[37] Some say the same of other sources to which the justices could turn, such as the profusion of pamphlets (heavily outnumbering the entire population) that argued for and against ratification of the new Constitution. But this mass of literature demonstrates not one but maybe dozens of understandings of what it all meant. In other words, the documents often fail to provide a single clear message.

Textualism

On the surface, textualism resembles original intent: it values the Constitution itself as a guide above all else. But this is where the similarity ends. In an effort to prevent the infusion of new meanings from sources outside the text of the Constitution, adherents of original intent seek to deduce constitutional truths by examining the *intended* meanings behind the words. Textualists, however, look no farther than the words of the Constitution to reach decisions.

This may seem similar to the original meaning approach we just considered, and there is certainly a commonality between the two approaches: both place emphasis on the words of the Constitution. But under the original meaning approach (Scalia's brand of textualism), it is fair game for justices to go beyond the literal meaning of the words and consider what they would have ordinarily meant to the people of that time. Other textualists, those we might call pure textualists or *literalists,* believe that justices ought to consider only the words in the constitutional text, and the words alone.

And it is these distinctions—between original intent and even meaning versus pure textualism—that can lead to some radically different results. To use the example of speech aimed at overthrowing the U.S. government, originalists might hold that the meaning or intent behind the First Amendment prohibits such expression. Those who consider themselves literalists, on the other hand, would scrutinize the words of the First Amendment—"Congress shall make no law . . . abridging the freedom of speech"—and construe them literally: *no law* means *no law.* Therefore, any statute infringing on speech, even a law that prohibits expression advocating the overthrow of the government, would violate the First Amendment.

Originalism and pure textualism sometimes overlap. When it comes to the right to privacy, particularly where it is leveraged to create other rights, such as legalized abortion, *some* originalists and literalists would reach the same conclusion: it does not exist. The former would argue that it was not the intent of the framers to confer privacy; the latter, that because the Constitution does not expressly mention this right, it does not exist.

Textual analysis is quite common in Supreme Court opinions. Many, if not most, look to the Constitution and ask what it says about the matter at hand, though Hugo Black is most closely associated with this view— at least in its pure form. During his thirty-four-year tenure on the Court, Justice Black continually emphasized his literalist philosophy. His own words best describe his position:

My view is, without deviation, without exception, without any ifs, buts, or whereases, that freedom of speech means that government shall not do anything to people . . . either for the views they have or the views they express or the words they speak or write. Some people would have you believe that this is a very radical position, and maybe it is. But all I am doing is following what to me is the clear wording of the First Amendment. . . . As I have said innumerable times before I simply believe that "Congress shall make no law" means Congress shall make no law. . . . Thus we have the absolute command of the First Amendment that no law shall be passed by Congress abridging freedom of speech or the press.[38]

---

37. Crosskey did, in fact, develop "a specialized dictionary of the eighteenth-century word-usages, and political and legal ideas." He believed that such a work was "needed for a true understanding of the Constitution." But some scholars have been skeptical of the understandings to which it led him, as many were highly "unorthodox." Bittker, "The Bicentennial of the Jurisprudence of Original Intent," 237–238. Some applauded Crosskey's conclusions. Charles E. Clark, for example, in "Professor Crosskey and the Brooding Omnipresence of Erie-Tompkins," *University of Chicago Law Review* 21 (1953): 24, called it "a major scholastic effort of our times." Others were appalled. See Julius Goebel Jr., "Ex Parte Clio," *Columbia Law Review* 54 (1954): 450. Goebel wrote, "[M]easured by even the least exacting of scholarly standards, [the work] is in the reviewer's opinion without merit."

---

38. Hugo L. Black, *A Constitutional Faith* (New York: Knopf, 1969), 45–46.

Why did Black advocate literalism? Like originalists, he viewed it as a value-free form of jurisprudence. If justices looked only at the words of the Constitution, their decisions would not reflect ideological or political values, but rather those of the document. Black's opinions provide good illustrations. Although he almost always supported claims of free *speech* against government challenges, he refused to extend constitutional protection to *expression* that was not strictly speech. He believed that activities such as flag burning and the wearing of armbands, even if calculated to express political views, fell outside the protections of the First Amendment.

Moreover, literalists maintain that their approach is superior to the doctrine of original intent. They say that some provisions of the Constitution are so transparent that were the government to violate them, justices could "almost instantaneously and without analysis identify the violation"; they would not need to undertake an extensive search to uncover the framers' understanding.[39] Often-cited examples include the "mathematical" provisions of the Constitution, such as the commands that the president's term be four years and that the president be at least thirty-five years old.

Despite the seeming logic of these justifications and the high regard many scholars have for Black, many have actively attacked his brand of jurisprudence. Some assert that it led him to take some rather odd positions, particularly in cases involving the First Amendment. Most analysts and justices—even those considered liberal—agree that obscene materials fall outside First Amendment protection and that states can prohibit the dissemination of such materials. But, in opinion after opinion, Black clung to the view that no publication could be banned on the grounds that it was obscene.

A second objection is that literalism can result in inconsistent outcomes. Was it really sensible for Black to hold that obscenity is constitutionally protected while other types of expression, such as the desecration of the flag, are not?

Segal and Spaeth raise yet a third problem with literalism: it presupposes a precision in the English language that does not exist. Not only may words, including those used by the framers, have multiple meanings, but also the meanings themselves may be contrary. As Segal and Spaeth note, the common legal word *sanction* means both to punish *and* to approve.[40] How, then, would a literalist construe it?

Finally, even when the words are crystal clear, pure textualism may not be on firm ground. Despite the precision of the mathematical provisions, law professor Frank Easterbrook has suggested that they, like all the others, are loaded with "reasons, goals, values, and the like."[41] The framers might have imposed the presidential age limit "as a percentage of average life expectancy," to ensure that presidents have a good deal of practical political experience before ascending to the presidency and little opportunity to engage in politicking after they leave, or "as a minimum number of years after puberty," to guarantee that they are sufficiently mature while not unduly limiting the pool of eligible candidates. Seen in this way, the words "thirty five years" in the Constitution may not have much value: they may be "simply the framers' shorthand for their more complex policies, and we could replace them by 'fifty years' or 'thirty years' without impairing the integrity of the constitutional structure."[42] More generally, as Justice Oliver Wendell Holmes Jr. once put it, "A word is not a crystal, transparent and unchanged, it is the skin of a living thought and may vary greatly in color and content according to the circumstances and the time in which it is used."[43]

Structural Reasoning

Textualist and originalist approaches tend to focus on particular words or clauses in the Constitution. Structural reasoning suggests that interpretation of these clauses should follow from, or at the least be consistent with, overarching structures or governing principles established in the Constitution—most notably, federalism and the separation of powers. Interestingly enough, these terms do not appear in the Constitution, but they "are familiar to any student of constitutional law"[44]— and will become second nature to you too as you work

---

39. We draw this material and the related discussion to follow from Mark V. Tushnet, "A Note on the Revival of Textualism," *Southern California Law Review* 58 (1985): 683.

40. Segal and Spaeth, *The Supreme Court and the Attitudinal Model Revisited,* 54.

41. Frank Easterbrook, "Statutes' Domains," *University of Chicago Law Review* 50 (1983): 536.

42. Tushnet, "A Note on the Revival of Textualism," 686.

43. *Towne v. Eisner* (1918).

44. Michael J. Gerhardt, Stephen M. Griffin, and Thomas D. Rowe Jr., *Constitutional Theory: Arguments and Perspectives,* 3rd ed. (Newark, NJ: LexisNexis, 2007), 321.

your way through the material in the pages to follow. The idea behind structuralism is that these structures or relationships are so important that judges and lawyers should read the Constitution to preserve them.

There are many famous examples of structural analyses, especially, as you would expect, in separation of powers and federalism cases. Charles Black, a leading proponent of structuralism, for example, points to *McCulloch v. Maryland* (1819) *(excerpted in chapters 3 and 6)*. Among the questions the Court addressed was whether a state could tax a federal entity—the Bank of the United States. Even though states have the power to tax, Chief Justice Marshall for the Court said the answer is "no," because the states could use this power to extinguish the bank. If states could do this, they would damage what Marshall believed to be "the warranted relational properties between the national government and the government of the states, with the structural corollaries of national supremacy."[45]

Here, Marshall invalidated a state action aimed at the federal government. Throughout this book, you will see the reverse: opinions that use structural arguments about the relationship between state power and federal power to invalidate federal action on the ground that it impinges on state functions. *National League of Cities v. Usery* (1976) and *Printz v. United States* (1997) *(excerpted in chapter 6)* are but two examples.

Despite their frequent appearance in federalism and separation of powers cases, structural arguments have their weaknesses. Primarily, as Philip Bobbitt notes, "while we all can agree on the presence of the various structures, we [bicker] when called upon to decide whether a particular result is necessarily inferred from their relationship."[46] What this means is that structural reasoning does not necessarily lead to a single answer in every case. *Immigration and Naturalization Service v. Chadha* (1983), involving the constitutionality of the legislative veto (used by Congress to veto decisions made by the executive branch), provides an example. Writing for the majority, Chief Justice Burger held that such a veto violated the constitutional doctrine of separation of powers; it eroded the "carefully defined limits of the power of each Branch" established by the framers. Writing in dissent, Justice White, too, relied in part on structural analysis, but he came to a very different

conclusion: the legislative veto fit compatibly with the separation of powers system because it ensured that Congress could continue to play "its role as the Nation's lawmaker" in the wake of the growth in the size of the executive branch.

The gap between Burger and White reflects, as we shall see, disagreement over the very nature of the separation of powers system, and similar disagreements arise over federalism. Hence, even when justices reason from structure, it is possible, even likely, that they will reach different conclusions.

Stare Decisis

Translated from Latin, the term *stare decisis* means "let the decision stand." What this concept suggests is that, as a general rule, jurists should decide cases on the basis of previously established rulings, or precedent. In shorthand terms, judicial tribunals should honor prior rulings.

The benefits of this approach are fairly evident. If justices rely on past cases to resolve current cases, some scholars argue, the law they generate becomes predictable and stable. Chief Justice Harlan F. Stone acknowledged the value of precedent in a somewhat more ironic way: "The rule of stare decisis embodies a wise policy because it is often more important that a rule of law be settled than that it be settled right."[47] The message, however, is the same: if the Court adheres to past decisions, it provides some direction to all who labor in the legal enterprise. Lower court judges know how they should and should not decide cases, lawyers can frame their arguments in accord with the lessons of past cases, legislators understand what they can and cannot enact or regulate, and so forth.

Precedent, then, can be an important and useful factor in Supreme Court decision making. Along these lines, it is interesting to note that the Court rarely reverses itself—it has done so fewer than three hundred times over its entire history. Even modern-day Courts, as table 1-2 shows, have been loath to overrule precedents. In the seven decades covered in the table, the Court has overturned only 159 precedents, or, on average, 2.7 per term. What is more, the justices almost always cite previous rulings in their decisions; indeed, it is the rare Court opinion that does not mention other cases.[48] Finally, several scholars have verified

45. Charles L. Black Jr., *Structure and Relationship in Constitutional Law* (Baton Rouge: Louisiana State University Press, 1969), 15.

46. Bobbitt, *Constitutional Fate*, 84.

47. *United States v. Underwriters Association* (1944).

48. See Jack Knight and Lee Epstein, "The Norm of Stare Decisis," *American Journal of Political Science* 40 (1996): 1018–1035.

that precedent helps to explain Court decisions in some areas of the law. In one study, analysts found that the Court reacted quite consistently to legal doctrine presented in more than fifteen years of death penalty litigation. Put differently, using precedent from past cases, the researchers could correctly categorize the outcomes (for or against the death penalty) in 75 percent of sixty-four cases decided since 1972.[49] Scholarly work considering precedent in search-and-seizure litigation has produced similar findings.[50]

Despite these data, we should not conclude that the justices necessarily follow this approach. Many allege that judicial appeal to precedent often is mere window dressing, used to hide ideologies and values, rather than a substantive form of analysis. There are several reasons for this allegation.

First, the Supreme Court has generated so much precedent that it is usually possible for justices to find support for any conclusion. By way of proof, turn to almost any opinion excerpted in this book and you probably will find the writers—both those for the majority and the dissenters—citing precedent.

Second, it may be difficult to locate the rule of law emerging in a majority opinion. To decide whether a previous decision qualifies as a precedent, judges and commentators often say, one must strip away the non-essentials of the case and expose the basic reasons for the Supreme Court's decision. This process is generally referred to as "establishing the principle of the case," or the ratio decidendi. Other points made in a given opinion—obiter dicta (any expression in an opinion that is unnecessary to the decision reached in the case or that relates to a factual situation other than the one actually before the court)—have no legal weight, and judges are not bound by them. It is up to courts to separate the ratio decidendi from dicta. Not only is this task difficult, but it also provides a way for justices to skirt precedent with which they do not agree. All they need to do is declare parts of it to be dicta. Or justices can brush aside even the ratio decidendi when it suits their interests. Because the Supreme Court, at least today, is so selective about the cases it decides, it probably would not take a case for which clear precedent

existed. Even in the past, two cases that were precisely identical probably would not be accepted. What this means is that justices can always deal with "problematic" ratio decidendi by distinguishing the case at hand from those that have already been decided.

A scholarly study of the role of precedent in Supreme Court decision making offers a third reason. Two political scientists hypothesized that if precedent matters, it ought to affect the subsequent decisions of members of the Court. If a justice dissented from a decision establishing a particular precedent, the same justice would not dissent from a subsequent application of the precedent. But that was not the case. Of the eighteen justices included in the study, only two occasionally subjugated their preferences to precedent.[51]

Finally, and most interesting, many justices recognize the limits of stare decisis in cases involving constitutional interpretation. Indeed, the justices often say that when constitutional issues are involved, stare decisis is a less rigid rule than it might normally be. This view strikes some as prudent, for the Constitution is difficult to amend, and judges make mistakes or they come to see problems quite differently as their perspectives change. As Justice Brandeis famously wrote,

Stare decisis is usually the wise policy. . . . But in cases involving the Federal Constitution, where correction through legislative action is practically impossible, this Court has often overruled its earlier decisions.[52]

Pragmatism

Whatever the role of precedent in constitutional interpretation, it is clear that the Court does not always feel bound to follow its own precedent. Perhaps a ruling was in error. Or perhaps circumstances have changed and the justices wish to announce a rule consistent with the new circumstances, even if it is inconsistent with the old rule. The justices might even consider the consequences of overturning a precedent or more generally of interpreting a precedent in a particular way. This approach is known as *pragmatic analysis,* and it

---

49. Tracey E. George and Lee Epstein, "On the Nature of Supreme Court Decision Making," *American Political Science Review* 86 (1992): 323–337.

50. Jeffrey A. Segal, "Predicting Supreme Court Cases Probabilistically: The Search and Seizure Cases, 1962–1984," *American Political Science Review* 78 (1984): 891–900.

51. Jeffrey A. Segal and Harold J. Spaeth, "The Influence of Stare Decisis on the Votes of U.S. Supreme Court Justices," *American Journal of Political Science* 40 (1996): 971–1003.

52. Justice Brandeis, dissenting in *Burnet v. Coronado Oil & Gas Co.* 285 U.S. 393 (1932). Whether the Justices actually follow this idea—that stare decisis policy is more flexible in constitutional cases—is a matter of debate. See Lee Epstein, William M. Landes, and Adam Liptak, "Departing from Precedent," *NYU Law Review* (2016).

TABLE 1-2 Precedents Overruled, 1953–2014 Terms

COURT ERA (TERMS)	NUMBER OF TERMS	NUMBER OF OVERRULED PRECEDENTS	AVERAGE NUMBER OF OVERRULINGS PER TERM
Warren Court (1953–1968)	16	43	2.7
Burger Court (1969–1985)	17	47	2.8
Rehnquist Court (1986–2004)	16	51	3.2
Roberts Court (2005–2014)	10	18	1.8

SOURCE: Calculated by the authors from data in the Supreme Court Database (http://supremecourtdatabase.org).

entails appraising alternative rulings by forecasting their consequences. Presumably, justices who engage in this form of analysis will select among plausible constitutional interpretations the one that has the best consequences and reject those that have the worst.

Pragmatism makes an appearance in many Supreme Court opinions, occasionally in the form of an explicit cost-benefit analysis in which the justices attempt to create rules, or analyze existing rules, so that they maximize benefits and minimize costs. Consider the exclusionary rule, which excludes from criminal proceedings evidence obtained in violation of the Fourth Amendment: Claims that the rule hampers the conviction of criminals have affected judicial attitudes, as Justice White frankly admitted in *United States v. Leon* (1984): "The substantial social costs exacted by the exclusionary rule for the vindication of Fourth Amendment rights have long been a source of concern." In *Leon* a majority of the justices applied a "cost-benefit" calculus to justify a "good faith" seizure by police on an invalid search warrant.

When you encounter cases that engage in this sort of analysis, you might ask the same questions raised by some critics of the approach: By what account of values should judges weigh costs and benefits? How do they take into account the different people whom a decision may simultaneously punish and reward?

Polls of Other Jurisdictions

Aside from turning to originalism, textualism, or other historical approaches, a justice might probe English traditions or early colonial or state practices to determine how public officials of the times—or of contemporary times—interpreted similar words or phrases.[53] The Supreme Court has frequently used such evidence.

When *Wolf v. Colorado* (1949) asked the Court whether the Fourth Amendment barred use in state courts of evidence obtained through an unconstitutional search, Justice Felix Frankfurter surveyed the law in all the states and in ten jurisdictions within the British Commonwealth. He used the information to bolster a conclusion that although the Constitution forbade unreasonable searches and seizures, it did not prohibit state officials from using such questionably obtained evidence against a defendant.

In 1952, however, *Rochin v. California* confronted the justices with the question of whether a state could use evidence it had obtained from a defendant by pumping his stomach—evidence admissible in the overwhelming majority of states. This time Frankfurter declined to call the roll. Instead, he declared that gathering evidence by a stomach pump was "conduct that shocks the conscience" whose fruits could not be used in either state or federal courts. When in 1961 *Mapp v. Ohio* overruled *Wolf* and held that state courts must exclude *all* unconstitutionally obtained evidence, the justices again surveyed the field. For the Court, Justice Tom C. Clark said, "While in 1949 almost two-thirds of the States were opposed to the exclusionary rule, now, despite the *Wolf* Case, more than half of those since passing upon it, by their own legislative or judicial decision, have wholly or partly adopted or adhered to the [rule]."

The point of these examples is not that Frankfurter or the Court was inconsistent, but rather that the method itself—although it offers insights—is far from foolproof. First, the Constitution of 1787, as it initially stood and has since been amended, rejects many English and some colonial and state practices. Second, even a steady stream of precedents from the states may signify nothing more than the fact that judges, too busy to give the issue much thought, imitated each other under the rubric of stare decisis.

---

53. We adopt the material in this section from Walter F. Murphy, C. Herman Pritchett, Lee Epstein, and Jack Knight, *Courts, Judges, and Politics,* 6th ed. (New York: McGraw-Hill, 2006).

Third, if justices are searching for original intent or understanding, it is difficult to imagine the relevance of what was in the minds of people in the eighteenth century to state practices in the twentieth and twenty-first centuries. Polls are useful if we want to know what other judges, now and in the recent past, have thought about the Constitution, writ large or small. Nevertheless, they say nothing about the correctness of those thoughts—and the correctness of a lower court's interpretation may be precisely the issue before the Supreme Court.

Despite these criticisms, the Supreme Court continues to take into account the practices of other U.S. jurisdictions, just as courts in other societies occasionally look to their counterparts elsewhere—including the U.S. Supreme Court—for guidance. The South African ruling in *The State v. Makwanyane* (1995) provides a vivid example: To determine whether the death penalty violated its nation's constitution, South Africa's Constitutional Court surveyed practices elsewhere, including those in the United States. At the end of the day, the justices decided not to follow the path taken by the U.S. Supreme Court, ruling instead that their constitution prohibited the state from imposing capital punishment. Rejection of U.S. practice was made all the more interesting in light of a speech delivered by Justice Harry Blackmun only a year before *Makwanyane*.[54] In that address, Blackmun chastised his colleagues for failing to take into account a decision of South Africa's court to dismiss a prosecution against a person kidnapped from a neighboring country. This ruling, Blackmun argued, was far more faithful to international conventions than the one the U.S. Supreme Court had reached in *United States v. Alvarez-Machain* (1992), which permitted U.S. agents to abduct a Mexican national.

Alvarez-Machain aside, the tendency seems to be growing for American justices to consider the rulings of courts abroad and practices elsewhere as they interpret the U.S. Constitution. This trend is particularly evident in opinions regarding capital punishment; justices opposed to this form of retribution often point to the nearly one hundred countries that have abolished the death penalty.

Whether this practice will become more widespread or filter into other legal areas is an intriguing question, and one likely to cause debate among the justices. Although some support efforts to expand their horizons beyond U.S. borders, others apparently agree with Justice Scalia, who has argued that "the views of other nations, however enlightened the Justices of this court may think them to be, cannot be imposed upon Americans through the Constitution."[55]

SUPREME COURT DECISION MAKING: REALISM

So far in our discussion we have not mentioned the justices' ideologies, their political party affiliations, or their personal views on various public policy issues. The reason is that legal approaches to Supreme Court decision making do not admit that these factors affect the way the Court arrives at its decisions. Instead, they suggest that justices divorce themselves from their personal and political biases and settle disputes based on the law. The approaches we consider below—recall, what some call more realistic or nonlegalistic approaches—posit a quite different vision of Supreme Court decision making. They argue that some of the forces that drive the justices are anything but legal in composition, and that it is unrealistic to expect justices to shed all their preferences and values or to ignore public opinion when they put on their black robes. Indeed, the justices are people like all of us, with strong and pervasive political biases and partisan attachments.

Because justices usually do not admit that they are swayed by the public or that they vote according to their ideologies, our discussion of realism is distinct from that of legalism. Here you will find little in the way of supporting statements from Court members, for it is an unusual justice indeed who admits to following anything but precedent, the intent of the framers, the words of the Constitution, and the like in deciding cases. Instead, we offer the results of decades of research by scholars who think that political and other extralegal factors shape judicial decisions. We organize these nonlegalistic explanations into three categories: (1) preference-based approaches, (2) strategic approaches, and (3) external forces. As you read the cases to come, you will have many opportunities to consider whether these scholarly accounts are persuasive.

---

54. "Justice Blackmun Addresses the ASIL Annual Dinner," American Society of International Law Newsletter, March 1994.

55. *Thompson v. Oklahoma* (1987); see also Scalia's dissent in *Atkins v. Virginia* (2002).

FIGURE 1-4   Percentage of Cases in Which Each Chief Justice Voted in the Liberal Direction, 1953–2014 Terms

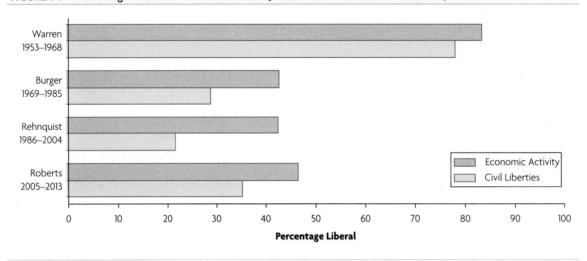

SOURCE: Calculated by the authors from data in the U.S. Supreme Court Database (http://supremecourtdatabase.org).

Preference-Based Approaches

Preference-based approaches see the justices as rational decision makers who hold certain values they would like to see reflected in the outcomes of Court cases. Two prevalent preference-based approaches stress the importance of judicial attitudes and roles.

Judicial Attitudes. Attitudinal approaches emphasize the importance of the justices' political ideologies. Typically, scholars examining the ideologies of the justices discuss the degree to which a justice is conservative or liberal—as in "Justice X holds conservative views on issues of criminal law" or "Justice Y holds liberal views on free speech." This school of thought maintains that when a case comes before the Court each justice evaluates the facts of the dispute and arrives at a decision consistent with his or her personal ideology.

C. Herman Pritchett was one of the first scholars to conduct a systematic study of the importance of the justices' personal attitudes.[56] Examining the Court during the 1930s and 1940s, Pritchett observed that dissent had become an institutionalized feature of judicial decisions. During the early 1900s, in no more than

20 percent of the cases did one or more justices file dissenting opinions; by the 1940s that figure was more than 60 percent. If precedent and other legal factors were the only factors driving Court rulings, why did various justices interpreting the same legal provisions consistently reach different results? Pritchett concluded that the justices were not following precedent but instead were "motivated by their own preferences."[57]

Pritchett's findings touched off an explosion of research on the influence of attitudes on Supreme Court decision making.[58] Much of this scholarship describes the liberal or conservative leanings of the various justices and attempts to predict their voting behavior based on their attitudinal preferences. To understand some of these differences, consider figure 1-4, which presents the voting records of the present chief justice, John G. Roberts Jr., and his three immediate predecessors: Earl Warren, Warren Burger, and William Rehnquist. The figure shows the percentage of times each voted in the liberal direction in two different issue areas: civil liberties and economic liberties.

56. C. Herman Pritchett, *The Roosevelt Court* (New York: Macmillan, 1948); and Pritchett, "Divisions of Opinion among Justices of the U.S. Supreme Court, 1939–1941," *American Political Science Review* 35 (1941): 890–898.

57. Pritchett, *The Roosevelt Court,* xiii.

58. The classic works in this area are Pritchett, *The Roosevelt Court*; Glendon Schubert, *The Judicial Mind* (Evanston, IL: Northwestern University Press, 1965); and David W. Rohde and Harold J. Spaeth, *Supreme Court Decision Making* (San Francisco: W. H. Freeman, 1976). For a lucid, modern-day treatment, see Segal and Spaeth, *The Supreme Court and the Attitudinal Model Revisited,* chaps. 3 and 8.

The data show dramatic differences among these chiefs, especially in cases involving civil liberties. Cases in this category include disputes over issues such as the First Amendment freedoms of religion, speech, and the press; the right to privacy; the rights of the criminally accused; and illegal discrimination. The liberal position is a vote in favor of the individual who is claiming a denial of these basic rights. Warren supports the liberal side in more than 80 percent of cases; Burger, Rehnquist, and Roberts do so in about one-third (or fewer) of such cases.

Economics cases involve challenges to the government's authority to regulate the economy. The liberal position supports an active role by the government in controlling business and economic activity. Here too the four chief justices show different ideological positions. Warren is the most liberal of the three, ruling in favor of government regulatory activity in better than 80 percent of the cases, while Burger, Rehnquist, and Roberts supported such government activity in fewer than half. In short, within particular issue areas, individual justices tend to show consistent ideological predispositions.

Moreover, we often hear that a particular Court is ideologically predisposed toward one side or the other. In a May 29, 2002, opinion piece, the *New York Times* said, "Chief Justice William Rehnquist and his fellow conservatives have made no secret of their desire to alter the balance of federalism, shifting power from Washington to the states." Three years later, on September 5, 2005, the *Times* headlined the chief justice's obituary "William H. Rehnquist, Architect of Conservative Court, Dies at 80." After President George W. Bush appointed Roberts to replace Rehnquist and a new associate justice, Samuel Alito, the press was quick to label both "reliable members of the conservative bloc." And now Sonia Sotomayor and Elena Kagan, President Obama's appointees, are often deemed "liberal." Sometimes an entire Court era is described in terms of its political preferences, such as the "liberal" Warren Court or the "conservative" Roberts Court. The data in figure 1-5 confirm that these labels have some basis in fact. Looking at the two lines from left to right, from the 1950s through the early 2000s, note the mostly downward trend, indicating the increased conservatism of the Court in economics and civil liberties cases. Note, though, the uptick in liberal civil liberties decisions during the 2014 term of the Roberts Court era. Whether this is a blip or trend remains to be seen. If it is the latter, the current Court would not be as conservative as many commentators have previously suggested.

Which raises the question: How valuable are the ideological terms used to describe particular justices or Courts in helping us understand judicial decision making? On one hand, knowledge of justices' ideologies can

FIGURE 1-5 Court Decisions on Economics and Civil Liberties, 1953–2014 Terms

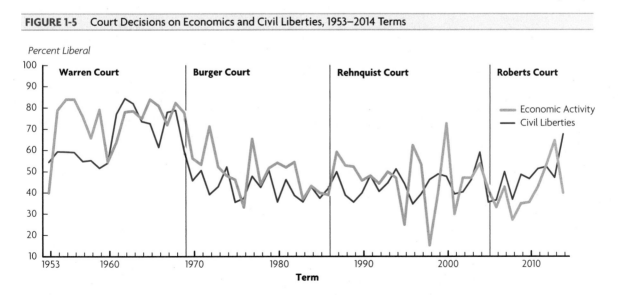

SOURCE: Calculated by the authors from data in the U.S. Supreme Court Database (http://supremecourtdatabase.org).

lead to fairly accurate predictions about their voting behavior. Suppose that the Roberts Court handed down a decision dealing with the death penalty and that the vote was 5–4 in favor of the criminal defendant. The most conservative members of that Court on death penalty cases are Chief Justice Roberts and Justices Antonin Scalia, Clarence Thomas, and Samuel Alito: they almost always vote against the defendant in death penalty cases. If we predicted that Roberts, Scalia, Thomas, and Alito cast the dissenting votes in our hypothetical death penalty case, we would almost certainly be right.[59]

On the other hand, preference-based approaches are not foolproof. First, how do we know if a particular justice is liberal or conservative? The answer typically is that we know a justice is liberal or conservative because he or she casts liberal or conservative votes. Scalia favors conservative positions on the Court because he is a conservative, and we know he is a conservative because he favors conservative positions in the cases he decides. This is circular reasoning indeed. Second, knowing that a justice is liberal or conservative or that the Court decided a case in a liberal or conservative way does not tell us much about the Court's (or the country's) policy positions. To say that *Roe v. Wade* (1973) is a liberal decision is to say little about the policies governing abortion in the United States. If it did, this book would be nothing more than a list of cases labeled liberal or conservative. But such labels would give us no sense of more than two hundred years of constitutional interpretation.

Finally, we must understand that ideological labels are occasionally time dependent, that they are bound to particular historical eras. In *Muller v. Oregon* (1908) the Supreme Court upheld a state law that set a maximum number on the hours women (but not men) could work. How would you, as a student in the twenty-first century, view such an opinion? You probably would classify it as conservative because it did not treat the sexes equally. But when it was decided most observers considered *Muller* a liberal ruling because it allowed the government to regulate business.

A related problem is that some decisions do not fall neatly into a single conservative–liberal dimension. In *Wisconsin v. Mitchell* (1993) the Court upheld a state law that increased the sentence for crimes if the defendant "intentionally selects the person against whom the crime is committed" on the basis of race, religion, national origin, sexual orientation, and other similar criteria. Is this ruling liberal or conservative? If you view the law as penalizing racial or ethnic hatred, you would likely see it as a liberal decision. If, however, you see the law as treating criminal defendants more harshly, the ruling is conservative.

Judicial Role. Another concept within the preference-based category is the judicial role, which scholars have defined as norms that constrain the behavior of jurists.[60] Some students of the Court argue that each justice has a view of his or her role, a view that is based far less on political ideology and far more on fundamental beliefs of what a good judge should do or what the proper role of the Court should be. Some scholars claim that jurists vote in accordance with these role conceptions.

Analysts typically discuss judicial roles in terms of activism and restraint. An activist justice believes that the proper role of the Court is to assert independent positions in deciding cases, to review the actions of the other branches vigorously, to be willing to strike down acts the justice believes are unconstitutional, and to impose far-reaching remedies for legal wrongs whenever necessary. Restraint-oriented justices take the opposite position. They believe that the Court should not become involved in the operations of the other branches unless absolutely necessary, that the benefit of the doubt should be given to actions taken by elected officials, and that the Court should impose remedies that are narrowly tailored to correct specific legal wrongs.

Based on these definitions, we might expect to find activist justices more willing than their opposites to strike down legislation. Therefore, a natural question to ask is this: To what extent have specific jurists practiced judicial activism or restraint? The data in table 1-3 address this question by reporting the votes of justices serving on the Court from the 1994 term through the 2014 term (and who are still on the Court) in cases in which the majority declared federal, state, or local legislation unconstitutional. Note the wide variation among the justices, even for the five who sat together and heard the same cases (Kennedy, Thomas, Scalia, Breyer, and Ginsburg). Of particular interest is that

59. We adopt this example from Jeffrey A. Segal and Harold J. Spaeth, *The Supreme Court and the Attitudinal Model* (New York: Cambridge University Press, 1993), 223.

60. See James L. Gibson, "Judges' Role Orientations, Attitudes, and Decisions," *American Political Science Review* 72 (1978): 911–924.

TABLE 1-3   Percentage of Votes to Declare Legislation Unconstitutional, 1994–2014 Terms

JUSTICE	FEDERAL LAWS	STATE AND LOCAL LAWS
Kennedy	92.2%	85.9%
Roberts	82.4	66.7
Thomas	76.5	58.6
Scalia	68.6	59.2
Alito	58.8	56.5
Sotomayor	57.1	71.4
Breyer	54.9	76.1
Ginsburg	52.9	71.8

SOURCE: Calculated by the authors from data in the Supreme Court Database (http://supremecourtdatabase.org).

NOTE: The figures shown indicate the percentage of cases in which each justice voted with the majority to declare legislation unconstitutional. The number of cases is 51 for federal laws and 71 for state and local laws. Some justices may not have participated in all cases. We do not show Elena Kagan because the numbers are too small to compute meaningful percentages. Roberts and Alito joined the Court in the 2005 term and Sotomayor in 2009.

some of the Court's conservative members—Kennedy, Scalia, and Thomas—were more likely to vote with the majority to strike down federal laws than were those on the left (Breyer and Ginsburg).

These patterns are suggestive: judicial activism and restraint do not necessarily equal judicial liberalism and conservatism. An activist judge need not be liberal, and a judge who practices restraint need not be conservative. It is also true that so-called liberal Courts are no more likely to strike down legislation than are so-called conservative Courts. During the liberal Warren Court, the Court invalidated 127 laws—or about 7.9 per term. During the more conservative Rehnquist years, the Court struck 119 laws—or about 7.4 per term. Because this difference is very small, it may call into question a strong relationship between ideology and judicial role.

Although scholars have used measures such as the number of laws struck down to assess the extent to which justices practice judicial activism or restraint, a question arises: To what extent does this information help us understand Supreme Court decision making? This question is difficult to answer because few scholars have studied the relationship between judicial roles and voting in a systematic way.

The paucity of scholarly work on judicial roles leads to a criticism of the approach: it is virtually impossible to separate roles from attitudes. When Scalia votes to uphold a law restricting access to abortions, can we conclude that he was practicing restraint? The answer, quite clearly, is no. It may be his attitude toward abortion—not restraint—that guides him to the law. Another criticism of role approaches is similar to that leveled at attitudinal factors—they tell us very little about the resulting policy in a case. Again, to say that *Roe v. Wade* was an activist decision because it struck down abortion laws nationwide is to say nothing about the policy content of the opinion.

Strategic Approaches

Strategic accounts of judicial decisions rest on a few simple propositions: justices may be primarily seekers of legal policy (as the attitudinal adherents claim) or they may be motivated by jurisprudential principles (as approaches grounded in law suggest), but they are not unconstrained actors who make decisions based solely on their own ideological attitudes or jurisprudential desires. Rather, justices are strategic actors who realize that their ability to achieve their goals—whatever those goals might be—depends on a consideration of the preferences of other relevant actors (such as their colleagues and members of other political institutions), the choices they expect others to make, and the institutional context in which they act. Scholars term this approach "strategic" because the ideas it contains are derived from the rational choice paradigm, on which strategic analysis is based and as it has been advanced by economists and political scientists working in other fields. Accordingly, we can restate the strategic argument in this way: we can best explain the choices of justices as strategic behavior and not merely as responses to ideological or jurisprudential values.[61]

Such arguments about Supreme Court decision making seem to be sensible because a justice can do very little alone. It takes a majority vote to decide a case and a majority agreeing on a single opinion to set precedent. Under such conditions, human interaction is important, and case outcomes—not to mention the rationale of decisions—can be influenced by the nature of relations among the members of the group.

Although scholars have not considered strategic approaches to the same degree that they have studied judicial attitudes, a number of influential works point

---

61. For more details on this approach, see Lee Epstein and Jack Knight, *The Choices Justices Make* (Washington, DC: CQ Press, 1998).

to their importance. Research begun in the 1960s and continuing today into the private papers of former justices consistently has shown that through intellectual persuasion, effective bargaining over opinion writing, informal lobbying, and so forth, justices have influenced the actions of their colleagues.[62]

How does strategic behavior manifest itself? One way is in the frequency of vote changes. During the deliberations that take place after oral arguments, the justices discuss the case and vote on it. These votes do not become final until the opinions are completed and the decision is made public *(see figure 1-1)*. Research has shown that between the initial vote on the merits of a case and the official announcement of the decision at least one vote switch occurs more than 50 percent of the time.[63]

A very recent example, as we already noted, is Chief Justice Roberts's change of heart over the constitutionality of the health-care law. Because of his vote switch, the Court ended up upholding key parts of the law by a vote of 5–4 rather than striking them by a vote of 5–4. This episode, along with the figure of 50 percent, indicates that justices change their minds—perhaps reevaluating their initial positions or succumbing to the persuasion of their colleagues—which seems inexplicable if we believe that justices are simply liberals or conservatives and always vote their preferences.

Vote shifts are just one manifestation of the interdependence of the Court's decision-making process. Another is the revision of opinions that occurs in almost every Court case.[64] As opinion writers try to accommodate their colleagues' wishes, their drafts may undergo five, ten, even fifteen revisions. Bargaining over the content of an opinion is important because it can significantly alter the policy ultimately expressed. A clear example is ***Griswold v. Connecticut*** (1965), in which the Court considered the constitutionality of a state law that prohibited the dissemination of birth control devices and information, even to married couples. In his initial draft of the majority opinion, Justice William O. Douglas struck down the law on the ground that it interfered with the First Amendment's right of association. A memorandum from Brennan convinced Douglas to alter his rationale and to establish the foundation for a right to privacy. "Had the Douglas draft been issued as the *Griswold* opinion of the Court, the case would stand as a precedent on the freedom of association" rather than serve as the landmark ruling it became.[65]

External Factors

In addition to internal bargaining, strategic approaches (as well as others) take account of political pressures that come from outside the Court. We consider three sources of such influence: public opinion, partisan politics, and interest groups. While reading about these sources of influence, keep in mind that one of the fundamental differences between the Supreme Court and the political branches is the lack of a direct electoral connection between the justices and the public. Once appointed, justices may serve for life. They are not accountable to the public and are not required to undergo any periodic reevaluation of their decisions. So why would they let the stuff of ordinary partisan politics, such as public opinion and interest groups, influence their opinions?

Public Opinion. To address this question, let us first look at public opinion as a source of influence on the Court. We know that the president and members of Congress are always trying to find out what the people are thinking. Conducting and analyzing public opinion polls is a never-ending task, and those who commission the polls have a good reason for this activity: the political branches are supposed to represent the people, and incumbents' can jeopardize their reelection prospects by straying too far from what the public

62. Walter F. Murphy, *Elements of Judicial Strategy* (Chicago: University of Chicago Press, 1964); David J. Danelski, "The Influence of the Chief Justice in the Decisional Process of the Supreme Court," in *The Federal Judicial System,* ed. Thomas P. Jahnige and Sheldon Goldman (New York: Holt, Rinehart & Winston, 1968); J. Woodford Howard, "On the Fluidity of Judicial Choice," *American Political Science Review* 62 (1968): 43–56; Epstein and Knight, *The Choices Justices Make*; Forrest Maltzman, Paul J. Wahlbeck, and James Spriggs, *Crafting Law on the Supreme Court: The Collegial Game* (New York: Cambridge University Press, 2000).

63. Saul Brenner, "Fluidity on the Supreme Court, 1956–1967," *American Journal of Political Science* 26 (1982): 388–390; Brenner, "Fluidity on the United States Supreme Court: A Re-examination," *American Journal of Political Science* 24 (1980): 526–535; Forrest Maltzman and Paul J. Wahlbeck, "Strategic Policy Considerations and Voting Fluidity on the Burger Court," *American Political Science Review* 90 (1996): 581–592.

64. Epstein and Knight, *The Choices Justices Make,* chap. 3.

65. See Bernard Schwartz, *The Unpublished Opinions of the Warren Court* (New York: Oxford University Press, 1985), chap. 7.

wants. But federal judges—including Supreme Court justices—are not dependent on pleasing the public to stay in office, and they do not serve in the same kind of representative capacity that legislators do.

Does that mean that the justices are not affected by public opinion? Some scholars assert that they are and offer three reasons for this claim.[66] First, because justices are political appointees, nominated and approved by popularly elected officials, it is logical that they should reflect, however subtly, the views of the majority. It is probably true that an individual radically out of step with either the president or the Senate would not be nominated, much less confirmed. Second, the Court, at least occasionally, views public opinion as a legitimate guide for decisions. It has even gone so far as to incorporate that consideration into some of its jurisprudential standards. For example, in evaluating whether certain kinds of punishments violate the Eighth Amendment's prohibition against cruel and unusual punishment, the Court proclaimed that it would look toward "evolving standards of decency," as defined by public sentiment.[67] The third reason relates to the Court as an institution. Put simply, the justices have no mechanism for enforcing their decisions. Instead, they depend on other political officials to support their positions and on general public compliance, especially when controversial Court opinions have ramifications beyond the particular concerns of the parties to the suits.

Certainly, we can think of cases that lend support to these claims—cases in which the Court seems to have embraced public opinion, especially under conditions of extreme national stress. One such case occurred during World War II. In *Korematsu v. United States* (1944) the justices endorsed the government's program to remove all Japanese Americans from the Pacific Coast states and relocate them to inland detention centers. It seems clear that the justices were swept up in the same wartime apprehensions as the rest of the nation. But it is equally easy to summon examples of the Court handing down rulings that fly in the face of what the public wants. The most obvious examples occurred after Franklin Roosevelt's 1932 election to the presidency. By choosing Roosevelt and a Democratic majority in

Congress, the voters sent a clear signal that they wanted the government to take vigorous action to end the Great Depression. The president and Congress responded with many laws—the so-called New Deal legislation—but the Court remained unmoved by the public's endorsement of Roosevelt and his legislation. In case after case, at least until 1937, the justices struck down many of the laws and administrative programs designed to get the nation's economy moving again.

And, in fact, some scholars remain unconvinced of the role of public opinion in Court decision making. After systematically analyzing the data, Helmut Norpoth and Jeffrey A. Segal conclude, "Does public opinion influence Supreme Court decisions? If the model of influence is of the sort where the justices set aside their own [ideological] preferences and abide by what they divine as the vox populi, our answer is a resounding no."[68] What Norpoth and Segal find instead is that Court appointments made by Richard Nixon in the early 1970s caused a "sizable ideological shift" in the direction of Court decisions (*see figure 1-5*). The entry of conservative justices created the illusion that the Court was echoing public opinion, and not that sitting justices modified their voting patterns to conform to the changing views of the public.

This finding reinforces yet another criticism of this approach: that public opinion affects the Court only indirectly through presidential appointments, not through the justices' reading of public opinion polls. This distinction is important, for if justices were truly influenced by the public, their decisions would change with the ebb and flow of opinion. But if they merely share their appointing president's ideology, which must mirror the majority of the citizens *at the time of the president's election,* their decisions will remain constant over time. They would not fluctuate, as public opinion often does.

The question of whether public opinion affects Supreme Court decision making is still open for discussion, as illustrated by a recent article, "Does Public Opinion Influence the Supreme Court? Possibly Yes (But We're Not Sure Why)."[69] The authors find that when the

---

66. See, for example, Barry Friedman, *The Will of the People* (New York: Farrar, Straus & Giroux, 2009); William Mishler and Reginald S. Sheehan, "The Supreme Court as a Counter-majoritarian Institution? The Impact of Public Opinion on Supreme Court Decisions," *American Political Science Review* 87 (1993): 87–101.

67. *Trop v. Dulles* (1958).

68. Helmut Norpoth and Jeffrey A. Segal, "Popular Influence in Supreme Court Decisions," *American Political Science Review* 88 (1994): 711–716.

69. Lee Epstein and Andrew D. Martin, "Does Public Opinion Influence the Supreme Court? Possibly Yes (But We're Not Sure Why)," *University of Pennsylvania Journal of Constitutional Law* 13 (2010): 263–281.

"mood" is liberal (or conservative), the Court is significantly more likely to issue liberal (or conservative) decisions. But why that is so, as the article's title suggests, is anyone's guess. It could be that the justices bend to the will of the people because the Court requires public support to remain an efficacious branch of government. Or it could be that "the people" include the justices. The justices do not respond to public opinion directly but rather respond to the same events or forces that affect the opinions of other members of the public. In 1921 Justice Benjamin Cardozo wrote, "The great tides and currents which engulf the rest of men do not turn aside in their course and pass the judge by."[70]

Partisan Politics. Public opinion may not be the only political factor that allegedly influences the justices. As Jonathan Casper wrote, we cannot overestimate "the importance of the political context in which the Court does its work." In his view, the statement that the Court follows the election returns "recognizes that the choices the Court makes are related to developments in the broader political system."[71] In other words, the political environment has an effect on Court behavior. In fact, many assert that the Court is responsive to the influence of partisan politics, both internally and externally.

On the inner workings of the Court, social scientists long have argued that political creatures inhabit the Court, that justices are not simply neutral arbiters of the law. Since 1789, the beginning of constitutional government in the United States, those who have ascended to the bench have come from the political institutions of government or, at the very least, have affiliated with particular political parties. Judicial scholars recognize that justices bring with them the philosophies of those partisan attachments. Just as the members of the present Court tend to reflect the views of the Republican Party or the Democratic Party, so too did the justices who came from the ranks of the Federalists and Jeffersonians. As one might expect, justices who affiliate with the Democratic Party tend to be more liberal in their decision making than those who are Republicans. Some commentators say that *Bush v. Gore* (2000), in which the Supreme Court issued a ruling that virtually ensured that George W.

Bush would become president, provides an example *(see chapter 4)*. In that case, five of the Court's seven Republican appointees "voted" for Bush, while its two Democrats "voted" for Gore.

Political pressures from the outside also can affect the Court. Although the justices have no electoral connection or mandate of responsiveness, the other institutions of government have some influence on judicial behavior, and, naturally, the direction of that influence reflects the partisan composition of those branches. The Court has always had a complex relationship with the president, a relationship that provides the president with several possible ways to influence judicial decisions. The president has some direct links with the Court, including (1) the power to nominate justices and shape the Court; (2) personal relationships with sitting justices, such as Franklin Roosevelt's with James Byrnes, Lyndon Johnson's with Abe Fortas, and Richard Nixon's with Warren Burger; and (3) the notion that the president, having been elected within the previous four years, may carry a popular mandate, reflecting citizens' preferences, which would affect the environment within which the Court operates.

A less direct source of influence is the executive branch, which operates under the president's command. The bureaucracy can assist the Court in implementing its policies, or it can hinder the Court by refusing to do so, a fact of which the justices are well aware. As a judicial body, the Supreme Court cannot implement or execute its own decisions. It often must depend on the executive branch to give its decisions legitimacy through action. The Court, therefore, may act strategically, anticipate the wishes of the executive branch, and respond accordingly to avoid a confrontation that could threaten its legitimacy. *Marbury v. Madison* (1803), in which the Court enunciated the doctrine of judicial review, is the classic example *(see chapter 2 for an excerpt)*. Some scholars suggest that the justices knew that, if they ruled a certain way, the Thomas Jefferson administration would not carry out the Court's orders. Because the Court believed that such a failure would threaten the legitimacy of judicial institutions, it crafted its opinion in a way that would not force the administration to take any action, but instead would send a message about its displeasure with the administration's politics.

Another indirect source of presidential influence is the office of the U.S. solicitor general. In addition to the SG's success as a petitioning party, the office can

---

70. Benjamin Cardozo, *The Nature of the Judicial Process* (New Haven, CT: Yale University Press, 1921), 168.

71. Jonathan Casper, *The Politics of Civil Liberties* (New York: Harper & Row, 1972), 293.

have an equally pronounced effect at the merits stage. In fact, data indicate that whether acting as an amicus curiae or as a party to a suit, the SG's office is generally able to convince the justices to adopt the position advocated by the SG.[72]

Presidential influence is also demonstrated in the kinds of arguments an SG brings into the Court. That is, SGs representing Democratic administrations tend to present more liberal arguments; those from the ranks of the Republican Party, more conservative arguments. The transition from George H. W. Bush's administration to Bill Clinton's provides an interesting illustration. Bush's SG had filed amicus curiae briefs—many of which took a conservative position—in a number of cases heard by the Court during the 1993–1994 term. Drew S. Days III, Clinton's first SG, rewrote at least four of those briefs to reflect the new administration's liberal posture. In one case, Days argued that the Civil Rights Act of 1991 should be applied retroactively, whereas the Bush administration had suggested that it should not be. In another, Days claimed trial attorneys could not systematically dismiss prospective jurors on the basis of sex; his predecessor had argued that such challenges were constitutional.

Congress, too—or so some argue—can influence Supreme Court decision making. Like the president, the legislature has many powers over the Court that the justices cannot ignore.[73] Some of these resemble presidential powers—the Senate's role in confirmation proceedings, the implementation of judicial decisions—but there are others. Congress can restrict the Court's jurisdiction to hear cases, enact legislation, or propose constitutional amendments to recast Court decisions, and hold judicial salaries constant. To forestall a congressional attack, the Court might accede to legislators' wishes. Often-cited instances include the Court's willingness to defer to the Radical Republican Congress after the Civil War and to approve New Deal legislation after Roosevelt proposed his Court-packing plan in 1937. Some argue that these examples represent anomalies, not the rule. The Court, they say, has no reason to respond strategically to Congress because it is so rare that the legislature threatens, much less takes action against, the judiciary. Indeed, Congress

has only infrequently removed the Supreme Court's jurisdiction to hear particular kinds of cases. The best-known example occurred just after the Civil War, and the most recent was in pursuance of the war on terrorism *(see chapter 2 for more details)*. You should keep this argument in mind as you read the cases that pit the Court against Congress and the president.

Interest Groups. In *Federalist* No. 78, Alexander Hamilton wrote that the U.S. Supreme Court was "to declare the sense of the law" through "inflexible and uniform adherence to the rights of the constitution and individuals." Despite this expectation, Supreme Court litigation has become political over time. We see manifestations of politics in virtually every aspect of the Court's work, from the nomination and confirmation of justices to the factors that influence their decisions, but perhaps the most striking example of this politicization is the incursion of organized interest groups into the judicial process.

Naturally, interest groups may not attempt to persuade the Supreme Court the same way lobbyists deal with Congress. It would be grossly improper for the representatives of an interest group to approach a Supreme Court justice directly. Instead, interest groups try to influence Court decisions by submitting amicus curiae briefs *(see box 1-2)*. Presenting a written legal argument to the Court allows an interest group to make its views known to the justices, even when the group is not a direct party to the litigation.

These days, it is a rare case before the U.S. Supreme Court that does not attract such submissions. In recent years, organized interests filed at least one amicus brief in more than 90 percent of all cases decided by full opinion between 2000 and 2015.[74] Some cases, particularly those involving controversial issues such as gun control legislation, abortion, and affirmative action, are especially attractive to interest groups. In *Regents of the University of California v. Bakke* (1978), involving admission of minority students to medical school, more than one hundred organizations filed fifty-eight amicus briefs: forty-two backing the university's admissions policy and sixteen supporting Bakke. The 2003 affirmative action case *Grutter v. Bollinger* drew eighty-four briefs, and from a wide range of interests: colleges and universities, *Fortune* 500 companies, and retired

---

72. See Epstein et al., *Supreme Court Compendium,* Tables 7-15 and 7-16.

73. See Gerald N. Rosenberg, "Judicial Independence and the Reality of Political Power," *Review of Politics* 54 (1992): 369–398.

74. See Epstein et al., *Supreme Court Compendium,* Table 7-22.

military officers, to name just a few.[75] And eighty-eight amicus briefs were submitted in *Fisher v. Texas,* the affirmative action case that highlighted the 2012 term. But it is not only cases of civil liberties and rights that attract interest group attention. In the 2012 challenge to the constitutionality of the Patient Protection and Affordable Care Act, the Court received more than one hundred amicus briefs. In addition to participating as amici, groups in record numbers are sponsoring cases—that is, providing litigants with attorneys and the money necessary to pursue their cases.

The explosion of interest group participation in Supreme Court litigation raises two questions. First, why do groups go to the Court? One answer is obvious: they want to influence the Court's decisions. But groups also go to the Supreme Court to achieve other, more subtle, ends. One is the setting of institutional agendas: by filing amicus curiae briefs at the case selection stage or by bringing cases to the Court's attention, organizations seek to influence the justices' decisions on which disputes to hear. Group participation also may serve as a counterbalance to other interests that have competing goals. So if Planned Parenthood, a pro-choice group, observes Life Legal Defense Foundation, a pro-life group, filing an amicus curiae brief in an abortion case (or vice versa), it too may enter the dispute to ensure that its side is represented in the proceedings. Finally, groups go to the Court to publicize their causes and their organizations. The NAACP (National Association for the Advancement of Colored People) Legal Defense Fund's legendary litigation campaign to end school segregation provides an excellent example. It not only resulted in a favorable policy decision in *Brown v. Board of Education* (1954) but also established the Legal Defense Fund as the foremost organizational litigant of this issue.

The second question is this: Do groups influence the outcomes of Supreme Court decisions?[76] This question has no simple answer. When interest groups participate on both sides, it is reasonable to speculate that one or more exerted some intellectual influence or at least that intervention of groups on the winning side neutralized the arguments of those who lost. To determine how

much influence any group or private party exerted, a researcher would have to interview all the justices who participated in the decision (and they do not grant such interviews), because even a direct citation to an argument advanced in one of the parties' or amici's briefs may indicate merely that a justice is seeking support for a conclusion he or she had already reached.

What we can say is that attorneys for some groups, such as the Women's Rights Project of the American Civil Liberties Union and the NAACP, are often more experienced, and their staffs more adept at research, than counsel for what Marc Galanter calls "one-shotters."[77] When he was chief counsel for the NAACP, Thurgood Marshall would solicit help from allied groups and orchestrate their cooperation on a case, dividing the labor among them by assigning specific arguments to each, while enlisting sympathetic social scientists to muster supporting data. Before going to the Supreme Court for oral argument, he would sometimes have a practice session with friendly law professors, each one playing the role of a particular justice and trying to pose the sorts of questions that justice would be likely to ask. Such preparation can pay off, but it need not be decisive. In oral argument, Allan Bakke's attorney displayed a surprising ignorance of constitutional law and curtly told one justice who tried to help him that he would like to argue the case his own way. Even with this poor performance, Bakke's side won.

Some evidence, however, suggests that attorneys working for interest groups are no more successful than private counsel. One study paired similar cases decided by the same district court judge, the same year, with the only major difference being that one case was sponsored by a group whereas the other was brought by attorneys unaffiliated with an organized interest. Despite Galanter's contentions about the obstacles confronting one-shotters, the study found no major differences between the two.[78]

In short, the debate over the influence of interest groups continues, and it is a debate that you will have ample opportunity to consider. Within the case excerpts in this volume, we often provide information

75. See Linda Greenhouse, "What Got into the Court?," *Maine Law Review* 57 (2005): 6. Greenhouse wrote that "more than 100 briefs, a record number, were filed" in the 2003 affirmative action cases. Our figure (84) for *Grutter* excludes briefs filed by individuals.

76. We adopt some of this material from Pritchett et al., *Courts, Judges, and Politics,* chap. 6.

77. Marc Galanter, "Why the 'Haves' Come Out Ahead: Speculations on the Limits of Legal Change," *Law and Society Review* 9 (1974): 95–160.

78. Lee Epstein and C. K. Rowland, "Debunking the Myth of Interest Group Invincibility in the Court," *American Political Science Review* 85 (1991): 205–217.

on the arguments of amici and attorneys so that you can compare these points with the justices' opinions.

CONDUCTING RESEARCH ON THE SUPREME COURT

As you can see, considerable disagreement exists in the scholarly and legal communities about how justices should interpret the Constitution, and even why they decide cases the way they do. These approaches show up in many of the Court's opinions in this book. Keep in mind, however, that the opinions are not presented here in full; the excerpts included here are intended to highlight the most important points of the various majority, dissenting, and concurring opinions. Occasionally, you may want to read the decisions in their entirety. Following is an explanation of how to find opinions and other kinds of information on the Court and its members.

Locating Supreme Court Decisions

U.S. Supreme Court decisions are published by various reporters. The four major reporters are (1) *U.S. Reports,* (2) *Lawyers' Edition,* (3) *Supreme Court Reporter,* and (4) *U.S. Law Week.* All contain the opinions of the Court, but they vary in the kinds of ancillary material they provide. As table 1-4 shows, the *Lawyers' Edition* contains excerpts of the briefs of attorneys submitted in orally argued cases, *U.S. Law Week* provides a topical index of cases on the Court's docket, and so forth.

Locating a case within these reporters is easy if you know the case citation. Case citations, as the table shows, take different forms, but they all work in roughly the same way. To see how, turn to page 274 to find an excerpt of *Mistretta v. United States* (1989). Directly under the case name is a citation: 488 U.S. 361, which means that *Mistretta v. United States* appears in volume 488, on page 361, of *U.S. Reports.*[79] The first set of numbers is the volume number, the U.S. is the form of citation for *U.S. Reports,* and the second set of numbers is the starting page of the case.

Mistretta v. United States also can be located in the three other reporters. The citations are as follows:

Lawyers' Edition: 102 L. Ed. 2d 714 (1989)

Supreme Court Reporter: 109 S. Ct. 647 (1989)

U.S. Law Week: 57 U.S.L.W. 4102 (1989)

Note that the abbreviations vary by reporter, but the citations parallel the *U.S. Reports* in that the first set of numbers is the volume number and the second set is the starting page number.

These days, however, many students turn to electronic sources to locate Supreme Court decisions. Several companies maintain databases of the decisions of federal and state courts, along with a wealth of other information. In some institutions these services—LexisNexis and Westlaw—are available only to law school students. If you are in another academic unit, check with your librarians to see if your school provides access, perhaps through Academic Universe (a subset of the LexisNexis service). Also, the Legal Information Institute at Cornell Law School (http://supct.law.cornell.edu/supct), FindLaw (www.findlaw.com/casecode/supreme.html), and now the Supreme Court itself (www.supremecourtus.gov)—to name just three—house Supreme Court opinions and offer an array of search capabilities. You can read the opinions online, have them e-mailed to you, or download them immediately. If a case we excerpt is located in these archives, we note the Web address after the case citation.

Locating Other Information on the Supreme Court and Its Members

As you might imagine, there is no shortage of reference material on the Court. Three good (print) starting points are the following:

1. *The Supreme Court Compendium: Data, Decisions, and Developments,* sixth edition, contains information on the following dimensions of Court activity: the Court's development, review process, opinions and decisions, judicial backgrounds, voting patterns, and impact.[80] You will find data as varied as the number of cases the Court decided during a particular term, the votes in the Senate on Supreme Court nominees, and the law schools the justices attended.

---

79. In this book, we list only the *U.S. Reports* cite because *U.S. Reports* is the official record of Supreme Court decisions. It is the only reporter published by the federal government; the other three are privately printed. Almost every law library has *U.S. Reports.* If your college or university does not have a law school, check with your librarians. If they have any Court reporter, it is probably *U.S. Reports.*

---

80. Epstein et al., *Supreme Court Compendium.*

TABLE 1-4   Reporting Systems

REPORTER/PUBLISHER	FORM OF CITATION (TERMS)	DESCRIPTION
United States Reports Government Printing Office	Dall. 1–4 (1790–1800) Cr. 1–15 (1801–1815) Wheat. 1–12 (1816–1827) Pet. 1–16 (1828–1843) How. 1–24 (1843–1861) Bl. 1–2 (1861–1862) Wall. 1–23 (1863–1875) U.S. 91–(1875–)	Contains official text of opinions of the Court. Includes tables of cases reported, cases and statutes cited, miscellaneous materials, and subject index. Includes most of the Court's decisions. Court opinions prior to 1875 are cited by the name of the reporter of the Court. For example, Dall. stands for Alexander J. Dallas, the first reporter.
United States Supreme Court Reports, Lawyers' Edition Lawyers' Cooperative Publishing Company	L. Ed. L. Ed. 2d	Contains official reports of opinions of the Court. Additionally, provides per curiam and other decisions not found elsewhere. Summarizes individual majority and dissenting opinions and counsel briefs.
Supreme Court Reporter West Publishing Company	S. Ct.	Contains official reports of opinions of the Court. Contains annotated reports and indexes of case names. Includes opinions of justices in chambers. Appears semimonthly.
United States Law Week Bureau of National Affairs	U.S.L.W.	Weekly periodical service containing full text of Court decisions. Includes four indexes: topical, table of cases, docket number table, and proceedings section. Contains summary of cases filed recently, journal of proceedings, summary of orders, arguments before the Court, argued cases awaiting decisions, review of Court's work, and review of Court's docket.

SOURCE: Lee Epstein, Jeffrey A. Segal, Harold J. Spaeth, and Thomas G. Walker, *The Supreme Court Compendium: Data, Decisions, and Developments,* 6th ed. (Thousand Oaks, CA: CQ Press, 2015), table 2-9. Dates of reporters are from David Savage, *Guide to the U.S. Supreme Court,* 5th ed. (Washington, DC: CQ Press, 2010).

2. *Guide to the U.S. Supreme Court,* fifth edition, provides a fairly detailed history of the Court. It also summarizes the holdings in landmark cases and provides brief biographies of the justices.[81]

3. *The Oxford Companion to the Supreme Court of the United States,* second edition, is an encyclopedia containing entries on the justices, important Court cases, the amendments to the Constitution, and so forth.[82]

The U.S. Supreme Court also gets a great deal of attention on the Internet. The Legal Information Institute (www.law.cornell.edu) is particularly useful. In addition to Supreme Court decisions, the Legal Information Institute contains links to various documents (such as the U.S. Code and state statutes), and to a vast array of legal indexes and libraries. If you are unable to find the material you are looking for here, you may locate it by clicking on one of the links.

Another worthwhile site is SCOTUSblog, a project of a law firm (www.scotusblog.com). Housed here are extensive commentaries on pending Court cases, as well as links to briefs filed by the parties and amici.

As already mentioned, you can listen to a number of oral arguments of the Court at the Oyez Project site (https://www.oyez.org). Oyez contains audio files of Supreme Court oral arguments for selected constitutional cases decided since the 1950s.

These are just a few of the many sites—perhaps hundreds—that contain information on the federal courts. But there is at least one other important electronic

---

81. David Savage, *Guide to the U.S. Supreme Court,* 5th ed. (Washington, DC: CQ Press, 2010).

82. Kermit Hall, ed., *The Oxford Companion to the Supreme Court of the United States,* 2nd ed. (New York: Oxford University Press, 2005).

source of information on the Court worthy of mention: the U.S. Supreme Court Database, developed by Harold J. Spaeth, a political scientist and lawyer. This resource provides a wealth of data beginning with the Vinson Court (1946 term) to the present. Among the many attributes of Court decisions it includes are the names of the courts that made the original decisions, the identities of the parties to the cases, the policy context of the cases, and the votes of each justice. Indeed, we deployed this database to create many of the charts and tables you have just read. You can obtain all the data and accompanying documentation, free of charge, at http://supremecourtdatabase.org.

In this chapter, we have examined Supreme Court procedures and attempted to shed some light on how and why justices make the choices they do. Our consideration of preference-based factors, for example, highlighted the role ideology plays in Court decision making, and our discussion of political explanations emphasized public opinion and interest groups. After reading this chapter, you may have concluded that the justices are relatively free to go about their business as they please. But, as we shall see in the next chapter, that is not necessarily so. Although Court members have a good deal of power and the freedom to exercise it, they also face considerable institutional obstacles. It is to the subjects of judicial power and constraints that we now turn.

ANNOTATED READINGS

In the text and footnotes, we mention many interesting studies on the Supreme Court. Our goal in each chapter's "Annotated Readings" section is to highlight a few books for the interested reader.

Lawrence Baum's *The Supreme Court,* 10th ed. (Washington, DC: CQ Press, 2011); and Linda Greenhouse's *The Supreme Court: A Very Short Introduction* (New York: Oxford University Press, 2012) provide modern-day introductions to the Court and its work. For insightful historical-political analyses, see Robert G. McCloskey's *The American Supreme Court* (Chicago: University of Chicago Press, 2004) and Barry Friedman's *The Will of the People* (New York: Farrar, Straus & Giroux, 2009). Several of the current justices have written books outlining their approaches to interpreting the Constitution. See Stephen Breyer's *Active Liberty: Interpreting Our Democratic Constitution* (New York: Knopf, 2005); and Antonin Scalia's *A Matter of Interpretation: Federal Courts and the Law* (Princeton, NJ: Princeton University Press, 1997), which includes responses from prominent legal scholars. For other studies of approaches to constitutional interpretation, see Philip Bobbitt, *Constitutional Fate: Theory of the Constitution* (New York: Oxford University Press, 1982); Richard H. Fallon Jr., *Implementing the Constitution* (Cambridge, MA: Harvard University Press, 2001); Michael J. Gerhardt, *The Power of Precedent* (New York: Oxford University Press, 2008); Leslie Friedman Goldstein, *In Defense of the Text* (Savage, MD: Rowman & Littlefield, 1991); Ronald Kahn, *The Supreme Court and Constitutional Theory* (Lawrence: University Press of Kansas, 1994); and Gary L. McDowell, *The Language of Law and the Foundations of American Constitutionalism* (New York: Cambridge University Press, 2010); Jack N. Rakove, *Original Meanings: Politics and Ideas in the Making of the Constitution* (New York: Vintage Books, 1996); Keith E. Whittington, *Constitutional Interpretation: Textual Meaning, Original Intent, and Judicial Review* (Lawrence: University Press of Kansas, 1999).

Noteworthy political science studies of judicial decision making (including case selection) are C. Herman Pritchett, *The Roosevelt Court* (New York: Macmillan, 1948); Glendon Schubert, *The Judicial Mind* (Evanston, IL: Northwestern University Press, 1965); Walter J. Murphy, *Elements of Judicial Strategy* (Chicago: University of Chicago Press, 1964); H. W. Perry Jr., *Deciding to Decide: Agenda Setting in the United States Supreme Court* (Cambridge, MA: Harvard University Press, 1991); Lee Epstein and Jack Knight, *The Choices Justices Make* (Washington, DC: CQ Press, 1998); Forrest Maltzman, Paul J. Wahlbeck, and James Spriggs, *Crafting Law on the Supreme Court: The Collegial Game* (New York: Cambridge University Press, 2000); Jeffrey A. Segal and Harold J. Spaeth, *The Supreme Court and the Attitudinal Model Revisited* (New York: Cambridge University Press, 2002); Stefanie A. Lindquist and Frank B. Cross, *Measuring Judicial Activism* (New York: Oxford University Press, 2009); Michael A. Bailey and Forrest Maltzman, *The Constrained Court: Law, Politics, and the Decisions Justices Make* (Princeton, NJ: Princeton University Press, 2011); Richard L. Pacelle Jr., Brett W. Curry, and Bryan W. Marshall, *Decision Making by the Modern Supreme Court* (New York: Cambridge University Press, 2011); Lee Epstein, William M. Landes, and Richard A. Posner, *The Behavior of Federal Judges: A Theoretical and Empirical Study of*

Rational Choice (Cambridge, MA: Harvard University Press, 2013).

On the work of interest groups and attorneys (including the solicitor general), see Ryan C. Black and Ryan J. Owens, *The Solicitor General and the United States Supreme Court: Executive Branch Influence and Judicial Decisions* (Cambridge: Cambridge University Press, 2012); Kevin T. McGuire, *The Supreme Court Bar: Legal Elites in the Washington Community* (Charlottesville: University of Virginia Press, 1993); Timothy R. Johnson, *Oral Arguments and the United States Supreme Court* (Albany: State University of New York Press, 2004); and Paul M. Collins Jr., *Friends of the Supreme Court: Interest Groups and Judicial Decision Making* (New York: Oxford University Press, 2008).

PART II   **Institutional Authority**

iStock/DanBrandenburg

Structuring the Federal System

ONE OF THE FIRST things everyone learns in an American government course is that two concepts undergird the U.S. constitutional system. The first is the separation of powers doctrine, under which each of the branches has a distinct function: the legislature makes the laws, the executive implements those laws, and the judiciary interprets them. The second concept is the notion of checks and balances: each branch of government imposes limits on the primary functions of the others. The Supreme Court may interpret laws and even strike them down as being in violation of the Constitution, but Congress can introduce legislation to override the Court's decision. If Congress takes action, then the president has the option of vetoing the proposed law. If that happens, Congress must decide whether to override the president's veto. Seen in this way, the rule of checks and balances inherent in the system of separation of powers suggests that policy in the United States emanates not from the separate actions of the branches of government but from the interaction among them.

A full understanding of the basics of institutional powers and constraints therefore requires a consideration of three important subjects. First, we must investigate the separation of powers doctrine and why the framers adopted it; we take up this subject in the following pages. Second, because of the unique role the judiciary plays in the American government system, we need to understand how the Court has interpreted its own powers (located in Article III of the Constitution) and the constraints on those powers, as well as those of Congress (Article I) and the president (Article II). We consider these matters in chapters 2, 3, and 4. Finally, we need to understand how the Court has dealt with situations in which the various institutions take on roles other than those ascribed to them in the Constitution (such as when the legislature exerts executive powers and vice versa) or when the Constitution is ambiguous about which branch has what powers (such as the power to make war). Chapter 5 takes up these important topics.

ORIGINS OF THE SEPARATION OF POWERS/ CHECKS AND BALANCES SYSTEM

Even a casual comparison of the Articles of Confederation with the Constitution reveals major differences in the way the two documents structured the national government *(see figure I-1)*. Under the articles, the powers of government were concentrated in the legislature, a unicameral Congress in which the states had equal voting powers. There was no executive or judicial branch separate and independent from the legislature. Issues of separation of powers and checks and balances were not particularly relevant to the articles, largely because the national government had almost no power to abuse. The states were capable of checking anything the central government proposed, and they provided whatever restraints the newly independent nation needed.

The government under the Articles of Confederation failed at least in part because it lacked sufficient power and authority to cope with the problems of the day. The requirements for amending the document were so restrictive that fundamental change within the articles proved impossible. When the Constitutional Convention met in Philadelphia in 1787, the delegates soon concluded that the articles had to be scrapped and replaced with a charter that would provide more effective power for the national government. The country had experienced conditions of economic decline, crippling taxation policies, interstate barriers to commerce, and isolated but alarming insurrections among the lower economic classes. The framers saw a newly structured national government as the only method of dealing with the problems besetting the nation in the aftermath of the Revolution.

But allocating significant power to the national government was not without its risks. Many of the framers feared the creation of a federal power capable of dominating the states and abusing individual liberties. It was apparent to all that the new government would have to be structured in a way that would minimize the potential for abuse and excess. The concept of the separation of powers and its twin, the idea of checks and balances, appealed to the framers as the best way to accomplish these necessary restraints.

The theory of separation of powers was not new to the framers. They had been introduced to it by the political philosophy of the day and by their own political experiences. The theories of James Harrington and Charles de Montesquieu were particularly influential in this respect. Harrington (1611–1677) was an English political philosopher whose emphasis on the importance of property found a sympathetic audience among the former colonists. His primary work, *Oceana*, published in 1656, was a widely read description of a model government. Incorporated into Harrington's ideal state was the notion that government powers ought to be divided into three parts. A Senate made up of the intellectual elite would propose laws; the people, guided by the Senate's wisdom, would enact the laws; and a magistrate would execute the laws. This system, Harrington argued, would impose an important balance that would maintain a stable government and protect property rights.

Harrington's concept of a separation of powers was less well developed than that later proposed by Montesquieu (1689–1755), a French political theorist. Many scholars consider his *Spirit of the Laws* (published as *De l'Esprit des Loix* in 1748), which was widely circulated during the last half of the eighteenth century, to be the classic treatise on the separation of powers philosophy. Montesquieu was concerned about government abuse of liberty. In his estimation, liberty could not long prevail if too much power accrued to a single ruler or a single branch of government. He warned, "When the legislative and executive powers are united in the same person, or the same body of magistrates, there can be no liberty. . . . Again, there is no liberty if the judicial power be not separated from the legislative and executive." Although Montesquieu's message was directed to the citizens of his own country, he found a more receptive audience in the United States.

The influence of these political thinkers was reinforced by the framers' political experiences. The settlers had come to the New World largely to escape the abuses of European governments. George III's treatment of the colonies taught them that executives were not to be trusted with too much power. The colonists also feared an independent and powerful judiciary, especially one not answerable to the people. The framers undoubtedly placed the most confidence in the legislature, but they knew it too had the potential of exceeding its proper bounds. The English experience during the reign of Oliver Cromwell was lesson enough that muting the power of the king did not necessarily lead to the elimination of government abuse. What the framers sought was balance, a system in which each branch of government would be strong enough to keep excessive power from flowing into the hands of any other single branch. This necessary balance, as John Adams pointed out in his *Defence of the Constitutions of Government of the United States of America* (1787–1788), would also have the advantage of being able to keep the power-hungry aristocracy in check and prevent the majority from taking rights away from the minority.

SEPARATION OF POWERS AND THE CONSTITUTION

The debates at the Constitutional Convention and the various plans that were presented for the delegates' consideration all focused on the issue of dividing government power among the three branches as well as between the national government and the states. A general fear of a concentration of power permeated all the discussions. James Madison noted, "The truth is, all men having power ought to be distrusted to a certain degree." The framers' solution to the difficult problem of expanding government power, and at the same time reducing the probability of abuse, was found in their proposed new Constitution of the United States.

Although the term *separation of powers* is nowhere to be found in the document, the Constitution plainly adopts the central tenets of the theory. A reading of the first lines of each of the first three articles—the vesting clauses—makes this point clearly:

All legislative Powers herein granted shall be vested in a Congress of the United States, which shall consist of a Senate and House of Representatives. [Article I]

The executive Power shall be vested in a President of the United States of America. [Article II]

The judicial Power of the United States, shall be vested in one supreme Court, and in such inferior Courts as the Congress may from time to time ordain and establish. [Article III]

In the scheme of government incorporated into the Constitution, the legislative, executive, and judicial powers resided in separate branches of government. Unless otherwise specified in the document, each branch was limited to the political function granted to it, and that function could not be exercised by either of the other two branches.

In addition to the separation of powers concept, the framers placed into the Constitution a number of mixed powers. That is, the document reserves certain functions for specific branches, but it also provides explicit checks on the exercise of those powers. As a consequence, each branch of government imposes limits on the primary functions of the others. A few examples illustrate this point:

- Congress has the right to pass legislation, but the president may veto the bills passed by Congress.
- The president may veto bills passed by Congress, but the legislature may override the president's veto.
- The president may make treaties with foreign powers, but the Senate must vote its approval of those treaties.
- The president is commander in chief of the army and navy, but Congress must pass legislation to raise armies, regulate the military, and declare war.

- The president may nominate federal judges, but the Senate must confirm them.
- The judiciary may interpret the law and even strike down laws as being in violation of the Constitution—a power the Court asserted for itself—but Congress may pass new legislation or propose constitutional amendments.
- Congress may pass laws, but the executive must enforce them.

In addition to these offsetting powers, the framers structured the branches so that the criteria and procedures for selecting the officials of the institutions differed, as did their tenures. Consequently, the branches all have slightly different sources of political power. In the original scheme these differences were even more pronounced than they are today.

In the original version of the Constitution, the two houses of Congress were politically dependent on different selection processes. Members of the House were, as they are today, directly elected by the people, and the seats were apportioned among the states on the basis of population. With terms of only two years, the representatives were required to go back to the people for review on a frequent and regular basis. Senators, on the other hand, were, and still are, representatives of whole states, with each state, regardless of size, having two members in the upper chamber. But senators originally were selected by the state legislatures, a system that was not changed until 1913, when the Seventeenth Amendment, which imposed popular election of senators, was ratified. The six-year, staggered terms of senators were intended to make the upper house less immediately responsive to the volatile nature of public opinion.

The Constitution dictated that the president be selected by the Electoral College, a group of political elites selected by the people or their representatives who would exercise judgment in casting their ballots among presidential candidates. Although the electors over time have ceased to perform any truly independent selection function, presidential selection remains a step away from direct popular election. The president's four-year term places the office squarely between the tenures conferred on representatives and senators. The original Constitution placed no limit on the number of terms a president could serve, but a two-term limit was observed by tradition until 1940 and was then imposed by constitutional amendment in 1951.

Differing altogether from the other two branches is the judiciary, which was assigned the least democratic selection system. The people have no direct role in the selection or retention of federal judges. Instead, the president nominates individuals for the federal bench, and the Senate confirms or rejects them. Once in office, federal judges serve for life, removable against their will only through impeachment. The intent of the framers was to make the judiciary independent. To do so, they created a system in which judges would not depend on the mood of the masses or on a single appointing power. Furthermore, judges would be accountable only to their own philosophies and consciences, with no periodic review or reassessment required.

Through a division of powers, an imposition of checks, and a variation in selection and tenure requirements, the framers hoped to achieve the balanced government they desired. This structure, they thought, would be the greatest protection against abuses of power and government violations of personal liberties and property rights. Many delegates to the Constitutional Convention considered this system of separation of powers a more effective method of protecting civil liberties than the formal pronouncements of a bill of rights.

Most political observers would conclude that the framers' invention has worked remarkably well. Through the years, the relative strengths of the branches have changed back and forth. At certain times, the judiciary has been exceptionally weak, such as during the pre-Marshall era and before the Civil War. At other times, the judiciary has been criticized as being too powerful, such as when it repeatedly blocked New Deal legislation in the 1930s or when it expanded civil liberties during the Warren Court era. The executive also has led the other branches in political power. Beginning with the tenure of Franklin Roosevelt and extending into the 1970s, references were often made to the "imperial presidency." But when one branch gains too much power and abuses occur, as in the case of Richard Nixon and the Watergate crisis, the system tends to reimpose the balance intended by the framers.

Nevertheless, debates continue over how best to approach the separation of powers system from a constitutional law perspective. In many of the cases that follow, especially those in chapter 5, you will see justices vacillate between formalist and functionalist approaches. Formalism emphasizes a basic idea behind the system: that the Constitution creates clear boundaries between and among the branches of government

by bestowing a primary power on each. Under this school of thought, federal judges and justices should not allow deviations from this plan unless the text of the Constitution permits them. Functionalism, in contrast, rejects strict divisions among the branches and emphasizes instead a more fluid system—one of shared rather than separated powers. On this account, as long as actions by Congress or the president do not result in the accumulation of too much power in any one branch, the federal courts should be flexible, enabling—not discouraging—experimentation.

CONTEMPORARY THINKING ON THE CONSTITUTIONAL SCHEME

The long-standing debate between functionalism and formalism is largely a normative debate—that is, it centers on how best to interpret the Constitution. As you read the cases to come and consider the logic behind the separation of powers doctrine, you may also want to take into account two contemporary descriptive frameworks for understanding relationships among the three branches of government.

First are the "separation of powers games" offered by law professor William Eskridge and political scientists John Ferejohn and Barry Weingast, among others.[1] These games typically operate under some simple assumptions about the goals of the various institutions of government and the way the political process works. According to this school of thought, the aim of the institutions of government is to see the government's policy—for our purposes, the ultimate state of the law—reflect the institutions' positions. Or, to put it another way, the branches want policy set as close as possible to their ideal or most preferred point. The problem—and here is where assumptions about the nature of the process, including the separation of powers doctrine, come in—is that the political institutions

---

1. William N. Eskridge Jr., "Reneging on History: Playing the Court/Congress/President Civil Rights Game," *California Law Review* 79 (1991): 613–684; Eskridge, "Overriding Supreme Court Statutory Interpretation Decisions," *Yale Law Journal* 101 (1991): 331–455; John A. Ferejohn and Barry Weingast, "Limitation of Statutes: Strategic Statutory Interpretation," *International Review of Law and Economics* 12 (1992): 263–279. See also Knight and Epstein, *The Choices Justices Make*; and Pablo T. Spiller and Rafael Gely, "Congressional Control or Judicial Independence: The Determinants of U.S. Supreme Court Labor-Relations Decisions," *RAND Journal of Economics* 23 (1992): 463–492.

FIGURE II-1   The Supreme Court as a Strategic National Policy Maker

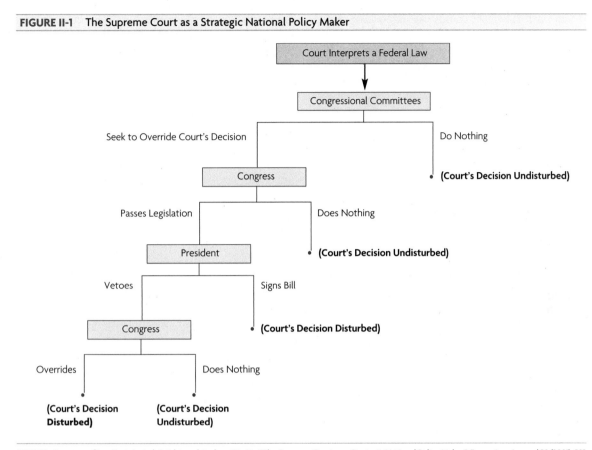

SOURCE: Courtesy of Lee Epstein, Jack Knight, and Andrew Martin, "The Supreme Court as a Strategic National Policy Maker," *Emory Law Journal* 50 (2001): 593.

do not make policy in isolation from one another. Rather, policy is set (or the game is played out) along the lines set out in figure II-1. In this example, the Supreme Court makes the first "move" when it interprets a congressional statute, a constitutional provision, and so forth. Congressional committees and other "gatekeepers" (majority party leaders) then must decide whether they want to introduce legislation to override the Court's decision; if they do, Congress must act by adopting the gatekeepers' recommendations, adopting a different version of it, or rejecting it. If Congress acts by passing legislation, then the president has the option of vetoing the law; the last move rests again with Congress, which must decide whether to override the president's veto.[2]

From these premises about the institutions' goals and about the sequence of play, perhaps you can see why the separation of powers doctrine is so important. Think about it this way. If the Supreme Court were the only American institution, it would merely set policy at its preferred point; it would not need to consider the positions of congressional gatekeepers, Congress as a whole, or the president. We know, however, that the Court is but one of several players in the game; therefore, it may take into account the preferences of others. If it sets the policy too far away from the position of, say, Congress, it could face an override. Congress might attempt to overturn the Court's decision with new legislation or "punish" the justices in other ways.

---

2. In Figure II-1 we depict a sequence in which the Court makes the first "move" and Congress the last. We could lay out other sequences and include other (or different) actors: we could construct

a scenario in which the Court moves first; Congress again goes next, but this time it proposes a constitutional amendment (rather than a law); and the states (not the president) have the last turn by deciding whether to ratify the amendment.

The last statement raises an interesting point: although the separation of powers games proposed by Eskridge and others are designed to cover instances when the Court interprets acts of Congress and it is clear that Congress and the president can modify Court decisions, some have suggested that the games may be applicable (though perhaps in a different form) to constitutional interpretation as well.[3] The reason is, as we consider in chapter 2, that the other branches possess various powers through which they can modify constitutional decisions or invoke various mechanisms to sanction the Court.

And that point brings us to the second approach, one that places emphasis on the "Constitution outside the Court." According to this account, the idea that only judges and justices interpret the Constitution is not only naive, but it also belies history. This at least was the argument Walter F. Murphy advanced more than twenty years ago when he asked, "Who shall interpret the Constitution?" His answer? Naturally, the courts, but not only the courts. The president, Congress, and even the people can also lay claim to playing a role in constitutional interpretation. Indeed, to Professor Murphy, that there is "no ultimate constitutional interpreter" is simply "a fact of American political life."[4] By way of example, Murphy points out that presidents of the stature of Thomas Jefferson, Andrew Jackson, and Abraham Lincoln were not willing to concede that they or Congress were obligated to accept the Supreme Court's constitutional interpretation as legally binding.

To say that contemporary scholars have rallied around Murphy's thinking is to seriously understate the case. Since the late 1990s, a multitude of volumes have dealt with how Congress and the president are involved

in constitutional interpretation.[5] That modern-day presidents, including George W. Bush and Barak Obama, have issued "signing statements" to express their interpretation of congressional legislation almost guarantees that more research will be forthcoming.[6]

Different as they may be, both approaches to the separation of powers system stress the role of all three branches of government in constitutional interpretation. The first emphasizes possible constraints on the Court imposed by the president and Congress. The second underscores that it is not only the Court that interprets the Constitution; the other institutions also can take and have taken on that task. As we explore the constitutional separation of powers/checks and balances system, keep in mind these contemporary accounts. Although our focus is on the Court's interpretation of various constitutional provisions, you will have a chance to consider the functions of the legislative and executive branches as well. You also will have ample opportunity to think about the extent to which the justices' perceptions of Congress and the president influence their decisions. In the coming pages we examine the significant political and legal clashes among the executive, legislative, and judicial branches, focusing on how the justices of the Supreme Court have interpreted and applied the Constitution to settle disputes. Throughout these constitutional controversies, what takes center stage are fundamental issues of institutional powers and the constraints placed on those powers.

3. See Lee Epstein, Jack Knight, and Andrew Martin, "The Supreme Court as a *Strategic* National Policy Maker," *Emory Law Journal* 50 (2001): 583–612; Rosenberg, "Judicial Independence and the Reality of Political Power"; Jeffrey A. Segal, Chad Westerland, and Stefanie A. Lindquist, "Congress, the Supreme Court and Judicial Review: Testing a Constitutional Separation of Powers Model," *American Journal of Political Science* 55 (2011): 89–104.

4. Murphy, "Who Shall Interpret the Constitution?"

5. See, for example, Larry Kramer, *The People Themselves: Popular Constitutionalism and Judicial Review* (New York: Oxford University Press, 2004); Mark Tushnet, *Taking the Constitution Away from the Courts* (Princeton, NJ: Princeton University Press, 1999); David P. Currie, *The Constitution in Congress: Democrats and Whigs, 1829–1861* (Chicago: University of Chicago Press, 2005); and. J. Mitchell Pickerill, *Constitutional Deliberation in Congress: The Impact of Judicial Review in a Separated System* (Durham, NC: Duke University Press, 2004).

6. Presidents may issue signing statements at the time they sign congressional bills. In such statements, they note their own interpretations of the laws or even assert their views of the "constitutional limits on the implementation" of some of the laws' provisions. For more on signing statements, see Philip J. Cooper, "George W. Bush, Edgar Allan Poe, and the Use and Abuse of Presidential Signing Statements," *Presidential Studies Quarterly* 35 (2005): 515–532; see also chapter 4 of this volume.

2 The Judiciary

ETWEEN 1932 AND 1983 Congress attached
legislative veto provisions to more than two
hundred laws. Although these provisions took
different forms, they usually authorized one house of
Congress to invalidate a decision of the executive
branch. One provision in the Immigration and
Nationality Act gave the U.S. attorney general power to
suspend the deportation of aliens, but Congress
reserved the authority to veto any such suspension by
a majority vote in either house. In *Immigration and
Naturalization Service v. Chadha* (1983), the U.S.
Supreme Court held that this device violated specific
clauses as well as general principles contained in the
U.S. Constitution. In doing so, as Justice Byron R.
White wrote in his dissent, the Court sounded the
"death knell" for the legislative veto.[1]

In many ways, the Court's action was less than startling. For two centuries federal courts have exerted
the power of judicial review—that is, the power to
review acts of government to determine their compatibility with the U.S. Constitution. And even though
the Constitution does not explicitly give them such
power, the courts' authority to do so has been challenged only occasionally. Today we take for granted
the notion that federal courts may review government

actions and strike them down if they violate constitutional mandates.

Nevertheless, when courts exert this power, as the
U.S. Supreme Court did in *Chadha,* they provoke
controversy. Look at it from this perspective:
Congress, composed of officials we *elect,* passed
these legislative veto provisions, which were then
rendered invalid by a Supreme Court of nine
unelected justices. Such an occurrence strikes some
people as quite odd, perhaps even antidemocratic.
Why should we Americans allow a branch of government over which we have no electoral control to
review and nullify the actions of the government
officials we elect to represent us?

The alleged antidemocratic nature of judicial review
is just one of many controversies surrounding the
practice. In this chapter, we review others—both in
theory and in practice. First, however, we explore the
circumstances leading to the adoption of Article III,
which outlines the contours of judicial power. To
understand the cases that follow—all of which examine the parameters of the judiciary's authority—it is
important to consider the framing of Article III. Next,
we turn to the development of judicial review in the
United States.

Judicial review is the primary weapon available to
the federal courts, the check they have on other
branches of government. Because this power can be
awesome in scope, many tend to emphasize it to the
neglect of factors that constrain its use, as well as other

---

1. It is worth noting that White's statement is true in theory but
not in practice. Since *Chadha,* Congress has continued to add legislative veto provisions to new laws. For more details, see Louis Fisher,
"The Legislative Veto: Invalidated, It Survives," *Law and Contemporary
Problems* 56 (1993): 273–293; and chapter 5 of this volume.

checks on the power of the Court. In the second and third parts of this chapter, we explore the limits on judicial power.

ESTABLISHMENT OF THE FEDERAL JUDICIARY

The federal judicial system is built on a foundation created by two major statements of the 1780s: Article III of the U.S. Constitution and the Judiciary Act of 1789. In this section, we consider both, with an emphasis on their content and the debates they provoked. Note, in particular, the degree to which the major controversies reflect more general concerns about federalism. Designing and fine-tuning the U.S. system of government required many compromises over the balance of power between the federal government and the states, and Article III and the Judiciary Act are no exceptions.

Article III

The framers of the Constitution spent days upon days debating the contents of Article I (dealing with the legislature) and Article II (centering on the executive), but they had comparatively little trouble drafting Article III. Indeed, it caused the least controversy of any major constitutional provision. Why? One reason is that the states and Great Britain had well-entrenched court systems, and the founders had firsthand knowledge of the workings of courts—knowledge they lacked about the other political institutions they were establishing. Second, thirty-four of the fifty-five delegates to the Constitutional Convention were lawyers or had some training in the law. They held a common vision of the *general* role courts should play in the new polity.[2]

Alexander Hamilton expressed that vision in *Federalist* No. 78, one of a series of papers designed to garner support for the ratification of the Constitution. Hamilton specifically referred to the judiciary as the "least dangerous branch" of government; he (and virtually all of the founders) saw the courts as legal, not political, bodies. He wrote, "If [judges] should be disposed to exercise WILL instead of JUDGMENT, the

consequence would equally be the substitution of their pleasure to that of the legislative body." The framers agreed on the need for judicial independence. They accomplished this goal by allowing judges to "hold their offices DURING GOOD BEHAVIOUR"—that is, giving them life tenure—rather than subjecting them to periodic public checks through the electoral process. The framers also concurred on the need to block Congress from reducing a federal judge's compensation during terms of continuous service. The compensation clause, located in Article III, implies judicial independence: the framers hoped to prevent members of the legislature upset with court decisions from punishing judges by cutting their pay.[3]

Federal judges continue to enjoy these protections, but many state court judges do not. In only three states do judges hold their jobs for life or until they reach a specified retirement age. In the remaining states judges must periodically face the electorate. In some states the voters decide whether to retain judges; in other states judges must be elected (or reelected), just as any other officials are. Either way, the practice of retaining or reelecting has raised interesting constitutional questions. In *Caperton v. A. T. Massey Coal Co.* (2009) *(excerpted in chapter 10),* the Court considered whether a judge should recuse himself from a case in which he has received substantial campaign contributions from a person with an interest in the outcome. The majority held that when there is a "serious risk of actual bias"—as it seemed clear in *Caperton*—failure to recuse amounts to a violation of the due process clause, which requires a "fair trial in a fair tribunal."

That the framers settled on life tenure for federal judges, and not some form of electoral or legislative

---

2. See Daniel A. Farber and Suzanna Sherry, *A History of the American Constitution,* 2nd ed. (St. Paul, MN: Thomson/West, 2005), 65.

3. Compensation clause cases are relatively rare, but one such dispute, *United States v. Hatter,* came before the Court in 2001. Here, the justices considered whether the clause prohibits the government from collecting certain Medicare and Social Security taxes from eight federal judges who were appointed before Congress extended the taxes to federal employees. Writing for the Court, Justice Stephen Breyer concluded that the compensation clause "does not prevent Congress from imposing a 'non-discriminatory tax laid generally' upon judges and other citizens, but it does prohibit taxation that singles out judges for specially unfavorable treatment. Consequently, we conclude that Congress may apply the Medicare tax—a nondiscriminatory tax—to then-sitting federal judges. The special retroactivity-related Social Security rules that Congress enacted in 1984, however, effectively singled out then-sitting federal judges for unfavorable treatment. Hence, we conclude that the Clause forbids the application of the Social Security tax to those judges."

check, and more generally shared a fundamental view of the role of the federal judiciary does not mean that they agreed on all the specifics. They had many debates over the structure of the American legal system. They agreed that there would be at least one federal court, the Supreme Court of the United States, but disagreed over the establishment of federal tribunals inferior to the Supreme Court. The Virginia Plan, which served as the basis for many of the proposals debated at the convention, suggested that Congress should establish lower federal courts. Delegates who favored a strong national government agreed with this plan, with some wanting to use Article III to create such courts.

But delegates favoring states' rights over those of the national government vehemently objected to the creation of any federal tribunals other than the U.S. Supreme Court. As one delegate, Pierce Butler of South Carolina, put it, "The people will not bear such an innovation. The states will revolt at such encroachments."[4] Instead of creating new federal courts, they proposed that the existing state courts should hear cases in the first instance, with an allowance for appeals to the U.S. Supreme Court. "This dispute," as Justice Hugo L. Black wrote in 1970, "resulted in compromise. One 'supreme Court' was created by the Constitution, and Congress was given the power to create other federal courts."[5] In other words, Article III does not establish a system of lower federal courts; rather, it gives Congress the option of doing so.

The First Congress (with its Federalist majority) took full advantage of Section 1 of Article III by immediately passing the Judiciary Act of 1789, which established lower federal courts. This action was not a surprise: because much of Article III—specifically Section 2, the longest part—defines the jurisdiction of federal courts that did not yet exist (or at least the jurisdiction that Congress could give them),[6] it is clear

that the majority of the founders anticipated the law. The framers outlined two types of jurisdiction that the federal courts might exercise: over cases involving certain subjects or over cases brought by certain parties. The framers also defined the jurisdiction of the U.S. Supreme Court in terms of its original and appellate authority *(see box 2-1).*

A second area of debate at the 1787 convention was the appointment of federal judges. Again, the debate focused on the Virginia Plan's suggestion that Congress appoint these judges. Some of the delegates backed the Virginia Plan, while others suggested that the Senate should make the appointments. Benjamin Franklin argued that perhaps lawyers should decide who would sit on the courts. After all, Franklin joked, the lawyers would select "the ablest of the profession in order to get rid of him, and share his practice among themselves."[7] Finally, the delegates decided that the appointment power should be given to the president, with the "advice and consent" of the Senate. Accordingly, the power to appoint federal judges is located in Article II, which lists the powers of the president. The Senate, however, takes the "advice and consent" phrase to mean that it must approve the president's nominees by a majority vote. And it has taken its part in the process quite seriously, rejecting outright 12 of the 160 nominations to the Supreme Court over the past two centuries—a greater number (proportionally speaking) than any other group of presidential appointees requiring senatorial approval

---

4. Quoted in Daniel A. Farber and Suzanna Sherry, *A History of the American Constitution,* 2nd edition (St. Paul, MN: Thomson/West, 2005), 70.

5. *Atlantic Coast Line Railroad Co. v. Brotherhood of Locomotive Engineers* (1970).

6. The traditional and still dominant view of Section 2 of Article III is that Congress is neither required to create federal courts nor required to provide such courts with the full range of jurisdiction over the cases listed in Section 2. See, for example, *Sheldon v. Sill* (1850), in which the Supreme Court wrote, "It must be admitted, that if the Constitution had ordained and established the inferior courts, and distributed to them their respective powers, they could

not be restricted or divested by Congress." But "because the Constitution did not do this, the Court concluded that Congress may withhold from any court of its creation jurisdiction of any of the enumerated controversies. Courts created by statute can have no jurisdiction other than that which the statute confers." Linda Mullenix, Martin H. Redish, and Georgene Vairo, *Understanding the Federal Courts and Jurisdiction* (New York: Matthew Bender, 1998), 7. Still, in *Martin v. Hunter's Lessee* (1816), Justice Story took the position that the Constitution required Congress to create the lower courts: "The language of the article throughout is manifestly designed to be mandatory upon the legislature. Its obligatory force is so imperative, that Congress could not, without a violation of its duty, have refused to carry it into operation." If this is so, then it seems reasonable to question the extent of Congress's discretion over the jurisdiction of the lower federal courts. Story's view has not been widely adopted, but see Akil Amar, "A Neo-Federalist View of Article III: Separating the Two Tiers of Federal Jurisdiction," *Boston University Law Review* 65 (1985): 205–274. See also our discussion of the Court's jurisdiction in this chapter.

7. Quoted in Farber and Sherry, *A History of the American Constitution,* 70.

BOX 2-1   JURISDICTION OF THE FEDERAL COURTS AS DEFINED IN ARTICLE III

Jurisdiction of the Lower Federal Courts

Subjects falling under their authority:

- Cases involving the U.S. Constitution, federal laws, and treaties
- Cases affecting ambassadors, public ministers, and consuls
- Cases of admiralty and maritime jurisdiction

Parties falling under their authority:

- United States
- Controversies between two or more states
- Controversies between a state and citizens of another state[1]
- Controversies between citizens of different states
- Controversies between citizens of the same state claiming lands under grants of different states
- Controversies between a state, or the citizens thereof, and foreign states, citizens, or subjects

Jurisdiction of the Supreme Court

Original jurisdiction:

- Cases affecting ambassadors, public ministers, and consuls
- Cases to which a state is a party

Appellate jurisdiction:

- Cases falling under the jurisdiction of the lower federal courts, "with such Exceptions, and under such Regulations as the Congress shall make."

1. In 1795 this was modified by the Eleventh Amendment, which removed from federal jurisdiction those cases in which a state is sued by the citizens of another state.

Another source of debate was James Madison's proposal for the creation of a council of revision, made up of Supreme Court justices and the president, with the power to veto legislative acts. Each time this idea was proposed, the delegates voted to defeat it. In *Marbury v. Madison* (1803), the first case we excerpt in this chapter, Chief Justice John Marshall in essence articulated such veto power for the Court. Those who take a dim view of Marshall's decision occasionally point to the delegates' rejection of the council of revision as proof that Marshall skirted the framers' intent.

At the end of the section on *Marbury v. Madison,* we consider debates over Marshall's holding. Here, we underscore that Article III—for the reasons just stated—did not establish any federal courts other than the U.S. Supreme Court. It was left up to Congress to create (or not) additional federal courts.[9] Dominated by Federalists, the First Congress did create new courts, giving some "flesh" to the "skeleton" that was Article III.[10]

Judiciary Act of 1789

The Judiciary Act of 1789 is a long and relatively complex law that, at its core, had two purposes. First, it sought to establish a federal court structure, which it accomplished by providing for the Supreme Court and circuit and district courts. Under the law, the Supreme Court was to have one chief justice and five associate justices. That the Court initially had six members illustrates an important point: Congress, not the U.S. Constitution, determines the number of justices on the Supreme Court. That number has been fixed at nine since 1869.

As figure 2-1 shows, the act also created thirteen district courts. Each of the eleven states that had ratified the Constitution received a court, with separate tribunals created for Maine and Kentucky, which were then parts

(see table 2-1). Another twenty-four Supreme Court nominations transmitted to the Senate were withdrawn, tabled, postponed, or otherwise not acted on.[8]

8. Presidents have sent 160 Supreme Court nominations to the Senate. Of these, according to the U.S. Senate's Web site (www.senate.gov/pagelayout/reference/nominations/Nominations.htm), 124

were confirmed, with 7 declining to serve. The Senate rejected 12. The rest failed to obtain confirmation because they were withdrawn, postponed, or otherwise not acted on. Note, however, that a withdrawal can become a successful appointment. After George W. Bush withdrew John G. Roberts's nomination to replace Sandra Day O'Connor, he nominated Roberts to serve as chief justice. The Senate confirmed Roberts, 78–22. For data on all nominations, see Epstein et al., *Supreme Court Compendium*, Table 4-15.

9. See note 6.

10. Russell R. Wheeler and Cynthia Harrison, *Creating the Federal Judicial System* (Washington, DC: Federal Judicial Center, 1989), 2.

TABLE 2-1   Presidential Nominees to the Supreme Court Rejected by the Senate

PRESIDENT	NOMINEE	DATE OF NOMINATION BY PRESIDENT	DATE OF REJECTION	VOTE	REASONS
Washington	John Rutledge	July 1, 1795	Dec. 15, 1795	10–14	Candidate's political views; mental health questions raised
Madison	Alexander Wolcott	Feb. 4, 1811	Feb. 13, 1811	9–24	Candidate's performance as a customs collector
Tyler	John C. Spencer	Jan. 9, 1844	Jan. 31, 1844	21–26	Partisan politics
Polk	George W. Woodward	Dec. 23, 1845	Jan. 22, 1846	20–29	Questions about candidate's political views
Buchanan	Jeremiah S. Black	Feb. 5, 1861	Feb. 21, 1861	25–26	Partisan politics; candidate's political views
Grant	Ebenezer R. Hoar	Dec. 15, 1869	Feb. 3, 1870	24–33	Candidate's political views
Cleveland	William B. Hornblower	Sept. 19, 1893	Jan. 15, 1894	24–30	Opposition from home state senator
Cleveland	Wheeler H. Peckham	Jan. 22, 1894	Feb. 16, 1894	32–41	Opposition from home state senator
Hoover	John J. Parker	Mar. 21, 1930	May 7, 1930	39–41	Questions about candidate's views toward civil rights and labor unions
Nixon	Clement Haynsworth Jr.	Aug. 18, 1969	Nov. 21, 1969	45–55	Ethical improprieties; opposition from labor and civil rights groups
Nixon	G. Harrold Carswell	Jan. 19, 1970	Apr. 8, 1970	45–51	Undistinguished judicial record; opposition from civil rights groups
Reagan	Robert H. Bork	July 1, 1987	Oct. 23, 1987	42–58	Candidate's political views; opposition from the liberal interest group community

SOURCES: David Savage, *CQ's Guide to the U.S. Supreme Court*, 4th ed. (Washington, DC: CQ Press, 2004); Lee Epstein, Jeffrey A. Segal, Harold J. Spaeth, and Thomas G. Walker, *The Supreme Court Compendium: Data, Decisions, and Developments*, 6th ed. (Thousand Oaks, CA: CQ Press, 2016), table 4-15; and Gregory A. Caldeira and John R. Wright, "Lobbying for Justice," in *Contemplating Courts*, ed. Lee Epstein (Washington, DC: CQ Press, 1995).

NOTE: This table includes only nominees rejected, with a vote, by the Senate. It excludes the twenty-four nominations that were transmitted to the Senate but ultimately withdrawn, tabled, postponed, or not acted on.

of Massachusetts and Virginia, respectively. District courts, then as now, were presided over by one judge. But the three newly established circuit courts were quite extraordinary in composition. Congress grouped the district courts—except those for Kentucky and Maine—geographically into the Eastern, Middle, and Southern Circuits and put one district court judge and two Supreme Court justices in charge of each. In other words, three judges would hear cases in the circuit courts. Today, appeals courts continue to hear cases in panels of three. However, these courts now have their own permanent judges, making regular participation by district court judges and Supreme Court justices unnecessary.

A second goal of the Judiciary Act was to specify the jurisdiction of the federal courts. Section 2 of Article III speaks broadly about the authority of federal courts, potentially giving them jurisdiction over cases involving particular parties or subjects or, in the case of the Supreme Court, original and appellate jurisdiction *(see box 2-1)*. The Judiciary Act provided more specific information, defining the parameters of authority for each of the newly established courts and for the U.S. Supreme Court. The district courts were to serve as trial courts, hearing cases involving admiralty issues, forfeitures and penalties, and petty federal crimes, as well as minor U.S. civil cases. Congress recognized that some of these courts would be busier than others and fixed judicial salaries accordingly. Delaware judges received only $800 per year for their services, while their counterparts in South Carolina, a coastal state that would generate many admiralty disputes, earned $1,800.[11]

---

11. Ibid., 6.

FIGURE 2-1   The Federal Court System under the Judiciary Act of 1789

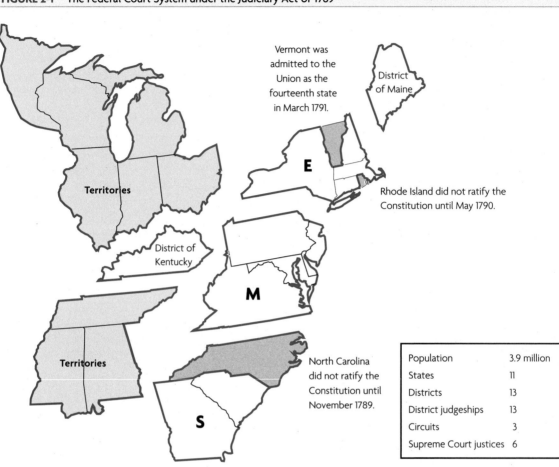

SOURCE: Russell R. Wheeler and Cynthia Harrison, *Creating the Federal Judicial System,* 3rd ed. (Washington, DC: Federal Judicial Center, 2005), 5.

NOTE: The Judiciary Act of 1789 created thirteen districts and placed eleven of them in three circuits: the Eastern, Middle, and Southern. Each district had a district court, which was a trial court with a single district judge and primarily admiralty jurisdiction. A circuit court also met in each district of the circuit and was composed of the district judge and two Supreme Court justices. The circuit courts exercised primarily diversity and criminal jurisdiction and heard appeals from the district courts in some cases. The districts of Maine and Kentucky (parts of the states of Massachusetts and Virginia, respectively) were part of no circuit; their district courts exercised both district and circuit court jurisdiction.

Unlike today, the circuit courts were trial courts with jurisdiction over cases involving citizens from different states and major federal criminal and civil cases. Congress also gave them limited appellate authority to hear major civil and admiralty disputes coming out of the district courts.

Finally, the 1789 act contained several provisions concerning the jurisdiction of the U.S. Supreme Court. Section 13 reiterated the Court's authority over suits in the first instance (its original jurisdiction) and gave the justices appellate jurisdiction over major civil disputes, those involving more than $2,000, which was a good deal of money back then. Section 13 also spoke about the Court's authority to issue writs of mandamus, which command a public official to carry out a particular act or duty: "The Supreme Court . . . shall have the power to issue . . . writs of *mandamus,* in cases warranted by the principles and usages of law, to any courts appointed, or persons holding office, under the authority of the United States." This matter may seem trivial, but, as we shall see, the Court's interpretation of this particular provision formed the centerpiece of *Marbury v. Madison.*

Another part of the act, Section 25, authorized the Supreme Court to review certain kinds of cases coming out of the states. Specifically, the Court could now hear appeals from the highest state courts if those tribunals upheld state laws against claims that the laws violated the Constitution or denied claims based on the U.S. Constitution, federal laws, or treaties.

At first glance, the components of the 1789 act—its establishment of a federal court system and of rules governing that system—appear to favor the Federalists' position. Recall that Anti-Federalist delegates at the Constitutional Convention did not want the document even to mention lower federal tribunals, much less to give Congress the authority to establish them. The 1789 act did that and more: it gave the Supreme Court the power to review state supreme court cases—surely an Anti-Federalist's worst nightmare! But it would be a mistake to believe that the act did not take into account the position taken by states' rights advocates. For example, the 1789 act used state lines as the boundaries for the district and circuit courts, even though the boundaries could have been defined in other ways.[12] That Congress tied the boundaries to the states may have been a concession to the Anti-Federalists, who wanted the judges of the federal courts to feel they were part of the legal and political cultures of the states.

Whichever side won or lost, passage of the 1789 Judiciary Act was a defining moment in American legal history. It established the first federal court system, one that is strikingly similar to that in effect today. And, as the following pages reveal, it paved the way for three landmark constitutional cases—*Marbury v. Madison, Martin v. Hunter's Lessee,* and *Cohens v. Virginia*—all of which centered on judicial review, the major power of the federal judiciary.

JUDICIAL REVIEW

Even though judicial review is a powerful tool of federal courts and there is some evidence that the framers intended courts to have it, it is not mentioned in the Constitution. Yet, even before ratification of the Constitution, courts in seven states, in at least eight cases, held that a state law violated a state constitution (or some other fundamental charter).[13] So, too, early in U.S. history, federal courts claimed it for themselves. In *Hylton v. United States* (1796), Daniel Hylton challenged the constitutionality of a 1793 federal tax on carriages. According to Hylton, the act violated the constitutional mandate that direct taxes must be apportioned on the basis of population. With only three justices participating, the Court upheld the act. But even by considering the challenge, the Court in effect reviewed the constitutionality of an act of Congress.

Not until 1803, however, would the Court invoke judicial review to strike down legislation it deemed incompatible with the U.S. Constitution. That decision came in the landmark case *Marbury v. Madison.* How does Chief Justice Marshall justify the Court's power to strike down legislation in light of the failure of the newly framed Constitution to provide it?

Marbury v. Madison

5 U.S. (1 Cranch) 137 (1803)

http://laws.findlaw.com/us/5/137.html

Vote: 4 (Chase, Marshall, Paterson, Washington)

    0

OPINION OF THE COURT: *Marshall*

NOT PARTICIPATING: *Cushing, Moore*

FACTS:

When voting in the presidential election of 1800 was over, it was apparent that Federalist president John Adams had lost after a long and bitter campaign, but it was not known who had won.[14] The Electoral College voting resulted in a tie between the Republican candidate, Thomas Jefferson, and his running mate, Aaron Burr, and the election had to be settled in the House of Representatives. In February 1801 the House elected Jefferson. This meant that the Federalists no longer

---

12. As Wheeler and Harrison note, "The creators of the federal judiciary might have established separate judicial administrative divisions that would ensure roughly equal allocation of workload and would be subject to realignment to maintain the allocation" (ibid.).

13. Saikrishna B. Prakash and John C. Yoo, "The Origins of Judicial Review," *University of Chicago Law Review* 70 (2003): 887–982.

14. For analyses of the events surrounding *Marbury*, see Jack Knight and Lee Epstein, "On the Struggle for Judicial Supremacy," *Law and Society Review* 30 (1996): 87–120; Dean Alfange Jr., "*Marbury v. Madison* and Original Understandings of Judicial Review: In Defense of Traditional Wisdom," *Supreme Court Review* (1994): 329–446.

controlled the presidency; they also lost their majority in Congress. Prior to the election, the Federalists controlled more than 56 percent of the 106 seats in the House and nearly 70 percent of the 32 seats in the Senate. After the election, those percentages declined to 35 percent and 44 percent, respectively.[15]

With these losses in the elected branches, the Federalists took steps to maintain control of the third branch of government, the judiciary. The lame-duck Congress enacted the Circuit Court Act of 1801, which created six new circuit courts and several district courts to accommodate the new states of Kentucky, Tennessee, and Vermont. These new courts required judges and support staff such as attorneys, marshals, and clerks. As a result, during the last six months of his term in office Adams made more than two hundred nominations, with sixteen judgeships (called the "midnight appointments" because of the rush to complete them before Adams's term expired) approved by the Senate during his last two weeks in office.

An even more important opportunity had arisen in December 1800, when the third chief justice of the United States, Federalist Oliver Ellsworth, resigned so that Adams—not Jefferson—could name his replacement. Adams first offered the post to John Jay, who had served as the first chief justice before leaving the Court to take the then-more-prestigious office of governor of New York. When Jay refused, Adams turned to his secretary of state, John Marshall, an ardent Federalist. The Senate confirmed Marshall in January 1801, but he also continued to serve as secretary of state.

In addition, the Federalist Congress passed the Organic Act of 1801, which authorized Adams to appoint forty-two justices of the peace for the District of Columbia. It was this seemingly innocuous law that set the stage for the dramatic case of *Marbury v. Madison.* In the confusion of the Adams administration's last days in office, Marshall, the outgoing secretary of state, failed to deliver some of these commissions. When the new administration came into office, James Madison, the new secretary of state, acting under orders from Jefferson, refused to deliver at least five commissions.[16]

Indeed, some years later, Jefferson explained the situation in this way:

I found the commissions on the table of the Department of State, on my entrance into office, and I forbade their delivery. Whatever is in the Executive offices is certainly deemed to be in the hands of the President, and in this case, was actually in my hands, because when I countermanded them, there was as yet no Secretary of State.[17]

As a result, in 1801 William Marbury and three others who were denied their commissions went directly to the Supreme Court and asked it to issue a writ of mandamus ordering Madison to deliver the commissions. Marbury thought he could take his case directly to the Court because Section 13 of the 1789 Judiciary Act gives the Court the power to issue writs of mandamus to anyone holding federal office. The relevant passage of Section 13 reads as follows:

The Supreme Court shall . . . have appellate jurisdiction from the circuit courts and courts of the several states, in the cases herein after specifically provided for; and shall have power to issue . . . mandamus in cases warranted by the principles and usages of law, to any courts appointed, or persons holding office, under the authority of the United States.

In this volatile political climate, Marshall, now serving as chief justice, was perhaps in the most tenuous position of all. On one hand, he had been a supporter of the Federalist Party, which now looked to him to "scold" the Jefferson administration. On the other, Marshall wanted to avoid a confrontation between the Jefferson administration and the Supreme Court, which not only seemed imminent but also could end in disaster for the Court and the struggling nation. In fact, Jefferson and his party were so annoyed with the Court for agreeing to hear the *Marbury* dispute that they began to consider impeaching Federalist judges—with two justices (Samuel Chase and Marshall himself) high on their lists. Note, too, the year in which the Court handed down the decision in *Marbury*; the case was not decided until two years after Marbury filed suit because Congress and the Jefferson administration had abolished the 1802 term of the Court.

15. Data are from the House's and Senate's Web sites: http://artandhistory.house.gov/house_history/partyDiv.aspx and http://www.senate.gov/history/partydiv.htm.

16. Historical accounts differ, but it seems that Jefferson decreased the number of Adams's appointments to justice of the peace positions to thirty from forty-two. Twenty-five of these thirty appointees received their commissions, but five, including William

Marbury, did not. See Francis N. Stites, *John Marshall* (Boston: Little, Brown, 1981), 84.

17. Quoted in Charles Warren, *The Supreme Court in United States History,* vol. 1 (Boston: Little, Brown, 1922), 244.

ARGUMENTS:

For the applicant, William Marbury:

- After the president has signed a commission for an office, it comes to the secretary of state. Nothing remains to be done except that the secretary perform those ministerial acts that the law imposes upon him. His duty is to seal, record, and deliver the commission. In such a case the appointment becomes complete by the signing and sealing; and the secretary does wrong if he withholds the commission.
- Congress has expressly given the Supreme Court the power of issuing writs of mandamus.
- Congress can confer original jurisdiction in cases other than those mentioned in the Constitution. The Supreme Court has entertained jurisdiction on mandamus in several cases—*United States v. Lawrence*, 3 U.S. 42 (1795), for example. In this case and in others, the power of the Court to issue writs of mandamus was taken for granted in the arguments of counsel on both sides. It appears there has been a legislative construction of the Constitution upon this point, and a judicial practice under it, since the formation of the government.

William Marbury

For Secretary of State James Madison:

(Madison and Jefferson intentionally did not appear in court to emphasize their position that the proceedings had no legitimacy. So it seems that Madison was unrepresented and no argument was made in his behalf.)

> **THE FOLLOWING OPINION OF THE COURT WAS DELIVERED BY THE CHIEF JUSTICE.**

The peculiar delicacy of this case, the novelty of some of its circumstances, and the real difficulty attending the points which occur in it, require a complete exposition of the principles, on which the opinion to be given by the court, is founded.

These principles have been, on the side of the applicant, very ably argued at the bar. In rendering the opinion of the court, there will be some departure in form, though not in substance, from the points stated in that argument.

In the order in which the court has viewed this subject, the following questions have been considered and decided.

1st. Has the applicant a right to the commission he demands?

2dly. If he has a right, and that right has been violated, do the laws of his country afford him a remedy?

John Marshall

Maryland Historical Society

Library of Congress

James Madison

Thomas Jefferson

3dly. If they do afford him a remedy, is it a *mandamus* issuing from this court?

The first object of enquiry is,

1st. Has the applicant a right to the commission he demands? . . .

In order to determine whether he is entitled to this commission, it becomes necessary to enquire whether he has been appointed to the office. For if he has been appointed, the law continues him in office for five years, and he is entitled to the possession of those evidences of office, which, being completed, became his property. . . .

These are the clauses of the constitution and laws of the United States, which affect this part of the case. They seem to contemplate three distinct operations:

1st. The nomination. This is the sole act of the President, and is completely voluntary.

2d. The appointment. This is also the act of the President, and is also a voluntary act, though it can only be performed by and with the advice and consent of the senate.

3d. The commission. To grant a commission to a person appointed, might perhaps be deemed a duty enjoined by the constitution. "He shall," says that instrument, "commission all the officers of the United States." . . .

The transmission of the commission, is a practice directed by convenience, but not by law. It cannot therefore be necessary to constitute the appointment which must precede it, and which is the mere act of the President. . . . A commission is transmitted to a person already appointed; not to a person to be appointed or not, as the letter enclosing the commission should happen to get into the post office and reach him in safety, or to miscarry. . . .

If the transmission of a commission be not considered as necessary to give validity to an appointment; still less is its acceptance. The appointment is the sole act of the President; the acceptance is the sole act of the officer, and is, in plain common sense, posterior to the appointment. . . .

Mr. Marbury, then, since his commission was signed by the President, and sealed by the secretary of state, was appointed; and as the law creating the office, gave the officer a right to hold for five years, independent of the Executive, the appointment was not revocable; but vested in the officer legal rights, which are protected by the laws of his country.

To withhold his commission, therefore, is an act deemed by the court not warranted by law, but violative of a vested legal right.

This brings us to the second enquiry; which is,

2dly. If he has a right, and that right has been violated, do the laws of his country afford him a remedy?

The very essence of civil liberty certainly consists in the right of every individual to claim the protection of the laws, whenever he receives an injury. One of the first duties of government is to afford that protection. In Great Britain, the King himself is sued in the respectful form of a petition, and he never fails to comply with the judgment of his court.

The government of the United States has been emphatically termed a government of laws, and not of men. It will certainly cease to deserve this high appellation, if the laws furnish no remedy for the violation of a vested legal right.

If this obloquy is to be cast on the jurisprudence of our country, it must arise from the peculiar character of the case. . . .

It behooves us, then, to inquire whether there be in its composition any ingredient which shall exempt from legal investigation or exclude the injured party from legal redress. . . .

Is it in the nature of the transaction? Is the act of delivering or withholding a commission to be considered as a mere political act belonging to the Executive department alone, for the performance of which entire confidence is placed by our Constitution in the Supreme Executive, and for any misconduct respecting which the injured individual has no remedy?

That there may be such cases is not to be questioned. But that every act of duty to be performed in any of the great departments of government constitutes such a case is not to be admitted. . . .

It follows, then, that the question whether the legality of an act of the head of a department be examinable in a court of justice or not must always depend on the nature of that act.

If some acts be examinable and others not, there must be some rule of law to guide the Court in the exercise of its jurisdiction.

In some instances, there may be difficulty in applying the rule to particular cases; but there cannot, it is believed, be much difficulty in laying down the rule.

By the Constitution of the United States, the President is invested with certain important political powers, in the exercise of which he is to use his own discretion, and is accountable only to his country in his political character and to his own conscience. To aid him in the performance of these duties, he is authorized to appoint certain officers, who act by his authority and in conformity with his orders.

In such cases, their acts are his acts; and whatever opinion may be entertained of the manner in which executive discretion may be used, still there exists, and can

exist, no power to control that discretion. The subjects are political. They respect the nation, not individual rights, and, being entrusted to the Executive, the decision of the Executive is conclusive. . . .

But when the Legislature proceeds to impose on that officer other duties; when he is directed peremptorily to perform certain acts; when the rights of individuals are dependent on the performance of those acts; he is so far the officer of the law, is amenable to the laws for his conduct, and cannot at his discretion, sport away the vested rights of others.

The conclusion from this reasoning is, that where the heads of departments are the political or confidential agents of the Executive, merely to execute the will of the President, or rather to act in cases in which the Executive possesses a constitutional or legal discretion, nothing can be more perfectly clear than that their acts are only politically examinable. But where a specific duty is assigned by law, and individual rights depend upon the performance of that duty, it seems equally clear that the individual who considers himself injured, has a right to resort to the laws of his country for a remedy.

If this be the rule, let us enquire how it applies to the case under the consideration of the court.

The power of nominating to the senate, and the power of appointing the person nominated, are political powers, to be exercised by the President according to his own discretion. When he has made an appointment, he has exercised his whole power, and his discretion has been completely applied to the case. If, by law, the officer be removable at the will of the President, then a new appointment may be immediately made, and the rights of the officer are terminated. But as a fact which has existed cannot be made never to have existed, the appointment cannot be annihilated; and consequently if the officer is by law not removable at the will of the President; the rights he has acquired are protected by the law, and are not resumable by the President. They cannot be extinguished by executive authority, and he has the privilege of asserting them in like manner as if they had been derived from any other source.

The question whether a right has vested or not, is, in its nature, judicial, and must be tried by the judicial authority. If, for example, Mr. Marbury had taken the oaths of a magistrate, and proceeded to act as one; in consequence of which a suit had been instituted against him, in which his defence had depended on his being a magistrate; the validity of his appointment must have been determined by judicial authority.

So, if he conceives that, by virtue of his appointment, he has a legal right, either to the commission which has been made out for him, or to a copy of that commission, it is equally a question examinable in a court, and the decision of the court upon it must depend on the opinion entertained of his appointment.

That question has been discussed, and the opinion is, that the latest point of time which can be taken as that at which the appointment was complete, and evidenced, was when, after the signature of the president, the seal of the United States was affixed to the commission.

It is then the opinion of the court,

1st. That by signing the commission of Mr. Marbury, the president of the United States appointed him a justice of peace, for the county of Washington in the district of Columbia; and that the seal of the United States, affixed thereto by the secretary of state, is conclusive testimony of the verity of the signature, and of the completion of the appointment; and that the appointment conferred on him a legal right to the office for the space of five years.

2dly. That, having this legal title to the office, he has a consequent right to the commission; a refusal to deliver which, is a plain violation of that right, for which the laws of his country afford him a remedy.

It remains to be enquired whether,

3dly. He is entitled to the remedy for which he applies.

The act to establish the judicial courts of the United States authorizes the supreme court "to issue writs of mandamus, in cases warranted by the principles and usages of law, to any courts appointed, or persons holding office, under the authority of the United States."

The secretary of state, being a person holding an office under the authority of the United States, is precisely within the letter of the description; and if this court is not authorized to issue a writ of mandamus to such an officer, it must be because the law is unconstitutional, and therefore absolutely incapable of conferring the authority, and assigning the duties which its words purport to confer and assign.

The constitution vests the whole judicial power of the United States in one supreme court, and such inferior courts as congress shall, from time to time, ordain and establish. This power is expressly extended to all cases arising under the laws of the United States; and consequently, in some form, may be exercised over the present case; because the right claimed is given by a law of the United States.

In the distribution of this power it is declared that "the supreme court shall have original jurisdiction in all cases affecting ambassadors, other public ministers and consuls, and those in which a state shall be a party. In all other cases, the supreme court shall have appellate jurisdiction."

It has been insisted, at the bar, that as the original grant of jurisdiction, to the supreme and inferior courts, is general, and the clause, assigning original jurisdiction to the supreme court, contains no negative or restrictive words; the power remains to the legislature, to assign original jurisdiction to that court in other cases than those specified in the article which has been recited; provided those cases belong to the judicial power of the United States.

If it had been intended to leave it in the discretion of the legislature to apportion the judicial power between the supreme and inferior courts according to the will of that body, it would certainly have been useless to have proceeded further than to have defined the judicial power, and the tribunals in which it should be vested. The subsequent part of the section is mere surplussage, is entirely without meaning, if such is to be the construction. If congress remains at liberty to give this court appellate jurisdiction, where the constitution has declared their jurisdiction shall be original; and original jurisdiction where the constitution has declared it shall be appellate; the distribution of jurisdiction, made in the constitution, is form without substance.

Affirmative words are often, in their operation, negative of other objects than those affirmed; and in this case, a negative or exclusive sense must be given to them or they have no operation at all.

It cannot be presumed that any clause in the constitution is intended to be without effect; and therefore such a construction is inadmissible, unless the words require it.

If the solicitude of the convention, respecting our peace with foreign powers, induced a provision that the supreme court should take original jurisdiction in cases which might be supposed to affect them; yet the clause would have proceeded no further than to provide for such cases, if no further restriction on the powers of congress had been intended. That they should have appellate jurisdiction in all other cases, with such exceptions as congress might make, is no restriction; unless the words be deemed exclusive of original jurisdiction.

When an instrument organizing fundamentally a judicial system, divides it into one supreme, and so many inferior courts as the legislature may ordain and establish; then enumerates its powers, and proceeds so far to distribute them, as to define the jurisdiction of the supreme court by declaring the cases in which it shall take original jurisdiction, and that in others it shall take appellate jurisdiction; the plain import of the words seems to be, that in one class of cases its jurisdiction is original, and not appellate;

in the other it is appellate, and not original. If any other construction would render the clause inoperative, that is an additional reason for rejecting such other construction, and for adhering to their obvious meaning.

To enable this court then to issue a mandamus, it must be shewn to be an exercise of appellate jurisdiction, or to be necessary to enable them to exercise appellate jurisdiction.

It has been stated at the bar that the appellate jurisdiction may be exercised in a variety of forms, and that if it be the will of the legislature that a mandamus should be used for that purpose, that will must be obeyed. This is true, yet the jurisdiction must be appellate, not original.

It is the essential criterion of appellate jurisdiction, that it revises and corrects the proceedings in a cause already instituted, and does not create that cause. Although, therefore, a mandamus may be directed to courts, yet to issue such a writ to an officer for the delivery of a paper, is in effect the same as to sustain an original action for that paper, and therefore seems not to belong to appellate, but to original jurisdiction. Neither is it necessary in such a case as this, to enable the court to exercise its appellate jurisdiction.

The authority, therefore, given to the supreme court, by the act establishing the judicial courts of the United States, to issue writs of mandamus to public officers, appears not to be warranted by the constitution; and it becomes necessary to enquire whether a jurisdiction, so conferred, can be exercised.

The question, whether an act, repugnant to the constitution, can become the law of the land, is a question deeply interesting to the United States; but, happily, not of an intricacy proportioned to its interest. It seems only necessary to recognise certain principles, supposed to have been long and well established, to decide it.

That the people have an original right to establish, for their future government, such principles as, in their opinion, shall most conduce to their own happiness, is the basis, on which the whole American fabric has been erected. The exercise of this original right is a very great exertion; nor can it, nor ought it to be frequently repeated. The principles, therefore, so established, are deemed fundamental. And as the authority, from which they proceed, is supreme, and can seldom act, they are designed to be permanent.

This original and supreme will organizes the government, and assigns, to different departments, their respective powers. It may either stop here; or establish certain limits not to be transcended by those departments.

The government of the United States is of the latter description. The powers of the legislature are defined, and limited; and that those limits may not be mistaken, or forgotten, the constitution is written. To what purpose are powers limited, and to what purpose is that limitation committed to writing, if these limits may, at any time, be passed by those intended to be restrained? The distinction, between a government with limited and unlimited powers, is abolished, if those limits do not confine the persons on whom they are imposed, and if acts prohibited and acts allowed, are of equal obligation. It is a proposition too plain to be contested, that the constitution controls any legislative act repugnant to it; or, that the legislature may alter the constitution by an ordinary act.

Between these alternatives there is no middle ground. The constitution is either a superior, paramount law, unchangeable by ordinary means, or it is on a level with ordinary legislative acts, and like other acts, is alterable when the legislature shall please to alter it.

If the former part of the alternative be true, then a legislative act contrary to the constitution is not law: if the latter part be true, then written constitutions are absurd attempts, on the part of the people, to limit a power, in its own nature illimitable.

Certainly all those who have framed written constitutions contemplate them as forming the fundamental and paramount law of the nation, and consequently the theory of every such government must be, that an act of the legislature, repugnant to the constitution, is void.

This theory is essentially attached to a written constitution, and is consequently to be considered, by this court, as one of the fundamental principles of our society. It is not therefore to be lost sight of in the further consideration of this subject.

If an act of the legislature, repugnant to the constitution, is void, does it, notwithstanding its invalidity, bind the courts, and oblige them to give it effect? Or, in other words, though it be not law, does it constitute a rule as operative as if it was a law? This would be to overthrow in fact what was established in theory; and would seem, at first view, an absurdity too gross to be insisted on. It shall, however, receive a more attentive consideration.

It is emphatically the province and duty of the judicial department to say what the law is. Those who apply the rule to particular cases, must of necessity expound and interpret that rule. If two laws conflict with each other, the courts must decide on the operation of each.

So if a law be in opposition to the constitution; if both the law and the constitution apply to a particular case, so that the court must either decide that case conformably to the law, disregarding the constitution; or conformably to the constitution, disregarding the law; the court must determine which of these conflicting rules governs the case. This is of the very essence of judicial duty.

If then the courts are to regard the constitution; and the constitution is superior to any ordinary act of the legislature; the constitution, and not such ordinary act, must govern the case to which they both apply.

Those then who controvert the principle that the constitution is to be considered, in court, as a paramount law, are reduced to the necessity of maintaining that courts must close their eyes on the constitution, and see only the law.

This doctrine would subvert the very foundation of all written constitutions. It would declare that an act, which, according to the principles and theory of our government, is entirely void; is yet, in practice, completely obligatory. It would declare, that if the legislature shall do what is expressly forbidden, such act, notwithstanding the express prohibition, is in reality effectual. It would be giving to the legislature a practical and real omnipotence, with the same breath which professes to restrict their powers within narrow limits. It is prescribing limits, and declaring that those limits may be passed at pleasure.

That it thus reduces to nothing what we have deemed the greatest improvement on political institutions—a written constitution—would of itself be sufficient, in America, where written constitutions have been viewed with so much reverence, for rejecting the construction. But the peculiar expressions of the constitution of the United States furnish additional arguments in favour of its rejection.

The judicial power of the United States is extended to all cases arising under the constitution.

Could it be the intention of those who gave this power, to say that, in using it, the constitution should not be looked into? That a case arising under the constitution should be decided without examining the instrument under which it arises?

This is too extravagant to be maintained.

In some cases then, the constitution must be looked into by the judges. And if they can open it at all, what part of it are they forbidden to read, or to obey?

There are many other parts of the constitution which serve to illustrate this subject.

It is declared that "no tax or duty shall be laid on articles exported from any state." Suppose a duty on the export of cotton, of tobacco, or of flour; and a suit instituted to recover it. Ought judgment to be rendered in such a case? ought the judges to close their eyes on the constitution, and only see the law?

The constitution declares that "no bill of attainder or *ex post facto* law shall be passed."

If, however, such a bill should be passed and a person should be prosecuted under it; must the court condemn to death those victims whom the constitution endeavours to preserve?

"No person," says the constitution, "shall be convicted of treason unless on the testimony of two witnesses to the same overt act, or on confession in open court."

Here the language of the constitution is addressed especially to the courts. It prescribes, directly for them, a rule of evidence not to be departed from. If the legislature should change that rule, and declare *one* witness, or a confession *out* of court, sufficient for conviction, must the constitutional principle yield to the legislative act?

From these, and many other selections which might be made, it is apparent, that the Framers of the constitution contemplated that instrument, as a rule for the government of *courts*, as well as of the legislature.

Why otherwise does it direct the judges to take an oath to support it? This oath certainly applies, in an especial manner, to their conduct in their official character. How immoral to impose it on them, if they were to be used as the instruments, and the knowing instruments, for violating what they swear to support!

The oath of office, too, imposed by the legislature, is completely demonstrative of the legislative opinion on this subject. It is in these words, "I do solemnly swear that I will administer justice without respect to persons, and do equal right to the poor and to the rich; and that I will faithfully and impartially discharge all the duties incumbent on me as according to the best of my abilities and understanding, agreeably to *the constitution*, and laws of the United States."

Why does a judge swear to discharge his duties agreeably to the constitution of the United States, if that constitution forms no rule for his government? if it is closed upon him, and cannot be inspected by him?

If such be the real state of things, this is worse than solemn mockery. To prescribe, or to take this oath, becomes equally a crime.

It is also not entirely unworthy of observation, that in declaring what shall be the supreme law of the land, the constitution itself is first mentioned; and not the laws of the United States generally, but those only which shall be made in pursuance of the constitution, have that rank.

Thus, the particular phraseology of the constitution of the United States confirms and strengthens the principle, supposed to be essential to all written constitutions, that a law repugnant to the constitution is void; and that courts, as well as other departments, are bound by that instrument.

The rule must be discharged.

Scholars differ about Marshall's opinion in *Marbury,* but supporters and critics alike acknowledge Marshall's shrewdness. As the great legal scholar Edward S. Corwin wrote,

Regarded merely as a judicial decision, the decision of *Marbury v. Madison* must be considered as most extraordinary, but regarded as a political pamphlet designed to irritate an enemy [Jefferson] to the very limit of endurance, it must be regarded a huge success.[18]

To see Corwin's point, we only have to think about the way the chief justice dealt with a most delicate political situation. By ruling against Marbury—who never did receive his judicial appointment *(see box 2-2)*—Marshall avoided a potentially devastating clash with Jefferson. But, by exerting the power of judicial review, Marshall sent the president a clear signal that the Court would be a major player in the American government. Other scholars, however, point out that judicial review emerged not because of some brilliant strategic move by Marshall in the face of intense political opposition, but because it was politically viable at the time. According to these scholars, Jefferson favored the establishment of judicial review and Marshall realized this. So Marshall simply took the rational course of action: deny Marbury his commission (which Jefferson desired) and articulate judicial review (a move that Jefferson also approved).[19]

BOX 2-2   AFTERMATH . . . *MARBURY v. MADISON*

FROM MEAGER beginnings, William Marbury gained political and economic influence in his home state of Maryland and became a strong supporter of John Adams and the Federalist Party. Unlike others of his day who rose in wealth through agriculture or trade, Marbury's path to prominence was banking and finance. At age thirty-eight he saw his appointment to be a justice of the peace as a public validation of his rising economic status and social prestige. Marbury never received his judicial position; instead, he returned to his financial activities, ultimately becoming the president of a bank in Georgetown. He died in 1835, the same year as Chief Justice John Marshall.

Other participants in the famous decision played major roles in the early history of our nation. Thomas Jefferson, who refused to honor Marbury's appointment, served two terms as chief executive, leaving office in 1809 as one of the nation's most revered presidents. James Madison, the secretary of state who carried out Jefferson's order depriving Marbury of his

judgeship, became the nation's fourth president, serving from 1809 to 1817. Following the *Marbury* decision, Chief Justice Marshall led the Court for an additional thirty-two years. His tenure was marked with fundamental rulings expanding the power of the judiciary and enhancing the position of the federal government relative to the states. He is rightfully regarded as history's most influential chief justice.

Although the *Marbury* decision established the power of judicial review, it is ironic that the Marshall Court never again used its authority to strike down a piece of congressional legislation. In fact, it was not until *Scott v. Sandford* (1857), more than two decades after Marshall's death, that the Court once again invalidated a congressional statute.

SOURCES: John A. Garraty, "The Case of the Missing Commissions," in *Quarrels That Have Shaped the Constitution*, rev. ed., ed. John A. Garraty (New York: Harper & Row, 1987); David F. Forte, "Marbury's Travail: Federalist Politics and William Marbury's Appointment as Justice of the Peace," *Catholic University Law Review* 45 (1996): 349–402.

---

18. Edward S. Corwin, "The Establishment of Judicial Review—II," *Michigan Law Review* 9 (1911): 292.

19. For more on this view, see Knight and Epstein, "On the Struggle for Judicial Supremacy."

Either way, the decision helped to establish Marshall's reputation as perhaps the greatest justice in Supreme Court history. As will be shown throughout this book, *Marbury* was just the first in a long line of seminal Marshall decisions. Most important here, *Marbury* asserted the Court's authority to review and strike down government actions that were incompatible with the Constitution. In Marshall's view, such authority, while not explicit in the Constitution, was clearly intended by the framers of that document. Was he correct? His opinion makes a plausible argument, but some judges and scholars have suggested otherwise. We review their assertions later in this chapter.

For now, it is worth noting that many countries have written judicial review into their constitutions, refusing to leave its establishment to chance *(see box 2-3)*. It is also the case that today's U.S. Supreme Court justices continue to cite *Marbury* with approval.

Consider, for example, the Court's decision in *City of Boerne v. Flores* (1997). At issue was the Religious Freedom Restoration Act of 1993 (RFRA), which Congress passed by overwhelming majorities in response to a 1990 Court decision, *Employment Division v. Smith*. RFRA directed the Court to adopt a particular standard of law in constitutional cases involving the free exercise clause of the First Amendment—a standard the Court had rejected in *Smith*.

In striking down Congress's effort at constitutional interpretation, the Court did not hesitate to cite *Marbury v. Madison*:

Our national experience teaches that the Constitution is preserved best when each part of the government respects both the Constitution and the proper actions and determinations of the other branches. When the Court has interpreted the Constitution, it has acted within the province of the Judicial Branch, which embraces the duty to say what the law is. *Marbury v. Madison*. When the political branches of the Government act against the background of a judicial interpretation of the Constitution already issued, it must be understood that in later cases and controversies the Court will treat its precedents with the respect due them under settled principles, including stare decisis, and contrary expectations must be disappointed. RFRA was designed to control cases and controversies, such as the one before us; but as the provisions of the federal statute

here invoked are beyond congressional authority, it is this Court's precedent, not RFRA, which must control.[20]

Three years later, in **Dickerson v. United States** (2000), the Court reiterated this message. At issue was a law Congress enacted in 1968 that was designed to overturn the Court's decision in *Miranda v. Arizona* (1966)—the decision that established the now-famous Miranda warning: "You have the right to remain silent; anything you say can and will be used against you." Once the justices held that *Miranda* announced a constitutional rule, they concluded that the 1968 congressional law was unconstitutional: "Congress may not legislatively supersede our decisions interpreting and applying the Constitution. See, e.g., **City of Boerne v. Flores** (1997)."

Judicial Review of State Court Decisions

In *Marbury* the Court addressed only the power to review acts of the federal government. Could the Court also exert judicial review over the states? Section 25 of the 1789 Judiciary Act suggested that it could. Recall from our discussion of the act that Congress authorized the Court to review appeals from the highest state courts, if those tribunals upheld state laws against challenges of unconstitutionality or denied claims based on the U.S. Constitution, federal laws, or treaties. But the mere existence of this statute did not necessarily mean that either state courts or the Supreme Court would follow it. After all, in *Marbury* the justices told Congress that it could not interpret Article III to expand the original jurisdiction of the Supreme Court—if that is, in fact, what Congress did. Would they say the same thing about Section 25, that Congress improperly read Article III to authorize the Court to review certain kinds of state court decisions?

Also to be considered was the potentially hostile reaction from the states, which in the 1780s and 1790s zealously guarded their power from federal encroachment. Even if the Court were to take advantage of its ability to review state court decisions, it was more than likely that they would disregard its rulings. Keep these

---

20. The battle over RFRA continued after *Boerne*. In 2000 Congress enacted another, albeit watered-down, version of the law, called the Religious Land Use and Institutionalized Persons Act, thereby generating the possibility that the Court might eventually approve part of what Congress wanted. Indeed, the Court upheld the law in *Cutter v. Wilkinson* (2005).

BOX 2-3 JUDICIAL REVIEW IN GLOBAL PERSPECTIVE

JUDICIAL AUTHORITY to invalidate acts of coordinate branches of government is not unique to the United States, although it is fair to say that the prestige of the U.S. Supreme Court has provided a model and incentive for other countries. By the middle of the nineteenth century, the Judicial Committee of the British Privy Council was functioning as a kind of constitutional arbiter for colonial governments within the British Empire—but not for the United Kingdom itself. Then in the late nineteenth century Canada, and in the first years of the twentieth Australia, created their own systems of constitutional review.

In the nineteenth century Argentina also modeled its Corte Suprema on that of the United States and even instructed its judges to pay special attention to precedents of the American tribunal. In the twentieth century Austria, India, Ireland, and the Philippines adopted judicial review, and variations of this power can be found in Norway, Switzerland, much of Latin America, and some countries in Africa.

After World War II the three defeated Axis powers—Italy, Japan, and (West) Germany—all institutionalized judicial review in their new constitutions. This development was due in part to revulsion regarding their recent experiences with unchecked political power and in part to the influence of American occupying authorities. Japan, where the constitutional document was largely drafted by Americans, follows the decentralized model of the United States: the power of constitutional review is diffused throughout the entire judicial system.[1] Any court of general jurisdiction can declare a legislative or executive act invalid.

Germany and Italy, and later Belgium, Portugal, and Spain, followed a centralized model first adopted in the Austrian constitution of 1920. Each country has a single constitutional court (although some sit in divisions or senates) that has a judicial monopoly on reviewing acts of government for their compatibility with the constitution. The most a lower court judge can do when a constitutional issue is raised is to refer the problem to the specialized constitutional court. *(See box 1-1.)*

After the Berlin Wall was torn down in 1989 and the Soviet Union disintegrated soon after, many Eastern European republics looked to judges' interpreting constitutional texts with bills of rights to protect their newfound liberties. Most opted for centralized systems of constitutional review, establishing ordinary tribunals and a separate constitutional court. They made this choice despite familiarity with John Marshall's argument for a decentralized court system in *Marbury*; namely, all judges may face the problem of a conflict between a statute or executive order on one hand and the terms of a constitutional document on the other. If judges cannot give preference to the constitutional provision over ordinary legislation or an executive act, they violate their oath to support the constitution.

The experiences of these tribunals have varied. The German Constitutional Court is largely regarded as a success story. In its first thirty-eight years, that tribunal invalidated 292 Bund (national) and 130 Land (state) laws, provoking frequent complaints that it "judicializes" politics.[2] The Court, however, has survived these attacks and has gone on to create a new and politically significant jurisprudence in the fields of federalism and civil liberties. The Russian Constitutional Court stood (or teetered) in stark contrast. It too began to make extensive use of judicial review to strike down government acts, but it quickly paid a steep price: in 1993 President Boris Yeltsin suspended the court's operations, and it did not resume its activities until nearly two years later.

1. Walter F. Murphy and Joseph Tanenhaus, eds., *Comparative Constitutional Law* (New York: St. Martin's Press, 1977), chaps. 1–6; C. Neal Tate and Torbjörn Vallinder, eds., *The Global Expansion of Judicial Power: The Judicialization of Politics* (New York: New York University Press, 1995).

2. Donald P. Kommens, *The Constitutional Jurisprudence of the Federal Republic of Germany*, 2nd ed. (Durham, NC: Duke University Press, 1997), 52.

SOURCE: Adapted from C. Herman Pritchett, Walter F. Murphy, Lee Epstein, and Jack Knight, *Courts, Judges, and Politics* (New York: McGraw-Hill, 2005), chap. 6.

issues in mind as you read *Martin v. Hunter's Lessee,* in which the Court sustained its power to review state court decisions that met the requirements of Section 25 (those upholding a state law against challenges of unconstitutionality or denying a claim based on the U.S. Constitution, federal laws, or treaties).

Martin v. Hunter's Lessee

14 U.S. (1 Wheat) 304 (1816)
http://laws.findlaw.com/us/14/304.html
Vote: 6 (Duvall, Johnson, Livingston, Story, Todd, Washington)
  0

OPINION OF THE COURT: *Story*
CONCURRING OPINION: *Johnson*
NOT PARTICIPATING: *Marshall*

FACTS:

Before the Revolutionary War, Lord Fairfax, a British loyalist, inherited a large tract of land in Virginia. When the war broke out, Fairfax, too old and frail to make the journey back to England, remained in Virginia. He died there in 1781 and left the property to his nephew, Denny Martin, a British subject residing in England, with the stipulation that Martin change his name to Fairfax.

The inheritance was complicated by a 1781 Virginia law that specified that no "enemy" could inherit land in the state. Virginia confiscated Fairfax's (also known as Martin's) property and began proceedings to sell it, including a plot to David Hunter.[21] Although Hunter was a real grantee, "he was a mere instrument of the state; the state managed the litigation completely." Because he believed he had rightfully inherited the land, Martin also began to sell off tracts—among the purchasers were John Marshall and his brother—resulting in a suit contesting title.

A lower Virginia state court upheld Martin's claim, but the highest court in Virginia reversed. When the case, *Fairfax's Devisee v. Hunter's Lessee* (1813), was appealed to the U.S. Supreme Court, only four justices heard it; Chief Justice Marshall recused himself due to the potential conflict of interest. In a 3–1 decision, the Court upheld Fairfax's claim, finding that the Virginia statute was unconstitutional because it conflicted with the 1783 Treaty of Paris, in which Congress promised to recommend to the states that they restore confiscated property to loyalists.

The U.S. Supreme Court ordered the Virginia Supreme Court to carry out its ruling. In response, the Virginia court, which did not consider itself subordinate to the Supreme Court, held hearings to determine whether it should comply. Eventually, it not only declined to follow the order but also struck down Section 25 of

---

21. William Winslow Crosskey, *Politics and the Constitution in the History of the United States*, vol. 2 (Chicago: University of Chicago Press, 1953), 788–789.

the Judiciary Act of 1789 as unconstitutional. The Virginia Supreme Court's decision was then appealed to the U.S. Supreme Court in the case of *Martin v. Hunter's Lessee*. Here the justices considered the question of whether Congress could expand their appellate jurisdiction, as it had done in Section 25.

ARGUMENTS:

For Denny Martin, heir at law and devisee of Fairfax:

- The uniform practice since the Constitution was adopted confirms the jurisdiction of the Court. The letters of Publius show that it was agreed, both by its friends and foes, that judicial power extends to this class of cases.
- This government is not a mere confederacy, like the old continental confederation. In its legislative, executive, and judicial authorities, it is a national government. Its judicial authority is analogous to its legislative: it alone has the power of making treaties; those treaties are declared to be the law of the land; and the judiciary of the United States is exclusively vested with the power of construing them.
- The state judiciaries are essentially incompetent to pronounce what is the law, not in the limited sphere of their territorial jurisdiction, but throughout the Union and the world.

For Hunter's Lessee:

- Under the Constitution, in which power was given to the federal government by the states, the U.S. Supreme Court can only review decisions of the lower federal courts.
- If the Supreme Court can exercise appellate jurisdiction over state courts, the sovereignty and independence of the states will be materially impaired.
- State court judges are men of integrity who take an oath to support the U.S. Constitution. They can be trusted to interpret it authoritatively.

STORY, J., DELIVERED THE OPINION OF THE COURT.

The questions involved in this judgment are of great importance and delicacy. Perhaps it is not too much to affirm, that, upon their right decision, rest some of the most solid principles which have hitherto been supposed to sustain and protect the constitution itself. The great respectability, too, of the court whose decisions we are called upon to review, and the entire deference which we entertain for the

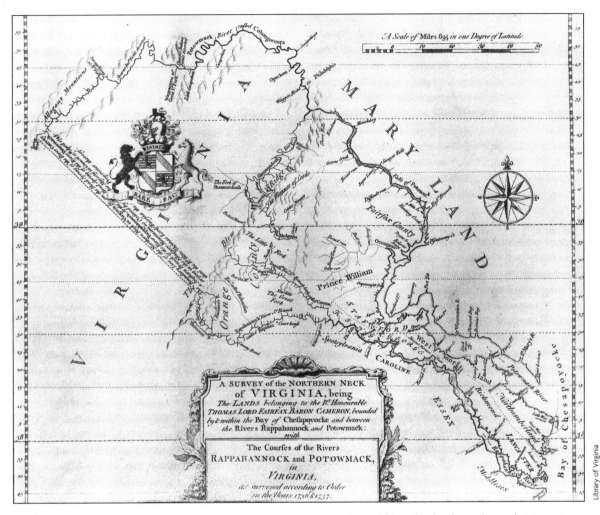

Martin v. Hunter's Lessee (1816) involved land in Virginia that the state had confiscated from a loyalist during the Revolutionary War. Justice Story wrote the landmark opinion establishing the Supreme Court's authority to reverse state court decisions involving federal laws or constitutional rights.

learning and ability of that court, add much to the difficulty of the task which has so unwelcomely fallen upon us. . . .

Before proceeding to the principal questions, it may not be unfit to dispose of some preliminary considerations which have grown out of the arguments at the bar.

The constitution of the United States was ordained and established, not by the states in their sovereign capacities, but emphatically, as the preamble of the constitution declares, by "the people of the United States." There can be no doubt that it was competent to the people to invest the general government with all the powers which they might deem proper and necessary; to extend or restrain these powers according to their own good pleasure, and to give them a paramount and supreme authority. As little

doubt can there be, that the people had a right to prohibit to the states the exercise of any powers which were, in their judgment, incompatible with the objects of the general compact; to make the powers of the state governments, in given cases, subordinate to those of the nation, or to reserve to themselves those sovereign authorities which they might not choose to delegate to either. The constitution was not, therefore, necessarily carved out of existing state sovereignties, nor a surrender of powers already existing in state institutions, for the powers of the states depend upon their own constitutions; and the people of every state had the right to modify and restrain them, according to their own views of policy or principle. On the other hand, it is perfectly clear that the sovereign powers vested in the state governments, by their respective constitutions, remained unaltered and unimpaired, except so far as they were granted to the government of the United States.

These deductions do not rest upon general reasoning, plain and obvious as they seem to be. They have been positively recognised by one of the articles in amendment of the constitution, which declares, that "the powers not delegated to the United States by the constitution, nor prohibited by it to the states, are reserved to the *states* respectively, or *to the people*."

The government, then, of the United States, can claim no powers which are not granted to it by the constitution, and the powers actually granted, must be such as are expressly given, or given by necessary implication. On the other hand, this instrument, like every other grant, is to have reasonable construction, according to the import of its terms; and where a power is expressly given in general terms, it is not to be restrained to particular cases, unless that construction grow out of the context expressly, or by necessary implication. The words are to be taken in their natural and obvious sense, and not in a sense unreasonably restricted or enlarged.

The constitution unavoidably deals in general language. It did not suit the purposes of the people, in framing this great charter of our liberties, to provide for minute specifications of its powers, or to declare the means by which those powers should be carried into execution. It was foreseen that this would be a perilous and difficult if not an impracticable, task. The instrument was not in ended to provide merely for the exigencies of a few years, but was to endure through a long lapse of ages, the events of which were locked up in the inscrutable purposes of Providence. It could not be foreseen what new changes and modifications of power might be indispensable to effectuate the general objects of the charter; and restrictions and specifications, which, at the present, might seem salutary, might, in the end, prove the overthrow of the system itself. Hence its powers are expressed in general terms, leaving to the legislature, from time to time, to adopt its own means to effectuate legitimate objects, and to mould and model the exercise of its powers, as its own wisdom, and the public interests, should require.

With these principles in view, principles in respect to which no difference of opinion ought to be indulged, let us now proceed to . . . the consideration of the great question as to the nature and extent of the appellate jurisdiction of the United States. . . . [A]ppellate jurisdiction is given by the constitution to the supreme court in all cases where it has not original jurisdiction; subject, however, to such exceptions and regulations as congress may prescribe. It is, therefore, capable of embracing every case enumerated in the constitution, which is not exclusively to be decided by way of original jurisdiction. But the exercise of appellate jurisdiction is far from being limited by the terms of the constitution to the supreme court. There can be no doubt that congress may create a succession of inferior tribunals, in each of which it may vest appellate as well as original jurisdiction. The judicial power is delegated by the constitution in the most general terms, and may, therefore, be exercised by congress under every variety of form, of appellate or original jurisdiction. And as there is nothing in the constitution which restrains or limits this power, it must, therefore, in all other cases, subsist in the utmost latitude of which, in its own nature, it is susceptible.

As, then, by the terms of the constitution, the appellate jurisdiction is not limited as to the supreme court, and as to this court it may be exercised in all other cases than those of which it has original cognizance, what is there to restrain its exercise over state tribunals in the enumerated cases? The appellate power is not limited by the terms of the third article to any particular courts. The words are, "the judicial power (which includes appellate power) shall extend *to all cases*," &c., and "in all other cases before mentioned the supreme court shall have appellate jurisdiction." It is the *case*, then, and not *the court*, that gives the jurisdiction. If the judicial power extends to the case, it will be in vain to search in the letter of the constitution for any qualification as to the tribunal where it depends. It is incumbent, then, upon those who assert such a qualification to show its existence by necessary implication. If the text be clear and distinct, no restriction upon its plain and obvious import ought to be admitted, unless the inference be irresistible.

If the constitution meant to limit the appellate jurisdiction to cases pending in the courts of the United States, it would necessarily follow that the jurisdiction of these courts would, in all the cases enumerated in the constitution, be exclusive of state tribunals. How otherwise could the jurisdiction extend to *all* cases arising under the constitution, laws, and treaties of the United States, or *to all cases* of admiralty and maritime jurisdiction? If some of these cases might be entertained by state tribunals, and no appellate jurisdiction as to them should exist, then the appellate power would not extend to *all*, but to *some*, cases. If state tribunals might exercise concurrent jurisdiction over all or some of the other classes of cases in the constitution without control, then the appellate jurisdiction of the United States might, as to such cases, have no real existence, contrary to the manifest intent of the constitution. Under such circumstances, to give effect to the judicial power, it must be construed to be exclusive; and this not only when the *casus faederis* [an event contemplated by a treaty] should arise directly, but when it should arise, incidentally, in cases pending in state courts. This construction would abridge the jurisdiction of such court far more than has been ever contemplated in any act of congress.

On the other hand, if, as has been contended, a discretion be vested in congress to establish, or not to establish, inferior courts at their own pleasure, and congress should not establish such courts, the appellate jurisdiction of the supreme court would have nothing to act upon, unless it could act upon cases pending in the state courts. Under such circumstances it must be held that the appellate power would extend to state courts; for the constitution is peremptory that it shall extend to certain enumerated cases, which cases could exist in no other courts. Any other construction, upon this supposition, would involve this strange contradiction, that a discretionary power vested in congress, and which they might rightfully omit to exercise, would defeat the absolute injunctions of the constitution in relation to the whole appellate power. . . .

It must, therefore, be conceded that the constitution not only contemplated, but meant to provide for cases within the scope of the judicial power of the United States, which might yet depend before state tribunals. It was foreseen that in the exercise of their ordinary jurisdiction, state courts would incidentally take cognizance of cases arising under the constitution, the laws, and treaties of the United States. Yet to all these cases the judicial power, by the very terms of the constitution, is to extend. It cannot extend by original jurisdiction if that was already rightfully and exclusively attached in the state courts, which (as has been already shown) may occur; it must, therefore, extend by appellate jurisdiction, or not at all. It would seem to follow that the appellate power of the United States must, in such cases, extend to state tribunals; and if in such cases, there is no reason why it should not equally attach upon all others within the purview of the constitution.

It has been argued that such an appellate jurisdiction over state courts is inconsistent with the genius of our governments, and the spirit of the constitution. That the latter was never designed to act upon state sovereignties, but only upon the people, and that if the power exists, it will materially impair the sovereignty of the states, and the independence of their courts. We cannot yield to the force of this reasoning; it assumes principles which we cannot admit, and draws conclusions to which we do not yield our assent.

It is a mistake that the constitution was not designed to operate upon states, in their corporate capacities. It is crowded with provisions which restrain or annul the sovereignty of the states in some of the highest branches of their prerogatives. The tenth section of the first article contains a long list of disabilities and prohibitions imposed upon the states. Surely, when such essential portions of state sovereignty are taken away, or prohibited to be exercised, it cannot be correctly asserted that the constitution does not act upon the states. The language of the constitution is also imperative upon the states as to the performance of many duties. It is imperative upon the state legislatures to make laws prescribing the time, places, and manner of holding elections for senators and representatives, and for electors of president and vice president. And in these, as well as some other cases, congress have a right to revise, amend, or supersede the laws which may be passed by state legislatures. . . . The courts of the United States can, without question, revise the proceedings of the executive and legislative authorities of the states, and if they are found to be contrary to the constitution, may declare them to be of no legal validity. Surely the exercise of the same right over judicial tribunals is not a higher or more dangerous act of sovereign power.

Nor can such a right be deemed to impair the independence of state judges. It is assuming the very ground in controversy to assert that they possess an absolute independence of the United States. In respect to the powers granted to the United States, they are not independent; they are expressly bound to obedience by the letter of the constitution; and if they should unintentionally transcend their authority, or misconstrue the constitution, there is no more reason for giving their judgments an absolute and irresistible force, than for giving it to the acts of the other coordinate departments of state sovereignty. . . .

It is further argued, that no great public mischief can result from a construction which shall limit the appellate power of the United States to cases in their own courts: first, because state judges are bound by an oath to support the constitution of the United States, and must be presumed to be men of learning and integrity; and, secondly, because congress must have an unquestionable right to remove all cases within the scope of the judicial power from the state courts to the courts of the United States, at any time before final judgment, though not after final judgment. As to the first reason—admitting that the judges of the state courts are, and always will be, of as much learning, integrity, and wisdom, as those of the courts of the United States (which we very cheerfully admit), it does not aid the argument. It is manifest that the constitution has proceeded upon a theory of its own, and given or withheld powers according to the judgment of the American people, by whom it was adopted. We can only construe its powers, and cannot inquire into the policy or principles which induced the grant of them. The constitution has presumed (whether rightly or wrongly we do not inquire) that state attachments, state prejudices, state jealousies, and state interests, might sometimes obstruct, or control, or be supposed to obstruct or control, the regular administration of justice. . . .

This is not all. A motive of another kind, perfectly compatible with the most sincere respect for state tribunals, might induce the grant of appellate power over their decisions. That motive is the importance, and even necessity of *uniformity* of decisions throughout the whole United States, upon all subjects within the purview of the constitution. Judges of equal learning and integrity, in different states, might differently interpret a statute, or a treaty of the United States, or even the constitution itself: If there were no revising authority to control these jarring and discordant judgments, and harmonize them into uniformity, the laws, the treaties, and the constitution of the United States would be different in different states, and might, perhaps, never have precisely the same construction, obligation, or efficacy, in any two states. The public mischiefs that would attend such a state of things would be truly deplorable; and it cannot be believed that they could have escaped the enlightened convention which formed the constitution. What, indeed, might then have been only prophecy, has now become fact; and the appellate jurisdiction must continue to be the only adequate remedy for such evils. . . .

On the whole, the court are of opinion, that the appellate power of the United States does extend to cases pending in the state courts; and that the 25th section of the judiciary act, which authorizes the exercise of this jurisdiction in the specified cases, by a writ of error, is supported by the letter and spirit of the constitution. We find no clause in that instrument which limits this power; and we dare not interpose a limitation where the people have not been disposed to create one. . . .

It is the opinion of the whole court, that the judgment of the court of appeals of Virginia, rendered on the mandate in this cause, be reversed, and the judgment of the district court, held at Winchester, be, and the same is hereby, affirmed.

With these words, the justices may have believed that the question was settled, but after they announced *Martin,* Virginia continued its assaults on the authority of the Supreme Court to review state actions. The issue was not settled until the case of *Cohens v. Virginia* (1821). The Cohen brothers were tried and convicted in Virginia for selling tickets for the District of Columbia lottery, a lottery that was authorized by an act of Congress but not by Virginia law. When the Cohens alleged that the federal law superseded the Virginia statute, the Supreme Court was again compelled to review a Virginia court's interpretation of a congressional act.

As in *Marbury,* the Court was faced with a difficult political situation. Virginia had refused to comply with the Court's earlier decision in *Martin.* The state's attorneys, including Philip P. Barbour, who later would serve on the U.S. Supreme Court, continued to argue that the Court could not review state court decisions because the states were sovereign entities. In particular, they turned to the Eleventh Amendment. That amendment overturned a 1793 Supreme Court decision, *Chisholm v. Georgia,* which had upheld the right of citizens of one state to bring suit, in the Supreme Court, against another state. The amendment says, "The Judicial power of the United States shall not be construed to extend to any suit in law or equity, commenced or prosecuted against one of the United States by Citizens of another State, or by Citizens or Subjects of any Foreign State." The attorneys argued that these words prohibited the Supreme Court from hearing appeals by citizens against their own states—regardless of what Section 25 said and even if the appeal involved a congressional act (as was the case here). Writing for a unanimous Court, Chief Justice Marshall disagreed:

The constitution and laws of a State, so far as they are repugnant to the constitution and laws of the United States, are absolutely void. These States are constituent parts of the United States. They are members of one great empire—for some purposes sovereign, for some purposes subordinate.

In a government so constituted, is it unreasonable that the judicial power should be competent to give efficacy to the constitutional laws of the legislature? . . .

We think it is not. We think that in a government acknowledgedly supreme, with respect to objects of vital interest to the nation, there is nothing inconsistent with sound reason, nothing incompatible with the nature of government, in making all its departments supreme, so far as respects those objects, and so far as is necessary to their attainment. The exercise of the appellate power over those judgments of the State tribunals which may contravene the constitution or laws of the United States, is, we believe, essential to the attainment of those objects.

By so ruling, Marshall reinforced the constitutionality of Section 25 of the Judiciary Act, held that the Eleventh Amendment did not preclude the Supreme Court from exercising jurisdiction over a federal question raised on appeal by citizens against their own states (in accord with Section 25), and ended the immediate dispute with Virginia. But neither *Martin* nor *Cohens* fully resolved questions concerning the role of federal courts vis-à-vis their state counterparts, nor did these cases end state challenges to the Court's authority.

In chapter 6 we have more to say about issues relating to federal court review of state court decisions. Here, we present just the basic contours of three (*see box 2-4*). The first centers directly on the Supreme Court and specifically its jurisdiction to hear appeals from state courts. Even after Congress, in 1916 and 1925, gave the Court discretion over whether to hear many sorts of disputes, it maintained provisions obligating the justices to review state court decisions invalidating federal laws or validating state laws challenged as inconsistent with federal law. Finally, in 1988, under pressure from the justices themselves, Congress eliminated these mandatory appeals, giving the Court nearly complete discretion over all state court decisions involving federal law. And, it is worth noting, the Supreme Court is quite selective about the kinds of state court decisions it will hear. Beginning with *Murdock v. City of Memphis* (1875), the Court has said that it will not review decisions interpreting state statutes and constitutional provisions unless the state court's interpretation implicates issues of federal law. Instead, the justices believe, state courts should interpret their own state laws and constitutions. This traditional view is the so-called adequate and independent state grounds test.[22]

The second issue centers on the supervisory powers of federal courts over their state counterparts and state officials. As box 2-4 shows, federal courts can issue injunctions to prevent state officials from implementing unconstitutional state laws; they can also review state court convictions via the habeas corpus procedure (petitions filed by people in custody to challenge their detention and to request a court to release them).

Finally, Congress has, on occasion, made other exceptions to the Eleventh Amendment. And, from *Cohens* through the 1980s, in case after case, the Court permitted these exceptions. In *Fitzpatrick v. Bitzer* (1976) the Court held that because the Fourteenth Amendment expressly gives Congress the power to enforce the amendment "by appropriate legislation," Congress could abrogate the Eleventh Amendment immunity from suit when attempting to enforce the Fourteenth. In *Pennsylvania v. Union Gas Co.* (1989) a divided Court held that the commerce clause of Article I permitted Congress to make an exception to the Eleventh Amendment's grant of immunity, stating that the power to regulate interstate commerce would be "incomplete without the authority to render States liable in damages." But, as we suggest in box 2-4, more-recent Courts have seriously cut back on these exceptions—much to the delight of those who support increased power for the states vis-à-vis the federal government. The first notable change came in *Seminole Tribe of Florida v. Florida* (1996), in which the Court overruled *Union Gas*. Writing for the Court, Chief Justice William H. Rehnquist held, "Even when the Constitution vests in Congress complete law-making authority over a particular area, the Eleventh Amendment prevents congressional authorization of suits by private parties against unconsenting States." In other words, the Court asserted that Article I of the Constitution does not permit Congress to abrogate the states' sovereign immunity from suits commenced or prosecuted in the federal courts. Three years later, the justices pushed *Seminole Tribe* even farther when they ruled in *Alden v. Maine* (1999) that Congress cannot subject nonconsenting states to private suits for damages even in their own courts. The Court continued this trend, ruling that Congress cannot make states liable for suits brought by state employees under federal age and disability

---

22. Because we discuss this approach in chapter 6, we want to note here only that this test is not as clear as it might seem because, occasionally, state court opinions rely on both federal and state law. So the question often emerges as to whether these kinds of

"ambiguous" decisions do or do not rest on adequate and independent state grounds.

BOX 2-4 SUPERVISION OF FEDERAL COURTS OVER THE STATES

Jurisdiction of the U.S. Supreme Court over State Court Decisions: Highlights

- Section 25 of the 1789 Judiciary Act. Gave the Court authority to review decisions from the highest state courts if those tribunals upheld state laws against challenges of unconstitutionality or denied claims based on the U.S. Constitution, federal laws, or treaties.
- *Murdock v. City of Memphis* (1875). Stated that the U.S. Supreme Court will not review decisions interpreting state statutes and constitutional provisions unless the state court's interpretation implicates issues of federal law. In other words, the justices believe that state courts should be the final arbiters of the meaning of their own laws and constitutions. This traditional view is called the "adequate and independent state grounds test": the Court will refrain from reviewing state court interpretations of state constitutions and law unless those decisions involve issues of federal law.
- Congressional Act of 1914. Opened the door to discretionary review by allowing the Court to review by certiorari state court decisions in favor of rights claimed under federal law; previously—for example, under Section 25 of the 1789 act—only state court decisions denying rights were reviewable.
- Administration of Justice Improvements Act of 1988. Eliminated virtually all of the Court's nondiscretionary jurisdiction. The Court was no longer obligated to review state court decisions involving federal law.

Other Mechanisms for Federal Court Supervision of States: Some Examples

- Injunctions. Beginning with *Osborn v. Bank of United States* (1824), the Court has said that federal courts may issue injunctions to prevent state officials from enforcing unconstitutional state provisions. The power of federal courts to do so was, during the Warren Court era, quite broad, but more recent Courts have limited it. In *Younger v. Harris* (1971) the justices said that federal courts should not enjoin state officials from enforcing their laws unless continued enforcement would irreparably harm the individuals seeking the enjoinment.
- Habeas corpus petitions. Federal courts have the ability to review state court convictions via habeas corpus petitions. Decisions of the Warren Court era loosened the requirements for filing such petitions in federal courts; subsequent decisions by the Republican-dominated Court restricted the scope of habeas corpus review, thereby reducing the supervisory role of federal courts.
- Congressional exceptions to the Eleventh Amendment. The Eleventh Amendment bars states from being sued in federal court without their express consent (see *Edelman v. Jordan,* 1974), but the Supreme Court allowed Congress to make exceptions to this rule. In *Fitzpatrick v. Bitzer* (1976), for example, the Court held that Congress could abrogate the Eleventh Amendment immunity from suit to enforce the Fourteenth Amendment, because the Fourteenth expressly empowers Congress to enforce the amendment "by appropriate legislation." And in *Pennsylvania v. Union Gas Co.* (1989) a divided Court held that Congress could make an exception to Eleventh Amendment immunity in order to fully exercise congressional authority granted by the commerce clause of Article I. In subsequent decisions, however, the Court cut back on some of these exceptions, as we explain in the text.

discrimination acts (*Kimel v. Florida Board of Regents,* 2000; *Board of Trustees of the University of Alabama v. Garrett,* 2001). In *Nevada Department of Human Resources v. Hibbs* (2003), however, the Court shifted its position when it held that state employees may bring suit under subparagraph (C) of the federal Family and Medical Leave Act of 1993, which enables employees to take up to twelve workweeks of unpaid leave annually to deal with a "serious health condition" of a spouse, child, or parent. Yet *Coleman v. Court of Appeals of Maryland* (2012) did not extend this exception to employees requesting self-care leave under subparagraph (D) of the act, because the sex-based discrimination that supports a subparagraph (C) suit is absent in (D).

Chapter 6 has more to say about sovereign immunity and other matters pertaining to the relationship between federal courts and the states, which during the 1990s and early 2000s were areas of focus as well as the causes of acrimonious debates among the justices. Indeed, underlying *Bush v. Gore* (2000) *(excerpted in chapter 4),* in which the justices effectively decided the outcome of the presidential election of 2000, are important questions about the ability and desirability of federal court review of state court decisions.

One clear implication of the brief discussion in this chapter is that the relationship between federal courts and the states has changed over time as a result of various Court rulings and congressional enactments. One thing that has not changed since the days of *Martin* and *Cohens,* however, is that states continue, on occasion, to challenge the authority of the Supreme Court to "interfere" in their business. And they have developed a variety of techniques to do so—as reactions to *Brown v. Board of Education* (1954) indicate. In the wake of that decision, which told states that they could not maintain segregated public schools, came the following responses (to name just a few):

- *Speech.* Public statements were made in defiance of the Court, such as Alabama governor George Wallace's often-cited declaration, "I draw the line in the dust and toss the gauntlet before the feet of tyranny and I say segregation now, segregation tomorrow, segregation forever," and Mississippi senator James Eastland's claim that the South "will not abide by or obey this legislative decision by a political court."
- *Legislation.* Reflecting the sentiment that "as long as we can legislate, we can segregate," Southern states passed 136 laws and state constitutional amendments aimed at preserving segregation. Examples include the Alabama legislature's declaration that the *Brown* decision was null and void, a Louisiana law that denied promotion or graduation to students of desegregated schools, and a Mississippi act that simply prohibited students from attending desegregated schools.
- *The Southern Manifesto.* A 1957 statement signed by ninety-six members of Congress from the South said, "We pledge ourselves to use all lawful means to bring about the reversal of [*Brown*]."
- *Threats of violence.* In 1957 Governor Orville Faubus of Arkansas had members of the National Guard stand at the entrance of Little Rock Central

High School to prevent black students from entering. He and other state officials claimed that they were not bound by *Brown.* This incident led to *Cooper v. Aaron* (1958), in which the justices took the opportunity to reaffirm their commitment to Marshall's words in *Marbury:* "It is emphatically the province and the duty of the judicial department to say what the law is."[23]

Judicial Review: Some Controversies

The reactions to *Brown* were extreme; the typical Supreme Court decision—even one that invalidates a state law—does not elicit such blatant defiance. Still, actions such as those noted above are suggestive: we know from the Court's opinion in *City of Boerne* that *Marbury* fixed, at least in the Court's eyes, the power of federal courts to exert judicial review over national actions, and *Martin* and *Cohens* established the Court's power of judicial review of state actions. In short, although specific decisions have met fierce resistance, the Court's role as a principal, but certainly not always *final,*[24] constitutional interpreter is now so firmly established that a Court decision can precipitate the resignation of a president, as it did in *United States v. Nixon* (1974) *(excerpted in chapter 4)* or the election of a president, as it did in *Bush v. Gore.* With the stroke of a pen, the Court can declare hundreds of federal statutory provisions unconstitutional, as it did in *Immigration and Naturalization Service v. Chadha* (1983) *(excerpted in chapter 5),* or invalidate almost every law in the country regulating abortion, as it did in *Roe v. Wade* (1973).

But what these and other momentous decisions did not do, and perhaps could not do, was put an end to the controversies surrounding judicial review. Some of the complaints regarding *Marbury* emerged while Marshall was still on the bench. Jefferson, for one, griped about the decision until his last days. In an 1823 letter he wrote,

---

23. These examples come from Gerald N. Rosenberg, *The Hollow Hope* (Chicago: University of Chicago Press, 1991); Richard Kluger, *Simple Justice* (New York: Knopf, 1975); and Bradley C. Canon and Charles A. Johnson, *Judicial Policies: Implementation and Impact,* 2nd ed. (Washington, DC: CQ Press, 1999).

24. We emphasize the word *final* because the extent to which the Court has or *should have* the last word in constitutional interpretation is a matter of considerable debate, especially when it comes to federal laws. Compare, for example, Larry D. Kramer, "Foreword: We the Court," *Harvard Law Review* 115 (2001): 4–168; and Prakash and Yoo, "The Origins of Judicial Review."

This practice of Judge Marshall, of travelling out of his case to prescribe what the law would be in a moot case not before the court, is very irregular and very censurable. . . . [In *Marbury v. Madison*] the Court determined at once, that being an original process, they had no cognizance of it; and therefore the question before them was ended. But the Chief Justice went on to lay down what the law would be, had they jurisdiction of the case, to wit: that they should command the delivery. The object was clearly to instruct any other court having the jurisdiction, what they should do if *Marbury* should apply to them. Besides the impropriety of this gratuitous interference, could anything exceed the perversion of law? . . . *Yet this case of Marbury and Madison is continually cited by bench and bar, as if it were settled law, without any animadversion on its being merely an obiter dissertation of the Chief Justice* [our italics].[25]

Strong words from one of our nation's most revered presidents!

But Jefferson was not the last to complain about Marshall's opinion. Some critics have picked apart specific aspects of the ruling, as Jefferson did. He argued that once Marshall ruled that the Court did not have jurisdiction to hear the case, he should have dismissed it. Another criticism of Marshall's opinion is that Section 13 of the 1789 Judiciary Act—which *Marbury* held unconstitutional—did not actually expand the Supreme Court's original jurisdiction. If this is so, then Marshall "had nothing to declare unconstitutional!"[26]

Other debates center on the Court's holding, in particular, on what legal scholar Alexander Bickel called the "countermajoritarian difficulty": Given our nation's fundamental commitment to a representative form of government, why should we allow a group of unelected officials to override the wishes of the people, as expressed by their elected officials?[27]

In other words, even though most Americans accept the fact that courts have the power of judicial review, many legal analysts still argue over whether they should. Let us consider some of the theoretical debates

surrounding judicial review, debates that fall into six categories: originalism, judicial self-restraint, democratic checks on the Court, judicial supremacy, public opinion, and protection of minority rights.[28]

Originalism. Perhaps the oldest—and yet still ongoing—debate concerns whether the Constitution's framers (or ratifiers, or Americans more generally) intended for the federal courts to exercise judicial review (or understood that they would). Chief Justice Marshall's affirmative view was a major justification in *Marbury* and *Cohens,* and some historical evidence exists to support it. Most important is that the framers had knowledge of judicial review. Although Marshall often is credited with its first full enunciation, the concept probably originated much earlier in England in *Dr. Bonham's Case* (1610). At issue was an act of Parliament that enabled physicians of the London College to authorize medical licenses and to punish persons practicing medicine without one. Convicted of violating the act, Dr. Bonham appealed his case to England's high court, the King's Bench. Writing for the court, Lord Chief Justice Sir Edward Coke struck down the act, noting in dictum, "It appears in our books, that in many cases, the common law will control acts of Parliament, and sometimes adjudge them to be utterly void." Coke's resounding declaration of the authority of the court to void parliamentary acts came at a critical point in British history. At a time when King James I was claiming tremendous authority, the court, in an otherwise trivial case, took the opportunity to assert its power.

By the early 1700s the concept of judicial review had fallen out of favor in England. Coke's writings, however, had a profound impact on the development of the American legal system, as best illustrated by the *Writs of Assistance Case* (1761), involving the legality of sweeping search warrants issued by the British Parliament in the name of the king. Arguing against such writs, James Otis, a Boston lawyer, relied on Coke's opinion in *Bonham* as precedent for his request. Otis lost the case, but his argument was not forgotten. Between 1776 and 1787, eight of the thirteen colonies incorporated judicial review into their constitutions, and, as we noted earlier, by 1789 seven state courts had

---

25. Andrew A. Lipscomb, ed., *The Writings of Thomas Jefferson,* vol. 15 (Washington, DC: Thomas Jefferson Memorial Association, 1905), 447–448.

26. Segal and Spaeth, *The Supreme Court and the Attitudinal Model Revisited,* 24. A counterargument is that people of the day must have considered Section 13 as expanding the Court's original jurisdiction, or else why would Marbury have brought his suit directly to the Supreme Court?

27. Alexander Bickel, *The Least Dangerous Branch of Government* (New York: Bobbs-Merrill, 1962).

28. These categories, with the exception of judicial supremacy, follow from David Adamany, "The Supreme Court," in *The American Courts: A Critical Assessment,* ed. John B. Gates and Charles A. Johnson (Washington, DC: CQ Press, 1991).

struck down as unconstitutional acts passed by their legislatures.

This background makes the question of why the framers left judicial review out of the Constitution even more perplexing. Some historians argue that the framers omitted it because they did not want to heighten controversy over Article III by inserting judicial review, not because they opposed the practice. To the contrary, they may have implicitly accepted it. Historians have established that more than half of the delegates to the Constitutional Convention approved of judicial review, including those generally considered to be the most influential. And some law professors point out that there seem to be no writings, whether for or against ratification, suggesting that the courts would not enjoy this power. There were, however, statements in its favor. Most famously, in *The Federalist Papers* Hamilton adamantly defended the concept, arguing that one branch of government must safeguard the Constitution and that the courts would be in the best position to undertake that responsibility. The suggestion here is, "[T]hough people disagreed on much else about the Constitution, all those who addressed judicial review agreed that the Constitution authorized the judiciary to ignore unconstitutional federal statutes."[29]

Even with all this evidence, many still argue that the framers did not intend for courts to review acts of the other branches. In support of this view, some point to the framers' rejection of the proposed council of revision, which would have been both composed of Supreme Court justices and the president, and permitted to veto legislative acts. Others note that even though some states adopted judicial review, their courts rarely exercised the power. When they did, public outcries typically followed, indicating that support for judicial review was not widespread. Moreover, the fact that some framers were concerned about writing judicial review into the Constitution could mean they believed that opposition to it was substantial enough to threaten the chances of ratification.[30]

What, then, can we conclude about the intent of the framers with regard to judicial review? Perhaps Edward Corwin said it best: "The people who say the framers intended it are talking nonsense, and the people who say they did not intend it are talking nonsense."[31]

---

29. Prakash and Yoo, "The Origins of Judicial Review," 928.

30. See Kramer, "Foreword."

31. Quoted in ibid., 13.

Judicial Self-Restraint. Another controversy surrounding judicial review involves the notion of judicial self-restraint. Today, as in the past, some legal analysts and judges contend that courts should defer to the elected branches of government unless they are reasonably certain that the actions of those branches have violated the Constitution.[32]

An early call for perhaps an even more extreme version of judicial self-restraint came in *Eakin v. Raub* (1825), in which John Gibson, a Pennsylvania Supreme Court justice, took issue with a seeming implication of *Marbury:* that the judiciary is the ultimate arbiter of the Constitution. Because Gibson's opinion provides an important counterpoint to Marshall's arguments in *Marbury,* we include here an excerpt from it. As you read it, consider whether you agree with Gibson's version of judicial self-restraint in light of the *Marbury* opinion.

Eakin v. Raub

12 SARGENT & RAWLE 330 (PA. 1825)

John Gibson was a well-regarded judge who served on the Pennsylvania Supreme Court for thirty-seven years and nearly obtained a seat on the U.S. Supreme Court. His dissent in *Eakin v. Raub* is significant not because it came in a case of any great moment—indeed, the facts are not particularly important. It is important because, as even scholars today maintain, it provides one of the finest rebuttals of Marshall's opinion in *Marbury v. Madison.*[33]

▶ GIBSON, J., dissenting.

I am aware, that a right to declare all unconstitutional acts void, without distinction as to either state or federal constitution, is generally held as a professional dogma; but I apprehend, rather as a matter of faith than of reason. It is not a little remarkable, that although the right in question has all along been claimed by the judiciary, no judge has ventured to discuss it, except Chief Justice Marshall; and if the argument of a jurist so distinguished for the strength of

---

32. For a history of judicial self-restraint—one claiming that Supreme Court justices did but no longer adhere to it—see Richard A. Posner, "The Rise and Fall of Judicial Self-Restraint," *California Law Review* 100 (2012): 519–556.

33. The excerpt of Gibson's dissent presented below comes from Melvin I. Urofsky, ed., *Documents of American Constitutional History,* vol. 1 (New York: Knopf, 1989), 183–185.

his ratiocinative powers be found inconclusive, it may fairly be set down to the weakness of the position which he attempts to defend. . . .

The constitution is said to be a law of superior obligation; and consequently, that if it were to come into collision with an act of the legislature, the latter would have to give way; this is conceded. But it is a fallacy, to suppose, that they can come into collision *before the judiciary.*

The constitution and the *right* of the legislature to pass the act, may be in collision; but is that a legitimate subject for judicial determination? If it be, the judiciary must be a peculiar organ, to revise the proceedings of the legislature, and to correct its mistakes; and in what part of the constitution are we to look for this proud preeminence? It is by no means clear, that to declare a law void, which has been enacted according to the forms prescribed in the constitution, is not a usurpation of legislative power. . . .

But it has been said to be emphatically the business of the judiciary, to ascertain and pronounce what the law is; and that this necessarily involves a consideration of the constitution. It does so: but how far? If the judiciary will inquire into anything beside the form of enactment, where shall it stop? There must be some point of limitation to such an inquiry; for no one will pretend, that a judge would be justifiable in calling for the election returns, or scrutinizing the qualifications of those who composed the legislature.

It will not be pretended, that the legislature has not, at least, an equal right with the judiciary to put a construction on the constitution; nor that either of them is infallible; nor that either ought to be required to surrender its judgment to the other. Suppose, then, they differ in opinion as to the constitutionality of a particular law; if the organ whose business it first is to decide on the subject, is not to have its judgment treated with respect, what shall prevent it from securing the preponderance of its opinion by the strong arm of power? The soundness of any construction which would bring one organ of the government into collision with another, is to be more than suspected; for where collision occurs, it is evident, the machine is working in a way the framers of it did not intend. . . .

But the judges are sworn to support the constitution, and are they not bound by it as the law of the land? The oath to support the constitution is not peculiar to the judges, but is taken indiscriminately by every officer of the government, and is designed rather as a test of the political principles of the man, than to bind the officer in the discharge of his duty: otherwise, it were difficult to determine, what operation it is to have in the case of a recorder of deeds, for instance, who, in the execution of his office, has nothing to do with the constitution. But granting it to relate to the official conduct of the judge, as well as every other officer, and not to his political principles, still, it must be understood in reference to supporting the constitution, *only as far as that may be involved in his official duty;* and consequently, if his official duty does not comprehend an inquiry into the authority of the legislature, neither does his oath. . . .

But do not the judges do a *positive act* in violation of the constitution, when they give effect to an unconstitutional law? Not if the law has been passed according to the forms established in the constitution. The fallacy of the question is, in supposing that the judiciary adopts the acts of the legislature as its own; whereas, the enactment of a law and the interpretation of it are not concurrent acts, and as the judiciary is not required to concur in the enactment, neither is it in the breach of the constitution which may be the consequence of the enactment; the fault is imputable to the legislature, and on it the responsibility exclusively rests. . . .

I am of the opinion that it rests with the people, in whom full and absolute sovereign power resides to correct abuses in legislation, by instructing their representatives to repeal the obnoxious act. What is wanting to plenary power in the government, is reserved by the people for their own immediate use; and to redress an infringement of their rights in this respect, would seem to be an accessory of the power thus reserved. It might, perhaps, have been better to vest the power in the judiciary; as it might be expected that its habits of deliberation, and the aid derived from the arguments of counsel, would more frequently lead to accurate conclusions. On the other hand, the judiciary is not infallible; and an error by it would admit of no remedy but a more distinct expression of the public will, through the extraordinary medium of a convention; whereas, an error by the legislature admits of a remedy by an exertion of the same will, in the ordinary exercise of the right of suffrage—a mode better calculated to attain the end, without popular excitement. It may be said, the people would probably not notice an error of their representatives. But they would as probably do so, as notice an error of the judiciary; and, beside, it is a postulate in the theory of our government, and the very basis of the superstructure, that the people are wise, virtuous, and competent to manage their own affairs. . . .

Twenty years after *Raub,* Gibson had a change of heart. In an 1845 opinion he suggested that state courts should exercise judicial review over the acts of political institutions located within their jurisdictions.[34] But if we take *Raub* on its face, the use of judicial review belies this notion of judicial restraint for which Gibson clamors. Recall the legislative veto case described earlier in this chapter. By even considering the issue, the Court placed itself squarely in the middle of an executive–legislative dispute; when it nullified the veto, it showed little deference to the wishes of the legislature. To this argument supporters of judicial review point to Marshall's decision in *Marbury,* Hamilton's assertion in *The Federalist Papers,* and so forth. They suggest that the government needs an umpire who will act neutrally and fairly in interpreting the constitutional strictures.

Again, the question of which position is correct has no absolute answer, only opinion. But what we do know is that U.S. Supreme Court justices—with a few exceptions, such as Oliver Wendell Holmes and Felix Frankfurter[35]—have not taken seriously the dictate of judicial self-restraint or, at the very least, have not let it interfere in their voting. Even those who profess a basic commitment to judicial deference have tended to allow their attitudes and values to dictate their decisions. That is, left-leaning justices tend to invalidate conservative laws, and right-leaning justices, liberal laws.[36]

Even so, there is some tendency to equate judicial self-restraint with conservatism and judicial activism with liberalism. Ronald Reagan, one of the most conservative presidents of the twentieth century, often asserted the need for judicial self-restraint, saying that, if he could, he would appoint a Court of Felix Frankfurters. But many note that what Reagan really wanted was a Court that would defer to legislatures if

the laws in question reflected conservative values and would overturn them otherwise.

Democratic Checks. A third controversy involves what David Adamany calls democratic checks on the Court. Although we consider these in more detail in the final section of this chapter (where we look at political constraints on the Court), here we outline the two sides of this debate. According to one side, judicial review is defensible on the ground that the Supreme Court—while lacking an explicit electoral connection—is subject to potential checks from the elected branches. If the Court overturns government acts in a way repugnant to the best interests of the people, Congress, the president, and even the states have a number of recourses. Acting in different combinations, they can ratify a constitutional amendment to overturn a decision, change the size of the Court, or remove the Court's appellate jurisdiction.

Some scholars suggest that the elected branches do not even need to use these weapons to influence the Court's decisions: the mere fact that they possess them may be enough. In other words, if the justices care about the ultimate state of the law or their own legitimacy, they might seek to accommodate the wishes of Congress rather than face the wrath of the legislators, which could lead to the reversal of their ruling or other forms of institutional retaliation.[37]

It is the existence of congressional threat, not its actual invocation, that may affect how the Court rules in a given case. This dynamic, in the eyes of some analysts, may explain why the justices rarely strike down acts of Congress. To see the point, consider *Mistretta v. United States* (1989) *(excerpted in chapter 5),* in which the Supreme Court scrutinized a law that sought to minimize judicial discretion in sentencing. The law created a sentencing commission charged with promulgating guidelines for federal judges to follow in handing down criminal sentences. Although some lower court judges refused to adopt the guidelines, arguing that they undermined judicial independence, the Supreme Court upheld the law. It is possible that the justices upheld the law because they agreed with it ideologically, or because precedent led them to that conclusion, and so forth. But it also may be true that

---

34. See ibid., 183.

35. And even over Frankfurter there is some debate. Compare Segal and Spaeth, *The Supreme Court and the Attitudinal Model,* 318; and Lee Epstein and William M. Landes, "Was There Ever Such a Thing as Judicial Self-Restraint?," *California Law Review* 100 (2012): 557–578. Segal and Spaeth argue that Frankfurter was "nothing more than a stalwart economic conservative who, along with his other economically oriented colleagues, used judicial restraint and judicial activism with equal facility to achieve his substantial policy objectives." Epstein and Landes, in line with the conventional view, find that throughout his career Frankfurter was highly reluctant to strike down federal laws, regardless of whether the laws were conservative or liberal.

36. See, for example, Epstein and Landes, "Was There Ever Such a Thing as Judicial Self-Restraint?"; Stefanie A. Lindquist and Frank B. Cross, *Measuring Judicial Activism* (New York: Oxford University Press, 2009).

37. See, generally, Eskridge, "Overriding Supreme Court Statutory Interpretation Decisions"; Segal, Westerland, and Lindquist, "Congress, the Supreme Court, and Judicial Review."

the justices wanted to avoid a congressional backlash and so acted in accord with legislators' wishes.

The problem with these arguments, according to some analysts, is twofold. First, explicit checks on the part of elected branches are so rarely invoked—only four amendments have overturned Court decisions, the Court's size has not been changed since 1869, and only infrequently has Congress removed the Court's appellate jurisdiction—that they do not constitute much of a threat. Second, although justices may vote in some constitutional cases in accordance with congressional preferences to avoid backlash, such cases may be the exception, not the rule. After all, some ask, why would the Court fear Congress when it so rarely takes action against Congress? *City of Boerne* illustrates the point: in rendering their opinion, the majority did not seem particularly concerned that the law had received substantial legislative support.

Judicial Supremacy. Related to debates over democratic checks are controversies about the relationship between judicial review and judicial supremacy.[38] To some scholars, it is one thing for the Court to assert its authority to invalidate acts of government. It is quite another, they argue, for the justices to take the next step and claim they have a monopoly on constitutional interpretation or that they are the final interpreters within the federal government. The two Rehnquist Court cases that came quite close to this position, *Dickerson* and *Boerne,* contain language that strongly asserts judicial supremacy in constitutional interpretation.

Why are these scholars (along with Judge Gibson in *Eakin*) so bothered by the idea of the Court as the "ultimate" arbiter of the Constitution? One reason is that it belies history. Both the president and Congress have engaged in constitutional interpretation from the nation's earliest days, and, according to David Currie, a leading authority on the subject, they actually performed the task better than the Supreme Court. In fact, after examining the early congressional record, Currie concluded that the "debates sparkled with brilliant insights about the meaning of constitutional provisions."[39]

Likewise, based on his analysis of Congress's handling of the Clinton impeachment, Mark Tushnet writes, "Congress can be, and frequently has been, a responsible interpreter of the Constitution."[40] Whether legislators are engaging in interpretation when they debate the document's meaning on the floor or in committee hearings is an interesting question. But it is certainly true that occasionally those debates, and perhaps the actions that result from them, became the last or only words on the meaning of specific constitutional provisions.

Another reason analysts take issue with the concept of judicial supremacy is this: even if the Court has the power to review the president's and Congress's interpretations, it does not necessarily follow that the Court should have the last word. Tushnet makes this point about *Boerne:*

> RFRA [the act at issue in *Boerne*] enacts an interpretation of what the free exercise clause means that we *know* is reasonable, because it was an interpretation that the Supreme Court itself articulated and applied for two decades. True, the Court today thinks that the older Court's interpretation—and Congress's—is not the best one. But . . . why should the Court's interpretation prevail?[41]

One response to Tushnet's question comes from *Marbury* itself: if we allow Congress to be the final arbiter of the Constitution, the document's meaning will change as the composition of Congress changes. No longer will it be a constitution; rather, it will be simple legislation to be interpreted as each Congress sees fit. Certainly, we could say the same about the Court—that as it experiences turnover in membership, its interpretation of the Constitution may change. But is it not the case that "stability in the law requires that someone have the last word and that giving the last word to the

---

38. We adopt some of the material to follow from Walter F. Murphy, C. Herman Pritchett, Lee Epstein, and Jack Knight, *Courts, Judges, and Politics* (New York: McGraw-Hill, 2005), chap. 12. See also Murphy, "Who Shall Interpret the Constitution?": 401.

39. David P. Currie, "Prolegomena for a Sampler: Extrajudicial Interpretation of the Constitution, 1789–1861," in *Congress and the Constitution,* ed. Neal Devins and Keith E. Whittington (Durham,

NC: Duke University Press, 2005), 24. See also Professor Currie's series of books on constitutional deliberation in Congress: *The Constitution in Congress: The Federalist Period, 1789–1801* (Chicago: University of Chicago Press, 1997); *The Constitution in Congress: The Jeffersonians, 1801–1829* (Chicago: University of Chicago Press, 2001); and *The Constitution in Congress: Democrats and Whigs, 1829–1861* (Chicago: University of Chicago Press, 2005).

40. Mark Tushnet, "Evaluating Congressional Constitutional Interpretation," in Devins and Whittington, *Congress and the Constitution,* 288; our italics. See also Tushnet, *Taking the Constitution Away from the Courts.*

41. Mark Tushnet, "The Story of *City of Boerne v. Flores:* Federalism, Rights, and Judicial Supremacy," in *Constitutional Law Stories,* ed. Michael C. Dorf (New York: Foundation Press, 2004), 522.

Court will get us more stability than Congress"?[42] Other scholars, in contrast to Tushnet, would suggest that the answer is yes, that the life-tenured justices are slower to undo their own interpretations than the electorally beholden members of Congress would be. As a result they are able to bring greater predictability to the law.

Public Opinion. A fifth debate about judicial review concerns public opinion and the Court. Those who support judicial review point to two aspects of the Court's relationship with the public. First, they argue that Court decisions are usually in harmony with public opinion; that is, even though the Court faces no real pressure to do so, it generally "follows the elections." Therefore, Americans need not fear that the Court will usurp their power because it does not exercise its power in a countermajoritarian fashion.

Empirical evidence, however, is mixed. After conducting an extensive investigation of the relationship between public opinion and the Court, Thomas R. Marshall concluded, "[T]he evidence suggests that the modern Court has been an essentially majoritarian institution. Where clear poll margins exist, three-fifths to two-thirds of Court rulings reflect the polls."[43] Yet, as he and others concede, the Court at times has handed down decisions well out of line with public preferences, such as its prohibition of prayer in school and its short-lived ban on the death penalty.[44]

Second, even if the Court is occasionally out of sync with the public, judicial review is important: when the Court reviews and affirms government acts, it can play the role of republican schoolmaster—educating the public and conferring legitimacy on those acts. Evidence suggests, however, that the Court does not and cannot serve this function because too few people actually know about any given Court decision, and, even if they do know, they do not necessarily shift their ideas to conform to the Court's opinions.

Research by Charles H. Franklin and Liane Kosaki provides an interesting example of the last point.[45]

They examined whether the Court's decision in ***Roe v. Wade*** (1973) changed citizens' opinions on abortion, reasoning that if the Court acted as a republican schoolmaster, the public would adopt more-liberal attitudes. Their data indicate, however, that no such change occurred. Instead, those who supported abortion rights before *Roe* became more pro-choice, while those opposed became more pro-life. In other words, the Court's decision served to solidify existing views and not to change attitudes.

Protection of Minority Rights. A final controversy concerns what role the Supreme Court should play in the American system of government. Those who support judicial review assert that the Court must have this power if it is to fulfill its most important constitutional assignment: protection of minority rights. By their very nature—the fact that they are elected—legislatures and executives reflect the interests of the majority and may take action that is blatantly unconstitutional. So that the majority cannot tyrannize a minority, it is necessary for the one branch of government that lacks any electoral connection to have the power of judicial review. This is a powerful argument, the truth of which has been demonstrated many times throughout American history. For example, when the legislatures of Southern states continued to enact segregation laws, it was the U.S. Supreme Court that struck the laws down as violative of the Constitution.

This position also has its share of problems. One is that it conflicts with the notion of the Court as a body that defers to the elected branches. Another is that empirical evidence suggests that some Supreme Courts have not used judicial review in this manner. According to Robert Dahl, many of the acts struck down by the Supreme Court before the 1960s were those that harmed a "privileged class," not disadvantaged minorities.[46] We saw similar decisions by the Rehnquist Court as well: in *City of Richmond v. J. A. Croson Co.* (1989) the justices struck down a city affirmative action program designed to help minority interests.

42. Ibid., 523. Tushnet, however, does not agree with this argument.

43. Thomas R. Marshall, *Public Opinion and the Supreme Court* (Boston: Unwin Hyman, 1989), 192.

44. For an excellent review of this literature, see Gregory A. Caldeira, "Courts and Public Opinion," in Gates and Johnson, *The American Courts.*

45. Charles H. Franklin and Liane Kosaki, "The Republican Schoolmaster: The U.S. Supreme Court, Public Opinion, and

Abortion," *American Political Science Review* 83 (1989): 751–771; see also Timothy R. Johnson and Andrew D. Martin, "The Public's Conditional Response to Supreme Court Decisions," *American Political Science Review* 92 (1998): 299–310.

46. Robert Dahl, "Decision-Making in a Democracy: The Supreme Court as a National Policy-Maker," *Journal of Public Law* 6 (1957): 279–295.

Judicial Review in Action. The controversies discussed above are important to the extent that they place the subject of judicial review within a theoretical context for debate. But they present debates that probably never will be resolved: as one side finds support for its position, the other always seems to follow suit.

Let us consider instead several issues arising from the way the Court actually has exercised the power of judicial review: the number of times it has invoked the power to strike laws and the significance of those decisions. As Lawrence Baum suggests, investigation of these issues can help us achieve a better understanding of judicial review and place it in a realistic context.[47] First, how often has the Court overturned a federal, state, or local law or ordinance? The data seem to indicate that the Court has made frequent use of the power, striking down close to fifteen hundred government acts since 1789. As Baum notes, however, those acts are but a "minute fraction" of the laws enacted at various levels of government. Since 1790, for example, Congress has passed more than sixty thousand laws, and the Court has struck down far less than 1 percent of them.

The more important question, then, may be that of significance: Does the Court tend to strike down important laws or relatively minor laws? Using *Scott v. Sandford (see chapter 6)* as an illustration, some argue that the Court, in fact, often strikes important legislation. Undoubtedly, the Court's opinion in *Scott* had major consequences. By ruling that Congress could not prohibit slavery in the territories and by striking down a law, the Missouri Compromise (which had already been repealed), the Court fed the growing divisions between the North and South and provided a major impetus for the Civil War. The decision also tarnished the prestige of the Court and the reputation of Chief Justice Roger B. Taney.

But how representative is *Scott*? Some other Court opinions striking down government acts have been almost as important—those nullifying state abortion and segregation laws, the federal child labor acts, and many pieces of New Deal legislation come to mind. But, as Baum astutely notes, "many of the Court's decisions declaring statutes unconstitutional have been unimportant."[48] *Monongahela Navigation Co. v.*

United States (1893) is an example. Here the Court struck down, on Fifth Amendment grounds, a law concerning the amount of money the United States would pay to companies for the "purchase or condemnation of a certain lock and dam in the Monongahela River."

Despite the rather ambiguous record, we can reach three conclusions about the Court's use of judicial review. First, although the Court has struck down some important acts of government—thereby demonstrating its muscle to the other branches and the states—it has not interfered with a good deal of their policy efforts. It is no wonder, then, that scholars believe that while judicial review allows the Court to play a major role in policy making, it certainly has not made the Court the dominant national policy maker.[49] Second, it is not necessarily the Court's use of judicial review that is significant. Rather, as is true with the presidential veto, the threat of its invocation may be its power. In either case, it is clear that without the power of judicial review the Court's role in our system of government would be far different and, perhaps, far slimmer than it is now.

Finally, given all the attention paid to judicial review, it is easy to forget that the power of courts to exercise it, and their judicial authority more generally, has substantial limits. In the next sections, we consider two: those that emanate from the Court's reading of Article III and those that stem more generally from the separation of powers system.

CONSTRAINTS ON JUDICIAL POWER: ARTICLE III

Article III—or the Court's interpretation of it—places three major constraints on the ability of federal tribunals to hear and decide cases: (1) courts must have authority to hear a case (jurisdiction), (2) the case must be appropriate for judicial resolution (justiciability), and (3) the appropriate party must bring the case (standing to sue). In what follows, we review doctrine surrounding these constraints. As you read this discussion, consider not only the Court's interpretation of its own limits, but also the justifications it offers. Note, in particular, how fluid these can be: some Supreme Courts tend to favor loose constructions of the rules,

---

47. Lawrence Baum, *The Supreme Court,* 9th ed. (Washington, DC: CQ Press, 2007), 163–170.

48. Ibid., 164.

49. Ibid., 170.

while others are anxious to enforce them. What factors might explain these different tendencies? Or, to put it another way, to what extent do these constraints limit the Court's authority?

Jurisdiction

According to Chief Justice Salmon P. Chase, "Without jurisdiction the court cannot proceed at all in any cause. Jurisdiction is power to declare the law, and when it ceases to exist, the only function remaining to the court is that of announcing the fact and dismissing the cause."[50] In other words, a court cannot hear a case unless it has the authority—the jurisdiction—to do so.

Article III, Section 2, defines the jurisdiction of U.S. federal courts. Lower courts have the authority to hear disputes involving particular parties and subject matter. The U.S. Supreme Court's jurisdiction is divided into original and appellate: the former are classes of cases that originate in the Court; the latter are those it hears after a lower court.

To what extent does jurisdiction actually constrain the federal courts? *Marbury v. Madison* provides some answers, although contradictory, to this question. Chief Justice Marshall informed Congress that it could not alter the original jurisdiction of the Court. Having reached this conclusion, perhaps Marshall should have merely dismissed the case on the ground that the Court lacked authority to hear it, but that is not what he did.

Marbury remains an authoritative ruling on original jurisdiction. The issue of appellate jurisdiction may be a bit more complex. Article III explicitly states that for those cases over which the Court does not have original jurisdiction, it "shall have appellate Jurisdiction . . . with such Exceptions, and under such Regulations as the Congress shall make." In other words, the exceptions clause seems to give Congress authority to alter the Court's appellate jurisdiction—including to subtract from it.

Would the justices agree? In *Ex parte McCardle* the Court addressed this question, examining whether Congress can use its power under the exceptions clause to *remove* the Court's appellate jurisdiction over a particular category of cases.

---

50. *Ex parte McCardle* (1869).

Ex parte McCardle

74 U.S. (7 Wall.) 506 (1869)
http://laws.findlaw.com/us/74/506.html
Vote: 8 (Chase, Clifford, Davis, Field, Grier, Miller, Nelson, Swayne)
    0

OPINION OF THE COURT: *Chase*

FACTS:

After the Civil War, the Radical Republican Congress imposed a series of restrictions on the South.[51] Known as the Reconstruction laws, they in effect placed the region under military rule. Journalist William McCardle opposed these measures and wrote editorials urging resistance to them. As a result, he was arrested for publishing allegedly "incendiary and libelous articles" and held for a trial before a military tribunal established under Reconstruction.

Because he was a civilian, not a member of any militia, McCardle claimed that he was being illegally held. He petitioned for a writ of habeas corpus under an 1867 act stipulating that federal courts had the power to grant writs of habeas corpus in all cases where any person was deprived of his or her liberty in violation of the Constitution, laws, or treaties of the United States. When this effort failed, McCardle appealed to the U.S. Supreme Court, which had gained appellate jurisdiction in such cases with passage of the 1867 law.

In early March 1868 *McCardle* "was very thoroughly and ably [presented] upon the merits" to the U.S. Supreme Court. It was clear to most observers that "no Justice was still making up his mind": the Court's sympathies, as was widely known, lay with McCardle.[52] But before the justices issued their decision, Congress, on March 27, 1868, enacted a law repealing the provision of the 1867 Habeas Corpus Act that gave the Supreme Court authority to hear appeals emanating from it; that is, Congress removed the Court's jurisdiction to hear appeals in cases like McCardle's. This move was meant either to punish the Court or to send it a strong message. Two years before *McCardle*, in 1866, the Court had invalidated President Abraham Lincoln's use of military tribunals in certain areas, and Congress did

---

51. See Lee Epstein and Thomas G. Walker, "The Role of the Supreme Court in American Society: Playing the Reconstruction Game," in *Contemplating Courts*, ed. Lee Epstein (Washington, DC: CQ Press, 1995), 315–346.

52. Charles Fairman, *History of the Supreme Court of the United States*, vol. 7, *Reconstruction and Reunion* (New York: Macmillan, 1971), 456.

not want to see the Court take similar action in this dispute.[53] The legislature felt so strongly on this issue that after President Andrew Johnson vetoed the 1868 repealer act, Congress overrode the veto.

The Court responded by redocketing the case for oral arguments in March 1869. During the arguments and in its briefs, the government contended that the Court no longer had authority to hear the case and should dismiss it.

ARGUMENTS:

For the appellant, William McCardle:

- According to the Constitution, the judicial power extends to "the laws of the United States." The Constitution also vests that judicial power in one Supreme Court. The jurisdiction of the Supreme Court, then, comes directly from the Constitution, not from Congress.
- Suppose that Congress never made any exceptions or any regulations regarding the Court's appellate jurisdiction. Under the argument that Congress must define when, where, and how the Supreme Court shall exercise its jurisdiction, what becomes of the "judicial power of the United States," given to the Supreme Court? It would cease to exist. But the Court is coexistent and co-ordinate with Congress, and must be able to exercise judicial power even if Congress passed no act on the subject.
- By interfering in a case that has already been argued and is under consideration by the Court, Congress is unconstitutionally exercising judicial power.

For the Appellee, United States:

- The Constitution gives Congress the power to "except" any or all of the cases mentioned in the jurisdiction clause of Article III from the appellate jurisdiction of the Supreme Court. It was clearly Congress's intention, in the repealer act, to exercise its power to except.
- The Court has no authority to pronounce any opinion or render any judgment in this cause because the act conferring the jurisdiction has been repealed, and so jurisdiction ceases.
- No court can act in any case without jurisdiction, and it does not matter at what period in the progress of the case the jurisdiction ceases. After it has ceased, no judicial act can be performed.

---

53. That action came in *Ex parte Milligan* (1866), discussed in chapter 5.

◉ THE CHIEF JUSTICE DELIVERED THE OPINION OF THE COURT.

It is unnecessary to consider whether, if Congress had made no exceptions and no regulations, this court might not have exercised general appellate jurisdiction under rules prescribed by itself. From among the earliest Acts of the first Congress, at its first session, was the Act of September 24th, 1789, to establish the judicial courts of the United States. That Act provided for the organization of this court, and prescribed regulations for the exercise of its jurisdiction. . . .

The exception to appellate jurisdiction in the case before us . . . is not an inference from the affirmation of other appellate jurisdiction. It is made in terms. The provision of the Act of 1867, affirming the appellate jurisdiction of this court in cases of habeas corpus, is expressly repealed. It is hardly possible to imagine a plainer instance of positive exception.

We are not at liberty to inquire into the motives of the Legislature. We can only examine into its power under the Constitution; and the power to make exceptions to the appellate jurisdiction of this court is given by express words.

What, then, is the effect of the repealing Act upon the case before us? We cannot doubt as to this. Without jurisdiction the court cannot proceed at all in any cause. Jurisdiction is power to declare the law, and when it ceases to exist, the only function remaining to the court is that of announcing the fact and dismissing the cause. And this is not less clear upon authority than upon principle. . . .

It is quite clear, therefore, that this . . . court cannot proceed to pronounce judgment in this case, for it has no longer jurisdiction of the appeal; and judicial duty is not less fitly performed by declining ungranted jurisdiction than in exercising firmly that which the Constitution and the laws confer. . . .

The appeal of the petitioner in this case must be dismissed for want of jurisdiction.

As we can see, the Court acceded and declined to hear the case. *McCardle* suggests that Congress has the authority to remove the Court's appellate jurisdiction as it deems necessary. As Justice Felix Frankfurter put it in 1949, "Congress need not give this Court any appellate power; it may withdraw appellate jurisdiction once conferred and it may do so even while a case is *sub judice* [before a judge]."[54] Former justice Owen J.

---

54. *National Mutual Insurance Co. v. Tidewater Transfer Co.* (1949).

Roberts, who apparently agreed with Frankfurter's assertion, proposed an amendment to the Constitution that would have deprived Congress of the ability to remove the Court's appellate jurisdiction.[55] In 1962, however, Justice William O. Douglas remarked, "There is a serious question whether the *McCardle* case could command a majority view today."[56] And even Chief Justice Chase himself suggested limits on congressional power in this area. After *McCardle* was decided, he noted that use of the exceptions clause was "unusual and hardly to be justified except upon some imperious public exigency."[57]

To this day, then, *McCardle*'s status remains an open question.[58] To Frankfurter and others in his camp, the *McCardle* precedent, not to mention the text of the exceptions clause, makes it quite clear that Congress can remove the Court's appellate jurisdiction.[59] And at least some members of the current Court seem to agree. In 2006, 137 years after the *McCardle* decision, the Court once again had occasion to consider a challenge to its appellate jurisdiction of petitions for writs of habeas corpus, this time in the case of a Yemeni national, Salim Ahmed Hamdan. Shortly after the Court agreed to hear Hamdan's case (**Hamdan v. Rumsfeld,** 2006), Congress enacted the Detainee Treatment Act (DTA) of 2005, which said "no court, justice, or judge shall have jurisdiction to hear or consider" habeas corpus petitions filed by detainees at Guantanamo Bay, Cuba. Although the act was silent about pending cases, the U.S. government believed

that the act removed the Supreme Court's jurisdiction to resolve Hamdan's suit and asked the justices to dismiss the writ of certiorari.

Some legal commentators thought that the justices might go along with the government and take the opportunity to reinforce *McCardle;* others argued that they would overturn it. The majority did neither. Justice Stevens, writing for himself and Justices Breyer, Ginsburg, Kennedy, and Souter, said that it was "unnecessary" to consider the various constitutional arguments because the DTA did not expressly cover pending cases. The three dissenters, Justices Alito, Scalia, and Thomas, deemed Stevens's reading of the DTA "patently erroneous." Believing that the law had "unambiguously" removed the Court's jurisdiction, they would have refrained from resolving the dispute.

Hamdan therefore tells us little about the current status of *McCardle*. But it does appear that at least three (and perhaps four) members of the Court endorse its holding. The fourth member would be Chief Justice Roberts, who recused himself from *Hamdan* because he had heard the case while serving on a federal court of appeals.

What arguments did Douglas make and others assert against *McCardle*'s viability? The first is that *McCardle* was something of an odd case, that the Court had no choice but to acquiesce to Congress if it wanted to retain its legitimacy in post–Civil War America. The pressures of the day, rather than the Constitution or the beliefs of the justices, may have led to the decision. Some commentators also suggest that *McCardle* does not square with American traditions: before *McCardle,* Congress had never stripped the Court's jurisdiction, and after *McCardle,* Congress did not take this step even in response to some of the Court's most controversial decisions such as **Roe v. Wade** and **Brown v. Board of Education,** as table 2-2 indicates.[60] The DTA was a notable exception, but neither in *Hamdan* nor in a subsequent case, **Boumediene v. Bush** (2008), did the Court directly address whether Congress could remove the Court's appellate jurisdiction. Instead, the Court's

---

55. See Owen J. Roberts, "Now Is the Time: Fortifying the Supreme Court's Independence," *American Bar Association Journal* 35 (1949): 1. The Senate approved the amendment in 1953, but the House tabled it. Cited in Gerald Gunther, *Constitutional Law,* 12th ed. (Westbury, NY: Foundation Press, 1991), 45.

56. *Glidden Co. v. Zdanok* (1962).

57. *Ex parte Yerger* (1869).

58. For a review of various answers, see Tara Leigh Grove, "The Structural Safeguards of Federal Jurisdiction," *Harvard Law Review* 124 (2011): 869–940.

59. Note that we deal only with the question directly flowing from *McCardle*—of whether Congress can remove the Supreme Court's appellate jurisdiction—not the related questions of whether it can strip jurisdiction from the lower federal courts or strip all federal jurisdiction. For interesting commentary on these questions, see Richard H. Fallon et al., *Hart & Wechsler's The Federal Courts and the Federal System,* 5th ed. (New York: Foundation Press, 2003); Gerald Gunther, "Congressional Power to Curtail Federal Court Jurisdiction: An Opinionated Guide to the Ongoing Debate," *Stanford Law Review* 36 (1984): 895–922.

60. Grove argues that this tradition follows the requirements of enacting legislation (primarily bicameralism and presentment) outlined in Article I. These "structural safeguards," she argues, "give competing political factions (even political minorities) considerable power to 'veto' legislation." And such factions are especially "likely to use their structural veto to block jurisdiction-stripping legislation favored by their opponents." Grove, "The Structural Safeguards of Federal Jurisdiction," 869.

TABLE 2-2   A Sample of Congressional Proposals Aimed at Limiting or Eliminating the U.S. Supreme Court's Appellate Jurisdiction

ISSUE	COURT DECISION PROVOKING PROPOSAL	PROPOSAL
Criminal confessions	*Miranda v. Arizona* (1966), in which the Court required police to read those under arrest a series of rights.	A 1968 proposal sought to remove the Court's jurisdiction to hear state cases involving the admissibility of confessions.
Abortion	*Roe v. Wade* (1973), in which the Supreme Court struck down state laws criminalizing abortion. Roe legalized abortion during the first two trimesters of pregnancy.	In the 1970s and 1980s several proposals sought to remove the Court's authority to hear abortion cases.
Pledge of Allegiance	*Newdow v. U.S. Congress* (2003), in which the U.S. Court of Appeals for the Ninth Circuit struck down the mandatory saying of the Pledge of Allegiance in public schools because the pledge has the phrase "under God."	A proposal in 2004 sought to remove the jurisdiction of the lower courts and the Supreme Court to hear any case on the constitutionality of the Pledge of Allegiance.
Gay rights	*Lawrence v. Texas* (2003), which struck down same-sex sodomy laws; *Obergefell v. Hodges* (2015), which invalidated state bans on same-sex marriage.	In 1996 Congress passed the Defense of Marriage Act (DOMA), which defines marriage as between one man and one woman. Either anticipating constitutional challenges to DOMA or in response to *Lawrence* (or both), a proposal in 2004 sought to remove the Court's appellate jurisdiction to decide on the constitutionality of DOMA. After the Court invalidated DOMA, in *United States v. Windsor* (2013) but before *Obergefell*, a bill was introduced in the House to "prevent the federal courts from hearing marriage cases."

SOURCE: Adapted from Kathleen M. Sullivan and Gerald Gunther, *Constitutional Law*, 15th ed. (New York: Foundation Press, 2004), 83–85; Tara Leigh Grove, "The Structural Safeguards of Federal Jurisdiction," *Harvard Law Review* 124 (2011): 869–940.

primary emphasis was on whether Congress had unconstitutionally suspended the writ of habeas corpus rather than the issue of jurisdiction stripping *(see chapter 5).*

Then there is the related claim that, taken to its extreme, jurisdiction stripping could render the Court virtually powerless. Would the framers have created an institution only to allow Congress to destroy it? Many scholars say no.

A final argument is that a case subsequent to *McCardle* may cast some doubt on the precedent it seemed to set. In *United States v. Klein* (1872) the Court considered an 1870 law in which Congress sought to impinge on the president's authority to issue executive amnesties. In particular, it required those who wished to recover property taken by the government during the Civil War to prove their loyalty, even if they had received a presidential pardon. In addition, the law withdrew the U.S. Supreme Court's (and a lower appellate court's) jurisdiction to hear such cases. Although the justices acknowledged that the exceptions clause gave Congress the right to remove their appellate jurisdiction "in a

particular class of cases," it could not do so only as "a means to an end." In previous cases, the Court had stated that the president had the power to grant pardons, and Congress was using the exceptions clause to skirt those decisions. If the Court allowed this, it would then permit Congress to "prescribe rules of decision to the Judicial Department . . . in cases pending before it," in violation of constitutional mandates requiring the separation of powers.

Still, *Klein* did not settle the issue. To see this, we need only compare the views of the three twentieth-century justices with whom we started this section—Frankfurter, Roberts, and Douglas—and recognize the ongoing debate within the legal community.

Justiciability

According to Article III, the federal courts' judicial power is restricted to "cases" and "controversies." Taken together, these words mean that litigation must be justiciable—appropriate or suitable for a federal tribunal to hear or to solve. As Chief Justice Earl Warren asserted, cases and controversies are two complementary but somewhat different limitations. In part those words limit the business of federal courts to questions presented in an adversary context and in a form historically viewed as capable of resolution through the judicial process. And in part those words define the role assigned to the judiciary in a tripartite allocation of power to assure that the federal courts will not intrude into areas committed to the other branches of government. Justiciability is the term of art employed to give expression to this dual limitation placed upon federal courts by the case-and-controversy doctrine.[61]

Although Warren also suggested that "justiciability is itself a concept of uncertain meaning and scope," he elucidated several characteristics of litigation that would render it nonjusticiable. In this section, we treat five: advisory opinions, collusive suits, mootness, ripeness, and political questions. In the following section we deal with another concept related to justiciability—standing to sue.

Advisory Opinions. A few states and some foreign countries require judges of the highest court to advise the executive or legislature, when so requested, as to their views on the constitutionality of a proposed policy. Since the time of Chief Justice John Jay, however, federal judges in the United States have refused to issue advisory opinions. They do not render advice in hypothetical suits because if litigation is abstract, it possesses no real controversy. The language of the Constitution does not prohibit advisory opinions as opinions, but the framers rejected a proposal that would have permitted the other branches of government to request judicial rulings "upon important questions of law, and upon solemn occasions." Madison was critical of this proposal on the ground that the judiciary should have jurisdiction only over "cases of a Judiciary Nature."[62]

The Supreme Court agreed. In July 1793, Secretary of State Thomas Jefferson asked the justices if they would be willing to address questions concerning the appropriate role America should play in the ongoing British–French war. Jefferson wrote that President George Washington "would be much relieved if he found himself free to refer questions [involving the war] to the opinions of the judges of the Supreme Court in the United States, whose knowledge . . . would secure us against errors dangerous to the peace of the United States."[63] Less than a month later the justices denied Jefferson's request, with a reply written directly to the president:

We have considered [the] letter written by your direction to us by the Secretary of State [regarding] the lines of separation drawn by the Constitution between the three departments of government. These being in certain respects checks upon each other, and our being judges of a court in the last resort, are considerations which afford strong arguments against the propriety of our extra-judicially deciding the questions alluded to, especially as the power given by the Constitution to the President, of calling on the heads of departments for opinions, seems to have been *purposely* as well as expressly united to the *executive* departments [italics provided].[64]

With these words, the justices sounded the death knell for advisory opinions: such opinions would violate the separation of powers principle embedded in the Constitution. The subject has resurfaced only a few times in U.S. history; in the 1930s, for example, President Franklin Roosevelt considered a proposal that would require the Court to issue advisory opinions on the constitutionality of federal laws. But Roosevelt quickly gave up on the idea, at least in part because of its dubious constitutionality.

Nevertheless, scholars still debate the Court's 1793 letter to Washington. Some agree with the justices' logic. Others assert that more institutional concerns were at work; perhaps the Court—out of concern for its institutional legitimacy—did not want to become embroiled in "political" disputes at this early phase in its development. Whatever the reason, all subsequent Courts have followed that 1793 precedent: requests for advisory opinions to the *U.S. Supreme Court* present nonjusticiable disputes.[65]

---

61. *Flast v. Cohen* (1968).

62. Quoted by Farber and Sherry, *A History of the American Constitution,* 65.

63. The full text of Jefferson's letter is in Henry M. Hart Jr. and Albert M. Sacks, *The Legal Process,* ed. William N. Eskridge Jr. and Philip P. Frickey (Westbury, NY: Foundation Press, 1994), 630–632.

64. Quoted in ibid., 637.

65. We emphasize the Supreme Court because some state courts do, in fact, issue advisory opinions. Also keep in mind that the Supreme Court allows a U.S. Court of Appeals to certify a "question or proposition of law on which it seeks instruction for the proper decision of a case." Supreme Court Rule 19. Answering certified questions is a form of advice, though it occurs within the context of a case or controversy in the lower court.

But this does not mean that justices have not found other ways of offering advice.[66] A few have sometimes offered political leaders' informal suggestions in private conversations or correspondence.[67] Furthermore, justices of the Supreme Court have often given advice in an institutional but indirect manner. The Judiciary Act of 1925, which granted the Court wide discretion in controlling its docket, was largely drafted by Justice Willis Van Devanter. Chief Justice William Howard Taft and several associate justices openly lobbied for its passage, "patrolling the halls of Congress," as Taft put it. In 1937, when the Senate was considering President Roosevelt's Court-packing plan, opponents arranged for Chief Justice Charles Evans Hughes to send a letter to Senator Burton K. Wheeler, advising him that increasing the number of justices would impede rather than facilitate the Court's work and that the justices' sitting in separate panels to hear cases—a procedure that increasing the number of justices was supposed to allow—would probably violate the constitutional command that there be one Supreme Court. It has become customary for chief justices to prepare annual reports on the state of the judiciary for Congress. Sometimes in these reports they explain not only what kind of legislation they believe would be good for the courts but also the likely impact of proposed legislation on the federal judicial system. In one of his addresses, Chief Roberts minced no words in "advising" the Senate to stop blocking judicial nominees and begin filling judicial vacancies posthaste or else many judicial districts would experience "acute difficulties."

Finally, justices have occasionally used their opinions to provide advice to decision makers. In *Regents of the University of California v. Bakke* (1978) the Court held that a state medical school's version of affirmative action had deprived a white applicant of equal protection of the laws by rejecting him in favor of minority applicants whom the school ranked lower on all the relevant academic criteria. But Justice Lewis F. Powell Jr.'s opinion proffered the advice that the kind of affirmative action program operated by Harvard University would be constitutionally acceptable.

Collusive Suits. A second corollary of justiciability is collusion. The Court will not decide cases in which the litigants (1) want the same outcome, (2) evince no real adversariness between them, or (3) are merely testing the law. Indeed, Chief Justice Taney once said that collusion is "contempt of the court, and highly reprehensible."[68]

Why the Court deems collusive suits nonjusticiable is well illustrated in *Muskrat v. United States* (1911). At issue here were several federal laws involving land distribution and appropriations to Native Americans. To determine whether these laws were constitutional, Congress enacted a statute authorizing David Muskrat and other Native Americans to challenge the land distribution law in court. This legislation also ordered the courts to give priority to Muskrat's suit and allowed the attorney general to defend his claim. Furthermore, Congress agreed to pay Muskrat's legal fees if his suit was successful. When the dispute reached the U.S. Supreme Court, the justices dismissed it. Justice William Day wrote,

[T]here is neither more nor less in this [litigation] than an attempt to provide for a judicial determination, final in this court, of the constitutional validity of an act of Congress. Is such a determination within the judicial power conferred by the Constitution, as the same has been interpreted and defined in the authoritative decisions to which we have referred? We think it is not. That judicial power, as we have seen, is the right to determine actual controversies arising between adverse litigants, duly instituted in courts of proper jurisdiction. The right to declare a law unconstitutional arises because an act of Congress relied upon by one or the other of such parties in determining their rights is in conflict with the fundamental law. The exercise of this, the most important and delicate duty of this court, is not given to it as a body with revisory power over the action of Congress, but because the rights of the litigants in justiciable controversies require the court to choose between the fundamental law and a law purporting to be enacted within constitutional authority, but in fact beyond the power delegated to the legislative branch of the Government. This attempt to obtain a judicial declaration of the validity of the act of Congress is not presented in a "case" or "controversy," to which, under the Constitution of the United States, the judicial power alone extends. It is true the United States is made a defendant to this action, but it has no interest adverse to the claimants. The object is not to assert a property right as against the

---

66. We adopt some of the material to follow from Murphy et al., *Courts, Judges, and Politics,* chap. 6.

67. See, for example, Stewart Jay, *Most Humble Servants: The Advisory Role of Early Judges* (New Haven, CT: Yale University Press, 1997).

---

68. *Lord v. Veazie* (1850).

Government, or to demand compensation for alleged wrongs because of action upon its part. The whole purpose of the law is to determine the constitutional validity of this class of legislation, in a suit not arising between parties concerning a property right necessarily involved in the decision in question, but in a proceeding against the Government in its sovereign capacity, and concerning which the only judgment required is to settle the doubtful character of the legislation in question.

The Court, however, has not always followed the *Muskrat* precedent. Indeed, several collusive suits resulted in landmark decisions, including *Pollock v. Farmers' Loan and Trust Co.* (1895), in which the Court declared the federal income tax unconstitutional. The litigants in this dispute, a bank and a stockholder in the bank, both wanted the same outcome—the demise of the tax *(see chapter 8)*. **Carter v. Carter Coal Co.** (1936) is also exemplary. Here the Court agreed to resolve a dispute over a major piece of New Deal legislation despite the fact that the litigants, a company president and the company, which included the president's father, both wanted the same outcome—the eradication of the legislation *(see chapter 7)*.

Why did the justices resolve these disputes? One answer is that the Court might overlook some element of collusion if the suit presents a real controversy or the potential for one. But some analysts see it differently. The temptation to set "good" public policy (or strike down "bad" public policy), they say, is sometimes too strong for the justices to follow their own rules. Then again, some commentators argue that they should resist. In 1913 the country ratified the Sixteenth Amendment to overturn *Pollock,* and the Court itself limited *Carter Coal* in the 1941 case of *United States v. Darby (see chapter 7)*.

Mootness. In general, the Court will not decide cases in which the controversy is no longer live by the time it reaches the Court's doorstep. **DeFunis v. Odegaard** (1974) is a clear example. Rejected for admission to the University of Washington Law School, Marco DeFunis Jr. brought suit against the school, alleging that it had engaged in reverse discrimination because it had denied him a place but accepted statistically less qualified minority students. In 1971 a trial court found merit in his claim and ordered that the university admit him. While DeFunis was in his second year of law school, the state's high court reversed the trial

judge's ruling. DeFunis then appealed to the U.S. Supreme Court. By that time, he had registered for his final quarter in school. In a per curiam opinion, the Court refused to rule on the merits of DeFunis's claim, asserting that it was moot:

Because [DeFunis] will complete his law school studies at the end of the term for which he has now registered regardless of any decision this Court might reach on the merits of this litigation, we conclude that the Court cannot, consistently with the limitations of Art. III of the Constitution, consider the substantive constitutional issues tendered by the parties.

In his dissent, Justice Brennan noted that DeFunis could conceivably not complete his studies that quarter, and so the issue was not necessarily moot. This suggests that the rules governing mootness are a bit fuzzier than the *DeFunis* majority opinion characterized them.

To see this possibility, consider another example: **Roe v. Wade** (1973), in which the Court legalized abortions performed during the first two trimesters of pregnancy. Norma McCorvey, also known as Roe, was pregnant when she filed suit in 1970, and by the time the Court handed down the decision in 1973, she had long since given birth and put her baby up for adoption. But the justices did not declare this case moot. Why not? What made *Roe* different from *DeFunis?*

The justices provided two legal justifications. First, DeFunis brought the litigation in his own behalf, but *Roe* was a class action—a lawsuit brought by one or more persons who represent themselves and all others similarly situated. Second, DeFunis had been admitted to law school, and he would "never again be required to run the gauntlet." Roe could become pregnant again; that is, pregnancy is a situation "capable of repetition, yet evading review." Are these reasonable points? Or is it possible, as some suspect, that the Court developed them to avoid particular legal issues? In either case, it is clear that the exceptions the Court has carved out can make mootness a rather slippery concept, open to interpretation by different justices and Courts.

Ripeness. Ripeness is the flip side of mootness. Whereas moot cases are brought too late, "unripe" cases are those that are brought too early. In other words, under existing Court interpretation, a case is nonjusticiable if the controversy is premature—has insufficiently gelled—for review. *United Public Workers v. Mitchell* (1947) is an often-cited example. In this case, government workers challenged the Hatch Act of 1940, which prohibits some types of federal employees from participating in political campaigns. But only one of the appellants had actually violated the act; the rest simply expressed an interest in working on campaigns. According to the justices, only the one employee had a ripe claim because "the power of courts, and ultimately of this Court to pass upon the constitutionality of acts of Congress arises only when the interests of the litigants require the use of this judicial authority for their protection against actual interference. A hypothetical threat is not enough. We can only speculate as to the kinds of political activity the appellants desire to engage in."

The justices echoed the sentiment of *Mitchell* in *International Longshoreman's Union v. Boyd* (1954). This case involved a 1952 federal law mandating that all aliens seeking admission into the United States from Alaska be "examined" as if they were entering from a foreign country. Believing that the law might affect seasonal American laborers working in Alaska temporarily, a union challenged the law. Writing for the Court, Justice Frankfurter dismissed the suit. In his view,

Appellants in effect asked [the Court] to rule that a statute the sanctions of which had not been set in motion against individuals on whose behalf relief was sought, because an occasion for doing so had not arisen, would not be applied to them if in the future such a contingency should arise. That is not a lawsuit to enforce a right; it is an endeavor to obtain a court's assurance that a statute does not govern hypothetical situations that may or may not make the challenged statute applicable. Determination of the . . . constitutionality of the legislation in advance of its immediate adverse effect in the context of a concrete case involves too remote and abstract an inquiry for the proper exercise of the judicial function.

In addition, the ripeness requirement mandates that a party exhaust all available administrative and lower court remedies before seeking review by the Supreme Court. Until these opportunities have been fully explored the case is not ready for the justices to hear.

Political Questions. Another type of nonjusticiable suit involves a political question. Chief Justice Marshall stated in *Marbury v. Madison,*

The province of the court is, solely, to decide on the rights of individuals, not to inquire how the executive, or executive officers, perform duties in which they have a discretion. Questions in their nature political, or which are, by the constitution and laws, submitted to the executive, can never be made in this court.

In other words, the Court recognizes that there is a class of questions the Court will not address because they are better solved by other branches of government, even though they may be constitutional in nature.

But what exactly constitutes a political question? The Court took its first stab at addressing this question in *Luther v. Borden* (1849). This case has its origins in the 1840s, when a number of Rhode Island citizens sought to persuade the legislature to change suffrage requirements (which mandated the ownership of property as a criterion for voting) or to hold a convention for the purpose of writing a constitution (which Rhode Island did not have, as it was still operating under its royal charter from King Charles II). When the government rejected these proposals, these citizens wrote their own constitution and created their own government. Meanwhile, the existing government issued a proclamation placing the entire state under martial law, and the governor warned citizens not to support the new constitution. He even contacted President John Tyler for help in suppressing the rebellion. Although Tyler did not send in federal troops, he agreed to do so if war broke out.

Eventually, the existing government managed to suppress the rebels, but one of them, Martin Luther, sued. Luther asserted that the Rhode Island Charter violated Article IV, Section 4, of the U.S. Constitution, which states, "The United States shall guarantee to every State in the Union a Republican Form of Government, and shall protect each of them against Invasion; and on Application of the Legislature or of the Executive (when the Legislature cannot be convened) against Domestic violence." Luther asked the Court to declare the charter government illegitimate and to supplant it with the new constitution.

The Supreme Court, however, refused to go along with Luther. Writing for the majority, Chief Justice Taney held that the Court should avoid deciding any question arising out of the guarantee clause because such questions are inherently "political." He based the opinion largely on the words of Article IV, which he believed governed relations between the states and the federal government, not governments and courts. In other words, because the clause omits mention of the Court, it is enforceable only by the president or Congress.

For the next hundred years or so, the Court maintained Taney's position: any case involving the guarantee clause constituted a nonjusticiable dispute. In the 1940s an issue came before the Court that presented it with an opportunity to rethink *Luther*. The issue was reapportionment, the way the states draw their legislative districts.

Under the U.S. Constitution, each state is allotted a certain number of seats in the House of Representatives based on the population of the state. Once that number has been determined, it is up to the state to map out the congressional districts. Article I specifies,

Representatives . . . shall be apportioned among the several States which may be included within this Union, according to their respective Numbers. . . . The actual Enumeration shall be made within three Years after the first Meeting of the Congress of the United States, and within every subsequent Term of ten Years, in such Manner as they shall by Law direct. The Number of Representatives shall not exceed one for every thirty Thousand, but each State shall have at Least one Representative.

Article I makes clear that a ten-year census determines the number of representatives each state receives. But no guidelines exist as to how those representatives are to be allocated or apportioned within a given state.

Most states redrew their congressional district lines as population shifts occurred within them around the middle of the twentieth century. The new maps meant creating greater parity for urban centers as citizens moved out of rural areas. Some states, however, ignored the population shifts and refused to reapportion seats. Over time, the results of their failure to do so became readily apparent. It was possible for two districts within the same state, each electing one member to the House, to have large differences in population.

Because malapportionment generally had the greatest effect on urban voters, grossly undervaluing their voting power, reform groups representing the interests of these voters began to bring litigation to force legislatures to reapportion. In one of the most important of these efforts, *Colegrove v. Green* (1946), they did so under Article IV. They argued that the failure

to reapportion legislative districts deprived some voters of their right to a republican form of government. By way of proof, plaintiffs indicated that a large statistical discrepancy existed between the voting power of citizens in urban areas and that of rural dwellers because the Illinois legislature had not reapportioned since 1901. The state parties, on the other hand, asked the court to dismiss the case on the ground that it raised "only political issues."

The Court agreed with the state. Writing for the Court, Justice Frankfurter dismissed *Colegrove* on the ground that legislative reapportionment within states was left open by the Constitution. If the Court intervened in this matter, it would be acting in a way "hostile to a democratic system." Put in different terms, reapportionment constituted a "political thicket" into which "courts ought not enter."

Less than two decades later, however, in *Baker v. Carr* (1962), the Court did, in fact, enter this thicket, holding that reapportionment was a justiciable issue. What brought about this change? And, more relevant here, what meaning does *Baker* have for the political question doctrine? In particular, does it overrule *Luther*, or does it merely change the interpretive context?

Baker v. Carr

369 U.S. 186 (1962)
http://laws.findlaw.com/us/369/186.html
Oral arguments are available at https://www.oyez.org.
Vote: 6 (Black, Brennan, Clark, Douglas, Stewart, Warren)
2 (Frankfurter, Harlan)

OPINION OF THE COURT: *Brennan*
CONCURRING OPINIONS: *Clark, Douglas, Stewart*
DISSENTING OPINIONS: *Frankfurter, Harlan*
NOT PARTICIPATING: *Whittaker*

FACTS:

As a result of the Court's decision in *Colegrove v. Green*, states that had not reapportioned since 1900 were under no federal constitutional mandate to do so, and disparities between the voting power of urban and rural citizens continued to grow. Figure 2-2 shows that a rural vote for the Tennessee legislature counted nearly four times as much as an urban vote.

Naturally, many citizens and organizations wanted to force legislatures to reapportion, but under *Colegrove* they could not do so using the guarantee clause. They looked, therefore, to another section of the Constitution,

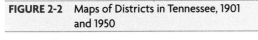

FIGURE 2-2 Maps of Districts in Tennessee, 1901 and 1950

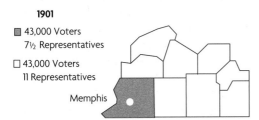

1901

☐ 43,000 Voters
7½ Representatives

☐ 43,000 Voters
11 Representatives

Memphis

Battle of the ballot: In 1901 Memphis, Tennessee, had as many people as eight nearby counties together and elected nearly the same number of representatives.

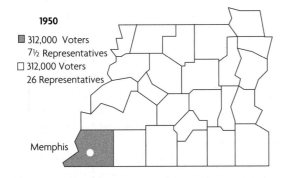

1950

☐ 312,000 Voters
7½ Representatives

☐ 312,000 Voters
26 Representatives

Memphis

By 1950 Memphis's population equaled that of twenty-four Tennessee counties. Under the state constitution the city should have gained more representatives, but it did not, so the rural vote counted almost four times as much as the urban. Reviewing city voters' complaint that this situation denied them equal protection of the laws, the Court in 1962 held that judges should hear and decide such claims under the Fourteenth Amendment (*Baker v. Carr*). Chief Justice Earl Warren looked back on this decision as the most important and influential in his sixteen years on the Court. It opened the way to enunciation (in *Reynolds v. Sims*) of the "one person, one vote" principle and its enforcement by court order in many related cases across the nation.

SOURCE: *Equal Justice under Law* (Washington, DC: Foundation of the Federal Bar Association, 1965), 108.

the Fourteenth Amendment's equal protection clause, which says that no state shall "deny to any person within its jurisdiction the equal protection of the laws." From this clause they made the argument that the failure to reapportion led to unequal treatment of voters.

Although this strategy represented a clever legal attempt to reframe the issue of reapportionment, when attorneys sought to apply it to the Tennessee situation, a lower federal district court dismissed their suit.[69]

69. For more on this, see Richard C. Cortner, "Strategies and Tactics of Litigants in Constitutional Cases," *Journal of Public Law* 17 (1968): 287–307; and Cortner, *The Apportionment Cases* (Knoxville: University of Tennessee Press, 1970).

Relying on *Colegrove* and other cases, that court held reapportionment to constitute a political question on which it could not rule.

ARGUMENTS:

For the Appellants, Charles W. Baker et al.:

- This case is distinguishable from *Colegrove* because in *Colegrove* the door to alternative relief, including relief by Congress, appeared to be open, whereas in this case, sixty years of history have demonstrated that these alternatives are not available to the appellants.

- This case should not be considered a nonjusticiable political question because there is a clear, mathematical standard by which the Court may determine whether appellants' votes have been discriminated against.

- Appellants have been denied the equal protection of the laws because their votes have been systematically discriminated against.

For the Appellees, Joe C. Carr,
Secretary of State, State of Tennessee, et al.:

- In the past, the Court has consistently stated that enforcement of the guaranty of a republican form of government is a political question and does not fall within its jurisdiction.

- Under the constitution of Tennessee, reapportionment has been specifically designated to the legislature and not to the courts.

MR. JUSTICE BRENNAN DELIVERED THE OPINION OF THE COURT.

In holding that the subject matter of this suit was not justiciable, the District Court relied on *Colegrove v. Green* . . . [and related cases]. The court stated: "From a review of these decisions there can be no doubt that the federal rule . . . is that the federal courts . . . will not intervene in cases of this type to compel legislative reapportionment." We understand the District Court to have read the cited cases as compelling the conclusion that since the appellants sought to have a legislative apportionment held unconstitutional, their suit presented a "political question" and was therefore nonjusticiable. We hold that this challenge to an apportionment presents no nonjusticiable "political question." The cited cases do not hold the contrary.

Of course the mere fact that the suit seeks protection of a political right does not mean it presents a political question. Such an objection "is little more than a play upon words." . . .

We hold that the claim pleaded here neither rests upon nor implicates the Guaranty Clause and that its justiciability is therefore not foreclosed by our decisions of cases involving that clause. The District Court misinterpreted *Colegrove v. Green* and other decisions of this Court on which it relied. . . . To show why we reject the argument based on the Guaranty Clause, we must examine the authorities under it. But because there appears to be some uncertainty as to why those cases did present political questions, and specifically as to whether this apportionment case is like those cases, we deem it necessary first to consider the contours of the "political question" doctrine. . . .

We have said that "In determining whether a question falls within [the political question] category, the appropriateness under our system of government of attributing finality to the action of the political departments and also the lack of satisfactory criteria for a judicial determination are dominant considerations." The nonjusticiability of a political question is primarily a function of the separation of powers. Much confusion results from the capacity of the "political question" label to obscure the need for case-by-case inquiry. Deciding whether a matter has in any measure been committed by the Constitution to another branch of government, or whether the action of that branch exceeds whatever authority has been committed, is itself a delicate exercise in constitutional interpretation, and is a responsibility of this Court as ultimate interpreter of the Constitution. To demonstrate this requires no less than to analyze representative cases and to infer from them the analytical threads that make up the political question doctrine. We shall then show that none of those threads catches this case.

Foreign relations: There are sweeping statements to the effect that all questions touching foreign relations are political questions. Not only does resolution of such issues frequently turn on standards that defy judicial application, or involve the exercise of a discretion demonstrably committed to the executive or legislature; but many such questions uniquely demand single-voiced statement of the Government's views. Yet it is error to suppose that every case or controversy which touches foreign relations lies beyond judicial cognizance. Our cases in this field seem invariably to show a discriminating analysis of the particular question posed, in terms of the history of its management by the

political branches, of its susceptibility to judicial handling in the light of its nature and posture in the specific case, and of the possible consequences of judicial action. For example, though a court will not ordinarily inquire whether a treaty has been terminated, since on that question "governmental action . . . must be regarded as of controlling importance," if there has been no conclusive "governmental action" then a court can construe a treaty and may find it provides the answer. Though a court will not undertake to construe a treaty in a manner inconsistent with a subsequent federal statute, no similar hesitancy obtains if the asserted clash is with state law. . . .

Dates of duration of hostilities: Though it has been stated broadly that "the power which declared the necessity is the power to declare its cessation, and what the cessation requires," here too analysis reveals isolable reasons for the presence of political questions, underlying this Court's refusal to review the political departments' determination of when or whether a war has ended. Dominant is the need for finality in the political determination, for emergency's nature demands "A prompt and unhesitating obedience." Moreover, "the cessation of hostilities does not necessarily end the war power. It was stated in *Hamilton v. Kentucky Distilleries & W. Co.* that the war power includes the power 'to remedy the evils which have arisen from its rise and progress' and continues during that emergency." But deference rests on reason, not habit. The question in a particular case may not seriously implicate considerations of finality—e.g., a public program of importance (rent control) yet not central to the emergency effort. Further, clearly definable criteria for decision may be available. In such case the political question barrier falls away. . . .

Validity of enactments: In *Coleman v. Miller* [1939] this Court held that the questions of how long a proposed amendment to the Federal Constitution remained open to ratification, and what effect a prior rejection had on a subsequent ratification, were committed to congressional resolution and involved criteria of decision that necessarily escaped the judicial grasp. Similar considerations apply to the enacting process: "The respect due to coequal and independent departments," and the need for finality and certainty about the status of a statute contribute to judicial reluctance to inquire whether, as passed, it complied with all requisite formalities. . . .

The status of Indian tribes: This Court's deference to the political departments in determining whether Indians are recognized as a tribe, while it reflects familiar attributes of political questions, also has a unique element in that the relation of the Indians to the United States is marked by peculiar and cardinal distinctions which exist no where else. . . . [The Indians are] domestic dependent nations . . . in a state of pupilage. . . .

Yet here, too, there is no blanket rule. While "It is for [Congress] . . . and not for the courts, to determine when the true interests of the Indian require his release from [the] condition of tutelage," . . . it is not meant by this that Congress may bring a community or body of people within the range of this power by arbitrarily calling them an Indian tribe. . . . Able to discern what is "distinctly Indian," the courts will strike down any heedless extension of that label. They will not stand impotent before an obvious instance of a manifestly unauthorized exercise of power.

It is apparent that several formulations which vary slightly according to the settings in which the questions arise may describe a political question, although each has one or more elements which identify it as essentially a function of the separation of powers. Prominent on the surface of any case held to involve a political question is found a textually demonstrable constitutional commitment of the issue to a coordinate political department; or a lack of judicially discoverable and manageable standards for resolving it; or the impossibility of deciding without an initial policy determination of a kind clearly for nonjudicial discretion; or the impossibility of a court's undertaking independent resolution without expressing lack of the respect due coordinate branches of government; or an unusual need for unquestioning adherence to a political decision already made; or the potentiality of embarrassment from multifarious pronouncements by various departments on one question.

Unless one of these formulations is inextricable from the case at bar, there should be no dismissal for nonjusticiability on the ground of a political question's presence. The doctrine of which we treat is one of "political questions," not one of "political cases." The courts cannot reject as "no lawsuit" a bona fide controversy as to whether some action denominated "political" exceeds constitutional authority. The cases we have reviewed show the necessity for discriminating inquiry into the precise facts and posture of the particular case, and the impossibility of resolution by any semantic cataloguing.

But it is argued that this case shares the characteristics of decisions that constitute a category not yet considered, cases concerning the Constitution's guaranty, in Art. IV, §4, of a republican form of government. A conclusion as to whether the case at bar does present a political question cannot be confidently reached until we have considered those cases with special care. We shall discover that Guaranty Clause claims involve those elements which define a "political question," and for that reason and no other, they are nonjusticiable. In particular, we shall discover that the nonjusticiability of such claims has nothing to do with their touching upon matters of state governmental organization.

Republican form of government: . . . Clearly, several factors were thought by the Court in *Luther* [*v. Borden*] to make the question there "political": the commitment to the other branches of the decision as to which is the lawful state government; the unambiguous action by the President, in recognizing the charter government as the lawful authority; the need for finality in the executive's decision; and the lack of criteria by which a court could determine which form of government was republican.

But the only significance that *Luther* could have for our immediate purposes is in its holding that the Guaranty Clause is not a repository of judicially manageable standards which a court could utilize independently in order to identify a State's lawful government. The Court has since refused to resort to the Guaranty Clause—which alone had been invoked for the purpose—as the source of a constitutional standard for invalidating state action. . . .

Just as the Court has consistently held that a challenge to state action based on the Guaranty Clause presents no justiciable question, so has it held, and for the same reasons, that challenges to congressional action on the ground of inconsistency with that clause present no justiciable question. . . .

We come, finally, to the ultimate inquiry whether our precedents as to what constitutes a nonjusticiable "political question" bring the case before us under the umbrella of that doctrine. A natural beginning is to note whether any of the common characteristics which we have been able to identify and label descriptively are present. We find none: The question here is the consistency of state action with the Federal Constitution. We have no question decided, or to be decided, by a political branch of government coequal with this Court. Nor do we risk embarrassment of our government abroad, or grave disturbance at home if we take issue with Tennessee as to the constitutionality of her action here challenged. Nor need the appellants, in order to succeed in this action, ask the Court to enter upon policy determinations for which judicially manageable standards are lacking. Judicial standards under the Equal Protection Clause are well developed and familiar, and it has been open to courts since the enactment of the Fourteenth Amendment to determine, if on the particular facts they must, that a discrimination reflects no policy, but simply arbitrary and capricious action.

This case does, in one sense, involve the allocation of political power within a State, and the appellants might conceivably have added a claim under the Guaranty Clause. Of course, as we have seen, any reliance on that clause would be futile. But because any reliance on the Guaranty Clause could not have succeeded it does not follow that appellants may not be heard on the equal protection claim which in fact they tender. True, it must be clear that the Fourteenth Amendment claim is not so enmeshed with those political question elements which render Guaranty Clause claims nonjusticiable as actually to present a political question itself. But we have found that not to be the case here. . . .

We conclude then that the nonjusticiability of claims resting on the Guaranty Clause which arises from their embodiment of questions that were thought "political," can have no bearing upon the justiciability of the equal protection claim presented in this case. Finally, we emphasize that it is the involvement in Guaranty Clause claims of the elements thought to define "political questions," and no other feature, which could render them nonjusticiable. . . .

. . . [T]he complaint's allegations of a denial of equal protection present a justiciable constitutional cause of action upon which appellants are entitled to a trial and a decision. The right asserted is within the reach of judicial protection under the Fourteenth Amendment.

The judgment of the District Court is reversed and the cause is remanded for further proceedings consistent with this opinion.

Reversed and remanded.

MR. JUSTICE CLARK, concurring.

I believe it can be shown that this case is distinguishable from earlier cases dealing with the distribution of political power by a State, that a patent violation of the Equal Protection Clause of the United States Constitution has been shown, and that an appropriate remedy may be formulated. . . .

Although I find the Tennessee apportionment statute offends the Equal Protection Clause, I would not consider intervention by this Court into so delicate a field if there

were any other relief available to the people of Tennessee. But the majority of the people of Tennessee have no "practical opportunities for exerting their political weight at the polls" to correct the existing "invidious discrimination." Tennessee has no initiative and referendum. I have searched diligently for other "practical opportunities" present under the law. I find none other than through the federal courts. The majority of the voters have been caught up in a legislative strait-jacket. Tennessee has an "informed, civically militant electorate" and "an aroused popular conscience," but it does not sear "the conscience of the people's representatives." This is because the legislative policy has riveted the present seats in the Assembly to their respective constituencies, and by the votes of their incumbents a reapportionment of any kind is prevented. The people have been rebuffed at the hands of the Assembly; they have tried the constitutional convention route, but since the call must originate in the Assembly it, too, has been fruitless. They have tried Tennessee courts with the same result, and Governors have fought the tide only to flounder. It is said that there is recourse in Congress and perhaps that may be, but from a practical standpoint this is without substance. To date Congress has never undertaken such a task in any State. We therefore must conclude that the people of Tennessee are stymied and without judicial intervention will be saddled with the present discrimination in the affairs of their state government.

MR. JUSTICE FRANKFURTER, whom MR. JUSTICE HARLAN joins, dissenting.

The Court today reverses a uniform course of decision established by a dozen cases, including one by which the very claim now sustained was unanimously rejected only five years ago. The impressive body of rulings thus cast aside reflected the equally uniform course of our political history regarding the relationship between population and legislative representation—a wholly different matter from denial of the franchise to individuals because of race, color, religion or sex. . . . Disregard of inherent limits in the effective exercise of the Court's "judicial Power" not only presages the futility of judicial intervention in the essentially political conflict of forces by which the relation between population and representation has time out of mind been, and now is, determined. It may well impair the Court's position as the ultimate organ of "the supreme Law of the Land" in that vast range of legal problems, often strongly entangled in popular feeling, on which this Court must pronounce. . . .

The present case involves all of the elements that have made the Guarantee Clause cases non-justiciable. It is, in effect, a Guarantee Clause claim masquerading under a different label. But it cannot make the case more fit for judicial action that appellants invoke the Fourteenth Amendment rather than Art. IV, §4, where, in fact, the gist of their complaint is the same—unless it can be found that the Fourteenth Amendment speaks with greater particularity to their situation. We have been admonished to avoid "the tyranny of labels." Art. IV, §4, is not committed by express constitutional terms to Congress. It is the nature of the controversies arising under it, nothing else, which has made it judicially unenforceable. Of course, if a controversy falls within judicial power, it depends "on how he [the plaintiff] casts his action," whether he brings himself within a jurisdictional statute. But where judicial competence is wanting, it cannot be created by invoking one clause of the Constitution rather than another. . . .

Here, appellants[] . . . complaint is that the basis of representation of the Tennessee Legislature hurts them. They assert that "a minority now rules in Tennessee," that the apportionment statute results in a "distortion of the constitutional system," that the General Assembly is no longer "a body representative of the people of the State of Tennessee," all "contrary to the basic principle of representative government. . . . " Accepting appellants' own formulation of the issue, one can know this handsaw from a hawk. Such a claim would be nonjusticiable not merely under Art. IV, §4, but under any clause of the Constitution, by virtue of the very fact that a federal court is not a forum for political debate.

But appellants, of course, do not rest on this claim *simpliciter*. In invoking the Equal Protection Clause, they assert that the distortion of representative government complained of is produced by systematic discrimination against them, by way of "a debasement of their votes. . . . " Does this characterization, with due regard for the facts from which it is derived, add anything to appellants' case?

At first blush, this charge of discrimination based on legislative underrepresentation is given the appearance of a more private, less impersonal claim, than the assertion that the frame of government is askew. Appellants appear as representatives of a class that is prejudiced as a class, in contradistinction to the polity in its entirety. However, the discrimination relied on is the deprivation of what appellants conceive to be their proportionate share of political influence. . . .

But they are permitted to vote and their votes are counted. They go to the polls, they cast their ballots, they send their representatives to the state councils. Their complaint is simply that the representatives are not sufficiently numerous or powerful—in short, that Tennessee has adopted a basis of representation with which they are dissatisfied. Talk of "debasement" or "dilution" is circular talk. One cannot speak of "debasement" or "dilution" of the value of a vote until there is first defined a standard of reference as to what a vote should be worth. What is actually asked of the Court in this case is to choose among competing bases of representation—ultimately, really, among competing theories of political philosophy—in order to establish an appropriate frame of government for the State of Tennessee and thereby for all the States of the Union. . . .

This is not a case in which a State has, through a device however oblique and sophisticated, denied Negroes or Jews or redheaded persons a vote, or given them only a third or a sixth of a vote. . . . What Tennessee illustrates is an old and still widespread method of representation—representation by local geographical division, only in part respective of population—in preference to others, others, forsooth, more appealing. Appellants contest this choice and seek to make this Court the arbiter of the disagreement. They would make the Equal Protection Clause the charter of adjudication, asserting that the equality which it guarantees comports, if not the assurance of equal weight to every voter's vote, at least the basic conception that representation ought to be proportionate to population, a standard by reference to which the reasonableness of apportionment plans may be judged.

To find such a political conception legally enforceable in the broad and unspecific guarantee of equal protection is to rewrite the Constitution. See *Luther v. Borden*. Certainly, "equal protection" is no more secure a foundation for judicial judgment of the permissibility of varying forms of representative government than is "Republican Form." Indeed since "equal protection of the laws" can only mean an equality of persons standing in the same relation to whatever governmental action is challenged, the determination whether treatment is equal presupposes a determination concerning the nature of the relationship. This, with respect to apportionment, means an inquiry into the theoretic base of representation in an acceptably republican state. For a court could not determine the equal protection issue without in fact first determining the Republican Form issue, simply because what is reasonable for equal protection purposes will depend upon what frame of government, basically, is allowed. To divorce "equal protection" from "Republican Form" is to talk about half a question. . . .

Manifestly, the Equal Protection Clause supplies no clearer guide for judicial examination of apportionment methods than would the Guarantee Clause itself. Apportionment, by its character, is a subject of extraordinary complexity, involving—even after the fundamental theoretical issues concerning what is to be represented in a representative legislature have been fought out or compromised—considerations of geography, demography, electoral convenience, economic and social cohesions or divergencies among particular local groups, communications, the practical effects of political institutions like the lobby and the city machine, ancient traditions and ties of settled usage, respect for proven incumbents of long experience and senior status, mathematical mechanics, censuses compiling relevant data, and a host of others. Legislative responses throughout the country to the reapportionment demands of the 1960 Census have glaringly confirmed that these are not factors that lend themselves to evaluations of a nature that are the staple of judicial determinations or for which judges are equipped to adjudicate by legal training or experience or native wit. And this is the more so true because in every strand of this complicated, intricate web of values meet the contending forces of partisan politics. The practical significance of apportionment is that the next election results may differ because of it. Apportionment battles are overwhelmingly party or intra-party contests. It will add a virulent source of friction and tension in federal-state relations to embroil the federal judiciary in them.

Baker v. Carr is important for a number of reasons. First, it opened the window for judicial resolution of reapportionment cases, which continue to appear on the Court's docket. Second, and more relevant here, is that, unlike *Luther,* it established elements for determining whether a dispute presented a political question. As Justice William Brennan wrote,

Prominent on the surface of any case held to involve a political question is found [1] a textually demonstrable constitutional commitment of the issue to a coordinate political department; or [2] a lack of judicially discoverable and manageable standards for resolving it; or [3] the impossibility of deciding without an initial policy determination of a kind clearly for nonjudicial discretion; or [4] the impossibility of a court's undertaking independent resolution without expressing lack of the respect due coordinate branches of government; or [5] an unusual need for unquestioning adherence to

a political decision already made; or [6] the potentiality of embarrassment from multifarious pronouncements by various departments on one question.

As our numbering indicates, this definition contains six characteristics, though they seem to fall under two rubrics.[70] First, the Court will look to the Constitution to see if there is a "textually demonstrable commitment" to another branch of government. The justices also consider whether particular questions should be left to another branch of government as a matter of prudence. This is where factors such as the lack of judicially discoverable standards, embarrassment, and so on come into play.

Note, however, that the definition does not dismiss the logic of *Luther* entirely; it just reworks it a bit. More to the point, Justice Brennan quite clearly states that claims invoking the guarantee clause possess the attributes of a political question (under his definition) and, therefore, are nonjusticiable.

But what else would fall under the definition? Although some analysts claim that *Baker* substantially weakened the political questions doctrine—a claim we explore at the end of this section—it did not lead to its complete demise. Over the years, various justices have used the doctrine to dismiss a range of substantive disputes, particularly those involving international relations. In **Goldwater v. Carter** (1979), which presented a challenge to President Jimmy Carter's unilateral termination of a U.S. treaty with Taiwan, the Court issued a per curiam remanding the case to the lower court with directions to dismiss the complaint. Justice Rehnquist concurred in the judgment, writing for himself and three others (Burger, Stewart, and Stevens) that the case presented a political question. In his view, it involved a foreign policy matter on which the Constitution provided no definitive answer. As such, it "should be left for resolution by the Executive and Legislative branches."

In *Nixon v. United States* (1993), however, the Court relied heavily on *Baker v. Carr* to examine a domestic issue—the impeachment of a federal judge who

---

70. For another way to consider the *Baker* elements, see Justice Sotomayor's concurring opinion in **Zivotofsky v. Clinton** (2012), in which she writes, "[T]he *Baker* factors reflect three distinct justifications for withholding judgment on the merits of a dispute." Sotomayor sees these as (1) textual commitment (*Baker* element 1), (2) "decisionmaking beyond courts' competence" (*Baker* elements 2 and 3), and (3) prudential considerations (*Baker* elements 4, 5, and 6).

claimed that the Senate used unconstitutional procedures in trying his case. As you read *Nixon,* take note of how the modern-day Court applied the political question doctrine. Also consider the mode of constitutional analysis it used; Chief Justice Rehnquist's opinion serves as an interesting example of the Court searching for the plain "meaning of the words" and the intent of the framers in interpreting a constitutional provision, the Senate's power to try impeachments.

Nixon v. United States

506 U.S. 224 (1993)
http://laws.findlaw.com/us/506/224.html
Oral arguments are available at https://www.oyez.org.
Vote: 9 (Blackmun, Kennedy, O'Connor, Rehnquist, Scalia, Souter, Stevens, Thomas, White)
      0

OPINION OF THE COURT: *Rehnquist*
CONCURRING OPINIONS: *Souter, Stevens, White*

FACTS:

Walter L. Nixon Jr. was appointed a U.S. district court judge for the Southern District of Mississippi by President Lyndon Johnson in 1968. In 1984 federal prosecutors began to investigate Judge Nixon's relationship with Hattiesburg entrepreneur Wiley Fairchild. They suspected that Fairchild had allowed Nixon to participate in a sweetheart oil and gas deal in return for Nixon's intervention in behalf of Fairchild's son, Drew, who was under state indictment for drug trafficking. Nixon, testifying before a federal grand jury, denied that he had discussed Drew Fairchild's case with the local district attorney or had intervened in any other way in the young man's behalf. In 1986 Nixon stood trial in a federal court for committing perjury in his grand jury testimony and for accepting an illegal gratuity. The jury acquitted Nixon of the illegal gratuity charge but convicted him on two counts of lying to the grand jury. He received a five-year prison term. Nixon, asserting his innocence on all charges, refused to resign from the bench and continued to receive his salary while serving his sentence.

The Judicial Conference of the United States, the policy-making body of the federal judiciary, recommended to the House of Representatives that Nixon be impeached. Impeachment is the only constitutionally permitted method of removing a federal judge from office. Following an investigation by the Judiciary Committee, the House voted 417–0 to impeach Nixon

U.S. district court judge Walter Nixon testifying during his 1989 Senate impeachment trial.

AP Images/Marcy Nighswander

for "high crimes and misdemeanors." The case then went to the Senate for trial. That body invoked its own rule, Impeachment Rule XI, under which the presiding officer appoints a committee of senators to "receive evidence and take testimony." The presiding officer appointed a special twelve-member bipartisan committee to hear the case and report to the full Senate.

As part of the deliberative process, the Senate committee examined briefs submitted by Nixon and the House impeachment managers, heard from ten witnesses, and allowed Nixon to "make a personal appeal." After four days of hearings, the committee recommended that Nixon be removed from office. In November 1989 the Senate voted 89–8 and 78–19 to convict Nixon on two articles of impeachment stemming from his grand jury testimony. The conviction officially stripped Nixon of his judgeship. By that time he had received an estimated $286,500 in salary since his federal court conviction.

Nixon responded by claiming in a federal lawsuit that Senate Rule XI violated the Constitution. He argued that the Senate procedure of having a committee—rather than the full Senate—hear his case violated Article I, Section 3, Clause 6, of the Constitution, which states that the "Senate shall have the sole power to try all Impeachments." The committee procedure, he alleged, prohibited the full Senate from participating in the evidentiary hearings. Unsuccessful in the lower courts, Nixon pursued his case to the U.S. Supreme Court.

ARGUMENTS:

For the petitioner, Walter L. Nixon:

- The words used in Article I, Section 3, of the Constitution state that the Senate is to "try" an impeachment "case" before senators who are "present" and "sitting" on "oath."
- If the Senate is permitted to use whatever rules it wishes in the impeachment of federal judges, then there is no check on this power and the legislature could very easily usurp judicial power.
- The word "sole" in Article I, Sec. 3, does not preclude judicial review of Senate impeachment procedures because the insertion of the word was simply a cosmetic edit by the Committee of Style.

For the respondents, United States et al.:

- The Constitution explicitly grants the Senate "sole Power" over the trial of impeachments, and therefore this case is not justiciable.
- There is no evidence in either the words of the Constitution or the Constitution's drafting history that would indicate that the framers intended to restrict how the Senate would receive evidence.

CHIEF JUSTICE REHNQUIST DELIVERED THE OPINION OF THE COURT.

Petitioner Walter L. Nixon, Jr., asks this Court to decide whether Senate Rule XI, which allows a committee of Senators to hear evidence against an individual who has been impeached and to report that evidence to the full Senate, violates the Impeachment Trial Clause, Art. I, §3, cl. 6. That Clause provides that the "Senate shall have the sole power to try all Impeachments." But before we reach the merits of such a claim, we must decide whether it is "justiciable," that is whether it is a claim that may be resolved by the courts. We conclude that it is not. . . .

A controversy is nonjusticiable—i.e., involves a political question—where there is a "textually demonstrable constitutional commitment of the issue to a coordinate political department; or a lack of judicially discoverable

and manageable standards for resolving it. . . ." *Baker v. Carr* (1962). But the courts must, in the first instance, interpret the text in question and determine whether and to what extent the issue is textually committed. As the discussion that follows makes clear, the concept of a textual commitment to a coordinate political department is not completely separate from the concept of a lack of judicially discoverable and manageable standards for resolving it; the lack of judicially manageable standards may strengthen the conclusion that there is a textually demonstrable commitment to a coordinate branch.

In this case, we must examine Art. I, §3, cl. 6, to determine the scope of authority conferred upon the Senate by the Framers regarding impeachment. It provides:

"The Senate shall have the sole Power to try all Impeachments. When sitting for that Purpose, they shall be on Oath or Affirmation. When the President of the United States is tried, the Chief Justice shall preside: And no Person shall be convicted without the Concurrence of two thirds of the Members present."

The language and structure of this Clause are revealing. The first sentence is a grant of authority to the Senate, and the word "sole" indicates that this authority is reposed in the Senate and nowhere else. The next two sentences specify requirements to which the Senate proceedings shall conform: the Senate shall be on oath or affirmation, a two-thirds vote is required to convict, and when the President is tried the Chief Justice shall preside.

Petitioner argues that the word "try" in the first sentence imposes by implication an additional requirement on the Senate in that the proceedings must be in the nature of a judicial trial. From there petitioner goes on to argue that this limitation precludes the Senate from delegating to a select committee the task of hearing the testimony of witnesses, as was done pursuant to Senate Rule XI. "'[T]ry' means more than simply 'vote on' or 'review' or 'judge.' In 1787 and today, trying a case means hearing the evidence, not scanning a cold record." Petitioner concludes from this that courts may review whether or not the Senate "tried" him before convicting him.

There are several difficulties with this position which lead us ultimately to reject it. The word "try," both in 1787 and later, has considerably broader meanings than those to which petitioner would limit it. Older dictionaries define try as "to examine" or "to examine as a judge." See 2 S. Johnson, *A Dictionary of the English Language* (1785). In more modern usage the term has various meanings. For example, try can mean "to examine or investigate judicially," "to conduct the trial of," or "to put to the test by experiment, investigation, or trial." *Webster's Third New International Dictionary* (1971). Petitioner submits that "try," as contained in T. Sheridan, *Dictionary of the English Language* (1796), means "to examine as a judge; to bring before a judicial tribunal." Based on the variety of definitions, however, we cannot say that the Framers used the word "try" as an implied limitation on the method by which the Senate might proceed in trying impeachments. "As a rule the Constitution speaks in general terms, leaving Congress to deal with subsidiary matters of detail as the public interests and changing conditions may require. . . . "

The conclusion that the use of the word "try" in the first sentence of the Impeachment Trial Clause lacks sufficient precision to afford any judicially manageable standard of review of the Senate's actions is fortified by the existence of the three very specific requirements that the Constitution does impose on the Senate when trying impeachments: the members must be under oath, a two-thirds vote is required to convict, and the Chief Justice presides when the President is tried. These limitations are quite precise, and their nature suggests that the Framers did not intend to impose additional limitations on the form of the Senate proceedings by the use of the word "try" in the first sentence.

Petitioner devotes only two pages in his brief to negating the significance of the word "sole" in the first sentence of Clause 6. As noted above, that sentence provides that "the Senate shall have the sole Power to try all Impeachments." We think that the word "sole" is of considerable significance. Indeed, the word "sole" appears only one other time in the Constitution—with respect to the House of Representatives' "*sole* Power of Impeachment." Art. I, §2, cl. 5 [our italics]. The common sense meaning of the word "sole" is that the Senate alone shall have authority to determine whether an individual should be acquitted or convicted. The dictionary definition bears this out. "Sole" is defined as "having no companion," "solitary," "being the only one," and "functioning . . . independently and without assistance or interference." *Webster's Third New International Dictionary* (1971). If the courts may review the actions of the Senate in order to determine whether that body "tried" an impeached official, it is difficult to see how the Senate would be "functioning . . . independently and without assistance or interference."

Nixon asserts that the word "sole" has no substantive meaning. To support this contention, he argues that the word is nothing more than a mere "cosmetic edit" added by the Committee of Style after the delegates had approved the substance of the Impeachment Trial Clause. There are two difficulties with this argument. First, accepting as we must the proposition that the Committee of Style had no authority from the Convention to alter the meaning of the Clause, we must presume that the Committee's reorganization or rephrasing accurately captured what the Framers meant in their unadorned language. That is, we must presume that the Committee did its job. This presumption is buttressed by the fact that the Constitutional Convention voted on, and accepted, the Committee of Style's linguistic version. . . . Second, carrying Nixon's argument to its logical conclusion would constrain us to say that the second to last draft would govern in every instance where the Committee of Style added an arguably substantive word. Such a result is at odds with the fact that the Convention passed the Committee's version, and with the well-established rule that the plain language of the enacted text is the best indicator of intent. . . .

The history and contemporary understanding of the impeachment provisions support our reading of the constitutional language. The parties do not offer evidence of a single word in the history of the Constitutional Convention or in contemporary commentary that even alludes to the possibility of judicial review in the context of the impeachment powers. This silence is quite meaningful in light of the several explicit references to the availability of judicial review as a check on the Legislature's power with respect to bills of attainder, *ex post facto* laws, and statutes.

The Framers labored over the question of where the impeachment power should lie. Significantly, in at least two considered scenarios the power was placed with the Federal Judiciary. Indeed, Madison and the Committee of Detail proposed that the Supreme Court should have the power to determine impeachments. Despite these proposals, the Convention ultimately decided that the Senate would have "the sole Power to Try all Impeachments." Art. I, §3, cl. 6. According to Alexander Hamilton, the Senate was the "most fit depositary of this important trust" because its members are representatives of the people. The Supreme Court was not the proper body because the Framers "doubted whether the members of the tribunal would, at all times, be endowed with so eminent a portion of fortitude as would be called for in the execution of so difficult a task" or whether the Court "would possess the degree of credit and authority" to carry out its judgment if it conflicted with the accusation brought by the Legislature—the people's representative. In addition, the Framers believed the Court was too small in number: "The awful discretion, which a court of impeachments must necessarily have, to doom to honor or to infamy the most confidential and the most distinguished characters of the community, forbids the commitment of the trust to a small number of persons."

There are two additional reasons why the Judiciary, and the Supreme Court in particular, were not chosen to have any role in impeachments. First, the Framers recognized that most likely there would be two sets of proceedings for individuals who commit impeachable offenses—the impeachment trial and a separate criminal trial. In fact, the Constitution explicitly provides for two separate proceedings. The Framers deliberately separated the two forums to avoid raising the specter of bias and to ensure independent judgments. . . . Certainly judicial review of the Senate's "trial" would introduce the same risk of bias as would participation in the trial itself.

Second, judicial review would be inconsistent with the Framers' insistence that our system be one of checks and balances. In our constitutional system, impeachment was designed to be the only check on the Judicial Branch by the Legislature. . . . Judicial involvement in impeachment proceedings, even if only for purposes of judicial review, is counterintuitive because it would eviscerate the "important constitutional check" placed on the Judiciary by the Framers.

Nevertheless, Nixon argues that judicial review is necessary in order to place a check on the Legislature. Nixon fears that if the Senate is given unreviewable authority to interpret the Impeachment Trial Clause, there is a grave risk that the Senate will usurp judicial power. The Framers anticipated this objection and created two constitutional safeguards to keep the Senate in check. The first safeguard is that the whole of the impeachment power is divided between the two legislative bodies, with the House given the right to accuse and the Senate given the right to judge. This split of authority "avoids the inconvenience of making the same persons both accusers and judges; and guards against the danger of persecution from the prevalency of a factious spirit in either of those branches." The second safeguard is the two-thirds supermajority vote requirement. Hamilton explained that "as the concurrence of two-thirds of the senate will be requisite to a condemnation, the security to innocence, from this additional circumstance, will be as complete as itself can desire."

In addition to the textual commitment argument, we are persuaded that the lack of finality and the difficulty of fashioning relief counsel against justiciability. See *Baker v. Carr*. We agree with the Court of Appeals that opening the door of judicial review to the procedures used by the Senate in trying impeachments would "expose the political

life of the country to months, or perhaps years, of chaos." This lack of finality would manifest itself most dramatically if the President were impeached. The legitimacy of any successor, and hence his effectiveness, would be impaired severely, not merely while the judicial process was running its course, but during any retrial that a differently constituted Senate might conduct if its first judgment of conviction were invalidated. Equally uncertain is the question of what relief a court may give other than simply setting aside the judgment of conviction. Could it order the reinstatement of a convicted federal judge, or order Congress to create an additional judgeship if the seat had been filled in the interim? . . .

We agree with Nixon that courts possess power to review either legislative or executive action that transgresses identifiable textual limits. . . . But we conclude, after exercising that delicate responsibility, that the word "try" in the Impeachment Clause does not provide an identifiable textual limit on the authority which is committed to the Senate.

For the foregoing reasons, the judgment of the Court of Appeals is

Affirmed.

JUSTICE SOUTER, concurring in the judgment.

Whatever considerations feature most prominently in a particular case, the political question doctrine is "essentially a function of the separation of powers," existing to restrain courts "from inappropriate interference in the business of the other branches of Government," and deriving in large part from prudential concerns about the respect we owe the political departments. Not all interference is inappropriate or disrespectful, however, and application of the doctrine ultimately turns, as Learned Hand put it, on "how importunately the occasion demands an answer."

This occasion does not demand an answer. The Impeachment Trial Clause commits to the Senate "the sole Power to try all Impeachments." . . . Other significant considerations confirm a conclusion that this case presents a nonjusticiable political question: the "unusual need for unquestioning adherence to a political decision already made," as well as "the potentiality of embarrassment from multifarious pronouncements by various departments on one question." As the Court observes, judicial review of an impeachment trial would under the best of circumstances entail significant disruption of government.

One can, nevertheless, envision different and unusual circumstances that might justify a more searching review of impeachment proceedings. If the Senate were to act in a manner seriously threatening the integrity of its results, convicting, say, upon a coin toss, or upon a summary determination that an officer of the United States was simply "'a bad guy,'" judicial interference might well be appropriate. In such circumstances, the Senate's action might be so far beyond the scope of its constitutional authority, and the consequent impact on the Republic so great, as to merit a judicial response despite the prudential concerns that would ordinarily counsel silence. "The political question doctrine, a tool for maintenance of governmental order, will not be so applied as to promote only disorder." *Baker [v. Carr]*.

The Court handed Judge Nixon a stinging defeat, and his circumstances did not improve much after the case *(see box 2-5)*. More generally, the Court ruled that Congress's procedures for impeachments are not subject to judicial review because they meet both prongs of the political questions doctrine: Article I of the Constitution assigns the task of impeachment to Congress, and judicial intrusion into impeachment proceedings could create confusion. Imagine the kinds of problems that would emerge if a U.S. president could challenge his impeachment in the federal courts. Would he still be president as his case made its way through the courts, or would his successor be the president? This is not a scenario for which the Court wanted to take responsibility. Even so, note Justice David Souter's caveat: the Court might not be so hesitant to review impeachment procedures if they "[threatened] the integrity of [the Senate's] results." But Justice John Paul Stevens, in a brief concurring opinion, disagreed: "Respect for a coordinate Branch of the Government forecloses any assumption that improbable hypotheticals like those mentioned by Justice Souter . . . will ever occur."

Despite the ruling in *Nixon*, the political questions doctrine remains controversial. Some scholars applaud decisions such as *Nixon* and suggest that the federal courts should continue to avoid cases that raise political questions. Indeed, in the view of these scholars, the Court does not make enough use of the doctrine. By way of example, they point not only to *Baker* but also to *Bush v. Gore* (2000) *(see chapter 4),* which they suggest the Court should have dismissed as raising a political question. To these observers, *Bush* is just the latest in a line of cases beginning with *Baker* that signal a

"weakening of the traditional 'political questions doctrine' and the expanded application of the equal protection clause to voting rights and democratic process." They say that the public should regard these cases as a dangerous trend on the Court's part—one reflecting "a broader conservative inclination to impose order on democratic politics."[71]

Other analysts vehemently disagree. Although they do not necessarily support the Court's decision in *Bush v. Gore,* they question any effort to revive a strong political questions doctrine. They believe that the Court has a responsibility to address constitutional questions, and the failure to do so is anathema to a *Marbury v. Madison*–type review.

Where the current Court will come down remains to be seen, although *Zivotofksy v. Clinton* (2012) may provide some clues. At issue in this case was a dispute over whether the passport of a U.S. citizen born in Jerusalem could list "Israel" as the country of birth rather than "Jerusalem." Under a State Department policy of long standing the answer was no, only Jerusalem could be listed, but under a federal law the answer was yes. The district court dismissed the case, holding that it presented a nonjusticiable political question regarding Jerusalem's political status. The D.C. Circuit Court affirmed, reasoning that Article II, which says that the president "shall receive ambassadors and other public ministers," gives the executive the exclusive power to recognize foreign sovereigns, and that the exercise of that power cannot be reviewed by the courts.

The Supreme Court disagreed. Writing for eight of the nine justices (Breyer dissented), Chief Justice Roberts had this to say:

In general, the Judiciary has a responsibility to decide cases properly before it, even those it "would gladly avoid." Our precedents have identified a narrow exception to that rule, known as the "political question" doctrine." [In a] controversy [that] involves a political question . . . we have held that a court lacks the authority to decide the dispute before it. . . .

The federal courts are not being asked to supplant a foreign policy decision of the political branches with the courts' own unmoored determination of what United States policy toward Jerusalem should be. Instead, Zivotofsky requests

---

71. See Howard Gillman, *The Votes That Counted* (Chicago: University of Chicago Press, 2001), 202.

> **BOX 2-5   AFTERMATH ... WALTER NIXON**

IN MARCH 1986 federal district court judge Walter L. Nixon Jr. was convicted of two counts of perjury for lying to a grand jury. He was sentenced to five years in prison. When his last appeal proved unsuccessful, Nixon entered a federal minimum security prison at Eglin Air Force Base in Florida. He served sixteen months before being released to a New Orleans halfway house in July 1989. Four months later, just eighteen days after the Senate removed him from office, Nixon was released on five years' probation.

Nixon had not heard any cases since his indictment in 1985 but, proclaiming his innocence, refused to resign from office. From 1985 until his removal by the Senate in 1989, Nixon was paid his $89,500 annual salary, even though he spent part of that time in a federal prison. The removal formally ended his tenure as a federal judge and terminated his salary. At about the same time, the Mississippi Supreme Court disbarred Nixon, so he could no longer practice law.

In 1990 Mississippi wildlife officials discovered Nixon and a former game warden in a field that was baited to attract wild turkeys. In Nixon's possession was a 12-gauge automatic shotgun. Nixon was charged with conspiracy to hunt wild birds with the aid of bait, a misdemeanor. More serious was his possession of a firearm, which violated the terms of his parole. The U.S. Parole Commission ordered Nixon to return to prison for four months; the punishment was relatively light because the shotgun had never been taken out of its zipped case.

Nixon's efforts to return to the practice of law were ultimately successful. In May 1993 the Mississippi Supreme Court considered Nixon's petition to be reinstated to the bar. The state bar association opposed the request, arguing that Nixon lacked the required moral character to practice law. A parade of public officials, including three former governors and three former state supreme court justices, urged the court to be lenient. The justices agreed to reactivate Nixon's license to practice law once he passed the state bar examination. Chief Justice Armis Hawkins said, "This petitioner has been whipped enough." Nixon passed and was readmitted to the practice of law in September 1993.

SOURCES: *Los Angeles Times*, May 21, 1993; Memphis Commercial Appeal, October 3, 1990; *New York Times*, April 28, 1990, September 26, 1993; *Washington Post*, February 7, 1986; *Washington Times*, November 22, 1989; various United Press International reports.

that the courts enforce a specific statutory right. To resolve his claim, the Judiciary must decide if Zivotofsky's interpretation of the statute is correct, and whether the statute is constitutional. This is a familiar judicial exercise.

Finding that the case did not present a political question, the Court sent the case back to the court of appeals to resolve the dispute.[72]

Do you agree with the Court's rationale? Does *Zivotofsky* sit comfortably with *Baker* and *Nixon?*

Standing to Sue

Another constraint on federal judicial power is the requirement that the party bringing a lawsuit have standing to sue: if the party bringing the litigation is not the appropriate party, the courts will not resolve the dispute. Put in somewhat different terms, "not every person with the money to bring a lawsuit is entitled to litigate the legality or constitutionality of government action in the federal courts."[73] According to the Court's interpretation of Article III, standing requires (1) that the party must have suffered a concrete injury or be in imminent danger of suffering such a loss, (2) that the injury must be "fairly traceable" to the challenged action of the defendant (usually the government in constitutional cases), and (3) that the party must show that a favorable court decision is likely to provide redress.[74] In general these three elements are designed, as Justice Brennan noted in *Baker,* "to assure ... concrete adverseness which sharpens the presentation of issues upon which the Court so largely depends for illumination of difficult constitutional questions."

72. After the court of appeals ruled against Zivotofsky, the case came back to the Supreme Court. It affirmed the lower court in *Zivotofsky v. Kerry* (2015) *(excerpted in chapter 5).*

73. C. Herman Pritchett, *The American Constitution* (New York: McGraw-Hill, 1959), 145.

74. See **Lujan v. Defenders of Wildlife** (1992), which lays out these three elements.

In many disputes, the litigants have little difficulty meeting the standing requirements mandated by Article III. A citizen who has been denied the right to vote on the basis of race, a criminal defendant sentenced to death, and a church member jailed for religious proselytizing would have sufficient standing to challenge the federal or state laws that may have deprived them of their rights. But what about parties who wish to challenge a government action on the ground that they are taxpayers? Such claims raise an important question: Does the mere fact that one pays taxes provide a sufficient basis for standing?

In general, the answer is no. In addition to the three constitutionally derived requirements, the Court has articulated several prudential considerations to govern standing. These do not strictly follow from Article III but rather from the Court's own view of the prudent administration of justice. Among the most prominent are those that limit—but do *not* absolutely prohibit, as we shall see—generalized grievance suits. In these suits, the parties do not have an injury that affects them in a "personal and individual way." Rather they have a "generally available grievance about government," with the only harm being to their—and every other citizen's—interest in applying appropriately the laws and constitution.[75] As such, should they win their case, they benefit no more directly or tangibly than all other citizens.

These general grievance suits come in several forms. Let's consider two: (1) taxpayer suits, which are brought by parties whose only injury is that they do not want the government to spend tax money in a particular way, and what we call (2) government-induced suits, which arise when legislators who voted against a law challenge its constitutionality or when the executive branch will not defend a law because it thinks the law violates the Constitution.

Taxpayer Suits. The Court first addressed taxpayer suits in *Frothingham v. Mellon* (1923). At issue was the Sheppard-Towner Maternity Act of 1921, in which Congress provided federal aid to the states to fund programs designed to reduce infant mortality rates. Although many progressive groups had lobbied for the law, other organizations viewed it as an unconstitutional intrusion into the family and into the rights of states, as they believed the Tenth Amendment of the Constitution

---

75. *Hollingsworth v. Perry* (2013).

guaranteed. They decided to challenge it and enlisted one among their ranks, Harriet Frothingham, to serve as a plaintiff. She was not receiving Sheppard-Towner Maternity Act aid; she was a taxpayer who did not want to see her tax dollars spent on the program. Her attorneys argued that she had sufficient grounds to bring suit.

The Court did not agree, holding that Frothingham lacked standing to bring the litigation. Justice George Sutherland wrote for the majority:

If one taxpayer may champion and litigate such a cause, then every other taxpayer may do the same, not only in respect of the statute here under review but also in respect of every other appropriation act and statute whose administration requires the outlay of public money, and whose validity may be questioned. The bare suggestion of such a result, with its attendant inconveniences, goes far to sustain the conclusion which we have reached, that a suit of this character cannot be maintained.

He also outlined an approach to standing:

The party . . . must be able to show not only that the statute is invalid but that he has sustained or is immediately in danger of sustaining some direct injury as the result of its enforcement, and not merely that he suffers in some indefinite way in common with people generally.

For the next forty years, *Frothingham* served as a major bar to taxpayer suits. Unless litigants could demonstrate that a government program injured them or threatened to do so—beyond the mere expenditure of tax dollars—they could not bring suit. In *Flast v. Cohen,* however, the Court relaxed that rule. Why? With what did the Court replace it?

Flast v. Cohen

392 U.S. 83 (1968)
http://laws.findlaw.com/us/392/83.html
Oral arguments are available at https://www.oyez.org.
Vote: 8 (Black, Brennan, Douglas, Fortas, Marshall, Stewart, Warren, White)
    1 (Harlan)

OPINION OF THE COURT: *Warren*
CONCURRING OPINIONS: *Douglas, Fortas, Stewart*
DISSENTING OPINION: *Harlan*

FACTS:

Seven taxpayers sought to challenge federal expenditures made under the Elementary and Secondary

Education Act of 1965. Under this law, states could apply to the federal government for grants to assist in the education of children from low-income families. They could, for example, obtain funds for the acquisition of textbooks, school library materials, and so forth. The taxpayers alleged that some of the funds disbursed under this act were used to finance "instruction in reading, arithmetic, and other subjects and for guidance in religious and sectarian schools." Such expenditures, they argued, violated the First Amendment's prohibition on religious establishment.

A three-judge district court dismissed their complaint. It reasoned that because the plaintiffs had suffered no real injury and because their only claim of standing rested "solely on their status as federal taxpayers," they failed to meet the criteria established in *Frothingham*.

ARGUMENTS:

For the appellants, Florence Flast et al.:
- The Court's precedent in *Frothingham* does not establish an absolute bar against taxpayers bringing suit concerning a federal expenditure.
- The factors that led to judicial restraint in *Frothingham* have no relevance to a suit brought under the First Amendment, as this one is.

For the appellees, Wilbur Cohen, secretary of Health, Education, and Welfare et al.:
- The case or controversy limitation of Article III requires that the Court uphold the principle that a federal taxpayer *qua* taxpayer, such as the appellant in this case, lacks standing to challenge specific expenditures of federal revenues.

MR. CHIEF JUSTICE WARREN DELIVERED THE OPINION OF THE COURT.

The "gist of the question of standing" is whether the party seeking relief has "alleged such a personal stake in the outcome of the controversy as to assure that concrete adverseness which sharpens the presentation of issues upon which the court so largely depends for illumination of difficult constitutional questions." *Baker v. Carr* (1962). In other words, when standing is placed in issue in a case, the question is whether the person whose standing is challenged is a proper party to request an adjudication of a particular issue and not whether the issue itself is justiciable. . . .

A taxpayer may or may not have the requisite personal stake in the outcome, depending upon the circumstances of the particular case. Therefore, we find no absolute bar in Article III to suits by federal taxpayers challenging allegedly unconstitutional federal taxing and spending programs. There remains, however, the problem of determining the circumstances under which a federal taxpayer will be deemed to have the personal stake and interest that impart the necessary concrete adverseness to such litigation so that standing can be conferred on the taxpayer *qua* taxpayer consistent with the constitutional limitations of Article III.

. . . [It] is not relevant that the substantive issues in the litigation might be nonjusticiable. However . . . it is both appropriate and necessary to look to the substantive issues for another purpose, namely, to determine whether there is a logical nexus between the status asserted and the claim sought to be adjudicated. . . .

The nexus demanded of federal taxpayers has two aspects to it. First, the taxpayer must establish a logical link between that status and the type of legislative enactment attacked. Thus, a taxpayer will be a proper party to allege the unconstitutionality only of exercises of congressional power under the taxing and spending clause of Art. I, §8, of the Constitution. It will not be sufficient to allege an incidental expenditure of tax funds in the administration of an essentially regulatory statute. . . . Secondly, the taxpayer must establish a nexus between that status and the precise nature of the constitutional infringement alleged. Under this requirement, the taxpayer must show that the challenged enactment exceeds specific constitutional limitations imposed upon the exercise of the congressional taxing and spending power and not simply that the enactment is generally beyond the powers delegated to Congress by Art. I, §8. When both nexuses are established, the litigant will have shown a taxpayer's stake in the outcome of the controversy and will be a proper and appropriate party to invoke a federal court's jurisdiction.

The taxpayer-appellants in this case have satisfied both nexuses to support their claim of standing under the test we announce today. Their constitutional challenge is made to an exercise by Congress of its power under Art. I, §8, to spend for the general welfare, and the challenged program involves a substantial expenditure of federal tax funds. In addition, appellants have alleged that the challenged expenditures violate the Establishment and Free Exercise Clauses of the First Amendment. Our history vividly illustrates that one of the specific evils feared by those who drafted the Establishment Clause and fought for its adoption was that the taxing and spending power would be used to favor one religion over another or to support religion in general. James Madison, who is generally recognized as the leading architect of the religion clauses of the First Amendment, observed in his famous Memorial and Remonstrance Against Religious Assessments that "the same authority which can force a citizen to contribute three pence only of his property for the support of any one establishment, may force him to conform to any other establishment in all cases what-so-ever." The concern of Madison and his supporters was quite clearly that religious liberty ultimately would be the victim if government could employ its taxing and spending powers to aid one religion over another or to aid religion in general. The Establishment Clause was designed as a specific bulwark against such potential abuses of governmental power, and that clause of the First Amendment operates as a specific constitutional limitation upon the exercise by Congress of the taxing and spending power conferred by Art. I, §8.

The allegations of the taxpayer in *Frothingham v. Mellon* were quite different from those made in this case, and the result in *Frothingham* is consistent with the test of taxpayer standing announced today. The taxpayer in *Frothingham* attacked a federal spending program and she, therefore, established the first nexus required. However, she lacked standing because her constitutional attack was not based on an allegation that Congress, in enacting the Maternity Act of 1921, had breached a specific limitation upon its taxing and spending power. . . . In essence, Mrs. Frothingham was attempting to assert the States' interest in their legislative prerogatives and not a federal taxpayer's interest in being free of taxing and spending in contravention of specific constitutional limitations imposed upon Congress' taxing and spending power.

We have noted that the Establishment Clause of the First Amendment does specifically limit the taxing and spending power conferred by Art. I, §8. Whether the Constitution contains other specific limitations can be determined only in the context of future cases. However, whenever such specific limitations are found, we believe a taxpayer will have a clear stake as a taxpayer in assuring that they are not breached by Congress. Consequently, we hold that a taxpayer will have standing consistent with Article III to invoke federal judicial power when he alleges that congressional action under the taxing and spending clause is in derogation of those constitutional provisions which operate to restrict the exercise of the taxing and spending power. The taxpayer's allegation in such cases would be that his tax money is being extracted and spent in violation of specific constitutional protections against such abuses of legislative power. Such an injury is appropriate for judicial redress, and the taxpayer has established the necessary nexus between his status and the nature of the allegedly unconstitutional action to support his claim of standing to secure judicial review. Under such circumstances, we feel confident that the questions will be framed with the necessary specificity, that the issues will be contested with the necessary adverseness and that the litigation will be pursued with the necessary vigor to assure that the constitutional challenge will be made in a form traditionally thought to be capable of judicial resolution. We lack that confidence in cases such as *Frothingham* where a taxpayer seeks to employ a federal court as a forum in which to air his generalized grievances about the conduct of government or the allocation of power in the Federal System.

While we express no view at all on the merits of appellants' claims in this case, their complaint contains sufficient allegations under the criteria we have outlined to give them standing to invoke a federal court's jurisdiction for an adjudication on the merits.

Reversed.

MR. JUSTICE HARLAN, dissenting.

The nub of my view is that the end result of *Frothingham v. Mellon* was correct, even though, like others, I do not subscribe to all of its reasoning and premises. Although I therefore agree with certain of the conclusions reached today by the Court, I cannot accept the standing doctrine that it substitutes for *Frothingham*, for it seems to me that this new doctrine rests on premises that do not withstand analysis. Accordingly, I respectfully dissent. . . .

The Court's analysis consists principally of the observation that the requirements of standing are met if a taxpayer has the "requisite personal stake in the outcome" of his suit. This does not, of course, resolve the standing problem; it merely restates it. The Court implements this standard with the declaration that taxpayers will be "deemed" to have the necessary personal interest if their suits satisfy two criteria: first, the challenged expenditure must form part of a federal spending program, and not merely be "incidental" to a regulatory program; and second, the constitutional provision under which the plaintiff claims must be a "specific limitation" upon Congress' spending powers. The difficulties with these criteria are many and severe, but it is enough for the moment to emphasize that they are not in any sense a measurement of any plaintiff's interest in the outcome of any suit. . . .

It is surely clear that a plaintiff's interest in the outcome of a suit in which he challenges the constitutionality of a federal expenditure is not made greater or smaller by the unconnected fact that the expenditure is, or is not, "incidental" to an "essentially regulatory" program. An example will illustrate the point. Assume that two independent federal programs are authorized by Congress, that the first is designed to encourage a specified religious group by the provision to it of direct grants-in-aid, and that the second is designed to discourage all other religious groups by the imposition of various forms of discriminatory regulation. Equal amounts are appropriated by Congress for the two programs. If a taxpayer challenges their constitutionality in separate suits, are we to suppose, as evidently does the Court, that his "personal stake" in the suit involving the second is necessarily smaller than it is in the suit involving the first, and that he should therefore have standing in one but not the other?

The Court's second criterion is similarly unrelated to its standard for the determination of standing. The intensity of a plaintiff's interest in a suit is not measured, even obliquely, by the fact that the constitutional provision under which he claims is, or is not, a "specific limitation" upon Congress' spending powers. Thus, among the claims in *Frothingham* was the assertion that the Maternity Act, deprived the petitioner of property without due process of law. The Court has evidently concluded that this claim did not confer standing because the Due Process Clause of the Fifth Amendment is not a specific limitation upon the spending powers. Disregarding for the moment the formidable obscurity of the Court's categories, how can it be said that Mrs. Frothingham's interests in her suit were, as a consequence of her choice of a constitutional claim, necessarily less intense than those, for example, of the present appellants? I am quite unable to understand how, if a taxpayer believes that a given public expenditure is unconstitutional, and if he seeks to vindicate that belief in a federal court, his interest in the suit can be said necessarily to vary according to the constitutional provision under which he states his claim. . . .

It seems to me clear that public actions, whatever the constitutional provisions on which they are premised, may involve important hazards for the continued effectiveness of the federal judiciary. Although I believe such actions to be within the jurisdiction conferred upon the federal courts by Article III of the Constitution, there surely can be little doubt that they strain the judicial function and press to the limit judicial authority. There is every reason to fear that unrestricted public actions might well alter the allocation of authority among the three branches of the Federal Government. It is not, I submit, enough to say that the present members of the Court would not seize these opportunities for abuse, for such actions would, even without conscious abuse, go far toward the final transformation of this Court into the Council of Revision which, despite Madison's support, was rejected by the Constitutional Convention. . . . We must as judges recall that, as Mr. Justice Holmes wisely observed, the other branches of the Government "are ultimate guardians of the liberties and welfare of the people in quite as great a degree as the courts." The powers of the federal judiciary will be adequate for the great burdens placed upon them only if they are employed prudently, with recognition of the strengths as well as the hazards that go with our kind of representative government.

Flast did not overrule *Frothingham;* in fact, the Court was careful to indicate that had the 1968 ruling been applied to *Frothingham,* the plaintiff still would have been unable to attain standing. But *Flast* substantially revised the 1923 precedent. If taxpayers could identify a logical link between their status and the legislation, and one between their status and a specific constitutional infringement, then they might have standing.

Flast symbolized what was at that time a general trend toward lowering barriers to access to federal courts. Twenty-two years earlier, Congress had passed the Administrative Procedure Act of 1946, which, among other things, provided that any person "suffering legal wrong because of agency action, or adversely affected or aggrieved within the meaning of a relevant statute, is entitled to judicial review thereof." Congress had been reacting to pressure from the American Bar Association and business organizations concerned about federal regulations, but other groups have been able to use this statute. *Association of Data Processing Service Organizations v. Camp* (1970) gave this provision a broad interpretation by specifically rejecting the old standing test of a "recognized legal interest."

But the days of easing standing requirements in taxpayer suits have apparently come to an end. Beginning in the mid-1970s and extending through today, the justices have restored strict standing requirements and limited access to federal courts. They have read *Flast* rather narrowly, restricting its reach to precisely the kind of suit at issue there—a challenge to the use of federal funds allegedly in violation of the First Amendment's ban of the government's establishment of religion. The Roberts Court's decision in *Hein v. Freedom from Religion Foundation* (2007) supplies an example. During the George W. Bush administration, the Freedom from Religion Foundation brought this establishment clause suit to challenge activities associated with the White House Office of Faith-Based and Community Initiatives. It claimed it had standing because its individual members were federal taxpayers opposed to executive branch use of congressional appropriations for activities that allegedly promoted religious community groups over secular organizations. The Supreme Court disagreed. Because these were executive branch programs, they did not meet the *Flast* standard. More broadly, Justice Alito noted in his judgment for the Court, "the payment of taxes is generally not enough to establish standing to challenge an action taken by the Federal Government." *Flast,* Alito wrote, was "a narrow exception." Such a reading led some scholars to assert that Court doctrine governing standing now resembles *Frothingham* rather than *Flast*. At the least, Justice Scalia suggested in a concurring opinion (joined by Thomas) in *Hein,* the Court's decision was inconsistent with *Flast*:

Today's opinion is, in one significant respect, entirely consistent with our previous cases addressing taxpayer standing to raise Establishment Clause challenges to government expenditures. Unfortunately, the consistency lies in the creation of utterly meaningless distinctions which separate the case at hand from the precedents that have come out differently, but which cannot possibly be (in any sane world) the reason it comes out differently. If this Court is to decide cases by rule of law rather than show of hands, we must surrender to logic and choose sides: Either *Flast v. Cohen* (1968) should be applied to (at a minimum) all challenges to the governmental expenditure of general tax revenues in a manner alleged to violate a constitutional provision specifically limiting the taxing and spending power, or *Flast* should be repudiated. For me, the choice is easy. *Flast* is wholly irreconcilable with the Article III restrictions on federal-court jurisdiction that this Court has repeatedly confirmed are embodied in the doctrine of standing.

Government-Based Suits. Whether this and other Roberts Court decisions leave *Flast* on life support, we

leave for you to determine.[76] What does seem to be true is that standing, like the other "constraints" on judicial power—jurisdiction and justiciability—is open to interpretation. This applies to taxpayer suits such as *Hein,* but also holds for government-inducted suits that raise standing questions.

To see this, let's consider two situations under which these suits can arise. In the first, legislators who voted against a law bring suit to challenge the law's constitutionality. This occurred in **Raines v. Byrd** (1997), involving the constitutionality of the Line Item Veto Act of 1996, which gave the president the ability to cancel certain tax and spending benefits after they were signed into law. Before the justices could decide whether the law was constitutional, they had to decide whether the six members of Congress—all opponents of the law—who had brought the suit had standing to challenge it.

Writing for the majority, Chief Justice Rehnquist concluded that they did not: The individual members of Congress "have alleged no injury to themselves as individuals [and] the institutional injury they allege is wholly abstract and widely dispersed. We . . . note that our conclusion neither deprives Members of Congress of an adequate remedy (since they may repeal the Act or exempt appropriations bills from its reach), nor forecloses the Act from constitutional challenge (by someone who suffers judicially cognizable injury as a result of the Act)."

In a dissenting opinion, Justice Stevens took issue with Rehnquist's conclusion:

The Line Item Veto Act purports to establish a procedure for the creation of laws that are truncated versions of bills that have been passed by the Congress and presented to the President for signature. If the procedure were valid, it would deny every Senator and every Representative any opportunity

---

76. See, e.g., **Arizona Christian School Tuition Organization v. Winn** (2011). The Court held that taxpayers lacked standing to challenge the use of tax credits to fund religious schools because the state's decision not to collect taxes created no nexus between the dissenting taxpayer and the religious establishment. Differentiating this case from *Flast,* the Court held that the state does not "extract and spend" the funds, rather the money goes directly from an individual to the schools. The dissent, written by Justice Kagan, expressed concern that the "novel distinction in standing law between appropriation and tax expenditure" threatened to eliminate all opportunities for taxpayers to challenge governmental financial support of religious institutions. Scalia concurred, writing that the taxpayers lacked standing based on Article III, rather than *Flast*.

to vote for or against the truncated measure that survives the exercise of the President's cancellation authority. Because the opportunity to cast such votes is a right guaranteed by the text of the Constitution, I think it clear that the persons who are deprived of that right by the Act have standing to challenge its constitutionality.

A year later, in *Clinton v. City of New York* (1998), the justices found that parties who had been affected when President Clinton exercised the line-item veto did have standing to challenge the act and decided the case on its merits *(see chapter 4).* But the very fact that these justices, in *Raines,* could reach such different conclusions underscores the notion that standing—like justiciability and jurisdiction—may be more fluid than it appears and than the Court sometimes lets on.

The same holds for a second type of government-induced suit, which occurs when the executive branch declines to defend a law because it believes the law is unconstitutional. The question these cases raise is whether anyone else can represent the government. Note the differing opinions that the majority and dissenters offer in *Hollingsworth v. Perry* (2013).

Republican State Senator Dennis Hollingsworth, who defended the constitutionality of California Proposition 8 under which the state recognized as legally valid only marriages between one woman and one man.

Hollingsworth v. Perry

570 U.S. ___ (2013)
http://caselaw.findlaw.com/us-supreme-court/12-144.html
Oral arguments are available at https://www.oyez.org.
Vote: 5 (Breyer, Ginsburg, Kagan, Roberts, Scalia)
    4 (Alito, Kennedy, Sotomayor, Thomas)
OPINION OF THE COURT: *Roberts*
DISSENTING OPINION: *Kennedy*

Sandy Stier (left) and Kris Perry, who challenged the constitutionality of California's ban on same-sex marriage.

FACTS:

In 2008 the California Supreme Court held that limiting marriage to opposite-sex couples violated the equal protection clause of the state's Constitution. In response, California voters passed a ballot initiative, known as Proposition 8 (or just Prop 8), that amended the state's Constitution to provide that "[o]nly marriage between a man and a woman is valid or recognized in California."

Kris Perry and Sandy Stier were a same-sex couple that wanted to marry in California. They and another same-sex couple filed suit in federal court, challenging Prop 8 under the due process and equal protection clauses of the U.S. Constitution's Fourteenth Amendment. Their complaint named as defendants California's governor, attorney general, and other officials responsible for enforcing California's marriage laws. Because the officials refused to defend the law, the district court allowed the initiative's official "proponents" (Hollingsworth and others) to intervene to defend it. After a bench trial, the district judge declared Prop 8 unconstitutional and permanently enjoined the California officials from enforcing the law.

While the California officials decided not to appeal the district court's decision, Prop 8's official proponents did. Before the U.S. Court of Appeals decided the case, the judges certified a question to the California Supreme Court: whether the official proponents of a ballot initiative have authority to assert the state's interest in defending the constitutionality of the initiative when public officials refuse to do so. The California Supreme Court responded yes:

In a postelection challenge to a voter-approved initiative measure, the official proponents of the initiative are authorized under California law to appear and assert the state's interest in the initiative's validity and to appeal a judgment invalidating the measure when the public officials who ordinarily defend the measure or appeal such a judgment decline to do so.

Relying on the state supreme court's response, the court of appeals concluded that the official proponents had standing under federal law to defend the constitutionality of Prop 8. States have the "prerogative, as independent sovereigns, to decide for themselves who may assert their interests," the court concluded.

On the merits of the suit, the court affirmed the district court. It held that Prop 8 was unconstitutional. The proponents, but again not state officials, asked the U.S. Supreme Court to reverse the circuit court's decision.

ARGUMENTS (ON STANDING):

For the petitioners, Dennis Hollingsworth et al.

1. A State unquestionably has standing to defend the constitutionality of its laws, and this Court's decisions establish that state law determines who is authorized to assert this interest on behalf of the State. The California Supreme Court has held that the proponents are authorized to assert this interest when public officials decline to defend an initiative.

2. In *Karcher v. May* (1987), this Court held that the presiding officers of the New Jersey Legislature were "proper" defendants in a case challenging the constitutionality of a state statute when the Attorney General declined to do so.

For the respondents, Kristin M. Perry et al.

1. Proponents have never contended that they would personally suffer any injury if gay men and lesbians were permitted to marry in California. Their mere desire to defend Proposition 8 is insufficient to satisfy standing requirements.

2. Proponents, who are not public officials, do not have a close relationship with the State like the state legislators did in *Karcher v. May* (1987).

CHIEF JUSTICE ROBERTS DELIVERED THE OPINION OF THE COURT.

The public is currently engaged in an active political debate over whether same-sex couples should be allowed to marry. That question has also given rise to litigation. In this case, petitioners, who oppose same-sex marriage, ask us to decide whether the Equal Protection Clause "prohibits the State of California from defining marriage as the union of a man and a woman." Respondents, same-sex couples who wish to marry, view the issue in somewhat different terms: For them, it is whether California—having previously recognized the right of same-sex couples to marry—may reverse that decision through a referendum.

Federal courts have authority under the Constitution to answer such questions only if necessary to do so in the course of deciding an actual "case" or "controversy." As used in the Constitution, those words do not include every sort of dispute, but only those "historically viewed as capable of resolution through the judicial process." *Flast v. Cohen* (1968). This is an essential limit on our power: It ensures that we act as judges, and do not engage in policymaking properly left to elected representatives.

For there to be such a case or controversy, it is not enough that the party invoking the power of the court have a keen interest in the issue. That party must also have "standing," which requires, among other things, that it have suffered a concrete and particularized injury. Because we find that petitioners do not have standing, we have no authority to decide this case on the merits, and neither did the Ninth Circuit. . . .

Article III of the Constitution confines the judicial power of federal courts to deciding actual "Cases" or "Controversies." One essential aspect of this requirement is that any person invoking the power of a federal court must demonstrate standing to do so. This requires the litigant to prove that he has suffered a concrete and particularized injury that is fairly traceable to the challenged conduct, and is likely to be redressed by a favorable judicial decision. *Lujan v. Defenders of Wildlife* (1992). In other words, for a federal court to have authority under the Constitution to settle a dispute, the party before it must seek a remedy for a personal and tangible harm. "The presence of a disagreement, however sharp and acrimonious it may be, is insufficient by itself to meet Art. III's requirements." . . .

Respondents initiated this case in the District Court against the California officials responsible for enforcing Proposition 8. The parties do not contest that respondents had Article III standing to do so. Each couple expressed a desire to marry and obtain "official sanction" from the State, which was unavailable to them given the declaration in Proposition 8 that "marriage" in California is solely between a man and a woman.

After the District Court declared Proposition 8 unconstitutional and enjoined the state officials named as defendants from enforcing it, however, the inquiry under Article III changed. Respondents no longer had any injury to redress—they had won—and the state officials chose not to appeal.

The only individuals who sought to appeal that order were petitioners, who had intervened in the District Court. But the District Court had not ordered them to do or refrain from doing anything. To have standing, a litigant must seek relief for an injury that affects him in a "personal and individual way." He must possess a "direct stake in the outcome" of the case. Here, however, petitioners had no "direct stake" in the outcome of their appeal. Their only interest in having the District Court order reversed was to vindicate the constitutional validity of a generally applicable California law.

We have repeatedly held that such a "generalized grievance," no matter how sincere, is insufficient to confer standing. A litigant "raising only a generally available grievance about government—claiming only harm to his and every citizen's interest in proper application of the Constitution and laws, and seeking relief that no more directly and tangibly benefits him than it does the public at large—does not state an Article III case or controversy." *Defenders of Wildlife.*

Petitioners argue that the California Constitution and its election laws give them a "'unique,' 'special,' and 'distinct' role in the initiative process—one 'involving both authority and responsibilities that differ from other supporters of the measure.'" True enough—but only when it comes to the process of enacting the law. Upon submitting the proposed initiative to the attorney general, petitioners became the official "proponents" of Proposition 8. As such, they were responsible for collecting the signatures required to qualify the measure for the ballot. After those signatures were collected, the proponents alone had the right to file the measure with election officials to put it on the ballot. Petitioners also possessed control over the arguments in favor of the initiative that would appear in California's ballot pamphlets.

But once Proposition 8 was approved by the voters, the measure became "a duly enacted constitutional amendment or statute." Petitioners have no role—special or otherwise—in the enforcement of Proposition 8. They therefore have no "personal stake" in defending its enforcement that is distinguishable from the general interest of every citizen of California.

Article III standing "is not to be placed in the hands of 'concerned bystanders,' who will use it simply as a 'vehicle for the vindication of value interests.'" No matter how deeply committed petitioners may be to upholding Proposition 8 or how "zealous [their] advocacy," that is not a "particularized" interest sufficient to create a case or controversy under Article III. *Defenders of Wildlife.* . . .

Petitioners contend that . . . they are "authorized under California law to appear and assert the state's interest" in the validity of Proposition 8. . . . As petitioners put it, they "need no more show a personal injury, separate from the State's indisputable interest in the validity of its law, than would California's Attorney General or did the legislative leaders held to have standing in *Karcher v. May* (1987).

In *Karcher*, we held that two New Jersey state legislators—Speaker of the General Assembly Alan Karcher and President of the Senate Carmen Orechio—could intervene in a suit against the State to defend the constitutionality of a New Jersey law, after the New Jersey attorney general had declined to do so. "Since the New Jersey Legislature had authority under state law to represent the State's interests in both the District Court and the Court of Appeals," we held that the Speaker and the President, in their official capacities, could vindicate that interest in federal court on the legislature's behalf.

Far from supporting petitioners' standing, however, *Karcher* is compelling precedent against it. The legislators in that case intervened in their official capacities as Speaker and President of the legislature. No one doubts that a State has a cognizable interest "in the continued enforceability" of its laws that is harmed by a judicial decision declaring a state law unconstitutional. To vindicate that interest or any other, a State must be able to designate agents to represent it in federal court. That agent is typically the State's attorney general. But state law may provide for other officials to speak for the State in federal court, as New Jersey law did for the State's presiding legislative officers in *Karcher*.

What is significant about *Karcher* is what happened after the Court of Appeals decision in that case. Karcher and Orechio lost their positions as Speaker and President, but nevertheless sought to appeal to this Court. We held that they could not do so. We explained that while they were able to participate in the lawsuit in their official capacities as presiding officers of the incumbent legislature, "since they no longer hold those offices, they lack authority to pursue this appeal."

The point of *Karcher* is not that a State could authorize private parties to represent its interests; Karcher and Orechio were permitted to proceed only because they were state officers, acting in an official capacity. As soon as they lost that capacity, they lost standing. Petitioners here hold no office and have always participated in this litigation solely as private parties. . . .

[P]etitioners are plainly not agents of the State—"formal" or otherwise. . . .

[The] most basic features of an agency relationship are missing here. Agency requires more than mere authorization to assert a particular interest. "An essential element of agency is the principal's right to control the agent's actions." Yet petitioners answer to no one; they decide for themselves, with no review, what arguments to make and how to make them. Unlike California's attorney general, they are not elected at regular intervals—or elected at all. No provision provides for their removal. . . .

"If the relationship between two persons is one of agency . . . , the agent owes a fiduciary obligation to the principal." But petitioners owe nothing of the sort to the people of California. Unlike California's elected officials, they have taken no oath of office. . . . They are free to pursue a purely ideological commitment to the law's constitutionality without the need to take cognizance of resource constraints, changes in public opinion, or potential ramifications for other state priorities. . . .

Neither the California Supreme Court nor the Ninth Circuit ever described the proponents as agents of the State, and they plainly do not qualify as such.

The dissent eloquently recounts the California Supreme Court's reasons for deciding that state law authorizes petitioners to defend Proposition 8. We do not "disrespect[ ]" or "disparage[ ]" those reasons. Nor do we question California's sovereign right to maintain an initiative process, or the right of initiative proponents to defend their initiatives in California courts, where Article III does not apply. But as the dissent acknowledges, standing in federal court is a question of federal law, not state law. And no matter its reasons, the fact that a State thinks a private party should have standing to seek relief for a generalized grievance cannot override our settled law to the contrary. . . .

We have never before upheld the standing of a private party to defend the constitutionality of a state statute when state officials have chosen not to. We decline to do so for the first time here.

Because petitioners have not satisfied their burden to demonstrate standing to appeal the judgment of the District Court, the Ninth Circuit was without jurisdiction to consider the appeal. The judgment of the Ninth Circuit is vacated, and the case is remanded with instructions to dismiss the appeal for lack of jurisdiction.

It is so ordered.

JUSTICE KENNEDY, with whom JUSTICE THOMAS, JUSTICE ALITO, and JUSTICE SOTOMAYOR join, dissenting.

The reasons the Supreme Court of California gave for its holding [that the official proponents of Prop 8 were authorized to appeal] have special relevance in the context of determining whether proponents have the authority to seek a federal-court remedy for the State's concrete, substantial, and continuing injury. As a class, official proponents are a small, identifiable group. Because many of their decisions must be unanimous, they are necessarily few in number. Their identities are public. Their commitment is substantial. They know and understand the purpose and operation of the proposed law, an important requisite in defending initiatives on complex matters such as taxation and insurance. Having gone to great lengths to convince voters to enact an initiative, they have a stake in the outcome and the necessary commitment to provide zealous advocacy.

Thus, in California, proponents play a "unique role . . . in the initiative process." . . . Proponents' authority under state law is not a contrivance. It is not a fictional construct. It is the product of the California Constitution and the California Elections Code. There is no basis for this Court to set aside the California Supreme Court's determination of state law. . . .

The Court concludes that proponents lack sufficient ties to the state government. It notes that they "are not elected," "answer to no one," and lack "'a fiduciary obligation'" to the State (quoting 1 Restatement (Third) of Agency). But what the Court deems deficiencies in the proponents' connection to the State government, the State Supreme Court saw as essential qualifications to defend the initiative system. The very object of the initiative system is to establish a lawmaking process that does not depend upon state officials. In California, the popular initiative is necessary to implement "the theory that all power of government ultimately resides in the people." The right to adopt initiatives has been described by the California courts as "one of the most precious rights of [the State's] democratic process." That historic role for the initiative system "grew out of dissatisfaction with the then governing public officials and a widespread belief that the people had lost control of the political process." The initiative's "primary purpose," then, "was to afford the people the ability to propose and to adopt constitutional amendments or statutory provisions that their elected public officials had refused or declined to adopt."

The California Supreme Court has determined that this purpose is undermined if the very officials the initiative process seeks to circumvent are the only parties who can defend an enacted initiative when it is challenged in a legal proceeding. Giving the Governor and attorney general this de facto veto will erode one of the cornerstones of the State's governmental structure. As a consequence, California finds it necessary to vest the responsibility and right to defend a voter-approved initiative in the initiative's proponents when the State Executive declines to do so.

Contrary to the Court's suggestion, this Court's precedents do not indicate that a formal agency relationship is necessary. In *Karcher v. May* (1987), the Speaker of the New Jersey Assembly (Karcher) and President of the New Jersey Senate (Orechio) intervened in support of a school moment-of-silence law that the State's Governor and attorney general declined to defend in court. In considering the question of standing, the Court looked to New Jersey law to determine whether Karcher and Orechio "had authority under state law to represent the State's interest in both the District Court and Court of Appeals." The Court concluded that they did. Because the "New Jersey Supreme Court ha[d] granted applications of the Speaker of the General Assembly and the President of the Senate to intervene as parties-respondent on behalf of the legislature in defense of a legislative enactment," the *Karcher* Court held that standing had been proper in the District Court and Court of Appeals. By the time the case arrived in this Court, Karcher and Orechio had lost their presiding legislative offices, without which they lacked the authority to represent the State under New Jersey law. This, the Court held, deprived them of standing. Here, by contrast, proponents' authority under California law is not contingent on officeholder status, so their standing is unaffected by the fact that they "hold no office" in California's Government. . . .

There is much irony in the Court's approach to justiciability in this case. A prime purpose of justiciability is to ensure vigorous advocacy, yet the Court insists upon litigation conducted by state officials whose preference is to lose the case. The doctrine is meant to ensure that courts are responsible and constrained in their power, but the Court's opinion today means that a single district court can make a decision with far-reaching effects that cannot be reviewed. And rather than honor the principle that justiciability exists to allow disputes of public policy to be resolved by the political process rather than the courts, here the Court refuses to allow a State's authorized representatives to defend the outcome of a democratic election. . . .

In the end, what the Court fails to grasp or accept is the basic premise of the initiative process. And it is this. The

essence of democracy is that the right to make law rests in the people and flows to the government, not the other way around. Freedom resides first in the people without need of a grant from government. The California initiative process embodies these principles and has done so for over a century. . . . In California and the 26 other States that permit initiatives and popular referendums, the people have exercised their own inherent sovereign right to govern themselves. The Court today frustrates that choice by nullifying, for failure to comply with the Restatement of Agency, a State Supreme Court decision holding that state law authorizes an enacted initiative's proponents to defend the law if and when the State's usual legal advocates decline to do so. The Court's opinion fails to abide by precedent and misapplies basic principles of justiciability. Those errors necessitate this respectful dissent.

The short-term impact of *Perry* was that it did not resolve one of the biggest constitutional questions in recent memory—whether states can prohibit the marriage of same-sex couples—because the appealing party lacked standing. (Of course, two years later the Court did answer the question in *Obergefell v. Hodges,* in which it invalidated bans on same-sex marriage.) In the longer term, the divergent opinions in *Perry* show that standing doctrine continues to remain open to interpretation.[77] The very fact that the majority and

---

77. On the same day the Court denied standing to the proponents of Prop 8, the Court issued an opinion in **United States v. Windsor** (2013). *Windsor* involved the constitutionality of a section of the Defense of Marriage Act (DOMA), which defined marriage as between a man and a woman for purposes of federal law. There the Court too confronted questions of standing: Because the Obama administration refused to defend the law's constitutionality, did the Bipartisan Legal Advisory Group (BLAG), a formal group within the House of Representatives, have standing to defend the law's constitutionality when it is the responsibility of the executive branch to do so? Without deciding whether BLAG had standing, the majority allowed the suit to proceed to its merits in part because the Obama administration was still enforcing the law (even though it would not defend its constitutionality). The Court also noted that "if the Executive's agreement with a plaintiff that a law is unconstitutional is enough to preclude judicial review," it would "undermine" the clear dictate of the separation-of-powers principle that "when an Act of Congress is alleged to conflict with the Constitution, '[i]t is emphatically the province and duty of the judicial department to say what the law is.'" *Marbury v. Madison.* The four dissenters took issue with these reasons. As Justice Alito wrote, "The United States clearly is not a proper petitioner in this case. The United States does not ask us to overturn the judgment of the court below or to alter that

dissenting justices in *Perry* could reach such different conclusions again shores up a theme we have emphasized throughout: although Article III places certain limits on the power of the federal judiciary, its language is vague enough to allow for a good deal of judicial latitude.

CONSTRAINTS ON JUDICIAL POWER AND THE SEPARATION OF POWERS SYSTEM

The jurisdiction, justiciability, and standing requirements place considerable constraints on the exercise of judicial power. Yet it is important to note that these doctrines largely come from the Court's own interpretation of Article III and its view of the proper role of the judiciary—the constraints are largely self-imposed. In *Ashwander v. Tennessee Valley Authority* (1936) Justice Louis Brandeis took the opportunity in a concurring opinion to provide a summary of the principles of judicial self-restraint as they pertain to constitutional interpretation *(see box 2-6)*. His goal was to delineate a set of rules that the Court should follow to avoid unnecessarily reaching decisions on the constitutionality of laws. In the course of outlining these "avoidance principles," he considered many of the constraints on judicial decision making we have reviewed in this section. More to the point, these "*Ashwander* Principles" serve as perhaps the best single statement of how the Court limits its own powers— and especially its exercise of judicial review.

Given the cases and materials you have just read, we wonder whether you think these are substantial constraints on the Court. Either way, it would be a mistake to conclude that the use of judicial power is limited only by self-imposed constraints. Rather, members of the executive and legislative branches also have expectations concerning the appropriate limits of judicial authority. If the justices are perceived as exceeding their role by failing to restrain the use of their own powers, a reaction from the political branches may occur.

What forms might such a reaction take? First, the other branches of government could attempt to alter constitutional policy established by the Court.

judgment in any way. Quite to the contrary, the United States argues emphatically in favor of the correctness of that judgment. We have never before reviewed a decision at the sole behest of a party that took such a position, and to do so would be to render an advisory opinion, in violation of Article III's dictates."

Although the Rehnquist Court shut down efforts to do so through simple legislation—for example, **City of Boerne v. Flores** and **Dickerson v. United States**—the other branches can propose constitutional amendments to overturn Court decisions. This constraint on the Court is especially effective because once an amendment is part of the Constitution, it is "constitutional," and the justices are bound by it. By the same token, once the amendment process is set in motion, the Court has been reluctant to interfere.

Consider *Coleman v. Miller* (1939), a case to which Justice Brennan made specific reference in his *Baker* opinion. In *Coleman* the Court considered the actions of the Kansas legislature over the child labor amendment. Proposed by Congress in 1924, the amendment stated, "The Congress shall have power to limit, regulate, and prohibit the labor of persons under eighteen years of age." In January 1925 Kansas legislators voted to reject the amendment. The issue arose again when the state senate reconsidered the amendment in January 1937. At that time the legislative body split, 20–20, with the lieutenant governor casting the decisive vote in favor of it. Members of the Kansas legislature (mostly those who had voted no) challenged the 1937 vote on two grounds: they questioned the ability of the lieutenant governor to break the tie and, more generally, the reconsideration of an amendment that previously had been rejected. Writing for the Court, Chief Justice Charles Evans Hughes refused to address these points. Rather, he asserted that the suit raised a political question. In his words, "the ultimate authority" over the amendment process was Congress, not the Court.

It is worth reiterating that Congress does not often propose constitutional amendments or even legislation to override the Court. Only four times has Congress succeeded in overriding the Court with a constitutional amendment, and attempts to overrule by simple legislation may be equally rare.[78] And when

---

78. But see James Meernik and Joseph Ignagni, "Judicial Review and Coordinate Construction of the Constitution": 41, *American Journal of Political Science*: 447–467 (1997). They state, "Congress often does reverse Supreme Court [constitutional] rulings." They claim that of the 569 cases in which the Court rendered unconstitutional a federal law, a state law, or executive order, Congress made 125 attempts to override by constitutional amendment or by statute. Of these, Congress succeeded in reversing the Court in 41. But it is uncertain whether Congress was attempting a reinterpretation of the Constitution, as it did in the Religious Freedom of Restoration Act, or trying to correct a constitutional defect identified by the Court.

BOX 2-6   JUSTICE BRANDEIS, CONCURRING IN *ASHWANDER v. TENNESSEE VALLEY AUTHORITY*

IN 1936 Justice Louis D. Brandeis delineated, in a concurring opinion in *Ashwander v. Tennessee Valley Authority*, a set of Court-formulated rules to avoid unnecessarily reaching decisions on the constitutionality of laws. A portion of his opinion setting forth those rules, minus case citations and footnotes, follows:

The Court developed, for its own governance in the cases confessedly within its jurisdiction, a series of rules under which it has avoided passing upon a large part of all the constitutional questions pressed upon it for decision. They are:

1. The Court will not pass upon the constitutionality of legislation in a friendly, non-adversary, proceeding, declining because to decide such questions "is legitimate only in the last resort, and as a necessity in the determination of real, earnest and vital controversy between individuals. It never was the thought that, by means of a friendly suit, a party beaten in the legislature could transfer to the courts an inquiry as to the constitutionality of the legislative act."

2. The Court will not "anticipate a question of constitutional law in advance of the necessity of deciding it." "It is not the habit of the Court to decide questions of a constitutional nature unless absolutely necessary to a decision of the case."

3. The Court will not "formulate a rule of constitutional law broader than is required by the precise facts to which it is to be applied."

4. The Court will not pass upon a constitutional question although properly presented by the record, if there is also present some other ground upon which the case may be disposed of. This rule has found most varied application. Thus, if a case can be decided on either of two grounds, one involving a constitutional question, the other a question of statutory construction or general law, the Court will decide only the latter. Appeals from the highest court of a state challenging its decision of a question under the Federal Constitution are frequently dismissed because the judgment can be sustained on an independent state ground.

5. The Court will not pass upon the validity of a statute upon complaint of one who fails to show that he is injured by its operation. Among the many applications of this rule, none is more striking than the denial of the right of challenge to one who lacks a personal or property right. Thus, the challenge by a public official interested only in the performance of his official duty will not be entertained. . . .

6. "The Court will not pass upon the constitutionality of a statute at the instance of one who has availed himself of its benefits."

7. "When the validity of an act of the Congress is drawn in question, and even if a serious doubt of constitutionality is raised, it is a cardinal principle that this Court will first ascertain whether a construction of the statute is fairly possible by which the question may be avoided."

---

the legislature attempts to direct the justices on how to adjudicate constitutional cases, they may decline to do so—as the majority's reaction in *Boerne* and *Dickerson* indicates. The more general point, however, is this: because Congress has, in the past, overridden the Court, there is no reason for justices to believe that the legislature would not do so in the future. This threat may be sufficient to constrain the justices, even in constitutional disputes.

Second, the elected branches possess various weapons that they could use to punish the Court. Congress can hold judicial salaries constant, impeach justices, change the size of the Court, and make "exceptions" to the Court's appellate jurisdiction. And these weapons can have an effect on the doctrine the Court produces. To see this point, we need only reconsider *Ex parte McCardle*. Perhaps to protect the Court's institutional legitimacy, the justices chose not to rule the way they really wanted—in favor of McCardle. Instead, they dismissed the suit, thereby lending credence to the notion that Congress can remove the Court's appellate jurisdiction as it deems necessary. In *Hamdan v. Rumsfeld*, however, a modern-day incarnation of *McCardle,* the justices proclaimed the jurisdictional question a nonissue: despite the president's arguments to the contrary, the majority claimed that Congress had not engaged in jurisdiction stripping, at least not over pending cases.

The mere existence of these congressional weapons, however, may serve to constrain policy-oriented justices from acting on their preferences. In *Marbury v. Madison*, Chief Justice Marshall—himself an Adams appointee—must have wanted to give Marbury his appointment. But, at the same time, Marshall was well aware of the serious repercussions of ordering the administration to do so. Jefferson made no secret of his disdain for Marshall, and with impeachment of the chief justice a distinct possibility in the president's (and Marshall's) mind, Marshall was confronted with a dilemma: vote his sincere political preferences and risk the institutional integrity of the Court (not to mention his own job), or act in a sophisticated fashion with regard to his political preferences (refuse to give Marbury his commission) and elevate judicial supremacy (establish judicial review) in a way that Jefferson could accept. Perhaps not so surprisingly, Marshall chose the latter course of action.

Finally, government actors can refuse, implicitly or explicitly, to implement particular constitutional decisions, thereby decreasing the Court's ability to create efficacious policy. *Immigration and Naturalization Service v. Chadha,* which we discussed at the beginning of this chapter, provides a case in point. Theoretically speaking, *Chadha* nullified on constitutional grounds the practice of legislative vetoes—that is, congressional rejection of policies produced by executive agencies. In practice, however, Congress has passed hundreds of new laws containing legislative vetoes since *Chadha,* and agencies continue to pay heed when Congress rejects their policies. The problem, so it seems, was that the Court fashioned a rule that was "unacceptable" to the other branches of government and, as a result, one that has been "eroded by open defiance and subtle evasion."[79] Why the Court would establish such an inefficacious rule is open to speculation, but the relevant point is simple enough: once the Court reached its decision, it had to depend on Congress to implement it. Because Congress failed to do so, the Court was unable to set long-term policy.

In sum, Article III is not the only source of constraint on the Court's power. The justices are fully aware that the president and Congress have the ability to impose such checks, and on occasion they may exercise their powers with at least some consideration of how other government actors may respond. Therefore, constraints on judicial power emanate not only from Article III and the Court's interpretation of it, but also from the constitutional separation of powers—a system giving each governmental branch a role in keeping the other branches within their legitimate bounds.

---

79. Fisher, "The Legislative Veto," 288.

ANNOTATED READINGS

For studies of judicial power, consult the citations in the footnotes in this chapter. Here we wish only to highlight several interesting books that explore the development of judicial power and how the Court interprets (or should interpret) its powers in Article III, along with the role the Court plays (or should play) in American society. These books include Alexander M. Bickel, *The Least Dangerous Branch* (New York: Bobbs-Merrill, 1962); Jesse H. Choper, *Judicial Review and the National Political Process* (Chicago: University of Chicago Press, 1980); Justin Crowe, *Building the Judiciary: Law, Courts, and the Politics of Institutional Development* (Princeton, NJ: Princeton University Press, 2012); John Hart Ely, *Democracy and Distrust* (Cambridge, MA: Harvard University Press, 1980); Thomas M. Franck, *Political Questions/Judicial Answers: Does the Rule of Law Apply in Foreign Affairs?* (Princeton, NJ: Princeton University Press, 2009); Scott Douglas Gerber, *A Distinct Judicial Power: The Origins of an Independent Judiciary* (New York: Oxford University Press, 2011); Larry D. Kramer, *The People Themselves: Popular Constitutionalism and Judicial Review* (New York: Oxford University Press, 2004); William Lasser, *The Limits of Judicial Power* (Chapel Hill: University of North Carolina Press, 1988); Philippa Strum, *The Supreme Court and Political Questions* (Tuscaloosa: University of Alabama Press, 1974); and Cass R. Sunstein, *One Case at a Time: Judicial Minimalism on the Supreme Court* (Cambridge, MA: Harvard University Press, 1999).

To greater and lesser extents, these works cover *Marbury v. Madison.* Books more explicitly about the case include Robert Lowry Clinton, Marbury v. Madison *and Judicial Review* (Lawrence: University Press of Kansas, 1989); William E. Nelson, Marbury v. Madison: *The Origins and Legacy of Judicial Review* (Lawrence: University Press of Kansas, 2000); and Cliff Sloan and David McKean, *The Great Decision: Jefferson, Adams, Marshall, and the Battle for the Supreme Court* (New York: Public Affairs, 2009).

3 The Legislature

ARTICLE I of the U.S. Constitution is its longest and most explicit. The founders spelled out in great detail the powers Congress did and did not have over its own operations and its authority to make laws. Reading through Article I, we might conclude that it could not be the source of much litigation. After all, given its specificity, how much room for interpretation could there be?

For cases involving Congress's authority over its internal affairs, this assumption would be accurate. The Supreme Court has heard relatively few cases touching on the first seven sections of Article I, which deal with the various qualifications for membership in Congress, the ability of the chambers to punish members, and certain privileges enjoyed by the members. On the relatively few of those on which the Court has ruled, it generally, though not always, has given the legislature wide latitude over its own business.

That assumption, however, is incorrect when we consider cases that deal directly with Congress's most basic power, the enactment of laws, and with its position in American government. Article I, Section 8, enumerates specifically the substantive areas in which Congress may legislate. But is it too specific, failing to foresee how congressional powers might need to be exercised in areas it does not cover? Section 8 provides Congress with the power to borrow and coin money, but not with the authority to make paper money for the payment of debts. Since 1792 congressional committees have held investigations and hearings, but no clause in Section 8 authorizes them to do so. In general, the Supreme Court has had to determine whether legislative action that is not explicitly covered in Article I falls within Congress's authority, and that is why the Court so often has examined statutes passed by Congress.

There is another reason. As we saw earlier, and as we shall see throughout this book, basic (and purposeful) tensions were built into the design of the government. Disputes occur between the branches of the federal government, between the federal government and the states, and between governments and individuals. Emanating from the basic principles underlying the structure of government—federalism, the separation of powers, and checks and balances—these conflicts have provided the stuff of myriad legal disputes, and the Court has been right in the middle of many of them.

This chapter examines how the justices have interpreted Article I of the Constitution.[1] It is divided into four sections: the first provides a historical overview of Article I, the second explores cases involving Congress's authority over its own structure and operations, and the third looks at the sources and scope of its lawmaking power. We end with a discussion of a topic that has generated considerable debate in recent years: constitutional deliberations within the federal legislature.

---

1. We focus generally in this chapter on the scope of Article I and related issues. In chapter 5 we consider relationships between the legislative and executive branches.

ARTICLE I: HISTORICAL OVERVIEW

Many issues led the colonists in America to rebel against England. An important one, sometimes neglected in treatments of the American Revolution, was the different ways the British and the colonists thought about legislative bodies such as Parliament. The British viewed legislatures as "deliberative bodies whose allegiance was to the nation rather than specific constituencies."[2] Underlying this view is the notion of "virtual" representation: "since the *interests* of all British citizens were represented in Parliament, the *citizens* themselves did not need to be." Therefore, the British reasoned, the colonists did not have to vote for members of Parliament because they were "virtually represented" within it. The Americans took quite a different stance. To them, legislators "were nothing more and nothing less than agents of their constituents." As John Adams wrote in 1776, the ideal legislature "should be in miniature an exact portrait of the people at large. It should think, feel, reason and act like them."

During the founding period, the American states created legislatures that reflected some of Adams's views of representation. Most states provided for short terms of office, with elections typically occurring every other year. They also mandated that legislatures have open sessions and publish their proceedings. Finally, many states actually gave their inhabitants the right to "instruct" their representatives on how to vote on certain issues. These and other measures were designed to keep legislators responsive to their constituents. Concerns about representation at the federal level also were present, as were suspicions about a national government that would be as powerful as England's. The unicameral Congress created by the Articles of Confederation had few important powers, and many of those it had it could not exercise without state compliance, which it seldom received *(see figure I-1)*.

The problems Congress and the nation faced under the Articles of Confederation made it clear to the delegates attending the Constitutional Convention of 1787 that a very different kind of legislature was necessary if the United States was to endure. But what form would that legislature take? And what powers would it have? These questions produced a great deal of discussion during the convention; indeed, debates over the structure and powers of Congress occupied more than half of the framers' time.

Structure and Composition of Congress

The Virginia Plan set the tone for the Constitutional Convention and became the backbone for Article I. Essentially, the plan called for a bicameral legislature, with the number of representatives in each house apportioned on the basis of state population. Under this scheme, the lower house (now the House of Representatives) would be elected by the people; the upper house (the Senate) would be chosen by the lower house based on recommendations from state legislatures.

The framers dealt with two aspects of the Virginia Plan with relative ease. Almost all agreed on the need for a bicameral legislature. Accord on this point was not surprising: by 1787 only four states had one-house legislatures. The plan for selecting the upper house provoked more discussion. Some thought that having the lower house elect the upper would make the Senate subservient to the House and upset the delicate checks and balances system. Instead, the delegates agreed that state legislatures should select the senators. (The Seventeenth Amendment to the Constitution, ratified in 1913, changed the method of selection; senators, like representatives, are now elected by the people.)

The third aspect of the Virginia Plan—the composition of the houses of Congress—generated some of the most acrimonious debates of the convention. As historians Alfred Kelly, Winfred Harbison, and Herman Belz put it,

Would the constituent units be the states, represented equally by delegates chosen by state legislatures, as the small-state group desired? Or would the constituent element be the people of the United States . . . with representation in both chambers apportioned according to population, as the large-state group wished?[3]

On one level, the answer to this question involved the straightforward motivation of self-interest. Naturally, the large states wanted both chambers to be based on population because they would send more representatives to the new Congress. The smaller

---

2. The discussion in this paragraph has been adopted from Farber and Sherry, *A History of the American Constitution,* 153–157.

3. Alfred H. Kelly, Winfred A. Harbison, and Herman Belz, *The American Constitution: Its Origins and Development,* 7th ed. (New York: W. W. Norton, 1991), 90.

states thought all states should have equal representation in both houses and regarded their plan as the only way to avoid tyranny by a majority. On another level, the issue of composition went to the core of the Philadelphia enterprise. The approach advocated by the small states would signify the importance of the states in the new system of government, while that put forth in the Virginia Plan would suggest that the federal government received its power directly from the people rather than from the states and was truly independent of the states.

It is no wonder, then, that the delegates had so much trouble resolving this issue: it defined the basic character of the new government. In the end they took the course of action that characterized many of their decisions—they agreed to disagree. Specifically, the delegates reached a compromise under which the House of Representatives would be constituted on the basis of population, and the Senate would have two delegates from each state.

Reaching this compromise was crucial to the success of the convention. Without it, the delegates may have disbanded without framing a constitution. But because the founders split the difference between the demands of the small and large states, they never fully dealt with the critical underlying issue: Do the people or the states empower the federal government? We address the impact of this lingering question on the development of the country in chapter 6. Here, we note that this question not only has been at the center of many disputes brought to the Supreme Court but also was a leading cause of the Civil War.

This compromise has also led to more specific controversies, centering on the very nature of representation. We know that in drafting Article I the framers clearly intended that representation in the House of Representatives would be based on population. Each state was allotted at least one representative, with additional seats based on the number of persons residing within the state's boundaries. The exact number of representatives per state was to be determined by a census of the population (beginning within three years of the First Congress and continuing at intervals of every ten years thereafter) and calculated by adding the number of "free persons" and "three-fifths of all other persons" (read: slaves). Passage of the Fourteenth Amendment changed this formula so that black people would be fully counted, and in 1911 and again in 1929 Congress set the size of the House at 435 members, where it

remains today. But even these steps did not end debates over representation. As late as 1992 the state of Montana sued, arguing that the formula Congress used to calculate representation unfairly denied it an additional representative.[4] Moreover, recall from chapter 2 that as population shifts occurred within states in the middle of the twentieth century, some states redrew their congressional district lines. For most, the new maps meant creating greater parity for urban centers as citizens moved out of rural areas. Other states, however, ignored these shifts and refused to reapportion seats. Over time, their failure meant that within a given state it was possible for two districts with large differences in population each to elect one member to the House. Beginning with *Baker v. Carr* (1962), the Court heard a series of challenges to legislative malapportionment, eventually creating the "one person, one vote" principle, which holds that "as nearly as is practicable one man's vote in a congressional election is to be worth as much as another's."[5]

With the articulation of this principle, the Court settled some controversies: so long as the one person, one vote principle is observed, the Supreme Court generally has allowed states freedom in constructing representational districts for members of the House of Representatives. But other controversies arose with time, in particular regarding the extent to which states may or should take race into account when they reapportion their districts. According to some analysts, creating districts with high concentrations of minority voters is the only way to increase minority representation in Congress. Others, including some civil rights advocates, have criticized such efforts, arguing that they do not offer real opportunities for increased minority representation. Even if the numbers of minority representatives grew to approximate the proportions of their respective minority groups in the general population, the argument goes, these representatives would still be too small in number to have any real clout in the legislature. These critics claim that only through changes in representational and institutional rules can minorities achieve political influence at the national level.[6] What is beyond debate is that the

---

4. *Department of Commerce v. Montana* (1992).

5. *Wesberry v. Sanders* (1964).

6. The Court has wrestled with the constitutional propriety of states purposefully drawing legislative district lines to ensure representation for minorities. During the 1970s and 1980s the Court

number of minority members of the House remains relatively small.

Powers of Congress

With the possible exceptions of reapportionment and term limits for members of Congress, which we cover later in the chapter, Americans today rarely debate issues concerning the structure and composition of Congress: most of us simply accept the arrangements outlined in the Constitution. Instead, we tend to concern ourselves with what Congress does or does not do, with its ability to change our lives—sometimes dramatically—through the exercise of its lawmaking powers. Should Congress increase taxes? Provide aid for the homeless? Authorize military action? Such questions—not structural points—generate heated debate among Americans.

In 1787 the situation was reversed. The framers argued over the makeup of the legislature but generally agreed about the particular powers it would have. This consensus probably reflected their experience under the Articles of Confederation: severe economic problems due in no small part, as the framers knew, to "congressional impotence."[7]

To correct these problems, Article I, Section 8, which lists seventeen specific powers the delegates gave to Congress, contains many provisions relating to the economy. Consider the problem of funding the government. Under the Articles of Confederation the legislature could not collect taxes from the people; instead, it had to rely on the less-than-dependable states to collect and forward taxes (from 1781 through 1783, the legislature requested $10 million from the states but received less than $2 million). In response, the first power given to Congress in the newly minted Constitution was to "lay and collect taxes." In all, six of the seventeen specific congressional powers enumerated in Section 8 deal with economic issues. The rest center on foreign relations, the military, and internal

matters such as the creation of courts, post offices, and so forth.

The framers agreed on these powers, but two others provoked controversy. The first concerned a proposal in the Virginia Plan to give Congress veto authority over state legislation. This idea had the strong support of James Madison, who argued, "[T]he propensity of the States to pursue their particular interests in opposition to the general interest . . . will continue to disturb the system, unless effectually controuled." Madison and others who supported the veto proposal were once again reacting to the problems produced by the Articles of Confederation. Because the federal government lacked coercive power over the states, cooperation among them was virtually nonexistent. They engaged in practices that hurt one another economically and, in general, acted more like thirteen separate countries than a union or even a confederation. But the majority of delegates thought that a congressional veto would "disgust all the States." Accordingly, they compromised with Article VI, the supremacy clause, which made the Constitution, U.S. laws, and treaties "the supreme law of the land," binding all judges in all the states to follow them.

The second source of controversy was this question: Would Congress be able to exercise powers that were not listed in Article I, Section 8, or was it limited to those explicitly enumerated? Some analysts would argue that the last clause of Article I, Section 8, the necessary and proper clause, addressed this question by granting Congress the power "[t]o make all Laws which shall be necessary and proper for carrying into Execution the foregoing Powers." But is that interpretation correct? Even after they agreed on the wording of that clause (with little debate), the delegates continued to discuss the issue. Delegate James McHenry of Maryland wrote about a conversation that occurred on September 6: "Spoke to Gov. Morris Fitzsimmons . . . to insert a power . . . enabling the legislature to erect piers for protection of shipping in winter. . . . Mr. Gov.: thinks it may be done under the words of [Article I]— 'and provide for the common defense and general welfare.'"[8] In other words, Fitzsimmons was arguing that one of Congress's enumerated powers (to provide for the common defense and general welfare) implied the power to erect piers. Under this argument, then, Congress could assert powers connected to, but beyond, those that were enumerated.

---

gave considerable leeway to state legislatures to take race into account. In the 1990s, however, the Court changed course sharply. In a series of cases, the justices ruled that the Constitution is violated when district lines are explainable only in terms of race and when racial factors clearly dominate more-traditional districting criteria. For a full discussion of this issue, see Lee Epstein and Thomas G. Walker, *Constitutional Law for a Changing America: Rights, Liberties, and Justice,* 9th ed. (Thousand Oaks, CA: CQ Press, 2016), chap. 14.

7. Farber and Sherry, *A History of the American Constitution,* 189.

---

8. Quoted in ibid., 199.

Because questions concerning the sources of congressional power and the role of the necessary and proper clause in particular are central to an understanding of the role Congress plays in American society, we shall return to them. At this point, however, we consider the Court's interpretation of the first parts of Article I, which lay out the structure of Congress and its authority over its own affairs.

CONGRESSIONAL AUTHORITY OVER INTERNAL AFFAIRS: INSTITUTIONAL INDEPENDENCE AND INTEGRITY

While the framers were debating Congress's structure and composition, they were also thinking about ways to safeguard the independence and integrity of the institution. Included in Article I are provisions dealing with the ability of the chambers to control who joins them and to punish those who do not behave in accord with their norms. Another section, the speech or debate clause, protects members from "harassment" by other institutions.

Would the Supreme Court interpret these provisions broadly, to give members of Congress a good deal of leeway, or more narrowly? One way to begin thinking about this question is to consider an interesting connection between the Court and Congress. Although we often conceptualize them as wholly separate entities, almost half the Court's members have had prior state or federal legislative experience, as table 3-1 shows. From this, we might think that those justices would empathize with the claims of Congress regarding the need for authority over its own affairs; indeed, the Court generally has acceded to legislative wishes— but not always. As you read what follows, think about the reasons the Court offers for its decisions. Furthermore, take note of the various coalitions that have emerged on different Courts. Have the justices with legislative experience exhibited a greater willingness to defer to Congress than those without this experience? Finally, note that appointing former legislators is mostly a phenomenon of the eighteenth and nineteenth centuries; the most recent justice who had served as a legislator was Sandra Day O'Connor (appointed in 1981). Do you detect a change in deference to Congress as the number of former legislators on the Court has dwindled? Or is there little connection between legislative experience and judicial rulings?

Membership in Congress: Seating and Discipline

In addition to specifying the structure and composition of Congress, Article I contains the requirements that must be met by all prospective members of the institution:

- A senator must be at least thirty years old and have been a citizen of the United States not less than nine years (Section 3, Clause 3).
- A representative must be at least twenty-five years old and have been a citizen not less than seven years (Section 2, Clause 2).
- Every member of Congress must be, when elected, an inhabitant of the state that he or she is to represent (Section 2, Clause 2; and Section 3, Clause 3).
- No one may be a member of Congress who holds any other "Office under the Authority of the United States" (Section 6, Clause 2).

Finally, Section 3 of the Fourteenth Amendment states that no person may be a senator or a representative who, having previously taken an oath as a member of Congress to support the Constitution, has engaged in rebellion against the United States or given aid or comfort to its enemies, unless Congress has removed such restriction by a two-thirds vote of both houses.

With only a few exceptions, these standards qua standards have not caused much controversy or litigation. Some legal questions, however, have arisen with respect to their relationship to Article I, Section 5, which reads, "Each House shall be the Judge of the Elections, Returns and Qualifications of its own Members." Several interpretations of this clause are possible. One is that it ought to be read in conjunction with the Article I requirements for members. That is, Congress cannot deny a duly elected person a seat in the institution unless that person fails to meet the specified criteria. Another interpretation is that Congress is free to develop additional qualifications, independent of those specified elsewhere.[9]

---

9. Note that this controversy—over the exclusion of duly elected members—stems from the first paragraph of Article I, Section 5. There is not much debate over whether Congress can censure or expel sitting members. The second paragraph of Article I, Section 5, is clear on this point: "Each House may determine the Rules of its Proceedings, punish its Members for disorderly Behaviour, and, with the Concurrence of two thirds, expel a member." The Court has not dealt directly with a dispute involving the punishment of members, such as censure or expulsion; rather, it has

TABLE 3-1   U.S. Supreme Court Justices Who Served in the U.S. Congress or in State Legislatures

JUSTICES APPOINTED IN THE 1700s (8 OF 12)

John Rutledge (South Carolina)

John Blair Jr. (Virginia)

Thomas Johnson (Maryland)

William Paterson (U.S. Senate; New Jersey)

Samuel Chase (Maryland)

Oliver Ellsworth (U.S. Senate; Connecticut)

Bushrod Washington (Virginia)

Alfred Moore (North Carolina)

JUSTICES APPOINTED IN THE 1800s (32 OF 44)

John Marshall (U.S. House; Virginia)

William Johnson (South Carolina)

Henry B. Livingston (New York)

Joseph Story (U.S. House; Massachusetts)

Gabriel Duvall (U.S. House; Maryland)

Smith Thompson (New York)

Robert Trimble (Kentucky)

John McLean (U.S. House; Ohio)

Henry Baldwin (U.S. House; Pennsylvania)

James M. Wayne (U.S. House; Georgia)

Roger B. Taney (Maryland)

Philip P. Barbour (U.S. House; Virginia)

John McKinley (U.S. House; U.S. Senate; Alabama)

Peter Daniel (Virginia)

Levi Woodbury (U.S. Senate; New Hampshire)

Benjamin R. Curtis (Massachusetts)

John A. Campbell (Alabama)

Nathan Clifford (U.S. House; Maine)

Noah H. Swayne (Ohio)

David Davis (Illinois)

Stephen J. Field (California)

Salmon P. Chase (U.S. Senate; Ohio)

William Strong (U.S. House; Pennsylvania)

Ward Hunt (New York)

Morrison R. Waite (Ohio)

William B. Woods (Ohio)

Stanley Matthews (U.S. Senate; Ohio)

Lucius Q. C. Lamar (U.S. House; U.S. Senate; Georgia)

Melville W. Fuller (Illinois)

Howell E. Jackson (U.S. Senate; Tennessee)

Edward D. White (U.S. Senate; Louisiana)

Joseph McKenna (U.S. House; California)

JUSTICES APPOINTED IN THE 1900s (12 OF 52)

William Moody (U.S. House; Massachusetts)

Willis Van Devanter (Wyoming)

Joseph R. Lamar (Georgia)

Mahlon Pitney (U.S. House; New Jersey)

George Sutherland (U.S. House; U.S. Senate; Utah)

Hugo L. Black (U.S. Senate; Alabama)

Stanley Reed (Kentucky)

James F. Byrnes (U.S. House; U.S. Senate; South Carolina)

Harold H. Burton (U.S. Senate; Ohio)

Fred M. Vinson (U.S. House; Kentucky)

Sherman Minton (U.S. Senate; Indiana)

Sandra Day O'Connor (Arizona)

JUSTICES APPOINTED IN THE 2000s (0 OF 4)

SOURCE: U.S. Supreme Court Justices Database, http://epstein.wustl.edu/research/justicesdata.html.

NOTE: State names indicate service in the legislature of the state. We count justices only once even if they have been appointed twice (as associate and chief).

For the better part of the nation's history, the Court did not resolve this debate,[10] even though Congress occasionally acted as if it could add qualifications or ignore them when they were not met. During the Civil War, Congress enacted the Test Oath Law of 1862, which required incoming members to

---

suggested that this is a broad privilege, best left to the judgment of the individual chambers. See, for example, *In re Chapman* (1897). This kind of action is rare in Congress: since 1787 it has censured twenty-seven members and expelled twenty. Congressional Quarterly, *Guide to Congress,* 6th ed. (Washington, DC: CQ Press, 2008), 1083–1097.

10. In the first case excerpted in this chapter, *Powell v. McCormack,* the House argued that the Court, in *Barry v. United States ex rel. Cunningham* (1929), suggested that regarding the elections, returns,

and qualification of members, each House could "render a judgment which is beyond the authority of any other tribunal to review." In *Powell,* the Court rejected this reading of *Barry,* stating it was not an essential component of the *Barry* ruling. The Court also pointed to another statement in *Barry:* that exercise of the "judging" power is subject "to the restraints imposed by or found in the implications of the Constitution."

TABLE 3-2   Duly Elected Members of Congress Excluded

CHAMBER (YEAR)	MEMBER-ELECT (PARTY-STATE)	GROUNDS FOR EXCLUSION
Senate (1793)	Albert Gallatin (D-Pa.)	Citizenship
House (1823)	John Bailey (Ind.-Mass.)	Residence
Senate (1849)	James Shields (D-Ill.)	Citizenship
House (1867)	John Y. Brown (D-Ky.)	Loyalty
House (1867)	John D. Young (D-Ky.)	Loyalty
House (1867)	John A. Wimpy (Ind.-Ga.)	Loyalty
House (1867)	W. D. Simpson (Ind.-S.C.)	Loyalty
Senate (1867)	Philip F. Thomas (D-Md.)	Loyalty
House (1870)	Benjamin F. Whittemore (R-S.C.)	Malfeasance
House (1900)	Brigham H. Roberts (D-Utah)	Polygamy
House (1919)	Victor L. Berger (Socialist-Wis.)	Sedition
House (1920)	Victor L. Berger (Socialist-Wis.)	Sedition
House (1967)	Adam C. Powell Jr. (D-N.Y.)	Misconduct

SOURCE: Congressional Quarterly, *Guide to Congress,* 7th ed. (Washington, DC: CQ Press, 2013).

"swear . . . that they had never voluntarily borne arms against the United States." Moreover, as shown in table 3-2, both the House and the Senate have refused to seat properly elected individuals, sometimes on extra-constitutional grounds. The Senate excluded Philip Thomas of Maryland on loyalty grounds when it was discovered that he had given money to his son when he became a soldier in the Confederate Army. The House refused to seat Brigham H. Roberts of Utah because he had been convicted of violating an antipolygamy law.

In the course of investigating the Roberts case, a congressional committee concluded that the framers "had not foreclosed the right of Congress to establish qualifications for membership other than those mentioned in the Constitution."[11] As table 3-2 shows, both houses subscribed to this theory. The question of whether the Supreme Court would follow suit remained largely unaddressed until 1969, when the Court decided *Powell v. McCormack* and responded to Congress's traditional approach to seating qualifications. What was the nature of that response? Did the Court simply defer to Congress's wishes?

Powell v. McCormack

395 U.S. 486 (1969)

http://laws.findlaw.com/us/395/486.html
Oral arguments are available at https://www.oyez.org.
Vote: 7 (Black, Brennan, Douglas, Harlan, Marshall, Warren, White)
  1 (Stewart)

OPINION OF THE COURT: *Warren*
CONCURRING OPINION: *Douglas*
DISSENTING OPINION: *Stewart*

FACTS:

Representative Adam Clayton Powell Jr. (D-N.Y.) was one of the most interesting and controversial people ever to serve in the U.S. Congress.[12] As pastor of the Abyssinian Baptist Church in Harlem, one of the nation's largest congregations, Powell had been a force within that New York City community since the 1930s. This influence only increased when he was elected to the House in 1944 after receiving nominations from both the Democratic and Republican Parties. He continued to be reelected by wide margins for the next twenty-five years.

By the early 1960s Powell had acquired sufficient seniority to chair the House Committee on Education

---

11. Congressional Quarterly, *Guide to Congress,* 7th ed. (Washington, DC: CQ Press, 2013), 1132.

12. We derive our account of this case largely from Thomas G. Walker, *American Politics and the Constitution* (North Scituate, MA: Duxbury Press, 1978), 132.

and Labor, but his relations with his colleagues were troubled. Other House members disliked his opulent, unconventional lifestyle, his unpredictable leadership, and his use of the media to suit his political ends. In addition, Powell became entangled in various legal controversies; for example, he refused to pay damages assessed against him in a defamation of character suit and actively sought to avert efforts to compel him to pay.

The Eighty-ninth Congress (1965–1966) launched an inquiry into Powell's activities, which yielded two major violations of House rules: Powell had used federal monies to fly a woman staff member with him on trips to his vacation home in the Bahamas and to pay his former wife a yearly salary of $20,000, even though she did not work in either his district or his Washington office, in accordance with law. Powell was reelected in November 1966, but the House refused to seat him pending further investigation.

Four months later, in March 1967, the new investigation reached two conclusions: (1) from a constitutional standpoint, Powell met the requirements for office: he was older than twenty-five, had been a citizen of the United States for seven years, and was an inhabitant of New York; and (2) Powell had sought to evade the fine associated with the defamation of character offense, had misused public funds, and had filed false expenditure reports. The committee recommended that Powell be seated as a member of Congress but that he be censured by the House, fined $40,000, and deprived of his seniority. The House rejected that recommendation and passed, 307–116, a resolution to exclude Powell from the House and direct Speaker John McCormack to notify the governor of New York that the seat was vacant. Powell, not one to accept such a decision lying down, responded. He and thirteen constituents filed a lawsuit against McCormack and other members of the House, claiming that the body's refusal to seat him violated the qualifications clause of the Constitution.

ARGUMENTS:

For the petitioner, Adam Clayton Powell Jr.:
- Because Powell meets the requirements for office, the House had no choice but to seat him. Article I, Section 5, which says, "Each House shall be the judge of the Elections, Returns and Qualifications of its own Members," is not implicated. It gives Congress no authority to exclude members who met the constitutional standards for office.
- It was the intent of the framers that Congress was to have no power to alter, add to, vary, or ignore constitutional qualification for membership.
- This Court has consistently emphasized that the right of the people to choose freely their representatives is the essence of a democratic society.

For the respondents, John W. McCormack et al.:
- The Court should read the qualifications clause and Section 5 separately. The action taken by the House was a proper exercise of the powers delegated to it by the Constitution under Section 5.
- This dispute presents a political question, which the Supreme Court should refrain from answering. Article I, Section 5, shows a textually demonstrable constitutional commitment to the House of the adjudicatory power to determine Powell's qualifications. Moreover, resolving this dispute would create a potentially embarrassing confrontation between the courts and Congress.

Speaker of the House John McCormack (left) and Representative Adam Clayton Powell walk in separate directions after conferring during the 1967 controversy over proposed disciplinary action against Powell for violating House rules.

▶ **MR. CHIEF JUSTICE WARREN DELIVERED THE OPINION OF THE COURT.**

After certiorari was granted, respondents filed a memorandum suggesting that . . . the case be dismissed as moot. On

January 3, 1969, the House of Representatives of the 90th Congress officially terminated, and petitioner Powell was seated as a member of the 91st Congress. Respondents insist that [because] Powell has now been seated, his claims are moot. Petitioners counter that [several] issues remain unresolved . . . [including] . . . whether Powell is entitled to salary withheld after his exclusion from the 90th Congress. We conclude that Powell's claim for back salary remains viable even though he has been seated in the 91st Congress, and thus find it unnecessary to determine whether the other issues have become moot.

Respondents maintain that even if this case is otherwise justiciable, it presents only a political question. It is well established that the federal courts will not adjudicate political questions. In *Baker v. Carr*, we noted that political questions are not justiciable primarily because of the separation of powers within the Federal Government. . . .

[Respondents contend that] this case presents a political question because under Art. I, §5, there has been a "textually demonstrable constitutional commitment" to the House of the "adjudicatory power" to determine Powell's qualifications. Thus it is argued that the House, and the House alone, has power to determine who is qualified to be a member.

In order to determine whether there has been a textual commitment to a coordinate department of the Government, we must interpret the Constitution. In other words, we must first determine what power the Constitution confers upon the House through Art. I, §5, before we can determine to what extent, if any, the exercise of that power is subject to judicial review. Respondents maintain that the House has broad power under §5, and, they argue, the House may determine which are the qualifications necessary for membership. On the other hand, petitioners allege that the Constitution provides that an elected representative may be denied his seat only if the House finds he does not meet one of the standing qualifications expressly prescribed by the Constitution. . . .

In order to determine the scope of any "textual commitment" under Art. I, §5, we necessarily must determine the meaning of the phrase to "be the Judge of the Qualifications of its own Members." Respondents insist . . . that a careful examination of the pre-Convention practices of the English Parliament and American colonial assemblies demonstrates that by 1787, a legislature's power to judge the qualifications of its members was generally understood to encompass exclusion or expulsion on the ground that an individual's character or past conduct rendered him unfit to serve. When the Constitution and the debates over its adoption are thus viewed in historical perspective, argue respondents, it becomes clear that the "qualifications" expressly set forth in the Constitution were not meant to limit the long-recognized legislative power to exclude or expel at will, but merely to establish "standing incapacities," which could be altered only by a constitutional amendment. Our examination of the relevant historical materials leads us to the conclusion that petitioners are correct and that the Constitution leaves the House without authority to exclude any person, duly elected by his constituents, who meets all the requirements for membership expressly prescribed in the Constitution. . . .

The Convention opened in late May 1787. . . .

On August 10, the Convention considered the Committee of Detail's proposal that the "Legislature of the United States shall have authority to establish such uniform qualifications of the members of each House, with regard to property, as to the said Legislature shall seem expedient." The debate on this proposal discloses much about the views of the Framers on the issue of qualifications. For example, James Madison urged its rejection, stating that the proposal would vest

"an improper & dangerous power in the Legislature. The qualifications of electors and elected were fundamental articles in a Republican Govt. and ought to be fixed by the Constitution. If the Legislature could regulate those of either, it can by degrees subvert the Constitution. A Republic may be converted into an aristocracy or oligarchy as well by limiting the number capable of being elected, as the number authorized to elect. . . . It was a power also, which might be made subservient to the views of one faction agst. another. Qualifications founded on artificial distinctions may be devised, by the stronger in order to keep out partizans of [a weaker] faction."

Significantly, Madison's argument was not aimed at the imposition of a property qualification as such, but rather at the delegation to the Congress of the discretionary power to establish any qualifications. . . .

Madison [also] referred to the British Parliament's assumption of the power to regulate the qualifications of both electors and the elected and noted that "the abuse they had made of it was a lesson worthy of our attention. They had made the changes in both cases subservient to their own views, or to the views of political or Religious parties." Shortly thereafter, the Convention rejected . . . the Committee's proposal. Later the same day, the Convention adopted without debate the provision authorizing each House to be "the judge of the . . . qualifications of its own members."

One other decision made the same day is very important to determining the meaning of Art. I, §5. When the delegates reached the Committee of Detail's proposal to empower each House to expel its members, Madison "observed that the right of expulsion . . . was too important to be exercised by a bare majority of a quorum: and in emergencies [one] faction might be dangerously abused." He therefore moved that "with the concurrence of two-thirds" be inserted. With the exception of one State, whose delegation was divided, the motion was unanimously approved without debate. . . . The importance of this decision cannot be overemphasized. None of the parties to this suit disputes that prior to 1787 the legislative powers to judge qualifications and to expel were exercised by a majority vote . . . Thus, the Convention's decision to increase the vote required to expel, because that power was "too important to be exercised by a bare majority," while at the same time not similarly restricting the power to judge qualifications, is compelling evidence that they considered the latter already limited by the standing qualifications previously adopted. . . .

The debates at the state conventions also demonstrate the Framers' understanding that the qualifications for members of Congress had been fixed in the Constitution. . . . In Virginia, [for example,] where the Federalists faced powerful opposition by advocates of popular democracy, Wilson Carey Nicholas, a future member of both the House and Senate and later Governor of the State, met the arguments that the new Constitution violated democratic principles with the following interpretation of Art. I, §2, cl. 2, as it respects the qualifications of the elected: "It has ever been considered a great security to liberty, that very few should be excluded from the right of being chosen to the legislature. This Constitution has amply attended to this idea. We find no qualifications required except those of age and residence, which create a certainty of their judgment being matured, and of being attached to their state." . . .

As clear as these statements appear, respondents dismiss them as "general statements . . . directed to other issues." They suggest that far more relevant is Congress' own understanding of its power to judge qualifications as manifested in post-ratification exclusion cases. Unquestionably, both the House and the Senate have excluded members-elect for reasons other than their failure to meet the Constitution's standing qualifications. For almost the first 100 years of its existence, however, Congress strictly limited its power to judge the qualifications of its members to those enumerated in the Constitution.

Congress was first confronted with the issue in 1807, when the eligibility of William McCreery was challenged because he did not meet additional residency requirements imposed by the State of Maryland. In recommending that he be seated, the [chairman of the] House Committee of Elections [explained]:

"The Committee of Elections considered the qualifications of members to have been unalterably determined by the Federal Convention, unless changed by an authority equal to that which framed the Constitution at first; that neither the State nor the Federal Legislatures are vested with authority to add to those qualifications, so as to change them. . . . Congress, by the Federal Constitution, are not authorized to prescribe the qualifications of their own members, but they are authorized to judge of their qualifications; in doing so, however, they must be governed by the rules prescribed by the Federal Constitution, and by them only. These are the principles on which the Election Committee have made up their report, and upon which their resolution is founded." . . .

At the conclusion of a lengthy debate, which tended to center on the more narrow issue of the power of the States to add to the standing qualifications set forth in the Constitution, the House agreed by a vote of 89 to 18 to seat Congressman McCreery.

There was no significant challenge to these principles for the next several decades. They came under heavy attack, however, "during the stress of civil war [but initially] the House of Representatives declined to exercise the power [to exclude], even under circumstances of great provocation." The abandonment of such restraint, however, was among the casualties of the general upheaval produced in war's wake. From that time until the present, congressional practice has been erratic; and on the few occasions when a member-elect was excluded although he met all the qualifications set forth in the Constitution, there were frequently vigorous dissents. . . .

Had these congressional exclusion precedents been more consistent, their precedential value still would be quite limited. That an unconstitutional action has been taken before surely does not render that same action any less unconstitutional at a later date. Particularly in view of the Congress' own doubts in those few cases where it did exclude members-elect, we are not inclined to give its precedents controlling weight. The relevancy of prior exclusion cases is limited largely to the insight they afford in correctly ascertaining the draftsmen's intent. Obviously, therefore, the precedential value of these cases tends to increase in proportion to their proximity to the Convention in 1787. And, what evidence we have of Congress' early understanding confirms our conclusion that the House is without power to exclude any member-elect who meets the Constitution's requirements for membership.

Had the intent of the Framers emerged from these materials with less clarity, we would nevertheless have been compelled to resolve any ambiguity in favor of a narrow construction of the scope of Congress' power to exclude members-elect. A fundamental principle of our representative democracy is, in Hamilton's words, "that the people should choose whom they please to govern them." As Madison pointed out at the Convention, this principle is undermined as much by limiting whom the people can select as by limiting the franchise itself. In apparent agreement with this basic philosophy, the Convention adopted his suggestion limiting the power to expel. To allow essentially that same power to be exercised under the guise of judging qualifications, would be to ignore Madison's warning. . . . Moreover, it would effectively nullify the Convention's decision to require a two-thirds vote for expulsion. Unquestionably, Congress has an interest in preserving its institutional integrity, but in most cases that interest can be sufficiently safeguarded by the exercise of its power to punish its members for disorderly behavior and, in extreme cases, to expel a member with the concurrence of two-thirds. In short, both the intention of the Framers, to the extent it can be determined, and an examination of the basic principles of our democratic system persuade us that the Constitution does not vest in the Congress a discretionary power to deny membership by a majority vote.

For these reasons, we have concluded that Art. I, §5, is at most a "textually demonstrable commitment" to Congress to judge only the qualifications expressly set forth in the Constitution. Therefore, the "textual commitment" formulation of the political question doctrine does not bar federal courts from adjudicating petitioners' claims. . . .

. . . Thus, there is no need to remand this case to determine whether he was entitled to be seated in the 90th Congress. Therefore, we hold that, since Adam Clayton Powell, Jr., was duly elected by the voters of the 18th Congressional District of New York and was not ineligible to serve under any provision of the Constitution, the House was without power to exclude him from its membership. . . .

It is so ordered.

MR. JUSTICE STEWART, *dissenting.*

I believe that events which have taken place since certiorari was granted in this case on November 18, 1968, have rendered it moot, and that the Court should therefore refrain from deciding the novel, difficult, and delicate constitutional questions which the case presented at its inception.

The essential purpose of this lawsuit by Congressman Powell and members of his constituency was to regain the seat from which he was barred by the 90th Congress. That purpose, however, became impossible of attainment on January 3, 1969, when the 90th Congress passed into history and the 91st Congress came into being. On that date, the petitioners' prayer for a judicial decree restraining enforcement of House Resolution No. 278 and commanding the respondents to admit Congressman Powell to membership in the 90th Congress became incontestably moot.

The petitioners assert that actions of the House of Representatives of the 91st Congress have prolonged the controversy raised by Powell's exclusion and preserved the need for a judicial declaration in this case. I believe, to the contrary, that the conduct of the present House of Representatives confirms the mootness of the petitioners' suit against the 90th Congress. Had Powell been excluded from the 91st Congress, he might argue that there was a "continuing controversy" concerning the exclusion attacked in this case. And such an argument might be sound even though the present House of Representatives is a distinct legislative body rather than a continuation of its predecessor, and though any grievance caused by conduct of the 91st Congress is not redressable in this action. But on January 3, 1969, the House of Representatives of the 91st Congress admitted Congressman Powell to membership, and he now sits as the Representative of the 18th Congressional District of New York. With the 90th Congress terminated and Powell now a member of the 91st, it cannot seriously be contended that there remains a judicial controversy between these parties over the power of the House of Representatives to exclude Powell and the power of a court to order him reseated.

Chief Justice Earl Warren's holding in *Powell* is indisputable: because Powell was duly elected and because he met the constitutional standards for membership, the House could not refuse to seat him. *(For Powell's fate after the Court's decision, see box 3-1.)* As

Warren emphatically noted, "Congress is limited to the standing qualifications prescribed in the Constitution." Note that Warren, on the basis of the intent of the framers of the Constitution, rejected McCormack's political question argument. But how would you square his decision with Chief Justice William H. Rehnquist's in *Nixon v. United States* (1993), discussed in chapter 2? Are the two reconcilable or contradictory?

Another question to ask yourself about *Powell* concerns its relevance for one of the more interesting present-day debates about Article I: Does the U.S. Constitution give states the power to enact term limits for members of the U.S. Congress? Opponents of term limits point to Article I's qualification clauses and use *Powell* to argue that those clauses fix the requirements for office—requirements that neither Congress nor the states may alter. Supporters, as we note below, offer a number of counterarguments to *Powell.* In 1995 the Supreme Court entered the fray in *U.S. Term Limits, Inc. v. Thornton,* excerpted below.

While reading Justice John Paul Stevens's opinion for the majority, compare it with Chief Justice Warren's in *Powell.* Does the majority's rationale in *U.S. Term Limits* square with Warren's reasoning? Also pay close attention to how both the majority and dissenting opinions deal with arguments following from originalism. Is *U.S. Term Limits* yet another example of the difficulty of applying this mode of analysis to actual cases? Finally, consider

this question: Would the Court have arrived at a different answer had the U.S. House of Representatives mustered the votes to propose a term limits amendment?

U.S. Term Limits, Inc. v. Thornton

514 U.S. 779 (1995)
http://laws.findlaw.com/us/514/779.html
Oral arguments are available at https://www.oyez.org.
Vote: 5 *(Breyer, Ginsburg, Kennedy, Souter, Stevens)*
    4 *(O'Connor, Rehnquist, Scalia, Thomas)*

OPINION OF THE COURT: *Stevens*
CONCURRING OPINION: *Kennedy*
DISSENTING OPINION: *Thomas*

FACTS:

In 1990 Colorado became the first state to limit terms for federal officeholders. Subsequently, twenty-three additional states passed term limit initiatives. *U.S. Term Limits* involved one of those initiatives. It originated in Arkansas, where in 1992 voters approved an amendment to the state constitution (Amendment 73) prohibiting from the ballot anyone seeking reelection who previously had served two terms in the U.S. Senate or three terms in the U.S. House of Representatives. It permitted anyone to be elected as a write-in candidate, presumably as a way of allowing for the reelection of a popular incumbent.

BOX 3-1 AFTERMATH . . . ADAM CLAYTON POWELL JR.

WHILE the House of Representatives debated what to do with him, Adam Clayton Powell Jr. spent most of 1967 on the island of Bimini in the Bahamas. He was unable to return to New York because of his refusal to pay court-ordered damages in a 1963 libel case and a pending contempt of court charge. He ultimately raised sufficient funds to satisfy the judgment and settled the contempt matter.

He ran for his vacated congressional seat in a special election in April 1967 and again in November 1968 regular elections, winning overwhelmingly both times. In January 1969, as the Supreme Court was about to hear arguments in the lawsuit challenging his 1967 exclusion from Congress, the House agreed to seat Powell but stripped him of his seniority and fined him $25,000 for misuse of funds. As a

result, Powell lost his position as chair of the House Committee on Education and Labor, a primary source of his political power.

About this same time Powell was diagnosed with cancer. Weakened by treatments for the disease, he ran for reelection in 1970 but was defeated by a 150-vote margin in the Democratic primary by Charles Rangel. The loss ended Powell's quarter century of service in Congress. In 1971 Powell, in declining health, retired from the pulpit of Harlem's Abyssinian Baptist Church and wrote his autobiography. He died on April 4, 1972, in Miami, Florida, at age sixty-four.

SOURCE: *American National Biography,* vol. 17 (New York: Oxford University Press, 1999), 773–775.

The amendment was to apply to all persons seeking reelection after January 1, 1993. About two months before that date, the League of Women Voters and various citizens of Arkansas, including U.S. Representative Ray Thornton, filed suit asking a state court to declare the amendment unconstitutional. Among the arguments they made in this court and later in the Arkansas Supreme Court was that Amendment 73 violated Article I of the U.S. Constitution. In particular, based on *Powell v. McCormack*, they claimed that the federal Constitution establishes the sole qualifications for federal office, and the states may not alter them. Arkansas and U.S. Term Limits, an organization supporting the amendment, responded by pointing to Section 4 of Article I: "The Times, Places and Manner of holding Elections for Senators and Representatives, shall be prescribed in each State by the Legislature thereof." In their view, this section—not the qualifications clauses—was applicable because term limits would regulate access to the ballot, not the qualifications for office. They further suggested that *Powell* spoke only about the ability of the U.S. House of Representatives, not of the states, to set qualifications. Finally, because the Constitution does not explicitly prohibit the states from setting qualifications for office, it is a power reserved to them under the Tenth Amendment.

The Arkansas courts disagreed. The lower court struck down the amendment as a violation of Article I, and in 1994 the state supreme court affirmed. According to that court, "The qualifications clauses fix the sole requirement for congressional service. This is not a power left to the states." With this defeat in hand, amendment proponents appealed to the U.S. Supreme Court, which agreed to hear the case.

ARGUMENTS:

For the petitioners, U.S. Term Limits, Inc., et al.:

- Amendment 73 does not set a qualification for office. Although it is designed to lessen the overwhelming election advantages enjoyed by incumbents, it does so only by not continuing to print such incumbents' names on ballots. It does not disqualify them from running, being elected, or serving in office. As a result, it is clear that Amendment 73 does not impose an additional qualification for congressional office.
- Qualifications for office are those attributes that are legal prerequisites to eligibility for office. Ballot access restrictions such as Amendment 73 are not qualifications.
- Even if the Arkansas Supreme Court were correct in its assertion that Amendment 73 added qualifications for holding congressional office, Article I still would not be violated. Article I, in both Sections 2 and 4, explicitly assigns the states broad power over congressional elections.[13]

For the respondents, Ray Thornton et al.:

- During the debates over the ratification of the proposed Constitution, opponents mounted unsuccessful efforts in several states to amend the document to provide for term limits for members of Congress—a limitation the framers had rejected during the Constitutional Convention.
- Petitioners and their supporters contend that the framers' rejection of term limits was meaningless and that anti-Federalist efforts to amend the Constitution to provide for rotation were entirely superfluous. These contentions are profoundly mistaken. As the antiratification forces clearly recognized two centuries ago, the text and structure of Article I preclude the imposition of additional qualifications for membership in Congress by any means other than by amending the Constitution.
- This Court acknowledged in *Powell v. McCormack* that the history surrounding the drafting and adoption of Article I reinforces what the text and structure reveal—that the framers eliminated term limits and other limitations and prescribed only a few and exclusive qualifications to ensure voters the widest possible choice of federal representatives. Amendment 73 seeks to circumscribe the choice of individual voters in federal elections and to disable permanently a specific class of candidates for Congress.

◆ JUSTICE STEVENS DELIVERED THE OPINION OF THE COURT.

Today's cases present a challenge to an amendment to the Arkansas State Constitution that prohibits the name of an otherwise eligible candidate for Congress from appearing on the general election ballot if that candidate has already served three terms in the House of Representatives or two terms in the Senate. The Arkansas Supreme Court held that the amendment violates the Federal Constitution. We

---

13. See also Table 1–1 in chapter 1, which provides additional arguments marshaled in this case.

agree with that holding. Such a state-imposed restriction is contrary to the "fundamental principle of our representative democracy," embodied in the Constitution, that "the people should choose whom they please to govern them." *Powell v. McCormack* (1969). Allowing individual States to adopt their own qualifications for congressional service would be inconsistent with the Framers' vision of a uniform National Legislature representing the people of the United States. If the qualifications set forth in the text of the Constitution are to be changed, that text must be amended. . . .

As the opinions of the Arkansas Supreme Court suggest, the constitutionality of Amendment 73 depends critically on the resolution of two distinct issues. The first is whether the Constitution forbids States from adding to or altering the qualifications specifically enumerated in the Constitution. The second is, if the Constitution does so forbid, whether the fact that Amendment 73 is formulated as a ballot access restriction rather than as an outright disqualification is of constitutional significance. Our resolution of these issues draws upon our prior resolution of a related but distinct issue: whether Congress has the power to add to or alter the qualifications of its Members.

Twenty-six years ago, in *Powell v. McCormack*, we reviewed the history and text of the Qualifications Clauses in a case involving an attempted exclusion of a duly elected Member of Congress. The principal issue was whether the power granted to each House in Art. I, §5, to judge the "Qualifications of its own Members" includes the power to impose qualifications other than those set forth in the text of the Constitution. In an opinion by Chief Justice Warren for eight Members of the Court, we held that it does not. Because of the obvious importance of the issue, the Court's review of the history and meaning of the relevant constitutional text was especially thorough. We therefore begin our analysis today with a . . . statement of what we decided in that case. . . .

Powell . . . establishes two important propositions: first, that the "relevant historical materials" compel the conclusion that, at least with respect to qualifications imposed by Congress, the Framers intended the qualifications listed in the Constitution to be exclusive; and second, that that conclusion is equally compelled by an understanding of the "fundamental principle of our representative democracy . . . 'that the people should choose whom they please to govern them.'" . . .

Unsurprisingly, the state courts and lower federal courts have similarly concluded that *Powell* conclusively resolved the issue whether Congress has the power to impose additional qualifications. [And] we reaffirm that the qualifications for service in Congress set forth in the text of the Constitution are "fixed," at least in the sense that they may not be supplemented by Congress.

Our reaffirmation of *Powell* does not necessarily resolve the specific questions presented in these cases. For petitioners argue that whatever the constitutionality of additional qualifications for membership imposed by Congress, the historical and textual materials discussed in *Powell* do not support the conclusion that the Constitution prohibits additional qualifications imposed by States. In the absence of such a constitutional prohibition, petitioners argue, the Tenth Amendment and the principle of reserved powers require that States be allowed to add such qualifications.

Before addressing these arguments, we find it appropriate to take note of the striking unanimity among the courts that have considered the issue. None of the overwhelming array of briefs submitted by the parties and amici has called to our attention even a single case in which a state court or federal court has approved of a State's addition of qualifications for a member of Congress. To the contrary, an impressive number of courts have determined that States lack the authority to add qualifications. . . . This impressive and uniform body of judicial decisions . . . indicates that the obstacles confronting petitioners are formidable indeed.

Petitioners argue that the Constitution contains no express prohibition against state-added qualifications, and that Amendment 73 is therefore an appropriate exercise of a State's reserved power to place additional restrictions on the choices that its own voters may make. We disagree for two independent reasons. First, we conclude that the power to add qualifications is not within the "original powers" of the States, and thus is not reserved to the States by the Tenth Amendment. Second, even if States possessed some original power in this area, we conclude that the Framers intended the Constitution to be the exclusive source of qualifications for members of Congress, and that the Framers thereby "divested" States of any power to add qualifications. . . .

Contrary to petitioners' assertions, the power to add qualifications is not part of the original powers of sovereignty that the Tenth Amendment reserved to the States. Petitioners' Tenth Amendment argument misconceives the nature of the right at issue because that Amendment could only "reserve" that which existed before. As Justice Story recognized, "the states can exercise no powers whatsoever, which exclusively spring out of the existence of the national government, which the Constitution does not delegate to them. . . . No state can say, that it has reserved, what it never possessed." . . .

With respect to setting qualifications for service in Congress, no such right existed before the Constitution was ratified. The contrary argument overlooks the revolutionary character of the government that the Framers conceived. Prior to the adoption of the Constitution, the States joined together under the Articles of Confederation. In that system, "the States retained most of their sovereignty, like independent nations bound together only by treaties." After the Constitutional Convention convened, the Framers were presented with, and eventually adopted a variation of, "a plan not merely to amend the Articles of Confederation but to create an entirely new government with a National Executive, National Judiciary, and a National Legislature." In adopting that plan, the Framers envisioned a uniform national system, rejecting the notion that the Nation was a collection of States, and instead creating a direct link between the National Government and the people of the United States. In that National Government, representatives owe primary allegiance not to the people of a State but to the people of a Nation. . . .

In short, as the Framers recognized, electing representatives to the National Legislature was a new right, arising from the Constitution itself. The Tenth Amendment thus provides no basis for concluding that the States possess reserved power to add qualifications to those that are fixed in the Constitution. Instead, any state power to set the qualifications for membership in Congress must derive not from the reserved powers of state sovereignty, but rather from the delegated powers of national sovereignty. In the absence of any constitutional delegation to the States of power to add qualifications to those enumerated in the Constitution, such a power does not exist.

Even if we believed that States possessed as part of their original powers some control over congressional qualifications, the text and structure of the Constitution, the relevant historical materials, and, most importantly, the "basic principles of our democratic system" all demonstrate that the Qualifications Clauses were intended to preclude the States from exercising any such power and to fix as exclusive the qualifications in the Constitution. . . .

The available affirmative evidence indicates the Framers' intent that States have no role in the setting of qualifications. . . .

We find compelling the complete absence in the ratification debates of any assertion that States had the power to add qualifications. In those debates, the question whether to require term limits, or "rotation," was a major source of controversy. The draft of the Constitution that was submitted for ratification contained no provision for rotation. In arguments that echo in the preamble to Arkansas' Amendment 73, opponents of ratification condemned the absence of a rotation requirement, noting that "there is no doubt that senators will hold their office perpetually; and in this situation, they must of necessity lose their dependence, and their attachments to the people." . . . At several ratification conventions, participants proposed amendments that would have required rotation.

The Federalists' responses to those criticisms and proposals addressed the merits of the issue, arguing that rotation was incompatible with the people's right to choose . . . . Hamilton argued that the representatives' need for reelection rather than mandatory rotation was the more effective way to keep representatives responsive to the people, because "when a man knows he must quit his station, let his merit be what it may, he will turn his attention chiefly to his own emolument."

Regardless of which side has the better of the debate over rotation, it is most striking that nowhere in the extensive ratification debates have we found any statement by either a proponent or an opponent of rotation that the draft constitution would permit States to require rotation for the representatives of their own citizens. . . .

Our conclusion that States lack the power to impose qualifications vindicates the same "fundamental principle of our representative democracy" that we recognized in *Powell*, namely that "the people should choose whom they please to govern them."

. . . [S]tate-imposed restrictions, unlike the congressionally imposed restrictions at issue in *Powell*, also violate [an] idea central to this basic principle: that the right to choose representatives belongs not to the States, but to the people. . . .

Petitioners attempt to overcome this . . . evidence against the States' power to impose qualifications by arguing that the practice of the States immediately after the adoption of the Constitution demonstrates their understanding that they possessed such power. One may properly question the extent to which the States' own practice is a reliable indicator of the contours of restrictions that the Constitution imposed on States, especially when no court has ever upheld a state-imposed qualification of any sort. . . . But petitioners' argument is unpersuasive even on its own terms. At the time of the Convention, "almost all the State Constitutions required members of their Legislatures to possess considerable property." Despite this near uniformity, only one State, Virginia, placed similar restrictions on members of Congress, requiring that a representative be . . . a "freeholder." Just 15 years after imposing a property qualification, Virginia replaced that requirement with a provision requiring that representatives be only "qualified according to the constitution of the United States." . . .

In sum, the available historical and textual evidence, read in light of the basic principles of democracy underlying the Constitution and recognized by this Court in *Powell*, reveal the Framers' intent that neither Congress nor the States should possess the power to supplement the exclusive qualifications set forth in the text of the Constitution.

Petitioners argue that, even if States may not add qualifications, Amendment 73 is constitutional because it is not such a qualification, and because Amendment 73 is a permissible exercise of state power to regulate the "Times, Places and Manner of Holding Elections." We reject these contentions.

Unlike §1 and §2 of Amendment 73, which create absolute bars to service for long-term incumbents running for state office, §3 merely provides that certain Senators and Representatives shall not be certified as candidates and shall not have their names appear on the ballot. They may run as write-in candidates and, if elected, they may serve. Petitioners contend that only a legal bar to service creates an impermissible qualification, and that Amendment 73 is therefore consistent with the Constitution. . . .

We need not decide whether petitioners' narrow understanding of qualifications is correct because, even if it is, Amendment 73 may not stand. As we have often noted, "'constitutional rights would be of little value if they could be . . . indirectly denied.'" The Constitution "nullifies sophisticated as well as simple-minded modes" of infringing on Constitutional protections.

In our view, Amendment 73 is an indirect attempt to accomplish what the Constitution prohibits Arkansas from accomplishing directly. As the plurality opinion of the Arkansas Supreme Court recognized, Amendment 73 is an "effort to dress eligibility to stand for Congress in ballot access clothing," because the "intent and the effect of Amendment 73 are to disqualify congressional incumbents from further service." . . . Indeed, it cannot be seriously contended that the intent behind Amendment 73 is other than to prevent the election of incumbents. The preamble of Amendment 73 states explicitly: "The people of Arkansas . . . herein limit the terms of elected officials." Sections 1 and 2 create absolute limits on the number of terms that may be served. There is no hint that §3 was intended to have any other purpose.

Petitioners do, however, contest the Arkansas Supreme Court's conclusion that the Amendment has the same practical effect as an absolute bar. They argue that the possibility of a write-in campaign creates a real possibility for victory, especially for an entrenched incumbent. One may reasonably question the merits of that contention. . . . But even if petitioners are correct that incumbents may occasionally win reelection as write-in candidates, there is no denying that the ballot restrictions will make it significantly more difficult for the barred candidate to win the election. In our view, an amendment with the avowed purpose and obvious effect of evading the requirements of the Qualifications Clauses by handicapping a class of candidates cannot stand. . . .

The merits of term limits, or "rotation," have been the subject of debate since the formation of our Constitution, when the Framers unanimously rejected a proposal to add such limits to the Constitution. The cogent arguments on both sides of the question that were articulated during the process of ratification largely retain their force today. Over half the States have adopted measures that impose such limits on some offices either directly or indirectly, and the Nation as a whole, notably by constitutional amendment, has imposed a limit on the number of terms that the President may serve. Term limits, like any other qualification for office, unquestionably restrict the ability of voters to vote for whom they wish. On the other hand, such limits may provide for the infusion of fresh ideas and new perspectives, and may decrease the likelihood that representatives will lose touch with their constituents. It is not our province to resolve this longstanding debate.

We are, however, firmly convinced that allowing the several States to adopt term limits for congressional service would effect a fundamental change in the constitutional framework. Any such change must come not by legislation adopted either by Congress or by an individual State, but rather—as have other important changes in the electoral process—through the Amendment procedures set forth in Article V. The Framers decided that the qualifications for service in the Congress of the United States be fixed in the Constitution and be uniform throughout the Nation. That decision reflects the Framers' understanding that Members of Congress are chosen by separate constituencies, but that they become, when elected, servants of the people of the United States. They are not merely delegates appointed by separate, sovereign States; they occupy offices that are integral and essential components of a single National Government. In the absence of a properly passed constitutional amendment, allowing individual States to craft their own qualifications for Congress would thus erode the structure envisioned by the Framers, a structure that was designed, in the words of the Preamble to our Constitution, to form a "more perfect Union."

The judgment is affirmed.

It is so ordered.

JUSTICE THOMAS, with whom THE CHIEF JUSTICE, JUSTICE O'CONNOR, and JUSTICE SCALIA join, dissenting.

It is ironic that the Court bases today's decision on the right of the people to "choose whom they please to govern them." Under our Constitution, there is only one State whose people have the right to "choose whom they please" to represent Arkansas in Congress. The Court holds, however, that neither the elected legislature of that State nor the people themselves (acting by ballot initiative) may prescribe any qualifications for those representatives. The majority therefore defends the right of the people of Arkansas to "choose whom they please to govern them" by invalidating a provision that won nearly 60% of the votes cast in a direct election and that carried every congressional district in the State.

I dissent. Nothing in the Constitution deprives the people of each State of the power to prescribe eligibility requirements for the candidates who seek to represent them in Congress. The Constitution is simply silent on this question. And where the Constitution is silent, it raises no bar to action by the States or the people.

Because the majority fundamentally misunderstands the notion of "reserved" powers, I start with some first principles. Contrary to the majority's suggestion, the people of the States need not point to any affirmative grant of power in the Constitution in order to prescribe qualifications for their representatives in Congress, or to authorize their elected state legislators to do so.

Our system of government rests on one overriding principle: all power stems from the consent of the people. To phrase the principle in this way, however, is to be imprecise about something important to the notion of "reserved" powers. The ultimate source of the Constitution's authority is the consent of the people of each individual State, not the consent of the undifferentiated people of the Nation as a whole. . . .

When they adopted the Federal Constitution, of course, the people of each State surrendered some of their authority to the United States (and hence to entities accountable to the people of other States as well as to themselves). They affirmatively deprived their States of certain powers and they affirmatively conferred certain powers upon the Federal Government. Because the people of the several States are the only true source of power, however, the Federal Government enjoys no authority beyond what the Constitution confers: the Federal Government's powers are limited and enumerated. In the words of Justice Black, "the United States is entirely a creature of the Constitution. Its power and authority have no other source."

In each State, the remainder of the people's powers—"the powers not delegated to the United States by the Constitution, nor prohibited by it to the States,"—are either delegated to the state government or retained by the people. The Federal Constitution does not specify which of these two possibilities obtains; it is up to the various state constitutions to declare which powers the people of each State have delegated to their state government. As far as the Federal Constitution is concerned, then, the States can exercise all powers that the Constitution does not withhold from them. The Federal Government and the States thus face different default rules: where the Constitution is silent about the exercise of a particular power—that is, where the Constitution does not speak either expressly or by necessary implication—the Federal Government lacks that power and the States enjoy it.

These basic principles are enshrined in the Tenth Amendment, which declares that all powers neither delegated to the Federal Government nor prohibited to the States "are reserved to the States respectively, or to the people." With this careful last phrase, the Amendment avoids taking any position on the division of power between the state governments and the people of the States: it is up to the people of each State to determine which "reserved" powers their state government may exercise. . . .

The majority begins by announcing an enormous and untenable limitation on the principle expressed by the Tenth Amendment. According to the majority, the States possess only those powers that the Constitution affirmatively grants to them or that they enjoyed before the Constitution was adopted; the Tenth Amendment "could only 'reserve' that which existed before." From the fact that the States had not previously enjoyed any powers over the particular institutions of the Federal Government established by the Constitution, the majority derives a rule precisely opposite to the one that the Amendment actually prescribes: "The states can exercise no powers whatsoever, which exclusively spring out of the existence of the national government, which the constitution does not delegate to them."

. . . Given the fundamental principle that all governmental powers stem from the people of the States, it would simply be incoherent to assert that the people of the States could not reserve any powers that they had not previously controlled.

The Tenth Amendment's use of the word "reserved" does not help the majority's position. If someone says that the power to use a particular facility is reserved to some group, he is not saying anything about whether that group has previously used the facility. He is merely saying that the people who control the facility have designated that group as the entity with authority to use it. The Tenth Amendment is similar: the people of the States, from whom all governmental powers stem, have specified that all powers not prohibited to the States by the Federal Constitution are reserved "to the States respectively, or to the people."

The majority is therefore quite wrong to conclude that the people of the States cannot authorize their state governments to exercise any powers that were unknown to the States when the Federal Constitution was drafted. Indeed, the majority's position frustrates the apparent purpose of the Amendment's final phrase. The Amendment does not pre-empt any limitations on state power found in the state constitutions, as it might have done if it simply had said that the powers not delegated to the Federal Government are reserved to the States. But the Amendment also does not prevent the people of the States from amending their state constitutions to remove limitations that were in effect when the Federal Constitution and the Bill of Rights were ratified. . . .

I take it to be established, then, that the people of Arkansas do enjoy "reserved" powers over the selection of their representatives in Congress. . . . Whatever one might think of the wisdom of this arrangement, we may not override the decision of the people of Arkansas unless something in the Federal Constitution deprives them of the power to enact such measures.

The majority settles on "the Qualifications Clauses" as the constitutional provisions that Amendment 73 violates. . . . [T]he Qualifications Clauses are merely straightforward recitations of the minimum eligibility requirements that the Framers thought it essential for every Member of Congress to meet. They restrict state power only in that they prevent the States from abolishing all eligibility requirements for membership in Congress. . . .

. . . To the extent that they bear on this case, the records of the Philadelphia Convention affirmatively support my unwillingness to find hidden meaning in the Qualifications Clauses, while the surviving records from the ratification debates help neither side. As for the post-ratification period, five States supplemented the constitutional disqualifications in their very first election laws. The historical evidence thus refutes any notion that the Qualifications Clauses were generally understood to be exclusive. Yet the majority must establish just such an understanding in order to justify its position that the Clauses impose unstated prohibitions on the States and the people. In my view, the historical evidence is simply inadequate to warrant the majority's conclusion that the Qualifications Clauses mean anything more than what they say.

The decision in *U.S. Term Limits v. Thornton*, coupled with the *Powell* ruling, authoritatively settled the issue of qualifications for congressional office. The Constitution's age, residency, and citizenship requirements are a complete statement of congressional eligibility standards. Neither Congress nor the states may add to or delete from those requirements. According to the Court, such alterations to the requirements for membership in the federal legislature could be imposed only by constitutional amendment.

The term limit question, however, remained a hot political topic—so much so that at least one state took direct action to circumvent the Court's decision. In response to *U.S. Term Limits,* voters in Missouri adopted an amendment (Article VIII) to their state constitution with the aim of bringing about a "congressional term limits amendment" to the federal Constitution. Article VIII required that the words "Disregarded Voters' Instruction on Term Limits" be put on the ballot near the name of any incumbent who had not taken specific actions in Congress to support a term limits amendment to the U.S. Constitution, and nonincumbents who had not taken a pledge to support term limits were to have the words "Declined to Pledge to Support Term Limits" printed on the ballot near their names. Donald Gralike, a nonincumbent candidate for the U.S. House of Representatives, challenged Missouri's Article VIII on federal constitutional grounds. And, in *Cook v. Gralike* (2001), he prevailed in the U.S. Supreme Court. Writing for the Court, Justice Stevens relied on the

BOX 3-2   PRIVILEGES AND IMMUNITIES FOR LEGISLATORS IN GLOBAL PERSPECTIVE

MOST democracies provide protection for legislators similar to the U.S. Constitution's speech or debate clause, but these countries have put their own twists on it. In Brazil, for example, legislators "shall enjoy civil and criminal immunity for any of their opinions, words and votes." The Brazilian Constitution also says that legislators may not be arrested "except in flagrante delicto [in the act of] for a non-bailable crime." But even then the police report is sent to the member's chamber, which decides on imprisonment by a majority vote. This is similar to Denmark's constitution: members cannot be "prosecuted or imprisoned in any manner," unless the legislature consents or the member is caught red-handed. The Israeli Constitution, in contrast, provides members of its legislature with immunity but the "particulars shall be prescribed by Law."

Some countries do have mechanisms for redress for people who believe they have been hurt by legislators. Australia provides an interesting example. Although members of its parliament are immune from defamation suits for statements they make on the floor, its senate allows people who believe they have been defamed to request that body to allow them to reply to such statements in the senate's published record.

SOURCES: The Constitute Project, at https://www.constituteproject .org/; George Thomas Kurian, *World Encyclopedia of Parliaments and Legislatures* (Washington, DC: Congressional Quarterly, 1998).

logic of his majority opinion in *Thornton* to conclude that Article VIII was an unconstitutional effort on the part of a state to add qualifications for office.

Speech or Debate Clause

The Court's reading of the Constitution in *Powell* protects those who have been duly elected to Congress and meet the qualifications of office from being excluded by members of their own branch. The Constitution also contains a safeguard against harassment or intimidation by the executive branch. Article I, Section 6, specifies:

The Senators and Representatives . . . shall in all Cases, except Treason, Felony, and Breach of the Peace, be privileged from Arrest during their Attendance at the Session of their respective Houses, and in going to and returning from the same; and for any Speech or Debate in either House, they shall not be questioned in any other Place.

Called the speech or debate clause, this privilege of membership derives from British practice. The English Parliament, during its struggles with the Crown, asserted that its members were immune from arrest during its sessions, and the English Bill of Rights embodies this guarantee.

The importance of the speech or debate clause's protection is undeniable: without it, a president could order the arrest of, or otherwise intimidate, members of Congress who disagree publicly with the administration.

The framers thought the statement was necessary "to protect the integrity of the legislative process by insuring the independence of individual legislators."[14] Other countries apparently share this sentiment. Whether in their constitutions or by law, many democracies throughout the world provide similar protection for their legislators *(see box 3-2)*.

The language of Article I, Section 6 of the U.S. Constitution has generated two kinds of constitutional questions: What is protected and who is protected? The Court first addressed the reach of the speech or debate clause in *Kilbourn v. Thompson* (1881). Though the justices dealt primarily with the scope of congressional investigations, they noted that the clause extends to

written reports presented . . . by its committees, to resolutions offered, which, though in writing, must be reproduced in speech, and to the act of voting, whether it is done vocally or by passing between the tellers. In short, to things generally done in a session [of Congress] by one of its members in relation to the business before it.

With only some minor modifications, *Kilbourn* remained the Court's most significant statement on the clause until 1972, when *Gravel v. United States* was decided. This case had important implications for both dimensions of Section 6: Who is protected and what is protected?

14. *United States v. Brewster* (1972).

Senator Mike Gravel whose release of the classified Pentagon Papers led to a major Supreme Court interpretation of the speech or debate clause.

Gravel v. United States

408 U.S. 606 (1972)
http://laws.findlaw.com/us/408/606.html
Oral arguments are available at https://www.oyez.org.
Vote: 5 (Blackmun, Burger, Powell, Rehnquist, White)
     4 (Brennan, Douglas, Marshall, Stewart)

OPINION OF THE COURT: *White*
DISSENTING OPINIONS: *Brennan, Douglas*
DISSENTING IN PART: *Stewart*

FACTS:

On June 29, 1971, Senator Mike Gravel (D-Alaska) held a public meeting of the Subcommittee on Buildings and Grounds, of which he was the chair. Before the hearing began, Gravel made a statement about the Vietnam War, noting that it was "relevant to his subcommittee . . . because of its effects upon the domestic economy and . . . the lack of federal funds to provide for adequate public facilities." He then read portions of a classified government document, now known as the Pentagon Papers, that provided a history of U.S. involvement in the war. After he finished, Gravel introduced the forty-seven-volume document into the committee's record and "arranged, without any personal profit to himself, for its verbatim publication by Beacon Press," a publishing division of the Unitarian Universalist Association. At the time, there were also reports in the press that members of Gravel's staff had talked with Howard Webber, director of MIT Press, about possible publication of the documents.

The Justice Department began an investigation to determine how the Pentagon Papers had been released. It requested a district court judge to convene a grand jury, which in turn subpoenaed Dr. Leonard Rodberg, an aide to Senator Gravel; Webber; and, later, the publisher of Beacon Press. Rodberg and Gravel asked the court to quash the subpoena. In their view, U.S. attorneys "intended to interrogate Dr. Rodberg" about "the actions of Senator Gravel and his aides in making available" the Pentagon Papers.

The government initially rejected all of Gravel's claims; it even argued that Gravel's actions remained outside constitutional protections. By the time the case reached the Supreme Court, however, the government had limited its charges to Gravel's aide and the publisher. Even so, *Gravel v. United States* continued to raise the classic questions: Who is covered and what is covered under the speech or debate clause?

ARGUMENTS:

For the petitioner, Mike Gravel:

- The interrogation of Rodberg would violate the speech or debate clause because its scope extends to aides. The realities of the modern-day legislative process require members of Congress to seek advice and assistance from their staff. Because forcing Rodberg to testify would be tantamount to having Gravel do so, both are protected.
- Forcing Webber and the publisher of Beacon Press to testify also would violate the speech or debate clause. Gravel's arrangements for private publication of the documents come under the protection of the speech or debate clause because those documents had been introduced in Congress.

For the respondent, United States:

- The language of the speech or debate clause, past precedents, and the intent of the framers all point to the same conclusion: its reach covers neither congressional aides nor arrangements with private publishers, even for material introduced into a subcommittee record.
- Abuses can arise when members of the House and Senate have the power to exempt others from criminal or civil laws.

◆ OPINION OF THE COURT BY MR. JUSTICE WHITE . . .

[T]he United States strongly urges that because the Speech or Debate Clause confers a privilege only upon "Senators and Representatives," Rodberg himself has no valid claim to constitutional immunity from grand jury inquiry. In our view, both courts below correctly rejected this position. We agree with the Court of Appeals that for the purpose of construing the privilege a Member and his aide are to be "treated as one." . . . [I]t is literally impossible, in view of the complexities of the modern legislative process, . . . for Members of Congress to perform their legislative tasks without the help of aides and assistants; the day-to-day work of such aides is so critical to the Members' performance that they must be treated as the latter's alter egos; and that if they are not so recognized, the central role of the Speech or Debate Clause—to prevent intimidation of legislators by the Executive and accountability before a possibly hostile judiciary—will inevitably be diminished and frustrated. . . .

Rather than giving the clause a cramped construction, the Court has sought to implement its fundamental purpose of freeing the legislator from executive and judicial oversight that realistically threatens to control his conduct as a legislator. We have little doubt that we are neither exceeding our judicial powers nor mistakenly construing the Constitution by holding that the Speech or Debate Clause applies not only to a Member but also to his aides insofar as the conduct of the latter would be a protected legislative act if performed by the Member himself. . . .

The United States fears the abuses that history reveals have occurred when legislators are invested with the power to relieve others from the operation of otherwise valid civil and criminal laws. But these abuses . . . are for the most part obviated if the privilege applicable to the aide is viewed . . . as the privilege of the Senator, and invocable only by the Senator or by the aide on the Senator's behalf, and if in all events the privilege available to the aide is confined to those services that would be immune legislative conduct if performed by the Senator himself. This view places beyond the Speech or Debate Clause a variety of services characteristically performed by aides for Members of Congress, even though within the scope of their employment. It likewise provides no protection for criminal conduct threatening the security of the person or property of others, whether performed at the direction of the Senator in preparation for or in execution of a legislative act or done without his knowledge or direction.

Neither does it immunize Senator or aide from testifying at trials or grand jury proceedings involving third-party crimes where the questions do not require testimony about or impugn a legislative act. Thus our refusal to distinguish between Senator and aide in applying the Speech or Debate Clause does not mean that Rodberg is for all purposes exempt from grand jury questioning.

We are convinced also that the Court of Appeals correctly determined that Senator Gravel's alleged arrangement with Beacon Press to publish the Pentagon Papers was not protected speech or debate within the meaning of Art. I, §6, cl. 1, of the Constitution. . . .

The heart of the Clause is speech or debate in either House. Insofar as the Clause is construed to reach other matters, they must be an integral part of the deliberative and communicative processes by which Members participate in committee and House proceedings with respect to the consideration and passage or rejection of proposed legislation or with respect to other matters which the Constitution places within the jurisdiction of either House. As the Court of Appeals put it, the courts have extended the privilege to matters beyond pure speech or debate in either House, but "only when necessary to prevent indirect impairment of such deliberations."

Here, private publication by Senator Gravel through the cooperation of Beacon Press was in no way essential to the deliberations of the Senate; nor does questioning as to private publication threaten the integrity or independence of the Senate by impermissibly exposing its deliberations to executive influence. The Senator had conducted his hearings; the record and any report that was forthcoming were available both to his committee and the Senate. Insofar as we are advised, neither Congress nor the full committee ordered or authorized the publication. We cannot but conclude that the Senator's arrangements with Beacon Press were not part and parcel of the legislative process. . . .

The Speech or Debate Clause does not in our view extend immunity to Rodberg, as a Senator's aide, from testifying before the grand jury about the arrangement between Senator Gravel and Beacon Press or about his own participation, if any, in the alleged transaction, so long as legislative acts of the Senator are not impugned. . . .

Rodberg's immunity . . . extends only to legislative acts as to which the Senator himself would be immune. The grand jury, therefore, if relevant to its investigation into the possible violations of the criminal law, . . . may require from Rodberg answers to questions relating to his or the Senator's arrangements, if any, with respect to republication or with respect to third-party conduct under valid investigation by the grand jury, as long as the questions do not implicate legislative action of the Senator. Neither do we perceive any constitutional or other privilege that shields Rodberg, any more than any other witness, from grand jury questions relevant to tracing the source of obviously highly classified documents that came into the Senator's possession and are the basic subject matter of inquiry in this case, as long as no legislative act is implicated by the questions.

Because the Speech or Debate Clause privilege applies both to Senator and aide, it appears to us that paragraph one of the order, alone, would afford ample protection of the privilege if it forbade questioning any witness, including Rodberg: (1) concerning the Senator's conduct, or the conduct of his aides, at the June 29, 1971, meeting of the subcommittee; (2) concerning the motives and purposes behind the Senator's conduct, or that of his aides, at that meeting; (3) concerning communications between the Senator and his aides during the term of their employment and related to said meeting or any other legislative act of the Senator; (4) except as it proves relevant to investigating possible third-party crime, concerning any act, in itself not criminal, performed by the Senator, or by his aides in the course of their employment, in preparation for the subcommittee hearing. We leave the final form of such an order to the Court of Appeals in the first instance, or, if that court prefers, to the District Court.

The judgment of the Court of Appeals is vacated and the cases are remanded to that court for further proceedings consistent with this opinion.

So ordered.

MR. JUSTICE STEWART, *dissenting in part.*
The Court . . . decides . . . that a Member of Congress may, despite the Speech or Debate Clause, be compelled to testify before a grand jury concerning the sources of information used by him in the performance of his legislative duties, if such an inquiry "proves relevant to investigating possible third-party crime." In my view, this ruling is highly dubious in view of the basic purpose of the Speech or Debate Clause—"to prevent intimidation [of members of Congress] by the executive and accountability before a possibly hostile judiciary."

Under the Court's ruling, a Congressman may be subpoenaed by a vindictive Executive to testify about informants who have not committed crimes and who have no knowledge of crime. Such compulsion can occur,

because the judiciary has traditionally imposed virtually no limitations on the grand jury's broad investigatory powers; grand jury investigations are not limited in scope to specific criminal acts, and standards of materiality and relevance are greatly relaxed. But even if the Executive had reason to believe that a Member of Congress had knowledge of a specific probable violation of law, it is by no means clear to me that the Executive's interest in the administration of justice must always override the public interest in having an informed Congress. Why should we not, given the tension between two competing interests, each of constitutional dimensions, balance the claims of the Speech or Debate Clause against the claims of the grand jury in the particularized contexts of specific cases? And why are not the Houses of Congress the proper institutions in most situations to impose sanctions upon a Representative or Senator who withholds information about crime acquired in the course of his legislative duties?

MR. JUSTICE BRENNAN, *with whom MR. JUSTICE DOUGLAS, and MR. JUSTICE MARSHALL, join, dissenting.*
My concern is with the narrow scope accorded the Speech or Debate Clause by today's decision. I fully agree with the Court that a Congressman's immunity under the Clause must also be extended to his aides if it is to be at all effective. . . .

[But] in holding that Senator Gravel's alleged arrangement with Beacon Press to publish the Pentagon Papers is not shielded from extra-senatorial inquiry by the Speech or Debate Clause, the Court adopts what for me is a far too narrow view of the legislative function. The Court seems to assume that words spoken in debate or written in congressional reports are protected by the Clause, so that if Senator Gravel had recited part of the Pentagon Papers on the Senate floor or copied them into a Senate report, those acts could not be questioned "in any other Place." Yet because he sought a wider audience, to publicize information deemed relevant to matters pending before his own committee, the Senator suddenly loses his immunity and is exposed to grand jury investigation and possible prosecution for the republication. The explanation for this anomalous result is the Court's belief that "Speech or Debate" encompasses only acts necessary to the internal deliberations of Congress concerning proposed legislation. "Here," according to the Court, "private publication by Senator Gravel through the cooperation of Beacon Press was in no way essential to the deliberations of the Senate." Therefore, "the Senator's arrangements with Beacon Press were not part and parcel of the legislative process."

Thus, the Court excludes from the sphere of protected legislative activity a function that I had supposed lay at the heart of our democratic system. I speak, of course, of the legislator's duty to inform the public about matters affecting the administration of government. That this "informing function" falls into the class of things "generally done in a session of the House by one of its members in relation to the business before it," *Kilbourn v. Thompson* (1881), was explicitly acknowledged by the Court in *Watkins v. United States* (1957). In speaking of the "power of the Congress to inquire into and publicize corruption, maladministration or inefficiency in agencies of the Government," the Court noted that "from the earliest times in its history, the Congress has assiduously performed an 'informing function' of this nature."

We need look no further than Congress itself to find evidence supporting the Court's observation in *Watkins*. Congress has provided financial support for communications between its Members and the public, including the franking privilege for letters, telephone and telegraph allowances, stationery allotments, and favorable prices on reprints from the Congressional Record. Congressional hearings, moreover, are not confined to gathering information for internal distribution, but are often widely publicized, sometimes televised, as a means of alerting the electorate to matters of public import and concern. The list is virtually endless, but a small sampling of contemporaneous hearings of this kind would certainly include . . . the 1966 hearings on automobile safety and the numerous hearings of the Senate Foreign Relations Committee on the origins and conduct of the war in Vietnam. In short, there can be little doubt that informing the electorate is a thing "generally done" by the Members of Congress "in relation to the business before it." . . .

Unlike the Court, therefore, I think that the activities of Congressmen in communicating with the public are legislative acts protected by the Speech or Debate Clause. I agree with the Court that not every task performed by a legislator is privileged; intervention before Executive departments is one that is not. But the informing function carries a far more persuasive claim to the protections of the Clause. It has been recognized by this Court as something "generally done" by Congressmen, the Congress itself has established special concessions designed to lower the cost of such communication, and, most important, the function furthers several well-recognized goals of representative government. To say in the

face of these facts that the informing function is not privileged merely because it is not necessary to the internal deliberations of Congress is to give the Speech or Debate Clause an artificial and narrow reading unsupported by reason.

Gravel provided some guidance for legislators: the speech or debate clause gave similar protection to the senator and the aide, but that protection was not absolute. Both senator and aide could be questioned for activities that had no direct connection to or "impinged upon" the legislative process.

Despite the specificity of the Court's ruling, it did not put an end to controversies under the speech or debate clause. Indeed, as illustrated in table 3-3, in the 1970s the Court decided several important issues that were left open by *Gravel*. In *United States v. Helstoski* (1979) the justices refused to allow prosecutors to introduce evidence into a court proceeding against a former member of Congress involving legislative activities. *Hutchinson v. Proxmire* (1979), however, was a defeat for congressional authority. Here, the Court examined a dispute arising when Senator William Proxmire (D-Wis.) on the floor of the Senate and later in a newsletter and on television, labeled Ronald R. Hutchinson's federally funded research virtually worthless and a waste of taxpayer money. Hutchinson brought a libel suit against Proxmire; when the case reached the Court the justices addressed the issue of whether the speech or debate clause immunized the senator from a libel proceeding on the ground that he had first made the remarks on the chamber's floor. The Court held that it did not:

A speech by Proxmire in the Senate would be wholly immune and would be available to other Members of Congress and the public in the Congressional Record. But neither the newsletters nor the press release was "essential to the deliberations of the Senate," and neither was part of the deliberative process.

Since *Proxmire*, speech or debate clause cases have not occupied much of the justices' attention, though exceptions occasionally arise. In 2008 the Justice Department asked the Court to review a decision by the U.S. Court of Appeals for the District of Columbia, holding that the speech or debate clause gave members

TABLE 3-3   Speech or Debate Clause Cases after *Gravel v. United States*

CASE	LEGAL QUESTION	COURT'S RESPONSE
United States v. Brewster (1972)	Does the speech or debate clause protect members of Congress from prosecution for alleged bribery to perform a legislative act?	The clause protects members from inquiry into legislative acts; it does not protect all conduct relating to the legislative process.
Doe v. McMillan (1973)	Does the speech or debate clause protect members (and their staff) and other persons who were involved in creating and distributing a report on the D.C. school system that identified, by name, specific children and did so in a negative way?	The clause offers absolute immunity to members and staff, but not to individuals who, acting under congressional authority, distributed the materials.
Eastland v. U.S. Servicemen's Fund (1975)	Does the speech or debate clause protect members against a suit brought by an organization to stop the implementation of a subpoena ordering a bank to produce certain records?	The clause offers absolute protection because the activities fall within the "legitimate legislative" sphere.
Davis v. Passman (1979)	Does the speech or debate clause protect a member against charges of sex discrimination?	The Court decided the case on Fifth Amendment grounds and reached no result on the member's claim that he was protected by the speech or debate clause.
United States v. Helstoski (1979)	Does the speech or debate clause protect a member against prosecution (for accepting bribes) when evidence introduced in that action hinges on past legislative acts?	The clause does not permit the introduction of evidence involving past legislative acts.
Hutchinson v. Proxmire (1979)	Does the speech or debate clause protect a member from a civil suit in response to negative statements made to the press and in newsletters about a government grant awardee's research?	The clause does not protect a member from a libel judgment when information is disseminated to the press and the public through newsletters.

of Congress some protection against searches—with warrants—of their congressional offices. The Justice Department was investigating Representative William Jefferson (D-La.) for allegedly taking bribes, and claimed that the court's ruling would impede its ability to enforce federal law against Jefferson and other lawmakers. The Supreme Court refused to hear the case, *U.S. v. Rayburn House Office Building Room 2113.*

LEGISLATIVE POWERS: SOURCES AND SCOPE

As we noted earlier, Section 8 of Article I contains a virtual laundry list of Congress's powers. These enumerated powers, covered in seventeen clauses, establish congressional authority to regulate commerce, to lay and collect taxes, to establish post offices, and so forth.

These enumerated powers qua powers pose few constitutional problems: because the Constitution names them, Congress clearly possesses them. It is when Congress exercises these powers that questions

can emerge. Some hinge on how to define the power—for example, Congress has the power to "regulate commerce among the states," but what does "commerce" mean? Other questions focus on whether congressional use of an enumerated power violates other constitutional provisions—say, the First Amendment or, more relevant to this volume, structures underlying the Constitution, such as the separation of powers system or federalism.

But what of other sources of legislative authority? For example, does the legislative branch have powers beyond those explicitly specified in the Constitution? Even though the framers may have left this question unaddressed, the Court has answered it affirmatively. As table 3-4 shows the Court has suggested that Congress possesses implied, amendment-enforcing, and inherent powers in addition to those explicitly mentioned in Article I. In this section, we examine the cases in which the Court has located those sources.

We also explore constraints on Congress's ability to exercise these powers. Just as the Court has placed limits on congressional exercise of its enumerated powers,

TABLE 3-4 Sources of Congressional Power

POWER[a]	DEFINED	ILLUSTRATION
Enumerated powers	Those that the Constitution expressly grants	Article I, Section 8. Includes the powers to borrow money, raise armies, and regulate commerce among the states.
Implied powers	Those that may be inferred from power expressly granted	Article I, Section 8, Clauses 2–17, in conjunction with Clause 18, the necessary and proper clause. For example, the enumerated power of raising and supporting armies leads to the implied power of operating a draft.
Amendment-enforcing powers	Those contained in some constitutional amendments that provide Congress with the ability to enforce them	Amendments 13, 14, and 15, for example, state that Congress shall have the power to enforce the article by "appropriate legislation."
Inherent powers	Those that do not depend on constitutional grants but grow out of national sovereignty	Foreign affairs. The national government would have foreign affairs powers even if the Constitution were silent, because these are powers that all nations have under international law. For example, the federal government can issue orders prohibiting U.S. businesses from selling arms to particular nations.

SOURCE: Adapted from Sue Davis and J. W. Peltason, Corwin and Peltason's *Understanding the Constitution*, 16th ed. (Belmont, CA: Wadsworth, 2004), 126.

a. Some analysts suggest that Congress also possesses resulting powers (those that result when several enumerated powers are added together) and inherited powers (those that Congress inherited from the British Parliament, such as the power to investigate).

it has constrained Congress's use of these others. For example, the Court has permitted Congress to conduct hearings and investigations (an unenumerated power), but it also has asserted that the power is not unlimited, that certain restrictions apply.

As you read the next cases, keep in mind not only the sources of legislative power, but also its scope. What limits has the Court placed on Congress and, more important, why? What pressures have been brought to bear on the justices in making their decisions?

Enumerated and Implied Powers

The Constitution's specific list of congressional powers leaves no doubt that Congress has these powers. In *Gibbons v. Ogden* (1824), when the Court was asked to interpret one of its powers, the power to regulate interstate commerce, Chief Justice John Marshall said,

The words [of the Constitution] are, "Congress shall have power to regulate commerce with foreign nations, and among the several States. . . ." The subject to be regulated is commerce, and our constitution being . . . *one of enumeration, and not of definition* [our italics], to ascertain the extent of the power, it becomes necessary to settle the meaning of the word.

In these two sentences, Marshall asserted that Congress indeed has the enumerated power to regulate commerce, but that the Court needed to define what that power entails. This point is important

because the fact that a power is written into the Constitution does not necessarily make the Court's task easier: often it must define how Congress can and cannot make use of that power, as we just suggested. Equally important, recall, is that Congress exercise its powers in ways that do not violate other constitutional provisions or doctrines.

In the chapters to come we consider these two issues as they relate to Congress's enumerated powers to regulate commerce and to tax, among others. For now, we can conclude that virtually no debate ever occurs over whether, in fact, Congress has the powers contained in Article I, Section 8.

Necessary and Proper Clause. The question that does deserve attention is whether Congress has more powers, or was intended to have more powers, than those specifically granted. And if so, how broad should they be? Those who look to the plain language of the Constitution or to the intent of the framers find few concrete answers, although both camps would point to the same clause. Article I, Section 8, Clause 18, provides that Congress shall have the power "to make all Laws which shall be necessary and proper for carrying into Execution the foregoing Powers, and all other Powers vested by this Constitution in the Government of the United States, or in any Department or Officer thereof."

Called by various names—the necessary and proper clause, the elastic clause, the sweeping clause—this provision was the subject of heated debate early in the nation's history. Many affiliated with the Federalist Party, which favored a strong national government, argued for a loose construction of the clause. In their view, the framers inserted it into the Constitution to provide Congress with some "flexibility"; in other words, Congress could exercise powers beyond those listed in the Constitution, those that were "necessary and proper" for implementing legislative activity. The Jeffersonians asserted the need for a strict interpretation of the clause; in their view, it constricted rather than expanded congressional powers. In other words, under the necessary and proper clause Congress could exercise only that power necessary to carry out its enumerated functions.

Which view would the Supreme Court adopt? Would it interpret the necessary and proper clause strictly or loosely? This was one of two major questions at the core of *McCulloch v. Maryland* (1819),[15] which many consider the Court's most important explication of congressional powers, as well as Chief Justice Marshall's finest. As you read this case, consider not only the Court's holding but also the language and logic of *McCulloch*. Why is it such an extraordinary statement?

McCulloch v. Maryland

17 U.S. (4 Wheat.) 316 (1819)
http://laws.findlaw.com/us/17/316.html
Vote: 6 (Duvall, Johnson, Livingston, Marshall, Story, Washington)
      0

OPINION OF THE COURT: *Marshall*
NOT PARTICIPATING: *Todd*

FACTS:

Although Americans take for granted the power of the federal government to operate a banking system—today called the Federal Reserve System—in the late eighteenth and early nineteenth centuries this topic was a political battleground. The first sign of controversy appeared in 1791 when George Washington's secretary of the Treasury, Alexander Hamilton, asked Congress to adopt a comprehensive economic plan for the new nation. Among the proposals was the creation of a Bank of the United States, which would receive deposits, disburse funds, and make loans; Congress responded with a bill authorizing the first federal bank.

When the bill arrived at President Washington's desk, however, he did not sign it immediately. He wanted to ascertain whether in fact Congress could create a bank, since it lacked explicit constitutional authority to do so. To this end he asked Hamilton, Secretary of State Thomas Jefferson, and Attorney General Edmund Randolph for their opinions on the bank's constitutionality.

Box 3-3 presents excerpts of Hamilton's and Jefferson's responses. We offer them not only because the two men reached different conclusions—Hamilton argued that the bank was constitutional, Jefferson that it was not—but also because the arguments represent the classic competing theories of congressional power. As historian Melvin I. Urofsky puts it, "Where Jefferson . . . argued that Congress could only do what the Constitution expressly permitted it do, Hamilton claims that Congress could do everything except what the Constitution specifically forbade."[16] The debates may also illustrate the limits of originalism as a method of constitutional interpretation. Does it seem odd that just four years after the writing of the Constitution, two of the nation's foremost leaders could have such different views? In his argument, Hamilton, in fact, noted that there was a "conflicting recollection" of a convention debate highly relevant to the bank issue.[17] In the end, Hamilton persuaded the president to sign the bill. Congress then created the First Bank of the United States in 1791 and granted it a twenty-year charter.

Nevertheless, the bank controversy did not disappear. As we illustrate in figure 3-1, which superimposes the bank's history (and that of its successor) on concurrent political and economic events, it is clear why the bank remained in the spotlight. Most important was that it became a symbol of the loose-construction, nationally oriented Federalist Party, which had lost considerable power from its heyday in the 1790s. Indeed, at the close of the eighteenth century, a strict-construction approach to congressional power was among the primary ideas endorsed by the Federalists' competitors, the Jeffersonian Republicans. Even though the bank had done an able job, to no one's

---

15. The other question involved federalism. See chapter 6.

16. Melvin I. Urofsky, *Supreme Decisions: Great Constitutional Cases and Their Impact* (Boulder, CO: Westview Press, 2012), 19.

17. One scholar notes that the framers rejected a proposal that would have allowed Congress to establish corporations; in fact, they did so in part because of the possibility that Congress would create banks. See Jethro K. Lieberman, *Milestones!* (St. Paul, MN: West, 1976), 19. Still, Hamilton argued that debate was unclear.

surprise the Republican Congress refused to renew its charter in 1811.

After the War of 1812, it became apparent even to the Republicans that Congress should recharter the bank. During the war the lack of a national bank for purposes of borrowing money and transferring funds became a source of embarrassment to the administration. Moreover, with the absence of a federal bank, state-chartered institutions flooded the market with worthless notes, contributing to economic problems throughout the country. Amid renewed controversy and cries for strict constructionism, Congress in 1816 created the Second Bank of the United States, granting it a twenty-year charter and $35 million in capital.

Some scholars have suggested that a challenge to the new bank was inevitable, primarily because the Supreme Court had never decided whether the first bank was constitutional. It is possible, however, that litigation would not have materialized had the second bank performed as well as its predecessor did, but it did not. It flourished during the postwar economic boom, mainly because it was fiscally aggressive and encouraged speculative investing. These practices caught up to bank officials when, in 1818, in anticipation of a recession, they began calling in the bank's outstanding loans. As a result, they caused overextended banks to fail throughout the South and West. To make matters worse, accusations of fraud and embezzlement were rampant in several of the bank's eighteen branches, particularly in Maryland, Pennsylvania, and Virginia. Among those most seriously implicated was James McCulloch, the cashier of the Baltimore branch bank and its main lobbyist in Washington. According to some accounts, his illegal financial schemes had cost the branch more than $1 million.

In response to these allegations, Congress began to hold hearings on the bank, and some states reacted by attempting to regulate branches located within their borders. Maryland mandated that branches of the bank in the state pay either a 2 percent tax on all banknotes or a fee of $15,000. When a state official came to collect from the Baltimore branch, McCulloch refused to pay and, by refusing, set the stage for a monumental confrontation between the United States and Maryland on not one but two major issues. The first involved the bank itself: Did Congress, in the absence of an explicit constitutional authorization, have the power to charter the bank? Second, did the state exceed its powers by seeking to tax a federal entity?

By the time the case reached the Supreme Court, it was clear that something significant was going to happen. The Court reporter noted that *McCulloch* involved "a constitutional question of great importance." The justices waived their rule that permitted only two attorneys per side "and allowed three each."[18] Oral arguments took nine days.

Both sides were ably represented. Some commentators praise Daniel Webster's oratory for the federal government's side as extraordinary, and we enumerate some of his claims below. But it was former attorney general and U.S. senator William Pinkney with whom the Court was most taken. Justice Joseph Story said later, "I never, in my whole life, heard a greater speech."[19] The gist of his arguments (and those of his colleagues) was familiar stuff; Pinkney largely reiterated Hamilton's original defense of the bank, particularly his interpretation of the necessary and proper clause.

Maryland's legal representation may have appeared less astute. According to one account, "it has been rumored" that one of the state's lawyers, Attorney General Luther Martin, "was drunk when he made his two-day-long argument. If he was, it apparently did not affect his acuity." For his side, he reiterated parts of Jefferson's argument against the bank, added some on the subject of states' rights, and read some of the speeches John Marshall had delivered at the Virginia convention.[20] Another attorney for the state, Joseph Hopkinson, seemed to take a somewhat different tack, as we detail below.

ARGUMENTS:

For the plaintiff in error, James McCulloch:

- The question of whether Congress constitutionally possesses the power to incorporate a bank arose after the adoption of the Constitution and was settled in the First Congress after extensive discussion. Arguments in the bank's favor were presented, with force, by Secretary of the Treasury Alexander Hamilton in his report to the president of the United States.

- Many of those who initially doubted the existence of the power to create the bank now view it as a

---

18. Quoted in Fred W. Friendly and Martha J. H. Elliot, *The Constitution: That Delicate Balance* (New York: Random House, 1984), 256.

19. Quoted in Lieberman, *Milestones!*, 122.

20. Farber and Sherry, *A History of the American Constitution*, 357.

BOX 3-3   JEFFERSON AND HAMILTON ON THE BANK OF THE UNITED STATES

Opinion on The Constitutionality of a National Bank (1791)

Thomas Jefferson

To take a single step beyond the boundaries . . . specially drawn around the powers of Congress, is to take possession of a boundless field of power, no longer susceptible of any definition.

The incorporation of a bank, and other powers assumed by this bill have not, in my opinion, been delegated to the U.S. by the Constitution.

I.   They are not among the powers specially enumerated, for these are

1.   A power to lay taxes for the purpose of paying the debts of the U.S. But no debt is paid by this bill, nor any tax laid. . . .

2.   "to borrow money." But this bill neither borrows money, nor ensures the borrowing of it. . . .

3.   "to regulate commerce with foreign nations, and among the states, and with the Indian tribes." To erect a bank, and to regulate commerce, are very different acts. . . ."

II.   Nor are they within either of the general phrases, which are the two following.

1.   "To lay taxes to provide for the general welfare of the U.S." that is to say "to lay taxes for the purpose of providing for the general welfare." For the laying of taxes is the power and the general welfare the purpose for which the power is to be exercised. They are not to lay taxes . . . for any purpose they please; but only to pay the debts or provide for the welfare of the Union. In like manner they are not to do anything they please to provide for the general welfare, but only to lay taxes for that purpose. To consider the latter phrase, not as describing the purpose of the first, but as giving a distinct and independent power to do any act they please, which might be for the good of the Union, would render all the preceding and subsequent enumerations of power completely useless. . . .

2.   The second general phrase is "to make all laws necessary and proper for carrying into execution the enumerated powers." But they can all be carried into execution without a bank. A bank therefore is not necessary, and consequently not authorised by this phrase.

It has been much urged that a bank will give great facility, or convenience in the collection of taxes. Suppose this were true: yet the constitution allows only the means which are "necessary" not those which are merely "convenient" for effecting the enumerated powers. If such a latitude of construction be allowed to this phrase as to give any non-enumerated power, it will go to every one, for there is no one which ingenuity may not torture into a convenience, in some way or other, to some one of so long a list of enumerated powers. It would swallow up all the delegated powers, and reduce the whole to one phrase as before observed. Therefore it was that the constitution restrained them to the necessary means, that is to say, to those means without which the grant of the power would be nugatory.

Opinion as to The Constitutionality of The Bank of The United States (1791)

Alexander Hamilton

[It seems to me] [t]hat every power vested in a government is in its nature sovereign, and includes, by force of the term, a right to employ all the means requisite and fairly applicable to the attainment of the ends of such power, and which are not precluded by restrictions and exceptions specified in the Constitution, or not immoral, or not contrary to the essential ends of political society. . . .

This general and indisputable principle puts at once an end to the abstract question, whether the United States have power to erect a corporation. . . . [I]t is unquestionably incident to sovereign power to erect corporations, and consequently to that of the United States, in relation to the objects intrusted to the management of the government....

It is not denied that there are implied [as] well as express powers, and that the ... implied powers are to be considered as delegated equally with express ones. Then it follows, that as a power of erecting a corporation may as well be implied as any other thing, it may as well be employed as an instrument or mean of carrying into execution any of the specified powers, as any other instrument or mean whatever. The only question must be ... whether the mean to be employed or in this instance, the corporation to be erected, has a natural relation to any of the acknowledged objects or lawful ends of the government. Thus a corporation may not be erected by Congress for superintending the police of the city of Philadelphia, because they are not authorized to regulate the police of that city. But one may be erected in relation to the collection of taxes, or to the trade with foreign countries, or to the trade between the States, or with the Indian tribes; because it is the province of the federal government to regulate those objects, and because it is incident to a general sovereign or legislative power to regulate a thing, to employ all the means which relate to its regulation to the best and greatest advantage....

To this mode of reasoning respecting the right of employing all the means requisite to the execution of the specified powers of the government, it is objected, that none but necessary and proper means are to be employed; and the Secretary of State maintains, that no means are to be considered as necessary but those without which the grant of the power would be nugatory....

It is essential to the being of the national government, that so erroneous a conception of the meaning of the word necessary should be exploded. Necessary often means no more than needful, requisite, incidental, useful, or conducive to. It is a common mode of expression to say, that it is necessary for a government or a person to do this or that thing, when nothing more is intended or understood, than that the interests of the government or person require, or will be promoted by, the doing of this or that thing.

The imagination can be at no loss for exemplifications of the use of the word in this sense. And it is the true one in which it is to be understood as used in the Constitution. The whole turn of the clause containing it indicates, that it was the intent of the Convention, by that clause, to give a liberal latitude to the exercise of the specified powers. The expressions have peculiar comprehensiveness. They are thought to make all laws necessary and proper for carrying into execution the foregoing powers....

To understand the word as the Secretary of State does, would be to depart from its obvious and popular sense, and to give it a restrictive operation, an idea never before entertained. It would be to give it the same force as if the word absolutely or indispensably had been prefixed to it.

Such a construction would beget endless uncertainty and embarrassment. The cases must be palpable and extreme, in which it could be pronounced, with certainty, that a measure was absolutely necessary, or one, without which, the exercise of a given power would be nugatory. There are few measures of any government which would stand so severe a test....

The only question is, whether [the government] has a right to [create the bank], in order to enable it the more effectually to accomplish ends which are in themselves lawful.

[A bank relates] to the power of collecting taxes, to that of borrowing money, to that of regulating trade between the States, and to those of raising and maintaining fleets and armies. To the two former the relation may be said to be immediate; ... and that it is clearly within the provision which authorizes the making of all needful rules and regulations.

SOURCE: Yale Law School, Lillian Goldman Law Library, The Avalon Project, http://avalon.law.yale.edu/18th_century/bank-ah.asp.

FIGURE 3-1 The History of the First and Second Banks of the United States

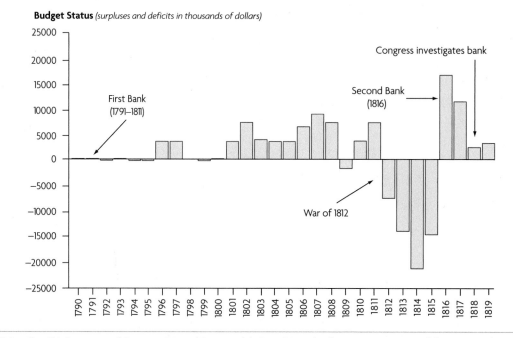

SOURCE: Data from U.S. Department of Commerce, *Historical Statistics of the United States* (Washington, DC: U.S. Bureau of the Census, 1975), 1104.

settled question. Because all the branches of government have been operating under the assumption that the bank is constitutional, it would seem almost too late to call it into question unless its repugnancy with the Constitution were plain.

- The bank's constitutionality is beyond dispute. Congress is authorized to pass all laws "necessary and proper" to carry into execution the powers conferred on it. These words, "necessary and proper" should be considered as synonymous. Necessary powers must mean such powers as are suitable and fitted to the object, the best and most useful in relation to the end proposed.

- A bank is a proper and suitable instrument to assist the operations of the government, in the collection and disbursement of revenue; in the occasional anticipations of taxes and imposts; and in the regulation of the actual currency, as being a part of the trade and exchange between the states.

For the defendant in error, State of Maryland et al.:

- The question of whether Congress has the constitutional power to incorporate the bank of the United States has, for many years, been the subject of

debate. Simply because the bank has existed for a long time does not mean that the subject is closed.

- It is agreed that no such power is expressly granted by the Constitution. It has been obtained by implication and asserted to exist, not of and by itself, but as an appendage to other granted powers, as necessary to carry them into execution. If the bank is not "necessary and proper" for this purpose, it has no foundation in our Constitution, and can have no support in this Court.

- A power, growing out of a necessity that may not be permanent, may also not be permanent. It relates to circumstances that change, in a state of things that may exist at one period and not at another. The argument might have been perfectly good, to show the necessity of a bank in 1791, and entirely fail now, when so many facilities for financial transactions abound, which did not exist then.

CHIEF JUSTICE MARSHALL DELIVERED THE OPINION OF THE COURT.

The constitution of our country, in its most interesting and vital parts, is to be considered; the conflicting powers of the government of the Union and of its members, as marked in that constitution, are to be discussed; and an opinion given, which may essentially influence the great operations of the government. No tribunal can approach such a question without a deep sense of its importance, and of the awful responsibility involved in its decision. But it must be decided peacefully, or remain a source of hostile legislation, perhaps of hostility of a still more serious nature; and if it is to be so decided, by this tribunal alone can the decision be made. On the Supreme Court of the United States has the constitution of our country devolved this important duty.

The first question . . . is, has Congress power to incorporate a bank? . . .

This government is acknowledged by all to be one of enumerated powers. The principle, that it can exercise only the powers granted to it, would seem too apparent to have required to be enforced by all those arguments which its enlightened friends, while it was depending before the people, found it necessary to urge. That principle is now universally admitted. But the question respecting the extent of the powers actually granted, is perpetually arising, and will probably continue to arise, as long as our system shall exist. . . .

Among the enumerated powers, we do not find that of establishing a bank or creating a corporation. But there is no phrase in the instrument which, like the articles of confederation, excludes incidental or implied powers; and which requires that everything granted shall be expressly and minutely described. Even the 10th amendment, which was framed for the purpose of quieting the excessive jealousies which had been excited, omits the word "expressly," and declares only that the powers "not delegated to the United States, nor prohibited to the states, are reserved to the states or to the people;" thus leaving the question, whether the particular power which may become the subject of contest has been delegated to the one government, or prohibited to the other, to depend on a fair construction of the whole instrument. . . . A constitution, to contain an accurate detail of all the subdivisions of which its great powers will admit, and of all the means by which they may be carried into execution, would partake of a prolixity of a legal code, and could scarcely be embraced by the human mind. It would probably never be understood by the public. Its nature, therefore, requires, that only its great outlines should be marked, its important objects designated, and the minor ingredients which compose those objects be deduced from the nature of the objects themselves. That this idea was entertained by the framers of the American constitution, is not only to be inferred from the nature of the instrument, but from the language. Why else were some of the limitations, found in the ninth section of the 1st article, introduced? It is also, in some degree, warranted by their having omitted to use any restrictive term which might prevent its receiving a fair and just interpretation. In considering this question, then, we must never forget that it is a constitution we are expounding.

Although, among the enumerated powers of government, we do not find the word "bank" or "incorporation," we find the great powers to lay and collect taxes; to borrow money; to regulate commerce; to declare and conduct a war; and to raise and support armies and navies. The sword and the purse, all the external relations, and no inconsiderable portion of the industry of the nation, are entrusted to its government. It can never be pretended that these vast powers draw after them others of inferior importance, merely because they are inferior. Such an idea can never be advanced. But it may with great reason be contended, that a government, entrusted with such ample powers, on the due execution of which the happiness and prosperity of the nation so vitally depends, must also be entrusted with ample means for their execution. The power being given, it is the interest of the nation to facilitate its execution. It can never be their interest, and cannot be presumed to have been their intention, to clog and embarrass its execution, by withholding the most appropriate means. . . .

The government which has a right to do an act, and has imposed on it the duty of performing that act, must, according to the dictates of reason, be allowed to select the means; and those who contend that it may not select any appropriate means, that one particular mode of effecting the object is excepted, take upon themselves the burden of establishing that exception.

The creation of a corporation, it is said, appertains to sovereignty. This is admitted. . . . The power of creating a corporation, though appertaining to sovereignty, is not, like the power of making war or levying taxes or of regulating commerce, a great substantive and independent power which cannot be implied as incidental to other powers or used as a means of executing them. It is never the end for which other powers are exercised, but a means by which other objects are accomplished. . . . The power of creating a corporation is never used for its own sake, but for the purpose of effecting something else. No sufficient reason is therefore perceived why it may not pass as incidental to those powers which are expressly given if it be a direct mode of executing them.

But the constitution of the United States has not left the right of Congress to employ the necessary means for the execution of the powers conferred on the government to general reasoning. To its enumeration of powers is added that of making "all laws which shall be necessary and proper, for carrying into execution the foregoing powers, and all other powers vested by this constitution, in the government of the United States, or in any department thereof."

The counsel for the State of Maryland have urged various arguments, to prove that this clause, though in terms a grant of power, is not so in effect; but is really restrictive of the general right, which might otherwise be implied, of selecting means for executing the enumerated powers. . . .

The word "necessary" is considered as controlling the whole sentence, and as limiting the right to pass laws for the execution of the granted powers, to such as are indispensable, and without which the power would be nugatory. That it excludes the choice of means, and leaves to Congress, in each case, that only which is most direct and simple.

Is it true that this is the sense in which the word "necessary" is always used? Does it always import an absolute physical necessity, so strong that one thing, to which another may be termed necessary, cannot exist without that other? We think it does not. If reference be had to its use, in the common affairs of the world, or in approved authors, we find that it frequently imports no more than that one thing is convenient, or useful, or essential to another. To employ the means necessary to an end, is generally understood as employing any means calculated to produce the end, and not as being confined to those single means, without which the end would be entirely unattainable. . . . Almost all compositions contain words which, taken in their rigorous sense, would convey a meaning different from that which is obviously intended. It is essential to just construction that many words which import something excessive should be understood in a more mitigated sense—in that sense which common usage justifies. The word "necessary" is of this description. It has not a fixed character peculiar to itself. It admits of all degrees of comparison, and is often connected with other words which increase or diminish the impression the mind receives of the urgency it imports. A thing may be necessary, very necessary, absolutely or indispensably necessary. To no mind would the same idea be conveyed by these several phrases. The comment on the word is well illustrated by the passage cited at the bar from the 10th section of the 1st article of the Constitution. It is, we think, impossible to compare the sentence which prohibits a State from laying "imposts, or duties on imports or exports, except what may be absolutely necessary for executing its inspection laws," with that which authorizes Congress "to make all laws which shall be necessary and proper for carrying into execution" the powers of the General Government without feeling a conviction that the convention understood itself to change materially the meaning of the word "necessary," by prefixing the word "absolutely." This word, then, like others, is used in various senses, and, in its construction, the subject, the context, the intention of the person using them are all to be taken into view.

Let this be done in the case under consideration. The subject is the execution of those great powers on which the welfare of a nation essentially depends. It must have been the intention of those who gave these powers, to insure, as far as human prudence could insure, their beneficial execution. This could not be done by confiding the choice of means to such narrow limits as not to leave it in the power of Congress to adopt any which might be appropriate, and which were conducive to the end. This provision is made in a constitution intended to endure for ages to come, and, consequently, to be adapted to the various crises of human affairs. To have prescribed the means by which government should, in all future time, execute its powers, would have been to change, entirely, the character of the instrument, and give it the properties of a legal code. It would have been an unwise attempt to provide, by immutable rules, for exigencies which, if foreseen at all, must have been seen dimly, and which can be best provided for as they occur. To have declared that the best means shall not be used, but those alone without which the power given would be nugatory, would have been to deprive the legislature of the capacity to avail itself of experience, to exercise its reason, and to accommodate its legislation to circumstances. . . .

The baneful influence of this narrow construction on all the operations of the government, and the absolute impracticability of maintaining it without rendering the government incompetent to its great objects, might be illustrated by numerous examples drawn from the constitution, and from our laws. . . .

In ascertaining the sense in which the word "necessary" is used in this clause of the constitution, we may derive some aid from that with which it is associated. Congress shall have power "to make all laws which shall be necessary and proper to carry into execution" the powers of the government. If the word "necessary" was used in that strict and rigorous sense for which the counsel for the State of

Maryland contend, it would be an extraordinary departure from the usual course of the human mind, as exhibited in composition, to add a word, the only possible effect of which is to qualify that strict and rigorous meaning; to present to the mind the idea of some choice of means of legislation not straightened and compressed within the narrow limits for which gentlemen contend. . . .

We admit, as all must admit, that the powers of the government are limited, and that its limits are not to be transcended. But we think the sound construction of the constitution must allow to the national legislature that discretion, with respect to the means by which the powers it confers are to be carried into execution, which will enable that body to perform the high duties assigned to it, in the manner most beneficial to the people. Let the end be legitimate, let it be within the scope of the constitution, and all means which are appropriate, which are plainly adapted to that end, which are not prohibited, but consist with the letter and spirit of the constitution, are constitutional.

That a corporation must be considered as a means not less usual, not of higher dignity, not more requiring a particular specification than other means, has been sufficiently proved. . . .

If a corporation may be employed indiscriminately with other means to carry into execution the powers of the government, no particular reason can be assigned for excluding the use of a bank, if required for its fiscal operations. To use one, must be within the discretion of Congress, if it be an appropriate mode of executing the powers of government. That it is a convenient, a useful, and essential instrument in the prosecution of its fiscal operations, is not now a subject of controversy. All those who have been concerned in the administration of our finances, have concurred in representing the importance and necessity; and so strongly have they been felt, that statesmen of the first class, whose previous opinions against it had been confirmed by every circumstance which can fix the human judgment, have yielded those opinions to the exigencies of the nation. Under the confederation, Congress, justifying the measure by its necessity, transcended perhaps its powers to obtain the advantage of a bank; and our own legislation attests the universal conviction of the utility of this measure. The time has passed away when it can be necessary to enter into any discussion in order to prove the importance of this instrument, as a means to effect the legitimate objects of the government.

But, were its necessity less apparent, none can deny its being an appropriate measure; and if it is, the degree of its necessity, as has been very justly observed, is to be discussed in another place. Should Congress, in the execution of its powers, adopt measures which are prohibited by the constitution; or should Congress, under the pretext of executing its powers, pass laws for the accomplishment of objects not entrusted to the government, it would become the painful duty of this tribunal, should a case requiring such a decision come before it, to say that such an act was not the law of the land. But where the law is not prohibited, and is really calculated to effect any of the objects entrusted to the government, to undertake here to inquire into the degree of its necessity, would be to pass the line which circumscribes the judicial department, and to tread on legislative ground. This court disclaims all pretensions to such a power. . . .

After the most deliberate consideration, it is the unanimous and decided opinion of this court that the act to incorporate the bank of the United States is a law made in pursuance of the constitution, and is a part of the supreme law of the land.

As we can see, Marshall adopted Hamilton's reasoning and the government's claims about the proper interpretation of the necessary and proper clause: "necessary" does not mean absolutely necessary or essential, as Jefferson argued, but rather convenient or useful, as Hamilton believed. Some even believed Marshall's opinion was a virtual transcript of the oral arguments presented by the federal attorneys. Given that Marshall issued *McCulloch* just three days after the case had been presented, it is more likely, as others suspect, that he had written the opinion the previous summer.

How did the public respond? Despite the Court's opinion upholding the bank, sentiment was decidedly against the cashier, James McCulloch *(see box 3-4)*. As for Marshall's opinion? Immediate reaction was interesting in that it focused less on the portion of the opinion we have dealt with here—congressional powers—and more on the federalism dimension, which we take up in chapter 6. Nevertheless, the long-term effect of Marshall's interpretation of the necessary and proper clause has been significant: Congress now exercises many powers not named in the Constitution but implied by it. In this way *McCulloch* is a landmark decision and one that might very well have accomplished Marshall's stated objective: to allow the Constitution "to endure for ages to come."

Before turning to one of those powers—the power to investigate—it is worth considering how contemporary

> **BOX 3-4   AFTERMATH . . . JAMES MCCULLOCH AND THE SECOND NATIONAL BANK**

JOHN MARSHALL'S opinion for a unanimous Court in *McCulloch v. Maryland* (1819) resolved the constitutional questions surrounding the Second Bank of the United States. The decision, however, did not diminish the strong public sentiment against Baltimore branch cashier James McCulloch (also known as M'Culloch or McCulloh), who had been accused of engaging with others in corruption and unchecked financial speculation. Negative newspaper articles and a congressional investigation into the affairs of the national bank led to claims that large amounts of money were unaccounted for or mishandled. On March 6, 1819, the same day the Court handed down the McCulloch decision, Langdon Cheves was installed as the new president of the national bank. Two months later Cheves relieved McCulloch of his duties, claiming that the Baltimore branch cashier had defrauded the bank of $1,671,221.87.

In July 1819 McCulloch, former branch president James Buchanan, and Baltimore businessman George Williams were indicted for conspiracy to defraud the bank of an amount exceeding $1.5 million. The indictment, instigated by Maryland attorney general Luther Martin, accused the defendants of "wickedly devising, contriving and intending, falsely, unlawfully, fraudulently, craftily and unjustly, and by indirect means, to cheat and impoverish" the bank. One observer at the time labeled the three "destroyers of widows and orphans." Among other schemes, the three accused men had operated a company that speculated in the bank's stock and were in a position to manipulate its value to their own advantage.

In April 1821 the trial court dismissed the charges on the ground that conspiracy to commit fraud was not a crime under common law or one specified by Maryland statute. Later that year, however, the Maryland Court of Appeals reversed, ordering a full trial on the charges. All along the three defendants argued that they might have committed certain indiscretions but that the bank's losses were the result of bad economic times rather than any criminal acts. In March 1823, McCulloch and Buchanan were found not guilty and the charges against Williams were dismissed.

Following his acquittal, James McCulloch began rebuilding his life and reputation. In 1825 he was elected to the state legislature representing Baltimore County, and the next year his legislative colleagues selected him to be Speaker of the Maryland House of Delegates. He was also active as a lobbyist for the city and county of Baltimore as well as for the Chesapeake and Ohio Canal Company. Ironically, McCulloch even served a term as director of the Maryland Penitentiary. In 1842 the Senate confirmed President John Tyler's nomination of McCulloch to be the first comptroller of the United States Treasury, a post he held for seven years. McCulloch died in 1861.

The Second Bank of the United States continued to do business after the *McCulloch* decision. In 1832 President Andrew Jackson, a fierce opponent of the bank, vetoed a congressional act extending the bank's charter. When its charter expired in 1836, the bank became a private institution under the laws of Pennsylvania. But it did not prosper. In 1839 it temporarily suspended payment on its obligations and then unsuccessfully fought a two-year battle for survival. Its assets were liquidated in 1841. From 1836 until 1913, when the Federal Reserve System was created, the United States operated without an effective central bank.

SOURCES: Bray Hammond, "Jackson, Biddle, and the Bank of the United States," *Journal of Economic History* 7 (May 1947): 1–23; Mark R. Killenbeck, *M'Culloch v. Maryland: Securing a Nation* (Lawrence: University Press of Kansas, 2006); Melvin I. Urofsky, *Supreme Decisions: Great Constitutional Cases and Their Impact* (Boulder, CO: Westview Press, 2012).

justices interpret Marshall's version of congressional authority under the necessary and proper clause. First, virtually all justices continue the Hamilton–Marshall tradition of defining "necessary" not as *absolutely* necessary but as convenient, useful, or beneficial to the exercise of congressional authority.

Second, the Court continues to be very (but not always) deferential to congressional determination that a law is "necessary." But it also has acknowledged that Congress's power is not unlimited, just as Marshall did. Recall the Chief's words:

Let the end be legitimate, let it be within the scope of the constitution, and all means which are appropriate, which are plainly adapted to that end, which are not prohibited, but consist with the letter and spirit of the constitution, are constitutional.

Does the Court continue to use this means–ends approach to the necessary and proper clause? Yes, but in a more specific form than Marshall puts it. In recent cases it has asked "whether the law constitutes a means that is rationally related [or reasonably adapted] to the implementation of a constitutionally enumerated power." *United States v. Comstock* (2010) provides an example.

At issue in *Comstock* was a law allowing a federal court, on the recommendation of the government, to order the civil commitment of a mentally ill, sexually dangerous, federal prisoner beyond the date he would otherwise be released. Writing for a 7–2 Court, Justice Breyer acknowledged that beyond federal crimes relating to "counterfeiting," "treason," or "Piracies and Felonies committed on the high Seas" or "against the Law of Nations," the Constitution does not explicitly mention "Congress' power to criminalize conduct [or] its power to imprison individuals who engage in that conduct, nor its power to enact laws governing prisons and prisoners." Still, Breyer maintained, Congress has "broad authority to do each of those things in the course of 'carrying into Execution' the enumerated powers 'vested by' the 'Constitution in the Government of the United States,'—authority granted by the Necessary and Proper Clause." In other words, the law at issue is rationally related to congressional power "to help ensure the enforcement of federal criminal laws [which even the first Congress] enacted in furtherance of its enumerated powers."

Only Justice Thomas, joined by Justice Scalia, dissented in *Comstock*. To them the law, while accomplishing an important end—protecting society from violent sex offenders—does not seem to execute *any* enumerated power. It rather piles one implied power on another in a way that Marshall would not have approved. To Thomas and Scalia, *McCulloch* demands that any implied power must follow plainly from, and not simply be vaguely related to, an enumerated end. Under their interpretation,

[F]ederal legislation is a valid exercise of Congress' authority under the [Necessary and Proper] Clause if it satisfies a two-part test: First, the law must be directed toward a "legitimate" end, which *McCulloch* defines as one "within the scope of the [C]onstitution"—that is, the powers expressly delegated to the Federal Government by some provision in the Constitution. Second, there must be a necessary and proper fit between the "means" (the federal law) and the "end" (the

enumerated power or powers) it is designed to serve. *McCulloch* accords Congress a certain amount of discretion in assessing means-end fit under this second inquiry. The means Congress selects will be deemed "necessary" if they are "appropriate" and "plainly adapted" to the exercise of an enumerated power, and "proper" if they are not otherwise "prohibited" by the Constitution and not "[in]consistent" with its "letter and spirit."

Thomas did not believe that the law at issue in *Comstock* met this test. Because the federal government could identify "no specific enumerated power or powers as a constitutional predicate for [the law]," it was not "'necessary and proper for carrying into Execution' one or more of those federal powers actually enumerated in the Constitution."

In *Comstock* Chief Justice Roberts was in the majority but, in *National Federation of Independent Business v. Sebelius* (2012), a case over the health-care law ("Obamacare") passed in 2010, Chief Justice Roberts seemed more sympathetic to limiting congressional power under the necessary and proper clause. We excerpt *National Federation of Independent Business* in chapter 7, so suffice it to note here that an important question in the case concerned the constitutionality of a provision in the law mandating that most people either buy health insurance or pay a penalty for not buying insurance. Among the government's arguments in defense of the provision was that it was "necessary," under the necessary and proper clause, because without it the government could not require insurance companies to cover people with preexisting conditions (a major goal of the health-care law). People would wait until they were sick to obtain insurance, and, without healthy people contributing, the system would go bankrupt. Roberts understood that the mandate was probably necessary but he rejected the idea that it was "proper." Why not? One of his reasons [21]—and the one that has generated a good deal of legal

---

21. As we will see in chapters 7 and 8, the government also argued that the individual mandate was a valid exercise of Congress's power to regulate commerce among the states and to tax. In making the necessary and proper clause argument, the government contended that the mandate was incident to the power to regulate commerce. Roberts rejected this argument on the ground that Congress was not regulating commercial activity; rather, it was compelling the uninsured to become active in a commercial market. And so, in addition to not be "proper," the mandate was not incident to the legitimate exercise of an enumerated power.

commentary—takes us back to Marshall's opinion in *McCulloch*. Recall Marshall's words:

The power of creating [the bank] is not, like the power of making war or levying taxes or of regulating commerce, a great substantive and independent power which cannot be implied as incidental to other powers or used as a means of executing them.

To Roberts, compelling people to buy insurance is, in fact, "a great substantive and independent power," not a power lesser than or incidental to an enumerated power. As a result, he concluded that the mandate was inconsistent with the "letter and spirit" of the Constitution, meaning it was not proper.

In so writing, Roberts did not overturn *Comstock*, which he continued to believe was warranted under the necessary and proper clause if only because the law was "narrow in scope" and pertained to those already in federal custody. On the other hand, he did not offer a specific rule to differentiate great and independent powers from lesser derivative powers. This caused Justice Ruth Bader Ginsburg to wonder, "How is a judge to decide, when ruling on the constitutionality of a federal statute, whether Congress employed an 'independent power' or merely a 'derivative' one. Whether the power used is 'substantive' or just 'incidental'? The instruction The Chief Justice, in effect, provides lower courts: You will know it when you see it."

From the different approaches in *Comstock* and *National Federation of Independent Business,* you can probably tell that the necessary and proper clause jurisprudence is somewhat murky, with clarification sure to come in future cases.[22] For now, consider whether the Thomas–Scalia and, possibly, Roberts approach squares with *McCulloch*. One way to think about this is to ask yourself whether Marshall would have upheld or struck the law at issue in *Comstock*. You can return to this question also when we consider the health-care case in more detail in the chapters to come.

Power to Investigate. Of all the implied powers that Congress asserts, the power to investigate merits close examination. Many think it is one of the major congressional powers. As Woodrow Wilson noted,

"The informing function of Congress should be preferred even to its legislative function." Another president, Harry Truman, concurred: "The power of investigation is one of the most important powers of Congress. The manner in which that power is exercised will largely determine the position and prestige of the Congress in the future." In addition, the scope of congressional authority in this area has been the subject of some rather interesting, perhaps conflicting, and most definitely controversial Supreme Court opinions.

What has never been controversial, however, is that Congress has the ability to conduct investigations. After all, to legislate effectively Congress must be able to gather information to determine whether new laws are necessary and, if so, how best to construct them. Although this is not an enumerated power, there is little question that legislatures can hold inquiries. Some analysts refer to the power to investigate as an inherent power that legislatures have by virtue of being legislatures. Others call it an inherited power that the British Parliament willed to Congress or, alternatively, an implied power. In any event, Congress took advantage of this privilege virtually from the beginning, holding its first investigation in 1792. Since then no period in American history has been without congressional investigations.

If the power of Congress to investigate is so well entrenched, what is controversial about the practice? We can point to several areas of dispute. One is the scope of the power: Into what subjects may Congress inquire? Another is subpoena power: May Congress summon witnesses and punish, by holding in contempt, those who do not cooperate with the investigating body? If so, what rights do witnesses have? In *Kilbourn v. Thompson* (1881), the justices attempted to provide some firm answers to these questions.

Kilbourn involved a House investigation into a private banking firm. An important witness, Hallett Kilbourn, refused to produce documents demanded by the inquiring committee. By a House order, he was held in contempt and jailed. When he was released, he sued various officials and representatives for false arrest. In his view, the investigation was not legitimate because, first, the House of Representatives "has no power whatever to punish for a contempt of its authority"; and second, the investigation concerned private, not public, matters. Kilbourn stated that he would resist "the naked, arbitrary power of the House to investigate private businesses in which nobody but me

---

22. See also *Zivotofsky v. Kerry* (2015) excerpted in chapter 5. You might want to ask yourself whether Justice Scalia's dissent in that case squares with the dissent he joined in *Comstock.*

and my customers have concern."[23] The House, in turn, claimed that power "undoubtedly exists, and when that body has formally exercised it, it must be presumed that it was rightfully exercised."[24]

On the one hand, the Supreme Court conceded that Congress can summon witnesses and punish for contempt, though this turned out to be was not much of a concession. As early as 1795 Congress jailed for contempt a man who had tried to bribe a member of Congress, and the Supreme Court theoretically approved of the practice as early as 1821, in *Anderson v. Dunn*. These rulings seem to reflect the view that the power to call and punish witnesses can be implied from the inherent nature of legislative authority. Congress is, by definition, a lawmaking institution, and an inherent quality of such an institution is the power to investigate. To function, therefore, Congress must have the authority to summon witnesses and punish those who do not comply, and both chambers have always availed themselves of this authority.

On the other hand, the justices seemed to agree with Kilbourn's arguments about the limited scope of the investigatory power. In what some have called a rather narrow ruling on legislative powers, the justices said that Congress could punish witnesses only if the inquiry itself was within the "legitimate cognizance" of the institution. Inquiries (1) must not "invade areas constitutionally reserved to the courts or the executive," (2) must deal "with subjects on which Congress could validly legislate," and (3) must suggest, in the resolutions authorizing the investigation, a "congressional interest in legislating on that subject."[25]

Under these limitations, Congress could hold inquiries only into subjects that are specifically grounded within its constitutional purview and, in particular, that the "private affairs of individuals," where the inquiry could result in "no valid legislation," did not fall into that category. As a result Kilbourn won his case because the resolution of the House of authorizing the investigation was "in excess of the power conferred on that body by the Constitution."

Four decades later the Court was once again called on to examine the scope of congressional investigative authority. As you read *McGrain v. Daugherty* (1927), consider its ruling in light of *Kilbourn*. Some think the justices substantially reworked the 1881 holding. Do you agree? If so, what did they change?

McGrain v. Daugherty

273 U.S. 135 (1927)
http://laws.findlaw.com/us/273/135.html
Vote: 8 (Brandeis, Butler, Holmes, McReynolds, Sanford, Sutherland, Taft, Van Devanter)
    0

OPINION OF THE COURT: *Van Devanter*
NOT PARTICIPATING: *Stone*

FACTS:

In 1922 Congress began an investigation of a huge scandal known as Teapot Dome. It involved the alleged bribery of public officials by private companies to obtain leasing rights to government-held oil reserves, including the Teapot Dome reserves in Wyoming. Initial inquiries centered on employees of the Department of the Interior, but Congress soon turned its attention to the Justice Department. It was thought that Attorney General Harry M. Daugherty was involved in fraudulent activities because he failed to prosecute wrongdoers. A Senate committee ordered the attorney general's brother, Mally S. Daugherty, to appear before it and to produce documents. Mally Daugherty was a bank president, and the committee suspected that he was involved in the scandal.

This suspicion grew stronger with the resignation of the attorney general and the subsequent refusal of his brother to appear before the committee. The Senate had Mally arrested. He, in turn, challenged the committee's authority to compel him—through arrest—to testify against his brother. Note how both the U.S. government and Daugherty attempted to use *Kilbourn* to frame their arguments.

ARGUMENTS:

For the appellant, John J. McGrain, Deputy Sergeant of Arms, U.S. Senate:
- Each house of Congress has the power to conduct an investigation in aid of legislative functions and to compel the attendance of witnesses and the production of materials that may throw light upon the subject of inquiry. This has been the practice of Congress for many years.

---

23. Quoted in Congressional Quarterly, *Guide to Congress,* 5th ed. (Washington, DC: CQ Press, 2000), 252.

24. The quotes in this paragraph come from the Court's summary of the parties' arguments.

25. See Pritchett, *Constitutional Law of the Federal System,* 191.

Members of the Senate investigating committee that sought to compel testimony from Mally Daugherty. From left, Burton K. Wheeler, George Moses, Smith Brookhart, Andrieus Jones, and Henry Ashurst.

- The investigation ordered by the Senate, in the course of which the testimony of Daugherty and the production of books and records of the bank of which he is president were required, was legislative in its character, as required by *Kilbourn v. Thompson.* In that way, this case is distinct from *Kilbourn* because it cannot possibly be said that the discovery of any facts showing neglect or failure on the part of the attorney general or his assistants to discharge their duty cannot be used by Congress as a basis for new legislation.[26]

For the appellee, Mally S. Daugherty:

- The investigation is not legislative but judicial in character; it is an attempt to prosecute, try, and determine the guilt or innocence of Daugherty. Except in cases of impeachment, Congress lacks such power, according to *Kilbourn v. Thompson.* The Senate cannot vest its committee with judicial power.
- The Senate, when acting in its legislative capacity, has no power to arrest in order to compel testimony.
- The Constitution does not grant Congress any power to compel testimony to aid it in formulating legislation. If, however, the Court holds that Congress has such power, then it must be shown what legislation Congress has in mind and that the evidence is pertinent to the proposed subject matter of the legislation.

---

26. McGrain's brief was written by Attorney General Harlan Fiske Stone, who had since been appointed a justice on the Court deciding the case.

◆ MR. JUSTICE VAN DEVANTER DELIVERED THE OPINION OF THE COURT.

We have given the case earnest and prolonged consideration because the principal questions involved are of unusual importance and delicacy. . . .

The first of the principal questions—the one which the witness particularly presses on our attention—is . . . whether the Senate—or the House of Representatives . . .—has power . . . to compel a private individual to appear before it or one of its committees and give testimony needed to enable it efficiently to exercise a legislative function belonging to it under the Constitution.

The Constitution provides for a Congress consisting of a Senate and House of Representatives and invests it with "all legislative powers" granted to the United States, and with power "to make all laws which shall be necessary and proper" for carrying into execution these powers and "all other powers" vested by the Constitution in the United States or in any department or officer thereof. . . . But there is no provision expressly investing either house with power to make investigations and exact testimony to the end that it may exercise its legislative function advisedly and effectively. So the question arises whether this power is so far incidental to the legislative function as to be implied.

In actual legislative practice, power to secure needed information by such means has long been treated as an attribute of the power to legislate. It was so regarded in the British Parliament and in the colonial Legislatures before the American Revolution; and a like view has prevailed and

Attorney General Harry M. Daugherty, whose brother Mally S. Daugherty refused to appear before the Senate to answer questions concerning the Teapot Dome scandal, in which both were implicated. In McGrain v. Daugherty the Court affirmed congressional power to investigate, even without an explicitly stated legislative purpose.

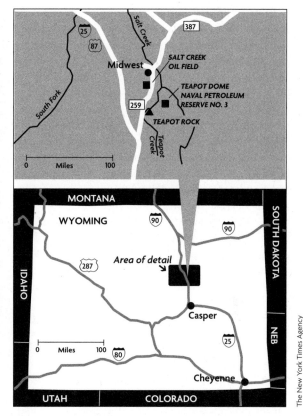

Map of Wyoming and detail showing the location of the U.S. Navy's oil reserves that, along with reserves in Elk Hills, California, were illegally leased to a private oil company.

been carried into effect in both houses of Congress and in most of the state Legislatures. . . .

. . . The state courts quite generally have held that the power to legislate carries with it by necessary implication ample authority to obtain information needed in the rightful exercise of that power, and to employ compulsory process for the purpose. . . .

[This Court has decided several cases that] are not decisive . . . [but] definitely settle two propositions . . . : One, that the two houses of Congress . . . possess, not only such powers as are expressly granted to them by the Constitution, but such auxiliary powers as are necessary and appropriate to make the express powers effective; and the other, that neither house is invested with "general" power to inquire into private affairs and compel disclosures, but only with such limited power of inquiry as is shown to exist when the rule of constitutional interpretation just stated is rightly applied. . . .

We are of opinion that the power of inquiry—with process to enforce it—is an essential and appropriate auxiliary

to the legislative function. . . . A legislative body cannot legislate wisely or effectively in the absence of information respecting the conditions which the legislation is intended to affect or change; and where the legislative body does not itself possess the requisite information—which not infrequently is true—recourse must be had to others who do possess it. Experience has taught that mere requests for such information often are unavailing, and also that information which is volunteered is not always accurate or complete; so some means of compulsion are essential to obtain what is needed. All this was true before and when the Constitution was framed and adopted. In that period the power of inquiry—with enforcing process—was regarded and employed as a necessary and appropriate attribute of the power to legislate—indeed, was treated as inhering in it. Thus there is ample warrant for thinking, as we do, that the constitutional provisions which commit the legislative function to the two houses are intended to include this attribute to the end that the function may be effectively exercised.

The contention is earnestly made on behalf of the witness that this power of inquiry, if sustained, may be abusively and oppressively exerted. If this be so, it affords no ground for denying the power. The same contention might be directed against the power to legislate, and of course would be unavailing. We must assume, for present purposes, that neither house will be disposed to exert the power beyond its proper bounds, or without due regard to the rights of witnesses. But if, contrary to this assumption, controlling limitations or restrictions are disregarded, the decision . . . in *Kilbourn v. Thompson* . . . point[s] to admissible measures of relief. And it is a necessary deduction from the decision . . . that a witness rightfully may refuse to answer where the bounds of the power are exceeded or the questions are not pertinent to the matter under inquiry.

We come now to the question whether it sufficiently appears that the purpose for which the witness's testimony was sought was to obtain information in aid of the legislative function. . . .

We are of opinion that . . . it sufficiently appears . . . that the object of the investigation and of the effort to secure the witness's testimony was to obtain information for legislative purposes.

It is quite true that the resolution directing the investigation does not in terms avow that it is intended to be in aid of legislation; but it does show that the subject to be investigated was . . . one on which legislation could be had and would be materially aided by the information which the investigation was calculated to elicit. This becomes manifest when it is reflected that the functions of the Department of Justice, the powers and duties of the Attorney General and the duties of his assistants, are all subject to regulation by congressional legislation, and that the department is maintained and its activities are carried on under such appropriations as in the judgment of Congress are needed from year to year.

The only legitimate object the Senate could have in ordering the investigation was to aid it in legislating; and we think the subject-matter was such that the presumption should be indulged that this was the real object. An express avowal of the object would have been better; but in view of the particular subject-matter was not indispensable. . . .

We conclude that the investigation was ordered for a legitimate object; that the witness wrongfully refused to appear and testify before the committee and was lawfully attached; [and] that the Senate is entitled to have him give testimony pertinent to the inquiry, either at its bar or before the committee.

McGrain is important for three reasons, corresponding to the three key questions about investigations: their scope, congressional power to punish, and the rights of witnesses. Beginning with the scope, the Justices articulated what some have called the proper legislative purpose test: Congress cannot hold a hearing unless there is a proper legislative purpose: "one on which legislation could be had and would be materially aided by the information which the investigation was calculated to elicit." This test follows from *Kilbourn*'s emphasis on Congress sticking to a subject on which it could validly legislate but some have argued that it is less rigid than the *Kilbourn* approach. Do you agree? You might ask yourself whether the *McGrain* Court would have allowed the investigation of Hallett Kilbourn.

Second, *McGrain* yet again but perhaps even more firmly established Congress's power to inquire and to enforce that power with the ability to punish as an implied power. The Court said, "Experience has taught that mere requests for such information often are unavailing . . . so some means of compulsion are essential to obtain what is needed." This statement was an important affirmation of a long-standing practice, as we hinted above. Since 1795 congressional committees had often invoked their power to punish, issuing more than 380 contempt citations over the years. When a committee does so, and if the parent chamber approves by a simple majority, the case is forwarded to a U.S. attorney for possible prosecution.[27]

Finally, and perhaps more important, *McGrain* provides some insight into the rights of witnesses. Even as it ruled against Daugherty, the Court held that witnesses may refuse to answer "where the bounds of the power are exceeded or the questions are not pertinent to the matter under inquiry."

This window of opportunity for witnesses to refuse to testify became quite important during World War II and in the postwar period when, out of fear of an influx of foreign ideologies into the United States, Congress embarked on a new type of investigation: the "inquisitorial panel." In short, the goal of congressional hearings on subversive activities was "exposure," not necessarily "information."

---

27. The executive branch has a (theoretical) duty to prosecute these cases but Congress cannot force the executive branch to do so. Should the executive branch decline to prosecute, Congress could attempt to file a civil suit compelling prosecution, but these suits could face dismissal on political question grounds (see chapter 2).

As discussed in box 3-5, this kind of "investigation" is similar to those held in the 1930s by the House Special Committee to Investigate Un-American Activities and in the 1940s and 1950s by Senator Joseph McCarthy (R-Wis.), and by the House Un-American Activities Committee (HUAC). McCarthy's committee and HUAC were especially controversial. At that time, the fear of communism was so pervasive that individuals summoned to testify before these committees lost their jobs, were placed on blacklists, and suffered other negative consequences. Moreover, many witnesses were sufficiently frightened of being branded communist sympathizers or supporters that they refused to testify or asserted a constitutional protection against so doing, which resulted in an unusually high number of contempt citations. Between 1792 and 1942, Congress had issued 108 contempt citations; from 1945 to 1957, fourteen committees presented 226 such citations to their respective chambers. HUAC alone held 144 "uncooperative" witnesses in contempt.[28]

In the late 1950s the Supreme Court decided two major cases involving the rights of witnesses to refuse to answer Congress's questions. While reading *Watkins v. United States* (1957) and *Barenblatt v. United States* (1959), think about this question: Did the Court treat the cases consistently? If not, what difference do you see?

Watkins v. United States

354 U.S. 178 (1957)
http://laws.findlaw.com/us/354/178.html
Oral arguments are available at https://www.oyez.org.
Vote: 6 (Black, Brennan, Douglas, Frankfurter, Harlan, Warren)
   1 (Clark)

OPINION OF THE COURT: *Warren*
CONCURRING OPINION: *Frankfurter*
DISSENTING OPINION: *Clark*
NOT PARTICIPATING: *Burton, Whittaker*

FACTS:

When the House Un-American Activities Committee was made a standing committee in 1945, Congress defined its authority in Rule XI as follows:

The Committee on Un-American Activities, as a whole or by subcommittee, is authorized to make from time to time

---

28. Congressional Quarterly, *Guide to Congress*, 3rd ed. (Washington, DC: Congressional Quarterly, 1982), 163.

investigations of (1) the extent, character, and objects of un-American propaganda activities in the United States, (2) the diffusion within the United States of subversive and un-American propaganda that is instigated from foreign countries or of a domestic origin and attacks the principle of the form of government as guaranteed by our Constitution, and (3) all other questions in relation thereto that would aid Congress in any necessary remedial legislation.

In the early 1950s HUAC took that mandate to mean that it could call witnesses to testify about Communist Party infiltration into American society and their involvement in that organization.

Watkins v. United States crystallized when the committee invoked a favorite modus operandi: asking a witness before it to "name names," to implicate others as Communist Party members. Two witnesses told the committee that John T. Watkins, who had been involved in various labor organizations such as the United Electrical, Radio and Machine Workers; and the United Auto Workers, was not only a Communist Party member but also a recruiter for the party.

When the committee subpoenaed Watkins in April 1954, he readily answered these allegations. Among his responses was the following:

I would like to make it clear that for a period of time from approximately 1942 to 1947 I cooperated with the Communist Party and participated in Communist activities to such a degree that some persons may honestly believe that I was a member of the party.

I have made contributions upon occasions to Communist causes. I have signed petitions for Communist causes. I attended caucuses at [a] . . . convention at which Communist Party officials were present.

Since I freely cooperated with the Communist Party I have no motive for making the distinction between cooperation and membership except for the simple fact that it is the truth. I never carried a Communist Party card. I never accepted discipline and indeed on several occasions I opposed their position.

The government conceded that in addressing questions pertaining to his own activities, it could "hardly . . . imagine" a more "complete and candid statement." But the government alleged that Watkins went astray because he refused to answer questions about the activities of others. When the committee read

BOX 3-5   INVESTIGATIONS OF "UN-AMERICANISM"

ONE OF THE MOST significant expansions of congressional investigative powers beyond direct legislative matters was the study of subversive movements after World War II. Instead of pursuing traditional lines of congressional inquiry—government operations and national social and economic problems—committees probed into the thoughts, actions, and associations of individuals and institutions.

The House Committee on Un-American Activities, also known as the House Un-American Activities Committee, or HUAC, was the premier example of these investigative panels. The committee was abolished in January 1975, ending thirty years of controversy over its zealous pursuit of subversives. Its long survival surprised many observers. From the outset, the panel, renamed the Internal Security Committee in 1969, was attacked by liberals and civil libertarians. Throughout the 1960s it withstood court suits challenging the constitutionality of its mandate and attempts in the House to end its funding. The deathblow finally came when the House Democratic Caucus, by voice vote in January 1975, transferred its functions to the House Judiciary Committee.

Early History

The first congressional investigation of un-American activities was authorized September 19, 1918, toward the close of World War I. That original mandate was to investigate the activities of German brewing interests. The investigation, conducted by the Senate Judiciary Committee, was expanded in 1919 to cover "any efforts . . . to propagate in this country the principles of any party exercising . . . authority in Russia . . . and . . . to incite the overthrow" of the U.S. government.

The House on May 12, 1930, set up the Special Committee to Investigate Communist Activities in the United States—the Fish Committee, nicknamed for its chair, Representative Hamilton Fish Jr. (R-N.Y.). On March 20, 1934, the House created the Special Committee on Un-American Activities, under Chair John W. McCormack (D-Mass.). On May 26, 1938, more than three years after McCormack's committee submitted its report, which covered Nazi as well as communist activities in the United States, the House set up another Special Committee on Un-American Activities under Chair Martin Dies Jr. (D-Texas). The committee, whose chair was avowedly anti-communist and anti–New Deal, was given a broad mandate to investigate subversion.

Dies focused his early investigations on organized labor groups, especially the Congress of Industrial Organizations, and set a tactical pattern that would guide the permanent Un-American Activities Committee, which was created in 1945. Friendly witnesses, who often met in secret with Dies as a one-man subcommittee, accused hundreds of people of supporting communist activities, but few of the accused were permitted to testify in rebuttal. The press treated Dies's charges sensationally, a practice that was to continue after World War II.

The Dies Committee was reconstituted in succeeding Congresses until 1945. That January, at the beginning of the Seventy-ninth Congress, it was renamed the House Committee on Un-American Activities and made a standing committee.

The next five years marked the peak of the committee's influence. In 1947 it investigated communism in the motion picture industry, with repercussions that lasted almost a decade. Its hearings resulted in the Hollywood blacklist that kept many writers and actors suspected of communist leanings out of work.

The committee's investigation in 1948 of State Department official Alger Hiss, and Hiss's subsequent conviction for perjury, established communism as a leading political issue and the committee as an important political force. The case against Hiss was vigorously developed by a young representative from Southern California, Richard Nixon.

The committee's tactics during this period included extensive use of contempt citations against unfriendly witnesses, some of whom pleaded their Fifth Amendment right against self-incrimination. In 1950 alone the House voted fifty-nine contempt citations, of which fifty-six had been recommended by the committee.

Senate Investigations

In the early 1950s the Un-American Activities Committee was overshadowed by Senate investigations conducted by Joseph R. McCarthy (R-Wis.), chair (1953–1954) of the Government Operations Committee's Permanent Investigations Subcommittee. McCarthy's investigation into alleged subversion in the U.S. Army—televised nationwide in 1954—intensified concerns over the use by Congress of its investigating powers and led to his censure by the Senate in 1954.

During the same period, the Senate Judiciary Committee's Internal Security Subcommittee, established in 1951, also investigated subversive influences in various fields, including government, education, labor unions, the United Nations, and the press.

SOURCE: Congressional Quarterly, *Guide to Congress*, 4th ed. (Washington, DC: CQ Press, 1991), 240.

to Watkins a list of names, some of whom he knew, and asked him to say whether they had been Communist Party members, Watkins said,

I refuse to answer certain questions that I believe are outside the proper scope of your committee's activities. I will answer any questions which this committee puts to me about myself. I will also answer questions about those persons whom I knew to be members of the Communist Party and whom I still believe are. I will not, however, answer any questions with respect to others with whom I associated in the past. I do not believe that any law in this country requires me to testify about persons who may in the past have been Communist Party members or otherwise engaged in Communist Party activity but who to my best knowledge and belief have long since removed themselves from the Communist movement.

Watkins then questioned the pertinence of the inquiries into others' activities to the committee's work:

I do not believe that such questions are relevant to the work of this committee, nor do I believe that this committee has the right to undertake the public exposure of persons because of their past activities. I may be wrong, and the committee

may have this power, but until and unless a court of law so holds and directs me to answer, I most firmly refuse to discuss the political activities of my past associates.

At that point, the committee chair responded to Watkins's question relating to pertinence:

This committee is set up by the House of Representatives to investigate subversion and subversive propaganda and to report to the House of Representatives for the purpose of remedial legislation.

The House of Representatives has by a very clear majority . . . directed us to engage in that type of work, and so we do, as a committee of the House of Representatives, have the authority, the jurisdiction, to ask you concerning your activities in the Communist Party, concerning your knowledge of any persons who are members of the Communist Party or who have been members of the Communist Party, and so, Mr. Watkins, you are directed to answer the question propounded to you by counsel.

When Watkins once again refused to respond, the committee chair reported the matter to the full House, which held Watkins in contempt and presented the case to a U.S. attorney for criminal prosecution. Watkins was

The House Un-American Activities Committee holds a press conference December 3, 1948, after a closed session. Standing are two committee investigators. Seated are several reporters and (left to right) Richard Nixon (R-Calif.), John Rankin (D-Miss.), and John McDowell (R-Pa.).

found guilty of "contempt of Congress," fined $100, and given a one-year suspended prison sentence.

ARGUMENTS:

For the petitioner, John T. Watkins:

- The congressional power to investigate is a limited power and does not encompass exposure for the sake of exposure. It is limited to investigation in aid of legislation. Otherwise the power is incompatible with our constitutional system, as previous decisions of the Court make clear.
- The questions that Watkins refused to answer fell beyond the language of the committee's authorization in part because the language does not authorize the committee to ask questions for exposure purposes.
- The committee's authorization is so vague that Watkins could not determine whether it authorized the questions he did not answer. Only by asserting the proposition that any connection with the Communist Party—whether many years ago and without engagement in subversive activities—was a proper subject for congressional investigation could Watkins conclude that the authorization was sufficiently clear to enable him to determine whether the questions were pertinent to the investigation.

For the respondent, United States:

- The committee was acting pursuant to a valid legislative purpose. The record of the hearing, along with the rule under which the committee operates, makes this clear.
- The inquiry would not have been invalid even if the committee's purpose had been merely to inform Congress and the public of communist activities in labor unions. Combating subversive activities by publicity does not necessarily mean that the inquiry would not also aid legislation. A disclosure that people loyal to a foreign government led certain organizations could be relevant in determining whether further legislation was needed.
- But even if the committee did not have legislation in mind in questioning Watkins and was concerned only with bringing information to Congress's and the public's attention, that would fit within the "informing function" of Congress, which is an inherent power of legislatures in representative governments.

◆ MR. CHIEF JUSTICE WARREN DELIVERED THE OPINION OF THE COURT.

We start with several basic premises on which there is general agreement. The power of the Congress to conduct investigations is inherent in the legislative process. That power is broad. It encompasses inquiries concerning the administration of existing laws, as well as proposed or possibly needed statutes. It includes surveys of defects in our social, economic or political system for the purpose of enabling the Congress to remedy them. It comprehends probes into departments of the Federal Government to expose corruption, inefficiency or waste. But, broad as is this power of inquiry, it is not unlimited. There is no general authority to expose the private affairs of individuals without justification in terms of the functions of the Congress. This was freely conceded by the Solicitor General in his argument of this case. Nor is the Congress a law enforcement or trial agency. These are functions of the executive and judicial departments of government. No inquiry is an end in itself; it must be related to, and in furtherance of, a legitimate task of the Congress. Investigations conducted solely for the personal aggrandizement of the investigators or to "punish" those investigated are indefensible.

It is unquestionably the duty of all citizens to cooperate with the Congress in its efforts to obtain the facts needed for intelligent legislative action. . . . This, of course, assumes that the constitutional rights of witnesses will be respected by the Congress as they are in a court of justice. The Bill of Rights is applicable to investigations as to all forms of governmental action. . . .

Abuses of the investigative process may imperceptibly lead to abridgment of protected freedoms. The mere summoning of a witness and compelling him to testify, against his will, about his beliefs, expressions or associations is a measure of governmental interference. And when those forced revelations concern matters that are unorthodox, unpopular, or even hateful to the general public, the reaction in the life of the witness may be disastrous. . . . Nor does the witness alone suffer the consequences. Those who are identified by witnesses and thereby placed in the same glare of publicity are equally subject to public stigma, scorn and obloquy. . . .

Accommodation of the congressional need for particular information with the individual and personal interest in privacy is an arduous and delicate task for any court. We do not underestimate the difficulties that would attend such an undertaking. It is manifest that despite the adverse effects which follow upon compelled disclosure of private matters, not all such inquiries are barred. *Kilbourn v. Thompson* [1881] teaches that such an investigation into individual affairs is invalid if unrelated to any legislative purpose. . . .

Petitioner has earnestly suggested that the difficult questions of protecting these rights from infringement by legislative inquiries can be surmounted in this case because there was no public purpose served in his interrogation. His conclusion is based upon the thesis that the Subcommittee was engaged in a program of exposure for the sake of exposure. . . .

The Government contends that the public interest at the core of the investigations of the Un-American Activities Committee is the need by the Congress to be informed of efforts to overthrow the Government by force and violence so that adequate legislative safeguards can be erected. From this core, however, the Committee can radiate outward infinitely to any topic thought to be related in some way to armed insurrection. The outer reaches of this domain are known only by the content of "un-American activities." . . .

It is, of course, not the function of this Court to prescribe rigid rules for the Congress to follow in drafting resolutions establishing investigating committees. That is a matter peculiarly within the realm of the legislature, and its decisions will be accepted by the courts up to the point where their own duty to enforce the constitutionally protected rights of individuals is affected. An excessively broad charter, like that of the House Un-American Activities Committee, places the courts in an untenable position if they are to strike a balance between the public need for a particular interrogation and the right of citizens to carry on their affairs free from unnecessary governmental interference. It is impossible in such a situation to ascertain whether any legislative purpose justifies the disclosures sought and, if so, the importance of that information to the Congress in furtherance of its legislative function. The reason no court can make this critical judgment is that the House of Representatives itself has never made it. Only the legislative assembly initiating an investigation can assay the relative necessity of specific disclosures.

Absence of the qualitative consideration of petitioner's questioning by the House of Representatives aggravates a serious problem, revealed in this case, in the relationship of congressional investigating committees and the witnesses who appear before them. Plainly these committees are restricted to the missions delegated to them, i.e., to acquire certain data to be used by the House or the Senate in coping with a problem that falls within its legislative sphere. No witness can be compelled to make disclosures on matters outside that area. This is a jurisdictional concept of pertinency drawn from the nature of a congressional committee's source of authority. . . . When the definition of jurisdictional pertinency is as uncertain and wavering as in the case of the Un-American Activities Committee, it becomes extremely difficult for the Committee to limit its inquiries to statutory pertinency. . . .

The problem attains proportion when viewed from the standpoint of the witness who appears before a congressional committee. He must decide at the time the questions are propounded whether or not to answer.

It is obvious that a person compelled to make this choice is entitled to have knowledge of the subject to which the interrogation is deemed pertinent. The "vice of vagueness" must be avoided here, as in all other crimes. There are several sources that can outline the "question under inquiry" in such a way that the rules against vagueness are satisfied. The authorizing resolution, the remarks of the chairman or members of the committee, or even the nature of the proceedings themselves, might sometimes make the topic clear. This case demonstrates, however, that these sources often leave the matter in grave doubt.

The authorizing resolution [could] itself so clearly declare the "question under inquiry" that a witness can understand the pertinency of questions asked him. The Government does not contend that the authorizing resolution of the Un-American Activities Committee could serve such a purpose. Its confusing breadth is amply illustrated by the innumerable and diverse questions into which the Committee has inquired under this charter since 1938. If the "question under inquiry" were stated with such sweeping and uncertain scope, we doubt that it would withstand an attack on the ground of vagueness.

[Also] the statement of the Committee Chairman in this case, in response to petitioner's protest, was woefully inadequate to convey sufficient information as to the pertinency of the questions to the subject under inquiry. Petitioner was thus not accorded a fair opportunity to determine whether he was within his rights in refusing to answer, and his conviction is necessarily invalid under the Due Process Clause of the Fifth Amendment. . . .

The conclusions we have reached in this case will not prevent the Congress, through its committees, from obtaining any information it needs for the proper fulfillment of its role in our scheme of government. . . . It is only those investigations that are conducted by use of compulsory process that give rise to a need to protect the rights of individuals against illegal encroachment. A measure of added care on the part of the House and the Senate in authorizing the use of compulsory process and by their committees in exercising that power would suffice. That is a small price to pay if it serves to uphold the principles of limited, constitutional government without constricting the power of the Congress to inform itself.

Reversed and remanded.

MR. JUSTICE FRANKFURTER, concurring.

The scope of inquiry that a committee is authorized to pursue must be defined with sufficiently unambiguous clarity to safeguard a witness from the hazards of vagueness in the enforcement of the criminal process against which the Due Process Clause protects. The questions must be put with relevance and definiteness sufficient to enable the witness to know whether his refusal to answer may lead to conviction for criminal contempt and to enable both the trial and the appellate courts readily to determine whether the particular circumstances justify a finding of guilt.

While implied authority for the questioning by the Committee, sweeping as was its inquiry, may be squeezed out of the repeated acquiescence by Congress in the Committee's inquiries, the basis for determining petitioner's guilt is not thereby laid. Prosecution for contempt of Congress presupposes an adequate opportunity for the defendant to have awareness of the pertinency of the information that he has denied to Congress. And the basis of such awareness must be contemporaneous with the witness' refusal to answer and not at the trial for it. Accordingly, the actual scope of the inquiry that the Committee was authorized to conduct and the relevance of the questions to that inquiry must be shown to have been luminous at the time when asked and not left, at best, in cloudiness. The circumstances of this case were wanting in these essentials.

MR. JUSTICE CLARK, dissenting.

It may be that at times the House Committee on Un-American Activities has, as the Court says, "conceived of its task in the grand view of its name." And, perhaps, as the Court indicates, the rules of conduct placed upon the Committee by the House admit of individual abuse and unfairness. But that is none of our affair. So long as the object of a legislative inquiry is legitimate and the questions propounded are pertinent thereto, it is not for the courts to interfere with the committee system of inquiry. To hold otherwise would be an infringement on the power given the Congress to inform itself, and thus a trespass upon the fundamental American principle of separation of powers. The majority has substituted the judiciary as the grand inquisitor and supervisor of congressional investigations. It has never been so. . . .

I think the Committee here was acting entirely within its scope and that the purpose of its inquiry was set out with "undisputable clarity." In the first place, [its charter] must be read as a whole, not dissected. It authorized investigation into subversive activity, its extent, character, objects, and diffusion. While the language might have been more explicit than using such words as "un-American," or phrases like "principle of the form of government," still these are fairly well understood terms. . . . Watkins' action at the hearing clearly reveals that he was well acquainted with the purpose of the hearing. It was to investigate Communist infiltration into his union. This certainly falls within the grant of authority from [its charter] and the House has had ample opportunity to limit the investigative scope of the Committee if it feels that the Committee has exceeded its legitimate bounds. . . .

The Court indicates that the questions propounded were asked for exposure's sake and had no pertile to the inquiry. It appears to me that they were entirely pertinent to the announced purpose of the Committee's inquiry. Undoubtedly Congress has the power to inquire into the subjects of communism and the Communist Party. As a corollary of the congressional power to inquire into such subject matter, the Congress, through its committees, can legitimately seek to identify individual members of the Party.

The pertinency of the questions is highlighted by the need for the Congress to know the extent of infiltration of communism in labor unions. . . . If the parties about whom Watkins was interrogated were Communists and collaborated with him, as a prior witness indicated, an entirely new area of investigation might have been opened up. Watkins' silence prevented the Committee from learning this information which could have been vital to its future investigation. The Committee was likewise entitled to elicit testimony showing the truth or falsity of the prior testimony of the witnesses who had involved Watkins and the union with collaboration with the Party. If the testimony was untrue a false picture of the relationship between the union and the Party leaders would have resulted. For these reasons there were ample indications of the pertinency of the questions.

Barenblatt v. United States

360 U.S. 109 (1959)
http://laws.findlaw.com/us/360/109.html
Oral arguments are available at https://www.oyez.org.
Vote: 5 *(Clark, Frankfurter, Harlan, Stewart, Whittaker)*
        4 *(Black, Brennan, Douglas, Warren)*

OPINION OF THE COURT: *Harlan*
DISSENTING OPINIONS: *Black, Brennan*

FACTS:

On February 25, 1953, a subcommittee of HUAC, operating under the same authority it had before the *Watkins* case (Rule XI), initiated a series of hearings called "Communist Methods of Infiltration (Education)." Before the hearings got under way, HUAC's chair stated that the committee's purpose would be to "ascertain the character, extent and objects of Communist Party activities . . . carried on by [teachers] who are subject to the directives and discipline of the Communist Party." More generally, he observed,

It has been fully established in testimony before congressional committees and before the courts of our land that the Communist Party of the United States is part of an international conspiracy which is being used as a tool or weapon by a foreign power to promote its own foreign policy and which has for its object the overthrow of the governments of all non-Communist countries, resorting to the use of force and violence, if necessary.

Among those testifying before the committee was Francis X. T. Crowley, who admitted that while he was a graduate student at the University of Michigan in 1950 he had belonged to a club with links to the Communist Party. He also told the committee that Lloyd Barenblatt, with whom he had shared an apartment, had been a member as well. Based on that information, in June 1954 the committee subpoenaed Barenblatt to testify before it. Since 1950 Barenblatt had been a psychology instructor at Vassar, but after he received the subpoena, the college refused to renew his contract.

Barenblatt told the committee that he had been a teaching fellow at Michigan, as Crowley had testified. He also admitted that he knew Crowley. But he refused to answer five questions about his activities:

1. Are you now a member of the Communist Party?

2. Have you ever been a member of the Communist Party?

3. Now, you have stated you knew Francis Crowley. Did you know Francis Crowley as a member of the Communist Party?

4. Were you ever a member of the Haldane Club of the Communist Party while at the University of Michigan?

5. Were you a member while a student of the University of Michigan Council of Arts, Sciences, and Professions?

The House held him in contempt for unlawfully refusing to answer these questions, and a U.S. attorney sought and obtained a conviction against him. On appeal to the Supreme Court, Barenblatt was represented by the American Civil Liberties Union.

ARGUMENTS:

For the petitioner, Lloyd Barenblatt:

- Based on *Watkins*, it is clear that the language of the legislation purportedly granting investigative authority to the House Committee was not sufficiently definite and specific to constitute a delegation of power; therefore, the committee lacks the authority to investigate by compulsory process.
- The committee's "excessively broad charter," to quote the Court in *Watkins*, makes it difficult to judge the pertinence of the questions. The committee's opening statement was an insufficient clarification because Barenblatt could not assess the reason why he was summoned.
- The questions infringed on Barenblatt's First Amendment right to expression and association.

For the respondent, United States:

- Although the Court in *Watkins* criticized the committee's authorizing resolution, it did not invalidate it. And now the Court must acknowledge that Congress was quite serious about investigating Communist Party infiltration, with the functions primarily falling to HUAC.
- Whatever justification there may be for criticism of HUAC's authorizing resolution as vague and imprecise, the resolution comes before the Court with a "persuasive gloss of legislative history" that shows beyond a doubt that the House wants the committee to investigate and report to the House on communism in its various aspects and facets, and the danger it poses to the United States.

MR. JUSTICE HARLAN DELIVERED THE OPINION OF THE COURT.

At the outset it should be noted that Rule XI authorized this Subcommittee to compel testimony within the framework of the investigative authority conferred on the Un-American Activities Committee. Petitioner contends that *Watkins v. United States* [1957] nevertheless held the grant of this power in all circumstances ineffective because of the vagueness of Rule XI in delineating the Committee jurisdiction to which its exercise was to be appurtenant. . . .

The *Watkins* case cannot properly be read as standing for such a proposition. A principal contention in *Watkins* was that the refusals to answer were justified because the requirement . . . that the questions asked be "pertinent to the question under inquiry" had not been satisfied. This Court reversed the conviction solely on that ground, holding that Watkins had not been adequately apprised of the subject matter of the Subcommittee's investigation or the pertinency thereto of the questions he refused to answer. . . .

Petitioner also contends, independently of *Watkins*, that the vagueness of Rule XI deprived the Subcommittee of the right to compel testimony in this investigation into Communist activity. . . . Granting the vagueness of the Rule, we may not read it in isolation from its long history in the House of Representatives. Just as legislation is often given meaning by the gloss of legislative reports, administrative interpretation, and long usage, so the proper meaning of an authorization to a congressional committee is not to be derived alone from its abstract terms unrelated to the definite content furnished them by the course of congressional actions. The Rule comes to us with a "persuasive gloss of legislative history," which shows beyond doubt that in pursuance of its legislative concerns in the domain of "national security" the House has clothed the Un-American Activities Committee with pervasive authority to investigate Communist activities in this country. . . .

In light of this . . . history it can hardly be seriously argued that the investigation of Communist activities generally, and the attendant use of compulsory process, was beyond the purview of the Committee's intended authority under Rule XI. . . .

Undeniably a conviction for contempt . . . cannot stand unless the questions asked are pertinent to the subject matter of the investigation. *Watkins v. United States*. But the factors which led us to rest decision on this ground in *Watkins* were very different from those involved here.

In *Watkins* the petitioner had made specific objection to the Subcommittee's questions on the ground of pertinency; the question under inquiry had not been disclosed in any illuminating manner; and the questions asked the petitioner were not only amorphous on their face, but in some instances clearly foreign to the alleged subject matter of the investigation—"Communism in labor."

. . . What we deal with here is whether petitioner was sufficiently apprised of "the topic under inquiry" thus authorized "and the connective reasoning whereby the precise questions asked relate[d] to it." In light of his prepared memorandum of constitutional objections there can be no doubt that this petitioner was well aware of the Subcommittee's authority and purpose to question him as it did. . . . The subject matter of the inquiry had been identified at the commencement of the investigation as Communist infiltration into the field of education. Just prior to petitioner's appearance before the Subcommittee, the scope of the day's hearings had been announced as "in the main communism in education and the experiences and background in the party by Francis X. T. Crowley. It will deal with activities in Michigan, Boston, and in some small degree, New York." . . . [P]etitioner refused to answer questions as to his own Communist Party affiliations, whose pertinency of course was clear beyond doubt. . . .

Our function, at this point, is purely one of constitutional adjudication in the particular case and upon the particular record before us, not to pass judgment upon the general wisdom or efficacy of the activities of this Committee in a vexing and complicated field.

The precise constitutional issue confronting us is whether the Subcommittee's inquiry into petitioner's past or present membership in the Communist Party transgressed the provisions of the First Amendment, which of course reach and limit congressional investigations.

. . . [T]he protections of the First Amendment, unlike a proper claim of the privilege against self-incrimination under the Fifth Amendment, do not afford a witness the right to resist inquiry in all circumstances. Where First Amendment rights are asserted to bar governmental interrogation resolution of the issue always involves a balancing by the courts of the competing private and public interests at stake in the particular circumstances shown. These principles were recognized in the *Watkins* case. . . .

The first question is whether this investigation was related to a valid legislative purpose, for Congress may not constitutionally require an individual to disclose his political relationships or other private affairs except in relation to such a purpose.

That Congress has wide power to legislate in the field of Communist activity in this Country, and to conduct appropriate investigations in aid thereof, is hardly debatable. The existence of such power has never been questioned by this Court. . . . Justification for its exercise in turn rests on the long and widely accepted view that the tenets of the Communist Party include the ultimate overthrow of the Government of the United States by force and violence, a view which has been given formal expression by the Congress. . . .

Nor can we accept the further contention that this investigation should not be deemed to have been in furtherance of a legislative purpose because the true objective of the Committee and of the Congress was purely "exposure." So long as Congress acts in pursuance of its constitutional power, the Judiciary lacks authority to intervene on the basis of the motives which spurred the exercise of that power. . . . The constitutional legislative power of Congress in this instance is beyond question.

Finally, the record is barren of other factors which in themselves might sometimes lead to the conclusion that the individual interests at stake were not subordinate to those of the state. . . .

We conclude that the balance between the individual and the governmental interests here at stake must be struck in favor of the latter, and that therefore the provisions of the First Amendment have not been offended.

MR. JUSTICE BLACK, with whom THE CHIEF JUSTICE and MR. JUSTICE DOUGLAS concur, dissenting.

The First Amendment says in no equivocal language that Congress shall pass no law abridging freedom of speech, press, assembly or petition. The activities of this Committee, authorized by Congress, do precisely that, through exposure, obloquy and public scorn. See *Watkins v. United States*. The Court does not really deny this fact but relies on . . . [t]he notion that despite the First Amendment's command Congress can abridge speech and association if this Court decides that the governmental interest in abridging speech is greater than an individual's interest in exercising that freedom. . . .

I do not agree that laws directly abridging First Amendment freedoms can be justified by a congressional or judicial balancing process. [Our previous cases cannot] be read as allowing legislative bodies to pass laws abridging freedom of speech, press and association merely because of hostility to views peacefully expressed in a place where the speaker had a right to be. Rule XI, on its face and as here applied, since it attempts inquiry into beliefs, not action—ideas and associations, not conduct—does just that.* . . .

---

* I do not understand the Court's opinion in *Watkins v. United States* to approve the type of balancing process adopted in the Court's opinion here. We did discuss in that case "the weight to

But even assuming what I cannot assume, that some balancing is proper in this case, I feel that the Court after stating the test ignores it completely. At most it balances the right of the Government to preserve itself, against Barenblatt's right to refrain from revealing Communist affiliations. Such a balance, however, mistakes the factors to be weighed. . . . [I]t completely leaves out the real interest in Barenblatt's silence, the interest of the people as a whole in being able to join organizations, advocate causes and make political "mistakes" without later being subjected to governmental penalties for having dared to think for themselves. It is this right, the right to err politically, which keeps us strong as a Nation. . . .

Finally, I think Barenblatt's conviction violates the Constitution because the chief aim, purpose and practice of the House Un-American Activities Committee, as disclosed by its many reports, is to try witnesses and punish them because they are or have been Communists or because they refuse to admit or deny Communist affiliations. The punishment imposed is generally punishment by humiliation and public shame. . . .

The same intent to expose and punish is manifest in the Committee's investigation which led to Barenblatt's conviction. The declared purpose of the investigation was to identify to the people of Michigan the individuals responsible for the, alleged, Communist success there. The Committee claimed that its investigation "uncovered" members of the Communist Party holding positions in the school systems in Michigan; that most of the teachers subpoenaed before the Committee refused to answer questions on the ground that to do so might result in self-incrimination, and that most of these teachers had lost their jobs. . . . It then stated that "the Committee on Un-American Activities approves of this action. . . ." The Court, today, barely mentions these statements, which, especially when read in the context of past reports by the Committee, show unmistakably what the Committee was

---

be ascribed to . . . the interest of the Congress in demanding disclosures from an unwilling witness." As I read, and still read, the Court's discussion of this problem in *Watkins* it was referring to the problems raised by *Kilbourn v. Thompson*, which held that legislative committees could not make roving inquiries into the private business affairs of witnesses. The Court, in *Kilbourn*, held that the courts must be careful to insure that, on balance, Congress did not unjustifiably encroach on an individual's private business affairs. Needless to say, an individual's right to silence in such matters is quite a different thing from the public's interest in freedom of speech and the test applicable to one has little, if anything, to do with the test applicable to the other.

doing. I cannot understand why these reports are deemed relevant to a determination of a congressional intent to investigate communism in education, but irrelevant to any finding of congressional intent to bring about exposure for its own sake or for the purposes of punishment.

I do not question the Committee's patriotism and sincerity in doing all this. I merely feel that it cannot be done by Congress under our Constitution. For, even assuming that the Federal Government can compel witnesses to testify as to Communist affiliations in order to subject them to ridicule and social and economic retaliation, I cannot agree that this is a legislative function. Such publicity is clearly punishment, and the Constitution allows only one way in which people can be convicted and punished. . . . Thus if communism is to be made a crime, and Communists are to be subjected to "pains and penalties," I would still hold this conviction bad, for the crime of communism, like all others, can be punished only by court and jury after a trial with all judicial safeguards. . . .

Ultimately, all the questions in this case really boil down to one—whether we as a people will try fearfully and futilely to preserve democracy by adopting totalitarian methods, or whether in accordance with our traditions and our Constitution we will have the confidence and courage to be free.

To return to our initial question: Did the Court treat the claims of *Barenblatt* and *Watkins* consistently? The majority in *Barenblatt* went to lengths to indicate that this case amounted to nothing more nor less than a "clarification" of *Watkins.* But many legal analysts, not to mention Justice Hugo L. Black's dissent, suggest that at minimum the justices backed away from *Watkins,* and others say that *Barenblatt* signaled a reversal of sorts of the earlier ruling.

If it was a reversal, how can we explain the shift, which occurred within a two-year period? There are two possibilities. The first takes us back to our discussion in chapter 2 about constraints on the Court imposed by the separation of powers system. On this account, *Barenblatt* constituted "a strategic withdrawal" because at the time the Court was under a good deal of pressure from the public and Congress.[29] In particular, *Watkins* and other "liberal" decisions on subversive activity and on discrimination, such as

Brown v. Board of Education (1954), made the Court the target of numerous congressional proposals. A few even sought to remove the Court's jurisdiction to hear cases involving subversive activities. According to some observers, the justices felt the heat and acceded to congressional pressure.

Another explanation is that personnel changes produced a more conservative Court, that *Barenblatt* was simply part of a trend ushered in by President Dwight Eisenhower's appointments of Charles Whittaker and Potter Stewart. By way of support, scholars point to the voting alignments in the two cases and to the general trend in the disposition of civil liberties cases. As Walter F. Murphy noted, during the 1956 term, which included *Watkins,* the Court ruled in favor of the civil liberties claim in 74 percent of the cases; that figure fell to 59 percent and 51 percent in the 1957 and 1958 terms, respectively.[30]

Either way, the explanations indicate the susceptibility of the Court to political influences outside and inside its chambers. As the dangers associated with the Cold War began to ebb, the justices again evinced a change of heart on the rights of witnesses. In case after case in the 1960s, they reversed the convictions of many whom Congress had cited for contempt. But their most significant decision involved not Congress but a state legislature. In *Gibson v. Florida Legislative Investigating Commission* (1963) the Court reversed the contempt conviction of a leader in the NAACP (National Association for the Advancement of Colored People) who refused to provide a committee with the organization's membership records. Theodore R. Gibson argued that doing so would abridge his First Amendment rights. The Supreme Court distinguished this dispute from *Barenblatt,* noting that the state had not sufficiently linked the NAACP to subversive activities and, therefore, had provided no compelling reason for wanting the membership lists. More generally, the Court said,

[T]his Court's prior holdings demonstrate that there can be no question that the State has power adequately to inform itself—through legislative investigation, if it so desires—in order to act and protect its legitimate and vital interests. . . . It is no less obvious, however, that the legislative power to investigate, broad as it may be, is not without limit. . . . [W]e hold . . . that groups which themselves are neither engaged in subversive or

---

29. C. Herman Pritchett, *Congress versus the Supreme Court, 1957–1960* (Minneapolis: University of Minnesota Press, 1961), 12.

30. Walter F. Murphy, *Congress and the Supreme Court* (Chicago: University of Chicago Press, 1962), 246.

other illegal or improper activities nor demonstrated to have any substantial connections with such activities are to be protected in their [First Amendment rights].

In essence, the Court sought to strike a balance between the rights of individuals and those of legislatures, no easy task because of the substantive nature of the power to investigate. Certainly, as HUAC's activities illustrate, the opportunities for abuse are plentiful, but when Congress invokes the investigation power in a responsible manner, it can serve as an important check on abuses of the system made by other actors. We have only to consider congressional hearings into the Watergate scandal, examined in chapter 4, to see the truth in this.

Amendment-Enforcing Power

The enumerated and implied powers we have considered so far come from Article I, Section 8: either Section 8 explicitly mentions them or they derive from the necessary and proper clause. Another important and frequently used source of legislative authority, amendment-enforcing power, comes from amendments to the Constitution. Seven (another, the Eighteenth Amendment, was repealed in 1933) contain some variant of the following language: *Congress shall have power to enforce, by appropriate legislation, the provisions of this article.* For example, the first section of the Fifteenth Amendment says, "The right of citizens of the United States to vote shall not be denied . . . on account of race," and this statement is followed by an enforcement provision: "The Congress shall have power to enforce this article by appropriate legislation."

Though this language seems straightforward enough, the justices have grappled with the meaning of the word *enforce*. On one level, the task seems easy: Presumably, the writers of this Reconstruction amendment, which was ratified in 1870, wanted Congress to implement its mandate. So at the very least Congress could "enforce" the amendment by passing laws that prevented the states from denying blacks the right to vote.

And this Congress did do. When, in the 1950s, many states, particularly those in the South, continued to impose barriers such as literacy tests, poll taxes, grandfather clauses, and primary rules aimed at excluding blacks from voting, Congress used its enforcement power under the Fifteenth Amendment to enact legislation to end these practices. The 1957 Civil Rights Act prohibited attempts to intimidate or prevent persons from voting in general or primary elections for federal offices, empowered the attorney general to seek an injunction when an individual was deprived or about to be deprived of the right to vote, gave the district courts jurisdiction over such proceedings, and provided that any person cited for contempt should be defended by counsel and allowed to compel witnesses to appear. Another act, passed three years later, enabled judges to appoint "referees" to help blacks register to vote.

Few analysts ever seriously questioned the constitutionality of these laws. Under the Fifteenth Amendment, Congress seemed to have the authority to ensure that states did not deny the right to vote, and because these acts were aimed at accomplishing that end, they were deemed appropriate under the language of Section 2 of the amendment.

Where harder questions about the enforcement power began to arise is when Congress wanted to use the power—not to remedy proven violations of the Fifteenth Amendment (and others), but to prevent future violations. These questions came in the mid-1960s, when voting rights advocates clamored for stronger laws. They claimed that the existing congressional legislation was inadequate, that the legal suits it authorized the attorney general to undertake were too expensive and not all that successful. Court rulings alone were insufficient to prompt major changes, they argued, because many local governments maintained seemingly nondiscriminatory voting laws but administered them in a discriminatory fashion. In other words, the South was following the letter, but not the spirit, of the laws. Voter registration figures for 1960 and 1964 support this observation: compared with voting-age whites, far lower percentages of nonwhites of voting age were registered to vote *(see table 3-5).*

Data of the sort displayed in table 3-5 convinced Congress that a more aggressive policy was required. The result was the Voting Rights Act of 1965, the most comprehensive—some say drastic—measure yet. Part of the act seemed designed to remedy proven violations of the Fifteenth Amendment by placing a nationwide ban on any standard, practice, or procedure that results in a denial of the right to vote on account of race, and authorizing legal action against states and subdivisions that do not comply. Sections 4 and 5 seemed different: they gave the federal government extraordinary power to prevent future violations of

TABLE 3-5 White and Nonwhite Voter Registration Statistics, 1960, 1964, 1970, 2000

PERCENTAGE OF VOTING-AGE POPULATION REGISTERED TO VOTE

STATE	1960		1964		1970		2000	
	WHITES	NONWHITES	WHITES	NONWHITES	WHITES	NONWHITES	WHITES	NONWHITES
Alabama	63.6	13.7	70.7	23.0	85.0	66.0	74.5	72.0
Arkansas	60.9	38.0	71.7	54.4	74.1	82.3	59.5	60.0
Florida	69.3	39.4	84.0	54.4	65.5	55.3	62.5	52.7
Georgia	56.8	29.3	74.5	44.0	71.7	57.2	59.3	66.3
Louisiana	76.9	31.3	80.4	32.0	77.0	57.4	77.5	73.5
Mississippi	63.9	5.2	70.7	6.7	82.1	71.0	72.2	73.7
North Carolina	92.1	39.1	92.5	46.8	68.1	51.3	67.9	62.9
South Carolina	57.1	13.7	78.5	38.8	62.3	56.1	68.2	68.6
Tennessee	73.0	59.1	72.9	69.4	78.5	71.6	61.9	64.9
Texas	42.5	35.5	53.2	57.7	62.0	72.6	61.8	69.5
Virginia	46.1	23.1	55.9	45.7	64.5	57.0	67.6	58.0
Averages	61.1	29.2	73.2	43.3	69.2	62.0	65.1	65.7

SOURCES: *Revolution in Civil Rights* (Washington, DC: Congressional Quarterly, 1965), 43, 74; and Lee Epstein, Jeffrey A. Segal, Harold J. Spaeth, and Thomas G. Walker, *The Supreme Court Compendium: Data, Decisions, and Developments, 6th ed.* (Thousand Oaks, CA: CQ Press, 2015).

NOTE. We use the term nonwhite because that is how the government reported voting data in the 1960s and 1970s. Now the Census Bureau, from where most of the data in the table derive, reports data on voters using the categories Black, Asian, Hispanic, and White. It also allows respondents to choose more than one race. We do not include data after 2000 because they may not be comparable with earlier figures. Overall in the South today about 70 percent of blacks and of whites reported that they were registered to vote.

the Fifteenth Amendment by regulating elections. Section 4 created a "triggering" or "coverage" formula to determine those states and political subdivisions that will be subject to additional scrutiny. The formula was based on the previous use of racially discriminatory practices and low voter registration or turnout. Section 5 created a procedure known as "preclearance": no jurisdiction that qualifies under the coverage formula can implement any changes in voting procedures until they are approved by the U.S. Justice Department or a three-judge district court in the District of Columbia. Also under the act, the U.S. government could send in federal examiners who, in turn, could order state officials to "register all persons found qualified to vote."

The Voting Rights Act of 1965 marked a dramatic change from earlier laws in which Congress simply provided mechanisms to enforce existing rights. Now it was issuing sanctions against states (the preclearance requirements) and allowing the attorney general to take action against certain areas, all in an effort to prevent future violations, despite the fact that no judicial body had found the states to be engaging in unconstitutional activity.

Did Congress's power to enforce amendments support such legislation? Was the legislation appropriate under the amendment's language? Given that the act constituted a dramatic intrusion of the federal government into state operations, it is not surprising that it was quickly challenged as an unconstitutional use of congressional power. As you read *South Carolina v. Katzenbach,* consider the Court's response, and not just its reaction to the 1965 act. How did it resolve the larger issue of the scope of Congress's amendment-enforcing power?

South Carolina v. Katzenbach

383 U.S. 301 (1966)

http://laws.findlaw.com/us/383/301.html
Oral arguments are available at https://www.oyez.org.
Vote: 8 (Brennan, Clark, Douglas, Fortas, Harlan, Stewart, Warren, White)
1 (Black)

OPINION OF THE COURT: *Warren*

CONCURRING/DISSENTING OPINION: *Black*

FACTS:

In accordance with the Voting Rights Act of 1965, the director of the Census Bureau sent the following notice to the attorney general in August 1965:

I have determined that in each of the following States less than 50 per centum of the persons of voting age residing therein voted in the presidential election of November 1964: Alabama, Alaska, Georgia, Louisiana, Mississippi, South Carolina, [and] Virginia.

These seven states, as well as parts of several others, met the criteria for coverage under the Voting Rights Act's remedial provisions.

Rather than accede to the federal government, South Carolina asked the U.S. Supreme Court, under its original jurisdiction, to find the act unconstitutional. Five of the other six states coming under the act's purview—Alaska did not participate—filed amicus curiae briefs in support of South Carolina. Representing the United States were Attorney General Nicholas Katzenbach and Solicitor General Thurgood Marshall. Nineteen states, mostly in the East and Midwest, submitted an amicus curiae brief supporting the U.S. government.[31] In contrast to their Southern counterparts, which supported South Carolina's states' rights position, they argued that "although a state has power to determine the qualifications for voting, such power may not be used to violate the Fourteenth and Fifteenth Amendments." The brief further stated, "Congress has power to enact appropriate legislation precluding the states from denying the right to vote on the basis of color."

ARGUMENTS:

For the plaintiff, State of South Carolina:
- The act is not "appropriate" to enforce the Fifteenth Amendment. Because the federal government is a government of delegated powers with limited authority, it can legislate only in a manner necessary and appropriate for the purposes it seeks to accomplish. This is an indeterminate sweep across the rights of South Carolina and its citizens. The law is designed to deal with "massive racial discrimination" in the right to vote, but it does not cover some areas where such discrimination exists, and it applies to some innocent states and subdivisions.

---

31. California and Illinois filed separate amicus curiae briefs in support of the act.

- As such, it violates the principle of equality of statehood. States that do not come under the act's coverage are free to administer literacy tests and other restrictions without suffering prohibitions on their sovereign rights and powers.
- The act creates an arbitrary and irrefutable presumption of a violation of the Fifteenth Amendment by South Carolina.

For the defendant, Nicholas Katzenbach:
- Under Section 2 of the Fifteenth Amendment, Congress has comprehensive authority to protect and enforce the citizen's right to vote free of racial discrimination and to adopt measures appropriate to that end. The choice of means is largely a question for Congress itself, as Chief Justice Marshall noted in McCulloch v. Maryland.
- The act does not interfere with powers reserved to the states. Congress does not rely on some inherent but unexpressed power. The grant of power is explicit in Section 2 of the Fifteenth Amendment.
- Using participation in the presidential election or the presence of barriers to the vote is not arbitrary. Congress has developed ample evidence that these are indicators of racial discrimination. The triggering conditions must be viewed as a single integrated measure for quickly halting devices designed to deny or abridge the right to vote on a account of race in violation of the Fifteenth Amendment.

MR. CHIEF JUSTICE WARREN DELIVERED THE OPINION OF THE COURT.

The Voting Rights Act was designed by Congress to banish the blight of racial discrimination in voting, which has infected the electoral process in parts of our country for nearly a century. The Act creates stringent new remedies for voting discrimination where it persists on a pervasive scale, and in addition the statute strengthens existing remedies for pockets of voting discrimination elsewhere in the country. Congress assumed the power to prescribe these remedies from §2 of the Fifteenth Amendment, which authorizes the National Legislature to effectuate by "appropriate" measures the constitutional prohibition against racial discrimination in voting. We hold that the sections of the Act which are properly before us are an appropriate means for carrying out Congress' constitutional responsibilities and are consonant with all other provisions of the Constitution. We therefore deny South

Carolina's request that enforcement of these sections of the Act be enjoined.

The constitutional propriety of the Voting Rights Act of 1965 must be judged with reference to the historical experience which it reflects. Before enacting the measure, Congress explored with great care the problem of racial discrimination in voting. . . .

Two points emerge vividly from the voluminous legislative history of the Act contained in the committee hearings and floor debates. First: Congress felt itself confronted by an insidious and pervasive evil which had been perpetuated in certain parts of our country through unremitting and ingenious defiance of the Constitution. Second: Congress concluded that the unsuccessful remedies which it had prescribed in the past would have to be replaced by sterner and more elaborate measures in order to satisfy the clear commands of the Fifteenth Amendment. . . .

. . . [P]rovisions of the Voting Rights Act of 1965 are challenged on the fundamental ground that they exceed the powers of Congress and encroach on an area reserved to the States by the Constitution. . . .

The objections to the Act which are raised under these provisions may therefore be considered only as additional aspects of the basic question presented by the case. Has Congress exercised its powers under the Fifteenth Amendment in an appropriate manner with relation to the States?

The ground rules for resolving this question are clear. The language and purpose of the Fifteenth Amendment, the prior decisions construing its several provisions, and the general doctrines of constitutional interpretation, all point to one fundamental principle. As against the reserved powers of the States, Congress may use any rational means to effectuate the constitutional prohibition of racial discrimination in voting. . . . We turn now to a more detailed description of the standards which govern our review of the Act.

Section 1 of the Fifteenth Amendment declares that "[t]he right of citizens of the United States to vote shall not be denied or abridged by the United States or by any State on account of race, color, or previous condition of servitude." This declaration has always been treated as self-executing and has repeatedly been construed, without further legislative specification, to invalidate state voting qualifications or procedures which are discriminatory on their face or in practice. Those decisions have been rendered with full respect for the general rule . . . that States "have broad powers to determine the conditions under which the right of suffrage may be exercised." The gist of the matter is that the Fifteenth Amendment supersedes contrary exertions of state power. "When a State exercises power wholly within the domain of state interest, it is insulated from federal judicial review. But such insulation is not carried over when state power is used as an instrument for circumventing a federally protected right."

South Carolina contends that the cases cited above are precedents only for the authority of the judiciary to strike down state statutes and procedures—that to allow an exercise of this authority by Congress would be to rob the courts of their rightful constitutional role. On the contrary, §2 of the Fifteenth Amendment expressly declares that "Congress shall have power to enforce this article by appropriate legislation." By adding this authorization, the Framers indicated that Congress was to be chiefly responsible for implementing the rights created in §1. "It is the power of Congress which has been enlarged. Congress is authorized to *enforce* the prohibitions by appropriate legislation. Some legislation is contemplated to make the [Civil War] amendments fully effective." Accordingly, in addition to the courts, Congress has full remedial powers to effectuate the constitutional prohibition against racial discrimination in voting.

Congress has repeatedly exercised these powers in the past, and its enactments have repeatedly been upheld. . . . On the rare occasions when the Court has found an unconstitutional exercise of these powers, in its opinion Congress had attacked evils not comprehended by the Fifteenth Amendment.

The basic test to be applied in a case involving §2 of the Fifteenth Amendment is the same as in all cases concerning the express powers of Congress with relation to the reserved powers of the States. Chief Justice Marshall laid down the classic formulation, 50 years before the Fifteenth Amendment was ratified:

"Let the end be legitimate, let it be within the scope of the constitution, and all means which are appropriate, which are plainly adapted to that end, which are not prohibited, but consist with the letter and spirit of the constitution, are constitutional." *McCulloch v. Maryland* [1819].

The Court has subsequently echoed his language in describing each of the Civil War Amendments:

"Whatever legislation is appropriate, that is, adapted to carry out the objects the amendments have in view, whatever tends to enforce submission to the prohibitions they contain, and to secure to all persons the enjoyment of perfect equality of civil rights and the equal protection of the laws against State denial or invasion, if not prohibited, is brought within the domain of congressional power." *Ex parte Virginia* [1880].

This language was again employed, nearly 50 years later, with reference to Congress' related authority under §2 of the Eighteenth Amendment.

We therefore reject South Carolina's argument that Congress may appropriately do no more than to forbid violations of the Fifteenth Amendment in general terms—that the task of fashioning specific remedies or of applying them to particular localities must necessarily be left entirely to the courts. Congress is not circumscribed by any such artificial rules under §2 of the Fifteenth Amendment. In the oft-repeated words of Chief Justice Marshall, referring to another specific legislative authorization in the Constitution, "This power, like all others vested in Congress, is complete in itself, may be exercised to its utmost extent, and acknowledges no limitations, other than are prescribed in the constitution." *Gibbons v. Ogden* [1824]. . . .

After enduring nearly a century of widespread resistance to the Fifteenth Amendment, Congress has marshalled an array of potent weapons against the evil, with authority in the Attorney General to employ them effectively. Many of the areas directly affected by this development have indicated their willingness to abide by any restraints legitimately imposed upon them. We here hold that the portions of the Voting Rights Act properly before us are a valid means for carrying out the commands of the Fifteenth Amendment. Hopefully, millions of non-white Americans will now be able to participate for the first time on an equal basis in the government under which they live. We may finally look forward to the day when truly "[t]he right of citizens of the United States to vote shall not be denied or abridged by the United States or by any State on account of race, color, or previous condition of servitude."

The bill of complaint is dismissed.

Bill dismissed.

MR. JUSTICE BLACK, concurring and dissenting.

Though . . . I agree with most of the Court's conclusions, I dissent from its holding that every part of §5 of the Act is constitutional. Section 4 (a), to which §5 is linked, suspends for five years all literacy tests and similar devices in those States coming within the formula of §4(b). Section 5 goes on to provide that a State covered by §4(b) can in no way amend its constitution or laws relating to voting without first trying to persuade the Attorney General of the United States or the Federal District Court for the District of Columbia that the new proposed laws do not have the purpose and will not have the effect of denying the right to vote to citizens on account of their race or color. I think this section is unconstitutional on at least two grounds.

(a) The Constitution gives federal courts jurisdiction over cases and controversies only. If it can be said that any case or controversy arises under this section which gives the District Court for the District of Columbia jurisdiction to approve or reject state laws or constitutional amendments, then the case or controversy must be between a State and the United States Government. But it is hard for me to believe that a justifiable controversy can arise in the constitutional sense from a desire by the United States Government or some of its officials to determine in advance what legislative provisions a State may enact or what constitutional amendments it may adopt. If this dispute between the Federal Government and the States amounts to a case or controversy it is a far cry from the traditional constitutional notion of a case or controversy as a dispute over the meaning of enforceable laws or the manner in which they are applied. And if by this section Congress has created a case or controversy, and I do not believe it has, then it seems to me that the most appropriate judicial forum for settling these important questions is this Court acting under its original Art. III, §2, jurisdiction to try cases in which a State is a party. At least a trial in this Court would treat the States with the dignity to which they should be entitled as constituent members of our Federal Union. . . .

(b) My second and more basic objection to §5 is that Congress has here exercised its power under §2 of the Fifteenth Amendment through the adoption of means that conflict with the most basic principles of the Constitution. As the Court says the limitations of the power granted under §2 are the same as the limitations imposed on the exercise of any of the powers expressly granted Congress by the Constitution. The classic formulation of these constitutional limitations was stated by Chief Justice Marshall when he said in *McCulloch v. Maryland*, "Let the end be legitimate, let it be within the scope of the constitution, and all means which are appropriate, *which are plainly adapted to that end, which are not prohibited, but consist with the letter and spirit of the constitution*, are constitutional" [our italics]. Section 5, by providing that some of the States cannot pass state laws or adopt state constitutional amendments without first being compelled to beg federal authorities to approve their policies, so distorts our constitutional structure of government as to render any distinction drawn in the Constitution between state and federal power almost meaningless. One of the most basic premises upon which our structure of government was founded was that the Federal Government was to have certain specific and limited powers and no others, and all other power was to be reserved either "to the States respectively, or to the people." Certainly if all the provisions of our Constitution which limit the power of the Federal Government and reserve other power to the States are to mean anything, they mean at least that the States have power to pass laws and amend their constitutions without first sending their officials hundreds of miles away to beg federal authorities to approve them. Moreover, it seems to me that §5 which gives federal officials power to veto state laws they do not like is in direct conflict with the clear command of our Constitution that "The United States shall guarantee to every State in this Union a Republican Form of Government." I cannot help but believe that the inevitable effect of any such law which forces any one of the States to entreat federal authorities in far-away places for approval of local laws before they can become effective is to create the impression that the State or States treated in this way are little more than conquered provinces. And if one law concerning voting can make the States plead for this approval by a distant federal court or the United States Attorney General, other laws on different subjects can force the States to seek the advance approval not only of the Attorney General but of the President himself or any other chosen members of his staff. It is inconceivable to me that such a radical degradation of state power was intended in any of the provisions of our Constitution or its Amendments. Of course I do not mean to cast any doubt whatever upon the indisputable power of the Federal Government to invalidate a state law once enacted and operative on the ground that it intrudes into the area of supreme federal power. But the Federal Government has heretofore always been content to exercise this power to protect federal supremacy by authorizing its agents to bring lawsuits against state officials once an operative state law has created an actual case and controversy. A federal law which assumes the power to compel the States to submit in advance any proposed legislation they have for approval by federal agents approaches dangerously near to wiping the States out as useful and effective units in the government of our country. I cannot agree to any constitutional interpretation that leads inevitably to such a result. . . .

In this and other prior Acts Congress has quite properly vested the Attorney General with extremely broad power to protect voting rights of citizens against discrimination on account of race or color. Section 5 viewed in this context is of very minor importance and in my judgment is likely to serve more as an irritant to the States than as an aid to the enforcement of the Act. I would hold §5 invalid for the reasons stated above with full confidence that the Attorney General has ample power to give vigorous, expeditious and effective protection to the voting rights of all citizens.

Katzenbach was a landmark opinion in two regards. First, it upheld the Voting Rights Act, which in turn had a marked effect on closing the gap between white and black voter registration rates. Throughout the United States, blacks and whites today report nearly equal registration rates of about 70 percent each, including in the South.

Second, and more relevant here, *Katzenbach* greatly enhanced Congress's amendment-enforcing power, placing it on the same level as implied powers. Indeed, the Court's standard for evaluating amendment-enforcing power, the words "appropriate legislation," is not so different from the one it uses to adjudicate under the necessary and proper clause. Not only does Chief Justice Warren cite *McCulloch v. Maryland* with approval, but also his logic reflects Marshall's. Compare Marshall's words: "Let the end be legitimate, let it be within the scope of the constitution, and all means which are appropriate . . . are constitutional," with Warren's: "Congress may use any rational means to effectuate the constitutional prohibition of racial discrimination in voting." To Warren, this included remedying proven violations, of course, but also preventing future violations through the preclearance mechanism.

But, just as is true for implied powers, the amendment-enforcing power is not without limits—a point the Warren Court's more conservative successors have made quite clear. Consider, first, the Rehnquist Court case of **City of Boerne v. Flores** (1997). At issue was the Religious Freedom Restoration Act of 1993 (RFRA), which Congress passed by overwhelming majorities in response to the Court's 1990 decision in *Employment Division v. Smith*. RFRA directed the Court to adopt a particular standard of law in constitutional cases involving the free exercise clause of the First Amendment—a standard the Court had rejected in *Smith*—that would presumably make it easier for people who believed that government had burdened their right to practice their religion to prevail in court. In passing some parts of RFRA, Congress relied on the

Fourteenth Amendment's enforcement provision. The first section of the Amendment reads, in relevant part, "No state shall . . . deprive any person of life, liberty, or property, without due process of law." Section 5, the enforcement provision, is nearly identical to the one in the Fifteenth Amendment: "The Congress shall have power to enforce, by appropriate legislation, the provisions of this article."

To the United States, which entered the case as an amicus curiae, RFRA was perfectly permissible because Congress was protecting one of the liberties, the free exercise of religion, which the Court had made applicable to the states by the Fourteenth Amendment's due process clause.

The Supreme Court disagreed. Although it acknowledged that "Congress can enact legislation under §5 [of the Fourteenth Amendment] enforcing the constitutional right to the free exercise of religion," it also said that "Congress cannot decree the substance of the Fourteenth Amendment's restrictions on the States. Legislation which alters the meaning of the Free Exercise Clause cannot be said to be enforcing the Clause."

How would the Court determine where to draw the line between legitimate use of the enforcement power—laws that remedy or prevent violations of an amendment—and those that are not—laws that alter (in this case, expand) the reach of constitutional provisions? The Court admitted that this was not an easy task and that Congress must be given "wide latitude," but it did provide a guideline.

There must be a congruence and proportionality between the injury to be prevented or remedied and the means adopted to that end. Lacking such a connection, legislation may become substantive in operation and effect. History and our case law support drawing the distinction, one apparent from the text of the Amendment.

According to the Court, the Voting Rights Act at issue in *Katzenbach* met this "congruent and proportional" standard but RFRA did not. Why? "In contrast to the record which confronted Congress and the judiciary in the voting rights cases," the Court wrote, "RFRA's legislative record lacks examples of modern instances of generally applicable laws passed because of religious bigotry." To the Court, the lack of modern-day examples of religious bigotry—not one law in forty years—showed that RFRA was so out of proportion to

a "remedial or preventive object that it cannot be understood as responsive to, or designed to prevent, unconstitutional behavior."[32] The link between the prohibited conduct and the constitutional violation was simply insufficient. As a result, the Court could only assume that the RFRA was designed to expand protections under the Fourteenth Amendment, and not to enforce existing protections.

The Roberts Court applied similar logic in *Shelby County v. Holder* (2013). This case takes us back to the Voting Rights Act of 1965. Recall that if states (or subdivisions) come under the coverage formula (Section 4 of the act), then they qualify for preclearance by the U.S. Justice Department or a special court (Section 5). Both Section 4 and Section 5 were seen as temporary measures that would expire in five years. But Congress extended the life of these provisions several times—most recently, enacting a twenty-five-year extension in 2006. Shelby County, a "covered" county in Alabama, brought suit, asking the district court to strike down Sections 4 and 5 as unconstitutional because the coverage formula that the Congress used in 2006 was based on 1965 racial discrimination data that no longer represented conditions in the affected states.

The Supreme Court did not strike down Section 5 of the law, but it did hold that Congress had exceeded its powers when it imposed restrictions on specific states based on forty-year-old data. Without saying as much, the majority's rationale seems to draw, in part, on the congruent and proportional analysis in the RFRA case: the 2006 reauthorization was not congruent and proportional because it imposed obligations on some states beyond those that the Constitution requires, without recent history or data showing that those requirements are necessary to prevent violations of the Fifteenth Amendment.

Writing in dissent, Justice Ginsburg took issue with this very claim:

The Court has time and again declined to upset legislation of this genre unless there was no or almost no evidence of unconstitutional action by States. See, e.g., *City of Boerne v. Flores* (1997) (legislative record "mention[ed] no episodes

---

32. Along similar lines, the Court noted that the Voting Rights Act was limited to those regions of the country "where voting discrimination had been most flagrant"; in the case of RFRA, no such limits existed. The act "is not designed to identify and counteract state laws likely to be unconstitutional because of their treatment of religion."

[of the kind the legislation aimed to check] occurring in the past 40 years"). No such claim can be made about the congressional record for the 2006 VRA [Voting Rights Act] reauthorization. Given a record replete with examples of denial or abridgment of a paramount federal right, the Court should have left the matter where it belongs: in Congress' bailiwick.

As of 2015 the future of coverage provision remains very much in doubt.[33] Though proposals have been introduced to remedy the Court's problems with the existing coverage formula, none has received serious attention in either the Senate or House.

Inherent Powers

In his position paper to President Washington over the constitutionality of the bank, Hamilton wrote, "[T]here are implied [as] well as express powers, and that the former are as effectually delegated as the latter." This much we have already discussed. But Hamilton also noted "another class of powers":

It will not be doubted, that if the United States should make a conquest of any of the territories of its neighbors, they would possess sovereign jurisdiction over the conquered territory. This would be rather a result, from the whole mass of the powers of the government, and from the nature of political society, than a consequence of either of the powers specially enumerated.

Hamilton referred to these as "resulting powers." Justice Story thought they could be another sort of implied power; for example, possessing sovereign jurisdiction over a conquered territory "could be deemed, if an incident to any, an incident to the power to make war." But Story was also quick to agree with Hamilton: there are powers, "nowhere declared in the Constitution," that are "natural incident(s), resulting from the sovereignty and character of the national government.[34]

Some scholars continue to refer to "resulting" powers, but in today's nomenclature we tend to think about Hamilton's and Story's versions as "inherent powers." The idea is that federal government has certain inherent powers that are neither explicit nor directly implied by the Constitution, but that somehow attach themselves to sovereign states (see table 3-4).

Some writers characterize the congressional power to investigate is an inherent, rather than implied, power, as we noted earlier. Earl Warren wrote as much in his majority opinion in *Watkins:* "The power of the Congress to conduct investigations is inherent in the legislative process." On this account, Congress is the lawmaking body, and an inherent quality of such an institution is the power to investigate.

Though the power of Congress to conduct investigations is not very controversial, the very notion of inherent powers is. Some argue that inherent powers cannot possibly conform with the vision of a federal government limited to its enumerated powers or those that can be inferred from them. As Madison wrote in *Federalist* No. 45, "The powers delegated by the proposed Constitution to the Federal Government, are few and defined. Those which are to remain in the State Governments are numerous and indefinite." The Tenth Amendment seems to echo Madison's sentiment: "The powers not delegated to the United States by the Constitution, nor prohibited by it to the States, are reserved to the States respectively, or to the people." Allowing the federal government to claim powers that it cannot trace back to the Constitution, some argue, runs the risk of a tyranny—an end the Constitution was designed to prevent.

And yet the Court has not rejected the idea that there are inherent powers. Many of the cases in this area pertain to claims of inherent presidential power, not congressional power, as we will see in chapters 4 and 5. There we will consider several cases in which a president claims to have special authority to run the nation and protect it during times of national emergency.

One case that we excerpt in chapter 4, *United States v. Curtiss-Wright Export Corp.* (1936), though, deserves mention here because it is among the Court's clearest statements of the inherent power of the federal government—including Congress.

At issue in *Curtiss-Wright* was a resolution passed by Congress in 1934 that gave President Franklin D. Roosevelt authority to prohibit the sale of arms to warring countries. Shortly thereafter, Roosevelt issued an order embargoing weapon sales to Bolivia and Paraguay. Curtiss-Wright, a company that built airplanes refused to comply with the order and tried to get around it by disguising bombers as passenger planes.

---

33. As does preclearance; after all, without a coverage formula, preclearance cannot exist.

34. Joseph Story, *Commentaries on the Constitution*, vol. 3, Chapter XXIV; available at http://constitution.org/js/js_324.htm.

Eventually, it got caught and was charged with violating the order.

Curtiss-Wright, in turn, challenged the constitutionality of the government's action. Among its arguments was that the 1934 resolution was invalid because Congress had given "uncontrolled" lawmaking "discretion" to the president. On this score, the company's reasoning appeared strong: in *Panama Refining Company v. Ryan* (1935) the Court had struck down a congressional act on the ground that the legislature had delegated its lawmaking authority to the president without sufficient guidelines.[35] In Curtiss-Wright's view, the 1934 resolution was no different from the law struck down in *Panama Refining*.

The U.S. government tried to distinguish the facts in this case from those in the 1935 decision, saying that the congressional delegation of power in *Panama Refining* involved domestic, not international, affairs. This distinction was important, in the government's argument, because "from the beginning of the government, in the conduct of foreign affairs, Congress has followed the practice of conferring upon the President power similar to that conferred by the present resolution." By way of example, U.S. attorneys indicated that as early as 1794 Congress had given the president the power to determine when embargoes should be laid "upon vessels in ports of the United States bound for foreign ports."

Though it is possible, even likely, that the Court would have struck down the congressional delegation in *Curtiss-Wright,* it agreed with the government on the difference between domestic and foreign relations. As Justice George Sutherland, who had gained substantial international policy-making experience in the 1920s,[36] wrote for the majority,

The two classes of powers are different, both in respect of their origin and their nature. The broad statement that the Federal government can exercise no powers except those specifically enumerated in the Constitution, and such implied powers as are necessary and proper to carry into effect the enumerated powers, is categorically true only in respect of our internal affairs. . . .

"The investment of the Federal government with the powers of external sovereignty," the Court continued, "did not depend upon the affirmative grants of the Constitution." Indeed, the majority went so far as to write,

The powers to declare and wage war, to conclude peace, to make treaties, to maintain diplomatic relations with other sovereignties, if they had never been mentioned in the Constitution, would have vested in the Federal government as necessary concomitants of nationality. . . . As a member of the family of nations, the right and power of the United States in that field are equal to the right and power of the other members of the international family. Otherwise, the United States is not completely sovereign. . . .

In other words, in the field of domestic affairs the federal government is limited to its enumerated and implied powers. But "authority over foreign affairs is an inherent power, which attaches automatically to the federal government as a sovereign entity, and derives from the Constitution only as the Constitution is the creator of that sovereign entity."[37] It is not Congress specifically but the federal government that enjoys complete authority over foreign relations, which is an inherent power of sovereign nations, one that is derived not from their charters, but from their status.

On what basis did the Court draw this distinction? In its view, the U.S. Constitution transferred some domestic powers from the states to the federal government, leaving some with the states or the people. That is why Congress cannot exercise authority over internal affairs beyond that which is explicitly enumerated or can be implied from that document. In contrast, no such transfer occurred or could have occurred for authority over foreign affairs: because the states never had such power to begin with, they could not bestow it on the federal government.

To be sure, there is support for the distinction the Court made between domestic and foreign affairs. We explore this subject in greater detail in chapters 4 and 5, but here we can say that some of the framers would have approved of *Curtiss-Wright*—including Hamilton. As he wrote in *Federalist* No. 23, "The circumstances that endanger the safety of nations are infinite, and for this reason no constitutional shackles can wisely be imposed on the power to which the care of it is committed." The

---

35. For more on *Panama Refining Company* and other delegation-of-powers cases, see chapter 5.

36. In 1921 he chaired the advisory committee of the U.S. delegation to the International Conference on the Limitation of Naval Armaments and the following year served as counsel in arbitration between the United States and Norway over shipping.

37. Pritchett, *Constitutional Law of the Federal System*, 305.

idea, in short, was not novel, and Sutherland had espoused it during his career.

But *Curtiss-Wright* also has provoked criticism. Some historians and legal scholars assert that Sutherland's historical analysis was inaccurate: "There is evidence that, after independence, at least some of the erstwhile colonies . . . considered themselves sovereign, independent states."[38] More relevant here, as we pointed out earlier, are the risks with allowing the government—Congress, the president, or both—to exercise "inherent powers," whether in the domestic or the foreign realm. At the very least, can it be that the language of the Tenth Amendment, which limits the federal government to its delegated powers, applies only to domestic powers and not to foreign affairs? *Curtiss-Wright* seems to teach this lesson, and it makes some analysts squirm.

Finally, we might raise questions about whether Sutherland's opinion remains authoritative doctrine. Have more-recent cases undercut its view that the federal government possesses extra-constitutional authority over foreign affairs that provide it with considerable leeway? You will have a chance to think about this when you read the next two chapters.

FEDERAL LEGISLATURE: CONSTITUTIONAL INTERPRETATIONS

Curtiss-Wright gives extraordinary authority to the federal government in the realm of foreign affairs, as you now know. But as you probably realize by now, the Court has also allowed Congress a good deal of leeway in domestic affairs, especially in disputes involving that body's power to regulate its own affairs and to enact legislation, even if a law intrudes on state operations.

The degree of deference the Court typically (but, again, not always) accords to Congress, some scholars argue, suggests the pervasiveness of congressional interpretation of the Constitution.[39] After all, when legislators debate and enact bills pursuant to the necessary and proper clause, they must interpret the word *proper*. Likewise, when they discuss legislation based on their amendment-enforcing powers, as they did in the Voting Rights Act at issue in *Katzenbach*, they must

agree on the meaning of the phrase *appropriate legislation*. That the Court more-than-occasionally defers to the legislature's interpretation implies that the justices recognize that they do not have a monopoly on constitutional interpretation.

It is also the case that most of the actions taken by Congress never reach the Supreme Court, thereby virtually ensuring that legislators have the last word. When Congress passed one of the most restrictive laws in American history, the Sedition Act of 1798, which prohibited writings or speech against the U.S. government, the Court had no opportunity to review its constitutionality before it expired in 1801. Likewise, during the Clinton impeachment proceedings in 1999, legislators made innumerable judgments about their powers—judgments the Court never reviewed.

Again, this is not to say that the Court never overturns congressional "interpretations." *Boerne* and *Shelby County* certainly prove otherwise. It is rather to say that most people, even Supreme Court justices, believe that Congress takes seriously the need to reach constitutional judgments as it goes about its lawmaking task.

But questions do arise over who should be the "ultimate interpreter" of the Constitution. As we discussed in chapter 2, the answer may be less obvious than you think. Not surprisingly, many justices have taken the position that it should be the Court. Chief Justice Charles Evans Hughes once said, "It is only from the Supreme Court that we can obtain a sane well-ordered interpretation of the Constitution." And, in cases such as *Boerne* and *Shelby County*, contemporary justices seem to agree. On the other hand, some commentators point out that there is no reason the Court should be the ultimate interpreter, and in fact Congress may be better suited to that task. After all, because members of Congress are elected, "switching final authority to interpret the Constitution from the Supreme Court to Congress would increase democratic inputs into constitutional interpretation."[40]

Based on your reading of the cases and narrative in this chapter, which side do you think is right? As you consider that question, keep in mind that commentators have also argued the president does (and should) play a role in constitutional interpretation. In the next two chapters, you will have an opportunity to consider how presidents have undertaken that task, and how the Court has responded.

---

38. Ibid., 23.

39. This section draws on Murphy, "Who Shall Interpret the Constitution?"; and chapters in Devins and Whittington, *Congress and the Constitution.*

---

40. Tushnet, "The Story of *City of Boerne v. Flores,* 524.

ANNOTATED READINGS

For discussion of Congress's authority over its structure and operations and the sources and scope of law-making power, see David Gray Adler and Larry N. George, eds., *The Constitution and the Conduct of American Foreign Policy* (Lawrence: University Press of Kansas, 1996); Richard E. Ellis, *Aggressive Nationalism; McCulloch v. Maryland and the Foundation of Federal Authority in the Young Republic* (New York: Oxford University Press, 2007); Gerald Gunther, ed., *John Marshall's Defense of* McCulloch v. Maryland (Stanford, CA: Stanford University Press, 1969); Chandler Davidson and Bernard Grofman, eds., *Quiet Revolution in the South: The Impact of the Voting Rights Act, 1965–1990* (Princeton, NJ: Princeton University Press, 1994); Ward E. Y. Elliott, *The Rise of Guardian Democracy: The Supreme Court's Role in Voting Rights Disputes, 1845–1969* (Cambridge, MA: Harvard University Press, 1974); Louis Henkin, *Foreign Affairs and the United States Constitution* (New York: Oxford University Press, 1996); Gary Lawson, Geoffrey P. Miller, Robert G. Natelson, and Guy I. Seidman, *The Origins of the Necessary and Proper Clause* (New York: Cambridge University Press, 2010); Mark R. Killenbeck, M'Culloch v. Maryland: *Securing a Nation* (Lawrence: University Press of Kansas, 2006); M. Nelson McGeary, *The Development of Congressional Investigative Power* (New York: Columbia University Press, 1940).

Books on Congress–Court relations and constitutional deliberations in Congress include Jeb Barnes, *Overruled? Legislative Overrides, Pluralism, and Contemporary Court–Congress Relations* (Stanford, CA: Stanford University Press, 2004); Campbell C. Colton and John F. Stack Jr., eds., *Congress Confronts the Court: The Struggle for Legitimacy and Authority in Lawmaking* (Lanham, MD: Rowman & Littlefield, 2001); David P. Currie, *The Constitution in Congress: The Federalist Period, 1789–1801* (Chicago: University of Chicago Press, 1997); Neal Devins and Keith E. Whittington, eds., *Congress and the Constitution* (Durham, NC: Duke University Press, 2005); Louis Fisher, *The Supreme Court and Congress: Rival Interpretations* (Washington, DC: CQ Press, 2009); Robert A. Katzmann, *Courts and Congress* (Washington, DC: Brookings Institution, 1997); Robert A. Katzmann, *Judges and Legislators: Toward Institutional Comity* (Washington, DC: Brookings Institution, 1988); Walter F. Murphy, *Congress and the Court* (Chicago: University of Chicago Press, 1962); Mitchell Pickerill, *Constitutional Deliberation in Congress: The Impact of Judicial Review in a Separated System* (Durham, NC: Duke University Press, 2004); C. Herman Pritchett, *Congress versus the Supreme Court, 1957–1960* (Minneapolis: University of Minnesota Press, 1961); John R. Schmidhauser and Larry L. Berg, *The Supreme Court and Congress* (New York: Free Press, 1972); Charles Warren, *Congress, the Constitution, and the Supreme Court* (Boston: Little, Brown, 1935).

4 The Executive

HE CONSTITUTION'S FRAMERS would have great trouble recognizing today's presidency. The sentiment of the Philadelphia convention was that the Articles of Confederation were flawed because they did not provide for an executive, but few delegates would have supported the far-reaching powers wielded by modern presidents. After what they had suffered under the British monarchy, many delegates had serious reservations about awarding too much authority to the executive branch. Those who supported the New Jersey Plan envisioned a plural executive in which two individuals would share the chief executive position as insurance against excessive power accruing to a single person. The framers would be amazed at the vast military resources over which the president serves as commander in chief, to say nothing of the hundreds of departments, agencies, and bureaus that constitute the executive branch.

Some of this growth likely traces to the rather loose wording of Article II. The article has neither the detail nor the precision of the framers' Article I description of the legislature; instead, it is dominated by issues of selection and removal and devotes less attention to powers and limitations. The wording is quite broad. Presidents are given the undefined "executive power" of the United States and are admonished to take care that the laws are "faithfully executed." Other grants of authority, such as the president's role as "Commander in Chief of the Army and Navy" and the preferential position given the chief executive in matters of foreign policy, allow for significant expansion.

The presidency also has grown in response to a changing world. As American society became more complex, the number of areas requiring government action mushroomed. Overwhelmed by these responsibilities, among other reasons, Congress delegated to the executive branch authority that the framers probably did not anticipate. In addition, the expanding importance of defense and foreign policy demanded a more powerful presidency.

As these changes took place, the Supreme Court was frequently called on to umpire disputes over the constitutional limits of executive authority. This chapter explores how the justices have interpreted Article II of the Constitution. It is divided into four sections. The first provides an overview of Article II, the second takes up the Supreme Court's general response to questions concerning presidential power, the third considers the domestic powers of the president, and the fourth explores the role of the president in foreign affairs.

ARTICLE II: BASIC CONSIDERATIONS

When the framers gathered in Philadelphia in 1787, they were uncertain about how to create an executive for the new nation.[1] They knew all too well the dangers of a strong executive. Indeed, widespread dissatisfaction

---

1. We adopt some of this discussion from Farber and Sherry, *A History of the American Constitution,* 107–110. Farber and Sherry contains excerpts of the debates over Article II.

with the British system led states, during the period from 1776 to 1778, to adopt constitutions that established weak governorships. State executives were given short terms of office, with few powers, and those few often shared with a council. By 1787, however, some states had become sufficiently dissatisfied with their weak governorships that they strengthened them. During the war with Britain, it had become apparent that state executives were too inexperienced and politically constrained to maintain an effective effort. Therefore, by the time the framers met, a range of executive systems existed in the states—from those that remained weak to those that were quite strong.

Which position would the founders take? To address this question, let us consider the two aspects of the executive with which they grappled: the structure of the presidency and executive powers.

The Structure of the Presidency

At the Constitutional Convention, the vast majority of discussions over Article II concerned not the powers of the executive, but the structure of the institution. The framers debated everything about the presidency, including selection, removal, tenure, and succession.

Selection of the President. The convention delegates considered several mechanisms for choosing the president, including, notably, selection by the national legislature. In the end they devised a novel solution: the Electoral College. Until then, the executives of most nations were chosen by bloodline, military power, or legislative selection *(see box 4-1)*. No other country had experimented with a system like the Electoral College apparatus created in Philadelphia. Perhaps because it had never been tried, the system, as we shall see, was plagued with defects that required correction over time.

The framers designed the Electoral College system to allow the general electorate to have some influence on the selection of the chief executive without resorting to direct popular election. Then, as now, the plan called for each state to select presidential electors equal in number to the state's delegates to the Senate and House of Representatives. The Constitution empowered the state legislatures to decide the method of choosing the electors. Popular election was always the most common method, but in the past some state legislatures voted for the electors. Article II disqualifies those who hold federal office from being electors but otherwise specifies no qualifications. The Electoral College system was based on the theory that the states would select as electors their most qualified citizens, who would exercise their best judgment in the selection of the president.

The Constitution mentions only three qualifications for presidential eligibility—citizenship, age, and residency. First, Article II requires that only individuals who are natural-born citizens may become president.[2] Naturalized citizens—those who attain citizenship after birth—are not eligible. Second, to be president a person must have reached the age of thirty-five. Third, the president must have been a resident of the United States for fourteen years. The Constitution made no mention of qualifications for vice president, but this oversight was corrected with the 1804 ratification of the Twelfth Amendment, which says that no person can serve as vice president who is not eligible to be president.

Under the original procedures detailed in Article II, the electors were to assemble in their respective state capitals on Election Day and cast votes for their presidential preferences. Each elector had two votes, no more than one of which could be cast for the candidate from the elector's home state. These ballots were then sent to the federal capital, where the president of the Senate opened them. The candidate receiving the most votes would be declared president, if the number of votes received was a majority of the number of electors. Article II anticipated two possible problems with this procedure: First, because the electors each cast two votes, it was possible for the balloting to result in a tie between two candidates. In this event, the Constitution stipulated that the House of Representatives should select one of the two. Second, if multiple candidates sought the presidency, it would be possible that no candidate would receive the required majority. In this case the House was to decide among the top five finishers in the Electoral College voting. In settling such disputed elections, each state delegation was to cast a single vote, rather than allowing the individual members to vote independently.

In the original scheme the vice president was selected right after the president. The formula for choosing the vice president was simple—the vice

---

2. The Constitution also allowed individuals who were citizens at the time the Constitution was adopted to be eligible to hold the presidency.

BOX 4-1   THE AMERICAN PRESIDENCY IN GLOBAL PERSPECTIVE

THE METHOD for selecting the president generated a good deal of discussion at the 1787 Constitutional Convention. The delegates considered and rejected several mechanisms, including selection by the national legislature. In the end the framers devised a novel solution: slates of electors equal to the congressional delegation of each state would elect the president.

In many countries—especially in Western Europe but also in Israel and Japan—chief executives are not chosen in elections separate from those of the legislative branch. In these parliamentary systems executives may be the leaders of parties that win legislative elections or are chosen by an elected legislature, as in Germany and the United Kingdom. Sometimes leaders continue to hold seats in the parliament. This practice is forbidden by the U.S. Constitution, which states, "[N]o Person holding any Office under the United States, shall be a Member of either House during his Continuance in Office."

Under the parliamentary system, if the electorate votes the ruling party in the legislature out of office, the executive also changes. Moreover, the executive is typically accountable to such a legislature: the membership may remove a leader after a vote of no confidence. Because of the importance of no-confidence votes, many nations have developed elaborate procedures for considering motions of no confidence. For example, the Italian parliament may not debate a no-confidence motion for more than three days, and the motion must be signed by at least one-tenth of the members of one house. In Germany a majority in the legislature may remove the chancellor, but only by simultaneously electing a successor.

SOURCE: George Thomas Kurian, *World Encyclopedia of Parliaments and Legislatures* (Washington, DC.: Congressional Quarterly, 1998).

---

president was the presidential candidate who received the second-highest number of electoral votes. If two or more candidates tied for second in the Electoral College voting, the Senate would select the vice president from among them.

The first two elections took place with no difficulty. In 1789 George Washington received one ballot from each of the 69 electors who participated and was elected president. John Adams became vice president because he received the next-highest number of electoral votes (thirty-four). History repeated itself in the election of 1792, with Washington receiving one vote from each of the 132 electors. Adams again gathered the next-highest number of votes (seventy-seven) and returned to the vice presidency.

The defects in the electoral system first became apparent with the election of 1796. By this time political parties had begun to develop, and this election was a contest between the incumbent Federalists and the Democratic-Republicans. With Washington declining to run for a third term, John Adams became the Federalist candidate, and Thomas Jefferson was the choice of those who wanted political change. Adams won the presidency with seventy-one electoral votes, and Jefferson, with sixty-eight, became vice president.

The nation therefore had a divided executive branch, with a president and vice president from different political parties.

Matters grew even worse with the 1800 election. The Democratic-Republicans were now the more popular of the two major parties, and they backed Jefferson for president and Aaron Burr for vice president. Electors committed to the Democratic-Republican candidates each cast one ballot for Jefferson and one for Burr. Although it was clear which man was running for which office, the method of selection did not allow for such distinctions. The result was that Jefferson and Burr each received seventy-three votes, and the election moved to the outgoing Federalist-dominated House of Representatives for settlement. Each of the sixteen states had a single vote, and a majority was required for election. On February 11, 1801, the first vote in the House was taken. Jefferson received eight votes and Burr six. Maryland and Vermont were unable to register a preference because their state delegations were evenly divided. The voting continued until the thirty-sixth ballot on February 17, when Jefferson received the support of ten state delegations and was named president, with Burr becoming vice president.

It was clear that the Constitution needed to be changed to avoid such situations. Congress proposed the Twelfth Amendment in 1803, and the states ratified it the next year. The amendment altered the selection system by separating the voting for president and vice president. Rather than casting two votes for president, electors would vote for a presidential candidate and then vote separately for a vice presidential candidate. The House and Senate continued to settle presidential and vice presidential elections in which no candidate received a majority, although the procedures for such elections also were modified by the amendment.

Presidential and vice presidential elections are still governed by the Twelfth Amendment, but the evolution of political parties and the reduction in the degree of independence exercised by presidential electors have made huge changes in the way the system operates. The Electoral College persists. Despite calls by some to replace it with direct popular election, proponents of this reform have never achieved enough strength to prompt Congress or the state legislatures to propose the necessary constitutional amendment. Historically, opposition to popular election has come from the smaller states, which enjoy more influence within the Electoral College system than they would under popular election reforms.

Indeed, until the 2000 election, most Americans were not concerned with reforming the presidential selection system. In modern times the Electoral College system had not produced a result at odds with the popular vote.[3] Texas governor George W. Bush assumed the presidency after capturing a majority of the Electoral College votes, although his opponent, Vice President Al Gore, narrowly won the popular vote. The election was so close that the result was not known until weeks after the balloting, when the Supreme Court's decision in *Bush v. Gore* (2000) settled the final issues that determined the outcome. The publicity surrounding this disputed election served as a national civics lesson in how the U.S. president is selected and sparked a widespread public debate on election reform. Consider the issue of reform as you read the excerpt below. Also consider another hotly debated question surrounding the case: To what degree did the justices allow their partisan preferences to enter into the decision? This question has arisen, in part, because five of the seven Republican justices cast their "ballots" for the candidate of their party, while both Democratic justices (Breyer and Ginsburg) "voted" for Gore.

Bush v. Gore

531 U.S. 98 (2000)
http://laws.findlaw.com/us/531/98.html
Oral arguments are available at https://www.oyez.org.
Vote: 5 (Kennedy, O'Connor, Rehnquist, Scalia, Thomas)
  4 (Breyer, Ginsburg, Souter, Stevens)

OPINION OF THE COURT: *Per Curiam*
CONCURRING OPINION: *Rehnquist*
DISSENTING OPINIONS: *Breyer, Ginsburg, Souter, Stevens*

FACTS:

The presidential election of November 7, 2000, was one of the closest races in American history. On election night it became clear that the battle between Governor Bush and Vice President Gore for the 270 electoral votes necessary for victory would be decided by the outcome in the state of Florida.

Initial vote counts in Florida gave Bush a lead of 1,780 votes out of 6 million cast. This narrow margin triggered an automatic machine recount held on November 10. The results gave Bush a victory, but the margin had slipped to a scant 250 votes, with absentee overseas ballots still to be counted. By this time charges and countercharges of voting irregularities led to lawsuits and political protests. As the various issues sorted themselves out over the ensuing days, the outcome of the election appeared to hinge on one major issue: large numbers of undercounted ballots in a select number of traditionally Democratic counties. Undercounted ballots were those for which vote-counting machines did not register a presidential preference. In many

---

3. Some political scientists argue that Richard Nixon won the popular vote in 1960. On this account, John F. Kennedy could have won the popular vote only if he was granted all the votes from Alabama that went to segregationist Democratic electors who had pledged to vote against Kennedy (and voted for Harry Byrd). In Alabama, voters received a separate vote for each elector, and the six anti-Kennedy electors each received more votes than the five pro-Kennedy electors. Because these electors were chosen in a primary, and because the voters in Alabama voted for the segregationists, who were anti-Kennedy, it seems difficult to claim them as Kennedy votes. If this is so, then the winner of the popular vote has lost four out of the last thirty-four presidential elections. For more on the popular vote in the 1960 presidential election, see Brian J. Gaines, "Popular Myths about Popular Vote–Electoral College Splits," *PS: Political Science and Politics* 34 (2001): 70–75.

The sequence of headlines that appeared in the **Orlando Sentinel** immediately after the election reflects the uncertainty and confusion that gripped Florida and the nation following the vote for president in 2000.

cases such undercounting was the result of a failure by the voter to pierce completely the computer punch-card ballot. In other cases, machine malfunction may have been the cause. Gore supporters demanded a hand recount of the undercounted ballots.

Three statutory deadlines imposed obstacles for the labor-intensive and time-consuming manual recounts. First, Florida law directed the secretary of state to certify the election results by November 18. Second, federal law (3 U.S.C. §5) provided that if all controversies and contests over a state's electors were resolved by December 12, the state's slate would be considered conclusive and beyond challenge (the so-called safe harbor provision). And third, federal law set December 18 as the date the electors would cast their ballots.

As the manual recounts proceeded, it became clear that the process would not be completed prior to the November 18 deadline for certification. Florida's Republican secretary of state, Katherine Harris, announced her intention to certify the vote on November 18 regardless of the ongoing recounts. Gore forces went to court to block her from doing so. A unanimous Florida Supreme Court, emphasizing that every vote cast should be counted, ruled that the recounts should continue and extended the certification date to November 26. Believing the Florida court had exceeded its authority, Bush's lawyers appealed this decision to the U.S. Supreme Court. On December 4 the justices set aside the Florida court's certification extension and asked the court to explain the reasoning behind its decision (*Bush v. Palm Beach County Canvassing Board,* 2000). In the meantime, Secretary Harris on November 26 certified Bush as winning the state by 537 votes.

Four days after the U.S. Supreme Court's decision, the Florida high court, in response to an appeal by Gore, ordered a new statewide manual recount of all undervotes to begin immediately. The recounts were to be conducted by local officials guided only by the instruction to determine voter intent on each ballot. Bush appealed this decision to the U.S. Supreme Court. On December 9 the justices scheduled the case for oral argument and ordered the recounts to stop pending a final decision. Both sides were well represented. Bush's attorney, Theodore Olson, had served as an assistant attorney general in the Reagan administration and, in private practice, had argued many cases before the Supreme Court. Gore's attorney was David Boies, a prominent litigator whose previous clients included George Steinbrenner and CBS. He had also helped the Justice Department win a major antitrust case against Microsoft. *(See box 4-2 on page194.)*

Two major issues dominated the case. First, did the Florida Supreme Court violate federal law by altering the election procedures in place prior to the election? Second, did the Florida Supreme Court violate the equal protection clause of the Fourteenth Amendment when it ordered a recount to take place without setting a single uniform standard for determining voter intent?

A badly divided Supreme Court issued its ruling on December 12. The per curiam opinion focuses on the equal protection claim.[4] The concurring and dissenting opinions include a wide range of views on the issues presented and debate what remedies should be imposed for any constitutional or statutory violations found.

ARGUMENTS:

For the petitioners, George W. Bush et al.:

- The Florida Supreme Court violated 3 U.S.C. §5, which states that appointments of electors are conclusive only if made pursuant to laws enacted prior to election day. By demanding that the recounts continue, the Florida Supreme Court is changing state law instead of interpreting state law.
- The new standards, procedures, and timetables established by the Florida Supreme Court for the selection of Florida's presidential electors are in conflict with the state legislature's plan for the resolution of election disputes. The court's new framework violates Article II, which vests in state legislatures the exclusive authority to regulate the appointment of presidential electors.
- The manual recount procedures newly concocted by the Florida Supreme Court are arbitrary, standardless, and subjective, and will necessarily vary in application, both across different counties and within individual counties, in violation of the equal protection clause of the Fourteenth Amendment. The equal protection clause forbids the state from treating similarly situated voters differently based merely on where they live.

---

4. A per curiam opinion represents the view of a majority of the justices, but, unlike most other Supreme Court opinions, it is unsigned. Per curiam opinions tend to be shorter than other opinions and are generally used for less-complicated cases, but this is not always so.

For the respondents, Albert Gore Jr. et al.:

- The federal law that petitioners accuse the Florida Supreme Court of violating supplies an option of safe harbor only if states choose to use it.
- In its ruling, the Florida court did not "make law" or establish any new legal standards that conflict with legislative enactments. Rather, the court engaged in a routine exercise of statutory interpretation that construed the Florida election code according to the legislature's designated manner for choosing electors in a statewide election.
- The Florida Supreme Court's judgment is fully consistent with equal protection. Petitioners' allegations about the way the manual recounts have been conducted have no support in the record and are based on unsubstantiated rumors, untested "evidence," and biased ex parte submissions. In fact, the recounts have been conducted in full public view by counting teams made up of representatives from different political parties, with the supervision of a canvassing board that includes a sitting county judge and review by the Florida judiciary. Supreme Court precedents emphasize the fundamental right of all qualified voters to cast their votes and to have their votes counted.

PER CURIAM.

The closeness of this election, and the multitude of legal challenges which have followed in its wake, have brought into sharp focus a common, if heretofore unnoticed, phenomenon. Nationwide statistics reveal that an estimated 2% of ballots cast do not register a vote for President for whatever reason, including deliberately choosing no candidate at all or some voter error, such as voting for two candidates or insufficiently marking a ballot. In certifying election results, the votes eligible for inclusion in the certification are the votes meeting the properly established legal requirements.

This case has shown that punch card balloting machines can produce an unfortunate number of ballots which are not punched in a clean, complete way by the voter. After the current counting, it is likely legislative bodies nationwide will examine ways to improve the mechanisms and machinery for voting.

The individual citizen has no federal constitutional right to vote for electors for the President of the United States unless and until the state legislature chooses a statewide election as the means to implement its power to appoint members of the Electoral College. U.S. Const., Art. II, §1. . . . [T]he State legislature's power to select the manner for appointing electors is plenary; it may, if it so chooses, select the electors itself, which indeed was the manner used by State legislatures in several States for many years after the Framing of our Constitution. History has now favored the voter, and in each of the several States the citizens themselves vote for Presidential electors. When the state legislature vests the right to vote for President in its people, the right to vote as the legislature has prescribed is fundamental; and one source of its fundamental nature lies in the equal weight accorded to each vote and the equal dignity owed to each voter. The State, of course, after granting the franchise in the special context of Article II, can take back the power to appoint electors.

The right to vote is protected in more than the initial allocation of the franchise. Equal protection applies as well to the manner of its exercise. Having once granted the right to vote on equal terms, the State may not, by later arbitrary and disparate treatment, value one person's vote over that of another. . . .

There is no difference between the two sides of the present controversy on these basic propositions. Respondents say that the very purpose of vindicating the right to vote justifies the recount procedures now at issue. The question before us, however, is whether the recount procedures the Florida Supreme Court has adopted are consistent with its obligation to avoid arbitrary and disparate treatment of the members of its electorate.

Much of the controversy seems to revolve around ballot cards designed to be perforated by a stylus but which, either through error or deliberate omission, have not been perforated with sufficient precision for a machine to count them. In some cases a piece of the card—a chad—is hanging, say by two corners. In other cases there is no separation at all, just an indentation.

The Florida Supreme Court has ordered that the intent of the voter be discerned from such ballots. For purposes of resolving the equal protection challenge, it is not necessary to decide whether the Florida Supreme Court had the authority under the legislative scheme for resolving election disputes to define what a legal vote is and to mandate a manual recount implementing that definition. The recount mechanisms implemented in response to the decisions of the Florida Supreme Court do not satisfy the minimum requirement for non-arbitrary treatment of voters necessary to secure the fundamental right. Florida's basic command for the count of legally cast votes is to consider the "intent of the voter." This is unobjectionable as an abstract proposition and a starting principle. The problem inheres in the absence of specific standards to ensure its equal application. The formulation of uniform rules to determine intent based on these recurring circumstances is practicable and, we conclude, necessary.

The law does not refrain from searching for the intent of the actor in a multitude of circumstances; and in some cases the general command to ascertain intent is not susceptible to much further refinement. In this instance, however, the question is . . . how to interpret the marks or holes or scratches on an inanimate object, a piece of cardboard or paper which, it is said, might not have registered as a vote during the machine count. The factfinder confronts a thing, not a person. The search for intent can be confined by specific rules designed to ensure uniform treatment.

The want of those rules here has led to unequal evaluation of ballots in various respects. As seems to have been acknowledged at oral argument, the standards for accepting or rejecting contested ballots might vary not only from county to county but indeed within a single county from one recount team to another.

The record provides some examples. A monitor in Miami-Dade County testified at trial that he observed that three members of the county canvassing board applied different standards in defining a legal vote. And testimony at trial also revealed that at least one county changed its evaluative standards during the counting process. Palm Beach County, for example, began the process with a 1990 guideline which precluded counting completely attached chads, switched to a rule that considered a vote to be legal if any light could be seen through a chad, changed back to the 1990 rule, and then abandoned any pretense of a *per se* rule, only to have a court order that the county consider dimpled chads legal. This is not a process with sufficient guarantees of equal treatment. . . .

The State Supreme Court ratified this uneven treatment. It mandated that the recount totals from two counties, Miami-Dade and Palm Beach, be included in the certified total. The court also appeared to hold *sub silentio* that the recount totals from Broward County, which were not completed until after the original November 14 certification by the Secretary of State, were to be considered part of the new certified vote totals even though the county certification was not contested by Vice President Gore. Yet each of the counties used varying standards to determine what was a legal vote. Broward County used a more forgiving standard than Palm Beach County, and uncovered almost three times as many new votes, a result markedly disproportionate to the difference in population between the counties. . . .

The recount process, in its features here described, is inconsistent with the minimum procedures necessary to protect the fundamental right of each voter in the special instance of a statewide recount under the authority of a single state judicial officer. Our consideration is limited to the present circumstances, for the problem of equal protection in election processes generally presents many complexities.

The question before the Court is not whether local entities, in the exercise of their expertise, may develop different systems for implementing elections. Instead, we are presented with a situation where a state court with the power to assure uniformity has ordered a statewide recount with minimal procedural safeguards. When a court orders a statewide remedy, there must be at least some assurance that the rudimentary requirements of equal treatment and fundamental fairness are satisfied. . . .

Upon due consideration of the difficulties identified to this point, it is obvious that the recount cannot be conducted in compliance with the requirements of equal protection and due process without substantial additional work. It would require not only the adoption (after opportunity for argument) of adequate statewide standards for determining what is a legal vote, and practicable procedures to implement them, but also orderly judicial review of any disputed matters that might arise. In addition, the Secretary of State has advised that the recount of only a portion of the ballots requires that the vote tabulation equipment be used to screen out undervotes, a function for which the machines were not designed. If a recount of overvotes were also required, perhaps even a second screening would be necessary. . . .

The Supreme Court of Florida has said that the legislature intended the State's electors to "participat[e] fully in the federal electoral process," as provided in 3 U.S.C. §5. That statute, in turn, requires that any controversy or contest that is designed to lead to a conclusive selection of electors be completed by December 12. That date is upon us, and there is no recount procedure in place under the State Supreme Court's order that comports with minimal constitutional standards. Because it is evident that any recount seeking to meet the December 12 date will be unconstitutional for the reasons we have discussed, we reverse the judgment of the Supreme Court of Florida ordering a recount to proceed.

Seven Justices of the Court agree that there are constitutional problems with the recount ordered by the Florida Supreme Court that demand a remedy. The only disagreement is as to the remedy. Because the Florida Supreme Court has said that the Florida Legislature intended to obtain the safe-harbor benefits of 3 U.S.C. §5, JUSTICE BREYER'S proposed remedy—remanding to the Florida Supreme Court for its ordering of a constitutionally proper contest until December 18—contemplates action in violation of the Florida election code, and hence could not be part of an "appropriate" order authorized by [Florida law].

None are more conscious of the vital limits on judicial authority than are the members of this Court, and none stand more in admiration of the Constitution's design to leave the selection of the President to the people, through their legislatures, and to the political sphere. When contending parties invoke the process of the courts, however, it becomes our unsought responsibility to resolve the federal and constitutional issues the judicial system has been forced to confront.

The judgment of the Supreme Court of Florida is reversed, and the case is remanded for further proceedings not inconsistent with this opinion.

CHIEF JUSTICE REHNQUIST, with whom JUSTICE SCALIA and JUSTICE THOMAS join, concurring.

We join the *per curiam* opinion. We write separately because we believe there are additional grounds that require us to reverse the Florida Supreme Court's decision.

We deal here not with an ordinary election, but with an election for the President of the United States. . . .

In most cases, comity and respect for federalism compel us to defer to the decisions of state courts on issues of state law. . . . But there are a few exceptional cases in which the Constitution imposes a duty or confers a power on a particular branch of a State's government. This is one of them. Article II, §1, cl. 2, provides that "[e]ach State shall appoint, in such Manner as the *Legislature* thereof may direct," electors for President and Vice President. Thus, the text of the election law itself, and not just its interpretation by the courts of the States, takes on independent significance. . . .

Art. II, §1, cl. 2, "convey[s] the broadest power of determination" and "leaves it to the legislature exclusively to define the method" of appointment. A significant departure from the legislative scheme for appointing Presidential electors presents a federal constitutional question. . . .

In Florida, the legislature has chosen to hold statewide elections to appoint the State's 25 electors. Importantly, the legislature has delegated the authority to run the elections and to oversee election disputes to the Secretary of

State (Secretary) and to state circuit courts.... In any election but a Presidential election, the Florida Supreme Court can give as little or as much deference to Florida's executives as it chooses.... But, with respect to a Presidential election, the court must be both mindful of the legislature's role under Article II in choosing the manner of appointing electors and deferential to those bodies expressly empowered by the legislature to carry out its constitutional mandate.

In order to determine whether a state court has infringed upon the legislature's authority, we necessarily must examine the law of the State as it existed prior to the action of the court. Though we generally defer to state courts on the interpretation of state law there are of course areas in which the Constitution requires this Court to undertake an independent, if still deferential, analysis of state law....

This inquiry does not imply a disrespect for state *courts* but rather a respect for the constitutionally prescribed role of state *legislatures*. To attach definitive weight to the pronouncement of a state court, when the very question at issue is whether the court has actually departed from the statutory meaning, would be to abdicate our responsibility to enforce the explicit requirements of Article II.

JUSTICE STEVENS, with whom JUSTICE GINSBURG and JUSTICE BREYER join, dissenting.

The Constitution assigns to the States the primary responsibility for determining the manner of selecting the Presidential electors. When questions arise about the meaning of state laws, including election laws, it is our settled practice to accept the opinions of the highest courts of the States as providing the final answers. On rare occasions, however, either federal statutes or the Federal Constitution may require federal judicial intervention in state elections. This is not such an occasion.

The federal questions that ultimately emerged in this case are not substantial. Article II provides that "[e]ach *State* shall appoint, in such Manner as the Legislature *thereof* may direct, a Number of Electors." It does not create state legislatures out of whole cloth, but rather takes them as they come—as creatures born of, and constrained by, their state constitutions.... The legislative power in Florida is subject to judicial review pursuant to Article V of the Florida Constitution, and nothing in Article II of the Federal Constitution frees the state legislature from the constraints in the state constitution that created it. Moreover, the Florida Legislature's own decision to employ a unitary code for all elections indicates that it intended

the Florida Supreme Court to play the same role in Presidential elections that it has historically played in resolving electoral disputes. The Florida Supreme Court's exercise of appellate jurisdiction therefore was wholly consistent with, and indeed contemplated by, the grant of authority in Article II....

Admittedly, the use of differing substandards for determining voter intent in different counties employing similar voting systems may raise serious concerns. Those concerns are alleviated—if not eliminated—by the fact that a single impartial magistrate will ultimately adjudicate all objections arising from the recount process....

What must underlie petitioners' entire federal assault on the Florida election procedures is an unstated lack of confidence in the impartiality and capacity of the state judges who would make the critical decisions if the vote count were to proceed. Otherwise, their position is wholly without merit. The endorsement of that position by the majority of this Court can only lend credence to the most cynical appraisal of the work of judges throughout the land. It is confidence in the men and women who administer the judicial system that is the true backbone of the rule of law. Time will one day heal the wound to that confidence that will be inflicted by today's decision. One thing, however, is certain. Although we may never know with complete certainty the identity of the winner of this year's Presidential election, the identity of the loser is perfectly clear. It is the Nation's confidence in the judge as an impartial guardian of the rule of law.

I respectfully dissent.

JUSTICE SOUTER, with whom JUSTICE BREYER joins and with whom JUSTICE STEVENS and JUSTICE GINSBURG join with regard to all but [the paragraphs dealing with the third issue], dissenting.

The Court should not have reviewed either *Bush v. Palm Beach County Canvassing Bd.* or this case, and should not have stopped Florida's attempt to recount all undervote ballots by issuing a stay of the Florida Supreme Court's orders during the period of this review. If this Court had allowed the State to follow the course indicated by the opinions of its own Supreme Court, it is entirely possible that there would ultimately have been no issue requiring our review, and political tension could have worked itself out in the Congress.... The case being before us, however, its resolution by the majority is another erroneous decision....

There are three issues: whether the State Supreme Court's interpretation of the statute providing for a contest of the state election results somehow violates 3 U.S.C. §5;

whether that court's construction of the state statutory provisions governing contests impermissibly changes a state law from what the State's legislature has provided, in violation of Article II, §1, cl. 2, of the national Constitution; and whether the manner of interpreting markings on disputed ballots failing to cause machines to register votes for President (the undervote ballots) violates the equal protection or due process guaranteed by the Fourteenth Amendment. None of these issues is difficult to describe or to resolve.

The 3 U.S.C. §5 issue is not serious. That provision sets certain conditions for treating a State's certification of Presidential electors as conclusive in the event that a dispute over recognizing those electors must be resolved in the Congress under 3 U.S.C. §15. Conclusiveness requires selection under a legal scheme in place before the election, with results determined at least six days before the date set for casting electoral votes. But no State is required to conform to §5 if it cannot do that (for whatever reason); the sanction for failing to satisfy the conditions of §5 is simply loss of what has been called its "safe harbor." And even that determination is to be made, if made anywhere, in the Congress.

The second matter here goes to the State Supreme Court's interpretation of certain terms in the state statute governing election "contests." . . . The issue is whether the judgment of the state supreme court has displaced the state legislature's provisions for election contests: is the law as declared by the court different from the provisions made by the legislature, to which the national Constitution commits responsibility for determining how each State's Presidential electors are chosen? See U.S. Const., Art. II, §1, cl. 2. . . . What Bush . . . argue[s], as I understand the contention, is that the interpretation of [Florida law] was so unreasonable as to transcend the accepted bounds of statutory interpretation, to the point of being a nonjudicial act and producing new law untethered to the legislative act in question. . . .

. . . [T]he interpretations by the Florida court raise no substantial question under Article II. That court engaged in permissible construction in determining that Gore had instituted a contest authorized by the state statute, and it proceeded to direct the trial judge to deal with that contest in the exercise of the discretionary powers generously conferred by [Florida law], to "fashion such orders as he or she deems necessary to ensure that each allegation in the complaint is investigated, examined, or checked, to prevent or correct any alleged wrong, and to provide any relief appropriate under such circumstances." . . .

It is only on the third issue before us that there is a meritorious argument for relief, as this Court's *Per Curiam* opinion recognizes. It is an issue that might well have been dealt with adequately by the Florida courts if the state proceedings had not been interrupted, and if not disposed of at the state level it could have been considered by the Congress in any electoral vote dispute. But because the course of state proceedings has been interrupted, time is short, and the issue is before us, I think it sensible for the Court to address it.

Petitioners have raised an equal protection claim, in the charge that unjustifiably disparate standards are applied in different electoral jurisdictions to otherwise identical facts. It is true that the Equal Protection Clause does not forbid the use of a variety of voting mechanisms within a jurisdiction, even though different mechanisms will have different levels of effectiveness in recording voters' intentions; local variety can be justified by concerns about cost, the potential value of innovation, and so on. But evidence in the record here suggests that a different order of disparity obtains under rules for determining a voter's intent that have been applied (and could continue to be applied) to identical types of ballots used in identical brands of machines and exhibiting identical physical characteristics (such as "hanging" or "dimpled" chads). I can conceive of no legitimate state interest served by these differing treatments of the expressions of voters' fundamental rights. The differences appear wholly arbitrary.

In deciding what to do about this, we should take account of the fact that electoral votes are due to be cast in six days. I would therefore remand the case to the courts of Florida with instructions to establish uniform standards for evaluating the several types of ballots that have prompted differing treatments, to be applied within and among counties when passing on such identical ballots in any further recounting (or successive recounting) that the courts might order.

Unlike the majority, I see no warrant for this Court to assume that Florida could not possibly comply with this requirement before the date set for the meeting of electors, December 18. . . . To recount these [disputed votes] manually would be a tall order, but before this Court stayed the effort to do that the courts of Florida were ready to do their best to get that job done. There is no justification for denying the State the opportunity to try to count all disputed ballots now.

I respectfully dissent.

JUSTICE GINSBURG, with whom JUSTICE STEVENS joins, and with whom JUSTICE SOUTER and JUSTICE BREYER join [except as to the portion of the opinion dealing with the equal protection claim], dissenting.

The extraordinary setting of this case has obscured the ordinary principle that dictates its proper resolution: Federal courts defer to state high courts' interpretations of their state's own law. This principle reflects the core of federalism, on which all agree. "The Framers split the atom of sovereignty. It was the genius of their idea that our citizens would have two political capacities, one state and one federal, each protected from incursion by the other." The Chief Justice's solicitude for the Florida Legislature comes at the expense of the more fundamental solicitude we owe to the legislature's sovereign. Were the other members of this Court as mindful as they generally are of our system of dual sovereignty, they would affirm the judgment of the Florida Supreme Court. . . .

The Court assumes that time will not permit "orderly judicial review of any disputed matters that might arise." But no one has doubted the good faith and diligence with which Florida election officials, attorneys for all sides of this controversy, and the courts of law have performed their duties. Notably, the Florida Supreme Court has produced two substantial opinions within 29 hours of oral argument. In sum, the Court's conclusion that a constitutionally adequate recount is impractical is a prophecy the Court's own judgment will not allow to be tested. Such an untested prophecy should not decide the Presidency of the United States.

JUSTICE BREYER, with whom JUSTICE STEVENS and JUSTICE GINSBURG join except as [to paragraphs 3–4 below], and with whom JUSTICE SOUTER joins [except as to the final paragraph of this excerpt], dissenting.

The Court was wrong to take this case. It was wrong to grant a stay. It should now vacate that stay and permit the Florida Supreme Court to decide whether the recount should resume.

The political implications of this case for the country are momentous. But the federal legal questions presented, with one exception, are insubstantial.

The majority raises three Equal Protection problems with the Florida Supreme Court's recount order: first, the failure to include overvotes in the manual recount; second, the fact that *all* ballots, rather than simply the undervotes, were recounted in some, but not all, counties; and third, the absence of a uniform, specific standard to guide the recounts. As far as the first issue is concerned, petitioners

presented no evidence, to this Court or to any Florida court, that a manual recount of overvotes would identify additional legal votes. The same is true of the second, and, in addition, the majority's reasoning would seem to invalidate any state provision for a manual recount of individual counties in a statewide election.

The majority's third concern does implicate principles of fundamental fairness. The majority concludes that the Equal Protection Clause requires that a manual recount be governed not only by the uniform general standard of the "clear intent of the voter," but also by uniform subsidiary standards (for example, a uniform determination whether indented, but not perforated, "undervotes" should count). The Florida Supreme Court ordered the inclusion of [one county's] undercounted "legal votes" even though those votes included ballots that were not perforated but simply "dimpled," while newly recounted ballots from other counties will likely include only votes determined to be "legal" on the basis of a stricter standard. In light of our previous remand, the Florida Supreme Court may have been reluctant to adopt a more specific standard than that provided for by the legislature for fear of exceeding its authority under Article II. However, since the use of different standards could favor one or the other of the candidates, since time was, and is, too short to permit the lower courts to iron out significant differences through ordinary judicial review, and since the relevant distinction was embodied in the order of the State's highest court, I agree that, in these very special circumstances, basic principles of fairness may well have counseled the adoption of a uniform standard to address the problem. In light of the majority's disposition, I need not decide whether, or the extent to which, as a remedial matter, the Constitution would place limits upon the content of the uniform standard.

Nonetheless, there is no justification for the majority's remedy, which is simply to reverse the lower court and halt the recount entirely. An appropriate remedy would be, instead, to remand this case with instructions that, even at this late date, would permit the Florida Supreme Court to require recounting *all* undercounted votes in Florida, including those from Broward, Volusia, Palm Beach, and Miami-Dade Counties, whether or not previously recounted prior to the end of the protest period, and to do so in accordance with a single-uniform substandard.

The majority justifies stopping the recount entirely on the ground that there is no more time. In particular, the majority relies on the lack of time for the Secretary to review and approve equipment needed to separate undervotes. But the majority reaches this conclusion in the absence of *any* record evidence that the recount could not have been completed in the time allowed by the Florida Supreme Court. The majority finds facts outside of the record on matters that state courts are in a far better position to address. Of course, it is too late for any such recount to take place by December 12, the date by which election disputes must be decided if a State is to take advantage of the safe harbor provisions of 3 U.S.C. §5. Whether there is time to conduct a recount prior to December 18, when the electors are scheduled to meet, is a matter for the state courts to determine. And whether, under Florida law, Florida could or could not take further action is obviously a matter for Florida courts, not this Court, to decide. . . .

I fear that in order to bring this agonizingly long election process to a definitive conclusion, we have not adequately attended to that necessary "check upon our own exercise of power," "our own sense of self-restraint." *United States v. Butler* (1936) (Stone, J., dissenting). Justice Brandeis once said of the Court, "The most important thing we do is not doing." What it does today, the Court should have left undone. I would repair the damage done as best we now can, by permitting the Florida recount to continue under uniform standards.

I respectfully dissent.

The Court's decision in *Bush v. Gore* became the final chapter in the presidential election controversy of 2000. By stopping the Florida recount, the Court removed Vice President Gore's last hope of capturing the state's twenty-five electoral votes and guaranteed that Governor Bush would become the next president *(see box 4-2)*.

BOX 4-2   AFTERMATH . . . *BUSH V. GORE*

THE ANNOUNCEMENT of the Supreme Court's decision in *Bush v. Gore* (2000) effectively ended the 2000 presidential election controversy. On December 13, 2000, the day after the justices ruled, Vice President Al Gore announced that he was ending his campaign: "I accept the finality of this outcome. . . . And tonight, for the sake of our unity as a people and the strength of our democracy, I offer my concession." Florida officials quickly certified the state's twenty-five electoral votes for Texas governor George W. Bush.

Florida's electoral votes gave Bush a total of 271 in the Electoral College, just one more than required to become the forty-third president of the United States. Bush became only the fourth president in U.S. history to win office while losing the popular vote to his chief opponent: Gore captured 48.39 percent of the popular vote, as opposed to Bush's 47.88 percent. Before Bush only John Quincy Adams in 1824, Rutherford B. Hayes in 1876, and Benjamin Harrison in 1888 had been elected president without leading in the popular vote count. (Some political scientists have argued that Richard Nixon won the popular vote in the election of 1960, but he lost the election to John F. Kennedy. See footnote 3.)

Because of the voting controversies in Florida, many states revised election laws and upgraded vote-counting equipment to avoid similar problems in future elections. The two Florida officials at the center of the controversy, Governor Jeb Bush and Secretary of State Katherine Harris, continued their political careers. Jeb Bush was reelected governor of Florida in 2002, and Harris won a congressional seat that same year. After serving two terms in the House, Harris lost her bid for a Senate seat. Theodore Olson, the lawyer who successfully argued Bush's case before the Supreme Court, was appointed solicitor general of the United States by the new president and served until 2004. In 2010 Olson and his former *Bush v. Gore* opponent, David Boies (Gore's lawyer), teamed up to challenge a California constitutional amendment banning same-sex marriage.

Gore seriously considered a rematch against President Bush in the 2004 elections, but in late 2002 he announced that he would not be a candidate for his party's nomination. He instead focused his efforts on environmental policy. *An Inconvenient Truth,* a documentary film on global warming that Gore wrote and narrated, won the 2006 Academy Award for Best Documentary. In 2007 he received the Nobel Peace Prize for his efforts to combat global climate change. President Bush was reelected to the presidency in 2004.

Public opinion polls taken after the Court's ruling in *Bush v. Gore* showed that a large majority of Americans accepted Bush as the legitimate president, and, contrary to many predictions, the polls failed to find any appreciable decline in public support for the Court because of its incursion into the presidential election. A Harris Poll taken in 2000 prior to the election found that 34 percent of the American people had "great confidence" in the Supreme Court. Harris repeated the poll in January 2001 and discovered virtually no change: 35 percent of the respondents expressed "great confidence" in the Court. Two years later the figure again was 34 percent.[1]

---

1. A summary of polling data on the public's confidence in the Supreme Court can be found in Lee Epstein, Jeffrey A. Segal, Harold J. Spaeth, and Thomas G. Walker, *The Supreme Court Compendium: Data Decisions, and Developments*, 6th ed. (Thousand Oaks, CA: CQ Press, 2016).

Although much of the nation was happy to see the election finally resolved, the Court's action caused intense debate in political and academic circles. Not only was there a question of whether the Supreme Court should have heard the case in the first place, but also many believed, for the reasons we noted earlier, that the justices' votes were excessively influenced by their own partisan preferences. Do you agree?

Removal. Although the framers spent some time dealing with presidential selection, they apparently agreed rather quickly about removal. If an incumbent president (or vice president) abuses the office, the Constitution provides for impeachment as the method of removal. Impeachment is a two-stage process. First, the House of Representatives investigates the charges against the incumbent. The Constitution stipulates that impeachment can occur only upon charges of "Treason, Bribery, or other High Crimes and Misdemeanors." Once convinced that there is sufficient evidence of such misconduct, the House passes articles of impeachment specifying the crimes charged and authorizing a trial. The second stage, the trial, takes place in the Senate, with the chief justice of the United States presiding. Conviction requires the agreement of two-thirds of the voting senators. The Constitution specifies that the chief justice shall preside over the Senate if it tries the president, but not when the vice president is being impeached. Could this mean that a vice president, acting as president of the Senate, may preside over his or her own impeachment? That is unlikely, but the procedures are not altogether clear because no vice president has ever been impeached by the House of Representatives. Finally, Congress may impose no penalty on a convicted official other than removal from office. The former officeholder may, however, be subject to separate criminal prosecution in the courts.

Congress has never removed a president from office, but three have barely escaped such a fate. Andrew Johnson was impeached by the House in 1868, and he survived his trial in the Senate by one vote. Richard Nixon was well on his way to being impeached in 1974 when he resigned from office. The House passed two articles of impeachment against Bill Clinton in 1998, and the Senate vote in February 1999 fell far short of the sixty-seven votes of guilt needed to convict. Because both the Nixon and Clinton episodes led to several important constitutional rulings on executive power, we have more to say about the circumstances surrounding these presidents' troubles in the coming pages.

Tenure and Succession. The Constitution sets the presidential term at four years. Originally, it placed no restriction on the number of terms a president could serve; George Washington began the tradition of a two-term limit when he announced at the end of his second term that he would not run again. Every president honored this tradition until Franklin Roosevelt sought election to a third term in 1940 and to a fourth term in 1944. In reaction, Congress proposed the Twenty-second Amendment, which held that no person could run for president after having served more than six years in that office. The states ratified the amendment in 1951.

In Article II the framers provided a mechanism for the replacement of the president in the event of death, resignation, or disability: the vice president assumes the powers and responsibilities of the office.[5] The Constitution further authorizes Congress to determine presidential succession if there is no sitting vice president when a vacancy occurs.

In 1965 Congress recommended additional changes in the Constitution to govern presidential succession. The need became apparent after Lyndon Johnson assumed the presidency following John F. Kennedy's

---

5. Nine sitting presidents have failed to complete their terms. Four (William Henry Harrison, Zachary Taylor, Warren G. Harding, and Franklin D. Roosevelt) died of natural causes, and four (Abraham Lincoln, James A. Garfield, William McKinley, and John F. Kennedy) were assassinated. One (Richard Nixon) resigned from office.

Although presidential approval is not required for amendments to be proposed or ratified, President Lyndon B. Johnson, surrounded by congressional leaders, signed the Twenty-fifth Amendment on February 23, 1967. The amendment authorized the president to nominate a new vice president when a vacancy in that office occurred. If Johnson had died or become disabled before the 1964 election, seventy-four-year-old Speaker John McCormack (far right) would have assumed the presidency. Next in the line of succession was the president pro tempore of the Senate, eighty-eight-year-old Carl Hayden (third from left, standing).

assassination in 1963. Johnson's ascension left the vice presidency vacant. If anything had happened to Johnson, the federal succession law dictated that next in line was the Speaker of the House, followed by the president pro tempore of the Senate *(see box 4-3)*. In 1965 the Speaker was John McCormack (D-Mass.) who was seventy-four years old, and the president pro tempore was Carl Hayden (D-Ariz.) who was eighty-eight. Neither would have been capable of handling the demands of the presidency. Congress proposed that the Constitution be amended to provide that when a vacancy occurs in the office of vice president, the president nominates a new vice president, who takes office upon confirmation by majority vote in both houses of Congress. The proposal also clarified procedures governing those times when a president is temporarily unable to carry out the duties of the office. The change was ratified by the states as the Twenty-fifth Amendment in 1967.

It was not long before the country used the procedures outlined in the Twenty-fifth Amendment. In 1973 Vice President Spiro Agnew resigned when he was charged with income tax evasion stemming from alleged corruption during his years as governor of Maryland. Nixon nominated, and Congress confirmed, Representative Gerald R. Ford of Michigan to become vice president. Just one year later, Nixon resigned the presidency, and Ford became the nation's first unelected chief executive. Ford selected Nelson Rockefeller, former governor of New York, to fill the new vacancy in the vice presidency.

Constitutional Powers of the President

The powers of the presidency are listed in Sections 2 and 3 of Article II, and, unlike presidential selection and succession, they are the same today as when

BOX 4-3   LINE OF SUCCESSION

O N MARCH 30, 1981, President Ronald Reagan was shot by would-be assassin John Hinckley outside a Washington hotel and rushed to an area hospital for surgery. Vice President George H. W. Bush was on a plane returning to Washington from Texas. Presidential aides and cabinet members gathered at the White House, where questions arose among them and the press corps about who was "in charge."[1] In the press briefing room Secretary of State Alexander M. Haig Jr. told the audience of reporters and live television cameras, "As of now, I am in control here in the White House, pending the return of the vice president.... Constitutionally, gentlemen, you have the president, the vice president, and the secretary of state."

Haig was, as many gleeful critics subsequently pointed out, wrong. The Constitution says nothing about who follows the vice president in the line of succession. The Succession Act of 1947 (later modified to reflect the creation of new departments) establishes congressional leaders and the heads of the departments, in the order the departments were created, as filling the line of succession that follows the vice president.

The line of succession is as follows:

vice president

Speaker of the House of Representatives

president pro tempore of the Senate

secretary of state

secretary of the Treasury

secretary of defense

attorney general

secretary of the interior

secretary of agriculture

secretary of commerce

secretary of labor

secretary of health and human services

secretary of housing and urban development

secretary of transportation

secretary of energy

secretary of education

secretary of veterans affairs

secretary of homeland security

A different "line"—not of succession to the presidency but of National Command Authority in situations of wartime emergency—was created according to the National Security Act of 1947. The command rules are detailed in secret presidential orders that each new president signs at the beginning of the term. Among other things, the orders authorize the secretary of defense to act as commander in chief in certain specific, limited situations in which neither the president nor the vice president is available. Presumably, such situations would follow a nuclear attack on Washington, D.C.

SOURCE: Michael Nelson, ed., *Guide to the Presidency*, 3rd ed. (Washington, DC: CQ Press, 2002), 409.

1. "Confusion Over Who Was in Charge Arose Following Reagan Shooting," *Wall Street Journal*, April 1, 1981.

they were drafted by the Philadelphia convention. Some of these powers are quite specific: the president has the power "to make Treaties, provided two thirds of the Senators present concur." Furthermore, the president "shall nominate, and by and with the Advice and Consent of the Senate, shall appoint Ambassadors, other public Ministers and Consuls, Judges of the supreme Court, and all other Officers of the United States." But a good deal of the wording in Article II is quite vague, as exemplified by the vesting clause: "The executive Power shall be vested in a President."[6] What did the framers mean by the term *executive power*? There are two possibilities: (1) a mere designation of office, or (2) a general grant of power.

The "mere designation" view holds that the first sentence of Article II simply summarizes the powers

6. Here we highlight one debate over the vesting clause. Another centers on the theory of the "unitary executive," which holds, under the vesting clause, that the president—and the president alone—controls the executive branch. We return to this theory when we consider the president's power of appointment and removal.

listed later on. That is, the president is limited to those specific grants of power contained in Sections 2 and 3 of Article II. This was the position James Madison implied in *Federalist* No. 51 and that President William Howard Taft advocated:

The true view of the Executive function is, as I conceive it, that the President can exercise no power which cannot be fairly and reasonably traced to some specific grant of power or justly implied and included within such express grant as proper and necessary to its exercise. Such specific grant must be either in the Federal Constitution or in an act of Congress passed in pursuance thereof. There is no undefined residuum of power which he can exercise because it seems to him to be in the public interest.[7]

Is there any constitutional or historical basis for this position? A common piece of support is based on pure logic: Why would the framers bother to list specific powers, as they did in Article II, if they meant for the president to have more powers than those they enumerated?

Alexander Hamilton in *Federalist* No. 70 and other advocates of the "general grant of power" view, which modern-day scholars call the stewardship theory or the prerogative or inherent powers approach, take a much different position. On their account, the president has all the powers listed in Article II plus those additional powers needed to run the nation—regardless of whether the Constitution specifically authorizes their exercise. In other words, as long as neither the Constitution nor Congress has restricted the president from doing something for the common good, the president may do it. Seen in this way, the term *executive power* in Article II is a general grant of power to the president, who must exercise that power in ways that best serve the nation. As President Theodore Roosevelt, an advocate of this view, put it,

The most important factor in getting the right spirit in my Administration, next to the insistence upon courage, honesty, and a genuine democracy of desire to serve the plain people, was my insistence upon the theory that the executive power was limited only by specific restrictions and prohibitions appearing in the Constitution or imposed by the Congress under its Constitutional powers. My view was that every executive officer, and above all every executive officer in high position, was a steward of the people bound actively and affirmatively to do all he could for the people, and not to content himself with the negative merit of keeping his talents undamaged in a napkin. I declined to adopt the view that what was imperatively necessary for the Nation could not be done by the President unless he could find some specific authorization to do it.[8]

How do proponents of this view justify it? One way is through an appeal to common sense: as the only national leader who is available twenty-four hours a day, the president must be able to exercise personal judgment in addressing any problems that may arise. To do so, the president must have the latitude to deal with situations that the framers never envisioned. Another response relies on the take care clause of Article II, Section 3, which states that the president shall be given the responsibility to "take Care that the Laws be faithfully executed." To carry out this command, adherents of the stewardship theory argue, the president must have powers that go beyond those explicitly enumerated in Article II.

If the debate between these two camps reminds you of the controversy between Jefferson and Hamilton over the creation of the Bank of the United States and, more generally, over congressional powers, you would not be wrong. Just as Jefferson argued that the Constitution limits Congress to enumerated powers, advocates of the mere designation approach suggest that the president can exercise only the powers listed in Article II. And just as Hamilton asserted that the necessary and proper clause of Article I provides Congress with some degree of flexibility, adherents of the stewardship theory argue that the take care clause of Article II enables the president to exercise powers beyond those listed in Article II.

---

7. William Howard Taft, *Our Chief Magistrate and His Powers* (New York: Columbia University, 1916), 139–140. Taft may have been a proponent of the "mere designation" view, but he did not advocate a weak president. In fact, Taft's opinion in *Myers v. United States* (1926) suggests that he was a proponent of the unitary executive theory, which we discuss later in the chapter.

---

8. Theodore Roosevelt, *An Autobiography* (New York: Macmillan, 1913), 371–372.

THE FAITHFUL EXECUTION OF THE LAWS: DEFINING THE CONTOURS OF PRESIDENTIAL POWER

Which view would the Court adopt? The justices provided one answer in the landmark case *In re Neagle* (1890).[9] The appeal presenting this case was based on one of the more bizarre and twisted stories in constitutional history. The dispute began some three decades before the case reached the Supreme Court. When the trial court reviewed the essential facts, the telling took more than five hundred pages. As you read this decision, consider the extent to which you think the Court's response was influenced by the fact that one of its own members had been threatened.

David S. Terry, former California state supreme court judge.

Sarah Althea Hill Terry, wife of David Terry and central figure in the dispute with Justice Stephen Field that led to the killing of her husband.

Stephen J. Field, associate justice of the U.S. Supreme Court, 1863–1897.

---

9. The docket title of this case is *Thomas Cunningham, Sheriff of the County of San Joaquin, California, Appellant v. David Neagle.*

An illustration depicting U.S. Deputy Marshal David Neagle, assigned to protect Justice Stephen Field, shooting David Terry in a railroad station restaurant in Lathrop, California, in 1889.

In re Neagle

135 U.S. 1 (1890)
http://laws.findlaw.com/us/135/1.html
Vote: 6 (Blatchford, Bradley, Brewer, Gray, Harlan, Miller)
    2 (Fuller, Lamar)
OPINION OF THE COURT: *Miller*
DISSENTING OPINION: *Lamar*
NOT PARTICIPATING: *Field*

FACTS:

Stephen J. Field and David S. Terry both went to California during the 1849 gold rush—Field from New England and Terry from the South. Both became judges on the California Supreme Court, with Terry its chief judge.[10] In 1859 a bitter dispute erupted between Judge Terry and David Broderick, a U.S. senator. Terry resigned his position, challenged Broderick to a duel, and killed him. Field had been a close friend of Broderick, and he vowed never to forget the killing.

---

10. For an account of the events surrounding this case, see Robert Kroninger, "The Justice and the Lady," in *Yearbook 1977 of the Supreme Court Historical Society* (Washington, DC: Supreme Court Historical Society, 1977), 11–19.

Field was then elevated to the chief justiceship of the state court, and four years later President Abraham Lincoln appointed him to the U.S. Supreme Court.

Terry went into private practice and eventually came to represent Sarah Althea Hill in a divorce action. Hill claimed to be the wife of William Sharon, a former U.S. senator from Nevada, who was a millionaire mine operator and hotel owner. Hill charged Sharon with adultery and sued for divorce, but Sharon denied ever having married her. Many believed that she was just another in a long series of mistresses Sharon had after his wife died. Sarah Hill claimed to have a document proving the marriage was valid, but during the divorce hearing the court ruled the document to be a forgery and dismissed her action.

When William Sharon died, his son Frederick took legal action to dismantle any claim Sarah Hill had to his father's estate. Attorney Terry by this time had fallen in love with his beautiful client (and perhaps with her potentially large inheritance) and married her. As luck would have it, in September 1888 Justice Field was assigned to a three-judge circuit court to decide the suit brought by Frederick Sharon against Sarah

Terry. When the judges announced their ruling in favor of Sharon, violence erupted in the courtroom. Sarah Terry shouted accusations that Field had been bribed to reach his decision. Field ordered the marshals to remove her, and David Terry, defending his wife, struck a marshal and knocked out a tooth. He also brandished a bowie knife, and Sarah attempted to pull a revolver from her purse. The marshals subdued both of them. Sarah Terry was sentenced to one month in jail for contempt, and David Terry to six months in jail.

During his imprisonment, Terry's hatred of Field festered. On several occasions and before numerous witnesses, he pledged to horsewhip and then kill Field if the justice ever returned to California. Sarah Terry also threatened to kill Field. In response, President Benjamin Harrison and the U.S. attorney general decided to provide protection for Justice Field on his next judicial visit to California. The administration authorized a federal marshal, David Neagle, to act as Field's bodyguard when the justice was on circuit court duty in California.

Field returned to California in the summer of 1889, and Neagle was with him at all times. Traveling from Los Angeles to San Francisco by train, Field disembarked at Lathrop to eat breakfast in the station dining room. The Terrys, who had been on the same train, entered the dining room and saw him. Sarah returned to the train to get her revolver, while David walked up behind Field, slapped him twice on the side of the face, and raised his fist for a third blow. Neagle immediately rose from his seat with his revolver drawn and ordered Terry to stop. Terry reached into his coat, and Neagle, fearing that he was going for a weapon, fired two shots, one to the chest and the other to the head, killing him. When Terry's body was searched, no weapons were found.

Sarah Terry, who was to spend her last forty-five years in a state mental institution, claimed that Neagle, in conspiracy with Field, murdered her husband. She was sufficiently convincing that the bodyguard was arrested and charged with murder. Charges also were filed against Field as an accomplice, but they were later dropped.

A federal court granted a writ of habeas corpus ordering state authorities to release Neagle, and California appealed. The issue before the Supreme Court was Neagle's legal authority to act as he did. The central question was whether the president, without congressional action, could issue an executive order through the U.S. attorney general to authorize a bodyguard to protect Justice Field.

ARGUMENTS:

For the appellant, Thomas Cunningham, Sheriff of San Joaquin County, California:

- Under California law, Neagle's rights to use force to protect Justice Field were limited to protecting him within the courthouse. Neither the president nor the attorney general has the power to authorize Neagle to guard Field outside the courthouse.
- If the president has any such power, what is its source? If the president has power, within the jurisdiction of the several states, to assign a bodyguard to all federal officials, he has power to place a marshal in the house of every American citizen to shield him from harm at the hands of his fellow citizens. And, if it has come to this, what use do we have for state governments?

For the appellee, David Neagle:

- The president is constitutionally required to "take care that the laws be faithfully executed," and that clause invests in the president implied powers beyond expressly listed executive powers in the Constitution, independent of congressional statutes.
- The doctrine of necessary and implied powers is not limited to Congress. On the contrary, because the Constitution invests the president with executive power and confers on him the power to "take care that the laws be faithfully executed," it gives him all power reasonably incident to exercise the executive function and necessary to enforce the laws. As long as the power has not been withheld from him by the Constitution and flows from the Constitution, the power is his.
- It was the duty of the executive branch to guard and protect the life of Justice Field in the discharge of his duty because protection of courts and judges is essential to the very existence of the government, as the framers emphasized in *The Federalist Papers*.

MR. JUSTICE MILLER DELIVERED THE OPINION OF THE COURT.

The justices of the Supreme Court have been members of the Circuit Courts of the United States ever since the organization of the government, and their attendance on the circuit and appearance at the places where the courts are held has always been thought to be a matter of importance. In order to enable him to perform this duty, Mr. Justice Field had to travel each year from Washington City, near the Atlantic coast, to San Francisco, on the Pacific coast. In doing this he was as much in the discharge of a duty imposed upon him by law as he was while sitting in court and trying cases. There are many duties which the judge performs outside of the court-room where he sits to pronounce judgment or to preside over a trial. The statutes of the United States, and the established practice of the courts, require that the judge perform a very large share of his judicial labors at what is called "chambers." This chamber work is as important, as necessary, as much a discharge of his official duty as that performed in the court-house. Important cases are often argued before the judge at any place convenient to the parties concerned, and a decision of the judge is arrived at by investigations made in his own room, wherever he may be, and it is idle to say that this is not as much the performance of judicial duty as the filing of the judgment with the clerk, and the announcement of the result in open court. . . .

Justice Field had not only left Washington and travelled the three thousand miles or more which were necessary to reach his circuit, but he had entered upon the duties of that circuit, had held the court at San Francisco for some time; and, taking a short leave of that court, had gone down to Los Angeles, another place where a court was to be held, and sat as a judge there for several days, hearing cases and rendering decisions. It was in the necessary act of returning from Los Angeles to San Francisco, by the usual mode of travel between the two places, where his court was still in session, and where he was required to be, that he was assaulted by Terry. . . .

The occurrence which we are called upon to consider was of so extraordinary a character that it is not to be expected that many cases can be found to cite as authority upon the subject. . . .

We have no doubt that Mr. Justice Field when attacked by Terry was engaged in the discharge of his duties as Circuit Justice of the Ninth Circuit, and was entitled to all the protection under those circumstances which the law could give him.

It is urged, however, that there exists no statute authorizing any such protection as that which Neagle was instructed to give Judge Field in the present case, and indeed no protection whatever against a vindictive or malicious assault growing out of the faithful discharge of his official duties; and that the language of section 753 of the Revised Statutes, that the party seeking the benefit of the writ of *habeas corpus* must in this connection show that he is "in custody for an act done or omitted in pursuance of a law of the United States," makes it necessary that upon this occasion it should be shown that the act for which Neagle is imprisoned was done by virtue of an act of

Congress. It is not supposed that any special act of Congress exists which authorizes the marshals or deputy marshals of the United States in express terms to accompany the judges of the Supreme Court through their circuits, and act as a bodyguard to them, to defend them against malicious assaults against their persons. But we are of opinion that this view of the statute is an unwarranted restriction of the meaning of a law designed to extend in a liberal manner the benefit of the writ of *habeas corpus* to persons imprisoned for the performance of their duty. And we are satisfied that if it was the duty of Neagle, under the circumstances, a duty which could only arise under the laws of the United States, to defend Mr. Justice Field from a murderous attack upon him, he brings himself within the meaning of the section we have recited. This view of the subject is confirmed by the alternative provision, that he must be in custody "for an act done or omitted in pursuance of a law of the United States or of an order, process, or decree of a court or judge thereof, or is in custody in violation of the Constitution or of a law or treaty of the United States."

In the view we take of the Constitution of the United States, any obligation fairly and properly inferable from that instrument, or any duty of the marshal to be derived from the general scope of his duties under the laws of the United States, is "a law" within the meaning of this phrase. It would be a great reproach to the system of government of the United States, declared to be within its sphere sovereign and supreme, if there is to be found within the domain of its powers no means of protecting the judges, in the conscientious and faithful discharge of their duties, from the malice and hatred of those upon whom their judgments may operate unfavorably. . . .

Where, then, are we to look for the protection which we have shown Judge Field was entitled to when engaged in the discharge of his official duties? Not to the courts of the United States; because, as has been more than once said in this court, in the division of the powers of government between the three great departments, executive, legislative and judicial, the judicial is the weakest for the purposes of self-protection and for the enforcement of the powers which it exercises. The ministerial officers through whom its commands must be executed are marshals of the United States, and belong emphatically to the executive department of the government. They are appointed by the President, with the advice and consent of the Senate. They are removable from office at his pleasure. They are subjected by act of Congress to the supervision and control of the Department of Justice, in the hands of one of the cabinet officers of the President, and their compensation is provided by acts of Congress. The same may be said of the district attorneys of the United States, who prosecute and defend the claims of the government in the courts.

The legislative branch of the government can only protect the judicial officers by the enactment of laws for that purpose, and the argument we are now combating assumes that no such law has been passed by Congress.

If we turn to the executive department of the government, we find a very different condition of affairs. The Constitution, section 3, Article 2, declares that the President "shall take care that the laws be faithfully executed," and he is provided with the means of fulfilling this obligation by his authority to commission all the officers of the United States, and, by and with the advice and consent of the Senate, to appoint the most important of them and to fill vacancies. He is declared to be commander in chief of the army and navy of the United States. The duties which are thus imposed upon him he is further enabled to perform by the recognition in the Constitution, and the creation by acts of Congress, of executive departments, which have varied in number from four or five to seven or eight, the heads of which are familiarly called cabinet ministers. These aid him in the performance of the great duties of his office, and represent him in a thousand acts to which it can hardly be supposed his personal attention is called, and thus he is enabled to fulfill the duty of his great department, expressed in the phrase that "he shall take care that the laws be faithfully executed." Is this duty limited to the enforcement of acts of Congress or of treaties of the United States according to their express terms, or does it include the rights, duties and obligations growing out of the Constitution itself, our international relations, and all the protection implied by the nature of the government under the Constitution? . . .

We cannot doubt the power of the President to take measures for the protection of a judge of one of the courts of the United States, who, while in the discharge of the duties of his office, is threatened with a personal attack which may probably result in his death, and we think it clear that where this protection is to be afforded through the civil power, the Department of Justice is the proper one to set in motion the necessary means of protection. . . .

But all these questions being conceded, it is urged against the relief sought by this writ of habeas corpus, that the question of the guilt of the prisoner of the crime of murder is a question to be determined by the laws of California, and to be decided by its courts, and that there exists no power in the government of the United States to take away

the prisoner from the custody of the proper authorities of the State of California and carry him before a judge of the court of the United States, and release him without a trial by jury according to the laws of the State of California. That the statute of the United States authorizes and directs such a proceeding and such a judgment in a case where the offence charged against the prisoner consists in an act done in pursuance of a law of the United States and by virtue of its authority, and where the imprisonment of the party is in violation of the Constitution and laws of the United States, is clear by its express language. . . .

It would seem as if the argument might close here. If the duty of the United States to protect its officers from violence, even to death, in discharge of the duties which its laws impose upon them, be established, and Congress has made the writ of habeas corpus one of the means by which this protection is made efficient, and if the facts of this case show that the prisoner was acting both under the authority of law, and the directions of his superior officers of the Department of Justice, we can see no reason why this writ should not be made to serve its purpose in the present case. . . .

The result at which we have arrived upon this examination is, that in the protection of the person and the life of Mr. Justice Field while in the discharge of his official duties, Neagle was authorized to resist the attack of Terry upon him; that Neagle was correct in the belief that without prompt action on his part the assault of Terry upon the judge would have ended in the death of the latter; that such being his well-founded belief, he was justified in taking the life of Terry, as the only means of preventing the death of the man who was intended to be his victim; that in taking the life of Terry, under the circumstances, he was acting under the authority of the law of the United States, and was justified in so doing; and that he is not liable to answer in the courts of California on account of his part in that transaction.

We therefore affirm the judgment of the Circuit Court authorizing his discharge from the custody of the sheriff of San Joaquin County.

MR. JUSTICE LAMAR (with whom concurred MR. CHIEF JUSTICE FULLER) dissenting.

[W]e deny that upon the facts of this record, [Neagle], as deputy marshal Neagle, or as private citizen Neagle, had any duty imposed on him by the laws of the United States growing out of the official character of Judge Field as a Circuit Justice. We deny that anywhere in this transaction, accepting throughout the appellee's version of the facts, he occupied in law any position other than what would have been occupied by any other person who should have interfered in the same manner, in any other assault of the same character, between any two other persons in that room. In short, we think that there was nothing whatever in fact of an official character in the transaction, whatever may have been the appellee's view of his alleged official duties and powers; and, therefore, we think that the courts of the United States have in the present state of our legislation no jurisdiction whatever in the premises, and that the appellee should have been remanded to the custody of the sheriff. . . .

The gravamen of this case is in the assertion that Neagle slew Terry in pursuance of a law of the United States. He who claims to have committed a homicide by authority must show the authority. If he claims the authority of law, then what law? And if a law, how came it to be a law? Somehow and somewhere it must have had an origin. Is it a law because of the existence of a special and private authority issued from one of the executive departments? So in almost these words is claimed in this case. Is it a law because of some constitutional investiture of sovereignty in the persons of judges who carry that sovereignty with them wherever they may go? Because of some power inherent in the judiciary to create for others a rule or law of conduct outside of legislation, which shall extend to the death penalty? So, also, in this case, . . . it is claimed. We dissent from both these claims. There can be no such law from either of those sources. The right claimed must be traced to legislation of Congress; else it cannot exist.

In *Neagle* the Court adopted the "general grant" perspective of executive power. The justices held that the president has the constitutional power to take those actions necessary to enforce the laws of the nation, even if the Constitution does not provide an explicit authorization for doing so.

Strong support from the Court for this view also came in an 1895 case, *In re Debs*. In May 1894 President Grover Cleveland sent troops into Chicago to stop striking train workers from obstructing the movement of the U.S. mails, and he had his attorney general secure a court injunction against the striking workers. When the workers defied the injunction and violence erupted, their leader, Eugene Debs, was cited for contempt. Debs, in turn, challenged the injunction, claiming that the president could not obtain it in the absence of explicit congressional authorization. The justices

disagreed: "Every government, entrusted, by the very terms of its being, with powers and duties to be exercised . . . for the general welfare, has the right to apply to its own courts for any proper assistance." Moreover, because the strike adversely affected the public, the president could forbid it.

Congressional Limitations on Executive Power

Debs and *Neagle* are examples of rulings that allow the president to take action without explicit approval from Congress or the Constitution—and, therefore, support the stewardship approach to the presidency. But the Court also has placed at least two types of limits on presidential prerogative.

The first—what we call the congressional limit—is well illustrated by *Youngstown Sheet & Tube Company v. Sawyer* (1952), also known as the Steel Seizure Case *(excerpted in chapter 5)*. In December 1951 the United Steelworkers Union announced that it would call a strike at the end of the month. Because the nation was engaged in a war in Korea and steel was needed in the production of arms and other military equipment, President Harry S. Truman was not about to let a strike shut down the mills. Only hours before the strike was to begin, Truman issued an executive order commanding Secretary of Commerce Charles Sawyer to seize the nation's steel mills and keep them in operation. Sawyer in turn ordered the mill owners to continue to run their facilities as operators for the United States.

Truman's seizure order cited no statutory authority for his action because there was none. Federal statutes permitted government seizure of industrial plants for certain specified reasons, but the settlement of a labor dispute was not one of them. In fact, the Taft-Hartley Act of 1947 rejected the idea that labor disputes could be resolved by such means. Instead, the act authorized the president to impose an eighty-day cooling-off period as a way to postpone any strike that seriously threatened the public interest. Truman, however, had little regard for the Taft-Hartley Act, which Congress had passed over his veto. The president ignored the cooling-off period alternative and took the direct action of seizing the mills. The inherent powers of the chief executive, he maintained, were enough to authorize the action.

A divided Supreme Court disagreed. Two members of the Court (Douglas and Black) adopted the mere designation or enumerated approach; they wrote, "The President's power, if any, to issue the order must stem either from an act of Congress or from the Constitution itself." Three justices (Vinson, Reed, and Minton) took the opposite position. In their opinion, the take care clause provided the president with a sufficient constitutional basis for his actions: he was taking steps that were in the best interest of the country until Congress could act. Finally, a plurality of four (Burton, Clark, Frankfurter, and Jackson) settled somewhere between the two extremes. Unlike Black and Douglas, they asserted that the president has powers beyond those enumerated in Article II. But, in contrast to Vinson, Reed, and Minton, they argued that President Truman could not seize the mills because he had acted against the "implied" desires of Congress. As Jackson put it in a landmark concurring opinion, "When the President takes measures incompatible with the expressed or implied will of Congress, his power is at the lowest ebb, for then he can rely only upon his own constitutional powers minus any constitutional powers of Congress over the matter."

Despite these divisions, the lesson from *Youngstown*—especially Jackson's concurrence—is clear: presidential powers may not be fixed, but the president can act against the will of Congress only if the President can show that the power he is asserting conclusively and exclusively belongs to him.[11] The situation confronting the Court becomes murkier, however, when Congress has not explicitly approved or disapproved of presidential action. We have more to say about that situation in the next chapter, in which we discuss the relative powers of the president and Congress over foreign affairs and in times of national emergencies, such as the 2001 terrorist attacks on New York City and Washington, D.C.

The Obligation to Enforce the Law

Another limit on presidential power centers on the lack of enforcement of the laws. Simply put, the Constitution obliges the president to enforce all the laws, not just those the administration supports. Although a number of presidents have been criticized for failing to carry out certain laws with sufficient enthusiasm, it would be difficult to prove that the chief executive had not satisfied the constitutional mandate of faithful execution. On rare occasions, however, a

president has openly refused to execute a law validly passed by Congress. In such cases court challenges are to be expected.

Congress passed the Federal Water Pollution Control Act Amendments of 1972 over President Nixon's veto. The act made federal money available to local governments for sewers and clean water projects. After losing the legislative battle, the president instructed the appropriate officials of his administration not to allot to local governments the full funds authorized by Congress.

New York City, which expected to be a recipient of these funds, filed suit against Russell Train, head of the Environmental Protection Agency, to force the administration to release the impounded money. In interpreting the legislation, the Supreme Court in **Train v. City of New York** (1975) found no congressional grant of discretion to the president that would allow him to decide how much of the appropriated money to allocate. In the absence of such a grant, the president's obligation was to carry out the terms of the statute. The Court held that the funds must be distributed according to the intent of Congress. The constitutional requirement of faithful execution of the laws means that the executive branch must enforce and administer the policies enacted by the legislature even if the president opposes them.

On the other hand, the historical record is full of instances in which administrations have chosen not to defend the constitutionality of particular federal laws. For example, in *Myers v. United States* (1926), which we will consider soon, the administration's solicitor general not only refused to defend the law at issue (curtailing presidential authority to fire a postmaster) but also argued against its constitutionality. And *Myers* is not all that unusual. Since 2004 alone the Justice Department has declined to defend statutes in nearly fifteen cases.[12] When the administration takes this position, criticism usually follows, as it did when Barack Obama's attorney general announced that the president would not defend the constitutionality of the Defense of Marriage Act (DOMA), which defines marriage for federal purposes as the legal union between one man and one woman.[13] The critics contend that the government has a duty to "take Care that the laws be faithfully Executed," even if

---

11. This happened in *Zivotofsky v. Kerry* (2015), in which the president claimed "exclusive" and "conclusive" power to "receive Ambassadors and other public Ministers." We shall consider this case in chapter 5.

12. Tony Mauro, "Government's 'Duty to Defend' Not a Given," *National Law Journal,* October 27, 2010.

13. **United States v. Windsor** (2013).

the president disagrees with those laws as a matter of policy. On the other side, presidents have argued that they take an oath to "preserve, protect, and defend" the Constitution and so have an obligation to make their own independent assessments of the constitutionality of federal laws, especially if they encroach on executive authority. In such a circumstance, the administration notifies Congress that it is not defending the law in question; Congress can then seek its own defense. In the case of DOMA, for example, the House of Representatives hired a former solicitor general, Paul Clement, to defend it.

DOMESTIC POWERS OF THE PRESIDENT

With this general discussion of executive power in mind, let us now turn to the specific powers of the president. In this section we examine domestic powers, and in the next we consider powers over foreign affairs. Treating the powers separately reflects the perspective of political scientists, who suggest that there are actually two "presidencies": one for domestic affairs and one for foreign policy. Although it is often hard to separate the two at times when one affects the other, differences remain. For example, some commentators argue that the president is generally more constrained—by the public, Congress, and even the Supreme Court—in domestic affairs than in the realm of foreign policy. As you read the material to come, as well as the cases and narrative in chapter 5, consider whether this division makes sense today. Has the Supreme Court approved greater presidential power over foreign policy? More generally, what approaches have the justices taken to the specific powers of the nation's chief executive?

Veto Power

Section 7 of Article I of the Constitution contains what has become known as the presentment clause. By its terms, after Congress passes a piece of legislation, it is sent to the president, who then has three options: sign it, veto it, or do nothing. If the president signs it, the bill becomes law. If he vetoes it, Congress can attempt to override him by the required two-thirds vote. If he does nothing, the bill becomes law after ten days, provided that Congress is in session; if Congress adjourns during the ten-day period, the bill is "pocket vetoed." Congress cannot override a pocket veto, but it can reintroduce the bill in its next session. Although

presidents do not often use the pocket veto (since 1789, only 1,066 times, or about five times a year) or, for that matter, their regular veto power (since 1789, 1,500 times, or about seven times a year), they typically regard their option to do so as important.[14] At the very least, a president can hold the veto out as a threat against a recalcitrant Congress, and Congress has generally been unwilling or unable to override a presidential veto. Of the 1,500 regular vetoes since 1789, only 110 have been overridden.

For much of American history, the veto power generated few constitutional disputes, but that is no longer true. Two issues relating to the veto have been the cause of major controversies. The first, which we discuss in some detail in chapter 5, is the legislative veto (when one or both houses of Congress attempt to veto decisions of the executive branch). The other is the line-item veto, which allowed the president to cancel particular taxing and spending provisions after they were signed into law. To understand why the line-item veto is controversial, think first about the way bills become laws: since the days of George Washington, Congress has passed laws and the president has had to decide whether to accept or reject them in their entirety. Most presidents have not been happy with this arrangement. Beginning with Ulysses S. Grant, virtually all have sought the ability to veto parts of a bill and accept others.

Among the rationales presidents have offered for the line-item veto, a common one is this: members of Congress must face periodic electoral checks, and they often include in the federal budget "pork-barrel projects"—projects designed solely to appease constituents—even though such projects waste money. Because members of Congress are unwilling to take fiscal responsibility and omit unnecessary spending from the budget, the argument goes, the president should take on this responsibility by being able to veto or "cancel" particular expenditures.

In 1996 Congress finally agreed and enacted the Line Item Veto Act, which allowed the president to cancel certain tax and spending benefits after they had been signed into law. In 1997 the Court heard a challenge to the act, *Raines v. Byrd,* but dismissed the case because, according to the Court, the members of Congress who brought the suit lacked standing *(see chapter 2)*. In his concurring opinion, Justice

---

14. Data in this paragraph are from "Summary of Bills Vetoed, 1789–Present," U.S. Senate Web site, http://www.senate.gov/reference/Legislation/Vetoes/vetoCounts.htm.

President Bill Clinton uses new power under the Line Item Veto Act to cancel two spending provisions and a special tax break on August 11, 1997. Groups challenging the law won a Supreme Court ruling declaring the act unconstitutional.

David Souter expressed his belief that the day would eventually come when a party would suffer a sufficient loss of federal funds to maintain a suit.

That day came the very next term. In *Clinton v. City of New York* (1998) the justices found that the litigants had standing to challenge the Line Item Veto Act, and the Court decided the case on its merits. What did the majority decide? Do the justices make a compelling case for their position?

Clinton v. City of New York

524 U.S. 417 (1998)
http://laws.findlaw.com/us/524/417.html
Oral arguments are available at https://www.oyez.org.
Vote: 6 (Ginsburg, Kennedy, Rehnquist, Souter, Stevens, Thomas)
    3 (Breyer, O'Connor, Scalia)

OPINION OF THE COURT: *Stevens*
CONCURRING OPINION: *Kennedy*
OPINION CONCURRING IN PART AND DISSENTING IN PART: *Scalia*
DISSENTING OPINION: *Breyer*

FACTS:

The Line Item Veto Act stated in part,

[T]he President may, with respect to any bill or joint resolution that has been signed into law pursuant to Article I, section 7, of the Constitution of the United States, cancel in whole—(1) any dollar amount of discretionary budget authority; (2) any item of new direct spending; or (3) any limited tax benefit; if the President—

(A) determines that such cancellation will—(i) reduce the Federal budget deficit; (ii) not impair any essential Government functions; and (iii) not harm the national interest; and

(B) notifies the Congress of such cancellation by transmitting a special message . . . within five calendar days (excluding Sundays) after the enactment of the law [to which the cancellation applies].

The act contained two other important provisions. First, although it gave the president the power to rescind various expenditures, it established a check on his ability to do so. Congress could consider "disapproval bills," which would render the president's cancellation "null and void." In other words, Congress could restore presidential cuts, but new congressional legislation would be subject to a presidential veto. Second, the act stated, "Any Member of Congress or any individual adversely affected by [this act] may bring an action, in the United States District Court for the District of Columbia, for declaratory judgment and injunctive relief on the ground that any provision of this part violates the Constitution."

On January 2, 1997, just one day after the act went into effect, six members of Congress who had voted against it brought suit in federal court against Secretary of the Treasury Robert E. Rubin and Franklin D. Raines, director of the Office of Management and Budget. The suit claimed that the act violated Article I of the Constitution because it "unconstitutionally expands the President's power" and "violates the requirements of bicameral passage and presentment by granting to the President, acting alone, the authority to 'cancel' and thus repeal provisions of federal law." The appellees further asserted that the act injured them "directly and concretely . . . in their official capacities" by (1) altering the legal and practical effect of all votes they may cast on bills containing such separately vetoable items, (2) divesting them of their constitutional role in the repeal of legislation, and (3) altering the constitutional balance of powers between the legislative and executive branches.

Attorneys for the executive branch officials argued that the legislators lacked standing to sue and that their claim was not ripe, meaning that the president had not yet used the new veto authority.

The lower court agreed with the members of Congress, and the executive branch officials appealed to the U.S. Supreme Court. Because the act directed the Court to hear as soon as possible any suit challenging its constitutionality, the justices established an expedited briefing schedule. They heard oral argument in *Raines v. Byrd* on May 27, 1997, a little more than a month after the lower court's decision.

But, as you know, the Court dismissed the case. Writing for the majority, Chief Justice William H. Rehnquist held that the suit was not a real case or controversy because members of Congress were "not the right" litigants. After the Court's decision, President Clinton invoked the line-item veto to cancel more than eighty items, including a provision of the Balanced Budget Act of 1997 that provided money for New York City hospitals and a section of the Taxpayer Relief Act of 1997 that gave a tax break to potato growers in Idaho. The affected parties immediately challenged these steps. Those in the first case were the City of New York, two hospital associations, one hospital, and two unions representing health-care employees. The parties in the second were a farmers' cooperative and one of its members.

A federal district court consolidated the cases, determined that at least one of the plaintiffs in each case had standing under Article III, and ruled that the Line Item Veto Act violated the presentment clause (Article I, Section 7, Clause 2). It also held that the law was an unconstitutional delegation of powers—an argument lawyers opposed to the line-item veto made before the Supreme Court. A majority on the Court thought it "unnecessary" to address this claim, but at least one of the justices, Kennedy in concurrence, seemed sympathetic. For this reason, we examine this aspect of *Clinton*, along with Kennedy's concurrence, in chapter 5.

ARGUMENTS:

For the appellants, William J. Clinton et al.:

- The Line Item Veto Act does not violate the presentment clause because the veto occurs after all the procedures in the presentment clause have been satisfied. Its title notwithstanding, the act does not authorize the president to sign into law some provisions of a tax or spending bill while "returning" other provisions to Congress. The president remains subject to the constitutional obligation to sign or return, in its entirety, a bill presented to him by Congress. His cancellation authority under the act comes into existence only after a tax or spending bill has been passed by both Houses of Congress and approved, in toto, by the president.

- The scope of authority vested in the president by the act is consistent both with historical practice and with this Court's decisions. Since 1789 Congress frequently has given the president discretion over the expenditure of appropriated funds. The Line Item Veto Act provides constitutionally sufficient limits on the president's exercise of discretion over federal spending. The act requires the president to cancel items "in whole" rather than in part and to devote any canceled amounts to deficit reduction, and it provides meaningful guidance to the president in his decision whether particular items should be canceled.

- Congress can specify that certain bills not be subject to cancellation, and that it failed to do so in this case must be construed to be congressional intent to offer cancellation as an option to the executive.

For the appellees, City of New York et al.:

- The procedure set forth in Article I requires that every bill adding, amending, or repealing any provision of federal law be passed in the same form by both Houses of Congress and presented to the president, who must sign, veto, or take no action with respect to each bill "in toto." These requirements were carefully designed to assure that federal laws have the consent of the people as expressed through their elected representatives.
- The presentment clause requires the president to act on the bill as a whole to protect the principle of bicameralism and to limit the president's power in the lawmaking process. Historically, this requirement has been clear since the first presidency, as found in Washington's writings.
- Although cancellation occurs after the procedures prescribed in the presentment clause, the act is merely an attempt to accomplish indirectly what the Constitution prohibits accomplishing directly.
- The "fundamental precept . . . is that the lawmaking function belongs to Congress . . . and may not be conveyed to another branch." The act violates that precept. The act allows the president the power to shape the law itself, which is a legislative power. The act also fails to provide an "intelligible principle" which would make delegation acceptable under the Court's delegation doctrine.

> ◀ **JUSTICE STEVENS DELIVERED THE OPINION OF THE COURT.**

Less than two months after our decision in [*Raines*], the President exercised his authority to cancel one provision in the Balanced Budget Act of 1997 and two provisions in the Taxpayer Relief Act of 1997. Appellees, claiming that they had been injured by two of those cancellations, filed these cases in the District Court. That Court again held the statute invalid and we again expedited our review. We now hold that these appellees have standing to challenge the constitutionality of the Act, and, reaching the merits, we

agree that the cancellation procedures set forth in the Act violate the Presentment Clause, Art. I, Sec. 7, cl. 2, of the Constitution. . . .

In both legal and practical effect, the President has amended two Acts of Congress by repealing a portion of each. "[R]epeal of statutes, no less than enactment, must conform with Art. I." *INS v. Chadha* (1983). There is no provision in the Constitution that authorizes the President to enact, to amend, or to repeal statutes. Both Article I and Article II assign responsibilities to the President that directly relate to the lawmaking process, but neither addresses the issue presented by these cases. The President "shall from time to time give to the Congress Information on the State of the Union, and recommend to their Consideration such Measures as he shall judge necessary and expedient. . . ." Art. II, Sec. 3. Thus, he may initiate and influence legislative proposals. Moreover, after a bill has passed both Houses of Congress, but "before it become[s] a Law," it must be presented to the President. If he approves it, "he shall sign it, but if not he shall return it, with his Objections to that House in which it shall have originated, who shall enter the Objections at large on their Journal, and proceed to reconsider it." Art. I, Sec. 7, cl. 2. His "return" of a bill, which is usually described as a "veto," is subject to being overridden by a two-thirds vote in each House.

There are important differences between the President's "return" of a bill pursuant to Article I, Sec. 7, and the exercise of the President's cancellation authority pursuant to the Line Item Veto Act. The constitutional return takes place before the bill becomes law; the statutory cancellation occurs after the bill becomes law. The constitutional return is of the entire bill; the statutory cancellation is of only a part. Although the Constitution expressly authorizes the President to play a role in the process of enacting statutes, it is silent on the subject of unilateral Presidential action that either repeals or amends parts of duly enacted statutes.

There are powerful reasons for construing constitutional silence on this profoundly important issue as equivalent to an express prohibition. The procedures governing the enactment of statutes set forth in the text of Article I were the product of the great debates and compromises that produced the Constitution itself. Familiar historical materials provide abundant support for the conclusion that the power to enact statutes may only "be exercised in accord with a single, finely wrought and exhaustively considered, procedure." *Chadha*. Our first President understood the text of the Presentment Clause as requiring that he either "approve all the parts of a Bill, or reject it in toto."

What has emerged in these cases from the President's exercise of his statutory cancellation powers, however, are truncated versions of two bills that passed both Houses of Congress. They are not the product of the "finely wrought" procedure that the Framers designed. . . .

. . . [O]ur decision rests on the narrow ground that the procedures authorized by the Line Item Veto Act are not authorized by the Constitution. The Balanced Budget Act of 1997 is a 500-page document that became "Public Law 105–33" after three procedural steps were taken: (1) a bill containing its exact text was approved by a majority of the Members of the House of Representatives; (2) the Senate approved precisely the same text; and (3) that text was signed into law by the President. The Constitution explicitly requires that each of those three steps be taken before a bill may "become a law." Art. I, Sec. 7. If one paragraph of that text had been omitted at any one of those three stages, Public Law 105–33 would not have been validly enacted. If the Line Item Veto Act were valid, it would authorize the President to create a different law—one whose text was not voted on by either House of Congress or presented to the President for signature. Something that might be known as "Public Law 105–33 as modified by the President" may or may not be desirable, but it is surely not a document that may "become a law" pursuant to the procedures designed by the Framers of Article I, Sec. 7, of the Constitution.

If there is to be a new procedure in which the President will play a different role in determining the final text of what may "become a law," such change must come not by legislation, but through the amendment procedures set forth in Article V of the Constitution. Cf. *U.S. Term Limits, Inc. v. Thornton* (1995).

The judgment of the District Court is

Affirmed.

JUSTICE SCALIA, with whom JUSTICE O'CONNOR joins, and with whom JUSTICE BREYER joins [in part], concurring in part and dissenting in part.

Insofar as the degree of political, "lawmaking" power conferred upon the Executive is concerned, there is not a dime's worth of difference between Congress' authorizing the President to cancel a spending item, and Congress' authorizing money to be spent on a particular item at the President's discretion. And the latter has been done since the Founding of the Nation. From 1789–1791, the First Congress made lump-sum appropriations for the entire Government—"sum[s] not exceeding" specified amounts for broad purposes. From a very early date, Congress also made permissive individual appropriations, leaving the decision whether to spend the money to the President's unfettered discretion. . . .

The short of the matter is this: had the Line Item Veto Act authorized the President to "decline to spend" any item of spending contained in the Balanced Budget Act of 1997, there is not the slightest doubt that authorization would have been constitutional. What the Line Item Veto Act does instead—authorizing the President to "cancel" an item of spending—is technically different. But the technical difference does not relate to the technicalities of the Presentment Clause, which have been fully complied with; and the doctrine of unconstitutional delegation, which is at issue here, is preeminently not a doctrine of technicalities. The title of the Line Item Veto Act, which was perhaps designed to simplify for public comprehension, or perhaps merely to comply with the terms of a campaign pledge, has succeeded in faking out the Supreme Court. The President's action it authorizes in fact is not a line-item veto, and thus does not offend Art. I, Sec. 7; and, insofar as the substance of that action is concerned, it is no different from what Congress has permitted the President to do since the formation of the Union.

JUSTICE BREYER, with whom JUSTICE O'CONNOR and JUSTICE SCALIA join [in part], dissenting.

I . . . do not agree with [the Court's] ultimate conclusion. In my view, the Line Item Veto Act does not violate any specific textual constitutional command, nor does it violate any implicit Separation of Powers principle. Consequently, I believe that the Act is constitutional. . . .

I recognize that the Act before us is novel. In a sense, it skirts a constitutional edge. But that edge has to do with means, not ends. The means chosen do not amount literally to the enactment, repeal, or amendment of a law. Nor, for that matter, do they amount literally to the "line item veto" that the Act's title announces. Those means do not violate any basic Separation of Powers principle. They do not improperly shift the constitutionally foreseen balance of power from Congress to the President. Nor, since they comply with Separation of Powers principles, do they threaten the liberties of individual citizens. They represent an experiment that may, or may not, help representative government work better. The Constitution, in my view, authorizes Congress and the President to try novel methods in this way. Consequently, with respect, I dissent.

When the opinion was announced, President Clinton said, "I am deeply disappointed with today's Supreme Court decision striking down the line-item veto. The decision is a defeat for all Americans—it deprives the President of a valuable tool for eliminating waste in the Federal budget and for enlivening the public debate over how to make the best use of public funds." Given the views of the six-person majority, however, it is unlikely that the Court will reverse itself any time in the near future.

Presidential Signing Statements

On occasion, presidents have expressed their opinions about particular bills at the time they sign them. In documents known as presidential signing statements, they typically point to provisions within the laws over which they have some concerns. A signing statement usually

1. Expresses the president's interpretation of the language of the law,

2. Announces constitutional limits on the implementation of some of the law's provisions, or

3. Indicates directions to executive branch officials as to how to administer the new law in an acceptable manner.[15]

When Congress passed the Balanced Budget and Emergency Deficit Act of 1985, a law designed to reduce budget deficits, President Ronald Reagan issued a signing statement. He expressed his view that the law was constitutionally defective because it gave power over the president to the comptroller general, an official removable only by Congress. Nearly two decades later, President George W. Bush issued a signing statement registering his objection to a 2002 law that directs the secretary of state to record, upon request, "Israel" as the place of birth on passports of U.S. citizens born in Jerusalem. To Bush, the law, which was meant to override State Department policy listing Jerusalem only and not Israel on passports, might interfere with the President's "constitutional authority . . . to recognize foreign states." Likewise, in 2011, after agreeing to

a budget compromise law, President Barack Obama declared his intention to ignore a section of the law that prohibited the use of appropriations for four executive branch "czars."

On what authority did Reagan, Bush, Obama, and other presidents issue these statements? Although the Constitution contains no specific authorization, some presidents have pointed to the take care clause of Article II, arguing that it counsels against executing provisions of a law that they believe are unconstitutional. "That, of course, means," as one commentator put it, that agencies charged with executing the law "are to act in the manner that the [president] considers appropriate as compared to the way the legislation sets forth the policy. In that sense, it is a kind of line-item veto."[16] It is also a form of constitutional interpretation by the president. Well before the Supreme Court can rule on a law, assuming it ever does, the president's views on the constitutionality of particular portions of it have been made public.

What have the justices had to say about this practice? Not much, as it turns out. Although signing statements have been the subject of lower court litigation, they have not faced a constitutional challenge in the Supreme Court. Moreover, the justices have virtually ignored these statements in their review of federal laws. In only a handful of cases has the Court cited, much less relied on, presidential signing statements to interpret legislation.

But change may be in the wind. Although presidents since James Monroe have issued signing statements, George W. Bush's use of the device was, in some regards, unique. He issued fewer statements on an annual basis than some of his predecessors, but he challenged more statutory provisions within individual statements and, more relevant for our purposes, frequently raised constitutional objections, as he did over the passport law. Only 18 percent of Bill Clinton's signing statements contained constitutional challenges to provisions of bills, compared to nearly 80 percent of Bush's.[17]

15. Cooper, "George W. Bush, Edgar Allen Poe, and the Use and Abuse of Presidential Signing Statements": 517. We adapt material in this section from this article. See also Cooper's book *By Order of the President: The Use and Abuse of Executive Direct Action* (Lawrence: University Press of Kansas, 2002).

16. Cooper, "George W. Bush," 517.

17. T. J. Halstead, "Presidential Signing Statements: Constitutional and Institutional Implications," Congressional Research Service Report for Congress, 2006 (a 2012 update of this report by Todd Garvey is available at http://www.fas.org/sgp/crs/natsec/RL33667 .pdf). See also Curtis A. Bradley and Eric A. Posner, "Signing Statements and Executive Power," *Constitutional Commentary* 23 (2007): 307–364.

As a candidate for president, Barack Obama criticized Bush's use of signing statements, and in his first three years as president he issued only 20 such statements, compared to Bush's 161 over eight years. Of Obama's twenty signing statements, ten contained constitutional challenges to the enacted law. In response to critics who claim that Obama has used signing statements in the same manner as the Bush administration, the Obama administration has argued that its use of signing statements has been rarer, based only on mainstream constitutional theories, and necessary for the president to articulate why certain provisions of laws are unconstitutional.[18]

The frequency of the use of signing statements by Bush and Obama has generated more awareness and commentary about the practice than ever before—with scholars and policy makers speaking out both for and against. Whether legal challenges or congressional action will follow, we cannot say.

What does seem clear—and this brings us to another development—is that pressure may be building within the Court to pay greater heed to the practice. In *Hamdan v. Rumsfeld* (2006), Justice Antonin Scalia, in critiquing the Court's use of legislative history to interpret a law, a practice he condemns, chided the majority for "wholly ignor[ing] the President's signing statement, which explicitly set forth his understanding" of the law at issue. An "understanding," we might add, with which Scalia agreed but the majority did not. Perhaps taking heed of Scalia's objection, the majority mentioned Bush's signing statement when the passport law was challenged in *Zivotofsky v. Kerry* (2015) *(excerpted in chapter 5),* though Justice Scalia, in dissent, did not.

So far, we are left with more questions than answers. Will the justices now become more attentive to signing statements when they interpret or review the constitutionality of federal laws? Should they? And what about the practice itself, especially its implications? Prior to a federal court decision, are presidents obligated to execute statutory provisions that they believe are unconstitutional? If so, should they not issue signing statements? Finally, does the use of signing statements undermine Marshall's view that it is the judiciary's job to say what the law is? We leave these questions to you

to consider as you read the material and cases to follow here and in the next chapter.

The Power of Appointment

For presidents to carry out the executive duties of the government effectively, they must be able to staff the various federal departments and offices with administrators who share their views and in whom they have confidence. This duty implies the power to appoint and the power to remove. The Constitution offers guidelines on the president's appointment power, but it is silent on the removal power.

Principal versus Inferior Officers. Article II, Section 2, contains what is known as the appointments clause. It specifies the president's authority to appoint major administrative and judicial officials, but it also allows Congress to allocate that authority to other bodies for minor administrative positions:

[The president] shall nominate, and by and with the Advice and Consent of the Senate, shall appoint Ambassadors, other public Ministers and Consuls, Judges of the supreme Court, and all other Officers of the United States, whose Appointments are not herein otherwise provided for, and which shall be established by Law: but the Congress may by Law vest the Appointment of such inferior Officers, as they think proper, in the President alone, in the Courts of Law, or in the Heads of Departments.

Article II, Section 2 concludes with what is known as the recess appointments clause:

The President shall have Power to fill up all Vacancies that may happen during the Recess of the Senate, by granting Commissions which shall expire at the End of their next Session.

Although these clauses seem detailed and specific enough, they have raised important constitutional questions. Let us consider two, one from each clause.

The first stems a line that the appointments clause draws between major (or principal) officers and inferior offices. Principal positions, according to the appointments clause, must be filled by presidential nomination and Senate confirmation, but selections of personnel to fill inferior positions may be made by some other means as determined by Congress. The question becomes how to distinguish between the two.

---

18. Charlie Savage, "Obama's Embrace of Bush Tactic Riles Congress," *New York Times,* August 8, 2009, A16; Charlie Savage, "Shift on Executive Power Lets Obama Bypass Rivals," *New York Times,* April 22, 2012, A1.

This is an important question because from time to time Congress establishes government positions that, for various reasons, are to be filled by an appointing authority other than the president. And on occasion, someone objects to the procedure on the ground that the position is too important for anyone other than the president to fill. Courts then must determine whether the official holds a principal position as an officer of the United States or is an inferior official.[19] If it is the former, then the president must make the appointment with the advice and consent of the Senate; if the latter, the power may be vested in the "President alone, in the Courts of Law, or in the Heads of Departments."

In *Morrison v. Olson* (1988), involving the creation of the office of special prosecutor, the Court attempted to delineate the difference between "inferior" and "principal" officers. Given the kinds of cases special prosecutors, or independent counsels, are appointed to investigate, are you convinced by the Court's analysis that this official is an "inferior officer" under the meaning of the appointments clause? Or is the Court taking a pragmatic approach, recognizing that it would be

unworkable for the president to appoint an official prosecuting crime and corruption in the executive branch?

Note too that the question of whether the special prosecutor is a principal or inferior officer is not the only one that *Morrison* addressed. The Court also considered the rather unique system of appointing the special prosecutor—one that involved federal judges. The appointments clause allows others to make appoint inferior officers, including "the Courts of Law." But, even assuming the special prosecutor is an inferior officer, does the clause allow judges to appoint members of another branch, such as the executive branch? In more general terms, does the appointments clause permit interbranch appointments?

Writing for the majority Chief Justice Rehnquist held not only that the special prosecutor is an inferior

---

19. See also *Buckley v. Valeo* (1976) for other questions relating to the appointment power. In this case, the justices heard a challenge to the constitutionality of the 1974 amendments to the Federal Election Campaign Act, which created the Federal Election Commission (FEC). The FEC was to enforce the law, conduct civil litigation, issue advisory opinions, and maintain records, among other responsibilities. Because of the Watergate scandal, Congress did not want the president alone to appoint the commission's eight members. Instead, the secretary of the Senate and the clerk of the House were ex officio members without the right to vote, and the president pro tempore of the Senate, the Speaker of the House, and the president each appointed two members, one Democrat and one Republican. Both houses of Congress had to confirm the six voting members.

This arrangement was challenged as a violation of the appointments clause: these officials had to be appointed either by the president with the advice and consent of the Senate or by "the President alone," the "Courts of Law," or the "Heads of Departments." Because four of the six commissioners were to be appointed by Congress—without any voice in their selection by the president, the courts, or any department head—challengers contended that the procedures violated the appointments clause. The Supreme Court partially agreed. With regard to the FEC's investigative powers, the Court had no problem with arrangement because investigative powers fall "in the same general category as those powers Congress might delegate to one of its own committees." But, in terms of the FEC's enforcement and other discretionary powers, the Court agreed with the challengers and invalidated the appointment procedures on the ground that those other powers do not operate "merely in the aid of congressional authority to legislate."

In Morrison v. Olson (1988) the Supreme Court rejected Assistant Attorney General Theodore Olson's constitutional challenge to the special prosecutor provisions of the Ethics in Government Act. In 2000 Olson served as George W. Bush's attorney in Bush v. Gore, *and he subsequently became U.S. solicitor general in the Bush administration.*

office but also that the interbranch appointment procedure is constitutional. These conclusions put him at odds with his fellow conservative, Justice Scalia. In dissent, Scalia accuses the majority of violating both the letter and the spirit of the separation of powers doctrine by depriving the president of all the executive powers vested in the office by the Constitution. This argument follows from a theory called the unitary executive, which claims to find support in the vesting clause of Article II: "The executive power shall be vested in a President of the United States of America." This language, according to proponents, implies that only the president is vested with the authority to carry out the laws in the executive branch, so only the president can appoint and remove officers exercising executive powers, including the special prosecutor.

Morrison v. Olson

487 U.S. 654 (1988)
http://laws.findlaw.com/us/487/654.html
Oral arguments are available at https://www.oyez.org.
Vote: 7 (Blackmun, Brennan, Marshall, O'Connor, Rehnquist, Stevens, White)
1 (Scalia)
OPINION OF THE COURT: Rehnquist
DISSENTING OPINION: Scalia
NOT PARTICIPATING: Kennedy

FACTS:

Because of the problems encountered in prosecuting the Watergate case, Congress included a provision in the Ethics in Government Act of 1978 dealing with the position of independent counsel (special prosecutor). The law provided for an independent counsel to investigate and, when necessary, to prosecute high-ranking officials of the government for violations of federal criminal laws. The independent counsel was to be chosen by a group of three federal judges, who would be appointed by the chief justice for two years and be known as the special division. The selection of independent counsels and the description of each counsel's jurisdiction would be the special division's only functions. It would carry out these responsibilities only after a preliminary investigation by the attorney general indicated that an independent counsel was necessary.

Once appointed, the independent counsel could exercise all the powers of the Justice Department. A counsel appointed under the act could be removed by the attorney general, but only for cause or disabilities that would substantially impair the counsel from completing the required duties. The federal district court could review such dismissals. The independent counsel's tenure otherwise would end when he or she declared the work to be completed or the special division concluded that the independent counsel's assigned tasks were accomplished.

In 1982 two House subcommittees investigated the activities of the Environmental Protection Agency and the Land and Natural Resources Division of the Justice Department. During that investigation the subcommittees asked the agencies to produce certain documents. A controversy flared up over whether the legislature could demand these documents from the executive branch, a dispute that was settled after contempt of Congress citations were made and lawsuits were filed. The following year the House Judiciary Committee began an investigation into the role of Justice Department officials in these events. Two years later, in 1985, the committee issued its report, which indicated that Assistant Attorney General Theodore B. Olson had provided false and misleading statements when he testified before the committee. Two other Justice Department officials were implicated in obstructing the committee's investigation. The committee requested that the attorney general initiate action for the appointment of an independent counsel to pursue these cases.

The special division appointed James McKay as independent counsel, but he resigned a month later. The judges then selected Alexia Morrison. Olson and the other targets of the investigation refused to cooperate with orders to produce evidence on the ground that the independent counsel provision of the Ethics in Government Act violated, among other clauses, the Constitution's appointments clause. As we detail below, they claimed that the independent counsel was not an "inferior officer" and therefore had to be appointed by the president, not by a group of three judges. The federal district court upheld the validity of the act, but the court of appeals reversed.

ARGUMENTS:

For the appellant, Alexia Morrison, independent counsel:

- Special prosecutors should be categorized as inferior officers because they are ranked lower than judges and department heads, are paid less than the attorney general, and are given duties for a single task and for a limited time.
- The term "inferior officer" in the appointments clause should be understood not in a hierarchical

sense, but in a functional sense. It is irrelevant that the special prosecutor is not subordinate to another officer.

- Nothing in the appointments clause prohibits cross-branch appointments; in fact, the clause specifically leaves Congress with discretion regarding appointments, and the Supreme Court has previously upheld cross-branch appointments.

For the appellees, Theodore B. Olson et al.:

- The act that created the office of special prosecutor violates the appointments clause of Article II because special prosecutors are not inferior officers, who are "subordinates of heads of the departments." Because not even the president can control special prosecutors, they are principal officers who must be appointed by the president.
- The framers vested executive power in the president because they envisioned a unitary executive as the best safeguard against tyranny. The act violates Article II's guarantee that the executive power is vested in one president required to take care that the laws are faithfully executed.

CHIEF JUSTICE REHNQUIST DELIVERED THE OPINION OF THE COURT.

The parties do not dispute that "[t]he Constitution for purposes of appointment . . . divides all its officers into two classes." "Principal officers are selected by the President with the advice and consent of the Senate. Inferior officers Congress may allow to be appointed by the President alone, by the heads of departments, or by the Judiciary." The initial question is, accordingly, whether appellant is an "inferior" or a "principal" officer. If she is the latter, as the Court of Appeals concluded, then the Act is in violation of the Appointments Clause.

The line between "inferior" and "principal" officers is one that is far from clear, and the Framers provided little guidance into where it should be drawn. . . . We need not attempt here to decide exactly where the line falls between the two types of officers, because in our view appellant clearly falls on the "inferior officer" side of that line. Several factors lead to this conclusion.

First, appellant is subject to removal by a higher Executive Branch official. Although appellant may not be "subordinate" to the Attorney General (and the President) insofar as she possesses a degree of independent discretion to exercise the powers delegated to her under the Act,

the fact that she can be removed by the Attorney General indicates that she is to some degree "inferior" in rank and authority. Second, appellant is empowered by the Act to perform only certain, limited duties. An independent counsel's role is restricted primarily to investigation and, if appropriate, prosecution for certain federal crimes. Admittedly, the Act delegates to appellant "full power and independent authority to exercise all investigative and prosecutorial functions and powers of the Department of Justice," but this grant of authority does not include any authority to formulate policy for the Government or the Executive Branch, nor does it give appellant any administrative duties outside of those necessary to operate her office. The Act specifically provides that in policy matters appellant is to comply to the extent possible with the policies of the Department.

Third, appellant's office is limited in jurisdiction. Not only is the Act itself restricted in applicability to certain federal officials suspected of certain serious federal crimes, but an independent counsel can only act within the scope of the jurisdiction that has been granted by the Special Division pursuant to a request by the Attorney General. Finally, appellant's office is limited in tenure. There is concededly no time limit on the appointment of a particular counsel. Nonetheless, the office of independent counsel is "temporary" in the sense that an independent counsel is appointed essentially to accomplish a single task, and when that task is over the office is terminated, either by the counsel herself or by action of the Special Division. Unlike other prosecutors, appellant has no ongoing responsibilities that extend beyond the accomplishment of the mission that she was appointed for and authorized by the Special Division to undertake. In our view, these factors relating to the "ideas of tenure, duration . . . and duties" of the independent counsel are sufficient to establish that appellant is an "inferior" officer in the constitutional sense. . . .

This does not, however, end our inquiry under the Appointments Clause. Appellees argue that even if appellant is an "inferior" officer, the Clause does not empower Congress to place the power to appoint such an officer outside the Executive Branch. They contend that the Clause does not contemplate congressional authorization of "interbranch appointments," in which an officer of one branch is appointed by officers of another branch. The relevant language of the Appointments Clause is worth repeating. It reads: " . . . but the Congress may by Law vest the Appointment of such inferior Officers, as they think proper, in the President alone, in the courts of Law, or in the Heads of Departments." On its face, the language of this "excepting clause" admits of no limitation on inter-branch appointments. Indeed, the inclusion of "as they think proper" seems clearly to give Congress significant discretion to determine whether it is "proper" to vest the appointment of, for example, executive officials in the "courts of Law." . . .

We also note that the history of the clause provides no support for appellees' position. Throughout most of the process of drafting the Constitution, the Convention con-centrated on the problem of who should have the authority to appoint judges. At the suggestion of James Madison, the Convention adopted a proposal that the Senate should have this authority, and several attempts to transfer the appointment power to the president were rejected. The August 6, 1787, draft of the Constitution reported by the Committee of Detail retained Senate appointment of Supreme Court Judges, provided also for Senate appoint-ment of ambassadors, and vested in the president the authority to "appoint officers in all cases not otherwise provided for by this Constitution." This scheme was main-tained until September 4, when the Committee of Eleven reported its suggestions to the Convention. This Committee suggested that the Constitution be amended to state that the president "shall nominate and by and with the advice and consent of the Senate shall appoint ambassadors, and other public Ministers, Judges of the Supreme Court, and all other Officers of the [United States], whose appoint-ments are not otherwise herein provided for." After the addition of "Consuls" to the list, the Committee's proposal was adopted, and was subsequently reported to the Convention by the Committee of Style. It was at this point, on September 15, that Gouverneur Morris moved to add the Excepting Clause to Art. II, §2. The one comment made on this motion was by Madison, who felt that the Clause did not go far enough in that it did not allow Congress to vest appointment powers in "Superior Officers below Heads of Departments." The first vote on Morris's motion ended in a tie. It was then put forward a second time, with the urging that "some such provision [was] too necessary, to be omitted." This time the proposal was adopted. As this discussion shows, there was little or no debate on the question of whether the Clause empowers Congress to provide for interbranch appointments, and there is nothing to suggest that the Framers intended to prevent Congress from having that power.

We do not mean to say that Congress' power to provide for interbranch appointments of "inferior officers" is unlimited. In addition to separation of powers concerns, which would arise if such provisions for appointment had the potential to impair the constitutional functions assigned to one of the branches, . . . Congress' decision to vest the appointment power in the courts would be improper if there was some "incongruity" between the functions normally performed by the courts and the per-formance of their duty to appoint. In this case, however, we do not think it impermissible for Congress to vest the power to appoint independent counsels in a specially cre-ated federal court. We thus disagree with the Court of Appeals' conclusion that there is an inherent incongruity about a court having the power to appoint prosecutorial officers. . . . Congress of course was concerned when it created the office of independent counsel with the con-flicts of interest that could arise in situations when the Executive Branch is called upon to investigate its own high-ranking officers. If it were to remove the appointing authority from the Executive Branch, the most logical place to put it was in the Judicial Branch. In the light of the Act's provision making the judges of the Special Division ineligible to participate in any matters relating to an inde-pendent counsel they have appointed, . . . we do not think that appointment of the independent counsels by the court runs afoul of the constitutional limitation on "incongru-ous" interbranch appointments.

Appellees next contend that the powers vested in the Special Division by the Act conflict with Article III of the Constitution. We have long recognized that by the express provision of Article III, the judicial power of the United States is limited to "Cases" and "Controversies." As a gen-eral rule, we have broadly stated that "executive or administrative duties of a nonjudicial nature may not be imposed on judges holding office under Art. III of the Constitution." The purpose of this limitation is to help ensure the independence of the Judicial Branch and to prevent the judiciary from encroaching into areas reserved for the other branches. With this in mind, we address in turn the various duties given to the Special Division by the Act.

Most importantly, the Act vests in the Special Division the power to choose who will serve as independent coun-sel and the power to define his or her jurisdiction. Clearly, once it is accepted that the Appointments Clause gives Congress the power to vest the appointment of officials such as the independent counsel in the "courts of Law," there can be no Article III objection to the Special Division's exercise of that power, as the power itself derives from the Appointments Clause, a source of authority for judicial action that is independent of Article III. . . .

In sum, we conclude today that it does not violate the Appointments Clause for Congress to vest the appointment of independent counsels in the Special Division; [and] that the powers exercised by the Special Division under the Act do not violate Article III. . . . The decision of the Court of Appeals is therefore

Reversed.

JUSTICE SCALIA, dissenting.

The present case began when the Legislative and Executive Branches became "embroiled in a dispute concerning the scope of the congressional investigatory power," which— as is often the case with such interbranch conflicts— became quite acrimonious. . . .

. . . The Court devotes most of its attention to such relatively technical details as the Appointments Clause and the removal power, addressing briefly and only at the end of its opinion the separation of powers. . . . I think that has it backwards. . . .

. . . Article II, §1, cl. 1, of the Constitution provides:

"The executive Power shall be vested in a President of the United States." . . . [T]his does not mean *some of* the executive power, but *all of* the executive power. It seems to me, therefore, that the decision of the Court of Appeals invalidating the present statute must be upheld on fundamental separation-of-powers principles if the following two questions are answered affirmatively: (1) Is the conduct of a criminal prosecution (and of an investigation to decide whether to prosecute) the exercise of purely executive power? (2) Does the statute deprive the President of the United States of exclusive control over the exercise of that power? Surprising to say, the Court appears to concede an affirmative answer to both questions, but seeks to avoid the inevitable conclusion that since the statute vests some purely executive power in a person who is not the President of the United States it is void.

The Court concedes that "[t]here is no real dispute that the functions performed by the independent counsel are 'executive,'" though it qualifies that concession by adding "in the sense that they are law enforcement functions that typically have been undertaken by officials within the Executive Branch." The qualifier adds nothing but atmosphere. In what *other* sense can one identify "the executive Power" that is supposed to be vested in the President (unless it includes everything the Executive Branch is given to do) *except* by reference to what has always and everywhere—if conducted by government at all—been conducted never by the legislature, never by the courts, and

always by the executive. There is no possible doubt that the independent counsel's functions fit this description. She is vested with the "full power and independent authority to exercise all *investigative and prosecutorial* functions and powers of the Department of Justice [and] the Attorney General." Governmental investigation and prosecution of crimes is a quintessentially executive function. See *United States v. Nixon* (1974).

As for the second question, whether the statute before us deprives the President of exclusive control over that quintessentially executive activity: the Court does not, and could not possibly, assert that it does not. That is indeed the whole object of the statute. Instead, the Court points out that the President, through his Attorney General, has at least *some* control. That concession is alone enough to invalidate the statute, but I cannot refrain from pointing out that the Court greatly exaggerates the extent of that "some" Presidential control. "Most importan[t]" among these controls, the Court asserts, is the Attorney General's "power to remove the counsel for 'good cause.'" This is somewhat like referring to shackles as an effective means of locomotion. . . .

. . . It effects a revolution in our constitutional jurisprudence for the Court, once it has determined that (1) purely executive functions are at issue here, and (2) those functions have been given to a person whose actions are not fully within the supervision and control of the President, nonetheless to proceed further to sit in judgment of whether "the President's need to control the exercise of [the independent counsel's] discretion is *so central* to the functioning of the Executive Branch" as to require complete control, whether the conferral of his powers upon someone else "*sufficiently* deprives the President of control over the independent counsel to interfere impermissibly with [his] constitutional obligation to ensure the faithful execution of the laws," and whether "the Act give[s] the Executive Branch *sufficient* control over the independent counsel to ensure that the President is able to perform his constitutionally assigned duties." It is not for us to determine, and we have never presumed to determine, how much of the purely executive powers of government must be within the full control of the President. The Constitution prescribes that they *all* are. . . .

Is it unthinkable that the President should have such exclusive power, even when alleged crimes by him or his close associates are at issue? No more so than that Congress should have the exclusive power of legislation, even when what is at issue is its own exemption from the burdens of certain laws. See Civil Rights Act of 1964, Title

VII . . . (prohibiting "employers," not defined to include the United States, from discriminating on the basis of race, color, religion, sex, or national origin). No more so than that this Court should have the exclusive power to pronounce the final decision on justiciable cases and controversies, even those pertaining to the constitutionality of a statute reducing the salaries of the Justices. See *United States v. Will* (1980). A system of separate and coordinate powers necessarily involves an acceptance of exclusive power that can theoretically be abused. . . . While the separation of powers may prevent us from righting every wrong, it does so in order to ensure that we do not lose liberty. The checks against any branch's abuse of its exclusive powers are twofold: First, retaliation by one of the other branch's use of its exclusive powers: Congress, for example, can impeach the executive who willfully fails to enforce the laws; the executive can decline to prosecute under unconstitutional statutes; and the courts can dismiss malicious prosecutions. Second, and ultimately, there is the political check that the people will replace those in the political branches (the branches more "dangerous to the political rights of the Constitution," Federalist No. 78) who are guilty of abuse. Political pressures produced special prosecutors—for Teapot Dome and for Watergate, for example—long before this statute created the independent counsel.

. . . What are the standards to determine how the balance is to be struck, that is, how much removal of Presidential power is too much? . . . Once we depart from the text of the Constitution, just where short of that do we stop? The most amazing feature of the Court's opinion is that it does not even purport to give an answer. It simply *announces*, with no analysis, that the ability to control the decision whether to investigate and prosecute the President's closest advisers, and indeed the President himself, is not "so central to the functioning of the Executive Branch" as to be constitutionally required to be within the President's control. Apparently that is so because we say it is so. Having abandoned as the basis for our decisionmaking the text of Article II that "the executive Power" must be vested in the President, the Court does not even attempt to craft a *substitute* criterion—a "justiciable standard," however remote from the Constitution—that today governs, and in the future will govern, the decision of such questions. Evidently, the governing standard is to be what might be called the unfettered wisdom of a majority of this Court, revealed to an obedient people on a case-by-case basis. This is not only not the government of laws that the Constitution established; it is not a government of laws at all. . . .

In sum, this statute does deprive the President of substantial control over the prosecutory functions performed by the independent counsel, and it does substantially affect the balance of powers. That the Court could possibly conclude otherwise demonstrates both the wisdom of our former constitutional system, in which the degree of reduced control and political impairment were irrelevant, since all purely executive power had to be in the President; and the folly of the new system of standardless judicial allocation of powers we adopt today.

The independent counsel statute upheld in *Morrison v. Olson* expired at the end of 1992. It was not reenacted because of partisan differences over an investigation into the Iran–Contra affair, a controversy involving members of the Reagan administration who allegedly offered to trade arms for the return of Americans held hostage in Lebanon. The independent counsel, Lawrence E. Walsh, aggressively pursued the case, but he was regarded by Republicans as excessively partisan. In addition, investigations such as that headed by Walsh had no effective spending limitations and had become unreasonably expensive. President George H. W. Bush, a Republican, threatened to veto reauthorization legislation.

In June 1994, however, a new independent counsel statute became law. The act received bipartisan support in Congress and was endorsed by President Clinton, the first chief executive to back independent counsel legislation. The new law imposed procedures modeled on the earlier statute: following the Justice Department's preliminary investigation into alleged wrongdoing by top administration officials, the attorney general was to petition a special three-judge federal court to appoint an independent counsel to pursue the matter. The law was invoked almost immediately to appoint Kenneth Starr to continue the investigation of Clinton's involvement in the Whitewater real estate business, which eventually led to his impeachment by the House in 1998.

The revised law received even more criticism than the earlier version. The special prosecutor's open-ended term of office, barely constrained use of prosecutorial power, and expensive operation doomed the prospects for renewing the statute yet again without significant reform. In short, Scalia's dissent in *Morrison* proved prophetic, and the legislation expired without reauthorization in 1999. Seen in this way, Olson may have lost his battle in the Court, but he won the war in

Congress. Moreover, Olson hardly disappeared from the political scene, serving as solicitor general of the United States from June 2001 to July 2004 *(see box 4-2)*.

Still, we should keep in mind that *Morrison* remains today an important standard for determining whether an officer is an inferior officer. But it is not the only one. Less than a decade after *Morrison,* Justice Scalia attempted to devise a new approach in his majority opinion *Edmond v. United States* (1997). After contending that "*Morrison* did not purport to set forth a definitive test for whether an office is 'inferior' under the Appointments Clause," he wrote,

Generally speaking, the term "inferior officer" connotes a relationship with some higher ranking officer or officers below the President: whether one is an "inferior" officer depends on whether he has a superior. It is not enough that other officers may be identified who formally maintain a higher rank, or possess responsibilities of a greater magnitude. If that were the intention, the Constitution might have used the phrase "lesser officer." Rather, in the context of a clause designed to preserve political accountability relative to important government assignments, *we think it evident that "inferior officers" are officers whose work is directed and supervised at some level by others who were appointed by presidential nomination with the advice and consent of the Senate.*

Even though Scalia's approach is more general than Rehnquist's, *Edmond* did not overrule *Morrison* and so today both approaches coexist. Had he applied his *Edmond* definition of "inferior" to the special prosecutor, do you think Scalia would have reached a different conclusion in Morrison? Why or why not?

Recess Appointments. In addition to outlining appointment procedures, Article II, Section 2 allows the president "to fill up all Vacancies that may happen during the Recess of the Senate," with the proviso that these appointments expire at the end of the next session. Why would the framers allow presidents to make these temporary "recess appointments"? Alexander Hamilton suggested a reason in *Federalist* No. 67:

[A]s it would have been improper to oblige [the Senate] to be continually in session for the appointment of officers, and as vacancies might happen in their recess, which it might be necessary for the public service to fill without delay, the . . . clause is evidently intended to authorize the President, singly, to make temporary appointments.

Keeping the government running at full capacity was of particular concern during the nineteenth century. Back then, the Senate's sessions were short and its recesses long. In some years, it was in session for less than half the year.[20]

In contemporary times sessions are longer and recesses shorter but presidents nonetheless continue to use their recess power. President Clinton made 139 recess appointments; Bush, 171; and Obama, 32 (through early 2015).[21] Some were intersession appointments, meaning they came during the recess between the two formal one-year sessions that each House of Congress holds. Other came during intra-sessions. (Intrasession breaks occur in the midst of a session when the Senate or House announces an "intrasession recess" by adopting a resolution stating that it will "adjourn" to a fixed date. That date could be a few days, weeks, or months away.) Moreover, it is worth noting, recess appointees have not just been executive officials but also judges—including fifteen justices of the Supreme Court (the last was Potter Stewart in 1958) and nearly thirty appellate court judges (the last was George W. Bush's recess of William Pryor in 2004).[22]

Why do modern-day presidents make inter- or intrasession recess appointments? Many would say that they, like Hamilton, are concerned about maintaining the administration of government. But another reason is more political: sidestepping the Senate. If the President thinks that the Senate might not confirm his nominee, he can use his recess power to install the nominee in a position, if only temporarily. Though he did not say so, perhaps Hamilton would have approved of this consideration. After all, he was concerned with the smooth operation of government, which would be difficult if the Senate failed to confirm candidates for important positions. Then again, Hamilton referred to the recess power as a "supplement" to the "ordinary" method of appointment, which, he wrote, is "confined to the President and Senate *jointly.*"

---

20. See Henry B. Hogue, "Recess Appointments: Frequently Asked Questions," *Congressional Research Service,* March 11, 2015. See also Appendix A to Justice Breyer's opinion in *Noel Canning.* It has the dates of all the intrasession and intersession recesses that Congress has taken since 1798.

21. Ibid.

22. Scott E. Graves and Robert M. Howard, *Justice Takes a Recess* (Plymouth, UK: Lexington Books, 2009).

Until the case of *National Labor Relations Board v. Noel Canning* (2014), there was no occasion for the Court to consider this or other issues related to the recess appointments clause. But, as Justice Breyer's opinion for the Court in *Noel Canning* makes clear, presidents and their advisers, along with members of Congress, did give thought to various interpretations that the wording of the clause could admit.

As you read *Noel Canning,* note how Justice Breyer makes use of this history, data drawn from historical sources, and practice, among other sources, to answer three questions about the recess power. Justice Scalia also makes use of history in his concurring opinion but comes to some very different conclusions. What are the differences between the two? Who makes the better case?

National Labor Relations Board v. Canning

573 U.S.__ (2014)
http://laws.findlaw.com/us/000/12–1281.html
Oral arguments are available at https//www.oyez.org
Vote: 9 (Alito, Breyer, Ginsburg, Kagan, Kennedy, Roberts, Scalia, Sotomayor, Thomas)
    0
OPINION OF THE COURT: Breyer
CONCURRING OPINION: Scalia

FACTS:

This case arises out of a labor dispute. The National Labor Relations Board (NLRB) found that Noel Canning, a Pepsi-Cola distribution company, had unlawfully refused to execute a collective-bargaining agreement with a labor union. Noel Canning, in turn, asked the Court of Appeals for the District of Columbia Circuit to set the Board's order aside. It claimed that the Board lacked a quorum because three of the five Board members had been invalidly appointed.

The three members in question were Sharon Block, Richard Griffin, and Terence Flynn. In 2011 President Obama had nominated each to the Board. As of January 2012, Flynn's nomination had been pending in the Senate awaiting confirmation for approximately a year. The nominations of the other two had been pending for a few weeks. On January 4, 2012, Obama, invoking the Recess Appointments Clause, appointed all three to the Board. The Recess Appointments Clause (Article II, Section 2, Clause 3) gives the president the power "to fill up all Vacancies that may happen during the Recess of the Senate."

Noel Canning argued that the appointments violated the Recess Appointments Clause. It noted that on December 17, 2011, the Senate had adopted a resolution providing that it would take a series of brief recesses beginning the following day. The Senate then proceeded to hold pro forma sessions ("with no business . . . transacted") every Tuesday and Friday until it returned for ordinary business on January 23, 2012. Noel Canning argued that because each pro forma session terminated the immediately preceding recess, the January 4 appointments were made during a three-day adjournment, which is not long enough to trigger the Recess Appointments Clause.

The U.S. Court of Appeals agreed that the appointments fell outside the scope of the Recess Clause, but for different reasons. It held that the phrase "the recess," as used in the Clause, does not include intrasession recesses, and that the phrase "vacancies that may happen during the recess" applies only to vacancies that first come into existence during a recess.

As a result, the Supreme Court addressed three questions: (1) whether "the recess" excludes intrasessions, as the lower court held, (2) whether "may happen" refers only to vacancies that arise during the recess, again as the lower court held, and (3) whether the Senate was in session or in recess during the pro forma sessions.

ARGUMENTS:

For the petitioner, NLRB:
- Intra-session recess appointments are necessary to serve the purposes of the recess appointment clause, and practice confirms this. Presidents have made thousands of intra-session appointments.
- Since the 1820s, the vast majority of Presidents have made recess appointments to fill vacancies that arose before a particular recess but continued to exist during that recess.
- The Senate is in "recess" for purposes when, for 20 days, a Senate order provides for only "pro forma" sessions at which "no business" is to be conducted. The mere possibility that the Senate might suspend its "no business" order during the 20-day period did not prevent that period from constituting a recess.

For the respondent, Noel Canning:
- Based on the text of the Constitution, the recess appointment power is limited to "*the recess*" between sessions.

- There can be no serious question that the text of the recess clause was originally understood to apply to vacancies that arise during the recess. Every known analysis prior to 1822 reaches that conclusion.
- The president cannot make recess appointments when the Senate is convening pro forma sessions every three days because pro forma sessions are actual sessions.

> **CHIEF JUSTICE BREYER DELIVERED THE OPINION OF THE COURT.**

Ordinarily the President must obtain "the Advice and Consent of the Senate" before appointing an "Office[r] of the United States." . . . U. S. Const., Art. II, §2, cl. 2. But the Recess Appointments Clause creates an exception. It gives the President alone the power "to fill up all Vacancies that may happen during the Recess of the Senate, by granting Commissions which shall expire at the End of their next Session." . . . Art. II, §2, cl. 3. We here consider three questions about the application of this Clause.

The first concerns the scope of the words "recess of the Senate." Does that phrase refer only to an inter-session recess (i.e., a break between formal sessions of Congress), or does it also include an intra-session recess, such as a summer recess in the midst of a session? We conclude that the Clause applies to both kinds of recess.

The second question concerns the scope of the words "vacancies that may happen." Does that phrase refer only to vacancies that first come into existence during a recess, or does it also include vacancies that arise prior to a recess but continue to exist during the recess? We conclude that the Clause applies to both kinds of vacancy.

The third question concerns calculation of the length of a "recess." The President made the appointments here at issue on January 4, 2012. At that time the Senate was in recess pursuant to a December 17, 2011, resolution providing for a series of brief recesses punctuated by "pro forma session[s]," with "no business . . . transacted," every Tuesday and Friday through January 20, 2012. . . . S. J., 112th Cong., 1st Sess., 923 (2011) (hereinafter 2011 S. J.). In calculating the length of a recess are we to ignore the pro forma sessions, thereby treating the series of brief recesses as a single, month-long recess? We conclude that we cannot ignore these pro forma sessions.

Our answer to the third question means that, when the appointments before us took place, the Senate was in the midst of a 3-day recess. Three days is too short a time to bring a recess within the scope of the Clause. Thus we conclude that the President lacked the power to make the recess appointments here at issue. . . .

Before turning to the specific questions presented, we shall mention two background considerations that we find relevant to all three. First, the Recess Appointments Clause sets forth a subsidiary, not a primary, method for appointing officers of the United States. [The primary method is presidential nomination followed by Senate confirmation.]

[T]he Recess Appointments Clause reflects the tension between, on the one hand, the President's continuous need for "the assistance of subordinates," *Myers v. United States*, (1926), and, on the other, the Senate's practice, particularly during the Republic's early years, of meeting for a single brief session each year. We seek to interpret the Clause as granting the President the power to make appointments during a recess but not offering the President the authority routinely to avoid the need for Senate confirmation.

Second, in interpreting the Clause, we put significant weight upon historical practice.

We recognize, of course, that . . . it is the "duty of the judicial department"—in a separation-of-powers case as in any other—"to say what the law is" *Marbury v. Madison* (1803). But it is equally true that the long standing "practice of the government" can inform our determination of "what the law is." . . .

There is a great deal of history to consider here. Presidents have made recess appointments since the beginning of the Republic. Their frequency suggests that the Senate and President have recognized that recess appointments can be both necessary and appropriate in certain circumstances. We have not previously interpreted the Clause, and, when doing so for the first time in more than 200 years, we must hesitate to upset the compromises and working arrangements that the elected branches of Government themselves have reached.

The first question concerns the scope of the phrase "the recess of the Senate." The Constitution provides for congressional elections every two years. And the 2-year life of each elected Congress typically consists of two formal 1-year sessions, each separated from the next by an "inter-session recess." The Senate or the House of Representatives announces an inter-session recess by approving a resolution stating that it will "adjourn sine die," i.e., without specifying a date to return (in which case Congress will reconvene when the next formal session is scheduled to begin).

The Senate and the House also take breaks in the midst of a session. The Senate or the House announces any such "intra-session recess" by adopting a resolution stating that it will "adjourn" to a fixed date, a few days or weeks or even months later. All agree that the phrase "the recess of the Senate" covers inter-session recesses. The question is whether it includes intra-session recesses as well.

In our view, the phrase "the recess" includes an intra-session recess of substantial length. Its words taken literally can refer to both types of recess. Founding-era dictionaries define the word "recess," much as we do today, simply as "a period of cessation from usual work." . . . The Oxford English Dictionary (hereinafter OED) citing 18th- and 19th-century sources for that definition of "recess." . . . The Founders themselves used the word to refer to intra-session, as well as to inter-session, breaks. . . .

We recognize that the word "the" in "the recess" might suggest that the phrase refers to the single break separating formal sessions of Congress. That is because the word "the" frequently (but not always) indicates "a particular thing." But the word can also refer "to a term used generically or universally." OED. The Constitution, for example, directs the Senate to choose a President pro tempore "in the Absence of the Vice-President" Art. I, §3, cl. 5. . . . Reading "the" generically in this way, there is no linguistic problem applying the Clause's phrase to both kinds of recess. And, in fact, the phrase "the recess" was used to refer to intra-session recesses at the time of the founding.

The constitutional text is thus ambiguous. And we believe the Clause's purpose demands the broader interpretation. The Clause gives the President authority to make appointments during "the recess of the Senate" so that the President can ensure the continued functioning of the Federal Government when the Senate is away. The Senate is equally away during both an inter-session and an intra-session recess, and its capacity to participate in the appointments process has nothing to do with the words it uses to signal its departure.

History also offers strong support for the broad interpretation. . . .

In all, between the founding and the Great Depression, Congress took substantial intra-session breaks (other than holiday breaks) in four years: 1867, 1868, 1921, and 1929. And in each of those years the President made intra-session recess appointments.

Since 1929, and particularly since the end of World War II, Congress has shortened its inter-session breaks as it has taken longer and more frequent intra-session breaks; Presidents have correspondingly made more intra-session recess appointments. Indeed, if we include military appointments, Presidents have made thousands of intra-session recess appointments. President Franklin Roosevelt, for example, commissioned Dwight Eisenhower as a permanent Major General during an intra-session recess; President Truman made Dean Acheson Under Secretary of State; and President George H. W. Bush reappointed Alan Greenspan as Chairman of the Federal Reserve Board. Justice Scalia does not dispute any of these facts. . . .

The upshot is that restricting the Clause to inter-session recesses would frustrate its purpose. It would make the President's recess-appointment power dependent on a formalistic distinction of Senate procedure. Moreover, the President has consistently and frequently interpreted the word "recess" to apply to intra-session recesses, and has acted on that interpretation. The Senate as a body has done nothing to deny the validity of this practice for at least three-quarters of a century. And three-quarters of a century of settled practice is long enough to entitle a practice to "great weight in a proper interpretation" of the constitutional provision. . . .

The greater interpretive problem is determining how long a recess must be in order to fall within the Clause. Is a break of a week, or a day, or an hour too short to count as a "recess"? . . .

Even the Solicitor General, arguing for a broader interpretation, acknowledges that there is a lower limit applicable to both kinds of recess. He argues that the lower limit should be three days by analogy to the Adjournments Clause of the Constitution. That Clause says: "Neither House, during the Session of Congress, shall, without the Consent of the other, adjourn for more than three days."

We agree with the Solicitor General that a 3-day recess would be too short. . . . A Senate recess that is so short that it does not require the consent of the House is not long enough to trigger the President's recess-appointment power.

That is not to say that the President may make recess appointments during any recess that is "more than three days." The Recess Appointments Clause seeks to permit the Executive Branch to function smoothly when Congress is unavailable. And though Congress has taken short breaks for almost 200 years, and there have been many thousands of recess appointments in that time, we have not found a single example of a recess appointment made during an intra-session recess that was shorter than 10 days. . . .

We therefore conclude, in light of historical practice, that a recess of more than 3 days but less than 10 days is presumptively too short to fall within the Clause. We add the word "presumptively" to leave open the possibility that some very unusual circumstance—a national catastrophe, for instance, that renders the Senate unavailable but calls for an urgent response—could demand the exercise of the recess-appointment power during a shorter break. . . . (It should go without saying—except that Justice Scalia compels us to say it—that political opposition in the Senate would not qualify as an unusual circumstance.) . . .

The second question concerns the scope of the phrase "vacancies that may happen during the recess of the Senate." Art. II, §2, cl. 3. All agree that the phrase applies to vacancies that initially occur during a recess. But does it also apply to vacancies that initially occur before a recess and continue to exist during the recess? In our view the phrase applies to both kinds of vacancy.

We believe that the Clause's language, read literally, permits, though it does not naturally favor, our broader interpretation. We concede that the most natural meaning of "happens" as applied to a "vacancy" (at least to a modern ear) is that the vacancy "happens" when it initially occurs. . . . But that is not the only possible way to use the word.

Thomas Jefferson wrote that the Clause is "certainly susceptible of [two] constructions." It "may mean 'vacancies that may happen to be' or 'may happen to fall'" during a recess. . . .

In any event, the linguistic question here is not whether the phrase can be, but whether it must be, read more narrowly. The question is whether the Clause is ambiguous. And the broader reading, we believe, is at least a permissible reading of a "'doubtful'" phrase. We consequently go on to consider the Clause's purpose and historical practice.

The Clause's purpose strongly supports the broader interpretation. That purpose is to permit the President to obtain the assistance of subordinate officers when the Senate, due to its recess, cannot confirm them. [T]he narrower interpretation would undermine this purpose. . . .

Examples are not difficult to imagine: An ambassadorial post falls vacant too soon before the recess begins for the President to appoint a replacement; the Senate rejects a President's nominee just before a recess, too late to select another. . . .

At the same time, we recognize one important purpose-related consideration that argues in the opposite direction. A broad interpretation might permit a President to avoid Senate confirmations as a matter of course. If the Clause gives the President the power to "fill up all vacancies" that occur before, and continue to exist during, the Senate's recess, a President might not submit any nominations to the Senate. He might simply wait for a recess and then provide all potential nominees with recess appointments. He might thereby routinely avoid the constitutional need to obtain the Senate's "advice and consent." . . .

While we concede that both interpretations carry with them some risk of undesirable consequences, we believe the narrower interpretation risks undermining constitutionally conferred powers more seriously and more often. It would prevent the President from making any recess appointment that arose before a recess, no matter who the official, no matter how dire the need, no matter how uncontroversial the appointment, and no matter how late in the session the office fell vacant. . . .

Historical practice over the past 200 years strongly favors the broader interpretation. The tradition of applying the Clause to pre-recess vacancies dates at least to President James Madison. . . .

Common sense also suggests that many recess appointees filled vacancies that arose before the recess began. We have compared the list of intra-session recess appointments in the Solicitor General's brief with the chart of congressional recesses. Where a specific date of appointment can be ascertained, more than half of those intra-session appointments were made within two weeks of the beginning of a recess. That short window strongly suggests that many of the vacancies initially arose prior to the recess. . . . Further, we have examined a random sample of the recess appointments made by our two most recent Presidents, and have found that almost all of those appointments filled pre-recess vacancies: Of a sample of 21 recess appointments, 18 filled pre-recess vacancies and only 1 filled a vacancy that arose during the recess in which he was appointed. The precise date on which 2 of the vacancies arose could not be determined. Taken together, we think it is a fair inference that a large proportion of the recess appointments in the history of the Nation have filled pre-existing vacancies.

Did the Senate object? Early on, there was some sporadic disagreement with the broad interpretation. . . .

[But] the Senate subsequently abandoned its hostility. . . .

[I]n 1940 Congress amended the Pay Act to authorize salary payments (with some exceptions) where (1) the "vacancy arose within thirty days prior to the termination of the session," (2) "at the termination of the session" a nomination was "pending," or (3) a nominee was "rejected by the Senate within thirty days prior to the termination of the session." All three circumstances concern a vacancy that did not initially occur during a recess but happened to exist during that recess. By paying salaries to this kind of recess appointee, the 1940 Senate (and later Senates) in effect supported the President's interpretation of the Clause.

The upshot is that the President has consistently and frequently interpreted the Recess Appointments Clause to apply to vacancies that initially occur before, but continue to exist during, a recess of the Senate. The Senate as a body has not countered this practice for nearly three-quarters of a century, perhaps longer. The tradition is long enough to entitle the practice "to great regard in determining the true construction" of the constitutional provision. And we are reluctant to upset this traditional practice where doing so would seriously shrink the authority that Presidents have believed existed and have exercised for so long.

In light of some linguistic ambiguity, the basic purpose of the Clause, and the historical practice we have described, we conclude that the phrase "all vacancies" includes vacancies that come into existence while the Senate is in session.

The third question concerns the calculation of the length of the Senate's "recess." On December 17, 2011, the Senate by unanimous consent adopted a resolution to convene "pro forma session[s]" only, with "no business . . . transacted," on every Tuesday and Friday from December 20, 2011, through January 20, 2012. At the end of each pro forma session, the Senate would "adjourn until" the following pro forma session. During that period, the Senate convened and adjourned as agreed. It held pro forma sessions on December 20, 23, 27, and 30, and on January 3, 6, 10, 13, 17, and 20; and at the end of each pro forma session, it adjourned until the time and date of the next.

The President made the recess appointments before us on January 4, 2012, in between the January 3 and the January 6 pro forma sessions. We must determine the significance of these sessions—that is, whether, for purposes of the Clause, we should treat them as periods when the Senate was in session or as periods when it was in recess. If the former, the period between January 3 and January 6 was a 3-day recess, which is too short to trigger the President's recess-appointment power. If the latter, however, then the 3-day period was part of a much longer recess during which the President did have the power to make recess appointments.

The Solicitor General argues that we must treat the pro forma sessions as periods of recess. He says that these "sessions" were sessions in name only because the Senate was in recess as a functional matter. The Senate, he contends, remained in a single, unbroken recess from January 3, when the second session of the 112th Congress began by operation of the Twentieth Amendment, until January 23, when the Senate reconvened to do regular business.

In our view, however, the pro forma sessions count as sessions, not as periods of recess. We hold that, for purposes of the Recess Appointments Clause, the Senate is in session when it says it is, provided that, under its own rules, it retains the capacity to transact Senate business. The Senate met that standard here.

The standard we apply is consistent with the Constitution's broad delegation of authority to the Senate to determine how and when to conduct its business. The Constitution explicitly empowers the Senate to "determine the Rules of its Proceedings." Art. I, §5, cl. 2. . . .

In addition, the Constitution provides the Senate with extensive control over its schedule. . . . This suggests that the Senate's determination about what constitutes a session should merit great respect. . . .

But our deference to the Senate cannot be absolute. [I]f the Senate had left the Capitol and "effectively given up . . . the business of legislating" then it might be in recess, even if it said it was not. In that circumstance, the Senate is not simply unlikely or unwilling to act upon nominations of the President. It is unable to do so. The purpose of the Clause is to ensure the continued functioning of the Federal Government while the Senate is unavailable. This purpose would count for little were we to treat the Senate as though it were in session even when it lacks the ability to provide its "advice and consent." Accordingly, we conclude that when the Senate declares that it is in session and possesses the capacity, under its own rules, to conduct business, it is in session for purposes of the Clause.

Applying this standard, we find that the pro forma sessions were sessions for purposes of the Clause. First, the Senate said it was in session. . . .

Second, the Senate's rules make clear that during its pro forma sessions, despite its resolution that it would conduct no business, the Senate retained the power to conduct business. . . .

By way of contrast, we do not see how the Senate could conduct business during a recess. It could terminate the recess and then, when in session, pass a bill. But in that case, of course, the Senate would no longer be in recess. It would be in session. And that is the crucial point. Senate rules make clear that, once in session, the Senate can act even if it has earlier said that it would not. . . .

The Recess Appointments Clause responds to a structural difference between the Executive and Legislative Branches: The Executive Branch is perpetually in operation, while the Legislature only acts in intervals separated by recesses. The purpose of the Clause is to allow the Executive to continue operating while the Senate is unavailable. We believe that the Clause's text, standing alone, is ambiguous. It does not resolve whether the

President may make appointments during intra-session recesses, or whether he may fill pre-recess vacancies. But the broader reading better serves the Clause's structural function. Moreover, that broader reading is reinforced by centuries of history, which we are hesitant to disturb. We thus hold that the Constitution empowers the President to fill any existing vacancy during any recess—intra-session or inter-session—of sufficient length.

Justice Scalia would render illegitimate thousands of recess appointments reaching all the way back to the founding era. More than that: Calling the Clause an "anachronism," he would basically read it out of the Constitution. He performs this act of judicial excision in the name of liberty. We fail to see how excising the Recess Appointments Clause preserves freedom. . . . [T]he Framers included the Recess Appointments Clause to preserve the "vigour of government" at times when an important organ of Government, the United States Senate, is in recess. Justice Scalia's interpretation of the Clause would defeat the power of the Clause to achieve that objective. . . .

Given our answer to the last question before us, we conclude that the Recess Appointments Clause does not give the President the constitutional authority to make the appointments here at issue. Because the Court of Appeals reached the same ultimate conclusion (though for reasons we reject), its judgment is affirmed.

It is so ordered.

JUSTICE SCALIA, concurring.

The first question presented is whether "the Recess of the Senate," during which the President's recess-appointment power is active, is (a) the period between two of the Senate's formal sessions, or (b) any break in the Senate's proceedings. I would hold that "the Recess" is the gap between sessions and that the appointments at issue here are invalid because they undisputedly were made during the Senate's session. The Court's contrary conclusion—that "the Recess" includes "breaks in the midst of a session,"—is inconsistent with the Constitution's text and structure, and it requires judicial fabrication of vague, unadministrable limits on the recess-appointment power (thus defined) that overstep the judicial role. . . .

A sensible interpretation of the Recess Appointments Clause should start by recognizing that the Clause uses the term "Recess" in contradistinction to the term "Session." . . .

In the founding era, the terms "recess" and "session" had well-understood meanings in the marking-out of legislative time. The life of each elected Congress typically consisted (as it still does) of two or more formal sessions separated by adjournments "sine die," that is, without a specified return date. The period between two sessions was known as "the recess."

To be sure, in colloquial usage both words, "recess" and "session," could take on alternative, less precise meanings. A session could include any short period when a legislature's members were "assembled for business," and a recess could refer to any brief "suspension" of legislative "business." . . . 2 N. Webster, American Dictionary of the English Language (1828). . . . But as even the majority acknowledges, the Constitution's use of "the word 'the' in 'the [R]ecess'" tends to suggest "that the phrase refers to the single break separating formal sessions." . . .

It is linguistically implausible to suppose—as the majority does—that the Clause uses one of those terms ("Recess") informally and the other ("Session") formally in a single sentence, with the result that an event can occur during both the "Recess" and the "Session." . . .

To avoid the absurd results that follow from its colloquial reading of "the Recess," the majority is forced to declare that some intra-session breaks—though undisputedly within the phrase's colloquial meaning—are simply "too short to trigger the Recess Appointments Clause." But it identifies no textual basis whatsoever for limiting the length of "the Recess," nor does it point to any clear standard for determining how short is too short. It is inconceivable that the Framers would have left the circumstances in which the President could exercise such a significant and potentially dangerous power so utterly indeterminate. . . .

Fumbling for some textually grounded standard, the majority seizes on the Adjournments Clause, which bars either House from adjourning for more than three days without the other's consent. According to the majority, that clause establishes that a 3-day break is always "too short" to trigger the Recess Appointments Clause. It goes without saying that nothing in the constitutional text supports that disposition. If (as the majority concludes) "the Recess" means a recess in the colloquial sense, then it necessarily includes breaks shorter than three days. And the fact that the Constitution includes a 3-day limit in one clause but omits it from the other weighs strongly against finding such a limit to be implicit in the clause in which it does not appear. In all events, the dramatically different contexts in which the two clauses operate make importing the 3-day limit from the Adjournments Clause into the Recess Appointments Clause "both arbitrary and mistaken."

And what about breaks longer than three days? The majority says that a break of four to nine days is "presumptively too short" but that the presumption may be rebutted in an "unusual circumstance," such as a "national catastrophe . . . that renders the Senate unavailable but calls for an urgent response." The majority must hope that the in terrorem effect of its "presumably too short" pronouncement will deter future Presidents from making any recess appointments during 4- to 9-day breaks and thus save us from the absurd spectacle of unelected judges evaluating (after an evidentiary hearing?) whether an alleged "catastrophe" was sufficiently "urgent" to trigger the recess-appointment power." . . .

As for breaks of 10 or more days: We are presumably to infer that such breaks do not trigger any "presumpt[ion]" against recess appointments, but does that mean the President has an utterly free hand? Or can litigants seek invalidation of an appointment made during a 10-day break by pointing to an absence of "unusual" or "urgent" circumstances necessitating an immediate appointment, albeit without the aid of a "presumpt[ion]" in their favor? Or, to put the question as it will present itself to lawyers in the Executive Branch: Can the President make an appointment during a 10-day break simply to overcome "political opposition in the Senate" despite the absence of any "national catastrophe," even though it "go[es] without saying" that he cannot do so during a 9-day break? Who knows? The majority does not say, and neither does the Constitution. . . .

An interpretation that calls for this kind of judicial adventurism cannot be correct. Indeed, if the Clause really did use "Recess" in its colloquial sense, then there would be no "judicially discoverable and manageable standard for resolving" whether a particular break was long enough to trigger the recess-appointment power, making that a nonjusticiable political question. . . .

For the foregoing reasons, the Constitution's text and structure unambiguously refute the majority's freewheeling interpretation of "the Recess." It is not plausible that the Constitution uses that term in a sense that authorizes the President to make unilateral appointments during any break in Senate proceedings, subject only to hazy, atextual limits crafted by this Court centuries after ratification. The majority, however, insists that history "offers strong support" for its interpretation. The historical practice of the political branches is, of course, irrelevant when the Constitution is clear. But even if the Constitution were thought ambiguous on this point, history does not support the majority's interpretation. . . .

. . . . Intra-session recess appointments were virtually unheard of for the first 130 years of the Republic, were deemed unconstitutional by the first Attorney General to address them, were not openly defended by the Executive

until 1921, were not made in significant numbers until after World War II, and have been repeatedly criticized as unconstitutional by Senators of both parties. It is astonishing for the majority to assert that this history lends "strong support" to its interpretation of the Recess Appointments Clause. And the majority's contention that recent executive practice in this area merits deference because the Senate has not done more to oppose it is utterly divorced from our precedent. "The structural interests protected by the Appointments Clause are not those of any one branch of Government but of the entire Republic," and the Senate could not give away those protections even if it wanted to. . . .

The second question presented is whether vacancies that "happen during the Recess of the Senate," which the President is empowered to fill with recess appointments, are (a) vacancies that arise during the recess, or (b) all vacancies that exist during the recess, regardless of when they arose. I would hold that the recess-appointment power is limited to vacancies that arise during the recess in which they are filled, and I would hold that the appointments at issue here—which undisputedly filled pre-recess vacancies—are invalid for that reason as well as for the reason that they were made during the session. The Court's contrary conclusion is inconsistent with the Constitution's text and structure, and it further undermines the balance the Framers struck between Presidential and Senatorial power. Historical practice also fails to support the majority's conclusion on this issue.

As the majority concedes, "the most natural meaning of 'happens' as applied to a 'vacancy' . . . is that the vacancy 'happens' when it initially occurs." The majority adds that this meaning is most natural "to a modern ear," but it fails to show that founding-era ears heard it differently. "Happen" meant then, as it does now, "[t]o fall out; to chance; to come to pass." 1 Johnson, *Dictionary of the English Language* 913. Thus, a vacancy that happened during the Recess was most reasonably understood as one that arose during the recess. It was, of course, possible in certain contexts for the word "happen" to mean "happen to be" rather than "happen to occur," as in the idiom "it so happens." But that meaning is not at all natural when the subject is a vacancy, a state of affairs that comes into existence at a particular moment in time.

[T]he majority's reading not only strains the Clause's language but distorts its constitutional role, which was meant to be subordinate. . . . The Senate's check on the President's appointment power was seen as vital because "'manipulation of official appointments' had long been one of the American revolutionary generation's greatest grievances against executive power." The unilateral power conferred on the President by the Recess Appointments Clause was therefore understood to be "nothing more than a supplement" to the "general method" of advice and consent. The Federalist No. 67.

If, however, the Clause had allowed the President to fill all pre-existing vacancies during the recess by granting commissions that would last throughout the following session, it would have been impossible to regard it—as the Framers plainly did—as a mere codicil to the Constitution's principal, power-sharing scheme for filling federal offices. On the majority's reading, the President would have had no need ever to seek the Senate's advice and consent for his appointments: Whenever there was a fair prospect of the Senate's rejecting his preferred nominee, the President could have appointed that individual unilaterally during the recess, allowed the appointment to expire at the end of the next session, renewed the appointment the following day, and so on ad infinitum. (Circumvention would have been especially easy if, as the majority also concludes, the President was authorized to make such appointments during any intra-session break of more than a few days.) It is unthinkable that such an obvious means for the Executive to expand its power would have been overlooked during the ratification debates. . . .

For the reasons just given, it is clear that the Constitution authorizes the President to fill unilaterally only those vacancies that arise during a recess, not every vacancy that happens to exist during a recess. Again, however, the majority says "[h]istorical practice" requires the broader interpretation. And again the majority is mistaken. Even if the Constitution were wrongly thought to be ambiguous on this point, a fair recounting of the relevant history does not support the majority's interpretation. . . .

. . . Washington's and Adams' Attorneys General read the Constitution to restrict recess appointments to vacancies arising during the recess, and there is no evidence that any of the first four Presidents consciously departed from that reading. The contrary reading was first defended by an executive official in 1823, was vehemently rejected by the Senate in 1863, was vigorously resisted by legislation in place from 1863 until 1940, and is arguably inconsistent with legislation in place from 1940 to the present. The Solicitor General has identified only about 100 appointments that have ever been made under the broader reading, and while it seems likely that a good deal more have been made in the last few decades, there is good reason to doubt that many were made before 1940 (since the

appointees could not have been compensated). I can conceive of no sane constitutional theory under which this evidence of "historical practice"—which is actually evidence of a long-simmering inter-branch conflict—would require us to defer to the views of the Executive Branch.

What the majority needs to sustain its judgment is an ambiguous text and a clear historical practice. What it has is a clear text and an at-best-ambiguous historical practice. Even if the Executive could accumulate power through adverse possession by engaging in a consistent and unchallenged practice over a long period of time, the oft-disputed practices at issue here would not meet that standard. Nor have those practices created any justifiable expectations that could be disappointed by enforcing the Constitution's original meaning. There is thus no ground for the majority's deference to the unconstitutional recess-appointment practices of the Executive Branch. . . .

It is not every day that we encounter a proper case or controversy requiring interpretation of the Constitution's structural provisions. Most of the time, the interpretation of those provisions is left to the political branches—which, in deciding how much respect to afford the constitutional text, often take their cues from this Court. We should therefore take every opportunity to affirm the primacy of the Constitution's enduring principles over the politics of the moment. Our failure to do so today will resonate well beyond the particular dispute at hand. Sad, but true: The Court's embrace of the adverse-possession theory of executive power (a characterization the majority resists but does not refute) will be cited in diverse contexts, including those presently unimagined, and will have the effect of aggrandizing the Presidency beyond its constitutional bounds and undermining respect for the separation of powers.

I concur in the judgment only.

After the Court issued its decision in *Noel Canning,* one journalist claimed that it was a "unanimous rebuke to President Obama."[23] Do you agree? You may want to consider that the opinion was hardly unanimous, despite the lack of dissents. Justice Scalia was so outraged by the majority's opinion that he took the very rare step of summarizing his *concurrence* from the bench. According to Scalia, "The majority practically bends over backwards to ensure that recess appointments will remain a powerful weapon in the president's arsenal."

23. Adam Liptak, "Supreme Court Rebukes Obama on Right of Appointment," *New York Times,* June 26, 2014, A1.

Which brings us to the question of whether *Noel Canning* was actually a major loss for presidential power. Scalia seems to think not. Why?

The Power of Remove

The president's need to have executive branch officials who support the administration's policy goals is only partially satisfied by the power to appoint. What is also required is the corollary—the discretionary right to remove administrative officials from office. This need may arise when a president's appointees do not carry out their duties the way the president wishes, or when an official appointed by a previous administration will not voluntarily step aside to make way for a nominee of the new president's choosing.

Article II, Section 4, of the Constitution specifies that "[t]he President, Vice President and all civil Officers of the United States, shall be removed from office on Impeachment for, and Conviction of, Treason, Bribery, or other high Crimes and Misdemeanors." Short of impeachment, however, the Constitution does not delineate procedures for removals. In the absence of constitutional guidelines, a lingering controversy has centered on whether administrative officials can be removed at the discretion of the president alone or whether Congress also must play a role.

The argument supporting presidential discretion holds that the chief executive must be free to remove those subordinates who fail to meet the president's expectations or who are not loyal to the administration's policy objectives. It would be unreasonable to require the approval of Congress before such officials could be dismissed. Such a requirement might well paralyze the executive branch, particularly when the legislature and the presidency are under the control of different political parties. Moreover, recall that in the view of proponents of the unitary executive doctrine, only the president is vested with the authority to execute the laws in the executive branch and only he can remove officers in "his" branch.

The argument for legislative participation in the process holds that the Constitution anticipates Senate action. If the president can appoint major executive department officials only with senatorial approval, it is reasonable to infer that the chief executive can remove administrators only by going through the same process and obtaining the advice and consent of the Senate. In *The Federalist Papers'* only reference to

the removal powers, in *Federalist* No. 77, Alexander Hamilton supported this view, stating flatly, "The consent of that body [the Senate] would be necessary to displace as well as to appoint." Hamilton argued that if the president and the Senate agreed that an official should be removed, the decision would be much better accepted than if the president acted alone. Hamilton also asserted that a new president should be restrained from removing an experienced official who had conducted his duties satisfactorily just because the president preferred to have a different person in the position.

Historical practice generally has rejected Hamilton's position. From the very beginning, Congress allowed the chief executive to remove administrative officials without Senate consent. In the First Congress James Madison proposed that three executive departments be created: the Foreign Affairs, Treasury, and War Departments. The creation of the Foreign Affairs (later State) Department received the most legislative attention. According to Madison's recommendation, the department was to have a secretary to be appointed by the president with the approval of the Senate who could be removed by the president alone. The House and the Senate held long, comprehensive debates on the removal power at that time and passed legislation allowing the secretary of state to be removed at the president's discretion without Senate approval.

At times, however, the legislature has asserted a right to participate in the removal process. The most notable example occurred with the passage of the Tenure of Office Act in 1867. This statute was enacted to restrict the powers of President Andrew Johnson, who took office after Lincoln's assassination in 1865. Following the Civil War, the Radical Republicans dominated Congress and had little use for Johnson, a Democrat from Tennessee. Congress did not want Johnson to be able to remove Lincoln's appointees. The Tenure of Office Act stipulated that the president could not remove high-ranking executive department heads without first obtaining the approval of the Senate. Johnson blatantly defied the statute by dismissing Secretary of War Edwin M. Stanton in August 1867 and appointing Ulysses S. Grant as interim secretary. The Senate ordered Stanton reinstated. Grant left office, and Stanton returned in January 1868. The next month Johnson fired Stanton again. The president's failure to comply with the law

In Myers v. United States, Chief Justice William Howard Taft, the only justice to have served previously as president, wrote an opinion strongly supporting the authority of the chief executive to remove executive branch officials without first obtaining Senate approval.

Myers v. United States

272 U.S. 52 (1926)
http://laws.findlaw.com/us/272/52.html
Vote: 6 (Butler, Sanford, Stone, Sutherland, Taft, Van Devanter)
   3 (Brandeis, Holmes, McReynolds)
OPINION OF THE COURT: *Taft*
DISSENTING OPINIONS: *Brandeis, Holmes, McReynolds*

FACTS:

Prior to its replacement by the United States Postal Service in 1970, the Post Office Department was considered a patronage agency. Postal officials, beginning with the postmaster general and continuing down to the local postmasters, were political appointees rewarded for loyal party service. In July 1917 President Woodrow Wilson, with the advice and consent of the Senate, appointed Frank S. Myers to be a first-class postmaster in Portland, Oregon, for a four-year term.

Toward the end of Wilson's administration, Postmaster General Albert Burleson obtained information that led him to believe that Myers had committed fraud in the course of his official duties. After considering the case, Wilson reached the same conclusion and was convinced that Myers should be removed from office. In January 1920 Burleson, on the president's orders, asked Myers to submit his resignation. When Myers ignored tradition and refused Wilson's request, the president ordered the postmaster general to fire him, an act that was carried out in February. Myers complained that his removal was illegal. The basis for his argument was an 1876 federal law that said, "Postmasters of the first, second and third classes shall be appointed and may be removed by the President by and with the advice and consent of the Senate and shall hold their offices for four years unless sooner removed or suspended according to law." Wilson strongly believed that his right to remove individuals from appointed office was not to be shared with Congress, and he had engaged in some bitter fights with Congress over this point.

Because Wilson had not received the approval of the Senate for the dismissal, Myers claimed to have been unlawfully fired. He sued for his unpaid salary from the date of his removal to the expiration of his four-year term, a claim of $8,838.71. During the period at issue, Myers accepted no other employment, and the Senate confirmed no other nominee for the position. After Myers died, his widow continued the legal action. The court of claims rejected Myers's suit, and an appeal came to the Supreme Court. After a detailed discussion

constituted one of the grounds upon which the House impeached him.

The Tenure of Office Act never had a judicial test. Once Johnson's term expired, the statute was weakened by amendment and then repealed in 1887. The Supreme Court finally faced this issue in 1926 when presented with an appeal from a fired postmaster. The Court's opinion came from Chief Justice Taft, who compiled one of the nation's most spectacular résumés. Among his positions were solicitor general, governor of the Philippines, secretary of war, president of the United States, and, finally, chief justice of the United States. Given Taft's rich experience in the executive branch and none as a legislator, we would expect, correctly, that he would support a broad interpretation of the president's removal powers and reject the notion that the Senate had the right to limit that discretion. His long, detailed opinion in *Myers v. United States,* combined with the dissenting opinions it provoked, filled 243 pages.

of the events surrounding Madison's proposals during the First Congress (the decision of 1789) and the controversy over the Tenure of Office Act, Chief Justice Taft explained the Court's decision in favor of presidential discretion in exercising the removal power.

ARGUMENTS:

For the appellant, Lois P. Myers for the estate of Frank S. Myers:

- Article II, Section 2, gives Congress discretion to vest the appointment of inferior officers in the president, courts, or heads of departments, and should be inferred to allow congressional participation in the removal of those same officers.
- The 1876 law is neither isolated nor eccentric; many congressional acts operate under the similar assumption that Congress has the power to prescribe the terms of removal from office of presidential appointees.
- The argument that the president cannot effectively execute the laws without the unrestricted power of removal begs the question. Congress makes the laws that the president must execute. The Constitution makes no vague grant of an executive prerogative to disregard legislative enactments.

For the appellee, United States:

- The president has full and complete power of removal under Article II, which vests the executive power in the president. Because the power to remove an officer of the executive branch is an executive duty, the president has full power of removal.
- If Congress has the power to prohibit the president from removing any executive official without its consent, the presidential office becomes dependent upon Congress, thereby impairing the system of checks and balances. If Congress can prohibit the president from removing a postmaster without its consent, then what is to stop Congress from prohibiting the president from removing a member of his cabinet without its consent?
- Suppose one political party dominated Congress and Congress made all incumbent cabinet members irremovable except with the consent of the Senate. If a president of a different party were elected, his power to do his job would be greatly impaired if not altogether destroyed. This would be the destruction of the presidential office as an independent branch of government.

◆ MR. CHIEF JUSTICE TAFT DELIVERED THE OPINION OF THE COURT.

This case presents the question whether under the Constitution the President has the exclusive power of removing executive officers of the United States whom he has appointed by and with the advice and consent of the Senate. . . .

The vesting of the executive power in the President was essentially a grant of the power to execute the laws. But the President alone and unaided could not execute the laws. He must execute them by the assistance of subordinates. This view has since been repeatedly affirmed by this court. As he is charged specifically to take care that they be faithfully executed, the reasonable implication, even in the absence of express words, was that as part of his executive power he should select those who were to act for him under his direction in the execution of the laws. The further implication must be, in the absence of any express limitation respecting removals, that as his selection of administrative officers is essential to the execution of the laws by him, so must be his power of removing those for whom he cannot continue to be responsible. It was urged that the natural meaning of the term "executive power" granted the President included the appointment and removal of executive subordinates. If such appointments and removals were not an exercise of the executive power, what were they? They certainly were not the exercise of legislative or judicial power in government as usually understood. . . .

. . . A veto by the Senate—a part of the legislative branch of the Government—upon removals is a much greater limitation upon the executive branch and a much more serious blending of the legislative with the executive than a rejection of a proposed appointment. It is not to be implied. The rejection of a nominee of the President for a particular office does not greatly embarrass him in the conscientious discharge of his high duties in the selection of those who are to aid him, because the President usually has an ample field from which to select for office, according to his preference, competent and capable men. The Senate has full power to reject newly proposed appointees whenever the President shall remove the incumbents. Such a check enables the Senate to prevent the filling of offices with bad or incompetent men or with those against whom there is tenable objection.

The power to prevent the removal of an officer who has served under the President is different from the authority to consent to or reject his appointment. When a nomination is made, it may be presumed that the Senate is, or may become, as well advised as to the fitness of the nominee as the President, but in the nature of things the defects in ability or intelligence or loyalty in the administration of the laws of one who has served as an officer under the President, are facts as to which the President, or his trusted subordinates, must be better informed than the Senate, and the power to remove him may, therefore, be regarded as confined, for very sound and practical reasons, to the governmental authority which has administrative control. The power of removal is incident to the power of appointment, not to the power of advising and consenting to appointment, and when the grant of the executive power is enforced by the express mandate to take care that the laws be faithfully executed, it emphasizes the necessity for including within the executive power as conferred the exclusive power of removal. . . .

Made responsible under the Constitution for the effective enforcement of the law, the President needs as an indispensable aid to meet it the disciplinary influence upon those who act under him of a reserve power of removal. But it is contended that executive officers appointed by the President with the consent of the Senate are . . . not his servants to do his will, and that his obligation to care for the faithful execution of the laws does not authorize him to treat them as such. The degree of guidance in the discharge of their duties that the President may exercise over executive officers varies with the character of their service as prescribed in the law under which they act. The highest and most important duties which his subordinates perform are those in which they act for him. In such cases they are exercising not their own but his discretion. This field is a very large one. It is sometimes described as political. Each head of a department is and must be the President's alter ego in the matters of that department where the President is required by law to exercise authority. . . .

In all such cases, the discretion to be exercised is that of the President in determining the national public interest and in directing the action to be taken by his executive subordinates to protect it. In this field his cabinet officers must do his will. He must place in each member of his official family, and his chief executive subordinates, implicit faith. The moment that he loses confidence in the intelligence, ability, judgment or loyalty of any one of them, he must have the power to remove him without delay. To require him to file charges and submit them to the consideration of the Senate might make impossible that unity and coordination in executive administration essential to effective action.

The duties of the heads of departments and bureaus in which the discretion of the President is exercised and which we have described, are the most important in the whole field of executive action of the Government. There is nothing in the Constitution which permits a distinction between the removal of the head of a department or a bureau, when he discharges a political duty of the President or exercises his discretion, and the removal of executive officers engaged in the discharge of their other normal duties. The imperative reasons requiring an unrestricted power to remove the most important of his subordinates in their most important duties must, therefore, control the interpretation of the Constitution as to all appointed by him.

But this is not to say that there are not strong reasons why the President should have a like power to remove his appointees charged with other duties than those above described. The ordinary duties of officers prescribed by statute come under the general administrative control of the President by virtue of the general grant to him of the executive power, and he may properly supervise and guide their construction of the statutes under which they act in order to secure that unitary and uniform execution of the laws which Article II of the Constitution evidently contemplated in vesting general executive power in the President alone. Laws are often passed with specific provision for the adoption of regulations by a department or bureau head to make the law workable and effective. The ability and judgment manifested by the official thus empowered, as well as his energy and stimulation of his subordinates, are subjects which the President must consider and supervise in his administrative control. Finding such officers to be negligent and inefficient, the President should have the power to remove them. Of course there may be duties so peculiarly and specifically committed to the discretion of a particular officer as to raise a question whether the President may overrule or revise the officer's interpretation of his statutory duty in a particular instance. Then there may be duties of a quasi-judicial character imposed on executive officers and members of executive tribunals whose decisions after hearing affect interests of individuals, the discharge of which the President can not in a particular case properly influence or control. But even in such a case he may consider the decision after its rendition as a reason for removing the officer, on the ground that the discretion regularly entrusted to that officer by statute has not been on the whole intelligently or wisely exercised. Otherwise he does not discharge his own constitutional duty of seeing that the laws be faithfully executed. . . .

We come now to consider an argument advanced and strongly pressed on behalf of the complainant, that this case concerns only the removal of a postmaster; that a postmaster is an inferior officer; that such an office was not included within the legislative decision of 1789, which related only to superior officers to be appointed by the President by and with the advice and consent of the Senate. . . .

The power to remove inferior executive officers, like that to remove superior executive officers, is an incident of the power to appoint them, and is in its nature an executive power. The authority of Congress given by the excepting clause to vest the appointment of such inferior officers in the heads of departments carries with it authority incidentally to invest the heads of departments with power to remove. It has been the practice of Congress to do so and this Court has recognized that power. . . . But the Court never has held, nor reasonably could hold, although it is argued to the contrary on behalf of the appellant, that the excepting clause enables Congress to draw to itself, or to either branch of it, the power to remove or the right to participate in the exercise of that power. To do this would be to go beyond the words and implications of that clause and to infringe the constitutional principle of the separation of governmental powers.

Assuming then the power of Congress to regulate removals as incidental to the exercise of its constitutional power to vest appointments of inferior officers in the heads of departments, certainly so long as Congress does not exercise that power, the power of removal must remain where the Constitution places it, with the President, as part of the executive power, in accordance with the legislative decision of 1789 which we have been considering. . . .

Our conclusion on the merits, sustained by the arguments before stated, is that Article II grants to the President the executive power of Government, i.e., the general administrative control of those executing the laws, including the power of appointment and removal of executive officers—a conclusion confirmed by his obligation to take care that the laws be faithfully executed; that Article II excludes the exercise of legislative power by Congress to provide for appointments and removals, except only as granted therein to Congress in the matter of inferior offices; that Congress is only given power to provide for appointments and removals of inferior officers after it has vested, and on condition that it does vest, their appointment in other authority than the President with the Senate's consent; that the provisions of the second section of Article II, which blend action by the legislative branch, or by part of it, in the work of the executive, are limitations to be strictly construed and not to be extended by implication; that the President's power of removal is further established as an incident to his specifically enumerated function of appointment by and with the advice of the Senate, but that such incident does not by implication extend to removals the Senate's power of checking appointments; and finally that to hold otherwise would make it impossible for the President, in case of political or other differences with the Senate or Congress, to take care that the laws be faithfully executed. . . .

When, on the merits, we find our conclusion strongly favoring the view which prevailed in the First Congress, we have no hesitation in holding that conclusion to be correct; and it therefore follows that the Tenure of Office Act of 1867, in so far as it attempted to prevent the President from removing executive officers who had been appointed by him by and with the advice and consent of the Senate, was invalid, and that subsequent legislation of the same effect was equally so.

For the reasons given, we must therefore hold that the provision of the law of 1876, by which the unrestricted power of removal of first class postmasters is denied to the President, is in violation of the Constitution, and invalid. This leads to an affirmance of the judgment of the Court of Claims.

The separate opinion of MR. JUSTICE McREYNOLDS.

Congress has long and vigorously asserted its right to restrict removals and there has been no common executive practice based upon a contrary view. The President has often removed, and it is admitted that he may remove, with either the express or implied assent of Congress; but the present theory is that he may override the declared will of the body. This goes far beyond any practice heretofore approved or followed; it conflicts with the history of the Constitution, with the ordinary rules of interpretation, and with the construction approved by Congress since the beginning and emphatically sanctioned by this court. To adopt it would be revolutionary. . . .

The federal Constitution is an instrument of exact expression. Those who maintain that Art. 2, Sec. 1, was intended as a grant of every power of executive nature not specifically qualified or denied, must show that the term "executive power" had some definite and commonly accepted meaning in 1787. This court has declared that it did not include all powers exercised by the King of England; and, considering the history of the period, none can say that it had then (or afterwards) any commonly accepted and practical definition. . . .

In any rational search for answer to the questions arising upon this record, it is important not to forget—

That this is a government of limited powers definitely enumerated and granted by a written Constitution. . . .

That the Constitution must be interpreted by attributing to its words the meaning which they bore at the time of its adoption and in view of commonly-accepted canons of construction, its history, early and long-continued practices under it, and relevant opinions of this court.

That the Constitution endows Congress with plenary powers "to establish post offices and post roads."

That exercising this power during the years from 1789 to 1836, Congress provided for postmasters and vested the power to appoint and remove all of them at pleasure in the Postmaster General.

That the Constitution contains no words which specifically grant to the President power to remove duly appointed officers. And it is definitely settled that he cannot remove those whom he has not appointed—certainly they can be removed only as Congress may permit.

That postmasters are inferior officers within the meaning of Art. II, Sec. 2, of the Constitution.

That from its first session to the last one Congress has often asserted its right to restrict the President's power to remove inferior officers, although appointed by him with consent of the Senate.

That many Presidents have approved statutes limiting the power of the executive to remove, and that from the beginning such limitations have been respected in practice. . . .

That the proceedings in the Constitutional Convention of 1787, the political history of the times, contemporaneous opinion, common canons of construction, the action of Congress from the beginning and opinions of this court, all oppose the theory that by vesting "the executive power" in the President the Constitution gave him an illimitable right to remove inferior officers. . . .

That to declare the President vested with indefinite and illimitable executive powers would extend the field of his possible action far beyond the limits observed by his predecessors and would enlarge the powers of Congress to a degree incapable of fair appraisement.

Considering all these things, it is impossible for me to accept the view that the President may dismiss, as caprice may suggest, any inferior officer whom he has appointed with consent of the Senate, notwithstanding a positive inhibition by Congress. In the last analysis that view has no substantial support, unless it be the polemic opinions expressed by Mr. Madison (and eight others) during the debate of 1789, when he was discussing questions relating to a "superior officer" to be appointed for an indefinite term. Notwithstanding his justly exalted reputation as one of the creators and early expounders of the Constitution, sentiments expressed under such circumstances ought not now to outweigh the conclusion which Congress affirmed by deliberate action while he was leader in the House and has consistently maintained down to the present year, the opinion of this court solemnly announced through the great Chief Justice more than a century ago, and the canons of construction approved over and over again.

Judgment should go for the appellant.

MR. JUSTICE BRANDEIS, dissenting.

May the President, having acted under the statute in so far as it creates the office and authorizes the appointment, ignore, while the Senate is in session, the provision which prescribes the condition under which a removal may take place?

It is this narrow question, and this only, which we are required to decide. . . . It is settled that, in the absence of a provision expressly providing for the consent of the Senate to a removal, the clause fixing the tenure will be construed as a limitation, not as a grant, and that, under such legislation, the President, acting alone, has the power of removal. But, in defining the tenure, this statute used words of grant. Congress clearly intended to preclude a removal without the consent of the Senate. . . .

The practice of Congress to control the exercise of the executive power of removal from inferior offices is evidenced by many statutes which restrict it in many ways besides the removal clause here in question. Each of these restrictive statutes became law with the approval of the President. Every President who has held office since 1861, except President Garfield, approved one or more of such statutes. Some of these statutes, prescribing a fixed term, provide that removal shall be made only for one of several specified causes. Some provide a fixed term, subject generally to removal for cause. Some provide for removal only after hearing. Some provide a fixed term, subject to removal for reasons to be communicated by the President to the Senate. Some impose the restriction in still other ways. . . .

The historical data submitted present a legislative practice, established by concurrent affirmative action of Congress and the President, to make consent of the Senate a condition of removal from statutory inferior, civil, executive offices to which the appointment is made for a fixed term by the President with such consent. They show that the practice has existed, without interruption, continuously for the last fifty-eight years; that, throughout this period, it has governed a great majority of all such offices; that the legislation applying the removal clause specifically to the office of postmaster was enacted more than half a century ago; and that recently the practice has, with the President's approval, been extended to several newly created offices. The data show further, that the insertion of the removal clause in acts creating inferior civil offices with fixed tenures is part of the broader legislative practice, which has prevailed since the formation of our government, to restrict or regulate in many ways both removal from and nomination to such offices. A persistent legislative practice which involves a delimitation of the respective powers of Congress and the President, and which has been so established and maintained, should be deemed tantamount to judicial construction, in the absence of any decision by any court to the contrary.

The persuasive effect of this legislative practice is strengthened by the fact that no instance has been found, even in the earlier period of our history, of concurrent affirmative action of Congress and the President which is inconsistent with the legislative practice of the last fifty-eight years to impose the removal clause. Nor has any instance been found of action by Congress which involves recognition in any other way of the alleged uncontrollable executive power to remove an inferior civil officer. The action taken by Congress in 1789 after the great debate does not present such an instance. The vote then taken did not involve a decision that the President had uncontrollable power. It did not involve a decision of the question whether Congress could confer upon the Senate the right, and impose upon it the duty, to participate in removals. It involved merely the decision that the Senate does not, in the absence of legislative grant thereof, have the right to share in the removal of an officer appointed with its consent; and that the President has, in the absence of restrictive legislation, the constitutional power of removal without such consent. Moreover, as Chief Justice Marshall recognized, the debate and the decision related to a high political office, not to inferior ones.

Nine years later the president's discretionary power to remove administrators was challenged again. This time the situation was somewhat different because the office involved had greater policy-making power than the local postmaster position at issue in *Myers*. Here, the fired officer was not a member of the regular executive branch departments but a member of the Federal Trade Commission (FTC), an independent regulatory board. Did these differences prompt the justices to rule differently on the president's removal power, or did the *Myers* precedent apply here as well?

Humphrey's Executor v. United States

295 U.S. 602 (1935)
http://laws.findlaw.com/us/295/602.html
Vote: 9 (Brandeis, Butler, Cardozo, Hughes, McReynolds, Roberts, Stone, Sutherland, Van Devanter)
   0
OPINION OF THE COURT: *Sutherland*

FACTS:

In 1914 Congress created the Federal Trade Commission (FTC) as an independent regulatory agency to enforce antitrust laws and prevent unfair methods of commercial competition. The statute called for the FTC to be staffed by five commissioners appointed by the president and confirmed by the Senate. Not more than three members could be of the same political party, and members were to serve staggered seven-year terms. These provisions were intended to increase the independence of the board and prevent its domination by the incumbent chief executive. The president could remove commissioners, but only for inefficiency, neglect of duty, or malfeasance in office. The commission had the powers of rule making, investigation, and enforcement.

In 1931 President Herbert Hoover named FTC commissioner William E. Humphrey to a second seven-year term, which would expire in 1938. When Franklin Roosevelt was elected in 1932, he made every effort to staff the executive branch with people who were committed to his New Deal programs for combating the Great Depression. The president wrote to Humphrey on July 25, 1933, asking him to resign from his post on the ground that "the aims and purposes of the Administration with respect to the work of the Commission can be carried out most effectively with personnel of my own selection." When Humphrey did not reply, the president wrote to him again on August 31: "You will, I know, realize that I do not feel that your mind and my mind go along together on either the policies or the administering of the Federal Trade Commission, and, frankly, I think it best for the people of this country that I should have a full confidence." Humphrey then told the president that he would not resign. In his third letter to Humphrey, dated October 7, Roosevelt wrote, "Effective as of this date you are hereby removed from the office of Commissioner of the Federal Trade Commission." The president did not rest his action on any of the statutory grounds for removing a commissioner; rather, he fired Humphrey because he did not approve of his positions on policy matters related to the jurisdiction of the FTC. Humphrey claimed he had been illegally removed.

Humphrey died in February 1934. His executor filed suit in the court of claims in behalf of Humphrey's estate to recover the salary lost between the date of his dismissal and his death. The administration argued on the basis of *Myers* that the president was free to remove executive officials at will. Humphrey's executor claimed that the law establishing the FTC placed constitutionally valid restraints on the president's discretion to remove officeholders. The court of claims asked the Supreme Court to answer two questions: Did the Federal Trade Commission Act restrict the president's removal power to those grounds cited in the statute? And, if so, is such a restriction constitutional?

ARGUMENTS:

For the plaintiff, Samuel F. Rathbun, as executor of the estate of William E. Humphrey, deceased:

- The duties and functions of the Federal Trade Commission are inconsistent with an unrestricted power of removal by the president. The FTC was intended to be an independent body. The power to remove an officer is the power to dominate him. The separation of powers theory is inconsistent with the domination of such an agency by the president through the exercise of an unrestricted removal power.
- In *Myers* the Court ruled that the Constitution gives the president the exclusive power to remove an executive officer appointed by him with the advice and consent of the Senate. This ruling has no application to an FTC commissioner who performs functions as an agent not only of the executive but also of the legislature and the courts.

For the defendant, United States:

- Limiting the removal power is an unconstitutional interference with the executive power of the president, as *Myers* held. The Supreme Court should adhere to precedent.
- No sound distinction can be drawn between this case and *Myers*. A limitation on the grounds of

removal is at least as substantial an interference with the executive power as is a requirement that the Senate participate in the removal.
- There is nothing in the nature and functions of the FTC to justify a departure from *Myers*. The functions the FTC performs are in no essential respects different from those performed by the heads of the departments.

MR. JUSTICE SUTHERLAND DELIVERED THE OPINION OF THE COURT.

First. The question first to be considered is whether, by the provisions of §1 of the Federal Trade Commission Act, . . . the President's power is limited to removal for the specific causes enumerated therein. . . .

The commission is to be non-partisan; and it must, from the very nature of its duties, act with entire impartiality. It is charged with the enforcement of no policy except the policy of the law. Its duties are neither political nor executive, but predominantly quasi-judicial and quasi-legislative. Like the Interstate Commerce Commission, its members are called upon to exercise the trained judgment of a body of experts "appointed by law and informed by experience."

The legislative reports in both houses of Congress clearly reflect the view that a fixed term was necessary to the effective and fair administration of the law. In the report to the Senate the Senate Committee on Interstate Commerce, in support of the bill which afterwards became the act in question, after referring to the provision fixing the term of office at seven years, so arranged that the membership would not be subject to complete change at any one time. . . .

The debates in both houses demonstrate that the prevailing view was that the commission was not to be "subject to anybody in the government but . . . only to the people of the United States"; free from "political domination or control" or the "probability or possibility of such a thing"; to be "separate and apart from any existing department of the government—not subject to the orders of the President."

More to the same effect appears in the debates, which were long and thorough and contain nothing to the contrary. While the general rule precludes the use of these debates to explain the meaning of the words of the statute, they may be considered as reflecting light upon its general purposes and the evils which it sought to remedy.

Thus, the language of the act, the legislative reports, and the general purposes of the legislation as reflected by the debates, all combine to demonstrate the Congressional intent to create a body of experts who shall gain experience by length of service—a body which shall be independent of executive authority, except in its selection, and free to exercise its judgment without the leave or hindrance of any other official or department of the government. To the accomplishment of these purposes, it is clear that Congress was of opinion that length and certainty of tenure would vitally contribute. And to hold that, nevertheless, the members of the commission continue in office at the mere will of the President, might be to thwart, in large measure, the very ends which Congress sought to realize by definitely fixing the term of office.

We conclude that the intent of the act is to limit the executive power of removal to the causes enumerated, the existence of none of which is claimed here; and we pass to the second question.

Second. To support its contention that the removal provision of §1, as we have just construed it, is an unconstitutional interference with the executive power of the President, the government's chief reliance is *Myers v. United States.* That case has been so recently decided, and the prevailing and dissenting opinions so fully review the general subject of the power of executive removal, that further discussion would add little to the value of the wealth of material there collected. These opinions examine at length the historical, legislative and judicial data bearing upon the question, beginning with what is called "the decision of 1789" in the first Congress and coming down almost to the day when the opinions were delivered. . . . Nevertheless, the narrow point actually decided was only that the President had power to remove a postmaster of the first class, without the advice and consent of the Senate as required by act of Congress. In the course of the opinion of the court, expressions occur which tend to sustain the government's contention, but these are beyond the point involved and, therefore, do not come within the rule of stare decisis. In so far as they are out of harmony with the views here set forth, these expressions are disapproved. . . .

The office of a postmaster is so essentially unlike the office now involved that the decision in the *Myers* case cannot be accepted as controlling our decision here. A postmaster is an executive officer restricted to the performance of executive functions. He is charged with no duty at all related to either the legislative or judicial power. The actual decision in the *Myers* case finds support in the theory that such an officer is merely one of the units in the executive department and, hence, inherently subject to the exclusive and illimitable power of removal by the Chief Executive, whose subordinate and aid he is. Putting aside dicta, which may be followed if sufficiently persuasive but which are not controlling, the necessary reach of the decision goes far enough to include all purely executive officers. It goes no farther;—much less does it include an officer who occupies no place in the executive department and who exercises no part of the executive power vested by the Constitution in the President.

The Federal Trade Commission is an administrative body created by Congress to carry into effect legislative policies embodied in the statute in accordance with the legislative standard therein prescribed, and to perform other specified duties as a legislative or as a judicial aid. Such a body cannot in any proper sense be characterized as an arm or an eye of the executive. Its duties are performed without executive leave and, in the contemplation of the statute, must be free from executive control. In administering the provisions of the statute in respect of "unfair methods of competition"—that is to say in filling in and administering the details embodied by that general standard—the commission acts in part quasi-legislatively and in part quasi-judicially. In making investigations and reports thereon for the information of Congress . . . in aid of the legislative power, it acts as a legislative agency. [The law also] authorizes the commission to act as a master in chancery under rules prescribed by the court, it acts as an agency of the judiciary. To the extent that it exercises any executive function—as distinguished from executive power in the constitutional sense—it does so in the discharge and effectuation of its quasi-legislative or quasi-judicial powers, or as an agency of the legislative or judicial departments of the government.

We think it plain under the Constitution that illimitable power of removal is not possessed by the President in respect of officers of the character of those just named. The authority of Congress, in creating quasi-legislative or quasi-judicial agencies, to require them to act in discharge of their duties independently of executive control cannot well be doubted; and that authority includes, as an appropriate incident, power to fix the period during which they shall continue in office, and to forbid their removal except for cause in the meantime. For it is quite evident that one who holds his office only during the pleasure of another, cannot be depended upon to maintain an attitude of independence against the latter's will.

The fundamental necessity of maintaining each of the three general departments of government entirely free from the control or coercive influence, direct or indirect, of either of the others, has often been stressed and is hardly open to serious question. So much is implied in the very fact of the separation of the powers of these departments by the Constitution; and in the rule which recognizes their essential co-equality. The sound application of a principle that makes one master in his own house precludes him from imposing his control in the house of another who is master there. . . .

The power of removal here claimed for the President falls within this principle, since its coercive influence threatens the independence of a commission, which is not only wholly disconnected from the executive department, but which, as already fully appears, was created by Congress as a means of carrying into operation legislative and judicial powers, and as an agency of the legislative and judicial departments. . . .

The result of what we now have said is this: Whether the power of the President to remove an officer shall prevail over the authority of Congress to condition the power by fixing a definite term and precluding a removal except for cause, will depend upon the character of the office; the *Myers* decision, affirming the power of the President alone to make the removal, is confined to purely executive officers; and as to officers of the kind here under consideration, we hold that no removal can be made during the prescribed term for which the officer is appointed, except for one or more of the causes named in the applicable statute.

To the extent that, between the decision in the Myers case, which sustains the unrestrictable power of the President to remove purely executive officers, and our present decision that such power does not extend to an office such as that here involved, there shall remain a field of doubt, we leave such cases as may fall within it for future consideration and determination as they may arise.

In *Humphrey's Executor* the Court distinguished between officials who exercise purely executive powers and those who carry out quasi-legislative and quasi-judicial functions. The former serve at the pleasure of the president and may be removed at his discretion. The latter may be removed only with procedures consistent with statutory conditions enacted by Congress.

Would Chief Justice Taft have agreed with this distinction? Or did his opinion in *Myers* suggest that he would have opposed any constraints on the presidential power to remove officials?

No matter what Taft might have thought, the *Humphrey's Executor* scheme was reaffirmed in *Wiener v. United States* (1958). The case involved a member of the War Claims Commission, a body that Congress established in 1948 to receive and adjudicate claims for compensating certain parties who suffered damages at the hands of the enemy in World War II. The statute created a three-member commission appointed by the president and confirmed by the Senate. The commission was scheduled to go out of existence two years after the deadline for filing claims, but, after some legislative extensions, the expiration date was changed to 1954. The statute contained no provisions for terms of office or procedures for removal.

President Truman appointed Myron Wiener to the commission in 1950. President Dwight D. Eisenhower, elected in 1952, wanted to replace the commission members with Republicans, and he requested the resignations of the incumbents. Eisenhower wrote to Wiener, "I regard it as in the national interest to complete the administration of the War Claims Act of 1948, as amended, with personnel of my own selection." When the incumbents refused to resign, Eisenhower ordered them dismissed and appointed their replacements. The Eisenhower appointees served in office as recess appointments. The Senate had not yet confirmed them when the commission ceased to exist. Wiener sued for the salary denied him from the date of his removal to the expiration of the commission. The court of claims ruled in favor of the government, and Wiener appealed to the Supreme Court.

Justice Felix Frankfurter, writing for a unanimous bench, reversed. The justices concluded that Wiener had been fired illegally. The war claims commissioners exercised quasi-judicial functions, and therefore the position was governed by the decision in *Humphrey's Executor* rather than *Myers*. Because Wiener did not exercise purely executive powers, Eisenhower had no power under the Constitution or the statute creating the commission to remove him. The *Wiener* decision is important because, by reaffirming *Humphrey's Executor,* it brought an authoritative close to questions regarding the extent of the president's power to remove officeholders at his discretion alone.

Executive Privilege: Protecting Presidential Confidentiality

Article II is silent on two potentially important and related questions pertaining to the president's roles as chief executive and commander in chief. The first, executive privilege, asks whether the president can refuse to supply the other branches of government with information about his activities. The second (covered in the next section) is immunity—whether and to what extent the president is protected from lawsuits while in office.

The executive privilege argument asserts that certain conversations, documents, and records are so closely tied to the sensitive duties of the president that they should remain confidential. Neither the legislature nor the judiciary should be allowed access to these materials without presidential consent, nor should the other branches be empowered to compel the president to hand over such items, especially those related to matters concerning national security or foreign policy. Executive privilege, it is argued, is inherent to the office of the president.

Although infrequently invoked, the privilege doctrine has been part of American history since the beginning of the nation. In some early disputes between the president and Congress, chief executives refused to provide certain information to the legislature. George Washington balked at giving the House of Representatives documents and correspondence pertaining to the Jay Treaty—a controversial treaty between the United States and Great Britain. In a message to the House, Washington wrote,

The nature of foreign negotiations requires caution, and their success must often depend on secrecy; and even when brought to a conclusion a full disclosure of all the measures, demands, or eventual concessions which may have been proposed or contemplated would be extremely impolitic; for this might have a pernicious influence on future negotiations, or produce immediate inconveniences, perhaps danger and mischief, in relation to other powers. The necessity of such caution and secrecy was one cogent reason for vesting the power of making treaties in the President, with the advice and consent of the Senate, the principle on which that body was formed confining it to a small number of members. To admit, then, a right in the House of Representatives to demand and to have as a matter of course all the papers respecting a negotiation with a foreign power would be to establish a dangerous precedent.[24]

Washington was hardly alone. During the investigation and trial of Aaron Burr, Thomas Jefferson cooperated with congressional information requests, but only up to a point. He refused to produce some items and later declined to testify at the trial even though he was subpoenaed. Other presidents, too, through the years have refused to comply with congressional requests for testimony. It is generally accepted that Congress does not have the power to compel the president to come before it to answer questions. Whether other executive department officials are covered by claims of privilege is a more open question.

The George W. Bush administration claimed the privilege a handful of times against congressional investigations—mostly after Democrats took control of both houses of Congress in 2006 and launched a series of investigations.[25] In 2012 President Obama asserted executive privilege in response to demands from House Republicans on the Committee on Oversight and Government Reform for information on a sting operation against Mexican drug cartel activities that had gone awry. Interestingly, when Obama came into office, he had to decide how to deal with a claim of executive privilege by his predecessor, President Bush, over the firing of U.S. attorneys in the face of a congressional subpoena. The Obama administration chose to negotiate an agreement whereby some of the requested documents and testimony would be provided, but only those documents from a specific period, and the testimony would not be in front of the public. Furthermore, the witnesses would not have to testify about communications to or from the president.

This is typical. In most instances, disputes over executive privilege are handled through negotiation between the executive branch and the institution requesting information. Only rarely have such disputes blown up into major court cases. When pushed to the limit, executive privilege claims rarely prevail, but when sensitive military or diplomatic matters requiring secrecy are involved, a president can expect to be on relatively safe ground in asserting executive privilege.

No case involving executive privilege has been more important than *United States v. Nixon* (1974). It

---

24. George Washington, message to the House regarding documents relative to the Jay Treaty, March 30, 1796, Yale Law School, Lillian Goldman Law Library, The Avalon Project, http://avalon.law.yale.edu/18th_century/gw003.asp.

25. Morton Rosenberg, "Presidential Claims of Executive Privilege: History, Law, Practice and Recent Developments," Order Code RL30319, CRS Report for Congress, 2008, updated August 21, 2008, http://www.fas.org/sgp/crs/secrecy/RL30319.pdf.

occurred at a time of great constitutional stress, when all three branches were locked in a fight about fundamental separation of powers issues.

The conflict ultimately was resolved when President Nixon resigned. Much of the impetus for breaking the constitutional deadlock came from the justices' unanimous decision in the *Nixon* case. Chief Justice Warren Burger's opinion for the Court reviewed the issues surrounding the executive privilege controversy and then rejected Nixon's invocation of the doctrine.

United States v. Nixon

418 U.S. 683 (1974)
http://laws.findlaw.com/us/418/683.html
Oral arguments are available at https://www.oyez.org.
Vote: 8 (Blackmun, Brennan, Burger, Douglas, Marshall, Powell, Stewart, White)
0
OPINION OF THE COURT: *Burger*
NOT PARTICIPATING: *Rehnquist*

FACTS:

This case was one of many court actions spawned by the Watergate scandal, which began on June 17, 1972, when seven men broke into the Democratic National Committee headquarters located in the Watergate complex in Washington, D.C. The men were apprehended and charged with criminal offenses. All had ties either to the White House or to the Committee to Re-elect the President. Five of the seven pleaded guilty, and two were convicted. At the end of the trial, one of the defendants, James McCord Jr., claimed that he had been pressured to plead guilty and that other people involved in the break-in had not been prosecuted. Many suspected that the break-in was only the tip of a very large iceberg of shady dealings and cover-ups engaged in by influential persons with close ties to the Nixon administration.

On May 17, 1973, the Senate began its investigation of the Watergate incident and the activities related to it. The star witness was John Dean III, special counsel to the president, who testified under a grant of immunity. Dean implicated high officials in the president's office, and he claimed that Nixon had known about the events and the subsequent cover-ups. As surprising as Dean's allegations were, the most shocking revelation came from Nixon adviser Alexander Butterfield, who testified that the president had installed a secret taping system that automatically recorded all conversations in the Oval Office. Obviously, the tape recordings held information that would settle the dispute between the witnesses

claiming White House involvement in the Watergate affair and the administration officials who denied it.

In addition to the Senate investigation, a special prosecutor was appointed to look into the Watergate affair. The first person to hold this position, Archibald Cox, asked the president to turn over the tapes. When Nixon declined, Cox went to court to get an order compelling him to deliver the materials. The district and appeals courts ruled in favor of Cox. Nixon then offered to release summaries of the recordings, but that did not satisfy Cox, who continued to pursue the tapes. In response, Nixon ordered that Cox be fired. When the two highest officials in the Justice Department resigned rather than comply with Nixon's order, Solicitor General Robert Bork became the acting attorney general and dismissed Cox. The firing and resignations, popularly known as the "Saturday night massacre," enraged the American people, and many began calling for the president's impeachment.

Leon Jaworski was appointed to take Cox's place. An attorney from Houston, Jaworski pursued the tapes with the same zeal as had Cox. Finally, Nixon relented and agreed to produce some of the materials. But when he did so the prosecutor found that the tapes had been heavily edited. One contained eighteen and one-half minutes of mysterious buzzing at a crucial point, indicating that conversation had been erased.

Jaworski obtained criminal indictments against several Nixon aides. Although no criminal charges were brought against the president, he was named in the indictment as a coconspirator. At about the same time, the House Judiciary Committee began an investigation into whether the president should be impeached.

The Judiciary Committee and Jaworski sought more of the tapes to review, but Nixon steadfastly refused to comply, claiming that it was his right under executive privilege to decide what would be released and what would remain secret. The district court issued a final subpoena duces tecum, an order to produce the tapes and other documents. Both the United States and Nixon requested that the Supreme Court review the case, and the justices accepted the case on an expedited basis, bypassing the court of appeals.

ARGUMENTS:

For the petitioner, United States:

- Courts, not the president, have final authority to determine the applicability and scope of claims of executive privilege.

GRAND JURY
Subpoena Duces Tecum

SUBPOENA DUCES TECUM
United States District Court
For the District of Columbia

Misc. #47-73

THE UNITED STATES
vs.

JOHN DOE

To: Richard M. Nixon, The White House, Washington, D. C., or any
subordinate officer, official, or employee with custody or
control of the documents or objects hereinafter described on
the attached schedule.

REPORT TO UNITED STATES DISTRICT
COURT HOUSE
*Between 3d Street and John Marshall Place
and on Constitution Avenue NW.*
Grand Jury Room 3
Washington, D.C.

FILED ✓

JUL 24 1973

JAMES F. DAVEY, Clerk

You are hereby commanded to attend before the Grand Jury of said Court on   Thursday
the   26th   day of   July   , 19 73 , at   10   o'clock   A. M., to testify
and to bring with you the documents or objects listed on the attached
sched- *WITNESS: The Honorable* John J. Sirica *Chief Judge of said Court, this*
ule.

23rd   day of   July   , 19 73 .
JAMES F. DAVEY, *Clerk.*

Archibald Cox
ARCHIBALD COX
Attorney for the United States

By   *Robert L. Line*
Deputy Clerk.

Form No. USA-9x-184   (Rev. 7-1-71)

34

This subpoena duces tecum was issued July 23, 1973. It ordered President Nixon or his representatives to appear before the federal grand jury on July 26 and to bring taped conversations relevant to the investigation of the Watergate affair.

This drawing illustrates Richard Nixon's attorney, James St. Clair, arguing the president's case before the Supreme Court in United States v. Nixon *(1974). The four justices are (left to right) Chief Justice Warren Burger, William J. Brennan Jr., Byron R. White, and Harry A. Blackmun. The empty chair at the far right belongs to Justice William Rehnquist, who recused himself because of his former duties as assistant attorney general in the Nixon administration.*

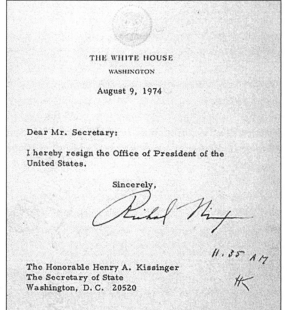

THE WHITE HOUSE
WASHINGTON

August 9, 1974

Dear Mr. Secretary:

I hereby resign the Office of President of the
United States.

Sincerely,

Richard Nixon

11.35 A M

The Honorable Henry A. Kissinger
The Secretary of State
Washington, D. C. 20520

With this one-sentence letter Richard Nixon became the first American president to resign from office.

- The framers deliberately created a system in which the president is not above the law; therefore, the president is subject to judicial orders requiring compliance with his clearly defined legal duty as a citizen of the United States.
- Qualified executive privilege exists to protect only the legitimate functioning of the government. In this case, there is a compelling public interest in disclosure that outweighs any possible benefit that executive privilege may bring to the functioning of government.

For the respondent, Richard Nixon:

- Executive privilege is inherent in the executive power. The president has a duty to faithfully execute the laws, which cannot be done without executive privilege to preserve the integrity of deliberations in the executive office.
- The doctrine of separation of powers dictates that each branch should be free of coercive control by the other branches. It follows that the judicial branch cannot compel production of material from the executive branch when the president has a privilege that he can exercise at his own discretion.
- Presidential conversations are presumptively privileged, unless there is a showing that the materials

are critical evidence with no effective substitute. The special prosecutor has not shown a compelling need for disclosure.

MR. CHIEF JUSTICE BURGER DELIVERED THE OPINION OF THE COURT.

[W]e turn to the claim that the subpoena should be quashed because it demands "confidential conversations between a President and his close advisors that it would be inconsistent with the public interest to produce." The first contention is a broad claim that the separation of powers doctrine precludes judicial review of a President's claim of privilege. The second contention is that if he does not prevail on the claim of absolute privilege, the court should hold as a matter of constitutional law that the privilege prevails over the subpoena *duces tecum*.

In the performance of assigned constitutional duties each branch of the Government must initially interpret the Constitution, and the interpretation of its powers by any branch is due great respect from the others. The President's counsel, as we have noted, reads the Constitution as providing an absolute privilege of confidentiality for all Presidential communications. Many decisions of this Court, however, have unequivocally reaffirmed the holding of *Marbury v. Madison* (1803) that "[i]t is emphatically the province and duty of the judicial department to say what the law is."

No holding of the Court has defined the scope of judicial power specifically relating to the enforcement of a subpoena for confidential Presidential communications for use in a criminal prosecution, but other exercises of power by the Executive Branch and the Legislative Branch have been found invalid as in conflict with the Constitution. *Powell v. McCormack* (1969); *Youngstown Sheet & Tube Co. v. Sawyer* (1952). . . .

Notwithstanding the deference each branch must accord the others, the "judicial Power of the United States" vested in the federal courts by Art. III, §1, of the Constitution can no more be shared with the Executive Branch than the Chief Executive, for example, can share with the Judiciary the veto power, or the Congress share with the Judiciary the power to override a Presidential veto. Any other conclusion would be contrary to the basic concept of separation of powers and the checks and balances that flow from the scheme of a tripartite government. We therefore reaffirm that it is the province and duty of this Court "to say what the law is" with respect to the claim of privilege presented in this case.

In support of his claim of absolute privilege, the President's counsel urges two grounds, one of which is common to all governments and one of which is peculiar to our system of separation of powers. The first ground is the valid need for protection of communications between high Government officials and those who advise and assist them in the performance of their manifold duties; the importance of this confidentiality is too plain to require further discussion. Human experience teaches that those who expect public dissemination of their remarks may well temper candor with a concern for appearances and for their own interests to the detriment of the decision making process. Whatever the nature of the privilege of confidentiality of Presidential communications in the exercise of Art. II powers, the privilege can be said to derive from the supremacy of each branch within its own assigned area of constitutional duties. Certain powers and privileges flow from the nature of enumerated powers; the protection of the confidentiality of Presidential communications has similar constitutional underpinnings.

The second ground asserted by the President's counsel in support of the claim of absolute privilege rests on the doctrine of separation of powers. Here it is argued that the independence of the Executive Branch within its own sphere insulates a President from a judicial subpoena in an ongoing criminal prosecution, and thereby protects confidential Presidential communications.

However, neither the doctrine of separation of powers, nor the need for confidentiality of high-level communications, without more, can sustain an absolute, unqualified Presidential privilege of immunity from judicial process under all circumstances. The President's need for complete candor and objectivity from advisers calls for great deference from the courts. However, when the privilege depends solely on the broad, undifferentiated claim of public interest in the confidentiality of such conversations, a confrontation with other values arises. Absent a claim of need to protect military, diplomatic, or sensitive national security secrets, we find it difficult to accept the argument that even the very important interest in confidentiality of Presidential communications is significantly diminished by production of such material for *in camera* inspection with all the protection that a district court will be obliged to provide.

The impediment that an absolute, unqualified privilege would place in the way of the primary constitutional duty of the Judicial Branch to do justice in criminal prosecutions would plainly conflict with the function of the courts under Art. III. In designing the structure of our Government and dividing and allocating the sovereign power among three co-equal branches, the Framers of the Constitution sought to provide a comprehensive system, but the separate powers were not intended to operate with absolute independence.... To read the Art. II powers of the President as providing an absolute privilege as against a subpoena essential to enforcement of criminal statutes on no more than a generalized claim of the public interest in confidentiality of nonmilitary and nondiplomatic discussions would upset the constitutional balance of "a workable government" and gravely impair the role of the courts under Art. III.

Since we conclude that the legitimate needs of the judicial process may outweigh Presidential privilege, it is necessary to resolve those competing interests in a manner that preserves the essential functions of each branch. The right and indeed the duty to resolve that question does not free the Judiciary from according high respect to the representations made on behalf of the President.

The expectation of a President to the confidentiality of his conversations and correspondence, like the claim of confidentiality of judicial deliberations, for example, has all the values to which we accord deference for the privacy of all citizens and, added to those values, is the necessity for protection of the public interest in candid, objective, and even blunt or harsh opinions in Presidential decision-making. A President and those who assist him must be free to explore alternatives in the process of shaping policies and making decisions and to do so in a way many would be unwilling to express except privately. These are the considerations justifying a presumptive privilege for Presidential communications. The privilege is fundamental to the operation of Government and inextricably rooted in the separation of powers under the Constitution....

But this presumptive privilege must be considered in light of our historic commitment to the rule of law. This is nowhere more profoundly manifest than in our view that "the twofold aim [of criminal justice] is that guilt shall not escape or innocence suffer." We have elected to employ an adversary system of criminal justice in which the parties contest all issues before a court of law. The need to develop all relevant facts in the adversary system is both fundamental and comprehensive. The ends of criminal justice would be defeated if judgments were to be founded on a partial or speculative presentation of the facts. The very integrity of the judicial system and public confidence in the system depend on full disclosure of all the facts, within the framework of the rules of evidence. To ensure that justice is done, it is imperative to the function of courts that compulsory process be available for the production of evidence needed either by the prosecution or by the defense. . . .

In this case the President challenges a subpoena served on him as a third party requiring the production of materials for use in a criminal prosecution; he does so on the claim that he has a privilege against disclosure of confidential communications. He does not place his claim of privilege on the ground they are military or diplomatic secrets. As to these areas of Art. II duties the courts have traditionally shown the utmost deference to Presidential responsibilities. . . . No case of the Court, however, has extended this high degree of deference to a President's generalized interest in confidentiality. Nowhere in the Constitution, as we have noted earlier, is there any explicit reference to a privilege of confidentiality, yet to the extent this interest relates to the effective discharge of a President's powers, it is constitutionally based.

The right to the production of all evidence at a criminal trial similarly has constitutional dimensions. The Sixth Amendment explicitly confers upon every defendant in a criminal trial the right "to be confronted with the witnesses against him" and "to have compulsory process for obtaining witnesses in his favor." Moreover, the Fifth Amendment also guarantees that no person shall be deprived of liberty without due process of law. It is the manifest duty of the courts to vindicate those guarantees, and to accomplish that it is essential that all relevant and admissible evidence be produced.

In this case we must weigh the importance of the general privilege of confidentiality of Presidential communications in performance of the President's responsibilities against the inroads of such a privilege on the fair administration of criminal justice. The interest in preserving confidentiality is weighty indeed and entitled to great respect. However, we cannot conclude that advisers will be moved to temper the candor of their remarks by the infrequent occasions of disclosure because of the possibility that such conversations will be called for in the context of a criminal prosecution.

On the other hand, the allowance of the privilege to withhold evidence that is demonstrably relevant in a criminal trial would cut deeply into the guarantee of due process of law and gravely impair the basic function of the courts. A President's acknowledged need for confidentiality in the communications of his office is general in nature, whereas the constitutional need for production of relevant evidence in a criminal proceeding is specific and central to the fair adjudication of a particular criminal case in the administration of justice. Without access to specific facts a criminal prosecution may be totally frustrated. The President's broad interest in confidentiality of communications will not be vitiated by disclosure of a limited number of conversations preliminarily shown to have some bearing on the pending criminal cases.

We conclude that when the ground for asserting privilege as to subpoenaed materials sought for use in a criminal trial is based only on the generalized interest in confidentiality, it cannot prevail over the fundamental demands of due process of law in the fair administration of criminal justice. The generalized assertion of privilege must yield to the demonstrated, specific need for evidence in a pending criminal trial.

The Court's ruling was clear. The people's interest in the fair administration of criminal justice outweighed the president's interest in confidentiality. Executive privilege was rejected as a justification for refusing to make the tapes available to the special prosecutor. The opinion, however, does not answer questions about exactly who can invoke executive privilege or how long the privilege would be in effect, if at all. Based on the majority's logic, do you think former presidents, high-ranking executive aides, or even the spouses of presidents could invoke executive privilege?

Nixon complied with the Court's ruling, knowing full well that it meant the end of his presidency. In obeying the Court order, he avoided provoking what many feared would be the most serious of all constitutional confrontations. What if Nixon had refused to comply? What if he had destroyed the tapes rather than turn them over? Who could have enforced sanctions on the president for doing so? Impeachment and conviction of the president probably would have been the only way to handle such a crisis. Whatever Nixon's culpability in Watergate and related matters, he spared the nation a crisis by bowing to the Supreme Court's interpretation of the Constitution. The Nixon tapes revealed substantial wrongdoing. It was clear that the House of Representatives would present articles of impeachment and the Senate would vote to remove Nixon from office. Rather than put himself and the nation through such an ordeal, Nixon resigned.

Immunity: Protecting the President from Lawsuit

Presidential immunity is a variation on the notion of executive privilege. It deals with the extent to which the president is protected from lawsuits while in office, and the subject raises many interesting questions. May

Library of Congress

Vice President Andrew Johnson, who had earlier served as a Democratic senator from Tennessee, assumed the presidency upon the assassination of Abraham Lincoln. Johnson's administration was characterized by fierce battles with the Radical Republicans in Congress. This conflict spawned several legal disputes, including Mississippi v. Johnson, *and led to the president's near removal from office.*

a president be ordered by a court to carry out certain executive actions, which are discretionary, or ministerial actions, which are performed as a matter of legal duty? Or conversely, may a president be restrained by a court from taking such actions? May a private party sue the president for damages that might have been suffered because of the president's actions or omissions? If so, may a court order the president to pay damages or provide some other restitution? If a doctrine of immunity exists, should it extend only to actions taken by presidents while in office? These questions place us in a quandary. To grant the president immunity from such legal actions may remove needed accountability. But to allow the chief executive to be subject to suit could make the execution of presidential duties impossible.

The Supreme Court's first significant venture into the area of executive immunity came in the aftermath of the Civil War. In *Mississippi v. Johnson* (1867) the Court was asked to enjoin the president from executing laws passed by Congress on the ground that the laws were unconstitutional. The justices unanimously concluded that the president was immune from such suits. Is this conclusion reasonable? Does the Court's distinction between executive and ministerial acts make sense? To what degree do you think the Court was responding to the political conditions of the times? Following the *Scott v. Sandford* decision in 1857, the Court's prestige was at an all-time low, and congressional power was overwhelmingly dominant. Was the decision of the Court in *Mississippi v. Johnson* just a convenient way for the justices to avoid an unwinnable conflict with Congress?

Mississippi v. Johnson

71 U.S. (4 WALL.) 475 (1867)
http://laws.findlaw.com/us/71/475.html
Vote: 9 (Chase, Clifford, Davis, Field, Grier, Miller, Nelson, Swayne, Wayne)
0
OPINION OF THE COURT: *Chase*

FACTS:

Following the Civil War, Congress passed a number of laws "for the more efficient government of the rebel states." Commonly known as the Reconstruction Acts of 1867, these laws imposed military rule over the Southern states until such time as loyal Republican governments could be established. Andrew Johnson, a Southerner from Tennessee, who had assumed the presidency after Lincoln's assassination, vetoed the legislation, but the Radical Republicans in Congress had sufficient votes to override him. Once the acts were part of federal law, the president had little choice but to enforce them, despite his belief that they were unconstitutional.

The state of Mississippi joined the fray. Applying directly to the Supreme Court, Mississippi sued Johnson, asking the justices to issue an order prohibiting him from enforcing the laws, which the state argued were unconstitutional.

ARGUMENTS:

For the petitioner, State of Mississippi:

- The president is not and should not be above the law. The Constitution gives the federal courts judicial power over *all* cases arising under the Constitution and makes no distinction as to the parties.

- In *Marbury v. Madison* the Court held that the secretary of state was subject to legal process for actions taken on behalf of the president. If the subordinate is liable for the acts of his principal, it follows that the principal should also be subject to the same legal process.
- The president was performing a purely ministerial action because there was no exercise of discretion in carrying out an act of Congress. Although, as the Court held in *Marbury*, the courts cannot control the actions of officers in discretionary duties, the executive is not above the law with regard to ministerial duties.

For the respondent, President Andrew Johnson:

- The president is the best judge of his duties to faithfully execute the laws, and the Court should not interfere and tell him what his duty is and compel him to perform it.
- The president cannot be treated as any other citizen in the legal process. The legal process, taken to its limits, could result in the president being imprisoned and the country left in turmoil.
- This case is distinguishable from any case involving subordinate executive officers because subordinate officers are easily reappointed and disruption to those offices would not disrupt the entire government.
- The president is beyond the control of any other branch of the government, and, under the Constitution, can be tried only by Congress. Only if he has been impeached can he appear before the courts—and then as an individual, not as a representative of the people.

▶ THE CHIEF JUSTICE DELIVERED THE OPINION OF THE COURT.

A motion was made, some days since, in behalf of the State of Mississippi, for leave to file a bill in the name of the State, praying this court perpetually to enjoin and restrain Andrew Johnson, President of the United States, and E. O. C. Ord, general commanding in the District of Mississippi and Arkansas, from executing, or in any manner carrying out, certain acts of Congress therein named.

The acts referred to are those of March 2d and March 23d, 1867, commonly known as the Reconstruction Acts.

The Attorney-General objected to the leave asked for, upon the ground that no bill which makes a President a defendant, and seeks an injunction against him to restrain the performance of his duties as President, should be allowed to be filed in this court.

This point has been fully argued, and we will now dispose of it.

We shall limit our inquiry to the question presented by the objection, without expressing any opinion on the broader issues discussed in argument, whether, in any case, the President of the United States may be required, by the process of this court, to perform a purely ministerial act under a positive law, or may be held amenable, in any case, otherwise than by impeachment for crime.

The single point which requires consideration is this: Can the President be restrained by injunction from carrying into effect an act of Congress alleged to be unconstitutional?

It is assumed by the counsel for the State of Mississippi, that the President, in the execution of the Reconstruction Acts, is required to perform a mere ministerial duty. In this assumption there is, we think, a confounding of the terms ministerial and executive, which are by no means equivalent in import.

A ministerial duty, the performance of which may, in proper cases, be required of the head of a department, by judicial process, is one in respect to which nothing is left to discretion. It is a simple, definite duty, arising under conditions admitted or proved to exist, and imposed by law.

The case of *Marbury v. Madison, Secretary of State*, furnishes an illustration. A citizen had been nominated, confirmed, and appointed a justice of the peace for the District of Columbia, and his commission had been made out, signed, and sealed. Nothing remained to be done except delivery, and the duty of delivery was imposed by law on the Secretary of State. It was held that the performance of this duty might be enforced by mandamus issuing from a court having jurisdiction.

So, in the case of *Kendall, Postmaster General v. Stockton & Stokes*, an act of Congress had directed the Postmaster General to credit Stockton & Stokes with such sums as the Solicitor of the Treasury should find due to them; and that officer refused to credit them with certain sums, so found due. It was held that the crediting of this money was a mere ministerial duty, the performance of which might be judicially enforced.

In each of these cases nothing was left to discretion. There was no room for the exercise of judgment. The law required the performance of a single specific act; and that performance, it was held, might be required by mandamus.

Very different is the duty of the President in the exercise of the power to see that the laws are faithfully executed, and among these laws the acts named in the bill. By the first of these acts he is required to assign generals to command in the several military districts, and to detail sufficient military force to enable such officers to discharge their duties under the law. By the supplementary act, other duties are imposed on the several commanding generals, and these duties must necessarily be performed under the supervision of the President as commander-in-chief. The duty thus imposed on the President is in no just sense ministerial. It is purely executive and political.

An attempt on the part of the judicial department of the government to enforce the performance of such duties by the President might be justly characterized, in the language of Chief Justice Marshall, as "an absurd and excessive extravagance."

It is true that in the instance before us the interposition of the court is not sought to enforce action by the Executive under constitutional legislation, but to restrain such action under legislation alleged to be unconstitutional. But we are unable to perceive that this circumstance takes the case out of the general principles which forbid judicial interference with the exercise of Executive discretion.

It was admitted in the argument that the application now made to us is without a precedent; and this is of much weight against it. . . .

The fact that no such application was ever before made in any case indicates the general judgment of the profession that no such application should be entertained.

It will hardly be contended that Congress can interpose, in any case, to restrain the enactment of an unconstitutional law; and yet how can the right to judicial interposition to prevent such an enactment, when the purpose is evident and the execution of that purpose certain, be distinguished, in principle, from the right to such interposition against the execution of such a law by the President?

The Congress is the legislative department of the government; the President is the executive department. Neither can be restrained in its action by the judicial department; though the acts of both, when performed, are, in proper cases, subject to its cognizance.

The impropriety of such interference will be clearly seen upon consideration of its possible consequences.

Suppose the bill filed and the injunction prayed for be allowed. If the President refuse obedience, it is needless to observe that the court is without power to enforce its process. If, on the other hand, the President complies with the order of the court and refuses to execute the acts of Congress, is it not clear that a collision may occur between the executive and legislative departments of the government? May not the House of Representatives impeach the President for such refusal? And in that case could this court interfere, in behalf of the President, thus endangered by compliance with its mandate, and restrain by injunction the Senate of the United States from sitting as a court of impeachment? Would the strange spectacle be offered to the public world of an attempt by this court to arrest proceedings in that court?

These questions answer themselves.

It is true that a State may file an original bill in this court. And it may be true, in some cases, that such a bill may be filed against the United States. But we are fully satisfied that this court has no jurisdiction of a bill to enjoin the President in the performance of his official duties; and that no such bill ought to be received by us.

It has been suggested that the bill contains a prayer that, if the relief sought cannot be had against Andrew Johnson, as President, it may be granted against Andrew Johnson as a citizen of Tennessee. But it is plain that relief as against the execution of an act of Congress by Andrew Johnson, is relief against its execution by the President. A bill praying an injunction against the execution of an act of Congress by the incumbent of the presidential office cannot be received, whether it describes him as President or as a citizen of a State.

The motion for leave to file the bill is, therefore,

Denied.

The holding in this case is plain. The president of the United States cannot be sued to prevent the carrying out of executive responsibilities. But the Supreme Court has allowed suits against the actions of lower-ranking executive officials. The very next year, the Court heard *Georgia v. Stanton* (1868), in which an injunction was sought to stop the secretary of war from enforcing the Reconstruction Acts. This suit also was unsuccessful, but it was decided on entirely different grounds—that it was a political question. The Court found no bar to suing an executive branch administrator, even at the cabinet level.

The decision in *Johnson* settled the issue of whether the president may be personally sued with respect to executive functions, but it did not answer the question of civil suits brought by private individuals who claim harm by a president's actions. If an incumbent president engages in activities that allegedly cause damages to private individuals, may the president be held accountable in a court of law? Or is the president immune from such suits? President Nixon found himself the object of such

Ricardo Watson

Ernest Fitzgerald sued President Richard Nixon after he was fired from his civilian job with the U.S. Air Force. Years later, the Supreme Court ruled against Fitzgerald.

a suit after he was involved in the dismissal of a federal employee. While reading the following decision, consider the differences between the absolute immunity doctrine articulated by Justice Lewis F. Powell and the approach advocated in Justice Byron R. White's dissenting opinion—that the scope of immunity is determined by function, not office.

Nixon v. Fitzgerald

457 U.S. 731 (1982)
http://laws.findlaw.com/us/457/731.html
Oral arguments are available at https://www.oyez.org.
Vote: 5 (Burger, O'Connor, Powell, Rehnquist, Stevens)
    4 (Blackmun, Brennan, Marshall, White)
OPINION OF THE COURT: *Powell*
CONCURRING OPINION: *Burger*
DISSENTING OPINIONS: *Blackmun, White*

FACTS:

A. Ernest Fitzgerald was a civilian management analyst for the U.S. Air Force. In November 1968 Fitzgerald testified before a congressional committee chaired by Senator William Proxmire (D-Wis.). Fitzgerald reported that cost overruns for the C-5A

transport plane might reach as high as $2 billion. In addition, he spoke about the technical problems the manufacturer had encountered in producing the aircraft. Needless to say, Fitzgerald's testimony was not well received by the Defense Department or military contractors.

Thirteen months later, in January 1970, Fitzgerald was removed from his job on the ground that a department reorganization had made a reduction in staff necessary. Fitzgerald believed he was fired in retaliation for his congressional appearance. The dismissal caused a great deal of concern among members of Congress, and Fitzgerald's story was widely reported in the media.

The question was whether the Nixon administration was trying to get rid of a troublemaking whistleblower. At a press conference the president said that he would look into the matter, and there appeared to be some attempt to find Fitzgerald another government position. That effort failed, perhaps because of an internal memorandum circulated by presidential aide Alexander Butterfield in which he concluded, "Fitzgerald is no doubt a topnotch cost expert, but he must be given very low marks in loyalty; and after all, loyalty is the name of the game. . . . [W]e should let him bleed, for a while at least."

Denied another government job, Fitzgerald began legal action, first complaining to the Civil Service Commission and then filing a suit for damages. When asked about the Fitzgerald matter, President Nixon responded, "I was totally aware that Mr. Fitzgerald would be fired or discharged or asked to resign. I approved it. . . . No, this was not a case of some person down the line deciding he should go. It was a decision that was submitted to me. I made it and I stick by it." The next day the president's office retracted his statements, explaining that Nixon had confused Fitzgerald with someone else. But, as revealed in the Watergate tapes, Nixon boasted privately that he gave the order to "get rid of that son of a bitch."

Fitzgerald's lawsuit was against a number of federal executive branch officials, including Nixon, who had resigned during the early stages of the lower court proceedings. Nixon's lawyers asserted that the former president should be removed from the suit on the ground of absolute executive immunity from legal actions based on his official conduct. The lower courts rejected the absolute immunity claim, and Nixon appealed.

ARGUMENTS:

For the petitioner, Richard Nixon:

- The framers intended to give the president absolute immunity from civil damage. The framers purposely chose to rely on checks and balances, public opinion, and the possibility of impeachment, instead of civil liability, to restrain the executive.
- The president's visibility makes him a vulnerable target for lawsuits filed for political motives.
- The separation of powers system justifies absolute immunity. The president needs to be free from judicial oversight to keep executive deliberations confidential and preserve the integrity of the office. Anything less than absolute immunity would overly involve courts in executive decision making.

For the respondent, A. Ernest Fitzgerald:

- Supreme Court precedent regarding state governors and cabinet officers dictates that qualified immunity applies only where it is functionally required, depending on the circumstances of each case. Immunity is dependent upon functions of an office, not upon the title of the office.
- The checks and balances system counsels against absolute immunity. If the president were absolutely immune, Congress would lose a reliable source of information on the activities of the executive branch, and the courts would not be able to protect individuals whose rights have been trampled by the president.
- Even if absolute immunity is available to the president, he must first show that he was acting within the scope of his authority. The president has failed to justify that he has constitutional power to remove inferior officers who were appointed by the head of a department.

JUSTICE POWELL DELIVERED THE OPINION OF THE COURT.

This case now presents the claim that the President of the United States is shielded by absolute immunity from civil damages liability. In the case of the President the inquiries into history and policy, though mandated independently by our cases, tend to converge. Because the Presidency did not exist through most of the development of common law, any historical analysis must draw its evidence primarily from our constitutional heritage and structure. Historical inquiry thus merges almost at its inception with the kind of

"public policy" analysis appropriately undertaken by a federal court. This inquiry involves policies and principles that may be considered implicit in the nature of the President's office in a system structured to achieve effective government under a constitutionally mandated separation of powers.

Here a former President asserts his immunity from civil damages claims of two kinds. He stands named as a defendant in a direct action under the Constitution and in two statutory actions under federal laws of general applicability. In neither case has Congress taken express legislative action to subject the President to civil liability for his official acts.

Applying the principles of our cases to claims of this kind, we hold that petitioner, as a former President of the United States, is entitled to absolute immunity from damages liability predicated on his official acts. We consider this immunity a functionally mandated incident of the President's unique office, rooted in the constitutional tradition of the separation of powers and supported by our history. . . .

The President occupies a unique position in the constitutional scheme. Article II, §1, of the Constitution provides that "[t]he executive Power shall be vested in a President of the United States. . . ." This grant of authority establishes the President as the chief constitutional officer of the Executive Branch, entrusted with supervisory and policy responsibilities of utmost discretion and sensitivity. These include the enforcement of federal law—it is the President who is charged constitutionally to "take Care that the Laws be faithfully executed"; the conduct of foreign affairs—a realm in which the Court has recognized that "[i]t would be intolerable that courts, without the relevant information, should review and perhaps nullify actions of the Executive taken on information properly held secret"; and management of the Executive Branch—a task for which "imperative reasons requir[e] an unrestricted power [in the President] to remove the most important of his subordinates in their most important duties."

In arguing that the President is entitled only to qualified immunity, the respondent relies on cases in which we have recognized immunity of this scope for governors and cabinet officers. We find these cases to be inapposite. The President's unique status under the Constitution distinguishes him from other executive officials.

Because of the singular importance of the President's duties, diversion of his energies by concern with private lawsuits would raise unique risks to the effective functioning of government. As is the case with prosecutors and judges—for whom absolute immunity now is established—a President must concern himself with matters likely to "arouse the most intense feelings." Yet, as our decisions have recognized, it is in precisely such cases that there exists the greatest public interest in providing an official "the maximum ability to deal fearlessly and impartially with" the duties of his office. This concern is compelling where the officeholder must make the most sensitive and far-reaching decisions entrusted to any official under our constitutional system. Nor can the sheer prominence of the President's office be ignored. In view of the visibility of his office and the effect of his actions on countless people, the President would be an easily identifiable target for suits for civil damages. Cognizance of this personal vulnerability frequently could distract a President from his public duties, to the detriment of not only the President and his office but also the Nation that the Presidency was designed to serve.

Courts traditionally have recognized the President's constitutional responsibilities and status as factors counseling judicial deference and restraint. For example, while courts generally have looked to the common law to determine the scope of an official's evidentiary privilege, we have recognized that the Presidential privilege is "rooted in the separation of powers under the Constitution." *United States v. Nixon* [1974]. It is settled law that the separation-of-powers doctrine does not bar every exercise of jurisdiction over the President of the United States. But our cases also have established that a court, before exercising jurisdiction, must balance the constitutional weight of the interest to be served against the dangers of intrusion on the authority and functions of the Executive Branch. When judicial action is needed to serve broad public interests—as when the Court acts, not in derogation of the separation of powers, but to maintain their proper balance, or to vindicate the public interest in an ongoing criminal prosecution—the exercise of jurisdiction has been held warranted. In the case of this merely private suit for damages based on a President's official acts, we hold it is not.

In defining the scope of an official's absolute privilege, this Court has recognized that the sphere of protected action must be related closely to the immunity's justifying purposes. Frequently our decisions have held that an official's absolute immunity should extend only to acts in performance of particular functions of his office. But the Court also has refused to draw functional lines finer than history and reason would support. In view of the special nature of the President's constitutional office and functions, we think

it appropriate to recognize absolute Presidential immunity from damages liability for acts within the "outer perimeter" of his official responsibility.

Under the Constitution and laws of the United States the President has discretionary responsibilities in a broad variety of areas, many of them highly sensitive. In many cases it would be difficult to determine which of the President's innumerable "functions" encompassed a particular action. In this case, for example, respondent argues that he was dismissed in retaliation for his testimony to Congress. The Air Force, however, has claimed that the underlying reorganization was undertaken to promote efficiency. Assuming that petitioner Nixon ordered the reorganization in which respondent lost his job, an inquiry into the President's motives could not be avoided under the kind of "functional" theory asserted both by respondent and the dissent. Inquiries of this kind could be highly intrusive.

Here respondent argues that petitioner Nixon would have acted outside the outer perimeter of his duties by ordering the discharge of an employee who was lawfully entitled to retain his job in the absence of "'such cause as will promote the efficiency of the service.'" Because Congress has granted this legislative protection, respondent argues, no federal official could, within the outer perimeter of his duties of office, cause Fitzgerald to be dismissed without satisfying this standard in prescribed statutory proceedings.

This construction would subject the President to trial on virtually every allegation that an action was unlawful, or was taken for a forbidden purpose. Adoption of this construction thus would deprive absolute immunity of its intended effect. It clearly is within the President's constitutional and statutory authority to prescribe the manner in which the Secretary will conduct the business of the Air Force. Because this mandate of office must include the authority to prescribe reorganizations and reductions in force, we conclude that petitioner's alleged wrongful acts lay well within the outer perimeter of his authority.

A rule of absolute immunity for the President will not leave the Nation without sufficient protection against misconduct on the part of the Chief Executive. There remains the constitutional remedy of impeachment. In addition, there are formal and informal checks on Presidential action that do not apply with equal force to other executive officials. The President is subjected to constant scrutiny by the press. Vigilant oversight by Congress also may serve to deter Presidential abuses of office, as well as to make credible the threat of impeachment. Other incentives to avoid misconduct may include a desire to earn reelection, the need to maintain prestige as an element of Presidential influence, and a President's traditional concern for his historical stature.

The existence of alternative remedies and deterrents establishes that absolute immunity will not place the President "above the law." For the President, as for judges and prosecutors, absolute immunity merely precludes a particular private remedy for alleged misconduct in order to advance compelling public ends.

For the reasons stated in this opinion, the decision of the Court of Appeals is reversed, and the case is remanded for action consistent with this opinion.

So ordered.

JUSTICE WHITE, with whom JUSTICE BRENNAN, JUSTICE MARSHALL, and JUSTICE BLACKMUN join, dissenting.

The four dissenting Members of the Court in *Butz v. Economou* (1978) argued that all federal officials are entitled to absolute immunity from suit for any action they take in connection with their official duties. That immunity would extend even to actions taken with express knowledge that the conduct was clearly contrary to the controlling statute or clearly violative of the Constitution. Fortunately, the majority of the Court rejected that approach: We held that although public officials perform certain functions that entitle them to absolute immunity, the immunity attaches to particular functions—not to particular offices. Officials performing functions for which immunity is not absolute enjoy qualified immunity; they are liable in damages only if their conduct violated well-established law and if they should have realized that their conduct was illegal.

The Court now applies the dissenting view in *Butz* to the Office of the President: A President, acting within the outer boundaries of what Presidents normally do, may, without liability, deliberately cause serious injury to any number of citizens even though he knows his conduct violates a statute or tramples on the constitutional rights of those who are injured. . . .

In declaring the President to be absolutely immune from suit for any deliberate and knowing violation of the Constitution or of a federal statute, the Court asserts that the immunity is "rooted in the constitutional tradition of the separation of powers and supported by our history." The decision thus has all the earmarks of a constitutional pronouncement—absolute immunity for the President's office is mandated by the Constitution. Although the Court appears to disclaim this, it is difficult to read the opinion coherently as standing for any narrower proposition: Attempts to subject the President to liability either by Congress through a statutory action or by the courts . . . would violate the separation of powers. Such a generalized absolute immunity cannot be sustained when examined in the traditional manner and in light of the traditional judicial sources. . . .

The functional approach to the separation-of-powers doctrine and the Court's more recent immunity decisions converge on the following principle: The scope of immunity is determined by function, not office. The wholesale claim that the President is entitled to absolute immunity in all of his actions stands on no firmer ground than did the claim that all Presidential communications are entitled to an absolute privilege, which was rejected in favor of a functional analysis, by a unanimous Court in *United States v. Nixon* (1974). Therefore, whatever may be true of the necessity of such a broad immunity in certain areas of executive responsibility, the only question that must be answered here is whether the dismissal of employees falls within a constitutionally assigned executive function, the performance of which would be substantially impaired by the possibility of a private action for damages. I believe it does not. . . .

Because of the importance of this case, it is appropriate to examine the reasoning of the majority opinion.

The opinion suffers from serious ambiguity even with respect to the most fundamental point: How broad is the immunity granted the President? The opinion suggests that its scope is limited by the fact that under none of the asserted causes of action "has Congress taken express legislative action to subject the President to civil liability for his official acts." We are never told, however, how or why congressional action could make a difference. It is not apparent that any of the propositions relied upon by the majority to immunize the President would not apply equally to such a statutory cause of action; nor does the majority indicate what new principles would operate to undercut those propositions.

. . . While the majority opinion recognizes that "[i]t is settled law that the separation-of-powers doctrine does not bar every exercise of jurisdiction over the President of the United States," it bases its conclusion, at least in part, on a suggestion that there is a special jurisprudence of the Presidency.

But in *United States v. Nixon* (1974), we upheld the power of a Federal District Court to issue a *subpoena duces tecum* against the President. In other cases we have enjoined executive officials from carrying out Presidential directives. See, *e.g., Youngstown Sheet & Tube Co. v. Sawyer* (1952). Not until this case has there ever been a suggestion that the mere formalism of the name appearing on the complaint was more important in resolving separation-of-powers problems than the substantive character of the judicial intrusion upon executive functions. . . .

Focusing on the actual arguments the majority offers for its holding of absolute immunity for the President, one finds surprisingly little. As I read the relevant section of the Court's opinion, I find just three contentions from which the majority draws this conclusion. Each of them is little more than a makeweight; together they hardly suffice to justify the wholesale disregard of our traditional approach to immunity questions.

First, the majority informs us that the President occupies a "unique position in the constitutional scheme," including responsibilities for the administration of justice, foreign affairs, and management of the Executive Branch. True as this may be, it says nothing about why a "unique" rule of immunity should apply to the President. . . .

Second, the majority contends that because the President's "visibility" makes him particularly vulnerable to suits for civil damages, a rule of absolute immunity is required. The force of this argument is surely undercut by the majority's admission that "there is no historical record of numerous suits against the President." . . .

Finally, the Court suggests that potential liability "frequently could distract a President from his public duties." Unless one assumes that the President himself makes the countless high-level executive decisions required in the administration of government, this rule will not do much to insulate such decisions from the threat of liability. The logic of the proposition cannot be limited to the President; its extension, however, has been uniformly rejected by this Court. . . . Furthermore, in no instance have we previously held legal accountability in itself to be an unjustifiable cost. The availability of the courts to vindicate constitutional and statutory wrongs has been perceived and protected as one of the virtues of our system of delegated and limited powers. . . .

The majority may be correct in its conclusion that "[a] rule of absolute immunity . . . will not leave the Nation without sufficient protection against misconduct on the part of the Chief Executive." Such a rule will, however, leave Mr. Fitzgerald without an adequate remedy for the harms that he may have suffered. More importantly, it will leave future plaintiffs without a remedy, regardless of the substantiality of their claims. The remedies in which the Court finds comfort were never designed to afford relief for individual harms. Rather, they were designed as political safety valves. Politics and history, however, are not the domain of the courts; the courts exist to assure each individual that he, as an individual, has enforceable rights that he may pursue to achieve a peaceful redress of his legitimate grievances.

I find it ironic, as well as tragic, that the Court would so casually discard its own role of assuring "the right of every individual to claim the protection of the laws," *Marbury v. Madison*, in the name of protecting the principle of separation of powers. Accordingly, I dissent.

In spite of the decisions in *Mississippi v. Johnson* and *Nixon v. Fitzgerald,* presidential immunity issues continue to appear—with *Clinton v. Jones* (1997) being the most recent example.

Clinton was surrounded by political intrigue and scandal. Paula Corbin Jones, a former state employee, had sued President Clinton for making "abhorrent" sexual advances in a Little Rock hotel room while he was governor of Arkansas. There were heated public arguments over whether this was a case of inexcusable sexual harassment or a groundless, politically motivated lawsuit designed to undermine and embarrass the president. Political rhetoric aside, the case presented a major constitutional issue: Can a sitting president be required to stand trial on allegations concerning his unofficial conduct? Jones's supporters argued that the president is not immune from lawsuit and that Jones, like any other citizen, had the right to a prompt judicial determination on her claims of being unlawfully treated. Clinton's supporters argued that the chief executive should not have to stand trial during his term of office. Allowing a trial to proceed would divert the president's attention from his official duties; the situation would be made worse by a potential rash of civil lawsuits following the trial. The Supreme Court settled the issue on May 27, 1997.

Clinton v. Jones

520 U.S. 681 (1997)
http://laws.findlaw.com/us/520/681.html
Oral arguments are available at https://www.oyez.org.
Vote: *9 (Breyer, Ginsburg, Kennedy, O'Connor, Rehnquist, Scalia, Souter, Stevens, Thomas)*
    0

OPINION OF THE COURT: *Stevens*
CONCURRING OPINION: *Breyer*

FACTS:

Bill Clinton was elected to the presidency in 1992 and reelected in 1996. Before becoming president, Clinton served as governor of Arkansas from 1979 to 1981 and from 1983 to 1992. In 1994 Paula Jones filed suit in federal district court in Arkansas against Clinton and Arkansas state trooper Danny Ferguson over an incident that was alleged to have occurred on May 8, 1991, at the Excelsior Hotel in Little Rock. On the day in question, Jones, then an employee of the state Industrial Development Commission, was working at the registration desk for a management conference at which Governor Clinton had delivered a speech. According to her allegations, Ferguson approached Jones and indicated that the governor wanted to see her. Ferguson then escorted her to Clinton's hotel suite, where Jones and the governor were left alone. The suit claimed that Clinton made "abhorrent" sexual advances to Jones, including exposing himself to her, touching her inappropriately, and making unwelcome sexual remarks. Jones said she rejected Clinton's suggestions, and he ceased his advances. As she was leaving the room, Jones alleged, Clinton said to her: "You are smart. Let's keep this between ourselves."

Jones's suit claimed that after she returned to her state job, her superiors began treating her rudely; she was ultimately transferred to another position that had little potential for advancement. She attributed this harsh treatment to retaliation for her rejection of the governor. The suit asked for actual damages of $75,000 and punitive damages of $100,000 in compensation for Clinton's violations of state and federal civil rights and sexual harassment laws.

Clinton denied the allegations and claimed the lawsuit was politically motivated. He filed motions asking the district court to dismiss the case on the ground of presidential immunity and to prohibit Jones from refiling the suit until after the end of his presidency. The district judge rejected the presidential immunity argument. Although she allowed pretrial discovery activities to proceed, the judge ordered that no trial would take place until Clinton was no longer president. Both Jones and Clinton appealed. Holding that "the President, like all other government officials, is subject to the same laws that apply to all other members of society," the court of appeals ruled that the trial should not be postponed. Clinton asked the Supreme Court to reverse the decision.

ARGUMENTS:

For the petitioner, William Jefferson Clinton:

- The framers and the Supreme Court have recognized that the president is unlike any other public official in that he has the sole responsibility for an entire branch of the federal government.
- Civil lawsuits would be distracting and disruptive not only to the president but also to the entire executive branch. To avoid offending the principle of separation of powers, judges should not be in the position of reviewing the president's priorities, which are inseparable from the priorities of the executive branch.
- Allowing this lawsuit will invite future lawsuits, disrupting government affairs even more.
- The Court should grant a temporary deferral of the case, which leaves the president still accountable for his conduct and does not place undue burdens on Jones.

Paula Corbin Jones, shown here at a 1998 news conference, brought a sexual harassment lawsuit against President Bill Clinton. The suit led the Supreme Court to confront the question of whether a president can be tried while still in office for conduct unrelated to official executive duties.

For the respondent, Paula Corbin Jones:

- There is no precedent for granting presidential immunity as a purely personal privilege for lawsuits unrelated to official presidential duties. Instead, *Nixon v. Fitzgerald* showed that presidents are not immune for acts outside official duties. This case does not involve executive branch communications or deliberations that need to be protected for the integrity of the branch.

- The separation of powers doctrine is concerned with the encroachment or aggrandizement of one branch at the expense of the other. The president has not shown that this lawsuit would have this effect.

- Deferral of the case would prolong the respondent's subjection to intense media scrutiny and would not hamper the effectiveness of the executive branch. The president has never been expected to personally execute every law, and presidents have always had time for personal commitments, including legal proceedings.

JUSTICE STEVENS DELIVERED THE OPINION OF THE COURT.

This case raises a constitutional and a prudential question concerning the Office of the President of the United States. Respondent, a private citizen, seeks to recover damages from the current occupant of that office based on actions allegedly taken before his term began. The President submits that in all but the most exceptional cases the Constitution requires federal courts to defer such litigation until his term ends and that, in any event, respect for the office warrants such a stay. Despite the force of the arguments supporting the President's submissions, we conclude that they must be rejected. . . .

Only three sitting Presidents have been defendants in civil litigation involving their actions prior to taking office. Complaints against Theodore Roosevelt and Harry Truman had been dismissed before they took office; the dismissals were affirmed after their respective inaugurations. Two companion cases arising out of an automobile accident were filed against John F. Kennedy in 1960 during the Presidential campaign. After taking office, he unsuccessfully argued that his status as Commander in Chief gave him a right to a stay under the Soldiers' and Sailors' Civil Relief Act of 1940. The motion for a stay was denied by the District Court, and the matter was settled out of court. Thus, none of those cases sheds any light on the constitutional issue before us.

The principal rationale for affording certain public servants immunity from suits for money damages arising out of their official acts is inapplicable to unofficial conduct. In cases involving prosecutors, legislators, and judges we have repeatedly explained that the immunity serves the public interest in enabling such officials to perform their designated functions effectively without fear that a particular decision may give rise to personal liability. . . .

That rationale provided the principal basis for our holding that a former President of the United States was "entitled to absolute immunity from damages liability predicated on his official acts," [*Nixon v.*] *Fitzgerald* [1982]. Our central concern was to avoid rendering the President "unduly cautious in the discharge of his official duties."

This reasoning provides no support for an immunity for unofficial conduct. As we explained in *Fitzgerald*, "the sphere of protected action must be related closely to the immunity's justifying purposes." Because of the President's broad responsibilities, we recognized in that case an immunity from damages claims arising out of official acts extending to the "outer perimeter of his authority." But we have never suggested that the President, or any other official, has an immunity that extends beyond the scope of any action taken in an official capacity.

Moreover, when defining the scope of an immunity for acts clearly taken within an official capacity, we have applied a functional approach. "Frequently our decisions have held that an official's absolute immunity should extend only to acts in performance of particular functions of his office." Hence, for example, a judge's absolute immunity does not extend to actions performed in a purely administrative capacity. As our opinions have made clear, immunities are grounded in "the nature of the function performed, not the identity of the actor who performed it."

Petitioner's effort to construct an immunity from suit for unofficial acts grounded purely in the identity of his office is unsupported by precedent.

We are also unpersuaded by the evidence from the historical record to which petitioner has called our attention. . . .

Petitioner's strongest argument supporting his immunity claim is based on the text and structure of the Constitution. He does not contend that the occupant of the Office of the President is "above the law," in the sense that his conduct is entirely immune from judicial scrutiny. The President argues merely for a postponement of the judicial proceedings that will determine whether he violated any law. His argument is grounded in the character of the office that was created by Article II of the Constitution, and relies on separation of powers principles that have structured our constitutional arrangement since the founding.

As a starting premise, petitioner contends that he occupies a unique office with powers and responsibilities so vast and important that the public interest demands that he devote his undivided time and attention to his public duties. He submits that—given the nature of the office—the doctrine of separation of powers places limits on the authority of the Federal Judiciary to interfere with the Executive Branch that would be transgressed by allowing this action to proceed.

We have no dispute with the initial premise of the argument. Former presidents, from George Washington to George Bush, have consistently endorsed petitioner's characterization of the office. . . .

It does not follow, however, that separation of powers principles would be violated by allowing this action to proceed. The doctrine of separation of powers is concerned with the allocation of official power among the three coequal branches of our Government. . . .

Of course the lines between the powers of the three branches are not always neatly defined. But in this case there is no suggestion that the Federal Judiciary is being asked to perform any function that might in some way be described as "executive." Respondent is merely asking the courts to exercise their core Article III jurisdiction to decide cases and controversies. Whatever the outcome of this case, there is no possibility that the decision will curtail the scope of the official powers of the Executive Branch. The litigation of questions that relate entirely to the unofficial conduct of the individual who happens to be the President poses no perceptible risk of misallocation of either judicial power or executive power.

Rather than arguing that the decision of the case will produce either an aggrandizement of judicial power or a narrowing of executive power, petitioner contends that—as a by product of an otherwise traditional exercise of judicial power—burdens will be placed on the President that will hamper the performance of his official duties. . . . As a factual matter, petitioner contends that this particular case—as well as the potential additional litigation that an affirmance of the Court of Appeals judgment might spawn—may impose an unacceptable burden on the President's time and energy, and thereby impair the effective performance of his office.

Petitioner's predictive judgment finds little support in either history or the relatively narrow compass of the issues raised in this particular case. As we have already noted, in the more than 200 year history of the Republic, only three sitting Presidents have been subjected to suits for their private actions. If the past is any indicator, it seems unlikely that a deluge of such litigation will ever engulf the Presidency. As for the case at hand, if properly managed by the District Court, it appears to us highly unlikely to occupy any substantial amount of petitioner's time.

Of greater significance, petitioner errs by presuming that interactions between the Judicial Branch and the Executive, even quite burdensome interactions, necessarily rise to the level of constitutionally forbidden impairment of the Executive's ability to perform its constitutionally mandated functions. . . . The fact that a federal court's exercise of its traditional Article III jurisdiction may significantly burden the time and attention of the Chief Executive is not sufficient to establish a violation of the Constitution. Two long-settled propositions, first announced by Chief Justice Marshall, support that conclusion.

First, we have long held that when the President takes official action, the Court has the authority to determine whether he has acted within the law. . . .

Second, it is also settled that the President is subject to judicial process in appropriate circumstances. Although Thomas Jefferson apparently thought otherwise, Chief Justice Marshall, when presiding in the treason trial of Aaron Burr, ruled that a *subpoena duces tecum* could be directed to the President. We unequivocally and emphatically endorsed Marshall's position when we held that President Nixon was obligated to comply with a subpoena commanding him to produce certain tape recordings of his conversations with his aides. *United States v. Nixon* (1974). As we explained, "neither the doctrine of separation of powers, nor the need for confidentiality of high level communications, without more, can sustain an absolute, unqualified Presidential privilege of immunity from judicial process under all circumstances."

Sitting Presidents have responded to court orders to provide testimony and other information with sufficient frequency that such interactions between the Judicial and Executive Branches can scarcely be thought a novelty. President Monroe responded to written interrogatories, President Nixon—as noted above—produced tapes in response to a subpoena *duces tecum*, President Ford complied with an order to give a deposition in a criminal trial, and President Clinton has twice given videotaped testimony in criminal proceedings. Moreover, sitting Presidents have also voluntarily complied with judicial requests for testimony. . . .

In sum, "[i]t is settled law that the separation of powers doctrine does not bar every exercise of jurisdiction over the President of the United States." *Fitzgerald.* If the

Judiciary may severely burden the Executive Branch by reviewing the legality of the President's official conduct, and if it may direct appropriate process to the President himself, it must follow that the federal courts have power to determine the legality of his unofficial conduct. The burden on the President's time and energy that is a mere by product of such review surely cannot be considered as onerous as the direct burden imposed by judicial review and the occasional invalidation of his official actions. We therefore hold that the doctrine of separation of powers does not require federal courts to stay all private actions against the President until he leaves office. . . .

. . . [W]e are persuaded that it was an abuse of discretion for the District Court to defer the trial until after the President leaves office. Such a lengthy and categorical stay takes no account whatever of the respondent's interest in bringing the case to trial. The complaint was filed within the statutory limitations period—albeit near the end of that period—and delaying trial would increase the danger of prejudice resulting from the loss of evidence, including the inability of witnesses to recall specific facts, or the possible death of a party.

The decision to postpone the trial was, furthermore, premature. The proponent of a stay bears the burden of establishing its need. . . . We think the District Court may have given undue weight to the concern that a trial might generate unrelated civil actions that could conceivably hamper the President in conducting the duties of his office. If and when that should occur, the court's discretion would permit it to manage those actions in such fashion (including deferral of trial) that interference with the President's duties would not occur. But no such impingement upon the President's conduct of his office was shown here.

We add a final comment on two matters that are discussed at length in the briefs: the risk that our decision will generate a large volume of politically motivated harassing and frivolous litigation, and the danger that national security concerns might prevent the President from explaining a legitimate need for a continuance.

We are not persuaded that either of these risks is serious. Most frivolous and vexatious litigation is terminated at the pleading stage or on summary judgment, with little if any personal involvement by the defendant. Moreover, the availability of sanctions provides a significant deterrent to litigation directed at the President in his unofficial capacity for purposes of political gain or harassment. History indicates that the likelihood that a significant number of such cases will be filed is remote. Although scheduling problems may arise, there is no reason to assume that the District Courts will be either unable to accommodate the President's needs or unfaithful to the tradition—especially in matters involving national security—of giving "the utmost deference to Presidential responsibilities." Several Presidents, including petitioner, have given testimony without jeopardizing the Nation's security. In short, we have confidence in the ability of our federal judges to deal with both of these concerns.

If Congress deems it appropriate to afford the President stronger protection, it may respond with appropriate legislation. . . . If the Constitution embodied the rule that the President advocates, Congress, of course, could not repeal it. But our holding today raises no barrier to a statutory response to these concerns.

The Federal District Court has jurisdiction to decide this case. Like every other citizen who properly invokes that jurisdiction, respondent has a right to an orderly disposition of her claims. Accordingly, the judgment of the Court of Appeals is affirmed.

It is so ordered.

JUSTICE BREYER, concurring in the judgment.

I agree with the majority that the Constitution does not automatically grant the President an immunity from civil lawsuits based upon his private conduct. Nor does the "doctrine of separation of powers . . . require federal courts to stay" virtually "all private actions against the President until he leaves office." Rather, as the Court of Appeals stated, the President cannot simply rest upon the claim that a private civil lawsuit for damages will "interfere with the constitutionally assigned duties of the Executive Branch . . . without detailing any specific responsibilities or explaining how or the degree to which they are affected by the suit." To obtain a postponement the President must "bea[r] the burden of establishing its need."

In my view, however, once the President sets forth and explains a conflict between judicial proceeding and public duties, the matter changes. At that point, the Constitution permits a judge to schedule a trial in an ordinary civil damages action (where postponement normally is possible without overwhelming damage to a plaintiff) only within the constraints of a constitutional principle—a principle that forbids a federal judge in such a case to interfere with the President's discharge of his public duties. I have no doubt that the Constitution contains such a principle applicable to civil suits, based upon Article II's vesting of the entire "executive Power" in a single individual, implemented through the Constitution's structural separation of powers, and revealed both by history and case precedent.

I recognize that this case does not require us now to apply the principle specifically, thereby delineating its contours; nor need we now decide whether lower courts are to apply it directly or categorically through the use of presumptions or rules of administration. Yet I fear that to disregard it now may appear to deny it. I also fear that the majority's description of the relevant precedents de-emphasizes the extent to which they support a principle of the President's independent authority to control his own time and energy. . . .

Case law, particularly, *Nixon v. Fitzgerald*, strongly supports the principle that judges hearing a private civil damages action against a sitting President may not issue orders that could significantly distract a President from his official duties. In *Fitzgerald*, the Court held that former President Nixon was absolutely immune from civil damage lawsuits based upon any conduct within the "outer perimeter" of his official responsibilities. . . .

The majority points to the fact that private plaintiffs have brought civil damage lawsuits against a sitting President only three times in our Nation's history; and it relies upon the threat of sanctions to discourage, and "the court's discretion" to manage, such actions so that "interference with the President's duties would not occur." I am less sanguine. Since 1960, when the last such suit was filed, the number of civil lawsuits filed annually in Federal District Courts has increased from under 60,000 to about 240,000; the number of federal district judges has increased from 233 to about 650; the time and expense associated with both discovery and trial have increased; an increasingly complex economy has led to increasingly complex sets of statutes, rules and regulations, that often create potential liability, with or without fault. And this Court has now made clear that such lawsuits may proceed against a sitting President. The consequence, as the Court warned in *Fitzgerald*, is that a sitting President, given "the visibility of his office," could well become "an easily identifiable target for suits for civil damages." The threat of sanctions could well discourage much unneeded litigation, but some lawsuits (including highly intricate and complicated ones) could resist ready evaluation and disposition; and individual district court procedural rulings could pose a significant threat to the President's official functions.

I concede the possibility that district courts, supervised by the Courts of Appeals and perhaps this Court, might prove able to manage private civil damage actions against sitting Presidents without significantly interfering with the discharge of Presidential duties—at least if they manage those actions with the constitutional problem in mind. Nonetheless, predicting the future is difficult, and I am skeptical. . . .

. . . The District Court in this case determined that the Constitution required the postponement of trial during the sitting President's term. It may well be that the trial of this case cannot take place without significantly interfering with the President's ability to carry out his official duties. Yet, I agree with the majority that there is no automatic temporary immunity and that the President should have to provide the District Court with a reasoned explanation of why the immunity is needed; and I also agree that, in the absence of that explanation, the court's postponement of the trial date was premature. For those reasons, I concur in the result.

The Court's conclusion that Jones's sexual harassment suit could proceed was a setback for President Clinton, who was by that time heavily involved in more serious controversies that ultimately led to his impeachment *(see box 4-4)*. In the end, Clinton and Jones reached an out-of-court monetary settlement of the dispute. Although the Jones case never went to trial, the Supreme Court's ruling that presidents while in office may be sued for unofficial conduct is a meaningful addition to the law of presidential immunity. It also remains controversial, with many scholars suggesting that it will prove damaging to the presidency. Do you agree? Or do you believe that the Clinton episode was so anomalous that we are unlikely to see anyone taking advantage of the Court's ruling?

The Power to Pardon

Executive power historically has included the authority to reduce or rescind criminal punishments in individual cases. The executive stands as the last source of mercy, capable of sparing a person when extraordinary circumstances warrant such action. European monarchs exercised this power long before the creation of the United States, so it is not surprising that the Constitutional Convention also gave it to the president. The wording of the pardon clause is straightforward: the president "shall have Power to grant Reprieves and Pardons for Offences against the United States, except in Cases of Impeachment."

A pardon erases all penalties and other legal effects of a criminal conviction. It is, as described by Chief Justice John Marshall, an act of grace. A person receiving a

> **BOX 4-4   AFTERMATH . . . *CLINTON V. JONES***

I N *Clinton v. Jones* (1997) the Supreme Court rejected President Bill Clinton's request to postpone a trial on Paula Jones's sexual harassment charges until his presidency ended. Thus began two years of intense legal difficulties for the president. Clinton was already under investigation by independent counsel Kenneth Starr for possible financial improprieties in the Whitewater matter, an Arkansas land deal that occurred prior to his presidency. That investigation coupled with the Jones lawsuit subjected Clinton to more-intense scrutiny than almost any other previous president had experienced.

While preparing their case, Jones's attorneys were made aware of a possible illicit relationship between Clinton and a young White House intern, Monica Lewinsky. Attempting to establish a pattern of wrongdoing, Jones's lawyers subpoenaed Lewinsky and the president. Lewinsky at first denied any sexual relationship with Clinton. On January 17, 1998, President Clinton gave a sworn deposition claiming that he had not had a sexual relationship with Lewinsky. Nine days later he made the same denial to the American people on national television. Taped telephone conversations between Lewinsky and her friend Linda Tripp, who had given the tapes to the independent counsel's office, revealed that a sexual relationship between Lewinsky and Clinton had occurred. Starr expanded his investigation to include an inquiry into the Lewinsky matter.

After receiving immunity from prosecution, Lewinsky changed her testimony, acknowledging a past relationship with the president. In August Clinton admitted to "a critical lapse of judgment" that had led to his affair with Lewinsky. By this time, other women had come forward claiming that Clinton had acted inappropriately with them. In November the president settled his legal dispute with Jones for $850,000 with no apology or admission of guilt.

Settling the case, however, did not end Clinton's troubles. In December the House of Representatives considered four articles of impeachment recommended by its Judiciary Committee. Two of the proposals passed: one charged Clinton with perjury, and the other alleged obstruction of justice. As a result, Bill Clinton became only the second president in U.S. history to be impeached.

In January 1999, with Chief Justice William Rehnquist presiding and the senators acting as a jury, the U.S. Senate tried Clinton on the two articles of impeachment. On February 12 the senators voted 55–45 to acquit Clinton on the perjury charge and 50–50 on the obstruction of justice charge, both falling far short of the 67 guilty votes required to remove the president from office. Throughout the impeachment process, public opinion ran decidedly in Clinton's favor.

Clinton's legal problems continued. U.S. judge Susan Webber Wright, who presided over the Jones lawsuit, found Clinton in contempt and fined him $90,000 for undermining "the integrity of the judicial system" by giving "false, misleading, and evasive answers that were designed to obstruct justice." In May 2000 the Arkansas Supreme Court initiated disbarment proceedings against him. But on January 19, 2001, his last full day in office, Clinton reached an agreement with the independent counsel in which he admitted wrongdoing and accepted a $25,000 fine and a five-year suspension of his license to practice law, thus settling the disbarment question.

Throughout all of these difficulties, Bill Clinton's presidency was surprisingly unaffected. Polls indicated that the public perceived Clinton as a man with serious personal character flaws, but he nevertheless received historically high approval ratings for the job he was doing as president.

SOURCES: *Los Angeles Times,* May 23, 2000; *Omaha World-Herald,* February 13, 1999; *New York Times,* February 13, 1999, July 30, 1999; *San Francisco Chronicle,* February 13, 1999.

---

complete pardon is released from serving any remaining sentence and has full civil rights restored. Legally, it is as if the individual had never committed the crime.[26] A reprieve, in contrast, is a presidential act that merely postpones the serving of a criminal penalty.

The president's power to grant pardons and reprieves is not absolute, however. The words of Article II restrict the president's authority to crimes against the United States, which means that the president may pardon only individuals charged with federal offenses, not those in violation of state criminal laws. The governors of the various states have similar pardoning or

---

26. See *Ex parte Garland* (1867).

clemency authority. Article II also prohibits the use of the pardoning power to nullify the effects of impeachment. And finally, the president may not impose a pardon on someone who refuses to accept it.[27]

Aside from these limits, the president is free to exercise the pardoning authority with full discretion, and some presidents have been quite generous in granting pardons. A pardon may completely void all criminal penalties for an offense or eliminate only a portion of the sentence. The president may place conditions on a pardon. In 1960 President Eisenhower spared army master sergeant Maurice Schick, a convicted murderer, from the death penalty on the condition that he be imprisoned for life without the possibility of parole.[28] A president may pardon individuals before or after they are tried for offenses or even before formal criminal charges are filed. A pardon may be granted to a single person or to an entire class of individuals. In 1795 George Washington granted amnesty to those who had participated in the Whiskey Rebellion, and in 1977 Jimmy Carter pardoned all Vietnam War draft evaders, an action that applied to an estimated 100,000 men.

For the most part, the Supreme Court has granted the chief executive great leeway in the exercise of the pardon power. *Ex parte Grossman* (1925) provides an example. The issue in this case was whether the president's pardon power extended to criminal contempt penalties imposed by a federal judge. Chief Justice Taft wrote the opinion of the Court. Taft, a former president, expressed strong support for a broad interpretation of the pardoning authority. In *Grossman,* note his use of history as a means of interpreting the Constitution.

Ex parte Grossman

267 U.S. 87 (1925)

http://laws.findlaw.com/us/267/87.html

Vote: 8 (Brandeis, Butler, Holmes, McReynolds, Sanford, Sutherland, Taft, Van Devanter)

0

OPINION OF THE COURT: *Taft*

FACTS:

On November 24, 1920, legal action was taken against Philip Grossman in the U.S. District Court for the Northern District of Illinois. He was charged with selling liquor at his place of business in violation of the National Prohibition Act. Government attorneys requested that the court issue an injunction prohibiting Grossman from any further violations, and two days later a judge issued the injunction. On January 11, 1921, the government filed charges against Grossman for violating the judge's order, claiming that he had continued to sell liquor at his establishment. The district court tried Grossman and found him guilty of criminal contempt of court for disobeying the order. The judge sentenced him to one year in prison and a fine of $1,000, and the sentence was upheld by the court of appeals.

In December 1923 President Calvin Coolidge issued a pardon in which he reduced Grossman's sentence to payment of the fine. Grossman accepted the pardon, paid the fine, and was released from prison. The district judge, however, refused to acknowledge the pardon on the ground that the president had no authority to commute a sentence for criminal contempt of court. He ordered Grossman to serve the remainder of his sentence. Grossman objected and filed a habeas corpus action against prison superintendent Ritchie Graham, demanding to be released.

ARGUMENTS:

For the petitioner, Philip Grossman:

- The Constitution should be read with the common meaning of each word at the time of its drafting. The common meaning of "offences" at the time included criminal contempt of court.

- Historically, the king of England exercised pardon power over contempt of court. There is no indication that the framers intended to change this power when they wrote the Constitution.

- There is no serious threat that the president would abuse the power to pardon a criminal contempt of court and impinge on the authority of the courts. Even if this were to happen, impeachment would be an appropriate remedy.

For the respondent, Ritchie V. Graham, superintendent of the Chicago House of Correction, Cook County, Ill.:

- The president has the power to pardon only statutory offenses against the United States.

- The language of the Constitution shows that pardonable offenses include only those subject to trial by jury.

---

27. *United States v. Wilson* (1833) and *Burdick v. United States* (1915). Later, however, the Court held that acceptance was not required when the president commuted a death sentence to life in prison (*Biddle v. Perovich,* 1927).

28. *Schick v. Reed* (1974).

- Allowing the president to pardon criminal contempt of court would violate the doctrine of separation of powers by impinging on the independence and authority of the judiciary.

MR. CHIEF JUSTICE TAFT DELIVERED THE OPINION OF THE COURT.

The argument for the respondent is that the President's power extends only to offenses against the United States and a contempt of Court is not such an offense, that offenses against the United States are not common law offenses but can only be created by legislative act, that the President's pardoning power is more limited than that of the King of England at common law, which was a broad prerogative and included contempts against his courts chiefly because the judges thereof were his agents and acted in his name; that the context of the Constitution shows that the word "offences" is used in that instrument only to include crimes and misdemeanors triable by jury and not contempts of the dignity and authority of the federal courts, and that to construe the pardon clause to include contempts of court would be to violate the fundamental principle of the Constitution in the division of powers between the Legislative, Executive and Judicial branches, and to take from the federal courts their independence and the essential means of protecting their dignity and authority.

The language of the Constitution cannot be interpreted safely except by reference to the common law and to British institutions as they were when the instrument was framed and adopted. The statesmen and lawyers of the Convention who submitted it to the ratification of the Conventions of the thirteen States, were born and brought up in the atmosphere of the common law, and thought and spoke in its vocabulary. They were familiar with other forms of government, recent and ancient, and indicated in their discussions earnest study and consideration of many of them, but when they came to put their conclusions into the form of fundamental law in a compact draft, they expressed them in terms of the common law, confident that they could be shortly and easily understood. . . .

The King of England before our Revolution, in the exercise of his prerogative, had always exercised the power to pardon contempts of court, just as he did ordinary crimes and misdemeanors and as he has done to the present day. In the mind of a common law lawyer of the eighteenth century the word pardon included within its scope the ending by the King's grace of the punishment of such derelictions,

whether it was imposed by the court without a jury or upon indictment, for both forms of trial for contempts were had. . . .

Nor is there any substance in the contention that there is any substantial difference in this matter between the executive power of pardon in our Government and the King's prerogative. The courts of Great Britain were called the King's Courts, as indeed they were; but for years before our Constitution they were as independent of the King's interference as they are today. The extent of the King's pardon was clearly circumscribed by law and the British Constitution, as the cases cited above show. The framers of our Constitution had in mind no necessity for curtailing this feature of the King's prerogative in transplanting it into the American governmental structures, save by excepting cases of impeachment; and even in that regard, as already pointed out, the common law forbade the pleading a pardon in bar to an impeachment. The suggestion that the President's power of pardon should be regarded as necessarily less than that of the King was pressed upon this Court . . . in *Ex parte William Wells*, [1855] but it did not prevail with the majority. . . .

Nothing in the ordinary meaning of the words "offences against the United States" excludes criminal contempts. That which violates the dignity and authority of federal courts such as an intentional effort to defeat their decrees justifying punishment violates a law of the United States, and so must be an offense against the United States. Moreover, this Court has held that the general statute of limitation which forbids prosecutions "for any offense unless instituted within three years next after such offense shall have been committed," applies to criminal contempts. . . .

. . . [C]riminal contempts of a federal court have been pardoned for eighty-five years. In that time the power has been exercised twenty-seven times. . . .

Executive clemency exists to afford relief from undue harshness or evident mistake in the operation or enforcement of the criminal law. The administration of justice by the courts is not necessarily always wise or certainly considerate of circumstances which may properly mitigate guilt. To afford a remedy, it has always been thought essential in popular governments, as well as in monarchies, to vest in some other authority than the courts power to ameliorate or avoid particular criminal judgments. It is a check entrusted to the executive for special cases. To exercise it to the extent of destroying the deterrent effect of judicial punishment would be to pervert it; but whoever is to make it useful must have full discretion to exercise it. Our

Constitution confers this discretion on the highest officer in the nation in confidence that he will not abuse it. An abuse in pardoning contempts would certainly embarrass courts, but it is questionable how much more it would lessen their effectiveness than a wholesale pardon of other offenses. If we could conjure up in our minds a President willing to paralyze courts by pardoning all criminal contempts, why not a President ordering a general jail delivery? A pardon can only be granted for a contempt fully completed. Neither in this country nor in England can it interfere with the use of coercive measures to enforce a suitor's right. The detrimental effect of excessive pardons of completed contempts would be in the loss of the deterrent influence upon future contempts. It is of the same character as that of the excessive pardons of other offenses. The difference does not justify our reading criminal contempts out of the pardon clause by departing from its ordinary meaning confirmed by its common law origin and long years of practice and acquiescence.

If it be said that the President, by successive pardons of constantly recurring contempts in particular litigation, might deprive a court of power to enforce its orders in a recalcitrant neighborhood, it is enough to observe that such a course is so improbable as to furnish but little basis for argument. Exceptional cases like this, if to be imagined at all, would suggest a resort to impeachment rather than to a narrow and strained construction of the general powers of the President.

The power of a court to protect itself and its usefulness by punishing contemnors is of course necessary, but it is one exercised without the restraining influence of a jury and without many of the guaranties which the bill of rights offers to protect the individual against unjust conviction. Is it unreasonable to provide for the possibility that the personal element may sometimes enter into a summary judgment pronounced by a judge who thinks his authority is flouted or denied? May it not be fairly said that in order to avoid possible mistake, undue prejudice or needless severity, the chance of pardon should exist at least as much in favor of a person convicted by a judge without a jury as in favor of one convicted in a jury trial? The pardoning by the President of criminal contempts has been practiced more than three-quarters of a century, and no abuses during all that time developed sufficiently to invoke a test in the federal courts of its validity.

It goes without saying that nowhere is there a more earnest will to maintain the independence of federal courts and the preservation of every legitimate safeguard of their effectiveness afforded by the Constitution than in this Court. But the qualified independence which they fortunately enjoy is not likely to be permanently strengthened by ignoring precedent and practice and minimizing the importance of the coordinating checks and balances of the Constitution.

The rule is made absolute and the petitioner is discharged.

Undoubtedly, the most controversial exercise of the pardon power to date was Gerald Ford's exoneration of Richard Nixon in 1974 *(see box 4-5)*. By resigning from office, Nixon kept all of the benefits the nation provides its former chief executives, but the resignation did not make him immune from a trial for Watergate-related crimes. The pardon covered any crimes Nixon may have committed during his entire tenure as chief executive, from January 20, 1969, through August 9, 1974. It was an extraordinary act: not only was Nixon the first president to be pardoned for possible wrongdoing, but he also received a blanket pardon covering almost six years and not restricted to any specific crimes or incidents. Furthermore, the pardon came before any formal criminal charges were brought against him. Ford's stated intent in granting the pardon was to begin to heal the nation by putting the Watergate scandal to rest.

Many people were appalled at the pardon, believing that if Nixon had committed criminal acts, he should be put on trial like any other citizen. They thought it was necessary for the former president to stand trial because his alleged wrongdoing had compromised the very foundation of the American government and violated the sacred trust of the people. The granting of this blanket protection to Nixon was so widely criticized that some analysts cite it as one reason Ford lost the 1976 election to Jimmy Carter.

Given the Supreme Court's interpretations of the pardon power, there was little doubt that Ford acted constitutionally. Few legal scholars thought a court challenge had any chance of success. Prevailing legal opinion, however, did not deter a Michigan attorney from filing suit against Ford to have the pardon declared unconstitutional. The dispute was heard and decided in federal district court and did not reach the Supreme Court. As you read the judge's opinion in *Murphy v. Ford,* notice how closely he ties his decision to the intention of the framers and to the precedents handed down by the Supreme Court.

BOX 4-5   NIXON PARDON PROCLAMATION

Following is the text of the proclamation by which President Gerald R. Ford, September 8, 1974, pardoned former president Richard Nixon:

Richard Nixon became the thirty-seventh President of the United States on January 20, 1969, and was re-elected in 1972 for a second term by the electors of forty-nine of the fifty states. His term in office continued until his resignation on August 9, 1974.

Pursuant to resolutions of the House of Representatives, its Committee on the Judiciary conducted an inquiry and investigation on the impeachment of the President extending over more than eight months. The hearings of the committee and its deliberations, which received wide national publicity over television, radio, and in printed media, resulted in votes adverse to Richard Nixon on recommended articles of impeachment.

As a result of certain acts or omissions occurring before his resignation from the office of President, Richard Nixon has become liable to possible indictment and trial for offenses against the United States. Whether or not he shall be so prosecuted depends on findings of the appropriate grand jury and on the discretion of the authorized prosecutor. Should an indictment ensue, the accused shall then be entitled to a fair trial by an impartial jury, as guaranteed to every individual by the Constitution.

It is believed that a trial of Richard Nixon, if it became necessary, could not fairly begin until a year or more has elapsed. In the meantime, the tranquility to which this nation has been restored by the events of recent weeks could be irreparably lost by the prospects of bringing to trial a former President of the United States. The prospects of such trial will cause prolonged and divisive debate over the propriety of exposing to further punishment and degradation a man who has already paid the unprecedented penalty of relinquishing the highest elective office in the United States.

Now, therefore, I, Gerald R. Ford, President of the United States, pursuant to the pardon power conferred upon me by Article II, Section 2, of the Constitution, have granted and by these presents do grant a full, free, and absolute pardon unto Richard Nixon for all offenses against the United States which he, Richard Nixon, has committed or may have committed or taken part in during the period from January 20, 1969, through August 9, 1974.

In witness whereof, I have hereunto set my hand this 8th day of September in the year of Our Lord Nineteen Hundred Seventy-Four, and of the Independence of the United States of America the 199th.

Murphy v. Ford

390 F. SUPP. 1372 (1975)
Decision of the U.S. District Court for the Western District of Michigan
Noel P. Fox, Chief Judge

FACTS:

F. Gregory Murphy, an attorney from Marquette, Michigan, filed suit against President Ford, asking the court to declare Ford's unconditional pardon of Richard Nixon void. Murphy contended that a pardon cannot constitutionally be granted to a person who has not been indicted or convicted and who has not been formally charged with any crime against the United States. The suit was heard by Judge Noel Fox, a Democrat appointed to the district court by President Kennedy.

CHIEF JUDGE FOX DELIVERED THE OPINION OF THE COURT.

In granting a pardon to Mr. Nixon, President Ford was not presuming to end the impeachment proceeding then pending in Congress. That was exclusively a Congressional affair. The impeachment exception to the Pardoning Power does not apply here.

The main issue is, did President Ford have the constitutional power to pardon former President Nixon for the latter's offenses against the United States?

In The Federalist No. 74, written in 1788 in support of the proposed Constitution, Alexander Hamilton explained why the Founding Fathers gave the President a discretionary power to pardon: "The principal argument for reposing the power of pardoning . . . [in] the Chief Magistrate," Hamilton wrote, "is this: in seasons of insurrection or rebellion, there are often critical moments, when a well-timed offer of pardon to the insurgents or rebels may restore the tranquillity of the commonwealth; and which, if suffered to pass unimproved, it may never be possible afterwards to recall."

Few would today deny that the period from the break-in at the Watergate in June 1972, until the resignation of President Nixon in August 1974, was a "season of insurrection or rebellion" by many actually in the Government. Since the end of 1970, various top officials of the Nixon Administration at times during this period deliberately and flagrantly violated the civil liberties of individual citizens and engaged in criminal violations of the campaign laws in order to preserve and expand their own and Nixon's personal power beyond constitutional limitations. When many illegal activities were threatened with exposure, some Nixon Administration officials formed and executed a criminal conspiracy to obstruct justice. Evidence now available suggests a strong probability that the Nixon Administration was conducting a covert assault on American liberty and an insurrection and rebellion against constitutional government itself, an insurrection and rebellion which might have succeeded but for timely intervention by a courageous free press, an enlightened Congress, and a diligent Judiciary dedicated to preserving the rule of law.

Certainly the summer and early fall of 1974 were a period of popular discontent, as the full extent of the Nixon Administration's misdeeds became known, and public trust in government virtually collapsed. After Mr. Nixon's resignation in August, the public clamor over the whole Watergate episode did not immediately subside; attention continued to focus on Mr. Nixon and his fate. When Mr. Ford became President, the executive branch was foundering in the wreckage of Watergate, and the country was in the grips of an apparently uncontrollable inflationary spiral and an energy crisis of unprecedented proportions.

Under these circumstances, President Ford concluded that the public interest required positive steps to end the divisions caused by Watergate and to shift the focus of attention from the immediate problem of Mr. Nixon to the hard social and economic problems which were of more lasting significance.

By pardoning Richard Nixon, who many believed was the leader of a conspiratorial insurrection and rebellion against American liberty and constitutional government, President Ford was taking steps, in the words of Alexander Hamilton in The Federalist, to *"restore the tranquillity of the commonwealth" by a "well-timed offer of pardon"* [our

italics] to the putative rebel leader. President Ford's pardon of Richard M. Nixon was thus within the letter and the spirit of the Presidential Pardoning Power granted by the Constitution. It was a prudent public policy judgment.

The fact that Mr. Nixon had been neither indicted nor convicted of an offense against the United States does not affect the validity of the pardon. *Ex parte Garland* (1867). In that case the Supreme Court considered the nature of the President's Pardoning Power, and the effect of a Presidential pardon. Mr. Justice Field, speaking for the court, said that the Pardoning Power is *"unlimited,"* except in cases of impeachment. "[The Power] extends to every offense known to the law, and may be exercised *at any time after its commission, either before legal proceedings are taken*, or during their pendency, or after conviction and judgment. . . . The benign prerogative of mercy reposed in [the President] cannot be fettered by any legislative restrictions.

"Such being the case, the inquiry arises as to the effect and operation of a pardon, and on this point all the authorities concur. A pardon reaches both the punishment prescribed for the offense and the guilt of the offender; and when the pardon is full, it releases the punishment and blots out of existence the guilt. . . . If granted before conviction, it prevents any of the penalties and disabilities consequent from conviction from attaching. . . .

"There is only this limitation to its operation: it does not restore offices forfeited, or property or interests vested in others in consequence of the conviction and judgment." . . . However, " . . . as the very essence of a pardon is forgiveness or remission of penalty, a pardon implies guilt; *it does not obliterate the fact of the commission of the crime and the conviction thereof; it does not wash out the moral stain; as has been tersely said; it involves forgiveness and not forgetfulness"* [our italics]. *Page v. Watson* [Florida Supreme Court, 1938].

The . . . motion to dismiss this action is hereby granted.

The power to pardon continues to be an important executive prerogative. Often it is used to extend mercy where, because of special circumstances, strict application of the law would lead to unjust results. At times, however, its use is controversial because of political implications. In December 1992, shortly after he had been defeated for reelection, President George H. W. Bush granted pardons to six former executive branch officials, including former secretary of defense Caspar Weinberger. Those pardoned were facing criminal charges for alleged illegal dealings with Iran. President Clinton also faced his share of criticism for his "eleventh hour" pardon of 140 individuals, including his former housing secretary, Henry Cisneros, for a total of 396 pardons during his administration. In contrast, though commentators questioned President George W. Bush's commutation of vice presidential adviser Lewis "Scooter" Libby's prison sentence for perjury and other crimes associated with the leaking of classified information, Bush issued only 189 pardons during his administration. As of mid-2015, President Obama has issued 64.

THE ROLE OF THE PRESIDENT IN FOREIGN POLICY

Perhaps the most significant authority given to the president is the power to create and carry out the nation's foreign policy. In this final section we review the ways the Constitution contemplates the president as the primary officer in conducting relations with other nations. In the next chapter we give special attention to the president's most important foreign policy power, the authority to wage war, and the conflicts that have arisen over the exercise of that power.

There can be no doubt that the Constitution confers on the president special authority over matters of foreign policy. A review of the powers the Constitution grants to the chief executive demonstrates why this is the case.

First, Article II, Section 2, assigns to the president the role of commander in chief of the army and navy. The foreign policy of a nation clearly is tied to its military capability: military power not only enables a nation to deter hostile actions from other countries, but also can be used as a credible threat to persuade other nations to follow certain preferred courses of action. Armed interventions and full-scale wars can be major elements in executing a nation's foreign policy. Modern military actions, both small and large, taken by the United States in Grenada, Panama, Afghanistan, Kuwait, Kosovo, Libya, and Iraq demonstrate the use of this power.

Second, Article II gives the president the sole authority to make treaties on behalf of the United States. These international agreements may cover almost any area of interaction among nations, including defense pacts, economic understandings, and human rights accords.

Third, the president selects the individuals to represent the United States in contacts with other nations. The power to appoint ambassadors and ministers influences U.S. relations with the leaders of other states.

Fourth, Article II, Section 3, provides that the president is the appropriate official to receive ambassadors and ministers from foreign nations.[29] When the president accepts the credentials of foreign emissaries, the act confers U.S. recognition on the governments they represent. This provision also suggests that when foreign diplomats communicate with the United States they must do so through the president.

The Supreme Court has endorsed the notion that by the sum of these powers the Constitution has entrusted the president with substantial authority for creating and implementing foreign policy. The broadest statement in this position comes in the case of *United States v. Curtiss-Wright Export Corp.* As you recall, we discussed this case in chapter 3 as an example of the Court endorsing the notion of inherent powers enjoyed by the federal government in the field of foreign relations. Justice George Sutherland's opinion for the Court also develops the president's constitutional position in matters of foreign policy.

United States v. Curtiss-Wright Export Corp.

299 U.S. 304 (1936)
http://laws.findlaw.com/us/299/304.html
Vote: 7 (Brandeis, Butler, Cardozo, Hughes, Roberts, Sutherland, Van
  Devanter)
  1 (McReynolds)
OPINION OF THE COURT: Sutherland
NOT PARTICIPATING: Stone

FACTS:

After Charles Lindbergh's 1927 transatlantic flight, the aviation industry began to boom. Americans were convinced that "flying . . . would take its place as the new mode of transportation."[30] As a result, many new companies, including Curtiss-Wright, formed to build aircraft.

---

29. This clause was the subject of a recent Supreme Court decision, *Zivotofsky v. Kerry* (2015), which we discuss at the end of this chapter and excerpt in the next.

30. We adopt this and what follows from Robert A. Divine, "The Case of the Smuggled Bombers," in *Quarrels That Have Shaped the Constitution*, rev. ed., ed. John A. Garraty (New York: Harper & Row, 1987).

Although it started off on a strong footing, Curtiss-Wright soon fell prey to the Great Depression, and in 1930–1931 it lost $13 million. To avoid going bankrupt, it looked beyond the United States into the foreign market, where money still could be made. Curtiss-Wright sold its wares not to other private companies but to foreign governments involved in military conflicts and in need of warplanes.

The company found a ready buyer in Bolivia, which since 1932 had been at war with Paraguay over the Chaco, a region east of Bolivia. Landlocked Bolivia was determined to take control of the Chaco to gain access to the Atlantic Ocean. It became an excellent customer of Curtiss-Wright, buying thirty-four planes in the early 1930s. The Chaco War enabled the company to survive the Depression.

Things began to turn sour in 1934. Books and articles appeared attacking companies such as Curtiss-Wright as "merchants of death." More important, the League of Nations wanted to put an end to the Chaco War and asked the United States to help. In response, President Franklin Roosevelt asked Congress to enact a resolution enabling him to prohibit the sale of arms to the warring countries, and on May 28, 1934, Congress did so.

[I]f the President finds that the prohibition of the sale of arms and munitions of war in the United States to those countries now engaged in armed conflict in the Chaco may contribute to the reestablishment of peace between those countries, and if after consultation with the governments of other American Republics and with their cooperation, as well as that of such other governments as he may deem necessary, he makes proclamation to that effect, it shall be unlawful to sell, except under such limitations and exceptions as the President prescribes, any arms or munitions of war in any place in the United States to the countries now engaged in that armed conflict, or to any person, company, or association acting in the interest of either country, until otherwise ordered by the President or by Congress.

Whoever sells any arms or munitions of war . . . shall . . . be punished by a fine not exceeding $10,000 or by imprisonment not exceeding two years, or both.

The day after passage of the joint resolution, Roosevelt issued an order embargoing weapon sales to Bolivia and Paraguay, and criminal sanctions immediately went into effect. Curtiss-Wright refused to comply with the order and tried to get around it by disguising bombers as passenger planes. Eventually, it got caught and was charged with violating the order. The company challenged the government's action.

On January 27, 1936, a grand jury returned an indictment against Curtiss-Wright Export Corporation charging that it had conspired to sell military equipment to Bolivia during the period covered by the first proclamation. Curtiss-Wright challenged the government's action as an unconstitutional delegation of legislative power to the executive branch.

The United States appealed to the Supreme Court. After explaining that Congress had not engaged in an unconstitutional delegation of power for the reasons we discussed in chapter 3, Justice Sutherland discussed the role the Constitution prescribes for the president in the area of foreign policy.

(We omit the arguments of the parties here because they focused almost exclusively on questions about the delegation of powers that we considered in chapter 3.)

MR. JUSTICE SUTHERLAND DELIVERED THE OPINION OF THE COURT.

[F]ederal power over external affairs in origin and essential character [not only is] different from that over internal affairs, but participation in the exercise of the power is significantly limited. In this vast external realm, with its important, complicated, delicate and manifold problems, the President alone has the power to speak or listen as a representative of the nation. He *makes* treaties with the advice and consent of the Senate; but he alone negotiates. Into the field of negotiation the Senate cannot intrude; and Congress itself is powerless to invade it. As [John] Marshall said in his great argument of March 7, 1800, in the House of Representatives, "The President is the sole organ of the nation in its external relations, and its sole representative with foreign nations." The Senate Committee on Foreign Relations at a very early day in our history (February 15, 1816), reported to the Senate, among other things, as follows:

"The President is the constitutional representative of the United States with regard to foreign nations. He manages our concerns with foreign nations and must necessarily be most competent to determine when, how, and upon what subjects negotiation may be urged with the greatest prospect of success. For his conduct he is responsible to the Constitution. The committee consider this responsibility the surest pledge for the faithful discharge of his duty. They think the interference of the Senate in the direction of foreign negotiations calculated to diminish that responsibility and thereby to impair the best security for the national safety. The nature of transactions with foreign nations, moreover, requires caution and unity of design, and their success frequently depends on secrecy and dispatch."

It is important to bear in mind that we are here dealing not alone with an authority vested in the President by an exertion of legislative power, but with such an authority plus the very delicate, plenary and exclusive power of the President as the sole organ of the federal government in the field of international relations—a power which does not require as a basis for its exercise an act of Congress, but which, of course, like every other governmental power, must be exercised in subordination to the applicable provisions of the Constitution. It is quite apparent that if, in the maintenance of our international relations, embarrassment—perhaps serious embarrassment—is to be avoided and success for our aims achieved, congressional legislation which is to be made effective through negotiation and inquiry within the international field must often accord to the President a degree of discretion and freedom from statutory restriction which would not be admissible were domestic affairs alone involved. Moreover, he, not Congress, has the better opportunity of knowing the conditions which prevail in foreign countries, and especially is this true in time of war. He has his confidential sources of information. He has his agents in the form of diplomatic, consular and other officials. Secrecy in respect of information gathered by them may be highly necessary, and the premature disclosure of it productive of harmful results. Indeed, so clearly is this true that the first President refused to accede to a request to lay before the House of Representatives the instructions, correspondence and documents relating to the negotiation of the Jay Treaty—a refusal the wisdom of which was recognized by the House itself and has never since been doubted. In his reply to the request, President Washington said:

"The nature of foreign negotiations requires caution, and their success must often depend on secrecy; and even when brought to a conclusion a full disclosure of all the measures, demands, or eventual concessions which may have been proposed or contemplated would be extremely impolitic: for this might have a pernicious influence on future negotiations, or produce immediate inconveniences, perhaps danger and mischief, in relation to other powers. The necessity of such caution and secrecy was one cogent reason for vesting the power of making treaties in the President, with the advice and consent of the Senate, the principle on which that body was formed confining it to a small number of members. To admit, then, a right in the House of Representatives to demand and to have as a matter of course all the papers respecting a negotiation with a foreign power would be to establish a dangerous precedent."

The marked difference between foreign affairs and domestic affairs in this respect is recognized by both houses of Congress in the very form of their requisitions for information from the executive departments. In the case of every department except the Department of State, the resolution *directs* the official to furnish the information. In the case of the State Department, dealing with foreign affairs, the President is *requested* to furnish the information "if not incompatible with the public interest." A statement that to furnish the information is not compatible with the public interest rarely, if ever, is questioned.

When the President is to be authorized by legislation to act in respect of a matter intended to affect a situation in foreign territory, the legislator properly bears in mind the important consideration that the form of the President's action—or, indeed, whether he shall act at all—may well depend, among other things, upon the nature of the confidential information which he has or may thereafter receive, or upon the effect which his action may have upon our foreign relations. This consideration, in connection with what we have already said on the subject, discloses the unwisdom of requiring Congress in this field of governmental power to lay down narrowly definite standards by which the President is to be governed. As this court said in *Mackenzie v. Hare* [1915], "As a government, the United States is invested with all the attributes of sovereignty. As it has the character of nationality it has the powers of nationality, especially those which concern its relations and intercourse with other countries. *We should hesitate long before limiting or embarrassing such powers.*" [italics provided]

In the light of the foregoing observations, it is evident that this court should not be in haste to apply a general rule which will have the effect of condemning legislation like that under review as constituting an unlawful delegation of legislative power. The principles which justify such legislation find overwhelming support in the unbroken legislative practice which has prevailed almost from the inception of the national government to the present day.

This opinion provides a strong statement—perhaps the strongest ever—of the president's power in foreign affairs. Note Justice Sutherland's words, which he adapted from a speech of then-Congressman John Marshall: the president is the "sole organ of the federal government in the field of international relations." To exercise his power, according to Sutherland, he does not "require . . . an act of Congress"; he is subordinate only to the Constitution.

Have subsequent Courts agreed? This is a question we explore in some detail in chapter 5 where we consider cases relating to the balance of power between the president and Congress in times of war and other national emergencies. For now, we can say that the answer is both yes and no.

Let's start with how the Court has undercut *Curtiss-Wright*. Chiefly, and in contrast to *Curtiss-Wright*, the justices have often reminded us that the Constitution does not leave the president completely unfettered in the pursuit of the nation's foreign policy. In fact, the framers were sufficiently concerned about the distribution of these foreign policy prerogatives that they gave the legislative branch certain powers to counterbalance those of the executive. The president is commander in chief of the military, yes, but Congress has the power to raise and support the army and the navy, make rules for the military, call up the militia, and declare war. The president has the constitutional authority to make treaties, but a treaty cannot take effect unless the Senate ratifies it by a two-thirds vote. The president appoints ambassadors and other foreign policy ministers, but the Senate must confirm them.

For this reason, today's justices often look to Congress when considering presidential action. Under an approach established in *Youngstown Sheet & Tube Co. v. Sawyer* (1952) *(excerpted in chapter 5)*, the president must show that a power is conclusively and exclusively his if he is taking action against Congress's will. In *Curtiss-Wright* the president and Congress were on the same page; Congress had authorized the president to issue the embargo. In *Youngstown,* they were not. When President Truman issued an executive order commanding his secretary of commerce to seize the nation's steel mills to keep workers from striking, the Court thought he had adopted a method that Congress had declined to adopt to settle labor strikes. Because the justices found that Truman could not point to any specific statutory or constitutional authority for his executive order, they invalidated it.

This does not mean the Court will always strike down presidential actions of which Congress does not approve. In another case we consider in chapter 5, *Zivotofsky v. Kerry* (2015), the Court upheld an executive action that Congress explicitly tried to overturn: the President did not want passports of U.S. citizens born in Jerusalem to list the country of birth as "Israel," whereas Congress had passed a law allowing Israel to be recorded. In this case the Court ruled for the president because he was able to point to a conclusive and exclusive power in Article II—the power to "receive Ambassadors and other public Ministers."

But even in *Zivotofsky,* the Court hardly ignored Congress's role in foreign affairs, and even more to the point took the opportunity to push back on *Curtiss-Wright*. After quoting language from *Curtiss-Wright* on the president's role as "the sole organ" of foreign affairs, the majority in *Zivotofsky* noted,

This description of the President's exclusive power was not necessary to the holding of *Curtiss-Wright*—which, after all, dealt with congressionally authorized action, not a unilateral Presidential determination. Indeed, *Curtiss-Wright* did not hold that the President is free from Congress' lawmaking power in the field of international relations. The President does have a unique role in communicating with foreign governments. . . . But whether the realm is foreign or domestic, it is still the Legislative Branch, not the Executive Branch, that makes the law. . . .

. . . It is not for the President alone to determine the whole content of the Nation's foreign policy.

Do you think Justice Sutherland would agree with this interpretation of his opinion?

Either way, and despite its repudiation of some of the language in *Curtiss-Wright,* we should keep in mind that the Court did rule for the president in *Zivotofsky.* Which brings us to the continuing vitality of *Curtiss-Wright:* as a general rule, the Court has been sympathetic to the executive branch when deciding disputes over the president's foreign policy role. For example, the justices have been rather lenient in the handling of the president's power to make treaties. In **Goldwater v. Carter** (1979) Senator Barry Goldwater (R-Ariz.) challenged President Carter's authority to terminate a defense treaty with Taiwan without the consent of the Senate. The Court refused to confront the constitutional issues raised by Goldwater, dismissing the case without even scheduling oral arguments.

With justices citing both political question and justiciability reasons, the Court found President Carter's actions to be related to his foreign relations authority and therefore not reviewable by the Court.

The Court also has supported the growing tendency of presidents to enter into executive agreements with other nations. Unlike treaties, these arrangements do not require Senate ratification (although many are made pursuant to legislation enabling the president to enter into certain agreements, including those involving trade or foreign aid or pursuant to the treaties themselves), so presidents often use them when they want to avoid the time-consuming and very public ratification process. But executive agreements have their limitations: federal law requires that the president inform Congress whenever such agreements are made, and they can be nullified by acts of Congress. Moreover, unlike treaties, executive agreements are not binding on future presidents without their consent.

As early as 1937, in **United States v. Belmont**, the Court not only endorsed the use of executive agreements but also blurred the distinction between such arrangements and fully ratified treaties. The Court held that the international agreements entered into by the president as part of the recognition of the Soviet Union had the force of law within the United States. The same set of agreements later was held to have sufficient force to supersede state law, just as treaties do.[31] Because of the advantages of executive agreements and their approval by the Court, presidents have grown to favor such agreements over treaties. During its first century the United States entered into 275 treaties and 265 executive agreements, but from 1945 through 2008 the nation concluded 1,056 treaties and 16,735 executive agreements. President George W. Bush alone entered into 1,998 executive agreements, but only 136 treaties. The Obama administration followed suit, with only 11 treaties and 422 agreements.[32]

In other areas, too, the justices have allowed the president to take actions in pursuit of American foreign policy that would be highly suspect in domestic affairs. **Haig v. Agee** (1981) provides an illustration. Philip Agee was an American citizen living in what was then West Germany. From 1957 to 1968 he worked for the Central Intelligence Agency (CIA) and was involved in covert intelligence gathering in foreign countries. During this period he acquired a vast knowledge of CIA operations and of agents in the field. After he left government service, Agee called a press conference to declare a personal war against the CIA, saying he would do everything he could to expose CIA agents and drive them out of the countries where they worked. Agee pursued this goal by traveling to various countries, using his contacts to identify CIA agents, and then exposing them. He published two books that revealed secret information about the activities of the agency and made public the identities of undercover CIA operatives.

In reaction, President Carter, through his secretary of state, revoked Agee's passport, thereby making it impossible for him to travel abroad legally. Agee claimed that the executive branch did not have the authority to revoke his passport. The Supreme Court, however, interpreted the powers of the president quite broadly and by a 7–2 vote rejected Agee's objections. The Court essentially agreed that the executive branch could use its power to issue passports—or not issue them—as a way of protecting the nation's foreign policy efforts.

The creation of foreign policy is just one aspect of the dealings of the United States with other countries. Another involves the power to wage war—a power that has taken on particular relevance since the terrorist attacks of September 11, 2001. We explore this issue in the next chapter, for, as our discussion there makes clear, it presents something of an invitation to struggle between the president and Congress and, occasionally, between the Court and the elected branches.

ANNOTATED READINGS

General treatments of Article II, executive authority, and theories of presidential power include Joseph Bessette and Jeffrey Tulis, eds., *The Constitutional Presidency* (Baltimore: Johns Hopkins University Press, 2009); Phillip J. Cooper, *By Order of the President: The Use and Abuse of Executive Direct Action* (Lawrence: University Press of Kansas, 2002); Edward S. Corwin, *The President: Office and Powers,* 5th rev. ed. (New York: New York University Press, 1984); Matthew J. Dickinson, *Bitter Harvest: FDR,*

---

31. *United States v. Pink* (1942). See also *Dames & Moore v. Regan* (1981).

32. Data for Obama are through 2010. Richard G. Niemi and Harold W. Stanley, *Vital Statistics on American Politics 2015–2016* (Thousand Oaks, CA: CQ Press, 2015), Table 9–1.

Presidential Power, and the Growth of the Presidential Branch (New York: Cambridge University Press, 1999); Eric A. Posner and Adrian Vermeule, *The Executive Unbound: After the Madisonian Republic* (New York: Oxford University Press, 2011); Robert Y. Shapiro, Martha Joynt Kumar, and Lawrence R. Jacobs, eds., *Presidential Power: Forging the Presidency for the Twenty-first Century* (New York: Columbia University Press, 2000).

Books covering more-specific domestic or foreign powers and related issues are Scott E. Graves and Robert M. Howard, *Justice Takes a Recess* (Plymouth, UK: Lexington Books, 2009); David Gray Adler and Larry N. George, eds., *The Constitution and the Conduct of American Foreign Policy* (Lawrence: University Press of Kansas, 1996); Raoul Berger, *Executive Privilege: A Constitutional Myth* (Cambridge, MA: Harvard University Press, 1974); Louis Fisher, *Presidential War Power,* 2nd ed. (Lawrence: University Press of Kansas, 2004); Michael J. Gerhardt, *The Federal Impeachment Process: A Constitutional and Historical Analysis* (Chicago: University of Chicago Press, 2000); Howard Gillman, *The Votes That Counted: How the Court Decided the 2000 Presidential Election* (Chicago: University of Chicago Press, 2001); Katy J.

Harriger, *Independent Justice: The Federal Special Prosecutor in American Politics* (Lawrence: University Press of Kansas, 1992); Louis Henkin, *Foreign Affairs and the Constitution* (Mineola, NY: Foundation Press, 1972); Scott M. Matheson, Bush v. Gore: *Exposing the Hidden Crisis in American Democracy* (Lawrence: University Press of Kansas, 2008); G. Calvin McKenzie, *The Politics of Presidential Appointments* (New York: Free Press, 1981); Merrill McLoughlin, ed., *The Impeachment and Trial of President Clinton* (New York: Random House, 1999); Richard A. Posner, *An Affair of State: The Investigation, Impeachment, and Trial of President Clinton* (Cambridge, MA: Harvard University Press, 1999); William H. Rehnquist, *Grand Inquests: The Historic Impeachments of Justice Samuel Chase and President Andrew Johnson* (New York: William Morrow, 1999); Mark J. Rozell and Clyde Wilcox, *The Clinton Scandal and the Future of American Government* (Washington, D.C.: Georgetown University Press, 2000); Mitchel A. Sollenberger, *The President Shall Nominate: How Congress Trumps Executive Power* (Lawrence: University Press of Kansas, 2008); Donald Grier Stephenson Jr., *Campaigns and the Court: The U.S. Supreme Court in Presidential Elections* (New York: Columbia University Press, 1999).

5 The Separation of Powers System in Action

IN THE PRECEDING three chapters we learned that the Constitution endows each branch of government with significant, but not unfettered, powers. But just how strong are the lines that divide the institutions? Consider these two examples:

- As part of its legislative responsibility, Congress must set penalties for crimes. And yet the legislature created a special sentencing commission, with members appointed by the president, to establish sentencing guidelines for federal offenses. May Congress turn over its legislative power to this commission?
- In the Immigration and Nationality Act, Congress gave the U.S. attorney general the power to make recommendations regarding the fate of aliens but kept for itself the power to veto decisions by the attorney general. May Congress take for itself an executive power—the power of the veto?

As we shall see, the answer to the first is yes and to the second is no. Why? We take up this question in the first part of the chapter, in which we consider two aspects of the separation of powers problem: when Congress gives other branches legislative power, and when it takes executive power for itself. These cases tend to implicate domestic affairs.

In the second part of the chapter, we turn to external affairs: international relations, war, and other national emergencies. As we noted at the end of chapter 4, the

power to wage war presents an "invitation to struggle" between the president and Congress because the Constitution provides each branch with significant and potentially overlapping powers. The president may be the "Commander in Chief of the Army and Navy," but Article I enables Congress to

- Provide for the common defense and general welfare of the country;
- Declare war;
- Raise and support armies;
- Provide and maintain a navy;
- Make rules to govern and regulate the land and naval forces;
- Provide for calling up the militia to carry out the laws of the nation, suppress insurrections, and repel invasions; and
- Provide for organizing, arming, and disciplining the militia.

It is no wonder, then, that disputes have arisen between the president and Congress—and that the Court has occasionally been asked to resolve the controversies. During the war on terrorism, the federal judiciary even became part of the controversy as the political branches took steps to remove it from resolving certain kinds of disputes. As you read the cases and narrative about external affairs, consider the justices' responses: Have they tended to side with one branch over another? What bearing have they had on presidential efforts to combat the threat of terrorism? How far can the president go without obtaining approval from the legislature? And what steps can the president take to circumvent the courts altogether?

DEBATES OVER THE SEPARATION OF POWERS SYSTEM

In our opening essay to Part II we pointed out two contemporary strands of thinking about the separation of powers system: formalism and functionalism. Both emphasize that all three branches of government contribute to constitutional interpretation. As you read the cases and narrative to come, you will see these approaches in action. When Congress gave itself the power to veto decisions by the attorney general, the majority of its members must have believed they were acting in accord with the Constitution. If they did not, they would be in violation of their oath of office to "support the Constitution of the United States." We could say the same of the president, who swears (or affirms) to "preserve, protect and defend the Constitution of the United States." When taking action, even action without congressional approval and even action later struck down by the Court, the president must believe that action is compatible with the Constitution. Whether Congress and the president do a good job as constitutional interpreters is a matter of some debate and one you will have many opportunities to consider in this chapter.

While you are reading the cases to come, also keep in mind the debate between formal and functional approaches to resolving separation of powers questions. Formalism emphasizes the idea that the Constitution creates clear boundaries between and among the branches of government by bestowing on each a primary power. Formalists believe that federal judges should not allow deviations from this plan unless the text of the Constitution permits them. Functionalism, in contrast, rejects strict divisions among the branches and emphasizes instead a more fluid system—one of shared rather than separated powers. Functionalists argue that all the Constitution prevents are extreme departures from the separation of powers, which could result in the accumulation of too much power in one branch of government. As long as actions by Congress or the president do not result in the tyranny of one

branch over the others, the federal courts should be flexible and enable—not discourage—experimentation.

We already have seen an example of this debate in action. In *Clinton v. City of New York* the Court struck down the line-item veto. The majority found that the line-item veto gave the president too much policy-making authority—authority that belongs to Congress. One of the dissenters, Justice Stephen Breyer, took a more functional approach when he argued that the veto did not infringe on the liberty of Americans by impermissibly concentrating too much power in the president. To the contrary—he believed that the veto represented "an experiment" that may "help representative government to work better."

In what follows, we present many more examples. As you read them, consider the various strengths and weaknesses of the two sides of the debate. Is formalism not only unrealistic but also undesirable because it may limit government's ability to act creatively in response to emerging problems? As for functionalism, we might raise questions about the Court's ability to judge whether a particular law will ultimately undermine the framers' plan to prevent any one branch from gaining too much power.

DOMESTIC POWERS

Our consideration of these and other matters begins with two actions that cross institutional boundaries in ways the framers might not have anticipated: when Congress delegates some of its authority to another branch of government, and when Congress tries to assert powers assigned to the executive and judicial branches.

Although the sections on these acts deal with different substantive material, you may note some commonalities in Court rulings. Pay careful attention to how the Court delineates constitutional interactions from the unconstitutional. Has it acted in a consistent manner? Have the justices grounded their opinions in constitutional language or philosophy, or have other factors—extralegal factors—had greater impact?

Delegation of Powers

Almost all discussions of the ability of Congress to delegate its lawmaking power begin with an old Latin maxim, *delegata potestas non potest delegari*, which means "a power once delegated cannot be redelegated." We could apply this statement to Congress in the following way: because the Constitution delegates to that institution all legislative powers—lawmaking authority—it cannot give such power to another body or person.

Why not? To answer that question, consider this example: Suppose that after you take the final examination in this course your instructor delegates the responsibility of grading the test papers to a teaching assistant (TA). Being busy with other work, the TA then delegates that task to a roommate who has never taken a constitutional law course. You would legitimately worry about the roommate's ability to grade your exam. But you might also wonder about accountability: Who would be responsible—the professor, the TA, or the roommate—if your final grade did not fairly reflect your work?[1] The same argument could be applied to the delegation of lawmaking power to a president in charge of executing laws who in turn hands authority over to a bureaucrat.

No political institution has, however, fully accepted the language of the Latin maxim—what is now commonly called the nondelegation doctrine. From the First Congress on, the legislature has delegated its power to other branches or even to nongovernmental entities. But why would Congress want to give away some of its power? One reason is that, like the professor in the example, Congress is often busy with other matters and must delegate some authority if it is to fulfill all of its responsibilities. Another is that Congress might be able to formulate general policies but lacks the expertise to fill in the details. As the job of governance becomes more technical and complex, this reason gains validity. *United States v. Curtiss-Wright Export Corp.* provides yet another reason: the need for flexibility. In *Curtiss-Wright,* Congress had given the president authority to issue an arms embargo if such an action would help to bring peace to warring South American nations. Congress recognized that once it enacts legislation it may have difficulty amending it, but that the problems covered by the legislation, such as in the *Curtiss-Wright* example, may require sustained attention. Finally, Congress might want to delegate for political reasons. Sotirios A. Barber noted, "A Congress of buck passers is one of the results of the electorate's tendency to reward politicians who are

responsive to its immediate wants, not [Congress's] considered constitutional duties."[2] In other words, to avoid dealing with certain "hot potato" issues, Congress might hand them off to others. The delegation of powers issue is tricky: although, in theory, Congress should not dole out its lawmaking authority, as a matter of practical and reasonable politics, it does so.

Not surprisingly, the Supreme Court has found itself enmeshed in this debate. As we saw in chapter 3's discussion of *Curtiss-Wright,* it has been asked to determine whether particular delegations of power are appropriate, constitutionally speaking, and, as in that case, the Court generally has upheld such delegations, even if they involve domestic issues. ***Wayman v. Southard*** (1825) was the Court's first major ruling on the delegation of domestic powers. This dispute, unlike most in this area, involved a congressional grant of lawmaking authority to the courts, not to the executive. The case asked the justices to determine whether a section of the 1789 Judiciary Act, which gave the courts power to "make and establish all necessary laws" for the conduct of judicial business, constituted a violation of the separation of powers doctrine and, as such, an unconstitutional delegation of power.

Writing for the Court in *Wayman,* Chief Justice John Marshall responded pragmatically. He sought to balance the letter of the Constitution with the practical concerns facing Congress when he formulated the following standard: the legislature must itself "entirely" regulate "important subjects," but for "those of less interest" it can enact a general provision and authorize "those who are to act under such general provisions to fill up the details." Put simply, Marshall established a different set of rules for the delegation of power, with the permissibility of delegation varying by the importance of the subject under regulation. Applying this standard to the delegation of power contained in the 1789 Judiciary Act, he found that Congress could grant courts authority to promulgate their own rules.

Wayman—in theory—created an important precedent for subsequent Courts to follow. We say "in theory" because for the next century or so the Supreme Court did not strike down a congressional delegation of power, but neither did it quite follow Marshall's standard. Rather, it took an even broader approach to this kind of case. In ***Hampton & Co. v. United States*** (1928)

---

1. Craig R. Ducat, *Constitutional Interpretation,* 8th ed. (Belmont, CA: Wadsworth/Thomson, 2004), 129.

2. Sotirios A. Barber, *On What the Constitution Means* (Baltimore: Johns Hopkins University Press, 1984), 177.

it let stand a grant of authority to the president that some suggest failed Marshall's standard. The Court examined the Fordney-McCumber Act of 1922, in which Congress established a tariff commission within the executive branch and permitted the president to increase or decrease tariffs on imported goods by as much as 50 percent. Because Congress gave the president (and the commission) virtually unlimited discretion to adjust rates, an import company challenged the act as a violation of the separation of powers doctrine. The company argued that Congress had provided the president with what was essentially lawmaking power. Writing for a unanimous Court, Chief Justice William Howard Taft—a former president of the United States—disagreed: "In determining what [Congress] may do in seeking assistance from another branch, the extent and character of that assistance must be fixed according to common sense and the inherent necessities of the governmental coordination." So long as Congress "shall lay down by legislative act an intelligible principle to which the person or body authorized to [exercise the delegated authority] is directed to conform," Taft wrote, "such legislative action is not a forbidden delegation of legislative power."

For nearly a decade the Court seemed quite willing to accept the so-called intelligible principle approach to congressional delegations. But in 1935 the Court dealt Congress and the president harsh blows when it struck down provisions of the National Industrial Recovery Act (NIRA) of 1933 as excessive delegations of power. Box 5-1 describes the circumstances surrounding these cases—***Panama Refining Company v. Ryan*** and *A. L. A. Schechter Poultry Corp. v. United States*—and the Court's rulings in them. *(For full details, see chapter 7.)* The NIRA was a major piece of the New Deal legislation designed to pull the nation out of the Great Depression. In *Panama* Congress had allowed the president to prohibit the shipment in interstate commerce of oil produced in excess of state quotas; in *Schechter* Congress had authorized the president to approve fair competition codes and standards if representatives of a particular industry recommended he do so. In both instances, the Court struck down the delegations of power as unconstitutional.

Because Congress passed the NIRA under its power to regulate interstate commerce, we take up the Court's reasons for these decisions from a somewhat different angle in chapter 7. For now, let us first consider these

cases from a delegation-of-powers perspective: Did earlier precedent, particularly *Wayman* and *Hampton,* necessarily lead to these outcomes? The Court undoubtedly thought so: by wide margins, it justified its opinions in *Panama* and *Schechter* as firmly grounded in past decisions. Eight of the nine justices agreed with the majority opinion in *Panama,* and the one dissenting justice, Benjamin Cardozo, joined the others in *Schechter,* noting that this law constituted "delegation running riot."

Was the Court on firm legal ground? One way to think about this question is to compare the Court's rulings here with those in *Wayman* and *Hampton.* Were the NIRA delegations of power more onerous than those in *Hampton?* Or did they not meet Marshall's standard in *Wayman?* Another is to consider the briefs and arguments in the 1935 cases. Before the Supreme Court decided *Panama,* a federal court of appeals had upheld the law as a constitutional use of congressional commerce powers and, in so doing, gave "very casual treatment to the delegation issue," noting simply that it met previously set standards. When the oil company appealed the decision, U.S. attorneys responded with a 195-page brief filed with the Supreme Court. Apparently, "lulled . . . into a false sense of security" by the lower court ruling and believing that "precedent [was] uniformly on their side," the United States devoted only three of those 195 pages to the delegation of powers issue. Indeed, the matter probably would not have been seriously considered had it not been for oral arguments. There, the lawyers for the oil company hammered away at both issues—the delegation of powers and the commerce clause—arguing that Congress had "laid down no rule or criterion to guide or limit the President in the orders that he may promulgate."[3]

Based on this sort of analysis, many scholars suggest that the justices were merely using the delegation of powers as an excuse to strike down New Deal legislation that they fundamentally and ideologically opposed.[4] Whether this is true we leave for you to

---

3. Peter H. Irons, *The New Deal Lawyers* (Princeton, NJ: Princeton University Press, 1982), 69, 70, 71, 93.

4. Perhaps now you can see why many thought Curtiss-Wright would win its case. It brought its challenge to a congressional delegation of power to the president in 1936, just one year after *Panama Refining Co.* and *Schechter Poultry.* Recall from chapter 3, though, that the Court upheld the delegation in *Curtiss-Wright* by differentiating between foreign and domestic affairs.

BOX 5-1 COURT'S DECISIONS IN *PANAMA* AND *SCHECHTER POULTRY*

	PANAMA REFINING CO. V. RYAN (JANUARY 7, 1935)	SCHECHTER POULTRY V. UNITED STATES (MAY 27, 1935)
Problem	The oil industry, as a result of overproduction to meet the demand for oil in the 1920s, began to ship "hot oil" (that which had been produced in excess of state quotas) across state lines as a way of dealing with falling prices.	The Great Depression indicated the need for greater regulation of various industries, particularly prohibitions on certain kinds of "unfair" competition.
Congressional solution	A provision of the NIRA permitted the president to prohibit the shipment of hot oil in interstate commerce.	The NIRA allowed the president, at the request of industrial trade associations, to approve codes for the entire industry. The codes would regulate trade practices, wages, hours, and other business activities within the industry. Trade associations and other industry groups had responsibility for drafting the codes, which were submitted to the president for approval. In the absence of recommendations from the private sector, the president was authorized to draft the codes himself. Once approved by the president, the codes had the force of law.
President's action	Issued an order prohibiting the shipment of oil produced in excess of state-established quotas.	Approved industry codes.
Specific dispute	Small oil companies challenged the quota system, alleging that it hurt independent, small producers.	The Schechter brothers challenged the Live Poultry Code, which established industry standards and set work hours.
Delegation of powers question	Did challenged sections of the NIRA constitute overly broad (and therefore unconstitutional) congressional delegations of power to the president?	
Majority opinion	Struck down the challenged section of the NIRA: "[I]n every case in which the question has been raised, the Court has recognized that there are limits of delegation which there is no constitutional authority to transcend. We think [the challenged section of the NIRA] goes beyond those limits. As to the transportation of oil production in excess of state permission, the Congress has declared no policy, has established no standard, has laid down no rule."	Struck down parts of the NIRA: "In view of the scope of [the] broad declaration and of the nature of the restrictions that are imposed, the discretion of the President in approving or prescribing codes, and thus enacting laws for the government of trade and industry throughout the country, is virtually unfettered. We think that the code-making authority . . . is an unconstitutional delegation of legislative power."
Cardozo's opinion[a]	In dissent: "My point of difference with the majority is narrow. I concede that to uphold the delegation there is need to discover in the terms of the act a standard reasonably clear whereby discretion must be governed. I deny that such a standard is lacking in respect of the prohibitions permitted by this section when the act . . . is considered as a whole."	Concurring: This is "delegation running riot."

a. We highlight Justice Cardozo's opinions in these cases because he was the only justice to write separately. (Justice Stone joined his concurrence in *Schechter*.)

...egated by Congress to Select Agencies

EXAMPLES OF SCOPE OF POWER

• Monitors the manufacture, import, transport, storage, and sale of $1 trillion worth of food, drugs, and cosmetics annually.
• Regulates the manufacture and distribution of food and drugs given to farm animals and pets.
• Adjudicates charges of unfair labor practices on the part of employers or unions.
• Enforces collective bargaining agreements.
• Regulates the transmission of gas, electricity, and oil in interstate commerce.
• Licenses and inspects private, municipal, and state hydroelectric projects.

Federal Energy
Regulatory Commission

decide. More important for now is that the rulings in *Panama* and *Schechter* represent anomalies. For reasons we offer later, by 1937 the Court had begun to uphold New Deal legislation, and by the end of the decade it was allowing for all sorts of delegations of power by Congress to a diverse range of executive agencies, some of which are listed in table 5-1.

What can we conclude about congressional delegations of power? Some analysts suggest that the Court's rulings in 1935 forced Congress to be more specific in the guidelines it sets out. Is that accurate? As noted in table 5-1, many executive agencies wield power that is as far-reaching as what the Court struck in the mid-1930s, but since 1936 the justices have not overturned a federal law explicitly on excessive delegation grounds. True, a few of the most suspect laws were never tested in the Court, but many observers have concluded that Congress can pretty much delegate as it sees fit.

An interesting example is *Mistretta v. United States* (1989), in which the Court scrutinized an act of Congress designed to minimize judicial discretion in sentencing. The Court's opinion takes us back to **Wayman v. Southard** and **Hampton & Co. v. United States.**

Mistretta v. United States

488 U.S. 361 (1989)
http://laws.findlaw.com/us/488/361.html
Oral arguments are available at https://www.oyez.org.
Vote: 8 (Blackmun, Brennan,[5] Kennedy, Marshall, O'Connor, Rehnquist,
    Stevens, White)
    1 (Scalia)

OPINION OF THE COURT: Blackmun
DISSENTING OPINION: Scalia

---

5. Brennan joined the majority in all but footnote 11 of its opinion, which dealt with the death penalty.

FACTS:

Concerned about wide disparities in sentences imposed by federal court judges, Congress enacted the Sentencing Reform Act of 1984, which created the U.S. Sentencing Commission as "an independent commission in the judicial branch of government." The commission was empowered to create sentencing guidelines for all federal offenses, to which lower court judges generally would be bound. It was to have seven members, nominated by the president and confirmed by the Senate. Three of its members, at minimum, were to be federal court judges, and no more than four members could be of the same political party.

The commission fulfilled its charge, promulgating sentencing guidelines for federal offenses, but the federal courts were not in agreement over the guidelines' constitutionality. More than 150 lower court judges found them constitutionally defective, while about 100 upheld them.

In *Mistretta v. United States* the lower federal court judge had upheld the plan, but the arguments of John Mistretta, who had been convicted of three counts of selling cocaine, were similar to those proffered by judges who did not approve of the guidelines. Of particular relevance here was Mistretta's charge that the act violated delegation of powers principles by giving the commission "excessive legislative authority."

ARGUMENTS:

For the petitioner, John M. Mistretta:

• The Sentencing Commission violates the principle of separation of powers because it includes Article III judges. The Constitution limits judges to deciding only actual cases or controversies. The unelected judges on the commission are making substantive law with political policy implications, which is a legislative function. Their involvement also weakens confidence in their impartiality.

- The president has too much control over the commission members through his appointment and removal powers, which threatens the independence of the judicial branch.

- The delegation of power is excessive because Congress did not provide an adequate intelligible principle for the commission to follow. Although Congress placed outer limits on the commission's task, the legislature gave commission members control of vast policy areas without directions and left fundamental policy decisions and substantive moral judgments to them.

For the respondent, United States:

- The text of the Constitution does not prohibit judges from serving in executive positions, and historically the practice has been accepted. Examination of the sentencing process is a neutral function, and having judges recuse themselves when necessary alleviates concerns about judicial impartiality.

- The president's removal power over the commission does not implicate the independence of the judiciary because the president is only authorized to remove the judges from their positions on the commission and cannot reach them as Article III judges.

- Congress provided detailed instructions to the commission, including the goals of punishment, structure of the sentencing guidelines, and general appropriateness and length of terms of imprisonment for various offenses and offenders. This is enough to be an intelligible principle for the commission.

JUSTICE BLACKMUN DELIVERED THE OPINION OF THE COURT.

Petitioner argues that in delegating the power to promulgate sentencing guidelines for every federal criminal offense to an independent Sentencing Commission, Congress has granted the Commission excessive legislative discretion in violation of the constitutionally based nondelegation doctrine. We do not agree.

The nondelegation doctrine is rooted in the principle of separation of powers that underlies our tripartite system of government. The Constitution provides that "[a]ll legislative Powers herein granted shall be vested in a Congress of the United States," and we long have insisted that "the integrity and maintenance of the system of government ordained by the Constitution" mandate that Congress generally cannot delegate its legislative power to another Branch. We also have recognized, however, that the separation-of-powers principle, and the nondelegation doctrine in particular, do not prevent Congress from obtaining the assistance of its coordinate Branches. In a passage now enshrined in our jurisprudence, Chief Justice Taft, writing for the Court, explained our approach to such cooperative ventures: "In determining what [Congress] may do in seeking assistance from another branch, the extent and character of that assistance must be fixed according to common sense and the inherent necessities of the governmental coordination." *J. W. Hampton, Jr., & Co. v. United States* (1928). So long as Congress "shall lay down by legislative act an intelligible principle to which the person or body authorized to [exercise the delegated authority] is directed to conform, such legislative action is not a forbidden delegation of legislative power."

Applying this "intelligible principle" test to congressional delegations, our jurisprudence has been driven by a practical understanding that in our increasingly complex society, replete with ever changing and more technical problems, Congress simply cannot do its job absent an ability to delegate power under broad general directives. . . .

Until 1935, this Court never struck down a challenged statute on delegation grounds. . . . After invalidating in 1935 two statutes as excessive delegations, see *Schechter Poultry Corp. v. United States* and *Panama Refining Co. v. Ryan*, we have upheld, again without deviation, Congress' ability to delegate power under broad standards.

In light of our approval of . . . broad delegations, we harbor no doubt that Congress' delegation of authority to the Sentencing Commission is sufficiently specific and detailed to meet constitutional requirements. Congress charged the Commission with three goals: to "assure the meeting of the purposes of sentencing as set forth" in the Act; to "provide certainty and fairness in meeting the purposes of sentencing, avoiding unwarranted sentencing disparities among defendants with similar records . . . while maintaining sufficient flexibility to permit individualized sentences," where appropriate; and to "reflect to the extent practicable, advancement in knowledge of human behavior as it relates to the criminal justice process." Congress further specified four "purposes" of sentencing that the Commission must pursue in carrying out its mandate: "to reflect the seriousness of the offense, to promote respect for the law, and to provide just punishment for the offense"; "to afford adequate deterrence to criminal conduct"; "to protect the public from further crimes of the defendant"; and "to provide the defendant with needed . . . correctional treatment."

In addition, Congress prescribed the specific tool—the guidelines system—for the Commission to use in regulating sentencing. More particularly, Congress directed the Commission to develop a system of "sentencing ranges" applicable "for each category of offense involving each category of defendant." . . .

To guide the Commission in its formulation of offense categories, Congress directed it to consider seven factors: the grade of the offense; the aggravating and mitigating circumstances of the crime; the nature and degree of the harm caused by the crime; the community view of the gravity of the offense; the public concern generated by the crime; the deterrent effect that a particular sentence may have on others; and the current incidence of the offense. Congress set forth 11 factors for the Commission to consider in establishing categories of defendants. These include the offender's age, education, vocational skills, mental and emotional condition, physical condition (including drug dependence), previous employment record, family ties and responsibilities, community ties, role in the offense, criminal history, and degree of dependence upon crime for a livelihood. Congress also prohibited the Commission from considering the "race, sex, national origin, creed, and socio-economic status of offenders," and instructed that the guidelines should reflect the "general inappropriateness" of considering certain other factors, such as current unemployment, that might serve as proxies for forbidden factors.

In addition to these overarching constraints, Congress provided even more detailed guidance to the Commission about categories of offenses and offender characteristics. Congress directed that guidelines require a term of confinement at or near the statutory maximum for certain crimes of violence and for drug offenses, particularly when committed by recidivists. Congress further directed that the Commission assure a substantial term of imprisonment for an offense constituting a third felony conviction, for a career felon, for one convicted of a managerial role in a racketeering enterprise, for a crime of violence by an offender on release from a prior felony conviction, and for an offense involving a substantial quantity of narcotics. . . . In other words, although Congress granted the Commission substantial discretion in formulating guidelines, in actuality it legislated a full hierarchy of punishment—from near maximum imprisonment, to substantial imprisonment, to some imprisonment, to alternatives—and stipulated the most important offense and offender characteristics to place defendants within these categories.

We cannot dispute petitioner's contention that the Commission enjoys significant discretion in formulating guidelines. The Commission does have discretionary authority to determine the relative severity of federal crimes and to assess the relative weight of the offender characteristics that Congress listed for the Commission to consider. . . . The Commission also has significant discretion to determine which crimes have been punished too leniently, and which too severely. Congress has called upon the Commission to exercise its judgment about which types of crimes and which types of criminals are to be considered similar for the purposes of sentencing.

But our cases do not at all suggest that delegations of this type may not carry with them the need to exercise judgment on matters of policy. . . .

The Act sets forth more than merely an "intelligible principle" or minimal standards. One court has aptly put it: "The statute outlines the policies which prompted establishment of the Commission, explains what the Commission should do and how it should do it, and sets out specific directives to govern particular situations."

Developing proportionate penalties for hundreds of different crimes by a virtually limitless array of offenders is precisely the sort of intricate, labor-intensive task for which delegation to an expert body is especially appropriate. Although Congress has delegated significant discretion to the Commission to draw judgments from its analysis of existing sentencing practice and alternative sentencing models, "Congress is not confined to that method of executing its policy which involves the least possible delegation of discretion to administrative officers." We have no doubt that in the hands of the Commission "the criteria which Congress has supplied are wholly adequate for carrying out the general policy and purpose" of the Act.

Affirmed.

JUSTICE SCALIA, dissenting.

While the products of the Sentencing Commission's labors have been given the modest name "Guidelines," they have the force and effect of laws, prescribing the sentences criminal defendants are to receive. A judge who disregards them will be reversed. I dissent from today's decision because I can find no place within our constitutional system for an agency created by Congress to exercise no governmental power other than the making of laws. . . .

The focus of controversy, in the long line of our so-called excessive delegation cases, has been whether the degree of generality contained in the authorization for exercise of executive or judicial powers in a particular field is so unacceptably high as to amount to a delegation of legislative powers. I say "so-called excessive delegation" because although that convenient terminology is often used, what is really at issue is whether there has been any delegation of legislative power, which occurs (rarely) when Congress authorizes the exercise of executive or judicial power without adequate standards. Strictly speaking, there is no acceptable delegation of legislative power. As John Locke put it almost 300 years ago, "[t]he power of the legislative being derived from the people by a positive voluntary grant and institution, can be no other, than what the positive grant conveyed, which being only to make laws, and not to make legislators, the legislative can have no power to transfer their authority of making laws, and place it in other hands." Or as we have less epigrammatically said: "That Congress cannot delegate legislative power to the President is a principle universally recognized as vital to the integrity and maintenance of the system of government ordained by the Constitution." In the present case, however, a pure delegation of legislative power is precisely what we have before us. It is irrelevant whether the standards are adequate, because they are not standards related to the exercise of executive or judicial powers; they are, plainly and simply, standards for further legislation.

The lawmaking function of the Sentencing Commission is completely divorced from any responsibility for execution of the law or adjudication of private rights under the law. It is divorced from responsibility for execution of the law not only because the Commission is not said to be "located in the Executive Branch" . . . but, more importantly, because the Commission neither exercises any executive power on its own, nor is subject to the control of the President who does. The only functions it performs, apart from prescribing the law, conducting the investigations useful and necessary for prescribing the law, and clarifying the intended application of the law that it prescribes are data collection and intragovernmental advice giving and education. These latter activities—similar to functions performed by congressional agencies and even congressional staff—neither determine nor affect private rights, and do not constitute an exercise of governmental power. See *Humphrey's Executor v. United States* [1935].

And the Commission's lawmaking is completely divorced from the exercise of judicial powers since, not being a court, it has no judicial powers itself, nor is it subject to the control of any other body with judicial powers. The power to make law at issue here, in other words, is not ancillary but quite naked. The situation is no different in principle from what would exist if Congress gave the same power of writing sentencing laws to a congressional agency such as the General Accounting Office, or to members of its staff.

The delegation of lawmaking authority to the Commission is, in short, unsupported by any legitimating theory to explain why it is not a delegation of legislative power. To disregard structural legitimacy is wrong in itself—but since structure has purpose, the disregard also has adverse practical consequences. In this case . . . the consequence is to facilitate and encourage judicially uncontrollable delegation. . . .

By reason of today's decision, I anticipate that Congress will find delegation of its lawmaking powers much more attractive in the future. If rulemaking can be entirely unrelated to the exercise of judicial or executive powers, I foresee all manner of "expert" bodies, insulated from the political process, to which Congress will delegate various portions of its lawmaking responsibility. How tempting to create an expert Medical Commission (mostly M.D.'s, with perhaps a few Ph.D.'s in moral philosophy) to dispose of such thorny, "no-win" political issues as the withholding of life-support systems in federally funded hospitals, or the use of fetal tissue for research. This is an undemocratic precedent that we set—not because of the scope of the delegated power, but because its recipient is not one of the three Branches of Government. The only governmental power the Commission possesses is the power to make law; and it is not the Congress.

Mistretta provides a nice example of the debate over functionalism versus formalism in separation of powers cases, with Justice Harry Blackmun's majority opinion favoring the former, and Justice Antonin Scalia's dissent, the latter. Blackmun acknowledges that Congress has delegated "significant" lawmaking power, but he is willing to allow the delegation, in part because the task at hand calls for a high degree of expertise. As Blackmun writes, "Developing proportionate penalties for hundreds of different crimes by a virtually limitless array of offenders is precisely the sort of intricate, labor-intensive task for which delegation to an expert body is especially appropriate." Scalia expresses deep misgivings about the extent and nature of the delegation here—lawmaking authority given to a commission located in the judicial branch—and where it may lead in the future. What is to prevent Congress from delegating most, if not all, of its lawmaking authority to an unaccountable commission, he wonders.

Mistretta is also interesting because it indicates that contemporary justices are no more likely to disallow delegations than their post–New Deal predecessors were.[6] It is consistent with a long line of decisions in which the Court has approved congressional delegation of power to the president or other executive officers.

But "no more likely" does not mean "totally unlikely." Recall that in *Clinton v. City of New York* (1998) the Court struck down the line-item veto as a violation of the presentment clause. Some of the briefs filed against the veto also challenged it as an unconstitutional delegation of power to the president, an argument the lower court found persuasive. As New York City's bar association wrote in an amicus curiae brief, the veto "rearranges the very structure of our government, taking significant responsibilities from Congress and transferring them to the Executive. The allocation of power between these branches is laid out in detail in the Constitution, and Congress cannot change that structure by legislative fiat." Perhaps not wishing to upset its long-standing doctrine on delegation of powers, the majority found it "unnecessary" to consider this claim. In a concurring opinion, however, Justice Kennedy seemed sympathetic:

That a congressional cession of power is voluntary does not make it innocuous. The Constitution is a compact enduring for more than our time, and one Congress cannot yield up its own powers, much less those of other Congresses to follow. Abdication of responsibility is not part of the constitutional design.

Whether Kennedy was simply responding to arguments made in this case or advocating a return to stricter enforcement of the nondelegation doctrine we cannot say. What seems beyond speculation is that this

issue will not vanish altogether in light of congressional incentives to delegate some lawmaking power to the executive.

Congress and the Exercise of Executive and Judicial Powers

The cases we discussed in the last section share a common thread: they involve cooperative relations between Congress and another branch of government, usually the executive. Congress was delegating some of its lawmaking authority—be it the establishment of tariff rates or the prohibition of the shipment of "hot oil"—to an executive desiring or perhaps even requesting such authority. But Congress is not always so eager to give away its powers; indeed, on many occasions and through different devices, it has sought to exercise authority over both the judicial and executive branches.

In chapters 2 and 3 we discussed a congressional attempt to take on judicial powers with passage of the Religious Freedom Restoration Act of 1993 (RFRA), the law at issue in *City of Boerne v. Flores* (1997). Aimed at undercutting the Court's 1990 decision in *Employment Division v. Smith*, RFRA directed the Court to use a particular standard of law to adjudicate First Amendment free exercise claims *(see chapters 2 and 3)*. But the justices would have none of it. Not only did the majority overturn RFRA, but it also rebuked the "political" branches for attempting to usurp judicial power:

Our national experience teaches that the Constitution is preserved best when each part of the government respects both the Constitution and the proper actions and determinations of the other branches. When the Court has interpreted the Constitution, it has acted within the province of the Judicial Branch, which embraces the duty to say what the law is. *Marbury v. Madison.* When the political branches of the Government act against the background of a judicial interpretation of the Constitution already issued, it must be understood that in later cases and controversies the Court will treat its precedents with the respect due them under settled principles, including stare decisis, and contrary expectations must be disappointed.

Have the justices extended such protection to the executive branch? To address this question, let us consider a device Congress developed to keep tabs on the executive: the so-called legislative veto. This kind of veto seems to flip the mandated lawmaking process.

---

6. For another contemporary example, see **Loving v. United States** (1996), in which the Court again noted, "Though in 1935 we struck down two delegations for lack of an intelligible principle, *A. L. A. Schechter Poultry Corp. v. United States* (1935), and *Panama Refining Co. v. Ryan* (1935), we have since upheld, without exception, delegations under standards phrased in sweeping terms."

Rather than following Article I procedures, meaning that both houses of Congress pass bills (bicameralism) and the president either signs or vetoes them (present-ment), under this practice the executive branch makes policies that Congress can veto by a vote of both houses, one house, or even a committee. It should come as no surprise that the legislative veto has been a source of contention between presidents and Congresses, with the former suggesting that it violates constitutional principles and the latter arguing that it represents a way to check all the lawmaking power Congress has delegated to the executive branch.

When it was first developed, the legislative veto was not all that contentious; to the contrary, it was part of a quid pro quo between Congress and President Herbert Hoover, who wanted "authority to reorganize the exec-utive branch without having to submit a bill to Congress." The legislature agreed to go along, but only if either the Senate or the House could turn down a reorganization plan. When Congress passed the 1933 legislative appropriations bill with that condition attached to it, the legislative veto was born.

Although Hoover had agreed to the provision, he was less than pleased when Congress actually used it the following year to veto part of the reorganization plan. His attorney general, William D. Mitchell, decried the legislative veto as a violation of the separa-tion of powers doctrine. That sort of sparring over the legislative veto continued through the early 1980s, but the patterns of debate were somewhat contradictory and confusing. On one hand, until 1972 Congress used the device rather sparingly, attaching it to only fifty-one laws. Furthermore, it did not seem to be a matter that either the president or Congress took very seri-ously. Scholars have observed that presidents rejected only a handful of laws solely because they contained legislative vetoes and that in those few instances Congress almost always repassed the bill without the veto provision.

On the other hand, some of the laws with a legisla-tive veto have been quite important, including the War Powers Resolution of 1973, under which Congress may direct the president to remove U.S. armed forces engaged in foreign hostilities when there is no declara-tion of war. Moreover, some presidents have objected to the legislative veto. Dwight D. Eisenhower loathed it, claiming that it violated "fundamental constitu-tional principles." Complaints grew louder after the Nixon presidency, when Congress sought to reassert itself over the executive and enacted sixty-two statutes with legislative vetoes between 1972 and 1979. In fact, in 1976 the House of Representatives came close to approving a proposal that would have made all rules enacted by all agencies subject to a legislative veto.

This issue came to a head during the Carter admin-istration. Jimmy Carter, like Eisenhower, despised leg-islative vetoes. Suggesting that he did not consider them binding, he had the Justice Department join *Immigration and Naturalization Service v. Chadha* as a test. The result was the first U.S. Supreme Court ruling centering specifically on the constitutionality of the legislative veto. As you read the opinions below, note that Chief Justice Warren Burger, writing for the majority, and Justice Byron White, in dissent, adopt wholly distinct approaches to separation of powers problems. Burger suggests that this sort of veto may be practical, but it is not constitutional. Why not? And why does White believe that the Court had committed a grave error?

Immigration and Naturalization Service v. Chadha; the U.S. House of Representatives v. Immigration and Naturalization Service; the U.S. Senate v. Immigration and Naturalization Service

462 U.S. 919 (1983)
http://laws.findlaw.com/us/462/919.html
Oral arguments are available at https://www.oyez.org.
Vote: 7 (Blackmun, Brennan, Burger, Marshall, O'Connor, Powell, Stevens)
    2 (Rehnquist, White)

OPINION OF THE COURT: Burger
CONCURRING OPINION: Powell
DISSENTING OPINIONS: Rehnquist, White

FACTS:

Jagdish Rai Chadha, an East Indian born in Kenya and holder of a British passport, was admitted into the United States in 1966 on a six-year student visa. More than a year after his visa expired, in October 1973, the Immigration and Naturalization Service ordered Chadha to attend a hearing and show cause why he should not be deported. After two such hearings, an immigration judge in June 1974 ordered a suspension of Chadha's deporta-tion, which meant that Chadha could stay in the United States, because he was of "good moral character" and would "suffer extreme hardship" if deported.

Acting under a provision of the Immigration and Nationality Act, the U.S. attorney general recommended to Congress that Chadha be allowed to remain in the United States in accordance with the judge's opinion. The act states,

Upon application by any alien who is found by the Attorney General to meet the requirements of . . . this section the Attorney General may in his discretion suspend deportation of such alien. If the deportation of any alien is suspended . . . a complete and detailed statement of the facts and pertinent provisions of the law in the case shall be reported to the Congress with the reasons for such suspension. Such reports shall be submitted on the first day of each calendar month in which Congress is in session.

Congress, in turn, had the authority to veto—by a resolution passed in either house—the attorney general's decision. The act specifies,

[I]f during the session of the Congress at which a case is reported, or prior to the close of the session of the Congress next following the session at which a case is reported, either the Senate or the House of Representatives passes a resolution stating in substance that it does not favor the suspension of such deportation, the Attorney General shall thereupon deport such alien or authorize the alien's voluntary departure at his own expense under the order of deportation in the manner provided by law. If, within the time above specified, neither the Senate nor the House of Representatives shall pass such a resolution, the Attorney General shall cancel deportation proceedings.

For a while it appeared as if Chadha's suspension of deportation was secure, but at the last moment Congress asserted its veto power. Congress had until December 19, 1975, to take action, and on December 12 the chair of a House committee introduced a resolution opposing the "granting of permanent residence in the United States to [six] aliens," including Chadha. Four days later the House of Representatives passed the motion. No debate or recorded vote occurred; indeed, it was never really clear why the chamber took the action.

That vote set the stage for a major showdown between Congress and the executive branch. Chadha filed a suit, first with the immigration court that reopened Chadha's deportation proceedings to implement the House's order and then with a federal court of appeals, asking that they declare the legislative veto unconstitutional. The Carter administration joined him to argue likewise. The president agreed with

Terrence McCarthy Photography

Jagdish Chadha, shown here with his wife, Therese Lorentz, and their two daughters, successfully challenged the constitutionality of the legislative veto during his legal efforts to avoid deportation.

Chadha's basic position, and administration attorneys thought his suit provided a great test case because it aptly displayed the problems with the legislative veto: in this case, as apparently in others, there was no debate, no recorded vote, and no approval by the Senate. Given the importance of the dispute, the court of appeals asked both the House and the Senate to file amicus curiae briefs supporting the veto practice, but in 1980 it ruled against their position, finding that the device violated separation of powers principles.

By the time the case was first argued before the Supreme Court, in February 1982, the Carter administration was out and the Reagan administration was in. During his 1980 campaign, Ronald Reagan claimed to support the legislative veto, but once in office, he instructed the attorney general to go forward with the *Chadha* case. The Justice Department presented the Court with several reasons the legislative veto violated the Constitution:

The Constitution explicitly requires that all congressional actions constituting the exercise of legislative power receive the concurrence of both Houses and be presented to the President for his approval or disapproval.

[The veto] violated the constitutional principle of separation of powers because it authorizes one House of Congress to participate in the execution of a previously enacted law.

The House and Senate, which had become parties to the suit, responded with an argument emphasizing a shared-powers approach to the separation doctrine:

The Constitution provides separately for each of the three Branches, and describes each Branch as vested with the respective functions of legislating, executing, and judging. But the Constitution does not say that the three great functions shall at all times be kept separate and independent of each other, or that the three functions can never be blended or mixed or delegated as among the three Branches. The notion of total separation of the powers "central or essential" to the operation of the three great departments is an illogical and impractical formulation of the separation doctrine, not a constitutional command.

They also noted that the legislative veto was a "pragmatic" and necessary device reflecting the realities of modern government.

The Court apparently had some difficulty sorting through these claims. After the first round of oral arguments, on the last day of the term, it ordered new arguments, which were held on the first day of the following term. But it took the Court until June 23—almost the whole term—to issue its decision. One reason for the delay was the delicate nature of the problem confronting the justices; indeed, during their initial conference over the case, Lewis Powell recorded Burger as saying the veto "issue is highly sensitive politically. Wish we could avoid the issue." After the Court voted to render legislative vetoes unconstitutional, a worried Chief Justice Burger circulated six drafts of his opinion, knowing that it was going to get "microscopic—and not always sympathetic!—scrutiny from across the park [that is, in Congress]."

ARGUMENTS:

For the Immigration and Naturalization Service et al.:

- In Article I, Sections 1 and 7, the Constitution is emphatic that all laws must receive bicameral approval. The framers expressly provided for procedures in situations in which they intended a departure from the bicameral process, but the legislative veto is not one of those.
- A one-house veto violates the doctrine of separation of powers because it gives power to Congress to usurp the powers of the executive branch. The act allows one house to overrule the attorney general in the executive branch and gives Congress final say over an executive action.
- If the act were upheld, Congress could incorporate the legislative veto into all future legislation, destroying the line between legislative and executive powers.

For the U.S. House and the U.S. Senate:

- The act merely delegates certain limited quasi-legislative functions to the attorney general, while retaining legislative power for Congress by reserving the power to make final decisions. Instead of an infringement of executive power, it is a restrained exercise of the congressional power to cancel deportations.
- Congress is not encroaching on any executive or judicial branch powers that were specifically given to the courts or the president in the Constitution. Therefore, this case is distinguishable from precedents finding impermissible delegation because those cases dealt with powers textually committed to the executive or judicial branches.
- The Constitution does not require the three branches be completely sealed from each other. Instead, it supports a blending of functions. Modern separation doctrine should reflect political realities; it should be pragmatic and flexible.

◗ CHIEF JUSTICE BURGER DELIVERED THE OPINION OF THE COURT.

We begin, of course, with the presumption that the challenged statute is valid. Its wisdom is not the concern of the courts; if a challenged action does not violate the Constitution, it must be sustained. . . .

By the same token, the fact that a given law or procedure is efficient, convenient, and useful in facilitating functions of government, standing alone, will not save it if it is contrary to the Constitution. Convenience and efficiency are not the primary objectives—the hallmarks—of democratic government and our inquiry is sharpened rather than blunted by the fact that congressional veto provisions are appearing with increasing frequency in statutes which delegate authority to executive and independent agencies. . . .

Justice White undertakes to make a case for the proposition that the one-House veto is a useful "political invention," and we need not challenge that assertion. . . . But policy arguments supporting even useful "political inventions" are subject to the demands of the Constitution which defines powers and . . . sets out just how those powers are to be exercised.

Explicit and unambiguous provisions of the Constitution prescribe and define the respective functions of the Congress and of the Executive in the legislative process. . . .

. . . [T]he purposes underlying the Presentment Clauses, Art. I, §7, cls 2, 3, and the bicameral requirement of Art. I, §1, and §7, cl 2, guide our resolution of the important question present in these cases. . . .

The records of the Constitutional Convention reveal that the requirement that all legislation be presented to the President before becoming law was uniformly accepted by the Framers. Presentment to the President and the Presidential veto were considered so imperative that the draftsmen took special pains to assure that these requirements could not be circumvented. . . .

The decision to provide the President with a limited and qualified power to nullify proposed legislation by veto was based on the profound conviction of the Framers that the powers conferred on Congress were the powers to be most carefully circumscribed. It is beyond doubt that lawmaking was a power to be shared by both Houses and the President. . . .

The bicameral requirement of Art. I, §§1, 7, was of scarcely less concern to the Framers than was the Presidential veto and indeed the two concepts are interdependent. By providing that no law could take effect without the concurrence of the prescribed majority of the Members of both Houses, the Framers reemphasized their belief . . . that legislation should not be enacted unless it has been carefully and fully considered by the Nation's elected officials. . . .

We see therefore that the Framers were acutely conscious that the bicameral requirement and the Presentment Clauses would serve essential constitutional functions. The President's participation in the legislative process was to protect the Executive Branch from Congress and to protect the whole people from improvident laws. The division of the Congress into two distinctive bodies assures that the legislative power would be exercised only after opportunity for full study and debate in separate settings. The President's unilateral veto power, in turn, was limited by the power of two-thirds of both Houses of Congress to overrule a veto thereby precluding final arbitrary action of one person. It emerges clearly that the prescription for legislative action in Art. I, §§1, 7, represents the Framers' decision that the legislative power of the Federal Government be exercised in accord with a single, finely wrought and exhaustively considered, procedure. . . .

Examination of the action taken here by one House pursuant to §244(c)(2) reveals that it was essentially legislative in purpose and effect. In purporting to exercise power defined in Art. I, §8, cl 4, to "establish an uniform Rule of Naturalization," the House took action that had the purpose and effect of altering the legal rights, duties, and relations of persons, including the Attorney General, Executive Branch officials and Chadha, all outside the Legislative Branch. . . .

The legislative character of the one-House veto in these cases is confirmed by the character of the congressional action it supplants. Neither the House of Representatives nor the Senate contends that, absent the veto provision in §244(c)(2), either one of them, or both of them acting together, could effectively require the Attorney General to deport an alien once the Attorney General, in the exercise of legislatively delegated authority, had determined the alien should remain in the United States. Without the challenged provision in §244(c)(2), this could have been achieved, if at all, only by legislation requiring deportation. Similarly, a veto by one House of Congress . . . cannot be justified as an attempt at amending the standards set out in §244(c)(2), or as a repeal of §244 as applied to Chadha. Amendment and repeal of statutes, no less than enactment, must conform with Art. I.

The nature of the decision implemented by the one-House veto in these cases further manifests its legislative character. . . . Congress made a deliberate choice to delegate to the Executive Branch . . . the authority to allow deportable aliens to remain in this country in certain specified circumstances. Congress must abide by its delegation of authority until that delegation is legislatively altered or revoked. . . .

Since it is clear that the action by the House . . . was an exercise of legislative power, that action was subject to the standards prescribed in Art. I. . . . To accomplish what has been attempted by one House of Congress in this case requires action in conformity with the express procedures of the Constitution's prescription for legislative action: passage by a majority of both Houses and presentment to the President.

The veto authorized by §244(c)(2) doubtless has been in many respects a convenient shortcut; the "sharing" with the Executive by Congress of its authority over aliens in this manner is, on its face, an appealing compromise. In purely practical terms, it is obviously easier for action to be taken by one House without submission to the President; but it is crystal clear from the records of the Convention, contemporaneous writings and debates, that the Framers ranked other values higher than efficiency. . . .

The choices we discern as having been made in the Constitutional Convention impose burdens on governmental processes that often seem clumsy, inefficient, even unworkable, but those hard choices were consciously made by men who had lived under a form of government that permitted arbitrary governmental acts to go unchecked. There is no support in the Constitution or decisions of this Court for the proposition that the cumbersomeness and delays often encountered in complying with explicit constitutional standards may be avoided, either by the Congress or by the President. With all the obvious flaws of delay, untidiness, and potential for abuse, we have not yet found a better way to preserve freedom than by making the exercise of power subject to the carefully crafted restraints spelled out in the Constitution.

We hold that the congressional veto provision . . . is unconstitutional.

Affirmed.

JUSTICE WHITE, dissenting.

Today the Court not only invalidates §244(c)(2) of the Immigration and Nationality Act, but also sounds the death knell for nearly 200 other statutory provisions in which Congress has reserved a "legislative veto." For this reason, the Court's decision is of surpassing importance. And it is for this reason that the Court would have been well advised to decide the cases, if possible, on the narrower grounds of separation of powers, leaving for full consideration the constitutionality of other congressional review statutes operating on such varied matters as war powers and agency rulemaking, some of which concern the independent regulatory agencies.

The prominence of the legislative veto mechanism in our contemporary political system and its importance to Congress can hardly be overstated. It has become a central means by which Congress secures the accountability of executive and independent agencies. Without the legislative veto, Congress is faced with a Hobson's choice: either to refrain from delegating the necessary authority, leaving itself with a hopeless task of writing laws with the requisite specificity to cover endless special circumstances across the entire policy landscape, or in the alternative, to abdicate its lawmaking function to the Executive Branch and independent agencies. To choose the former leaves major national problems unresolved; to opt for the latter risks unaccountable policymaking by those not elected to fill that role. Accordingly, over the past five decades, the legislative veto has been placed in nearly 200 statutes. The device is known in every field of governmental concern: reorganization, budgets, foreign affairs, war powers, and regulation of trade, safety, energy, the environment, and the economy. . . .

I do not suggest that all legislative vetoes are necessarily consistent with separation-of-powers principles. A legislative check on an inherently executive function . . . poses an entirely different question. But the legislative veto device here—and in many other settings—is far from an instance of legislative tyranny over the Executive. It is a necessary check on the unavoidably expanding power of the agencies, both Executive and independent, as they engage in exercising authority delegated by Congress.

I regret that I am in disagreement with my colleagues on the fundamental questions that these cases present. But even more I regret the destructive scope of the Court's holding. It reflects a profoundly different conception of the Constitution than that held by the courts which sanctioned the modern administrative state. Today's decision strikes down in one fell swoop provisions in more laws enacted by Congress than the Court has cumulatively invalidated in its history. I fear it will now be more difficult to "insur[e] that the fundamental policy decisions in our society will be made not by an appointed official but by the body immediately responsible to the people," *Arizona v. California* (1963) (Harlan, J., dissenting in part). I must dissent.

In theory, the Court banished legislative vetoes from the government system because they undermined the spirit and letter of the Constitution. In practice, however, the chief justice was correct to be concerned: since *Chadha*, Congress has passed more than four hundred new laws containing legislative vetoes. But even more important is that the practice continues even in the absence of specific legislation—agencies and departments still abide by congressional rejections of policy.[7]

Why has the Court's opinion resulted in such blatant noncompliance? More to the point, why do executive agencies and departments continue to respect the wishes of Congress, even though they need not? One reason is purely pragmatic: because departments and agencies depend on Congress for fiscal support, they relent, fearing retaliation from Congress. Another reason is that implied by Justice White in his dissenting opinion: *Chadha* "did not, and could not, eliminate the conditions that gave rise to the legislative veto: the desire of executive officials for broad delegations of power, and the insistence of Congress that it control those delegations without having to pass another public law."[8]

In this particular instance, then, the executive branch may have won the battle but surely lost the war, as the legislative veto continues to operate. Perhaps the Court was the biggest loser: its decision offered a "solution" that was obviously "unacceptable to the political branches" and, as a result, will continue to "be eroded by open defiance and subtle evasion."[9]

Such a reaction, however, has not prevented the Court from involving itself in reviewing other actions by or acts of Congress challenged on separation of powers grounds. As we saw in chapter 4 and as touched on in box 5-2, in many other separation of powers cases the Court has authoritatively ruled for one of the political branches over the other.

---

7. Fisher, "The Legislative Veto." Fisher has updated the data and reports the figure of more than four hundred through 2004. In 1996 Congress took a stab at correcting some the constitutional deficiencies of the existing legislative veto. Under the Congressional Review Act of 1996, Congress may rescind an agency rule by passing a resolution of disapproval, which cannot be filibustered, by a majority vote in both houses. Such a resolution must be presented to and approved by the president. Because the president must approve of the "veto," this practice would seem to lack teeth: it would be unusual for a president to sign a disapproval resolution against his own agencies. Yet it could be a valuable tool during presidential-party transitions (e.g., from Bush to Obama), enabling Congress to "fast-track" rescissions of agency rules. See Charlie Savage, "Democrats Look for Ways to Undo Late Bush Administration Rules," *New York Times*, January 11, 2009, A10; and Note, "The Mysteries of the Congressional Review Act," *Harvard Law Review* 122 (2009): 2162–2183.

8. Louis Fisher, *American Constitutional Law* (New York: McGraw-Hill, 1990), 231. For another perspective on this case, see William N. Eskridge Jr. and John Ferejohn, "The Article I, Section 7 Game," *Georgetown Law Journal* 80 (1992): 523–563.

9. Fisher, *American Constitutional Law*, 281.

An important example comes in *Bowsher v. Synar* (1986), in which Congress again sought to exercise a power given to the president—the responsibility and authority to enforce the laws. The suit involved a challenge to the constitutionality of certain provisions of the Balanced Budget and Emergency Deficit Control Act of 1985, better known as the Gramm-Rudman-Hollings Act. While reading this case, keep in mind the discussions of legislative power in chapter 3. Did the Court make clear the distinction between legislative and executive functions? Was the Court's response to this statute reasonable, or was Justice White correct when he argued in dissent that the majority invalidated an important piece of legislation on the basis of a trivial objection, placing formalism above practicality?

Bowsher v. Synar

478 U.S. 714 (1986)
http://laws.findlaw.com/us/478/714.html
Oral arguments are available at https://www.oyez.org.
Vote: 7 (Brennan, Burger, Marshall, O'Connor, Powell, Rehnquist, Stevens)
2 (Blackmun, White)

OPINION OF THE COURT: Burger
CONCURRING OPINION: Stevens
DISSENTING OPINIONS: Blackmun, White

FACTS:

President Reagan signed the Balanced Budget and Emergency Deficit Control Act, popularly known as the Gramm-Rudman-Hollings bill, into law December 12, 1985. The legislation attempted to control the federal budget deficit by imposing automatic budget cuts when members of Congress were unable or unwilling to exercise sufficient fiscal restraint. The law established maximum budget deficit levels for each year beginning in 1986. The size of the deficit was to decrease each year until fiscal 1991, when no deficit would be allowed. If the federal budget deficit in any year exceeded the maximum allowed, across-the-board budget cuts would automatically be imposed.

Triggering the cuts involved steps to be taken by several government officials. First, the director of the Office of Management and Budget (OMB) and the director of the Congressional Budget Office (CBO) would independently estimate the projected deficit with program-by-program calculations. Second, these estimates would be jointly reported to the comptroller general of the United States. Third, the comptroller general would review the OMB and CBO reports and

---

BOX 5-2   SEPARATION OF POWERS CASES: THE BATTLES OF THE 1970s–2000s

DURING THE 1970s and 1980s the Supreme Court found itself unusually busy reviewing acts of Congress that were challenged as infringing on the separation of powers implicit in the Constitution. More often than not, the Court agreed with the challenge and struck down the law as impinging on the sphere of the executive or the courts.

The Court's decisions in these cases include the following:

- ***Buckley v. Valeo*** (1976). The 1974 Federal Election Campaign Act Amendments infringed on executive power by giving Congress the power to appoint four of the five members of the Federal Election Commission, which would enforce the law.
- *Bowsher v. Synar* (1986). Congress infringed on presidential prerogatives when it included in the 1985 Balanced Budget and Emergency Deficit Control Act a provision giving the comptroller general, an officer removable from office only by Congress, the power to tell the president where to cut federal spending.
- *Morrison v. Olson* (1988). The 1978 Ethics in Government Act did not usurp executive power when it authorized a panel of judges to appoint independent prosecutors to investigate charges of misconduct by high government officials.

One explanation for the increase in this kind of litigation during this period is that it stemmed from divided government, meaning that the president and Congress were of different political parties. President Bill Clinton, however, found that relations could be contentious even when his party was in control of Congress. Some of the squabbles were leftovers from previous administrations but had implications for the Clinton presidency. In *Dalton v. Specter* (1994) the Court considered a challenge by Senator Arlen Specter (R-Pa.) to a 1991 decision, reached

by an independent commission and finalized by the George H. W. Bush administration, to close a Philadelphia naval base. By the time the case reached the Supreme Court, the battle pitted Specter against the Clinton administration, which supported the base-closing law. The Supreme Court refused to review the president's decision.

Dalton was not the only legislative-executive battle of the 1990s that made its way to the courts. In ***Raines v. Byrd*** (1997), recall from chapter 2, members of Congress challenged the constitutionality of the Line Item Veto Act, which allowed the president to veto specific spending provisions. The justices ruled that they could not decide the question because the suit was not brought by parties who suffered a direct injury as a consequence of such a veto. When President Clinton began using the line-item veto, the conditions became ripe for a new lawsuit, *Clinton v. City of New York*, to settle this separation of powers issue.

George W. Bush faced severe criticism from Democrats over his administration's foreign policy almost from the beginning of his presidency. He did not, however, experience many court battles on the domestic front, even after the Democrats took control of Congress in the 2006 midterm elections. That was not the case with issues related to the war on terrorism, as detailed later in the chapter. But, as *Raines* indicates, it is difficult for U.S. legislators to challenge the constitutionality of particular actions. This is not the case, we might note, in many other countries, where legislators (or groups of legislators) can take their claims directly to a constitutional court *(see box 1-1).* There are no standing requirements that bar them from so doing, as their constitutions specifically enable legislators and, in many instances, executives to bring suits.

SOURCES: Excerpted and adapted from David Savage, *Guide to the U.S. Supreme Court,* 5th ed. (Washington, DC: CQ Press, 2010); and Holly Idelson and Pat Towell, "House and Supreme Court Take Hands-Off Stance," *Congressional Quarterly Weekly Report,* May 28, 1994, 1404.

---

issue a final report with recommendations. Fourth, the comptroller general would send the report to the president, who would issue an order mandating the automatic budget cuts recommended by the comptroller.

The statute's reliance on the comptroller general for the execution of this law presented a potential constitutional problem. The comptroller general heads the Government Accountability Office (GAO; then named the General Accounting Office), an agency created by Congress in 1921 to provide independent audits of the financial activities of executive agencies. The GAO is located within the legislative branch, and the comptroller general, although appointed by the president, is an employee of Congress, not the White House. Moreover, this official can be removed from office only by impeachment or by a joint resolution of Congress for one of several specified causes. Under traditional views of the separation of powers, no legislative officer may exercise executive authority.

Just hours after the bill was signed, Representative Mike Synar (D-Okla.), who had voted against it, filed suit against Comptroller General Charles A. Bowsher to have the law declared unconstitutional. At the same time, the National Treasury Employees Union took legal action to have the statute declared void. A three-judge district court struck down the statutory provisions that permitted an enforcement role for the comptroller general. Bowsher, on behalf of Congress, appealed.

ARGUMENTS:

For the appellant, Charles A. Bowsher, comptroller general of the United States:

- The 1921 act creating the GAO was designed to make it independent of both political branches and to make the comptroller general an independent officer of the United States appointed for a fifteen-year nonrenewable term by the president and confirmed by the Senate. As an independent officer, the comptroller general was delegated functions performed since 1789 by the comptroller of the Treasury—functions that are administrative and judicial.

- The Court should apply the logic of *Humphrey's Executor v. United States,* holding that commissioners of an agency are independent of the president

Comptroller General Charles A. Bowsher (left), given enforcement authority under the Balanced Budget and Emergency Deficit Control Act of 1985, was sued by Representative Mike Synar (D-Okla.) (right), who challenged the constitutionality of the law.

Terry Ashe/The LIFE Images Collection/Getty Images

The Washington Times/Landov

despite the president's power to remove commissioners for cause. Similarly, congressional power to remove the comptroller general for cause does not necessarily lead to the comptroller general's subservience to Congress.

- The functions of the comptroller general center on fact-finding and reporting. Because this Court has upheld delegations that include functions that entail broader policy judgments, delegation of ministerial functions should also be upheld.

For the appellees, Mike Synar, member of Congress, et al.:

- The entire purpose of delegating powers to the comptroller general is for Congress to avoid political accountability; no one member of Congress wants to be responsible for spending cuts or more taxes. This is not a pragmatic necessity that can properly justify a delegation of power.
- The act gives the comptroller general the power to execute critical aspects of the act and make decisions that are binding on the president and the entire executive branch. The separation of powers prohibits the comptroller general from this level of involvement in the execution of the act. First, he is an officer of the legislative branch and is subject to removal by Congress. Second, only the president or an officer who serves at his pleasure can make binding decisions on the president and the executive branch.
- The Court has said that some functions are so central to the legislative branch that they cannot be delegated. Here, the Constitution explicitly and exclusively designates the delegated power, the power of the purse, to Congress.
- The nature of the comptroller general's work is to predict the future state of the economy, not merely to report on its current state. This task is replete with political judgments that should be left to the president and Congress.

CHIEF JUSTICE BURGER DELIVERED THE OPINION OF THE COURT.

The question presented by these appeals is whether the assignment by Congress to the Comptroller General of the United States of certain functions under the Balanced Budget and Emergency Deficit Control Act of 1985 violates the doctrine of separation of powers. . . .

Appellants urge that the Comptroller General performs his duties independently and is not subservient to Congress. We agree with the District Court that this contention does not bear close scrutiny. . . .

It is clear that Congress has consistently viewed the Comptroller General as an officer of the Legislative Branch. The Reorganization Acts of 1945 and 1949, for example, both stated that the Comptroller General and the GAO are "a part of the legislative branch of the Government." Similarly, in the Accounting and Auditing Act of 1950, Congress required the Comptroller General to conduct audits "as an agent of the Congress."

Over the years, the Comptrollers General have also viewed themselves as part of the Legislative Branch. In one of the early Annual Reports of Comptroller General, the official seal of his office was described as reflecting

"the independence of judgment to be exercised by the General Accounting Office, subject to the control of the legislative branch. . . . The combination represents an agency of the Congress independent of other authority auditing and checking the expenditures of the Government as required by law and subjecting any questions arising in that connection to quasi-judicial determination."

Later, Comptroller General Warren, who had been a Member of Congress for 15 years before being appointed Comptroller General, testified: "During most of my public life, . . . I have been a member of the legislative branch. Even now, although heading a great agency, it is an agency of the Congress, and *I am an agent of the Congress*" [our italics]. And, in one conflict during Comptroller General McCarl's tenure, he asserted his independence of the Executive Branch, stating:

"Congress . . . is . . . the only authority to which there lies an appeal from the decision of this office. . . ."

Against this background, we see no escape from the conclusion that, because Congress has retained removal authority over the Comptroller General, he may not be entrusted with executive powers. The remaining question is whether the Comptroller General has been assigned such powers in the Balanced Budget and Emergency Deficit Control Act of 1985.

The primary responsibility of the Comptroller General under the instant Act is the preparation of a "report." This report must contain detailed estimates of projected federal revenues and expenditures. The report must also specify the reductions, if any, necessary to reduce the deficit to the target for the appropriate fiscal year. The reductions must be set forth on a program-by-program basis.

In preparing the report, the Comptroller General is to have "due regard" for the estimates and reductions set forth in a joint report submitted to him by the Director of CBO and the Director of OMB, the President's fiscal and budgetary adviser. However, the Act plainly contemplates that the Comptroller General will exercise his independent judgment and evaluation with respect to those estimates. The Act also provides that the Comptroller General's report "shall explain fully any differences between the contents of such report and the report of the Directors."

Appellants suggest that the duties assigned to the Comptroller General in the Act are essentially ministerial and mechanical so that their performance does not constitute "execution of the law" in a meaningful sense. On the contrary, we view these functions as plainly entailing execution of the law in constitutional terms. Interpreting a law enacted by Congress to implement the legislative mandate is the very essence of "execution" of the law. Under §251, the Comptroller General must exercise judgment concerning facts that affect the application of the Act. He must also interpret the provisions of the Act to determine precisely what budgetary calculations are required. Decisions of that kind are typically made by officers charged with executing a statute.

The executive nature of the Comptroller General's functions under the Act is revealed in §252(a)(3) which gives the Comptroller General the ultimate authority to determine the budget cuts to be made. Indeed, the Comptroller General commands the President himself to carry out, without the slightest variation (with exceptions not relevant to the constitutional issues presented), the directive of the Comptroller General as to the budget reductions. . . .

Congress of course initially determined the content of the Balanced Budget and Emergency Deficit Control Act; and undoubtedly the content of the Act determines the nature of the executive duty. However, as [*Immigration and Naturalization Service v.*] *Chadha* [1983] makes clear, once Congress makes its choice in enacting legislation, its participation ends. Congress can thereafter control the execution of its enactment only indirectly—by passing new legislation. By placing the responsibility for execution of the Balanced Budget and Emergency Deficit Control Act in the hands of an officer who is subject to removal only by itself, Congress in effect has retained control over the execution of the Act and has intruded into the executive function. The Constitution does not permit such intrusion.

Affirmed.

JUSTICE WHITE, dissenting.

The Court, acting in the name of separation of powers, takes upon itself to strike down the Gramm-Rudman-Hollings Act, one of the most novel and far-reaching legislative responses to a national crisis since the New Deal. The basis of the Court's action is a solitary provision of another statute that was passed over 60 years ago and has lain dormant since that time. I cannot concur in the Court's action. Like the Court, I will not purport to speak to the wisdom of the policies incorporated in the legislation the Court invalidates; that is a matter for the Congress and the Executive, *both* of which expressed their assent to the statute barely half a year ago. I will, however, address the wisdom of the Court's willingness to interpose its distressingly formalistic view of separation of powers as a bar to the attainment of governmental objectives through the means chosen by the Congress and the President in the legislative process established by the Constitution. Twice in the past four years I have expressed my view that the Court's recent efforts to police the separation of powers have rested on untenable constitutional propositions leading to regrettable results. See *Northern Pipeline Construction Co. v. Marathon Pipe Line Co.* (1982) (WHITE, J., Dissenting); *INS v. Chadha* (1983) (WHITE, J., Dissenting). Today's result is even more misguided. . . . [T]he Court's decision rests on a feature of the legislative scheme that is of minimal practical significance and that presents no substantial threat to the basic scheme of separation of powers. In attaching dispositive significance to what should be regarded as a triviality, the Court neglects what has in the past been recognized as a fundamental principle governing consideration of disputes over separation of powers:

> "The actual art of governing under our Constitution does not and cannot conform to judicial definitions of the power of any of its branches based on isolated clauses or even single Articles torn from context. While the Constitution diffuses power the better to secure liberty, it also contemplates that practice will integrate the dispersed powers into a workable government." Youngstown Sheet & Tube Co. v. Sawyer (1952) (Jackson, J., concurring).

Bowsher supplied a clear declaration of the boundaries between legislative and executive authority, but the decision had little impact on the legislation. Congress, anticipating a lawsuit, had written into the law certain "fallback" mechanisms to enforce the budget restrictions if any part of the original plan failed a constitutional challenge. This plan removed the comptroller general from any enforcement activity, which eliminated the constitutional violation.

Two years later the Court again considered a dispute in which Congress was accused of interfering with executive power. In the wake of the Watergate scandal, Congress set up a process for selecting an independent counsel to investigate and prosecute high-ranking government officials for federal crimes. This move resulted in *Morrison v. Olson,* which you read in chapter 4.

Morrison, as we stressed, is known for detailing the characteristics of "inferior" versus "principal" officers, but the opinion also addressed the proper separation of the legislative and executive branches. Similar to the situation in *Bowsher,* Congress had restricted removal of the special prosecutor to the attorney general, who may fire the special prosecutor only for "good cause." Ted Olson argued that this amounted to an interference with the president's power to control subordinates and that Congress was unconstitutionally grabbing executive power.

The Court ultimately rejected Olson's arguments. In so doing, it attempted to distinguish *Morrison* from *Bowsher:*

Unlike *Bowsher* . . . this case does not involve an attempt by Congress itself to gain a role in the removal of executive officials other than its established powers of impeachment and conviction. The Act instead puts the removal power squarely in the hands of the Executive Branch; an independent counsel may be removed from office, "only by the personal action of the Attorney General, and only for good cause." There is no requirement of congressional approval of the Attorney General's removal decision, though the decision is subject to judicial review.

The Court also dealt with Olson's argument that the special prosecutor act violated the separation of powers because it interfered with the role of the executive branch:

Time and again we have reaffirmed the importance in our constitutional scheme of the separation of governmental powers into the three coordinate branches. . . . [T]he system of separated powers and checks and balances established in the Constitution was regarded by the Framers as "a self-executing safeguard against the encroachment or aggrandizement of one branch at the expense of the other." We

have not hesitated to invalidate provisions of law which violate this principle. On the other hand, we have never held that the Constitution requires that the three Branches of Government "operate with absolute independence." . . .

We observe . . . that this case does not involve an attempt by Congress to increase its own powers at the expense of the Executive Branch. Unlike . . . *Bowsher v. Synar,* this case simply does not pose a "dange[r] of congressional usurpation of Executive Branch functions." Indeed, with the exception of the power of impeachment—which applies to all officers of the United States—Congress retained for itself no powers of control or supervision over an independent counsel. The Act does empower certain members of Congress to request the Attorney General to apply for the appointment of an independent counsel, but the Attorney General has no duty to comply with the request, although he must respond within a certain time limit. Other than that, Congress' role under the Act is limited to receiving reports or other information and oversight of the independent counsel's activities, functions that we have recognized generally as being incidental to the legislative functions of Congress.

Are you convinced by the Court's arguments in *Morrison?* Does the majority make a good case for distinguishing *Bowsher?* Do the *Morrison* justices bring a more functional approach to bear than the *Bowsher* justices? Or are both equally apt?

POWERS OVER FOREIGN AFFAIRS

The cases we have considered so far mostly involve questions pertaining to the separation of powers in cases of domestic politics. This should not be taken to mean, however, that such questions arise only in domestic disputes. Indeed, questions concerning the constitutional authority over external affairs—including the power to conduct and wage war—have plagued the nation from the very beginning.

Even today, many such questions remain unresolved. Because war and conditions of national emergency customarily demand quick action, they rarely afford those involved sufficient time for the dispassionate consideration of legal questions. When national survival is at stake or the country's relations with other nations are in jeopardy and emotions are running high, it may be willing to ignore rules about limitations on government power that would be insisted on in peacetime.[10] Once the crisis has passed, the nation turns to other matters, and questions of war do not again capture its attention until the next threat occurs.

Constitutional War Powers

The constitutional authority to send troops into combat has always sparked controversy. As we noted at the beginning of this chapter, the root of the problem is that the legislative and executive branches both have powers that can be interpreted as controlling the commitment of military forces to combat. The case for presidential control is based on the following passage: "The President shall be Commander in Chief of the Army and Navy of the United States, and of the Militia of the several States, when called into the actual Service of the United States" (Article II, Section 2). Proponents of congressional dominance over the making of war rest their case on these words:

The Congress shall have Power . . .

To declare War, grant Letters of Marque and Reprisal, and make Rules concerning Captures on Land and Water;

To raise and support Armies, but no Appropriation of Money to that Use shall be for a longer Term than two Years;

To provide and maintain a Navy;

To make Rules for the Government and Regulation of the land and naval Forces;

To provide for calling forth the Militia to execute the Laws of the Union, suppress Insurrections and repel Invasions. (Article I, Section 8.)

The distribution of war-making powers as determined by the framers envisioned a situation in which Congress would raise and support military forces when necessary and provide the general rules governing those forces. By granting Congress the power to declare war, the Constitution anticipates that the legislature should determine when military force is to be used. Once the military is raised and war is declared, executive power becomes dominant, consistent with the philosophy that waging war successfully requires that a single official be in charge.

This allocation of powers was more realistic at the end of the eighteenth century than it is today. At the time the framers considered these issues, the United States was a remote nation far removed from the frequent wars in Europe. It took weeks for vessels to cross the Atlantic, allowing plenty of time for Congress to debate the question of initiating hostilities. Most delegates at the Constitutional Convention did not even anticipate the establishment of a standing military.

Today, with the rapid deployment of troops, airpower, and intercontinental missiles, hostile conditions demand quick and decisive actions. The nation expects the president to act immediately to repel an attack and to worry about congressional approval later.

The United States has initiated hundreds of military actions without declarations of war. President John Adams took the first such action when he authorized military strikes against French privateers. Most of these undeclared actions have been quick rather than prolonged conflicts, but two major long-term military efforts, the Korean War and the Vietnam War, were conducted without any formal declaration of war. In fact, Congress has taken the positive action of declaring a state of war only five times in the nation's history:[11]

1. The War of 1812 against Great Britain

2. The Mexican War in 1846

3. The Spanish-American War in 1898

4. World War I in 1917

5. World War II in 1941

Occasionally, military actions begin and end so quickly that the president's move allows no time for congressional approval; an example is President Clinton's authorization of missile strikes on targets in Afghanistan and Sudan in 1998. When military actions have extended over greater periods, Congress often has given approval through means other than a formal declaration of war. This approval may come in the form of a resolution authorizing the president to conduct military action, such as the 1964 Tonkin Gulf Resolution that granted President Lyndon Johnson authority to

---

10. Clinton L. Rossiter, *Constitutional Dictatorship: Crisis Government in the Modern Democracies* (Princeton, NJ: Princeton University Press, 1948).

11. Congress also declared a state of war during the Civil War, but this conflict is technically classified as an internal rebellion rather than a true war between independent nations.

use force to repel attacks on U.S. forces and to forestall future aggression. Similarly, on January 12, 1991, Congress passed a joint resolution authorizing President George H. W. Bush to use force against Iraq, giving its approval to the Persian Gulf conflict in words just short of a formal declaration of war. Just days after the terrorist attacks on New York City and Washington, D.C., on September 11, 2001, the legislature passed a joint resolution authorizing President George W. Bush to use "United States Armed Forces against those responsible for the recent attacks launched against the United States." A little more than a year later, in October 2002, it voted in favor of a similar resolution, the Authorization for Use of Military Force Against Iraq (AUMF), enabling Bush to use military force against Iraq, although some suggest that the resolution did not authorize the war that later ensued. Finally, Congress can give indirect approval to the president in the form of continuing congressional appropriations to support military action. In the wake of September 11, Congress approved a bill authorizing $40 billion for various military operations and disaster relief.

But Congress has not abdicated its constitutional authority to approve war; in fact, the legislature has insisted that the president consult it on all military actions. In 1973 Congress passed the War Powers Resolution over Nixon's veto. This legislation acknowledges the right of the president to undertake limited military action without first obtaining formal approval from Congress but requires the president to file a formal report with Congress within forty-eight hours of initiating hostilities. Military action under this act is limited to sixty days with a possible thirty-day extension. If the president wishes to pursue military activity beyond these limits, prior congressional consent is required. Although the legislation was designed to impose restrictions on the president, most experts believe the law actually expands the chief executive's right to employ military force. The AUMF may provide an example. It contains language requiring the president to submit to Congress "a report on matters relevant to this joint resolution" at least "once every 60 days." But it also states, "The President is authorized to use the Armed Forces of the United States as he determines to be necessary and appropriate in order to— (1) defend the national security of the United States against the continuing threat posed by Iraq; and (2) enforce all relevant United Nations Security Council resolutions regarding Iraq."

What role does the judiciary play in times of war? Because it must wait for an appropriate case to be filed before it can act, and because of its slow, deliberative procedures, the judicial branch is less capable than the other two branches of taking a leading role in matters of war and national emergency. Furthermore, the Constitution gives the courts no specified authority in these areas. The judiciary is, however, sometimes called on to decide if government power is being used legitimately or if constitutional limits have been exceeded. In times of war and national emergency, the executive branch may find it necessary to take actions that would be unlawful at other times. The limits of the Constitution may be stretched to respond to the crisis. When legal disputes arise from such situations, the courts may become active participants in determining the government's legitimate authority. But it is also true, as we saw in chapter 2, that political actors have sometimes attempted to reduce or even eliminate the federal judiciary's participation in suits related to the crisis at hand.

In what follows, we consider the Court's responses to litigation arising during four periods of threat: the Civil War, World War II, the Korean conflict, and foreign policy in the Mideast. In the last section, we explain the steps President George W. Bush and his administration took to combat terrorism—some of which the Obama administration also followed—and the Court's reactions. As you read the contemporary material, try to assess the justices' positions on President Bush's claims about the importance of strong executive authority in times of crisis. Did the justices' decisions support the administration? Or does the answer to that question depend on the particular actions at issue in the litigation, whether the president had support from Congress, or other factors?

Civil War

If it is a generally recognized constitutional doctrine that government may exercise more power during times of war and national emergency than during times of peace and security, what is not evident from this rather vague statement is at what point the government's extraordinary powers are activated. This question came to the Supreme Court in the *Prize Cases* in 1863. The disputes giving rise to these cases present the most fundamental questions of the constitutional allocation of the war powers. When does war begin? Who has power to initiate war? What war powers may the president pursue without a formal declaration from Congress?

The Prize Cases

67 U.S. (22 Bl.) 635 (1863)
http://laws.findlaw.com/us/67/635.html
Vote: 5 (Davis, Grier, Miller, Swayne, Wayne)
    4 (Catron, Clifford, Nelson, Taney)

OPINION OF THE COURT: *Grier*
DISSENTING OPINION: *Nelson*

FACTS:

Abraham Lincoln was elected president in November 1860. Before his inauguration on March 4, 1861, seven Southern states seceded from the Union, and Lincoln knew that he had to act quickly and decisively to preserve the nation. Beginning in mid-April, shortly after the first shots were fired at Fort Sumter, Lincoln imposed a naval blockade of Southern ports. He took this action unilaterally, without seeking the prior approval of Congress, which did not enact a formal declaration of hostilities until July 13 and did not ratify Lincoln's blockade until August 6.

Prior to July 13, Union war vessels seized four ships trading with the Confederacy. The owners of the captured ships brought suit to recover their property, claiming that Lincoln had no authority to institute a blockade in the absence of a congressional declaration of war and that the seizures were illegal. Among other matters, the justices confronted this important constitutional issue: Did the president have the right to institute a blockade of ports under the control of persons in armed rebellion against the government before Congress had acted? Lincoln believed he did, on the grounds that a state of insurrection existed as a result of the shots at Fort Sumter and that he had the responsibility, under various constitutional provisions, to protect the country.

ARGUMENTS:

For the claimants, ship owners:

• For ships to be captured via blockades as prizes of war, there must be a war. Article I, Section 8, of the Constitution explicitly gives Congress the power to declare war. Because Congress never declared war, there was no official war or blockade.

• The president's powers are limited to those granted to him in the Constitution. He is empowered to use the nation's army and navy against insurrections or invasions, as Congress has provided, but exercising those powers alone does not amount to war.

• The Constitution plainly distinguishes between "war" and "insurrection," treating foreign disturbances distinctly from domestic disturbances. Because the blockade was in reaction to hostility from states in the Union, the disturbance was an insurrection, not a war.

For the libellants, United States:

• War is the exercise of force by political bodies against each other for the purpose of coercion. War is a state of things, not just a legislative act, and can exist without official declaration by either side.

• Historically, a civil war exists whenever the regular course of justice is interrupted by revolt or rebellion, so that the courts cannot be kept open.

• Practical necessity demands that the president be allowed some leeway to use his war powers without waiting for Congress to act first. The president must be able to protect the country from sudden attacks at times when Congress might not be assembled or be able to respond in time.

MR. JUSTICE GRIER DELIVERED THE OPINION OF THE COURT.

Had the President a right to institute a blockade of ports in possession of persons in armed rebellion against the Government, on the principles of international law, as known and acknowledged among civilized States? . . .

By the Constitution, Congress alone has the power to declare a national or foreign war. It cannot declare war against a State, or any number of States, by virtue of any clause in the Constitution. The Constitution confers on the President the whole Executive power. He is bound to take care that the laws be faithfully executed. He is Commander-in-chief of the Army and Navy of the United States, and of the militia of the several States when called into the actual service of the United States. He has no power to initiate or declare a war either against a foreign nation or a domestic State. But by the Acts of Congress of February 28th, 1795, and 3d of March, 1807, he is authorized to call out the militia and use the military and naval forces of the United States in case of invasion by foreign nations, and to suppress insurrection against the government of a State or of the United States.

If a war be made by invasion of a foreign nation, the President is not only authorized but bound to resist force

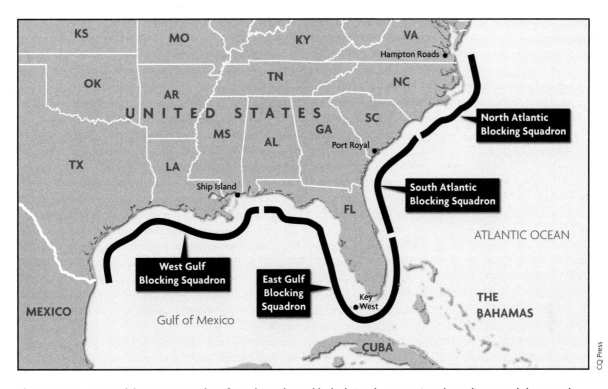

The Prize Cases examined the constitutionality of Lincoln's orders to blockade Southern ports in order to disrupt trade between the Confederacy and foreign nations. As this map illustrates, the federal operation was divided into four regional blockading units: the North Atlantic Blockading Squadron based at Hampton Roads, Virginia; the South Atlantic Squadron at Port Royal, South Carolina; the Eastern Gulf Squadron at Key West, Florida; and the Western Gulf Squadron at Pensacola, Florida, and Ship Island, Mississippi.

by force. He does not initiate the war, but is bound to accept the challenge without waiting for any special legislative authority. And whether the hostile party be a foreign invader, or States organized in rebellion, it is none the less a war, although the declaration of it be *"unilateral."* . . .

This greatest of civil wars was not gradually developed by popular commotion, tumultuous assemblies, or local unorganized insurrections. However long may have been its previous conception, it nevertheless sprung forth suddenly from the parent brain, a Minerva in the full panoply of *war.* The President was bound to meet it in the shape it presented itself, without waiting for Congress to baptize it with a name; and no name given to it by him or them could change the fact.

It is not the less a civil war, with belligerent parties in hostile array, because it may be called an "insurrection" by one side, and the insurgents be considered as rebels or traitors. It is not necessary that the independence of the revolted province or State be acknowledged in order to constitute it a party belligerent in a war according to the law of nations. Foreign nations acknowledge it as war by a declaration of neutrality. The condition of neutrality cannot exist unless there be two belligerent parties. . . .

The law of nations is also called the law of nature; it is founded on the common consent as well as the common sense of the world. It contains no such anomalous doctrine as that which this Court are now for the first time desired to pronounce, to wit, that insurgents who have risen in rebellion against their sovereign, expelled her Courts, established a revolutionary government, organized armies, and commenced hostilities, are not *enemies* because they are *traitors;* and a war levied on the Government by traitors, in order to dismember and destroy it, is not a *war* because it is an "insurrection."

Whether the President in fulfilling his duties, as Commander-in-chief, in suppressing an insurrection, has met with such armed hostile resistance, and a civil war of such alarming proportions as will compel him to accord to them the character of belligerents, is a question to be decided *by him,* and this Court must be governed by the decisions and acts of the political department of the Government to which this power was entrusted. "He must determine what degree of force the crisis demands." The proclamation of blockade is itself official and conclusive evidence to the Court that a state of war existed which demanded and authorized a recourse to such a measure, under the circumstances peculiar to the case. . . .

. . . [T]herefore we are of the opinion that the President had a right, *jure belli*, to institute a blockade of ports in possession of the States in rebellion, which neutrals are bound to regard.

MR. JUSTICE NELSON, dissenting. [MR. CHIEF JUSTICE TANEY, MR. JUSTICE CATRON, and MR. JUSTICE CLIFFORD concurred in the dissenting opinion of MR. JUSTICE NELSON.]

Th[e] great and pervading change in the existing condition of a country, and in the relations of all her citizens or subjects, external and internal, from a state of peace, is the immediate effect and result of a state of war, and hence the same code which has annexed to the existence of a war all these disturbing consequences has declared that the right of making war belongs exclusively to the supreme or sovereign power of the State.

This power in all civilized nations is regulated by the fundamental laws or municipal constitution of the country.

By our constitution, this power is lodged in Congress. Congress shall have power "to declare war, grant letters of marque and reprisal, and make rules concerning captures on land and water." . . .

It is not to be denied . . . that if a civil war existed between that portion of the people in organized insurrection to overthrow this Government at the time this vessel and cargo were seized, and if she was guilty of a violation of the blockade, she would be lawful prize of war. But before this insurrection against the established Government can be dealt with on the footing of a civil war, within the meaning of the law of nations and the Constitution of the United States, and which will draw after it belligerent rights, it must be recognized or declared by the war-making power of the Government. No power short of this can change the legal status of the Government or the relations of its citizens from that of peace to a state of war, or bring into existence all those duties and obligations of neutral third parties growing out of a state of war. The war power of the Government must be exercised before this changed condition of the Government and people and of neutral third parties can be admitted. There is no difference in this respect between a civil or a public war. . . .

Now, in one sense, no doubt this is war, and may be a war of the most extensive and threatening dimensions and effects, but it is a statement simply of its existence in a material sense, and has no relevancy or weight when the question is what constitutes war in a legal sense, in the sense of the law of nations, and of the Constitution of the United States? For it must be a war in this sense to attach to it all the consequences that belong to belligerent rights. Instead, therefore, of inquiring after armies and navies, and victories lost and won, or organized rebellion against the general Government, the inquiry should be into the law of nations and into the municipal fundamental laws of the Government. For we find there that to constitute a civil war in the sense in which we are speaking, before it can exist in contemplation of law, it must be recognized or declared by the sovereign power of the State, and which sovereign power by our Constitution is lodged in the Congress of the United States—civil war, therefore, under our system of government, can exist only by an act of Congress, which requires the assent of two of the great departments of the Government, the Executive and Legislative.

We have thus far been speaking of the war power under the Constitution of the United States, and as known and recognized by the law of nations. But we are asked, what would become of the peace and integrity of the Union in case of an insurrection at home or invasion from abroad if this power could not be exercised by the President in the recess of Congress, and until that body could be assembled?

The framers of the Constitution fully comprehended this question, and provided for the contingency. . . . The Constitution declares that Congress shall have power "to provide for calling forth the militia to execute the laws of the Union, suppress insurrections, and repel invasions." Another clause, "that the President shall be Commander-in-chief of the Army and Navy of the United States, and of the militia of the several States when called into the actual service of United States;" and, again, "He shall take care that the laws shall be faithfully executed." Congress passed laws on this subject in 1792 and 1795.

[These and other acts] did not, and could not under the Constitution, confer on the President the power of declaring war against a State of this Union, or of deciding that war existed, and upon that ground authorize the capture and confiscation of the property of every citizen of the State whenever it was found on the waters. The laws of war, whether the war be civil or inter gentes . . . convert every citizen of the hostile State into a public enemy, and treat him accordingly, whatever may have been his previous conduct. This great power over the business and property of the citizen is reserved to the legislative department by the express words of the Constitution. It cannot be delegated or surrendered to the Executive. Congress alone can determine whether war exists or should be declared, and until they have acted, no citizen of the State can be punished in his person or property unless he has committed some offence against a law of Congress passed before the act was committed which made it a crime and defined the punishment. The penalty of confiscation for the acts of others with which he had no concern cannot lawfully be inflicted.

Upon the whole, after the most careful consideration of this case which the pressure of other duties has admitted, I am compelled to the conclusion that no civil war existed between this Government and the States in insurrection till recognized by the Act of Congress 13th of July, 1861; that the President does not possess the power under the Constitution to declare war or recognize its existence within the meaning of the law of nations, which carries with it belligerent rights, and thus change the country and all its citizens from a state of peace to a state of war; that this power belongs exclusively to the Congress of the United States, and, consequently, that the President had no power to set on foot a blockade under the law of nations, and that the capture of the vessel and cargo in this case, and in all cases before us in which the capture occurred before the 13th of July, 1861, for breach of blockade, or as enemies' property, are illegal and void, and that the decrees of condemnation should be reversed and the vessel and cargo restored.

Lincoln's actions were supported by the slightest of majorities. Three of the justices who voted to endorse the validity of the blockade were his own appointees, Samuel Miller, Noah Swayne, and David Davis. They were joined by two Democrats, Robert Grier of Pennsylvania and James Wayne, a Georgian who remained loyal to the Union. The decision is significant for expanding the right of the president to take military action without waiting for congressional approval. It further established that a state of war comes into existence when certain conditions are present, not when the legislature declares that it exists. The decision, however, did not fully settle the issue. The arguments raised in the majority and dissenting opinions in this case seem to reappear whenever a controversy over the power to conduct war arises.

The blockade was only the first of Lincoln's acts of questionable constitutionality. In *Ex parte Milligan* the

justices addressed another, this one concerning the president's actions suppressing civil liberties.[12] The ruling came after Lincoln's death and the war's conclusion. Do you think the Court's decision would have been different had the case been heard when hostilities were at their peak and Confederate troops were scoring successes on the battlefield?

Ex parte Milligan

71 U.S. (24 Wall.) 2 (1866)
http://laws.findlaw.com/us/71/2.html
Vote: 9 (Chase, Clifford, Davis, Field, Grier, Miller, Nelson, Swayne, Wayne)
   0

OPINION OF THE COURT: *Davis*
CONCURRING OPINION: *Chase*

FACTS:

The Civil War was unlike other wars Americans had faced: the enemies were fellow Americans, not foreigners. The conflict touched almost every part of the nation, and Lincoln particularly worried about the presence of Confederate supporters in the Northern and border states. These individuals were capable of aiding the Southern forces without joining the Confederate Army. Of special concern were the large numbers of Southern sympathizers, known as Copperheads, who were active in Illinois, Indiana, Missouri, and Ohio. Combating these civilian enemies posed a difficult problem for the president. Lincoln decided that the Union was more important than the procedural rights of individuals. Consequently, he gave his military commanders broad powers to arrest civilians suspected of engaging in traitorous activities. These suspects were to be tried in military courts.

In those parts of the country where hostilities were not occurring, however, the army had no legal authority to arrest and try civilians. State and federal courts were in full operation and were capable of trying civilians charged with treason or any other crime. Before civilians could be tried by military courts, a state of martial law had to be declared, and for that to happen the right of habeas corpus had to be suspended. Habeas corpus is a legal procedure with roots extending far back into English legal history; it permits an arrested person to have a judge determine whether the detention is legal. If

---

12. For a description of the events leading up to the Court's decision, see Allan Nevins, "The Case of the Copperhead Conspirator," in Garraty, *Quarrels That Have Shaped the Constitution.*

the court determines that there are no legal grounds for the arrest, it may order the release of the detained individual. Habeas corpus is essential to the doctrine of checks and balances because it gives the judiciary the right to intervene if the executive branch abuses the law enforcement power.

Article I, Section 9, of the Constitution provides for the suspension of habeas corpus in the following words: "The Privilege of the Writ of Habeas Corpus shall not be suspended, unless when in Cases of Rebellion or Invasion the public Safety may require it." This provision posed two problems for Lincoln. First, the suspension provision is found in Article I, which outlines legislative, not executive, powers. And second, if the civilian courts are in full operation and no armed hostilities are taking place in the area, the public safety probably does not demand a suspension of habeas corpus procedures.

These obstacles did not stop the president. Several times during the war he issued orders expanding military control over civilian areas, permitting military arrests and trials of civilians, and suspending habeas corpus. Congress later endorsed some of these actions. Arrests of suspected traitors and conspirators were common and often based on little evidence. Were such actions constitutional under the war powers doctrine? The Court addressed this question in *Ex parte Milligan* (1866), a decision of great importance in defining the wartime powers of the chief executive.

Lambdin P. Milligan was an attorney residing in northeastern Indiana. As a member of the Democratic Party, with strong states' rights beliefs, he was sympathetic toward the Confederate cause. He openly organized groups and gave speeches in support of the South. He also was involved in efforts to persuade men not to join the Union Army. At one point Milligan and his fellow Copperheads were suspected of hatching a plan to raid prisoner-of-war camps in Illinois, Indiana, and Ohio and to release the imprisoned Confederate soldiers, who would then take control of the three states. Federal military investigators followed Milligan closely and kept records of his activities and contacts.

On October 5, 1864, under orders from General Alvin Hovey, commander of the Union Army in Indiana, federal agents arrested Milligan at his home. They also arrested four of Milligan's fellow Confederate sympathizers. Sixteen days later Hovey placed Milligan on trial before a military tribunal in Indianapolis. He was found guilty and sentenced to be hanged on May 19, 1865. On May 2, less than a month after the war ended with General Robert E. Lee's surrender at Appomattox, President Andrew Johnson, who had succeeded Lincoln, sustained the order that Milligan be executed. In response, Milligan's attorneys filed for a writ of habeas corpus in federal circuit court, claiming that Milligan should not have been tried by a military tribunal and that the president should not have suspended the writ of habeas corpus. Uncertain of how

Courtesy of The Indiana State Library

The Union Army military commission that tried Lambdin P. Milligan and his fellow conspirators in October 1864.

to apply the law, the circuit judges requested that the Supreme Court resolve certain questions regarding the legal authority of a military commission to try and sentence Milligan.

Nine months later, in March 1866, the Court heard the *Milligan* case. Oral arguments took place at a time of heightened political tension. Relations were strained between Johnson, who supported a moderate position toward the reintroduction of the Southern states into the Union, and the Radical Republicans in Congress, who demanded a stricter Reconstruction policy. A majority of the justices opposed the military trials at issue in *Milligan,* but there was concern about possible congressional retaliation if the justices struck a blow against military authority. The Court at this point was quite vulnerable, having suffered a decline in prestige because of the infamous decision in *Scott v. Sandford* (1857). But the justices had a potential ally in Johnson. The president opposed the use of military tribunals, and the Radicals had not yet gained sufficient strength to override a veto of a congressional act. The Court announced its decision in *Milligan* on April 3, 1866, but did not issue formal opinions until eight months later.

ARGUMENTS:

For the petitioner, Lambdin P. Milligan:

- The power to suspend the writ of habeas corpus belongs to Congress, not the president. Article I grants the power to Congress only; there is no analogous language in Article II. The debates of the framers support this claim, as do the laws of England upon which our Constitution is based.
- The Constitution was written with distrust of the executive; the framers divided war powers to keep the executive in check. It is illogical to assume that the framers intended to give the president absolute control over regions under martial law when they denied him the basic power to raise and support an army and navy.
- Historically, legislation regarding military commissions has specified that they have jurisdiction only over military personnel and spies in times of war or rebellion. Milligan was a civilian in a peaceful state where the courts were open, their processes uninterrupted, and the civil laws had full power.
- The plain text of the Fifth Amendment shows that military commissions apply only to persons "in the land or naval services, or in the militia when in

Indiana Historical Society, P0411

Five Southern sympathizers were charged with treason by military authorities. The question of the constitutionality of their arrests and trials before a military commission was settled by the Supreme Court in Ex parte Milligan (1866). Clockwise from top: William A. Bowles, Andrew Humphreys, Stephen Horsey, H. Heffren, and Lambdin P. Milligan.

actual service, in time of war or public danger." The last phrase shows that the amendment applies in times of war as well as peace.

For the respondent, United States:

- The president derives authority to suspend the writ of habeas corpus from his constitutional power as commander in chief.
- The Constitution limits the presidential war power by granting Congress the powers to declare war and raise armies. Once war begins, however, the presidential war power must be unlimited to allow the president to meet new challenges that the slow movement of legislative action cannot meet.
- Jurisdiction of the military tribunal does not depend on residency in the rebel states; the commander in chief has power to establish military districts where

needed and to arrest and punish anyone who aids the enemy.

- The Second, Fourth, Fifth, and Sixth Amendments should be construed as peacetime provisions that fall silent in times of war. The framers neither put nor intended limits on the president's power to conduct war.

MR. JUSTICE DAVIS DELIVERED THE OPINION OF THE COURT.

During the late wicked Rebellion, the temper of the times did not allow that calmness in deliberation and discussion so necessary to a correct conclusion of a purely judicial question. *Then*, considerations of safety were mingled with the exercise of power; and feelings and interests prevailed which are happily terminated. *Now* that the public safety is assured, this question, as well as all others, can be discussed and decided without passion or the admixture of any element not required to form a legal judgment. We approach the investigation of this case, fully sensible of the magnitude of the inquiry and the necessity of full and cautious deliberation. . . .

The controlling question in the case is this: Upon the *facts* stated in Milligan's petition, and the exhibits filed, had the military commission mentioned in it *jurisdiction*, legally, to try and sentence him? Milligan, not a resident of one of the rebellious states, or a prisoner of war, but a citizen of Indiana for twenty years past, and never in the military or naval service, is, while at his home, arrested by the military power of the United States, imprisoned, and, on certain criminal charges preferred against him, tried, convicted, and sentenced to be hanged by a military commission, organized under the direction of the military commander of the military district of Indiana. Had this tribunal the *legal* power and authority to try and punish this man?

No graver question was ever considered by this court, nor one which more nearly concerns the rights of the whole people, for it is the birthright of every American citizen when charged with crime, to be tried and punished according to law. . . . By that Constitution and the laws authorized by it this question must be determined. The provisions of that instrument on the administration of criminal justice are too plain and direct, to leave room for misconstruction or doubt of their true meaning. Those applicable to this case are found in that clause of the original Constitution which says, "That the trial of all crimes, except in case of impeachment, shall be by jury"; . . .

. . . The Constitution of the United States is a law for rulers and people, equally in war and in peace, and covers with the shield of its protection all classes of men, at all times, and under all circumstances. No doctrine, involving more pernicious consequences, was ever invented by the wit of man than that any of its provisions can be suspended during any of the great exigencies of government. Such a doctrine leads directly to anarchy or despotism, but the theory of necessity on which it is based is false; for the government, within the Constitution, has all the powers granted to it, which are necessary to preserve its existence; as has been happily proved by the result of the great effort to throw off its just authority.

Have any of the rights guaranteed by the Constitution been violated in the case of Milligan? and if so, what are they?

Every trial involves the exercise of judicial power; and from what source did the military commission that tried him derive their authority? Certainly no part of the judicial power of the country was conferred on them; because the Constitution expressly vests it "in one supreme court and such inferior courts as the Congress may from time to time ordain and establish," and it is not pretended that the commission was a court ordained and established by Congress. They cannot justify on the mandate of the President; because he is controlled by law, and has his appropriate sphere of duty, which is to execute, not to make, the laws; and there is "no unwritten criminal code to which resort can be had as a source of jurisdiction."

But it is said that the jurisdiction is complete under the "laws and usages of war."

It can serve no useful purpose to inquire what those laws and usages are, whence they originated, where found, and on whom they operate; they can never be applied to citizens in states which have upheld the authority of the government, and where the courts are open and their process unobstructed. This court has judicial knowledge that in Indiana the Federal authority was always unopposed, and its courts always open to hear criminal accusations and redress grievances; and no usage of war could sanction a military trial there for any offence whatever of a citizen in civil life, in nowise connected with the military service. Congress could grant no such power; and to the honor of our national legislature be it said, it has never been provoked by the state of the country even to attempt its exercise. One of the plainest constitutional provisions was, therefore, infringed when Milligan was tried by a court not ordained and established by Congress, and not composed of judges appointed during good behavior.

Why was he not delivered to the Circuit Court of Indiana to be proceeded against according to law? . . .

. . . All other persons, citizens of states where the courts are open, if charged with crime, are guaranteed the inestimable privilege of trial by jury. This privilege is a vital principle, underlying the whole administration of criminal justice; it is not held by sufferance, and cannot be frittered away on any plea of state or political necessity. When peace prevails, and the authority of the government is undisputed, there is no difficulty of preserving the safeguards of liberty; for the ordinary modes of trial are never neglected, and no one wishes it otherwise; but if society is disturbed by civil commotion—if the passions of men are aroused and the restraints of law weakened, if not disregarded—these safeguards need, and should receive, the watchful care of those intrusted with the guardianship of the Constitution and laws. In no other way can we transmit to posterity unimpaired the blessings of liberty, consecrated by the sacrifices of the Revolution.

It is claimed that martial law covers with its broad mantle the proceedings of this military commission. The proposition is this: that in a time of war the commander of an armed force (if in his opinion the exigencies of the country demand it, and of which he is to judge), has the power, within the lines of his military district, to suspend all civil rights and their remedies, and subject citizens as well as soldiers to the rule of his will; and in the exercise of his lawful authority cannot be restrained, except by his superior officer or the President of the United States.

If this position is sound to the extent claimed, then when war exists, foreign or domestic, and the country is subdivided into military departments for mere convenience, the commander of one of them can, if he chooses, within his limits, on the plea of necessity, with the approval of the Executive, substitute military force for and to the exclusion of the laws, and punish all persons, as he thinks right and proper, without fixed or certain rules.

The statement of this proposition shows its importance; for, if true, republican government is a failure, and there is an end of liberty regulated by law. Martial law, established on such a basis, destroys every guarantee of the Constitution, and effectually renders the "military independent of and superior to the civil power"—the attempt to do which by the King of Great Britain was deemed by our fathers such an offence, that they assigned it to the world as one of the causes which impelled them to declare their independence. Civil liberty and this kind of martial law cannot endure together; the antagonism is irreconcilable; and, in the conflict, one or the other must perish.

This nation, as experience has proved, cannot always remain at peace, and has no right to expect that it will always have wise and humane rulers, sincerely attached to the principles of the Constitution. Wicked men, ambitious of power, with hatred of liberty and contempt of law, may fill the place once occupied by Washington and Lincoln; and if this right is conceded, and the calamities of war again befall us, the dangers to human liberty are frightful to contemplate. If our fathers had failed to provide for just such a contingency, they would have been false to the trust reposed in them. . . .

It is essential to the safety of every government that, in a great crisis, like the one we have just passed through, there should be a power somewhere of suspending the writ of habeas corpus. In every war, there are men of previously good character, wicked enough to counsel their fellow-citizens to resist the measures deemed necessary by a good government to sustain its just authority and overthrow its enemies; and their influence may lead to dangerous combinations. In the emergency of the times, an immediate public investigation according to law may not be possible; and yet, the peril to the country may be too imminent to suffer such persons to go at large. Unquestionably, there is then an exigency which demands that the government, if it should see fit in the exercise of a proper discretion to make arrests, should not be required to produce the persons arrested in answer to a writ of habeas corpus. The Constitution goes no further. It does not say after a writ of habeas corpus is denied a citizen, that he shall be tried otherwise than by the course of the common law; if it had intended this result, it was easy by the use of direct words to have accomplished it. The illustrious men who framed that instrument were guarding the foundations of civil liberty against the abuses of unlimited power; they were full of wisdom, and the lessons of history informed them that a trial by an established court, assisted by an impartial jury, was the only sure way of protecting the citizen against oppression and wrong. Knowing this, they limited the suspension to one great right, and left the rest to remain forever inviolable. But, it is insisted that the safety of the country in time of war demands that this broad claim for martial law shall be sustained. If this were true, it could be well said that a country, preserved at the sacrifice of all the cardinal principles of liberty, is not worth the cost of preservation. Happily, it is not so.

It will be borne in mind that this is not a question of the power to proclaim martial law, when war exists in a community and the courts and civil authorities are overthrown. Nor is it a question what rule a military commander, at the head of his army, can impose on states in rebellion to cripple their resources and quell the insurrection. The jurisdiction claimed is much more extensive. The necessities of the service, during the late Rebellion, required that the loyal states should be placed within the limits of certain military districts and commanders appointed in them; and, it is urged, that this, in a military sense, constituted them the theatre of military operations; and, as in this case, Indiana had been and was again threatened with invasion by the enemy, the occasion was furnished to establish martial law. The conclusion does not follow from the premises. If armies were collected in Indiana, they were to be employed in another locality, where the laws were obstructed and the national authority disputed. On her soil there was no hostile foot; if once invaded, that invasion was at an end, and with it all pretext for martial law. Martial law cannot arise from a threatened invasion. The necessity must be actual and present; the invasion real, such as effectually closes the courts and deposes the civil administration.

It is difficult to see how the safety of the country required martial law in Indiana. If any of her citizens were plotting treason, the power of arrest could secure them, until the government was prepared for their trial, when the courts were open and ready to try them. It was as easy to protect witnesses before a civil as a military tribunal; and as there could be no wish to convict, except on sufficient legal evidence, surely an ordained and established court was better able to judge of this than a military tribunal composed of gentlemen not trained to the profession of the law.

THE CHIEF JUSTICE delivered the following opinion:

[T]he opinion . . . as we understand it, asserts not only that the military commission held in Indiana was not authorized by Congress, but that it was not in the power of Congress to authorize it, from which it may be thought to follow that Congress has no power to indemnify the officers who composed the commission against liability in civil courts for acting as members of it.

We cannot agree to this.

We agree in the proposition that no department of the government of the United States—neither President, nor Congress, nor the Courts—possesses any power not given by the Constitution.

We assent fully to all that is said in the opinion of the inestimable value of the trial by jury, and of the other constitutional safeguards of civil liberty. And we concur also in what is said of the writ of habeas corpus and of its suspension, with two reservations: (1) that, in our judgment, when the writ is suspended, the Executive is authorized to arrest, as well as to detain, and (2) that there are cases in which, the privilege of the writ being suspended, trial and punishment by military commission, in states where civil courts are open, may be authorized by Congress, as well as arrest and detention.

We think that Congress had power, though not exercised, to authorize the military commission which was held in Indiana.

We do not think it necessary to discuss at large the grounds of our conclusions. We will briefly indicate some of them.

The Constitution itself provides for military government, as well as for civil government. And we do not understand it to be claimed that the civil safeguards of the Constitution have application in cases within the proper sphere of the former.

What, then, is that proper sphere? Congress has power to raise and support armies, to provide and maintain a navy, to make rules for the government and regulation of the land and naval forces, and to provide for governing such part of the militia as may be in the service of the United States.

It is not denied that the power to make rules for the government of the army and navy is a power to provide for trial and punishment by military courts without a jury. It has been so understood and exercised from the adoption of the Constitution to the present time. . . .

We by no means assert that Congress can establish and apply the laws of war where no war has been declared or exists.

Where peace exists, the laws of peace must prevail. What we do maintain is that, when the nation is involved in war, and some portions of the country are invaded, and all are exposed to invasion, it is within the power of Congress to determine in what states or district such great and imminent public danger exists as justifies the authorization of military tribunals for the trial of crimes and offences against the discipline or security of the army or against the public safety. . . .

We cannot doubt that, in such a time of public danger, Congress had power under the Constitution to provide for the organization of a military commission and for trial by that commission of persons engaged in this conspiracy. The fact that the Federal courts were open was regarded by Congress as a sufficient reason for not exercising the power, but that fact could not deprive Congress of the right to exercise it. Those courts might be open and undisturbed in the execution of their functions, and yet wholly incompetent to

BOX 5-3 AFTERMATH ... LAMBDIN P. MILLIGAN

BEGINNING with his October 1864 arrest for disloyal practices and continuing throughout the controversy over his activities, Lambdin Milligan claimed that the charges were a fantasy created by the Republicans for political gain. By the time the Supreme Court reversed his conviction and death sentence, Milligan had spent eighteen months in prison. Upon his release, he returned to his hometown of Huntington, Indiana, where he was received as a local hero. Two decades earlier Milligan had moved with his family to the Indiana town from Ohio to farm and practice law. He had also been active in local Democratic Party politics, unsuccessfully running for Congress and governor.

Milligan immediately sought revenge for the treatment he had received at the hands of the military. He filed suit for trespass and false imprisonment against James Slack, a local attorney who first urged that he be arrested; General Alvin Hovey, who had ordered his arrest; and twenty-two others involved in his prosecution. The jury decided in favor of Milligan, but the law placed a $5 ceiling on damages awarded in such cases, limiting the satisfaction he received from his judicial victory.

Milligan ran a successful legal practice in Huntington for an additional thirty years. He retired in 1897 at the age of eighty-five. He died two years later, only three months after the death of his second wife.

SOURCE: Mark C. Carnes, ed., *American National Biography*, vol. 15 (New York: Oxford University Press, 1999), 529–530.

avert threatened danger or to punish, with adequate promptitude and certainty, the guilty conspirators. . . .

Mr. Justice WAYNE, Mr. Justice SWAYNE, and Mr. Justice MILLER concur with me in these views.

Although the Court's decision was unanimous as to Milligan's claim of illegal imprisonment, the justices split on the power of the government to suspend habeas corpus under the conditions presented in the case. A majority of five (Clifford, Davis, Field, Grier, and Nelson) held that neither the president nor Congress, acting separately or in agreement, could suspend the writ of habeas corpus as long as the civilian courts were in full operation and the area was not a combat zone. In a concurring opinion joined by Miller, Swayne, and Wayne, Chief Justice Chase argued that although the president did not have the power to establish these military tribunals, Congress did.

Before the Court handed down its ruling in this case, President Johnson commuted Milligan's sentence to life in prison, a sentence he was serving under General Hovey in an Ohio prison when the case was decided. Milligan was released from custody in April 1866 *(see box 5-3)*.

World War II

As we already have seen, the restriction of civil liberties during time of war is not uncommon. Nations pressed for their very survival may feel compelled to deny basic liberties to insure against the efforts of traitors and saboteurs. World War II was no exception. During that period the government took many steps that amounted to suppressions of rights and liberties. The most infamous of such actions, which we discuss shortly, was the internment of Americans of Japanese descent.

Yet another action paralleled the one at issue in *Milligan*: the use of military tribunals. In 1941 federal authorities captured eight Nazi saboteurs who had illegally entered the country. All had previously lived in the United States, and one claimed to be a U.S. citizen. President Franklin D. Roosevelt, in his capacity as president and commander in chief of the army and navy, and acting what he believed to be authority granted to him by Congress under the Articles of War,[13] ordered the saboteurs to be tried by a military tribunal. The Germans filed for a writ of habeas corpus, claiming that the president had no authority to subject them to military trial and that they, like Milligan, had the right to be tried in the civilian courts.

13. Article I of the Constitution gives Congress the power to "To make Rules for the Government and Regulation of the land and naval Force." Under this power, Congress enacted the Articles of War in 1806. The system of military justice continued to operate under the Articles of War (with revisions) until 1950 when Congress passed the Uniform Code of Military Justice, which went into effect in 1951 and replaced the Articles of War.

In ***Ex parte Quirin*** (1942), however, the justices unanimously upheld the government's authority to try these men by military tribunal. Why did the Court reach a decision seemingly inconsistent with the precedent set in *Milligan*? According to the justices, the Nazi saboteurs were unlawful combatants. Contrary to the laws of war, they secretly and illegally entered the country without uniform for the purpose of gathering military information or destroying life and property. As such, the saboteurs had no right to be treated as prisoners of war but could be subject to trial by military tribunal. Milligan, by comparison, was an American citizen, permanently residing in the United States, and not a military combatant in service to the enemy. The *Quirin* Court also emphasized that Congress had explicitly approved of the use of military commissions in the Articles of War. In a case we discuss later in this chapter, in ***Hamdan v. Rumsfeld*** (2006), Justice Stevens took issue with the *Quirin* Court's conclusion that Congress gave its approval to the military commissions, deeming it "controversial."

Other commentators suggest that the circumstances surrounding the two earlier cases help explain the different result: *Milligan* was decided after the war was over, whereas *Quirin* came down "during the darkest days of World War II," as Chief Justice William H. Rehnquist wrote.[14]

Rehnquist is probably right: It did not help the Nazis that they, unlike Milligan, were captured and tried during one of the most desperate times of the war when public opinion toward Germany was especially hostile. Six of the eight saboteurs were sentenced to death, and the remaining two received long prison terms in return for their cooperation with federal authorities.

Until recently this case provoked less criticism and notoriety than litigation associated with the internment of Japanese Americans, but it is worthy of our consideration. The final section of this chapter discusses President George W. Bush's authorization of the use of military tribunals for foreign nationals suspected of terrorism, giving *Quirin* and *Milligan* new relevance.

We leave it to you to ponder these and other possibilities. You might want to consider also the contemporary reaction to *Quirin,* which was, as

Prisoner Richard Quirin, thirty-four, is escorted on July 12, 1942, to the courtroom in the Justice Department building where he and seven other accused Nazi saboteurs stood trial before a special military commission.

Rehnquist suggests, decidedly against the saboteurs. If anything, Americans were "disappointed" that the Court even took the case, believing that the eight should be "shot on sight."[15] But subsequent responses have cast the whole episode, including the Court's decision, in a different light. A decade or so after the decision, Justice Felix Frankfurter deemed it "not a happy precedent." Legal scholar John Frank, who served as a clerk to Justice Hugo Black at the time the Court decided *Quirin,* said simply, "The Court allowed itself to be stampeded," presumably by the Roosevelt administration.[16] Despite these reactions, *Quirin* remains good law, as the Court has never overruled it. Keep this point in mind when we return to the subject of military tribunals in the last section of this chapter.

However negatively history has treated *Quirin,* the reactions are relatively mild compared with those

14. William H. Rehnquist, *All the Laws but One: Civil Liberties in Wartime* (New York: Knopf, 1998), 221.

15. Alpheus T. Mason, "Inter Arma Silent Leges," *Harvard Law Review* 69 (1955): 815.

16. The quotes in this paragraph come from Tony Mauro, "A Mixed Precedent for Military Tribunals," *Legal Times,* November 19, 2001.

evoked by the Court's decision in *Korematsu v. United States* (1944), one of the Japanese American internment cases. Read Justice Black's decision carefully. Does he make a convincing case that the conditions of war stretch the Constitution to the point that exclusion orders based on race or national origin are permissible? How can you explain the fact that some of the justices who were the most sympathetic to civil liberties causes—Black, Harlan Fiske Stone, Douglas, and Wiley Rutledge—voted to approve the military orders? Compare Black's opinion with the dissents of Justice Frank Murphy, who emphasizes the racial foundations of the policy, and Justice Robert Jackson, who stresses the possible long-term consequences of construing the Constitution to uphold the government's actions.

Korematsu v. United States

323 U.S. 214 (1944)

http://laws.findlaw.com/us/323/214.html

Vote: 6 (Black, Douglas, Frankfurter, Reed, Rutledge, Stone)
3 (Jackson, Murphy, Roberts)

OPINION OF THE COURT: *Black*

CONCURRING OPINION: *Frankfurter*

DISSENTING OPINIONS: *Jackson, Murphy, Roberts*

FACTS:

The origins of *Korematsu* lie in Japan's bombing of Pearl Harbor on December 7, 1941, which touched off a wave of anti-Japanese hysteria in the United States. In the early weeks of the Pacific war the Japanese fleet demonstrated remarkable strength and power, and the United States feared that Japanese forces were planning an invasion of the West Coast. The large numbers of people of Japanese ancestry living on the coast also became a matter of concern. Many thought that among the Japanese American population were significant numbers of people sympathetic to the Japanese war effort, people who might aid the enemy in an invasion of the United States.

To prevent such an occurrence, on February 19, 1942, President Roosevelt issued Executive Order 9066, which applied to all people of Japanese background residing on the West Coast. His initial command placed all Japanese Americans under a tight curfew that required them to stay in their homes between 8:00 P.M. and 6:00 A.M. and to register for future relocation. This order was followed by the much harsher orders to evacuate Japanese Americans from the Pacific Coast area and move them to inland detention centers. The first of these, Civilian Exclusion

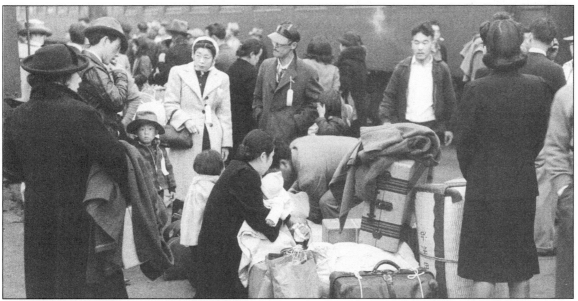

Library of Congress

During World War II thousands of Japanese Americans were removed from their jobs and homes and relocated to internment camps. In 1988, more than four decades after the war, Congress appropriated $20,000 in compensation for each of the 75,000 surviving internees.

Order 34, came on May 3. It was not issued directly by Roosevelt, but by Lieutenant General John L. DeWitt, the commanding general of the Western Defense Command. The secretary of war had authorized DeWitt to issue the order pursuant to Roosevelt's executive order of February 19, which Congress had ratified in March.

The program made no attempt to distinguish the loyal from the disloyal or the citizen from the noncitizen—it affected all persons of Japanese ancestry. The government interned an estimated 110,000 Japanese American citizens and resident aliens, some for as long as four years.[17] These actions spawned a number of important lawsuits.

In 1943 the Supreme Court heard a challenge to the curfew regulations brought by Gordon Hirabayashi, an American citizen of Japanese descent. He was a native of Washington State and a pacifist of the Quaker faith. At the time he challenged the government actions, he was a senior at the University of Washington. In *Hirabayashi v. United States* (1943) the Supreme Court unanimously upheld the constitutionality of the curfew program. For the Court, Chief Justice Harlan Fiske Stone explained that the war powers doctrine gave the government ample authority to impose the restrictions. The grave and threatening conditions of war made the racially based program constitutionally acceptable.

The following year the Court heard *Korematsu v. United States* (1944), an appeal attacking the most serious denial of the civil liberties of Japanese Americans— the orders removing them to detention camps. Fred Korematsu was arrested May 30, 1942, by San Leandro, California, police for being on the public streets in violation of the government's evacuation orders. Korematsu was a native-born American whose parents had immigrated to the United States from Japan. He grew up in the San Francisco area. Rejected for military service for health reasons, he worked in the defense industry as a welder. When arrested, he tried to convince police that he was of Spanish Hawaiian origin. He had undergone plastic surgery to make his racial characteristics less pronounced in an effort to avoid the anti-Japanese discrimination he feared because of his engagement to an Italian American

woman.[18] After the arrest, representatives of the American Civil Liberties Union approached Korematsu and offered to defend him and challenge the validity of the evacuation program. The Japanese-American Citizens League also lent support.

ARGUMENTS:

For the petitioner, Fred Toyosaburo Korematsu:

- The congressional law, proclamations, and orders are unconstitutional because they deprive Korematsu of rights accorded to other citizens of the United States without due process of law in violation of the Fifth Amendment. These include the right to "live and work where he will" (*Allegeyer v. Louisiana*), "to establish a home" (*Meyer v. Nebraska*), and to "freedom of movement" (*Williams v. Fears*).

- The government's actions deny Korematsu equal protection of the laws; they discriminate on the basis of race. Although the equal protection clause of the Fourteenth Amendment applies to the states, for purposes of equal protection the due process clause of the Fifth Amendment, which applies to the federal government, and the Fourteenth Amendment clause are identical. The utter inequality at issue here violates the due process clause, which in the United States cannot mean one law for one citizen and another for another citizen. Prejudice, not military necessity, inspired the internments.

- The government's actions also violate the petitioner's Sixth Amendment rights. The government's actions subject him to deportation and internment without informing him of the nature and cause of any accusations against him and without affording him a fair trial.

For the respondent, United States:

- The order was a valid exercise of the war power. This Court ruled in *Hirabayashi* that the joint war power of the president and Congress is sufficiently broad to cover a measure for which there is "any substantial basis" to conclude that a "protective measure is necessary to meet the threat of sabotage and espionage."

- A substantial basis exists to conclude that some persons of Japanese ancestry, although American

---

17. See Peter H. Irons, *Justice at War: The Story of the Japanese American Internment Cases* (New York: Oxford University Press, 1983).

18. Ibid., 93–99.

citizens, had formed an attachment to and sympathy and enthusiasm for Japan. It would be impossible to have quickly and accurately distinguished these persons from other Japanese Americans.

MR. JUSTICE BLACK DELIVERED THE OPINION OF THE COURT.

It should be noted, to begin with, that all legal restrictions which curtail the civil rights of a single racial group are immediately suspect. That is not to say that all such restrictions are unconstitutional. It is to say that courts must subject them to the most rigid scrutiny. Pressing public necessity may sometimes justify the existence of such restrictions; racial antagonism never can. . . .

In the light of the principles we announced in the *Hirabayashi* case, we are unable to conclude that it was beyond the war power of Congress and the Executive to exclude those of Japanese ancestry from the West Coast war area at the time they did. True, exclusion from the area in which one's home is located is a far greater deprivation than constant confinement to the home from 8 P.M. to 6 A.M. Nothing short of apprehension by the proper military authorities of the gravest imminent danger to the public safety can constitutionally justify either. But exclusion from a threatened area, no less than curfew, has a definite and close relationship to the prevention of espionage and sabotage. The military authorities, charged with the primary responsibility of defending our shores, concluded that curfew provided inadequate protection and ordered exclusion. They did so, as pointed out in our *Hirabayashi* opinion, in accordance with Congressional authority to the military to say who should, and who should not, remain in the threatened areas.

In this case the petitioner challenges the assumptions upon which we rested our conclusions in the *Hirabayashi* case. He also urges that by May 1942, when Order No. 34 was promulgated, all danger of Japanese invasion of the West Coast had disappeared. After careful consideration of these contentions we are compelled to reject them.

Here, as in the *Hirabayashi* case, " . . . we cannot reject as unfounded the judgment of the military authorities and of Congress that there were disloyal members of that population, whose number and strength could not be precisely and quickly ascertained. We cannot say that the warmaking branches of the Government did not have ground for believing that in a critical hour such persons could not readily be isolated and separately dealt with, and constituted a menace to the national defense and safety, which

demanded that prompt and adequate measures be taken to guard against it."

Like curfew, exclusion of those of Japanese origin was deemed necessary because of the presence of an unascertained number of disloyal members of the group, most of whom we have no doubt were loyal to this country. It was because we could not reject the finding of the military authorities that it was impossible to bring about an immediate segregation of the disloyal from the loyal that we sustained the validity of the curfew order as applying to the whole group. In the instant case, temporary exclusion of the entire group was rested by the military on the same ground. The judgment that exclusion of the whole group was for the same reason a military imperative answers the contention that the exclusion was in the nature of group punishment based on antagonism to those of Japanese origin. That there were members of the group who retained loyalties to Japan has been confirmed by investigations made subsequent to the exclusion. Approximately five thousand American citizens of Japanese ancestry refused to swear unqualified allegiance to the United States and to renounce allegiance to the Japanese Emperor, and several thousand evacuees requested repatriation to Japan.

We uphold the exclusion order as of the time it was made and when the petitioner violated it. In doing so, we are not unmindful of the hardships imposed by it upon a large group of American citizens. But hardships are part of war, and war is an aggregation of hardships. All citizens alike, both in and out of uniform, feel the impact of war in greater or lesser measure. Citizenship has its responsibilities as well as its privileges, and in time of war the burden is always heavier. Compulsory exclusion of large groups of citizens from their homes, except under circumstances of direst emergency and peril, is inconsistent with our basic governmental institutions. But when under conditions of modern warfare our shores are threatened by hostile forces, the power to protect must be commensurate with the threatened danger. . . .

It is said that we are dealing here with the case of imprisonment of a citizen in a concentration camp solely because of his ancestry, without evidence or inquiry concerning his loyalty and good disposition towards the United States. Our task would be simple, our duty clear, were this a case involving the imprisonment of a loyal citizen in a concentration camp because of racial prejudice. Regardless of the true nature of the assembly and relocation centers—and we deem it unjustifiable to call them concentration camps with all the ugly connotations that term implies—we are dealing specifically with nothing but an exclusion order. To cast this case into outlines of racial prejudice, without reference to the real military dangers which were presented, merely confuses the issue. Korematsu was not excluded from the Military Area because of hostility to him or his race. He *was* excluded because we are at war with the Japanese Empire, because the properly constituted military authorities feared an invasion of our West Coast and felt constrained to take proper security measures, because they decided that the military urgency of the situation demanded that all citizens of Japanese ancestry be segregated from the West Coast temporarily, and finally, because Congress, reposing its confidence in this time of war in our military leaders—as inevitably it must—determined that they should have the power to do just this. There was evidence of disloyalty on the part of some, the military authorities considered that the need for action was great, and time was short. We cannot—by availing ourselves of the calm perspective of hindsight—now say that at that time these actions were unjustified.

Affirmed.

MR. JUSTICE FRANKFURTER, concurring.

The provisions of the Constitution which confer on the Congress and the President powers to enable this country to wage war are as much part of the Constitution as provisions looking to a nation at peace. And we have had recent occasion to quote approvingly the statement of former Chief Justice Hughes that the war power of the Government is "the power to wage war successfully." *Hirabayashi v. United States.* Therefore, the validity of action under the war power must be judged wholly in the context of war. That action is not to be stigmatized as lawless because like action in times of peace would be lawless. To talk about a military order that expresses an allowable judgment of war needs by those entrusted with the duty of conducting war as "an unconstitutional order" is to suffuse a part of the Constitution with an atmosphere of unconstitutionality. The respective spheres of action of military authorities and of judges are of course very different. But within their sphere, military authorities are no more outside the bounds of obedience to the Constitution than are judges within theirs. To recognize that military orders are "reasonably expedient military precautions" in time of war and yet to deny them constitutional legitimacy makes of the Constitution an instrument for dialectic subtleties not reasonably to be attributed to the hard-headed Framers, of whom a majority had had actual participation in war. If a military order such as that under review does not transcend the means appropriate for conducting war, such action by the military is as constitutional as would be any authorized action by the Interstate Commerce Commission within the limits of the constitutional power to regulate commerce. And being an exercise of the war power explicitly granted by the Constitution for safeguarding the national life by prosecuting war effectively, I find nothing in the Constitution which denies to Congress the power to enforce such a valid military order by making its violation an offense triable in the civil courts. To find that the Constitution does not forbid the military measures now complained of does not carry with it approval.

MR. JUSTICE MURPHY, dissenting.

This exclusion of "all persons of Japanese ancestry, both alien and non-alien," from the Pacific Coast area on a plea of military necessity in the absence of martial law ought not to be approved. Such exclusion goes over "the very brink of constitutional power" and falls into the ugly abyss of racism.

In dealing with matters relating to the prosecution and progress of a war, we must accord great respect and consideration to the judgments of the military authorities who are on the scene and who have full knowledge of the military facts. The scope of their discretion must, as a matter of necessity and common sense, be wide. And their judgments ought not to be overruled lightly by those whose training and duties ill-equip them to deal intelligently with matters so vital to the physical security of the nation.

At the same time, however, it is essential that there be definite limits to military discretion, especially where martial law has not been declared. Individuals must not be left impoverished of their constitutional rights on a plea of military necessity that has neither substance nor support. Thus, like other claims conflicting with the asserted constitutional rights of the individual, the military claim must subject itself to the judicial process of having its reasonableness determined and its conflicts with other interests reconciled. "What are the allowable limits of military discretion, and whether or not they have been overstepped in a particular case, are judicial questions."

The judicial test of whether the Government, on a plea of military necessity, can validly deprive an individual of any of his constitutional rights is whether the deprivation is reasonably related to a public danger that is so "immediate, imminent, and impending" as not to admit of delay and not to permit the intervention of ordinary constitutional processes to alleviate the danger. Civilian Exclusion Order

No. 34, banishing from a prescribed area of the Pacific Coast "all persons of Japanese ancestry, both alien and non-alien," clearly does not meet that test. Being an obvious racial discrimination, the order deprives all those within its scope of the equal protection of the laws as guaranteed by the Fifth Amendment. It further deprives these individuals of their constitutional rights to live and work where they will, to establish a home where they choose and to move about freely. In excommunicating them without benefit of hearings, this order also deprives them of all their constitutional rights to procedural due process. Yet no reasonable relation to an "immediate, imminent, and impending" public danger is evident to support this racial restriction which is one of the most sweeping and complete deprivations of constitutional rights in the history of this nation in the absence of martial law.

It must be conceded that the military and naval situation in the spring of 1942 was such as to generate a very real fear of invasion of the Pacific Coast, accompanied by fears of sabotage and espionage in that area. The military command was therefore justified in adopting all reasonable means necessary to combat these dangers. In adjudging the military action taken in light of the then apparent dangers, we must not erect too high or too meticulous standards; it is necessary only that the action have some reasonable relation to the removal of the dangers of invasion, sabotage and espionage. But the exclusion, either temporarily or permanently, of all persons with Japanese blood in their veins has no such reasonable relation. And that relation is lacking because the exclusion order necessarily must rely for its reasonableness upon the assumption that *all* persons of Japanese ancestry may have a dangerous tendency to commit sabotage and espionage and to aid our Japanese enemy in other ways. It is difficult to believe that reason, logic or experience could be marshalled in support of such an assumption.

That this forced exclusion was the result in good measure of this erroneous assumption of racial guilt rather than bona fide military necessity is evidenced by the Commanding General's Final Report on the evacuation from the Pacific Coast area. In it he refers to all individuals of Japanese descent as "subversive," as belonging to "an enemy race" whose "racial strains are undiluted," and as constituting "over 112,000 potential enemies . . . at large today" along the Pacific Coast. . . .

The main reasons relied upon by those responsible for the forced evacuation, therefore, do not prove a reasonable relation between the group characteristics of Japanese Americans and the dangers of invasion, sabotage and espionage. The reasons appear, instead, to be largely an accumulation of much of the misinformation, half-truths and insinuations that for years have been directed against Japanese Americans by people with racial and economic prejudices— the same people who have been among the foremost advocates of the evacuation. A military judgment based upon such racial and sociological considerations is not entitled to the great weight ordinarily given the judgments based upon strictly military considerations. Especially is this so when every charge relative to race, religion, culture, geographical location, and legal and economic status has been substantially discredited by independent studies made by experts in these matters.

The military necessity which is essential to the validity of the evacuation order thus resolves itself into a few intimations that certain individuals actively aided the enemy, from which it is inferred that the entire group of Japanese Americans could not be trusted to be or remain loyal to the United States. . . . To give constitutional sanction to that inference in this case, however well-intentioned may have been the military command on the Pacific Coast, is to adopt one of the cruelest of the rationales used by our enemies to destroy the dignity of the individual and to encourage and open the door to discriminatory actions against other minority groups in the passions of tomorrow. . . .

Moreover, there was no adequate proof that the Federal Bureau of Investigation and the military and naval intelligence services did not have the espionage and sabotage situation well in hand during this long period. Nor is there any denial of the fact that not one person of Japanese ancestry was accused or convicted of espionage or sabotage after Pearl Harbor while they were still free, a fact which is some evidence of the loyalty of the vast majority of these individuals and of the effectiveness of the established methods of combatting these evils. It seems incredible that, under these circumstances, it would have been impossible to hold loyalty hearings for the mere 112,000 persons involved—or at least for the 70,000 American citizens—especially when a large part of this number represented children and elderly men and women. Any inconvenience that may have accompanied an attempt to conform to procedural due process cannot be said to justify violations of constitutional rights of individuals.

I dissent, therefore, from this legalization of racism. Racial discrimination in any form and in any degree has no justifiable part whatever in our democratic way of life. It is unattractive in any setting but it is utterly revolting among a free people who have embraced the principles set forth in the Constitution of the United States. All residents of this nation are kin in some way by blood or culture to a foreign land. Yet they are primarily and necessarily a part of the new and distinct civilization of the United States. They must accordingly be treated at all times as the heirs of the American experiment and as entitled to all the rights and freedoms guaranteed by the Constitution.

MR. JUSTICE JACKSON, dissenting.

Korematsu was born on our soil, of parents born in Japan. The Constitution makes him a citizen of the United States by nativity and a citizen of California by residence. No claim is made that he is not loyal to this country. There is no suggestion that apart from the matter involved here he is not law-abiding and well disposed. Korematsu, however, has been convicted of an act not commonly a crime. It consists merely of being present in the state whereof he is a citizen, near the place where he was born, and where all his life he has lived.

Even more unusual is the series of military orders which made this conduct a crime. They forbid such a one to remain, and they also forbid him to leave. They were so drawn that the only way Korematsu could avoid violation was to give himself up to the military authority. This meant submission to custody, examination, and transportation out of the territory, to be followed by indeterminate confinement in detention camps.

A citizen's presence in the locality, however, was made a crime only if his parents were of Japanese birth. Had Korematsu been one of four—the others being, say, a German alien enemy, an Italian alien enemy, and a citizen of American-born ancestors, convicted of treason but out on parole—only Korematsu's presence would have violated the order. The difference between their innocence and his crime would result, not from anything he did, said, or thought, different than they, but only in that he was born of different racial stock.

Now, if any fundamental assumption underlies our system, it is that guilt is personal and not inheritable. Even if all of one's antecedents had been convicted of treason, the Constitution forbids its penalties to be visited upon him, for it provides that "no attainder of treason shall work corruption of blood, or forfeiture except during the life of the person attainted." But here is an attempt to make an otherwise innocent act a crime merely because this prisoner is the son of parents as to whom he had no choice, and belongs to a race from which there is no way to resign. If Congress in peace-time legislation should enact such a criminal law, I should suppose this Court would refuse to enforce it. . . .

It would be impracticable and dangerous idealism to expect or insist that each specific military command in an area of probable operations will conform to conventional tests of constitutionality. When an area is so beset that it must be put under military control at all, the paramount consideration is that its measures be successful, rather than legal. The armed services must protect a society, not merely its Constitution. The very essence of the military job is to marshal physical force, to remove every obstacle to its effectiveness, to give it every strategic advantage. Defense measures will not, and often should not, be held within the limits that bind civil authority in peace. No court can require such a commander in such circumstances to act as a reasonable man; he may be unreasonably cautious and exacting. Perhaps he should be. But a commander in temporarily focusing the life of a community on defense is carrying out a military program; he is not making law in the sense the courts know the term. He issues orders, and they may have a certain authority as military commands, although they may be very bad as constitutional law.

But if we cannot confine military expedients by the Constitution, neither would I distort the Constitution to approve all that the military may deem expedient. This is what the Court appears to be doing, whether consciously or not. I cannot say, from any evidence before me, that the orders of General DeWitt were not reasonably expedient military precautions, nor could I say that they were. But even if they were permissible military procedures, I deny that it follows that they are constitutional. If, as the Court holds, it does follow, then we may as well say that any military order will be constitutional and have done with it.

The limitation under which courts always will labor in examining the necessity for a military order are illustrated by this case. How does the Court know that these orders have a reasonable basis in necessity? No evidence whatever on that subject has been taken by this or any other court. There is sharp controversy as to the credibility of the DeWitt report. So the Court, having no real evidence before it, has no choice but to accept General DeWitt's own unsworn, self-serving statement, untested by any cross-examination, that what he did was reasonable. And thus it will always be when courts try to look into the reasonableness of a military order.

In the very nature of things, military decisions are not susceptible of intelligent judicial appraisal. They do not pretend to rest on evidence, but are made on information that often would not be admissible and on assumptions that could not be proved. Information in support of an order could not be disclosed to courts without danger that it would reach the enemy. Neither can courts act on communications made in confidence. Hence, courts can never have any real alternative to accepting the mere declaration of the authority that issued the order that it was reasonably necessary from a military viewpoint.

Much is said of the danger to liberty from the Army program for deporting and detaining these citizens of Japanese extraction. But a judicial construction of the due process clause that will sustain this order is a far more subtle blow to liberty than the promulgation of the order itself. A military order, however unconstitutional, is not apt to last longer than the military emergency. Even during that period a succeeding commander may revoke it all. But once a judicial opinion rationalizes such an order to show that it conforms to the Constitution, or rather rationalizes the Constitution to show that the Constitution sanctions such an order, the Court for all time has validated the principle of racial discrimination in criminal procedure and of transplanting American citizens. The principle then lies about like a loaded weapon ready for the hand of any authority that can bring forward a plausible claim of an urgent need. . . .

I should hold that a civil court cannot be made to enforce an order which violates constitutional limitations even if it is a reasonable exercise of military authority.

 BOX 5-4 AFTERMATH . . . FRED KOREMATSU

FOLLOWING his arrest and conviction in 1942 for refusing to leave his Northern California home in compliance with President Franklin D. Roosevelt's evacuation orders, Fred T. Korematsu was sentenced to five years' probation. He was also sent with other Japanese Americans to an isolated internment camp in Topaz, Utah. After the war, he returned to his home in San Leandro, California, married, and continued his work as a welder.

Almost forty years later, documents were discovered providing evidence that officials of the U.S. Navy and the Justice Department had intentionally deceived the Supreme Court by suppressing information showing that Japanese Americans posed no threat during World War II. Based on this new evidence, lawyers representing Korematsu filed a legal action to clear his name. In November 1983 a federal district court in San Francisco overturned Korematsu's conviction. Charges against Gordon Hirabayashi for violating a curfew imposed on Japanese Americans, upheld by the Supreme Court in 1942, were similarly reversed by a Seattle federal court in 1986. These legal actions helped fuel a movement that led Congress in 1988 to approve $20,000 in reparations for each living Japanese American who was interned during the war.

In 1998 President Bill Clinton awarded Korematsu, then seventy-eight years old, the Presidential Medal of Freedom, the nation's highest civilian award. "In the long history of our country's constant search for justice," Clinton said, "some names of ordinary citizens stand for millions of souls. Plessy, Brown, Parks. To that distinguished

President Bill Clinton stands with Fred Korematsu after awarding him the Presidential Medal of Freedom on January 15, 1998.

list, today we add the name of Fred Korematsu." Korematsu died in Marin County, California, on March 30, 2005, at the age of eighty-six.

SOURCES: *New York Times*, January 31, 1983, November 11, 1983, August 11, 1988, February 19, 1992; *San Francisco Chronicle*, January 16, 1998.

The courts can exercise only the judicial power, can apply only law, and must abide by the Constitution, or they cease to be civil courts and become instruments of military policy. . . .

My duties as a justice as I see them do not require me to make a military judgment as to whether General DeWitt's evacuation and detention program was a reasonable military necessity. I do not suggest that the courts should have attempted to interfere with the Army in carrying out its task. But I do not think they may be asked to execute a military expedient that has no place in law under the Constitution. I would reverse the judgment and discharge the prisoner.

The *Korematsu* decision was softened, but only slightly, by *Ex parte Endo* (1944), handed down the same day. In that case Mitsuye Endo had been caught escaping from a detention center for Japanese Americans. She had, however, gone through the appropriate government procedures and had been classified as loyal to the United States. The justices ruled in her favor, holding that the government does not have the authority to detain persons whose loyalty has been established. The *Korematsu* decision has been severely criticized, and in 1988 Congress approved $20,000 in reparations for each living Japanese American who was interned during the war *(see box 5-4)*.

Korean Conflict

During the war in Korea the justices were called on to decide the constitutional validity of yet another executive action taken in the name of the war powers doctrine, but this case involved property rights rather than civil liberties. As you read Justice Black's opinion for the Court in *Youngstown Sheet & Tube Co. v. Sawyer* (1952), compare it to his opinion in *Korematsu*. Both involved actions the president took to strengthen war efforts. Does it make sense to you that the Court approved the detention of more than 110,000 individuals on the basis of national origin but ruled that the government could not take nominal possession of the steel mills? Note the analysis provided in Justice Jackson's concurring opinion, in which he lays out an approach for deciding questions of presidential power in relation to congressional action. Consider, too, the dissenting opinion of Chief Justice Frederick Vinson, who concludes that the national emergency justified the president's actions.

© Bettman/Corbis

The attorney representing the steel industry, John W. Davis Jr. (left), arriving at the Supreme Court on May 13, 1952, with acting attorney general Philip B. Perlman. Davis was the Democratic nominee for the presidency in 1924, capturing 29 percent of the popular vote in a loss to Calvin Coolidge. He later represented the school board defendants in the 1954 school desegregation cases.

Youngstown Sheet & Tube Co. v. Sawyer

343 U.S. 579 (1952)
http://laws.findlaw.com/us/343/579.html
Vote: 6 (Black, Burton, Clark, Douglas, Frankfurter, Jackson)
  3 (Minton, Reed, Vinson)
OPINION OF THE COURT: *Black*
CONCURRING OPINIONS: *Burton, Clark, Douglas, Frankfurter, Jackson*
DISSENTING OPINION: *Vinson*

FACTS:

In 1951 a labor dispute began in the American steel industry. In December the United Steelworkers Union announced that it would call a strike at the end of that month, when its contract with the steel companies expired. For the next several months the Federal Mediation and Conciliation Service and the Federal Wage Stabilization Board tried to work out a settlement, but without success. On April 4, 1952, the union said that its strike would begin on April 9.

President Harry S. Truman was not about to let a strike hit the steel industry. The nation was engaged in a war in Korea, and steel was needed to produce arms and other military equipment. Only hours before the strike was to begin, Truman issued an executive order commanding Secretary of Commerce Charles Sawyer to seize the nation's steel mills and keep them in operation. Sawyer in turn ordered the mill owners to continue to run their facilities as operators for the United States.

Truman's seizure order cited no statutory authority for his action because there was none. Federal statutes allowed government seizure of industrial plants for certain specified reasons, but the settlement of a labor dispute was not one of them. In fact, the Taft-Hartley Act of 1947 rejected the idea that labor disputes could be resolved by such means. Instead, the act authorized the president to impose an eighty-day cooling-off period as a way to postpone any strike that seriously threatened the public interest. Truman, however, had little regard for the Taft-Hartley Act, which Congress had passed over his veto. The president ignored the cooling-off period alternative and took the direct action of seizing the mills. The inherent powers of the chief executive, he maintained, were enough to authorize the action.

Congress might have improved the president's legal ground by immediately passing legislation authorizing such seizures retroactively, but it did not. The mill owners complied with the seizure orders under protest and filed suit in federal court to have Truman's action declared unconstitutional. The district court ruled in favor of the steel industry, enjoining the secretary from seizing the plants, but the same day the court of appeals stayed the injunction.

ARGUMENTS:

For the petitioners, Youngstown Sheet & Tube Co. et al.:

- The president's action was inconsistent with and contrary to the remedy Congress expressly provided in the Taft-Hartley Act. There was and could be no valid reason for disregarding the congressional remedy.
- The seizure was not an action taken to meet a sudden national emergency in a situation where no other remedy was available. It was taken with the goal of settling a labor dispute by executive fiat when another remedy was available. Petitioners

stand ready to settle the strike in the manner prescribed by Congress.
- The Constitution does not give the president the power to seize the petitioners' property. The seizure cannot be justified by the president's power as commander in chief because that power is limited to a command or executive function. The president's military functions do not cover any power to legislate on the war or related questions.
- If executive action is not authorized by the Constitution or by Congress—as is the case here—it is invalid. There is no place under the Constitution for the concept of inherent powers.

For the respondent, United States:

- The president took action, temporary in nature, to meet a critical emergency. In so doing, he acted in the discharge of his constitutional function as chief executive and as commander in chief and of his unique constitutional responsibility for the conduct of foreign affairs. In short, he used his constitutional powers to deal with an emergency situation.
- In addition to the general grant of executive power in Article II, Section 1, and the powers stemming from the commander in chief clause, the president has a duty to "take Care that the Laws be faithfully executed." In *In re Neagle* the Court made clear that this clause is available to the president to justify actions taken in the interests of carrying out national policy and protecting the nation's security.
- American history and case law for 150 years support the conclusion that the president has, as the Court noted in *Hirabayashi*, a "wide scope for the exercise of judgment and discretion" in determining the nature and extent of threats to the United States.
- The Taft-Hartley Act was not intended to be either an exclusive or a mandatory means of dealing with labor disputes that threaten the security of the United States. In the Defense of Production Act of 1950, Congress wrote, "It is the intent of Congress, in order to . . . maintain uninterrupted production, that there be effective procedures for the settlement of labor disputes affecting national defense."

MR. JUSTICE BLACK DELIVERED THE OPINION OF THE COURT.

We are asked to decide whether the President was acting within his constitutional power when he issued an order directing the Secretary of Commerce to take possession of and operate most of the Nation's steel mills. The mill owners argue that the President's order amounts to lawmaking, a legislative function which the Constitution has expressly confided to the Congress and not to the President. The Government's position is that the order was made on findings of the President that his action was necessary to avert a national catastrophe which would inevitably result from a stoppage of steel production, and that in meeting this grave emergency the President was acting within the aggregate of his constitutional powers as the Nation's Chief Executive and the Commander in Chief of the Armed Forces of the United States. . . .

The President's power, if any, to issue the order must stem either from an act of Congress or from the Constitution itself. There is no statute that expressly authorizes the President to take possession of property as he did here. Nor is there any act of Congress to which our attention has been directed from which such a power can fairly be implied. Indeed, we do not understand the Government to rely on statutory authorization for this seizure. . . .

It is clear that if the President had authority to issue the order he did, it must be found in some provision of the Constitution. And it is not claimed that express constitutional language grants this power to the President. The contention is that presidential power should be implied from the aggregate of his powers under the Constitution. Particular reliance is placed on provisions in Article II which say that "The executive Power shall be vested in a President . . ."; that "he shall take Care that the Laws be faithfully executed"; and that he "shall be Commander in Chief of the Army and Navy of the United States."

The order cannot properly be sustained as an exercise of the President's military power as Commander in Chief of the Armed Forces. The Government attempts to do so by citing a number of cases upholding broad powers in military commanders engaged in day-to-day fighting in a theater of war. Such cases need not concern us here. Even though "theater of war" be an expanding concept, we cannot with faithfulness to our constitutional system hold that the Commander in Chief of the Armed Forces has the ultimate power as such to take possession of private property in order to keep labor disputes from stopping production. This is a job for the Nation's lawmakers, not for its military authorities.

Nor can the seizure order be sustained because of the several constitutional provisions that grant executive power to the President. In the framework of our Constitution, the President's power to see that the laws are faithfully executed refutes the idea that he is to be a lawmaker. The Constitution limits his functions in the lawmaking process to the recommending of laws he thinks wise and the vetoing of laws he thinks bad. And the Constitution is neither silent nor equivocal about who shall make laws which the President is to execute. The first section of the first article says that "All legislative Powers herein granted shall be vested in a Congress of the United States. . . ." After granting many powers to the Congress, Article I goes on to provide that Congress may "make all Laws which shall be necessary and proper for carrying into Execution the foregoing Powers, and all other Powers vested by this Constitution in the Government of the United States, or in any Department or Officer thereof."

The President's order does not direct that a congressional policy be executed in a manner prescribed by Congress—it directs that a presidential policy be executed in a manner prescribed by the President. The preamble of the order itself, like that of many statutes, sets out reasons why the President believes certain policies should be adopted, proclaims these policies as rules of conduct to be followed, and again, like a statute, authorizes a government official to promulgate additional rules and regulations consistent with the policy proclaimed and needed to carry that policy into execution. The power of Congress to adopt such public policies as those proclaimed by the order is beyond question. It can authorize the taking of private property for public use. It can make laws regulating the relationships between employers and employees, prescribing rules designed to settle labor disputes, and fixing wages and working conditions in certain fields of our economy. The Constitution does not subject this lawmaking power of Congress to presidential or military supervision or control.

It is said that other Presidents without congressional authority have taken possession of private business enterprises in order to settle labor disputes. But even if this be true, Congress has not thereby lost its exclusive constitutional authority to make laws necessary and proper to carry out the powers vested by the Constitution "in the Government of the United States, or any Department or Officer thereof."

The Founders of this Nation entrusted the lawmaking power to the Congress alone in both good and bad times. It would do no good to recall the historical events, the fears of power and the hopes for freedom that lay behind their choice. Such a review would but confirm our holding that this seizure order cannot stand.

The judgment of the District Court is

Affirmed.

MR. JUSTICE JACKSON, concurring in the judgment and opinion of the Court.

That comprehensive and undefined presidential powers hold both practical advantages and grave dangers for the country will impress anyone who has served as legal adviser to a President in time of transition and public anxiety. While an interval of detached reflection may temper teachings of that experience, they probably are a more realistic influence on my views than the conventional materials of judicial decision which seem unduly to accentuate doctrine and legal fiction. But, as we approach the question of presidential power, we half overcome mental hazards by recognizing them. The opinions of judges, no less than executives and publicists, often suffer the infirmity of confusing the issue of a power's validity with the cause it is invoked to promote, of confounding the permanent executive office with its temporary occupant. The tendency is strong to emphasize transient results upon policies—such as wages or stabilization—and lose sight of enduring consequences upon the balanced power structure of our Republic.

A judge, like an executive adviser, may be surprised at the poverty of really useful and unambiguous authority applicable to concrete problems of executive power as they actually present themselves. Just what our forefathers did envision, or would have envisioned had they foreseen modern conditions, must be divined from materials almost as enigmatic as the dreams Joseph was called upon to interpret for Pharaoh. A century and a half of partisan debate and scholarly speculation yields no net result but only supplies more or less apt quotations from respected sources on each side of any question. They largely cancel each other. And court decisions are indecisive because of the judicial practice of dealing with the largest questions in the most narrow way.

The actual art of governing under our Constitution does not, and cannot, conform to judicial definitions of the power of any of its branches based on isolated clauses, or even single Articles torn from context. While the Constitution diffuses power the better to secure liberty, it also contemplates that practice will integrate the dispersed powers into a workable government. It enjoins upon its branches separateness but interdependence, autonomy but reciprocity. Presidential powers are not fixed but fluctuate depending upon their disjunction or conjunction with those of Congress. We may well begin by a somewhat over-simplified grouping of practical situations in which a President may doubt, or others may challenge, his powers, and by distinguishing roughly the legal consequences of this factor of relativity.

1. When the President acts pursuant to an express or implied authorization of Congress, his authority is at its maximum, for it includes all that he possesses in his own right plus all that Congress can delegate. . . .

2. When the President acts in absence of either a congressional grant or denial of authority, he can only rely upon his own independent powers, but there is a zone of twilight in which he and Congress may have concurrent authority, or in which its distribution is uncertain. Therefore, congressional inertia, indifference or quiescence may sometimes, at least as a practical matter, enable, if not invite, measures on independent presidential responsibility. In this area, any actual test of power is likely to depend on the imperatives of events and contemporary imponderables rather than on abstract theories of law.

3. When the President takes measures incompatible with the expressed or implied will of Congress, his power is at its lowest ebb, for then he can rely only upon his own constitutional powers minus any constitutional powers of Congress over the matter. Courts can sustain exclusive presidential control in such a case only by disabling the Congress from acting upon the subject. Presidential claim to a power at once so conclusive and preclusive must be scrutinized with caution, for what is at stake is the equilibrium established by our constitutional system.

Into which of these classifications does this executive seizure of the steel industry fit? It is eliminated from the first by admission, for it is conceded that no congressional authorization exists for this seizure. . . .

Can it then be defended under flexible tests available to the second category? It seems clearly eliminated from that class because Congress has not left seizure of private property an open field but has covered it by three statutory policies inconsistent with this seizure. . . .

This leaves the current seizure to be justified only by the severe tests under the third grouping, where it can be supported only by any remainder of executive power after subtraction of such powers as Congress may have over the subject. In short, we can sustain the President only by holding that seizure of such strike-bound industries is within his domain and beyond control by Congress. Thus, this Court's first review of such seizures occurs under circumstances which leave presidential power most vulnerable to attack and in the least favorable of possible constitutional postures.

I did not suppose, and I am not persuaded, that history leaves it open to question, at least in the courts, that the executive branch, like the Federal Government as a whole, possesses only delegated powers. The purpose of the

Constitution was not only to grant power, but to keep it from getting out of hand. However, because the President does not enjoy unmentioned powers does not mean that the mentioned ones should be narrowed by a niggardly construction. Some clauses could be made almost unworkable, as well as immutable, by refusal to indulge some latitude of interpretation for changing times. I have heretofore, and do now, give to the enumerated powers the scope and elasticity afforded by what seem to be reasonable, practical implications, instead of the rigidity dictated by a doctrinaire textualism.

The Solicitor General seeks the power of seizure in three clauses of the Executive Article, the first reading, "The executive Power shall be vested in a President of the United States of America." Lest I be thought to exaggerate, I quote the interpretation which his brief puts upon it: "In our view, this clause constitutes a grant of all the executive powers of which the Government is capable." If that be true, it is difficult to see why the forefathers bothered to add several specific items, including some trifling ones.

. . . I cannot accept the view that this clause is a grant in bulk of all conceivable executive power, but regard it as an allocation to the presidential office of the generic powers thereafter stated.

The clause on which the Government next relies is that "The President shall be Commander in Chief of the Army and Navy of the United States. . . ." These cryptic words have given rise to some of the most persistent controversies in our constitutional history. Of course, they imply something more than an empty title. But just what authority goes with the name has plagued presidential advisers who would not waive or narrow it by nonassertion, yet cannot say where it begins or ends. . . .

I cannot foresee all that it might entail if the Court should indorse this argument. Nothing in our Constitution is plainer than that declaration of a war is entrusted only to Congress. Of course, a state of war may, in fact, exist without a formal declaration. But no doctrine that the Court could promulgate would seem to me more sinister and alarming than that a President whose conduct of foreign affairs is so largely uncontrolled, and often even is unknown, can vastly enlarge his mastery over the internal affairs of the country by his own commitment of the Nation's armed forces to some foreign venture. . . .

The third clause in which the Solicitor General finds seizure powers is that "he shall take Care that the Laws be faithfully executed. . . . That authority must be matched against words of the Fifth Amendment that "No person shall be . . . deprived of life, liberty or property, without due process of law. . . ." One gives a governmental authority that reaches so far as there is law, the other gives a private right that authority shall go no farther. These signify about all there is of the principle that ours is a government of laws, not of men, and that we submit ourselves to rulers only if under rules.

The Solicitor General lastly grounds support of the seizure upon nebulous, inherent powers never expressly granted, but said to have accrued to the office from the customs and claims of preceding administrations. The plea is for a resulting power to deal with a crisis or an emergency according to the necessities of the case, the unarticulated assumption being that necessity knows no law.

Loose and irresponsible use of adjectives colors all nonlegal and much legal discussion of presidential powers. "Inherent" powers, "implied" powers, "incidental" powers, "plenary" powers, "war" powers and "emergency" powers are used, often interchangeably and without fixed or ascertainable meanings.

The vagueness and generality of the clauses that set forth presidential powers afford a plausible basis for pressures within and without an administration for presidential action beyond that supported by those whose responsibility it is to defend his actions in court. The claim of inherent and unrestricted presidential powers has long been a persuasive dialectical weapon in political controversy. While it is not surprising that counsel should grasp support from such unadjudicated claims of power, a judge cannot accept self-serving press statements of the attorney for one of the interested parties as authority in answering a constitutional question, even if the advocate was himself. But prudence has counseled that actual reliance on such nebulous claims stop short of provoking a judicial test.

The Solicitor General, acknowledging that Congress has never authorized the seizure here, says practice of prior Presidents has authorized it. He seeks color of legality from claimed executive precedents, chief of which is President Roosevelt's seizure on June 9, 1941, of the California plant of the North American Aviation Company. Its superficial similarities with the present case, upon analysis, yield to distinctions so decisive that it cannot be regarded as even a precedent, much less an authority for the present seizure.

The appeal, however, that we declare the existence of inherent powers *ex necessitate* to meet an emergency asks us to do what many think would be wise, although it is something the forefathers omitted. They knew what emergencies were, knew the pressures they engender for authoritative action, knew, too, how they afford a ready pretext for usurpation. We may also suspect that they suspected that emergency powers would tend to kindle emergencies. Aside from suspension of the privilege of the writ of habeas corpus in time of rebellion or invasion, when the public safety may require it, they made no express provision for exercise of extraordinary authority because of a crisis. I do not think we rightfully may so amend their work, and, if we could, I am not convinced it would be wise to do so, although many modern nations have forthrightly recognized that war and economic crises may upset the normal balance between liberty and authority. . . .

But [contemporary foreign experience] suggests that emergency powers are consistent with free government only when their control is lodged elsewhere than in the Executive who exercises them. That is the safeguard that would be nullified by our adoption of the "inherent powers" formula. Nothing in my experience convinces me that such risks are warranted by any real necessity, although such powers would, of course, be an executive convenience.

In the practical working of our Government, we already have evolved a technique within the framework of the Constitution by which normal executive powers may be considerably expanded to meet an emergency. Congress may and has granted extraordinary authorities which lie dormant in normal times but may be called into play by the Executive in war or upon proclamation of a national emergency. . . .

In view of the ease, expedition and safety with which Congress can grant and has granted large emergency powers, certainly ample to embrace this crisis, I am quite unimpressed with the argument that we should affirm possession of them without statute. Such power either has no beginning or it has no end. If it exists, it need submit to no legal restraint. I am not alarmed that it would plunge us straightway into dictatorship, but it is at least a step in that wrong direction. . . .

I cannot be brought to believe that this country will suffer if the Court refuses further to aggrandize the presidential office, already so potent and so relatively immune from judicial review, at the expense of Congress.

But I have no illusion that any decision by this Court can keep power in the hands of Congress if it is not wise and timely in meeting its problems. A crisis that challenges the President equally, or perhaps primarily, challenges Congress. If not good law, there was worldly wisdom in the maxim attributed to Napoleon that "The tools belong to the man who can use them." We may say that power to legislate for emergencies belongs in the hands of Congress, but only Congress itself can prevent power from slipping through its fingers.

MR. CHIEF JUSTICE VINSON, with whom MR. JUSTICE REED and MR. JUSTICE MINTON join, dissenting.

Those who suggest that this is a case involving extraordinary powers should be mindful that these are extraordinary times. A world not yet recovered from the devastation of World War II has been forced to face the threat of another and more terrifying global conflict.

Accepting in full measure its responsibility in the world community, the United States was instrumental in securing adoption of the United Nations Charter, approved by the Senate by a vote of 89 to 2. The first purpose of the United Nations is to "maintain international peace and security, and to that end: to take effective collective measures for the prevention and removal of threats to the peace, and for the suppression of acts of aggression or other breaches of the peace. . . ." In 1950, when the United Nations called upon member nations "to render every assistance" to repel aggression in Korea, the United States furnished its vigorous support. For almost two full years, our armed forces have been fighting in Korea, suffering casualties of over 108,000 men. Hostilities have not abated. The "determination of the United Nations to continue its action in Korea to meet the aggression" has been reaffirmed. Congressional support of the action in Korea has been manifested by provisions for increased military manpower and equipment and for economic stabilization. . . .

In the Defense Production Act of 1950, Congress granted the powers requested and, *in addition*, granted power to stabilize prices and wages and to provide for settlement of labor disputes arising in the defense program. The Defense Production Act was extended in 1951, a Senate Committee noting that in the dislocation caused by the programs for purchase of military equipment "lies the seed of an economic disaster that might well destroy the military might we are straining to build." Significantly, the Committee examined the problem "in terms of just one commodity, steel," and found "a graphic picture of the over-all inflationary danger growing out of reduced civilian supplies and rising incomes." Even before Korea, steel production at levels above theoretical 100% capacity was not capable of supplying civilian needs alone. Since Korea, the tremendous military demand for steel has far exceeded the increases in productive capacity. This Committee emphasized that the shortage of steel, even with the mills operating at full capacity, coupled with increased civilian purchasing power, presented grave danger of disastrous inflation. . . .

A review of executive action demonstrates that our Presidents have on many occasions exhibited the leadership contemplated by the Framers when they made the President Commander in Chief, and imposed upon him the trust to "take Care that the Laws be faithfully executed." With or without explicit statutory authorization, Presidents have at such times dealt with national emergencies by acting promptly and resolutely to enforce legislative programs, at least to save those programs until Congress could act. Congress and the courts have responded to such executive initiative with consistent approval. . . .

The broad executive power granted by Article II to an officer on duty 365 days a year cannot, it is said, be invoked to avert disaster. Instead, the President must confine himself to sending a message to Congress recommending action. Under this messenger-boy concept of the Office, the President cannot even act to preserve legislative programs from destruction so that Congress will have something left to act upon. There is no judicial finding that the executive action was unwarranted because there was in fact no basis for the President's finding of the existence of an emergency for, under this view, the gravity of the emergency and the immediacy of the threatened disaster are considered irrelevant as a matter of law.

Seizure of plaintiffs' property is not a pleasant undertaking. Similarly unpleasant to a free country are the draft which disrupts the home and military procurement which causes economic dislocation and compels adoption of price controls, wage stabilization and allocation of materials. The President informed Congress that even a temporary Government operation of plaintiffs' properties was "thoroughly distasteful" to him, but was necessary to prevent immediate paralysis of the mobilization program. Presidents have been in the past, and any man worthy of the Office should be in the future, free to take at least interim action necessary to execute legislative programs essential to survival of the Nation. A sturdy judiciary should not be swayed by the unpleasantness or unpopularity of necessary executive action, but must independently determine for itself whether the President was acting, as required by the Constitution, to "take Care that the Laws be faithfully executed."

Youngstown is interesting in at least two regards. First, the justices were sharply divided over the nature of executive power—a subject we covered in chapter 4. Two members of the Court (Douglas and Black) adopted the "mere designation" or enumerated approach, writing, "The President's power, if any, to issue the order must stem either from an act of Congress or from the Constitution itself." Three justices (Vinson, Stanley Reed, and Sherman Minton) took the opposite position. In their opinion, the take care clause of Article II provided the president with a sufficient constitutional basis for his actions: he was taking steps that were in the best interest of the country until Congress could act. Finally, a plurality of four (Frankfurter, Jackson, Harold Burton, and Tom C. Clark) settled somewhere between the two extremes. Jackson's concurrence is especially interesting. Although he seems to read the vesting clause of Article II as a mere designation of office, as do Black and Douglas (as well as to refute *In re Neagle*'s notion of inherent powers), Jackson concedes that other clauses in Article II can and should be interpreted flexibly to accommodate the modern presidency. But, in contrast to the dissenters, he and his three colleagues argue that President Truman could not seize the mills because he had acted against the "implied" desires of Congress. As Jackson puts it, "When the President takes measures incompatible with the expressed or implied will of Congress, his power is at its lowest ebb, for then he can rely only upon his own constitutional powers minus any constitutional powers of Congress over the matter." In other words, when the president is at odds with Congress, he must show that he alone has conclusive and exclusive power, and Congress has none (since Congress withdrew whatever it has).

A second interesting point is this: although it is typically the majority opinion that establishes precedent for the nation, in *Youngstown* legal analysts regard Jackson's concurrence as the most important statement coming out of the case. Indeed, some scholars deem it the most important concurrence ever written. The explanation, it seems, is that Jackson provided a useful framework for dealing with presidential power vis-à-vis Congress.

Foreign Policy in the Middle East

Would the Court adopt the Jackson framework in similar cases in times of national emergency? *Dames & Moore v. Regan* (1981) and *Zivotofsky v. Kerry* (2015), both involving foreign policy toward the Middle East, provide some answers.

In *Dames,* the justices considered an appeal based on a serious foreign policy problem from the Carter administration—the Iran hostage crisis. *Dames &*

Moore involved the power of the president to seize Iranian assets and use them as a bargaining chip to help resolve an international stalemate. To preserve the assets under his control, President Carter disallowed any lawsuits by U.S. citizens and corporations, requesting that the assets be used to pay off judgments against Iran. Was the president acting within his legitimate foreign policy powers? Or was Dames & Moore Company correct in arguing that he had gone too far? As you read the opinion, compare it with the views expressed in *Youngstown*. See how closely Rehnquist—a former law clerk to Justice Jackson—ties his opinion to both Black's majority views and Jackson's concurrence in *Youngstown*.

Dames & Moore v. Regan

453 U.S. 654 (1981)
http://laws.findlaw.com/us/453/654.html
Oral arguments are available at https://www.oyez.org.
Vote: 9 (Blackmun, Brennan, Burger, Marshall, Powell, Rehnquist, Stevens, Stewart, White)
   0

OPINION OF THE COURT: *Rehnquist*

OPINION CONCURRING IN PART: *Stevens*

OPINION CONCURRING IN PART AND DISSENTING IN PART: *Powell*

FACTS:

On November 4, 1979, Iranians seized the American embassy in Tehran, captured its diplomatic personnel, and held them hostage. In response, President Carter invoked the International Economic Emergency Powers Act and froze all assets of the Iranian government and its agencies within the jurisdiction of the United States. As part of the regulations enforcing the order, the Treasury Department ruled that unless otherwise stipulated the seized Iranian assets were protected against judgments, decrees, or attachments by U.S. courts.

On December 19 Dames & Moore Company filed suit in federal district court against the government of Iran, the Atomic Energy Organization of Iran, and a number of Iranian banks. The suit claimed that the company had been under contract with the Iranian Atomic Energy Organization to conduct site inspections for a proposed nuclear power facility and had not been fully paid for its services. Dames & Moore contended that the Iranians still owed the company almost $3.5 million and asked the court to grant it the back payments plus interest. Furthermore, Dames & Moore

wanted the district court to attach Iranian assets in the United States to ensure payment of the judgment.

The crisis ended in January 1981 when the United States and Iran reached an agreement and the hostages were released. As part of the settlement the United States agreed to terminate all American lawsuits involving the frozen Iranian assets. A special Iran–United States Claims Tribunal was established to settle disputes over the Iranian assets; the tribunal's judgments were to be final and enforceable in the courts of any nation. To implement these arrangements, the day before he left office President Carter ordered that all frozen Iranian assets be moved to the Federal Reserve Bank in New York for ultimate transfer back to Iran, with a portion set aside for payment of Claims Tribunal judgments. In February 1981 President Reagan issued executive orders reaffirming Carter's actions.

With these orders in effect, the district court denied attachments against the Iranian assets to pay Dames & Moore. The company then filed a suit against Secretary of the Treasury Donald Regan. The district court ruled in favor of the government, and the Supreme Court accepted the company's appeal, using expedited procedures to bring the case immediately before the justices.

ARGUMENTS:

For the petitioner, Dames & Moore:

- No president has ever done what has been attempted here. A review of the cases and international agreements cited by the government reveals no executive settlement of a commercial claim of a private American citizen against a foreign state pending in an American court at the time of settlement.

- The president exceeded his constitutional and statutory power by removing Iranian assets from possible attachment by the federal courts. The president does not have any inherent authority to settle or remove enforceable claims of Americans properly before Article III courts by executive agreement.

- The International Emergency Economic Powers Act authorizes temporary blocking and freezing of foreign property. But when read against the background of its predecessor statute, the Trading with the Enemy Act, the IEEPA [International Economic Emergency Powers Act] does not authorize the president permanently to transfer foreign property away from American creditors and back to a hostile power.

For the respondents, Donald T. Regan, Secretary of the Treasury, et al.:

- As Justice Jackson noted in *Youngstown Sheet & Tube Co.*, presidential power is at its maximum when exercised with the express or implied authorization of Congress, as is the case here. The president's actions were completely consistent with the language, purposes, and background of the IEEPA.
- In enacting the IEEPA Congress recognized the necessity for the president to possess the authority to control dispositions of alien property in an effort to deal with external threats to the national security, foreign policy, or economy of the United States.
- The president has and has long exercised the authority under the Constitution to settle the claims of American nationals against a foreign country by executive agreement. This power has been approved by Congress and the Court (see *United States v. Pink* [1942]).

JUSTICE REHNQUIST DELIVERED THE OPINION OF THE COURT.

The parties and the lower courts . . . have all agreed that much relevant analysis is contained in *Youngstown Sheet & Tube Co. v. Sawyer* (1952). Justice Black's opinion for the Court in that case, involving the validity of President Truman's effort to seize the country's steel mills in the wake of a nationwide strike, recognized that "[t]he President's power, if any, to issue the order must stem either from an act of Congress or from the Constitution itself." Justice Jackson's concurring opinion elaborated in a general way the consequences of different types of interaction between the two democratic branches in assessing Presidential authority to act in any given case. When the President acts pursuant to an express or implied authorization from Congress, he exercises not only his powers but also those delegated by Congress. In such a case the executive action "would be supported by the strongest of presumptions and the widest latitude of judicial interpretation, and the burden of persuasion would rest heavily upon any who might attack it." When the President acts in the absence of congressional authorization he may enter "a zone of twilight in which he and Congress may have concurrent authority, or in which its distribution is uncertain." In such a case the analysis becomes more complicated, and the validity of the President's action, at least so far as separation-of-powers principles are concerned, hinges on a consideration of all the circumstances which might shed light on the views of the Legislative Branch toward such action, including "congressional inertia, indifference or quiescence." Finally, when the President acts in contravention of the will of Congress, "his power is at its lowest ebb," and the Court can sustain his actions "only by disabling the Congress from acting upon the subject."

Although we have in the past found and do today find Justice Jackson's classification of executive actions into three general categories analytically useful. . . . Justice Jackson himself recognized that his three categories represented "a somewhat over-simplified grouping," and it is doubtless the case that executive action in any particular instance falls, not neatly in one of three pigeonholes, but rather at some point along a spectrum running from explicit congressional authorization to explicit congressional prohibition. This is particularly true as respects cases such as the one before us, involving responses to international crises the nature of which Congress can hardly have been expected to anticipate in any detail. . . .

Although we have declined to conclude that the IEEPA or the Hostage Act directly authorizes the President's suspension of claims for the reasons noted, we cannot ignore the general tenor of Congress' legislation in this area in trying to determine whether the President is acting alone or at least with the acceptance of Congress. As we have noted, Congress cannot anticipate and legislate with regard to every possible action the President may find it necessary to take or every possible situation in which he might act. Such failure of Congress specifically to delegate authority does not, "especially . . . in the areas of foreign policy and national security," imply "congressional disapproval" of action taken by the Executive. On the contrary, the enactment of legislation closely related to the question of the President's authority in a particular case which evinces legislative intent to accord the President broad discretion may be considered to "invite" "measures on independent presidential responsibility," *Youngstown* (Jackson, J., concurring). At least this is so where there is no contrary indication of legislative intent and when, as here, there is a history of congressional acquiescence in conduct of the sort engaged in by the President. . . .

Crucial to our decision today is the conclusion that Congress has implicitly approved the practice of claim settlement by executive agreement. This is best demonstrated by Congress' enactment of the International Claims Settlement Act of 1949. The Act had two purposes: (1) to allocate to United States nationals funds received in the course of an executive claims settlement with Yugoslavia, and (2) to provide a procedure whereby funds resulting from future settlements could be distributed. To achieve these ends Congress created the International Claims Commission, now the Foreign Claims Settlement Commission, and gave it jurisdiction to make final and binding decisions with respect to claims by United States nationals against settlement funds. By creating a procedure to implement future settlement agreements, Congress placed its stamp of approval on such agreements. Indeed, the legislative history of the Act observed that the United States was seeking settlements with countries other than Yugoslavia and that the bill contemplated settlements of a similar nature in the future. . . .

In addition to congressional acquiescence in the President's power to settle claims, prior cases of this Court have also recognized that the President does have some measure of power to enter into executive agreements without obtaining the advice and consent of the Senate. In *United States v. Pink,* for example, the Court upheld the validity of the Litvinov Assignment, which was part of an Executive Agreement whereby the Soviet Union assigned to the United States amounts owed to it by American nationals so that outstanding claims of other American nationals could be paid. . . .

Just as importantly, Congress has not disapproved of the action taken here. Though Congress has held hearings on the Iranian Agreement itself, Congress has not enacted legislation or even passed a resolution, indicating its displeasure with the Agreement. Quite the contrary, the relevant Senate Committee has stated that the establishment of the Tribunal is "of vital importance to the United States." We are thus clearly not confronted with a situation in which Congress has in some way resisted the exercise of Presidential authority.

Finally, we re-emphasize the narrowness of our decision. We do not decide that the President possesses plenary power to settle claims, even as against foreign governmental entities. . . . But where, as here, the settlement of claims has been determined to be a necessary incident to the resolution of a major foreign policy dispute between our country and another, and where, as here, we can conclude that Congress acquiesced in the President's action, we are not prepared to say that the President lacks the power to settle such claims.

Affirmed.

The *Dames & Moore* decision underscores the same principle that the Court articulated almost a half century earlier in *Curtiss-Wright*—the president is the primary government authority over matters of foreign

policy. Yet those powers are not as unlimited as perhaps *Curtiss-Wright* suggested. As emphasized in *Youngstown* and *Dames & Moore,* the president stands on much firmer constitutional ground when acting with the assent of Congress, which Rehnquist thought was the case in the *Dames & Moore* dispute. But even that, as we shall see, is no guarantee that the justices will uphold what they believe to be unconstitutional actions on the part of the political branches.

What about the reverse, when Congress and the president are at odds? Does this automatically spell disaster for the president? Following Jackson's formulation in *Youngstown,* the Court said no in the interesting case of *Zivotofsky v. Kerry* (2015). As you read the excerpt below note how a seemingly small dispute over passport regulation turned into an interesting case pitting the President against Congress for control over foreign policy. Also notice how the justices make use of textual, historical, and structural arguments to shore up their positions.

Zivotofsky v. Kerry, Secretary of State

576 U.S. ___ (2015)
http://caselaw.findlaw.com/us-supreme-court/13–628.html
Oral arguments are available at https://www.oyez.org.
Vote: 6 (Breyer, Ginsburg, Kagan, Kennedy, Sotomayor, and Thomas)
    3 (Alito, Roberts, Scalia)

OPINION OF THE COURT: *Kennedy*

**OPINION CONCURRING IN THE JUDGMENT IN PART AND
    DISSENTING IN PART: *Thomas***

DISSENTING OPINIONS: *Roberts, Scalia*

Ari Zivotofsky (r) with his nine-year-old son Menachem. Menachem's passport was at the center of a dispute between Congress and the President over whether Americans born in Jerusalem should have their birthplaces listed as "Jerusalem" or "Israel."

FACTS:

Jerusalem's political status has long been, and remains, a delicate issue in current international affairs—with, over the years, Israel and Palestine, among others, asserting full or partial sovereignty over the city.

In 1948 President Truman formally recognized Israel in a signed statement of "recognition," but that statement did not recognize Israeli sovereignty over Jerusalem. Since then, no U.S. president has issued an official statement or declaration acknowledging any country's sovereignty over Jerusalem. Instead, the executive branch has maintained that "the status of Jerusalem . . . should be decided not unilaterally but in consultation with all concerned."

State Department policy on passports and consular reports of births abroad reflects the president's position. The department's Foreign Affairs Manual (FAM) instructs its employees to record the place of birth on a passport as the "country [having] present sovereignty over the actual area of birth." If a citizen objects to the country listed as sovereign, he or she may list the city or town of birth rather than the country. The FAM, however, does not allow citizens to list a sovereign that conflicts with executive branch policy. Because the United States does not recognize any country as having sovereignty over Jerusalem, the FAM instructs employees to record the place of birth for citizens born there as "Jerusalem."

In 2002 Congress passed the act at issue here, the Foreign Relations Authorization Act. Section 214 of the Act is titled "United States Policy with Respect to Jerusalem as the Capital of Israel." The subsection that lies at the heart of this case, §214(d), addresses passports. That subsection seeks to override the FAM by allowing citizens born in Jerusalem to list their place of birth as "Israel." §214(d) states, "[f]or purposes of the registration of birth, certification of nationality, or issuance of a passport of a United States citizen born in the city of Jerusalem, the Secretary shall, upon the request of the citizen or the citizen's legal guardian, record the place of birth as Israel."

When he signed the act into law, President George W. Bush issued a signing statement declaring his position that §214 would, "if construed as mandatory rather than advisory, impermissibly interfere with the President's constitutional authority to formulate the position of the United States, speak for the Nation in international affairs, and determine the terms on which recognition is given to foreign states." The president concluded, "U.S. policy regarding Jerusalem has not changed."

Some parties were not reassured by the president's statement. A cable from the U.S. consulate in Jerusalem noted that the Palestine Liberation Organization Executive Committee, Fatah Central Committee, and the Palestinian Authority Cabinet had all issued statements claiming that §214 "undermines the role of the U.S. as a sponsor of the peace process." In the Gaza Strip and elsewhere residents marched in protest.

In response the secretary of state advised diplomats to express their understanding of "Jerusalem's importance to both sides and to many others around the world." He noted his belief that America's "policy towards Jerusalem" had not changed.

In 2002 Menachem Binyamin Zivotofsky was born to U.S. citizens living in Jerusalem. In December of that year, Zivotofsky's mother visited the American Embassy in Tel Aviv to request both a passport and a consular report of birth abroad for her son. She asked that his country of birth be listed as "Israel." The embassy clerks explained that, pursuant to State Department policy, the passport would list only "Jerusalem." Zivotofsky's parents objected and, as his guardians, brought suit on Menachem's behalf in a federal district court.

Zivotofsky claimed that 214(d) gave him the right to have "Israel" recorded as his place of birth in his passport. The secretary of state responded that the case presented a non-justiciable political question or, in the alternative, that §214 violated the Constitution by interfering with the president's constitutional power to "receive Ambassadors and other public Ministers," which embraced the power to recognize a foreign sovereign.

The district court dismissed the case, ***Zivotofsky v. Clinton*** (2012), on the grounds that it raised a political question *(see chapter 2)*. After the court of appeals affirmed, the case went to the Supreme Court in 2012. By an 8–1 vote (with only Justice Breyer dissenting), the Court vacated and remanded the case, holding that "the Judiciary must decide if Zivotofsky's interpretation of the statute is correct, and whether the statute is constitutional"—not whether Jerusalem is, in fact, part of Israel.

On remand the court of appeals agreed with the secretary of state (and the president), ruling that

214(d) unconstitutionally infringed on the president's authority to grant formal recognition to a foreign sovereign. Zivotofsky again appealed to the U.S. Supreme Court, which granted certiorari in 2014.

(Note: In the lower courts, Zivotofsky waived any argument that his consular report of birth abroad should be treated differently than his passport. As a result, the majority addressed only Zivotofsky's passport argument. Justice Thomas, however, differentiated between passports and consular reports in his opinion concurring in part and dissenting in part.)

ARGUMENTS:

For the petitioner, Menachem Binyamin Zivotofsky:

1. Justice Jackson's concurring opinion in *Youngstown Sheet & Tube Co. v. Sawyer* has been adopted by this Court as "the accepted framework for evaluating executive action in this [foreign-policy] area." This case falls within Justice Jackson's third category.

2. Congress frequently and routinely legislates, pursuant to explicit constitutional authority, in areas that affect foreign nations. One example is immigration law.

3. There is no "Recognition Clause" in the United States Constitution. The President is merely assigned the ceremonial duty of receiving foreign ambassadors. And even if there is, history indicates that Congress has engaged in legislative recognition of foreign governments and participated in the recognition process.

For the respondent, John Kerry, Secretary of State:

1. The Constitution's text and structure, as well as historical practice, establish that the President has exclusive authority to recognize foreign states and their governments, as well as the territorial limits of their sovereignty.

2. By contrast, the Constitution makes no provision for the Congress to participate in recognition decisions, or to override the President's decisions.

3. The executive historically has been understood to possess inherent constitutional authority to determine passport content as it pertains to the conduct of diplomacy. §214(d), which purports to establish "United States policy with respect to Jerusalem as

the capital of Israel," encroaches on the President's exclusive constitutional authority to recognize foreign sovereigns.

JUSTICE KENNEDY DELIVERED THE OPINION OF THE COURT.

A delicate subject lies in the background of this case. That subject is Jerusalem. Questions touching upon the history of the ancient city and its present legal and international status are among the most difficult and complex in international affairs. In our constitutional system these matters are committed to the Legislature and the Executive, not the Judiciary. As a result, in this opinion the Court does no more, and must do no more, than note the existence of international debate and tensions respecting Jerusalem. Those matters are for Congress and the President to discuss and consider as they seek to shape the Nation's foreign policies. . . .

The Court addresses two questions to resolve the interbranch dispute now before it. First, it must determine whether the President has the exclusive power to grant formal recognition to a foreign sovereign. Second, if he has that power, the Court must determine whether Congress can command the President and his Secretary of State to issue a formal statement that contradicts the earlier recognition. The statement in question here is a congressional mandate that allows a United States citizen born in Jerusalem to direct the President and Secretary of State, when issuing his passport, to state that his place of birth is "Israel." . . .

In considering claims of Presidential power this Court refers to Justice Jackson's familiar tripartite framework from *Youngstown Sheet & Tube Co. v. Sawyer* (1952) (concurring opinion). The framework divides exercises of Presidential power into three categories: First, when "the President acts pursuant to an express or implied authorization of Congress, his authority is at its maximum, for it includes all that he possesses in his own right plus all that Congress can delegate." Second, "in absence of either a congressional grant or denial of authority" there is a "zone of twilight in which he and Congress may have concurrent authority," and where "congressional inertia, indifference or quiescence may" invite the exercise of executive power. Finally, when "the President takes measures incompatible with the expressed or implied will of Congress . . . he can rely only upon his own constitutional powers minus any constitutional powers of Congress over the matter." To succeed in this third category, the President's asserted power must be both "exclusive" and "conclusive" on the issue.

In this case the Secretary contends that §214(d) infringes on the President's exclusive recognition power by "requiring the President to contradict his recognition position regarding Jerusalem in official communications with foreign sovereigns." In so doing the Secretary acknowledges the President's power is "at its lowest ebb." *Youngstown.* Because the President's refusal to implement §214(d) falls into Justice Jackson's third category, his claim must be "scrutinized with caution," and he may rely solely on powers the Constitution grants to him alone.

To determine whether the President possesses the exclusive power of recognition the Court examines the Constitution's text and structure, as well as precedent and history bearing on the question.

Recognition is a "formal acknowledgement" that a particular "entity possesses the qualifications for statehood" or "that a particular regime is the effective government of a state." . . .

Despite the importance of the recognition power in foreign relations, the Constitution does not use the term "recognition," either in Article II or elsewhere. The Secretary asserts that the President exercises the recognition power based on the Reception Clause, which directs that the President "shall receive Ambassadors and other public Ministers." Art. II, §3. As Zivotofsky notes, the Reception Clause received little attention at the Constitutional Convention. In fact, during the ratification debates, Alexander Hamilton claimed that the power to receive ambassadors was "more a matter of dignity than of authority," a ministerial duty largely "without consequence." *The Federalist* No. 69.

At the time of the founding, however, prominent international scholars suggested that receiving an ambassador was tantamount to recognizing the sovereignty of the sending state. It is a logical and proper inference, then, that a Clause directing the President alone to receive ambassadors would be understood to acknowledge his power to recognize other nations.

This in fact occurred early in the Nation's history when President Washington recognized the French Revolutionary Government by receiving its ambassador. After this incident the import of the Reception Clause became clear—causing Hamilton to change his earlier view. He wrote that the Reception Clause "includes th[e power] of judging, in the case of a revolution of government in a foreign country, whether the new rulers are competent organs of the national will, and ought to be recognised, or not." As a result, the Reception Clause provides support, although not the sole authority, for the President's power to recognize other nations.

The inference that the President exercises the recognition power is further supported by his additional Article II powers. It is for the President, "by and with the Advice and Consent of the Senate," to "make Treaties, provided two thirds of the Senators present concur." Art. II, §2, cl. 2. In addition, "he shall nominate, and by and with the Advice and Consent of the Senate, shall appoint Ambassadors" as well as "other public Ministers and Consuls."

As a matter of constitutional structure, these additional powers give the President control over recognition decisions. . . .

The text and structure of the Constitution grant the President the power to recognize foreign nations and governments. The question then becomes whether that power is exclusive. The various ways in which the President may unilaterally effect recognition—and the lack of any similar power vested in Congress—suggest that it is. So, too, do functional considerations. Put simply, the Nation must have a single policy regarding which governments are legitimate in the eyes of the United States and which are not. Foreign countries need to know, before entering into diplomatic relations or commerce with the United States, whether their ambassadors will be received; whether their officials will be immune from suit in federal court; and whether they may initiate lawsuits here to vindicate their rights. These assurances cannot be equivocal.

Recognition is a topic on which the Nation must "speak . . . with one voice." That voice must be the President's. Between the two political branches, only the Executive has the characteristic of unity at all times. And with unity comes the ability to exercise, to a greater degree, "[d]ecision, activity, secrecy, and dispatch." *The Federalist* No. 70 (A. Hamilton). The President is capable, in ways Congress is not, of engaging in the delicate and often secret diplomatic contacts that may lead to a decision on recognition. He is also better positioned to take the decisive, unequivocal action necessary to recognize other states at international law. These qualities explain why the Framers listed the traditional avenues of recognition—receiving ambassadors, making treaties, and sending ambassadors—as among the President's Article II powers.

The President since the founding has exercised this unilateral power to recognize new states—and the Court has endorsed the practice. See *United States v. Pink* (1942). Texts and treatises on international law treat the President's word as the final word on recognition. In light of this authority all six judges who considered this case in the Court of Appeals agreed that the President holds the exclusive recognition power.

It remains true, of course, that many decisions affecting foreign relations—including decisions that may determine the course of our relations with recognized countries—require congressional action. Congress may "regulate Commerce with foreign Nations," "establish an uniform Rule of Naturalization," "define and punish Piracies and Felonies committed on the high Seas, and Offences against the Law of Nations," "declare War," "grant Letters of Marque and Reprisal," and "make Rules for the Government and Regulation of the land and naval Forces." U. S. Const., Art. I, §8. In addition, the President cannot make a treaty or appoint an ambassador without the approval of the Senate. Art. II, §2, cl. 2. The President, furthermore, could not build an American Embassy abroad without congressional appropriation of the necessary funds. Art. I, §8, cl. 1. Under basic separation-of-powers principles, it is for the Congress to enact the laws, including "all Laws which shall be necessary and proper for carrying into Execution" the powers of the Federal Government. §8, cl. 18.

In foreign affairs, as in the domestic realm, the Constitution "enjoins upon its branches separateness but interdependence, autonomy but reciprocity." *Youngstown* (Jackson, J., concurring). Although the President alone effects the formal act of recognition, Congress' powers, and its central role in making laws, give it substantial authority regarding many of the policy determinations that precede and follow the act of recognition itself. If Congress disagrees with the President's recognition policy, there may be consequences. Formal recognition may seem a hollow act if it is not accompanied by the dispatch of an ambassador, the easing of trade restrictions, and the conclusion of treaties. And those decisions require action by the Senate or the whole Congress.

In practice, then, the President's recognition determination is just one part of a political process that may require Congress to make laws. The President's exclusive recognition power encompasses the authority to acknowledge, in a formal sense, the legitimacy of other states and governments, including their territorial bounds. Albeit limited, the exclusive recognition power is essential to the conduct of Presidential duties. The formal act of recognition is an executive power that Congress may not qualify. If the President is to be effective in negotiations over a formal recognition determination, it must be evident to his counterparts abroad that he speaks for the Nation on that precise question.

A clear rule that the formal power to recognize a foreign government subsists in the President therefore serves a necessary purpose in diplomatic relations. All this, of course, underscores that Congress has an important role in other aspects of foreign policy, and the President may be bound by any number of laws Congress enacts. In this way ambition counters ambition, ensuring that the democratic will of the people is observed and respected in foreign affairs as in the domestic realm. See *The Federalist* No. 51 (J. Madison). . . .

The Secretary urges the Court to define the executive power over foreign relations in even broader terms. He contends that under the Court's precedent the President has "exclusive authority to conduct diplomatic relations," along with "the bulk of foreign-affairs powers." In support of his submission that the President has broad, undefined powers over foreign affairs, the Secretary quotes *United States v. Curtiss-Wright Export Corp.*, which described the President as "the sole organ of the federal government in the field of international relations." This Court declines to acknowledge that unbounded power. A formulation broader than the rule that the President alone determines what nations to formally recognize as legitimate—and that he consequently controls his statements on matters of recognition—presents different issues and is unnecessary to the resolution of this case.

The *Curtiss-Wright* case does not extend so far as the Secretary suggests. In *Curtiss-Wright*, the Court considered whether a congressional delegation of power to the President was constitutional. Congress had passed a joint resolution giving the President the discretion to prohibit arms sales to certain militant powers in South America. The resolution provided criminal penalties for violation of those orders. The Court held that the delegation was constitutional, reasoning that Congress may grant the President substantial authority and discretion in the field of foreign affairs. Describing why such broad delegation may be appropriate, the opinion stated:

"In this vast external realm, with its important, complicated, delicate and manifold problems, the President alone has the power to speak or listen as a representative of the nation. He makes treaties with the advice and consent of the Senate; but he alone negotiates. Into the field of negotiation the Senate cannot intrude; and Congress itself is powerless to invade it."

This description of the President's exclusive power was not necessary to the holding of *Curtiss-Wright*—which, after all, dealt with congressionally authorized action, not a unilateral Presidential determination. Indeed, Curtiss-Wright did not hold that the President is free from Congress' lawmaking power in the field of international relations. The President does have a unique role in communicating with foreign governments. . . . But whether the realm is foreign or domestic, it is still the Legislative Branch, not the Executive Branch, that makes the law.

Having examined the Constitution's text and this Court's precedent, it is appropriate to turn to accepted understandings and practice. In separation-of-powers cases this Court has often "put significant weight upon historical practice." Here, history is not all on one side, but on balance it provides strong support for the conclusion that the recognition power is the President's alone. As Zivotofsky argues, certain historical incidents can be interpreted to support the position that recognition is a shared power. But the weight of historical evidence supports the opposite view, which is that the formal determination of recognition is a power to be exercised only by the President. . . .

The first debate over the recognition power arose in 1793, after France had been torn by revolution. Once the Revolutionary Government was established, Secretary of State Jefferson and President Washington, without consulting Congress, authorized the American Ambassador to resume relations with the new regime. Soon thereafter, the new French Government proposed to send an ambassador, Citizen Genet, to the United States. Members of the President's Cabinet agreed that receiving Genet would be a binding and public act of recognition. They decided, however, both that Genet should be received and that consultation with Congress was not necessary. Congress expressed no disagreement with this position, and Genet's reception marked the Nation's first act of recognition—one made by the President alone. . . .

President Carter recognized the People's Republic of China (PRC) as the government of China, and derecognized the Republic of China, located on Taiwan. As to the status of Taiwan, the President "acknowledge[d] the Chinese position" that "Taiwan is part of China," but he did not accept that claim. The President proposed a new law defining how the United States would conduct business with Taiwan. After extensive revisions, Congress passed, and the President signed, the Taiwan Relations Act. The Act (in a simplified summary) treated Taiwan as if it were a legally distinct entity from China—an entity with which the United States intended to maintain strong ties.

Throughout the legislative process, however, no one raised a serious question regarding the President's exclusive authority to recognize the PRC—or to decline to grant formal recognition to Taiwan. . . .

This history confirms the Court's conclusion in the instant case that the power to recognize or decline to recognize a foreign state and its territorial bounds resides in the President alone. For the most part, Congress has respected the Executive's policies and positions as to formal recognition. At times, Congress itself has defended the President's constitutional prerogative. Over the last 100 years, there has been scarcely any debate over the President's power to recognize foreign states. In this respect the Legislature, in the narrow context of recognition, on balance has acknowledged the importance of speaking "with one voice." The weight of historical evidence indicates Congress has accepted that the power to recognize foreign states and governments and their territorial bounds is exclusive to the Presidency.

As the power to recognize foreign states resides in the President alone, the question becomes whether §214(d) infringes on the Executive's consistent decision to withhold recognition with respect to Jerusalem. . . .

If the power over recognition is to mean anything, it must mean that the President not only makes the initial, formal recognition determination but also that he may maintain that determination in his and his agent's statements. This conclusion is a matter of both common sense and necessity. If Congress could command the President to state a recognition position inconsistent with his own, Congress could override the President's recognition determination. . . . [I]f Congress could alter the President's statements on matters of recognition or force him to contradict them, Congress in effect would exercise the recognition power.

As Justice Jackson wrote in *Youngstown*, when a Presidential power is "exclusive," it "disabl[es] the Congress from acting upon the subject." Here, the subject is quite narrow: The Executive's exclusive power extends no further than his formal recognition determination. But as to that determination, Congress may not enact a law that directly contradicts it. This is not to say Congress may not express its disagreement with the President in myriad ways. For example, it may enact an embargo, decline to confirm an ambassador, or even declare war. But none of these acts would alter the President's recognition decision.

If Congress may not pass a law, speaking in its own voice, that effects formal recognition, then it follows that it may not force the President himself to contradict his earlier statement. That congressional command would not only prevent the Nation from speaking with one voice but also prevent the Executive itself from doing so in conducting foreign relations.

Although the statement required by §214(d) would not itself constitute a formal act of recognition, it is a mandate that the Executive contradict his prior recognition determination in an official document issued by the Secretary of State. . . .

The flaw in §214(d) is further underscored by the undoubted fact that the purpose of the statute was to infringe on the recognition power—a power the Court now holds is the sole prerogative of the President. The statute is titled "United States Policy with Respect to Jerusalem as the Capital of Israel." The House Conference Report proclaimed that §214 "contains four provisions related to the recognition of Jerusalem as Israel's capital." And, indeed, observers interpreted §214 as altering United States policy regarding Jerusalem—which led to protests across the region. From the face of §214, from the legislative history, and from its reception, it is clear that Congress wanted to express its displeasure with the President's policy by, among other things, commanding the Executive to contradict his own, earlier stated position on Jerusalem. This Congress may not do.

It is true, as Zivotofsky notes, that Congress has substantial authority over passports. . . .

The problem with §214(d), however, lies in how Congress exercised its authority over passports. It was an improper act for Congress to "aggrandiz[e] its power at the expense of another branch" by requiring the President to contradict an earlier recognition determination in an official document issued by the Executive Branch. To allow Congress to control the President's communication in the context of a formal recognition determination is to allow Congress to exercise that exclusive power itself. As a result, the statute is unconstitutional.

In holding §214(d) invalid the Court does not question the substantial powers of Congress over foreign affairs in general or passports in particular. This case is confined solely to the exclusive power of the President to control recognition determinations, including formal statements by the Executive Branch acknowledging the legitimacy of a state or government and its territorial bounds. Congress cannot command the President to contradict an earlier recognition determination in the issuance of passports.

The judgment of the Court of Appeals for the District of Columbia Circuit is

Affirmed.

JUSTICE BREYER, concurring.
I continue to believe that this case presents a political question inappropriate for judicial resolution. See *Zivotofsky v. Clinton* (2012) (BREYER, J., dissenting). But because precedent precludes resolving this case on political question grounds, I join the Court's opinion.

JUSTICE THOMAS, concurring in the judgment in part and dissenting in part.
Our Constitution allocates the powers of the Federal Government over foreign affairs in two ways. First, it expressly identifies certain foreign affairs powers and vests them in particular branches, either individually or jointly. Second, it vests the residual foreign affairs powers of the Federal Government—i.e., those not specifically enumerated in the Constitution—in the President by way of Article II's Vesting Clause.

Rather than adhere to the Constitution's division of powers, the Court relies on a distortion of the President's recognition power to hold both of these parts of §214(d) unconstitutional. Because I cannot join this faulty analysis, I concur only in the portion of the Court's judgment holding §214(d) unconstitutional as applied to passports. I respectfully dissent from the remainder of the Court's judgment. . . .

The Constitution specifies a number of foreign affairs powers and divides them between the political branches. . . .

These specific allocations, however, cannot account for the entirety of the foreign affairs powers exercised by the Federal Government. Neither of the political branches is expressly authorized, for instance, to communicate with foreign ministers, to issue passports, or to repel sudden attacks. Yet the President has engaged in such conduct, with the support of Congress, since the earliest days of the Republic.

The President's longstanding practice of exercising unenumerated foreign affairs powers reflects a constitutional directive that "the President ha[s] primary responsibility—along with the necessary power—to protect the national security and to conduct the Nation's foreign relations." *Hamdi v. Rumsfeld.* Specifically, the Vesting Clause of Article II provides that "[t]he executive Power shall be vested in a President of the United States." Art. II, §1. This Clause is notably different from the Vesting Clause of Article I, which provides only that "[a]ll legislative Powers herein granted shall be vested in a Congress of the United States," Art. I, §1. By omitting the words "herein granted" in Article II, the Constitution indicates that the "executive Power" vested in the President is not confined to those powers expressly identified in the document. Instead, it includes all powers originally understood as falling within the "executive Power" of the Federal Government. . . .

[I]t is unsurprising that those who ratified the Constitution understood the "executive Power" vested by Article II to include those foreign affairs powers not otherwise allocated in the Constitution. James Iredell, for example, told the North Carolina ratifying convention that, under the new Constitution, the President would "regulate all intercourse with foreign powers" and act as the "primary agent" of the United States, though no specific allocation of foreign affairs powers in the document so provided. . . .

Early practice of the founding generation also supports this understanding of the "executive Power." Upon taking office, President Washington assumed the role of chief diplomat; began to direct the Secretary of Foreign Affairs who, under the Articles of Confederation, had reported to the Congress; and established the foreign policy of the United States. At the same time, he respected Congress' prerogatives to declare war, regulate foreign commerce, and appropriate funds. . . .

For its part, Congress recognized a broad Presidential role in foreign affairs. It created an "Executive department" called the "Department of Foreign Affairs," with a Secretary wholly subordinate to the President. . . .

The statutory provision at issue implicates the President's residual foreign affairs power. Section 214(d) instructs the Secretary of State, upon request of a citizen born in Jerusalem (or that citizen's legal guardian), to list that citizen's place of birth as Israel on his passport and consular report of birth abroad, even though it is the undisputed position of the United States that Jerusalem is not a part of Israel. The President argues that this provision violates his foreign affairs powers generally and his recognition power specifically. Zivotofsky rejoins that Congress passed §214(d) pursuant to its enumerated powers and its action must therefore take precedence.

Neither has it quite right. The President is not constitutionally compelled to implement §214(d) as it applies to passports because passport regulation falls squarely within his residual foreign affairs power and Zivotofsky has identified no source of congressional power to require the President to list Israel as the place of birth for a citizen born in Jerusalem on that citizen's passport. Section 214(d) can, however, be constitutionally applied to consular reports of birth abroad because those documents do not fall within the President's foreign affairs authority but do fall within Congress' enumerated powers over naturalization.

In the Anglo-American legal tradition, passports have consistently been issued and controlled by the body exercising executive power—in England, by the King; in the colonies, by the Continental Congress; and in the United States, by President Washington and every President since. . . .

That the President has the power to regulate passports under his residual foreign affairs powers does not, however, end the matter, for Congress has repeatedly legislated on the subject of passports. These laws have always been narrow in scope. For example, Congress enacted laws prohibiting the issuance of passports to noncitizens, created an exception to that rule for "persons liable to military duty," and then eliminated that exception. . . .

As with any congressional action, however, such legislation is constitutionally permissible only insofar as it is promulgated pursuant to one of Congress' enumerated powers. I must therefore address whether Congress had constitutional authority to enact §214(d)'s regulation of passports. . . .

The Constitution contains no Passport Clause, nor does it explicitly vest Congress with "plenary authority over passports." Because our Government is one of enumerated powers, "Congress has no power to act unless the Constitution authorizes it to do so." *United States v. Comstock* (2010) (THOMAS, J., dissenting). And "[t]he Constitution plainly sets forth the 'few and defined' powers that Congress may exercise." A "passport power" is not one of them. . . .

JUSTICE SCALIA would locate Congress' power to enact the passport directive of §214(d) in Congress' power under the Necessary and Proper Clause to bring into effect its enumerated power over naturalization. As an initial matter, he asserts that "[t]he naturalization power . . . enables Congress to furnish the people it makes citizens with papers verifying their citizenship," yet offers no support for this interpretation of a clause that, by its terms, grants Congress only the "Power. . . . To establish an uniform Rule of Naturalization," U. S. Const., Art. I, §8, cl. 4. He then concludes that, if Congress can grant such documents, "it may also require these [documents] to record his birthplace as 'Israel'" pursuant to its power under the Necessary and Proper Clause. But this theory does not account for the President's power to act in this area, nor does it confront difficult questions about the application of the Necessary and Proper Clause in the case of conflict among the branches. . . .

Because the President has residual foreign affairs authority to regulate passports and because there appears to be no congressional power that justifies §214(d)'s application to passports, Zivotofsky's challenge to the Executive's designation of his place of birth on his passport must fail.

Although the consular report of birth abroad shares some features with a passport, it is historically associated with naturalization, not foreign affairs. In order to establish a "uniform Rule of Naturalization," Congress must be able to identify the categories of persons who are eligible for naturalization, along with the rules for that process. Congress thus has always regulated the "acquisition of citizenship by being born abroad of American parents . . . in the exercise of the power conferred by the Constitution to establish a uniform rule of naturalization." . . .

The consular report of birth abroad is well suited to carrying into execution the power conferred on Congress in the Naturalization Clause. The report developed in response to Congress' requirement that children born abroad to U. S. citizens register with the consulate or lose their citizenship. And it continues to certify the acquisition of U. S. citizenship at birth by a person born abroad to a U. S. citizen. . . .

Because regulation of the consular report of birth abroad is justified as an exercise of Congress' powers under the Naturalization and Necessary and Proper Clauses and does not fall within the President's foreign affairs powers, §214(d)'s treatment of that document is constitutional.

CHIEF JUSTICE ROBERTS, with whom JUSTICE ALITO joins, dissenting.

Today's decision is a first: Never before has this Court accepted a President's direct defiance of an Act of Congress in the field of foreign affairs. We have instead stressed that the President's power reaches "its lowest ebb" when he contravenes the express will of Congress, "for what is at stake is the equilibrium established by our constitutional system." *Youngstown Sheet & Tube Co. v. Sawyer* (1952) (Jackson, J., concurring). . . .

Ultimately, the only power that could support the President's position is the one the majority purports to reject: the "exclusive authority to conduct diplomatic relations." The Government offers a single citation for this allegedly exclusive power: *United States v. Curtiss-Wright Export Corp.* (1936). But as the majority rightly acknowledges, *Curtiss-Wright* did not involve a claim that the Executive could contravene a statute; it held only that he could act pursuant to a legislative delegation.

The expansive language in *Curtiss-Wright* casting the President as the "sole organ" of the Nation in foreign affairs certainly has attraction for members of the Executive Branch. The Solicitor General invokes the case no fewer than ten times in his brief. But our precedents have never accepted such a sweeping understanding of executive power. . . .

Resolving the status of Jerusalem may be vexing, but resolving this case is not. Whatever recognition power the President may have, exclusive or otherwise, is not implicated by §214(d). It has not been necessary over the past 225 years to definitively resolve a dispute between Congress and the President over the recognition power. Perhaps we could have waited another 225 years. But instead the majority strains to reach the question based on the mere possibility that observers overseas might misperceive the significance of the birthplace designation at issue in this case. And in the process, the Court takes the perilous step—for the first time in our history—of allowing the President to defy an Act of Congress in the field of foreign affairs.

I respectfully dissent.

JUSTICE SCALIA, with whom THE CHIEF JUSTICE and JUSTICE ALITO join, dissenting.

This case arises out of a dispute between the Executive and Legislative Branches about whether the United States should treat Jerusalem as a part of Israel. The Constitution contemplates that the political branches will make policy about the territorial claims of foreign nations the same way they make policy about other international matters: The President will exercise his powers on the basis of his views, Congress its powers on the basis of its views. That is just what has happened here. . . .

Before turning to Presidential power under Article II, I think it well to establish the statute's basis in congressional power under Article I. Congress's power to "establish an uniform Rule of Naturalization," Art. I, §8, cl. 4, enables it to grant American citizenship to someone born abroad. The naturalization power also enables Congress to furnish the people it makes citizens with papers verifying their citizenship—say a consular report of birth abroad (which certifies citizenship of an American born outside the United States) or a passport (which certifies citizenship for purposes of international travel). As the Necessary and Proper Clause confirms, every congressional power "carries with it all those incidental powers which are necessary to its complete and effectual execution." Even on a miserly understanding of Congress's incidental authority, Congress may make grants of citizenship "effectual" by providing for the issuance of certificates authenticating them. . . .

No doubt congressional discretion in executing legislative powers has its limits; Congress's chosen approach must be not only "necessary" to carrying its powers into execution, but also "proper." Congress thus may not transcend boundaries upon legislative authority stated or implied elsewhere in the Constitution. But . . . §214(d) does not transgress any such restriction.

The Court frames this case as a debate about recognition. Recognition is a sovereign's official acceptance of a status under international law. . . .

[But] §214(d) has nothing to do with recognition. Section 214(d) does not require the Secretary to make a formal declaration about Israel's sovereignty over Jerusalem. And nobody suggests that international custom infers acceptance of sovereignty from the birthplace designation on a passport or birth report, as it does from bilateral treaties or exchanges of ambassadors. Recognition would preclude the United States (as a matter of international law) from later contesting Israeli sovereignty over Jerusalem. But making a notation in a passport or birth report does not encumber the Republic with any international obligations. It leaves the Nation free (so far as international law is concerned) to change its mind in the future. That would be true even if the statute required all passports to list "Israel." But in fact it requires only those passports to list "Israel" for which the citizen (or his guardian) requests "Israel"; all the rest, under the Secretary's policy, list "Jerusalem." It is utterly impossible for this deference to private requests to constitute an act that unequivocally manifests an intention to grant recognition. . . .

In the final analysis, the Constitution may well deny Congress's power to recognize—the power to make an international commitment accepting a foreign entity as a state, a regime as its government, a place as a part of its territory, and so on. But whatever else §214(d) may do, it plainly does not make (or require the President to make) a commitment accepting Israel's sovereignty over Jerusalem. . . .

JUSTICE THOMAS's concurrence deems §214(d) constitutional to the extent it regulates birth reports, but unconstitutional to the extent it regulates passports. The concurrence finds no congressional power that would extend to the issuance or contents of passports. Including the power to regulate foreign commerce—even though passports facilitate the transportation of passengers, "a part of our commerce with foreign nations." Including the power over naturalization—even though passports issued to citizens, like birth reports, "have the same force and effect as proof of United States citizenship as certificates of naturalization." . . . The concurrence's stingy interpretation of the enumerated powers forgets that the Constitution does not "partake of the prolixity of a legal code," that "only its great outlines [are] marked, its important objects designated, and the minor ingredients which compose those objects [left to] be deduced from the nature of the objects themselves." McCulloch. It forgets, in other words, "that it is a constitution we are expounding."

Defending Presidential primacy over passports, the concurrence says that the royal prerogative in England included the power to issue and control travel documents akin to the modern passport. Perhaps so, but that power was assuredly not exclusive. . . .

That brings me, in analytic crescendo, to the concurrence's suggestion that even if Congress's enumerated powers otherwise encompass §214(d), and even if the President's power to regulate the contents of passports is not exclusive, the law might still violate the Constitution, because it "conflict[s]" with the President's passport policy. It turns the Constitution upside-down to suggest that in areas of shared authority, it is the executive policy that preempts the law, rather than the other way around. Congress may make laws necessary and proper for carrying into execution the President's powers, Art. I, §8, cl. 18, but the President must "take Care" that Congress's legislation "be faithfully executed," Art. II, §3. And Acts of Congress made in pursuance of the Constitution are the "supreme Law of the Land"; acts of the President (apart from treaties) are not. Art. VI, cl. 2. . . .

A President empowered to decide all questions relating to [international disputes about statehood and territory], immune from laws embodying congressional disagreement with his position, would have uncontrolled mastery of a vast share of the Nation's foreign affairs.

That is not the chief magistrate under which the American People agreed to live when they adopted the national charter. . . .

I dissent.

What should we make of *Zivotofsky*? First, it provides direct evidence that Justice Jackson's third category will not always lead the Court to nullify presidential action (as it did in *Youngstown*). Here the president was able to demonstrate that his power to recognize foreign governments belonged exclusively to him, and for that reason the Court invalidated §214(d) as an encroachment on his power. Second, and despite ruling in the president's favor, Justice Kennedy acknowledged the role that Congress plays in foreign affairs: "It remains true . . . that many decisions affecting foreign relations—including decisions that may determine the course of our relations with recognized

BOX 5-5   THE WAR AGAINST TERRORISM IN GLOBAL PERSPECTIVE

IN FIGHTING the war against terrorism, the United States has taken a number of steps that intrude on rights and liberties. In the text we note some of these steps, as well as arguments for and against them.

Worth noting here is that the United States is not the only democracy that has enacted measures designed to combat terrorist activities. Others throughout the world have passed or are considering laws in the name of national security that also may repress rights.

- Canada. The Canadian parliament has adopted several measures that raise the concerns of civil libertarians. One allowed law enforcement officials to detain foreign terrorism suspects indefinitely without disclosing the evidence against them. After the Canadian Supreme Court struck down the law, the government introduced new legislation that would allow detention without a warrant if the detention was deemed necessary to prevent a terrorist act.
- Denmark. Denmark's antiterror laws ban financing of radical groups and give police new powers to eavesdrop electronically on suspected radicals. Danish intelligence officers have stepped up "preventive talks" with potential radicals.
- France. Under a law that took effect in 2004, France bans "ostentatious" religious symbols in schools. Most people believed the law was aimed at the hijab (the headscarf worn by many Muslim women and girls), but most voters supported the ban. France also has undertaken an antiterrorism campaign that includes surveillance of mosques and

raids for unrelated reasons (such as tax inspections) on places where Muslims in particular are found (such as halal butchers' shops). Terrorist suspects can be detained for up to four days without being charged.
- Italy. After the July 2005 London bombings carried out by Islamic extremists, the Italian parliament approved a new antiterrorism law that permits authorities to conduct surveillance of the Internet and phone networks, to interrogate suspects without lawyers being present, to impose prison sentences and fines on persons who purposely hide their faces in public, and to implement more-expeditious methods for expelling illegal immigrants who pose a security threat to the country.
- United Kingdom. The British government has introduced several proposals designed to tighten existing terrorism laws: ban certain Islamist organizations; close mosques believed to be sources of terrorist agitation and recruitment; streamline the process by which clerics deemed to be radical would be deported, potentially to countries that practice torture; strip naturalized radicals of their British citizenship; and create closed pretrial hearings at which secret evidence could be introduced. In a setback to the government, Britain's highest court ruled that evidence obtained through torture could not be used at trial.

SOURCES: *Washington Post;* Freedom House (http://www.freedom-house.org).

---

countries—require congressional action." He even went so far as to cut back on some of *Curtiss-Wright's* broad claims about presidential power, as we noted in chapter 4. Chief Justice Roberts, in his dissenting opinion, was even more direct: "The expansive language in *Curtiss-Wright* casting the President as the 'sole organ' of the Nation in foreign affairs certainly has attraction for members of the Executive Branch. [The brief for Kerry] invokes the case no fewer than ten times in his brief. But our precedents have never accepted such a sweeping understanding of executive power."

Which brings us to our last point: *Zivotofsky,* once again, provides an opportunity to consider different approaches to the balance of power between the president and Congress in the real world of foreign affairs. Of the range of views presented in the opinions—majority, concurring, and dissenting—which do you find most compelling? As you consider this question, reflect not only on the cases we have covered in this chapter but also on those we covered in chapter 3 (especially on the necessary and proper clause) and in chapter 4 (theories of presidential power, along with *Curtiss-Wright*).

The War on Terrorism

All of this material, too, has relevance for post–September 11 America. In the process of waging a "war on terrorism"—a battle that may endure far longer than any other conflict Americans have experienced—the George W. Bush administration sent military forces into two countries, Afghanistan and Iraq. The president also took steps to restrict the rights and liberties of Americans and foreigners alike. To some observers, these steps amounted to little more than the kinds of actions often taken by leaders, both in the United States and abroad, when confronted with threats to national security (see box 5-5 on page 329). In interpreting Article II, the administration took a unilateral approach. It argued that the president has complete authority within his purview—including the execution of his military powers—to pursue whatever actions he thinks best regardless of whether Congress has authorized them or not, and courts may not review those actions.[19] Others believe that President Bush's measures went too far.

Which side has the better case? To develop answers to this question, let us consider the steps Congress and the president took after the September 11 attacks.[20] First, just one week later, Congress enacted a resolution, the AUMF, authorizing the president to "use all necessary and appropriate force against those nations, organizations, or persons he determines planned, authorized, committed, or aided the terrorist attacks" or "harbored such organizations or persons, in order to prevent any future acts of international terrorism against the United States by such nations, organizations or persons." Acting under the AUMF, in October 2001 the president ordered U.S. armed forces to Afghanistan to battle the al-Qaeda terrorist network, which was behind the attacks, and the Taliban regime, which supported al-Qaeda.

Several weeks after that, President Bush issued an order titled Detention, Treatment, and Trial of Certain Non-Citizens in the War Against Terrorism, which was designed to accomplish two ends. First, the administration wanted to detain enemies of the United States (persons believed by the president to be members of al-Qaeda and persons involved in acts of international terrorism against the United States or who knowingly harbored such terrorists) in a naval detention center at Guantanamo Bay, Cuba, for the duration of the hostilities. The United States had taken this same action with enemies captured during other hostilities, but, under its reading of the Geneva conventions, it did not feel bound to accord these "enemy combatants" the same treatment that the United States had accorded other prisoners.[21] Taking this step meant that the administration could interrogate detainees in whatever manner it felt appropriate and not necessarily in accord with the conventions. Also notable is that the government understood that the war on terrorism might continue indefinitely, meaning that it could hold the detainees indefinitely. Second, the administration's order said that any individual subject to the order, when tried, would be tried by a military commission, not in a state or federal court. Under such a commission, the accused could be deprived of many of the rights normally afforded accused persons, such as the rights to remain silent, to be present at their own proceedings, and to review the government's evidence. Moreover, the president's order prohibited a detainee from seeking review of the military commission's decision in a federal court through a writ of habeas corpus or "any other remedy."

On what grounds did the administration justify the terms of the order? It made two kinds of arguments.

---

19. The Bush administration's positions are closely associated with John Yoo, a law professor who worked in the administration. In Yoo's words, "Long-standing U.S. practice recognizes that the president, as commander in chief, plays the leading role in wartime. Presidents have started wars without congressional authorization, and they have exercised complete control over military strategy and tactics. They can act with a speed, unity and secrecy that the other branches of government cannot match. By contrast, legislatures are large, diffuse and slow. Their collective design may make them better for deliberating over policy, but at the cost of delay and lack of resolve.... As an official in the Bush administration's Justice Department from 2001 to 2003, I argued that the president had the constitutional power to act, alone if necessary, to defend the country from another attack." For a more scholarly exposition of the unitary executive theory, see Christopher S. Yoo, Steven G. Calabresi, and Anthony J. Colangelo, "The Unitary Executive in the Modern Era, 1945–2004," *Iowa Law Review* 90 (2005): 601–731.

20. This section draws on James E. Pfander's *One Supreme Court* (New York: Oxford University Press, 2009). We also make use of Lee Epstein, Daniel E. Ho, Gary King, and Jeffrey A. Segal, "The Supreme Court during Crisis: How War Affects Only Nonwar Cases," *New York University Law Review* 80 (April 2005): 1–116.

21. The Geneva conventions are a series of four international agreements designed, among other things, to provide protections to civilians during armed conflicts and to those no longer participating in such disputes, including wounded and sick members of the armed forces and prisoners of war. Since the last convention came into effect in 1950, 194 nations, including the United States, have ratified the Geneva conventions.

TABLE 5-2   Cases Growing Out of the War on Terrorism

CASE NAME AND DATE	CIRCUMSTANCES TRIGGERING THE DISPUTE	COURT'S DECISION
Hamdi v. Rumsfeld (2004)	Hamdi, an American citizen, was captured on a battlefield in Afghanistan and held in a U.S. military prison. The government claimed he was an "enemy combatant" and that it could hold him indefinitely without formal charges. His father filed a petition for habeas corpus, claiming the continued detention violated Hamdi's constitutional right to due process of law.	In a judgment of the Court, Justice O'Connor found that the congressional resolution authorizing the use of military force (the AUMF) authorized Hamdi's detention. But a majority of the Court ruled that, as a U.S. citizen, Hamdi was entitled to challenge his classification as an "enemy combatant" in a federal court.
Rasul v. Bush (2004)	The relatives of two Australians and twelve Kuwaitis held at naval detention facilities at Guantanamo Bay in Cuba filed habeas corpus petitions on the detainees' behalf, claiming they were illegally incarcerated. The lower federal courts dismissed the lawsuits, holding that the federal courts have no jurisdiction outside the United States.	The Court reversed. It held that aliens detained at Guantanamo could seek review of their detention by filing habeas corpus petitions in the U.S. Court of Appeals in Washington, D.C.
Hamdan v. Rumsfeld (2006)	Hamdan, held at Guantanamo, was to be tried by a military tribunal in accord with the president's order. Hamdan's attorney argued that his client should not be tried by a military tribunal and that the procedures adopted to try him were inconsistent with the basic tenets of military and international law, including the principle that a defendant must be permitted to see and hear the evidence against him.	After the Court agreed to hear Hamdan's case, Congress passed the Detainee Treatment Act of 2005 (DTA), which said that no court could exercise habeas jurisdiction over those detained as enemy combatants. If a special military tribunal (set up in response to the *Rasul* and *Hamdi* decisions) had found the detainee to be an "enemy combatant," the detainee could appeal his detention to the U.S. Court of Appeals in Washington, D.C., as could those convicted by military tribunals. Based on the DTA, the government asked the Court to dismiss the suit because it lacked appellate jurisdiction. The Court declined on the grounds that the DTA did not expressly cover pending cases. The Court outlawed the use of military commissions, saying that Congress had not authorized the commissions and even in war the "Executive is bound to comply with the Rule of Law."
Boumediene v. Bush (2008)	Months after *Hamdan,* Congress passed the Military Commission Act (MCA), which authorized the use of military commissions for suspected terrorists. The MCA denied federal courts jurisdiction to hear the detainees' habeas corpus applications.	Based in part on their review of the history and origins of the writ of habeas corpus, the justices held that Guantanamo detainees have a right to challenge their detention in the federal courts. They struck down the part of the MCA that stripped the federal courts of the power to hear habeas petitions. The majority asserted that the DTA had not provided an adequate substitute for the writ.

NOTE: Excerpts of the cases in this table appear either in this volume or in the online case archive.

First, the administration said it did not require congressional authorization for its actions. Under its interpretation of presidential wartime authority and Supreme Court decisions, it believed that Article II provided the executive with plenary authority to detain the enemy combatants. This is a position embraced by some of the cases and opinions we have considered, especially *Curtiss-Wright* and Thomas's concurrence in

Zivotofsky (though the latter antedated Bush's order). But it is an argument that Justice Jackson's concurrence in *Youngstown Sheet & Tube* could be seen to reject. There was another problem too with Bush's claim of authority to hold enemy combatants (at least those who were U.S. citizens) without formal charges: a federal law (18 U.S.C. §4001(a)): that said, "No citizen shall be imprisoned or otherwise detained by the

United States except pursuant to an Act of Congress." This law was enacted to overturn an act of the Cold Act era, the Emergency Detention Act of 1950, which had authorized the attorney general, in time of emergency, to detain anyone reasonably thought likely to engage in espionage or sabotage. Congress replaced it with 18 U.S.C. §4001(a) in 1971 out of fear that the 1950 law could "authorize a repetition of the World War II internment of citizens of Japanese ancestry."[22] Congress meant to preclude another episode like the one described in *Korematsu v. United States*, 323 U.S. 214 (1944).

In the face of these potential difficulties, the administration had a back-up argument. Government lawyers claimed that §4001(a) was, in fact, satisfied because Congress had in fact authorized the use of detentions through the AUMF, its resolution authorizing the use of military force.

How did the Court respond to these actions and arguments by the administration and to legislation Congress later passed to support the president's order? Not particularly enthusiastically, as table 5-2 on page 331 and *Hamdi v. Rumsfeld* (2004) suggest.

Hamdi v. Rumsfeld

542 U.S. 507 (2004)
http://laws.findlaw.com/us/542/507.html
Oral arguments may be found at https://www.oyez.org.
On the question of the validity of Hamdi's detention:
Vote: 5 (Breyer, Kennedy, O'Connor, Rehnquist, Thomas)
    4 (Ginsburg, Scalia, Souter, Stevens)
On the question of Hamdi's access to courts and lawyers:
Vote: 8 (Breyer, Ginsburg, Kennedy, O'Connor, Rehnquist, Scalia, Souter, Stevens)
    1 (Thomas)

OPINION ANNOUNCING THE JUDGMENT OF THE COURT: *O'Connor*

OPINION CONCURRING IN PART, DISSENTING IN PART, AND CONCURRING IN JUDGMENT: *Souter*

DISSENTING OPINIONS: *Scalia, Thomas*

FACTS:

One week after the September 11, 2001, al-Qaeda terrorist attacks on the United States, Congress passed the Authorization for Use of Military Force (AUMF) resolution, which gave the president authority to "use all necessary and appropriate force against those nations, organizations, or persons he determines planned, authorized, committed, or aided the terrorist attacks"

---

22. See Justice Souter's opinion in *Hamdi v. Rumsfeld*.

or "harbored such organizations or persons, in order to prevent any future acts of international terrorism against the United States." On the basis of this congressional grant of authority, President Bush ordered American armed forces to Afghanistan to attack al-Qaeda and the Taliban regime that supported it.

During this military effort, Afghan elements supporting the United States captured twenty-year-old Yaser Esam Hamdi and delivered him to U.S. forces. Hamdi was an American citizen by virtue of his birth in Louisiana, but his family had moved to Saudi Arabia when he was a child. After being interrogated in Afghanistan, Hamdi was transferred first to the U.S. naval base at Guantanamo Bay, Cuba, then to military prisons in Norfolk, Virginia, and Charleston, South Carolina. The government claimed that Hamdi was an "enemy combatant" and as such could be held indefinitely without formal charges, court proceedings, access to counsel, or the freedom to communicate with anyone beyond the prison walls.

In 2004 the Supreme Court upheld the military detention of Yaser Hamdi, a U.S. citizen captured during hostilities in Afghanistan, but also ruled that Hamdi must be given an opportunity to rebut the government's designation of him as an "enemy combatant."

AP Photo/Asharq al-Awsat

In June 2002 Hamdi's father, Esam Fouad Hamdi, filed a petition for habeas corpus on behalf of his son against Secretary of Defense Donald Rumsfeld, claiming the continued detention without formal charges or access to lawyers or the courts violated the younger Hamdi's constitutional right to due process of law. Hamdi's father argued that his son was not engaged in military activity but had gone to Afghanistan as a relief worker. The United States countered that Hamdi had received military training in Afghanistan and had joined a Taliban unit prior to his capture in a theater of war. The government's allegations as to Hamdi's participation in Taliban activities were submitted in the form of a statement by Michael Mobbs, a Defense Department official. This document, referred to as the Mobbs Declaration, contained little in the way of direct factual evidence.

After a series of hearings at the district and circuit court levels, the U.S. Court of Appeals for the Fourth Circuit ruled in favor of the government's position, holding that Hamdi could be detained and was entitled only to the limited judicial determination of whether the government had acted properly under its war powers.

ARGUMENTS:

For the petitioner, Yaser Esam Hamdi et al.:

- Well acquainted with the danger posed by the government's power to effect detention, the founders enshrined the power to suspend the writ of habeas corpus in Article I and limited its exercise to cases of rebellion or invasion. It ensures that the executive cannot discard the judicial process and imprison citizens at its pleasure; only Congress has the power to suspend the Great Writ.
- The Constitution gives the executive no inherent power to detain citizens indefinitely during war or peace. While the commander in chief clause necessarily entails plenary executive authority in areas of actual fighting, the power over citizens incident to this authority is only temporary. The executive enjoys the authority to detain citizens seized in areas of actual fighting for only a limited period of time as required by military necessity. Once the citizen is removed from the area of actual fighting, the Constitution requires statutory authorization to hold that citizen indefinitely.
- Federal law (18 U.S.C. § 4001(a)) makes clear that only Congress can authorize the prolonged detention of citizens.

For the respondents, Donald Rumsfeld, Secretary of Defense, et al.:

- In our constitutional system, the responsibility for waging war is committed to the political branches. In time of war, the president, as commander in chief, has the authority to capture and detain enemy combatants for the duration of hostilities. That includes enemy combatants presumed to be United States citizens. See *Ex parte Quirin* (1942).
- The president's determination that an individual is an enemy combatant is entitled to the utmost deference by a court.
- Hamdi's detention is bolstered by, and by no means contrary to, the actions of Congress. Congress has affirmed the type of classic wartime detention at issue in this case. Immediately following the September 11 attacks, Congress not only recognized by statute that "the President has authority under the Constitution to take action to deter and prevent acts of international terrorism against the United States" but also explicitly backed the president's use of "all necessary and appropriate force" in connection with the current conflict. The AUMF satisfies the requirements of 18 U.S.C. §4001(a); it is authorization of the detention of citizens and noncitizens alike.

JUSTICE O'CONNOR ANNOUNCED THE JUDGMENT OF THE COURT AND DELIVERED AN OPINION, IN WHICH THE CHIEF JUSTICE, JUSTICE KENNEDY, AND JUSTICE BREYER JOIN.

At this difficult time in our Nation's history, we are called upon to consider the legality of the Government's detention of a United States citizen on United States soil as an "enemy combatant" and to address the process that is constitutionally owed to one who seeks to challenge his classification as such. . . . We hold that although Congress authorized the detention of combatants in the narrow circumstances alleged here, due process demands that a citizen held in the United States as an enemy combatant be given a meaningful opportunity to contest the factual basis for that detention before a neutral decisionmaker. . . .

The threshold question before us is whether the Executive has the authority to detain citizens who qualify as "enemy combatants." There is some debate as to the proper scope of this term, and the Government has never provided any court with the full criteria that it uses in classifying individuals as such. It has made clear, however, that, for purposes of this case, the "enemy combatant" that it is seeking to detain is an individual who, it alleges, was "'part of or supporting forces hostile to the United States or coalition partners'" in Afghanistan and who "'engaged in an armed conflict against the United States'" there. We therefore answer only the narrow question before us: whether the detention of citizens falling within that definition is authorized.

The Government maintains that no explicit congressional authorization is required, because the Executive possesses plenary authority to detain pursuant to Article II of the Constitution. We do not reach the question whether Article II provides such authority, however, because we agree with the Government's alternative position, that Congress has in fact authorized Hamdi's detention, through the AUMF [the Authorization for Use of Military Force resolution]. . . . and that the AUMF satisfied §4001(a)'s requirement that a detention be "pursuant to an Act of Congress."

The AUMF authorizes the President to use "all necessary and appropriate force" against "nations, organizations, or persons" associated with the September 11, 2001, terrorist attacks. There can be no doubt that individuals who fought against the United States in Afghanistan as part of the Taliban, an organization known to have supported the al Qaeda terrorist network responsible for those attacks, are individuals Congress sought to target in passing the AUMF. We conclude that detention of individuals falling into the limited category we are considering, for the duration of the particular conflict in which they were captured, is so fundamental and accepted an incident to war as to be an exercise of the "necessary and appropriate force" Congress has authorized the President to use.

The capture and detention of lawful combatants and the capture, detention, and trial of unlawful combatants, by "universal agreement and practice," are "important incident[s] of war." *Ex parte Quirin* [1942]. The purpose of detention is to prevent captured individuals from returning to the field of battle and taking up arms once again. . . .

There is no bar to this Nation's holding one of its own citizens as an enemy combatant. In *Quirin*, one of the detainees, Haupt, alleged that he was a naturalized United States citizen. We held that "[c]itizens who associate themselves with the military arm of the enemy government, and with its aid, guidance and direction enter this country bent on hostile acts, are enemy belligerents within the meaning of . . . the law of war." . . . A citizen, no less than an alien, can be "part of or supporting forces hostile to the United States or coalition partners" and "engaged in an armed

conflict against the United States"; such a citizen, if released, would pose the same threat of returning to the front during the ongoing conflict.

In light of these principles, it is of no moment that the AUMF does not use specific language of detention. Because detention to prevent a combatant's return to the battlefield is a fundamental incident of waging war, in permitting the use of "necessary and appropriate force," Congress has clearly and unmistakably authorized detention in the narrow circumstances considered here.

Hamdi objects, nevertheless, that Congress has not authorized the *indefinite* detention to which he is now subject. . . . As the Government concedes, "given its unconventional nature, the current conflict is unlikely to end with a formal cease-fire agreement." The prospect Hamdi raises is therefore not far-fetched. If the Government does not consider this unconventional war won for two generations, and if it maintains during that time that Hamdi might, if released, rejoin forces fighting against the United States, then the position it has taken throughout the litigation of this case suggests that Hamdi's detention could last for the rest of his life.

It is a clearly established principle of the law of war that detention may last no longer than active hostilities.

Hamdi contends that the AUMF does not authorize indefinite or perpetual detention. Certainly, we agree that indefinite detention for the purpose of interrogation is not authorized. Further, we understand Congress' grant of authority for the use of "necessary and appropriate force" to include the authority to detain for the duration of the relevant conflict, and our understanding is based on longstanding law-of-war principles. If the practical circumstances of a given conflict are entirely unlike those of the conflicts that informed the development of the law of war, that understanding may unravel. But that is not the situation we face as of this date. Active combat operations against Taliban fighters apparently are ongoing in Afghanistan. The United States may detain, for the duration of these hostilities, individuals legitimately determined to be Taliban combatants who "engaged in an armed conflict against the United States." If the record establishes that United States troops are still involved in active combat in Afghanistan, those detentions are part of the exercise of "necessary and appropriate force," and therefore are authorized by the AUMF.

Ex parte Milligan (1866) does not undermine our holding about the Government's authority to seize enemy combatants. . . . In that case, the Court made repeated reference to the fact that its inquiry into whether the military tribunal had jurisdiction to try and punish Milligan turned in large part on the fact that Milligan was not a prisoner of war, but a resident of Indiana arrested while at home there. That fact was central to its conclusion. Had Milligan been captured while he was assisting Confederate soldiers by carrying a rifle against Union troops on a Confederate battlefield, the holding of the Court might well have been different. The Court's repeated explanations that Milligan was not a prisoner of war suggest that had these different circumstances been present he could have been detained under military authority for the duration of the conflict, whether or not he was a citizen. . . .

Even in cases in which the detention of enemy combatants is legally authorized, there remains the question of what process is constitutionally due to a citizen who disputes his enemy-combatant status. . . .

Though they reach radically different conclusions on the process that ought to attend the present proceeding, the parties begin on common ground. All agree that, absent suspension, the writ of habeas corpus remains available to every individual detained within the United States. Only in the rarest of circumstances has Congress seen fit to suspend the writ. At all other times, it has remained a critical check on the Executive, ensuring that it does not detain individuals except in accordance with law. All agree suspension of the writ has not occurred here. . . .

. . . [A]s critical as the Government's interest may be in detaining those who actually pose an immediate threat to the national security of the United States during ongoing international conflict, history and common sense teach us that an unchecked system of detention carries the potential to become a means for oppression and abuse of others who do not present that sort of threat. See *Ex parte Milligan*. . . . We reaffirm today the fundamental nature of a citizen's right to be free from involuntary confinement by his own government without due process of law, and we weigh the opposing governmental interests against the curtailment of liberty that such confinement entails.

On the other side of the scale are the weighty and sensitive governmental interests in ensuring that those who have in fact fought with the enemy during a war do not return to battle against the United States. . . . [T]he law of war and the realities of combat may render such detentions both necessary and appropriate, and our due process analysis need not blink at those realities. Without doubt, our Constitution recognizes that core strategic matters of war making belong in the hands of those who are best positioned and most politically accountable for making them.

The Government also argues at some length that its interests in reducing the process available to alleged enemy combatants are heightened by the practical difficulties that would accompany a system of trial-like process. In its view, military officers who are engaged in the serious work of waging battle would be unnecessarily and dangerously distracted by litigation half a world away, and discovery into military operations would both intrude on the sensitive secrets of national defense and result in a futile search for evidence buried under the rubble of war. To the extent that these burdens are triggered by heightened procedures, they are properly taken into account in our due process analysis.

Striking the proper constitutional balance here is of great importance to the Nation during this period of ongoing combat. But it is equally vital that our calculus not give short shrift to the values that this country holds dear or to the privilege that is American citizenship. It is during our most challenging and uncertain moments that our Nation's commitment to due process is most severely tested; and it is in those times that we must preserve our commitment at home to the principles for which we fight abroad. . . .

We therefore hold that a citizen-detainee seeking to challenge his classification as an enemy combatant must receive notice of the factual basis for his classification, and a fair opportunity to rebut the Government's factual assertions before a neutral decisionmaker. These essential constitutional promises may not be eroded.

At the same time, the exigencies of the circumstances may demand that, aside from these core elements, enemy combatant proceedings may be tailored to alleviate their uncommon potential to burden the Executive at a time of ongoing military conflict. Hearsay, for example, may need to be accepted as the most reliable available evidence from the Government in such a proceeding. Likewise, the Constitution would not be offended by a presumption in favor of the Government's evidence, so long as that presumption remained a rebuttable one and fair opportunity for rebuttal were provided. Thus, once the Government puts forth credible evidence that the habeas petitioner meets the enemy combatant criteria, the onus could shift to the petitioner to rebut that evidence with more persuasive evidence that he falls outside the criteria. A burden-shifting scheme of this sort would meet the goal of ensuring that the errant tourist, embedded journalist, or local aid worker has a chance to prove military error while giving due regard to the Executive once it has put forth meaningful support for its conclusion that the detainee is in fact an enemy combatant. . . .

We think it unlikely that this basic process will have the dire impact on the central functions of warmaking that the Government forecasts. The parties agree that initial captures on the battlefield need not receive the process we have discussed here; that process is due only when the determination is made to *continue* to hold those who have been seized. . . . While we accord the greatest respect and consideration to the judgments of military authorities in matters relating to the actual prosecution of a war, and recognize that the scope of that discretion necessarily is wide, it does not infringe on the core role of the military for the courts to exercise their own time-honored and constitutionally mandated roles of reviewing and resolving claims like those presented here. . . .

In so holding, we necessarily reject the Government's assertion that separation of powers principles mandate a heavily circumscribed role for the courts in such circumstances. Indeed, the position that the courts must forgo any examination of the individual case and focus exclusively on the legality of the broader detention scheme cannot be mandated by any reasonable view of separation of powers, as this approach serves only to *condense* power into a single branch of government. We have long since made clear that a state of war is not a blank check for the President when it comes to the rights of the Nation's citizens. . . . Likewise, we have made clear that, unless Congress acts to suspend it, the Great Writ of habeas corpus allows the Judicial Branch to play a necessary role in maintaining this delicate balance of governance, serving as an important judicial check on the Executive's discretion in the realm of detentions. . . .

. . . Plainly, the "process" Hamdi has received is not that to which he is entitled under the Due Process Clause.

There remains the possibility that the standards we have articulated could be met by an appropriately authorized and properly constituted military tribunal. . . .

Hamdi asks us to hold that the Fourth Circuit also erred by denying him immediate access to counsel upon his detention and by disposing of the case without permitting him to meet with an attorney. Since our grant of certiorari in this case, Hamdi has been appointed counsel, with whom he has met for consultation purposes on several occasions, and with whom he is now being granted unmonitored meetings. He unquestionably has the right to access to counsel in connection with the proceedings on remand. No further consideration of this issue is necessary at this stage of the case.

The judgment of the United States Court of Appeals for the Fourth Circuit is vacated, and the case is remanded for further proceedings.

It is so ordered.

JUSTICE SOUTER, with whom JUSTICE GINSBURG joins, concurring in part, dissenting in part, and concurring in the judgment.

The threshold issue is how broadly or narrowly to read §4001(a), . . . the tone of which is severe: "No citizen shall be imprisoned or otherwise detained by the United States except pursuant to an Act of Congress." . . . The fact that Congress intended to guard against a repetition of the World War II internments when it . . . gave us §4001(a) provides a powerful reason to think that §4001(a) was meant to require clear congressional authorization before any citizen can be placed in a cell. . . .

Under this principle of reading §4001(a) robustly to require a clear statement of authorization to detain, [the government's arguments do not] suffice to justify Hamdi's detention. . . .

The Government's claim, accepted by the Court, that the terms of [AUMF] are adequate to authorize detention of an enemy combatant . . . fails to . . . satisfy §4001(a) as read to require a clear statement of authority to detain. Since the [AUMF] was adopted one week after the attacks of September 11, 2001, it naturally speaks with some generality, but its focus is clear, and that is on the use of military power. It is fairly read to authorize the use of armies and weapons, whether against other armies or individual terrorists. But . . . it never so much as uses the word detention, and there is no reason to think Congress might have perceived any need to augment Executive power to deal with dangerous citizens within the United States, given the well-stocked statutory arsenal of defined criminal offenses covering the gamut of actions that a citizen sympathetic to terrorists might commit. . . .

Because I find Hamdi's detention . . . unauthorized by the Force Resolution, I would not reach any questions of what process he may be due in litigating disputed issues in a proceeding under the habeas statute or prior to the habeas enquiry itself. For me, it suffices that the Government has failed to justify holding him in the absence of a further Act of Congress, criminal charges, [or] a showing that the detention conforms to the laws of war. . . .

Since this disposition does not command a majority of the Court, however, the need to give practical effect to the conclusions of eight members of the Court rejecting the Government's position calls for me to join with the plurality in ordering remand on terms closest to those I would impose. Although I think litigation of Hamdi's status as an enemy combatant is unnecessary, the terms of the plurality's remand will allow Hamdi to offer evidence that he is not an enemy combatant, and he should at the least have the benefit of that opportunity

It should go without saying that in joining with the plurality to produce a judgment, I do not adopt the plurality's resolution of constitutional issues that I would not reach. It is not that I could disagree with the plurality's determinations (given the plurality's view of the [AUMF]) that someone in Hamdi's position is entitled at a minimum to notice of the Government's claimed factual basis for holding him, and to a fair chance to rebut it before a neutral decision maker; nor, of course, could I disagree with the plurality's affirmation of Hamdi's right to counsel. On the other hand, I do not mean to imply agreement that the Government could claim an evidentiary presumption casting the burden of rebuttal on Hamdi or that an opportunity to litigate before a military tribunal might obviate or truncate enquiry by a court on habeas.

Subject to these qualifications, I join with the plurality in a judgment of the Court vacating the Fourth Circuit's judgment and remanding the case.

JUSTICE SCALIA, with whom
JUSTICE STEVENS joins, dissenting.

This case brings into conflict the competing demands of national security and our citizens' constitutional right to personal liberty. Although I share the Court's evident unease as it seeks to reconcile the two, I do not agree with its resolution.

Where the Government accuses a citizen of waging war against it, our constitutional tradition has been to prosecute him in federal court for treason or some other crime. Where the exigencies of war prevent that, the Constitution's Suspension Clause, Art. I, §9, cl.2, allows Congress to relax the usual protections temporarily. Absent suspension, however, the Executive's assertion of military exigency has not been thought sufficient to permit detention without charge. No one contends that the congressional Authorization for Use of Military Force, on which the Government relies to justify its actions here, is an implementation of the Suspension Clause. Accordingly, I would reverse the decision below. . . .

JUSTICE O'CONNOR, writing for a plurality of this Court, asserts that captured enemy combatants (other than those suspected of war crimes) have traditionally been detained until the cessation of hostilities and then released. That is probably an accurate description of wartime practice with respect to enemy *aliens*. The tradition with respect to American citizens, however, has been quite different. Citizens aiding the enemy have been treated as traitors subject to the criminal process. . . .

. . . [T]he reasoning and conclusion of [*Ex parte*] *Milligan* logically cover the present case. The Government justifies imprisonment of Hamdi on principles of the law of war and admits that, absent the war, it would have no such authority. But if the law of war cannot be applied to citizens where courts are open, then Hamdi's imprisonment without criminal trial is no less unlawful than Milligan's trial by military tribunal. . . .

The proposition that the Executive lacks indefinite wartime detention authority over citizens is consistent with the Founders' general mistrust of military power permanently at the Executive's disposal. . . .

. . . Hamdi is entitled to a habeas decree requiring his release unless (1) criminal proceedings are promptly brought, or (2) Congress has suspended the writ of habeas corpus. A suspension of the writ could, of course, lay down conditions for continued detention, similar to those that today's opinion prescribes under the Due Process Clause. But there is a world of difference between the people's representatives' determining the need for that suspension (and prescribing the conditions for it), and this Court's doing so.

The plurality finds justification for Hamdi's imprisonment in the Authorization for Use of Military Force. . . .

This is not remotely a congressional suspension of the writ, and no one claims that it is. . . . The Suspension Clause of the Constitution, which carefully circumscribes the conditions under which the writ can be withheld, would be a sham if it could be evaded by congressional prescription of requirements *other than the common-law requirement of committal for criminal prosecution* that render the writ, though available, unavailing. If the Suspension Clause does not guarantee the citizen that he will either be tried or released, unless the conditions for suspending the writ exist and the grave action of suspending the writ has been taken; if it merely guarantees the citizen that he will not be detained unless Congress by ordinary legislation says he can be detained; it guarantees him very little indeed. . . .

Several limitations give my views in this matter a relatively narrow compass. They apply only to citizens, accused of being enemy combatants, who are detained within the territorial jurisdiction of a federal court. This is not likely to be a numerous group. . . . Where the citizen is captured outside and held outside the United States, the constitutional requirements may be different. Moreover, even within the United States, the accused citizen-enemy combatant may lawfully be detained once prosecution is in progress or in contemplation. . . .

I frankly do not know whether these tools are sufficient to meet the Government's security needs, including the need to obtain intelligence through interrogation. It is far beyond my competence, or the Court's competence, to determine that. But it is not beyond Congress's. If the situation demands it, the Executive can ask Congress to authorize suspension of the writ—which can be made subject to whatever conditions Congress deems appropriate, including even the procedural novelties invented by the plurality today. To be sure, suspension is limited by the Constitution to cases of rebellion or invasion. But whether the attacks of September 11, 2001, constitute an "invasion," and whether those attacks still justify suspension several years later, are questions for Congress rather than this Court. If civil rights are to be curtailed during wartime, it must be done openly and democratically, as the Constitution requires, rather than by silent erosion through an opinion of this Court. . . .

Many think it not only inevitable but entirely proper that liberty give way to security in times of national crisis— that, at the extremes of military exigency, *inter arma silent leges*. Whatever the general merits of the view that war silences law or modulates its voice, that view has no place in the interpretation and application of a Constitution designed precisely to confront war and, in a manner that accords with democratic principles, to accommodate it. Because the Court has proceeded to meet the current emergency in a manner the Constitution does not envision, I respectfully dissent.

JUSTICE THOMAS, *dissenting*.

The Executive Branch, acting pursuant to the powers vested in the President by the Constitution and with explicit congressional approval, has determined that Yaser Hamdi is an enemy combatant and should be detained. This detention falls squarely within the Federal Government's war powers, and we lack the expertise and capacity to second guess that decision. As such, petitioners' habeas challenge should fail, and there is no reason to remand the case. The plurality reaches a contrary conclusion by failing adequately to consider basic principles of the constitutional structure as it relates to national security and foreign affairs. . . .

I do not think that the Federal Government's war powers can be balanced away by this Court. Arguably, Congress could provide for additional procedural protections, but until it does, we have no right to insist upon them. But even if I were to agree with the general approach the plurality takes, I could not accept the particulars. The plurality utterly fails to account for the Government's compelling interests and for our own institutional inability to weigh competing concerns correctly. I respectfully dissent.

Note that Justice Sandra Day O'Connor, writing for Chief Justice Rehnquist and Justices Kennedy and Breyer in *Hamdi*, refused to rely on the administration's claim of plenary executive powers, holding instead that the AUMF authorized the detention of enemy combatants (even if they were U.S. citizens). She reasoned that because the justification for detention is to prevent hostile combatants from returning to the battlefield, detention powers were necessary and appropriate to fight the war, and were implied under the AUMF. Justice Clarence Thomas agreed that the government could detain Hamdi, but on different grounds. He was the only member of the Court who seemed to endorse the president's view that, as president, he had "inherent" authority to detain enemies. To Thomas, the detention power "falls squarely within the Federal Government's war powers."

Four justices voted for Hamdi on the detention issue, but for different reasons. Justices David Souter and Ruth Bader Ginsburg believed the AUMF had not authorized the detentions. To support their position, they turned to §4001(a), which, recall, provides that "no citizen shall be imprisoned or otherwise detained by the United States except pursuant to an Act of Congress." To Souter and Ginsburg, the AUMF "never so much as uses the word detention," much less authorizes them. Scalia and Stevens agreed but believed the problem was even broader. They argued that the government can detain citizens only through the criminal justice system or by suspending the writ of habeas corpus, which the AUMF had not done.

Although the justices divided over Hamdi's detention, they were nearly unanimous in their belief that "a state of war is not a blank check for the President when it comes to the rights of the Nation's citizens." They ruled that even though the government could detain Hamdi as an enemy combatant, he was entitled to challenge his classification and to be afforded "a fair opportunity to rebut the Government's factual assertions before a neutral decisionmaker." But Hamdi never received that opportunity. Following the Court's decision, his lawyers and the government reached an agreement that allowed him to return to Saudi Arabia in exchange for renouncing his American citizenship.

Hamdi answered questions about the rights of U.S. citizens who are captured during military conflict, but it did not address similar issues with respect to noncitizens. The justices considered this aspect of the president's war powers in **Rasul v. Bush** (2004), decided the same day as *Hamdi. Rasul* centered on the status of some six hundred men who had been captured during hostilities in Afghanistan and transported to Guantanamo. The prisoners were detained without formal charges and without access to courts or attorneys. The relatives of two Australians and twelve Kuwaitis filed habeas corpus petitions on the detainees' behalf claiming they were illegally incarcerated. The lower federal courts dismissed these lawsuits, holding that the federal courts have no jurisdiction outside the United States. The relatives of the detainees requested Supreme Court review.

A six-justice majority reversed, ruling that U.S. law confers jurisdiction on the federal courts over such habeas corpus petitions. Federal authority extends to areas under the control of the United States, such as the Guantanamo naval base, as well as to the military custodians of the detainees. Under the Court's decision, incarcerated captives, whether American citizens or aliens, have the right to challenge their imprisonment in federal court.

The decision in *Rasul* was based on an interpretation of federal statutes, not on the Constitution. The ruling is important, however, because it allows access to the courts where the constitutional validity of the detainees' continued imprisonment may be challenged.

Hamdi and *Rasul* dealt with the government's power to detain suspected terrorists and limit challenges in the federal courts to their detention. But they were not the Court's last words on the executive power in the war against terrorism. Just as Lincoln and Roosevelt resorted to military tribunals or commissions, so too did President Bush. And just as during those earlier wartime administrations—recall *Milligan* and *Quirin*—the president's actions were challenged. In **Hamdan v. Rumsfeld** (2006) the Court considered the order issued by President Bush that subjected "enemy combatants" to military commissions.

Justice Stevens, writing for the majority, outlawed the use of these commissions, reiterating the view that

even during wars the "Executive is bound to comply with the Rule of Law."[23] The Court did not, however, entirely shut the door. Part of the majority's concern about the commissions was that Congress had not authorized them. But under the Court's ruling, as Justice Breyer noted, "[n]othing prevents the President from returning to Congress to seek the authority he believes necessary." And, in fact, the administration took that step—with success. Within months of the Court's decision in *Hamdan,* Congress passed the Military Commissions Act (MCA), which authorized the use of military commissions for trying suspected terrorists and denied federal courts jurisdiction to hear the detainees' habeas corpus applications.

Based in part on their review of the history and origins of the writ of habeas corpus, the justices struck down parts of the law in **Boumediene v. Bush** (2008). In a closely divided vote, they held that the Guantanamo Bay detainees have a right to challenge their imprisonment in the federal courts. Writing for the majority, Justice Kennedy declared, "The laws and Constitution are designed to survive, and remain in force, in extraordinary times. Liberty and security can be reconciled; and in our system they are reconciled within the framework of the law. The Framers decided that habeas corpus, a right of first importance, must be a part of that framework, a part of that law." He held that "if the privilege of habeas corpus is to be denied to the detainees now before us, Congress must act in accordance with the requirements of the Suspension Clause." In the view of the majority, the procedures outlined in the DTA did not provide an adequate substitute for the "privilege" of habeas corpus.

---

23. In addition to the issue of the constitutionality of the military commissions, *Hamdan* raised a jurisdictional issue. Shortly after the Court agreed to hear *Hamdan*, on December 30, 2005, Congress enacted the Detainee Treatment Act (DTA), which said that "no court, justice, or judge shall have jurisdiction to hear or consider" habeas corpus petitions filed by Guantanamo detainees. Although the act was silent about pending cases, the Bush administration believed that it removed the Supreme Court's jurisdiction to resolve Hamdan's suit. Accordingly, the administration asked the justices to dismiss the writ of certiorari. In light of the government's request, some commentators thought that *Hamdan* presented an opportunity for the Court to clarify its ruling in *Ex parte McCardle (excerpted in chapter 2)* and, more generally, the appropriate reading of the exceptions clause. But Justice Stevens, writing for himself and Justices Breyer, Ginsburg, Kennedy, and Souter, said that it was "unnecessary" to consider the various constitutional arguments about *McCardle* and the exceptions clause because the DTA did not expressly cover pending cases. Justices Scalia and Alito, in contrast, believed that Congress had taken away the Court's jurisdiction to hear the case.

The four dissenters objected strongly to Kennedy's analysis. Justice Scalia wrote, "The game of bait-and-switch that today's opinion plays upon the Nation's Commander in Chief will make the war harder on us. It will almost certainly cause more Americans to be killed." President Bush remarked that his administration would "abide by the Court's decision," but he did not agree with it.

What are the lessons of *Hamdi, Rasul, Hamdan,* and *Boumediene*—all four of which the executive lost in part or in full? Are they in line with other cases you have read in this chapter? Is the central idea one that follows from Jackson's concurrence in *Youngstown,* that in the interest of the nation's security, the justices may be willing to allow the president to take actions during times of war that they would otherwise prohibit, but generally only if the president has the backing of Congress? If so, do you agree that this is the appropriate way for the justices to proceed? On one hand, why would legislative approval be so important if the president believes he is acting in the country's best interest? On the other, should the Court allow the president, even with Congress's support, to curtail rights and liberties? Keep in mind that in *Boumediene,* the Court took the position that it should not: Congress had approved of the detentions, but the Court still ruled against the executive.

Whether this is an appropriate role for the Court to play in wartime remains an open question, and the justices will no doubt continue to mull it over in the decades to come. Certainly, if history is any indication, President Bush will not be the last president to claim broad constitutional authority for the executive in such circumstances. It is worth noting, in fact, that upon taking office, Barack Obama's administration continued at least some of the policies promulgated during the Bush years. Although the Obama Justice Department dropped the term *enemy combatant,* it continued to assert authority to detain terrorist suspects who "substantially supported terrorist organizations.

ANNOTATED READINGS

Books on the domestic context of separation of powers problems include Sotirios A. Barber, *The Constitution and the Delegation of Congressional Power* (Chicago: University of Chicago Press, 1975); Barbara H. Craig, *Chadha: The Story of an Epic Constitutional Struggle* (New York: Oxford University Press, 1988); Jessica Korn, *The Power of Separation: American Constitutionalism and the Myth of Legislative Veto* (Princeton, NJ: Princeton University Press, 1998).

Books on foreign policy and war include Howard Ball, *Bush, the Detainees, and the Constitution: The Battle over Presidential Power in the War on Terrorism* (Lawrence: University Press of Kansas, 2007); John Hart Ely, *War and Responsibility: Constitutional Lessons of Vietnam and Its Aftermath* (Princeton, NJ: Princeton University Press, 1993); Louis Fisher, *Nazi Saboteurs on Trial: A Military Tribunal and American Law* (Lawrence: University Press of Kansas, 2003); Louis Fisher, *Presidential War Power,* 2nd ed. (Lawrence: University Press of Kansas, 2004); Louis Henkin, *Foreign Affairs and the Constitution* (New York: Oxford University Press, 1996); Peter Irons, *Justice at War: The Story of the Japanese American Internment Cases* (New York: Oxford University Press, 1983); Elizabeth D. Leonard, *Lincoln's Avengers: Justice, Revenge, and Reunion after the Civil War* (New York: W. W. Norton, 2004); Maeva Marcus, *Truman and the Steel Seizure Case: The Limits of Presidential Power* (Durham, NC: Duke University Press, 1994); Scott M. Matheson, *Presidential Constitutionalism in Perilous Times* (Cambridge, MA: Harvard University Press, 2009); Christopher May, *In the Name of War: Judicial Review and the War Powers since 1918* (Cambridge, MA: Harvard University Press, 1989); Brian McGinty, *Lincoln and the Court* (Cambridge, MA: Harvard University Press, 2008); Eric A. Posner and Adrian Vermeule, *Terror in the Balance: Security, Liberty, and the Courts* (New York: Oxford University Press, 2007); William H. Rehnquist, *All the Laws but One: Civil Liberties in Wartime* (New York: Knopf, 1998); W. Taylor Reveley III, *War Powers of the President and Congress* (Charlottesville: University of Virginia Press, 1981); Martin S. Sheffer, *The Judicial Development of Presidential War Powers* (Westport, CT: Praeger, 1999); Gordon Silverstein, *Imbalance of Powers: Constitutional Interpretation and the Making of American Foreign Policy* (New York: Oxford University Press, 1996); and Geoffrey R. Stone, *War and Liberty: An American Dilemma* (New York: W. W. Norton, 2007).

For works on the writ of habeas corpus, see Eric M. Freedman, *Habeas Corpus: Rethinking the Great Writ of Liberty* (New York: New York University Press, 2003); Nancy J. King and Joseph L. Hoffmann, *Habeas for the Twenty-first Century: Uses, Abuses, and the Future of the Great Writ* (Chicago: University of Chicago Press, 2011); and Justin J. Wert, *Habeas Corpus in America: The Politics of Individual Rights* (Lawrence: University Press of Kansas, 2011).

PART III

Nation–State Relations

iStock/DanBrandenburg

Allocating Government Power

Allocating Government Power

IF WE WERE TO CATALOG the types of governments that exist in the world today, we would have a fairly diverse list. Some are unitary systems in which power is located in a central authority that may or may not mete out power to its subdivisions. Others are virtually the opposite, with authority resting largely in local governments and only certain powers reserved to national authority. When the framers drafted the Constitution, they had to make some basic decisions about the allocation of government power between the states and the national government they were creating. Their choice, generally speaking, was federalism: a system in which "a constitution divides governmental power between a central government and one or more subdivisional governments, giving each substantial functions."[1]

That decision turned out to be a good one, and we reap the advantages of it today. For example, because the government is multilayered, Americans have many points of access to influence the system. If your state enacts legislation you do not like, you might find grounds to challenge it in federal court or lobby your representative in Congress urging federal action to counter it. You could even "vote with your feet" and move to a state that has laws you prefer. Moreover, the

system provides for further checks on the exercise of government power because federal, state, and even local systems are all involved in policy making. Finally, it encourages experimentation and provides for flexibility. Justice Louis Brandeis once wrote, "It is one of the happy incidents of the federal system that a single courageous State may, if its citizens choose, serve as a laboratory; and try novel social and economic experiments without risk to the rest of the country."[2] Because of their proximity to many problems, state and local governments may be better positioned to fashion effective public policy than is the federal government. If successful, such policy innovations may be copied in other states or even adopted nationwide. The states were first to implement tougher laws to discourage drunk driving, policies to protect workers' rights, welfare reforms, and so forth. Other problems, such as those associated with foreign policy, are better left to the national government, which can act in behalf of the entire country.

But federalism is not perfect. It can add considerable inefficiency to government operations. The implementation of certain kinds of policies might require the coordination of the national government, fifty state governments, and numerous subdivisions, which inevitably slows down the process.

For our purposes, the most relevant concern about federalism is its complexity. It is quite difficult for citizens

---

1. J. W. Peltason, *Corwin and Peltason's Understanding the Constitution,* 14th ed. (Fort Worth, TX: Harcourt Brace, 1997), 17. See also J. W. Peltason and Sue Davis, *Corwin and Peltason's Understanding the Constitution,* 15th ed. (Fort Worth, TX: Harcourt Brace, 2000), chap. 1.

2. Dissent in *New State Ice Co. v. Liebmann,* 285 U.S. 262 at 311 (1932).

to keep abreast of such a decentralized system. People may not understand which level of government makes specific policies. In addition, government may seem so remote to some citizens that they may not even know the names of their representatives. At the other end of the spectrum, governments sometimes do not understand or abide by the boundaries of their own power. American history is full of examples of allegations by states that the federal government has gone too far in regulating "their" business; indeed, this was one issue over which the Civil War, the most extreme disagreement, was fought.

Yet, in most circumstances, it is neither war that has resolved these disputes nor the entities themselves that have shed light on their complexities. Rather, since the nation's founding, the U.S. Supreme Court has played a substantial role in delineating and defining the contours of American federalism. The chapters that follow discuss why and how the Court has done so. Chapter 6 focuses on the various theories of federal–state relations with which the Court has dealt. Chapters 7 and 8 consider the exercise of government power over the most contentious issues: the regulation of commerce and the power to tax and spend.

But first, let us explore several issues emanating from our discussion so far: the kind of system the framers adopted, the amending of that system, and its complexity, which often leads to the involvement of "neutral" arbiters—judges and Supreme Court justices.

THE FRAMERS AND FEDERALISM

We have already mentioned that the framers selected federalism from among several alternative forms of government, although the word *federalism* does not appear in the Constitution. The founders had some general vision of the sort of government they wanted or, more to the point, the sort they did not want. They rejected a unitary system as wholly incompatible with basic values and traditions already existing within the states. They also rejected a confederation in which power would reside with the states; after all, that is what they had under the Articles of Confederation, the charter they came to Philadelphia to revise.

How to divide power, then, became the delegates' central concern. In the end, they wrote into the document a rather elaborate "pattern of allocation." What does this system look like? In other words, who gets

what? Table III-1 depicts the allocation of powers emanating from the Constitution. As we can see, the different levels of government have some exclusive and some concurrent powers, but they are also prohibited from operating in certain spheres.

Despite the framers' attempt to allocate power, ambiguity resulted. One source of confusion was the question of constitutional relationships; that is, in the parlance of the eighteenth century, the framers looked at the Constitution as a contract, but a contract between whom? Some commentators argue that it specifies the relationship between the people and the national government, and that the former empower the latter. Justice Joseph Story wrote,

The constitution of the United States was ordained and established, not by the states in their sovereign capacities, but emphatically, as the preamble of the constitution declares, by "the people of the United States." . . . The constitution was not, therefore, necessarily carved out of existing state sovereignties, nor a surrender of powers already existing in state institutions.[3]

Others suggest that the contract is between the states and the nation. In a 1798 resolution of the Virginia Assembly, James Madison wrote,

That this Assembly doth explicitly and peremptorily declare that it views the powers of the Federal Government as resulting from the compact, to which the States are parties, as limited by the plain sense and intention of the instrument constituting that compact; as no further valid than they are authorized by the grants enumerated in that compact; and that in case of deliberate, palpable, and dangerous exercise of other powers not granted by the said compact, the States, who are the parties thereto, have the right, and are in duty bound, to interpose for arresting the progress of the evil, and for maintaining within their respective limits, the authorities, rights, and liberties appertaining to them.[4]

This debate is not abstract: it has real consequences. In its most violent incarnation, the Civil War, Southern leaders took Madison's logic to its limit. They argued that the Constitution represented a contract between the states and the federal government, with the states creating the national government. When the federal

---

3. *Martin v. Hunter's Lessee,* 14 U.S. (1 Wheat) 304 at 324–325 (1816).

4. Reprinted in Urofsky, *Documents of American Constitutional and Legal History,* , 159.

TABLE III-I The Constitutional Allocation of Government Power

POWERS SPECIFIED WITHIN THE CONSTITUTION OR BY COURT INTERPRETATION

POWERS EXCLUSIVE TO THE NATIONAL GOVERNMENT	POWERS EXCLUSIVE TO STATE GOVERNMENTS	CONCURRENT POWERS TO BOTH FEDERAL AND STATE GOVERNMENTS
Coin money	Run elections	Tax
Regulate interstate and foreign commerce	Regulate intrastate commerce	Borrow money
Tax imports	Establish republican forms of state and local governments	Establish courts
Make treaties	Protect public health, safety, and morals	Charter banks and corporations
Make all laws "necessary and proper"	All powers not delegated to the national government or denied to the states by the Constitution	Make and enforce laws
Make war		Take property (power of eminent domain)
Regulate postal system		

POWERS DENIED BY THE CONSTITUTION OR BY COURT INTERPRETATION

EXPRESSLY PROHIBITED TO THE NATIONAL GOVERNMENT	EXPRESSLY PROHIBITED TO STATE GOVERNMENT	EXPRESSLY PROHIBITED TO BOTH
Tax exports	Tax imports and exports	Pass bills of attainder
Change state boundaries	Coin money	Pass ex post facto laws
	Enter into treaties	Grant titles of nobility
	Impair obligation of contracts	Impose religious tests
		Pass laws in conflict with the Bill of Rights and subsequent amendments

SOURCES: Adapted from J. W. Peltason, Corwin and Peltason's *Understanding the Constitution*, 14th ed. (Fort Worth, TX: Harcourt Brace, 1997), 20–22; and C. Herman Pritchett, *Constitutional Law of the Federal System* (Englewood Cliffs, NJ: Prentice Hall, 1984), 58.

government—controlled by the Northern states—abrogated its end of the agreement, the contract was no longer valid. The Civil War ended that particular dispute, but the principle continued to flare up in less extreme but important forms. The refusal of some Southern states to abide by federal civil rights laws is one example.

This problem continues to manifest itself, largely because the Constitution supports both sides and therefore neither. Those who favor the national government–people approach point to the document's preamble: "*We the people* [our italics] of the United States . . . do ordain and establish this Constitution." To support the national government–state argument, proponents turn to the language of Article VII, that the ratification of nine states "shall be sufficient for the Establishment of this Constitution *between the States* [our italics] so ratifying." When issues related to the contractual nature of

the Constitution arise, therefore, many look to the Supreme Court to resolve them. As we shall see in the next chapter, different Courts have approached this debate in varying ways, adopting one view over the other at distinct points in American history.

THE TENTH AND ELEVENTH AMENDMENTS

Arguments over who the parties to the constitutional contract are may never be fully resolved, but another point of ambiguity was thought so onerous that it could not be left to interpretation. That area is the balance of power between the states and the federal government. The original charter, in the view of some, placed too much authority with the federal government. In particular, states' rights advocates pointed to two clauses in the Constitution as working against their interests.

The first is the necessary and proper clause: Congress has the power "To make all Laws which shall be necessary and proper for carrying into Execution [its] Powers, and all other Powers vested by this Constitution in the Government of the United States, or in any Department or Officer thereof."

The other is the supremacy clause: "This Constitution, and the Laws of the United States which shall be made in Pursuance thereof; and all Treaties made, or which shall be made, under the Authority of the United States, shall be the supreme Law of the Land; and the Judges in every State shall be bound thereby, any Thing in the Constitution or Laws of any State to the Contrary notwithstanding."

These clauses seem to allocate a great deal of power to the national government. Yet, as Madison wrote in *Federalist* No. 45,

The powers delegated by the proposed Constitution to the Federal Government, are few and defined. Those which are to remain in the State Governments are numerous and indefinite. The former will be exercised principally on external objects, as war, peace, negotiation, and foreign commerce; with which last the power of taxation will for the most part be connected. The powers reserved to the several States will extend to all the objects, which, in the ordinary course of affairs, concern the lives, liberties and properties of the people; and the internal order, improvement, and prosperity of the State.

Nevertheless, states remained concerned that the national government would attempt to cut into their power and sovereignty, and the language of the Constitution did little to allay their fears. At worst, it suggested that the federal institutions would always be supreme; at best, it was highly ambiguous. Even Madison recognized its lack of clarity when he wrote in *Federalist* No. 39,

The proposed Constitution therefore . . . is in strictness neither a national nor a federal Constitution; but a composition of both. In its foundation it is federal, not national; in the sources from which the ordinary powers of the Government are drawn, it is partly federal, and partly national: in the operation of these powers, it is national, not federal. In the extent of them, again, it is federal; not national: And finally in the authoritative mode of introducing amendments, it is neither wholly federal, nor wholly national.

Madison clearly thought this ambiguity was an asset of the new system of government, an advantage that made it fit compatibly into the overall philosophies of separation of powers and checks and balances. But this argument proved insufficient; when the perceived unfair balance of power proved to be an obstacle to the ratification of the Constitution, those favoring its adoption promised to remedy it.

This remedy took the form of the Tenth Amendment, which—depending on the interpretation—seems quite different from the rest of the Bill of Rights. The first nine amendments deal mainly with the rights of the people vis-à-vis the federal government, such as the First Amendment: "Congress shall make no law respecting an establishment of religion." But the Tenth Amendment states, "The powers not delegated to the United States by the Constitution, nor prohibited by it to the States, are reserved to the States respectively, or to the people." With these words in place, states' rights advocates were mollified, at least temporarily. To be sure, some understood the Tenth Amendment to do little more than to affirm that the Constitution created a federal government limited to its "delegated" powers. In the view of some states' rights advocates, however, the amendment established the rights of states, creating a protected area—an enclave—for state power.[5]

We will have many opportunities to explore this debate in the chapters to come. For now, it is worth noting that supporters of state authority quickly learned that the Tenth Amendment did not offer the states complete protection against federal encroachment. Just three years after the amendment was ratified, the Supreme Court in ***Chisholm v. Georgia*** (1793) upheld the authority of the federal courts to hear cases brought against a state by citizens of another state. The idea that the fortunes of a state could be decided by a federal tribunal was unacceptable to state power advocates. They demanded constitutional protection against such intrusions. The result was the Eleventh Amendment, ratified in 1795, which restricted the power of the federal courts to hear disputes brought against a state by the citizens of another state or by citizens of other nations. As history would quickly

---

5. For more on the Tenth Amendment as an enclave, see Martin H. Redish, *The Constitution as Political Structure* (New York: Oxford University Press, 1995). Redish rejects this interpretation of the amendment.

show, however, neither the Tenth nor the Eleventh Amendment settled the perennial question of the proper distribution of political power between the federal government and the states.

Why not? Given the elaborate system of American federalism depicted in table III-1, why is the division of power the center of so much controversy? In part, the answer takes us back to the contractual nature of the Constitution. As we shall see in the following chapter, which explores general theoretical approaches to federalism, the Court has had some difficulty determining the parties to the contract, and its confusion encouraged litigation. In more concrete terms, no matter how elaborate the design, the contract does not (and perhaps cannot) address the range of real disputes that arise between nation and state.

Indeed, the irony here is that the complexity of the system, coupled with the language of the Constitution, is what fosters the need for interpretation. We often must ask, Where do state powers begin and federal powers end, and vice versa? States have the authority to regulate intrastate commerce, and the federal government regulates interstate commerce, but is it so easy to delineate those boundaries? Which entity controls the manufacturing of goods in one state that are shipped to another? And, more to the point, what happens when the state and federal governments have different ideas regarding how to regulate the manufacturing?

If that problem is not enough, compare the constitutional language of the Tenth Amendment with that of the necessary and proper and supremacy clauses. The supremacy clause prohibits states from passing laws that directly conflict with the Constitution, federal laws, and so forth. But so often the issues are not that clear. Is the federal authority supreme only in its sphere of operations—those activities where it has clear constitutional mandates—as some argue the Tenth Amendment dictates? Or is it the case that every time the federal government enters into a particular realm, it automatically preempts the actions of states? Or does the answer depend on the intent of Congress—that is, whether it intended to preempt state action?

It should be clear that American federalism is something of a two-edged sword. On one hand, the balance of power the framers created pacified those who were opposed to ratifying the Constitution, and this balance continues to define the contours of the U.S. system of government. On the other hand, the complexity of federalism has given rise to tensions between the levels of government, often leading to disputes that require settlement by the courts. It may be that the system has been resilient because it constantly requires fresh interpretation. But we will leave that for you to decide as we now turn to how the Supreme Court has formulated theories and specific rulings in response to two distinct but interrelated issues: the general contours of state–federal relations and the important powers of commerce and taxing and spending.

6 Federalism

URING THE 1960s Congress amended the Fair Labor Standards Act (FLSA) of 1938 to require state governments to pay virtually all their employees a specified minimum wage and to compensate them for overtime work. Were these amendments constitutional, or had Congress interfered with state authority and autonomy? The answer depends on how we view the letter and spirit of the Constitution. We would reach very different conclusions depending on whether we subscribed to the dual or cooperative approach to nation–state relations *(see table 6-1)*.

Proponents of dual federalism would want the Court to strike down the law. As advocates of states' rights, they would argue that the Constitution represents an agreement between the states and the federal government in which the states empower the central government and that, therefore, states are not subservient to the federal government. In other words, because each state is supreme within its own sphere, the federal government could no more impose minimum wage requirements on states than the states could impose them on the federal government. To back their theory, dual federalists invoke the Tenth Amendment, arguing that it creates an "enclave" of states' rights that Congress may not invade—especially if Congress encroaches on a traditional state function.[1]

Cooperative federalism takes the opposite view. Proponents argue that the people, not the states, created and animated the federal government. This view holds that the supremacy clause and the necessary and proper clause, not the Tenth Amendment, control the balance of power between the federal government and the states. That amendment, according to cooperative federalism, grants no additional powers to the states. It serves only to emphasize that the federal government is limited to the powers the Constitution assigns to it. As long as Congress bases the law regulating wages and hours on an enumerated (or implied) power, the law passes constitutional muster. The Tenth Amendment creates no bar, or so the argument goes.

The history of nation–state relations issues before the Supreme Court has been characterized by swings back and forth between variants of cooperative federalism and dual federalism. In fact, a sharply divided Supreme Court voted 5 to 4 to strike down the amendments to the Fair Labor Standards Act (FLSA) of 1976. The case was *National League of Cities v. Usery*, in which the majority held that the provisions violated the Tenth Amendment and were an unconstitutional interference with states. Just nine years later, however, in another 5–4 decision, the Court upheld the maximum hours and minimum wage provisions of the law in *Garcia v. San Antonio Metropolitan Transit Authority* (1985), which effectively overruled the 1976 decision.

In this chapter we explore four aspects of the constitutional division of power between the federal

---

1. See Redish, *The Constitution as Political Structure*. The idea here is that even if Congress possessed the power, it would be unable to exercise it if it impinged on the "enclave."

TABLE 6-1 A Comparison of Dual and Cooperative Federalism

	DUAL FEDERALISM	COOPERATIVE FEDERALISM
General view	Operates under the assumption that the two levels of government are coequal sovereigns, each supreme within its own sphere.	Operates under the assumption that the national government is supreme even if its actions touch state functions. States and the federal government are "partners," but the latter largely sets policy for the nation.
View of the Constitution	Is a compact among the states and a contract between the states and the federal government.	Rejects view of it as a "compact"; the people, not the states, empower the national government.
Constitutional support	Tenth Amendment reserves certain powers to the states and thus limits the national government to those powers specifically delegated to it.	Tenth Amendment does not provide additional powers to the states.
	Necessary and proper clause is to be read narrowly.	Necessary and proper clause is to be read expansively.
		Supremacy clause means that the national government is supreme within its own sphere, even if its actions touch on state functions.

government and the states. First, we examine the doctrinal cycle of nation–state relations, tracing the historical swings between cooperative and dual federalism. Second, we look at the Eleventh Amendment and the doctrine of sovereign immunity, which promote the status of the states by shielding them from lawsuits. Next, we address new judicial federalism, an approach to the division of authority between state and federal judiciaries that arose during the 1980s and strengthened the role of state courts. We end the chapter with a discussion of a recurring issue of federalism: What happens when both the states and the federal government want to regulate the same activity?

THE DOCTRINAL CYCLE OF NATION–STATE RELATIONS

The Court's about-face from *National League of Cities* to *Garcia* is not an anomaly in this area of the law; rather, it is a symptom of the general confusion that has surrounded American federalism since the eighteenth century. As depicted in table 6-2, throughout U.S. history the Supreme Court's allegiance has shifted from cooperative federalism to dual federalism (or one of their variants) and back again. As a consequence the justices have moved between states' rights and national supremacy positions over time. *(See table 6-2.)*

From our introduction to this part of the book, you learned that the Tenth Amendment was included in the Bill of Rights to allay concerns that the national

TABLE 6-2 Doctrinal Cycles of Nation–State Relations

COURT ERA	GENERAL APPROACH ADOPTED
Marshall Court (1801–1835)	Cooperative federalism: as long as Congress can ground a law in its enumerated or implied powers, the Tenth Amendment does not serve as a bar.
Taney Court (1835–1864)	Dual federalism (states' rights).
Civil War/ Reconstruction Courts (1865–1895)	Cooperative federalism.
Laissez-faire Courts (1896–1936)	Dual federalism, grounded in laissez-faire philosophy.
Post–New Deal Courts (1937–1969)	Cooperative federalism.
Burger Court (1969–1986)	Weakening support for cooperative federalism with occasional decisions supporting dual federalism (*National League of Cities v. Usery*, 1976). New judicial federalism.
Rehnquist and Roberts Courts (1986–present)	Limited dual federalism, a milder form of dual federalism: states cannot be treated as administrative units of the federal government.

government would run roughshod over the states. Vexing from the start, however, has been the question of how to interpret its words: "The powers not delegated to the United States by the Constitution, nor prohibited by it to the States, are reserved to the States respectively, or to the people." As the discussion above suggests, to dual federalists it is a states' rights amendment—one that creates an enclave that protects states from unwarranted federal intrusions. To cooperative federalists, it does little more than confirm that the Constitution created a federal government limited to its "delegated" powers. Disputes over these competing views raise questions that implicate the very nature of the Constitution.

As we review the doctrinal cycles in the following pages, we highlight those disputes where a state has claimed that actions of the federal government directly impinge on the constitutional authority of the state or where the federal government had similar complaints about state actions. In chapters 7 and 8 we broaden our discussion by exploring federalism's effects on the regulation of commerce and the exercise of the fiscal powers of taxation and spending. It has been within these policy areas that some of the most significant federalism battles have been fought.

The Marshall Court and the Rise of National Supremacy

An ardent Federalist, Chief Justice John Marshall was true to his party's tenets over the course of his long career on the Court. In case after case (in particular, **Cohens v. Virginia**, 1821), he was more than willing to elevate the powers of the federal government above those of the states—even when he knew that some states were questioning the authority of the Court or failing to respect its decisions.

Such behavior may not be unusual in new democracies, as our discussion of the problems of the Russian Constitutional Court demonstrates *(see box 6-1)*. But that did not deter Marshall from making a number of important statements on national supremacy—with perhaps the most significant coming in *McCulloch v. Maryland* (1819). In chapter 3 we saw how Marshall used this case to assert that Congress has implied powers. Here, we shall see that *McCulloch* also served as Marshall's vehicle to expound the notion of national supremacy; note in particular his view of the Tenth Amendment. We offer a brief review of the essential facts to remind you of the issues in this case.

McCulloch v. Maryland

17 U.S. (4 Wheat.) 316 (1819)
http://laws.findlaw.com/us/17/316.html
Vote: 6 (Duvall, Johnson, Livingston, Marshall, Story, Washington)
   0

OPINION OF THE COURT: *Marshall*
NOT PARTICIPATING: *Todd*

FACTS:

Congress established the Second Bank of the United States in 1816. Because of inefficiency and corruption, the bank was very unpopular, and many blamed it for the nation's economic problems. To show its displeasure, the Maryland legislature passed a law saying that banks operating in the state that were not chartered by the state—in other words, the national bank—could issue banknotes only on special paper, which the state taxed. The Maryland law was clearly a state attack on an operation of the federal government. Was it constitutional for the state to use its authority to block a federal program? This question became a legal dispute when James McCulloch, the cashier of the Baltimore branch of the Bank of the United States, refused to pay the tax and Maryland took legal action to enforce its law. The United States challenged the constitutionality of the Maryland tax, and in return Maryland disputed the constitutionality of the bank.[2]

ARGUMENTS:

For the plaintiff in error, James McCulloch:

- The necessary and proper clause justifies the establishment of the bank. It allows Congress to use all usual and suitable means of executing its constitutional powers. Congress has the power to raise revenue to support the government, and a bank is a suitable means to exercise that power.
- Under the supremacy clause, the laws of the United States are supreme and control all state constitutions and legislation.
- Allowing states to tax the bank implicitly allows them to control the federal government, even to the point of its destruction. That possibility was precisely the situation the framers wished to avoid. They did not intend for the federal government to operate upon the discretion of the states.

---

2. The first part of the opinion deals with the question of whether Congress had the power to create the bank. See the excerpt in chapter 3. The second part deals with the constitutionality of the Maryland tax. Marshall clearly delineates this division.

BOX 6-1   FEDERALISM AND JUDICIAL POWER IN GLOBAL PERSPECTIVE

AS OUR DISCUSSIONS of *McCulloch v. Maryland* in this chapter and in chapter 2 illustrate, the states of the United States zealously guarded their power from federal encroachment during Chief Justice Marshall's tenure. The justices were well aware of the possibility that at least some states would disregard their decisions, and, in fact, some did.

As it turns out, the U.S. Supreme Court is not the only judicial tribunal to face such challenges. Quite early in its history, the Russian Constitutional Court confronted a similar lack of respect from its country's republics.

Created in 1991, the Russian court was given substantial powers, including the ability to review the constitutionality of all state (republic) actions (in the absence of a concrete dispute) at the request of various executive and legislative bodies. In other words, if a member of Russia's parliament or even the president believed that a republic was violating constitutional mandates, he or she could bring the claim directly to the court, which could then issue a ruling.

In March 1992 a group of Russian legislators took advantage of this right to challenge an action of Tatarstan, a republic within the Russian Federation. Specifically, they argued that a referendum Tatarstan hoped to put to its citizens was unconstitutional. The referendum asked whether the citizens agreed or disagreed "that the Tatarstan Republic is a sovereign state and a party to international law, basing its relations with the Russian Federation as partners."

The justices accepted the case and scheduled hearings, which Tatarstan officials refused to attend. After hearing the arguments, the justices held that, in fact, the referendum violated several constitutional provisions, especially those establishing national supremacy: "The denial of the supremacy of federal laws over the laws of members of the federation is contrary to the constitutional status of the republics in a federated state and precludes the establishment of a law-governed state."

When the Tatar government decided to ignore the ruling, the justices requested that their chair (chief justice), Valerii Zor'kin, persuade parliament to seek compliance with their decision. The parliament issued a resolution that supported the court's ruling and requested that the president enforce it. That was insufficient, however, to deter Tatarstan from going ahead with its referendum about a week later, and a majority of the voters cast ballots in favor of the measure.

To be sure, the U.S. Supreme Court continues to confront challenges from the states, but blatant disregard for its decisions is unusual today. Whether the Russian Constitutional Court will be able to attain a similar status is a question only time can answer. As of this writing, however, the court remains a relatively weak institution. A recent dissertation concluded that the court's authority has actually decreased over time, "particularly with the regions in the Russian federal system."

SOURCES: Herman Schwartz, *The Struggle for Constitutional Justice in Post-Communist Europe* (Chicago: University of Chicago Press, 2000); Robert Sharlet, "The Russian Constitutional Court: The First Term," *Post-Soviet Affairs* 9 (1993): 1–39; Julia Wishnevsky, "Russian Constitutional Court: A Third Branch of Government?," RFE/RL Research Report 2 (1993): 1; Sabrina Lyne Pinnell, "The Russian Constitutional Court: An Analysis of Its Evolution within a Developing Federal System" (PhD dissertation, University of California, Santa Barbara, 2007).

For the defendant in error, state of Maryland et al.:
- The Tenth Amendment ensures that all powers not expressly enumerated to the federal government are reserved to the states. The federal government has enumerated powers to collect taxes, borrow money, and pay public debts, but a bank fulfills none of those ends. Therefore, it is beyond the scope of congressional power and is a power reserved to the states.
- This interpretation of the Tenth Amendment is supported by the history of the Constitution, which was ratified as a compact between states, not by the people as one aggregate mass.

- The necessary and proper clause should be interpreted as a restriction on Congress's power to choose the means of executing its enumerated powers. The framers said "necessary *and* proper," instead of "necessary *or* proper," to avoid granting general and unlimited discretion to the federal government.
- Taxation is an acknowledged power of the states, and states have sovereign power to tax, independent of the Constitution. The Constitution prohibits states only from taxing imposts or tonnage duties, and therefore states may tax anything else.

MR. CHIEF JUSTICE MARSHALL DELIVERED THE OPINION OF THE COURT.

The constitution of our country, in its most interesting and vital parts, is to be considered; the conflicting powers of the government of the Union and of its members, as marked in that constitution, are to be discussed; and an opinion given, which may essentially influence the great operations of the government. . . .

In discussing this . . . the counsel for the state of Maryland have deemed it of some importance, in the construction of the constitution, to consider that instrument not as emanating from the people, but as the act of sovereign and independent states. The powers of the general government, it has been said, are delegated by the states, who alone are truly sovereign; and must be exercised in subordination to the states, who alone possess supreme dominion.

It would be difficult to sustain this proposition. The convention which framed the constitution was indeed elected by the state legislatures. But the instrument, when it came from their hands, was a mere proposal, without obligation, or pretensions to it. It was reported to the then existing Congress of the United States, with a request that it might "be submitted to a convention of delegates, chosen in each state by the people thereof, under the recommendation of its legislature, for their assent and ratification." This mode of proceeding was adopted; and by the convention, by Congress, and by the state legislatures, the instrument was submitted to the people. They acted upon it in the only manner in which they can act safely, effectively, and wisely, on such a subject, by assembling in convention. It is true, they assembled in their several states—and where else should they have assembled? No political dreamer was ever wild enough to think of breaking down the lines which separate the states, and of compounding the American people into one common mass. Of consequence, when they act, they act in their states. But the measures they adopt do not, on that account, cease to be the measures of the people themselves, or become the measures of the state governments. . . .

The government of the Union, then . . . is, emphatically, and truly, a government of the people. . . .

It is the government of all; its powers are delegated by all; it represents all, and acts for all. Though any one state may be willing to control its operations, no state is willing to allow others to control them. The nation, on those subjects on which it can act, must necessarily bind its component parts. But this question is not left to mere reason; the

people have, in express terms, decided it by saying, "this constitution, and the laws of the United States, which shall be made in pursuance thereof," "shall be the supreme law of the land," and by requiring that the members of the state legislatures, and the officers of the executive and judicial departments of the states shall take the oath of fidelity to it. The government of the United States, then, though limited in its powers, is supreme; and its laws, when made in pursuance of the constitution, form the supreme law of the land, "anything in the constitution or laws of any State to the contrary notwithstanding."

Among the enumerated powers, we do not find that of establishing a bank or creating a corporation. But there is no phrase in the instrument which, like the articles of confederation, excludes incidental or implied powers; and which requires that everything granted shall be expressly and minutely described. Even the 10th amendment, which was framed for the purpose of quieting the excessive jealousies which had been excited, omits the word "expressly," and declares only that the powers "not delegated to the United States, nor prohibited to the states, are reserved to the states or to the people"; thus leaving the question, whether the particular power which may become the subject of contest has been delegated to the one government, or prohibited to the other, to depend on a fair construction of the whole instrument. The men who drew and adopted this amendment had experienced the embarrassments resulting from the insertion of this word in the articles of confederation, and probably omitted it to avoid those embarrassments. A constitution, to contain an accurate detail of all the subdivisions of which its great powers will admit, and of all the means by which they may be carried into execution, would partake of a prolixity of a legal code, and could scarcely be embraced by the human mind. It would probably never be understood by the public. Its nature, therefore, requires, that only its great outlines should be marked, its important objects designated, and the minor ingredients which compose those objects be deduced from the nature of the objects themselves. That this idea was entertained by the framers of the American constitution, is not only to be inferred from the nature of the instrument, but from the language. . . .

After this declaration, it can scarcely be necessary to say that the existence of state banks can have no possible influence on the question. No trace is to be found in the constitution of an intention to create a dependence of the government of the Union on those of the states, for the execution of the great powers assigned to it. Its means are adequate to its ends; and on those means alone was it expected to rely for the accomplishment of its ends. To impose on it the necessity of resorting to means which it cannot control, which another government may furnish or withhold, would render its course precarious; the result of its measures uncertain, and create a dependence on other governments, which might disappoint its most important designs and is incompatible with the language of the constitution. But were it otherwise, the choice of means implies a right to choose a national bank in preference to state banks, and Congress alone can make the election.

After the most deliberate consideration, it is the unanimous and decided opinion of this court that the act to incorporate the bank of the United States is a law made in pursuance of the constitution, and is part of the supreme law of the land. . . .

It being the opinion of the court, that the act incorporating the bank is constitutional; and that the power of establishing a branch in the State of Maryland might be properly exercised by the bank itself, we proceed to inquire . . . whether the State of Maryland may, without violating the constitution, tax that branch? . . .

The argument on the part of the State of Maryland, is, not that the States may directly resist a law of Congress, but that they may exercise their acknowledged powers upon it, and that the constitution leaves them this right in the confidence that they will not abuse it.

That the power to tax involves the power to destroy; that the power to destroy may defeat and render useless the power to create; that there is a plain repugnance, in conferring on one government a power to control the constitutional measures of another, which other, with respect to those very measures, is declared to be supreme over that which exerts the control, are propositions not to be denied. But all inconsistencies are to be reconciled by the magic of the word Confidence. Taxation, it is said, does not necessarily and unavoidably destroy. To carry it to the excess of destruction would be an abuse, to presume which, would banish that confidence which is essential to all government.

But is this a case of confidence? Would the people of any one State trust those of another with a power to control the most insignificant operations of their State government? We know they would not. Why, then, should we suppose that the people of any one State should be willing to trust those of another with a power to control the operations of a government to which they have confided their most important and most valuable interests? In the legislature of the Union alone, are all represented. The legislature

of the Union alone, therefore, can be trusted by the people with the power of controlling measures which concern all, in the confidence that it will not be abused. This, then, is not a case of confidence, and we must consider it as it really is.

If we apply the principle for which the State of Maryland contends, to the constitution generally, we shall find it capable of changing totally the character of that instrument. We shall find it capable of arresting all the measures of the government, and of prostrating it at the foot of the States. The American people have declared their constitution, and the laws made in pursuance thereof, to be supreme; but this principle would transfer the supremacy, in fact, to the States.

If the States may tax one instrument, employed by the government in the execution of its powers, they may tax any and every other instrument. They may tax the mail; they may tax the mint; they may tax patent rights; they may tax the papers of the custom-house; they may tax judicial process; they may tax all the means employed by the government, to an excess which would defeat all the ends of government. This was not intended by the American people. They did not design to make their government dependent on the States. . . .

It has also been insisted, that, as the power of taxation in the general and State governments is acknowledged to be concurrent, every argument which would sustain the right of the general government to tax banks chartered by the States, will equally sustain the right of the States to tax banks chartered by the general government.

But the two cases are not on the same reason. The people of all the States have created the general government, and have conferred upon it the general power of taxation. The people of all the States, and the States themselves, are represented in Congress, and, by their representatives, exercise this power. When they tax the chartered institutions of the States, they tax their constituents; and these taxes must be uniform. But, when a State taxes the operations of the government of the United States, it acts upon institutions created, not by their own constituents, but by people over whom they claim no control. It acts upon the measures of a government created by others as well as themselves, for the benefit of others in common with themselves. The difference is that which always exists, and always must exist, between the action of the whole on a part, and the action of a part on the whole—between the laws of a government declared to be supreme, and those of a government which, when in opposition to those laws, is not supreme.

But if the full application of this argument could be admitted, it might bring into question the right of Congress to tax the State banks, and could not prove the right of the States to tax the Bank of the United States.

The court has bestowed on this subject its most deliberate consideration. The result is a conviction that the states have no power, by taxation or otherwise, to retard, impede, burden, or in any manner control the operations of the constitutional laws enacted by Congress to carry into execution the powers vested in the general government. This is, we think, the unavoidable consequence of that supremacy which the constitution has declared.

We are unanimously of opinion that the law passed by the legislature of Maryland, imposing a tax on the Bank of the United States, is unconstitutional and void.

Constitutional scholars regard *McCulloch* as an unequivocal statement of national power over the states. Its strength lies in Marshall's treatment of the three relevant constitutional provisions: the necessary and proper clause, the Tenth Amendment, and the supremacy clause.

First, as you may recall from chapter 3, according to *McCulloch* the necessary and proper clause permits Congress to pass legislation implied by its enumerated functions, bounded chiefly in this way: "Let the end be legitimate, let it be within the scope of the constitution, and all means which are appropriate, which are plainly adapted to that end, which are not prohibited, but consist with the letter and spirit of the constitution, are constitutional."[3]

Second, because the Tenth Amendment reserves to the states or to the people only power that has not been delegated (expressly or otherwise) to Congress, it stands as no significant bar to Congress's exercise of its powers, including those that are implied. Given Marshall's treatment of the necessary and proper clause, implied powers seem quite expansive. This also seems to be an explicit rejection of the "enclave" approach to the Tenth Amendment.

---

3. Also recall from the excerpt in chapter 3 that Marshall declared, "Should Congress, in the execution of its powers, adopt measures which are prohibited by the Constitution, or should Congress, under the pretext of executing its powers, pass laws for the accomplishment of objects not intrusted to the Government, it would become the painful duty of this tribunal, should a case requiring such a decision come before it, to say that such an act was not the law of the land."

Third, the supremacy clause places the national government at the top within its sphere of operation, a sphere that again, according to Marshall's interpretation of the necessary and proper clause, is expansive. If the supremacy clause means anything, it means that no state may "retard, impede, burden, or in any manner control the operations of the constitutional laws enacted by Congress." Note, too, Marshall's view of the constitutional arrangement. As one would expect, he fully endorses the position that the charter represents a contract between the federal government and the people—not the states.

McCulloch's holdings—supporting congressional creation of the bank and negating state taxation of it— were not particularly surprising. Most observers thought the Marshall Court would rule the way it did. It was the chief justice's language and the constitutional theories he offered that sparked a serious debate in a states' rights newspaper, the *Richmond Enquirer*. The argument started just weeks after *McCulloch* was decided, as a barrage of states' rights advocates wrote letters to the newspaper's editor condemning the ruling. Apparently concerned that if their views took hold, the Union would revert back to its form under the Articles of Confederation, Marshall took an unusual step for a Supreme Court justice: he responded to his critics. Initially, he wrote two articles, carried by a Philadelphia newspaper, defending *McCulloch*. But when an old enemy, Spencer Roane, the Virginia Supreme Court judge who was the target of the Court's decision in *Martin v. Hunter's Lessee* (1816), launched an unbridled attack, Marshall responded with nine essays published under the pseudonym "A Friend of the Constitution."[4]

The Taney Court and States' Rights

While Marshall was chief justice of the United States, it was his view of nation–state relations, not Roane's, that prevailed. But their dispute foreshadowed a series of events that took place from the 1830s through the 1860s, events that would change the country forever (*see table 6-3*). The first occurred in November 1832. After Congress passed a tariff act that the South thought unfairly burdensome, South Carolina adopted an ordinance that nullified the federal law. Several

---

4. For records of these essays, see Gerald Gunther, ed., *John Marshall's Defense of* McCulloch v. Maryland (Stanford, CA: Stanford University Press, 1969).

TABLE 6-3 Selected Events Leading to the Civil War

DATE	EVENT	RESULT
November 1832	South Carolina passes ordinance of nullification.	Suggests that states can nullify acts of the federal government and, if necessary, secede from the Union.
December 1832	Jackson issues proclamation warning South Carolina against secession.	Temporarily halts secession crisis, as no state follows South Carolina's lead.
December 1835	Jackson nominates Taney to be chief justice of the United States.	The Senate delays confirming Taney, a former slaveholder, until 1836.
May 1854	Congress repeals the Missouri Compromise.	Allows territories with or without slavery to enter the Union.
March 1857	*Scott v. Sandford* is announced.	Increases tension between the North and South, as the former loudly denounces the decision.
November 1860	Lincoln is elected president.	South proclaims that secession is inevitable.
December 1860	South Carolina passes ordinance of secession.	South Carolina votes to secede from the Union. Within a few weeks, six other states follow suit.

days later, the state said it was prepared to enforce its nullification by military force and, if necessary, secession from the Union. It is not surprising that South Carolina took the lead in the battle for state sovereignty. The state was the home of John C. Calhoun, a former vice president of the United States and an outspoken proponent of slavery and states' rights. Indeed, Calhoun is best remembered as an advocate of the doctrine of concurrent majorities, a view that would provide states with a veto over federal policies. This doctrine was the underpinning for South Carolina's ordinance of nullification.

The president, Andrew Jackson, was no great nationalist; rather, he believed that states' rights were not incompatible with the powers of the federal government. But even he took issue with South Carolina's ordinance. Just a month after the state acted, as table 6-3 illustrates, Jackson issued a proclamation warning the state that it could not secede from the Union. The president's action infuriated South Carolina, but it temporarily averted a major crisis, as no other state attempted to act on the nullification doctrine.

Another event that would have major implications was Chief Justice Marshall's death in 1835 and Roger Taney's ascension to the chief justiceship. In some ways, Marshall and Taney were alike. Both had begun their political careers in their respective states— Virginia and Maryland—and then held major positions within the executive branch of the national government. Both were committed partisan activists. The difference was that they were committed to opposing conceptions of government structure, particularly of nation–state relations. In contrast to Marshall's Federalist sentiments, Taney was a Jacksonian Democrat, a full believer in the ideas espoused by President Jackson, under whom he had served as attorney general, secretary of war, and secretary of the Treasury, and who had appointed him chief justice. The two chief justices' views on the Bank of the United States provide a clear example of their political ideas in action. In 1819 Marshall lent his full support to the bank; in 1832 Taney helped write President Jackson's veto message on the bank's recharter:

It is maintained by the advocates of the bank that its constitutionality in all its features ought to be considered as settled by precedent and by the decision of the Supreme Court. To this conclusion I can not assent. Mere precedent is a dangerous source of authority, and should not be regarded as deciding questions of constitutional power except where the acquiescence of the people and the States can be considered as well settled.

Had Taney been Jackson's only appointment to the Court, the course of federalism might not have been altered. But that was not the case. Table 6-4 shows that by 1841 Joseph Story was the only justice remaining from the Marshall Court that decided *McCulloch*. The others, like Taney, were schooled in Jacksonian democracy. It

TABLE 6-4 From the Marshall Court to the Taney Court

MARSHALL COURT (1819)	TANEY COURT (1841)
Marshall	Taney
Livingston	Thompson
Story	Story
Washington	Baldwin
Duval	Daniel
Johnson	Wayne
Todd	McLean
	Catron
	McKinley

Dred Scott

was, as R. Kent Newmyer has noted, no longer "the Marshall Court. But, then again it was not the age of Marshall."[5] This observation holds on two levels: doctrinally and politically. The Taney Court ushered in substantial legal changes, especially in federal–state relations. Although there is no true Taney corollary to Marshall's opinion in *McCulloch,* examples of Taney's views abound. In many opinions he explicated the doctrine of dual federalism, that national and state governments are equivalent sovereigns within their own spheres of operation. Unlike Marshall, he read the Tenth Amendment in a broad sense, asserting that it did, in fact, reserve to the states certain powers and limited the power of the federal government over the states.

Early Taney Court decisions were not politically controversial. They may have represented a break from previous doctrine, but they matched the tenor of the times. Although Jackson had his feuds with the states (as his battle with South Carolina illustrates), his general philosophical approach to federalism and governance aligned with popular opinion. The issue of slavery was another matter. It had been the cause of acrimony at the Philadelphia convention in 1787, and animosity between the North and the South had continued. The country remained united only through compromises, such as the "three-fifths" plan in the U.S. Constitution, by which a slave was counted as three-fifths of a person for purposes of determining state populations, and the Missouri Compromise of 1820,

which provided a plan for slavery in newly admitted states and the territories. By the 1850s old battles were heating up; for example, after California was admitted to the Union as a free state, South Carolina once again issued a secession call.

Slavery, therefore, represented the most immediate concern of the day, splitting the nation into two ideological camps. On a different level, however, it was a symptom of a larger problem: the growing resistance of Southern states to federal supremacy. As the North's criticism of slavery became more vocal, calls for secession or, at the very least, for adoption of Calhoun's "concurrent majority" doctrine, became more widespread in the South.

It was at this critical moment that the Taney Court interceded in both issues—slavery and federal supremacy—by planting its feet firmly in the states' rights camp. With its decision in the infamous case of *Scott v. Sandford,* the Court may have contributed to the collapse of the Union. Also, as you read Taney's opinion in this case, note his theory of the nature of the constitutional contract. How do his views differ from Marshall's in *McCulloch?*

---

5. R. Kent Newmyer, *The Supreme Court under Marshall and Taney* (New York: Crowell, 1968), 94.

Scott v. Sandford

60 U.S. (19 How.) 393 (1857)

http://laws.findlaw.com/us/60/393.html

Vote: 7 (Campbell, Catron, Daniel, Grier, Nelson, Taney, Wayne)

2 (Curtis, McLean)

OPINION OF THE COURT: *Taney*

CONCURRING OPINIONS: *Campbell, Catron, Daniel, Grier, Nelson, Wayne*

DISSENTING OPINIONS: *Curtis, McLean*

FACTS:

Dred Scott was born into slavery in Virginia about 1795.[6] His original owner was Peter Blow, a plantation owner. Although the title to Scott would be transferred several times, Blow's family remained connected to Scott throughout his life.

Blow moved to St. Louis with his family and slaves in 1827. In 1833, after Blow's death, Scott was sold to John Emerson, a surgeon in the U.S. Army. The following year Emerson took Scott to the free state of Illinois, and in 1836 to the Upper Louisiana Territory, which was to remain free of slavery under the Missouri Compromise of 1820. While in the Wisconsin Territory, Scott married Harriet Robinson, also a slave. They had two daughters.

Eventually, Scott and Emerson returned to Missouri, but the doctor died shortly thereafter, and title to Scott transferred to his widow, E. Irene Sanford Emerson.[7] She had little need for a slave and hired him out to other families in St. Louis. Scott, however, was a poor worker and produced little income. Irene Emerson then moved to Massachusetts, leaving Scott and his family behind. She married Calvin Clifford Chaffee, a New England abolitionist, without telling him that she held title to a slave in St. Louis.[8]

---

6. Sources for the facts of this case are *National Cyclopaedia of American Biography,* vol. 2 (New York: James T. White, 1892), 306–307; *Dictionary of American Biography,* vol. 8 (New York: Charles Scribner's Sons, 1935), 488–489; *American National Biography,* vol. 19 (New York: Oxford University Press, 1999), 487–489. Original documents relating to the case are available at "The Revised Dred Scott Case Collection," Washington University http://digital.wustl .edu/dredscott/.

7. The name Sanford was misspelled Sandford in the official records.

8. Just prior to the Court's decision in *Scott v. Sandford,* an embarrassed Calvin Chaffee discovered his wife's previous owner-ship of the slave. When the justices ruled against Scott, Chaffee and Sanford transferred title to Scott to Taylor Blow, another son of his original owner. They did so to facilitate Scott's emancipation. Under state law, a Missouri slave could be freed only if the owner was a

In 1846 Henry T. Blow, wealthy son of Scott's original owner, initiated a lawsuit in Missouri state courts to gain Scott's freedom. Blow and Scott believed that Scott no longer had slave status because he had lived on free soil. While the courts considered this petition, Scott remained in the custody of the St. Louis sheriff and was hired out at $5 per month.

Scott received a favorable decision at the trial court level but lost in the Missouri Supreme Court. When state courts rejected Scott's bid for emancipation, Blow arranged for Scott's ownership to be transferred to Irene Chaffee's brother, John Sanford of New York. This sale allowed Scott to take his case to federal court under diversity of citizenship jurisdiction—Scott was a citizen of Missouri and Sanford was a citizen of New York. Sanford argued that the suit should be dismissed because members of the "African race" could not be citizens. The lower federal courts seemed perplexed by the issue. In the end, they ruled in favor of Sanford but suggested that for legal purposes Scott may be a citizen. From 1854 to 1857, while the federal courts considered his cause, Scott lived in St. Louis with virtually no restraints on his freedom.

By the time the case arrived at the U.S. Supreme Court for final judgment in 1856, the facts and the political situation had become increasingly complex. In 1854, under mounting pressure, Congress had repealed the Missouri Compromise, replacing it with legislation declaring congressional neutrality on the issue of slavery. Given this new law and the growing tensions between the North and the South and the free and slave states, some observers speculated that the Court would decline to decide the case: it had become too controversial and political.

For at least a year, the Court chose that route. Historians, in fact, have suggested that after hearing the case the justices wanted simply to affirm the state court's decision, thereby evading the issue of slavery and citizenship for blacks. But when Justice James Wayne, a Jackson appointee from Georgia, insisted that the Court deal with these concerns, the majority of the others—including Chief Justice Taney, a former slave-holder—went along. Waiting until after the presidential

---

Missouri citizen. Blow emancipated Dred Scott and his family on May 26, 1857, just two and a half months after the Supreme Court's ruling. By this time, Scott had become a local celebrity in St. Louis. He spent the rest of his life as a porter at the Barum Hotel. He lived just over a year as a free man, dying of tuberculosis on September 17, 1858. Henry Blow paid for his funeral and burial in St. Louis.

election, a very divided Court (nine separate opinions were written) announced its decision.

ARGUMENTS:[9]

For the plaintiff in error, Dred Scott:

- Scott is entitled to freedom under the Missouri Compromise, the congressional emancipation act that prohibited citizens from holding and owning slaves in the Louisiana Purchase territories. Because he was living in emancipated territories, Congress emancipated him.
- Scott is also entitled to freedom under Illinois state emancipation law. He was taken to Illinois and thereupon was made free, and the mere fact that he was taken back to Missouri does not revert him back to a state of slavery.
- Art. IV, Sect. 3, Cl. 2, of the Constitution gives Congress the power to "to dispose of and make all needful rules and regulations respecting the territory or other property belonging to the United States," which includes regulating slavery in all territories of the nation.

For the defendant in error, John F. A. Sanford:

- Considering the debates during the drafting of the Constitution, it is clear that the framers did not intend for the word *citizen* to encompass people of the African race. Even if Scott were a citizen of a state, he would not be a citizen of the United States under the Constitution. Therefore, he does not have the right to sue in a court of the United States, and the Court has no jurisdiction over this case.
- The Supreme Court had previously set precedent establishing that the freedom or servitude of a slave returning to a slave state from a free state depends on the laws of the original home state. Following precedent, the Court has no jurisdiction to revise state court holdings on state law.
- The plain text of the Constitution protects the right to slave ownership, and for this reason, the Missouri Compromise is unconstitutional.

---

9. *U.S. Reports* contains the following statement about arguments in this case: "The reporter regrets that want of room will not allow him to give the arguments of counsel; but he regrets it the less, because the subject is thoroughly examined in the opinion of the court, the opinions of the concurring judges, and the opinions of the judges who dissented from the judgment of the court." Not only are the arguments not recorded in *U.S. Reports* (as they often were for nineteenth-century cases), but we also cannot locate briefs. Accordingly, we follow the reporter's advice and develop arguments from the Court's opinion.

▶ MR. CHIEF JUSTICE TANEY DELIVERED THE OPINION OF THE COURT.

The question is simply this: can a negro whose ancestors were imported into this country and sold as slaves, become a member of the political community formed and brought into existence by the Constitution of the United States, and as such become entitled to all the rights, and privileges, and immunities, guarantied by that instrument to the citizen. One of which rights is the privilege of suing in a court of the United States in the cases specified in the Constitution. . . .

The words "people of the United States" and "citizens" are synonymous terms, and mean the same thing. They both describe the political body, who, according to our republican institutions, form the sovereignty, and who hold the power and conduct the government through their representatives. . . . The question before us is, whether ["negroes"] compose a portion of this people, and are constituent members of this sovereignty. We think they are not, and that they are not included, and were not intended to be included, under the word "citizens" in the Constitution, and can, therefore, claim none of the rights and privileges which that instrument provides for and secures to citizens of the United States. On the contrary, they were at that time considered as a subordinate and inferior class of beings, who had been subjugated by the dominant race, and whether emancipated or not, yet remained subject to their authority, and had no rights or privileges but such as those who held the power and the government might choose to grant them.

It is not the province of the court to decide upon the justice or injustice, the policy or impolicy of these laws. The decision of that question belonged to the political or lawmaking power; to those who formed the sovereignty and framed the Constitution. The duty of the court is to interpret the instrument they have framed, with the best lights we can obtain on the subject, and to administer it as we find it, according to its true intent and meaning when it was adopted. . . .

. . . [We] must not confound the rights of citizenship which a State may confer within its own limits and the rights of citizenship as a member of the Union. It does not by any means follow, because he has all the rights and privileges of a citizen of a State, that he must be a citizen of the United States. He may have all of the rights and privileges of the citizen of a State and yet not be entitled to the rights and privileges of a citizen in any other State. . . . Each State may still confer them upon an alien, or anyone it thinks proper, or upon any class or description of persons, yet he would not be a citizen in the sense in which that word is used in the Constitution of the United States. . . .

It becomes necessary, therefore, to determine who were citizens of the several States when the Constitution was adopted. . . .

In the opinion of the court, the legislation and histories of the times, and the language used in the Declaration of Independence, show, that neither the class of persons who had been imported as slaves, nor their descendants, whether they had become free or not, were then acknowledged as a part of the people, nor intended to be included in the general words used in that memorable instrument.

It is difficult at this day to realize the state of public opinion in relation to that unfortunate race, which prevailed in the civilized and enlightened portions of the world at the time of the Declaration of Independence, and when the Constitution of the United States was framed and adopted. . . .

They had for more than a century before been regarded as beings of an inferior order, and altogether unfit to associate with the white race, either in social or political relations; and so far inferior, that they had no rights which the white man was bound to respect; and that the negro might justly and lawfully be reduced to slavery for his benefit. He was bought and sold, and treated as an ordinary article of merchandise and traffic, whenever a profit could be made by it. This opinion was at that time fixed and universal in the civilized portion of the white race. . . .

The legislation of the different colonies furnishes positive and indisputable proof of this fact. . . .

. . . [T]hese laws . . . [which] were still in force when the Revolution began and are a faithful index to the state of feeling towards the class of persons of whom they speak, show that a perpetual and impassable barrier was intended to be erected between the white race and the one which they had reduced to slavery, and governed as subjects with absolute and despotic power, and which they then looked upon as so far below them in the scale of created beings, that intermarriages between white persons and negroes or mulattoes were regarded as unnatural and immoral, and punished as crimes, not only in the parties, but in the person who joined them in marriage. And no distinction in this respect was made between the free negro or mulatto and the slave, but this stigma, of the deepest degradation, was fixed upon the whole race. . . .

This state of public opinion had undergone no change when the Constitution was adopted, as is equally evident from its provisions and language. . . .

. . . [T]here are two clauses in the Constitution which point directly and specifically to the negro race as a separate class of persons, and show clearly that they were not regarded as a portion of the people or citizens of the Government then formed.

One of these clauses reserves to each of the thirteen States the right to import slaves until the year 1808, if it thinks proper. . . . And by the other provision the States pledge themselves to each other to maintain the right of property of the master, by delivering up to him any slave who may have escaped from his service, and be found within their respective territories. By the first above-mentioned clause, therefore, the right to purchase and hold this property is directly sanctioned and authorized for twenty years by the people who framed the Constitution. And by the second, they pledge themselves to maintain and uphold the right of the master in the manner specified, as long as the Government they then formed should endure. And these two provisions show, conclusively, that neither the description of persons therein referred to, nor their descendants, were embraced in any of the other provisions of the Constitution; for certainly these two clauses were not intended to confer on them or their posterity the blessings of liberty, or any of the personal rights so carefully provided for the citizen. . . .

No one, we presume, supposes that any change in public opinion or feeling, in relation to this unfortunate race, in the civilized nations of Europe or in this country, should induce the court to give to the words of the Constitution a more liberal construction in their favor than they were intended to bear when the instrument was framed and adopted. Such an argument would be altogether inadmissible in any tribunal called on to interpret it. If any of its provisions are deemed unjust, there is a mode prescribed in the instrument itself by which it may be amended; but while it remains unaltered, it must be construed now as it was understood at the time of its adoption. It is not only the same in words, but the same in meaning, and delegates the same powers to the Government, and reserves and secures the same rights and privileges to the citizen; and as long as it continues to exist in its present form, it speaks not only in the same words, but with the same meaning and intent with which it spoke when it came from the hands of its framers, and was voted on and adopted by the people of the United States. . . .

What the construction was at that time we think can hardly admit of doubt. . . .

And upon a full and careful consideration of the subject, the court is of opinion that, upon the facts stated in the plea in abatement, Dred Scott was not a citizen of Missouri within the meaning of the Constitution of the United States, and not entitled as such to sue in its courts;

and, consequently, that the Circuit Court had no jurisdiction of the case, and that the judgment on the plea in abatement is erroneous. . . .

We proceed, therefore, to inquire whether the facts relied on by the plaintiff entitled him to his freedom. . . .

. . . [T]he difficulty which meets us at the threshold of this part of the inquiry is whether Congress was authorized to pass [the Missouri Compromise] under any of the powers granted to it by the Constitution; for if the authority is not given by that instrument, it is the duty of this court to declare it void and inoperative, and incapable of conferring freedom upon any one who is held as a slave under the laws of any one of the States.

The counsel for the plaintiff has laid much stress upon that article in the Constitution which confers on Congress the power "to dispose of and make all needful rules and regulations respecting the territory or other property belonging to the United States"; but, in the judgment of the court, that provision has no bearing on the present controversy, and the power there given, whatever it may be, is confined, and was intended to be confined, to the territory which at that time belonged to, or was claimed by, the United States, and was within their boundaries as settled by the Treaty with Great Britain, and can have no influence upon a territory afterwards acquired from a foreign government. It was a special provision for a known and particular Territory, and to meet a present emergency, and nothing more. . . .

The language used in the clause, the arrangement and combination of the powers, and the somewhat unusual phraseology it uses when it speaks of the political power to be exercised in the government of the territory, all indicate the design and meaning of the clause to be such as we have mentioned. It does not speak of any territory, nor of Territories, but uses language which, according to its legitimate meaning, points to a particular thing. The power is given in relation only to the territory of the United States—that is, to a territory then in existence, and then known or claimed as the territory of the United States. It begins its enumeration of powers by that of disposing, in other words, making sale of the lands, or raising money from them, which, as we have already said, was the main object of the cession, and which is accordingly the first thing provided for in the article. It then gives the power which was necessarily associated with the disposition and sale of the lands—that is, the power of making needful rules and regulations respecting the territory. And whatever construction may now be given to these words, everyone, we think, must admit that they are not the words usually employed by statesmen in giving supreme power of legislation. They

are certainly very unlike the words used in the power granted to legislate over territory which the new Government might afterwards itself obtain by cession from a State, either for its seat of Government or for forts, magazines, arsenals, dockyards, and other needful buildings.

This brings us to examine by what provision of the Constitution the present Federal Government under its delegated and restricted powers, is authorized to acquire territory outside of the original limits of the United States, and what powers it may exercise therein over the person or property of a citizen of the United States, while it remains a territory, and until it shall be admitted as one of the States of the Union. . . .

There is certainly no power given by the Constitution to the Federal Government to establish or maintain colonies bordering on the United States or at a distance to be ruled and governed at its own pleasure, nor to enlarge its territorial limits in any way except by the admission of new States.

Taking this rule to guide us, it may be safely assumed that citizens of the United States who migrate to a Territory belonging to the people of the United States cannot be ruled as mere colonists, dependent upon the will of the General Government and to be governed by any laws it may think proper to impose. The principle upon which our Governments rest and upon which alone they continue to exist, is the union of States, sovereign and independent within their own limits in their internal and domestic concerns, and bound together as one people by a General Government, possessing certain enumerated and restricted powers delegated to it by the people of the several States, and exercising supreme authority within the scope of the powers granted to it throughout the dominion of the United States. A power, therefore, in the General Government to obtain and hold colonies and dependent territories over which they might legislate without restriction would be inconsistent with its own existence in its present form. Whatever it acquires, it acquires for the benefit of the people of the several States who created it. It is their trustee acting for them, and charged with the duty of promoting the interests of the whole people of the Union in the exercise of the powers specifically granted.

Upon these considerations, it is the opinion of the court that the Act of Congress which prohibited a citizen from holding and owning property of this kind in the territory of the United States north of the line therein mentioned, is not warranted by the Constitution, and is therefore void; and that neither Dred Scott himself, nor any of his family, were made free by being carried into this territory; even if they had been carried there by the owner, with the intention of becoming a permanent resident. . . .

Upon the whole, therefore, it is the judgment of this court, that it appears by the record before us that the plaintiff in error is not a citizen of Missouri, in the sense in which that word is used in the Constitution; and that the Circuit Court of the United States, for that reason, had no jurisdiction in the case, and could give no judgment in it.

Its judgment for the defendant must, consequently, be reversed, and a mandate issued directing the suit to be dismissed for want of jurisdiction.

MR. JUSTICE CURTIS, dissenting.

To determine whether any free persons, descended from Africans held in slavery, were citizens of the United States under the Confederation, and consequently at the time of the adoption of the Constitution of the United States, it is only necessary to know whether any such persons were citizens of either of the States under the Confederation, at the time of the adoption of the Constitution.

Of this there can be no doubt. At the time of the ratification of the Articles of Confederation, all free native-born inhabitants of the States of New Hampshire, Massachusetts, New York, New Jersey, and North Carolina, though descended from African slaves, were not only citizens of those States, but such of them as had the other necessary qualifications possessed the franchise of electors, on equal terms with other citizens. . . .

Did the Constitution of the United States deprive them or their descendants of citizenship?

That Constitution was ordained and established by the people of the United States, through the action, in each State, of those persons who were qualified by its laws to act thereon, in behalf of themselves and all other citizens of that State. In some of the States, as we have seen, colored persons were among those qualified by law to act on this subject. These colored persons were not only included in the body of "the people of the United States," by whom the Constitution was ordained and established, but in at least five of the States they had the power to act, and doubtless did act, by their suffrages, upon the question of its adoption. It would be strange, if we were to find in that instrument anything which deprived of their citizenship any part of the people of the United States who were among those by whom it was established.

I can find nothing in the Constitution which, proprio vigore [by its own force], deprives of their citizenship any class of persons who were citizens of the United States at the time of its adoption, or who should be native-born citizens of any State after its adoption; nor any power enabling Congress to disfranchise persons born on the soil of any State, and entitled to citizenship of such State by its Constitution and laws. And my opinion is, that, under the Constitution of the United States, every free person born on the soil of a State, who is a citizen of that State by force of its Constitution or laws, is also a citizen of the United States.

Taney's opinion held that Scott was still a slave for the following reasons: First, although Scott could become a citizen of a state, he could not be considered, in a legal sense, to be a citizen of the United States; the nation's history and the words of the Constitution and other documents foreclosed that possibility. As a result, Scott could not sue in federal courts. Second, Congress had no constitutional power to regulate slavery in the territories (in reaching this result, the Court struck down the Missouri Compromise, which Congress had already repealed); the Constitution protects the right to property, a category that, according to Taney, included slaves. Third, the status of slaves depended on the law of the state to which they voluntarily returned, regardless of where they had been. Because the Missouri Supreme Court ruled that Scott was a slave, the U.S. Supreme Court would follow suit. Embedded in these holdings is a strong commitment to dual federalism. Although Taney did not explicitly cite the Tenth Amendment, his use of its language made clear that he viewed it as a brake on the federal government.

Scott was decided as the nation was on the verge of collapse (*see table 6-3*). Taney's holding, coupled with his vision of the nature of the federal–state relationship, rather than calming matters, probably added fuel to the fire. From the perspective of Northerners and abolitionists, the opinion was among the most evil and heinous the Court ever issued. Opponents of slavery used the ruling to rally support for their position; they took aim at Taney and the Court, claiming that the institution was so pro-South that it could not be taken seriously. Northern newspapers aroused anti-Court sentiment around the country with stories about the decision. As one wrote,

The whole slavery agitation was reopened by the proceedings in the Supreme Court today, and that tribunal voluntarily introduced itself into the political arena. . . . Much feeling is excited by this decree, and the opinion is freely expressed that a new element of sectional strife has been wantonly imposed upon the country.[10]

---

10. Quoted by Charles Warren in *The Supreme Court in United States History,* vol. 2 (Boston: Little, Brown, 1926), 304.

Members of Congress lambasted the Court for the raw and unnecessary display of judicial power it had exercised in striking down the Missouri Compromise. A history on the period asserted, "Never has the Supreme Court been treated with such ineffable contempt, and never has that tribunal so often cringed before the clamor of the mob."[11] As for the chief justice, his reputation was forever tarnished. Even after his death, Congress resisted commissioning a bust of him to sit beside those of other chief justices in the Capitol's Supreme Court room. At the time, Senator Charles Sumner said, "I object to that; that now an emancipated country should make a bust to the author of the Dred Scott decision. . . . [T]he name of Taney is to be hooted down the page of history. Judgment is beginning now; and an emancipated country will fasten upon him the stigma which he deserves."[12]

To Southerners, *Scott* was a cause for celebration. Indeed, Taney's notions of slavery and dual federalism appeared in a more energized form just a few years later when South Carolina issued its Declaration of the Causes of Secession. President Abraham Lincoln presented precisely the opposite view—the Marshall approach—in his 1861 inaugural address, but his words could not prevent the outbreak of war.

At its core the Civil War was not only about slavery but also about the supremacy of the national government over the states. It was the culmination of the debates between the Federalists and Anti-Federalists, between Marshall and Roane, and so forth. When the Union won the war, it seemed to have also won the debate over the nature of federal–state relations. In the immediate aftermath of the battle, the Court acceded, though not willingly, to congressional power over the defeated region.

The Post–Civil War Era and the Return of Dual Federalism

Once the Civil War concluded Congress moved swiftly to embed into the Constitution the victories that Union armies had won on the battlefield. Three constitutional amendments were proposed and ratified. The Thirteenth and Fifteenth Amendments focused on issues of slavery and race. The Thirteenth (1865) put an official end to slavery and the Fifteenth (1870) barred the denial voting rights on account of race. The Fourteenth Amendment (1968) shifted much governmental authority from the states to the federal government. It also directly overruled Taney's *Dred Scott* opinion by declaring, "All persons born or naturalized in the United States, and subject to the jurisdiction thereof, are citizens of the United States and of the State wherein they reside." As a consequence, United States citizenship became superior to state citizenship. Constitutionally, the dual federalism of the Jacksonian era had ended.

Did the conclusion of the Civil War and the rise of national supremacy mean that Taney's dual federalism had seen its last days? Indeed, it remained under wraps for several decades but then resurfaced in a somewhat different form as the nation became engulfed in the Industrial Revolution and the rise of big business. From the 1890s to the 1930s laissez-faire economic philosophies ruled the day. The Supreme Court's decisions during this period generally favored business interests by invalidating laws that regulated commerce and the economy. The Tenth Amendment was frequently relied on to justify striking down federal legislation.

Even outside the sphere of commerce and business, the Court once again began articulating the philosophy of dual federalism. Take, for example, the justices' decision in *Coyle v. Smith* (1911). This dispute involved a congressional directive telling a newly admitted state where it must locate its capital. Did Congress's power to admit new states extend to placing such conditions on statehood? Or was the congressional order an unconstitutional intrusion into state sovereignty? As you read Justice Lurton's opinion note the vivid language of dual federalism, including the position that the national government is a "union of states" and that the states must be "equal in power, dignity and authority, each competent to exert that residuum of sovereignty not delegated to the United States by the Constitution itself." Lurton goes so far to declare that "without the States in union, there could be no such political body as the United States." Finally, notice the Court's narrow interpretation of Congress's implied powers.

---

11. Quoted by Bernard Schwartz in A *History of the Supreme Court* (New York: Oxford University Press, 1993), 154.

12. *Congressional Globe* (23 February 1865) 38th Cong., 2d sess., 1012. It was not until 1874 that busts of Samuel Chase and Roger Taney were approved "without debate." See Warren, *The Supreme Court in United States History*, 393–394.

Coyle v. Smith

221 U.S. 559 (1911)
http://laws.findlaw.com/us/221/559.html
Vote: 7 (Day, Harlan, Hughes, Lamar, Lurton, Van Devanter, White)
    2 (Holmes, McKenna)

OPINION OF THE COURT: *Lurton*

FACTS:

Article IV, section 3 of the Constitution authorizes Congress to admit new states. On June 16, 1906, Congress exercised this power by passing the Enabling Act inviting the Oklahoma territory to join the Union. The invitation, however, came with certain conditions. One of those conditions required that the state capital be in Guthrie, where territorial capital was located, and that the state refrain from relocating the capital or making any provisions for relocation before 1913. The terms of the Enabling Act were to be "irrevocable."

Why this restriction was imposed is a bit uncertain, but it seemingly had to do with a Republican-dominated Congress granting statehood to a heavily Democratic territory. The city of Guthrie, however, was Oklahoma's lone Republican stronghold.

The territory accepted the terms of the invitation, and in 1907 Oklahoma became the forty-sixth state. But just three years later the state's voters supported a measure to move the capital to Oklahoma City. Democratic governor Charles Haskell and the state legislature did not wait until 1913 to take action on the voters' wishes, but immediately enacted implementing legislation and began securing the necessary funds to effect the relocation.

W. H. Coyle, a large Guthrie landowner who would suffer economic losses if the capital were to be moved, filed suit against Oklahoma secretary of state Thomas Smith to block the relocation. Oklahoma's supreme court upheld the state's actions, and Coyle requested Supreme Court review.

ARGUMENTS:

For the petitioner, W. H. Coyle:
- Congress's constitutional authority to admit states is absolute, and in its discretion it can impose whatever conditions it deems appropriate.
- Congress has a history of imposing such conditions, often doing so to ensure that new states adhere to the constitutional obligation to have a "republican form of government."
- Oklahoma freely agreed to the provisions of the Enabling Act. Those provisions are irrevocable.

For the respondent, Thomas P. Smith, Oklahoma secretary of state:
- In requiring Oklahoma to yield a portion of its state sovereignty, Congress violated the constitutional principle of state equality under which all states stand on equal footing.
- Congress cannot deny a state its police powers, which include the authority to locate the state capital where it can most effectively serve the state's citizens.
- A state cannot be bound by unconstitutional provisions contained in an agreement imposed by Congress.

MR. JUSTICE LURTON DELIVERED THE OPINION OF THE COURT.

The only question for review by us is whether the provision of the enabling act was a valid limitation upon the power of the State after its admission which overrides any subsequent state legislation repugnant thereto.

The power to locate its own seat of government and to determine when and how it shall be changed from one place to another, and to appropriate its own public funds for that purpose, are essentially and peculiarly state powers. That one of the original thirteen States could now be shorn of such powers by an act of Congress would not be for a moment entertained. The question then comes to this: can a State be placed upon a plane of inequality with its sister States in the Union if the Congress chooses to impose conditions which so operate at the time of its admission? . . .

The power of Congress in respect to the admission of new States is found in the third section of the fourth Article of the Constitution. That provision is that "New States may be admitted by the Congress into this Union." The only expressed restriction upon this power is that no new State shall be formed within the jurisdiction of any other State, nor by the junction of two or more States, or parts of States, without the consent of such States, as well as of the Congress.

But what is this power? It is not to admit political organizations which are less or greater, or different in dignity or power, from those political entities which constitute the Union. It is, as strongly put by counsel, a "power to admit States."

The definition of "a State" is found in the powers possessed by the original States which adopted the Constitution, a definition emphasized by the terms employed in all subsequent acts of Congress admitting new States into the Union. The first two States admitted into the Union were the States of Vermont and Kentucky, one as of March 4, 1791, and the other as of June 1, 1792. No terms or conditions were exacted from either. Each act declares that the State is admitted "as a new and *entire member* of the United States of America." Emphatic and significant as is the phrase admitted as "an entire member," even stronger was the declaration upon the admission in 1796 of Tennessee, as the third new State, it being declared to be "one of the United States of America," "on an equal footing with the original States in all respects whatsoever," phraseology which has ever since been substantially followed in admission acts, concluding with the Oklahoma act, which declares that Oklahoma shall be admitted "on an equal footing with the original States."

The power is to admit "new States into *this* Union."

"This Union" was and is a union of States, equal in power, dignity and authority, each competent to exert that residuum of sovereignty not delegated to the United States by the Constitution itself. To maintain otherwise would be to say that the Union, through the power of Congress to admit new States, might come to be a union of States unequal in power, as including States whose powers were restricted only by the Constitution, with others whose powers had been further restricted by an act of Congress accepted as a condition of admission. Thus, it would result, first, that the powers of Congress would not be defined by the Constitution alone, but in respect to new States, enlarged or restricted by the conditions imposed upon new States by its own legislation admitting them into the Union; and, second, that such new States might not exercise all of the powers which had not been delegated by the Constitution, but only such as had not been further bargained away as conditions of admission.

The argument that Congress derives from the duty of "guaranteeing to each State in this Union a republican form of government" power to impose restrictions upon a new State which deprives it of equality with other members of the Union, has no merit. . . . [I]t obviously does not confer power to admit a new State which shall be any less a State than those which compose the Union. . . .

. . . The constitutional provision concerning the admission of new States is not a mandate, but a power to be exercised with discretion. From this alone, it would follow that Congress may require, under penalty of denying admission, that the organic laws of a new State at the time of admission shall be such as to meet its approval. A constitution thus supervised by Congress would, after all, be a constitution of a State, and, as such, subject to alteration and amendment by the State after admission. Its force would be that of a state constitution, and not that of an act of Congress. . . .

So far as this court has found occasion to advert to the effect of enabling acts as affirmative legislation affecting the power of new States after admission, there is to be found no sanction for the contention that any State may be deprived of any of the power constitutionally possessed by other States, as States, by reason of the terms in which the acts admitting them to the Union have been framed. . . .

. . . [W]hen a new State is admitted into the Union, it is so admitted with all of the powers of sovereignty and jurisdiction which pertain to the original States, and that such powers may not be constitutionally diminished, impaired or shorn away by any conditions, compacts or stipulations embraced in the act under which the new State came into the Union which would not be valid and effectual if the subject of congressional legislation after admission. . . .

. . . The legislation in the Oklahoma enabling act relating to the location of the capital of the State, if construed as forbidding a removal by the State after its admission as a State, is referable to no power granted to Congress over the subject, and if it is to be upheld at all, it must be implied from the power to admit new States. If power to impose such a restriction upon the general and undelegated power of a State be conceded as implied from the power to admit a new State, where is the line to be drawn against restrictions imposed upon new States? The insistence finds no support in the decisions of this court. . . .

Has Oklahoma been admitted upon an equal footing with the original States? If she has, she, by virtue of her jurisdictional sovereignty as such a State, may determine for her own people the proper location of the local seat of government. She is not equal in power to them if she cannot.

In *Texas v. White* [1869] Chief Justice Chase said in strong and memorable language that, "the Constitution, in all of its provisions, looks to an indestructible Union, composed of indestructible States."

In *Lane County v. Oregon* [1869], he said:

"The people of the United States constitute one nation, under one government, and this government, within the scope of the powers with which it is invested, is supreme. On the other hand, the people of each State compose a State having its own government, and endowed with all the functions essential to separate and independent existence. The States disunited might continue to exist. Without the States in union, there could be no such political body as the United States."

To this we may add that the constitutional equality of the States is essential to the harmonious operation of the scheme upon which the Republic was organized. When that equality disappears, we may remain a free people, but the Union will not be the Union of the Constitution.

Judgment affirmed.

The immediate dispute in *Coyle v. Smith* was a relatively narrow one. The admission of a new state, after all, is an uncommon occurrence. Importantly, however, the dual federalism principles articulated in *Coyle*, including an elevated protection of states' rights and a narrow construction of federal authority, can be readily found in other areas of constitutional importance during this era. Most significant were the Court's decisions on the regulation of commerce.

Article I grants Congress the power "to regulate commerce . . . among the several States," leaving purely intrastate commerce to be governed by the states. Although this division of authority appears to be a logical one, the distinction between interstate commerce and intrastate commerce is subject to interpretation. From the 1890s into the 1930s, the Supreme Court narrowly constructed the meaning of interstate commerce and under the Tenth Amendment vigorously protected the authority of the states to regulate commercial activity outside that definition. Underlying these dual federalism rulings, of course, was a strong adherence to the antiregulatory, laissez-faire philosophy of that era.

In *United States v. E. C. Knight Co.* (1895), for example, the Court struck down a federal antitrust effort in the sugar industry on the ground that enterprises such as manufacturing and refining take place within state boundaries and therefore qualify as intrastate commerce not subject to federal regulation. This was true, the Court said, in spite of the fact that the manufactured products may subsequently be shipped to other states. Interstate commerce does not begin, according to Chief Justice Fuller's opinion for the Court, until the manufactured goods "commence their final movement from the State of their origin to that of their destination." The manufacturing stage, therefore, remained under the regulatory powers of the states.

In *Hammer v. Dagenhardt* (1918) the justices applied these same principles in considering the constitutionality of the Federal Child Labor Act of 1915.

The law prohibited the shipment in interstate commerce of factory goods made by children under the age of fourteen or by children ages fourteen to sixteen who worked more than eight hours a day. Congress had attempted to keep child labor within its constitutional authority by targeting the interstate shipment of such goods, but the Court saw the statute for what it really was: an effort intended to eliminate child labor in the manufacturing stage. Writing for a divided Court, Justice William R. Day stated that the law was "repugnant to the Constitution" in two ways: "It not only transcends the authority delegated to Congress over commerce, but also exerts a power as to a purely local matter to which the Federal authority does not extend." Taking an enclave approach to the Tenth Amendment, Day wrote,

In interpreting the Constitution it must never be forgotten that the nation is made up of states, to which are intrusted the powers of local government. And to them and to the people the powers not expressly delegated to the national government are reserved. The power of the states to regulate their purely internal affairs by such laws as seem wise to the local authority is inherent, and has never been surrendered to the general government. To sustain this statute would not be, in our judgment, a recognition of the lawful exertion of congressional authority over interstate commerce, but would sanction an invasion by the Federal power of the control of a matter purely local in its character, and over which no authority has been delegated to Congress in conferring the power to regulate commerce among the states.

Day's opinion was a clear endorsement of dual federalism, but to some commentators its analysis of the Tenth Amendment rests on tenuous grounds. First, in its adoption of the enclave approach to the amendment it rejects Marshall's logic in *McCulloch*: if the federal government is exercising one of its enumerated or implied powers, the Tenth Amendment has no role to play; it does not provide additional protections to the states. And second, as C. Herman Pritchett points out, Justice Day misstated the Tenth Amendment: it does not contain the word *expressly*. In so doing, he not only ignored Marshall's reasoning in *McCulloch*—it was critical to Marshall's interpretation of congressional powers that the word *expressly* did not appear—but he also might have ignored the history surrounding the Tenth Amendment. When

Congress considered it, one representative proposed to "add the word 'expressly' so as to read 'the powers not expressly delegated by this Constitution.'" James Madison and others objected, and the motion was defeated.[13] So Day assumed "a position that was historically inaccurate."[14]

Decisions such as *E. C. Knight* and *Hammer* were compatible with the legal and political opinion of the day. The Court's willingness to embrace a free enterprise philosophy reflected the general mood of Americans, many of whom were benefiting financially from the vigorous growth of the economy. By the 1930s, however, the Court's laissez-faire, dual federalism philosophy met stiff opposition. When the Great Depression seized the nation following the stock market crash of 1929, the people demanded government action to solve the economic crisis. In 1932 they elected President Franklin Roosevelt and Democratic majorities in Congress. Roosevelt promoted his "New Deal" program that included unprecedented federal control of commerce and the economy. Many elements of the New Deal were inconsistent with the Court's view of interstate commerce and the role of the Tenth Amendment. The result was an inevitable clash between the Supreme Court and the political branches.

Between 1935 and 1936 the Court struck down a number of major legislative enactments, including codes of fair completion for various industries (*Schechter Poultry v. United States,* 1935); production, price, and labor regulations for the nation's mines (***Carter v. Carter Coal***, 1936); and limitations on agricultural acreage planted (*United States v. Butler,* 1936). These decisions were based on specific violations of congressional authority along with Tenth Amendment intrusions into the powers reserved for the states.

This exercise of judicial review led to a historic confrontation between the Court and the president, during which Roosevelt even proposed to alter the structure of the Court in order to appoint new justices with philosophies more consistent with the president's view of federal authority. The battle ended in 1937 when, in *National Labor Relations Board v. Jones & Laughlin Steel Corporation,* the Court shifted position and began taking a more generous view of the role of the federal government in economic regulation and a narrower view of the powers reserved to the states. (The conflict between the Court and the political branches and how that conflict was resolved is covered in detail in chapter 7.)

The year 1937 marks the end of a nearly half-century of Court adherence to a dual federalism philosophy. It is important to understand, however, that the dual federalism of this period differed from the dual federalism of the Taney Court. For Chief Justice Taney dual federalism was a means of equalizing state and federal power. During the 1890s through the 1930s dual federalism was seen as part of a laissez-faire philosophy to curtail federal regulation and promote free enterprise capitalism.

The (Re)Emergence of National Supremacy: Cooperative Federalism

Although the Court's abandonment of dual federalism began in 1937, the death knell rang most loudly with the decision in *United States v. Darby* (1941). For reasons we explain in chapter 7, *Darby* is a significant modern-day statement of Congress's power under the commerce clause, but here we focus on *Darby's* equally important interpretation of the Tenth Amendment.

Darby involved a challenge to an important piece of New Deal legislation, the Fair Labor Standards Act (FLSA). Passed in 1938 under Congress's power to regulate interstate commerce, the law provided that all employers "engaged in interstate commerce, or in the production of goods for that commerce" must pay all their employees a minimum wage of twenty-five cents per hour and not permit employees to work longer than forty-four hours per week without paying them one and one-half times their regular pay for their overtime hours. Fred W. Darby, the owner of a lumber company, was indicted for violating the law.

Darby did not dispute the charges. Rather, invoking the logic of *Hammer,* he argued against a broad interpretation of congressional powers and a narrow approach to the Tenth Amendment. The government responded that the Tenth Amendment merely reserves to the states "the powers not delegated to the United States." This, the government argued, is merely a statement of fact that adds no new powers to the states and does not limit the authority that has been given to the federal government.

13. Farber and Sherry, *A History of the American Constitution,* 343.

14. Pritchett, *Constitutional Law of the Federal System,* 60–61.

Writing for a unanimous Court, Justice Stone agreed with the government's position. Not only did he uphold the FLSA, but he also overruled *Hammer:*

The conclusion is inescapable that *Hammer v. Dagenhart* was a departure from the principles which have prevailed in the interpretation of the Commerce Clause both before and since the decision and that such vitality, as a precedent, as it then had has long since been exhausted. It should be and now is overruled.

As for *Darby*'s Tenth Amendment argument, Stone wrote,

Our conclusion is unaffected by the Tenth Amendment which provides: "The powers not delegated to the United States by the Constitution nor prohibited by it to the states are reserved to the states respectively or to the people." The amendment states but a truism that all is retained which has not been surrendered. There is nothing in the history of its adoption to suggest that it was more than declaratory of the relationship between the national and state governments as it had been established by the Constitution before the amendment or that its purpose was other than to allay fears that the new national government might seek to exercise powers not granted, and that the states might not be able to exercise fully their reserved powers.

From the beginning and for many years the amendment has been construed as not depriving the national government of authority to resort to all means for the exercise of a granted power which are appropriate and plainly adapted to the permitted end.

Justice Stone's opinion in *Darby* brought the Court back full circle to Marshall's view of nationalism. Not only did *Darby* explicitly overrule *Hammer* and uphold the FLSA, but it also gutted attempts to use the Tenth Amendment as an enclave of states' rights. The Court denied that the amendment constituted a tool that litigants could wield to build up state authority that they could then use to challenge the federal government's proper exercise of enumerated and implied powers. According to Justice Stone, and supported by a surprisingly unanimous Court, the Tenth Amendment was "but a truism."

For the next thirty-five years dual federalism was out and Stone's version of cooperative federalism was in. Under this doctrine, at least theoretically, the various levels of government shared policy-making responsibilities. In practice, it meant, as Stone's opinion implies, that the national government took the lead in formulating many policy goals, which it expected state and local officials to implement. Consistent with this new approach, the Court generally deferred to Congress in establishing economic regulatory policy. By the 1960s the federal government reigned supreme.

But change was in the wind. The election of Richard Nixon to the presidency in 1968 was an indication of growing dissatisfaction with an increasingly expansive federal government. Although Nixon was not a strong supporter of dual federalism, he favored increased state participation in federal programs. When it came to judicial appointments, Nixon desired justices who exercised judicial restraint generally and leaned toward a law-and-order posture in particular. Such individuals also tended to have greater sympathy for the role of state governments than did the post–New Deal era justices who preceded them. Nixon had the good fortune of being able to appoint a new chief justice, Warren Burger, and three associate justices, enough to alter the ideological makeup of the Court.

The first significant sign of change occurred with the announcement of the Court's ruling in ***National League of Cities v. Usery*** (1976), the case with which we introduced this chapter. *National League* centered once again on the FLSA, which the Court had upheld in *United States v. Darby*. This case crystallized when Congress in 1974 expanded the scope of the FLSA to require the state governments to pay all their employees the minimum wage and to disallow them from working in excess of maximum hours requirements. This, of course, represented a major change in the scope of the law. It was one thing for Congress to use its commerce power authority to regulate wages and hours for workers in the private sector, but it was a much different matter for the federal government to dictate how state governments must treat their own state employees.

Various cities and states challenged the constitutionality of the new amendments. In particular, they argued that the amendments represented a "collision" between federal expansion and states' rights in violation of the Tenth Amendment.

In their scrutiny of the FLSA, the four Nixon appointees plus Justice Potter Stewart provided an undeniable signal that dual federalism—in the form of a revival of the Tenth Amendment enclave—was far from dead. Writing for the Court, Justice Rehnquist struck down the new extension of the FLSA as impinging on state sovereignty. Rehnquist's opinion did not question the validity of federal regulation of private employers. He concluded, however, that when Congress is regulating the states as states—even if the law falls within one of Congress's enumerated or implied powers—the Tenth Amendment enclave comes into play. "There are attributes of sovereignty attaching to every state government," he wrote, "which may not be impaired by Congress, not because Congress may lack an affirmative grant of legislative authority to reach the matter, but because the Constitution prohibits it from exercising the authority in that manner."

Where is the line separating constitutional from unconstitutional federal intrusions into state business? Rehnquist provided an answer when he wrote, "Congress may not exercise that power so as to force directly upon the States its choices as to how essential decisions regarding the conduct of integral governmental functions are to be made." "While clearly not delineating these functions," Joseph Kobylka has observed, "the Court did say that they must be 'essential to [the] separate and independent existence of the states.'"[15] Examples of functions outside congressional authority and "well within the area of traditional operations of state and local governments" included firefighting, police protection, sanitation, public health, and parks and recreation.

Writing in dissent, Justice Brennan took great issue with Rehnquist's analysis. He accused Rehnquist of ignoring *Darby* and subsequent cases when he used the Tenth Amendment to protect states. Brennan argued that as long as Congress is not interfering with individual rights and liberties and is properly exercising one of its constitutional powers—here to regulate commerce among the states—the Court should uphold the regulation; the Tenth Amendment provides no additional rights to the states. This approach made sense to Brennan because states are already protected in Congress, which, of course, is composed of representatives from the states.

As it turned out, Brennan, and not Rehnquist, would win the battle (at least in the short term) when the Court overruled *National League of Cities* in *Garcia v. San Antonio Metropolitan Transit Authority* (1985). Part of the problem with *National League,* as Justice Blackmun explained, was that it was difficult for the Court to distinguish traditional and essential state functions from those that are nontraditional and less essential. But, in upholding the federal law, did Blackmun give too much deference to Congress?

---

15. Joseph F. Kobylka, "The Court, Justice Blackmun, and Federalism," *Creighton Law Review* 19 (1985–1986): 21.

Garcia v. San Antonio Metropolitan Transit Authority

469 U.S. 528 (1985)
http://laws.findlaw.com/us/469/528.html
Oral arguments are available at https://www.oyez.org.
Vote: 5 (Blackmun, Brennan, Marshall, Stevens, White)
  4 (Burger, O'Connor, Powell, Rehnquist)

OPINION OF THE COURT: *Blackmun*
DISSENTING OPINIONS: *Powell, O'Connor, Rehnquist*

FACTS:

Garcia was virtually a carbon copy of *National League of Cities.* That latter case arose when Congress in 1974 expanded the scope of the FLSA and brought virtually all state public employees, who were excluded in the original legislation, under its reach. Various cities and states and two organizations representing their collective interests, the National League of Cities and the National Governors' Conference, challenged the constitutionality of the new amendments. In particular, they argued that the amendments represented a "collision" between federal expansion and states' rights in violation of the Tenth Amendment. The Court, in *National League of Cities,* agreed.

Garcia, too, centered on amendments to the FLSA, in this case amendments that obligated states to meet minimum wage and overtime requirements for almost all public employees. The facts, however, were a bit more complicated than those in *National League of Cities.*

The San Antonio Transit System (SATS) began operation in 1959. At first the mass transit system was a moneymaking venture, but by 1969 it was operating at a loss and turned to the federal government for assistance. The federal Urban Mass Transit Administration (UMTA) provided it with a $4 million grant. In 1978 the city replaced SATS with the San Antonio Metropolitan Transit Authority (SAMTA), which also was subsidized by federal grants. Between 1970 and 1980 the transit system received more than $51 million, or 40 percent of its costs, from the federal government. The case started in 1979 when, "in response to a specific inquiry about the applicability of the FLSA to employees of SAMTA," the U.S. Department of Labor issued an opinion holding that SAMTA must abide by the act's wage provisions. SAMTA filed a challenge to the department's holding, and Joe G. Garcia and other SAMTA employees, in turn, initiated a suit against their employer for overtime pay.

When this case and a companion, *Donovan v. San Antonio Metropolitan Transit Authority,* reached the U.S. Supreme Court, SAMTA relied heavily on *National League of Cities.* It argued that "transit is a traditional [city] function," and, as the operator of that function, it was not covered by FLSA amendments. The U.S. government and Garcia countered by arguing that *National League of Cities* was not necessarily applicable. In their view, application of the FLSA to public transit did not violate the Tenth Amendment because (1) operation of a transit system is not a traditional government function, and (2) operation of a transit system is not a core government function that must be exempted from federal commerce power legislation to preserve the states' independence.

ARGUMENTS:

For the appellant, Joe G. Garcia:

- Transit is not a traditional government function; instead it is traditionally a private business enterprise that has always been subject to federal labor regulation. Exempting state-run transit systems from regulation because of the Tenth Amendment would encourage state takeover of all transit systems in order to avoid regulation. That is clearly not the intended purpose of the Tenth Amendment.
- *National League of Cities v. Usery* limits federal authority only to the extent necessary to preserve state sovereignty in essential state functions. State sovereignty is most directly expressed in lawmaking and law enforcement powers, not in the state's provision of particular goods and services. In this case, the provision of service is in question, not lawmaking or law enforcement powers.
- Funding from the federal government made possible the state's entry into the public transit arena. Therefore, the public transit systems are cooperative efforts of the federal government and the state. It would be illogical to conclude that the very federal aid that helped create this system is not subject to federal regulation.

For the appellee, San Antonio Metropolitan Transit Authority:

- *National League of Cities v. Usery* established precedent that state power to determine wages and hours is an attribute of state sovereignty. In this case, the very same act that threatened state sovereignty in *National League* is again in question. The Tenth Amendment protects against this.

- Transit is a traditional state function because it is purely local, has a long history of state and local regulation through their power to regulate street transportation, and historically has not been subject to federal regulation any more than any of the activities protected in *National League.*
- The transit system is indistinguishable from the hospitals that were exempted from federal regulation in *National League.* Both have roots in the private sector, and both receive significant funding from the government.
- The federal government is really making an argument about its spending power, not its commerce clause power. It is clear from *National League* that federal funding is irrelevant in determining whether an activity is protected.

JUSTICE BLACKMUN DELIVERED THE OPINION OF THE COURT.

We revisit in these cases an issue raised in *National League of Cities v. Usery* (1976). In that litigation, this Court, by a sharply divided vote, ruled that the Commerce Clause does not empower Congress to enforce the minimum-wage and overtime provisions of the Fair Labor Standards Act (FLSA) against the States "in areas of traditional government functions." Although *National League of Cities* supplied some examples of "traditional governmental functions," it did not offer a general explanation of how a "traditional" function is to be distinguished from a "nontraditional" one. Since then, federal and state courts have struggled with the task, thus imposed, of identifying a traditional function for purposes of state immunity under the Commerce Clause.

In the present cases, a Federal District Court concluded that municipal ownership and operation of a mass-transit system is a traditional governmental function and thus, under *National League of Cities,* is exempt from the obligations imposed by the FLSA. Faced with the identical question, three Federal Courts of Appeals and one state appellate court have reached the opposite conclusion.

Our examination of this "function" standard applied in these and other cases over the last eight years now persuades us that the attempt to draw the boundaries of state regulatory immunity in terms of "traditional governmental function" is not only unworkable but is also inconsistent with established principles of federalism and, indeed, with those very federalism principles on which *National League of Cities* purported to rest. That case, accordingly, is overruled. . . .

The central theme of *National League of Cities* was that the States occupy a special position in our constitutional system and that the scope of Congress' authority under the Commerce Clause must reflect that position. Of course, the Commerce Clause by its specific language does not provide any special limitation on Congress' actions with respect to the States. It is equally true, however, that the text of the Constitution provides the beginning rather than the final answer to every inquiry into questions of federalism, for "[b]ehind the words of the constitutional provisions are postulates which limit and control." *National League of Cities* reflected the general conviction that the Constitution precludes "the National Government [from] devour[ing] the essentials of state sovereignty." In order to be faithful to the underlying federal premises of the Constitution, courts must look for the "postulates which limit and control."

What has proved problematic is not the perception that the Constitution's federal structure imposes limitations on the Commerce Clause, but rather the nature and content of those limitations. One approach to defining the limits on Congress' authority to regulate the States under the Commerce Clause is to identify certain underlying elements of political sovereignty that are deemed essential to the States' "separate and independent existence." This approach obviously underlay the Court's use of the "traditional governmental function" concept in *National League of Cities*. It also has led to the separate requirement that the challenged federal statute "address matters that are indisputably 'attribute[s]' of state sovereignty.'" . . . The opinion did not explain what aspects of such decisions made them such an "undoubted attribute," and the Court since then has remarked on the uncertain scope of the concept. The point of the inquiry, however, has remained to single out particular features of a State's internal governance that are deemed to be intrinsic parts of state sovereignty.

We doubt that courts ultimately can identify principled constitutional limitations on the scope of Congress' Commerce Clause powers over the States merely by relying on *a priori* definitions of state sovereignty. In part, this is because of the elusiveness of objective criteria for "fundamental" elements of state sovereignty, a problem we have witnessed in the search for "traditional governmental functions." There is, however, a more fundamental reason: the sovereignty of the States is limited by the Constitution itself. A variety of sovereign powers, for example, are withdrawn from the States by Article I, §10. Section 8 of the same Article works an equally sharp contraction of state sovereignty by authorizing Congress to exercise a wide range of legislative powers and (in conjunction with the Supremacy Clause of Article VI) to displace contrary state legislation. . . .

The States unquestionably do "retai[n] a significant measure of sovereign authority." They do so, however, only to the extent that the Constitution has not divested them of their original powers and transferred those powers to the Federal Government. . . .

As a result, to say that the Constitution assumes the continued role of the States is to say little about the nature of that role. . . . With rare exceptions, like the guarantee, in Article IV, §3, of state territorial integrity, the Constitution does not carve out express elements of state sovereignty that Congress may not employ its delegated powers to displace. . . . The power of the Federal Government is a "power to be respected" as well, and the fact that the States remain sovereign as to all powers not vested in Congress or denied them by the Constitution offers no guidance about where the frontier between state and federal power lies. In short, we have no license to employ freestanding conceptions of state sovereignty when measuring congressional authority under the Commerce Clause.

When we look for the States' "residuary and inviolable sovereignty," *The Federalist* No. 39 (J. Madison), in the shape of the constitutional scheme, rather than in predetermined notions of sovereign power, a different measure of state sovereignty emerges. Apart from the limitation on federal authority inherent in the delegated nature of Congress' Article I powers, the principal means chosen by the Framers to ensure the role of the States in the federal system lies in the structure of the Federal Government itself. It is no novelty to observe that the composition of the Federal Government was designed in large part to protect the States from overreaching by Congress. The Framers thus gave the States a role in the selection both of the Executive and the Legislative Branches of the Federal Government. The States were vested with indirect influence over the House of Representatives and the Presidency by their control of electoral qualifications and their role in Presidential elections. U.S. Const., Art. I, §2, and Art. II, §1. They were given more direct influence in the Senate, where each State received equal representation and each Senator was to be selected by the legislature of his State. Art. I, §3. The significance attached to the States' equal representation in the Senate is underscored by the prohibition of any constitutional amendment divesting a State of equal representation without the State's consent. Art. V. . . .

The effectiveness of the federal political process in preserving the States' interests is apparent even today in the course of federal legislation. . . . [T]he States have been able to direct a substantial proportion of federal revenues into their own treasuries in the form of general and program-specific grants in aid. . . . As a result, federal grants now account for about one-fifth of state and local government expenditures. The States have obtained federal funding for such services as police and fire protection, education, public health and hospitals, parks and recreation, and sanitation. . . . The fact that some federal statutes such as the FLSA extend general obligations to the States cannot obscure the extent to which the political position of the States in the federal system has served to minimize the burdens that the States bear under the Commerce Clause.

We realize that changes in the structure of the Federal Government have taken place since 1789, not the least of which has been the substitution of popular election of Senators by the adoption of the Seventeenth Amendment in 1913, and that these changes may work to alter the influence of the States in the federal political process. Nonetheless, against this background, we are convinced that the fundamental limitation that the constitutional scheme imposes on the Commerce Clause to protect the "States as States" is one of process, rather than one of result. Any substantive restraint on the exercise of Commerce Clause powers must find its justification in the procedural nature of this basic limitation, and it must be tailored to compensate for possible failings in the national political process, rather than to dictate a "sacred province of state autonomy."

Insofar as the present cases are concerned, then, we need go no further than to state that we perceive nothing in the overtime and minimum-wage requirements of the FLSA, as applied to SAMTA, that is destructive of state sovereignty or violative of any constitutional provision. SAMTA faces nothing more than the same minimum-wage and overtime obligations that hundreds of thousands of other employers, public as well as private, have to meet. . . .

Of course, we continue to recognize that the States occupy a special and specific position in our constitutional system and that the scope of Congress' authority under the Commerce Clause must reflect that position. But the principal and basic limit on the federal commerce power is that inherent in all congressional action—the built-in restraints that our system provides through state participation in federal governmental action. The political process ensures that laws that unduly burden the States

will not be promulgated. In the factual setting of these cases the internal safeguards of the political process have performed as intended. . . .

We do not lightly overrule recent precedent. We have not hesitated, however, when it has become apparent that a prior decision has departed from a proper understanding of congressional power under the Commerce Clause. Due respect for the reach of congressional power within the federal system mandates that we do so now.

National League of Cities v. Usery (1976) is overruled. The judgment of the District Court is reversed, and these cases are remanded to that court for further proceedings consistent with this opinion.

It is so ordered.

JUSTICE POWELL, with whom THE CHIEF JUSTICE, JUSTICE REHNQUIST, and JUSTICE O'CONNOR join, dissenting.

Whatever effect the Court's decision may have in weakening the application of *stare decisis*, it is likely to be less important than what the Court has done to the Constitution itself. A unique feature of the United States is the federal system of government guaranteed by the Constitution and implicit in the very name of our country. Despite some genuflecting in the Court's opinion to the concept of federalism, today's decision effectively reduces the Tenth Amendment to meaningless rhetoric when Congress acts pursuant to the Commerce Clause. . . .

Today's opinion does not explain how the States' role in the electoral process guarantees that particular exercises of the Commerce Clause power will not infringe on residual state sovereignty. Members of Congress are elected from the various States, but once in office, they are Members of the Federal Government. Although the States participate in the Electoral College, this is hardly a reason to view the President as a representative of the States' interest against federal encroachment. . . . The Court offers no reason to think that this pressure will not operate when Congress seeks to invoke its powers under the Commerce Clause, notwithstanding the electoral role of the States.

The Court apparently thinks that the States' success at obtaining federal funds for various projects and exemptions from the obligations of some federal statutes is indicative of the "effectiveness of the federal political process in preserving the States' interests. . . ." But such political success is not relevant to the question whether the political processes are the proper means of enforcing constitutional limitations. The fact that Congress generally does not transgress constitutional limits on its power to reach state activities does not make judicial review any less necessary to rectify the cases in which it does do so. The States' role in our system of government is a matter of constitutional law, not of legislative grace.

More troubling than the logical infirmities in the Court's reasoning is the result of its holding, i.e., that federal political officials, invoking the Commerce Clause, are the sole judges of the limits of their own power. This result is inconsistent with the fundamental principles of our constitutional system. See, e.g., *The Federalist* No. 78 (Hamilton). At least since *Marbury v. Madison* (1803), it has been the settled province of the federal judiciary "to say what the law is" with respect to the constitutionality of Acts of Congress. In rejecting the role of the judiciary in protecting the States from federal overreaching, the Court's opinion offers no explanation for ignoring the teaching of the most famous case in our history.

JUSTICE O'CONNOR, with whom JUSTICE POWELL and JUSTICE REHNQUIST join, dissenting.

It is worth recalling the . . . passage in *McCulloch v. Maryland* (1819) that lies at the source of the recent expansion of the commerce power. "Let the end be legitimate, let it be within the scope of the constitution," Chief Justice Marshall said, "and all means which are appropriate, which are plainly adapted to that end, which are not prohibited, but consist with the letter *and spirit* of the constitution, are constitutional" [emphasis added]. The *spirit* of the Tenth Amendment, of course, is that the States will retain their integrity in a system in which the laws of the United States are nevertheless supreme.

It is not enough that the "end be legitimate"; the means to that end chosen by Congress must not contravene the spirit of the Constitution. Thus many of this Court's decisions acknowledge that the means by which national power is exercised must take into account concerns for state autonomy. . . . The operative language of these cases varies, but the underlying principle is consistent: state autonomy is a relevant factor in assessing the means by which Congress exercises its powers.

This principle requires the Court to enforce affirmative limits on federal regulation of the States to complement the judicially crafted expansion of the interstate commerce power. *National League of Cities v. Usery* represented an attempt to define such limits. The Court today rejects *National League of Cities* and washes its hands of all efforts to protect the States. In the process, the Court opines that unwarranted federal encroachments on state authority are and will remain "'horrible possibilities that never happen in the real world.'" There is ample reason to believe to the contrary.

The last two decades have seen an unprecedented growth of federal regulatory activity, as the majority itself acknowledges. . . . Today, as federal legislation and coercive grant programs have expanded to embrace innumerable activities that were once viewed as local, the burden of persuasion has surely shifted, and the extraordinary has become ordinary. For example, recently the Federal Government has, with this Court's blessing, undertaken to tell the States the age at which they can retire their law enforcement officers, and the regulatory standards, procedures, and even the agenda which their utilities commissions must consider and follow. The political process has not protected against these encroachments on state activities, even though they directly impinge on a State's ability to make and enforce its laws. With the abandonment of *National League of Cities*, all that stands between the remaining essentials of state sovereignty and Congress is the latter's underdeveloped capacity for self-restraint.

The problems of federalism in an integrated national economy are capable of more responsible resolution than holding that the States as States retain no status apart from that which Congress chooses to let them retain. The proper resolution, I suggest, lies in weighing state autonomy as a factor in the balance when interpreting the means by which Congress can exercise its authority on the States as States. It is insufficient, in assessing the validity of congressional regulation of a State pursuant to the commerce power, to ask only whether the same regulation would be valid if enforced against a private party. That reasoning, embodied in the majority opinion, is inconsistent with the spirit of our Constitution. It remains relevant that a State is being regulated, as *National League of Cities* and every recent case have recognized. . . .

It has been difficult for this Court to craft bright lines defining the scope of the state autonomy protected by *National League of Cities*. Such difficulty is to be expected whenever constitutional concerns as important as federalism and the effectiveness of the commerce power come into conflict. Regardless of the difficulty, it is and will remain the duty of this Court to reconcile these concerns in the final instance. That the Court shuns the task today by appealing to the "essence of federalism" can provide scant comfort to those who believe our federal system requires something more than a unitary, centralized government. I would not shirk the duty acknowledged by

National League of Cities and its progeny, and I [along with Justice Rehnquist believe] that this Court will in time again assume its constitutional responsibility.

I respectfully dissent.

After *Garcia*, with the Tenth Amendment relegated back to "truism" status, it looked as if this contentious area of law was, at long last, settled. *National League* was but an anomalous blip; *Garcia* was now the law of the land. But it was not to remain so. *Garcia* proved to be the last major articulation of cooperative federalism of the post–New Deal period. Though *National League of Cities* would not return in full form, neither would the Court fully abide by *Garcia*'s highly deferential approach to congressional power, nor would it completely discard the Tenth Amendment enclave.

Return of (a Milder Form of) Dual Federalism

Given the cyclical history of debates over the proper form of American federalism, it should come as no surprise that *Garcia* did not settle the issue. Justice Sandra Day O'Connor's predicted in *Garcia* that the principles of *National League of Cities* would return one day "to command the support of a majority of the Court." Her forecast proved partially correct.

Change came about largely because of membership shifts on the Court. In the early 1990s five justices departed, including two members of the five-justice *Garcia* majority, William Brennan and Thurgood Marshall. In addition, William Rehnquist, a strong supporter of state authority, became chief justice. New members, appointed by Presidents Reagan and George H. W. Bush, sufficiently changed the makeup of the Court to prompt observers to look for a rekindling of the federalism debate.

The first indication that the balance of power had shifted occurred in *New York v. United States* (1992). This decision involved one of the most important federalism questions of the 1990s: May the federal government constitutionally command the states to carry out federal policy? The Court's position was announced by Justice O'Connor. Consider the framework she lays out to resolve federalism disputes. Is this framework—especially her use of the Tenth Amendment—compatible with the Court's decision in *Garcia?*

New York v. United States

505 U.S. 144 (1992)
http://laws.findlaw.com/us/505/144.html
Oral arguments are available at https://www.oyez.org.
Vote: 6 (Kennedy, O'Connor, Rehnquist, Scalia, Souter, Thomas)
　　3 (Blackmun, Stevens, White)

OPINION OF THE COURT: *O'Connor*
DISSENTING OPINIONS: *Stevens, White*

FACTS:

In 1980 Congress passed the Low-Level Radioactive Waste Policy Act. The law was a response to the growing problem of the disposal of radioactive waste generated by private industry, government, hospitals, and research institutions. When the act was passed, disposal sites existed only in Nevada, South Carolina, and Washington, but these states were increasingly uncomfortable accepting radioactive waste from the other forty-seven. Moreover, the existing sites were approaching capacity. The 1980 statute and its subsequent 1985 amendments declared each state responsible for radioactive waste within its borders and encouraged states to develop disposal sites or enter into interstate compacts to develop regional disposal programs. To give the other states sufficient time to develop alternatives, the three existing sites were required to continue accepting out-of-state waste until 1992. The law allowed the Nevada, South Carolina, and Washington sites to impose a surcharge when accepting waste that originated in states that had not yet complied with the act.

Congress included in the act three types of incentives to encourage the states to comply with the law. First were monetary incentives: 25 percent of the surcharges collected at the three existing disposal sites would be transferred to the secretary of energy, who would distribute the funds to states that were complying with the statute. Second were access incentives: the longer a state failed to comply with the law, the higher the surcharge that would be imposed on that state's waste brought to the existing sites. Ultimately, the operational sites could deny noncomplying states access to the sites. Third were what the Court deemed the "most severe" incentives—those that followed from the "take title" provision of the law: after 1996 any state that had not developed an in-state disposal site or had not entered into a regional compact for that purpose would be required to take title of radioactive waste generated inside the state and be fully responsible for it.

In 1990 New York filed suit challenging the constitutionality of the waste disposal law. The state claimed that the incentive provisions violated, among other provisions, the Tenth Amendment.[16] The federal government defended the law and was supported by a group of states that were already participating in the program. Lower courts upheld the law.

ARGUMENTS:

For the petitioner, state of New York:
- Judicial review is needed under the Tenth Amendment and the principles of federalism because the act, particularly the "take title" provision, imposes unconditional affirmative obligations on the states and only on the states.
- This case is distinguishable from *Garcia v. San Antonio Metropolitan Transit Authority,* in which the law at issue applied to both private entities and states and concerned an activity that the states had voluntarily undertaken. Here, the act compels the states to act without their consent, depriving them of their sovereignty.
- The states are deprived of the opportunity to make an independent choice as to whether the federal funds outweigh the burden compliance with the federal scheme.

For the respondents, United States et al.:
- The 1985 act does not require the state to enact or enforce any federally mandated regulatory program and does not intrude impermissibly on state sovereignty. To the contrary, it leaves the states with a number of options. New York could contract with a regional interstate compact to ensure that its generators can dispose of the state's waste elsewhere.
- The act was the result of cooperative federalism, and New York was an active participant in its drafting and enactment. The process provided the state ample opportunity to contribute, and the resulting act generally conformed to New York's recommendations. The state's claim that the act leaves it politically powerless is baseless.
- This Court's decisions established that the Constitution permits some types of federal directives addressed directly to the states, especially in areas of intense federal interest. The serious issue of interstate disposal of radioactive waste, and the disputes among states which arose around this issue, qualify as areas of intense federal interest.

JUSTICE O'CONNOR DELIVERED THE OPINION OF THE COURT.

This case implicates one of our Nation's newest problems of public policy and perhaps our oldest question of constitutional law. The public policy issue involves the disposal of radioactive waste: In this case, we address the constitutionality of three provisions of the Low-Level Radioactive Waste Policy Amendments Act of 1985. The constitutional question is as old as the Constitution: It consists of discerning the proper division of authority between the Federal Government and the States. We conclude that while Congress has substantial power under the Constitution to encourage the States to provide for the disposal of the radioactive waste generated within their borders, the Constitution does not confer upon Congress the ability simply to compel the States to do so. We therefore find that only two of the Act's three provisions at issue are consistent with the Constitution's allocation of power to the Federal Government. . . .

. . . At least as far back as *Martin v. Hunter's Lessee* (1816), the Court has resolved questions "of great importance and delicacy" in determining whether particular sovereign powers have been granted by the Constitution to the Federal Government or have been retained by the States. . . .

These questions can be viewed in either of two ways. In some cases, the Court has inquired whether an Act of Congress is authorized by one of the powers delegated to Congress in Article I of the Constitution. See, e.g., *McCulloch v. Maryland* (1819). In other cases, the Court has sought to determine whether an Act of Congress invades the province of state sovereignty reserved by the Tenth Amendment. See, e.g., *Garcia v. San Antonio Metropolitan Transit Authority* (1985). In a case like this one, involving the division of authority between federal

---

16. New York also argued that the act was inconsistent with the guarantee clause, which directs the United States to "guarantee to every State in this Union a Republican Form of Government." Recall from chapter 2 that, beginning in *Luther v. Borden* (1849), the Court seemed to suggest that claims under the guarantee clause present nonjusticiable political questions. New York's attorneys marshaled scholarly arguments suggesting that under some circumstances the Court should address questions following from the guarantee clause. See, for example, Deborah Jones Merritt, "The Guarantee Clause and State Autonomy: Federalism for a Third Century," *Columbia Law Review* 88 (1988): 1–78. Justice O'Connor declined to enter this debate.

and state governments, the two inquiries are mirror images of each other. If a power is delegated to Congress in the Constitution, the Tenth Amendment expressly disclaims any reservation of that power to the States; if a power is an attribute of state sovereignty reserved by the Tenth Amendment, it is necessarily a power the Constitution has not conferred on Congress.

It is in this sense that the Tenth Amendment "states but a truism that all is retained which has not been surrendered." *United States v. Darby* (1941). . . .

Congress exercises its conferred powers subject to the limitations contained in the Constitution. Thus, for example, under the Commerce Clause, Congress may regulate publishers engaged in interstate commerce, but Congress is constrained in the exercise of that power by the First Amendment. The Tenth Amendment likewise restrains the power of Congress, but this limit is not derived from the text of the Tenth Amendment itself, which, as we have discussed, is essentially a tautology. Instead, the Tenth Amendment confirms that the power of the Federal Government is subject to limits that may, in a given instance, reserve power to the States. The Tenth Amendment thus directs us to determine, as in this case, whether an incident of state sovereignty is protected by a limitation on an Article I power.

The benefits of this federal structure have been extensively catalogued elsewhere, but they need not concern us here. Our task would be the same even if one could prove that federalism secured no advantages to anyone. It consists not of devising our preferred system of government, but of understanding and applying the framework set forth in the Constitution.

This framework has been sufficiently flexible over the past two centuries to allow for enormous changes in the nature of government. The Federal Government undertakes activities today that would have been unimaginable to the Framers in two senses; first, because the Framers would not have conceived that any government would conduct such activities; and second, because the Framers would not have believed that the Federal Government, rather than the States, would assume such responsibilities. Yet the powers conferred upon the Federal Government by the Constitution were phrased in language broad enough to allow for the expansion of the Federal Government's role. Among the provisions of the Constitution that have been particularly important in this regard, three concern us here.

First, the Constitution allocates to Congress the power "[t]o regulate Commerce . . . among the several States."

The volume of interstate commerce and the range of commonly accepted objects of government regulation have, however, expanded considerably in the last 200 years, and the regulatory authority of Congress has expanded along with them. As interstate commerce has become ubiquitous, activities once considered purely local have come to have effects on the national economy, and have accordingly come within the scope of Congress' commerce power.

Second, the Constitution authorizes Congress "to pay the Debts and provide for the . . . general Welfare of the United States." As conventional notions of the proper objects of government spending have changed over the years, so has the ability of Congress to "fix the terms on which it shall disburse federal money to the States." While the spending power is "subject to several general restrictions articulated in our cases," these restrictions have not been so severe as to prevent the regulatory authority of Congress from generally keeping up with the growth of the federal budget.

The Court's broad construction of Congress' power under the Commerce and Spending Clauses has of course been guided, as it has with respect to Congress' power generally, by the Constitution's Necessary and Proper Clause, which authorizes Congress "[t]o make all Laws which shall be necessary and proper for carrying into Execution the foregoing Powers."

Finally, the Constitution provides that "the Laws of the United States . . . shall be the supreme Law of the Land . . . any Thing in the Constitution or Laws of any State to the Contrary notwithstanding." As the Federal Government's willingness to exercise power within the confines of the Constitution has grown, the authority of the States has correspondingly diminished to the extent that federal and state policies have conflicted.

The actual scope of the Federal Government's authority with respect to the States has changed over the years, therefore, but the constitutional structure underlying and limiting that authority has not. In the end, just as a cup may be half empty or half full, it makes no difference whether one views the question at issue in this case as one of ascertaining the limits of the power delegated to the Federal Government under the affirmative provisions of the Constitution or one of discerning the core of sovereignty retained by the States under the Tenth Amendment. Either way, we must determine whether any of the three challenged provisions of the Low-Level Radioactive Waste Policy Amendments Act of 1985 oversteps the boundary between federal and state authority.

Petitioners do not contend that Congress lacks the power to regulate the disposal of low level radioactive waste. Space in radioactive waste disposal sites is frequently sold by residents of one State to residents of another. Regulation of the resulting interstate market in waste disposal is therefore well within Congress' authority under the Commerce Clause. . . . Petitioners contend only that the Tenth Amendment limits the power of Congress to regulate in the way it has chosen. Rather than addressing the problem of waste disposal by directly regulating the generators and disposers of waste, petitioners argue, Congress has impermissibly directed the States to regulate in this field.

Most of our recent cases interpreting the Tenth Amendment have concerned the authority of Congress to subject state governments to generally applicable laws. The Court's jurisprudence in this area has traveled an unsteady path. See *National League of Cities v. Usery* (1976) (state employers are not subject to Fair Labor Standards Act); *Garcia v. San Antonio Metropolitan Transit Authority* (1985) (overruling *National League of Cities*) This case presents no occasion to apply or revisit the holdings of any of these cases, as this is not a case in which Congress has subjected a State to the same legislation applicable to private parties.

This case instead concerns the circumstances under which Congress may use the States as implements of regulation; that is, whether Congress may direct or otherwise motivate the States to regulate in a particular field or a particular way. Our cases have established a few principles that guide our resolution of the issue.

As an initial matter, Congress may not simply "commandee[r] the legislative processes of the States by directly compelling them to enact and enforce a federal regulatory program." . . .

. . . While Congress has substantial powers to govern the Nation directly, including in areas of intimate concern to the States, the Constitution has never been understood to confer upon Congress the ability to require the States to govern according to Congress' instructions. . . .

Indeed, the question whether the Constitution should permit Congress to employ state governments as regulatory agencies was a topic of lively debate among the Framers. . . .

In the end, the Convention opted for a Constitution in which Congress would exercise its legislative authority directly over individuals, rather than over States. This choice was made clear to the subsequent state ratifying conventions. Oliver Ellsworth, a member of the Connecticut delegation in Philadelphia, explained the distinction to his State's convention: "This Constitution does not attempt to coerce sovereign bodies, states, in their political capacity. . . . But this legal coercion singles out the . . . individual." Charles Pinckney, another delegate at the Constitutional Convention, emphasized to the South Carolina House of Representatives that, in Philadelphia, "the necessity of having a government which should at once operate upon the people, and not upon the states, was conceived to be indispensable by every delegation present." . . .

In providing for a stronger central government, therefore, the Framers explicitly chose a Constitution that confers upon Congress the power to regulate individuals, not States. . . . [T]he Court has consistently respected this choice. We have always understood that, even where Congress has the authority under the Constitution to pass laws requiring or prohibiting certain acts, it lacks the power directly to compel the States to require or prohibit those acts. The allocation of power contained in the Commerce Clause, for example, authorizes Congress to regulate interstate commerce directly; it does not authorize Congress to regulate state governments' regulation of interstate commerce. . . .

This is not to say that Congress lacks the ability to encourage a State to regulate in a particular way, or that Congress may not hold out incentives to the States as a method of influencing a State's policy choices. Our cases have identified a variety of methods, short of outright coercion, by which Congress may urge a State to adopt a legislative program consistent with federal interests. Two of these methods are of particular relevance here.

First, under Congress' spending power, "Congress may attach conditions on the receipt of federal funds." Such conditions must (among other requirements) bear some relationship to the purpose of the federal spending; otherwise, of course, the spending power could render academic the Constitution's other grants and limits of federal authority. Where the recipient of federal funds is a State, as is not unusual today, the conditions attached to the funds by Congress may influence a State's legislative choices. [*South Dakota v.*] *Dole* was one such case: the Court found no constitutional flaw in a federal statute directing the Secretary of Transportation to withhold federal highway funds from States failing to adopt Congress' choice of a minimum drinking age. Similar examples abound.

Second, where Congress has the authority to regulate private activity under the Commerce Clause, we have recognized Congress' power to offer States the choice of regulating that activity according to federal standards or having state law pre-empted by federal regulation. This arrangement, which has been termed "a program of cooperative federalism," is replicated in numerous federal statutory schemes [including] the Clean Water Act . . . (Clean Water Act "anticipates a partnership between the States and the Federal Government, animated by a shared objective"). . . .

By either of these two methods, as by any other permissible method of encouraging a State to conform to federal policy choices, the residents of the State retain the ultimate decision as to whether or not the State will comply. If a State's citizens view federal policy as sufficiently contrary to local interests, they may elect to decline a federal grant. If state residents would prefer their government to devote its attention and resources to problems other than those deemed important by Congress, they may choose to have the Federal Government, rather than the State, bear the expense of a federally mandated regulatory program, and they may continue to supplement that program to the extent state law is not pre-empted. Where Congress encourages state regulation, rather than compelling it, state governments remain responsive to the local electorate's preferences; state officials remain accountable to the people.

By contrast, where the Federal Government compels States to regulate, the accountability of both state and federal officials is diminished. If the citizens of New York, for example, do not consider that making provision for the disposal of radioactive waste is in their best interest, they may elect state officials who share their view. That view can always be pre-empted under the Supremacy Clause if it is contrary to the national view, but, in such a case, it is the Federal Government that makes the decision in full view of the public, and it will be federal officials that suffer the consequences if the decision turns out to be detrimental or unpopular. But where the Federal Government directs the States to regulate, it may be state officials who will bear the brunt of public disapproval, while the federal officials who devised the regulatory program may remain insulated from the electoral ramifications of their decision. Accountability is thus diminished when, due to federal coercion, elected state officials cannot regulate in accordance with the views of the local electorate in matters not preempted by federal regulation.

With these principles in mind, we turn to the three challenged provisions of the Low-Level Radioactive Waste Policy Amendments Act of 1985. . . .

The Act comprises three sets of "incentives" for the States to provide for the disposal of low level radioactive

waste generated within their borders. We consider each in turn. . . .

[Justice O'Connor upheld the first set of incentives—the monetary incentives—as within congressional authority under the commerce and spending clauses. She wrote, "Because the first set of incentives is supported by affirmative constitutional grants of power to Congress, it is not inconsistent with the Tenth Amendment." She also upheld the access incentives because they fall within Congress's commerce power and "do not intrude on the sovereignty reserved to the States by the Tenth Amendment." Justice O'Connor wrote: "The affected States are not compelled by Congress to regulate, because any burden caused by a State's refusal to regulate will fall on those who generate waste and find no outlet for its disposal, rather than on the State as a sovereign. A State whose citizens do not wish it to attain the Act's milestones may devote its attention and its resources to issues its citizens deem more worthy; the choice remains at all times with the residents of the State, not with Congress. The State need not expend any funds, or participate in any federal program, if local residents do not view such expenditures or participation as worthwhile. Nor must the State abandon the field if it does not accede to federal direction; the State may continue to regulate the generation and disposal of radioactive waste in any manner its citizens see fit." She then moved to the take-title provision.]

The take-title provision is of a different character. This third so-called "incentive" offers States, as an alternative to regulating pursuant to Congress' direction, the option of taking title to and possession of the low level radioactive waste generated within their borders and becoming liable for all damages waste generators suffer as a result of the States' failure to do so promptly. In this provision, Congress has crossed the line distinguishing encouragement from coercion. . . .

The take-title provision offers state governments a "choice" of either accepting ownership of waste or regulating according to the instructions of Congress. Respondents do not claim that the Constitution would authorize Congress to impose either option as a freestanding requirement. On one hand, the Constitution would not permit Congress simply to transfer radioactive waste from generators to state governments. Such a forced transfer, standing alone, would in principle be no different than a congressionally compelled subsidy from state governments to radioactive waste producers. The same is true of the provision requiring the States to become liable for the generators' damages. Standing alone, this provision would be indistinguishable from an Act of Congress directing the States to assume the liabilities of certain state residents. Either type of federal action would "commandeer" state governments into the service of federal regulatory purposes, and would, for this reason, be inconsistent with the Constitution's division of authority between federal and state governments. On the other hand, the second alternative held out to state governments—regulating pursuant to Congress' direction—would, standing alone, present a simple command to state governments to implement legislation enacted by Congress. . . . [T]he Constitution does not empower Congress to subject state governments to this type of instruction.

Because an instruction to state governments to take title to waste, standing alone, would be beyond the authority of Congress, and because a direct order to regulate, standing alone, would also be beyond the authority of Congress, it follows that Congress lacks the power to offer the States a choice between the two. Unlike the first two sets of incentives, the take-title incentive does not represent the conditional exercise of any congressional power enumerated in the Constitution. In this provision, Congress has not held out the threat of exercising its spending power or its commerce power; it has instead held out the threat, should the States not regulate according to one federal instruction, of simply forcing the States to submit to another federal instruction. A choice between two unconstitutionally coercive regulatory techniques is no choice at all. Either way, "the Act commandeers the legislative processes of the States by directly compelling them to enact and enforce a federal regulatory program," an outcome that has never been understood to lie within the authority conferred upon Congress by the Constitution.

Respondents emphasize the latitude given to the States to implement Congress' plan. The Act enables the States to regulate pursuant to Congress' instructions in any number of different ways. States may avoid taking title by contracting with sited regional compacts, by building a disposal site alone or as part of a compact, or by permitting private parties to build a disposal site. States that host sites may employ a wide range of designs and disposal methods, subject only to broad federal regulatory limits. This line of reasoning, however, only underscores the critical alternative a State lacks: a State may not decline to administer the federal program. No matter which path the State chooses, it must follow the direction of Congress.

The take-title provision appears to be unique. No other federal statute has been cited which offers a state government no option other than that of implementing legislation enacted by Congress. Whether one views the take-title provision as lying outside Congress' enumerated powers or as infringing upon the core of state sovereignty reserved by the Tenth Amendment, the provision is inconsistent with the federal structure of our Government established by the Constitution. . . .

. . . [T]he Constitution protects us from our own best intentions: it divides power among sovereigns and among branches of government precisely so that we may resist the temptation to concentrate power in one location as an expedient solution to the crisis of the day. The shortage of disposal sites for radioactive waste is a pressing national problem, but a judiciary that licensed extraconstitutional government with each issue of comparable gravity would, in the long run, be far worse.

States are not mere political subdivisions of the United States. State governments are neither regional offices nor administrative agencies of the Federal Government. The positions occupied by state officials appear nowhere on the Federal Government's most detailed organizational chart. The Constitution instead "leaves to the several States a residuary and inviolable sovereignty," reserved explicitly to the States by the Tenth Amendment.

Whatever the outer limits of that sovereignty may be, one thing is clear: the Federal Government may not compel the States to enact or administer a federal regulatory program. The Constitution . . . does not . . . authorize Congress simply to direct the States to provide for the disposal of the radioactive waste generated within their borders. While there may be many constitutional methods of achieving regional self-sufficiency in radioactive waste disposal, the method Congress has chosen is not one of them. The judgment of the Court of Appeals is accordingly

Affirmed in part and reversed in part.

JUSTICE WHITE, with whom JUSTICE BLACKMUN and JUSTICE STEVENS join, concurring in part and dissenting in part.

Curiously absent from the Court's analysis is any effort to place the take-title provision within the overall context of the legislation. As . . . this opinion suggests, the 1980 and 1985 statutes were enacted against a backdrop of national concern over the availability of additional low-level radioactive waste disposal facilities. Congress could have pre-empted the field by directly regulating the disposal of this waste pursuant to its powers under the Commerce and Spending Clauses, but instead it unanimously assented to the States' request for congressional ratification of agreements to which they had acceded. As the floor statements of Members of Congress reveal, the States wished to take the lead in achieving a solution to this problem and agreed among themselves to the various incentives and penalties implemented by Congress to ensure adherence to the various deadlines and goals. The chief executives of the States proposed this approach, and I am unmoved by the Court's vehemence in taking away Congress' authority to sanction a recalcitrant unsited State now that New York has reaped the benefits of the sited States' concessions. . . .

I am convinced that, seen as a term of an agreement entered into between the several States, this measure proves to be less constitutionally odious than the Court opines. . . .

I would also submit, in this connection, that the Court's attempt to carve out a doctrinal distinction for statutes that purport solely to regulate state activities is especially unpersuasive after *Garcia*. It is true that, in that case, we considered whether a federal statute of general applicability—the Fair Labor Standards Act—applied to state transportation entities, but our most recent statements have explained the appropriate analysis in a more general manner. Just last Term, for instance, Justice O'Connor wrote . . . that "this Court in *Garcia* has left primarily to the political process the protection of the States against intrusive exercises of Congress' Commerce Clause powers."

. . . [T]herefore, the more appropriate analysis should flow from *Garcia*, even if this case does not involve a congressional law generally applicable to both States and private parties. In *Garcia*, we stated the proper inquiry: "[W]e are convinced that the fundamental limitation that the constitutional scheme imposes on the Commerce Clause to protect the 'States as States' is one of process, rather than one of result. Any substantive restraint on the exercise of Commerce Clause powers must find its justification in the procedural nature of this basic limitation, and it must be tailored to compensate for possible failings in the national political process, rather than to dictate a 'sacred province of state autonomy.'" Where it addresses this aspect of respondents' argument, the Court tacitly concedes that a failing of the political process cannot be shown in this case, because it refuses to rebut the unassailable arguments that the States were well able to look after themselves in the legislative process that culminated in the 1985 Act's passage. Indeed, New York acknowledges that its "congressional delegation participated in the drafting and enactment of both the 1980 and the 1985 Acts." The Court rejects this process-based argument by resorting to generalities and platitudes about the purpose of federalism being to protect individual rights.

Ultimately, I suppose, the entire structure of our federal constitutional government can be traced to an interest in establishing checks and balances to prevent the exercise of tyranny against individuals. But these fears seem extremely far distant to me in a situation such as this. We face a crisis of national proportions in the disposal of low-level radioactive waste, and Congress has acceded to the wishes of the States by permitting local decisionmaking, rather than imposing a solution from Washington. New York itself participated and supported passage of this legislation at both the gubernatorial and federal representative levels, and then enacted state laws specifically to comply with the deadlines and timetables agreed upon by the States in the 1985 Act. For me, the Court's civics lecture has a decidedly hollow ring at a time when action, rather than rhetoric, is needed to solve a national problem.

In *New York v. United States* the Supreme Court once again explicated the delicate relationship between the federal government and the states, a relationship that becomes more complex with the growth of problems as serious as the disposal of nuclear waste. The majority clearly stated that the Constitution does not allow the federal government to command the states to pass legislation to implement federal policy. The federal government may provide incentives for the states to act, but the constitutional division of authority between the general government and the various states is offended when the states are compelled to act. The decision also indicated the presence of a majority concerned with preserving the traditional role of the states.

Still, O'Connor's opinion was not a complete return to the logic of *National League of Cities*. Rather, O'Connor gave a narrow reading to *Garcia*, as Justice White's dissent suggests. Under her interpretation, *Garcia* simply held the states to the same standards as private employers. But when a problem is "uniquely governmental," as is the disposal of radioactive waste, the Tenth Amendment prohibits Congress from compelling the states to act, from "commandeering state legislatures."

Seen in this way, the Court's decision in *New York* signaled that those sympathetic to preserving the traditional role of the states now formed a majority. Five years later the same majority ruled when the Court handed down its decision in *Printz v. United States*

(1997), another case concerning the proper relationship between the central government and the states.

The lawsuit involved the Brady Handgun Violence Prevention Act, a gun control act that Congress passed in 1993. A provision in that statute obligated local law enforcement officials to play a role in the law's implementation. The case raised a question related to the one addressed in *New York:* May Congress compel local political officials to carry out federal legislation?

Printz v. United States

521 U.S. 898 (1997)
http://laws.findlaw.com/us/521/898.html
Oral arguments are available at https://www.oyez.org.
Vote: 5 (Kennedy, O'Connor, Rehnquist, Scalia, Thomas)
      4 (Breyer, Ginsburg, Souter, Stevens)

OPINION OF THE COURT: *Scalia*

CONCURRING OPINIONS: *O'Connor, Thomas*

DISSENTING OPINIONS: *Breyer, Souter, Stevens*

FACTS:

The Gun Control Act of 1968 forbids firearms dealers to transfer firearms to convicted felons, unlawful users of controlled substances, fugitives from justice, persons judged to be mentally defective, persons dishonorably discharged from the military, persons who have renounced their citizenship, and persons who have committed certain acts of domestic violence. In 1993 Congress amended the Gun Control Act with the Brady Handgun Violence Prevention Act. This act required the attorney general to establish, by November 30, 1998, a national database allowing for an instant background check on anyone attempting to buy a handgun. In the interim, the Brady Act allowed gun dealers to sell firearms to buyers who already possessed state handgun permits or who lived in states with existing instant background check systems.

In states where these two alternatives were not possible, the act required certain actions by the local chief law enforcement officer (CLEO). It mandated that CLEOs receive firearm purchase forms from gun dealers and make a reasonable effort within five business days to verify that any proposed sale was not to a person unqualified under the law. Essentially, the act required local CLEOs to conduct background checks on all potential gun purchasers. When CLEOs determined that any particular proposed sale would violate the law, they were required upon request to submit a

written report to the proposed purchaser stating the reasons for that determination. If CLEOs found no reason for objecting to a sale, they were required to destroy all records pertaining to it. These mandated responsibilities were to terminate in 1998 once the federal instant background check program became operative.

Jay Printz, sheriff of Ravalli County, Montana, and Richard Mack, sheriff of Graham County, Arizona, filed separate suits challenging the constitutionality of the Brady Act's interim provisions. They argued that the federal government had no authority to command state or local officials to administer a federal program. In each case the district court declared the act unconstitutional to the extent that it forced state officers to

James S. Brady, former press secretary for President Reagan, who was wounded during an assassination attempt on the president, listens as President Clinton speaks before signing the Brady Bill gun control legislation in 1993.

Stephanie Sinclair/VII

Richard Mack, sheriff of Graham County, Arizona, who, along with Sheriff Jay Printz of Ravalli County, Montana, challenged the constitutionality of those provisions of the Brady Bill that required local law enforcement officials to conduct background checks on prospective handgun purchasers.

carry out federal policies. Other provisions of the law were left untouched. The court of appeals disagreed, finding no provisions of the law to violate the Constitution. The Supreme Court accepted the cases for review. Although the decision immediately affected a temporary provision that was scheduled to expire in 1998, it involved a meaningful constitutional issue.

ARGUMENTS:

For the petitioner, Jay Printz, sheriff of Ravalli County:
- *New York v. United States* established that Congress cannot order states to enact or administer a federal regulatory program without violating the Tenth Amendment. Historically, the authority for defining and enforcing criminal laws lies with the states. Criminal law enforcement has been a fundamental element of state sovereignty. Drafting state employees for federal enforcement duty is unprecedented.

- The commerce clause cannot justify conscripting local CLEOs into federal law enforcement, because CLEOs are not engaged in or connected to interstate commerce. Attempts to argue that regulation will ultimately affect commerce and therefore is justifiable under the commerce clause have been struck down in earlier cases.

- Article II of the Constitution provides that the president, not CLEOs, shall faithfully execute the laws. The careful system of checks and balances in the U.S. system of government is disrupted by having local CLEOs enforce federal laws, without any of the safeguards against abuse of power that were built into the Constitution.

For the respondent, United States:
- This case is distinguishable from *New York v. United States.* In that case, Congress commandeered the states' legislative process by requiring the states to legislate their own solution. In this case, the federal government is asking only for local assistance in implementing a comprehensive federal policy.

- Congress may find it necessary and proper to enlist local officials in limited, non-policy-making aspects of the implementation of federal law. Congress has done this in the past, beginning with the First Congress requiring court clerks to help register aliens seeking citizenship.

- The act does not pose substantial burdens on the states or the CLEOs, so it does not threaten the separate and independent existence of the states. The act imposes only temporary and minimal duties on local officeholders and grants them discretion in determining how to meet those responsibilities.

- Because the regulated activity is legitimately subject to federal regulation under the commerce clause, the only question before the Court is whether the means chosen are reasonably related to the ends. Petitioner has not claimed that the means are an irrational means to the ends.

JUSTICE SCALIA DELIVERED THE OPINION OF THE COURT.

The question presented in these cases is whether certain interim provisions of the Brady Handgun Violence Prevention Act, commanding state and local law enforcement officers to conduct background checks on prospective handgun purchasers and to perform certain related tasks, violate the Constitution. . . .

. . . [T]he Brady Act purports to direct state law enforcement officers to participate, albeit only temporarily, in the administration of a federally enacted regulatory scheme. . . .

The petitioners here object to being pressed into federal service, and contend that congressional action compelling state officers to execute federal laws is unconstitutional. Because there is no constitutional text speaking to this precise question, the answer to the CLEOs' challenge must be sought in historical understanding and practice, in the structure of the Constitution, and in the jurisprudence of this Court. . . .

Petitioners contend that compelled enlistment of state executive officers for the administration of federal programs is, until very recent years at least, unprecedented. The Government contends, to the contrary, that "the earliest Congresses enacted statutes that required the participation of state officials in the implementation of federal laws." . . .

The Government's contention demands our careful consideration, since early congressional enactments "provid[e] 'contemporaneous and weighty evidence' of the Constitution's meaning." . . . Conversely if, as petitioners contend, earlier Congresses avoided use of this highly attractive power, we would have reason to believe that the power was thought not to exist. . . .

Not only do the enactments of the early Congresses, as far as we are aware, contain no evidence of an assumption that the Federal Government may command the States' executive power in the absence of a particularized constitutional authorization, they contain some indication of precisely the opposite assumption. On September 23, 1789—the day before its proposal of the Bill of Rights—the First Congress enacted a law aimed at obtaining state assistance of the most rudimentary and necessary sort for the enforcement of the new Government's laws: the holding of federal prisoners in state jails at federal expense. Significantly, the law issued not a command to the States' executive, but a recommendation to their legislatures. Congress "recommended to the legislatures of the several States to pass laws, making it expressly the duty of the keepers of their gaols [jails], to receive and safe keep therein all prisoners committed under the authority of the United States." . . .

In addition to early legislation, the Government also appeals to other sources we have usually regarded as indicative of the original understanding of the Constitution. It points to portions of *The Federalist* which . . . [state]

that Congress will probably "make use of the State officers and State regulations, for collecting" federal taxes, *The Federalist* No. 36 (A. Hamilton), and predicted that "the eventual collection [of internal revenue] under the immediate authority of the Union, will generally be made by the officers, and according to the rules, appointed by the several States" (J. Madison). The Government also invokes the *Federalist's* more general observations that the Constitution would "enable the [national] government to employ the ordinary magistracy of each [State] in the execution of its laws," No. 27 (A. Hamilton), and that it was "extremely probable that in other instances, particularly in the organization of the judicial power, the officers of the States will be clothed in the correspondent authority of the Union," No. 45 (J. Madison). But none of these statements necessarily implies—what is the critical point here—that Congress could impose these responsibilities *without the consent of the States.* They appear to rest on the natural assumption that the States would consent to allowing their officials to assist the Federal Government, an assumption proved correct by the extensive mutual assistance the States and Federal Government voluntarily provided one another in the early days of the Republic, including voluntary *federal implementation of state law.* . . .

. . . We turn next to consideration of the structure of the Constitution, to see if we can discern among its "essential postulate[s]" a principle that controls the present cases. . . .

It is incontestable that the Constitution established a system of "dual sovereignty." Although the States surrendered many of their powers to the new Federal Government, they retained "a residuary and inviolable sovereignty," *The Federalist* No. 39 (J. Madison). . . . Residual state sovereignty was also implicit, of course, in the Constitution's conferral upon Congress of not all governmental powers, but only discrete, enumerated ones, which implication was rendered express by the Tenth Amendment's assertion that "[t]he powers not delegated to the United States by the Constitution, nor prohibited by it to the States, are reserved to the States respectively, or to the people."

The Framers' experience under the Articles of Confederation had persuaded them that using the States as the instruments of federal governance was both ineffectual and provocative of federal-state conflict. . . . [T]he Framers rejected the concept of a central government that would act upon and through the States, and instead designed a system in which the state and federal governments would exercise concurrent authority over the people—who were, in Hamilton's words, "the only proper objects of government," *The Federalist* No. 15. . . . The great innovation of this design was that-our citizens would have two political capacities, one state and one federal, each protected from incursion by the other. . . . The Constitution thus contemplates that a State's government will represent and remain accountable to its own citizens. As Madison expressed it: "[T]he local or municipal authorities form distinct and independent portions of the supremacy, no more subject, within their respective spheres, to the general authority than the general authority is subject to them, within its own sphere." *The Federalist* No. 39.

This separation of the two spheres is one of the Constitution's structural protections of liberty. "Just as the separation and independence of the coordinate branches of the Federal Government serve to prevent the accumulation of excessive power in any one branch, a healthy balance of power between the States and the Federal Government will reduce the risk of tyranny and abuse from either front." . . . To quote Madison once again:

In the compound republic of America, the power surrendered by the people is first divided between two distinct governments, and then the portion allotted to each subdivided among distinct and separate departments. Hence a double security arises to the rights of the people. The different governments will control each other, at the same time that each will be controlled by itself. The *Federalist* No. 51

We have thus far discussed the effect that federal control of state officers would have upon the first element of the "double security" alluded to by Madison: the division of power between State and Federal Governments. It would also have an effect upon the second element: the separation and equilibration of powers between the three branches of the Federal Government itself. The Constitution does not leave to speculation who is to administer the laws enacted by Congress; the President, it says, "shall take Care that the Laws be faithfully executed," personally and through officers whom he appoints. . . . The Brady Act effectively transfers this responsibility to thousands of CLEOs in the 50 States, who are left to implement the program without meaningful Presidential control (if indeed meaningful Presidential control is possible without the power to appoint and remove). The insistence of the Framers upon unity in the Federal Executive—to insure both vigor and accountability—is well known. See *The Federalist* No. 70 (A. Hamilton). That unity would be shattered, and the power of the President would be subject to reduction, if Congress could act as effectively without the President as with him, by simply requiring state officers to execute its laws.

The dissent of course resorts to the last, best hope of those who defend *ultra vires* congressional action, the Necessary and Proper Clause. It reasons that the power to regulate the sale of handguns under the Commerce Clause, coupled with the power to "make all Laws which shall be necessary and proper for carrying into Execution the foregoing Powers," conclusively establishes the Brady Act's constitutional validity, because the Tenth Amendment imposes no limitations on the exercise of *delegated* powers but merely prohibits the exercise of powers "*not* delegated to the United States." What destroys the dissent's Necessary and Proper Clause argument, however, is not the Tenth Amendment but the Necessary and Proper Clause itself. When a "La[w] . . . for carrying into Execution" the Commerce Clause violates the principle of state sovereignty reflected in the various constitutional provisions we mentioned earlier it is not a "La[w] . . . *proper* for carrying into Execution the Commerce Clause." and is thus, in the words of *The Federalist*, "merely [an] ac[t] of usurpation" which "deserve[s] to be treated as such." *The Federalist* No. 33 (A. Hamilton).

Finally, and most conclusively in the present litigation, we turn to the prior jurisprudence of this Court. . . .

. . . In *New York* [*v. United States* we held that] "The Federal Government . . . may not compel the States to enact or administer a federal regulatory program." . . .

The Government contends that *New York* is distinguishable on the following ground: unlike the "take title" provisions invalidated there, the background check provision of the Brady Act does not require state legislative or executive officials to make policy, but instead issues a final directive to state CLEOs. . . .

The Government's distinction between "making" law and merely "enforcing" it, between "policymaking" and mere "implementation," is an interesting one. . . . [But] [e]xecutive action that has utterly no policymaking component is rare, particularly at an executive level as high as a jurisdiction's chief law enforcement officer. Is it really true that there is no policymaking involved in deciding, for example, what "reasonable efforts" shall be expended to conduct a background check? . . .

The Government also maintains that requiring state officers to perform discrete, ministerial tasks specified by Congress does not violate the principle of *New York* because it does not diminish the accountability of state or federal officials. This argument fails even on its own terms. By forcing state governments to absorb the financial burden of implementing a federal regulatory program, Members of Congress can take credit for "solving" problems without having to ask their constituents to pay for the solutions with higher federal taxes. And even when the States are not forced to absorb the costs of implementing a federal program, they are still put in the position of taking the blame for its burdensomeness and for its defects. . . .

We held in *New York* [*v. United States*] that Congress cannot compel the States to enact or enforce a federal regulatory program. Today we hold that Congress cannot circumvent that prohibition by conscripting the State's officers directly. The Federal Government may neither issue directives requiring the States to address particular problems, nor command the States' officers, or those of their political subdivisions, to administer or enforce a federal regulatory program. [S]uch commands are fundamentally incompatible with our constitutional system of dual sovereignty. Accordingly, the judgment of the Court of Appeals for the Ninth Circuit is reversed. Accordingly, the judgment of the Court of Appeals for the Ninth Circuit is reversed.

It is so ordered.

JUSTICE THOMAS, concurring.

In my "revisionist" view, the Federal Government's authority under the Commerce Clause, which merely allocates to Congress the power "to regulate Commerce . . . among the several states," does not extend to the regulation of wholly intrastate, point of sale transactions. Absent the underlying authority to regulate the intrastate transfer of firearms, Congress surely lacks the corollary power to impress state law enforcement officers into administering and enforcing such regulations. . . .

Even if we construe Congress' authority to regulate interstate commerce to encompass those intrastate transactions that "substantially affect" interstate commerce, I question whether Congress can regulate the particular transactions at issue here. The Constitution, in addition to delegating certain enumerated powers to Congress, places whole areas outside the reach of Congress' regulatory authority. The First Amendment, for example, is fittingly celebrated for preventing Congress from "prohibiting the free exercise" of religion or "abridging the freedom of speech." The Second Amendment similarly appears to contain an express limitation on the government's authority. . . . This Court has not had recent occasion to consider the nature of the substantive right safeguarded by the Second Amendment. If, however, the Second Amendment is read to confer a personal right to "keep and bear arms," a colorable argument exists that the Federal Government's

regulatory scheme, at least as it pertains to the purely intrastate sale or possession of firearms, runs afoul of that Amendment's protections.

JUSTICE STEVENS, with whom JUSTICE SOUTER, JUSTICE GINSBURG, and JUSTICE BREYER join, dissenting.

When Congress exercises the powers delegated to it by the Constitution, it may impose affirmative obligations on executive and judicial officers of state and local governments as well as ordinary citizens. This conclusion is firmly supported by the text of the Constitution, the early history of the Nation, decisions of this Court, and a correct understanding of the basic structure of the Federal Government.

These cases do not implicate the more difficult questions associated with congressional coercion of state legislatures addressed in *New York v. United States* (1992). Nor need we consider the wisdom of relying on local officials rather than federal agents to carry out aspects of a federal program, or even the question whether such officials may be required to perform a federal function on a permanent basis. The question is whether Congress, acting on behalf of the people of the entire Nation, may require local law enforcement officers to perform certain duties during the interim needed for the development of a federal gun control program. . . .

The text of the Constitution provides a sufficient basis for a correct disposition of this case.

Article I, §8, grants the Congress the power to regulate commerce among the States. Putting to one side the revisionist views expressed by Justice Thomas in his concurring opinion in *United States v. Lopez* (1995), there can be no question that that provision adequately supports the regulation of commerce in handguns effected by the Brady Act. Moreover, the additional grant of authority in that section of the Constitution "[t]o make all Laws which shall be necessary and proper for carrying into Execution the foregoing Powers" is surely adequate to support the temporary enlistment of local police officers in the process of identifying persons who should not be entrusted with the possession of handguns. In short, the affirmative delegation of power in Article I provides ample authority for the congressional enactment.

Unlike the First Amendment, which prohibits the enactment of a category of laws that would otherwise be authorized by Article I, the Tenth Amendment imposes no restriction on the exercise of delegated powers. . . .

The Amendment confirms the principle that the powers of the Federal Government are limited to those affirmatively granted by the Constitution, but it does not purport to limit the scope or the effectiveness of the exercise of powers that are delegated to Congress. Thus, the Amendment provides no support for a rule that immunizes local officials from obligations that might be imposed on ordinary citizens. . . .

There is not a clause, sentence, or paragraph in the entire text of the Constitution of the United States that supports the proposition that a local police officer can ignore a command contained in a statute enacted by Congress pursuant to an express delegation of power enumerated in Article I. . . .

. . . [T]he Court's reasoning [also] contradicts *New York v. United States.*

That decision squarely approved of cooperative federalism programs, designed at the national level but implemented principally by state governments. *New York* disapproved of a particular *method* of putting such programs into place, not the *existence* of federal programs implemented locally. . . .

The provision of the Brady Act that crosses the Court's newly defined constitutional threshold is more comparable to a statute requiring local police officers to report the identity of missing children to the Crime Control Center of the Department of Justice than to an offensive federal command to a sovereign state. If Congress believes that such a statute will benefit the people of the Nation, and serve the interests of cooperative federalism better than an enlarged federal bureaucracy, we should respect both its policy judgment and its appraisal of its constitutional power.

Accordingly, I respectfully dissent.

JUSTICE SOUTER, dissenting.

In deciding these cases, which I have found closer than I had anticipated, it is *The Federalist* that finally determines my position. I believe that the most straightforward reading of No. 27 is authority for the Government's position here, and that this reading is both supported by No. 44 and consistent with Nos. 36 and 45.

Hamilton in No. 27 first notes that because the new Constitution would authorize the National Government to bind individuals directly through national law, it could "employ the ordinary magistracy of each [State] in the execution of its laws." Were he to stop here, he would not necessarily be speaking of anything beyond the possibility of cooperative arrangements by agreement. But he then addresses the combined effect of the proposed Supremacy Clause, and state officers' oath requirement, and he states that "the Legislatures, Courts and Magistrates of the respective members will be incorporated into the operations of the national government, as far as its just and constitutional authority extends; and will be rendered auxiliary to the enforcement of its laws." The natural reading of this language is not merely that the officers of the various branches of state governments may be employed in the performance of national functions; Hamilton says that the state governmental machinery "will be incorporated" into the Nation's operation, and because the "auxiliary" status of the state officials will occur because they are "bound by the sanctity of an oath," I take him to mean that their auxiliary functions will be the products of their obligations thus undertaken to support federal law, not of their own, or the States,' unfettered choices.

Madison in No. 44 supports this reading in his commentary on the oath requirement. He asks why state magistrates should have to swear to support the National Constitution, when national officials will not be required to oblige themselves to support the state counterparts. His answer is that national officials "will have no agency in carrying the State Constitutions into effect. The members and officers of the State Governments, on the contrary, will have an essential agency in giving effect to the Federal Constitution." . . .

In the light of all these passages, I cannot persuade myself that the statements from No. 27 speak of anything less than the authority of the National Government, when exercising an otherwise legitimate power (the commerce power, say), to require state "auxiliaries" to take appropriate action.

Because of the scheduled date for the national background check system to become operative, *Printz* had little impact on gun control. The decision, however, gave a clear indication of the Rehnquist Court's position on federalism. Five conservative justices, all appointees of Republican presidents, Ronald Reagan and George H. W. Bush, expressed their commitment to maintaining the view that the states are not merely administrative units of the federal government. Justice Antonin Scalia, for the majority, invoked the term *dual sovereignty* to describe the constitutionally mandated division of power between the central government and the states. Justice John Paul Stevens, writing for the four liberal justices in dissent, explicitly endorsed "cooperative federalism." (As we shall see, precisely this same pattern of voting emerged in the Rehnquist Court's interpretation of the Eleventh Amendment.)

What of the Rehnquist Court's successor, the Roberts Court? Although significant personnel changes have occurred since *New York* and *Printz,* the Court's federalism jurisprudence seems to be relatively stable. Perhaps most instructive of this point is the Court's complex ruling on the constitutionality of the Patient Protection and Affordable Care Act of 2010 (the federal health-care law widely known as "Obamacare"), *National Federation of Independent Business v. Sebelius* (2012). As we shall see in chapters 7 and 8, five justices (the conservatives) did not believe that the act's requirement that most Americans purchase health insurance was a valid exercise of congressional commerce power, but five (the four liberals plus Roberts) nonetheless upheld the so-called individual mandate as within Congress's power under the taxing clause of Article I.

At the same time, as we detail in chapter 8, seven justices (all but Ginsburg and Sotomayor) agreed that another section of the law—expanding Medicaid coverage—put too much coercive pressure on the states. As Chief Justice Roberts wrote, "Congress has no authority to order the States to regulate according to its instructions. Congress may offer the States grants and require the States to comply with accompanying conditions, but the States must have a genuine choice whether to accept the offer. The States are given no such choice in this case: They must either accept a basic change in the nature of Medicaid, or risk losing all Medicaid funding." Though Roberts did not cite the Tenth Amendment, his opinion echoed the claim of the challenging states: that the threatened loss of all federal Medicaid funding violated the Tenth Amendment by coercing them into complying with the Medicaid expansion.

Still, the Supreme Court's shift back toward dual federalism should not be interpreted as a return to the pre–Civil War days of Roger Taney or to the laissez-faire philosophies that were popular prior to the New Deal. Rather, in cases such as *New York, Printz,* and *Sebelius,* the majority sought to remind us that under the U.S. constitutional system the states retain significant independent sovereignty. Congress may achieve its goals by cooperating with the states or by providing incentives to encourage states to participate in the administration of federally established policies, but the federal government may not commandeer the states and order them to carry out federal directives.

THE ELEVENTH AMENDMENT AND SOVEREIGN IMMUNITY

An important element in our understanding of federalism is the principle of sovereign immunity. The origins of this doctrine can be traced back several centuries into the early development of English common law. Sovereign immunity initially was based on the notion that all law flows from the king and that the courts are the king's creation. Therefore, the king can do no wrong under the law (*rex non potest peccare*) and consequently he cannot be held accountable in the courts he created. As the law developed, sovereign immunity came to mean that a government cannot be sued in its own courts unless it gives consent. When the colonists settled in America, sovereign immunity was a generally accepted legal doctrine. Even before the formation of the federal government, state governments claimed sovereign immunity protection from lawsuits in their own courts; and when the federal government was created it was universally understood that it, too, enjoyed sovereign immunity protection. Importantly, sovereign immunity is not granted by the Constitution, but is considered to emanate from the very essence of statehood.

During the process of ratifying the Constitution, concern was expressed that federal judicial power would extend to suits brought against states by citizens of other states or even by foreign countries. In *Federalist* No. 81 Alexander Hamilton tried to put such fears to rest: "It is inherent in the nature of sovereignty not to be amenable to the suit of an individual without its consent." In other words, sovereign immunity would protect a state from suits to which it did not consent.

Quite early on, however, it appeared that the United States would not adhere to this principle. As we noted in chapter 2, in 1793 the Supreme Court accepted original jurisdiction in ***Chisholm v. Georgia,*** a suit brought against the state of Georgia by two citizens of South Carolina trying to collect a debt. This action was based on Article III's authorization for federal courts to adjudicate controversies "between a State and Citizens of another State." Congress and the states strongly opposed the Court's action and reacted quickly by adopting the Eleventh Amendment, which gives states immunity from being sued, without their consent, in federal courts by "Citizens of another State, or by Citizens or Subjects of any Foreign State."

Soon afterward, however, the Supreme Court gave the Eleventh Amendment a "stingy" reading. In his opinion in **Cohens v. Virginia** (1821), Chief Justice Marshall stated his belief that the Eleventh Amendment did not preclude citizens from bringing suit in federal court against their own state. That view held sway with the Court until the post–Civil War case of *Hans v. Louisiana* (1890). The Court, in *Hans,* was aware of Marshall's "observation" in *Cohens* but deemed it dicta, "unnecessary to the decision," and therefore not binding. It went on to conclude that the Eleventh Amendment does, in fact, prohibit suits brought in federal court by citizens against their own state unless the state grants consent. According to the Court, even though the text of the amendment does not mention suits by a state's own citizens, it would be "anomalous"—especially given the furor over *Chisholm*—that a state may be sued in the federal courts by its own citizens in cases arising under the Constitution or federal laws but could not be sued under similar circumstances by the citizens of other states, or of a foreign state.

Although *Hans* seemed to expand the reach of state sovereign immunity, Congress, with the blessing of the Supreme Court, attempted to contract it. This trend continued into the 1980s. In case after case, the Court allowed Congress to make exceptions to the sovereign immunity established in the Eleventh Amendment. In *Fitzpatrick v. Bitzer* (1976) the Court held that because the Fourteenth Amendment expressly authorizes Congress to enforce the amendment "by appropriate legislation," Congress could, when exercising that authority, abrogate the states' immunity from suit under the Eleventh Amendment. Similarly, in *Pennsylvania v. Union Gas Co.* (1989) a divided Court ruled that the commerce clause (Article I, Section 8) permitted Congress to make an exception to the Eleventh Amendment's grant of immunity, holding that the power to regulate commerce "among the several States" would be "incomplete without the authority to render States liable in damages." These decisions, favoring federal power over state interests, were consistent with the philosophy of cooperative federalism that was accepted by the justices at that time.

But in 1996 the Court overruled *Union Gas* in **Seminole Tribe of Florida v. Florida**, a case involving the Indian Gaming Regulatory Act. This act requires that states negotiate in good faith with Native American tribes over gambling activities. If a tribe thinks a state is not doing so, the act permits the tribe to bring suit in a federal court to compel the state to negotiate in good faith. Writing for the Court, Chief Justice Rehnquist stated, "Even when the Constitution vests in Congress complete law-making authority over a particular area, the Eleventh Amendment prevents congressional authorization of suits by private parties

Sun Journal photo by Russ Dillingham

In Alden v. Maine *the U.S. Supreme Court ruled that state workers such as Julio Martinez, left, Linda Maher, and Joe DeFilipp of Maine could not sue the state for federal labor law violations.*

against unconsenting States." In other words, the Court asserted that the specific terms of Article I of the constitutional text do not permit Congress to abrogate the states' immunity from suits commenced or prosecuted in the federal courts.

Would the Court push *Seminole Tribe* even farther, holding that Congress cannot subject nonconsenting states to private suits for damages even in their own courts? This question was at the heart of *Alden v. Maine.*

Alden v. Maine

527 U.S. 706 (1999)
http://laws.findlaw.com/us/527/706.html
Oral arguments are available at https://www.oyez.org.
Vote: 5 (Kennedy, O'Connor, Rehnquist, Scalia, Thomas)
    4 (Breyer, Ginsburg, Souter, Stevens)

OPINION OF THE COURT: *Kennedy*
DISSENTING OPINION: *Souter*

The Eleventh Amendment bars states from being sued in federal court without their express consent. The Supreme Court, despite the ruling in *Hans,* allowed Congress to make some exceptions to this general rule. Congress took advantage of these decisions, occasionally abrogating the Eleventh Amendment immunity from suit. The Fair Labor Standards Act (FLSA), for example, enables state employees to bring federal suits against their states.

In 1992 sixty-five probation officers took advantage of this provision and sued their employer, the state of Maine, in federal district court for violating overtime pay provisions of the FLSA. While the suit was pending, the Supreme Court reversed course. In *Seminole Tribe of Florida* it held that Article I does not permit Congress to abrogate the states' sovereign immunity from suits commenced or prosecuted in the federal courts. This decision, in turn, led the district court to dismiss the probation officers' suit.

Not willing to give up the battle, the officers took their claim to a Maine state court. Even though the FLSA enables employees to bring suit against their states in state courts, the trial court dismissed the suit on the basis of sovereign immunity, and the Maine Supreme Judicial Court affirmed.

When the officers appealed to the Supreme Court, the justices were confronted with this question: Do the powers delegated to Congress under Article I include the power to subject nonconsenting states to private suits for damages in state courts? Because the text of the Eleventh Amendment, which itself was a response to the Supreme Court's decision in *Chisholm,* speaks only of federal judicial power, the majority turned to history and tradition to derive an answer.

ARGUMENTS:

For the petitioners, John H. Alden et al.:

- The supremacy clause makes clear that a state court cannot refuse to hear this case by relying on the sovereign immunity defense asserted by the state. It makes a federal law as much the law in the states as laws passed by the state legislature, and it charges state courts with a responsibility to enforce that law. This rule applies equally to actions against a state.

- There is no federal constitutional principle of state sovereign immunity that overrides a state court's duty under the supremacy clause to enforce federal law. The Eleventh Amendment, by its text, limits only "the Judicial power of the United States" and does not apply to suits brought in state court.

For the respondent, state of Maine:

- A basic right of the states is that they cannot be sued in their own courts without their consent. This right existed when the Constitution was ratified; it was made an explicit part of the Constitution when the Eleventh Amendment was adopted. It is as essential a component of state sovereignty today as it was two hundred years ago.

- Although the Eleventh Amendment specifically refers to the judicial power of the United States and so cannot resolve the federalism issues raised in this case, the Supreme Court has never interpreted the Eleventh Amendment by a mechanical, textual interpretation. Instead, the Court has indicated that the Eleventh Amendment memorializes a fundamental principle of federalism: state immunity from suit exists as an attribute of sovereignty independent of the Eleventh Amendment.

- The Civil War amendments represent the only exception to this principle.

 **JUSTICE KENNEDY DELIVERED THE OPINION OF THE COURT.**

In this case we must determine whether Congress has the power, under Article I, to subject nonconsenting States to private suits in their own courts. [T]he fact that the Eleventh Amendment by its terms limits only "[t]he Judicial power of the United States" does not resolve the question. . . .

In determining whether there is "compelling evidence" that this derogation of the States' sovereignty is "inherent in the constitutional compact," we [discuss] history, practice, . . . and the structure of the Constitution.

We look first to evidence of the original understanding of the Constitution. Petitioners contend that because the ratification debates and the events surrounding the adoption of the Eleventh Amendment focused on the States' immunity from suit in federal courts, the historical record gives no instruction as to the founding generation's intent to preserve the States' immunity from suit in their own courts.

We believe, however, that the founders' silence is best explained by the simple fact that no one, not even the Constitution's most ardent opponents, suggested the document might strip the States of the immunity. In light of the overriding concern regarding the States' war-time debts, together with the well known creativity, foresight, and vivid imagination of the Constitution's opponents, the silence is most instructive. It suggests the sovereign's right to assert immunity from suit in its own courts was a principle so well established that no one conceived it would be altered by the new Constitution. . . .

. . . The . . . furor raised by *Chisholm*, and the speed and unanimity with which the Amendment was adopted . . . underscore the jealous care with which the founding generation sought to preserve the sovereign immunity of the States. . . .

Our historical analysis is supported by early congressional practice. . . . Although early Congresses enacted various statutes authorizing federal suits in state court, we have discovered no instance in which they purported to authorize suits against nonconsenting States in these fora. . . .

Not only were statutes purporting to authorize private suits against nonconsenting States in state courts not enacted by early Congresses, statutes purporting to authorize such suits in any forum are all but absent from our historical experience. . . .

Our final consideration is whether a congressional power to subject nonconsenting States to private suits in their own courts is consistent with the structure of the Constitution. We look both to the essential principles of federalism and to the special role of the state courts in the constitutional design.

Although the Constitution grants broad powers to Congress, our federalism requires that Congress treat the States in a manner consistent with their status as residuary sovereigns and joint participants in the governance of the Nation. See, *e.g., United States v. Lopez* [1995]; *Printz* [*v. United States*, 1997]; *New York* [*v. United States*, 1992]. The founding generation thought it "neither becoming nor convenient that the several States of the Union, invested with that large residuum of sovereignty which had not been delegated to the United States, should be summoned as defendants to answer the complaints of private persons." The principle of sovereign immunity preserved by constitutional design "thus accords the States the respect owed them as members of the federation." Petitioners contend that immunity from suit in federal court suffices to preserve the dignity of the States. Private suits against nonconsenting States, however, present "the indignity of subjecting a State to the coercive process of judicial tribunals at the instance of private parties," regardless of the forum. Not only must a State defend or default but also it must face the prospect of being thrust, by federal fiat and against its will, into the disfavored status of a debtor, subject to the power of private citizens to levy on its treasury or perhaps even government buildings or property which the State administers on the public's behalf.

In some ways, of course, a congressional power to authorize private suits against nonconsenting States in their own courts would be even more offensive to state sovereignty than a power to authorize the suits in a federal forum. Although the immunity of one sovereign in the courts of another has often depended in part on comity or agreement, the immunity of a sovereign in its own courts has always been understood to be within the sole control of the sovereign itself. A power to press a State's own courts into federal service to coerce the other branches of the State, furthermore, is the power first to turn the State against itself and ultimately to commandeer the entire political machinery of the State against its will and at the behest of individuals. Such plenary federal control of state governmental processes denigrates the separate sovereignty of the States.

It is unquestioned that the Federal Government retains its own immunity from suit not only in state tribunals but also in its own courts. In light of our constitutional system recognizing the essential sovereignty of the States, we are reluctant to conclude that the States are not entitled to a reciprocal privilege.

Underlying constitutional form are considerations of great substance. Private suits against nonconsenting

States—especially suits for money damages—may threaten the financial integrity of the States. It is indisputable that, at the time of the founding, many of the States could have been forced into insolvency but for their immunity from private suits for money damages. Even today, an unlimited congressional power to authorize suits in state court to levy upon the treasuries of the States for compensatory damages, attorney's fees, and even punitive damages could create staggering burdens, giving Congress a power and a leverage over the States that is not contemplated by our constitutional design. The potential national power would pose a severe and notorious danger to the States and their resources. . . .

Congress cannot abrogate the States' sovereign immunity in federal court; were the rule to be different here, the National Government would wield greater power in the state courts than in its own judicial instrumentalities. . . .

The constitutional privilege of a State to assert its sovereign immunity in its own courts does not confer upon the State a concomitant right to disregard the Constitution or valid federal law. The States and their officers are bound by obligations imposed by the Constitution and by federal statutes that comport with the constitutional design. We are unwilling to assume the States will refuse to honor the Constitution or obey the binding laws of the United States. The good faith of the States thus provides an important assurance that "[t]his Constitution, and the Laws of the United States which shall be made in Pursuance thereof . . . shall be the supreme Law of the Land." U.S. Const., Art. VI.

Sovereign immunity, moreover, does not bar all judicial review of state compliance with the Constitution and valid federal law. Rather, certain limits are implicit in the constitutional principle of state sovereign immunity.

The first of these limits is that sovereign immunity bars suits only in the absence of consent. Many States, on their own initiative, have enacted statutes consenting to a wide variety of suits. The rigors of sovereign immunity are thus "mitigated by a sense of justice which has continually expanded by consent the suability of the sovereign." Nor, subject to constitutional limitations, does the Federal Government lack the authority or means to seek the States' voluntary consent to private suits.

The States have consented, moreover, to some suits pursuant to the plan of the Convention or to subsequent constitutional amendments. In ratifying the Constitution, the States consented to suits brought by other States or by the Federal Government. A suit which is commenced and prosecuted against a State in the name of the United States

by those who are entrusted with the constitutional duty to "take Care that the Laws be faithfully executed," U.S. Const., Art. II, §3, differs in kind from the suit of an individual: While the Constitution contemplates suits among the members of the federal system as an alternative to extralegal measures, the fear of private suits against nonconsenting States was the central reason given by the founders who chose to preserve the States' sovereign immunity. Suits brought by the United States itself require the exercise of political responsibility for each suit prosecuted against a State, a control which is absent from a broad delegation to private persons to sue nonconsenting States.

We have held also that in adopting the Fourteenth Amendment, the people required the States to surrender a portion of the sovereignty that had been preserved to them by the original Constitution, so that Congress may authorize private suits against nonconsenting States pursuant to its §5 enforcement power. By imposing explicit limits on the powers of the States and granting Congress the power to enforce them, the Amendment "fundamentally altered the balance of state and federal power struck by the Constitution." When Congress enacts appropriate legislation to enforce this Amendment, federal interests are paramount, and Congress may assert an authority over the States which would be otherwise unauthorized by the Constitution. *Fitzpatrick* [*v. Bitzer*, 1976]. . . .

The second important limit to the principle of sovereign immunity is that it bars suits against States but not lesser entities. The immunity does not extend to suits prosecuted against a municipal corporation or other governmental entity which is not an arm of the State. The principle of sovereign immunity as reflected in our jurisprudence strikes the proper balance between the supremacy of federal law and the separate sovereignty of the States. Established rules provide ample means to correct ongoing violations of law and to vindicate the interests which animate the Supremacy Clause. That we have, during the first 210 years of our constitutional history, found it unnecessary to decide the question presented here suggests a federal power to subject nonconsenting States to private suits in their own courts is unnecessary to uphold the Constitution and valid federal statutes as the supreme law.

The sole remaining question is whether Maine has waived its immunity. The State of Maine "regards the immunity from suit as 'one of the highest attributes inherent in the nature of sovereignty,'" and adheres to the general rule that "a specific authority conferred by an enactment of the legislature is requisite if the sovereign is to be taken as having shed the protective mantle of immunity." Petitioners have not attempted to establish a waiver of immunity under this standard. Although petitioners contend the State has discriminated against federal rights by claiming sovereign immunity from this FLSA suit, there is no evidence that the State has manipulated its immunity in a systematic fashion to discriminate against federal causes of action. To the extent Maine has chosen to consent to certain classes of suits while maintaining its immunity from others, it has done no more than exercise a privilege of sovereignty concomitant to its constitutional immunity from suit. The State, we conclude, has not consented to suit. . . .

. . . Although the Constitution begins with the principle that sovereignty rests with the people, it does not follow that the National Government becomes the ultimate, preferred mechanism for expressing the people's will. The States exist as a refutation of that concept. In choosing to ordain and establish the Constitution, the people insisted upon a federal structure for the very purpose of rejecting the idea that the will of the people in all instances is expressed by the central power, the one most remote from their control. The Framers of the Constitution did not share our dissenting colleagues' belief that the Congress may circumvent the federal design by regulating the States directly when it pleases to do so, including by a proxy in which individual citizens are authorized to levy upon the state treasuries absent the States' consent to jurisdiction. . . .

The judgment of the Supreme Judicial Court of Maine is

Affirmed.

JUSTICE SOUTER, with whom JUSTICE STEVENS, JUSTICE GINSBURG, and JUSTICE BREYER join, dissenting.

The National Constitution formally and finally repudiated the received political wisdom that a system of multiple sovereignties constituted the "great solecism of an imperium in imperio." Once "the atom of sovereignty" had been split, the general scheme of delegated sovereignty as between the two component governments of the federal system was clear, and was succinctly stated by Chief Justice Marshall: "In America, the powers of sovereignty are divided between the government of the Union, and those of the States. They are each sovereign, with respect to the objects committed to it, and neither sovereign with respect to the objects committed to the other." *McCulloch v. Maryland* (1819).

Hence the flaw in the Court's appeal to federalism. The State of Maine is not sovereign with respect to the national objective of the FLSA. It is not the authority that promulgated the FLSA, on which the right of action in this case depends. That authority is the United States acting through the Congress, whose legislative power under Article I of the Constitution to extend FLSA coverage to state employees has already been decided, see *Garcia v. San Antonio Metropolitan Transit Authority* (1985), and is not contested here. . . .

. . . [T]here is much irony in the Court's profession that it grounds its opinion on a deeply rooted historical tradition of sovereign immunity, when the Court abandons a principle nearly as inveterate, and much closer to the hearts of the Framers: that where there is a right, there must be a remedy. . . . The generation of the Framers thought the principle so crucial that several States put it into their constitutions. And when Chief Justice Marshall asked about Marbury, "If he has a right, and that right has been violated, do the laws of his country afford him a remedy?" *Marbury v. Madison* (1803), the question was rhetorical, and the answer clear:

"The very essence of civil liberty certainly consists in the right of every individual to claim the protection of the laws, whenever he receives an injury. One of the first duties of government is to afford that protection. In Great Britain the king himself is sued in the respectful form of a petition, and he never fails to comply with the judgment of his court."

Yet today the Court has no qualms about saying frankly that the federal right to damages afforded by Congress under the FLSA cannot create a concomitant private remedy. The right was "made for the benefit of" petitioners; they have been "hindered by another of that benefit"; but despite what has long been understood as the "necessary consequence of law," they have no action. It will not do for the Court to respond that a remedy was never available where the right in question was against the sovereign. A State is not the sovereign when a federal claim is pressed against it, and even the English sovereign opened itself to recovery and, unlike Maine, provided the remedy to complement the right. To the Americans of the founding generation it would have been clear (as it was to Chief Justice Marshall) that if the King would do right, the democratically chosen Government of the United States could do no less. The Chief Justice's contemporaries might well have reacted to the Court's decision today in the words spoken by Edmund Randolph when responding to the objection to jurisdiction in *Chisholm:* "[The framers] must have viewed human rights in their essence, not in their mere form."

The Court has swung back and forth with regrettable disruption on the enforceability of the FLSA against the

States, but if the present majority had a defensible position one could at least accept its decision with an expectation of stability ahead. As it is, any such expectation would be naive. The resemblance of today's state sovereign immunity to the *Lochner* era's industrial due process is striking. The Court began this century by imputing immutable constitutional status to a conception of economic self-reliance that was never true to industrial life and grew insistently fictional with the years, and the Court has chosen to close the century by conferring like status on a conception of state sovereign immunity that is true neither to history nor to the structure of the Constitution. I expect the Court's late essay into immunity doctrine will prove the equal of its earlier experiment in laissez-faire, the one being as unrealistic as the other, as indefensible, and probably as fleeting.

The Court's *Alden* decision rejected Congress's attempt to penetrate Maine's sovereign immunity shield by authorizing aggrieved parties to sue the state in state court. That left the probation workers in an impossible situation. Although federal law provided state government employees certain rights, the *Seminole Tribe* decision barred them from taking their claims to federal court, and in *Alden* the justices ruled that sovereign immunity prohibited them from suing the state in state court. This, the dissenters pointed out, created a legal wrong with no legal remedy.

The Court's ruling in *Alden* was a strong statement in favor of the protections provided state governments by sovereign immunity. The 5–4 vote in the case, however, indicated that the majority was somewhat fragile. In subsequent decisions the justices usually (but not always) remained reasonably loyal to the position articulated in *Alden*. In **Kimel v. Florida Board of Regents** (2000), for example, the *Alden* majority held that Congress could not make states liable for suits brought in federal court under the federal Age Discrimination in Employment Act. And in **Board of Trustees of the University of Alabama v. Garrett** (2001) the same five justices ruled that state employees cannot sue their employers in federal court for violations of the Americans with Disabilities Act of 1990.

Something of a break in this trend came from the Court in a 2003 statement on the Eleventh Amendment. In **Nevada Department of Human Resources v. Hibbs** the justices surprised observers when they held that states are not immune from suits brought in federal court by their employees under the federal Family and Medical Leave Act of 1993, which provides employees with up to twelve workweeks of unpaid leave annually in the event of the onset of a "serious health condition" in the employee's spouse and for other reasons. One purpose of the act, according to Congress, was "to minimize the potential for employment discrimination on the basis of sex by ensuring generally that leave is available on a gender-neutral basis and to promote the goal of equal employment opportunity for women and men." Congress believed the act was necessary because "due to the nature of the roles of men and women in our society, the primary responsibility for family caretaking often falls on women, and such responsibility affects the working lives of women more than it affects the working lives of men."

Chief Justice Rehnquist explained why the Court rejected the state's claim of immunity from suit in this case but not in *Kimel* and *Garrett*. Specifically, he noted that discrimination based on age and disability receives a lower level of scrutiny than do classifications based on gender, and this law—unlike those at issue in *Kimel* and *Garrett*—is aimed at minimizing gender discrimination. Rehnquist concluded, "The States' record of unconstitutional participation in, and fostering of, gender-based discrimination in the administration of leave benefits is weighty enough to justify the enactment of [the law]" under Congress's Fourteenth Amendment enforcement powers. This was not the case in *Garrett* and *Kimel*.

Given the care Rehnquist took to differentiate *Hibbs* from *Kimel* and other modern Eleventh Amendment rulings, it seemed likely that *Hibbs* represented an exception, not the start of a trend. This supposition received support in 2012 when the Court appeared to revert to its earlier positions. In *Coleman v. Court of Appeals of Maryland* the justices took up the issue of whether Congress properly abrogated a state's Eleventh Amendment sovereign immunity when it passed a section of the Family and Medical Leave Act of 1993. By a 5–4 vote the justices held that a man who was allegedly fired by the Maryland Court of Appeals after he requested sick leave under the self-care provisions of the act could not sue the state for damages in federal court. The evidence, Justice Kennedy wrote, failed to show a relevant pattern of state constitutional violations sufficient to justify Congress's authority to subject the state to federal lawsuit.

In the end, the centuries-old sovereign immunity doctrine provides federal and state governments considerable protection from citizen lawsuits. Unless it gives consent, the federal government cannot be sued in either federal or state court. State sovereign immunity, supplemented by the Eleventh Amendment, extends to state governments similar protections against private lawsuits. The sovereign immunity enjoyed by the states applies only to the state government itself and not to political subdivisions such as cities, counties, or school districts. Federal and state governments voluntarily have reduced the practical effects of sovereign immunity by passing legislation granting permission to be sued over a variety of litigation categories. The Federal Tort Claims Act, for example, permits citizens who have been wrongfully injured by persons acting on behalf of the United States government to sue for damages in federal court.

NEW JUDICIAL FEDERALISM

Federalism issues are not confined to conflicts over the actions of legislators and executives. Federal–state relations questions frequently arise in the judicial branch as well. Often this is due to legal conflicts that implicate both state and federal laws. For example, if a magazine seller is charged by state authorities of selling obscene materials in violation of state law, the accused may offer a defense that his actions are protected by the federal Constitution's First Amendment freedom of expression. As a consequence, various stages of the subsequent legal actions may occur in either federal or state court with the judges required to interpret or apply both state and federal laws. This gives rise to the potential for conflict between state and federal courts.

Such conflicts are limited by the principle of comity: the mutual respect that the two court systems owe to each. This principle requires federal judges to follow state interpretations of state law and to respect, but not necessarily defer to, state judges' interpretations of federal statutes and the Constitution. As Laurence H. Tribe explains, the principles of federalism require that federal courts further "the twin policies of preserving the integrity of state law and respecting the institutional autonomy of state judicial systems."[17]

Following that principle, the Court in *Murdock v. City of Memphis* (1875) said that it would not review state decisions unless the state court's interpretation implicated issues of federal law. This traditional view is called the "adequate and independent state grounds test": so long as a state court decision rests on adequate and independent state grounds, the Supreme Court will not resolve either the state or the federal issue in the case. Consequently, state courts are entitled to interpret their own statutes and constitutional provisions, and if their reasoning rests on adequate and independent state grounds, their decisions are not subject to review by federal courts.[18]

Until the 1970s the adequate and independent doctrine caused little concern among litigants and interest groups seeking expansive interpretations of constitutional rights. As we noted in chapter 1, in the 1950s and 1960s the U.S. Supreme Court, under the leadership of Earl Warren, was among the most liberal in modern American history. In decision after decision, it sought to protect the disadvantaged in society. During the heyday of that Court (1962–1968 terms), when the justices were ruling for disadvantaged societal interests in more than 75 percent of their cases, "the notion of a state court [being] more liberal than the Supreme Court was oxymoronic."[19]

This situation changed dramatically when President Richard Nixon had the opportunity to replace some of the most liberal members of the Warren Court. His choice of Warren Burger for chief justice was particularly effective: Earl Warren supported the claims of criminal defendants and other societal "underdogs" in more than three-quarters of the Court's cases, but his successor supported such claims only about 30 percent of the time.

It is not surprising that commentators perceived that the Burger Court had reduced protection of certain constitutional rights. Warren Court holdovers, particularly Justices Brennan and Marshall, shared

---

17. Laurence H. Tribe, *American Constitutional Law,* 2nd ed. (New York: Foundation Press, 1988), 196–197.

18. As Abrahamson and Gutman explain, the Court had two justifications for promulgating this doctrine: a respect for the independence of state judiciaries and a desire to avoid "issuing . . . opinions that discuss and answer legal questions unnecessary to the resolution of the case," otherwise known as advisory opinions. Shirley S. Abrahamson and Diane S. Gutman, "The New Judicial Federalism: State Constitutions and State Courts," *Judicature* 71 (1987), 88–99. See *Herb v. Pitcairn* (1945), in which the Court discusses its rationale for the "adequate and independent state grounds test."

19. Harold J. Spaeth, "Burger Court Review of State Court Civil Liberties Decisions," *Judicature* 68 (1985): 285.

this perception. They were disappointed with the Burger Court's drift toward conservatism. To offset it, they argued that states may permissibly invoke their own constitutional guarantees and laws to extend the protection of liberties and rights beyond the level provided by the federal Constitution as the Burger Court was interpreting it.[20] That Brennan and Marshall would offer this argument makes sense, given the existing state of doctrine governing the Court's responsibility to review state court decisions interpreting state statutory and constitutional provisions—the adequate and independent state grounds test.

In Brennan and Marshall's thinking, state court judges could use their constitutions and laws to reach liberal decisions—or, at least, decisions more liberal than those of the Burger Court—and, under the adequate and independent standard test, the Supreme Court would refrain from reviewing (overturning) them. By relying more on state courts than federal courts, litigants representing liberal civil liberties interests would also avoid having their cases heard by the lower federal courts, which were increasingly staffed by conservative Nixon appointees.

In order for Brennan and Marshall's suggestions to take hold, litigants would have to allege a violation of state law and initiate their claims in state court; state judges would need to rely on state law to reach their conclusions. The result would be an enhanced role for state courts in determining the rights of their citizens. This elevation in the importance of state courts was referred to as the "new judicial federalism."[21]

Just as Brennan and Marshall's arguments were beginning to gain some traction in the legal community,[22] their conservative colleagues stepped directly into the debate. As you read the excerpts from *Michigan v. Long* (1983), consider whether the Burger Court's approach to the adequate and independent grounds test contributed to new judicial federalism, as some scholars argue, or compromised it, as others assert.

---

20. See, for example, Brennan's dissent (joined by Marshall) in *Michigan v. Mosley* (1975).

21. Abrahamson and Gutman, "The New Judicial Federalism."

22. In an influential *Harvard Law Review* article, Brennan presented an extended version of his *Mosley* dissent directly to the legal community. See William J. Brennan Jr., "State Constitutions and the Protection of Individual Rights," *Harvard Law Review* 90 (1977): 489–504.

Michigan v. Long

463 U.S. 1032 (1983)
http://laws.findlaw.com/us/463/1032.html
Oral arguments are available at https://www.oyez.org.
Vote: 6 (Blackmun, Burger, O'Connor, Powell, Rehnquist, White)
   3 (Brennan, Marshall, Stevens)

OPINION OF THE COURT: *O'Connor*
CONCURRING OPINION: *Blackmun*
DISSENTING OPINIONS: *Brennan, Stevens*

FACTS:

Under the adequate and independent state grounds test, the Supreme Court refrains from reviewing state court interpretations of state constitutions and laws unless those decisions involve issues of federal law. This test is not as clear as it might seem because, occasionally, state court opinions rely on both federal and state law. So the question often emerges as to whether these kinds of "ambiguous" decisions do or do not rest on adequate and independent state grounds.

Addressing this question has proved to be a vexing task for the justices, and the results have been inconsistent. Prior to *Michigan v. Long,* the Court had used several methods of responding to appeals about which there was ambiguity as to whether the state court had decided the case on adequate and independent state grounds. These methods included dismissing the case, vacating the decision and sending it back to the state court for clarification of the grounds on which the decision rested, directing the litigant to obtain such clarification from the state, and making an independent determination whether the state court relied on federal or state laws/constitutions.

In *Long* the Supreme Court tried to clarify its approach to the adequate and independent state grounds test. The case involved the constitutionality of a police search of David Long's car, which resulted in the seizure of a substantial amount of marijuana. A lower state court found Long guilty of possessing controlled substances, but the Michigan Supreme Court reversed his conviction. The state high court held that the officers' search of the car violated both the Fourth Amendment of the U.S. Constitution and Article I, Section 11, of the Michigan Constitution. These two constitutional provisions share nearly identical language in describing search and seizure rights.

That the Michigan Supreme Court used the state constitution to reach a liberal decision—one that favored the criminally accused—was just the kind of action Brennan and Marshall had wanted, but the court's opinion contained a glitch. Because the Michigan Supreme Court rested its decision on both the federal and state constitutions, the ruling fell into the "ambiguous" zone: Did it rest on sufficiently independent and adequate state grounds so that the U.S. Supreme Court should refuse to examine it? Or was the invocation of the U.S. Constitution grounds enough for Supreme Court review? In what follows, we excerpt those parts of the opinions that deal with these questions.

ARGUMENTS:

For the petitioner, state of Michigan:

- The Michigan Supreme Court made a reference to Article I, Section 11, of the Michigan Constitution, but the decision was made on the basis of the Fourth Amendment of the U.S. Constitution. The court discussed only federal cases dealing with the Fourth Amendment.
- If the Michigan Supreme Court had applied Michigan law, it would allow the search at issue here. Michigan case law on the reasonableness of searches bears a strong relationship to the Fourth Amendment.

For the respondent, David Long:

- The Court lacks jurisdiction to hear this case. The decision of the Michigan Supreme Court rests on adequate state law ground. The state courts in Michigan have consistently imposed a higher standard under the state constitutional provisions relating to search and seizure than the U.S. Supreme Court has adopted under the Fourth Amendment.
- At minimum the question of whether the state court rested its decision on state or federal law is uncertain enough that the Court should remand the case for clarification.

JUSTICE O'CONNOR DELIVERED THE OPINION OF THE COURT.

In *Terry v. Ohio* (1968), we upheld the validity of a protective search for weapons in the absence of probable cause to arrest because it is unreasonable to deny a police officer the right "to neutralize the threat of physical harm," when he possesses an articulable suspicion that an individual is armed and dangerous. We did not, however, expressly address whether such a protective search for weapons could extend to an area beyond the person in the absence of probable cause to arrest. In the present case, respondent

David Long was convicted for possession of marihuana found by police in the passenger compartment and trunk of the automobile that he was driving. The police searched the passenger compartment because they had reason to believe that the vehicle contained weapons potentially dangerous to the officers. We hold that the protective search of the passenger compartment was reasonable under the principles articulated in *Terry* and other decisions of this Court. We also examine Long's argument that the decision below rests upon an adequate and independent state ground, and we decide in favor of our jurisdiction. . . .

. . . [W]e must consider Long's argument that we are without jurisdiction to decide this case because the decision below rests on an adequate and independent state ground. The court below referred twice to the State Constitution in its opinion, but otherwise relied exclusively on federal law. Long argues that the Michigan courts have provided greater protection from searches and seizures under the State Constitution than is afforded under the Fourth Amendment, and the references to the State Constitution therefore establish an adequate and independent ground for the decision below.

It is, of course, "incumbent upon this Court . . . to ascertain for itself . . . whether the asserted non-federal ground independently and adequately supports the judgment." Although we have announced a number of principles in order to help us determine whether various forms of references to state law constitute adequate and independent state grounds, we openly admit that we have thus far not developed a satisfying and consistent approach for resolving this vexing issue. . . . In some instances, we have taken the strict view that if the ground of decision was at all unclear, we would dismiss the case. In other instances, we have vacated, or continued a case in order to obtain clarification about the nature of a state court decision. In more recent cases, we have ourselves examined state law to determine whether state courts have used federal law to guide their application of state law or to provide the actual basis for the decision that was reached. . . .

This *ad hoc* method of dealing with cases that involve possible adequate and independent state grounds is antithetical to the doctrinal consistency that is required when sensitive issues of federal-state relations are involved. Moreover, none of the various methods of disposition that we have employed thus far recommends itself as the preferred method that we should apply to the exclusion of others, and we therefore determine that it is appropriate to reexamine our treatment of this jurisdictional issue in order to achieve the consistency that is necessary. . . .

Respect for the independence of state courts, as well as avoidance of rendering advisory opinions, have been the cornerstones of this Court's refusal to decide cases where there is an adequate and independent state ground. It is precisely because of this respect for state courts, and this desire to avoid advisory opinions, that we do not wish to continue to decide issues of state law that go beyond the opinion that we review, or to require state courts to reconsider cases to clarify the grounds of their decisions. Accordingly, when, as in this case, a state court decision fairly appears to rest primarily on federal law, or to be interwoven with the federal law, and when the adequacy and independence of any possible state law ground is not clear from the face of the opinion, we will accept as the most reasonable explanation that the state court decided the case the way it did because it believed that federal law required it to do so. If a state court chooses merely to rely on federal precedents as it would on the precedents of all other jurisdictions, then it need only make clear by a plain statement in its judgment or opinion that the federal cases are being used only for the purpose of guidance, and do not themselves compel the result that the court has reached. In this way, both justice and judicial administration will be greatly improved. If the state court decision indicates clearly and expressly that it is alternatively based on bona fide separate, adequate, and independent grounds, we, of course, will not undertake to review the decision.

This approach obviates in most instances the need to examine state law in order to decide the nature of the state court decision, and will at the same time avoid the danger of our rendering advisory opinions. It also avoids the unsatisfactory and intrusive practice of requiring state courts to clarify their decisions to the satisfaction of this Court. We believe that such an approach will provide state judges with a clearer opportunity to develop state jurisprudence unimpeded by federal interference, and yet will preserve the integrity of federal law. . . .

Our review of the decision below under this framework leaves us unconvinced that it rests upon an independent state ground. Apart from its two citations to the State Constitution, the court below relied *exclusively* on its understanding of *Terry* and other federal cases. Not a single state case was cited to support the state court's holding that the search of the passenger compartment was unconstitutional. Indeed, the court declared that the search in this case was unconstitutional because "[the] Court of Appeals erroneously applied the principles of *Terry v. Ohio* . . . to the search of the interior of the vehicle in this case." The references to the State Constitution

in no way indicate that the decision below rested on grounds in any way *independent* from the state court's interpretation of federal law. Even if we accept that the Michigan Constitution has been interpreted to provide independent protection for certain rights also secured under the Fourth Amendment, it fairly appears in this case that the Michigan Supreme Court rested its decision primarily on federal law.

Rather than dismissing the case, or requiring that the state court reconsider its decision on our behalf solely because of a mere possibility that an adequate and independent ground supports the judgment, we find that we have jurisdiction in the absence of a plain statement that the decision below rested on an adequate and independent state ground. It appears to us that the state court "felt compelled by what it understood to be federal constitutional considerations to construe . . . its own law in the manner it did." . . .

The judgment of the Michigan Supreme Court is reversed and the case is remanded for further proceedings not inconsistent with this opinion.

It is so ordered.

JUSTICE STEVENS, dissenting.

The jurisprudential questions presented in this case are far more important than the question whether the Michigan police officer's search of respondent's car violated the Fourth Amendment. The case raises profoundly significant questions concerning the relationship between two sovereigns—the State of Michigan and the United States of America.

The Supreme Court of the State of Michigan expressly held "that the deputies' search of the vehicle was proscribed by the Fourth Amendment to the United States Constitution and *art 1, §11 of the Michigan Constitution*" [emphasis added]. The state law ground is clearly adequate to support the judgment, but the question whether it is independent of the Michigan Supreme Court's understanding of federal law is more difficult. Four possible ways of resolving that question present themselves: (1) asking the Michigan Supreme Court directly, (2) attempting to infer from all possible sources of state law what the Michigan Supreme Court meant, (3) presuming that adequate state grounds are independent unless it clearly appears otherwise, or (4) presuming that adequate state grounds are not independent unless it clearly appears otherwise. This Court has, on different occasions, employed each of the first three approaches; never until today has it even hinted at the fourth. In order to "achieve the consistency that is necessary," the Court today undertakes a reexamination of all the possibilities. It rejects the first approach as inefficient and unduly burdensome for state courts, and rejects the second approach as an inappropriate expenditure of our resources. Although I find both of those decisions defensible in themselves, I cannot accept the Court's decision to choose the fourth approach over the third—to presume that adequate state grounds are intended to be dependent on federal law unless the record plainly shows otherwise. I must therefore dissent.

If we reject the intermediate approaches, we are left with a choice between two presumptions: one in favor of our taking jurisdiction, and one against it. Historically, the latter presumption has always prevailed. . . . The Court today points out that in several cases we have weakened the traditional presumption by using the other two intermediate approaches identified above. Since those two approaches are now to be rejected, however, I would think that *stare decisis* would call for a return to historical principle. Instead, the Court seems to conclude that because some precedents are to be rejected, we must overrule them all.

Even if I agreed with the Court that we are free to consider as a fresh proposition whether we may take presumptive jurisdiction over the decisions of sovereign States, I could not agree that an expansive attitude makes good sense. It appears to be common ground that any rule we adopt should show "respect for state courts, and [a] desire to avoid advisory opinions." And I am confident that all Members of this Court agree that there is a vital interest in the sound management of scarce federal judicial resources. All of those policies counsel against the exercise of federal jurisdiction. They are fortified by my belief that a policy of judicial restraint—one that allows other decisional bodies to have the last word in legal interpretation until it is truly necessary for this Court to intervene—enables this Court to make its most effective contribution to our federal system of government. . . .

The Court offers only one reason for asserting authority over cases such as the one presented today: "an important need for uniformity in federal law [that] goes unsatisfied when we fail to review an opinion that rests primarily upon federal grounds and where the independence of an alleged state ground is not apparent from the four corners of the opinion." Of course, the supposed need to "review an opinion" clashes directly with our oft-repeated reminder that "our power is to correct wrong judgments, not to revise

opinions." The clash is not merely one of form: the "need for uniformity in federal law" is truly an ungovernable engine. That same need is no less present when it is perfectly clear that a state ground is both independent and adequate. In fact, it is equally present if a state prosecutor announces that he believes a certain policy of nonenforcement is commanded by federal law. Yet we have never claimed jurisdiction to correct such errors, no matter how egregious they may be, and no matter how much they may thwart the desires of the state electorate. We do not sit to expound our understanding of the Constitution to interested listeners in the legal community; we sit to resolve disputes. If it is not apparent that our views would affect the outcome of a particular case, we cannot presume to interfere.

Finally, I am thoroughly baffled by the Court's suggestion that it must stretch its jurisdiction and reverse the judgment of the Michigan Supreme Court in order to show "[respect] for the independence of state courts." . . .

I respectfully dissent.

Writing for the Court in *Long,* Justice O'Connor—a former state court judge—offered a new approach for applying the adequate and independent state grounds standard to ambiguous state court decisions. In such cases the Supreme Court would now presume that the state decision rested on federal grounds.[23] Should state judges desire to avoid this presumption, O'Connor wrote, they "need only make clear by a plain statement in [their] judgment that the federal cases are being used only for the purpose of guidance, and do not themselves compel the result the court has reached." For if they indicate "clearly and expressly" that their decisions are "based on bona fide separate, adequate, and independent state grounds," then the Court will "not undertake to review the decision."

Naturally, the majority justified this new approach to the adequate and independent state grounds test as a reasonable way to resolve the "vexing issue" of ambiguous state decisions. Even Justice Stevens, in his dissent, did not take issue with the notion that a clear approach to this area of the law was needed. He simply disliked the one O'Connor fashioned, as did many other commentators, who asserted that the majority's solution was ideologically grounded, designed to provide the conservative justices with a way to oppose the liberal state

---

23. Abrahamson and Gutman, "The New Judicial Federalism," 97.

courts' new course. The decision in *Long* shores up this point: by invoking this new approach—the presumption that a state court decision rested on federal grounds—to the independent and adequate state grounds standard, the Court was able to review and overturn a liberal (here, pro-defendant) state court decision.

Although this new test allowed the Supreme Court to uphold Long's conviction, it also gave a large assist to new judicial federalism. O'Connor's opinion essentially provided state judges specific instructions on how to avoid Supreme Court review. The Supreme Court would not accept for review a lower court decision that included a clear statement that the ruling was based on state law alone. If federal precedents were cited, the court would have to make clear that such decisions were used for guidance only and were not relied on for the court's final conclusions.

Under the Court's new approach, the *Long* outcome could have been much different. Long claimed that the search of his automobile violated both federal and state constitutions. The state supreme court could have ruled in Long's favor by finding a violation of state search and seizure provisions alone. Doing so would have removed the need for the state court even to address the federal constitutional claim. An explicit statement to that effect would have satisfied the Supreme Court's new independent and adequate grounds test and precluded federal court review of the decision.

Are state courts taking advantage of this opportunity? There are certainly examples that they have. Take, for instance, the Massachusetts Supreme Judicial Court's decision in *Goodridge v. Department of Public Health* (2003). In that case fourteen individuals filed legal action against the state claiming that the Massachusetts prohibition against same-sex marriage violated their rights. The state trial court ruled against them, but on appeal the state supreme court reversed. The decision was based on the court's conclusion that the Massachusetts marriage laws deprived the plaintiffs of their rights to due process of law and equal treatment under the law as guaranteed by the Massachusetts state constitution. By relying on the Massachusetts constitution alone, the court removed the possibility of the state appealing the decision to the U.S. Supreme Court where a very different outcome would have been possible. As a result, same-sex marriages became a legal reality in Massachusetts a dozen years before the U.S. Supreme Court reached the same conclusion in *Obergefell v. Hodges* (2015).

NATIONAL PREEMPTION OF STATE LAWS

One of the more important recurring issues of federalism arises when both state and federal governments lay claim to regulation of the same activity. The supremacy clause seems to offer an easy answer to such conflicts: if Congress passes legislation with the intent of occupying a certain issue area and precluding state involvement in that area, then any state legislation that "stands as an obstacle" must fall. The federal statute preempts state involvement, even if Congress and the states exercise concurrent authority over the subject in question. The problem is that federal laws usually do not specify whether Congress intended to preclude state action. When disputes arise over this ambiguity, the judiciary is often called on to determine whether Congress desires to exercise exclusive or concurrent jurisdiction.

For certain subjects, the Supreme Court has found the task easy. There is little question, in the Court's view, that when Congress acts in the area of foreign affairs, it does so exclusively even if its actions touch on areas over which states have some authority. The Court made this point quite clear in *State of Missouri v. Holland*. In this case, the federal government entered into a treaty with Great Britain, but a direct conflict between state and federal laws arose when Congress passed legislation to implement the provisions of that treaty.

State of Missouri v. Holland

252 U.S. 416 (1920)
http://laws.findlaw.com/us/252/416.html
Vote: 7 (Brandeis, Clark, Day, Holmes, McKenna, McReynolds, White)
    2 (Pitney, Van Devanter)
OPINION OF THE COURT: *Holmes*

FACTS:

In 1913 Congress enacted legislation to protect certain species of migratory birds in danger of extinction, but the act was struck down as an unconstitutional use of the power to regulate interstate commerce. Three years later, the United States and Great Britain entered into a treaty that addressed a similar concern. The treaty noted that many species of migratory birds "traversed certain parts of the United States and of Canada, that they were of great value as a source of food and in destroying insects injurious to vegetation, but were in danger of extermination through lack of adequate protection." Britain and the United States agreed that their "law-making bodies" should take steps to prevent the extinction of these birds. To give effect to this agreement, Congress in 1918 enacted another law, the Migratory Bird Treaty Act, which prohibited anyone from "killing, capturing, or selling" any species of birds cited in the treaty.

Missouri challenged the act, bringing suit against a U.S. game warden, Ray P. Holland, to prevent him from enforcing it. The state argued that the law infringed on states' rights regardless of whether it was based in congressional commerce power or in treaty-making authority.

ARGUMENTS:

For the appellant, the state of Missouri:

- Under the ancient law, feudal law, and the common law in England, the absolute control of wild game was a part of sovereignty. When the American colonies became "free and independent states," the power to control the taking of wild game passed to the states.
- The 1918 act is the same as the 1913 law that the lower courts struck down. Congress was merely using its treaty power as a vehicle to interfere with rights reserved to the states under the Tenth Amendment.
- If Congress can use treaties to take over powers reserved to the state, the president and Senate could control the laws of a state relating to health and internal trade; prescribe law regarding elections; force the introduction and sale of alcohol and drugs, however injurious to the health and well-being of a state; cede to a foreign power a state; and destroy the securities of liberty and property as effectually as the most tyrannical government ever formed.

For the appellee, Ray P. Holland, U.S. game warden:

- Aside from the treaty, a migratory bird law falls under the government's power to regulate commerce between the states.
- The Constitution expressly gives Congress the power to enact laws as may be necessary to give effect to treaties.
- The power of Congress to legislate to make treaties effective is not limited to the subjects over which it has power in purely domestic affairs. The situations are different. In the domestic sphere, Americans are citizens with dual sovereignties, each supreme within its own sphere. But in foreign relations, Americans are part of one government, which is invested with the powers that belong to independent nations.

MR. JUSTICE HOLMES DELIVERED THE OPINION OF THE COURT.

[T]he question raised is the general one whether the treaty and statute are void as an interference with the rights reserved to the states.

To answer this question it is not enough to refer to the 10th Amendment, reserving the powers not delegated to the United States, because by article 2, §2, the power to make treaties is delegated expressly, and by article 6, treaties made under the authority of the United States, along with the Constitution and laws of the United States, made in pursuance thereof, are declared the supreme law of the land. If the treaty is valid, there can be no dispute about the validity of the statute under article 1, §8, as a necessary and proper means to execute the powers of the government. The language of the Constitution as to the supremacy of treaties being general, the question before us is narrowed to an inquiry into the ground upon which the present supposed exception is placed.

It is said that a treaty cannot be valid if it infringes the Constitution; that there are limits, therefore, to the treaty-making power; and that one such limit is that what an act of Congress could not do unaided, in derogation of the powers reserved to the states, a treaty cannot do. An earlier act of Congress that attempted by itself, and not in pursuance of a treaty, to regulate the killing of migratory birds within the states, had been held bad in the district court. *United States v. Shauver; United States v. McCullagh.* Those decisions were supported by arguments that migratory birds were owned by the states in their sovereign capacity, for the benefit of their people, and that . . . this control was one that Congress had no power to displace. The same argument is supposed to apply now with equal force.

Whether the two cases cited were decided rightly or not, they cannot be accepted as a test of the treaty power. Acts of Congress are the supreme law of the land only when made in pursuance of the Constitution, while treaties are declared to be so when made under the authority of the United States. It is open to question whether the authority of the United States means more than the formal acts prescribed to make the convention. We do not mean to imply that there are no qualifications to the treaty-making power; but they must be ascertained in a different way. It is obvious that there may be matters of the sharpest exigency for the national well-being that an act of Congress could not deal with, but that a treaty followed by such an act could, and it is not lightly to be assumed that, in matters requiring national action, "a power which must belong to and somewhere reside in every civilized government" is not to be found. *Andrews v. Andrews* (1903). What was said in that case with regard to the powers of the states applies with equal force to the powers of the nation in cases where the states individually are incompetent to act. We are not yet discussing the particular case before us, but only are considering the validity of the test proposed. With regard to that, we may add that when we are dealing with words that also are a constituent act, like the Constitution of the United States, we must realize that they have called into life a being the development of which could not have been foreseen completely by the most gifted of its begetters. It was enough for them to realize or to hope that they had created an organism; it has taken a century and has cost their successors much sweat and blood to prove that they created a nation. The case before us must be considered in the light of our whole experience, and not merely in that of what was said a hundred years ago. The treaty in question does not contravene any prohibitory words to be found in the Constitution. The only question is whether it is forbidden by some invisible radiation from the general terms of the 10th Amendment. We must consider what this country has become in deciding what that amendment has reserved.

The state, as we have intimated, founds its claim of exclusive authority upon an assertion of title to migratory birds,—an assertion that is embodied in statute. No doubt it is true that, as between a state and its inhabitants, the state may regulate the killing and sale of such birds, but it does not follow that its authority is exclusive of paramount powers. To put the claim of the state upon title is to lean upon a slender reed. Wild birds are not in the possession of anyone; and possession is the beginning of ownership. The whole foundation of the state's rights is the presence within their jurisdiction of birds that yesterday had not arrived, tomorrow may be in another state, and in a week a thousand miles away. If we are to be accurate, we cannot put the case of the state upon higher ground than that the treaty deals with creatures that for the moment are within the state borders, that it must be carried out by officers of the United States within the same territory, and that, but

for the treaty, the state would be free to regulate this subject itself.

As most of the laws of the United States are carried out within the states, and as many of them deal with matters which, in the silence of such laws, the state might regulate, such general grounds are not enough to support Missouri's claim. Valid treaties, of course, "are as binding within the territorial limits of the states as they are effective throughout the dominion of the United States." No doubt the great body of private relations usually falls within the control of the state, but a treaty may override its power. . . .

Here a national interest of very nearly the first magnitude is involved. It can be protected only by national action in concert with that of another power. The subject-matter is only transitorily within the state, and has no permanent habitat therein. But for the treaty and the statute, there soon might be no birds for any powers to deal with. We see nothing in the Constitution that compels the government to sit by while a food supply is cut off and the protectors of our forests and of our crops are destroyed. It is not sufficient to rely upon the states. The reliance is vain, and were it otherwise, the question is whether the United States is forbidden to act. We are of opinion that the treaty and statute must be upheld.

Decree affirmed.

Justice Holmes's opinion was narrowly drawn; he focused on the matter at hand. Even so, his message was clear: when Congress acts in the area of foreign affairs, it does so exclusively even if its actions touch on areas over which states have some authority. Eight decades later the Rehnquist Court reiterated this basic message in a case dealing with trade with Burma. Unlike *Missouri v. Holland,* however, this case involves state and federal policies that shared the same basic objective: to apply economic sanctions on a nation that repressed the democratic rights of its people.

Crosby v. National Foreign Trade Council

530 U.S. 363 (2000)
http://laws.findlaw.com/us/530/363.html
Oral arguments are available at https://www.oyez.org.
Vote: 9 (Breyer, Ginsburg, Kennedy, O'Connor, Rehnquist, Scalia, Souter, Stevens, Thomas)
0

OPINION OF THE COURT: *Souter*
OPINION CONCURRING IN JUDGMENT: *Scalia*

FACTS:

In June 1996 Massachusetts passed a law barring state entities from buying goods or services from companies doing business with Burma.[24] The law defines "doing business with Burma" to cover any person (including a business)

(a)   Having a principal place of business in Burma;

(b)   Providing financial services to the government of Burma;

(c)   Promoting the importation or sale from Burma of gems, timber, oil, gas, or other related products, commerce in which is largely controlled by the government of Burma; or

(d)   Providing any goods or services to the government of Burma.

In September, three months after the Massachusetts law was enacted, Congress passed a statute imposing a set of mandatory and conditional sanctions on Burma. The federal act has five basic parts, three of which are substantive and two procedural. First, it imposes three sanctions directly on Burma. It bans all aid to the Burmese government except for humanitarian assistance, counternarcotics efforts, and promotion of human rights and democracy. These restrictions are to remain in effect "until such time as the President determines and certifies to Congress that Burma has made measurable and substantial progress in improving human rights practices and implementing democratic government." Second, the federal act authorizes the president to impose further sanctions subject to certain conditions. He may prohibit "United States persons" from "new investment" in Burma, and shall do so if he determines and certifies to Congress that the Burmese government has physically harmed, rearrested, or exiled Daw Aung San Suu Kyi (the Burmese opposition leader who was awarded the Nobel Peace Prize in 1991) or has committed "large-scale repression of or violence against

the Democratic opposition." Third, the statute directs the president to work to develop "a comprehensive, multilateral strategy to bring democracy to and improve human rights practices and the quality of life in Burma."

In the procedural provisions of the federal statute, the fourth section requires the president to report periodically to certain congressional committee chairs on the progress toward democratization and better living conditions in Burma as well as on the development of the required strategy. The fifth part of the federal act authorizes the president "to waive, temporarily

Three Burmese monks stand in front of the U.S. Supreme Court on March 22, 2000, to demonstrate their support for Massachusetts's "selective purchasing" law. The law, which condemns Burma's human rights record and all but prohibits state government purchases from companies operating there, was overturned by the Court in 2000.

Tim Sloan/AFP/Getty Images

---

24. The state law refers to Burma or Myanmar. The military regime that runs the Union of Burma changed the name of the country to Myanmar, but the democratically elected opposition continues to call the country Burma. According to the U.S. State Department, "Out of support for the democratically elected leaders, the U.S. Government likewise uses Burma."

or permanently, any sanction [under the federal act] . . . if he determines and certifies to Congress that the application of such sanction would be contrary to the national security interests of the United States."

On May 20, 1997, President Clinton issued Executive Order 13047, in which he certified that the government of Burma had "committed large-scale repression of the democratic opposition in Burma" and found that the Burmese government's actions and policies constituted "an unusual and extraordinary threat to the national security and foreign policy of the United States," a threat characterized as a national emergency. The president then prohibited new investment in Burma "by United States persons," any approval or facilitation by a United States person of such new investment by foreign persons, and any transaction meant to evade or avoid the ban. Subsequently, Congress imposed mandatory and conditional sanctions on Burma.

Because several members of the National Foreign Trade Council, a nonprofit corporation representing companies engaged in foreign commerce, were affected by the state act, the council brought a federal suit against Massachusetts. The district court held that the state law "unconstitutionally impinged on the federal government's exclusive authority to regulate foreign affairs," and the First Circuit Court of Appeals affirmed. When the Supreme Court heard this case on appeal, the United States government participated as amicus curiae urging the justices to strike down the Massachusetts law.

ARGUMENTS:

For the petitioner, Stephen Crosby, Massachusetts secretary of administration and finance:

- For more than two hundred years, Massachusetts and other states have used boycotts to support the "natural, essential, and unalienable rights" of people around the world. The Massachusetts law is similar to the many divestment and selective purchasing laws enacted by state and local governments in the 1980s concerning South Africa.
- Nothing in the U.S. Constitution denies states the right to apply a moral standard to their spending decisions or requires states to trade with dictators.
- The federal law does not preempt; rather, it implicitly permits state selective purchasing laws regarding Burma. The Court should presume that the state law is valid given the historical importance of the ability of states to make their own spending decisions. Simply because a federal law

in the foreign affairs realm is at issue does not change the presumption.

For the respondent, National Foreign Trade Council:

- For more than two hundred years, the federal government has employed sanctions against merchants as part of its foreign policy strategy. These sanctions express disapproval of other nations and their policies and use economic leverage as a means of bringing about change in their conduct.
- The framers wanted to ensure that the Constitution reserves such foreign policy decisions exclusively to the federal government, and this Court has agreed. To allow the state action here would be to undermine national foreign policy and put Americans at risk.
- The law violates the commerce clause by discriminating against companies engaged in commerce with Burma. There is no question that the state law conflicts with the federal law imposing sanctions on Burma. The state disrupts the careful balance created by federal policy.

JUSTICE SOUTER DELIVERED THE OPINION OF THE COURT.

The issue is whether the Burma law of the Commonwealth of Massachusetts, restricting the authority of its agencies to purchase goods or services from companies doing business with Burma, is invalid under the Supremacy Clause of the National Constitution owing to its threat of frustrating federal statutory objectives. We hold that it is. . . .

A fundamental principle of the Constitution is that Congress has the power to preempt state law. Art. VI, cl. 2. Even without an express provision for preemption, we have found that state law must yield to a congressional Act in at least two circumstances. When Congress intends federal law to "occupy the field," state law in that area is preempted. And even if Congress has not occupied the field, state law is naturally preempted to the extent of any conflict with a federal statute. We will find preemption where it is impossible for a private party to comply with both state and federal law and where "under the circumstances of [a] particular case, [the challenged state law] stands as an obstacle to the accomplishment and execution of the full purposes and objectives of Congress." What is a sufficient obstacle is a matter of judgment, to be informed by examining the federal statute as a whole and identifying its purpose and intended effects:

"For when the question is whether a Federal act overrides a state law, the entire scheme of the statute must of course be considered and that which needs must be implied is of no less force than that which is expressed. If the purpose of the act cannot otherwise be accomplished—if its operation within its chosen field else must be frustrated and its provisions be refused their natural effect—the state law must yield to the regulation of Congress within the sphere of its delegated power." [*Savage v. Jones*, 1912]

Applying this standard, we see the state Burma law as an obstacle to the accomplishment of Congress's full objectives under the federal Act. We find that the state law undermines the intended purpose and "natural effect" of at least three provisions of the federal Act, that is, its delegation of effective discretion to the President to control economic sanctions against Burma, its limitation of sanctions solely to United States persons and new investment, and its directive to the President to proceed diplomatically in developing a comprehensive, multilateral strategy towards Burma.

First, Congress clearly intended the federal act to provide the President with flexible and effective authority over economic sanctions against Burma. Although Congress immediately put in place a set of initial sanctions, it authorized the President to terminate any and all of those measures upon determining and certifying that there had been progress in human rights and democracy in Burma. It invested the President with the further power to ban new investment by United States persons, dependent only on specific Presidential findings of repression in Burma. And, most significantly, Congress empowered the President "to waive, temporarily or permanently, any sanction [under the federal act] . . . if he determines and certifies to Congress that the application of such sanction would be contrary to the national security interests of the United States."

This express investiture of the President with statutory authority to act for the United States in imposing sanctions with respect to the government of Burma, augmented by the flexibility* to respond to change by suspending sanctions in the interest of national security,

recalls Justice Jackson's observation in *Youngstown Sheet & Tube Co. v. Sawyer* (1952): "When the President acts pursuant to an express or implied authorization of Congress, his authority is at its maximum, for it includes all that he possesses in his own right plus all that Congress can delegate." Within the sphere defined by Congress, then, the statute has placed the President in a position with as much discretion to exercise economic leverage against Burma, with an eye toward national security, as our law will admit. And it is just this plenitude of Executive authority that we think controls the issue of preemption here. The President has been given this authority not merely to make a political statement but to achieve a political result, and the fullness of his authority shows the importance in the congressional mind of reaching that result. It is simply implausible that Congress would have gone to such lengths to empower the President if it had been willing to compromise his effectiveness by deference to every provision of state statute or local ordinance that might, if enforced, blunt the consequences of discretionary Presidential action.

And that is just what the Massachusetts Burma law would do in imposing a different, state system of economic pressure against the Burmese political regime. . . . [T]he state statute penalizes some private action that the federal Act (as administered by the President) may allow, and pulls levers of influence that the federal Act does not reach. But the point here is that the state sanctions are immediate. This unyielding application undermines the President's intended statutory authority by making it impossible for him to restrain fully the coercive power of the national economy when he may choose to take the discretionary action open to him, whether he believes that the national interest requires sanctions to be lifted, or believes that the promise of lifting sanctions would move the Burmese regime in the democratic direction. Quite simply, if the Massachusetts law is enforceable the President has less to offer and less economic and diplomatic leverage as

---

*Statements by the sponsors of the federal Act underscore the statute's clarity in providing the President with flexibility in implementing its Burma sanctions policy. See statement of principal sponsor Sen. Cohen, emphasizing importance of providing "the administration flexibility in reacting to changes, both positive and negative, with respect to the behavior of the [Burmese regime]"; statement of cosponsor Sen. McCain, describing the federal act as "giv[ing] the President, who, whether Democrat or Republican, is

charged with conducting our Nation's foreign policy, some flexibility." . . . These sponsors chose a pliant policy with the explicit support of the Executive. See, letter from Barbara Larkin, Assistant Secretary, Legislative Affairs, U.S. Department of State to Sen. Cohen: "We believe the current and conditional sanctions which your language proposes are consistent with Administration policy. As we have stated on several occasions in the past, we need to maintain our flexibility to respond to events in Burma and to consult with Congress on appropriate responses to ongoing and future development there."

a consequence. In *Dames & Moore v. Regan* (1981), we used the metaphor of the bargaining chip to describe the President's control of funds valuable to a hostile country; here, the state Act reduces the value of the chips created by the federal statute. It thus "stands as an obstacle to the accomplishment and execution of the full purposes and objectives of Congress."

Congress manifestly intended to limit economic pressure against the Burmese Government to a specific range. The federal Act confines its reach to United States persons, imposes limited immediate sanctions, places only a conditional ban on a carefully defined area of "new investment," and pointedly exempts contracts to sell or purchase goods, services, or technology. These detailed provisions show that Congress's calibrated Burma policy is a deliberate effort "to steer a middle path."

The State has set a different course, and its statute conflicts with federal law at a number of points by penalizing individuals and conduct that Congress has explicitly exempted or excluded from sanctions. While the state Act differs from the federal in relying entirely on indirect economic leverage through third parties with Burmese connections, it otherwise stands in clear contrast to the congressional scheme in the scope of subject matter addressed. It restricts all contracts between the State and companies doing business in Burma. . . . It is specific in targeting contracts to provide financial services, and general goods and services, to the Government of Burma, and thus prohibits contracts between the State and United States persons for goods, services, or technology, even though those transactions are explicitly exempted from the ambit of new investment prohibition when the President exercises his discretionary authority to impose sanctions under the federal Act. . . .

. . . [T]he state Act is at odds with the President's intended authority to speak for the United States among the world's nations in developing a "comprehensive, multilateral strategy to bring democracy to and improve human rights practices and the quality of life in Burma." Congress called for Presidential cooperation with . . . other countries in developing such a strategy, directed the President to encourage a dialogue between the government of Burma and the democratic opposition, and required him to report to the Congress on the progress of his diplomatic efforts. As with Congress's explicit delegation to the President of power over economic sanctions, Congress's express command to the President to take the initiative for the United States among the international community

invested him with the maximum authority of the National Government, cf. *Youngstown Sheet & Tube Co.* in harmony with the President's own constitutional powers, U.S. Const., Art. II, §2, cl. 2 ("[The President] shall have Power, by and with the Advice and Consent of the Senate, to make Treaties" and "shall appoint Ambassadors, other public Ministers and Consuls"); §3 ("[The President] shall receive Ambassadors and other public Ministers"). This clear mandate and invocation of exclusively national power belies any suggestion that Congress intended the President's effective voice to be obscured by state or local action.

Again, the state Act undermines the President's capacity, in this instance for effective diplomacy. It is not merely that the differences between the state and federal Acts in scope and type of sanctions threaten to complicate discussions; they compromise the very capacity of the President to speak for the Nation with one voice in dealing with other governments. We need not get into any general consideration of limits of state action affecting foreign affairs to realize that the President's maximum power to persuade rests on his capacity to bargain for the benefits of access to the entire national economy without exception for enclaves fenced off willy-nilly by inconsistent political tactics. When such exceptions do qualify his capacity to present a coherent position on behalf of the national economy, he is weakened, of course, not only in dealing with the Burmese regime, but in working together with other nations in hopes of reaching common policy and "comprehensive" strategy. . . .

[The state] contends that the failure of Congress to preempt the state Act demonstrates implicit permission. The State points out that Congress has repeatedly declined to enact express preemption provisions aimed at state and local sanctions, and it calls our attention to the large number of such measures passed against South Africa in the 1980s, which various authorities cited have thought were not preempted. The State stresses that Congress was aware of the state Act in 1996, but did not preempt it explicitly when it adopted its own Burma statute. The State would have us conclude that Congress's continuing failure to enact express preemption implies approval, particularly in light of occasional instances of express preemption of state sanctions in the past.

The argument is unconvincing on more than one level. A failure to provide for preemption expressly may reflect nothing more than the settled character of implied preemption doctrine that courts will dependably apply, and in any event, the existence of conflict cognizable under the

Supremacy Clause does not depend on express congressional recognition that federal and state law may conflict. The State's inference of congressional intent is unwarranted here, therefore, simply because the silence of Congress is ambiguous. Since we never ruled on whether state and local sanctions against South Africa in the 1980s were preempted or otherwise invalid, arguable parallels between the two sets of federal and state Acts do not tell us much about the validity of the latter.

Because the state Act's provisions conflict with Congress's specific delegation to the President of flexible discretion, with limitation of sanctions to a limited scope of actions and actors, and with direction to develop a comprehensive, multilateral strategy under the federal Act, it is preempted, and its application is unconstitutional, under the Supremacy Clause.

The judgment of the Court of Appeals for the First Circuit is affirmed.

It is so ordered.

JUSTICE SCALIA, with whom JUSTICE THOMAS joins, concurring in the judgment.

It is perfectly obvious on the face of this statute that Congress, with the concurrence of the President, intended to "provid[e] the President with flexibility in implementing its Burma sanctions policy." I therefore see no point in devoting a footnote [footnote 9] to the interesting (albeit unsurprising) proposition that "[s]tatements by the sponsors of the federal Act" show that they shared this intent and that a statement in a letter from a State Department officer shows that flexibility had "the explicit support of the Executive." . . .

Of course even if . . . the Court's invocations of legislative history were not utterly irrelevant, I would still object to them, since neither the statements of individual Members of Congress (ordinarily addressed to a virtually empty floor), nor Executive statements and letters addressed to congressional committees, nor the nonenactment of other proposed legislation, is a reliable indication of what a majority of both Houses of Congress intended when they voted for the statute before us. The *only* reliable indication of *that* intent—the only thing we know for sure can be attributed to *all* of them—is the words of the bill that they voted to make law. In a way, using unreliable legislative history to confirm what the statute plainly says anyway (or what the record plainly shows) is less objectionable since, after all, it has absolutely no effect upon the outcome. But in a way, this utter lack of necessity makes it even worse. . . .

. . . [I]t tells future litigants that, even when a statute is clear on its face, and its effects clear upon the record, statements from the legislative history may help (and presumably harm) the case. If so, they must be researched and discussed by counsel—which makes appellate litigation considerably more time consuming, and hence considerably more expensive, than it need be. This to my mind outweighs the arguable good that may come of such persistent irrelevancy, at least when it is indulged in the margins: that it may encourage readers to ignore our footnotes.

For this reason, I join only the judgment of the Court.

Crosby is an interesting case for several reasons, among them Scalia's concurring opinion. Scalia demonstrates his interest in reaching decisions based on the clear language in laws without delving into the intent of their framers or legislative history.

Furthermore, as in *Holland* the justices held that states were preempted from taking action in the areas of foreign affairs. And, if this holding needed any additional reinforcement, the Court provided it in **American Insurance Association v. Garamendi** (2003). This case considered a California law that required any insurer doing business in the state to disclose information about all policies sold in Europe between 1920 and 1945 by the company itself or anyone "related" to it. The aim of the law was to ensure that Holocaust victims or their heirs could take direct action on their own behalf to receive payment on their insurance policies. The American Insurance Association, joined by the United States as an amicus curiae, challenged the law on the ground that it interfered with the federal government's conduct of foreign relations and thus is preempted.

Writing for the majority, Justice David Souter agreed with this argument. He noted that the federal government's position "expressed unmistakably in the executive agreements signed by the President with Germany and Austria, has been to encourage European insurers to work . . . to develop acceptable claim procedures" rather than to encourage lawsuits. "California," Souter noted, "has taken a different tack of providing regulatory sanctions to compel disclosure and payment, supplemented by a new cause of action for Holocaust survivors if the other sanctions should fail." He continued,

The situation created by the California legislation calls to mind the impact of the Massachusetts Burma law on the effective exercise of the President's power, as recounted in the statutory preemption case, *Crosby v. National Foreign Trade Council* (2000). [The California law's] economic compulsion to make public disclosure employs "a different, state system of economic pressure," and in doing so undercuts the President's diplomatic discretion and the choice he has made exercising it. . . . The law thus "compromise[s] the very capacity of the President to speak for the Nation with one voice in dealing with other governments" to resolve claims against European companies arising out of World War II.

In *Holland, Crosby,* and *Garamendi*, the Court delivered a clear message to the states. State laws that impinge on the federal government's foreign policy powers are not likely to receive a favorable treatment by the Court. Most preemption disputes, however, involve domestic matters. In recent decades the Court's docket almost every year has included at least one preemption dispute. Table 6-5 provides examples of some of the more important domestic preemption cases the Court has decided.

Arizona v. United States (2012) is one of the more controversial of the Court's recent preemption decisions. The case focused on the nation's immigration laws, a policy area with both foreign and domestic components. States in the nation's southwestern region have experienced large numbers of immigrants from Latin American nations, with a significant portion entering the United States unlawfully. Most observers agree that federal policies designed to deal with the influx of unauthorized aliens have been largely ineffective, but political deadlocks have doomed reform attempts. Residents of the states along the border with Mexico have sharply criticized federal inaction and long complained that they have been forced to bear the brunt of the social and economic costs associated with the problem.

In 2010 the state of Arizona passed legislation granting state law enforcement officials new authority to enforce federal laws against those unlawfully residing within its borders. The federal government immediately reacted by filing a lawsuit claiming that the Arizona statute unconstitutionally encroached on federal authority. This constitutional dispute had enormous political, economic, and humanitarian implications.

In reading Justice Kennedy's majority opinion in this case, pay special attention to his discussion of

On January 25, 2012, Arizona governor Janice Brewer and President Barack Obama have a heated immigration policy exchange on the tarmac of the Phoenix-Mesa Gateway Airport. Two years earlier, Arizona passed the Support Our Law Enforcement and Neighborhoods Act "to discourage and deter unlawful entry" into the United States. In 2012 the Supreme Court struck down major portions of the law on the ground that federal statutes preempted them.

federalism and his review of standards used by the Court to settle preemption disputes.

Arizona v. United States

567 U.S. _____ (2012)
http://laws.findlaw.com/us/000/11–182.html
Oral arguments are available at https://www.oyez.org.
Vote: 5 (Breyer, Ginsburg, Kennedy, Roberts, Sotomayor)
3 (Alito, Scalia, Thomas)

OPINION OF THE COURT: *Kennedy*

OPINIONS CONCURRING IN PART AND DISSENTING IN PART: *Alito, Scalia, Thomas*

NOT PARTICIPATING: *Kagan*

FACTS:

Faced with large numbers of unauthorized aliens within its borders and frustrated by the federal government's inability to resolve the nation's immigration issues, the Arizona legislature in 2010 passed S.B. 1070, the Support Our Law Enforcement and Neighborhoods Act. The stated purpose of the legislation was to "discourage and deter the unlawful entry and presence of aliens and economic activity by persons unlawfully present in the United States." The law established a state policy of "attrition through enforcement."

TABLE 6–5 Examples of Domestic Policy Preemption Decisions

CASE	QUESTION	HOLDING (VOTE)
Florida Lime & Avocado Growers, Inc. v. Paul (1963)	Is California's requirement of minimum oil content for avocados preempted by federal regulations that certify as mature avocados that have lower levels of oil?	No (5–4). Brennan, for the majority, concluded, "There is neither such actual conflict between the two schemes of regulation that both cannot stand in the same area, nor evidence of a congressional design to pre-empt the field."
City of Burbank v. Lockheed Air Terminal (1973)	Is a Burbank ordinance that prohibits the takeoff of aircraft between 11:00 P.M. and 7:00 A.M. preempted by federal laws regulating the aviation industry?	Yes (5–4). The pervasively national nature of the airline industry requires preemption of local regulations by federal law.
Pacific Gas and Electric Company v. State Energy Resources Conservation and Development Commission (1983)	Does the federal Atomic Energy Act preempt a California law imposing a statewide moratorium on the certification of nuclear energy plants for reasons other than safety?	No (9–0). Although "the Federal Government has occupied the entire field of nuclear safety concerns," such preemption would prevent only those state moratoriums that had as their rationale safety concerns. Since California provided other, nonsafety reasons for its action, the law is valid.
Silkwood v. Kerr-McGee (1984)	Does the Atomic Energy Act preempt a state tort law system that allows for the award of punitive damages for harm caused by the escape of plutonium from a federally licensed nuclear facility?	No (5–4). Although such awards may influence the safety decisions that are at the heart of the Atomic Energy Act, there is no evidence that Congress intended to preempt state tort law remedies. Absent such a congressional intent, the state tort remedy is valid.
Wisconsin Public Intervenor v. Mortier (1991)	Does the Federal Insecticide, Fungicide, and Rodenticide Act, a comprehensive regulatory law enforced by the Environmental Protection Agency, preempt regulation of pesticides by local governments?	No (9–0). The states' historic powers are not superseded by federal law unless that is the clear and manifest purpose of Congress. Compliance with both local and federal regulations is not a physical impossibility.
Cipollone v. Liggett Group (1992)	Do the federally required warnings on cigarette packages preempt states from allowing lawsuits filed by individuals for damages arising from cigarette-related illnesses?	No (7–2). Federal warning requirements preempt state warning laws. Damage suits under state law may not be filed based on a failure of manufacturers to warn adequately. However, suits may be filed against manufacturers on grounds other than adequate warning.
Lorillard Tobacco Co. v. Reilly (2000)	Does a federal cigarette advertising act that prescribes mandatory health warnings for cigarette packaging and advertising preempt the attorney general of Massachusetts from promulgating regulations on cigarette advertising and sales?	Yes (5–4). According to the Court, "Congress pre-empted state cigarette advertising regulations . . . because they would upset federal legislative choices to require specific warnings and to impose the ban on cigarette advertising in electronic media in order to address concerns about smoking and health."
Riegel v. Medtronic (2008)	Does premarketing approval by the U.S. Food and Drug Administration of medical devices (such as replacement heart valves and pacemakers) preempt state damage suits against such devices' manufacturers?	Yes (8–1). In the Medical Device Amendments of 1976, Congress expressly preempted these suits, which "disrupt the federal scheme."
Wyeth v. Levine (2009)	Does U.S. Food and Drug Administration approval of a company's drug labels preempt state lawsuits claiming that the labels failed to provide adequate and effective warnings?	No (6–3). Surely, according to the Court, if "Congress thought [these state suits] posed an obstacle to its objectives, it would have enacted an express pre-emption at some point." Instead, Congress "evidently determined that [state lawsuits] provide appropriate relief for injured consumers."
National Meat Association v. Harris (2012)	Does a California law regulating the slaughter of livestock for human consumption conflict with provisions of the Federal Meat Inspection Act?	Yes. (9–0). The federal law regulates the handling of livestock through the entire slaughtering process. California's law endeavors to regulate the same process, but imposes different requirements.

The law had four provisions of constitutional concern. First, Section 3 made failure to carry federally required alien registration documents a state crime. Second, Section 5(C) made it a state crime for unauthorized aliens to apply for work or to work as employees or independent contractors in Arizona. Third, Section 6 authorized police to make a warrantless arrest of any person if the officer had probable cause to believe that the person had committed a deportable offense. And fourth, Section 2(B) required state law enforcement officers to check the immigration status of any lawfully stopped person whom the officer reasonably suspected of being an unauthorized immigrant.

Before S.B. 1070 could take effect, the federal government filed suit against the state of Arizona and Governor Janice Brewer, claiming that federal immigration law preempted S.B. 1070 and that the law was therefore unconstitutional on its face. The federal district court ruled in favor of the United States and issued a preliminary injunction against enforcement of the law. The court of appeals affirmed, and the Supreme Court granted review.

ARGUMENTS:

For the petitioners, the state of Arizona and Arizona Governor Janice Brewer:

- S.B. 1070 does not impose its own substantive immigration standards; it simply uses state resources to enforce existing federal rules.
- Under our system of cooperative federalism, the laws of the United States can be enforced by either federal or state officers unless Congress specifically states otherwise. Congress has not done so.
- Congress has established policies for cooperative actions between the federal government and the states on immigration matters. This indicates that Congress has not implied that federal law preempts the immigration field.

For the respondent, United States:

- Under the Constitution, the national government has plenary authority to admit aliens to this country, to prescribe the terms under which they may remain, and, if necessary, to remove them. Because those decisions involve other countries' citizens, they necessarily implicate "important and delicate" considerations of foreign policy.
- Congress has set forth a single federal framework governing aliens' obligations. The state cannot, in the name of enforcing a federal obligation, claim the right to punish aliens who the executive branch has decided not to prosecute based on important considerations consistent with the Immigration and Naturalization Act.
- In enforcing immigration laws, the federal government welcomes the cooperation and assistance of state and local officers. Sections of S.B. 1070, however, make cooperation impossible by authorizing local officers to take actions that might not be consistent with the federal government's priorities.

◤ JUSTICE KENNEDY DELIVERED THE OPINION OF THE COURT.

The Government of the United States has broad, undoubted power over the subject of immigration and the status of aliens. This authority rests, in part, on the National Government's constitutional power to "establish an uniform Rule of Naturalization," and its inherent power as sovereign to control and conduct relations with foreign nations.

The federal power to determine immigration policy is well settled. Immigration policy can affect trade, investment, tourism, and diplomatic relations for the entire Nation, as well as the perceptions and expectations of aliens in this country who seek the full protection of its laws. Perceived mistreatment of aliens in the United States may lead to harmful reciprocal treatment of American citizens abroad.

It is fundamental that foreign countries concerned about the status, safety, and security of their nationals in the United States must be able to confer and communicate on this subject with one national sovereign, not the 50 separate States. This Court has reaffirmed that "[o]ne of the most important and delicate of all international relationships . . . has to do with the protection of the just rights of a country's own nationals when those nationals are in another country." Hines v. Davidowitz (1941).

Federal governance of immigration and alien status is extensive and complex. Congress has specified categories of aliens who may not be admitted to the United States. Unlawful entry and unlawful reentry into the country are federal offenses. Once here, aliens are required to register with the Federal Government and to carry proof of status on their person. Failure to do so is a federal misdemeanor. Federal law also authorizes States to deny noncitizens a range of public benefits, and it imposes sanctions on employers who hire unauthorized workers. . . .

Discretion in the enforcement of immigration law embraces immediate human concerns. Unauthorized workers trying to support their families, for example, likely pose less danger than alien smugglers or aliens who commit a serious crime. The equities of an individual case may turn on many factors, including whether the alien has children born in the United States, long ties to the community, or a record of distinguished military service. Some discretionary decisions involve policy choices that bear on this Nation's international relations. . . . The dynamic nature of relations with other countries requires the Executive Branch to ensure that enforcement policies are consistent with this Nation's foreign policy with respect to these and other realities. . . .

The pervasiveness of federal regulation does not diminish the importance of immigration policy to the States. Arizona bears many of the consequences of unlawful immigration. Hundreds of thousands of deportable aliens are apprehended in Arizona each year. Unauthorized aliens who remain in the State comprise, by one estimate, almost six percent of the population. And in the State's most populous county, these aliens are reported to be responsible for a disproportionate share of serious crime. . . .

These concerns are the background for the formal legal analysis that follows. The issue is whether, under preemption principles, federal law permits Arizona to implement the state-law provisions in dispute.

Federalism, central to the constitutional design, adopts the principle that both the National and State Governments have elements of sovereignty the other is bound to respect. From the existence of two sovereigns follows the possibility that laws can be in conflict or at cross-purposes. The Supremacy Clause provides a clear rule that federal law "shall be the supreme Law of the Land; and the Judges in every State shall be bound thereby, any Thing in the Constitution or Laws of any State to the Contrary notwithstanding." Under this principle, Congress has the power to preempt state law. See *Crosby v. National Foreign Trade Council* (2000); *Gibbons v. Ogden* (1824). There is no doubt that Congress may withdraw specified powers from the States by enacting a statute containing an express preemption provision.

State law must also give way to federal law in at least two other circumstances. First, the States are precluded from regulating conduct in a field that Congress, acting within its proper authority, has determined must be regulated by its exclusive governance. The intent to displace state law altogether can be inferred from a framework of regulation "so pervasive . . . that Congress left no room for the States to supplement it" or where there is a "federal interest . . . so dominant that the federal system will be assumed to preclude enforcement of state laws on the same subject." *Rice v. Santa Fe Elevator Corp.* (1947).

Second, state laws are preempted when they conflict with federal law. This includes cases where "compliance with both federal and state regulations is a physical impossibility," and those instances where the challenged state law "stands as an obstacle to the accomplishment and execution of the full purposes and objectives of Congress," *Hines*. In preemption analysis, courts should assume that "the historic police powers of the States" are not superseded "unless that was the clear and manifest purpose of Congress." *Rice*; see *Wyeth v. Levine* (2009).

The four challenged provisions of the state law each must be examined under these preemption principles.

Section 3

Section 3 of S. B. 1070 creates a new state misdemeanor. It forbids the "willful failure to complete or carry an alien registration document . . . in violation of 8 United States Code section 1304(e) or 1306(a)." In effect, §3 adds a state-law penalty for conduct proscribed by federal law. The United States contends that this state enforcement mechanism intrudes on the field of alien registration, a field in which Congress has left no room for States to regulate.

The Court discussed federal alien-registration requirements in *Hines v. Davidowitz*. In 1940, as international conflict spread, Congress added to federal immigration law a "complete system for alien registration." The new federal law struck a careful balance. It punished an alien's willful failure to register but did not require aliens to carry identification cards. There were also limits on the sharing of registration records and fingerprints. The Court found that Congress intended the federal plan for registration to be a "single integrated and all-embracing system." Because this "complete scheme . . . for the registration of aliens" touched on foreign relations, it did not allow the States to "curtail or complement" federal law or to "enforce additional or auxiliary regulations." As a consequence, the Court ruled that Pennsylvania could not enforce its own alien-registration program.

The present regime of federal regulation is not identical to the statutory framework considered in *Hines*, but it remains comprehensive. . . .

The framework enacted by Congress leads to the conclusion here, as it did in *Hines*, that the Federal Government has occupied the field of alien registration. The federal statutory directives provide a full set of standards governing alien registration, including the punishment for noncompliance. It was designed as a "harmonious whole." Where Congress occupies an entire field, as it has in the field of alien registration, even complementary state regulation is impermissible. Field preemption reflects a congressional decision to foreclose any state regulation in the area, even if it is parallel to federal standards. See *Silkwood v. Kerr-McGee Corp.* (1984).

Federal law makes a single sovereign responsible for maintaining a comprehensive and unified system to keep track of aliens within the Nation's borders. If §3 of the Arizona statute were valid, every State could give itself independent authority to prosecute federal registration violations, "diminish[ing] the [Federal Government]'s control over enforcement" and "detract[ing] from the 'integrated scheme of regulation' created by Congress." *Wisconsin Dept. of Industry v. Gould Inc.* (1986). Even if a State may make violation of federal law a crime in some instances, it cannot do so in a field (like the field of alien registration) that has been occupied by federal law. . . .

These specific conflicts between state and federal law simply underscore the reason for field preemption. As it did in *Hines*, the Court now concludes that, with respect to the subject of alien registration, Congress intended to preclude States from "complement[ing] the federal law, or enforc[ing] additional or auxiliary regulations." Section 3 is preempted by federal law.

Section 5(C)

Unlike §3, which replicates federal statutory requirements, §5(C) enacts a state criminal prohibition where no federal counterpart exists. The provision makes it a state misdemeanor for "an unauthorized alien to knowingly apply for work, solicit work in a public place or perform work as an employee or independent contractor" in Arizona. Violations can be punished by a $2,500 fine and incarceration for up to six months. The United States contends that the provision upsets the balance struck by the Immigration Reform and Control Act of 1986 (IRCA) and must be preempted as an obstacle to the federal plan of regulation and control. . . .

. . . Congress enacted IRCA as a comprehensive framework for "combating the employment of illegal aliens." *Hoffman Plastic Compounds, Inc. v. NLRB* (2002). The law makes it illegal for employers to knowingly hire, recruit, refer, or continue to employ unauthorized workers. It also requires every employer to verify the employment authorization status of prospective employees. These requirements are enforced through criminal penalties and

an escalating series of civil penalties tied to the number of times an employer has violated the provisions.

This comprehensive framework does not impose federal criminal sanctions on the employee side (i.e., penalties on aliens who seek or engage in unauthorized work). . . .

The legislative background of IRCA underscores the fact that Congress made a deliberate choice not to impose criminal penalties on aliens who seek, or engage in, unauthorized employment. . . . IRCA's framework reflects a considered judgment that making criminals out of aliens engaged in unauthorized work—aliens who already face the possibility of employer exploitation because of their removable status—would be inconsistent with federal policy and objectives. . . .

The ordinary principles of preemption include the well-settled proposition that a state law is preempted where it "stands as an obstacle to the accomplishment and execution of the full purposes and objectives of Congress." *Hines.* Under §5(C) of S. B. 1070, Arizona law would interfere with the careful balance struck by Congress with respect to unauthorized employment of aliens. Although §5(C) attempts to achieve one of the same goals as federal law—the deterrence of unlawful employment—it involves a conflict in the method of enforcement. The Court has recognized that a "[c]onflict in technique can be fully as disruptive to the system Congress enacted as conflict in overt policy." *Motor Coach Employees v. Lockridge* (1971). The correct instruction to draw from the text, structure, and history of IRCA is that Congress decided it would be inappropriate to impose criminal penalties on aliens who seek or engage in unauthorized employment. It follows that a state law to the contrary is an obstacle to the regulatory system Congress chose. Section 5(C) is preempted by federal law.

Section 6

Section 6 of S. B. 1070 provides that a state officer, "without a warrant, may arrest a person if the officer has probable cause to believe . . . [the person] has committed any public offense that makes [him] removable from the United States." The United States argues that arrests authorized by this statute would be an obstacle to the removal system Congress created.

As a general rule, it is not a crime for a removable alien to remain present in the United States. See *INS v. Lopez-Mendoza* (1984). If the police stop someone based on nothing more than possible removability, the usual predicate for an arrest is absent. When an alien is suspected of being removable, a federal official issues an administrative document called a Notice to Appear. The form does not authorize an arrest. Instead, it gives the alien information about the proceedings, including the time and date of the removal hearing. If an alien fails to appear, an *in absentia* order may direct removal.

The federal statutory structure instructs when it is appropriate to arrest an alien during the removal process. For example, the Attorney General can exercise discretion to issue a warrant for an alien's arrest and detention "pending a decision on whether the alien is to be removed from the United States." And if an alien is ordered removed after a hearing, the Attorney General will issue a warrant. . . . [W]arrants are executed by federal officers who have received training in the enforcement of immigration law. . . .

Section 6 attempts to provide state officers even greater authority to arrest aliens on the basis of possible removability than Congress has given to trained federal immigration officers. Under state law, officers who believe an alien is removable by reason of some "public offense" would have the power to conduct an arrest on that basis regardless of whether a federal warrant has issued or the alien is likely to escape. This state authority could be exercised without any input from the Federal Government about whether an arrest is warranted in a particular case. This would allow the State to achieve its own immigration policy. The result could be unnecessary harassment of some aliens (for instance, a veteran, college student, or someone assisting with a criminal investigation) whom federal officials determine should not be removed.

This is not the system Congress created. . . .

By authorizing state officers to decide whether an alien should be detained for being removable, §6 violates the principle that the removal process is entrusted to the discretion of the Federal Government. A decision on removability requires a determination whether it is appropriate to allow a foreign national to continue living in the United States. Decisions of this nature touch on foreign relations and must be made with one voice. . . .

Congress has put in place a system in which state officers may not make warrantless arrests of aliens based on possible removability except in specific, limited circumstances. By nonetheless authorizing state and local officers to engage in these enforcement activities as a general matter, §6 creates an obstacle to the full purposes and objectives of Congress. Section 6 is preempted by federal law.

Section 2(B)

Section 2(B) of S. B. 1070 requires state officers to make a "reasonable attempt . . . to determine the immigration status" of any person they stop, detain, or arrest on some other legitimate basis if "reasonable suspicion exists that the person is an alien and is unlawfully present in the United States." The law also provides that "[a]ny person who is arrested shall have the person's immigration status determined before the person is released." . . .

Three limits are built into the state provision. First, a detainee is presumed not to be an alien unlawfully present in the United States if he or she provides a valid Arizona driver's license or similar identification. Second, officers "may not consider race, color or national origin . . . except to the extent permitted by the United States [and] Arizona Constitution[s]." Third, the provisions must be "implemented in a manner consistent with federal law regulating immigration, protecting the civil rights of all persons and respecting the privileges and immunities of United States citizens."

The United States and its *amici* contend that, even with these limits, the State's verification requirements pose an obstacle to the framework Congress put in place. The first concern is the mandatory nature of the status checks. The second is the possibility of prolonged detention while the checks are being performed. . . .

The nature and timing of this case counsel caution in evaluating the validity of §2(B). The Federal Government has brought suit against a sovereign State to challenge the provision even before the law has gone into effect. There is a basic uncertainty about what the law means and how it will be enforced. At this stage, without the benefit of a definitive interpretation from the state courts, it would be inappropriate to assume §2(B) will be construed in a way that creates a conflict with federal law. As a result, the United States cannot prevail in its current challenge. This opinion does not foreclose other preemption and constitutional challenges to the law as interpreted and applied after it goes into effect. . . .

The National Government has significant power to regulate immigration. With power comes responsibility, and the sound exercise of national power over immigration depends on the Nation's meeting its responsibility to base its laws on a political will informed by searching, thoughtful, rational civic discourse. Arizona may have understandable frustrations with the problems caused by illegal immigration while that process continues, but the State may not pursue policies that undermine federal law.

The United States has established that §§3, 5(C), and 6 of S. B. 1070 are preempted. It was improper, however, to enjoin §2(B) before the state courts had an opportunity to construe it and without some showing that enforcement of the provision in fact conflicts with federal immigration law and its objectives.

The judgment of the Court of Appeals for the Ninth Circuit is affirmed in part and reversed in part. The case is remanded for further proceedings consistent with this opinion.

It is so ordered.

JUSTICE SCALIA, concurring in part and dissenting in part.

The United States is an indivisible "Union of sovereign States." Today's opinion, approving virtually all of the Ninth Circuit's injunction against enforcement of the four challenged provisions of Arizona's law, deprives States of what most would consider the defining characteristic of sovereignty: the power to exclude from the sovereign's territory people who have no right to be there. Neither the Constitution itself nor even any law passed by Congress supports this result. . . .

As is often the case, discussion of the dry legalities that are the proper object of our attention suppresses the very human realities that gave rise to the suit. Arizona bears the brunt of the country's illegal immigration problem. Its citizens feel themselves under siege by large numbers of illegal immigrants who invade their property, strain their social services, and even place their lives in jeopardy. Federal officials have been unable to remedy the problem, and indeed have recently shown that they are unwilling to do so. Thousands of Arizona's estimated 400,000 illegal immigrants—including not just children but men and women under 30—are now assured immunity from enforcement, and will be able to compete openly with Arizona citizens for employment.

Arizona has moved to protect its sovereignty—not in contradiction of federal law, but in complete compliance with it. The laws under challenge here do not extend or revise federal immigration restrictions, but merely enforce those restrictions more effectively. If securing its territory in this fashion is not within the power of Arizona, we should cease referring to it as a sovereign State. I dissent.

JUSTICE THOMAS, concurring in part and dissenting in part.

I agree with Justice Scalia that federal immigration law does not pre-empt any of the challenged provisions of S. B. 1070. I reach that conclusion, however, for the simple reason that there is no conflict between the "ordinary meanin[g]" of the relevant federal laws and that of the four provisions of Arizona law at issue here. . . .

Despite the lack of any conflict between the ordinary meaning of the Arizona law and that of the federal laws at issue here, the Court holds that various provisions of the Arizona law are pre-empted because they "stan[d] as an obstacle to the accomplishment and execution of the full purposes and objectives of Congress." I have explained [concurring opinion in *Wyeth v. Levine* (2009) and dissenting opinion in *Haywood v. Drown* (2009)] that the "purposes and objectives" theory of implied pre-emption is inconsistent with the Constitution because it invites courts to engage in freewheeling speculation about congressional purpose that roams well beyond statutory text. Under the Supremacy Clause, pre-emptive effect is to be given to congressionally enacted laws, not to judicially divined legislative purposes. Thus, even assuming the existence of some tension between Arizona's law and the supposed "purposes and objectives" of Congress, I would not hold that any of the provisions of the Arizona law at issue here are pre-empted on that basis.

JUSTICE ALITO, concurring in part and dissenting in part.

I agree with the Court that §2(B) is not pre-empted. That provision does not authorize or require Arizona law enforcement officers to do anything they are not already allowed to do under existing federal law. The United States' argument that §2(B) is pre-empted, not by any federal statute or regulation, but simply by the Executive's current enforcement policy is an astounding assertion of federal executive power that the Court rightly rejects.

I also agree with the Court that §3 is pre-empted by virtue of our decision in *Hines v. Davidowitz* (1941). Our conclusion in that case that Congress had enacted an "all-embracing system" of alien registration and that States cannot "enforce additional or auxiliary regulations" forecloses Arizona's attempt here to impose additional, state-law penalties for violations of the federal registration scheme.

While I agree with the Court on §2(B) and §3, I part ways on §5(C) and §6. The Court's holding on §5(C) is inconsistent with *De Canas v. Bica* (1976), which held that employment regulation, even of aliens unlawfully present in the country, is an area of traditional state concern. Because state police powers are implicated here, our precedents require us to presume that federal law does not displace state law unless Congress' intent to do so is clear and manifest. I do not believe Congress has spoken with the requisite clarity to justify invalidation of §5(C). Nor do I believe that §6 is invalid. Like §2(B), §6 adds virtually nothing to the authority that Arizona law enforcement officers already exercise. And whatever little authority they have gained is consistent with federal law.

Having discussed in this chapter the general dimensions of federalism and the doctrinal cycles that have characterized the Supreme Court's interpretation of it, we will turn our attention in the next two chapters to the authority of government to regulate commerce and to tax and spend. It is in these two policy realms that some of the most significant and controversial disputes over the division of federal and state powers have occurred.

ANNOTATED READINGS

General books on federalism, including the founding period and *McCulloch v. Maryland,* are Robert Allen, *The Ordeal of the Constitution: The Antifederalists and the Ratification Struggle of 1787–1788* (Norman: University of Oklahoma Press, 1966); Raoul Berger, *Federalism: The Founders' Design* (Norman: University of Oklahoma Press, 1987); Erwin Chemerinsky, *Enhancing Government: Federalism for the 21st Century* (Palo Alto, CA: Stanford University Press, 2008); Richard E. Ellis, *Aggressive Nationalism:* McCulloch v. Maryland *and the Foundation of Federal Authority in the Young Republic* (New York: Oxford University Press, 2007); Malcolm M. Feeley and Edward Rubin, *Federalism: Political Identity and Tragic Compromise* (Ann Arbor: University of Michigan Press, 2008); Gerald Gunther, ed., *John Marshall's Defense of* McCulloch v. Maryland (Stanford, CA: Stanford University Press, 1969); Alison L. LaCroix, *The Ideological Origins of American Federalism* (Cambridge, MA: Harvard University Press, 2011); Laura Langer, *Judicial Review in State Supreme Courts: A Comparative Study* (Albany, NY: State University Press of America, 2002); Alpheus Mason, *The States Rights Debate: Anti-Federalism and the Constitution* (Englewood Cliffs, NJ: Prentice Hall, 1964); Robert F. Nagel, *The Implosion of American Federalism* (New York: Oxford University Press, 2001); John D. Nugent, *Safeguarding Federalism: How States Protect Their Interests in National Policy Making* (Norman: University of Oklahoma Press, 2009); John R. Schmidhauser, *The Supreme Court as Final Arbiter in Federal-State Relations, 1789–1957* (Chapel Hill: University of North Carolina Press, 1958); and Eric N. Waltenburg and Bill Swinford, *Litigating Federalism: The States before the U.S. Supreme Court* (Westport, CT: Greenwood Press, 1999).

On the Tenth and Eleventh Amendments, new judicial federalism (and the role of state supreme courts), and preemption, see William W. Buzbee, ed., *Preemption Choice: The Theory, Law, and Reality of Federalism's Core Question* (Cambridge: Cambridge University Press, 2009); Mark R. Killenbeck, ed., *The Tenth Amendment and State Sovereignty* (Lanham, MD: Rowman & Littlefield, 2002); and John V. Orth, *The Judicial Power of the United States: The Eleventh Amendment in American History* (New York: Oxford University Press, 1987).

7 The Commerce Power

ONSIDER the following laws:

- The Sherman Anti-Trust Act, designed to outlaw monopolies that attempt to dominate particular industries and eliminate all competition
- The Fair Labor Standards Act, aimed at ensuring that employers pay their employees fair wages and that employers do not force employees to work unreasonable numbers of hours
- The Civil Rights Act of 1964, which prohibits certain forms of discrimination on the basis of race, color, religion, or national origin

These three laws may cover different subjects, but they are alike in one important regard: Congress enacted them under its power "to regulate Commerce . . . among the several States."

Given the importance of these and the many other laws Congress has passed under its commerce power, it is no wonder that these few words have resulted in many controversies and substantial litigation. Concern over the exercise of the power to regulate commerce was present at the Constitution's birth and continues today. At each stage of the nation's development from a former colony isolated from the world's commercial centers to a country wielding vast economic power, legal disputes of great significance tested the powers of

government to regulate the economy. During certain periods, such as John Marshall's chief justiceship, the decisions of the Supreme Court enhanced the role of the federal government in promoting economic development. At other times, however, such as the period immediately following the Great Depression, the Court's interpretations thwarted the government's attempts to overcome economic collapse. From the earliest days of the nation, battles over the commerce power have raised basic questions: What is regulation? What is commerce? What is commerce among the states (now called interstate commerce)? What powers of commercial regulation does the Constitution grant to the federal government, and what powers remain with the states?

Rather than address these questions individually, in this chapter we explore the development of the commerce power chronologically. We take this approach because, as we have just suggested, the Court has answered such questions in various ways in different eras, sometimes enhancing the federal government's power and sometimes curtailing it. These phases tend to correspond to the cyclical debate between dual and cooperative federalism that we considered in chapter 6. Keep in mind, however, that at times justices who adopt the tools of the dual federalism approach—especially the Tenth Amendment and narrower approaches to defining interstate commerce—are more committed to an antiregulation regime than they are to states' rights.

FOUNDATIONS OF THE COMMERCE POWER

A primary reason the Constitutional Convention was called was the inability of the government under the Articles of Confederation to control the country's commercial activity effectively. Economic conditions were dismal following the Revolutionary War. The national and state governments were deeply in debt. The tax base of the newly independent nation was minimal, and commerce was undeveloped, leaving property taxes and customs duties as the primary sources of government funds.

The states were almost exclusively in charge of economic regulation. To raise enough revenue to pay their debts, the states imposed substantial taxes on land, placing farmers in an economically precarious condition. The states also erected trade barriers and imposed duties on the importation of foreign goods. Although these policies were enacted in part to promote the states' domestic businesses, the result was a general strangulation of commercial activity. Several states printed their own money and passed statutes canceling debts. With each of the states working independently, the national economy continued to slide into stagnation, and, for all practical purposes, the central government was powerless to respond effectively.

When agrarian interests reached their economic breaking point—culminating in the 1787 march on the federal arsenal at Springfield, Massachusetts, by a makeshift army of farmers led by Revolutionary War veteran Daniel Shays and others—it was clear that something had to be done. Congress called for a convention to reconsider the status of the Articles of Confederation, a convention that ultimately resulted in the drafting of the United States Constitution.

Commerce and the Constitutional Convention

The delegates to the Constitutional Convention recognized the necessity of giving the power to regulate the economy to the central government. The nation could no longer tolerate the individual states' pursuit of independent policies, each having a different impact on the country's economic health. To that end, Article I of the Constitution removed certain powers from the states and gave the federal government powers it did not have under the Articles of Confederation. States could not print money, impair the obligation of contracts, or tax imports or exports. The federal government obtained the authority necessary to impose uniform regulations for the national economy. Among the powers granted to the central government were the authority to tax and impose customs duties, to spend and borrow, to develop and protect a single monetary system, and to regulate bankruptcies. Most important was the authority to regulate interstate and foreign commerce. Article I, Section 8, states: "The Congress shall have the Power . . . to regulate Commerce with foreign Nations, and among the several States, and with the Indian Tribes."

The need for Congress to speak for the nation with a single voice on these matters was clear to the framers. Even Alexander Hamilton and James Madison, who disagreed on many questions of federalism, were in accord on the necessity of the central government to control interstate and foreign commerce. Hamilton wrote in *The Federalist Papers* No. 22:

In addition to the defects already enumerated in the existing federal system, there are others of not less importance which concur in rendering it altogether unfit for the administration of the affairs of the Union.

The want of a power to regulate commerce is by all parties allowed to be of the number.

In *Federalist* No. 42 Madison took a similar position, arguing that the experience of the United States under the articles, as well as that of European countries, demonstrated that a central government without broad powers over the nation's commerce was destined to fail.

Congress quickly seized on the authority to regulate commerce with other nations. Almost immediately, it imposed import duties as a means of raising revenue. The constitutional grant in this area was clear: the power to regulate foreign commerce, as well as other matters of foreign policy, was given unambiguously to the national government, and the role of the states was eliminated. Since ratification, the states have challenged congressional supremacy over foreign commerce only on rare occasions.

The power to regulate interstate commerce, however, was a different story. Congress was slow in responding to this grant of authority, and federal officials continued to view business as an activity occurring within the borders of the individual states. In fact,

Congress did not pass comprehensive legislation governing commerce among the states until the Interstate Commerce Act of 1887.

Marshall Defines the Commerce Power

The commerce clause gives Congress the power to "regulate Commerce . . . among the Several states." But what do these terms—"regulate," "commerce," and "among"—mean? The history of the commerce clause is replete with disputes over definitions. Is "commerce" limited to buying and selling goods, or is its meaning broad enough to include other activities, such as manufacturing and production? What about "among"? How should we distinguish *inter*state commerce, which, according to the Constitution, the federal government regulates, from *intra*state commerce, over which the states may retain regulatory power? Problems associated with such distinctions were difficult enough in the early years, but they became even more complex as the economy grew and the country changed from agrarian to industrialized. As many constitutional law cases illustrate, disputes over commercial regulatory authority often involve power struggles between the national government and the states.

Disputes over the meaning of the commerce clause came to the Supreme Court even during the early years of nationhood. The justices probed the constitutional definition of "commerce" and the proper division of federal and state power to regulate it. Of the commerce cases decided by the Supreme Court in those early decades, none was more important than *Gibbons v. Ogden* (1824). This dispute involved some of the nation's most prominent and powerful businessmen and attorneys. A great deal was at stake, both economically and politically. In his opinion for the Court, Chief Justice Marshall responded to the fundamental problems of defining the power to regulate commerce among the states. His answers to the questions presented in this case are still very much a part of our constitutional fabric.

Gibbons v. Ogden

22 U.S. (9 Wheat.) 1 (1824)
http://laws.findlaw.com/us/22/1.html
Vote: 6 (Duvall, Johnson, Marshall, Story, Todd, Washington)
   0

OPINION OF THE COURT: *Marshall*
CONCURRING OPINION: *Johnson*
NOT PARTICIPATING: *Thompson*

Aaron Ogden

Thomas Gibbons

FACTS:

This complicated litigation can be traced back to 1798, when the New York legislature granted the wealthy and prominent Robert R. Livingston a monopoly to operate steamboats on all waters within the state, including the two most important commercial waterways, New York Harbor and the Hudson River. New York officials did not see the monopoly grant as particularly important because no one had yet developed a steamship that could operate reliably and profitably. Livingston, however, joined forces with Robert Fulton, and together they produced a commercially viable steamship. This mode of transportation became extremely popular and very profitable for the partners. When they obtained a similar monopoly over the port of New Orleans in 1811, they had significant control over the nation's two most important harbors.

The rapid westward expansion taking place at that time fueled the need for modern transportation systems. The Livingston-Fulton monopoly, however, put a damper on the use of steam engines in the evolution of such a system. The New York monopoly was so strong and so vigorously enforced that retaliatory laws were enacted by other states, which refused to let steam-powered vessels from New York use their waters. Especially hostile relations developed between New York and New Jersey, and violence between the crews of rival companies became common. Livingston died in 1813, followed two years later by Fulton, but their monopoly lived on.

Aaron Ogden, a former governor of New Jersey, and Thomas Gibbons, a successful Georgia lawyer, entered into a partnership to carry passengers between New York City and Elizabethtown, New Jersey. Ogden had purchased the right to operate in New York waters from the Livingston-Fulton monopoly, and Gibbons had a federal permit issued under the 1793 Coastal Licensing Act to operate steamships along the coast. With these grants of authority the two partners could carry passengers between New York and New Jersey. The leaders of the New York monopoly, however, pressured Ogden to terminate his relationship with Gibbons and to join them. As a result, the Ogden-Gibbons partnership dissolved.

Gibbons then joined forces with Cornelius Vanderbilt, and they began a fierce competition with Ogden and the New York monopoly interests. Gibbons and Vanderbilt entered New York waters in violation of the monopoly whenever they could, picking up as much New York business as possible. In response, Ogden successfully convinced the New York courts to enjoin Gibbons from entering New York waters. Gibbons appealed this ruling to the U.S. Supreme Court.

To press their case, Gibbons and Vanderbilt acquired the services of two of the best lawyers of the day, William Wirt and Daniel Webster. Wirt, the attorney general of the United States, argued that the federal permit issued to Gibbons took precedence over any state-issued monopoly, and therefore Gibbons had the right to enter New York waters. Webster took a more radical position, explicitly stating that the commerce clause of the Constitution gave Congress near exclusive power over commerce and that the state-granted monopoly was a violation of that clause. Ogden's lawyer responded that navigation was not commerce under the meaning of the Constitution but instead was an intrastate enterprise left to the states to regulate. The oral arguments in the case lasted four and a half days.

ARGUMENTS:

For the appellant, Thomas Gibbons:

- Although not all regulations that might affect commerce are exclusively in the power of Congress, the power exercised by the state in this case is a federal power that did not remain with the states in the Constitution.

- The power to regulate commerce is crucial to the nation's well-being. In establishing the Constitution, the people understood this and transferred the commerce power from the states to the federal government so that a uniform and general system could be maintained. What is regulated here is not the commerce of the several states, respectively, but the commerce of the United States.

- The inevitable consequence of this analysis is that Congress may establish ferries and turnpikes and may regulate in other ways that touch the interior of states.

For the respondent, Aaron Ogden:

- The Constitution provides for limited and expressly delegated powers, which can be exercised only as granted, or in the cases enumerated. This principle, which distinguishes the national from the state governments, follows from the fact that the Constitution itself is a delegation of power, not a restriction of power previously possessed and from the express stipulation in the Tenth Amendment. The Constitution must be construed strictly with regard to the powers expressly granted. Every portion of power not granted must remain with the states.

- The practice of the states shows that the commerce power has always been considered concurrent. New York has passed numerous laws that are regulations of commerce with foreign nations, with other states, and with the Indian tribes. The state may exercise its power, so long as its laws do not interfere with any right exercised under the Constitution or laws of the United States.

- The commerce power is not only concurrent, but is limited in Congress. It does not extend to the regulation of the internal commerce of any state because terms used in the grant of power are "among the several States." Internal commerce is that which is carried on within the limits of a state.

- The state law does not even regulate commerce; it regulates internal trade and the right of navigation within a state. This belongs exclusively to the states, even though it incidentally may affect the right of intercourse between the states.

> ▶ **MR. CHIEF JUSTICE MARSHALL DELIVERED THE OPINION OF THE COURT.**

The appellant contends that this decree is erroneous, because the laws which purport to give the exclusive privilege it sustains, are repugnant to the constitution and laws of the United States.

They are said to be repugnant—

To that clause in the constitution which authorizes Congress to regulate commerce. . . .

The words are, "Congress shall have power to regulate commerce with foreign nations, and among the several States, and with the Indian tribes."

The subject to be regulated is commerce; and our constitution being . . . one of enumeration, and not of definition, to ascertain the extent of the power, it becomes necessary to settle the meaning of the word. The counsel for the appellee would limit it to traffic, to buying and selling, or the interchange of commodities, and do not admit that it comprehends navigation. This would restrict a general term, applicable to many objects, to one of its significations. Commerce, undoubtedly, is traffic, but it is something more: it is intercourse. It describes the commercial intercourse between nations, and parts of nations, in all its branches, and is regulated by prescribing rules for carrying on that intercourse. The mind can scarcely conceive a system for regulating commerce between nations, which shall exclude all laws concerning navigation, which shall be silent on the admission of the vessels of the one nation into the ports of the other, and be confined to prescribing rules for the conduct of individuals, in the actual employment of buying and selling, or of barter.

If commerce does not include navigation, the government of the Union has no direct power over that subject, and can make no law prescribing what shall constitute American vessels, or requiring that they shall be navigated by American seamen. Yet this power has been exercised from the commencement of the government, has been exercised with the consent of all, and has been understood by all to be a commercial regulation. All America understands, and has uniformly understood, the word "commerce," to comprehend navigation. It was so understood, and must have been so understood, when the constitution was framed. The power over commerce, including navigation, was one of the primary objects for which the people of America adopted their government, and must have been contemplated in forming it. The convention must have used the word in that sense, because all have understood it in that sense; and the attempt to restrict it comes too late. . . .

Daniel Webster's 1821 handwritten note to Cornelius Vanderbilt acknowledging receipt of a $500 retainer to represent Thomas Gibbons in the case of Gibbons v. Ogden.

The word used in the constitution, then, comprehends, and has been always understood to comprehend, navigation within its meaning; and a power to regulate navigation, is as expressly granted, as if that term had been added to the word "commerce."

To what commerce does this power extend? The constitution informs us, to commerce "with foreign nations, and among the several States, and with the Indian tribes."

It has, we believe, been universally admitted, that these words comprehend every species of commercial intercourse between the United States and foreign nations. No sort of trade can be carried on between this country and any other, to which this power does not extend. It has been truly said, that commerce, as the word is used in the constitution, is a unit, every part of which is indicated by the term.

If this be the admitted meaning of the word, in its application to foreign nations, it must carry the same meaning throughout the sentence, and remain a unit, unless there be some plain intelligible cause which alters it.

The subject to which the power is next applied, is to commerce "among the several States." The word "among" means intermingled with. A thing which is among others, is intermingled with them. Commerce among the States, cannot stop at the external boundary line of each State, but may be introduced into the interior.

It is not intended to say that these words comprehend that commerce, which is completely internal, which is carried on between man and man in a State, or between different parts of the same State, and which does not extend to or affect other States. Such a power would be inconvenient, and is certainly unnecessary.

Comprehensive as the word "among" is, it may very properly be restricted to that commerce which concerns more States than one. The phrase is not one which would probably have been selected to indicate the completely interior traffic of a State, because it is not an apt phrase for that purpose; and the enumeration of the particular classes of commerce, to which the power was to be extended, would not have been made, had the intention been to extend the power to every description. The enumeration presupposes something not enumerated; and that something, if we regard the language or the subject of the sentence, must be the exclusively internal commerce of a State. The genius and character of the whole government seem to be, that its action is to be applied to all the external concerns of the nation, and to those internal concerns which affect the States generally; but not to those which are completely within a particular State, which do not affect other States, and with which it is not necessary to interfere, for the purpose of executing some of the general powers of the government. The completely internal commerce of a State, then, may be considered as reserved for the State itself.

But, in regulating commerce with foreign nations, the power of Congress does not stop at the jurisdictional lines of the several States. It would be a very useless power, if it could not pass those lines. The commerce of the United States with foreign nations, is that of the whole United States. Every district has a right to participate in it. The deep streams which penetrate our country in every direction, pass through the interior of almost every State in the Union, and furnish the means of exercising this right. If Congress has the power to regulate it, that power must be exercised whenever the subject exists. If it exists within the States, if a foreign voyage may commence or terminate at a port within a State, then the power of Congress may be exercised within a State.

This principle is, if possible, still more clear, when applied to commerce "among the several States." They either join each other, in which case they are separated by a mathematical line, or they are remote from each other, in which case other States lie between them. What is commerce "among" them; and how is it to be conducted? Can a trading expedition between two adjoining States, commence and terminate outside of each? And if the trading intercourse be between two States remote from each other, must it not commence in one, terminate in the other, and probably pass through a third? Commerce among the States must, of necessity, be commerce with the States. . . .

We are now arrived at the inquiry—What is this power?

It is the power to regulate; that is, to prescribe the rule by which commerce is to be governed. This power, like all others vested in Congress, is complete in itself, may be exercised to its utmost extent, and acknowledges no limitations, other than are prescribed in the constitution. . . . If, as has always been understood, the sovereignty of Congress, though limited to specified objects, is plenary as to those objects, the power over commerce with foreign nations, and among the several States, is vested in Congress as absolutely as it would be in a single government, having in its constitution the same restrictions on the exercise of the power as are found in the constitution of the United States. The wisdom and the discretion of Congress, their identity with the people, and the influence which their constituents possess at elections, are, in this, as in many other instances, as that, for example, of declaring war, the sole restraints on which they have relied, to secure them from its abuse. They are the restraints on which the people must often rely solely, in all representative governments.

The power of Congress, then, comprehends navigation, within the limits of every State in the Union; so far as that navigation may be, in any manner, connected with "commerce with foreign nations, or among the several States, or with the Indian tribes." It may, of consequence, pass the jurisdictional line of New York, and act upon the very waters to which the prohibition now under consideration applies.

But it has been urged with great earnestness, that, although the power of Congress to regulate commerce with foreign nations, and among the several States, be co-extensive with the subject itself, and have no other limits than are prescribed in the constitution, yet the States may severally exercise the same power, within their respective jurisdictions. In support of this argument, it is said, that they possessed it as an inseparable attribute of sover-eignty, before the formation of the constitution, and still retain it, except so far as they have surrendered it by that instrument; that this principle results from the nature of the government, and is secured by the tenth amendment; that an affirmative grant of power is not exclusive, unless in its own nature it be such that the continued exercise of it by the former possessor is inconsistent with the grant, and that this is not of that description.

The appellant, conceding these postulates, except the last, contends, that full power to regulate a particular sub-ject, implies the whole power, and leaves no residuum; that a grant of the whole is incompatible with the existence of a right in another to any part of it. . . .

In discussing the question, whether this power is still in the States, in the case under consideration, we may dis-miss from it the inquiry, whether it is surrendered by the mere grant to Congress, or is retained until Congress shall exercise the power. We may dismiss that inquiry, because it has been exercised, and the regulations which Congress deemed it proper to make, are now in full operation. The sole question is, can a State regulate commerce with for-eign nations and among the States, while Congress is regu-lating it?

The counsel for the respondent answer this question in the affirmative, and rely very much on the restrictions in the 10th section, as supporting their opinion. . . .

It has been contended by the general counsel for the appellant, that, as the word "to regulate" implies in its nature, full power over the thing to be regulated, it excludes, necessarily, the action of all others that would perform the same operation on the same thing. That regulation is designed for the entire result, applying to those parts which remain as they were, as well as to those which are altered. It produces a uniform whole, which is as much disturbed and deranged by changing what the regulating power designs to leave untouched, as that on which it has operated.

There is great force in this argument, and the Court is not satisfied that it has been refuted.

Since, however, in exercising the power of regulating their own purely internal affairs, whether of trading or police, the States may sometimes enact laws, the validity of which depends on their interfering with, and being con-trary to, an act of Congress passed in pursuance of the constitution, the Court will enter upon the inquiry, whether the laws of New York, as expounded by the highest tribu-nal of that State, have, in their application to this case, come into collision with an act of Congress, and deprived a citizen of a right to which that act entitles him. Should this collision exist, it will be immaterial whether those laws were passed in virtue of a concurrent power "to regu-late commerce with foreign nations and among the several States," or, in virtue of a power to regulate their domestic trade and police. In one case and the other, the acts of New York must yield to the law of Congress; and the decision sustaining the privilege they confer, against a right given by a law of the Union, must be erroneous. . . .

But the framers of our constitution foresaw this state of things, and provided for it, by declaring the supremacy not only of itself, but of the laws made in pursuance of it. The nullity of any act, inconsistent with the constitution, is pro-duced by the declaration, that the constitution is the supreme law. The appropriate application of that part of the clause which confers the same supremacy on laws and treaties, is to such acts of the State Legislatures as do not transcend their powers, but, though enacted in the execu-tion of acknowledged State powers, interfere with, or are contrary to the laws of Congress, made in pursuance of the constitution, or some treaty made under the authority of the United States. In every such case, the act of Congress, or the treaty, is supreme; and the law of the State, though enacted in the exercise of powers not controverted, must yield to it. . . .

But all inquiry into this subject seems to the Court to be put completely at rest, by the act already mentioned, enti-tled, "An act for the enrolling and licensing of steam boats."

This act authorizes a steam boat employed, or intended to be employed, only in a river or bay of the United States, owned wholly or in part by an alien, resident within the

United States, to be enrolled and licensed as if the same belonged to a citizen of the United States.

This act demonstrates the opinion of Congress, that steam boats may be enrolled and licensed, in common with vessels using sails. They are, of course, entitled to the same privileges, and can no more be restrained from navigating waters, and entering ports which are free to such vessels, than if they were wafted on their voyage by the winds, instead of being propelled by the agency of fire. The one element may be as legitimately used as the other, for every commercial purpose authorized by the laws of the Union; and the act of a State inhibiting the use of either to any vessel having a license under the act of Congress, comes, we think, in direct collision with that act.

Like his opinions in *Marbury* and *McCulloch,* Marshall's opinion in *Gibbons* laid a constitutional foundation that remains in place today. The decision made several important points. First, commerce involves more than buying and selling: it also includes the commercial intercourse between nations and states, and therefore transportation and navigation clearly fall within the definition of commerce. Second, commerce among the states begins in one state and ends in another; it does not stop when the act of crossing a state border is completed. Consequently, commerce that occurs within a state may be part of a larger interstate process. Third, once an act is considered part of interstate commerce, Congress, according to the Constitution, may regulate it. The power to regulate interstate commerce is complete and has no limitation other than what may be found in other constitutional provisions. But note that Marshall rejects Ogden's argument that the Tenth Amendment serves as such a limit. In line with his opinion in *McCulloch,* Marshall does not find that the amendment creates an "enclave" of state power. Instead, he emphasizes that Congress is limited to its delegated powers (*see chapter 6*)—in this case, the power to regulate interstate commerce, however broadly defined. This brings us to the fourth point: because the text of the commerce clause limits congressional power to regulate commerce among the states, the power to regulate commerce that occurs completely within the boundaries of a single state and does not extend to or affect other states belongs to the states.

Gibbons v. Ogden was a substantial victory for national power. It broadly construed the terms *regulate,* "Commerce," and "Commerce . . . among the several States" (or interstate commerce). But Marshall did not go as far as Daniel Webster had urged. The opinion asserts only that Congress has complete power to regulate interstate commerce and that federal regulations are superior to any state laws. The decision does not answer the question of the legitimacy of states regulating interstate commerce in the absence of federal action. That controversy was left for future justices to decide.

ATTEMPTS TO DEFINE THE COMMERCE POWER IN THE WAKE OF THE INDUSTRIAL REVOLUTION

Marshall provided a clear, if expansive, framework for the exercise of congressional commerce power, but the national legislature did not take immediate advantage of this broad interpretation of its authority. As a result, commerce clause cases did not become major items on the Supreme Court's agenda until the second half of the nineteenth century. By that time, small intrastate businesses were giving way to large interstate corporations. Industrial expansion blossomed, and the interstate railroad and pipeline systems were well under way. The infamous captains of industry were creating large monopolistic trusts that dominated huge segments of the national economy, squeezing out small businesses and discouraging new entrepreneurs. The industrial combines that controlled the railroads also, in effect, ruled agriculture and other interests that relied on the rails to transport goods to market. This commercial growth brought great prosperity to some, but it also caused horrendous social problems. Children worked in sweatshops, and unsafe working conditions and low wages plagued employees of all ages, eventually leading to the formation of labor unions.

In light of these developments, Congress sought to exert some control over both the economic and the social concerns following from the rise of big business. To deal with the former, it passed several laws—aimed at regulating business practices—based in its commerce power. In the case of social problems, it began to make use of the commerce clause as a federal police power—that is, the government's authority to regulate for the health, safety, morals, and general welfare of its citizens.

Critics immediately attacked Congress for exceeding its constitutional authority. Their primary argument was that the laws regulated intrastate activity, not "Commerce . . . among the several States," and so Congress had overstepped its power; the regulation of intrastate activity was reserved to the states under the Tenth Amendment. In the social realm, they also questioned whether laws motivated by morality considerations were an appropriate exercise of the commerce power and whether laws that prohibited particular kinds of activities—for example, shipping lottery tickets across state lines—fell within Congress's power "to regulate" commerce.

In what follows, we consider the Court's response to these arguments, beginning with the debate over intra- versus interstate commerce, and moving next to the use of commerce as a federal police power. As you read the cases, consider whether the developing doctrine was compatible with Marshall's foundational decision in *Gibbons*.

Defining Interstate Commerce

As we just noted, in the wake of the rise of big business, Congress passed several laws based on its commerce power. Two are particularly notable: the Interstate Commerce Act of 1887, which established a mechanism for regulating the nation's interstate railroads, and the Sherman Anti-Trust Act of 1890 (hereafter Sherman Act), which was designed to break up monopolies that restrained trade. Business interests challenged both, primarily on the ground that they were regulations not of interstate commerce, but rather of intrastate activity, which was the purview of the states, not Congress.

Even with Marshall's decision in *Gibbons,* discriminating between inter- and intrastate commerce was not easy. The Supreme Court faced a significant number of appeals that asked the justices to clarify whether the national legislature had overstepped its bounds and regulated commerce that was purely intrastate. To say that the Court had difficulty developing a coherent doctrine is an understatement.

Manufacturing and Its Relationship to Interstate Commerce. The Court's endorsement of the federal power to regulate transportation, navigation, and instruments of commerce did not extend initially to the attempts by Congress to impose effective antitrust legislation. The targets of the antitrust statutes were the monopolies that controlled basic industries and choked out all competition. During the late 1800s these trusts grew to capture and exercise dominance over many industries, including oil, meatpacking, sugar, and steel. The Sherman Act was Congress's first attempt to break up these anticompetitive combines. It outlawed all contracts and combinations of companies that had the effect of restraining trade and commerce or eliminating competition.

For the antitrust law to be fully effective, however, its provisions had to cover the manufacturing and processing stages of commercial activity, which raised a serious constitutional problem. In earlier cases the Court had ruled that manufacturing was essentially a local activity and not part of interstate commerce. In *Veazie v. Moor* (1853) the Court had labeled it a far-reaching "pretension" to suggest that the federal power over interstate commerce extended to manufacturing. Later, in **Kidd v. Pearson** (1888), the Court took an even stronger stand. At issue was an Iowa statute that outlawed the production of alcoholic beverages. The law was challenged on the ground that the liquor being manufactured was intended for interstate shipment and sale, and consequently, the state was unconstitutionally regulating interstate commerce.

Speaking for the Court, Justice Lucius Q. C. Lamar rejected the attack, arguing,

No distinction is more popular to the common mind, or more clearly expressed in economic and political literature, than that between manufactures and commerce. Manufacture is transformation—the fashioning of raw materials into a change of form for use. The functions of commerce are different. The buying and selling and the transportation incident thereto constitute commerce.

Could the new antitrust law be applied to manufacturing? Or had Congress exceeded its constitutional authority in regulating production? These questions were answered in *United States v. E. C. Knight Co.* (1895), a battle over the federal government's attempts to break up the sugar trust.

United States v. E. C. Knight Co.

156 U.S. 1 (1895)
http://laws.findlaw.com/us/156/1.html
Vote: 8 (Brewer, Brown, Field, Fuller, Gray, Jackson, Shiras, White)
   1 (Harlan)

OPINION OF THE COURT: *Fuller*
DISSENTING OPINION: *Harlan*

FACTS:

At the end of the nineteenth century, six companies dominated the American sugar refining industry. The largest was American Sugar Refining Company, which had control of about 65 percent of the nation's refining capacity. Four Pennsylvania refiners shared 33 percent of the market, and a Boston company had a scant 2 percent. In March 1892 American Sugar entered into agreements that allowed it to acquire the four Pennsylvania refineries, including E. C. Knight Company, giving it absolute control over 98 percent of the sugar refining business in the United States.

The federal government sued to have the acquisition agreements canceled. According to Justice Department attorneys, the sugar trust operated as a monopoly in restraint of trade in violation of the Sherman Act. Attorneys for American Sugar and the acquired companies held that the law did not apply to sugar refining because that activity is manufacturing subject to state, not federal, control.

E. C. Knight was the Court's first antitrust case. The outcome was crucial to the government's attempts to break up powerful monopolies. Some observers have charged that Attorney General Richard Olney failed to provide the best prosecution of the case. Olney was not a dedicated trustbuster; he had opposed the passage of the antitrust act and later worked for its repeal.[1]

ARGUMENTS:

For the appellant, United States:

- The power to control the manufacturing of sugar is a monopoly over an important good, which cannot be enjoyed by most Americans unless it is shipped in interstate commerce. As a result, the federal government, in the exercise of its power to regulate commerce, may prohibit monopolies directly and set aside the instruments that have created them.

- The products of these refineries were sold and distributed among the states; therefore, all the companies were engaged in trade or commerce with several states and other nations.

For the appellee, E. C. Knight Co.:

- Congress's commerce clause power does not extend to articles that are manufactured simply because they are manufactured with an intent to sell later to citizens of the same state or another. No article is

1. Savage, *Guide to the U.S. Supreme Court,* 102.

part of trade or commerce, which can be regulated by Congress, until it is put in the way of transit. Congress can only regulate trade and commerce between the states (contracts to buy, sell, exchange goods to be transported, the actual transportation, and the instrumentalities of transportation). There is, in short, a distinction between manufacturing and commerce.

- If businesses agree that they will not transport goods from one state to another, they make a contract in restraint of trade between the states. If, however, they simply agree that they will not manufacture goods within a certain state, even if this results in no trade with other states in the goods, Congress cannot interfere because the agreement pertains to manufacturing, not commerce.

MR. CHIEF JUSTICE FULLER DELIVERED THE OPINION OF THE COURT.

The fundamental question is, whether conceding that the existence of a monopoly in manufacture is established by the evidence, that monopoly can be directly suppressed under the act of Congress in the mode attempted by this bill.

It cannot be denied that the power of a State to protect the lives, health, and property of its citizens, and to preserve good order and the public morals, "the power to govern men and things within the limits of its dominion," is a power originally and always belonging to the States, not surrendered by them to the general government, not directly restrained by the Constitution of the United States, and essentially exclusive. The relief of the citizens of each State from the burden of monopoly and the evils resulting from the restraint of trade among such citizens was left with the States to deal with, and this court has recognized their possession of that power even to the extent of holding that an employment or business carried on by private individuals, when it becomes a matter of such public interest and importance as to create a common charge or burden upon the citizen; in other words, when it becomes a practical monopoly, to which the citizen is compelled to resort and by means of which a tribute can be exacted from the community, is subject to regulation by state legislative power. On the other hand, the power of Congress to regulate commerce among the several States is also exclusive. The Constitution does not provide that interstate commerce shall be free, but, by the grant of this exclusive power to regulate it, it was left free except as Congress might impose restraints. Therefore it has been determined that the failure of Congress to exercise this exclusive power in any case is an expression of its will that the subject shall be free from restrictions or impositions upon it by the several States, and if a law passed by a State in the exercise of its acknowledged powers comes into conflict with that will, the Congress and the State cannot occupy the position of equal opposing sovereignties, because the Constitution declares its supremacy and that of the laws passed in pursuance thereof; and that which is not supreme must yield to that which is supreme. "Commerce, undoubtedly, is traffic," said Chief Justice Marshall, "but it is something more; it is intercourse. It describes the commercial intercourse between nations and parts of nations in all its branches, and is regulated by prescribing rules for carrying on that intercourse." That which belongs to commerce is within the jurisdiction of the United States, but that which does not belong to commerce is within the jurisdiction of the police power of the State.

The argument is that the power to control the manufacture of refined sugar is a monopoly over a necessary of life, to the enjoyment of which by a large part of the population of the United States interstate commerce is indispensable, and that, therefore, the general government in the exercise of the power to regulate commerce may repress such monopoly directly and set aside the instruments which have created it. But this argument cannot be confined to necessaries of life merely, and must include all articles of general consumption. Doubtless the power to control the manufacture of a given thing involves in a certain sense the control of its disposition, but this is a secondary and not the primary sense; and although the exercise of that power may result in bringing the operation of commerce into play, it does not control it, and affects it only incidentally and indirectly. Commerce succeeds to manufacture, and is not a part of it. The power to regulate commerce is the power to prescribe the rule by which commerce shall be governed, and is a power independent of the power to suppress monopoly. But it may operate in repression of monopoly whenever that comes within the rules by which commerce is governed or whenever the transaction is itself a monopoly of commerce.

It is vital that the independence of the commercial power and of the police power, and the delimitation between them, however sometimes perplexing, should always be recognized and observed, for while the one furnishes the strongest bond of union, the other is essential to the preservation of the autonomy of the States as required by our dual form of government; and acknowledged evils, however grave and urgent they may appear to be, had better be borne, than the risk be run, in the effort to suppress them, of more serious consequences by resort to expedients of even doubtful constitutionality.

It will be perceived how far-reaching the proposition is that the power of dealing with a monopoly directly may be exercised by the general government whenever interstate or international commerce may be ultimately affected. The regulation of commerce applies to the subjects of commerce and not to matters of internal police. Contracts to buy, sell, or exchange goods to be transported among the several States, the transportation and its instrumentalities, and articles bought, sold, or exchanged for the purposes of such transit among the States, or put in the way of transit, may be regulated, but this is because they form part of interstate trade or commerce. The fact that an article is manufactured for export to another State does not of itself make it an article of interstate commerce, and the intent of the manufacturer does not determine the time when the article or product passes from the control of the States and belongs to commerce. This was so ruled in *Coe v. Errol* [1886], in which the question before the court was whether certain logs cut at a place in New Hampshire and hauled to a river town for the purpose of transportation to the State of Maine were liable to be taxed like other property in the State of New Hampshire. Mr. Justice Bradley, delivering the opinion of the court, said: "Does the owner's state of mind in relation to the goods, that is, his intent to export them, and his partial preparation to do so, exempt them from taxation? This is the precise question for solution. . . . There must be a point of time when they cease to be governed exclusively by the domestic law and begin to be governed and protected by the national law of commercial regulation, and that moment seems to us to be a legitimate one for this purpose, in which they commence their final movement from the State of their origin to that of their destination."

And again, in *Kidd v. Pearson*, where the question was discussed whether the right of a State to enact a statute prohibiting within its limits the manufacture of intoxicating liquors, except for certain purposes, could be overthrown by the fact that the manufacturer intended to export the liquors when made, it was held that the intent of the manufacturer did not determine the time when the article or product passed from the control of the State and belonged to commerce, and that, therefore, the statute, in omitting to except from its operation the manufacture of intoxicating liquors within the limits of the State for export, did not constitute an unauthorized interference with the right of Congress to regulate commerce. . . .

Contracts, combinations, or conspiracies to control domestic enterprise in manufacture, agriculture, mining, production in all its forms, or to raise or lower prices or wages, might unquestionably tend to restrain external as well as domestic trade, but the restraint would be an indirect result, however inevitable and whatever its extent, and such result would not necessarily determine the object of the contract, combination, or conspiracy.

Again, all the authorities agree that in order to vitiate a contract or combination it is not essential that its result should be a complete monopoly; it is sufficient if it really tends to that end and to deprive the public of the advantages which flow from free competition. Slight reflection will show that if the national power extends to all contracts and combinations in manufacture, agriculture, mining, and other productive industries, whose ultimate result may affect external commerce, comparatively little of business operations and affairs would be left for state control.

It was in the light of well-settled principles that the act of July 2, 1890, was framed. Congress did not attempt thereby to assert the power to deal with monopoly directly as such; or to limit and restrict the rights of corporations created by the States or the citizens of the States in the acquisition, control, or disposition of property; or to regulate or prescribe the price or prices at which such property or the products thereof should be sold; or to make criminal the acts of persons in the acquisition and control of property which the States of their residence or creation sanctioned or permitted. Aside from the provisions applicable where Congress might exercise municipal power, what the law struck at was combinations, contracts, and conspiracies to monopolize trade and commerce among the several States or with foreign nations; but the contracts and acts of the defendants related exclusively to the acquisition of the Philadelphia refineries and the business of sugar refining in Pennsylvania, and bore no direct relation to commerce between the States or with foreign nations. The object was manifestly private gain in the manufacture of the commodity, but not through the control of interstate or foreign commerce. It is true that the bill alleged that the products of these refineries were sold and distributed among the several States, and that all the companies were engaged in trade or commerce with the several States and with foreign nations; but this was no more than to say that trade and commerce served manufacture to fulfill its function. Sugar was refined for sale, and sales were probably made at Philadelphia for consumption, and undoubtedly for resale by the first purchasers throughout Pennsylvania and other States, and refined sugar was also forwarded by the companies to other States for sale. Nevertheless it does not follow that an attempt to monopolize, or the actual monopoly of, the manufacture was an attempt, whether executory or consummated, to monopolize commerce, even though, in order to dispose of the product, the instrumentality of commerce was necessarily invoked. There was nothing in the proofs to indicate any intention to put a restraint upon trade or commerce, and the fact, as we have seen, that trade or commerce might be indirectly affected was not enough to entitle complainants to a decree. . . .

Decree affirmed.

MR. JUSTICE HARLAN, dissenting.

In my judgment, the citizens of the several States composing the Union are entitled, of right, to buy goods in the State where they are manufactured, or in any other State, without being confronted by an illegal combination whose business extends throughout the whole country, which by the law everywhere is an enemy to the public interests, and which prevents such buying, except at prices arbitrarily fixed by it. I insist that the free course of trade among the States cannot coexist with such combinations. When I speak of trade I mean the buying and selling of articles of every kind that are recognized articles of interstate commerce. Whatever improperly obstructs the free course of interstate intercourse and trade, as involved in the buying and selling of articles to be carried from one State to another, may be reached by Congress, under its authority to regulate commerce among the States. The exercise of that authority so as to make trade among the States, in all recognized articles of commerce, absolutely free from unreasonable or illegal restrictions imposed by combinations, is justified by an express grant of power to Congress and would redound to the welfare of the whole country. I am unable to perceive that any such result would imperil the autonomy of the States, especially as that result cannot be attained through the action of any one State.

Undue restrictions or burdens upon the purchasing of goods, in the market for sale, to be transported to other States, cannot be imposed even by a State without violating the freedom of commercial intercourse guaranteed by the Constitution. But if a *State* within whose limits the business of refining sugar is exclusively carried on may not constitutionally impose burdens upon purchases of sugar *to be transported to other States*, how comes it that combinations of corporations or individuals, within the same State, may not be prevented by the national government from putting unlawful restraints upon the purchasing of that article *to be carried from the State in which such purchases are made?* If the national power is competent to repress State action in restraint of interstate trade as it may be involved in purchases of refined sugar to be transported from one State to another State, surely it ought to be deemed sufficient to prevent unlawful restraints attempted to be imposed by combinations of corporations or individuals upon those identical purchases; otherwise, illegal combinations of corporations or individuals may—so far as national power and interstate commerce are concerned—do, with impunity, what no State can do. . . .

To the general government has been committed the control of commercial intercourse among the States, to the end that it may be free at all times from any restraints except such as Congress may impose or permit for the benefit of the whole country. The common government of all the people is the only one that can adequately deal with a matter which directly and injuriously affects the entire commerce of the country, which concerns equally all the people of the Union, and which, it must be confessed, cannot be adequately controlled by any one State. Its authority should not be so weakened by construction that it cannot reach and eradicate evils that, beyond all question, tend to defeat an object which that government is entitled, by the Constitution, to accomplish.

Chief Justice Melville W. Fuller's opinion shows the initial development of the Court's focus on the extent to which the various stages of business affect interstate commerce. Proponents of federal regulation often argued that if an intrastate economic activity—whether manufacturing and production or shipment and distribution—had any effect on interstate commerce, Congress could regulate it. The Supreme Court rejected this position in *E. C. Knight.* To the Court, commerce is different from manufacturing and production because "commerce succeeds to manufacture, and is not a part of it." As a result, manufacturing affects interstate commerce only indirectly and Congress may not regulate it; rather, it is a local matter that is up to the states to regulate. Federal authority becomes activated only when the intrastate activity has a *direct* effect on interstate commerce. In the sugar trust case, Fuller concluded that the challenged monopoly of refining facilities had only an indirect effect on interstate commerce and therefore was not

subject to federal regulation. While the distinction between direct and indirect effects could be interpreted various ways, conservative Courts continued to use it to strike down other federal regulatory attempts. Indeed, the distinction took center stage in the Court's opinion in *Schechter Poultry Corp. v. United States,* in which, as we shall see, the justices struck down a major piece of Roosevelt's New Deal legislation.

Although *E. C. Knight* removed manufacturing from the authority of the Sherman Act, it did not doom federal antitrust efforts. In fact, when the monopolistic activity was not manufacturing, the Court was quite willing to apply the law. For example, the Court held that companies engaged in production and interstate sale of pipe came under the sections of the Sherman Act.[2] In 1904 the Court went even farther, ruling in **Northern Securities Company v. United States** that stock transactions creating a holding company (the result of an effective merger between the Northern Pacific and Great Northern Railroad companies) were subject to Sherman Act scrutiny. In spite of these applications of the antitrust law, *E. C. Knight* set an important precedent, declaring manufacturing to be outside the definition of interstate commerce. This ruling later would be extended, with serious repercussions, to bar many of the New Deal programs passed to combat the Great Depression. It was only at such a time of economic collapse that the wisdom expressed in Justice John Marshall Harlan's dissent in *E. C. Knight* became apparent: the federal government must be empowered to regulate economic evils that are injurious to the nation's commerce and that a single state is incapable of eradicating.

The Shreveport Doctrine. The regulation of the railroads provided the Court an early opportunity to refine the definition of interstate commerce. The first railroads were small local operations regulated by the states, but as interstate rail systems developed, the justices held that their regulation was rightfully a federal responsibility.[3] Congress responded by passing the Interstate Commerce Act of 1887, which created the Interstate Commerce Commission (ICC) to regulate railroads and set rates. The Court approved the constitutionality of the commission but later stripped it of its

---

2. *Addyston Pipe and Steel Co. v. United States* (1899).

3. *Wabash, St. Louis & Pacific Railway Co. v. Illinois* (1886).

ability to set rates.[4] In 1906 Congress revised the authority and procedures of the commission and reestablished its rate-setting power.

The Court's decision in *Houston, E. & W. Texas Railway Co. v. United States* (1914), better known as the *Shreveport Rate Case,* firmly established congressional power over the nation's rails. This dispute arose from competition among three railroad companies to serve various cities in Texas. Two were based in Texas, one in Houston and the other in Dallas, and the third competitor operated out of Shreveport, Louisiana. The Texas Railroad Commission regulated the Texas companies because their operations were exclusively intrastate, but the Shreveport company came under the jurisdiction of the ICC. Difficulties arose when the Texas regulators set rates substantially lower than did the ICC. The motive behind these lower rates was clear: the Texas commission wanted to encourage intrastate trade and to discourage Texas companies from taking their business to Shreveport. The rates placed the Shreveport railroad at a distinct disadvantage in competing for the Texas market. In response, the ICC ordered the intrastate Texas rates to be raised to the interstate levels. When the commission's authority to set intrastate rail rates was challenged, the Supreme Court ruled in favor of the ICC, articulating what became known as the Shreveport doctrine. The Court held that the federal government had the power to regulate intrastate commerce when a failure to regulate would cripple, retard, or destroy interstate commerce. According to Justice Charles Evans Hughes's opinion for the Court,

The fact that [these] carriers are instruments of intrastate commerce, as well as of interstate commerce, does not derogate from the complete and paramount authority of Congress over the latter, or preclude the Federal power from being exerted to prevent the intrastate operations of such carriers from being made a means of injury to that which has been confided to Federal care. Wherever the interstate and intrastate transactions of carriers are so related that the government of the one involves the control of the other, it is Congress, and not the state, that is entitled to prescribe the final and

dominant rule, for otherwise Congress would be denied the exercise of its constitutional authority, and the state, and not the nation, would be supreme within the national field.

It was clear to Hughes that the regulatory power of the federal government extends to those aspects of intrastate commerce that have such a close and substantial relation to interstate traffic that control is essential to protect the security and efficiency of interstate commerce.

The Stream of Commerce Doctrine. Government efforts to break up the meatpacking trust presented a different constitutional challenge. The corporations that dominated the meat industry, such as Armour, Cudahy, and Swift, ruled the nation's stockyards, which stood at the throat of the meat-distribution process. Western ranchers sent their livestock to the stockyards to be sold, butchered, and packed for shipment to consumers in the East. Livestock brokers, known as commission men, received the animals at the stockyards and sold them to the meatpacking companies for the ranchers. Consequently, when the meatpacking trust acquired control of the stockyards and the commission men who worked there, it was in a position to direct where the ranchers sent their stock, fix meat prices, demand unreasonably low rates for transporting stock, and decide when to withhold meat from the market. The government believed these actions constituted a restraint of trade in violation of the Sherman Act. The meatpackers argued that their control over the stockyards was an intrastate matter to be regulated by the states.

The Court settled the dispute in *Swift & Company v. United States* (1905), in which Justice Oliver Wendell Holmes held for a unanimous Court that the Sherman Act applied to the stockyards. The commercial sale of beef, the justice reasoned, began when the cattle left the range and did not terminate until final sale. The fact that the cattle stopped at the stockyards, midpoint in this commercial enterprise, did not mean that they were removed from interstate commerce. Holmes's opinion develops what has become known as the "stream of commerce doctrine," which allows federal regulation of interstate commerce from the point of its origin to the point of its termination. Interruptions in the course of that interstate commerce do not suspend the right of Congress to regulate. *Stafford v. Wallace,* an

---

4. *Interstate Commerce Commission v. Brimson* (1894); *Interstate Commerce Commission v. Cincinnati, New Orleans & Texas Pacific Railway Co.* (1897); *Interstate Commerce Commission v. Alabama-Midland Railway Co.* (1897).

appeal based on another federal assault on the meat-packing combines, develops the doctrine more fully.

Stafford v. Wallace

258 U.S. 495 (1922)
http://laws.findlaw.com/us/258/495.html
Vote: 7 (Brandeis, Clarke, Holmes, McKenna, Pitney, Taft, Van Devanter)
   1 (McReynolds)
OPINION OF THE COURT: *Taft*
NOT PARTICIPATING: *Day*

FACTS:

Armed with the *Swift & Company* precedent, Congress in 1921 passed the Packers and Stockyard Act. This legislation attempted to go beyond antitrust considerations in regulating the meatpacking industry. In addition to making it unlawful for the packers to fix prices or engage in monopolistic practices, the law forbade meatpackers in interstate commerce to engage in any unfair, discriminatory, or deceptive practices. It required all stockyard dealers and commission men to register with the secretary of agriculture. The transactions at the stockyards had to conform to a schedule of charges open for public inspection. Fees and charges could be changed only after ten days' notice to the secretary. Congress delegated to the Agriculture Department the authority to make rules and regulations to carry out the act, set stockyard rates, and prescribe record-keeping procedures for stockyard officials.

   Stafford and Company, a corporation engaged in commercial transactions of cattle, sued Secretary of Agriculture Henry Wallace, asking the courts to enjoin his enforcement of the act. The lower court refused to issue the requested injunction, and the company appealed.

ARGUMENTS:

For the appellants, T. F. Stafford et al.:

- The lower court's decision rests on the following syllogism: "the stockyards themselves are instrumentalities of interstate commerce," and the dealers in livestock at the yards are "engaged in or participating in that commerce within the stockyards"; accordingly, the dealers are engaged in interstate commerce, which Congress can regulate. Both the premise and conclusion are wrong. The dealers are not engaged in "commerce within the stockyards." They buy and sell livestock for others, which is something separate and distinct from interstate commerce. It is not affected by whether the shipment originates within the state or out of state. The transportation ceases when the livestock reaches the stockyards, and it does not begin again, if ever, until after the services of appellants have been fully performed.

- If the appellants are engaged in interstate commerce solely because they perform a service concerning livestock that may be shipped in interstate commerce, so too are the men who feed the cattle, and so on. If Congress can regulate these activities—that is, all the incidents connected with that commerce—the entire sphere of mercantile activity would exclude state control over contracts and commerce that are purely domestic in their nature.

For the appellees, Henry Wallace, secretary of agriculture, et al.:

- Various Court decisions have established the power of Congress to regulate all instrumentalities by which interstate commerce is carried on or conducted. The appellant's business, which offers terminal facilities at one of the world's largest livestock markets, is embraced within those instrumentalities of interstate commerce just as if it were an integral part of a great railroad system.

- The question here is not whether the appellants should be covered by the Packers and Stockyard Act by judicial interpretation but whether Congress had the power to designate them and their transactions as part of the "current of commerce" and therefore covered by the act. The answer is yes because they form as much a part of the "current of commerce" as the railroads or the stockyards company. See *Swift*.

MR. CHIEF JUSTICE TAFT DELIVERED THE OPINION OF THE COURT.

The object to be secured by the act is the free and unburdened flow of live stock from the ranges and farms of the West and the Southwest through the great stockyards and slaughtering centers on the borders of that region, and thence in the form of meat products to the consuming cities of the country in the Middle West and East, or, still as live stock, to the feeding places and fattening farms in the Middle West or East for further preparation for the market.

   The chief evil feared is the monopoly of the packers, enabling them unduly and arbitrarily to lower prices to the shipper who sells, and unduly and arbitrarily to increase the price to the consumer who buys. Congress thought that the power to maintain this monopoly was aided by control of the stockyards. Another evil which it sought to provide against by the act, was exorbitant charges, duplication of commissions, deceptive practices in respect of prices, in the passage of the live stock through the stockyards, all made possible by collusion between the stockyards management and the commission men, on the one hand, and the packers and dealers on the other. Expenses incurred in the passage through the stockyards necessarily reduce the price received by the shipper, and increase the price to be paid by the consumer. If they be exorbitant or unreasonable, they are an undue burden on the commerce which the stockyards are intended to facilitate. Any unjust or deceptive practice or combination that unduly and directly enhances them is an unjust obstruction to that commerce. . . .

The stockyards are not a place of rest or final destination. Thousands of head of live stock arrive daily by carload and trainload lots, and must be promptly sold and disposed of and moved out to give place to the constantly flowing traffic that presses behind. The stockyards are but a throat through which the current flows, and the transactions which occur therein are only incident to this current from the West to the East, and from one State to another. Such transactions cannot be separated from the movement to which they contribute and necessarily take on its character. The commission men are essential in making the sales without which the flow of the current would be obstructed, and this, whether they are made to packers or dealers. The dealers are essential to the sales to the stock farmers and feeders. The sales are not in this aspect merely local transactions. They create a local change of title, it is true, but they do not stop the flow; they merely change the private interests in the subject of the current, not interfering with, but, on the contrary, being indispensable to its continuity. The origin of the live stock is in the West, its ultimate destination known to, and intended by, all engaged in the business is in the Middle West and East either as meat products or stock for feeding and fattening. This is the definite and well-understood course of business. The stockyards and the sales are necessary factors in the middle of this current of commerce.

The act, therefore, treats the various stockyards of the country as great national public utilities to promote the flow of commerce from the ranges and farms of the West to the consumers in the East. It assumes that they conduct a business affected by a public use of a national character and subject to national regulation. That it is a business within the power of regulation by legislative action needs

no discussion. . . . Nor is there any doubt that in the receipt of live stock by rail and in their delivery by rail the stockyards are an interstate commerce agency. The only question here is whether the business done in the stockyards between the receipt of the live stock in the yards and the shipment of them therefrom is a part of interstate commerce, or is so associated with it as to bring it within the power of national regulation. A similar question has been before this court and had great consideration in *Swift & Co. v. United States.* The judgment in that case gives a clear and comprehensive exposition which leaves to us in this case little but the obvious application of the principles there declared. . . .

The application of the commerce clause of the Constitution in the *Swift Case* was the result of the natural development of interstate commerce under modern conditions. It was the inevitable recognition of the great central fact that such streams of commerce from one part of the country to another which are ever flowing are in their very essence the commerce among the States and with foreign nations which historically it was one of the chief purposes of the Constitution to bring under national protection and control. This court declined to defeat this purpose in respect of such a stream and take it out of complete national regulation by a nice and technical inquiry into the noninterstate character of some of its necessary incidents and facilities when considered alone and without reference to their association with the movement of which they were an essential but subordinate part.

The principles of the *Swift Case* have become a fixed rule of this court in the construction and application of the commerce clause. . . .

Of course, what we are considering here is not a bill in equity or an indictment charging conspiracy to obstruct interstate commerce, but a law. The language of the law shows that what Congress had in mind primarily was to prevent such conspiracies by supervision of the agencies which would be likely to be employed in it. If Congress could provide for punishment or restraint of such conspiracies after their formation through the Anti-Trust Law as in the *Swift Case,* certainly it may provide regulation to prevent their formation. . . .

As already noted, the word "commerce" when used in the act is defined to be interstate and foreign commerce. Its provisions are carefully drawn to apply only to those practices and obstructions which in the judgment of Congress are likely to affect interstate commerce prejudicially. Thus construed and applied, we think the act clearly within congressional power and valid.

Other objections are made to the act and its provisions as violative of other limitations of the Constitution, but the only one seriously pressed was that based on the Commerce Clause and we do not deem it necessary to discuss the others.

The orders of the District Court refusing the interlocutory injunctions are

Affirmed.

The stream of commerce precedents set in the *Swift* and *Stafford* stockyards cases were applied later to other regulatory schemes. Most notable was *Chicago Board of Trade v. Olsen* (1923), which brought the grain exchanges under the rubric of interstate commerce. Such decisions broadened the power of the federal government to control the economy.

But, we hasten to note, the Court continued to find that certain commercial activities exerted too little direct impact on interstate commerce to justify congressional control. The most prominent among these were manufacturing and processing. The 1895 sugar trust case of *E. C. Knight* established this principle and was reinforced in 1918 by *Hammer v. Dagenhart,* the child labor case. *Hammer,* excerpted later in this chapter, provides an example of the Court's use during this period of the Tenth Amendment to limit federal regulatory power; it also, as we shall see, illustrates the Court's use of the production/distribution distinction of *E. C. Knight* to narrow Congress's ability to use the commerce clause as a federal police power.

Regulating Commerce as a Federal Police Power

Challenging laws as regulating intrastate, not interstate, commerce was only one approach taken to resist federal regulatory efforts during this period. Business interests also attacked certain kinds of laws as beyond congressional commerce power on the ground that they regulated morality and not commerce. They claimed that Congress was inappropriately using the commerce clause as a federal police power. As we noted earlier, the term *police power* refers to the general authority of a government to regulate for the health, safety, morals, and general welfare of its citizens. The states possessed general police powers prior to the adoption of the federal Constitution and retained them when the national government was created. Consequently, states may pass laws for the

general welfare without any specific grant of power to do so. As long as the legislation does not run afoul of specific constitutional limitations (such as the Bill of Rights), the states are free to act.

The federal government, on the other hand, is a government of delegated powers. It does not possess any general police power. For an act of Congress to be valid, it must rest on a specific grant of authority—an enumerated, implied, or inherent power. Madison described the situation aptly in *Federalist* No. 45: the "powers delegated by the proposed Constitution to the federal government are few and defined. Those which are to remain in the State governments are numerous and indefinite."

Consider prostitution, which was at issue in *Hoke v. United States* (1913). Based on its police powers, a state could pass legislation outlawing prostitution without any justification necessary. The federal government, however, could pass such a law only if Congress could justify it as an exercise of a delegated power. Consequently, we have the dispute in *Hoke* over whether a law making it a criminal violation to take "any woman or girl" across state lines "for the purpose of prostitution or debauchery, or for any other immoral purpose" was a valid exercise of the power to regulate interstate commerce.

So, while most of the battles over the meaning of interstate commerce have been largely economic—*Gibbons* and *E. C. Knight* provide examples—*Hoke* illustrates that the regulation of commerce can be structured in a way that affects matters of health, safety, and morals. But are regulations of this sort constitutional? Congress framed the law at issue in *Hoke,* known as the Mann Act, as an exercise of its commerce power. But the legislators may have been motivated by moral, rather than commercial, considerations. Is this an appropriate exercise of the commerce power? May Congress legitimately use the commerce clause as a means of exercising an authority at the national level similar to the states' police powers? A related consideration is that many of these laws, including the Mann Act, prohibit particular activities. Are "prohibitions" regulations within the meaning of the commerce clause?

Marshall's opinion in *Gibbons* is suggestive. Recall his words: "Th[e] [commerce] power, like all others vested in Congress, is complete in itself, may be exercised to its utmost extent, and acknowledges no limitations, other than are prescribed in the constitution." In other words, if an activity falls under the definition of commerce among the states, then Congress has the right to regulate it as long as the regulation does not violate a constitutional limitation (such as the First Amendment). The commerce clause itself imposes no limitations on the motivations for such legislation.

Would subsequent Courts agree? *Champion v. Ames* provides an initial response. The case demonstrates, first, that the power to "regulate" commerce includes the power to *prohibit* certain activities. It also shows how Congress can use the commerce power to depress certain activities it deems unacceptable. This goal is much different from those that are present when Congress regulates commerce for economic reasons.

As you read Justice John Marshall Harlan's opinion for the Court, notice the expansive terms he uses to describe the commerce power. Does he convince you that Congress can use the commerce clause to include the power to prohibit what Congress thought was an immoral trade? The four dissenters did not think so. They argued that Congress was not regulating commerce at all; instead, it was trying to prohibit lotteries, a matter for the police powers of the state to address.

Champion v. Ames

188 U.S. 321 (1903)
http://laws.findlaw.com/us/188/321.html
Vote: 5 (Brown, Harlan, Holmes, McKenna, White)
      4 (Brewer, Fuller, Peckham, Shiras)
OPINION OF THE COURT: *Harlan*
DISSENTING OPINION: *Fuller*

FACTS:

In 1895 Congress passed a statute prohibiting lottery tickets from being imported from abroad, transported across state lines or sent through the mail. United States Marshal John Ames arrested Charles Champion in Chicago on charges that he had arranged for a shipment of lottery tickets, supposedly printed in Paraguay, to be transported from Texas to California by Wells Fargo. When federal authorities attempted to transport Champion to Texas to stand trial on the charges, he filed for a writ of habeas corpus challenging his arrest. He alleged that Congress acted unconstitutionally when it passed the lottery ticket law.

ARGUMENTS:

For the appellant, Charles Champion:

- The power to regulate lotteries, and to permit or prohibit the sale of lottery tickets, is exclusively a police power reserved to the states. The suppression of lotteries is not an exercise of any power the Constitution commits to Congress and so violates the Tenth Amendment.

- The law can be sustained only as an exercise of the commerce power. But it is not a regulation of commerce; it is a suppression of an alleged evil. Sending lottery tickets is not a transaction within the scope of the commerce power. And it cannot be doubted that the intention and purpose of Congress was to suppress lotteries.

- Although the law may be necessary to suppress lotteries, it has no relation to interstate commerce and, therefore, is not "necessary and proper for carrying into execution" the power to regulate commerce among the states.

For the appellee, John C. Ames, U.S. marshal:

- Lottery tickets are articles of commerce in the sense that they are things that are the subjects of barter and sale.

- Whether an article is or is not an article of commerce is dependent not on its noxiousness or usefulness, nor on whether the states have prohibited it within their borders in the exercise of their police power, but on whether such articles have been, in the ordinary and usual channels of trade, the subjects of purchase and sale. Any article that people buy or sell is an article of commerce and comes under the power of Congress when its exchange is interstate.

- The power to prohibit is absolute, and the legislature is the final judge of the wisdom of its exercise.

MR. JUSTICE HARLAN DELIVERED THE OPINION OF THE COURT.

What is the import of the word "commerce" as used in the Constitution? It is not defined by that instrument. Undoubtedly, the carrying from one State to another by independent carriers of things or commodities that are ordinary subjects of traffic, and which have in themselves a recognized value in money, constitutes interstate commerce. But does not commerce among the several States include something more? Does not the carrying from one State to another, by independent carriers, of lottery tickets that entitle the holder to the payment of a certain amount of money therein specified also constitute commerce among the States? . . .

The leading case under the commerce clause of the Constitution is *Gibbons v. Ogden*. Referring to that clause, Chief Justice Marshall said: " . . . This power, like all others vested in Congress, is *complete in itself*, may be exercised *to its utmost extent*, and acknowledges *no limitations, other than are prescribed in the Constitution*. These are expressed in plain terms, and do not affect the questions which arise in this case or which have been discussed at the bar. If, as has always been understood, the sovereignty of Congress, though limited to specified objects, is plenary as to those objects, the power over commerce with foreign nations, and among the several States, is vested in Congress *as absolutely as it would be in a single government, having in its constitution the same restrictions on the exercise of the power as are found in the Constitution of the United States*." . . .

. . . [P]rior adjudications . . . sufficiently indicate the grounds upon which this court has proceeded when determining the meaning and scope of the commerce clause. They show that commerce among the States embraces navigation, intercourse, communication, traffic, the transit of persons, and the transmission of messages by telegraph. They also show that the power to regulate commerce among the several States is vested in Congress as absolutely as it would be in a single government, having in its constitution the same restrictions on the exercise of the power as are found in the Constitution of the United States; that such power is plenary, complete in itself, and may be exerted by Congress to its utmost extent, subject *only* to such limitations as the Constitution imposes upon the exercise of the powers granted by it; and that in determining the character of the regulations to be adopted Congress has a large discretion which is not to be controlled by the courts, simply because, in their opinion, such regulations may not be the best or most effective that could be employed.

We come then to inquire whether there is any solid foundation upon which to rest the contention that Congress may not regulate the carrying of lottery tickets from one State to another, at least by corporations or companies whose business it is, for hire, to carry tangible property from one State to another. . . .

We are of opinion that lottery tickets are subjects of traffic and therefore are subjects of commerce, and the regulation of the carriage of such tickets from State to State, at least by independent carriers, is a regulation of commerce among the several States. . . .

It is to be remarked that the Constitution does not define what is to be deemed a legitimate regulation of interstate commerce. In *Gibbons v. Ogden* it was said that the power to regulate such commerce is the power to prescribe the rule by which it is to be governed. But this general observation leaves it to be determined, when the question comes before the court, whether Congress in prescribing a particular rule has exceeded its power under the Constitution. While our Government must be acknowledged by all to be one of enumerated powers, the Constitution does not attempt to set forth all the means by which such powers may be carried into execution. It leaves to Congress a large discretion as to the means that may be employed in executing a given power. . . .

If a State, when considering legislation for the suppression of lotteries within its own limits, may properly take into view the evils that inhere in the raising of money, in that mode, why may not Congress, invested with the power to regulate commerce among the several States, provide that such commerce shall not be polluted by the carrying of lottery tickets from one State to another? In this connection it must not be forgotten that the power of Congress to regulate commerce among the States is plenary, is complete in itself, and is subject to no limitations except such as may be found in the Constitution. What provision in that instrument can be regarded as limiting the exercise of the power granted? What clause can be cited which, in any degree, countenances the suggestion that one may, of right, carry or cause to be carried from one State to another that which will harm the public morals? We cannot think of any clause of that instrument that could possibly be invoked by those who assert their right to send lottery tickets from State to State except the one providing that no person shall be deprived of his liberty without the due process of law. We have said that the liberty protected by the Constitution embraces the right to be free in the enjoyment of one's faculties; "to be free to use them in all lawful ways; to live and work where he will; to earn his livelihood by any lawful calling; to pursue any livelihood or avocation, and for that purpose to enter into all contracts that may be proper." But surely it will not be said to be a part of any one's liberty, as recognized by the supreme law of the land, that he shall be allowed to introduce into commerce among the States an element that will be confessedly injurious to the public morals. . . .

Besides, Congress, by that act, does not assume to interfere with traffic or commerce in lottery tickets carried on exclusively within the limits of any State, but has in view only commerce of that kind among the several States. It has not assumed to interfere with the completely internal affairs of any State, and has only legislated in respect of a matter which concerns the people of the United States. As a State may, for the purpose of guarding the morals of its own people, forbid all sales of lottery tickets within its limits, so Congress, for the purpose of guarding the people of the United States against the "widespread pestilence of lotteries" and to protect the commerce which concerns all the States, may prohibit the carrying of lottery tickets from one State to another. . . .

The whole subject is too important, and the questions suggested by its consideration are too difficult of solution to justify any attempt to lay down a rule for determining in advance the validity of every statute that may be enacted under the commerce clause. We decide nothing more in the present case than that lottery tickets are subjects of traffic among those who choose to sell or buy them; that the carriage of such tickets by independent carriers from one State to another is therefore interstate commerce; that under its power to regulate commerce among the several States Congress—subject to the limitations imposed by the Constitution upon the exercise of the powers granted—has plenary authority over such commerce, and may prohibit the carriage of such tickets from State to State; and that legislation to that end, and of that character, is not inconsistent with any limitation or restriction imposed upon the exercise of the powers granted to Congress.

The judgment is

Affirmed.

MR. CHIEF JUSTICE FULLER, with whom concur
MR. JUSTICE BREWER, MR. JUSTICE SHIRAS, and
MR. JUSTICE PECKHAM, dissenting.

The naked question is whether the prohibition by Congress of the carriage of lottery tickets from one State to another by means other than the mails is within the powers vested in that body by the Constitution of the United States. That the purpose of Congress in this enactment was the suppression of lotteries cannot reasonably be denied. That purpose is avowed in the title of the act, and is its natural and reasonable effect, and by that its validity must be tested.

The power of the State to impose restraints and burdens on persons and property in conservation and promotion of the public health, good order and prosperity is a power originally and always belonging to the States, not surrendered by them to the General Government nor directly restrained by the Constitution of the United States, and essentially exclusive, and the suppression of lotteries

as a harmful business falls within this power, commonly called of police.

It is urged, however, that because Congress is empowered to regulate commerce between the several States, it, therefore, may suppress lotteries by prohibiting the carriage of lottery matter. Congress may indeed make all laws necessary and proper for carrying the powers granted to it into execution, and doubtless an act prohibiting the carriage of lottery matter would be necessary and proper to the execution of a power to suppress lotteries; but that power belongs to the States and not to Congress. To hold that Congress has general police power would be to hold that it may accomplish objects not entrusted to the General Government, and to defeat the operation of the Tenth Amendment, declaring that: "The powers not delegated to the United States by the Constitution, nor prohibited by it to the States, are reserved to the States respectively, or to the people."

Champion set the precedent that Congress may indeed use the commerce clause in much the same manner as states use their police powers. In the years following *Champion,* the legislature passed a number of laws designed to accomplish social, not economic, goals through the exercise of the commerce power. In 1906 Congress passed the Meat Inspection Act and the Pure Food and Drug Act, which prohibited contaminated foods from interstate commerce. Five years later the Supreme Court upheld the Food and Drug Act as a proper exercise of the commerce power.[5] In 1910, as a method of curtailing interstate prostitution rings, Congress passed the Mann Act, as we mentioned above. In *Hoke* the Court unanimously ruled that the federal government has the authority under the commerce clause to prohibit taking women across state lines for purposes of prostitution or other immoral activities. In addition, Congress passed various laws that federalized criminal activity that extends beyond the boundaries of a single state. Kidnapping that crosses state lines, interstate transportation of stolen property, and even interstate flight to avoid prosecution are all federal crimes because of Congress's power to regulate commerce among the states.

And yet, just when it seemed that the Court would continue to allow Congress to develop federal police powers via the commerce clause, it dealt Congress a significant blow in the case of *Hammer v. Dagenhart* (1918).

---

5. *Hipolite Egg Company v. United States* (1911).

Young girls working in a clothing factory. Congressional attempts to curb child labor by taxing the items produced were repeatedly rebuffed by the Supreme Court.

Library of Congress

Hammer v. Dagenhart

247 U.S. 251 (1918)
http://laws.findlaw.com/us/247/251.html
Vote: 5 (Day, McReynolds, Pitney, Van Devanter, White)
  4 (Brandeis, Clarke, Holmes, McKenna)

OPINION OF THE COURT: *Day*
DISSENTING OPINION: *Holmes*

FACTS:

In the 1880s America entered the industrial age, which was characterized by the unfettered growth of the private sector economy. The Industrial Revolution changed the United States for the better in countless ways, but it also had a downside. Lacking any significant government controls, many businesses had less-than-benevolent relations with their workers. Some forced employees to work more than fourteen hours a day at absurdly low wages and under dreadful conditions. They also had no qualms about employing children under the age of sixteen.

Americans were divided over these practices. On one side were the entrepreneurs, stockholders, and others who gained from worker exploitation. By employing children, paying low wages, and providing no benefits, they minimized expenses and maximized profits. On the other side were the progressives, reformist groups, and individuals who sought to persuade the states and the federal government to enact laws to protect workers. These two camps repeatedly clashed in their struggle to attain diametrically opposed policy ends.[6]

One of the first battles came in 1915, when Congress began consideration of a bill to prohibit the shipment in interstate commerce of factory products made by children under the age of fourteen or by children ages fourteen to sixteen who worked more than

6. We derive what follows from Lee Epstein, *Conservatives in Court* (Knoxville: University of Tennessee Press, 1985); and Stephen B. Wood, *Constitutional Politics in the Progressive Era* (Chicago: University of Chicago Press, 1968).

eight hours a day. Numerous progressive groups supported the legislation, but it faced substantial opposition from employer associations such as the Executive Committee of Southern Cotton Manufacturers. This group was made up of militant mill owners who organized in 1915 solely to defeat federal child labor legislation. After months of legislative battles, Congress finally passed the legislation, known as the Keating-Owen Child Labor Act of 1916. The committee's leader, David Clark, vowed that his group would challenge the constitutionality of the act in court. He retained the services of a corporate law firm that held a laissez-faire philosophy to argue the committee's case. He then sought the right test case to challenge the law. Eventually, he decided on a suit against the Fidelity Manufacturing Company.

The case he brought was perfect for the committee's needs. Roland Dagenhart and his two minor sons were employed at Fidelity, a cotton mill in North Carolina. Under state law, each of Dagenhart's sons was permitted to work up to eleven hours a day. Under the new federal act, however, the older boy could work only eight hours, and the younger one could not work at all. Not only were the facts relating to the Dagenharts advantageous, but Clark also secured the cooperation of the company, which had equal disdain for the law, in planning the litigation. One month before the effective date of the law, the company posted the new federal regulations on its door and "explained" to affected employees that they would be unable to continue to work. A week later, having already secured the consent of the Dagenharts and the factory, the committee's attorneys filed an injunction against the company and William C. Hammer, a federal prosecutor, to prevent enforcement of the law.

Within a month, the district court heard arguments and ruled the act unconstitutional. The judge did not write an opinion, but when he handed down his decision he fully agreed with the committee's arguments, suggesting that the federal government had usurped state power.

Once the district court stayed enforcement of the act, both the committee and the U.S. Justice Department began to plan the strategies they would use before the U.S. Supreme Court. The committee argued that Congress had no authority to impose its policies on the states. The government's defense was led by Solicitor General John W. Davis. One of the great attorneys of the day, he made a strong case for the law, although he probably personally opposed it. Not only did he argue that the regulation of child labor fell squarely within Congress's purview, but he also supplied the Court with data indicating that the states themselves had sought to eliminate the exploitation of young children by employers. His brief pointed out that only three states placed no age limit on factory employees, and only ten allowed those between the ages of fourteen and sixteen to work. We detail additional arguments below.

ARGUMENTS:

For the appellant, William C. Hammer, U.S. attorney:
- The commerce clause authorizes Congress to "regulate commerce among the several states." Here, the statute is clearly a regulation, and it applies only to the actual transportation of products out of state, not to the intrastate activity of manufacturing. Supreme Court precedent has clarified that transportation of goods is clearly within the meaning of "commerce." Therefore, the statute is wholly within the bounds of congressional commerce power.
- Unfair competition concerns also justify the act. States cannot limit child labor without raising the costs of manufacturing within their borders, which puts them at an economic disadvantage. The federal government is the only body that is able to enact a uniform law to prevent business practices that lead to unfair competition.
- The question of states' rights is irrelevant if the statute is found to be valid exercise of congressional power under the commerce clause.

For the appellee, Roland Dagenhart:
- In their writings, the framers made clear that the purpose of the commerce clause was not to grant a positive power to the federal government. Rather, it was viewed as a provision designed to prevent injustices committed in commerce by the states.
- Legislative history shows that the purpose of the act is to prevent child labor, not to protect or promote commerce. Congress is attempting to regulate the pretransportation conditions of labor, not the actual transportation of the goods. That is beyond the scope of the commerce clause, and Congress may not do indirectly what it is prohibited to do directly.
- Any consequences of child labor are local, so they may be regulated only by the state. The Tenth Amendment reserves the right to exercise police power over intrastate matters to the states.

It is . . . contended that the authority of Congress may be exerted to control interstate commerce in the shipment of child-made goods because of the effect of the circulation of such goods in other states where the evil of this class of labor has been recognized by local legislation, and the right to thus employ child labor has been more rigorously restrained than in the state of production. In other words, that the unfair competition thus engendered may be controlled by closing the channels of interstate commerce to manufacturers in those states where the local laws do not meet what Congress deems to be the more just standard of other states.

There is no power vested in Congress to require the states to exercise their police power so as to prevent possible unfair competition. Many causes may co-operate to give one state, by reason of local laws or conditions, an economic advantage over others. The commerce clause was not intended to give to Congress a general authority to equalize such conditions. In some of the states laws have been passed fixing minimum wages for women; in others the local law regulates the hours of labor of women in various employments. Business done in such states may be at an economic disadvantage when compared with states which have no such regulations; surely, this fact does not give Congress the power to deny transportation in interstate commerce to those who carry on business where the hours of labor and the rate of compensation for women have not been fixed by a standard in the use in other states and approved by Congress.

The grant of power to Congress over the subject of interstate commerce was to enable it to regulate such commerce, and not to give it authority to control the states in their exercise of the police power over local trade and manufacture.

The grant of authority over a purely Federal matter was not intended to destroy the local power always existing and carefully reserved to the states in the 10th Amendment to the Constitution. . . .

That there should be limitations upon the right to employ children in mines and factories in the interest of their own and the public welfare, all will admit. That such employment is generally deemed to require regulation is shown by the fact that the brief of counsel states that every state in the Union has a law upon the subject, limiting the right to thus employ children. In North Carolina, the state wherein is located the factory in which the employment was had in the present case, no child under twelve years of age is permitted to work.

. . . The maintenance of the authority of the states over matters purely local is as essential to the preservation of our institutions as is the conservation of the supremacy of the Federal power in all matters intrusted to the nation by the Federal Constitution.

In interpreting the Constitution it must never be forgotten that the nation is made up of states, to which are intrusted the powers of local government. And to them and to the people the powers not expressly delegated to the national government are reserved. The power of the states to regulate their purely internal affairs by such laws as seem wise to the local authority is inherent, and has never been surrendered to the general government. To sustain this statute would not be, in our judgment, a recognition of the lawful exertion of congressional authority over interstate commerce, but would sanction an invasion by the Federal power of the control of a matter purely local in its character, and over which no authority has been delegated to Congress in conferring the power to regulate commerce among the states.

We have neither authority nor disposition to question the motives of Congress in enacting this legislation. The purposes intended must be attained consistently with constitutional limitations, and not by an invasion of the powers of the states. This court has no more important function than that which devolves upon it the obligation to preserve inviolate the constitutional limitations upon the exercise of authority, Federal and state, to the end that each may continue to discharge, harmoniously with the other, the duties intrusted to it by the Constitution.

In our view the necessary effect of this act is, by means of a prohibition against the movement in interstate commerce of ordinary commercial commodities, to regulate the hours of labor of children in factories and mines within the states,—a purely state authority. Thus the act in a twofold sense is repugnant to the Constitution. It not only transcends the authority delegated to Congress over commerce, but also exerts a power as to a purely local matter to which the Federal authority does not extend. The far-reaching result of upholding the act cannot be more plainly indicated than by pointing out that if Congress can thus regulate matters intrusted to local authority by prohibition of the movement of commodities in interstate commerce, all freedom of commerce will be at an end, and the power of the states over local matters may be eliminated, and thus our system of government be practically destroyed.

For these reasons we hold that this law exceeds the constitutional authority of Congress. It follows that the decree of the District Court must be affirmed.

MR. JUSTICE HOLMES, dissenting.

The act does not meddle with anything belonging to the states. They may regulate their internal affairs and their domestic commerce as they like. But when they seek to send their products across the state line they are no longer within their rights. If there were no Constitution and no Congress their power to cross the line would depend upon their neighbors. Under the Constitution such commerce belongs not to the states, but to Congress to regulate. It may carry out its views of public policy whatever indirect effect they may have upon the activities of the states. Instead of being encountered by a prohibitive tariff at her boundaries, the state encounters the public policy of the United States which it is for Congress to express. The public policy of the United States is shaped with a view to the benefit of the nation as a whole. . . . The national welfare as understood by Congress may require a different attitude within its sphere from that of some self-seeking state. It seems to me entirely constitutional for Congress to enforce its understanding by all the means at its command.

If William Day's opinion was a total victory for the Executive Committee, it meant little to the Dagenharts *(see box 7-1)*. More important is what it meant for congressional power under the commerce clause. First, it perpetuated that distinction drawn in *E. C. Knight* between the manufacturing and the production of goods, which the Court regarded as intrastate commerce and therefore to be regulated only by the states, and their shipment in interstate commerce, which Congress could regulate. In *Hammer* the Court saw the law as a regulation of the manufacturing stage rather than a regulation of interstate commerce. Seen in this way, some say the decision was not so much a rejection of the power of Congress to regulate social matters as it was a reminder that the justices would treat these types of laws in the way as they did the Anti-Trust Law at issue in *E. C. Knight:* Congress must show that it is not regulating manufacturing or production. On the other hand, Day seemed to reprimand Congress for using the commerce power to invade state police power. As he wrote, "The grant of power to Congress over the subject of interstate commerce was to enable it to regulate such commerce, and not to give it authority to control the states in their exercise of the police power over local trade and manufacture." This is related to another

---

> ### BOX 7-1   AFTERMATH . . . REUBEN DAGENHART
>
> **F**IVE YEARS after the Supreme Court's decision in *Hammer v. Dagenhart* striking down the child labor law, a journalist interviewed Reuben Dagenhart, whose father had sued to prevent Congress from interfering with his sons' jobs in a North Carolina cotton mill. Reuben was twenty when he was interviewed. Excerpts follow:
>
> "What benefit . . . did you get out of the suit which you won in the United States Supreme Court?"
>
> "I don't see that I got any benefit. I guess I'd be a lot better off if they hadn't won it.
>
> "Look at me! A hundred and five pounds, a grown man, and no education. I may be mistaken, but I think the years I've put in the cotton mills have stunted my growth. They kept me from getting any schooling. I had to stop school after the third grade and now I need the education I didn't get."
>
> "Just what did you and John get out of that suit then?" he was asked.
>
> "Why, we got some automobile rides when them big lawyers from the North was down here. Oh yes, and they bought both of us a Coca-Cola! That's all we got out of it."
>
> "What did you tell the judge when you were in court?"
>
> "Oh, John and me was never in court. Just Paw was there. John and me was just little kids in short pants. I guess we wouldn't have looked like much in court. . . . We were working in the mill while the case was going on."
>
> Reuben hasn't been to school in years, but his mind has not been idle.
>
> "It would have been a good thing for all the kids in this state if that law they passed had been kept. Of course, they do better now than they used to. You don't see so many babies working in the factories, but you see a lot of them that ought to be going to school."
>
> SOURCE: *Labor*, November 17, 1923, 3, quoted in Leonard F. James, ed., *The Supreme Court in American Life*, 2nd ed. (Glenview, IL: Scott, Foresman, 1971), 74.

striking aspect of *Hammer:* the Court's use of the Tenth Amendment as, seemingly, an independent brake on the commerce power.

THE SUPREME COURT AND THE NEW DEAL

The Supreme Court's related moves of narrowing the definition of commerce and invoking the Tenth Amendment in *E. C. Knight* and *Hammer* probably reflected less a commitment to states' rights than a willingness on the part of the Court to embrace a free enterprise philosophy. If so, this matched the general mood of the public, as at least some Americans were benefiting so much from the economic boom of the 1920s that they opposed regulation. Calvin Coolidge famously put it this way: "After all, the chief business of the American people is business."

This changed almost overnight when the New York Stock Exchange crashed on October 29, 1929. The crash set in motion a series of events that shook the American economy and drove the nation into a deep depression. For the next two years, the stock market continued to tumble, with the Standard & Poor's Industrial Average falling 75 percent. The gross national product declined 27 percent over three years, and the unemployment rate rose from a healthy 3.2 percent in 1929 to a catastrophic 24.9 percent in 1933.

The Republican Party, which had been victorious in the November 1928 elections, controlled the White House and both houses of Congress. The party attempted to cope with the Great Depression by following the laissez-faire philosophy of government that it had followed prior to the stock market crash, but that approach was no longer working; the economic forces against which the Republicans were fighting were enormous. A different political approach was necessary to battle the collapse, and the American people were demanding such a change. They got it, as we detail below, with the election of a Democratic president and Congress in the 1932 elections.

While some of the Court's decisions, such as *Swift* and *Stafford,* seemed to give the government more power to regulate the economy, others, such as *E. C. Knight* and *Hammer,* were obstacles, limiting Congress's ability to cope effectively with a full-scale economic collapse. And at least initially the justices of the Supreme Court were unwilling to remove them. This situation touched off one of history's most dramatic confrontations between the Court and the president, and it permanently altered the allocation of government powers.

The Depression and Political Change

In the 1932 presidential election, voters rejected incumbent Herbert Hoover and swept Democratic candidate Franklin D. Roosevelt into office by a huge margin. With new Democratic majorities in the House and Senate, the president began combating the Depression with policies he called the New Deal. The overwhelming Democratic margins in Congress gave Roosevelt all the political clout he needed to gain approval of his radical new approach to boosting the economy. His programs were so popular with the American people that in 1936 they reelected Roosevelt by an even greater margin and provided him with even larger Democratic majorities in Congress, reducing the Republicans almost to minor party status. Clearly, the severe economic events following the 1929 crash triggered substantial political change, with the legislative and executive branches experiencing wholesale partisan shifts *(see table 7-1).*

The U.S. Supreme Court, however, did not change. In 1929, just before the stock market crash, the Court membership was six Republicans and three Democrats. The economic conservatives (Butler, McReynolds, Sanford, Sutherland, Taft, and Van Devanter) were in control, outnumbering the justices more sympathetic to political and economic change (Brandeis, Holmes, and Stone). By 1932 the Court had three new justices. Former justice Charles Hughes, who had resigned his seat in 1916 to seek the presidency, succeeded William Howard Taft as chief justice; Benjamin Cardozo took Holmes's seat; and Owen Roberts replaced Edward Sanford. Although these changes reduced the Republican majority to five, it created no appreciable change in the ideological balance of the Court. Hoover filled all three of these vacancies, which occurred before Roosevelt took office. Inaugurated in March 1933, Roosevelt had no opportunity to name a Supreme Court justice until Willis Van Devanter retired in June 1937. Roosevelt's first appointment, Hugo Black, assumed his seat in August of that year. Not until 1940 did the Court have a majority appointed from the period after Roosevelt's first election.

In the executive branch, however, Roosevelt was able to assemble a cadre of young, creative people to devise novel ways of approaching the ailing economy,

TABLE 7-1   The Great Depression and Political Change

	1929	1931	1933	1935	1937
House of Representatives					
No. of Democratic seats	163	216	313	332	333
No. of Republican seats	267	218	117	103	89
Senate					
No. of Democratic senators	39	47	59	69	75
No. of Republican senators	56	48	36	25	17
Presidency					
Incumbent	Hoover (R)	—	Roosevelt (D)	—	Roosevelt (D)
% of popular vote	58.2	—	57.4	—	60.8
Electoral vote margin	444–87	—	472–59	—	523–8
Supreme Court					
Republican justices	6	6	5	5	5
Number of new appointments over previous two years	0	2	1	0	0

NOTE: These data depict the change in political representation in the three branches of the federal government following the 1929 stock market crash and the deepening depression that continued over the next several years. Members of the House and one-third of the senators were elected the previous November. The data on presidential election margins are based on previous November's elections. Supreme Court information is as of January of the designated years.

and these New Deal Democrats quickly set out to develop, enact, and implement their programs. Congress passed the first legislation, the Emergency Banking Act of 1933, just five days after Roosevelt's inauguration, and a string of statutes designed to control all major sectors of the nation's economy followed (see box 7-2). In adopting these programs, Congress relied on a number of constitutional powers, including the powers to tax, spend, and regulate interstate and foreign commerce.

The new political majority that dominated the legislative and executive branches called for the government to take an active role in economic regulation. The Supreme Court remained firmly in the control of representatives of the old order, with views on the relationship of government and the economy at odds with those of the political branches. A clash between the president and the Court was inevitable.

The Court Attacks the New Deal

As soon as the New Deal programs came into being, conservative business interests began to challenge their constitutional validity. In just two years the appeals started to reach the Court's doorstep. Beginning in 1935 and lasting for two long, tense years, the Court and the New Deal Democrats fought over the constitutionality of an expanded federal role in managing the economy.

During this period, the justices struck down a number of important New Deal statutes. Of ten major programs, the Supreme Court approved only two—the Tennessee Valley Authority and the emergency monetary laws. Four hard-line conservative justices—Pierce Butler, James McReynolds, George Sutherland, and Willis Van Devanter—formed the heart of the Court's opposition. Many thought their obstruction of New Deal initiatives would bring about the nation's ruin. As a consequence, they became known as the Four Horsemen of the Apocalypse, a biblical reference to the end of the world in the Book of Revelation. Two of the four, Butler and McReynolds, were Democrats (see box 7-3).

Naturally, these four justices by themselves could not declare void any act of Congress. They needed the vote of at least one other justice. As box 7-4 indicates, they had little trouble attracting others to their cause. Of the eight major 1935–1936 decisions in which they struck down congressional policies, three were by 5–4 votes in which Justice Roberts joined the four conservatives. In one additional case, both Roberts and Chief Justice Hughes voted with them. But in three of these significant decisions, the Court was unanimous, with even the liberals, Brandeis, Cardozo, and Stone, voting to strike down the challenged legislation.

The first salvo in the war between the two branches occurred on January 7, 1935, when the Court

BOX 7-2 NEW DEAL LEGISLATION

THE Roosevelt Democrats moved on the nation's economic problems with great speed after the president took the oath of office on March 4, 1933. Listed below are the major economic actions passed during his first term. Note how many were enacted within the first one hundred days of the new administration.

March 9, 1933	Emergency Banking Act
March 31, 1933	Civilian Conservation Corps created
May 12, 1933	Agricultural Adjustment Act
May 12, 1933	Federal Emergency Relief Act
May 18, 1933	Tennessee Valley Authority created
June 5, 1933	Nation taken off gold standard
June 13, 1933	Home Owners Loan Corporation created
June 16, 1933	Federal Deposit Insurance Corporation created
June 16, 1933	Farm Credit Administration created
June 16, 1933	National Industrial Recovery Act
January 30, 1934	Dollar devalued
June 6, 1934	Securities and Exchange Commission authorized
June 12, 1934	Reciprocal Tariff Act
June 19, 1934	Federal Communications Commission created
June 27, 1934	Railroad Retirement Act
June 28, 1934	Federal Housing Administration authorized
April 8, 1935	Works Progress Administration created
July 5, 1935	National Labor Relations Act
August 14, 1935	Social Security Act
August 26, 1935	Federal Power Commission created
August 30, 1935	National Bituminous Coal Conservation Act
February 19, 1936	Soil Conservation and Domestic Allotment Act

BOX 7-3 THE FOUR HORSEMEN

Willis Van Devanter (1910–1937)

Republican from Wyoming. Born 1859. University of Cincinnati Law School. Wyoming state legislator and state supreme court judge. Federal appeals court judge. Appointed by William Howard Taft.

James Clark McReynolds (1914–1941)

Democrat from Tennessee. Born 1862. University of Virginia Law School. United States attorney general. Appointed by Woodrow Wilson.

George Sutherland (1922–1938)

Republican from Utah. Born 1862. University of Michigan Law School. State legislator, U.S. representative, U.S. senator. Appointed by Warren G. Harding.

Pierce Butler (1922–1939)

Democrat from Minnesota. Born 1866. No law school, studied privately. Corporate attorney. Appointed by Warren G. Harding.

Library of Congress

BOX 7-4   THE SUPREME COURT AND THE NEW DEAL

Listed below are eight major decisions handed down by the Supreme Court in 1935 and 1936 declaring parts of the New Deal legislative program unconstitutional.

CASE (DECISION DATE)	ACTS RULED UNCONSTITUTIONAL (GROUNDS)	MAJORITY	DISSENT
Panama Refining Co. v. Ryan (January 7, 1935)	Portions of the National Industrial Recovery Act (improper delegation of congressional powers)	Brandeis, Butler, Hughes, McReynolds, Roberts, Stone, Sutherland, Van Devanter	Cardozo
Railroad Retirement Board v. Alton Railroad Co. (May 6, 1935)	Railroad Retirement Act of 1934 (exceeded commerce clause powers; Fifth Amendment due process violations)	Butler, McReynolds, Roberts, Sutherland, Van Devanter	Brandeis, Cardozo, Hughes, Stone
A. L. A. Schechter Poultry Corp. v. United States (May 27, 1935)	Portions of the National Industrial Recovery Act (a regulation of intrastate commerce and improper delegation of congressional power)	Brandeis, Butler, Cardozo, Hughes, McReynolds, Roberts, Stone, Sutherland, Van Devanter	
Louisville Bank v. Radford (May 27, 1935)	Frazier-Lemke Act of 1934 extending bankruptcy relief (Fifth Amendment property rights)	Brandeis, Butler, Cardozo, Hughes, McReynolds, Roberts, Stone, Sutherland, Van Devanter	
Hopkins Savings Association v. Cleary (December 12, 1935)	Home Owners Loan Act of 1933 (Tenth Amendment)	Brandeis, Butler, Cardozo, Hughes, McReynolds, Roberts, Stone, Sutherland, Van Devanter	
United States v. Butler (January 6, 1936)	Agricultural Adjustment Act (taxing and spending power violations)	Butler, Hughes, McReynolds, Roberts, Sutherland, Van Devanter	Brandeis, Cardozo, Stone
Carter v. Carter Coal Co. (May 18, 1936)	Bituminous Coal Conservation Act (a regulation of intrastate commerce; improper delegation of congressional power)	Butler, McReynolds, Roberts, Sutherland, Van Devanter	Brandeis, Cardozo, Hughes, Stone
Ashton v. Cameron County District Court (May 25, 1936)	Municipal Bankruptcy Act (Tenth Amendment; Fifth Amendment property rights)	Butler, McReynolds, Roberts, Sutherland, Van Devanter	Brandeis, Cardozo, Hughes, Stone

announced its decision in *Panama Refining Company v. Ryan.* By an 8–1 vote the justices struck down a section of the National Industrial Recovery Act of 1933 (NIRA) as an improper delegation of congressional power to the executive branch. The section in question was a major New Deal weapon for regulating the oil industry. It gave the president the power to prohibit interstate shipment of oil and petroleum products that were produced or stored in a manner illegal under state law. The justices found fault with the act because it did not provide sufficiently clear standards to guide the executive branch; rather, it gave the president almost unlimited discretion in applying the prohibitions. *Panama Refining* was the first case in which the Court

struck down legislation because it was an improper delegation of power. *(See chapter 5 for more on the delegation of powers.)*

Although the decision in *Panama Refining* was restricted to the delegation question and did not focus on Congress's interstate commerce authority, it promised bad days ahead for the administration. Not only was the decision a disappointment for the president, but also the vote was lopsided. Justice Cardozo alone voted to approve the law.

The Court dropped its biggest bomb on the New Deal four months later. The justices voted 5–4 on May 6 to declare the Railroad Retirement Act of 1934 an unconstitutional violation of the commerce clause and the due process clause of the Fifth Amendment.[7] Then, on May 27—a date that became known as Black Monday—the justices announced three significant blows to the administration's efforts to fight the Depression, all by unanimous votes. First, in *Humphrey's Executor v. United States,* the Court declared that the president did not have the power to remove a member of the Federal Trade Commission (FTC). Second, the justices invalidated the 1934 Frazier-Lemke Act, which had provided mortgage relief, especially to farmers.[8] Finally, in *A. L. A. Schechter Poultry Corp. v. United States* the Court handed the president his most stinging defeat by declaring major portions of the NIRA unconstitutional as an improper delegation of legislative power and a violation of the commerce clause.

A. L. A. Schechter Poultry Corp. v. United States

295 U.S. 495 (1935)

http://laws.findlaw.com/us/295/495.html

Vote: 9 (Brandeis, Butler, Cardozo, Hughes, McReynolds, Roberts, Stone, Sutherland, Van Devanter)

    0

OPINION OF THE COURT: *Hughes*

CONCURRING OPINION: *Cardozo*

FACTS:

Congress passed the National Industrial Recovery Act (NIRA), the most far-reaching and comprehensive of all the New Deal legislation, on June 16, 1933. Applying to every sector of American industry, the NIRA called for the creation of codes of fair competition for business. The codes would regulate trade practices, wages, hours, and other business activities within various industries. Trade associations and other industry groups had the responsibility for drafting the codes, which were submitted to the president for approval. In the absence of the private sector's recommendations, the president was authorized to draft codes himself. Once approved by the president, the codes had the force of law, and violators faced fines and even jail.

The NIRA was vulnerable to constitutional challenge on two grounds. First, it set almost no standards for the president to use in approving or drafting the codes. Congress had handed Roosevelt a blank check to bring all of American industry into line with his views of what was best for economic recovery. Second,

the law regulated what at that time was considered intrastate commerce.

The *Schechter* case involved a challenge to the NIRA poultry codes, focusing on the industry in New York, the nation's largest chicken market.[9] This market clearly was operating in interstate commerce, as 96 percent of the poultry sold in New York came from out-of-state suppliers. The industry was riddled with graft and plagued by deplorable health and sanitation conditions. The Live Poultry Code approved by President Roosevelt set a maximum workweek of forty hours and a minimum hourly wage of fifty cents. In addition, the code established a health inspection system, regulations to govern slaughtering procedures, and compulsory record keeping.

A. L. A. Schechter Poultry Corporation, owned by Joseph, Martin, Aaron, and Alex Schechter, was a poultry slaughtering business in Brooklyn. Slaughterhouse operators such as the Schechters purchased large numbers of live chickens from local poultry dealers who imported the fowl from out of state to be killed and dressed for sale.

Government officials found the Schechters in violation of the Poultry Code on numerous counts: They ignored the code's wage and hour provisions, failed to comply with government record-keeping requirements, and did not conform to the slaughter regulations. Their worst offense, however, was selling unsanitary poultry that the government found unfit for human consumption. For this reason, *Schechter Poultry* became known as the "sick chicken case."

The government obtained indictments against the Schechter Poultry Corporation and the four brothers on sixty counts of violating the code, and the jury found them guilty of nineteen. Each of the brothers was sentenced to a short jail term. They appealed unsuccessfully to the court of appeals and then pressed their case to the U.S. Supreme Court, asserting that the NIRA was unconstitutional on improper delegation and commerce clause grounds.

ARGUMENTS:

For the petitioners, A. L. A. Schechter Poultry Corp. et al.:

- The act attempts to override and ignore not only the limitations of the commerce clause but also the prohibition against illegal delegation of legislative power.

---

7. *Railroad Retirement Board v. Alton Railroad Co.* (1935).

8. *Louisville Bank v. Radford* (1935).

9. For a good discussion of the *Schechter* case, see Irons, *The New Deal Lawyers,* chap. 5.

It is a bold and unparalleled law that is drastic in character.

- The act is an illegal delegation of power because Congress has set up no intelligible policies to govern the president and no standards to guide and restrict his action.
- The act exceeds the commerce power because, according to existing precedent, production—whether by way of manufacture, mining, farming, or any other activity—is not commerce and is not subject to regulation under the commerce clause. To hold otherwise, as decisions of the Court make clear, would destroy our dual system of government and allow the federal government to nationalize industry.

For the respondent, United States:

- Under the Court's decisions, the act's provisions are within the commerce power of the Congress. Petitioners' slaughtering business is so closely related to interstate movement that it makes no difference what parts of their business are "in" interstate commerce and what parts are less "in" but still necessary to its functioning.
- The effect of petitioners' practices on the national price and on the interstate movement of poultry is the same as the effect of the local activities at issue in *Stafford v. Wallace*. The New York market dominates the live poultry industry and determines the prices in other markets, as well as the prices received by shippers and farmers.
- Petitioners' practices also affect the quality and volume of poultry shipped in interstate commerce, another reason for federal regulation. Because consumers are unable to distinguish good poultry from unfit poultry, they distrust the market and buy less poultry. It is estimated that if unfit poultry were excluded from the market by effectively prohibiting its sale in New York, the consumption and shipment of poultry would increase by about 20 percent.
- Even if the practices here in normal economic times would have only an indirect effect upon interstate commerce, economic conditions are such that they now substantially burden interstate commerce because we are in a period of overproduction, cutthroat competition, unemployment, and reduced buying power. Only Congress can deal with the causes contributing to these problems. It would be impossible for the states to take quick and uniform action.

A. L. A. Schechter (center) of Schechter Poultry Corporation with his attorneys Joseph Heller (left) and Frederick Wood, May 2, 1935.

© Bettmann/Corbis

MR. CHIEF JUSTICE HUGHES DELIVERED THE OPINION OF THE COURT.

The question of the delegation of legislative power. We recently had occasion to review the pertinent decisions and the general principles which govern the determination of this question. The Constitution provides that "All legislative powers herein granted shall be vested in a Congress of the United States, which shall consist of a Senate and House of Representatives." Art. I, §1. And the Congress is authorized "To make all laws which shall be necessary and proper for carrying into execution" its general powers. Art. I, §8, par. 18. The Congress is not permitted to abdicate or to transfer to others the essential legislative functions with which it is thus vested. . . .

Section 3 of the Recovery Act is without precedent. It supplies no standards for any trade, industry or activity. It does not undertake to prescribe rules of conduct to be applied to particular states of fact determined by appropriate administrative procedure. Instead of prescribing rules of conduct, it authorizes the making of codes to prescribe them. For that legislative undertaking, §3 sets up no standards, aside from the statement of the general aims of rehabilitation, correction and expansion described in section one. In view of the scope of that broad declaration, and of the nature of the few restrictions that are imposed, the discretion of the President in approving or prescribing codes, and thus enacting laws for the government of trade and industry throughout the country, is virtually unfettered. We think that the code-making authority thus conferred is an unconstitutional delegation of legislative power.

. . . The question of the application of the provisions of the Live Poultry Code to intrastate transactions. . . . This aspect of the case presents the question whether the particular provisions of the Live Poultry Code, which the defendants were convicted for violating and for having conspired to violate, were within the regulating power of Congress.

These provisions relate to the hours and wages of those employed by defendants in their slaughterhouses in Brooklyn and to the sales there made to retail dealers and butchers.

(1) Were these transactions "*in*" interstate commerce? Much is made of the fact that almost all the poultry coming to New York is sent there from other States. But the code provisions, as here applied, do not concern the transportation of the poultry from other States to New York, or the transactions of the commission men or others to whom it is consigned, or the sales made by such consignees to defendants. When defendants had made their purchases, whether at the West Washington Market in New York City or at the railroad terminals serving the City, or elsewhere, the poultry was trucked to their slaughterhouses in Brooklyn for local disposition. The interstate transactions in relation to that poultry then ended. Defendants held the poultry at their slaughterhouse markets for slaughter and local sale to retail dealers and butchers who in turn sold directly to consumers. Neither the slaughtering nor the sales by defendants were transactions in interstate commerce.

The undisputed facts thus afford no warrant for the argument that the poultry handled by defendants at their slaughterhouse markets was in a "*current*" or "*flow*" of interstate commerce and was thus subject to congressional regulation. The mere fact that there may be a constant flow of commodities into a State does not mean that the flow continues after the property has arrived and has become commingled with the mass of property within the State and is there held solely for local disposition and use. So far as the poultry here in question is concerned; the flow in interstate commerce had ceased. The poultry had come to a permanent rest within the State. It was not held, used, or sold by defendants in relation to any further transactions in interstate commerce and was not destined for transportation to other States. Hence, decisions which deal with a stream of interstate commerce—where goods come to rest within a State temporarily and are later to go forward in interstate commerce—and with the regulations of transactions involved in that practical continuity of movement, are not applicable here.

(2) Did the defendants' transactions directly "*affect*" interstate commerce so as to be subject to federal regulation? The power of Congress extends not only to the regulation of transactions which are part of interstate commerce, but to the protection of that commerce from injury. It matters not that the injury may be due to the conduct of those engaged in intrastate operations. Thus, Congress may protect the safety of those employed in interstate transportation "no matter what may be the source of the dangers which threaten it." We said in *Second Employers' Liability Cases*, that it is the "effect upon interstate commerce," not "the source of the injury," which is "the criterion of congressional power." We have held that, in dealing with common carriers engaged in both interstate and intrastate commerce, the dominant authority of Congress necessarily embraces the right to control

their intrastate operations in all matters having such a close and substantial relation to interstate traffic that the control is essential or appropriate to secure the freedom of that traffic from interference or unjust discrimination and to promote the efficiency of the interstate service. And combinations and conspiracies to restrain interstate commerce, or to monopolize any part of it, are none the less within the reach of the Anti-Trust Act because the conspirators seek to attain their end by means of intrastate activities. . . .

In determining how far the federal government may go in controlling intrastate transactions upon the ground that they "affect" interstate commerce, there is a necessary and well-established distinction between direct and indirect effects. The precise line can be drawn only as individual cases arise, but the distinction is clear in principle. Direct effects are illustrated by the railroad cases we have cited, as, *e.g.*, the effect of failure to use prescribed safety appliances on railroads which are the highways of both interstate and intrastate commerce, injury to an employee engaged in interstate transportation by the negligence of an employee engaged in an intrastate movement, the fixing of rates for intrastate transportation which unjustly discriminate against interstate commerce. But where the effect of intrastate transactions upon interstate commerce is merely indirect, such transactions remain within the domain of state power. If the commerce clause were construed to reach all enterprises and transactions which could be said to have an indirect effect upon interstate commerce, the federal authority would embrace practically all the activities of the people and the authority of the State over its domestic concerns would exist only by sufferance of the federal government. Indeed, on such a theory, even the development of the State's commercial facilities would be subject to federal control. As we said in the *Minnesota Rate Cases:* "In the intimacy of commercial relations, much that is done in the superintendence of local matters may have an indirect bearing upon interstate commerce. The development of local resources and the extension of local facilities may have a very important effect upon communities less favored and to an appreciable degree alter the course of trade. The freedom of local trade may stimulate interstate commerce, while restrictive measures within the police power of the State enacted exclusively with respect to internal business, as distinguished from interstate traffic, may in their reflex or indirect influence diminish the latter and reduce the volume of articles transported into or out of the State."

The distinction between direct and indirect effects has been clearly recognized in the application of the Anti-Trust Act. Where a combination or conspiracy is formed, with the intent to restrain interstate commerce or to monopolize any part of it, the violation of the statute is clear. But where that intent is absent, and the objectives are limited to intrastate activities, the fact that there may be an indirect effect upon interstate commerce does not subject the parties to the federal statute, notwithstanding its broad provisions. . . .

. . . [T]he distinction between direct and indirect effects of intrastate transactions upon interstate commerce must be recognized as a fundamental one, essential to the maintenance of our constitutional system. Otherwise, as we have said, there would be virtually no limit to the federal power and for all practical purposes we should have a completely centralized government. We must consider the provisions here in question in the light of this distinction.

The question of chief importance relates to the provisions of the Code as to the hours and wages of those employed in defendants' slaughterhouse markets. It is plain that these requirements are imposed in order to govern the details of defendants' management of their local business. The persons employed in slaughtering and selling in local trade are not employed in interstate commerce. Their hours and wages have no direct relation to interstate commerce. The question of how many hours these employees should work and what they should be paid differs in no essential respect from similar questions in other local businesses which handle commodities brought into a State and there dealt in as a part of its internal commerce. This appears from an examination of the considerations urged by the Government with respect to conditions in the poultry trade. Thus, the Government argues that hours and wages affect prices; that slaughterhouse men sell at a small margin above operating costs; that a slaughterhouse operator paying lower wages or reducing his cost by exacting long hours of work, translates his saving into lower prices; that this results in demands for a cheaper grade of goods; and that the cutting of prices brings about a demoralization of the price structure. Similar conditions may be adduced in relation to other businesses. The argument of the Government proves too much. If the federal government may determine the wages and hours of employees in the internal commerce of a State, because of their relation to cost and prices and their indirect effect upon interstate commerce, it would seem that a similar control might be exerted over other elements of cost, also affecting prices, such as the number of employees, rents, advertising, methods of doing business, etc. All the processes of production and distribution that enter into cost could likewise be controlled. If the cost of doing an intrastate business is in itself the permitted object of federal control, the extent of the regulation of cost would be a question of discretion and not of power.

The Government also makes the point that efforts to enact state legislation establishing high labor standards have been impeded by the belief that unless similar action is taken generally, commerce will be diverted from the States adopting such standards, and that this fear of diversion has led to demands for federal legislation on the subject of wages and hours. The apparent implication is that the federal authority under the commerce clause should be deemed to extend to the establishment of rules to govern wages and hours in intrastate trade and industry generally throughout the country, thus overriding the authority of the States to deal with domestic problems arising from labor conditions in their internal commerce.

It is not the province of the Court to consider the economic advantages or disadvantages of such a centralized system. It is sufficient to say that the Federal Constitution does not provide for it. Our growth and development have called for wide use of the commerce power of the federal government in its control over the expanded activities of interstate commerce, and in protecting that commerce from burdens, interferences, and conspiracies to restrain and monopolize it. But the authority of the federal government may not be pushed to such an extreme as to destroy the distinction, which the commerce clause itself establishes, between commerce "among the several States" and the internal concerns of a State. The same answer must be made to the contention that is based upon the serious economic situation which led to the passage of the Recovery Act—the fall in prices, the decline in wages and employment, and the curtailment of the market for commodities. Stress is laid upon the great importance of maintaining wage distributions which would provide the necessary stimulus in starting "the cumulative forces making for expanding commercial activity." Without in any way disparaging this motive, it is enough to say that the recuperative efforts of the federal government must be made in a manner consistent with the authority granted by the Constitution.

We are of the opinion that the attempt through the provisions of the Code to fix the hours and wages of employees of defendants in their intrastate business was not a valid exercise of federal power.

The other violations for which defendants were convicted related to the making of local sales. Ten counts, for violation of the provision as to "straight killing," were for permitting customers to make "selections of individual chickens taken from particular coops and half coops." Whether or not this practice is good or bad for the local trade, its effect, if any, upon interstate commerce was only indirect. The same may be said of violations of the Code by intrastate transactions consisting of the sale "of an unfit chicken" and of sales which were not in accord with the ordinances of the City of New York. The requirement of reports as to prices and volumes of defendants' sales was incident to the effort to control their intrastate business. . . .

On both the grounds we have discussed, the attempted delegation of legislative power, and the attempted regulation of intrastate transactions which affect interstate commerce only indirectly, we hold the code provisions here in question to be invalid and that the judgment of conviction must be reversed.

MR. JUSTICE CARDOZO, concurring.

The delegated power of legislation which has found expression in this code is not canalized within banks that keep it from overflowing. It is unconfined and vagrant. . . .

This is delegation running riot. . . .

The code does not confine itself to the suppression of methods of competition that would be classified as unfair according to accepted business standards or accepted norms of ethics. It sets up a comprehensive body of rules to promote the welfare of the industry, if not the welfare of the nation, without reference to standards, ethical or commercial, that could be known or predicted in advance of its adoption. . . . Even if the statute itself had fixed the meaning of fair competition by way of contrast with practices that are oppressive or unfair, the code outruns the bounds of the authority conferred. What is excessive is not sporadic or superficial. It is deep-seated and pervasive. The licit and illicit sections are so combined and welded as to be incapable of severance without destructive mutilation.

But there is another objection, far-reaching and incurable, aside from any defect of unlawful delegation.

If this code had been adopted by Congress itself, and not by the President on the advice of an industrial association, it would even then be void, unless authority to adopt it is included in the grant of power "to regulate commerce with foreign nations, and among the several States." United States Constitution, art. 1, 8, cl. 3.

I find no authority in that grant for the regulation of wages and hours of labor in the intrastate transactions that make up the defendants' business. As to this feature of the case, little can be added to the opinion of the court. There is a view of causation that would obliterate the distinction between what is national and what is local in the activities of commerce. . . .

I am authorized to state that MR. JUSTICE STONE joins in this opinion.

The decision in *Schechter* closely paralleled the *E. C. Knight* ruling and rejected the application of the stream of commerce doctrine. In *E. C. Knight* the Court held that sugar refining was a manufacturing stage not part of interstate commerce and, therefore, the federal government could not regulate it. Similarly, in *Schechter* the Court classified the slaughtering and local sale of chickens as intrastate commerce. The stream of commerce evident in the stockyards decisions did not apply. In *Schechter* the interstate movement of the poultry had ceased. Once the distributor had sold to local processors like the Schechters' company, the chickens had reached their state of final destination and became a part of intrastate commerce. Also consistent with *E. C. Knight*, the justices concluded that the poultry slaughter business had only an indirect effect on interstate commerce.

Through the remaining months of 1935 and into 1936, the Court continued to strike down federal legislation designed to cope with the Depression. In some cases the Court found the statutes defective for violating the federal taxing and spending power or for depriving individuals of their right to property without due process of law, topics we cover in later chapters. No matter what the reason for the decision, the Court throughout this period was concerned with congressional actions that went beyond constitutional authority to regulate interstate commerce. Congress could not constitutionally legislate local business activity, such as manufacturing, processing, or refining, unless it had a direct effect on interstate commerce. The Court supported congressional regulation when the commerce was in movement from one state to another, but, as demonstrated in *Schechter*, the justices were unwilling to allow Congress to act on commerce after it had completed its interstate journey. *Schechter* examined when interstate commerce ends; in May 1936 the Court taught the administration a lesson in when interstate commerce begins, with its decision in *Carter v. Carter Coal Company.*

Congress passed the Bituminous Coal Conservation Act in August 1935, following the *Schechter* decision. This law replaced the NIRA coal codes, which had been reasonably effective in bringing some stability to the depressed coal industry. The new act called for the establishment of a commission empowered to develop regulations regarding fair competition, production, wages, hours, and labor relations. The commission included representatives from coal producers, coal miners, and the public. To fund the program, Congress imposed a tax at the mines of 15 percent of the value of the coal produced. As was not the case with the NIRA codes, compliance with the new code regulations was voluntary. There was, however, an incentive for joining the program. Companies who participated were given a rebate of 90 percent of the taxes levied by the act.

James W. Carter and other shareholders urged their company, Carter Coal, not to participate in the program. The board of directors did not want to join, but it believed that the company could not afford to pay the 15 percent tax and forgo the participation rebate. Carter and the stockholders sued to prevent the company from joining the program on the ground that the Coal Act was unconstitutional. Of Carter's several attacks on the law, the most deadly was the charge that coal mining was not interstate commerce.

By a 5–4 vote the justices struck down the law. The majority held that coal mining was not interstate commerce because the activity occurred within a single state. The stream of commerce doctrine was inapplicable because the movement of the coal to other states had not yet begun. Furthermore, the justices concluded that the production of coal did not have a direct effect on interstate commerce. For these reasons, the Court invalidated federal regulation of coal mining. But *Carter v. Carter Coal* was to be Roosevelt's last major defeat at the hands of the Four Horsemen and their allies.

The Court-Packing Plan

The Court entered its summer recess in 1936 having completed a year and a half of dealing with Roosevelt's legislative program and striking down several of the New Deal's most important programs. The Four Horsemen constituted a solid bloc, and in major cases these justices could count on the support of at least one other—usually Owen Roberts. Roosevelt was understandably frustrated with what he viewed as the Court's obstructionism; he was also impatient that no vacancies had occurred that he might fill with appointees sympathetic to the New Deal.

In the national elections of 1936, few doubted that Roosevelt would be reelected and that the Democrats would continue to control Congress.[10] The only question was how big the margin was going to be. Roosevelt won by a landslide, capturing 98 percent of the electoral votes. His Republican opponent, Alf Landon of Kansas, carried only Maine and Vermont. The congressional elections were also a triumph for the Democrats. When the legislature reconvened in early 1937, they controlled approximately 80 percent of the seats in both houses. With such an impressive mandate from the people and such strong party support in Congress, Roosevelt was willing to proceed with his planned attack on the Court. If no vacancies on the Supreme Court occurred naturally, Roosevelt would try to create some.

On February 5, 1937, the president announced his plan to reorganize the federal court system. His proposed legislation was predicated, at least formally, on the argument that the judiciary was too overworked and understaffed to carry out its duties effectively. His idea was to expand the number of lower court judgeships; streamline federal jurisdiction, especially with respect to cases having constitutional significance; and adopt a flexible method of temporarily moving lower court judges from their normal duties to districts with case backlogs (see box 7-5).

To many observers these administrative reforms were little more than a smoke screen for Roosevelt's proposals concerning the Supreme Court. The president asked Congress to authorize the creation of one new seat on the Court for every justice who had attained the age of seventy but remained in active service. Up to six new justices could be appointed in this way, bringing the potential size of the Court to a maximum of fifteen. At the time of his proposal, six sitting justices were older than seventy. If Roosevelt could appoint six New Deal advocates to the Court, they probably could attract the votes of at least two others and form a majority that

would give constitutional approval to the president's programs. Although Roosevelt attempted to justify his idea on the ground that the advanced age of several sitting justices called for the addition of younger, more-vigorous colleagues, everyone saw the plan for what it was—an attempt to pack the Court.

Reaction was not favorable.[11] Public opinion polls taken during the course of the debate over the plan reveal that at no time did a majority of Americans support Roosevelt's proposal (see figure 7-1). Members of the organized bar were overwhelmingly opposed. Even with large Democratic majorities in both houses of Congress, Roosevelt had difficulty selling his proposal to the legislature. Chief Justice Hughes wrote a public letter criticizing the proposal to Senator Burton Wheeler of Montana, a leader of Democrats opposing the president.[12] The press expressed sharp disapproval. In spite of the general support the people gave Roosevelt and the New Deal, they did not appreciate his tampering with the structure of government to get his way. Roosevelt's response to this unexpected criticism was to go directly to the people to press his case, and in doing so he became a little more open about his objectives. In his radio broadcast the president explained his proposal and urged the American public to support it.

The Switch in Time That Saved Nine

The battle in Congress over the president's plan was closely fought.[13] A continuation of the confrontation, however, was averted in large measure by the actions of the justices themselves. On March 29, 1937, just twenty days after the president's broadcast, the Court signaled that changes were in the making. The first indication was the 5–4 decision in *West Coast Hotel v. Parrish* (1937), which upheld the validity of a Washington State law regulating wages and working conditions for women and children.

10. Not everyone predicted a Roosevelt victory. The *Literary Digest* published a famous poll during that election year forecasting a Roosevelt defeat. The poll has become universally regarded as a classic case of defective research procedures. Within months after the election, the *Literary Digest* was defunct.

11. See Gregory A. Caldeira, "Public Opinion and the U.S. Supreme Court: FDR's Court-Packing Plan," *American Political Science Review* 81 (December 1987): 1139–1153.

12. The letter from Hughes to Wheeler, dated March 21, 1937, is reprinted in Joan Biskupic and Elder Witt, *Guide to the U.S. Supreme Court,* 3rd ed. (Washington, DC: Congressional Quarterly, 1997), 1039–1040.

13. See William E. Leuchtenburg, "The Origins of Franklin D. Roosevelt's 'Court-Packing' Plan," *in Supreme Court Review 1966,* ed. *Philip B. Kurland* (Chicago: University of Chicago Press, 1966), 347–400; and Leuchtenburg, *Franklin D. Roosevelt and the New Deal, 1932–1940* (New York: Harper & Row, 1963).

BOX 7-5   EXCERPTS FROM THE WHITE HOUSE BROADCAST, MARCH 9, 1937

TONIGHT, sitting at my desk in the White House, I make my first radio report to the people in my second term of office....

Last Thursday I described the American form of Government as a three horse team provided by the Constitution to the American people so that their field might be plowed. The three horses are, of course, the three branches of government—the Congress, the Executive and the Courts. Two of the horses are pulling in unison today; the third is not. Those who have intimated that the President of the United States is trying to drive that team overlook the simple fact that the President, as Chief Executive, is himself one of the three horses.

It is the American people themselves who are in the driver's seat.

It is the American people themselves who want the furrow plowed.

It is the American people themselves who expect the third horse to pull in unison with the other two....

When the Congress has sought to stabilize national agriculture, to improve the conditions of labor, to safeguard business against unfair competition, to protect our national resources, and in many other ways, to serve our clearly national needs, the majority of the Court has been assuming the power to pass on the wisdom of these Acts of the Congress—and to approve or disapprove the public policy written into these laws....

The Court...has improperly set itself up as a third House of the Congress—a super-legislature, as one of the Justices has called it—reading into the Constitution words and implications which are not there, and which were never intended to be there.

We have, therefore, reached the point as a Nation where we must take action to save the Constitution from the Court and the Court from itself. We must find a way to take an appeal from the Supreme Court to the Constitution itself. We want a Supreme Court which will do justice under the Constitution—not over it. In our Courts we want a government of laws and not of men.

I want—as all Americans want—an independent judiciary as proposed by the framers of the Constitution. That means a Supreme Court that will enforce the Constitution as written—that will refuse to amend the Constitution by the arbitrary exercise of judicial power—amendment by

judicial say-so. It does not mean a judiciary so independent that it can deny the existence of facts universally recognized....

What is my proposal? It is simply this: whenever a Judge or Justice of any Federal Court has reached the age of seventy and does not avail himself of the opportunity to retire on a pension, a new member shall be appointed by the President then in office, with the approval, as required by the Constitution, of the Senate of the United States.

That plan has two chief purposes. By bringing into the Judicial system a steady and continuing stream of new and younger blood, I hope, first, to make the administration of all Federal justice speedier and, therefore, less costly; secondly, to bring to the decision of social and economic problems younger men who have had personal experience and contact with modern facts and circumstances under which average men have to live and work. This plan will save our national Constitution from hardening of the judicial arteries.

The number of Judges to be appointed would depend wholly on the decision of present Judges now over seventy, or those who would subsequently reach the age of seventy.

If, for instance, any one of the six Justices of the Supreme Court now over the age of seventy should retire as provided under the plan, no additional place would be created. Consequently, although there never can be more than fifteen, there may be only fourteen, or thirteen, or twelve. And there may be only nine.

There is nothing novel or radical about this idea. It seeks to maintain the Federal bench in full vigor. It has been discussed and approved by many persons of high authority ever since a similar proposal passed the House of Representatives in 1869....

The statute would apply to all the Courts in the Federal system. There is general approval so far as the lower Federal courts are concerned. The plan has met opposition only so far as the Supreme Court of the United States itself is concerned. If such a plan is good for the lower courts it certainly ought to be equally good for the highest Court from which there is no appeal.

Those opposing this plan have sought to arouse prejudice and fear by crying that I am seeking to "pack" the

Supreme Court and that a baneful precedent will be established.

What do they mean by the words "packing the Court"?

Let me answer this question with a bluntness that will end all honest misunderstanding of my purposes.

If by that phrase "packing the Court" it is charged that I wish to place on the bench spineless puppets who would disregard the law and would decide specific cases as I wished them to be decided, I make this answer—that no President fit for his office would appoint, and no Senate of honorable men fit for their office would confirm, that kind of appointees to the Supreme Court.

But if by that phrase the charge is made that I would appoint and the Senate would confirm Justices worthy to sit beside present members of the Court who understand those modern conditions—that I will appoint Justices who will not undertake to override the judgment of the Congress on legislative policy—that I will appoint Justices who will act as Justices and not as legislators—if the appointment of such Justices can be called "packing the Courts," then I say that I and with me the vast majority of the American people favor doing just that thing—now.

Is it a dangerous precedent for the Congress to change the number of the Justices? The Congress has always had, and will have, that power. The number of Justices has been changed several times before—in the Administrations of John Adams and Thomas Jefferson—both signers of the Declaration of Independence—Andrew Jackson, Abraham Lincoln and Ulysses S. Grant....

We think it so much in the public interest to maintain a vigorous judiciary that we encourage the retirement of elderly Judges by offering them a life pension at full salary. Why then should we leave the fulfillment of this public policy to chance or make it dependent upon the desire or prejudice of any individual Justice?

It is the clear intention of our public policy to provide for a constant flow of new and younger blood into the Judiciary. Normally every President appoints a large number of District and Circuit Judges and a few members of the Supreme Court. Until my first term practically every President of the United States had appointed at least one member of the Supreme Court. President Taft appointed five members and named a Chief Justice—President Wilson three—President Harding four including

a Chief Justice—President Coolidge one—President Hoover three including a Chief Justice.

Such a succession of appointments should have provided a Court well-balanced as to age. But chance and the disinclination of individuals to leave the Supreme bench have now given us a Court in which five Justices will be over seventy-five years of age before next June and one over seventy. Thus a sound public policy has been defeated.

I now propose that we establish by law an assurance against any such ill-balanced Court in the future. I propose that hereafter, when a Judge reaches the age of seventy, a new and younger Judge shall be added to the Court automatically. In this way I propose to enforce a sound public policy by law instead of leaving the composition of our Federal Courts, including the highest, to be determined by chance or the personal decision of individuals.

If such a law as I propose is regarded as establishing a new precedent—is it not a most desirable precedent?

Like all lawyers, like all Americans, I regret the necessity of this controversy. But the welfare of the United States, and indeed of the Constitution itself, is what we all must think about first. Our difficulty with the Court today rises not from the Court as an institution but from human beings within it. But we cannot yield our constitutional destiny to the personal judgment of a few men who, being fearful of the future, would deny us the necessary means of dealing with the present.

This plan of mine is no attack on the Court; it seeks to restore the Court to its rightful and historic place in our system of Constitutional Government and to have it resume its high task of building anew on the Constitution "a system of living law." . . .

During the past half century the balance of power between the three great branches of the Federal Government has been tipped out of balance by the Courts in direct contradiction of the high purposes of the framers of the Constitution. It is my purpose to restore that balance. You who know me will accept my solemn assurance that in a world in which democracy is under attack, I seek to make American democracy succeed.

SOURCE: Fireside Chat, March 9, 1937.

FIGURE 7-1   Public Support for Roosevelt's 1937 Court-Packing Plan

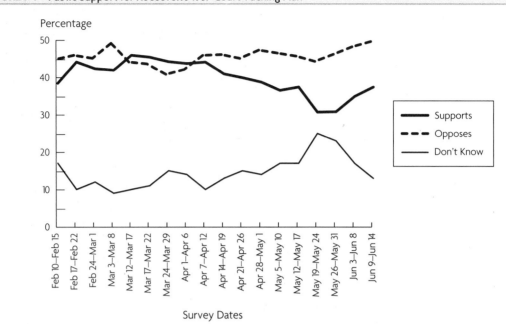

SOURCE: Lee Epstein, Jeffrey A. Segal, Harold Spaeth, and Thomas G. Walker, *The Supreme Court Compendium: Data, Decisions, and Developments*, 6th ed. (Thousand Oaks, CA: Sage/CQ Press, 2015), table 8–30.

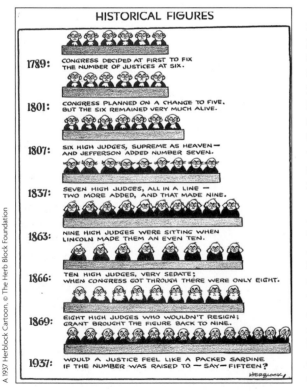

"Historical Figures"—a 1937 Herblock cartoon, copyright by The Herb Block Foundation.

Although this case involved a state law rather than a federal statute and concerned issues of substantive due process rather than the commerce clause, it had great significance. Aside from the doctrinal importance of the case, discussed in chapter 10, it signaled a change in the Court's voting coalitions. Justice Roberts, so long an ally of the Four Horsemen, deserted the conservatives and voted with the liberal bloc to approve the legislation. Just months earlier Roberts had voted with the conservatives in a 5–4 decision striking down a New York law that was nearly identical to the one he now approved.[14]

Two weeks later Roberts proved that his *West Coast Hotel* vote was not an aberration. On April 12 the Court issued its ruling in *National Labor Relations Board (NLRB) v. Jones & Laughlin Steel Corporation.* Once again Roberts joined Hughes, Brandeis, Cardozo, and Stone to form a majority, this time upholding a major piece of New Deal legislation. The decision may be the most important economic ruling of the twentieth century. In it the Court announced a break from the past and ushered in a new era in the constitutional relationship between the government and the economy.

---

14. *Morehead v. New York ex rel. Tipaldo* (1936).

National Labor Relations Board v. Jones & Laughlin Steel Corporation

301 U.S. 1 (1937)
http://laws.findlaw.com/us/301/1.html
Vote: 5 (Brandeis, Cardozo, Hughes, Roberts, Stone)
         4 (Butler, McReynolds, Sutherland, Van Devanter)
OPINION FOR THE COURT: *Hughes*
DISSENTING OPINION: *McReynolds*

FACTS:

In 1935 Congress passed the National Labor Relations Act, more commonly known as the Wagner Act. The purpose of the legislation was to help workers achieve gains in wages and working conditions through the collective bargaining process. The act's primary aim was to protect the rights of employees to organize and join labor unions and to provide a means for the enforcement of those rights. The law authorized the creation of the National Labor Relations Board (NLRB), which was empowered to hear complaints of unfair labor practices and impose certain corrective measures. The act was based on the power of Congress to regulate interstate commerce and on the assertion that labor unrest and strikes ("industrial strife") caused interruptions in such commerce that Congress had the right to prevent.

Jones & Laughlin was one of the nation's largest steel producers. Its operations were fully integrated, extending into many states and involving every aspect of steel production, from mining through production and distribution. Complaints were filed against the company for engaging in unfair labor practices at its plant in Aliquippa, Pennsylvania. The charges included discriminating against workers who wanted to join a labor union. The NLRB ruled against the company and ordered it to reinstate ten workers who had been dismissed because of their union activities. The company refused, claiming that the Wagner Act was unconstitutional. Steel production facilities, according to the company, were engaged in a manufacturing activity that had been declared by the Supreme Court to be intrastate commerce and thus outside Congress's regulatory authority. The lower courts, applying existing Supreme Court precedent, ruled in favor of the company, and the NLRB appealed.

ARGUMENTS:

For the petitioner, National Labor Relations Board:

- The act is a legitimate exercise of preventive power: it deals with the causes of the burden (here, industrial strife) on interstate commerce in anticipation of their probable effect, in much the same way as did the act at issue in *Stafford v. Wallace*. The law attempts to eliminate only those practices "affecting commerce." This phrase "affecting commerce" is defined in the law as "in commerce, or burdening or obstructing commerce or the free flow of commerce, or having led or tending to lead to a labor dispute burdening or obstructing commerce or the free flow of commerce." These words are patterned on language from the Court's commerce clause decisions.

- *Schechter Poultry* and *Carter Coal* do not apply here. In *Schechter* the Court rejected arguments that wages and hours in local industry affected interstate commerce through an intricate chain of economic causes and effects; any effect was indirect. In *Carter Coal* the Court held that the effect of wage cutting on interstate commerce was also indirect. The law at issue in *Carter Coal* also had collective bargaining provisions, which were included mostly to provide a means for regulating wages. The National Labor Relations Act, in contrast, is designed solely to eliminate the burden on interstate commerce caused by industrial strife, which affects commerce directly, without an intervening condition.

For the respondent, Jones & Laughlin Steel Corporation:

- The act, although disguised as a regulation of interstate commerce, is a regulation of labor. Under *Schechter Poultry,* the commerce clause cannot be used to legislate labor relations, which do not constitute a part of interstate commerce.

- Congress has tried to evade this distinction by limiting the act to transactions "affecting commerce," although the provisions are broad enough to cover almost every employment relation. To reach the conclusion that firing a few production employees has a consequential effect on interstate commerce, the government must pile assumption on assumption. This statute is a labor law, not a regulation of commerce, and it does not help to sustain the pretext that an indirect connection exists between the two.

- Decisions such as *Stafford v. Wallace* are not applicable here. Stockyards are instrumentalities of interstate commerce in much the same way as are the actual carriers of interstate commerce. The regulated activities in this and other cases were in the stream of commerce and exerted a direct effect on its flow. This doctrine does not apply to production activities that may indirectly affect the stream of commerce, as *Carter Coal* makes clear.

◢ **MR. CHIEF JUSTICE HUGHES DELIVERED THE OPINION OF THE COURT.**

First. The Scope of the Act.—The Act is challenged in its entirety as an attempt to regulate all industry, thus invading the reserved powers of the States over their local concerns. It is asserted that the references in the Act to interstate and foreign commerce are colorable at best; that the Act is not a true regulation of such commerce or of matters which directly affect it but on the contrary has the fundamental object of placing under the compulsory supervision of the federal government all industrial labor relations within the nation. . . .

If this conception of terms, intent and consequent inseparability were sound, the Act would necessarily fall by reason of the limitation upon the federal power which inheres in the constitutional grant, as well as because of the explicit reservation of the Tenth Amendment. The authority of the federal government may not be pushed to such an extreme as to destroy the distinction, which the commerce clause itself establishes, between commerce "among the several States" and the internal concerns of a State. That distinction between what is national and what is local in the activities of commerce is vital to the maintenance of our federal system. . . .

We think it clear that the National Labor Relations Act may be construed so as to operate within the sphere of constitutional authority. The jurisdiction conferred upon the Board, and invoked in this instance, is found in §10 (a), which provides:

"Sec. 10 (a). The Board is empowered, as hereinafter provided, to prevent any person from engaging in any unfair labor practice (listed in section 8 . . .) affecting commerce. The critical words of this provision, prescribing the limits of the Board's authority in dealing with the labor practices, are 'affecting commerce.' The Act specifically defines the 'commerce' to which it refers (§2 (6) . . .):

"The term 'commerce' means trade, traffic, commerce, transportation, or communication among the several States, or between the District of Columbia or any Territory of the United States and any State or other Territory, or between any foreign country and any State, Territory, or the District of Columbia, or within the District of Columbia or any Territory, or between points in the same State but through any other State or any Territory or the District of Columbia or any foreign country."

There can be no question that the commerce thus contemplated by the Act (aside from that within a Territory or the District of Columbia) is interstate and foreign commerce in the constitutional sense. The Act also defines the term "affecting commerce" (§2 (7) . . .):

"The term 'affecting commerce' means in commerce, or burdening or obstructing commerce or the free flow of commerce or having led or tending to lead to a labor dispute burdening or obstructing commerce or the free flow of commerce."

This definition is one of exclusion as well as inclusion. The grant of authority to the Board does not purport to extend to the relationship between all industrial employees and employers. Its terms do not impose collective bargaining upon all industry regardless of effects upon interstate and foreign commerce. It purports to reach only what may be deemed to burden or obstruct that commerce and, thus qualified, it must be construed as contemplating the exercise of control within constitutional bounds. It is a familiar principle that acts which directly burden or obstruct interstate or foreign commerce, or its free flow, are within the reach of the congressional power. Acts having that effect are not rendered immune because they grow out of labor disputes. It is the effect upon commerce, not the source of the injury, which is the criterion. Whether or not particular action does affect commerce in such a close and intimate fashion as to be subject to federal control, and hence to lie within the authority conferred upon the Board, is left by the statute to be determined as individual cases arise. We are thus to inquire whether in the instant case the constitutional boundary has been passed.

Second. The Unfair Labor Practices in Question.— . . . [T]he statute goes no further than to safeguard the right of employees to self-organization and to select representatives of their own choosing for collective bargaining or other mutual protection without restraint or coercion by their employer.

That is a fundamental right. Employees have as clear a right to organize and select their representatives for lawful purposes as the respondent has to organize its business and select its own officers and agents. Discrimination and coercion to prevent the free exercise of the right of employees to self-organization and representation is a proper subject for condemnation by competent legislative authority. Long ago we stated the reason for labor organizations. We said that they were organized out of the necessities of the situation; that a single employee was helpless in dealing with an employer; that he was dependent ordinarily on his daily wage for the maintenance of himself and family; that if the employer refused to pay him the wages that he thought fair, he was nevertheless unable to leave the employ and resist arbitrary and unfair treatment; that union was essential to give laborers opportunity to deal on an equality with their employer. We reiterated these views when we had under consideration the Railway Labor Act of 1926. Fully recognizing the legality of collective action on the part of employees in order to safeguard their proper interests, we said that Congress was not required to ignore this right but could safeguard it. Congress could seek to make appropriate collective action of employees an instrument of peace rather than of strife. We said that such collective action would be a mockery if representation were made futile by interference with freedom of choice. Hence the prohibition by Congress of interference with the selection of representatives for the purpose of negotiation and conference between employers and employees, "instead of being an invasion of the constitutional right of either, was based on the recognition of the rights of both." We have reasserted the same principle in sustaining the application of the Railway Labor Act as amended in 1934.

*Third. The Application of the Act to Employees Engaged in Production.—The Principle Involved.—*Respondent says that whatever may be said of employees engaged in interstate commerce, the industrial relations and activities in the manufacturing department of respondent's enterprise are not subject to federal regulation. The argument rests upon the proposition that manufacturing in itself is not commerce.

The Government distinguishes these cases. The various parts of respondent's enterprise are described as interdependent and as thus involving "a great movement of iron ore, coal and limestone along well-defined paths to the steel mills, thence through them, and thence in the form of steel products into the consuming centers of the country—a definite and well-understood course of business." It is urged that these activities constitute a "stream" or "flow" of commerce, of which the Aliquippa manufacturing plant is the focal point, and that industrial strife at that point would cripple the entire government. Reference is made to our decision sustaining the Packers and Stockyards Act. . . .

We do not find it necessary to determine whether these features of defendant's business dispose of the asserted analogy to the "stream of commerce" cases. The instances in which that metaphor has been used are but particular, and not exclusive, illustrations of the protective power which the Government invokes in support of the present Act. The congressional authority to protect interstate commerce from burdens and obstructions is not limited to transactions which can be deemed to be an essential part of a "flow" of interstate or foreign commerce. Burdens and obstructions may be due to injurious action springing from other sources. The fundamental principle is that the power to regulate commerce is the power to enact "all appropriate legislation" for "its protection and advancement"; to adopt measures "to promote its growth and insure its safety"; "to foster, protect, control and restrain." That power is plenary and may be exerted to protect interstate commerce "no matter what the source of the dangers which threaten it." Although activities may be intrastate in character when separately considered, if they have such a close and substantial relation to interstate commerce that their control is essential or appropriate to protect that commerce from burdens and obstructions, Congress cannot be denied the power to exercise that control. . . .

It is thus apparent that the fact that the employees here concerned were engaged in production is not determinative. The question remains as to the effect upon interstate commerce of the labor practice involved. . . .

*Fourth. Effects of the Unfair Labor Practice in Respondent's Enterprise.—*Giving full weight to respondent's contention with respect to a break in the complete continuity of the "stream of commerce" by reason of respondent's manufacturing operations, the fact remains that the stoppage of those operations by industrial strife would have a most serious effect upon interstate commerce. In view of respondent's far-flung activities, it is idle to say that the effect would be indirect or remote. It is obvious that it would be immediate and might be catastrophic. We are asked to shut our eyes to the plainest facts of our national life and to deal with the question of direct and indirect effects in an intellectual vacuum. Because there may be but indirect and remote effects upon interstate commerce in connection with a host of local enterprises throughout the country, it does not follow that other industrial activities do not have such a close and intimate relation to interstate commerce as to make the presence of industrial strife a matter of the most urgent national concern. When industries organize themselves on a national scale, making their relation to interstate commerce the dominant factor in their activities, how can it be maintained that their industrial labor relations constitute a forbidden field into which Congress may not enter when it is necessary to protect interstate commerce from the paralyzing consequences of industrial war? We have often said that interstate commerce itself is a practical conception. It is equally true that interferences with that commerce must be appraised by a judgment that does not ignore actual experience.

Experience has abundantly demonstrated that the recognition of the right of employees to self-organization and to have representatives of their own choosing for the purpose of collective bargaining is often an essential condition of industrial peace. Refusal to confer and negotiate has been one of the most prolific causes of strife. This is such an outstanding fact in the history of labor disturbances that it is a proper subject of judicial notice and requires no citation of instances. . . . These questions have frequently engaged the attention of Congress and have been the subject of many inquiries. The steel industry is one of the great basic industries of the United States, with ramifying activities affecting interstate commerce at every point. The Government aptly refers to the steel strike of 1919–1920 with its far-reaching consequences. The fact that there appears to have been no major disturbance in that industry in the more recent period did not dispose of the possibilities of future and like dangers to interstate commerce which Congress was entitled to foresee and to exercise its protective power to forestall. It is not necessary again to detail the facts as to respondent's enterprise. Instead of being beyond the pale, we think that it presents in a most striking way the close and intimate relation which a manufacturing industry may have to interstate commerce and we have no doubt that Congress had constitutional authority to safeguard the right of respondent's employees to self-organization and freedom in the choice of representatives for collective bargaining. . . .

Reversed.

MR. JUSTICE McREYNOLDS delivered the following dissenting opinion in the cases preceding:
MR. JUSTICE VAN DEVANTER, MR. JUSTICE SUTHERLAND, MR. JUSTICE BUTLER and I are unable to agree with the decisions just announced. . . .

Considering the far-reaching import of these decisions, the departure from what we understand has been consistently ruled here, and the extraordinary power confirmed to a Board of three [the NLRB], the obligation to present our views becomes plain. . . .

The precise question for us to determine is whether in the circumstances disclosed Congress has power to authorize what the Labor Board commanded the respondents to do. Stated otherwise, in the circumstances here existing could Congress by statute direct what the Board has ordered? . . .

The argument in support of the Board affirms: "Thus the validity of any specific application of the preventive measures of this Act depends upon whether industrial strife resulting from the practices in the particular enterprise under consideration would be of the character which Federal power could control if it occurred. If strife in that enterprise could be controlled, certainly it could be prevented."

Manifestly that view of Congressional power would extend it into almost every field of human industry. With striking lucidity, fifty years ago, *Kidd v. Pearson* declared: "If it be held that the term [commerce with foreign Nations, and among the several States] includes the regulation of all such manufactures as are intended to be the subject of commercial transactions in the future, it is impossible to deny that it would also include all productive industries that contemplate the same thing. The result would be that Congress would be invested, to the exclusion of the States, with the power to regulate, not only manufactures, but also agriculture, horticulture, stock raising, domestic fisheries, mining—in short, every branch of human activity." This doctrine found full approval in *United States v. E. C. Knight Co.*, *Schechter Poultry Corp. v. United States*, and *Carter v. Carter Coal Co.*, where the authorities are collected and principles applicable here are discussed. . . .

The Constitution still recognizes the existence of states with indestructible powers; the Tenth Amendment was supposed to put them beyond controversy.

We are told that Congress may protect the "stream of commerce" and that one who buys raw material without the state, manufactures it therein, and ships the output to another state is in that stream. Therefore it is said he may be prevented from doing anything which may interfere with its flow.

This, too, goes beyond the constitutional limitations heretofore enforced. If a man raises cattle and regularly delivers them to a carrier for interstate shipment, may Congress prescribe the conditions under which he may employ or discharge helpers on the ranch? The products of a mine pass daily into interstate commerce; many things are brought to it from other states. Are the owners and miners within the power of Congress in respect of the miners' tenure and discharge? May a mill owner be prohibited from closing his factory or discontinuing his business because so to do would stop the flow of products to and from his plant in interstate commerce? May employees in a factory be restrained from quitting work in a body because this will close the factory and thereby stop the flow of commerce? May arson of a factory be made a Federal offense whenever this would interfere with such flow? If the business cannot continue with the existing wage scale, may Congress command a reduction? If the ruling of the Court just announced is adhered to these questions suggest some of the problems certain to arise. . . .

There is no ground on which reasonably to hold that refusal by a manufacturer, whose raw materials come from states other than that of his factory and whose products are regularly carried to other states, to bargain collectively with employees in his manufacturing plant, directly affects interstate commerce. In such business, there is not one but two distinct movements or streams in interstate transportation. The first brings in raw material and there ends. Then follows manufacture, a separate and local activity. Upon completion of this, and not before, the second distinct movement or stream in interstate commerce begins and the products go to other states. Such is the common course for small as well as large industries. It is unreasonable and unprecedented to say the commerce clause confers upon Congress power to govern the relations between employers and employees in these local activities. In *Schechter*'s case we condemned as unauthorized by the commerce clause assertion of federal power in respect of commodities which had come to rest after interstate transportation. And, in *Carter*'s case, we held Congress lacked the power to regulate labor relations in respect of commodities before interstate commerce has begun.

It is gravely stated that experience teaches that if an employer discourages membership in "any organization of any kind" "in which employees participate, and which exists for the purpose in whole or in part of dealing with employers concerning grievances, labor disputes, wages, rates of pay, hours of employment or conditions of work," discontent may follow and this in turn may lead to a strike, and as the outcome of the strike there may be a block in the stream of interstate commerce. Therefore Congress may inhibit the discharge! Whatever effect any cause of discontent may ultimately have upon commerce is far too indirect to justify Congressional regulation. Almost anything—marriage, birth, death—may in some fashion affect commerce.

That Congress has power by appropriate means, not prohibited by the Constitution, to prevent direct and material interference with the conduct of interstate commerce is settled doctrine. But the interference struck at must be direct and material, not some mere possibility contingent on wholly uncertain events; and there must be no impairment of rights guaranteed. . . .

The things inhibited by the Labor Act relate to the management of a manufacturing plant—something distinct from commerce and subject to the authority of the state.

And this may not be abridged because of some vague possibility of distant interference with commerce. . . .

The right to contract is fundamental and includes the privilege of selecting those with whom one is willing to assume contractual relations. This right is unduly abridged by the Act now upheld. A private owner is deprived of power to manage his own property by freely selecting those to whom his manufacturing operations are to be entrusted. We think this cannot lawfully be done in circumstances like those here disclosed.

It seems clear to us that Congress has transcended the powers granted.

Justice Owen Roberts. He cast critical votes in 1937 Supreme Court cases that expanded the authority of the federal government to regulate the economy.

The decisions in *West Coast Hotel v. Parrish* and *NLRB v. Jones & Laughlin Steel* took the energy out of Roosevelt's drive to pack the Court. It no longer appeared necessary, as the Court now was looking with greater approval at state and federal legislation to correct the failing economy. In addition, on May 18,

1937, Justice Van Devanter, a consistent foe of Roosevelt's New Deal programs, announced that he would retire from the Court at the end of the term. At long last the president would have an opportunity to put a justice of his own choosing on the Court.

On June 7 the Senate Judiciary Committee recommended that the Court-packing bill not be passed. To the president's great displeasure, seven of the ten senators signing the report were Democrats. Majority Leader Joseph Robinson (D-Ark.), mounted a last-ditch effort on behalf of the president, advocating a compromise plan that would have raised the threshold age for replacing the justices from seventy to seventy-five years. Robinson made considerable progress in forging a coalition to pass this modified plan, but the effort stalled when he died from a heart attack on July 14.[15]

Much has been said and written about Justice Roberts's change in position. At the time, it was described as "the switch in time that saved nine," because his move from the conservative to the liberal wing of the Court was largely responsible for killing the Court-packing plan and preserving the Court as a nine-justice institution. Such a characterization is not flattering for a judge, who is not supposed to make decisions on the basis of external political pressures. Nevertheless, it would certainly be understandable for a justice to rethink his views if the future of the Court as an institution were at stake.

More-contemporary analyses of Roberts's switch point out that the notion that he caved in to the pressures of the president's plan is overly simplistic. Although the decision in *West Coast Hotel* was announced after Roosevelt sent his proposal to Congress, it was argued and initially voted on weeks before the president made his plans public. Roosevelt had kept the Court-packing proposal carefully under wraps before he announced it, and the likelihood that the justices had advance knowledge of it is slight. Furthermore, Roberts was not a doctrinaire conservative. Although he joined the Court's right wing in several important decisions, he did not have the laissez-faire zeal of the Four Horsemen. In fact, Roberts

had voted on a number of occasions in support of state efforts to combat economic problems.[16] Some observers now conclude that Roberts's change of position was primarily a matter of his growing disenchantment with the hard-line conservative view and that he followed "his sound judicial intuition to a well-reasoned position in keeping with the public interest."[17] As for Roberts's own explanation, he maintained traditional judicial silence. When asked in a 1946 interview why he had altered his position, he deflected the question by responding, "Who knows what causes a judge to decide as he does? Maybe the breakfast he had has something to do with it."[18] Whatever the reasons for his switch, it broke the conservatives' domination of the Court.

Consolidating the New Interpretation of the Commerce Power

Justice Van Devanter's retirement was followed over the next four years by the retirements of Justices Sutherland and Brandeis and the deaths of Justices Cardozo and Butler. By 1940 Franklin Roosevelt had appointed a majority of the sitting justices. And in 1941 Justice McReynolds, the last of the Four Horsemen, also retired.

With *NLRB v. Jones & Laughlin Steel* showing the way, the increasingly liberal Court upheld a number of New Deal programs. It also continued to expand the concept of interstate commerce. Gone were the old notions that production, manufacturing, mining, and processing were exclusively intrastate affairs with insufficient direct effects on interstate commerce to activate federal commerce powers. Precedents such as *E. C. Knight, Hammer, Panama Refining, Schechter Poultry,* and *Carter Coal* were substantially overruled or discredited, or severely limited *(see box 7-6)*.

Of all the cases during this period, two are considered among the Court's most important statements on congressional commerce power: *United States v. Darby* (1941) and *Wickard v. Filburn* (1942). Not only do they provide insight into modern-era commerce

---

15. For a full account of the events surrounding this compromise plan, see William E. Leuchtenburg, "FDR's Court-Packing Plan: A Second Life, a Second Death," *Duke Law Journal* (June-September 1985): 673–689.

16. See, for example, his opinion for the Court in *Nebbia v. New York* (1934).

17. Merlo J. Pusey, "Justice Roberts' 1937 Turnaround," in *Yearbook of the Supreme Court Historical Society* (Washington, DC: Supreme Court Historical Society, 1983), 107.

18. Ibid., 106.

BOX 7-6   SUPREME COURT EXPANSION OF THE COMMERCE POWERS, 1937–1942

DECISION	RULING
NLRB v. Friedman-Harry Marks Clothing Company (1937)	The National Labor Relations Act applies to a company engaged in the manufacturing of clothing.
NLRB v. Fruehauf Trailer Company (1937)	The National Labor Relations Act applies to a company engaged in the manufacturing of trailers.
Steward Machine v. Davis (1937)	Unemployment provisions of the Social Security Act are constitutional.
Helvering v. Davis (1937)	Old-age benefits provisions of the Social Security Act are constitutional.
Santa Cruz Fruit Packing v. NLRB (1938)	The National Labor Relations Act applies to a fruit-packing company even though only 37 percent of its product is sold in interstate commerce.
Consolidated Edison Company v. NLRB (1938)	The National Labor Relations Act applies to a power company even though all of its power is sold in state.
NLRB v. Fainblatt (1939)	The National Labor Relations Act applies to a small garment manufacturer even though all of its goods are sold in state.
United States v. Rock Royal Cooperative (1939)	Legislation allowing the secretary of agriculture to set milk prices paid to farmers is constitutional.
Mulford v. Smith (1939)	Tobacco production quotas set by the secretary of agriculture under the Agricultural Adjustment Act of 1938 are constitutional.
United States v. Darby (1941)	Congressional action prohibiting shipment in interstate commerce of goods in violation of federal wage and hour laws is constitutional.
Wickard v. Filburn (1942)	The provision of the Agricultural Adjustment Act allowing the secretary of agriculture to regulate an individual's planting wheat on his own property for on-farm consumption is constitutional.

---

clause doctrine, but they also serve to illustrate how far the Court had moved from its pre-1937 idea of interstate commerce. As you read *Darby,* keep in mind decisions such as *Hammer v. Dagenhart,* in which the Court struck down an act prohibiting the shipment in interstate commerce of products made by children. Regulating child labor, the Court reasoned, was not "expressly" delegated to the federal government and so, by virtue of the Tenth Amendment, belonged to the states. As you compare *Wickard* to earlier rulings, recall that in *E. C. Knight* a sugar trust that controlled 98 percent of the nation's sugar refining was considered to be operating in intrastate commerce. And in *Carter v. Carter Coal,* the entire coal mining industry was said to be outside the power of Congress to regulate interstate commerce. How do these industries compare with Roscoe Filburn's farm *(p. 463)?*

United States v. Darby

312 U.S. 100 (1941)
http://laws.findlaw.com/us/312/100.html
Vote: *8 (Black, Douglas, Frankfurter, Hughes, Murphy, Reed, Roberts, Stone)*
    0
OPINION OF THE COURT: *Stone*

FACTS:

In 1938 Congress, under its power to regulate interstate commerce, enacted a major piece of New Deal legislation, the Fair Labor Standards Act (FLSA). It provided that all employers "engaged in interstate commerce, or in the production of goods for that commerce" must pay all their employees a minimum wage of twenty-five cents per hour and not permit employees to work longer than forty-four hours per week without paying them one and one-half times their regular pay for their overtime hours. In November

1939 the federal government sought and obtained an indictment against Fred W. Darby for violating the FLSA. The indictment alleged that Darby, the owner of a lumber company, was engaged in the production and manufacturing of goods shipped out of state, but that he had not abided by either of the FLSA's principal pay requirements.

Darby did not dispute the charges but invoked the logic of *Hammer v. Dagenhart* and other pre-1937 cases. The government responded with legal and pragmatic arguments.

ARGUMENTS:

For the appellant, United States:

- The meaning of the phrase *interstate commerce* at the time the commerce clause was drafted included manufacturing and the entire economy. Therefore, Congress is empowered by the Constitution to regulate all of these areas.
- Due to interstate commercial competition, no one state can require higher labor standards in the absence of a uniform federal law. Employers with lower labor standards would have an unfair advantage in interstate competition, and only the national government can pragmatically act on the problem. The lumber industry well illustrates the problem of the inability of the states to ensure adequate labor conditions: more than 57 percent of the lumber produced enters into interstate commerce from forty-five of the states.
- The commerce clause power should be assessed by what it regulates, not by what it affects. Intrastate acts lie within the power of Congress when it is necessary to effectively control interstate transactions, and Congress need not wait until transportation begins to protect the flow of commerce.
- Since *McCulloch* the Court has recognized that the Tenth Amendment is not a limit on the powers of the federal government. That doctrine has not been overruled, and it cannot be overruled by implication by the recent cases suggesting otherwise.

For the appellee, Fred W. Darby:

- The act is an unconstitutional attempt to regulate the conditions surrounding the production of goods and commodities; it is not a regulation of interstate commerce within the delegated power to Congress under the commerce clause.
- The government's argument is an indirect attack upon the dual system of government established by the framers. Allowing the federal government to control anything related to economic issues is directly contrary to the doctrine that the federal government is a government of limited and enumerated powers. The Tenth Amendment guarantees that certain powers are reserved to the states and the people.
- The mere fact that individual states cannot adequately protect the markets outside their borders for the sale of their products does not give the national government unqualified power to regulate competition in those interstate markets.

MR. JUSTICE STONE DELIVERED THE OPINION OF THE COURT.

The two principal questions raised by the record in this case are, first, whether Congress has constitutional power to prohibit the shipment in interstate commerce of lumber manufactured by employees whose wages are less than a prescribed minimum or whose weekly hours of labor at that wage are greater than a prescribed maximum [Section 15(1)], and, second, whether it has power to prohibit the employment of workmen in the production of goods "for interstate commerce" at other than prescribed wages and hours [Section 15(a)(2)]. . . .

The prohibition of shipment of the proscribed goods in interstate commerce. Section 15(a)(1) prohibits, and the indictment charges, the shipment in interstate commerce, of goods produced for interstate commerce by employees whose wages and hours of employment do not conform to the requirements of the Act. [T]he only question arising under the commerce clause with respect to such shipments is whether Congress has the constitutional power to prohibit them.

While manufacture is not, of itself, interstate commerce, the shipment of manufactured goods interstate is such commerce, and the prohibition of such shipment by Congress is indubitably a regulation of the commerce. The power to regulate commerce is the power "to prescribe the rule by which commerce is governed." *Gibbons v. Ogden.* It extends not only to those regulations which aid, foster and protect the commerce, but embraces those which prohibit it. It is conceded that the power of Congress to prohibit transportation in interstate commerce includes noxious articles, *Lottery Case, Hoke v. United States . . . ,* kidnapped persons and articles, such as intoxicating liquor or convict made goods, traffic in which is forbidden or restricted by the laws of the state of destination.

But it is said that the present prohibition falls within the scope of none of these categories; that, while the prohibition is nominally a regulation of the commerce, its motive or purpose is regulation of wages and hours of persons engaged in manufacture, the control of which has been reserved to the states. . . . [It is said that] under the guise of a regulation of interstate commerce, [Congress] undertakes to regulate wages and hours within the state contrary to the policy of the state which has elected to leave them unregulated.

The power of Congress over interstate commerce "is complete in itself, may be exercised to its utmost extent, and acknowledges no limitations other than are prescribed in the Constitution." *Gibbons v. Ogden*. That power can neither be enlarged nor diminished by the exercise or non-exercise of state power. Congress, following its own conception of public policy concerning the restrictions which may appropriately be imposed on interstate commerce, is free to exclude from the commerce articles whose use in the states for which they are destined it may conceive to be injurious to the public health, morals or welfare, even though the state has not sought to regulate their use.

Such regulation is not a forbidden invasion of state power merely because either its motive or its consequence is to restrict the use of articles of commerce within the states of destination, and is not prohibited unless by other Constitutional provisions. It is no objection to the assertion of the power to regulate interstate commerce that its exercise is attended by the same incidents which attend the exercise of the police power of the states.

The motive and purpose of the present regulation are plainly to make effective the Congressional conception of public policy that interstate commerce should not be made the instrument of competition in the distribution of goods produced under substandard labor conditions, which competition is injurious to the commerce and to the states from and to which the commerce flows. The motive and purpose of a regulation of interstate commerce are matters for the legislative judgment upon the exercise of which the Constitution places no restriction, and over which the courts are given no control. . . .

In the more than a century which has elapsed since the decision of *Gibbons v. Ogden*, these principles of constitutional interpretation have been so long and repeatedly recognized by this Court as applicable to the Commerce Clause that there would be little occasion for repeating them now were it not for the decision of this Court twenty-two years ago in *Hammer v. Dagenhart*. In that case, it was held by a bare majority of the Court, over the powerful

and now classic dissent of Mr. Justice Holmes setting forth the fundamental issues involved, that Congress was without power to exclude the products of child labor from interstate commerce. The reasoning and conclusion of the Court's opinion there cannot be reconciled with the conclusion which we have reached, that the power of Congress under the Commerce Clause is plenary to exclude any article from interstate commerce subject only to the specific prohibitions of the Constitution.

Hammer v. Dagenhart has not been followed. The distinction on which the decision was rested, that Congressional power to prohibit interstate commerce is limited to articles which in themselves have some harmful or deleterious property—a distinction which was novel when made and unsupported by any provision of the Constitution—has long since been abandoned. . . .

The conclusion is inescapable that *Hammer v. Dagenhart* was a departure from the principles which have prevailed in the interpretation of the Commerce Clause both before and since the decision, and that such vitality, as a precedent, as it then had, has long since been exhausted. It should be, and now is, overruled.

Validity of the wage and hour requirements. Section 15(a)(2) [requires] employers to conform to the wage and hour provisions with respect to all employees engaged in the production of goods for interstate commerce. As appellee's employees are not alleged to be "engaged in interstate commerce," the validity of the prohibition turns on the question whether the employment, under other than the prescribed labor standards, of employees engaged in the production of goods for interstate commerce is so related to the commerce, and so affects it, as to be within the reach of the power of Congress to regulate it. . . .

The obvious purpose of the Act was not only to prevent the interstate transportation of the proscribed product, but to stop the initial step toward transportation, production with the purpose of so transporting it. Congress was not unaware that most manufacturing businesses shipping their product in interstate commerce make it in their shops without reference to its ultimate destination, and then, after manufacture, select some of it for shipment interstate and some intrastate, according to the daily demands of their business, and that it would be practically impossible, without disrupting manufacturing businesses, to restrict the prohibited kind of production to the particular pieces of lumber, cloth, furniture or the like which later move in interstate, rather than intrastate, commerce.

There remains the question whether such restriction on the production of goods for commerce is a permissible exercise of the commerce power. The power of Congress over interstate commerce is not confined to the regulation of commerce among the states. It extends to those activities intrastate which so affect interstate commerce or the exercise of the power of Congress over it as to make regulation of them appropriate means to the attainment of a legitimate end, the exercise of the granted power of Congress to regulate interstate commerce. *See McCulloch v. Maryland.*

While this Court has many times found state regulation of interstate commerce, when uniformity of its regulation is of national concern, to be incompatible with the Commerce Clause even though Congress has not legislated on the subject, the Court has never implied such restraint on state control over matters intrastate not deemed to be regulations of interstate commerce or its instrumentalities even though they affect the commerce. In the absence of Congressional legislation on the subject, state laws which are not regulations of the commerce itself or its instrumentalities are not forbidden, even though they affect interstate commerce.

But it does not follow that Congress may not, by appropriate legislation, regulate intrastate activities where they have a substantial effect on interstate commerce. A recent example is the National Labor Relations Act for the regulation of employer and employee relations in industries in which strikes, induced by unfair labor practices named in the Act, tend to disturb or obstruct interstate commerce. *See National Labor Relations Board v. Jones & Laughlin Steel Corp.* But, long before the adoption of the National Labor Relations Act, this Court had many times held that the power of Congress to regulate interstate commerce extends to the regulation through legislative action of activities intrastate which have a substantial effect on the commerce or the exercise of the Congressional power over it. In such legislation, Congress has sometimes left it to the courts to determine whether the intrastate activities have the prohibited effect on the commerce, as in the Sherman Act. . . . In passing on the validity of legislation of the class last mentioned, the only function of courts is to determine whether the particular activity regulated or prohibited is within the reach of the federal power.

Congress having by the present Act adopted the policy of excluding from interstate commerce all goods produced for the commerce which do not conform to the specified labor standards, it may choose the means reasonably adapted to the attainment of the permitted end even though they involve control of intrastate activities. Such legislation has often been sustained with respect to powers other than the commerce power granted to the national government when the means chosen, although not themselves within the granted power, were nevertheless deemed appropriate aids to the accomplishment of some purpose within an admitted power of the national government. A familiar like exercise of power is the regulation of intrastate transactions which are so commingled with or related to interstate commerce that all must be regulated if the interstate commerce is to be effectively controlled. *Shreveport Case.*

We think also that §15(a)(2), now under consideration, is sustainable independently of §15(a)(1), which prohibits shipment or transportation of the proscribed goods. As we have said, the evils aimed at by the Act are the spread of substandard labor conditions through the use of the facilities of interstate commerce for competition by the goods so produced with those produced under the prescribed or better labor conditions, and the consequent dislocation of the commerce itself caused by the impairment or destruction of local businesses by competition made effective through interstate commerce. The Act is thus directed at the suppression of a method or kind of competition in interstate commerce which it has, in effect, condemned as "unfair," . . . made effective through interstate commerce.

The Sherman Act and the National Labor Relations Act are familiar examples of the exertion of the commerce power to prohibit or control activities wholly intrastate because of their effect on interstate commerce. . . .

The means adopted by §15(a)(2) for the protection of interstate commerce by the suppression of the production of the condemned goods for interstate commerce is so related to the commerce, and so affects it, as to be within the reach of the commerce power. Congress, to attain its objective in the suppression of nationwide competition in interstate commerce by goods produced under substandard labor conditions, has made no distinction as to the volume or amount of shipments in the commerce or of production for commerce by any particular shipper or producer. It recognized that, in present day industry, competition by a small part may affect the whole, and that the total effect of the competition of many small producers may be great. The legislation, aimed at a whole, embraces all its parts.

So far as *Carter v. Carter Coal Co.* is inconsistent with this conclusion, its doctrine is limited in principle by the decisions under the Sherman Act and the National Labor Relations Act, which we have cited and which we follow.

Our conclusion is unaffected by the Tenth Amendment, which provides:

The powers not delegated to the United States by the Constitution, nor prohibited by it to the States, are reserved to the States respectively, or to the people.

The amendment states but a truism that all is retained which has not been surrendered. There is nothing in the history of its adoption to suggest that it was more than declaratory of the relationship between the national and state governments as it had been established by the Constitution before the amendment, or that its purpose was other than to allay fears that the new national government might seek to exercise powers not granted, and that the states might not be able to exercise fully their reserved powers.

From the beginning and for many years, the amendment has been construed as not depriving the national government of authority to resort to all means for the exercise of a granted power which are appropriate and plainly adapted to the permitted end. *McCulloch v. Maryland.* . . .

Reversed.

Wickard v. Filburn

317 U.S. 111 (1942)
http://laws.findlaw.com/us/317/111.html
Vote: 9 (Black, Byrnes, Douglas, Frankfurter, Jackson, Murphy, Reed, Roberts, Stone)
       0

OPINION OF THE COURT: *Jackson*

FACTS:

The 1938 Agricultural Adjustment Act, as amended, allowed the secretary of agriculture to establish production limits for various grains. Under these limits, acreage allotments were assigned to the individual farmer. The purpose of the law was to stop wild swings in grain prices by eliminating surpluses and shortfalls.

Roscoe Filburn owned a small farm in Montgomery County, Ohio. For many years he raised dairy cattle and chickens, selling the milk, poultry, and eggs the farm produced. He also raised winter wheat on a small portion of his farm. He sold some wheat and used the rest to feed his cattle and chickens, make flour for home consumption, and produce seeds for the next planting.

In July 1940 Secretary of Agriculture Claude R. Wickard set the wheat production limits for the 1941 crop. Filburn was allotted 11.1 acres to be planted in wheat with a yield of 20.1 bushels per acre. He planted not only his allotted acres but also some other land to produce the wheat for home consumption. In total Filburn planted 23 acres in wheat, from which he harvested 239 bushels more than the government allowed him. For this excess planting Filburn was fined $117.11. He refused to pay the fine, claiming that Congress had exceeded its powers under the commerce clause by regulating the planting by an individual of wheat on his own property for on-farm consumption. The lower court ruled in Filburn's favor, and Secretary Wickard appealed.

ARGUMENTS:

For the appellant, Claude R. Wickard, secretary of agriculture, et al.:

• The quota on wheat is a valid exercise of the commerce power. That the law penalizes excess wheat, which is available for marketing but is consumed as feed, seed, or household food, does not make it invalid. Because excessive wheat affects national price and supply, Congress reasonably concluded that orderly interstate marketing and reasonable

Roscoe Filburn, the Ohio farmer who unsuccessfully argued that Congress lacked the constitutional power to regulate the production of wheat intended for on-farm consumption.

Courtesy of Mary Lou Spurgeon

interstate prices could best be achieved if the quota system applied to all wheat available for marketing and not just to that actually sold.

- The quota system was also adopted because of the practical difficulties in devising an enforcement system limited to wheat sold. It would be impossible for the government to check on all sales by the more than 1 million wheat producers. Under the current system enforcement is feasible because all the government needs to know is the amount of acreage planted by the farmer and the average yield per acre.

- Under the Constitution, Congress can choose whatever means it deems appropriate and necessary to carry out its policy of keeping excess wheat off the interstate market under its commerce clause power.

For the appellee, Roscoe Filburn:

- Neither interstate nor intrastate commerce, nor an intermingling between the two, is at issue here. It involves wheat that a farmer may consume on his own farm for food, seed, or feed. It at no time moves into commerce between the states, nor even in a state. It is under the control of the farmer and has not moved into any channel of trade; it is private property.

- The government insists that wheat used on a farm for the farmer's own purposes is in competition with commercial feed and seeds. This is too absurd to take seriously. This is akin to saying that because person A manufactures a radio, A cannot use the radio in his own home but must instead buy a radio from person B so that B can continue his business and B must buy a radio from A to keep A in business. Neither party can have the benefit of his own product.

MR. JUSTICE JACKSON DELIVERED THE OPINION OF THE COURT.

It is urged that under the Commerce Clause of the Constitution, Article I, §8, clause 3, Congress does not possess the power it has in this instance sought to exercise. The question would merit little consideration since our decision in *United States v. Darby* sustaining the federal power to regulate production of goods for commerce, except for the fact that this Act extends federal regulation to production not intended in any part for commerce but wholly for consumption on the farm. The Act includes a definition of "market" and its derivatives, so that as related

to wheat, in addition to its conventional meaning, it also means to dispose of "by feeding (in any form) to poultry or livestock which, or the products of which, are sold, bartered, or exchanged, or to be so disposed of." Hence, marketing quotas not only embrace all that may be sold without penalty but also what may be consumed on the premises. Wheat produced on excess acreage is designated as "available for marketing" as so defined, and the penalty is imposed thereon. Penalties do not depend upon whether any part of the wheat, either within or without the quota, is sold or intended to be sold. The sum of this is that the Federal Government fixes a quota including all that the farmer may harvest for sale or for his own farm needs, and declares that wheat produced on excess acreage may neither be disposed of nor used except upon payment of the penalty, or except it is stored as required by the Act or delivered to the Secretary of Agriculture.

Appellee says that this is a regulation of production and consumption of wheat. Such activities are, he urges, beyond the reach of Congressional power under the Commerce Clause, since they are local in character, and their effects upon interstate commerce are at most "indirect." In answer the Government argues that the statute regulates neither production nor consumption, but only marketing; and, in the alternative, that if the Act does go beyond the regulation of marketing it is sustainable as a "necessary and proper" implementation of the power of Congress over interstate commerce.

The Government's concern lest the Act be held to be a regulation of production or consumption, rather than of marketing, is attributable to a few dicta and decisions of this Court which might be understood to lay it down that activities such as "production," "manufacturing," and "mining" are strictly "local" and, except in special circumstances which are not present here, cannot be regulated under the commerce power because their effects upon interstate commerce are, as matter of law, only "indirect." Even today, when this power has been held to have great latitude, there is no decision of this Court that such activities may be regulated where no part of the product is intended for interstate commerce or intermingled with the subjects thereof. We believe that a review of the course of decision under the Commerce Clause will make plain, however, that questions of the power of Congress are not to be decided by reference to any formula which would give controlling force to nomenclature such as "production" and "indirect" and foreclose consideration of the actual effects of the activity in question upon interstate commerce.

At the beginning Chief Justice Marshall described the federal commerce power with a breadth never yet exceeded. *Gibbons v. Ogden.* He made emphatic the embracing and penetrating nature of this power by warning that effective restraints on its exercise must proceed from political rather than from judicial processes.

For nearly a century, however, decisions of this Court under the Commerce Clause dealt rarely with questions of what Congress might do in the exercise of its granted power under the Clause, and almost entirely with the permissibility of state activity which it was claimed discriminated against or burdened interstate commerce. During this period there was perhaps little occasion for the affirmative exercise of the commerce power, and the influence of the Clause on American life and law was a negative one, resulting almost wholly from its operation as a restraint upon the powers of the states. In discussion and decision the point of reference, instead of being what was "necessary and proper" to the exercise by Congress of its granted power, was often some concept of sovereignty thought to be implicit in the status of statehood. Certain activities such as "production," "manufacturing," and "mining" were occasionally said to be within the province of state governments and beyond the power of Congress under the Commerce Clause.

It was not until 1887, with the enactment of the Interstate Commerce Act, that the interstate commerce power began to exert positive influence in American law and life. This first important federal resort to the commerce power was followed in 1890 by the Sherman Anti-Trust Act and, thereafter, mainly after 1903, by many others. These statutes ushered in new phases of adjudication, which required the Court to approach the interpretation of the Commerce Clause in the light of an actual exercise by Congress of its power thereunder.

When it first dealt with this new legislation, the Court adhered to its earlier pronouncements, and allowed but little scope to the power of Congress. *United States v. Knight Co.* These earlier pronouncements also played an important part in several of the five cases in which this Court later held that Acts of Congress under the Commerce Clause were in excess of its power.

Even while important opinions in this line of restrictive authority were being written, however, other cases called forth broader interpretations of the Commerce Clause destined to supersede the earlier ones, and to bring about a return to the principles first enunciated by Chief Justice Marshall in *Gibbons v. Ogden.* . . .

Whether the subject of the regulation in question was "production," "consumption," or "marketing" is . . . not material for purposes of deciding the question of federal power before us. That an activity is of local character may help in a doubtful case to determine whether Congress intended to reach it. The same consideration might help in determining whether in the absence of Congressional action it would be permissible for the state to exert its power on the subject matter, even though in so doing it to some degree affected interstate commerce. But even if appellee's activity be local and though it may not be regarded as commerce, it may still, whatever its nature, be reached by Congress if it exerts a substantial economic effect on interstate commerce, and this irrespective of whether such effect is what might at some earlier time have been defined as "direct" or "indirect." . . .

The effect of consumption of home-grown wheat on interstate commerce is due to the fact that it constitutes the most variable factor in the disappearance of the wheat crop. Consumption on the farm where grown appears to vary in an amount greater than 20 per cent of average production. The total amount of wheat consumed as food varies but relatively little, and use as seed is relatively constant.

The maintenance by government regulation of a price for wheat undoubtedly can be accomplished as effectively by sustaining or increasing the demand as by limiting the supply. The effect of the statute before us is to restrict the amount which may be produced for market and the extent as well to which one may forestall resort to the market by producing to meet his own needs. That appellee's own contribution to the demand for wheat may be trivial by itself is not enough to remove him from the scope of federal regulation where, as here, his contribution, taken together with that of many others similarly situated, is far from trivial.

It is well established by decisions of this Court that the power to regulate commerce includes the power to regulate the prices at which commodities in that commerce are dealt in and practices affecting such prices. One of the primary purposes of the Act in question was to increase the market price of wheat, and to that end to limit the volume thereof that could affect the market. It can hardly be denied that a factor of such volume and variability as home-consumed wheat would have a substantial influence on price and market conditions. This may arise because being in marketable condition such wheat overhangs the market and, if induced by rising prices, tends to flow into the market and check price increases. But if we assume that it is never marketed, it supplies a need of the man who grew it which would otherwise be reflected by purchases in the open market. Homegrown wheat in this sense competes with wheat in commerce. The stimulation of commerce is a use of the regulatory function quite as definitely as prohibitions or restrictions thereon. This record leaves us in no doubt that Congress may properly have considered that wheat consumed on the farm where grown, if wholly outside the scheme of regulation, would have a substantial effect in defeating and obstructing its purpose to stimulate trade therein at increased prices. . . .

Reversed.

THE ERA OF EXPANSIVE COMMERCE CLAUSE JURISPRUDENCE

With the *Darby* and *Wickard* decisions, the Court entered a new era of commerce clause interpretation. The justices no longer considered relevant issues such as direct versus indirect effects, manufacturing/ production versus distribution, or stream of commerce concerns. They made clear, as Stone wrote in *Darby,* that "[t]he power of Congress over interstate commerce is not confined to the regulation of commerce among the states. It extends to those activities intrastate which so affect interstate commerce or the exercise of the power of Congress over it as to make regulation of them appropriate means to the attainment of a legitimate end, the exercise of the granted power of Congress to regulate interstate commerce."

Why would the Court allow Congress to regulate activities that were purely local in nature when the commerce clause speaks only of activities "among the several States"? Stone's invocation of the language of *McCulloch* provides the answer. For Congress to regulate the interstate activities, it may be "necessary and proper" for it to regulate the local activities. This, according to Stone, was the case in *Darby,* and according to Jackson it held in *Wickard,* too. If every farmer acted as Filburn did, it would affect demand for wheat, which, in turn, would have a substantial effect in "defeating and obstructing" the congressional regulatory scheme of stabilizing prices. As Jackson put it, that Filburn's "own contribution to the demand for wheat may be trivial by itself is not enough to remove him from the scope of federal regulation where, as here, his contribution, taken together with that of many other similarly situated, is far from trivial." Under this approach very little commercial activity could be defined as purely intrastate. For, as *Darby, Wickard,*

and the commerce clause cases to come in the 1960s and 1970s suggest, as long as the local activities are part of a class of activities that *Congress decides* in the aggregate have a substantial effect on interstate commerce, Congress may regulate. Finally, as our emphasis on "Congress decides" suggests, no longer would the Court decide whether the local activities, taken in the aggregate, substantially affect interstate commerce in fact, but only whether Congress reasonably thinks it does (or whether it has a "rational basis" for so concluding, as more-modern Courts have termed it). This approach sat comfortably with the Court's new approach to economic legislation, whether passed by Congress or by the states *(see chapter 10).*

Note too *Darby*'s return to the Court's approach in *Gibbons,* that the power of Congress over interstate commerce "is complete in itself, may be exercised to its utmost extent, and acknowledges no limitations other than are prescribed in the constitution." To the *Darby* Court, Congress was free to use its commerce power as a federal police power, excluding from "commerce articles whose use in the states for which they are destined it may conceive to be injurious to the public health, morals or welfare." A law falling into this category, as Stone wrote, is "not a forbidden invasion of state power merely because either its motive or its consequence is to restrict the use of articles of commerce within the states of destination, and is not prohibited unless by other Constitutional provisions." But, to Stone, other "constitutional provisions" do not include the Tenth Amendment. In contrast to the Court's approach in *Hammer,* the Tenth Amendment is not an enclave to which the litigants can turn when Congress is making constitutional use of its commerce power; it is but a "truism."

Taken together, these cases gave Congress substantial authority to regulate under the commerce clause without fear of the Court invalidating its legislation. Congress took great advantage of this new deference by enacting a vast number of laws that earlier Courts might have considered outside the definition of interstate commerce and thus federal purview.

Many of these were in the economic realm, but with the expansive definition of interstate commerce that occurred after 1937 came a commensurate expansion of the federal police powers. These changes gave Congress sufficient power to combat social problems that it otherwise would have been unable to fight effectively.

Modern civil rights laws provide a good example. The constitutional protections against discrimination are found primarily in the equal protection clause of the Fourteenth Amendment and the due process clause of the Fifth, which have erected powerful barriers against invidious discrimination. But their exclusive target is discrimination perpetuated by the government. The words of the Fourteenth Amendment are clear: "Nor shall any state . . . deny to any person within its jurisdiction the equal protection of the laws." Nothing in the Fifth or Fourteenth Amendments prohibits discrimination by private parties. These amendments were not intended to prohibit a private citizen from being discriminatory, but only to bar discriminatory government action. Although the Fourteenth Amendment includes a clause giving Congress the authority to enforce the provision with appropriate legislation, the Supreme Court has ruled that such enforcement legislation may not extend beyond the scope of the amendment itself. Consequently, the amendment does not empower Congress to regulate private discriminatory behavior.

When the civil rights activists of the 1950s and 1960s campaigned for the elimination of discriminatory conditions, high on their list was the eradication of discrimination by private parties who operated public accommodations. The movement targeted the owners of hotels, restaurants, movie theaters, recreation areas, and transportation systems. With the decision in *Brown v. Board of Education* (1954), governments could no longer maintain laws mandating segregation of such facilities, but private operators could still impose discrimination on their own. In the South, where segregation was the way of life, no one expected the states to pass civil rights statutes prohibiting private parties from discriminating. Therefore, civil rights advocates pressured Congress to act.

Congress responded by enacting the Civil Rights Act of 1964, the most comprehensive legislation of its type ever passed. The act, as amended, is still the nation's strongest statute aimed at eliminating discrimination. The primary authority for passing this groundbreaking legislation, however, was not a clause in the Bill of Rights or one of the Civil War amendments, but the commerce clause. Because the Court had treated commerce clause legislation favorably since 1937, members of Congress had confidence that the Civil Rights Act would withstand a legal challenge. Opponents of the legislation argued that Congress had

misused its power to regulate commerce by invoking it to justify a civil rights law. Obviously, they said, the framers, many of whom owned slaves, did not intend the power to regulate commerce among the states to be used to enact civil rights legislation.

Was Congress on solid ground in doing so? The primary test of the law's constitutionality was *Heart of Atlanta Motel, Inc. v. United States* (1964). As you read this case, note Justice Tom C. Clark's description of how racial discrimination has a negative impact on interstate commerce. Also note the Court's expansive view of interstate commerce and its conclusion that the commerce clause can be used to combat moral wrongs.

Heart of Atlanta Motel, Inc. v. United States

379 U.S. 241 (1964)
http://laws.findlaw.com/us/379/241.html
Oral arguments are available at https://www.oyez.org.
Vote: 9 (Black, Brennan, Clark, Douglas, Goldberg, Harlan, Stewart, Warren, White)
0

OPINION OF THE COURT: *Clark*
CONCURRING OPINIONS: *Black, Douglas, Goldberg*

FACTS:

Title II of the 1964 Civil Rights Act in its original form prohibited discrimination on the basis of race, color, religion, or national origin by certain public accommodations that operated in or affected interstate commerce. The accommodations specifically included were as follows:

1. Inns, hotels, motels, or other lodging facilities of five rooms or more. Because they served the traveling public, these facilities were considered part of interstate commerce by definition.

2. Restaurants and cafeterias, if they served interstate travelers or if a substantial portion of their food or other products had moved in interstate commerce.

3. Motion picture houses, if they presented films that had moved in interstate commerce.

4. Any facility physically located within any of the other covered accommodations, which included operations such as hotel shops and theater snack bars.

The Heart of Atlanta Motel was a 216-room facility in Atlanta, Georgia, owned by a group of investors led by Moreton Rolleston Jr. Located near the commercial center of the city, it had easy access to two interstate highways and two major state roads. The motel advertised for business in national publications and maintained more than fifty billboards and highway signs around the state. Both the government and the motel agreed that the facility met the act's definition of a public accommodation in interstate commerce.

The motel admitted that prior to the enactment of the civil rights law it practiced a policy of racial discrimination. Furthermore, it acknowledged that it intended to continue its policy of not serving African Americans. To secure its right to do so, the motel filed suit to have the 1964 Civil Rights Act declared unconstitutional.

ARGUMENTS:

For the appellant, Heart of Atlanta Motel, Inc.:

- The Court should not construe the Constitution in the way it thinks the framers of the Constitution, if living, would today. The Court should construe the Constitution in accord with the intentions of the framers at the time it was drawn and with the intentions of those who adopted it at the time.
- The framers' intentions were clear: to limit the powers of the federal government to those delegated in the Constitution with all others reserved to the states. If the Court allows this broad use of commerce power, there is no limit on Congress. It can regulate every person and every business as it sees fit.
- Congress has not even established any standards to determine if a motel is in or materially affects interstate commerce. It might just as well have confiscated all motels and nationalized them on the ground that they are in interstate commerce.

For the appellees, United States et al.:

- Based on the Court's decision in *NLRB,* Congress has the power to regulate local activities that might have a substantial and harmful effect on interstate commerce. Based on *Wickard,* the effect on commerce need not be determined solely by the effect on the parties to the litigation. Congress (and the Court) may consider whether the party's contribution, aggregated with others similarly situated, will have an adverse effect on commerce.
- As *Champion* makes clear, Congress, in exercising its power to foster interstate commerce, may touch on subjects of social or moral wrong, in addition to their adverse economic effects.

- Congress's fact-finding shows that, under these precedents, Title II is a valid exercise of Congress's power to regulate interstate commerce. Discrimination in public accommodations imposes a burden on movement in interstate commerce, and discrimination in hotels and motels serving transient guests imposes burdens on interstate travel.
- Race discrimination is not only a social and moral issue but also a national and economic issue. Testimony shows that because African Americans may be forced to find lodging in places far removed from their route of travel due to discrimination by hotels, the number of persons engaging in interstate travel is diminished.

MR. JUSTICE CLARK DELIVERED THE OPINION OF THE COURT.

The Basis of Congressional Action.

While the Act as adopted carried no congressional findings the record of its passage through each house is replete with evidence of the burdens that discrimination by race or color places upon interstate commerce. This testimony included the fact that our people have become increasingly mobile with millions of people of all races traveling from State to State; that Negroes in particular have been the subject of discrimination in transient accommodations, having to travel great distances to secure the same; that often they have been unable to obtain accommodations and have had to call upon friends to put them up overnight; and that these conditions had become so acute as to require the listing of available lodging for Negroes in a special guidebook which was itself "dramatic testimony to the difficulties" Negroes encounter in travel. These exclusionary practices were found to be nationwide, the Under Secretary of Commerce testifying that there is "no question that this discrimination in the North still exists to a large degree" and in the West and Midwest as well. This testimony indicated a qualitative as well as a quantitative effect on interstate travel by Negroes. The former was the obvious impairment of the Negro traveler's pleasure and convenience that resulted when he continually was uncertain of finding lodging. As for the latter, there was evidence that this uncertainty stemming from racial discrimination had the effect of discouraging travel on the part of a substantial portion of the Negro community. This was the conclusion not only of the Under Secretary of Commerce but also of the Administrator of the Federal Aviation Agency who wrote the Chairman of the Senate Commerce

Committee that it was his "belief that air commerce is adversely affected by the denial to a substantial segment of the traveling public of adequate and desegregated public accommodations." We shall not burden this opinion with further details since the voluminous testimony presents overwhelming evidence that discrimination by hotels and motels impedes interstate travel.

The Power of Congress over Interstate Travel.

The power of Congress to deal with these obstructions depends on the meaning of the Commerce Clause. Its meaning was first enunciated 140 years ago by the great Chief Justice John Marshall in *Gibbons v. Ogden* (1824), in these words:

"The subject to be regulated is commerce; and . . . to ascertain the extent of the power, it becomes necessary to settle the meaning of the word. The counsel for the appellee would limit it to traffic, to buying and selling, or the interchange of commodities . . . but it is something more: it is intercourse . . . between nations, and parts of nations, in all its branches, and is regulated by prescribing rules for carrying on that intercourse.

"To what commerce does this power extend? The constitution informs us, to commerce 'with foreign nations and among the several States, and with the Indian tribes.'

"It has, we believe, been universally admitted, that these words comprehend every species of commercial intercourse. . . . No sort of trade can be carried on . . . to which this power does not extend.

"The subject to which the power is next applied, is to commerce 'among the several States.' The word 'among' means intermingled." . . .

In short, the determinative test of the exercise of power by the Congress under the Commerce Clause is simply whether the activity sought to be regulated is "commerce which concerns more States than one" and has a real and substantial relation to the national interest. Let us now turn to this facet of the problem.

That the "intercourse" of which the Chief Justice spoke included the movement of persons through more States than one was settled as early as 1849, in the *Passenger Cases*, where Mr. Justice McLean stated: "That the transportation of passengers is a part of commerce is not now an open question." Again in 1913 Mr. Justice McKenna, speaking for the Court, said: "Commerce among the States, we have said, consists of intercourse and traffic between their citizens, and includes the transportation of persons and property. . . . Nor does it make any difference whether the transportation is commercial in character." . . .

The same interest in protecting interstate commerce which led Congress to deal with segregation in interstate carriers and the white-slave traffic has prompted it to extend the exercise of its power to gambling; to criminal enterprises; to deceptive practices in the sale of products; to fraudulent security transactions; to misbranding of drugs; to wages and hours; to members of labor unions; to crop control; to discrimination against shippers; to the protection of small business from injurious price cutting; to resale price maintenance; to professional football; and to racial discrimination by owners and managers of terminal restaurants.

That Congress was legislating against moral wrongs in many of these areas rendered its enactments no less valid. In framing Title II of this Act Congress was also dealing with what it considered a moral problem. But that fact does not detract from the overwhelming evidence of the disruptive effect that racial discrimination has had on commercial intercourse. It was this burden which empowered Congress to enact appropriate legislation, and, given this basis for the exercise of its power, Congress was not restricted by the fact that the particular obstruction to interstate commerce with which it was dealing was also deemed a moral and social wrong.

It is said that the operation of the motel here is of a purely local character. But . . . the power of Congress to promote interstate commerce also includes the power to regulate the local incidents thereof, including local activities in both the States of origin and destination, which might have a substantial and harmful effect upon that commerce. One need only examine the evidence which we have discussed above to see that Congress may—as it has—prohibit racial discrimination by motels serving travelers, however "local" their operations may appear. . . .

We, therefore, conclude that the action of the Congress in the adoption of the Act as applied here to a motel which concededly serves interstate travelers is within the power granted it by the Commerce Clause of the Constitution, as interpreted by this Court for 140 years. It may be argued that Congress could have pursued other methods to eliminate the obstructions it found in interstate commerce caused by racial discrimination. But this is a matter of policy that rests entirely with the Congress not with the courts. How obstructions in commerce may be removed—what means are to be employed—is within the sound and exclusive discretion of the Congress. It is subject only to one caveat—that the means chosen by it must be reasonably adapted to the end permitted by the Constitution. We cannot say that its choice here was not so adapted. The Constitution requires no more.

Affirmed.

Employing the same sweeping language as the Court used in *Wickard* and especially *Darby,* Justice Clark's opinion gave Congress broad powers to use the commerce clause as authority to regulate moral wrongs that occur in interstate commerce. The Heart of Atlanta Motel complied with the Court's decision *(see box 7-7),* and a new era of civil rights in public accommodations began. The Court's interpretation of the commerce clause turned that provision into one of the most powerful weapons in the federal government's regulatory arsenal.

Although this broad interpretation of Congress's regulatory powers under the commerce clause had become generally accepted, it is important to note that

---

BOX 7-7   AFTERMATH . . . HEART OF ATLANTA MOTEL

THE HEART OF ATLANTA MOTEL, built in 1956, was owned by a group of Atlanta investors. One of the co-owners was Moreton Rolleston Jr., a former lieutenant commander in the U.S. Navy and a longtime Atlanta lawyer. Rolleston was a strong supporter of racial segregation. It was no coincidence, therefore, that the Heart of Atlanta Motel refused to serve black customers and that the motel did not cooperate with a consortium of fourteen downtown hotels whose owners agreed in 1963 to accommodate conventions that included blacks.

Moreton Rolleston Jr.

Leviton-Atlanta: Jay

When it appeared certain that Congress would pass the 1964 Civil Rights Act, Rolleston, who also served as the motel's attorney, prepared a lawsuit to challenge its constitutionality. He filed the suit just two hours after President Lyndon Johnson signed the bill into law.

In August 1964, after losing in the district court, the owners complied with the court's ruling and began operating the motel on an integrated basis. At the same time, they pressed an appeal to the U.S. Supreme Court. Rolleston, arguing before the justices, claimed that the Civil Rights Act was an unconstitutional intrusion by the federal government into an area reserved to the states and a violation of the rights of business owners. When the Supreme Court unanimously upheld the law on December 14, 1964, Rolleston lamented, "The decision opens the frightful door to unlimited power of a centralized government in Washington, in which the individual citizen and his personal liberty are of no importance."

Several years later Rolleston bought out his fellow investors and became the motel's sole owner. In 1973 the motel was sold and razed. A large, modern hotel now occupies the land where the Heart of Atlanta Motel once stood.

Rolleston continued to practice law in Atlanta well into his eighties. In 2000 he was briefly a Republican candidate for the U.S. Senate. Seven years later, the Georgia Supreme Court disbarred the eighty-nine-year-old Rolleston for abusing the legal process by excessive litigation in a property dispute that was ongoing for more than two decades. The legal battle included Rolleston's attempts to stop film producer and actor Tyler Perry from building a 30,000-square-foot mansion on a seventeen-acre riverfront parcel of land that Rolleston claimed to own, a claim that the courts repeatedly rejected. In addition, Rolleston lost a $5.4 million malpractice ruling in 1995, and he suffered a $4.1 million judgment in 1998. In defiance of the disbarment action, Rolleston pledged to continue practicing law.

Rolleston died on August 19, 2013, at the age of ninety-five.

SOURCES: Richard C. Cortner, *Civil Rights and Public Accommodations: The Heart of Atlanta Motel and McClung Cases* (Lawrence: University Press of Kansas, 2001); *Atlanta Journal-Constitution,* May 14, 1991; May 16, 1991; December 25, 1991; March 23, 1995; February 8, 1996; March 5, 1998; August 8, 2000; October 10, 2007; October 24, 2007; burial records, Arlington Memorial Park, Sandy Springs, Georgia.

even in the 1960s and 1970s, individual justices occasionally expressed doubts about the expansiveness of the modern definitions of interstate commerce. An example is Hugo Black's reaction to the Court's decision in **Daniel v. Paul** (1969). At issue was the application of federal regulations to the Lake Nixon Club, a small recreational facility located in a rural area of Arkansas on county roads far from any interstate highway. To avoid having to comply with desegregation laws, owner Euell Paul operated it as a private club, charging a nominal membership fee of twenty-five cents for participation in activities such as swimming, dancing, picnicking, and boating. The club served a local clientele: there was no evidence that any interstate traveler had ever used it. The Court ruled that the club operated in interstate commerce for the following reasons: (1) it advertised for business in publications known to be read by some interstate travelers; (2) it leased fifteen paddleboats from an Oklahoma company; (3) it owned a jukebox and records that, while purchased from an Arkansas company, had been manufactured out of state; and (4) three out of the four items sold at the snack bar (e.g., bread and soft drinks) contained ingredients from out of state.

This reasoning was too much for Justice Black. Although he opposed the racial policies of the club, Black refused to accept the conclusion that this "sleepy hollow" was engaged in interstate commerce. The Court's decision, he argued, was "stretching the Commerce Clause so as to give the Federal Government complete control over every little remote country place of recreation in every nook and cranny of every precinct and county in every one of the 50 states. This goes too far for me." His dissent was ironic given that Black was the first of the ardent New Deal justices.

Justice Potter Stewart had a similar reaction in *Perez v. United States* (1971). This case involved the Consumer Credit Protection Act, which Congress passed under its commerce clause power to criminalize extortionate means to collect payments on loans. Congress based its use of the commerce clause on its conclusion that "loan sharks"—lenders who use threats of violence to ensure the repayment of loans—are in a class largely controlled by organized crime, which exerts an adverse effect on interstate commerce. Alcides Perez was convicted under the act for attempting to extort money from the owner of a butcher shop. Perez challenged the law, claiming that Congress may not use its commerce power to regulate purely local loan-sharking.

The Supreme Court disagreed. Writing for a majority of eight, Justice William O. Douglas began by setting out his understanding of what the Court had said about the reach of the commerce clause:

The Commerce Clause reaches, in the main, three categories of problems. First, the use of channels of interstate or foreign commerce which Congress deems are being misused. Second, protection of the instrumentalities of interstate commerce. Third, those activities affecting commerce. It is with this last category that we are here concerned.

By "channels . . . being misused," Douglas meant, for example, using airline routes to ship stolen goods or interstate highways to transport people who have been kidnapped. (*Champion v. Ames* provides another example.) The "instrumentalities" of interstate commerce follow from, among other cases, the *Shreveport Rate Case* and include things (or even persons) that move in the channels of interstate commerce. Neither of these ideas is especially controversial.[19] Even in *E. C. Knight* the Court held that "transportation and its instrumentalities" are appropriate subjects of the commerce power.

The chief concerns in *Perez,* as in so many cases, are raised by Douglas's last category. How do we know whether an activity that seems local, such as the activity at issue here, affects commerce? For Douglas, the answer lay in the Court's post–New Deal decisions in *NLRB, Wickard,* and *Darby:* Congress had concluded that loan-sharking, although a purely local activity, had, by virtue of being part of a "class of activities," a substantial effect on interstate commerce, and that was enough to sustain the law.

Justice Stewart cast the lone dissent in the case. He agreed that Congress can use its commerce clause power to protect the instrumentalities and channels of commerce and to regulate intrastate activities that have a substantial effect on interstate commerce. But, echoing Black in **Daniel v. Paul,** he was concerned that under this law "a man can be convicted without any proof of interstate movement, of the use of the facilities of interstate commerce, or of facts showing that his conduct affected interstate commerce." He continued, "The Framers of the Constitution never intended that

---

19. As Justice Scalia wrote in *Gonzales v. Raich* (2005), "The first two categories are self-evident, since they are the ingredients of interstate commerce itself. See *Gibbons v. Ogden* (1824)."

the National Government might define as a crime and prosecute such wholly local activity through the enactment of federal criminal laws." This power, in Stewart's view, belonged to the states unless Congress could "rationally have concluded that loan-sharking is an activity with interstate attributes that distinguish it in some substantial respect from other local crime." In short, it was not enough for Stewart to say simply that loan-sharking has some interstate characteristics because "all crime is a national problem" and Congress cannot regulate "all crime."

Still, in spite of these occasional complaints that the Court had erased the distinction between inter- and intrastate commerce, the justices remained wedded to a broad interpretation of the congressional commerce power. The post–New Deal approach reflects Justice Cardozo's dissent in **Carter v. Carter Coal Company,** in which he said the commerce power is "as broad as the need that evokes it."

LIMITS ON THE COMMERCE POWER: THE REPUBLICAN COURT ERA

As the nation entered the 1990s, commerce clause jurisprudence seemed to be a settled matter. Since the 1937 decision in *NLRB v. Jones & Laughlin Steel Corporation,* the Court had persevered in its commitment to cooperative federalism and loyalty to an expansive view of

the federal government's commerce powers. As late as 1985, the Court in *San Antonio Metropolitan Transit Authority (SAMTA) v. Garcia* had made a major statement supportive of continuing in this vein.

Under the surface, however, the prospects for change were mounting. The Court's vote in *Garcia* was 5–4 and, therefore, vulnerable to the impact of personnel changes. The four justices who dissented in *Garcia* were all Republican appointees, and the nation had turned decidedly in the direction of the Republicans by electing presidents of that party in three successive elections (1980, 1984, and 1988). Republican President Ronald Reagan had the opportunity to appoint four new justices to the Court and George H. W. Bush added two more. The most consequential of those appointments was Bush's 1991 selection of conservative justice Clarence Thomas to replace the retiring Thurgood Marshall, a member of the *Garcia* majority. This appointment tipped the scales in favor of justices who were sympathetic to the interests of the states and less supportive of expansive federal regulation. Table 7-2 illustrates the effect of those personnel changes, beginning with the decision in *Garcia* and continuing over six subsequent major federalism/commerce decisions through 2012.

The first indication that the balance of power had shifted occurred in *New York v. United States* (1992), just one year after the appointment of Justice Thomas. You may recall from our reading of that case in chapter 6

TABLE 7-2   Support for Expansive Federal Commerce Power in Key Cases after *Garcia*

GARCIA V. SAMTA (1985)	*N.Y. V. U.S.* (1992)	*U.S. V. LOPEZ* (1995)	*PRINTZ V. U.S.* (1997)	*U.S. V. MORRISON* (2000)	*GONZALES V. RAICH* (2005)	*NATIONAL FEDERATION OF INDEPENDENT BUSINESS V. SEBELIUS* (2012)
Brennan (D)→	Souter (R)	Souter	Souter	Souter	Souter→	Sotomayor (D)
Blackmun (R)	Blackmun→	Breyer (D)	Breyer	Breyer	Breyer	Breyer
Stevens (R)	Stevens	Stevens	Stevens	Stevens	Stevens→	Kagan (D)
White (D)	White→	Ginsburg (D)	Ginsburg	Ginsburg	Ginsburg	Ginsburg
Marshall (D)→	Thomas (R)	Thomas	Thomas	Thomas	Thomas	Thomas
Burger (R)	Rehnquist	Rehnquist	Rehnquist	Rehnquist	Rehnquist→	Roberts (R)
O'Connor (R)	O'Connor	O'Connor	O'Connor	O'Connor	O'Connor→	Alito (R)
Powell (R)	Kennedy (R)	Kennedy	Kennedy	Kennedy	Kennedy	Kennedy
Rehnquist (R)	Scalia (R)	Scalia	Scalia	Scalia	Scalia	Scalia

NOTE: Justices whose names appear in bold generally support a more expansive view of the commerce power than do those whose names are in plain font. Justices whose names are underlined were in the majority. Votes in *Sebelius* are classified on the basis of the Commerce Clause portion of the decision. R = Republican appointee; D = Democratic appointee.

that the majority struck down a federal law that mandated that states adopt a particular radioactive waste policy. The justices held that the Constitution does not allow the federal government to command the states to pass legislation to implement federally preferred policies. The Court's decision in *New York* signaled that those sympathetic to preserving the traditional role of the states now formed a majority.

Even so, the Court's decision in *United States v. Lopez* (1995) came as somewhat of a surprise. For the first time since the battles over the New Deal, the justices invalidated a federal statute as falling outside the authority granted to Congress by the commerce clause.[20] In addition to explaining the rationale for this outcome, Chief Justice Rehnquist's majority opinion nicely reviews the evolution of the Court's commerce clause doctrine.

United States v. Lopez

514 U.S. 549 (1995)
http://laws.findlaw.com/us/514/549.html
Oral arguments are available at https://www.oyez.org.
Vote: 5 (Kennedy, O'Connor, Rehnquist, Scalia, Thomas)
    4 (Breyer, Ginsburg, Souter, Stevens)
OPINION OF THE COURT: Rehnquist
CONCURRING OPINIONS: Kennedy, Thomas
DISSENTING OPINIONS: Breyer, Souter, Stevens

FACTS:

On March 10, 1992, Alfonso Lopez Jr. came to Edison High School carrying a concealed .38 caliber handgun and five rounds of ammunition. Acting on an anonymous tip, officials at the San Antonio school confronted the twelfth-grade student, and he admitted having the weapon. Lopez claimed that he had been given the gun by an individual who instructed him to deliver it to a third person. The gun was to be used in gang-related activities. Lopez was arrested for violating the federal Gun-Free School Zones Act of 1990.

Lopez, who had no record of previous criminal activity, was convicted in federal district court and sentenced to six months in prison, two years of supervised release, and a $50 fine. His attorneys appealed to the Fifth Circuit Court of Appeals, claiming that

---

20. Keep in mind that in *National League of Cities* and *New York* the Court invalidated the federal laws not because they were beyond Congress's power to regulate interstate commerce but because they violated the Tenth Amendment.

Congress had no constitutional authority to pass the Gun-Free School Zones Act. Attorneys for the United States countered by arguing that the law was an appropriate exercise of congressional power to regulate interstate commerce. The appeals court held in favor of Lopez, and the government asked the Supreme Court to review that ruling.

Congress passed the Gun-Free School Zones Act—section 922(q) of chapter 18 of the United States Code—in 1990. In passing the act, Congress did not issue any findings showing a relationship between gun possession on school property and commerce. The federal government argued that such findings should not be required, that it would be sufficient if Congress could reasonably conclude that gun-related violence in schools affects interstate commerce directly or indirectly. Lopez argued that the simple possession of a weapon on school grounds is not a commercial activity that reasonably falls under commerce clause jurisdiction. Furthermore, the regulation of crime and education are traditional areas of state, not federal, jurisdiction.

ARGUMENTS:

For the petitioner, United States:

- Under the commerce clause and based on past decisions, Congress is empowered to regulate even intrastate, noneconomic activity that, in the aggregate, exerts a substantial impact on interstate commerce.
- All Congress must show is that it could rationally have concluded that gun possession on or near school premises affects interstate commerce.
- There is an abundant basis from which Congress could reasonably determine that the conduct regulated in the law affects interstate commerce. For example, the need for insurance spreads the economic consequences of violent crime throughout the nation. In addition, violent crime affects interstate commerce by reducing the willingness of people to travel to areas they think are unsafe.
- Congress also had grounds for concluding that the presence of guns in schools poses an unacceptable threat to the proper functioning of primary and secondary education. For the last decade or so, the importance of education to national productivity and economic competitiveness was the subject of extensive national concern and debate.

For the respondent, Alfonso Lopez Jr.:

- Under the Supreme Court's decision in *Perez v. United States* (1971), congressional jurisdiction under the commerce clause reaches, in the main, three categories: (1) the use of channels of interstate or foreign commerce: (2) protection of the instrumentalities of interstate commerce: and (3) those activities affecting interstate commerce. This case involves only the third *Perez* category.

- Congress must demonstrate a substantial link between the object of its regulation and interstate commerce. Here, Congress failed to provide any link between interstate commerce and possession of a firearm.

- Even if the Court finds that Congress need not have made formal or informal findings or even have concrete evidence of an effect on commerce when passing the Gun-Free School Zones Act, the act is still unconstitutional. In *Gibbons,* Chief Justice Marshall recognized that Congress's power under the commerce clause does not extend to "exclusively internal commerce of a State." The power to regulate commerce, however broad, is not unlimited. Because it regulates internal, noneconomic activity without a substantial connection to interstate commerce, the Gun-Free School Zones Act exceeds those limits.

CHIEF JUSTICE REHNQUIST DELIVERED THE OPINION OF THE COURT.

In the Gun-Free School Zones Act of 1990, Congress made it a federal offense "for any individual knowingly to possess a firearm at a place that the individual knows, or has reasonable cause to believe, is a school zone." The Act neither regulates a commercial activity nor contains a requirement that the possession be connected in any way to interstate commerce. We hold that the Act exceeds the authority of Congress "[t]o regulate Commerce . . . among the several States." . . .

We start with first principles. The Constitution creates a Federal Government of enumerated powers. As James Madison wrote, "[t]he powers delegated by the proposed Constitution to the federal government are few and defined. Those which are to remain in the State governments are numerous and indefinite." This constitutionally mandated division of authority "was adopted by the Framers to ensure protection of our fundamental liberties." *Gregory v. Ashcroft* (1991). . . .

. . . The Court, through Chief Justice Marshall, first defined the nature of Congress' commerce power in *Gibbons v. Ogden* (1824):

"Commerce, undoubtedly, is traffic, but it is something more: it is intercourse. It describes the commercial intercourse between nations, and parts of nations, in all its branches, and is regulated by prescribing rules for carrying on that intercourse."

The commerce power "is the power to regulate; that is, to prescribe the rule by which commerce is to be governed. This power, like all others vested in Congress, is complete in itself, may be exercised to its utmost extent, and acknowledges no limitations, other than are prescribed in the constitution." Id. . . .

For nearly a century thereafter, the Court's Commerce Clause decisions dealt but rarely with the extent of Congress' power, and almost entirely with the Commerce Clause as a limit on state legislation that discriminated against interstate commerce. . . . Under this line of precedent, the Court held that certain categories of activity such as "production," "manufacturing," and "mining" were within the province of state governments, and thus were beyond the power of Congress under the Commerce Clause. See *Wickard v. Filburn* (1942) (describing development of Commerce Clause jurisprudence).

In 1887, Congress enacted the Interstate Commerce Act, and in 1890, Congress enacted the Sherman Antitrust Act. These laws ushered in a new era of federal regulation under the commerce power. When cases involving these laws first reached this Court, we imported from our negative Commerce Clause cases the approach that Congress could not regulate activities such as "production," "manufacturing," and "mining." See, *e.g., United States v. E. C. Knight Co.* (1895); *Carter v. Carter Coal Co.* (1936). Simultaneously, however, the Court held that, where the interstate and intrastate aspects of commerce were so mingled together that full regulation of interstate commerce required incidental regulation of intrastate commerce, the Commerce Clause authorized such regulation. See, *e.g., Houston, E. & W. T. R. Co. v. United States* (1914) (Shreveport Rate Cases).

In *A. L. A. Schechter Poultry Corp. v. United States* (1935), the Court struck down regulations that fixed the hours and wages of individuals employed by an intrastate business because the activity being regulated related to interstate commerce only indirectly. In doing so, the Court characterized the distinction between direct and indirect effects of intrastate transactions upon interstate commerce as "a fundamental one, essential to the maintenance of our constitutional system." Activities that affected interstate commerce directly were within Congress' power; activities that affected interstate commerce indirectly were beyond Congress' reach. The justification for this formal distinction was rooted in the fear that otherwise "there would be virtually no limit to the federal power and for all practical purposes we should have a completely centralized government."

Two years later, in the watershed case of *NLRB v. Jones & Laughlin Steel Corp.* (1937), the Court upheld the National Labor Relations Act against a Commerce Clause challenge, and in the process, departed from the distinction between "direct" and "indirect" effects on interstate commerce. The Court held that intrastate activities that "have such a close and substantial relation to interstate commerce that their control is essential or appropriate to protect that commerce from burdens and obstructions" are within Congress' power to regulate.

In *United States v. Darby* (1941), the Court upheld the Fair Labor Standards Act, stating:

"The power of Congress over interstate commerce is not confined to the regulation of commerce among the states. It extends to those activities intrastate which so affect interstate commerce or the exercise of the power of Congress over it as to make regulation of them appropriate means to the attainment of a legitimate end, the exercise of the granted power of Congress to regulate interstate commerce."

In *Wickard v. Filburn*, the Court upheld the application of amendments to the Agricultural Adjustment Act of 1938 to the production and consumption of homegrown wheat. The *Wickard* Court explicitly rejected earlier distinctions between direct and indirect effects on interstate commerce, stating:

"[E]ven if appellee's activity be local and though it may not be regarded as commerce, it may still, whatever its nature, be reached by Congress if it exerts a substantial economic effect on interstate commerce, and this irrespective of whether such effect is what might at some earlier time have been defined as 'direct' or 'indirect.'"

The *Wickard* Court emphasized that although Filburn's own contribution to the demand for wheat may have been trivial by itself, that was not "enough to remove him from the scope of federal regulation where, as here, his contribution, taken together with that of many others similarly situated, is far from trivial."

Jones & Laughlin Steel, Darby, and *Wickard* ushered in an era of Commerce Clause jurisprudence that greatly expanded the previously defined authority of Congress under that Clause. In part, this was a recognition of the great changes that had occurred in the way business was carried on in this country. Enterprises that had once been local or at most regional in nature had become national in scope. But the doctrinal change also reflected a view that earlier Commerce Clause cases artificially had constrained the authority of Congress to regulate interstate commerce.

But even these modern-era precedents which have expanded congressional power under the Commerce Clause confirm that this power is subject to outer limits. In *Jones & Laughlin Steel*, the Court warned that the scope of the interstate commerce power "must be considered in the light of our dual system of government and may not be extended so as to embrace effects upon interstate commerce so indirect and remote that to embrace them, in view of our complex society, would effectually obliterate the distinction between what is national and what is local and create a completely centralized government." See also *Darby* (Congress may regulate intrastate activity that has a "substantial effect" on interstate commerce); *Wickard* (Congress may regulate activity that "exerts a substantial economic effect on interstate commerce"). Since that time, the Court has heeded that warning and undertaken to decide whether a rational basis existed for concluding that a regulated activity sufficiently affected interstate commerce. . . .

Consistent with this structure, we have identified three broad categories of activity that Congress may regulate under its commerce power. First, Congress may regulate the use of the channels of interstate commerce. Second, Congress is empowered to regulate and protect the instrumentalities of interstate commerce, or persons or things in interstate commerce, even though the threat may come only from intrastate activities. Finally, Congress' commerce authority includes the power to regulate those activities having a substantial relation to interstate commerce.

Within this final category, admittedly, our case law has not been clear whether an activity must "affect" or "substantially affect" interstate commerce in order to be within Congress' power to regulate it under the Commerce Clause. We conclude, consistent with the great weight of our case law, that the proper test requires an analysis of whether the regulated activity "substantially affects" interstate commerce.

We now turn to consider the power of Congress, in the light of this framework, to enact 922(q). The first two categories of authority may be quickly disposed of: 922(q) is not a regulation of the use of the channels of interstate commerce, nor is it an attempt to prohibit the interstate transportation of a commodity through the channels of commerce; nor can 922(q) be justified as a regulation by which Congress has sought to protect an instrumentality of interstate commerce or a thing in interstate commerce. Thus, if 922(q) is to be sustained, it must be under the third category as a regulation of an activity that substantially affects interstate commerce.

First, we have upheld a wide variety of congressional Acts regulating intrastate economic activity where we have concluded that the activity substantially affected interstate commerce. Examples include the regulation of intrastate coal mining, intrastate extortionate credit transactions, restaurants utilizing substantial interstate supplies, inns and hotels catering to interstate guests, and production and consumption of home-grown wheat. These examples are by no means exhaustive, but the pattern is clear. Where economic activity substantially affects interstate commerce, legislation regulating that activity will be sustained. . . .

Section 922(q) is a criminal statute that by its terms has nothing to do with "commerce" or any sort of economic enterprise, however broadly one might define those terms. Section 922(q) is not an essential part of a larger regulation of economic activity, in which the regulatory scheme could be undercut unless the intrastate activity were regulated. It cannot, therefore, be sustained under our cases upholding regulations of activities that arise out of or are connected with a commercial transaction, which viewed in the aggregate, substantially affects interstate commerce.

Second, 922(q) contains no jurisdictional element which would ensure, through case-by-case inquiry, that the firearm possession in question affects interstate commerce. For example, in *United States v. Bass* (1971), the Court interpreted former 18 U.S.C. 1202(a), which made it a crime for a felon to "receiv[e], posses[s], or transpor[t] in commerce or affecting commerce . . . any firearm." The Court interpreted the possession component of 1202(a) to require an additional nexus to interstate commerce both because the statute was ambiguous and because "unless Congress conveys its purpose clearly, it will not be deemed to have significantly changed the federal-state balance." . . . Unlike the statute in *Bass*, 922(q) has no express jurisdictional element which might limit its reach to a discrete set of firearm possessions that additionally have an explicit connection with or effect on interstate commerce.

Although as part of our independent evaluation of constitutionality under the Commerce Clause we of course consider legislative findings, and indeed even congressional committee findings, regarding effect on interstate commerce, the Government concedes that "[n]either the statute nor its legislative history contain[s] express congressional findings regarding the effects upon interstate commerce of gun possession in a school zone." We agree with the Government that Congress normally is not required to make formal findings as to the substantial burdens that an activity has on interstate commerce. But to the extent that congressional findings would enable us to evaluate the legislative judgment that the activity in question substantially affected interstate commerce, even though no such substantial effect was visible to the naked eye, they are lacking here. . . .

The Government's essential contention, *in fine*, is that we may determine here that 922(q) is valid because possession of a firearm in a local school zone does indeed substantially affect interstate commerce. The Government argues that possession of a firearm in a school zone may result in violent crime and that violent crime can be expected to affect the functioning of the national economy in two ways. First, the costs of violent crime are substantial, and, through the mechanism of insurance, those costs are spread throughout the population. Second, violent crime reduces the willingness of individuals to travel to areas within the country that are perceived to be unsafe. The Government also argues that the presence of guns in schools poses a substantial threat to the educational process by threatening the learning environment. A handicapped educational process, in turn, will result in a less productive citizenry. That, in turn, would have an adverse effect on the Nation's economic well-being. As a result, the Government argues that Congress could rationally have concluded that 922(q) substantially affects interstate commerce.

We pause to consider the implications of the Government's arguments. The Government admits, under its "costs of crime" reasoning, that Congress could regulate not only all violent crime, but all activities that might lead to violent crime, regardless of how tenuously they relate to interstate commerce. Similarly, under the Government's "national productivity" reasoning, Congress could regulate any activity that it found was related to the economic productivity of individual citizens: family law (including marriage, divorce, and child custody), for example. Under the theories that the Government presents in support of 922(q), it is difficult to perceive any limitation on federal power, even in areas such as criminal law enforcement or education where States historically have been sovereign. Thus, if we were to accept the Government's arguments, we are hard-pressed to posit any activity by an individual that Congress is without power to regulate. . . .

Admittedly, a determination whether an intrastate activity is commercial or noncommercial may in some cases result in legal uncertainty. But, so long as Congress' authority is limited to those powers enumerated in the Constitution, and so long as those enumerated powers are interpreted as having judicially enforceable outer limits, congressional legislation under the Commerce Clause always will engender "legal uncertainty." . . .

These are not precise formulations, and in the nature of things they cannot be. But we think they point the way to a correct decision of this case. The possession of a gun in a local school zone is in no sense an economic activity that might, through repetition elsewhere, substantially affect any sort of interstate commerce. Respondent was a local student at a local school; there is no indication that he had recently moved in interstate commerce, and there is no requirement that his possession of the firearm have any concrete tie to interstate commerce.

To uphold the Government's contentions here, we would have to pile inference upon inference in a manner that would bid fair to convert congressional authority under the Commerce Clause to a general police power of the sort retained by the States. Admittedly, some of our prior cases have taken long steps down that road, giving great deference to congressional action. The broad language in these opinions has suggested the possibility of additional expansion, but we decline here to proceed any further. To do so would require us to conclude that the Constitution's enumeration of powers does not presuppose something not enumerated, and that there never will be a distinction between what is truly national and what is truly local. This we are unwilling to do. For the foregoing reasons the judgment of the Court of Appeals is

Affirmed.

JUSTICE BREYER, with whom JUSTICE STEVENS, JUSTICE SOUTER, and JUSTICE GINSBURG join, dissenting.

The issue in this case is whether the Commerce Clause authorizes Congress to enact a statute that makes it a crime to possess a gun in, or near, a school. In my view, the statute falls well within the scope of the commerce power as this Court has understood that power over the last half-century.

In reaching this conclusion, I apply three basic principles of Commerce Clause interpretation. First, the power to "regulate Commerce . . . among the several States" encompasses the power to regulate local activities insofar as they significantly affect interstate commerce. . . . I use the word "significant" because the word "substantial" implies a somewhat narrower power than recent precedent suggests. But, to speak of "substantial effect" rather than "significant effect" would make no difference in this case.

Second, in determining whether a local activity will likely have a significant effect upon interstate commerce, a court must consider, not the effect of an individual act (a single instance of gun possession), but rather the cumulative effect of all similar instances (i.e., the effect of all guns possessed in or near schools).

Third, the Constitution requires us to judge the connection between a regulated activity and interstate commerce, not directly, but at one remove. Courts must give Congress a degree of leeway in determining the existence of a significant factual connection between the regulated activity and interstate commerce—both because the Constitution delegates the commerce power directly to Congress and because the determination requires an empirical judgment of a kind that a legislature is more likely than a court to make with accuracy. The traditional words "rational basis" capture this leeway. Thus, the specific question before us, as the Court recognizes, is not whether the "regulated activity sufficiently affected interstate commerce," but, rather, whether Congress could have had "a rational basis" for so concluding.

I recognize that we must judge this matter independently. "[S]imply because Congress may conclude that a particular activity substantially affects interstate commerce does not necessarily make it so." And, I also recognize that Congress did not write specific "interstate commerce" findings into the law under which Lopez was convicted. Nonetheless, as I have already noted, the matter that we review independently (*i.e.*, whether there is a "rational basis") already has considerable leeway built into it. And, the absence of findings, at most, deprives a statute of the benefit of some extra leeway. This extra deference, in principle, might change the result in a close case, though, in practice, it has not made a critical legal difference. . . .

Applying these principles to the case at hand, we must ask whether Congress could have had a rational basis for finding a significant (or substantial) connection between gun-related school violence and interstate commerce . . . . As long as one views the commerce connection, not as a "technical legal conception," but as "a practical one," *Swift & Co. v. United States* (1905), the answer to this question must be yes. . . .

For one thing, reports, hearings, and other readily available literature make clear that the problem of guns in and around schools is widespread and extremely serious. . . . Congress obviously could have thought that guns and learning are mutually exclusive. And, Congress could therefore have found a substantial educational problem—teachers unable to teach, students unable to learn—and concluded that guns near schools contribute substantially to the size and scope of that problem.

Having found that guns in schools significantly undermine the quality of education in our Nation's classrooms, Congress could also have found, given the effect of education upon interstate and foreign commerce, that gun-related violence in and around schools is a commercial, as well as a human, problem. Education, although far more than a matter of economics, has long been inextricably intertwined with the Nation's economy. . . .

In recent years the link between secondary education and business has strengthened, becoming both more direct and more important. Scholars on the subject report that technological changes and innovations in management techniques have altered the nature of the workplace so that more jobs now demand greater educational skills. . . .

Increasing global competition also has made primary and secondary education economically more important. . . . Indeed, Congress has said, when writing other statutes, that "functionally or technologically illiterate" Americans in the work force "erod[e]" our economic "standing in the international marketplace," and that "our Nation is . . . paying the price of scientific and technological illiteracy, with our productivity declining, our industrial base ailing, and our global competitiveness dwindling."

Finally, there is evidence that, today more than ever, many firms base their location decisions upon the presence, or absence, of a work force with a basic education. . . .

The economic links I have just sketched seem fairly obvious. Why then is it not equally obvious, in light of those links, that a widespread, serious, and substantial physical threat to teaching and learning also substantially threatens the commerce to which that teaching and learning is inextricably tied? That is to say, guns in the hands of six percent of inner-city high school students and gun-related violence throughout a city's schools must threaten the trade and commerce that those schools support. The only question, then, is whether the latter threat is (to use the majority's terminology) "substantial." And, the evidence of (1) the extent of the gun-related violence problem, (2) the extent of the resulting negative effect on classroom learning, and (3) the extent of the consequent negative commercial effects, when taken together, indicate a threat to trade and commerce that is "substantial." At the very least, Congress could rationally have concluded that the links are "substantial."

Specifically, Congress could have found that gun-related violence near the classroom poses a serious economic threat (1) to consequently inadequately educated workers who must endure low paying jobs, and (2) to communities and businesses that might (in today's "information society") otherwise gain, from a well-educated work force, an important commercial advantage, of a kind that location near a railhead or harbor provided in the past. . . . The violence related facts, the educational facts, and the economic facts, taken together, make this conclusion rational. And, because under our case law, the sufficiency of the constitutionally necessary Commerce Clause link between a crime of violence and interstate commerce turns simply upon size or degree, those same facts make the statute constitutional.

The majority's holding—that 922 falls outside the scope of the Commerce Clause—creates three serious legal problems. First, the majority's holding runs contrary to modern Supreme Court cases that have upheld congressional actions despite connections to interstate or foreign commerce that are less significant than the effect of school violence. . . .

The second legal problem the Court creates comes from its apparent belief that it can reconcile its holding with earlier cases by making a critical distinction between "commercial" and noncommercial "transaction[s]." That is to say, the Court believes the Constitution would distinguish between two local activities, each of which has an identical effect upon interstate commerce, if one, but not the other, is "commercial" in nature. . . .

The third legal problem created by the Court's holding is that it threatens legal uncertainty in an area of law that, until this case, seemed reasonably well settled. . . .

In sum, to find this legislation within the scope of the Commerce Clause would permit "Congress . . . to act in terms of economic . . . realities." . . . Upholding this legislation would do no more than simply recognize that Congress had a "rational basis" for finding a significant connection between guns in or near schools and (through their effect on education) the interstate and foreign commerce they threaten. For these reasons, I would reverse the judgment of the Court of Appeals. Respectfully, I dissent.

Just how far-reaching was *United States v. Lopez*? How did it fit into the Court's evolving commerce clause jurisprudence? Some interpreted it quite narrowly, simply as a warning to Congress that it must justify its legislation by showing the relationship between the activities regulated and interstate commerce. Had Congress explicitly demonstrated that it was responding to the negative impact school violence has on the economy, they asserted, it is likely that the Court would have found no fault with the law. These commentators saw the decision as little more than a detour and not a full-scale retreat from the body of commerce clause jurisprudence that flows almost seamlessly from *NLRB v. Jones & Laughlin Steel Corporation* onward (the Tenth Amendment cases of *National League of Cities* and *New York v. United States* being the chief exceptions).

Others viewed the decision as more sweeping, and as a signal that the Court would no longer allow Congress to regulate whatever it wished on the ground that all activities somehow affect interstate commerce. These critics concluded that *Lopez* was not an isolated ruling; rather, it should be considered in conjunction with *New York v. United States* (1992) and *Printz v. United States* (1997) *(both excerpted in chapter 6)*— other decisions in which a majority of the Court ruled against federal action that was seen as encroaching on the states.

The justices themselves seemed divided on what the case represented. In their concurring opinions, Justice Anthony Kennedy called *Lopez* a "limited holding," but Justice Clarence Thomas declared that it was time "to modify our Commerce Clause jurisprudence." The Court's 5–4 vote contributed additional uncertainty. Whether *Lopez* was an aberration or a signal that the Court was following Thomas's advice became clearer five years later, when the Court issued its decision in *United States v. Morrison*.

United States v. Morrison

529 U.S. 598 (2000)
http://laws.findlaw.com/us/529/598.html
Oral arguments are available at https://www.oyez.org.
Vote: 5 (Kennedy, O'Connor, Rehnquist, Scalia, Thomas)
  4 (Breyer, Ginsburg, Souter, Stevens)
OPINION OF THE COURT: *Rehnquist*
CONCURRING OPINION: *Thomas*
DISSENTING OPINIONS: *Breyer, Souter*

FACTS:

Not long after Christy Brzonkala enrolled at Virginia Polytechnic Institute (Virginia Tech) in the fall of 1994, she met Antonio Morrison and James Crawford,

members of the university's varsity football team. Brzonkala alleged that within thirty minutes of meeting Morrison and Crawford, she was assaulted and repeatedly raped by the two young men. She claimed that the attack caused her to become severely emotionally disturbed and depressed. In early 1995 she filed a complaint under Virginia Tech's sexual assault policy. At the subsequent hearing Morrison admitted having sexual contact with Brzonkala and claimed that even though she had twice told him no, the sexual activity was ultimately consensual.

The Judicial Committee found insufficient evidence against Crawford, but it found Morrison guilty of sexual assault and sentenced him to an immediate suspension from the university for two semesters. Morrison appealed this decision, and, because of procedural technicalities, the university retried Morrison under its abusive conduct policy. This time Morrison was found guilty of "using abusive language" and sentenced once more to a two-semester suspension. Morrison again appealed. The university provost set aside Morrison's punishment. She concluded that it was "excessive" when compared with other convictions under the abusive conduct policy. Morrison's final punishment was probation and minimal counseling.

Brzonkala then filed suit in federal district court against Morrison, Crawford, and Virginia Tech under 42 U.S.C. 13981, the Violence Against Women Act of 1994, which provided a federal civil remedy for the victims of gender-motivated violence. The district court held that Congress lacked the authority to pass this particular provision under either the commerce clause or the Fourteenth Amendment. A divided court of appeals affirmed that conclusion. The United States intervened in the suit to defend the validity of the statute. Because the court of appeals had invalidated a federal statute on constitutional grounds, the Supreme Court granted certiorari.

The justices concluded that Congress did not have the power to enact the challenged statute under the Fourteenth Amendment. In the portion of the decision excerpted here, the Court addresses Congress's authority to enact this legislation under the commerce clause.

ARGUMENTS:

For the petitioner, United States:

• The law is an appropriate exercise of Congress's power under the commerce clause. After four years of investigation, Congress found that gender-motivated violence burdens the national economy and inter-state commerce by making women fear for their safety in the workplace and by imposing increased medical and other costs on victims, their employers and insurers, and state and local governments. All of those burdens were documented in the extensive legislative record.

- Congress's commerce power is not confined to the regulation of those intrastate activities that are "commercial" or "economic" in nature. It is not the character of the activity but the substantiality of its impact on interstate commerce that determines whether the activity may be regulated under the commerce clause, as was suggested in *Lopez*. Even so, the act is connected to economic activity because the gender-motivated violence remedied occurs at, or en route to, workplaces, retail establishments, and interstate transportation terminals as well as in other settings.

For the respondent, Antonio J. Morrison:

- Congress cannot regulate felonious conduct under its commerce power because the activity being regulated is wholly noneconomic in nature. In *Lopez* the Court emphasized the noneconomic nature of the activity being regulated.

- Petitioner's arguments would give Congress the power to pass virtually any legislation at all because all human activity has economic consequences of one kind or another. That was the federalism concern at the core of *Lopez*. Ultimately, the government's argument amounts to the proposition that Congress should be able to regulate any problem it deems sufficiently important. Morrison has a right to be free from an overreaching Congress, just as he has the right to be free from a Congress that would pass a law abridging freedom of speech.

CHIEF JUSTICE REHNQUIST DELIVERED THE OPINION OF THE COURT.

Due respect for the decisions of a coordinate branch of Government demands that we invalidate a congressional enactment only upon a plain showing that Congress has exceeded its constitutional bounds. With this presumption of constitutionality in mind, we turn to the question whether §13981 falls within Congress' power under Article I, §8, of the Constitution. Brzonkala and the United States rely upon the third clause of the Article, which gives Congress power "[t]o regulate Commerce with foreign Nations, and among the several States, and with the Indian Tribes."

As we discussed at length in [*United States v.*] *Lopez* [1995], our interpretation of the Commerce Clause has changed as our Nation has developed. We need not repeat that detailed review of the Commerce Clause's history here; it suffices to say that, in the years since *NLRB v. Jones & Laughlin Steel Corp.* (1937), Congress has had considerably greater latitude in regulating conduct and transactions under the Commerce Clause than our previous case law permitted.

Lopez emphasized, however, that even under our modern, expansive interpretation of the Commerce Clause, Congress' regulatory authority is not without effective bounds.

"[E]ven [our] modern-era precedents which have expanded congressional power under the Commerce Clause confirm that this power is subject to outer limits. In Jones & Laughlin Steel, the Court warned that the scope of the interstate commerce power 'must be considered in the light of our dual system of government and may not be extended so as to embrace effects upon interstate commerce so indirect and remote that to embrace them, in view of our complex society, would effectually obliterate the distinction between what is national and what is local and create a completely centralized government.'"

As we observed in *Lopez*, modern Commerce Clause jurisprudence has "identified three broad categories of activity that Congress may regulate under its commerce power." "First, Congress may regulate the use of the channels of interstate commerce." "Second, Congress is empowered to regulate and protect the instrumentalities of interstate commerce, or persons or things in interstate commerce, even though the threat may come only from intrastate activities." "Finally, Congress' commerce authority includes the power to regulate those activities having a substantial relation to interstate commerce, . . . i.e., those activities that substantially affect interstate commerce."

Petitioners do not contend that these cases fall within either of the first two of these categories of Commerce Clause regulation. They seek to sustain §13981 as a regulation of activity that substantially affects interstate commerce. . . .

Since *Lopez* most recently canvassed and clarified our case law governing this third category of Commerce Clause regulation, it provides the proper framework for conducting the required analysis of §13981. In *Lopez*, we held that the Gun-Free School Zones Act of 1990, which made it a federal crime to knowingly possess a firearm in a school zone, exceeded Congress' authority under the Commerce Clause. Several significant considerations contributed to our decision.

First, we observed that [the Gun-Free School Zones Act] was "a criminal statute that by its terms has nothing to do with 'commerce' or any sort of economic enterprise, however broadly one might define those terms." . . .

. . . *Lopez*'s review of Commerce Clause case law demonstrates that in those cases where we have sustained federal regulation of intrastate activity based upon the activity's substantial effects on interstate commerce, the activity in question has been some sort of economic endeavor.

The second consideration that we found important . . . was that the statute contained "no express jurisdictional element which might limit its reach to a discrete set of firearm possessions that additionally have an explicit connection with or effect on interstate commerce." . . .

Third, we noted that neither [the Gun-Free School Zones Act] "nor its legislative history contain[s] express congressional findings regarding the effects upon interstate commerce of gun possession in a school zone." While "Congress normally is not required to make formal findings as to the substantial burdens that an activity has on interstate commerce," the existence of such findings may "enable us to evaluate the legislative judgment that the activity in question substantially affect[s] interstate commerce, even though no such substantial effect [is] visible to the naked eye."

Finally, our decision in *Lopez* rested in part on the fact that the link between gun possession and a substantial effect on interstate commerce was attenuated. The United States argued that the possession of guns may lead to violent crime, and that violent crime "can be expected to affect the functioning of the national economy in two ways. First, the costs of violent crime are substantial, and, through the mechanism of insurance, those costs are spread throughout the population. Second, violent crime reduces the willingness of individuals to travel to areas within the country that are perceived to be unsafe." The Government also argued that the presence of guns at schools poses a threat to the educational process, which in turn threatens to produce a less efficient and productive workforce, which will negatively affect national productivity and thus interstate commerce.

We rejected these "costs of crime" and "national productivity" arguments because they would permit Congress to "regulate not only all violent crime, but all activities that might lead to violent crime, regardless of how tenuously they relate to interstate commerce." . . .

" . . . Thus, if we were to accept the Government's arguments, we are hard pressed to posit any activity by an individual that Congress is without power to regulate." [*Lopez.*]

With these principles underlying our Commerce Clause jurisprudence as reference points, the proper resolution of the present cases is clear. Gender-motivated crimes of violence are not, in any sense of the phrase, economic activity. While we need not adopt a categorical rule against aggregating the effects of any noneconomic activity in order to decide these cases, thus far in our Nation's history our cases have upheld Commerce Clause regulation of intrastate activity only where that activity is economic in nature.

Like the Gun-Free School Zones Act at issue in *Lopez*, §13981 contains no jurisdictional element establishing that the federal cause of action is in pursuance of Congress' power to regulate interstate commerce. . . .

In contrast with the lack of congressional findings that we faced in *Lopez*, §13981 is supported by numerous findings regarding the serious impact that gender-motivated violence has on victims and their families. But the existence of congressional findings is not sufficient, by itself, to sustain the constitutionality of Commerce Clause legislation. As we stated in *Lopez*, "'[S]imply because Congress may conclude that a particular activity substantially affects interstate commerce does not necessarily make it so.'" Rather, "'[w]hether particular operations affect interstate commerce sufficiently to come under the constitutional power of Congress to regulate them is ultimately a judicial rather than a legislative question, and can be settled finally only by this Court.'"

. . . Congress' findings are substantially weakened by the fact that they rely so heavily on a method of reasoning that we have already rejected as unworkable if we are to maintain the Constitution's enumeration of powers. Congress found that gender-motivated violence affects interstate commerce

"by deterring potential victims from traveling interstate, from engaging in employment in interstate business, and from transacting with business, and in places involved in interstate commerce; . . . by diminishing national productivity, increasing medical and other costs, and decreasing the supply of and the demand for interstate products."

Given these findings and petitioners' arguments, the concern that we expressed in *Lopez* that Congress might use the Commerce Clause to completely obliterate the

Constitution's distinction between national and local authority seems well founded. . . . If accepted, petitioners' reasoning would allow Congress to regulate any crime as long as the nationwide, aggregated impact of that crime has substantial effects on employment, production, transit, or consumption. Indeed, if Congress may regulate gender-motivated violence, it would be able to regulate murder or any other type of violence since gender-motivated violence, as a subset of all violent crime, is certain to have lesser economic impacts than the larger class of which it is a part.

Petitioners' reasoning, moreover, will not limit Congress to regulating violence but may, as we suggested in *Lopez*, be applied equally as well to family law and other areas of traditional state regulation since the aggregate effect of marriage, divorce, and childrearing on the national economy is undoubtedly significant. Congress may have recognized this specter when it expressly precluded §13981 from being used in the family law context. Under our written Constitution, however, the limitation of congressional authority is not solely a matter of legislative grace.

We accordingly reject the argument that Congress may regulate noneconomic, violent criminal conduct based solely on that conduct's aggregate effect on interstate commerce. The Constitution requires a distinction between what is truly national and what is truly local. In recognizing this fact we preserve one of the few principles that has been consistent since the Clause was adopted. The regulation and punishment of intrastate violence that is not directed at the instrumentalities, channels, or goods involved in interstate commerce has always been the province of the States. Indeed, we can think of no better example of the police power, which the Founders denied the National Government and reposed in the States, than the suppression of violent crime and vindication of its victims. . . .

Petitioner Brzonkala's complaint alleges that she was the victim of a brutal assault. . . . If the allegations here are true, no civilized system of justice could fail to provide her a remedy for the conduct of respondent Morrison. But under our federal system that remedy must be provided by the Commonwealth of Virginia, and not by the United States. The judgment of the Court of Appeals is

Affirmed.

JUSTICE SOUTER, with whom JUSTICE STEVENS, JUSTICE GINSBURG, and JUSTICE BREYER join, dissenting.
The Court says both that it leaves Commerce Clause precedent undisturbed and that the Civil Rights Remedy of the Violence Against Women Act of 1994 exceeds Congress's power under that Clause. I find the claims irreconcilable and respectfully dissent.

Our cases, which remain at least nominally undisturbed, stand for the following propositions. Congress has the power to legislate with regard to activity that, in the aggregate, has a substantial effect on interstate commerce. The fact of such a substantial effect is not an issue for the courts in the first instance, but for the Congress, whose institutional capacity for gathering evidence and taking testimony far exceeds ours. By passing legislation, Congress indicates its conclusion, whether explicitly or not, that facts support its exercise of the commerce power. The business of the courts is to review the congressional assessment, not for soundness but simply for the rationality of concluding that a jurisdictional basis exists in fact. Any explicit findings that Congress chooses to make, though not dispositive of the question of rationality, may advance judicial review by identifying factual authority on which Congress relied. Applying those propositions in these cases can lead to only one conclusion.

One obvious difference from *United States v. Lopez* (1995) is the mountain of data assembled by Congress, here showing the effects of violence against women on interstate commerce. Passage of the Act in 1994 was preceded by four years of hearings, which included testimony from physicians and law professors; from survivors of rape and domestic violence; and from representatives of state law enforcement and private business. The record includes reports on gender bias from task forces in 21 States, and we have the benefit of specific factual findings in the eight separate Reports issued by Congress and its committees over the long course leading to enactment. . . .

Congress thereby explicitly stated the predicate for the exercise of its Commerce Clause power. Is its conclusion irrational in view of the data amassed? True, the methodology of particular studies may be challenged, and some of the figures arrived at may be disputed. But the sufficiency of the evidence before Congress to provide a rational basis for the finding cannot seriously be questioned. . . .

The Act would have passed muster at any time between *Wickard* [*v. Filburn*] in 1942 and *Lopez* in 1995, a period in which the law enjoyed a stable understanding that congressional power under the Commerce Clause, complemented by the authority of the Necessary and Proper Clause, extended to all activity that, when aggregated, has a substantial effect on interstate commerce. . . .

The fact that the Act does not pass muster before the Court today is therefore proof, to a degree that *Lopez* was not, that the Court's nominal adherence to the substantial effects test is merely that. Although a new jurisprudence has not emerged with any distinctness, it is clear that some congressional conclusions about obviously substantial, cumulative effects on commerce are being assigned lesser values than the once-stable doctrine would assign them. These devaluations are accomplished not by any express repudiation of the substantial effects test or its application through the aggregation of individual conduct, but by supplanting rational basis scrutiny with a new criterion of review. . . .

All of this convinces me that today's ebb of the commerce power rests on error, and at the same time leads me to doubt that the majority's view will prove to be enduring law. There is yet one more reason for doubt. Although we sense the presence of [*Carter v.*] *Carter Coal* [1936], *Schechter* [*Poultry v. United States*, 1935], and [*National League of Cities v.*] *Usery* [1976] once again, the majority embraces them only at arm's-length. Where such decisions once stood for rules, today's opinion points to considerations by which substantial effects are discounted. Cases standing for the sufficiency of substantial effects are not overruled; cases overruled since 1937 are not quite revived. The Court's thinking betokens less clearly a return to the conceptual straitjackets of *Schechter* and *Carter Coal* and *Usery* than to something like the unsteady state of obscenity law between *Redrup v. New York* (1967) and *Miller v. California* (1973), a period in which the failure to provide a workable definition left this Court to review each case ad hoc. As our predecessors learned then, the practice of such ad hoc review cannot preserve the distinction between the judicial and the legislative, and this Court, in any event, lacks the institutional capacity to maintain such a regime for very long. This one will end when the majority realizes that the conception of the commerce power for which it entertains hopes would inevitably fail the test expressed in Justice Holmes's statement that "[t]he first call of a theory of law is that it should fit the facts." The facts that cannot be ignored today are the facts of integrated national commerce and a political relationship between States and Nation much affected by their respective treasuries and constitutional modifications adopted by the people. The federalism of some earlier time is no more adequate to account for those facts today than the theory of laissez-faire was able to govern the national economy 70 years ago.

The importance of *United States v. Morrison* extended far beyond the main participants in the dispute *(see box 7-8)*. By the same 5–4 vote as occurred in

Lopez and using the same reasoning, the Supreme Court struck down the Violence Against Women Act. Four months later the justices in *Jones v. United States* (2000) held that a federal criminal statute against arson, passed pursuant to the interstate commerce power, could not be applied to a man who tossed a Molotov cocktail into his cousin's house. Because the target of the arson was a private residence not used in any commercial activity, the Court concluded that Congress under the commerce clause had no authority to regulate.[21]

The opinions in *Lopez, Morrison,* and *Jones,* taken together with other Rehnquist Court federalism and taxation decisions, provide some indication of the Court's modified commerce clause jurisprudence *(see box 7-9)*. Following the New Deal revolution, the federal government was given wide latitude to regulate in the name of interstate commerce, but now the Court seemed to be cautioning that the commerce clause does not give Congress a blank check to regulate all activity in the name of commerce. In contrast to the New Deal case of *Darby,* the Court asserted that the Tenth Amendment could stand as a barrier to laws passed under the commerce clause if they commandeered the states, as in *Printz.* And in contrast to a case like *Garcia,* the Court in *Lopez* and *Morrison* now suggested that a federal law may be constitutionally suspect if it does not regulate an economic activity that, in the aggregate, substantially affects interstate commerce.

The importance of this evolution in doctrine remains to be seen. Although the Court has enunciated a revised interpretation of the commerce power, its application of that standard in no way resembles the breadth of the Court's attack on federal authority in the period prior to 1937. In fact, some of its decisions have been quite

---

21. The Court reinforced this revised view of the federal commerce power in **Solid Waste Agency of Northern Cook County v. United States Army Corps of Engineers** (2001), a case presenting a factual story very different from those challenging the authority of Congress to regulate gun possession, rape, or arson. At issue was an application of the federal Clean Water Act. A consortium of twenty-three Chicago-area cities attempted to develop a solid waste facility on a 533-acre parcel that previously had been used as a sand and gravel pit operation. The site included a series of small ponds, some permanent and others seasonal. The Army Corps of Engineers claimed that federal approval was necessary before development could take place because the ponds were habitats for migratory birds that crossed state lines. The Court, in another 5–4 ruling, held that the Corps' action impinged on the states' traditional power over land and water use, and that there was no evidence that Congress's regulation of navigable waters extended to abandoned gravel pits.

➤ BOX 7-8   AFTERMATH . . . *UNITED STATES V. MORRISON*

CHRISTY BRZONKALA, a former high school basketball player, arrived at Virginia Tech in 1994 with the goal of becoming a sports nutritionist. Antonio Morrison and James Crawford were members of the highly ranked Virginia Tech football team. They had dreams of careers in athletics, perhaps even in professional football. The ambitions of all three were shattered as the result of an incident in a dorm room on a September evening just one month after the school year began, when, as Brzonkala claimed, Morrison and Crawford gang-raped her. What followed was a tangled legal battle ending in the Supreme Court's decision in *United States v. Morrison* (2000). By the time the Supreme Court issued its opinion, the case had evolved into a federalism controversy over the extent to which Congress can regulate under its interstate commerce powers. Left behind were the lives of the three principals in the case.

AP Photo

Christy Brzonkala, with one of her attorneys, Kathryn Rodgers of the NOW Legal Defense Fund.

Brzonkala initially failed to tell anyone about the alleged assault. After several months of rarely leaving her room, performing poorly in her courses, and abusing thyroid medication, she came forward with her story. The university refused to expel Morrison and Crawford, and Brzonkala dropped out of college and moved back to her family's home in Fairfax County, Virginia. She resumed her academic career at George Mason University, but remained there only briefly. She then moved to Washington, D.C., and found work as a waitress. Brzonkala's suit against the university for sex discrimination was settled out of court. Virginia Tech agreed to pay her $75,000 but admitted no wrongdoing. In 2000 the National Organization for Women, which had supported Brzonkala's legal efforts, bestowed on her its Women of Courage Award.

The football players argued that they were unfairly charged. Morrison claimed that his sexual encounter with Brzonkala was consensual, and Crawford said that he left the room before any sexual activity occurred. Although police investigated the incident, neither Morrison nor Crawford was charged with any criminal offense.

The university placed Morrison on probation, but he was allowed to remain in school. Not long thereafter he was suspended from the football team following his arrest during a bar brawl. He transferred to Hampton University but returned to Virginia Tech a semester later. He did not play football again. He ultimately received a degree in human nutrition, foods, and exercise. After graduating, Morrison pursued a career as an athletic trainer but found it difficult to find employment. He claimed that racial factors were partially responsible for the unfair treatment he received and the damage his reputation suffered.

Crawford was later convicted of an unrelated sexual assault and disorderly conduct after an altercation in a parking lot. He was stripped of his football scholarship and left the university. He returned to his home state of Florida and began working in retail.

Although the Supreme Court held that the federal government had acted unconstitutionally in passing the Violence Against Women Act, Brzonkala was free to take her suit against Morrison and Crawford to state court. Brzonkala and her attorneys, however, said there was little chance that they would do so. Such a suit would be for monetary damages, and even if it were successful, Morrison and Crawford had little means of satisfying any judgment against them.

SOURCES: *Baltimore Sun*, January 8, 2000; *Washington Post*, May 20, 2000.

---

consistent with its earlier post–New Deal jurisprudence. One example is *Gonzales v. Raich* (2005), a controversial ruling on the validity of state laws that allow the medical use of marijuana. Under vigorous attack from the dissenters, the majority applied the precedent of *Wickard v. Filburn* and other post–New Deal doctrine.

BOX 7-9   EVOLUTION OF INTERSTATE COMMERCE DOCTRINE

MARSHALL INTERPRETATION

Gibbons v. Ogden (1824)
Marshall opinion for a 6–0 Court

Commerce begins in one state and ends in another. It does not stop when the act of crossing a state border is completed. Commerce occurring within a state may be part of a larger interstate process.

SHREVEPORT DOCTRINE

Shreveport Rate Case (1914)
Hughes opinion for a 7–2 Court

Congress may regulate intrastate commerce when it is intertwined with interstate commerce and when a failure to regulate intrastate commerce would injure interstate commerce.

STREAM OF COMMERCE DOCTRINE

Swift & Company v. United States (1905)
Holmes opinion for a 9–0 Court

Stafford v. Wallace (1922)
Taft opinion for a 7–1 Court

An article in interstate commerce does not lose its status until it reaches its final destination. Stopping along the way to its terminal sale does not remove an article from the stream of interstate commerce.

MANUFACTURING EXCLUDED FROM INTERSTATE COMMERCE

United States v. E. C. Knight Co. (1895)
Fuller opinion for an 8–1 Court

Schechter Poultry v. United States (1935)
Hughes opinion for a 9–0 Court

Carter v. Carter Coal Co. (1936)
Sutherland opinion for a 5–4 Court

Manufacturing, processing, and mining activities are local by nature and not a part of interstate commerce. Their effect on interstate commerce is indirect. That an article is intended for interstate commerce does not make its manufacture part of interstate commerce. "Commerce succeeds to manufacture, and is not a part of it."

MODERN INTERPRETATION OF INTERSTATE COMMERCE

NLRB v. Jones & Laughlin Steel Corporation (1937)
Hughes opinion for a 5–4 Court

Congress may enact all appropriate legislation to protect, advance, promote, and ensure interstate commerce. "Although activities may be intrastate in character when separately considered, if they have such a close and substantial relation to interstate commerce that their control is essential or appropriate to protect that commerce from burdens and obstructions, Congress cannot be denied the power to exercise that control."

United States v. Darby (1941)
Stone opinion for an 8–0 Court

"The power of Congress over interstate commerce is not confined to the regulation of commerce among the states. It extends to those intrastate activities that so affect interstate commerce or the exercise of the power of Congress over it as to make regulation of them an appropriate means to the attainment of a legitimate end, the exercise of the granted power of Congress to regulate interstate commerce."

Wickard v. Filburn (1942)
Jackson opinion for a 9–0 Court

Even if an activity is local and not regarded as commerce, "it may still, whatever its nature, be reached by Congress if it exerts a substantial economic effect on interstate commerce, and this is irrespective of whether such effect is what might at some earlier time have been defined as "direct" or "indirect." ... That [an individual's] own contribution [to interstate commerce] may be trivial by itself is not enough to remove him from the scope of federal regulation where [his] contribution, taken together with that of many others similarly situated, is far from trivial."

Gonzales v. Raich (2005)
Stevens opinion for a 6–3 Court

"In assessing the scope of Congress' authority under the Commerce Clause, we stress that the task before us is a modest one. We need not determine whether [the] activities, taken in the aggregate, substantially affect interstate commerce in fact, but only whether a 'rational basis' exists for so concluding."

MODERN COMMERCE POWER LIMITATIONS

United States v. Lopez (1995)
Rehnquist opinion for a 5–4 Court

United States v. Morrison (2000)
Rehnquist opinion for a 5–4 Court

Federal legislation is constitutionally suspect if it does not regulate an economic activity that, in the aggregate, substantially affects interstate commerce.

National Federation of Independent Business v. Sebelius (2012)
Roberts opinion for a 5–4 Court

"The power to regulate commerce presupposes the existence of commercial activity to be regulated." Congress cannot compel individuals "to become active in commerce by purchasing a product," even if their failure to do so affects interstate commerce.

AP Photo/Noah Berger

Angel Raich, shown here at a 2004 press conference, sued to block the U.S. attorney general from enforcing the federal Controlled Substances Act against her. Raich, suffering from a brain tumor and other serious medical conditions, used marijuana under California's Compassionate Use Act to combat her pain and discomfort.

AP Photo/Rich Pedrocelli

Diane Monson joined Angel Raich in asking the Supreme Court to uphold California's medicinal marijuana law. Monson, under a physician's direction, regularly used marijuana to alleviate chronic and severe back pain.

Gonzales v. Raich

545 U.S. 1 (2005)
http://laws.findlaw.com/us/545/1.html
Oral arguments are available at https://www.oyez.org.
Vote: 6 (Breyer, Ginsburg, Kennedy, Scalia, Souter, Stevens)
    3 (O'Connor, Rehnquist, Thomas)

OPINION OF THE COURT: *Stevens*
OPINION CONCURRING IN JUDGMENT: *Scalia*
DISSENTING OPINIONS: *O'Connor, Thomas*

FACTS:

In 1996 California voters passed Proposition 215, commonly known as the Compassionate Use Act. The law allowed seriously ill state residents to use marijuana for medical purposes. The act also created an exemption from criminal prosecution for patients, physicians, and caregivers who cultivate and possess marijuana for medical reasons.

Californian Angel Raich suffered from more than ten serious and possibly life-threatening medical conditions, including an inoperable brain tumor. On the advice of her doctor she used marijuana to help ease her suffering. Too ill to produce her own supply, Raich depended on two caregivers to grow and provide marijuana without charge.

Diane Monson, another California resident following her physician's advice, had been using marijuana in compliance with the Compassionate Use Act for about five years to combat chronic back pain caused by a degenerative disease of the spine. She grew about six cannabis plants to maintain a supply of the drug.

In 2002 county deputy sheriffs and federal drug agents came to Monson's home. After an investigation, the local officials found no evidence of illegal activity under California law. The federal agents, however, concluded that Monson's possession of marijuana violated the federal Controlled Substances Act. They seized and destroyed her marijuana plants.

Raich and Monson brought a lawsuit against Attorney General Alberto Gonzales and the head of the U.S. Drug Enforcement Administration to bar enforcement of the Controlled Substances Act to the extent that it prevented them from obtaining and possessing marijuana for medical purposes. The federal government claimed that its constitutional power to regulate commerce was sufficiently broad to regulate the use of the substance. Raich and Monson argued that the federal commerce power does not extend to the medical use of marijuana, a purely local and noncommercial activity regulated by state law. They further claimed that their marijuana plants were grown and processed only with water, nutrients, supplies, and equipment originating in California. The court of appeals ruled in favor of Raich and Monson, and the federal government asked the Supreme Court to reverse.

ARGUMENTS:

For the petitioners, Alberto R. Gonzales, attorney general, et al.:

- Congress has the power under the commerce clause, coupled with the necessary and proper clause, to regulate local activity that substantially affects interstate commerce (see *Wickard* and *Darby*). Congress's determination that local activity with respect to a product substantially affects interstate commerce or could interfere with Congress's objective in regulating the interstate market of that product is entitled to substantial deference.

- Because marijuana trafficking is a commercial activity that occurs in interstate and foreign commerce and affects interstate commerce, Congress has the power under the commerce clause to regulate all commercial marijuana activity, including commercial possession, manufacture, and distribution that occurs wholly intrastate (see *Lopez*).

- The act also constitutionally regulates intrastate manufacture and possession of marijuana for personal use and the distribution of those substances without charge. Congress has concluded that regulation of all intrastate drug activity "is essential to the effective control" of interstate drug trafficking and that regulation of intrastate drug activity was a reasonably necessary means to accomplish its comprehensive regulation of the interstate market in controlled substances.

For the respondents, Angel McClary Raich et al.:

- This case is and always has been about state sovereignty and federalism. The issue is whether the federal government may criminalize wholly intrastate, noncommercial conduct that is expressly authorized by the state in an exercise of its broad powers to define criminal law, regulate medical practice, and protect the lives of its citizens. In *Lopez* and *Morrison* the Court invalidated federal statutes that were consistent with achievement of goals shared by all the states.

- The government's argument goes beyond the outer limits of *Wickard*, which involved regulation of commercial farming activity. The respondents' activity is not commercial, and the link between it and interstate commerce is, at best, attenuated. In addition, prohibiting respondents' activity is not essential to a larger regulation of interstate economic activity.

JUSTICE STEVENS DELIVERED THE OPINION OF THE COURT.

California is one of at least nine States that authorize the use of marijuana for medicinal purposes. The question presented in this case is whether the power vested in Congress by Article I, §8, of the Constitution "[t]o make all Laws which shall be necessary and proper for carrying into Execution" its authority to "regulate Commerce with foreign Nations, and among the several States" includes the power to prohibit the local cultivation and use of marijuana in compliance with California law. . . .

Respondents in this case do not dispute that passage of the CSA [Controlled Substances Act], as part of the Comprehensive Drug Abuse Prevention and Control Act, was well within Congress' commerce power. Nor do they contend that any provision or section of the CSA amounts to an unconstitutional exercise of congressional authority. Rather, respondents' challenge is actually quite limited; they argue that the CSA's categorical prohibition of the manufacture and possession of marijuana as applied to the intrastate manufacture and possession of marijuana for medical purposes pursuant to California law exceeds Congress' authority under the Commerce Clause.

In assessing the validity of congressional regulation, none of our Commerce Clause cases can be viewed in isolation. As charted in considerable detail in *United States v. Lopez* [1995], our understanding of the reach of the Commerce Clause, as well as Congress' assertion of authority thereunder, has evolved over time. . . .

. . . [We have now] identified three general categories of regulation in which Congress is authorized to engage under its commerce power. First, Congress can regulate the channels of interstate commerce. *Perez v. United States* (1971). Second, Congress has authority to regulate and protect the instrumentalities of interstate commerce, and persons or things in interstate commerce. *Ibid.* Third, Congress has the power to regulate activities that substantially affect interstate commerce. *Ibid.; NLRB v. Jones &*

Laughlin Steel Corp. (1937). Only the third category is implicated in the case at hand.

Our case law firmly establishes Congress' power to regulate purely local activities that are part of an economic "class of activities" that have a substantial effect on interstate commerce. See, *e.g.*, *Perez*; *Wickard v. Filburn* (1942). As we stated in *Wickard*, "even if appellee's activity be local and though it may not be regarded as commerce, it may still, whatever its nature, be reached by Congress if it exerts a substantial economic effect on interstate commerce." We have never required Congress to legislate with scientific exactitude. When Congress decides that the "'total incidence'" of a practice poses a threat to a national market, it may regulate the entire class. In this vein, we have reiterated that when "'a general regulatory statute bears a substantial relation to commerce, the *de minimis* character of individual instances arising under that statute is of no consequence.'"

Our decision in *Wickard* is of particular relevance. . . .

Wickard . . . establishes that Congress can regulate purely intrastate activity that is not itself "commercial," in that it is not produced for sale, if it concludes that failure to regulate that class of activity would undercut the regulation of the interstate market in that commodity.

The similarities between this case and *Wickard* are striking. Like the farmer in *Wickard*, respondents are cultivating, for home consumption, a fungible commodity for which there is an established, albeit illegal, interstate market. Just as the Agricultural Adjustment Act was designed "to control the volume [of wheat] moving in interstate and foreign commerce in order to avoid surpluses . . ." and consequently control the market price, a primary purpose of the CSA is to control the supply and demand of controlled substances in both lawful and unlawful drug markets. In *Wickard*, we had no difficulty concluding that Congress had a rational basis for believing that, when viewed in the aggregate, leaving home-consumed wheat outside the regulatory scheme would have a substantial influence on price and market conditions. Here too, Congress had a rational basis for concluding that leaving home-consumed marijuana outside federal control would similarly affect price and market conditions.

More concretely, one concern prompting inclusion of wheat grown for home consumption in the 1938 Act was that rising market prices could draw such wheat into the interstate market, resulting in lower market prices. The parallel concern making it appropriate to include marijuana grown for home consumption in the CSA is the likelihood that the high demand in the interstate market will draw such marijuana into that market. While the diversion of homegrown wheat tended to frustrate the federal interest in stabilizing prices by regulating the volume of commercial transactions in the interstate market, the diversion of homegrown marijuana tends to frustrate the federal interest in eliminating commercial transactions in the interstate market in their entirety. In both cases, the regulation is squarely within Congress' commerce power because production of the commodity meant for home consumption, be it wheat or marijuana, has a substantial effect on supply and demand in the national market for that commodity. . . .

In assessing the scope of Congress' authority under the Commerce Clause, we stress that the task before us is a modest one. We need not determine whether respondents' activities, taken in the aggregate, substantially affect interstate commerce in fact, but only whether a "rational basis" exists for so concluding. Given the enforcement difficulties that attend distinguishing between marijuana cultivated locally and marijuana grown elsewhere and concerns about diversion into illicit channels, we have no difficulty concluding that Congress had a rational basis for believing that failure to regulate the intrastate manufacture and possession of marijuana would leave a gaping hole in the CSA. Thus, as in *Wickard*, when it enacted comprehensive legislation to regulate the interstate market in a fungible commodity, Congress was acting well within its authority to "make all Laws which shall be necessary and proper" to "regulate Commerce . . . among the several States." That the regulation ensnares some purely intrastate activity is of no moment. As we have done many times before, we refuse to excise individual components of that larger scheme.

To support their contrary submission, respondents rely heavily on two of our more recent Commerce Clause cases. In their myopic focus, they overlook the larger context of modern-era Commerce Clause jurisprudence preserved by those cases. Moreover, even in the narrow prism of respondents' creation, they read those cases far too broadly. Those two cases, of course, are *Lopez* and [*United States v.*] *Morrison* [2000]. . . .

Unlike those at issue in *Lopez* and *Morrison*, the activities regulated by the CSA are quintessentially economic. "Economics" refers to "the production, distribution, and consumption of commodities." Webster's *Third New International Dictionary* 720 (1966). The CSA is a statute that regulates the production, distribution, and consumption of commodities for which there is an established, and lucrative, interstate market. Prohibiting the intrastate possession or manufacture of an article of commerce is a rational (and commonly utilized) means of regulating commerce in that product. . . . Because the CSA is a statute that directly regulates economic, commercial activity, our opinion in *Morrison* casts no doubt on its constitutionality. . . .

The exemption for cultivation by patients and caregivers can only increase the supply of marijuana in the California market. The likelihood that all such production will promptly terminate when patients recover or will precisely match the patients' medical needs during their convalescence seems remote; whereas the danger that excesses will satisfy some of the admittedly enormous demand for recreational use seems obvious. Moreover, that the national and international narcotics trade has thrived in the face of vigorous criminal enforcement efforts suggests that no small number of unscrupulous people will make use of the California exemptions to serve their commercial ends whenever it is feasible to do so. Taking into account the fact that California is only one of at least nine States to have authorized the medical use of marijuana, . . . Congress could have rationally concluded that the aggregate impact on the national market of all the transactions exempted from federal supervision is unquestionably substantial.

. . . Thus the case for the exemption comes down to the claim that a locally cultivated product that is used domestically rather than sold on the open market is not subject to federal regulation. Given the findings in the CSA and the undisputed magnitude of the commercial market for marijuana, our decisions in *Wickard v. Filburn* and the later cases endorsing its reasoning foreclose that claim. . . .

. . . [T]he judgment of the Court of Appeals must be vacated. The case is remanded for further proceedings consistent with this opinion.

It is so ordered.

JUSTICE SCALIA, concurring in the judgment.

I agree with the Court's holding that the Controlled Substances Act (CSA) may validly be applied to respondents' cultivation, distribution, and possession of marijuana for personal, medicinal use. I write separately because my understanding of the doctrinal foundation on which that holding rests is, if not inconsistent with that of the Court, at least more nuanced.

Since *Perez v. United States* (1971), our cases have mechanically recited that the Commerce Clause permits congressional regulation of three categories: (1) the channels of interstate commerce; (2) the instrumentalities of interstate commerce, and persons or things in interstate commerce; and (3) activities that "substantially affect"

interstate commerce. The first two categories are self-evident, since they are the ingredients of interstate commerce itself. See *Gibbons v. Ogden* (1824). The third category, however, is different in kind, and its recitation without explanation is misleading and incomplete.

It is misleading because, unlike the channels, instrumentalities, and agents of interstate commerce, activities that substantially affect interstate commerce are not themselves part of interstate commerce, and thus the power to regulate them cannot come from the Commerce Clause alone. Rather, as this Court has acknowledged since at least *United States v. Coombs* (1838), Congress's regulatory authority over intrastate activities that are not themselves part of interstate commerce (including activities that have a substantial effect on interstate commerce) derives from the Necessary and Proper Clause. And the category of "activities that substantially affect interstate commerce," *Lopez*, is incomplete because the authority to enact laws necessary and proper for the regulation of interstate commerce is not limited to laws governing intrastate activities that substantially affect interstate commerce. Where necessary to make a regulation of interstate commerce effective, Congress may regulate even those intrastate activities that do not themselves substantially affect interstate commerce.

JUSTICE O'CONNOR, with whom the CHIEF JUSTICE and JUSTICE THOMAS join . . . , dissenting.

We enforce the "outer limits" of Congress' Commerce Clause authority not for their own sake, but to protect historic spheres of state sovereignty from excessive federal encroachment and thereby to maintain the distribution of power fundamental to our federalist system of government. One of federalism's chief virtues, of course, is that it promotes innovation by allowing for the possibility that "a single courageous State may, if its citizens choose, serve as a laboratory; and try novel social and economic experiments without risk to the rest of the country." *New State Ice Co. v. Liebmann* (1932) (Brandeis, J., dissenting).

This case exemplifies the role of States as laboratories. The States' core police powers have always included authority to define criminal law and to protect the health, safety, and welfare of their citizens. Exercising those powers, California (by ballot initiative and then by legislative codification) has come to its own conclusion about the difficult and sensitive question of whether marijuana should be available to relieve severe pain and suffering. Today the Court sanctions an application of the federal Controlled Substances Act that extinguishes that experiment, without any proof that the personal cultivation, possession, and use of marijuana for medicinal purposes, if economic activity in the first place, has a substantial effect on interstate commerce and is therefore an appropriate subject of federal regulation. In so doing, the Court announces a rule that gives Congress a perverse incentive to legislate broadly pursuant to the Commerce Clause—nestling questionable assertions of its authority into comprehensive regulatory schemes—rather than with precision. That rule and the result it produces in this case are irreconcilable with our decisions in *Lopez* and *United States v. Morrison* (2000). . . .

The Court's definition of economic activity is breathtaking. It defines as economic any activity involving the production, distribution, and consumption of commodities. And it appears to reason that when an interstate market for a commodity exists, regulating the intrastate manufacture or possession of that commodity is constitutional either because that intrastate activity is itself economic, or because regulating it is a rational part of regulating its market. . . . [T]he Court's definition of economic activity for purposes of Commerce Clause jurisprudence threatens to sweep all of productive human activity into federal regulatory reach.

The Court uses a dictionary definition of economics to skirt the real problem of drawing a meaningful line between "what is national and what is local." It will not do to say that Congress may regulate noncommercial activity simply because it may have an effect on the demand for commercial goods, or because the noncommercial endeavor can, in some sense, substitute for commercial activity. Most commercial goods or services have some sort of privately producible analogue. Home care substitutes for daycare. Charades games substitute for movie tickets. Backyard or windowsill gardening substitutes for going to the supermarket. To draw the line wherever private activity affects the demand for market goods is to draw no line at all, and to declare everything economic. . . .

The Government has not overcome empirical doubt that the number of Californians engaged in personal cultivation, possession, and use of medical marijuana, or the amount of marijuana they produce, is enough to threaten the federal regime. Nor has it shown that Compassionate Use Act marijuana users have been or are realistically likely to be responsible for the drug's seeping into the market in a significant way. . . .

Relying on Congress' abstract assertions, the Court has endorsed making it a federal crime to grow small amounts of marijuana in one's own home for one's own medicinal use. This overreaching stifles an express choice by some

States, concerned for the lives and liberties of their people, to regulate medical marijuana differently. If I were a California citizen, I would not have voted for the medical marijuana ballot initiative; if I were a California legislator I would not have supported the Compassionate Use Act. But whatever the wisdom of California's experiment with medical marijuana, the federalism principles that have driven our Commerce Clause cases require that room for experiment be protected in this case. For these reasons I dissent.

JUSTICE THOMAS, dissenting.

Respondents Diane Monson and Angel Raich use marijuana that has never been bought or sold, that has never crossed state lines, and that has had no demonstrable effect on the national market for marijuana. If Congress can regulate this under the Commerce Clause, then it can regulate virtually anything—and the Federal Government is no longer one of limited and enumerated powers. . . .

Even the majority does not argue that respondents' conduct is itself "Commerce among the several States." Monson and Raich neither buy nor sell the marijuana that they consume. They cultivate their cannabis entirely in the State of California—it never crosses state lines, much less as part of a commercial transaction. Certainly no evidence from the founding suggests that "commerce" included the mere possession of a good or some purely personal activity that did not involve trade or exchange for value. In the early days of the Republic, it would have been unthinkable that Congress could prohibit the local cultivation, possession, and consumption of marijuana. . . .

Moreover, even a Court interested more in the modern than the original understanding of the Constitution ought to resolve cases based on the meaning of words that are actually in the document. Congress is authorized to regulate "Commerce," and respondents' conduct does not qualify under any definition of that term. The majority's opinion only illustrates the steady drift away from the text of the Commerce Clause. There is an inexorable expansion from "'commerce,'" to "commercial" and "economic" activity, and finally to all "production, distribution, and consumption" of goods or services for which there is an "established . . . interstate market." Federal power expands, but never contracts, with each new locution. The majority is not interpreting the Commerce Clause, but rewriting it. . . .

. . . The majority's rush to embrace federal power "is especially unfortunate given the importance of showing respect for the sovereign States that comprise our Federal Union." Our federalist system, properly understood, allows

California and a growing number of other States to decide for themselves how to safeguard the health and welfare of their citizens. I would affirm the judgment of the Court of Appeals. I respectfully dissent.

Although the decision in *Raich* still allows federal agents to prosecute medical marijuana cases, in October 2009 the Obama administration announced that it would no longer prosecute such cases *if* the individuals involved are in compliance with state law. The decision of some states, beginning with Colorado and Washington, to remove bans on recreational use of marijuana certainly widens the policy gap between the legalizing states and the federal government. Clearly, under *Gonzales v. Raich* the federal government can enforce federal laws prohibiting the distribution and possession of marijuana no matter what state law provides. For the present, federal authorities have chosen not to prosecute such violations. Whether that nonenforcement policy will continue for the long term remains to be seen.

Raich demonstrates that *Lopez, Morrison,* and *Jones* should not be seen as a wholesale repudiation of commerce clause jurisprudence as it has developed since 1937. Rather, the six-justice majority in *Raich,* which included conservatives Scalia and Kennedy, held fast to the precedent set in *Wickard v. Filburn:* the production of commercially viable items, when considered in the aggregate, has a sufficiently substantial relationship with interstate commerce to trigger the use of congressional regulatory authority. But when Congress under the commerce clause attempts to regulate noneconomic activity (such as gun possession, rape, or arson) without showing that the regulation is a necessary part of a broader regulation of interstate commerce, it may impermissibly infringe on powers reserved for the states.

The justices were faced with a legal dispute in 2012 that required them to go well beyond the distinction between economic and noneconomic activity. In *National Federation of Independent Business v. Sebelius,* the Court considered whether Congress has the power to regulate economic *inactivity.* At issue

On February 25, 2010, key figures in the debate over proposed health-care reforms met at Blair House in Washington but were unsuccessful at finding common ground. One month later President Obama signed into law the Patient Protection and Affordable Care Act after it had passed on a nearly straight party-line vote, with congressional Democrats supporting the law and Republicans opposed. From left, President Barack Obama and Secretary of Health and Human Services Kathleen Sebelius (both Democrats), Senate Minority Leader Mitch McConnell (R-Ky.), and House Minority Leader John Boehner (R-Ohio).

was the constitutionality of the Patient Protection and Affordable Care Act of 2010. The attacked legislation imposed comprehensive reforms on the nation's medical care and health insurance sectors. The law was exceptionally controversial and became a political issue that affected the 2010 and 2012 congressional and presidential elections. A core question in the case was whether Congress constitutionally can require unwilling individuals to purchase health insurance.

In deciding the case the justices examined congressional powers under the commerce clause, the necessary and proper clause, and the taxing and spending clauses. In the following excerpt, we provide the Court's analysis of congressional authority to enact the health-care law under the commerce clause and the necessary and proper clause. As you will see, the majority concludes that these constitutional provisions do not empower Congress to regulate commercial inactivity. But the commerce clause ruling did not settle the case. As we will see in chapter 8, the health insurance purchase requirement, while not constitutional under the commerce power, was found to be a valid regulation under Congress's authority to tax and spend.

National Federation of Independent Business v. Sebelius

567 U.S. _____ (2012)
http://laws.findlaw.com/us/000/11-393.html
Oral arguments are available at https://www.oyez.org.
Vote on the commerce clause challenge to the Affordable Care Act:
  5 (Alito, Kennedy, Roberts, Scalia, Thomas)
  4 (Breyer, Ginsburg, Kagan, Sotomayor)
OPINION ANNOUNCING THE JUDGMENT OF
  THE COURT AND THE OPINION OF THE COURT: *Roberts*
OPINION CONCURRING IN PART
  AND DISSENTING IN PART: *Ginsburg*
JOINT OPINION CONCURRING ON THE COMMERCE
  CLAUSE ISSUE BUT DISSENTING FROM THE FINAL
  CASE OUTCOME: *Alito, Kennedy, Scalia, and Thomas*
DISSENTING OPINION: *Thomas*

FACTS:

In 2010 Congress passed the Patient Protection and Affordable Care Act (ACA). The purpose of the law was to increase the number of Americans covered by health insurance and to decrease the cost of health care. The law was passed along partisan lines, with Democrats supporting the bill and Republicans opposed. The American public also was closely divided

over the policies to be implemented by the act. The legislation was quite complex, with the statute running more than nine hundred pages in length. It introduced major changes in the health insurance industry, expanded insurance coverage and benefits, eliminated coverage limitations for preexisting conditions, and significantly expanded Medicaid.

At the heart of the ACA is a requirement known as the "individual mandate" (also known as the "minimum coverage" requirement). This provision directs that most Americans purchase "minimum essential" health insurance coverage for themselves and their dependents if they do not receive such coverage from their employers. Those who do not comply with this provision are required to make a "shared responsibility" payment to the federal government. The act provides that this "penalty" will be paid to the Internal Revenue Service and "shall be assessed and collected in the same manner" as tax penalties. The mandate was intended to ensure that health costs are evenly distributed throughout the population and to prohibit individuals from refusing to buy health insurance until they develop medical conditions requiring treatment.

Almost immediately after President Obama signed the bill into law, a series of lawsuits were filed challenging the constitutionality of the ACA. The lower federal courts reached differing opinions on the validity of the law. In order to resolve this conflict, the Supreme Court granted a petition to review a decision of the Eleventh Circuit Court of Appeals striking down portions of the law but allowing the balance of the statute to remain in effect. The appealed decision involved a suit initiated by the National Federation of Independent Business, twenty-six state governments, and several individuals against Kathleen Sebelius, then secretary of health and human services.

Challengers of the law argued that Congress exceeded its commerce clause powers by compelling individuals to purchase insurance when they may not wish to do so. Commercial inactivity, they argued, is not commerce. Secretary Sebelius responded that health care is an integral part of the national economy. Therefore, the commerce clause and the necessary and proper clause give Congress ample authority to enact a comprehensive health-care law that includes an individual mandate. She asserted that the ACA was also a legitimate action under Congress's constitutional power to tax and spend. In another line of attack, the challengers claimed that the expansion of the federal

Medicaid program unconstitutionally infringed on the powers of the states.

In the excerpted material appearing here, we focus exclusively on the question of whether the individual mandate provision can legitimately rest on Congress's power to regulate interstate commerce and the necessary and proper clause. In the next chapter we will return to this decision and highlight arguments related to the authority of Congress to tax and spend.

For the petitioners, National Federation of Independent Business et al.:

- The individual mandate is an unprecedented law that rests on an extraordinary and unbounded assertion of federal power.
- The Constitution grants Congress the power to regulate commerce, not the power to compel individuals to enter into commerce.
- The federal government may not save the individual mandate by resorting to the necessary and proper clause. The mandate is not a law for carrying into execution the commerce power. It is a law for carrying into execution an independent power that the Constitution does not grant to the federal government.

For the respondents, Health and Human Services Secretary Kathleen Sebelius et al.:

- Congress has authority under the commerce and necessary and proper clauses to enact the minimum coverage provision. The Affordable Care Act expands access to health care services and controls health care costs. The minimum coverage provision plays a critical role in that comprehensive regulatory scheme by regulating how health care consumption is financed.
- The act's minimum coverage provision is a particularly well-adapted means of accomplishing Congress's concededly legitimate ends. It is necessary to effectuate Congress's comprehensive reforms of the insurance market and is itself an economic regulation of the timing and method of financing health care services. This provision regulates economic activity that substantially affects interstate commerce. Its links to interstate commerce are tangible, direct, and strong.
- There is no textual support in the commerce clause for the opponents' "inactivity" limitation. Furthermore, the uninsured as a class are active in the market for health care, which they regularly seek and obtain.

> **CHIEF JUSTICE ROBERTS ANNOUNCED THE JUDGMENT OF THE COURT AND DELIVERED . . . AN OPINION WITH RESPECT TO [THE COMMERCE CLAUSE CHALLENGE TO THE INDIVIDUAL MANDATE].**

In our federal system, the National Government possesses only limited powers; the States and the people retain the remainder. Nearly two centuries ago, Chief Justice Marshall observed that "the question respecting the extent of the powers actually granted" to the Federal Government "is perpetually arising, and will probably continue to arise, as long as our system shall exist." *McCulloch v. Maryland* (1819). In this case we must again determine whether the Constitution grants Congress powers it now asserts, but which many States and individuals believe it does not possess. Resolving this controversy requires us to examine both the limits of the Government's power, and our own limited role in policing those boundaries.

The Federal Government "is acknowledged by all to be one of enumerated powers." Ibid. That is, rather than granting general authority to perform all the conceivable functions of government, the Constitution lists, or enumerates, the Federal Government's powers. Congress may, for example, "coin Money," "establish Post Offices," and "raise and support Armies." Art. I, §8, cls. 5, 7, 12. The enumeration of powers is also a limitation of powers, because "[t]he enumeration presupposes something not enumerated." *Gibbons v. Ogden* (1824). The Constitution's express conferral of some powers makes clear that it does not grant others. And the Federal Government "can exercise only the powers granted to it." *McCulloch.*

. . . If no enumerated power authorizes Congress to pass a certain law, that law may not be enacted, even if it would not violate any of the express prohibitions in the Bill of Rights or elsewhere in the Constitution.

. . . The Federal Government has expanded dramatically over the past two centuries, but it still must show that a constitutional grant of power authorizes each of its actions. See, e.g., *United States v. Comstock* (2010).

The same does not apply to the States, because the Constitution is not the source of their power. . . . The States thus can and do perform many of the vital functions of modern government—punishing street crime, running public schools, and zoning property for development, to name but a few—even though the Constitution's text does not authorize any government to do so. Our cases refer to this general power of governing, possessed by the States but not by the Federal Government, as the "police power." See, e.g., *United States v. Morrison* (2000). . . .

This case concerns . . . powers that the Constitution does grant the Federal Government, but which must be read carefully to avoid creating a general federal authority akin to the police power. The Constitution authorizes Congress to "regulate Commerce with foreign Nations, and among the several States, and with the Indian Tribes." Our precedents read that to mean that Congress may regulate "the channels of interstate commerce," "persons or things in interstate commerce," and "those activities that substantially affect interstate commerce." *Morrison.* The power over activities that substantially affect interstate commerce can be expansive. That power has been held to authorize federal regulation of such seemingly local matters as a farmer's decision to grow wheat for himself and his livestock, and a loan shark's extortionate collections from a neighborhood butcher shop. See *Wickard v. Filburn* (1942); *Perez v. United States* (1971). . . .

The reach of the Federal Government's enumerated powers is broader still because the Constitution authorizes Congress to "make all Laws which shall be necessary and proper for carrying into Execution the foregoing Powers." We have long read this provision to give Congress great latitude in exercising its powers: "Let the end be legitimate, let it be within the scope of the constitution, and all means which are appropriate, which are plainly adapted to that end, which are not prohibited, but consist with the letter and spirit of the constitution, are constitutional." *McCulloch.*

Our permissive reading of these powers is explained in part by a general reticence to invalidate the acts of the Nation's elected leaders. . . .

Our deference in matters of policy cannot, however, become abdication in matters of law. "The powers of the legislature are defined and limited; and that those limits may not be mistaken, or forgotten, the constitution is written." *Marbury v. Madison* (1803). Our respect for Congress's policy judgments thus can never extend so far as to disavow restraints on federal power that the Constitution carefully constructed. . . . And there can be no question that it is the responsibility of this Court to enforce the limits on federal power by striking down acts of Congress that transgress those limits. *Marbury v. Madison.*

The questions before us must be considered against the background of these basic principles. . . .

The Government's . . . argument is that the individual mandate is a valid exercise of Congress's power under the Commerce Clause and the Necessary and Proper Clause. According to the Government, the health care market is characterized by a significant cost-shifting problem.

Everyone will eventually need health care at a time and to an extent they cannot predict, but if they do not have insurance, they often will not be able to pay for it. Because state and federal laws nonetheless require hospitals to provide a certain degree of care to individuals without regard to their ability to pay, hospitals end up receiving compensation for only a portion of the services they provide. To recoup the losses, hospitals pass on the cost to insurers through higher rates, and insurers, in turn, pass on the cost to policy holders in the form of higher premiums. Congress estimated that the cost of uncompensated care raises family health insurance premiums, on average, by over $1,000 per year. . . .

The Government contends that the individual mandate is within Congress's power because the failure to purchase insurance "has a substantial and deleterious effect on interstate commerce" by creating the cost-shifting problem. . . .

Given its expansive scope, it is no surprise that Congress has employed the commerce power in a wide variety of ways to address the pressing needs of the time. But Congress has never attempted to rely on that power to compel individuals not engaged in commerce to purchase an unwanted product. Legislative novelty is not necessarily fatal; there is a first time for everything. But sometimes "the most telling indication of [a] severe constitutional problem . . . is the lack of historical precedent" for Congress's action. *Free Enterprise Fund v. Public Company Accounting Oversight Bd.* (2010). At the very least, we should "pause to consider the implications of the Government's arguments" when confronted with such new conceptions of federal power. *Lopez.*

The Constitution grants Congress the power to "regulate Commerce." The power to regulate commerce presupposes the existence of commercial activity to be regulated. If the power to "regulate" something included the power to create it, many of the provisions in the Constitution would be superfluous. For example, the Constitution gives Congress the power to "coin Money," in addition to the power to "regulate the Value thereof." And it gives Congress the power to "raise and support Armies" and to "provide and maintain a Navy," in addition to the power to "make Rules for the Government and Regulation of the land and naval Forces." If the power to regulate the armed forces or the value of money included the power to bring the subject of the regulation into existence, the specific grant of such powers would have been unnecessary. The language of the Constitution reflects the natural understanding that the power to regulate assumes there is already something to be regulated.

Our precedent also reflects this understanding. As expansive as our cases construing the scope of the commerce power have been, they all have one thing in common: They uniformly describe the power as reaching "activity." . . .

The individual mandate, however, does not regulate existing commercial activity. It instead compels individuals to become active in commerce by purchasing a product, on the ground that their failure to do so affects interstate commerce. Construing the Commerce Clause to permit Congress to regulate individuals precisely because they are doing nothing would open a new and potentially vast domain to congressional authority. Every day individuals do not do an infinite number of things. In some cases they decide not to do something; in others they simply fail to do it. Allowing Congress to justify federal regulation by pointing to the effect of inaction on commerce would bring countless decisions an individual could potentially make within the scope of federal regulation, and—under the Government's theory—empower Congress to make those decisions for him.

Applying the Government's logic to the familiar case of *Wickard v. Filburn* shows how far that logic would carry us from the notion of a government of limited powers. In *Wickard*, the Court famously upheld a federal penalty imposed on a farmer for growing wheat for consumption on his own farm. That amount of wheat caused the farmer to exceed his quota under a program designed to support the price of wheat by limiting supply. The Court rejected the farmer's argument that growing wheat for home consumption was beyond the reach of the commerce power. It did so on the ground that the farmer's decision to grow wheat for his own use allowed him to avoid purchasing wheat in the market. That decision, when considered in the aggregate along with similar decisions of others, would have had a substantial effect on the interstate market for wheat.

Wickard has long been regarded as "perhaps the most far reaching example of Commerce Clause authority over intrastate activity," *Lopez*, but the Government's theory in this case would go much further. . . . The farmer in *Wickard* was at least actively engaged in the production of wheat, and the Government could regulate that activity because of its effect on commerce. The Government's theory here would effectively override that limitation, by establishing that individuals may be regulated under the Commerce Clause whenever enough of them are not doing something the Government would have them do.

Indeed, the Government's logic would justify a mandatory purchase to solve almost any problem. To consider a different example in the health care market, many Americans do not eat a balanced diet. That group makes up a larger percentage of the total population than those without health insurance. The failure of that group to have a healthy diet increases health care costs, to a greater extent than the failure of the uninsured to purchase insurance. Those increased costs are borne in part by other Americans who must pay more, just as the uninsured shift costs to the insured. Congress addressed the insurance problem by ordering everyone to buy insurance. Under the Government's theory, Congress could address the diet problem by ordering everyone to buy vegetables.

People, for reasons of their own, often fail to do things that would be good for them or good for society. Those failures—joined with the similar failures of others—can readily have a substantial effect on interstate commerce. Under the Government's logic, that authorizes Congress to use its commerce power to compel citizens to act as the Government would have them act.

That is not the country the Framers of our Constitution envisioned. . . . Congress already enjoys vast power to regulate much of what we do. Accepting the Government's theory would give Congress the same license to regulate what we do not do, fundamentally changing the relation between the citizen and the Federal Government.

To an economist, perhaps, there is no difference between activity and inactivity; both have measurable economic effects on commerce. But the distinction between doing something and doing nothing would not have been lost on the Framers, who were "practical statesmen," not metaphysical philosophers. . . . The Framers gave Congress the power to regulate commerce, not to compel it, and for over 200 years both our decisions and Congress's actions have reflected this understanding. There is no reason to depart from that understanding now.

The Government sees things differently. It argues that because sickness and injury are unpredictable but unavoidable, "the uninsured as a class are active in the market for health care, which they regularly seek and obtain." The individual mandate "merely regulates how individuals finance and pay for that active participation—requiring that they do so through insurance, rather than through attempted self-insurance with the back-stop of shifting costs to others." . . .

The individual mandate's regulation of the uninsured as a class is, in fact, particularly divorced from any link to existing commercial activity. The mandate primarily affects healthy, often young adults who are less likely to need significant health care and have other priorities for spending their money. It is precisely because these individuals, as an actuarial class, incur relatively low health care costs that the mandate helps counter the effect of forcing insurance companies to cover others who impose greater costs than their premiums are allowed to reflect. If the individual mandate is targeted at a class, it is a class whose commercial inactivity rather than activity is its defining feature.

The Government, however, claims that this does not matter. The Government regards it as sufficient to trigger Congress's authority that almost all those who are uninsured will, at some unknown point in the future, engage in a health care transaction. . . .

The proposition that Congress may dictate the conduct of an individual today because of prophesied future activity finds no support in our precedent. . . .

Everyone will likely participate in the markets for food, clothing, transportation, shelter, or energy; that does not authorize Congress to direct them to purchase particular products in those or other markets today. The Commerce Clause is not a general license to regulate an individual from cradle to grave, simply because he will predictably engage in particular transactions. . . .

The Government says that health insurance and health care financing are "inherently integrated." But that does not mean the compelled purchase of the first is properly regarded as a regulation of the second. No matter how "inherently integrated" health insurance and health care consumption may be, they are not the same thing: They involve different transactions, entered into at different times, with different providers. And for most of those targeted by the mandate, significant health care needs will be years, or even decades, away. The proximity and degree of connection between the mandate and the subsequent commercial activity is too lacking to justify an exception of the sort urged by the Government. The individual mandate forces individuals into commerce precisely because they elected to refrain from commercial activity. Such a law cannot be sustained under a clause authorizing Congress to "regulate Commerce."

The Government next contends that Congress has the power under the Necessary and Proper Clause to enact the individual mandate because the mandate is an "integral part of a comprehensive scheme of economic regulation." . . .

The power to "make all Laws which shall be necessary and proper for carrying into Execution" the powers enumerated in the Constitution vests Congress with authority to enact provisions "incidental to the [enumerated] power,

and conducive to its beneficial exercise." *McCulloch.* Although the Clause gives Congress authority to "legislate on that vast mass of incidental powers which must be involved in the constitution," it does not license the exercise of any "great substantive and independent power[s]" beyond those specifically enumerated. Instead, the Clause is "'merely a declaration, for the removal of all uncertainty, that the means of carrying into execution those [powers] otherwise granted are included in the grant.'" *Kinsella v. United States ex rel. Singleton* (1960).

As our jurisprudence under the Necessary and Proper Clause has developed, we have been very deferential to Congress's determination that a regulation is "necessary." We have thus upheld laws that are "'convenient, or useful' or 'conducive' to the authority's 'beneficial exercise.'" *Comstock.* But we have also carried out our responsibility to declare unconstitutional those laws that undermine the structure of government established by the Constitution. Such laws, which are not "consist[ent] with the letter and spirit of the constitution," *McCulloch,* are not "proper [means] for carrying into Execution" Congress's enumerated powers. Rather, they are, "in the words of The Federalist, 'merely acts of usurpation' which 'deserve to be treated as such.'" *Printz v. United States* (1997).

Applying these principles, the individual mandate cannot be sustained under the Necessary and Proper Clause as an essential component of the insurance reforms. Each of our prior cases upholding laws under that Clause involved exercises of authority derivative of, and in service to, a granted power. For example, we have upheld provisions permitting continued confinement of those already in federal custody when they could not be safely released, *Comstock.* The individual mandate, by contrast, vests Congress with the extraordinary ability to create the necessary predicate to the exercise of an enumerated power.

This is in no way an authority that is "narrow in scope," *Comstock,* or "incidental" to the exercise of the commerce power, *McCulloch.* Rather, such a conception of the Necessary and Proper Clause would work a substantial expansion of federal authority. No longer would Congress be limited to regulating under the Commerce Clause those who by some preexisting activity bring themselves within the sphere of federal regulation. Instead, Congress could reach beyond the natural limit of its authority and draw within its regulatory scope those who otherwise would be outside of it. Even if the individual mandate is "necessary" to the Act's insurance reforms, such an expansion of federal power is not a "proper" means for making those reforms effective. . . .

Just as the individual mandate cannot be sustained as a law regulating the substantial effects of the failure to purchase health insurance, neither can it be upheld as a "necessary and proper" component of the insurance reforms. The commerce power thus does not authorize the mandate.

JUSTICE GINSBURG, with whom JUSTICE SOTOMAYOR joins, and with whom JUSTICE BREYER and JUSTICE KAGAN join . . . concurring in part, concurring in the judgment in part, and dissenting in part.

Unlike The Chief Justice, . . . I would hold . . . that the Commerce Clause authorizes Congress to enact the minimum coverage provision. . . .

Since 1937, our precedent has recognized Congress' large authority to set the Nation's course in the economic and social welfare realm. See *United States v. Darby* (1941); *NLRB v. Jones & Laughlin Steel Corp.* (1937). The Chief Justice's crabbed reading of the Commerce Clause harks back to the era in which the Court routinely thwarted Congress' efforts to regulate the national economy in the interest of those who labor to sustain it. It is a reading that should not have staying power.

In enacting the Patient Protection and Affordable Care Act (ACA), Congress comprehensively reformed the national market for health-care products and services. By any measure, that market is immense. Collectively, Americans spent $2.5 trillion on health care in 2009, accounting for 17.6% of our Nation's economy. Within the next decade, it is anticipated, spending on health care will nearly double.

The health-care market's size is not its only distinctive feature. Unlike the market for almost any other product or service, the market for medical care is one in which all individuals inevitably participate. Virtually every person residing in the United States, sooner or later, will visit a doctor or other health-care professional. . . .

When individuals make those visits, they face another reality of the current market for medical care: its high cost. In 2010, on average, an individual in the United States incurred over $7,000 in health-care expenses. Over a lifetime, costs mount to hundreds of thousands of dollars. . . .

Although every U.S. domiciliary will incur significant medical expenses during his or her lifetime, the time when care will be needed is often unpredictable. . . .

To manage the risks associated with medical care—its high cost, its unpredictability, and its inevitability—most people in the United States obtain health insurance. . . .

Not all U.S. residents, however, have health insurance. In 2009, approximately 50 million people were uninsured, either by choice or, more likely, because they could not afford private insurance and did not qualify for government aid. As a group, uninsured individuals annually consume more than $100 billion in health-care services, nearly 5% of the Nation's total. Over 60% of those without insurance visit a doctor's office or emergency room in a given year.

The large number of individuals without health insurance, Congress found, heavily burdens the national health-care market. . . . Unlike markets for most products, however, the inability to pay for care does not mean that an uninsured individual will receive no care. Federal and state law, as well as professional obligations and embedded social norms, require hospitals and physicians to provide care when it is most needed, regardless of the patient's ability to pay.

As a consequence, medical-care providers deliver significant amounts of care to the uninsured for which the providers receive no payment. In 2008, for example, hospitals, physicians, and other health-care professionals received no compensation for $43 billion worth of the $116 billion in care they administered to those without insurance.

Health-care providers do not absorb these bad debts. Instead, they raise their prices, passing along the cost of uncompensated care to those who do pay reliably: the government and private insurance companies. In response, private insurers increase their premiums, shifting the cost of the elevated bills from providers onto those who carry insurance. The net result: Those with health insurance subsidize the medical care of those without it. As economists would describe what happens, the uninsured "free ride" on those who pay for health insurance.

The size of this subsidy is considerable. Congress found that the cost-shifting just described "increases family [insurance] premiums by on average over $1,000 a year." Higher premiums, in turn, render health insurance less affordable, forcing more people to go without insurance and leading to further cost-shifting. . . .

States cannot resolve the problem of the uninsured on their own. . . .

Aware that a national solution was required, . . . Congress enacted the ACA, a solution that retains a robust role for private insurers and state governments. To make its chosen approach work, however, Congress had to use some new tools, including a requirement that most individuals obtain private health insurance coverage. . . . [B]y employing these tools, Congress was able to achieve a practical, altogether reasonable, solution. . . .

. . . Congress passed the minimum coverage provision as a key component of the ACA to address an economic and social problem that has plagued the Nation for decades: the large number of U.S. residents who are unable or unwilling to obtain health insurance. Whatever one thinks of the policy decision Congress made, it was Congress' prerogative to make it. Reviewed with appropriate deference, the minimum coverage provision, allied to the guaranteed-issue and community-rating prescriptions, should survive measurement under the Commerce and Necessary and Proper Clauses.

The Commerce Clause, it is widely acknowledged, "was the Framers' response to the central problem that gave rise to the Constitution itself." Under the Articles of Confederation, the Constitution's precursor, the regulation of commerce was left to the States. This scheme proved unworkable, because the individual States, understandably focused on their own economic interests, often failed to take actions critical to the success of the Nation as a whole. . . . The Framers' solution was the Commerce Clause, which, as they perceived it, granted Congress the authority to enact economic legislation "in all Cases for the general Interests of the Union, and also in those Cases to which the States are separately incompetent." . . .

Consistent with the Framers' intent, we have repeatedly emphasized that Congress' authority under the Commerce Clause is dependent upon "practical" considerations, including "actual experience." We afford Congress the leeway "to undertake to solve national problems directly and realistically."

Until today, this Court's pragmatic approach to judging whether Congress validly exercised its commerce power was guided by two familiar principles. First, Congress has the power to regulate economic activities "that substantially affect interstate commerce." *Gonzales v. Raich* (2005). This capacious power extends even to local activities that, viewed in the aggregate, have a substantial impact on interstate commerce.

Second, we owe a large measure of respect to Congress when it frames and enacts economic and social legislation. When appraising such legislation, we ask only (1) whether Congress had a "rational basis" for concluding that the regulated activity substantially affects interstate commerce, and (2) whether there is a "reasonable connection between the regulatory means selected and the asserted ends." In answering these questions, we presume the statute under review is constitutional and may strike it down only on a "plain showing" that Congress acted irrationally.

Straightforward application of these principles would require the Court to hold that the minimum coverage provision is proper Commerce Clause legislation. Beyond

dispute, Congress had a rational basis for concluding that the uninsured, as a class, substantially affect interstate commerce. Those without insurance consume billions of dollars of health-care products and services each year. Those goods are produced, sold, and delivered largely by national and regional companies who routinely transact business across state lines. The uninsured also cross state lines to receive care. Some have medical emergencies while away from home. Others, when sick, go to a neighboring State that provides better care for those who have not prepaid for care.

Not only do those without insurance consume a large amount of health care each year; critically, as earlier explained, their inability to pay for a significant portion of that consumption drives up market prices, foists costs on other consumers, and reduces market efficiency and stability. Given these far-reaching effects on interstate commerce, the decision to forgo insurance is hardly inconsequential or equivalent to "doing nothing"; it is, instead, an economic decision Congress has the authority to address under the Commerce Clause.

The minimum coverage provision, furthermore, bears a "reasonable connection" to Congress' goal of protecting the health-care market from the disruption caused by individuals who fail to obtain insurance. By requiring those who do not carry insurance to pay a toll, the minimum coverage provision gives individuals a strong incentive to insure. This incentive, Congress had good reason to believe, would reduce the number of uninsured and, correspondingly, mitigate the adverse impact the uninsured have on the national health-care market.

Congress also acted reasonably in requiring uninsured individuals, whether sick or healthy, either to obtain insurance or to pay the specified penalty. As earlier observed, because every person is at risk of needing care at any moment, all those who lack insurance, regardless of their current health status, adversely affect the price of health care and health insurance. . . .

Rather than evaluating the constitutionality of the minimum coverage provision in the manner established by our precedents, The Chief Justice relies on a newly minted constitutional doctrine. The commerce power does not, The Chief Justice announces, permit Congress to "compe[l] individuals to become active in commerce by purchasing a product."

The Chief Justice's novel constraint on Congress' commerce power gains no force from our precedent and for that reason alone warrants disapprobation. But even assuming, for the moment, that Congress lacks authority under the Commerce Clause to "compel individuals not engaged in commerce to purchase an unwanted product," such a limitation would be inapplicable here. Everyone will, at some point, consume health-care products and services. Thus, if The Chief Justice is correct that an insurance-purchase requirement can be applied only to those who "actively" consume health care, the minimum coverage provision fits the bill. . . .

Our decisions . . . acknowledge Congress' authority, under the Commerce Clause, to direct the conduct of an individual today (the farmer in *Wickard*, stopped from growing excess wheat; the plaintiff in *Raich*, ordered to cease cultivating marijuana) because of a prophesied future transaction (the eventual sale of that wheat or marijuana in the interstate market). Congress' actions are even more rational in this case, where the future activity (the consumption of medical care) is certain to occur, the sole uncertainty being the time the activity will take place. . . .

In any event, The Chief Justice's limitation of the commerce power to the regulation of those actively engaged in commerce finds no home in the text of the Constitution or our decisions. Article I, §8, of the Constitution grants Congress the power "[t]o regulate Commerce . . . among the several States." Nothing in this language implies that Congress' commerce power is limited to regulating those actively engaged in commercial transactions. . . .

For the reasons explained above, the minimum coverage provision is valid Commerce Clause legislation. When viewed as a component of the entire ACA, the provision's constitutionality becomes even plainer.

The Necessary and Proper Clause "empowers Congress to enact laws in effectuation of its [commerce] powe[r] that are not within its authority to enact in isolation." Hence, "[a] complex regulatory program . . . can survive a Commerce Clause challenge without a showing that every single facet of the program is independently and directly related to a valid congressional goal." "It is enough that the challenged provisions are an integral part of the regulatory program and that the regulatory scheme when considered as a whole satisfies this test."

Recall that one of Congress' goals in enacting the Affordable Care Act was to eliminate the insurance industry's practice of charging higher prices or denying coverage to individuals with preexisting medical conditions. The commerce power allows Congress to ban this practice, a point no one disputes.

Congress knew, however, that simply barring insurance companies from relying on an applicant's medical history would not work in practice. Without the individual mandate, Congress learned, guaranteed-issue and community-rating requirements would trigger an adverse-selection death-spiral in the health-insurance market: Insurance premiums would skyrocket, the number of uninsured would increase, and insurance companies would exit the market. When complemented by an insurance mandate, on the other hand, guaranteed issue and community rating would work as intended, increasing access to insurance and reducing uncompensated care. The minimum coverage provision is thus an "essential par[t] of a larger regulation of economic activity"; without the provision, "the regulatory scheme [w]ould be undercut." *Raich*. Put differently, the minimum coverage provision, together with the guaranteed-issue and community-rating requirements, is "'reasonably adapted' to the attainment of a legitimate end under the commerce power": the elimination of pricing and sales practices that take an applicant's medical history into account.

Asserting that the Necessary and Proper Clause does not authorize the minimum coverage provision, The Chief Justice focuses on the word "proper." A mandate to purchase health insurance is not "proper" legislation, The Chief Justice urges, because the command "undermine[s] the structure of government established by the Constitution." If long on rhetoric, The Chief Justice's argument is short on substance. . . .

The Chief Justice [does not] pause to explain *why* the power to direct either the purchase of health insurance or, alternatively, the payment of a penalty collectible as a tax is more far-reaching than other implied powers this Court has found meet under the Necessary and Proper Clause. These powers include the power to enact criminal laws; the power to imprison, including civil imprisonment, see, *e.g.*, *Comstock*; and the power to create a national bank, see *McCulloch*.

In failing to explain why the individual mandate threatens our constitutional order, The Chief Justice disserves future courts. How is a judge to decide, when ruling on the constitutionality of a federal statute, whether Congress employed an "independent power" or merely a "derivative" one. Whether the power used is "substantive" or just "incidental"? The instruction The Chief Justice, in effect, provides lower courts: You will know it when you see it. . . .

In the early 20th century, this Court regularly struck down economic regulation enacted by the peoples' representatives in both the States and the Federal Government. See, *e.g.*, *Carter Coal Co.*, *Dagenhart*, *Lochner v. New York* (1905). The Chief Justice's Commerce Clause opinion, and even more so the joint dissenters' reasoning, bear a disquieting resemblance to those long-overruled decisions.

Joint Opinion of JUSTICE SCALIA, JUSTICE KENNEDY, JUSTICE THOMAS, and JUSTICE ALITO, dissenting.

Congress has set out to remedy the problem that the best health care is beyond the reach of many Americans who cannot afford it. It can assuredly do that, by exercising the powers accorded to it under the Constitution. The question in this case, however, is whether the complex structures and provisions of the Patient Protection and Affordable Care Act go beyond those powers. We conclude that they do.

. . . What is absolutely clear, affirmed by the text of the 1789 Constitution, by the Tenth Amendment ratified in 1791, and by innumerable cases of ours in the 220 years since, is that there are structural limits upon federal power—upon what it can prescribe with respect to private conduct, and upon what it can impose upon the sovereign States. . . .

That clear principle carries the day here. The striking case of *Wickard v. Filburn* (1942), which held that the economic activity of growing wheat, even for one's own consumption, affected commerce sufficiently that it could be regulated, always has been regarded as the *ne plus ultra* of expansive Commerce Clause jurisprudence. To go beyond that, and to say the failure to grow wheat (which is not an economic activity, or any activity at all) nonetheless affects commerce and therefore can be federally regulated, is to make mere breathing in and out the basis for federal prescription and to extend federal power to virtually all human activity. . . .

Article I, §8, of the Constitution gives Congress the power to "regulate Commerce . . . among the several States." The Individual Mandate in the Act commands that every "applicable individual shall for each month beginning after 2013 ensure that the individual, and any dependent of the individual who is an applicable individual, is covered under minimum essential coverage." If this provision "regulates" anything, it is the failure to maintain minimum essential coverage. One might argue that it regulates that failure by requiring it to be accompanied by payment of a penalty. But that failure—that abstention from commerce—is not "Commerce." To be sure, purchasing insurance is "Commerce"; but one does not regulate commerce that does not exist by compelling its existence. . . .

. . . Congress has impressed into service third parties, healthy individuals who could be but are not customers of the relevant industry, to offset the undesirable consequences of the regulation. Congress' desire to force these individuals to purchase insurance is motivated by the fact that they are further removed from the market than unhealthy individuals with pre-existing conditions, because they are less likely to need extensive care in the near future. If Congress can reach out and command even those furthest removed from an interstate market to participate in the market, then the Commerce Clause becomes a font of unlimited power, or in Hamilton's words, "the hideous monster whose devouring jaws . . . spare neither sex nor age, nor high nor low, nor sacred nor profane." *The Federalist* No. 3. . . .

Wickard v. Filburn has been regarded as the most expansive assertion of the commerce power in our history. A close second is *Perez v. United States* (1971), which upheld a statute criminalizing the eminently local activity of loan-sharking. Both of those cases, however, involved commercial activity. To go beyond that, and to say that the failure to grow wheat or the refusal to make loans affects commerce, so that growing and lending can be federally compelled, is to extend federal power to virtually everything. All of us consume food, and when we do so the Federal Government can prescribe what its quality must be and even how much we must pay. But the mere fact that we all consume food and are thus, sooner or later, participants in the "market" for food, does not empower the Government to say when and what we will buy. That is essentially what this Act seeks to do with respect to the purchase of health care. It exceeds federal power.

What should we make of the health-care decision? It is important to realize that while Roberts held that the mandate could not be sustained as an exercise of congressional commerce power, he did uphold it as a tax, as we will see in chapter 8. Moreover, even the holding on the commerce power may not be so far-reaching, because Congress has rarely forced people into commerce.[22] Finally, even if Congress does pass another law of this kind, it is not altogether clear that the Court would stand by the distinction drawn by Justice Roberts: it could adopt Ginsburg's dissenting position. For, as we have seen, commerce clause doctrine has not moved in a straight line; rather, it has varied greatly depending on the philosophies of the sitting justices.

---

22. Rarely is not never. For some early examples, see Einer Elhauge, "If Health Insurance Mandates Are Unconstitutional, Why Did the Founding Fathers Back Them?," *New Republic*, April 13, 2012.

COMMERCE POWER OF THE STATES

Resolving the question of federal power over interstate and foreign commerce leaves unsettled the question of state commercial regulation. Marshall wrote in *Gibbons* that commerce completely internal to the state that does not extend to or affect other states is reserved for state regulation. This grant of power was substantial prior to the Civil War, when most commercial activity was distinctly local and subject to state regulation. But with the Industrial Revolution and improved transportation systems, business quickly became interstate in nature. Finally, the Supreme Court's 1937 redefinition of interstate commerce left little that met Marshall's notion of commerce that is "completely internal."

If the regulation of any business activity that affects interstate commerce were the exclusive preserve of the federal government, the role of the states would be minimal indeed. But this is not the case. The decisions of the Supreme Court have left a substantial sphere of authority for the states to regulate commerce. The dividing line between federal and state power, however, has varied over time as the Court has struggled to formulate an appropriate doctrine to govern this difficult area of federal–state relations.

Doctrine of Selected Exclusiveness

Constructing the parameters of state power began in 1829 with the decision in ***Willson v. Black-Bird Creek Marsh Company.***[23] The dispute involved a Delaware law that authorized the building of a dam on a creek to stop water from entering a local marsh. Thompson Willson owned and operated a vessel that was federally licensed under the Coastal Licensing Act of 1793, the same legislation under which Thomas Gibbons had operated his steamboats. Willson objected to the dam as an impediment to commerce on a navigable stream. His ship purposefully rammed the dam, causing it considerable damage. The dam's owner took legal action against Willson, and the state courts ruled against Willson, who appealed, claiming that the Delaware law authorizing the dam was in conflict with the Constitution. He argued that only Congress had

the power to pass a law permitting the construction of an impediment to commerce on a navigable stream.

Chief Justice Marshall, speaking for the Court, rejected Willson's position. The justices concluded that, in the absence of federal laws to the contrary, the police powers of the state to regulate for the health and general welfare of its citizens were sufficient to authorize the dam. Indeed, Congress had not enacted any legislation dealing with commercial streams and the problems associated with marshland. "If congress had passed any act . . . the object of which was to control state legislation over those small navigable creeks into which the tide flows," Marshall's opinion stated, "we should feel not much difficulty in saying that a state law coming in conflict with such act would be void." The Court's decision in *Willson* began to carve out an area of state authority over commerce that is not purely intrastate, but where the boundaries of that authority were not yet settled.

With Marshall's death in 1835, his successor, Chief Justice Roger Taney, was left with the task of more sharply defining the commerce powers of the states. Taney was far more sympathetic to the states than Marshall had been, and it is not surprising that the rulings of the Taney era strike a balance between federal and state authority. The Taney Court first grappled with the problem in ***Mayor of New York v. Miln*** (1837), a case that had been carried over from the last Marshall term.

The dispute arose over the validity of New York's Passenger Act of 1824, which was designed to curb the flow of foreign indigents into the state. The law required the masters of incoming ships to supply the mayor of New York with comprehensive information on all passengers. This material was necessary for the city to enforce a regulation that allowed it to exclude people likely to require public assistance. Ship captains who did not comply were liable for fines and penalties of $75 per passenger. In addition, the law required that passengers who were refused entry be returned to their point of origin at the shipowner's expense. George Miln, who had a financial interest in a ship called *The Emily*, was fined when the ship's master refused to comply with the law. Miln protested the stiff $7,500 penalty on the ground that regulating foreign commerce was the exclusive jurisdiction of Congress, leaving no room for state action.

The Supreme Court upheld the New York law. In doing so, the justices did everything possible to avoid the complicated commerce issues the case presented. Instead, the Court followed the lead taken by Marshall

---

23. Disputes over the power of the states to impose taxes on interstate and foreign commerce actually had begun two years earlier in *Brown v. Maryland* (1827). We discuss the taxation issues in chapter 8, where the fiscal authority to tax and spend is our focus.

in *Willson* and focused on the state's police powers. According to Justice Philip Barbour's majority opinion, the states have the sovereign power to regulate for the well-being of their residents. That power is complete and unqualified. In the absence of federal commercial legislation to the contrary, there is nothing to bar the state from using its police authority, even if it affects foreign commerce as in the matter here. In fact, Barbour argued that it was the duty of the state to protect its citizens from the financial obligations that would result from admitting "multitudes of poor persons, who come from foreign countries without possessing the means of supporting themselves." As a consequence, a state may use its police powers to ward off the "moral pestilence of paupers, vagabonds, and possibly convicts." The Court has long since abandoned this attitude toward the poor.[24]

What the *Miln* decision revealed is the Taney Court's readiness to support state regulations in the absence of federal action. This thinking was consistent with the dual federalism philosophy of that time *(see chapter 6)*. But because the Court relied so heavily on the police powers, it failed to develop a complete doctrine of state commercial authority.

The *License Cases* of 1847 further revealed the difficulty the Taney Court had in crafting an adequate policy for the commerce powers of the states. These appeals came from New Hampshire, Rhode Island, and Massachusetts, where the legislatures had passed statutes licensing and taxing alcoholic beverages.[25] The regulations applied to domestic liquors as well as imported alcoholic beverages. Once again the Court upheld the laws as exercises of state police power, but the justices were badly divided as to rationale. No majority opinion was reached, an unusual occurrence for that time. In fact, six justices wrote opinions. All supported the state laws, but the highly fractionalized opinions provided no authoritative guidance for the states.

---

24. *Edwards v. California* (1941) effectively overruled *Miln*. In *Edwards* the justices struck down an "anti-Okie" law passed to discourage large numbers of people from Oklahoma and other states from moving into California in an effort to escape the economic depression caused by the effects of the Dust Bowl in the central states. The Court found that the law violated the right of citizens to travel freely among the various states.

25. The *License Cases* (1847) is the collective name given to the cases *Peirce v. New Hampshire*, *Fletcher v. Rhode Island*, and *Thurlow v. Massachusetts*.

Two years later the Court heard arguments in *Smith v. Turner* and *Norris v. Boston*, which are known as the *Passenger Cases* (1849). These appeals tested the constitutionality of New York and Massachusetts laws seeking to regulate foreigners coming into the United States. The legislation was intended to discourage indigent immigrants and to provide for the treatment of individuals who arrived for entry in a diseased condition. The laws included provisions for taxing, bonding, and record keeping. The New York law taxed each incoming ship $1.00–$1.50 per passenger. These fees were used to fund a hospital to treat arriving immigrants. The Massachusetts law prohibited the importation of passengers who were indigent or had physical or mental disabilities. In addition, Massachusetts charged arriving ships $2.00 for each passenger, with the proceeds going to a fund for immigrants who later required public assistance. George Smith and James Norris were British shipmasters. Smith landed in New York City with 290 immigrant passengers, and Norris docked in Boston with 19. Both protested the constitutionality of the taxes on commerce clause grounds.

The Court found these cases difficult to resolve. In fact, they were argued three times, and still the justices had trouble reaching a majority decision. Finally, by a 5–4 vote, the Court struck down the laws as being in conflict with the authority of Congress to regulate foreign commerce. The five justices in the majority each wrote an opinion. The four dissenters, led by Taney, adhered to the view that such regulations to protect a state's citizens from indigent and sick immigrants were within the states' police powers.

The *Passenger Cases* left the law unsettled. Not only was the decision in conflict with previous rulings, but also the Court had failed to produce an opinion supported by a majority of the justices. This situation demanded a ruling that would authoritatively explain the constitutional division between federal and state commerce powers, but instead many questions remained unanswered. Did Congress have the exclusive power to regulate interstate and foreign commerce, leaving no authority for the states? Could the states regulate such commerce only if Congress had failed to enact any relevant legislation? Was the commerce power concurrent? Could Congress delegate its regulatory power to the states? Three years after the *Passenger Cases*, in *Cooley v. Board of Wardens*, the justices issued a ruling that resolved some of the confusion.

Library of Congress

Philadelphia's ordinance regulating the use of pilots in the city's harbor was challenged as an infringement on the commerce power of the federal government. The Supreme Court upheld the ordinance in Cooley v. Board of Wardens, *stating that some aspects of interstate and foreign commerce are essentially local and can be regulated locally if Congress has not already passed laws to the contrary.*

Cooley v. Board of Wardens

53 U.S. (12 How.) 299 (1852)
http://laws.findlaw.com/us/53/299.html
Vote: 7 (Catron, Curtis, Daniel, Grier, McKinley, Nelson, Taney)
    2 (McLean, Wayne)

OPINION OF THE COURT: *Curtis*
CONCURRING OPINION: *Daniel*
DISSENTING OPINION: *McLean*

FACTS:

Based on its power over interstate and foreign commerce, Congress passed a statute in 1789 pertaining to the regulation of ports. The legislation said that until Congress acted otherwise, state and local authorities would continue to control the nation's ports and harbors. In 1803 Pennsylvania passed a port regulation law requiring that all vessels hire a local pilot to guide ships in and out of the Port of Philadelphia. Shipowners who did not comply were fined. The money from these fines was placed in a "charitable fund for the distressed or decayed pilots, their widows and children."

Aaron Cooley owned a vessel that sailed into Philadelphia without hiring a local pilot. The port's Board of Wardens took legal action against him, and Cooley was fined. He responded by claiming that the Pennsylvania law was unconstitutional; only Congress, he asserted, could regulate the port because the harbor was an integral part of interstate and foreign commerce, and the states had no constitutional authority to set regulations for such commerce. By implication, Cooley also was challenging the 1789 act of Congress that had delegated the powers to the states. The Pennsylvania Supreme Court upheld the law and the fine, and Cooley pressed his case to the U.S. Supreme Court.

ARGUMENTS:

For the plaintiff in error, Aaron B. Cooley:

- The Pennsylvania law violates the commerce clause because the power to regulate interstate and foreign commerce is exclusive to Congress. Regulations of navigation are regulations of commerce and within the jurisdiction of Congress.

- In legislation of the type at issue here, Congress can neither confer on the states powers not given them by the Constitution nor enable them to legislate on subjects clearly within the powers of Congress.

For the defendants in error, the Board of Wardens of the Port of Philadelphia et al.:

- The Pennsylvania law does not violate the commerce clause because the law does not regulate commerce. It was passed pursuant to the exercise of powers by the state—powers that the states never surrendered: to control their ports and to protect the property and lives of their citizens.
- The law is local in character and is an exercise of state police power designed to aid, not to regulate, commerce. See *City of New York v. Miln.*
- Even if the law is a regulation of commerce, the power of Congress is not exclusive. Because Congress has passed no conflicting legislation, the state law is valid.

◥ MR. JUSTICE CURTIS DELIVERED THE OPINION OF THE COURT.

That the power to regulate commerce includes the regulation of navigation, we consider settled. And when we look to the nature of the service performed by pilots, to the relations which that service and its compensations bear to navigation between the several States, and between the ports of the United States and foreign countries, we are brought to the conclusion, that the regulation of the qualifications of pilots, of the modes and times of offering and rendering their services, of the responsibilities which shall rest upon them, of the powers they shall possess, of the compensation they may demand, and of the penalties by which their rights and duties may be enforced, do constitute regulations of navigation, and consequently of commerce, within the just meaning of this clause of the Constitution. . . .

Nor should it be lost sight of, that this subject of the regulation of pilots and pilotage has an intimate connection with, and an important relation to the general subject of commerce with foreign nations and among the several States, over which it was one main object of the Constitution to create a national control. Conflicts between the laws of neighboring States, and discriminations favorable or adverse to commerce with particular foreign

nations, might be created by State laws regulating pilotage, deeply affecting that equality of commercial rights, and that freedom from State interference, which those who formed the Constitution were so anxious to secure, and which the experience of more than half a century has taught us to value so highly. . . .

It becomes necessary, therefore, to consider whether this law of Pennsylvania, being a regulation of commerce, is valid.

The act of Congress of the 7th of August, 1789, sect. 4, is as follows:

"That all pilots in the bays, inlets, rivers, harbors, and ports of the United States shall continue to be regulated in conformity with the existing laws of the States, respectively, wherein such pilots may be, or with such laws as the States may respectively hereafter enact for the purpose, until further legislative provision shall be made by Congress."

If the law of Pennsylvania, now in question, had been in existence at the date of this act of Congress, we might hold it to have been adopted by Congress, and thus made a law of the United States, and so valid. Because this act does, in effect, give the force of an act of Congress, to the then existing State laws on this subject, so long as they should continue unrepealed by the State which enacted them.

But the law on which these actions are founded was not enacted till 1803. What effect then can be attributed to so much of the act of 1789, as declares, that pilots shall continue to be regulated in conformity, "with such laws as the States may respectively hereafter enact for the purpose, until further legislative provision shall be made by Congress"?

If the States were divested of the power to legislate on this subject by the grant of the commercial power to Congress, it is plain this act could not confer upon them power thus to legislate. If the Constitution excluded the States from making any law regulating commerce, certainly Congress cannot regrant, or in any manner reconvey to the States that power. And yet this act of 1789 gives its sanction only to laws enacted by the States. This necessarily implies a constitutional power to legislate; for only a rule created by the sovereign power of a State acting in its legislative capacity, can be deemed a law, enacted by a State; and if the State has so limited its sovereign power that it no longer extends to a particular subject, manifestly it cannot, in any proper sense, be said to enact laws thereon. Entertaining these views we are brought directly and unavoidably to the consideration of the question, whether the grant of the commercial power to Congress, did *per se* deprive the States of all power to regulate pilots. This question has never been decided by this court, nor, in our judgment, has any case depending upon all the considerations which must govern this one, come before this court. The grant of commercial power to Congress does not contain any terms which expressly exclude the States from exercising an authority over its subject matter. If they are excluded it must be because the nature of the power, thus granted to Congress, requires that a similar authority should not exist in the States. If it were conceded on the one side, that the nature of this power, like that to legislate for the District of Columbia, is absolutely and totally repugnant to the existence of similar power in the States, probably no one would deny that the grant of the power to Congress, as effectually and perfectly excludes the States from all future legislation on the subject, as if express words had been used to exclude them. And on the other hand, if it were admitted that the existence of this power in Congress, like the power of taxation, is compatible with the existence of a similar power in the States, then it would be in conformity with the contemporary exposition of the Constitution (*Federalist*, No. 32) and with the judicial construction, given from time to time by this court, after the most deliberate consideration, to hold that the mere grant of such a power to Congress, did not imply a prohibition on the States to exercise the same power; that it is not the mere existence of such a power, but its exercise by Congress, which may be incompatible with the exercise of the same power by the States, and that the States may legislate in the absence of congressional regulations.

The diversities of opinion, therefore, which have existed on this subject, have arisen from the different views taken of the nature of this power. But when the nature of a power like this is spoken of, when it is said that the nature of the power requires that it should be exercised exclusively by Congress, it must be intended to refer to the subjects of that power, and to say they are of such a nature as to require exclusive legislation by Congress. Now the power to regulate commerce, embraces a vast field, containing not only many, but exceedingly various subjects, quite unlike in their nature; some imperatively demanding a single uniform rule, operating equally on the commerce of the United States in every port; and some, like the subject now in question, as imperatively demanding that diversity, which alone can meet the local necessities of navigation.

Either absolutely to affirm, or deny that the nature of this power requires exclusive legislation by Congress, is to lose sight of the nature of the subjects of this power, and to assert concerning all of them, what is really applicable but to a part. Whatever subjects of this power are in their nature national, or admit only of one uniform system, or plan of regulation, may justly be said to be of such a nature as to require exclusive legislation by Congress. That this cannot be affirmed of laws for the regulation of pilots and pilotage is plain. The act of 1789 contains a clear and authoritative declaration by the first Congress, that the nature of this subject is such, that until Congress should find it necessary to exert its power, it should be left to the legislation of the States; that it is local and not national; that it is likely to be the best provided for, not by one system, or plan of regulations, but by as many as the legislative discretion of the several States should deem applicable to the local peculiarities of the ports within their limits.

Viewed in this light, so much of this act of 1789 as declares that pilots shall continue to be regulated "by such laws as the States may respectively hereafter enact for that purpose," instead of being held to be inoperative, as an attempt to confer on the States a power to legislate, of which the Constitution had deprived them, is allowed an appropriate and important signification. It manifests the understanding of Congress, at the outset of the government, that the nature of this subject is not such as to require its exclusive legislation. The practice of the States, and of the national government, has been in conformity with this declaration, from the origin of the national government to this time; and the nature of the subject when examined, is such as to leave no doubt of the superior fitness and propriety, not to say the absolute necessity, of different systems of regulation, drawn from local knowledge and experience, and conformed to local wants. How then can we say, that by the mere grant of power to regulate commerce, the States are deprived of all the power to legislate on this subject, because from the nature of the power the legislation of Congress must be exclusive. . . .

It is the opinion of a majority of the court that the mere grant to Congress of the power to regulate commerce, did not deprive the States of power to regulate pilots, and that although Congress has legislated on this subject, its legislation manifests an intention, with a single exception, not to regulate this subject, but to leave its regulation to the several States. To these precise questions, which are all we are called on to decide, this opinion must be understood to be confined. It does not extend to the question what other subjects, under the commercial power, are within the exclusive control of Congress, or may be regulated by the States in the absence of all congressional legislation; nor to the general question how far any regulation of a subject by Congress, may be deemed to operate as an exclusion of all legislation by the States upon the same subject. We decide the precise questions before us, upon what we deem sound principles, applicable to this particular subject in the state in which the legislation of Congress has left it. We go no further. . . .

We are of opinion that this State law was enacted by virtue of a power, residing in the State to legislate; that it is not in conflict with any law of Congress; that it does not interfere with any system which Congress has established by making regulations, or by intentionally leaving individuals to their own unrestricted action; that this law is therefore valid, and the judgment of the Supreme Court of Pennsylvania in each case must be affirmed.

Justice Benjamin Curtis's opinion in *Cooley* nicely outlines the basic constitutional principles governing the state's power to regulate commerce. From this decision and those that preceded it, we can begin to build some understanding of how far the states may go in regulating commercial enterprise:

1. The states retain the power to regulate purely intrastate commerce.

2. Congress has the power to regulate interstate and foreign commerce. When it exercises this power, any contrary state laws are preempted.

3. The power of Congress to regulate interstate and foreign commerce is exclusive over those elements of commercial activity that are national in scope or require uniform regulation.

4. Those elements of interstate and foreign commerce that are not national in scope or do not require uniformity, and that have not been regulated by Congress, may be subject to state authority, including the states' police powers.

This division of authority is known as the doctrine of selected exclusiveness. It designates certain aspects of interstate and foreign commerce over which the powers of Congress are exclusive, allowing no state action. This exclusiveness, however, is not complete; in the absence of federal legislation, states may regulate some local business activity affecting interstate commerce. The regulation of the Philadelphia port is an obvious part of interstate and foreign commerce where local harbor conditions require state supervision.

State Burdens on Interstate Commerce: The Dormant Commerce Clause

Under the Articles of Confederation the states often imposed protective barriers that obstructed interstate business activity and impeded the growth of the national economy. To protect against such state policies, the framers gave Congress the authority to regulate interstate and foreign commerce. The goal was to promote free and robust commercial activity. Under the doctrine of selective exclusiveness, however, the states retained some powers to regulate commerce and potentially could use those powers to thwart the purposes of the commerce clause.

In 1803 John Marshall, writing in *Marbury v. Madison,* declared, "Affirmative words are often, in their operation, negative of other objects than those affirmed." Almost two centuries later, Justice John Paul Stevens echoed this proposition, noting in *Quill Corp. v. North Dakota* (1992), "[T]he Commerce Clause is more than an affirmative grant of power; it has a negative sweep as well." Over the years the justices have often applied this principle to the state regulation of commercial activity: the affirmative grant of power to the federal government to regulate interstate and foreign commerce implies that the states are prohibited from regulating in ways that are detrimental to the national economy—even if Congress does not explicitly bar them from doing so. The Court, therefore, creates a balancing situation. In the absence of federal laws to the contrary, states for valid reasons may regulate local commercial activities, but those regulations may not negatively and unreasonably affect interstate commerce.

The justices refer to this interpretation as the "dormant" or "negative" commerce clause. This jurisprudence recognizes that although the commerce clause is a positive grant of power to the federal government, it carries with it a negative command against certain state actions. The Court has been particularly concerned with state policies that either burden interstate and foreign commerce or discriminate against them in favor of state interests. Applying the dormant commerce clause approach, such state regulations are contrary to the Constitution.

State Burdens on Interstate Commerce. Among the essentially local aspects of interstate commerce are matters of public safety. Interstate trucking provides a good illustration. The use of trucks for the transportation of goods is an integral part of interstate commerce, but trucks use local roads that are the state's concern. One of the primary elements of a state's police powers is regulation to ensure the safety of its citizens, and safety regulations may impose a burden on interstate commerce.

The Supreme Court addressed this conflict in 1938 in **South Carolina State Highway Department v. Barnwell Brothers.** For purposes of public safety and to prevent damage to the state's highways, the South Carolina legislature passed a statute prohibiting certain trucks from using the highways. No truck with a gross weight in excess of twenty thousand pounds or a width greater than ninety inches was permitted. Barnwell Brothers Trucking Company challenged the regulation as an unreasonable burden on interstate commerce. Evidence presented at trial showed that between 85 percent and 90 percent of all interstate trucks were ninety-six inches wide and weighed more than the prescribed limit. Only four other states had weight limits as low as South Carolina's, and none had width restrictions as severe. Based on this information, the trial court ruled that the state law was an unconstitutional burden on the flow of interstate commerce.

The Supreme Court reversed. Justice Stone's opinion for the Court noted that "[t]he commerce clause, by its own force, prohibits discrimination against interstate commerce, whatever its form or method." States consequently are prohibited from giving a preference to intrastate businesses at the expense of interstate commerce or placing unreasonable burdens on out-of-state businesses. Stone, however, wrote, "There are matters of local concern, the regulation of which unavoidably involves some regulation of interstate commerce but which, because of their local character and their number and diversity, may never be fully dealt with by Congress." The regulation of such matters, in the absence of federal legislation, is best left to the states. Congress has recognized this situation by allowing state and local governments to have a say in the regulation of highways, ports, harbors, rivers, and docks. Congress also has not prohibited certain quarantine laws imposed by the states. Naturally, Congress may act in any of these areas when it determines that uniform national legislation is required.

In their 7–0 decision the justices held that South Carolina's regulation of trucks using the state highways fell into this category. Because of an absence of federal legislation over highway safety and because the state regulations applied to vehicles in intra- and interstate

commerce equally, the state law was not in violation of the Constitution.

Still, *Barnwell Brothers* left a number of issues unresolved: How far may a state go in regulating interstate commerce for safety purposes? How much of a burden may be imposed on the free flow of commerce among the states to achieve greater safety? Were the highways, which the states built, owned, and maintained, a special case, or did state authority similarly extend to other areas of interstate commerce? The justices took another look at these issues in *Southern Pacific Company v. Arizona* (1945). Once again Stone wrote the opinion for the Court, but this time the outcome was different. Was *Southern Pacific* consistent with *Barnwell Brothers*, or did the Court modify its position?

Southern Pacific Company v. Arizona

325 U.S. 761 (1945)
http://laws.findlaw.com/us/325/761.html
Vote: 7 (Frankfurter, Jackson, Murphy, Reed, Roberts, Rutledge, Stone)
    2 (Black, Douglas)
OPINION FOR THE COURT: Stone
DISSENTING OPINIONS: Black, Douglas

FACTS:

On May 16, 1912, the Arizona legislature passed the Train Limit Law, making it unlawful for any individual or corporation to operate a train with more than fourteen passenger cars or seventy freight cars within the state. Violators were subject to fines. In 1940 the state brought a legal action against Southern Pacific Company, which acknowledged operating passenger and freight trains in excess of the state limits. The company argued that the state law was unconstitutional because it conflicted with the commerce clause.

The jury returned a verdict for the company, but the state supreme court reversed, holding that Arizona was free to enact such regulations because Congress had not legislated the length of railroad trains. The Arizona law was a safety measure that could be justified as an exercise of the state's police powers to act in the interests of local health, safety, and well-being. The railroad appealed the ruling to the U.S. Supreme Court, arguing that the state law placed an undue burden on the flow of interstate commerce. In presenting its case, Southern Pacific enjoyed the support of two powerful allies: the U.S. government and the Association of American Railroads submitted amicus curiae briefs attacking the constitutionality of the state law.

For the appellant, Southern Pacific Company:

- The state law violates the commerce clause because it regulates a matter of national, not solely local, concern. Only Congress can determine whether a uniform system of regulation is needed, and only Congress can enact such measures. The power to regulate commerce is necessarily exclusive when it is exercised over subjects that are national in character or require a single plan of regulation.

- The Court must strike down the state law because it frustrates the principal goals of the commerce clause as outlined in previous decisions: to preserve the interests of the nation against conflicting and discriminatory state legislation and to guard against obstructions of the free flow of commerce. This law imposes a serious burden on interstate commerce by hindering efficient train service.

- The law invades a field of regulation of commerce that Congress fully occupies, as previous federal laws regulating trains indicate. Congressional silence or inaction over the matter here is the same as a declaration that interstate commerce should remain free and unobstructed.

For the appellee, state of Arizona:

- The state law does not invade a national field exclusively reserved to Congress. It has a real relation to the safety and protection of Arizona's citizens and is not an area in which Congress has regulated.

- It is up to Congress, not the courts, to determine whether a state can exercise its reserved police powers in a way that might indirectly affect interstate commerce. Congress does this by permissibly occupying a field under its commerce power, which it has not done here. But even the courts have recognized that states have legitimately regulated in areas that require regulation until Congress intervenes.

- Whether the state law imposes an impermissible burden on interstate commerce is a question Congress, not the courts, should address through appropriate legislative means. Even so, the financial burden is not as substantial as appellant contends.

▶ MR. CHIEF JUSTICE STONE DELIVERED THE OPINION OF THE COURT.

Although the commerce clause conferred on the national government power to regulate commerce, its possession of the power does not exclude all state power of regulation. Ever since *Willson v. Black-Bird Creek Marsh Co.* and *Cooley v. Board of Wardens*, it has been recognized that, in the absence of conflicting legislation by Congress, there is a residuum of power in the state to make laws governing matters of local concern which nevertheless in some measure affect interstate commerce or even, to some extent, regulate it. Thus the states may regulate matters which, because of their number and diversity, may never be adequately dealt with by Congress. *Cooley v. Board of Wardens, South Carolina Highway Dept. v. Barnwell Bros.* When the regulation of matters of local concern is local in character and effect, and its impact on the national commerce does not seriously interfere with its operation, and the consequent incentive to deal with them nationally is slight, such regulation has been generally held to be within state authority.

But ever since *Gibbons v. Ogden*, the states have not been deemed to have authority to impede substantially the free flow of commerce from state to state, or to regulate those phases of the national commerce which, because of the need of national uniformity, demand that their regulation, if any, be prescribed by a single authority. Whether or not this long-recognized distribution of power between the national and the state governments is predicated upon the implications of the commerce clause itself, or upon the presumed intention of Congress, where Congress has not spoken, the result is the same.

In the application of these principles some enactments may be found to be plainly within and others plainly without state power. But between these extremes lies the infinite variety of cases, in which regulation of local matters may also operate as a regulation of commerce, in which reconciliation of the conflicting claims of state and national power is to be attained only by some appraisal and accommodation of the competing demands of the state and national interests involved.

For a hundred years it has been accepted constitutional doctrine that the commerce clause, without the aid of Congressional legislation, thus affords some protection from state legislation inimical to the national commerce and that in such cases, where Congress has not acted, this Court, and not the state legislature, is under the commerce clause the final arbiter of the competing demands of state and national interests.

Congress has undoubted power to redefine the distribution of power over interstate commerce. It may either permit the states to regulate the commerce in a manner which would otherwise not be permissible, or exclude state regulation even of matters of peculiarly local concern which nevertheless affect interstate commerce.

But in general Congress has left it to the courts to formulate the rules thus interpreting the commerce clause in its application, doubtless because it has appreciated the destructive consequences to the commerce of the nation if their protection were withdrawn, and has been aware that in their application state laws will not be invalidated without the support of relevant factual material which will "afford a sure basis" for an informed judgment. Meanwhile, Congress has accommodated its legislation, as have the states, to these rules as an established feature of our constitutional system. There has thus been left to the states wide scope for the regulation of matters of local state concern, even though it in some measure affects the commerce, provided it does not materially restrict the free flow of commerce across state lines, or interfere with it in matters with respect to which uniformity of regulation is of predominant national concern.

Hence the matters for ultimate determination here are the nature and extent of the burden which the state regulation of interstate trains, adopted as a safety measure, imposes on interstate commerce, and whether the relative weights of the state and national interests involved are such as to make inapplicable the rule, generally observed, that the free flow of interstate commerce and its freedom from local restraints in matters requiring uniformity of regulation are interests safeguarded by the commerce clause from state interference. . . .

The findings show that the operation of long trains, that is trains of more than fourteen passenger and more than seventy freight cars, is standard practice over the main lines of the railroads of the United States, and that, if the length of trains is to be regulated at all, national uniformity in the regulation adopted, such as only Congress can prescribe, is practically indispensable to the operation of an efficient and economical national railway system. On many railroads passenger trains of more than fourteen cars and freight trains of more than seventy cars are operated, and on some systems freight trains are run ranging from one hundred and twenty-five to one hundred and sixty cars in length. Outside of Arizona, where the length of trains is not restricted, appellant runs a substantial proportion of long trains. In 1939 on its comparable route for through traffic through Utah and Nevada from 66 to 85% of its freight trains were over seventy cars in length and over 43% of its passenger trains included more than fourteen passenger cars.

In Arizona, approximately 93% of the freight traffic and 95% of the passenger traffic is interstate. Because of the Train Limit Law appellant is required to haul over 30% more trains in Arizona than would otherwise have been necessary. The record shows a definite relationship between operating costs and the length of trains, the increase in length resulting in a reduction of operating costs per car. The additional cost of operation of trains complying with the Train Limit Law in Arizona amounts for the two railroads traversing that state to about $1,000,000 a year. The reduction in train lengths also impedes efficient operation. More locomotives and more manpower are required; the necessary conversion and reconversion of train lengths at terminals and the delay caused by breaking up and remaking long trains upon entering and leaving the state in order to comply with the law, delays the traffic and diminishes its volume moved in a given time, especially when traffic is heavy. . . .

The unchallenged findings leave no doubt that the Arizona Train Limit Law imposes a serious burden on the interstate commerce conducted by appellant. It materially impedes the movement of appellant's interstate trains through that state and interposes a substantial obstruction to the national policy proclaimed by Congress, to promote adequate, economical and efficient railway transportation service. Enforcement of the law in Arizona, while train lengths remain unregulated or are regulated by varying standards in other states, must inevitably result in an impairment of uniformity of efficient railroad operation because the railroads are subjected to regulation which is not uniform in its application. Compliance with a state statute limiting train lengths requires interstate trains of a length lawful in other states to be broken up and reconstituted as they enter each state according as it may impose varying limitations upon train lengths. The alternative is for the carrier to conform to the lowest train limit restriction of any of the states through which its trains pass, whose laws thus control the carriers' operations both within and without the regulating state.

Although the seventy car maximum for freight trains is the limitation which has been commonly proposed, various bills introduced in the state legislatures provided for maximum freight train lengths of from fifty to one hundred and twenty-five cars, and maximum passenger train lengths of from ten to eighteen cars. With such laws in force in states which are interspersed with those having no limit on train lengths, the confusion and difficulty with which interstate operations would be burdened under the varied system of state regulation and the unsatisfied need for uniformity in such regulation, if any, are evident. . . .

We think, as the trial court found, that the Arizona Train Limit Law, viewed as a safety measure, affords at most slight and dubious advantage, if any, over unregulated train lengths, because it results in an increase in the number of trains and train operations and the consequent increase in train accidents of a character generally more severe than those due to slack action. Its undoubted effect on the commerce is the regulation, without securing uniformity, of the length of trains operated in interstate commerce, which lack is itself a primary cause of preventing the free flow of commerce by delaying it and by substantially increasing its cost and impairing its efficiency. In these respects the case differs from those where a state, by regulatory measures affecting the commerce, has removed or reduced safety hazards without substantial interference with the interstate movement of trains. Such are measures abolishing the car stove, requiring locomotives to be supplied with electric headlights, providing for full train crews, and for the equipment of freight trains with cabooses. . . .

Here we conclude that the state does go too far. Its regulation of train lengths, admittedly obstructive to interstate train operation, and having a seriously adverse effect on transportation efficiency and economy, passes beyond what is plainly essential for safety since it does not appear that it will lessen rather than increase the danger of accident. Its attempted regulation of the operation of interstate trains cannot establish nationwide control such as is essential to the maintenance of an efficient transportation system, which Congress alone can prescribe. The state interest cannot be preserved at the expense of the national interest by an enactment which regulates interstate train lengths without securing such control, which is a matter of national concern. To this the interest of the state here asserted is subordinate. . . .

Reversed.

MR. JUSTICE BLACK, dissenting.

[T]he determination of whether it is in the interest of society for the length of trains to be governmentally regulated is a matter of public policy. Someone must fix that policy—either the Congress, or the state, or the courts. A century and a half of constitutional history and government admonishes this Court to leave that choice to the elected legislative representatives of the people themselves, where it properly belongs both on democratic principles and the requirements of efficient government. . . .

Representatives elected by the people to make their laws, rather than judges appointed to interpret those laws, can best determine the policies which govern the people. That at least is the basic principle on which our democratic society rests. I would affirm the judgment of the Supreme Court of Arizona.

MR. JUSTICE DOUGLAS, dissenting.

I have expressed my doubts whether the courts should intervene in situations like the present and strike down state legislation on the grounds that it burdens interstate commerce. My view has been that the courts should intervene only where the state legislation discriminated against interstate commerce or was out of harmony with laws which Congress had enacted. It seems to me particularly appropriate that that course be followed here. For Congress has given the Interstate Commerce Commission broad powers of regulation over interstate carriers. The Commission is the national agency which has been entrusted with the task of promoting a safe, adequate, efficient, and economical transportation service. It is the expert on this subject. It is in a position to police the field. And if its powers prove inadequate for the task, Congress, which has paramount authority in this field, can implement them.

Chief Justice Stone's opinion in *Southern Pacific* is a strong declaration of how state requirements affect the flow of interstate traffic and commerce. Under the dormant commerce clause doctrine, the Constitution leaves no room for state legislation that is inimical to national commerce, even if the subject of that regulation has not been touched by federal legislation. A state law that obstructs interstate commerce, going beyond what is clearly necessary for safety regulation, cannot stand in the face of the commerce clause.

State Discrimination against Interstate Commerce.
Even though the Court's decisions in *Barnwell Brothers* and *Southern Pacific* deal with transportation and distribution activities, the principles set down in those cases also apply to state regulations that place burdens on other aspects of interstate commerce, especially a state's attempt to protect local businesses by discriminating against interstate commerce. In *Hunt v. Washington State Apple Advertising Commission* the justices confronted a state regulation that restricted the kind of information that could be displayed on containers of

out-of-state agricultural products. The state claimed that the rule was an exercise of the police powers to protect its citizens from fraud and deception. Does the state make a convincing case, or is the regulation nothing more than a way to prevent interstate commerce from having a negative impact on local producers?

Hunt v. Washington State Apple Advertising Commission

432 U.S. 333 (1977)
http://laws.findlaw.com/us/432/333.html
Oral arguments are available at https://www.oyez.org.
Vote: 8 (Blackmun, Brennan, Burger, Marshall, Powell, Stevens, Stewart, White)
0

OPINION OF THE COURT: *Burger*
NOT PARTICIPATING: *Rehnquist*

FACTS:

In 1972 the North Carolina Board of Agriculture adopted a regulation that required all closed containers of apples shipped into the state to display either the U.S. Department of Agriculture (USDA) grade or nothing at all. It barred information based on the grading systems of the states in which the apples were grown. The reason for the regulation, according to North Carolina, which has a substantial apple industry, was to ensure that all apples coming into the state used the same grading system, thereby removing the danger that multiple systems would confuse purchasers and lead to deception and fraud in the market. No other state had such a regulation.

Through their industry advertising commission, apple growers in Washington State challenged the North Carolina regulations. Washington grows approximately 30 percent of the nation's apples and is responsible for roughly half of all apples shipped in interstate commerce. Because the industry is so important to that state, it has taken steps to enhance its reputation by imposing a strict mandatory inspection and grading system. Washington's standards are higher than the USDA's, and the grading system has widespread acceptance in the apple trade.

The Washington commission asked North Carolina to alter its regulation or to allow certain exceptions. When North Carolina refused, the commission sued to have the regulation declared unconstitutional. The federal trial court found that the regulation violated the commerce clause, and North Carolina governor James Hunt, on behalf of the state, appealed to the U.S. Supreme Court.

ARGUMENTS:

For the appellants, James B. Hunt Jr., governor of North Carolina, et al.:

- If the law imposes burdens on the sale of Washington apples in North Carolina, the local benefits of North Carolina's valid exercise of its police power outweigh those burdens. North Carolina is protecting its citizens—and indeed all Americans—from fraud and deception in the marketing of apples.
- The law accomplishes this goal of uniformity in an evenhanded manner because it applies to all apples sold in closed containers in the state without regard to their point of origin.
- Many Court decisions have held that not every state law imposing burdens on interstate commerce is unconstitutional. Especially when states act to protect their citizens from fraud and deception in the marketing of food, the residuum of power left to the states is particularly broad.

For the appellee, Washington State Apple Advertising Commission:

- The law unreasonably burdens interstate commerce in three ways. First, it clearly discriminates against interstate commerce in favor of local growers. Second, it denies Washington growers the ability to use the widely accepted quality grading system and diminishes the marketing advantage the state's industry had earned. Third, North Carolina's regulation increases the cost of interstate commerce by requiring out-of-state growers to package their North Carolina–bound products differently from those being sent to the other states.

▶ MR. CHIEF JUSTICE BURGER DELIVERED THE OPINION OF THE COURT.

We turn . . . to the appellant's claim that the District Court erred in holding that the North Carolina statute violated the Commerce Clause insofar as it prohibited the display of Washington State grades on closed containers of apples shipped into the State. Appellants do not really contest the District Court's determination that the challenged statute burdened the Washington apple industry by increasing its costs of doing business in the North Carolina market and causing it to lose accounts there. Rather, they maintain that any such burdens on the interstate sale of Washington apples were far outweighed by the local benefits flowing from what they contend was a valid exercise of North Carolina's inherent police powers designed to protect its citizenry from fraud and deception in the marketing of apples.

Prior to the statute's enactment, appellants point out, apples from 13 different States were shipped into North Carolina for sale. Seven of those States, including the State of Washington, had their own grading system which, while differing in their standards, used similar descriptive labels (*e.g.*, fancy, extra fancy, etc.). This multiplicity of inconsistent grades, as the District Court itself found, posed dangers of deception and confusion not only in the North Carolina market, but in the Nation as a whole. The North Carolina statute, appellants claim, was enacted to eliminate this source of deception and confusion by replacing the numerous state grades with a single uniform standard. Moreover, it is contended that North Carolina sought to accomplish this goal of uniformity in an evenhanded manner as evidenced by the fact that its statute applies to all apples sold in closed containers in the State without regard to their point of origin. Nonetheless, appellants argue that the District Court gave "scant attention" to the obvious benefits flowing from the challenged legislation and to the long line of decisions from this Court holding that the State possesses "broad powers" to protect local purchasers from fraud and deception in the marketing of foodstuffs.

As the appellants properly point out, not every exercise of state authority imposing some burden on the free flow of commerce is invalid. Although the Commerce Clause acts as a limitation upon state power even without congressional implementation, our opinions have long recognized that,

"in the absence of conflicting legislation by Congress, there is a residuum of power in the state to make laws governing matters of local concern which nevertheless in some measure affect interstate commerce or even, to some extent, regulate it." *Southern Pacific Co. v. Arizona* (1945).

Moreover, as appellants correctly note, that "residuum" is particularly strong when the State acts to protect its citizenry in matters pertaining to the sale of foodstuffs. By the same token, however, a finding that state legislation furthers matters of legitimate local concern, even in the health and consumer protection areas, does not end the inquiry. Such a view, we have noted, "would mean that the Commerce Clause of itself imposes no limitations on state action . . . save for the rare instance where a state artlessly discloses an avowed purpose to discriminate against interstate goods." *Dean Milk Co. v. Madison* (1951). Rather, when such state legislation comes into conflict with the Commerce Clause's overriding requirement of a

national "common market," we are confronted with the task of effecting an accommodation of the competing national and local interests. We turn to that task.

As the District Court correctly found, the challenged statute has the practical effect of not only burdening interstate sales of Washington apples, but also discriminating against them. This discrimination takes various forms. The first, and most obvious, is the statute's consequence of raising the costs of doing business in the North Carolina market for Washington apple growers and dealers, while leaving those of their North Carolina counterparts unaffected. As previously noted, this disparate effect results from the fact that North Carolina apple producers, unlike their Washington competitors, were not forced to alter their marketing practices in order to comply with the statute. They were still free to market their wares under the USDA grade or none at all as they had done prior to the statute's enactment. Obviously, the increased costs imposed by the statute would tend to shield the local apple industry from the competition of Washington apple growers and dealers who are already at a competitive disadvantage because of their great distance from the North Carolina market.

Second, the statute has the effect of stripping away from the Washington apple industry the competitive and economic advantages it has earned for itself through its expensive inspection and grading system. The record demonstrates that the Washington apple-grading system has gained nationwide acceptance in the apple trade. Indeed, it contains numerous affidavits from apple brokers and dealers located both inside and outside of North Carolina who state their preference, and that of their customers, for apples graded under the Washington, as opposed to the USDA, system because of the former's greater consistency, its emphasis on color, and its supporting mandatory inspections. Once again, the statute had no similar impact on the North Carolina apple industry and thus operated to its benefit.

Third, by prohibiting Washington growers and dealers from marketing apples under their State's grades, the statute has a leveling effect which insidiously operates to the advantage of local apple producers. As noted earlier, the Washington State grades are equal or superior to the USDA grades in all corresponding categories. Hence, with free market forces at work, Washington sellers would normally enjoy a distinct market advantage vis-à-vis local producers in those categories where the Washington grade is superior. However, because of the statute's operation, Washington apples which would otherwise qualify for and be sold under the superior Washington grades will now have to be marketed under their inferior USDA counterparts. Such "down-grading" offers the North Carolina apple industry the very sort of protection against competing out-of-state products that the Commerce Clause was designed to prohibit. At worst, it will have the effect of an embargo against those Washington apples in the superior grades as Washington dealers withhold them from the North Carolina market. At best, it will deprive Washington sellers of the market premium that such apples would otherwise command.

Despite the statute's facial neutrality, the Commission suggests that its discriminatory impact on interstate commerce was not an unintended byproduct and there are some indications in the record to that effect. The most glaring is the response of the North Carolina Agriculture Commissioner to the Commission's request for an exemption following the statute's passage in which he indicated that before he could support such an exemption, he would "want to have the sentiment from our apple producers *since they were mainly responsible for this legislation being passed . . .*" [emphasis added]. Moreover, we find it somewhat suspect that North Carolina singled out only closed containers of apples, the very means by which apples are transported in commerce, to effectuate the statute's ostensible consumer protection purpose when apples are not generally sold at retail in their shipping containers. However, we need not ascribe an economic protection motive to the North Carolina Legislature to resolve this case; we conclude that the challenged statute cannot stand insofar as it prohibits the display of Washington State grades even if enacted for the declared purpose of protecting consumers from deception and fraud in the marketplace.

When discrimination against commerce of the type we have found is demonstrated, the burden falls on the State to justify it both in terms of the local benefits flowing from the statute and the unavailability of nondiscriminatory alternatives adequate to preserve the local interests at stake. North Carolina has failed to sustain that burden on both scores.

The several States unquestionably possess a substantial interest in protecting their citizens from confusion and deception in the marketing of foodstuffs, but the challenged statute does remarkably little to further that laudable goal at least with respect to Washington apples and grades. The statute, as already noted, permits the marketing of closed containers of apples under *no* grades at all. Such a result can hardly be thought to eliminate the problems of deception and confusion created by the multiplicity of differing state grades; indeed, it magnifies them by depriving purchasers of all information concerning the quality of the contents of closed apple containers. Moreover, although the

statute is ostensibly a consumer protection measure, it directs its primary efforts, not at the consuming public at large, but at apple wholesalers and brokers who are the principal purchasers of closed containers of apples. And those individuals are presumably the most knowledgeable individuals in this area. Since the statute does nothing at all to purify the flow of information at the retail level, it does little to protect consumers against the problems it was designed to eliminate. Finally, we note that any potential for confusion and deception created by the Washington grades was not of the type that led to the statute's enactment. Since Washington grades are in all cases equal or superior to their USDA counterparts, they could only "deceive" or "confuse" a consumer to his benefit, hardly a harmful result.

In addition, it appears that nondiscriminatory alternatives to the outright ban of Washington State grades are readily available. For example, North Carolina could effectuate its goal by permitting out-of-state growers to utilize state grades only if they also marked their shipments with the applicable USDA label. In that case, the USDA grade would serve as a benchmark against which the consumer could evaluate the quality of the various state grades. If this alternative was for some reason inadequate to eradicate problems caused by state grades inferior to those adopted by the USDA, North Carolina might consider banning those state grades which, unlike Washington's, could not be demonstrated to be equal or superior to the corresponding USDA categories. Concededly, even in this latter instance, some potential for "confusion" might persist. However, it is the type of "confusion" that the national interest in the free flow of goods between the States demands be tolerated.

The judgment of the District Court is

Affirmed.

The *Southern Pacific* and *Washington State Apple* cases are but two examples from a long line of decisions in which the Court has cast a disapproving eye on state laws that discriminate against interstate commerce or place an unreasonable burden on it. Other examples are summarized in box 7-10.

It would be a mistake to conclude, however, that all state regulations that discriminate against interstate products are unconstitutional. In several cases, including *Hughes v. Oklahoma* (1979) and *New Energy Co. of Indiana v. Limbach* (1988), the Court has allowed such unequal treatment under two conditions. First, Congress may pass legislation that permits discrimination by the states and thereby removes the restrictions

---

✳ **BOX 7-10 EXAMPLES OF SUPREME COURT DECISIONS STRIKING DOWN STATE AND LOCAL RESTRICTIONS ON INTERSTATE COMMERCE**

CASE	LAW DECLARED UNCONSTITUTIONAL
Edwards v. California (1941)	California law making it a crime knowingly to bring an indigent into the state
Dean Milk Company v. Madison (1951)	Madison, Wisconsin, city ordinance discriminating against milk produced out of state
Bibb v. Navajo Freight Lines (1959)	Illinois statute requiring a particular mud flap on all trucks and outlawing a conventional mud flap legal in forty-five other states
Pike v. Bruce Church (1970)	Arizona law requiring that all Arizona-grown cantaloupes be packaged inside the state
Great Atlantic and Pacific Tea Company v. Cottrell (1976)	Mississippi law banning milk produced in Louisiana in response to Louisiana's refusal to sign a reciprocity agreement
Raymond Motor Transit v. Rice (1978)	Wisconsin regulation prohibiting from the state's highways double trucks exceeding sixty-five feet in length
Philadelphia v. New Jersey (1978)	New Jersey ban on the importation and dumping of out-of-state garbage
Hughes v. Oklahoma (1979)	Oklahoma law outlawing the transportation of Oklahoma-grown minnows for out-of-state sale
Kassell v. Consolidated Freightways (1981)	Iowa law banning sixty-five-foot double trucks from the state's highways
New England Power Company v. New Hampshire (1982)	New Hampshire prohibition against selling domestically produced power to out-of-state interests
Healy v. Beer Institute (1989)	Connecticut law requiring out-of-state beer distributors to show that the prices charged inside Connecticut are not higher than prices charged in bordering states
State of Wyoming v. State of Oklahoma (1992)	Oklahoma law mandating that electrical utility companies purchase at least 10 percent of their coal from Oklahoma mining operations
C & A Carbone, Inc. v. Town of Clarkstown, New York (1994)	Clarkston, New York, city ordinance requiring that all nonhazardous solid waste within the town be sent to a local transfer station, forbidding such waste to be shipped to out-of-state facilities
Camps Newfound/Owatoona v. Town of Harrison (1997)	Maine statute singling out institutions that served mostly state residents for beneficial tax treatment and penalizing those institutions that did primarily interstate business
Granholm v. Heald (2005)	Michigan law allowing state residents to order wine from in-state wineries and have it directly shipped to their homes, but to prohibit such purchases and deliveries from out-of-state wineries
Comptroller of the Treasury of Maryland v. Wynne (2015)	Maryland law that includes a county income tax system that taxes income state residents earn out of state without crediting the taxes paid to the state in which the income was earned

---

imposed by the negative commerce clause. Second, the justices have allowed discrimination against interstate commerce when the states can advance a legitimate local purpose that cannot be adequately served by reasonable nondiscriminatory alternatives.

Maine v. Taylor (1986) involves a dispute over a state law that bans importation of a commodity while allowing the sale of the same article produced within the state. Maine argues that Congress approved the prohibition and that the law is a necessary environmental health regulation. Does the state offer a sufficiently strong case that its trade barrier is not offensive to the Constitution, or is the state using the police power as a means of protecting a domestic industry against interstate competition?

Maine v. Taylor

477 U.S. 131 (1986)
http://laws.findlaw.com/us/477/131.html
Oral arguments are available at https://www.oyez.org.
Vote: 8 (Blackmun, Brennan, Burger, Marshall, O'Connor, Powell, Rehnquist, White)
  1 (Stevens)

OPINION OF THE COURT: Blackmun
DISSENTING OPINION: Stevens

FACTS:

Maine passed a law prohibiting the importation of any live fish to be used as bait in any of the state's inland waters. The state said the law was to protect indigenous fish from parasites and diseases that are common among imported baitfish and to prevent the introduction of fish that might be detrimental to the state's ecology. Coupled with this state law was the Lacey Act, a federal statute that, among other things, made it a crime to transport any fish or wildlife in violation of state laws.

In a clear violation of the state statute, Robert J. Taylor, operator of a bait business in Maine, imported 158,000 live golden shiners. The fish were intercepted at the state border, and the federal government indicted Taylor for violating the Lacey Act. In his defense, Taylor attacked the constitutionality of the Maine law. He claimed that the ban on the interstate shipment of baitfish was a direct violation of the commerce clause. Maine intervened to defend its statute. In a hearing before a U.S. magistrate, Maine introduced testimony showing that the law served a legitimate local purpose that could not be adequately served by reasonable nondiscriminatory alternatives. The judge and later a U.S. district court agreed that the state had met its burden and upheld its law. But the court of appeals, also considering the purpose and possible alternatives, reversed. The reversal cast doubt on the state's claim that its law served a legitimate local purpose on the grounds that the law was unique and had an "aura of economic protectionism." Even if it assumed the law had a legitimate local purpose, the court held that less-discriminatory alternatives existed, including the inspection of the fish before they are released into Maine waters. Maine and the United States petitioned the U.S. Supreme Court to review the case.

ARGUMENTS:

For the appellant, state of Maine:

- Congress, in enacting the Lacey Act, encouraged the enactment of statutes such as Maine's.
- The law satisfies the purpose and alternative requirements, as the magistrate and later district court judge found. The court of appeals' decision to the contrary is at odds with evidence that the lower court found persuasive. Under existing case law (and the rules of civil procedure) courts of appeals are not free to set aside findings of fact by the lower court unless they are clearly erroneous, which they are not in this case.

For the appellee, Robert J. Taylor:

- When a state law discriminates against interstate commerce in a way that is not incidental or even-handed, the state must show that its law serves a legitimate local purpose and that no reasonable alternative exists to promote the purpose without discriminating against commerce. Because the state has shown neither, the law violates the commerce clause.
- The state has not demonstrated that its law serves a legitimate local purpose that outweighs the national interest in the free flow of commerce throughout the United States. At trial an expert indicated that the dangers posed by parasites may be overstated.
- Even if the law served a legitimate local purpose, the court of appeals was right to rule that Maine has not taken advantage of less discriminatory alternatives.

▶ JUSTICE BLACKMUN DELIVERED THE OPINION OF THE COURT.

Once again, a little fish has caused a commotion. See *Hughes v. Oklahoma* (1979); *TVA v. Hill* (1978); *Cappaert v. United States* (1976). The fish in this case is the golden shiner, a species of minnow commonly used as live bait in sport fishing. . . .

The Commerce Clause of the Constitution grants Congress the power "[t]o regulate Commerce with foreign Nations, and among the several States, and with the Indian Tribes." Art. I, §8, cl. 3. "Although the Clause thus speaks in terms of powers bestowed upon Congress, the Court long has recognized that it also limits the power of the States to erect barriers against interstate trade." Maine's statute restricts interstate trade in the most direct manner possible, blocking all inward shipments of live baitfish at the State's border. Still, as both the District Court and the Court of Appeals recognized, this fact alone does not render the law unconstitutional. The limitation imposed by the Commerce Clause on state regulatory power "is by no means absolute," and "the States retain authority under their general police powers to regulate matters of 'legitimate local concern,' even though interstate commerce may be affected."

In determining whether a State has overstepped its role in regulating interstate commerce, this Court has distinguished between state statutes that burden interstate transactions only incidentally, and those that affirmatively discriminate against such transactions. While statutes in the first group violate the Commerce Clause only if the burdens they impose on interstate trade are "clearly excessive in relation to the putative local benefits," statutes in the second group are subject to more demanding scrutiny. The Court explained in *Hughes v. Oklahoma* that once a state law is shown to discriminate against interstate commerce "either on its face or in practical effect," the burden falls on the State to demonstrate both that the statute "serves a legitimate local purpose," and that this purpose could not be served as well by available nondiscriminatory means. . . .

No matter how one describes the abstract issue whether "alternative means could promote this local purpose as well without discriminating against interstate commerce," *Hughes v. Oklahoma*, the more specific question whether scientifically accepted techniques exist for the sampling and inspection of live baitfish is one of fact, and the District Court's finding that such techniques have not been devised cannot be characterized as clearly erroneous. Indeed, the record probably could not support a contrary finding. Two prosecution witnesses testified to the lack of such procedures, and appellee's expert conceded the point, although he disagreed about the need for such tests. That Maine has allowed the importation of other freshwater fish after inspection hardly demonstrates that the District Court clearly erred in crediting the corroborated and uncontradicted expert testimony that standardized inspection techniques had not yet been developed for baitfish. . . .

After reviewing the expert testimony . . . we cannot say that the District Court clearly erred in finding that substantial scientific uncertainty surrounds the effect that baitfish parasites and nonnative species could have on Maine's fisheries. Moreover, we agree with the District Court that Maine has a legitimate interest in guarding against imperfectly understood environmental risks, despite the possibility that they may ultimately prove to be negligible. "[T]he constitutional principles underlying the commerce clause cannot be read as requiring the State of Maine to sit idly by and wait until potentially irreversible environmental damage has occurred or until the scientific community agrees on what disease organisms are or are not dangerous before it acts to avoid such consequences."

Nor do we think that much doubt is cast on the legitimacy of Maine's purposes by what the Court of Appeals took to be signs of protectionist intent. Shielding in-state industries from out-of-state competition is almost never a legitimate local purpose, and state laws that amount to "simple economic protectionism" consequently have been subject to a "virtually *per se* rule of invalidity." But there is little reason in this case to believe that the legitimate justifications the State has put forward for its statute are merely a sham or a "*post hoc* rationalization." . . .

The Commerce Clause significantly limits the ability of States and localities to regulate or otherwise burden the flow of interstate commerce, but it does not elevate free trade above all other values. As long as a State does not needlessly obstruct interstate trade or attempt to "place itself in a position of economic isolation," it retains broad regulatory authority to protect the health and safety of its citizens and the integrity of its natural resources. The evidence in this case amply supports the District Court's findings that Maine's ban on the importation of live baitfish serves legitimate local purposes that could not adequately be served by available nondiscriminatory alternatives. This is not a case of arbitrary discrimination against interstate commerce; the record suggests that Maine has legitimate reasons "apart from their origin, to treat [out-of-state baitfish] differently." The judgment of the Court of Appeals setting aside appellee's conviction is therefore reversed.

JUSTICE STEVENS, dissenting.

There is something fishy about this case. Maine is the only State in the Union that blatantly discriminates against out-of-state baitfish by flatly prohibiting their importation. Although golden shiners are already present and thriving in Maine (and, perhaps not coincidentally, the subject of a flourishing domestic industry), Maine excludes golden shiners grown and harvested (and, perhaps not coincidentally, sold) in other States. This kind of stark discrimination against out-of-state articles of commerce requires rigorous justification by the discriminating State. "When discrimination against commerce of the type we have found is demonstrated, the burden falls on the State to justify it both in terms of the local benefits flowing from the statute and the unavailability of nondiscriminatory alternatives adequate to preserve the local interests at stake." *Hunt v. Washington State Apple Advertising Comm'n* (1977).

. . . [T]he Court concludes that uncertainty about possible ecological effects from the possible presence of parasites and nonnative species in shipments of out-of-state shiners suffices to carry the State's burden of proving a legitimate public purpose. The Court similarly concludes that the State has no obligation to develop feasible inspection procedures that would make a total ban unnecessary. It seems clear, however, that the presumption should run the other way. Since the State engages in obvious discrimination against out-of-state commerce, it should be put to its proof. Ambiguity about dangers and alternatives should actually defeat, rather than sustain, the discriminatory measure.

This is not to derogate the State's interest in ecological purity. But the invocation of environmental protection or public health has never been thought to confer some kind of special dispensation from the general principle of non-discrimination in interstate commerce. "A different view, that the ordinance is valid simply because it professes to be a health measure, would mean that the Commerce Clause of itself imposes no restraints on state action other than those laid down by the Due Process Clause, save for the rare instance where a state artlessly discloses an avowed purpose to discriminate against interstate goods." If Maine wishes to rely on its interest in ecological preservation, it must show that interest, and the infeasibility of other alternatives, with far greater specificity. Otherwise, it must further that asserted interest in a manner far less offensive to the notions of comity and cooperation that underlie the Commerce Clause.

Significantly, the Court of Appeals, which is more familiar with Maine's natural resources and with its legislation than we are, was concerned by the uniqueness of Maine's ban. That court felt, as I do, that Maine's unquestionable natural splendor notwithstanding, the State has not carried its substantial burden of proving why it cannot meet its environmental concerns in the same manner as other States with the same interest in the health of their fish and ecology.

I respectfully dissent.

Maine v. Taylor illustrates a successful attempt on the part of a state to gain approval of a statute that clearly discriminated against interstate commerce. Because of the implications of the Lacey Act and the environmental interests at stake, the Court found ample reason to forgo the standard prohibitions imposed by the dormant commerce clause. Such efforts, however, do not always end with victory for state interests. *Granholm v. Heald* (2005) provides an illustration. As you read this case, consider whether the states' arguments are compelling. Also ask yourself, Did the precedent set in *Maine v. Taylor* govern this case, or did the Court find sufficient differences to justify an alternative outcome?

Granholm v. Heald

544 U.S. 460 (2005)
http://laws.findlaw.com/us/544/460.html
Oral arguments are available at https://www.oyez.org.
Vote: 5 (Breyer, Ginsburg, Kennedy, Scalia, Souter)
    4 (O'Connor, Rehnquist, Stevens, Thomas)

OPINION OF THE COURT: *Kennedy*
DISSENTING OPINIONS: *O'Connor, Thomas*

FACTS:

This case consolidates two appeals—one from Michigan, the other from New York—involving challenges to the constitutionality of certain wine sales regulations. Both states operate three-tier regulatory systems that separately license wine producers, wholesalers, and retailers. Although the specifics of the two schemes differ, both lead to the same result: in-state wineries may legally sell and ship their products directly to residents of that state, but, either by direct prohibition or the imposition of prohibitive costs, out-of-state wineries may not. Consequently, Michigan consumers can buy wine directly from a Michigan winery and have it delivered to their homes, but they cannot have wine purchased from an out-of-state vineyard shipped to their residences.

A coalition of several wine producers who relied on direct consumer sales and private individuals who wanted to purchase wines from out-of-state sources challenged the constitutionality of these regulations on the ground that they discriminate against interstate commerce in violation of the commerce clause. In response, the states argued that they were not attempting to promote domestic wineries but instead were legislating to protect minors from easy access to alcohol and to facilitate the collection of liquor taxes. They also claimed that the Twenty-first Amendment permits such discriminatory legislation. In addition, the states argued that Congress expressed its support for such state regulations when it passed the Webb-Kenyon Act of 1913. In that statute Congress prohibited the importation of alcohol into any state in violation of that state's laws.

The Sixth Circuit Court of Appeals struck down the Michigan regulations, but the Second Circuit Court of Appeals upheld the constitutionality of the New York law. The U.S. Supreme Court accepted the appeals to resolve the conflict between the findings of the two lower appellate courts.

ARGUMENTS:

For the petitioners, Jennifer M. Granholm, governor of Michigan, et al.:

- The Twenty-first Amendment gives the states broad power to adopt any reasonable regulation on the importation of alcoholic beverages for use by their residents. It was designed to create an exception to the dormant commerce clause, giving the states the same power over alcohol traffic that the commerce clause gives to the traffic of all other products. As long as the laws bear a rational connection to their regulatory objectives and do not violate other provisions of the Constitution, they are constitutional.

- Congress reaffirmed this power by exercising its power under the commerce clause to enact and reenact the Webb-Kenyon Act.
- Michigan's differential treatment of foreign and domestic wineries reflects an entirely rational legislative judgment. In-state wineries may ship directly to consumers because these wineries are subject to effective oversight and regulation. Michigan cannot, as a practical matter, check the backgrounds, inspect the records, or otherwise monitor the regulatory compliance of out-of-state wineries.

For the respondents, Eleanor Heald et al.:

- Michigan's law amounts to classic discrimination within the meaning of the dormant commerce clause: "differential treatment of in-state and out-of-state economic interests that benefits the former and burdens the latter."
- The Supreme Court has made clear that the same nondiscrimination principle applies to the sale of alcoholic products. The Twenty-first Amendment does not allow states to violate core commerce clause principles by explicitly discriminating against out-of-state alcohol producers. The Webb-Kenyon Act does not confer upon the states the power to discriminate against interstate commerce; it merely mirrors the language of the Twenty-first Amendment.
- The Court has left open the possibility that a state may discriminate against interstate commerce "by showing that it advances a legitimate local purpose that cannot be adequately served by reasonable non-discriminatory alternatives." Michigan has not met this test. Michigan asserts that the discrimination is necessary to prevent the sale of wine to minors, prevent loss of revenue, and protect public health and safety, but has not supported this assertion with any proof. In fact, the Federal Trade Commission has found that the twenty-six states that allow direct shipping have encountered none of these problems.

■ JUSTICE KENNEDY DELIVERED THE OPINION OF THE COURT.

Time and again this Court has held that, in all but the narrowest circumstances, state laws violate the Commerce Clause if they mandate "differential treatment of in-state and out-of-state economic interests that benefits the former and burdens the latter." *Oregon Waste Systems, Inc. v. Department of Environmental Quality of Ore.* (1994). This rule is essential to the foundations of the Union. The mere fact of nonresidence should not foreclose a producer in one State from access to markets in other States. States may not enact laws that burden out-of-state producers or shippers simply to give a competitive advantage to in-state businesses. This mandate "reflect[s] a central concern of the Framers that was an immediate reason for calling the Constitutional Convention: the conviction that in order to succeed, the new Union would have to avoid the tendencies toward economic Balkanization that had plagued relations among the Colonies and later among the States under the Articles of Confederation." *Hughes v. Oklahoma* (1979). . . .

Laws of the type at issue in the instant cases contradict these principles. They deprive citizens of their right to have access to the markets of other States on equal terms. The perceived necessity for reciprocal sale privileges risks generating the trade rivalries and animosities, the alliances and exclusivity, that the Constitution and, in particular, the Commerce Clause were designed to avoid. . . . The current patchwork of laws—with some States banning direct shipments altogether, others doing so only for out-of-state wines, and still others requiring reciprocity—is essentially the product of an ongoing, low-level trade war. Allowing States to discriminate against out-of-state wine "invite[s] a multiplication of preferential trade areas destructive of the very purpose of the Commerce Clause." *Dean Milk Co. v. Madison* (1951). . . .

State laws that discriminate against interstate commerce face "a virtually per se rule of invalidity." *Philadelphia v. New Jersey* (1978). The Michigan and New York laws by their own terms violate this proscription. The two States, however, contend their statutes are saved by §2 of the Twenty-first Amendment, which provides:

"The transportation or importation into any State, Territory, or possession of the United States for delivery or use therein of intoxicating liquors, in violation of the laws thereof, is hereby prohibited."

The States' position is inconsistent with our precedents and with the Twenty-first Amendment's history. Section 2 does not allow States to regulate the direct shipment of wine on terms that discriminate in favor of in-state producers. . . .

The aim of the Twenty-first Amendment was to allow States to maintain an effective and uniform system for controlling liquor by regulating its transportation, importation, and use. The Amendment did not give States the authority to pass nonuniform laws in order to discriminate against out-of-state goods, a privilege they had not enjoyed at any earlier time. . . .

Our more recent cases, furthermore, confirm that the Twenty-first Amendment does not supersede other provisions of the Constitution and, in particular, does not displace the rule that States may not give a discriminatory preference to their own producers. . . .

Our determination that the Michigan and New York direct-shipment laws are not authorized by the Twenty-first Amendment does not end the inquiry. We still must consider whether either State regime "advances a legitimate local purpose that cannot be adequately served by reasonable nondiscriminatory alternatives." *New Energy Co. of Ind.* [*v. Limbach*, 1988]. The States offer two primary justifications for restricting direct shipments from out-of-state wineries: keeping alcohol out of the hands of minors and facilitating tax collection. . . .

The States, aided by several amici, claim that allowing direct shipment from out-of-state wineries undermines their ability to police underage drinking. Minors, the States argue, have easy access to credit cards and the Internet and are likely to take advantage of direct wine shipments as a means of obtaining alcohol illegally.

The States provide little evidence that the purchase of wine over the Internet by minors is a problem. Indeed, there is some evidence to the contrary. . . . Without concrete evidence that direct shipping of wine is likely to increase alcohol consumption by minors, we are left with the States' unsupported assertions. Under our precedents, which require the "clearest showing" to justify discriminatory state regulation, *C & A Carbone, Inc.* [*v. Clarkstown*, 1994], this is not enough. . . .

The States' tax-collection justification is also insufficient. Increased direct shipping, whether originating in state or out of state, brings with it the potential for tax evasion. . . .

In summary, the States provide little concrete evidence for the sweeping assertion that they cannot police direct shipments by out-of-state wineries. Our Commerce Clause cases demand more than mere speculation to support discrimination against out-of-state goods. The "burden is on the State to show that 'the *discrimination* is demonstrably justified,'" *Chemical Waste Management, Inc. v. Hunt* (1992) (emphasis in original). The Court has upheld state regulations that discriminate against interstate commerce only after finding, based on concrete record evidence, that a State's nondiscriminatory alternatives will prove unworkable. Michigan and New York have not satisfied this exacting standard.

States have broad power to regulate liquor under §2 of the Twenty-first Amendment. This power, however, does not allow States to ban, or severely limit, the direct shipment of out-of-state wine while simultaneously authorizing direct shipment by in-state producers. If a State chooses to allow direct shipment of wine, it must do so on evenhanded terms. Without demonstrating the need for discrimination, New York and Michigan have enacted regulations that disadvantage out-of-state wine producers. Under our Commerce Clause jurisprudence, these regulations cannot stand.

It is so ordered.

JUSTICE THOMAS, with whom THE CHIEF JUSTICE, JUSTICE STEVENS, and JUSTICE O'CONNOR join, dissenting.

The Court devotes much attention to the Twenty-first Amendment, yet little to the terms of the Webb-Kenyon Act. This is a mistake, because that Act's language displaces any negative Commerce Clause barrier to state regulation of liquor sales to in-state consumers.

The Webb-Kenyon Act immunizes from negative Commerce Clause review the state liquor laws that the Court holds are unconstitutional. The Act "prohibit[s]" any "shipment or transportation" of alcoholic beverages "into any State" when those beverages are "intended, by any person interested therein, to be received, possessed, sold, or in any manner used . . . in violation of any law of such State." State laws that regulate liquor imports in the manner described by the Act are exempt from judicial scrutiny under the negative Commerce Clause, as this Court has long held. . . .

The Michigan and New York direct-shipment laws are within the Webb-Kenyon Act's terms and therefore do not run afoul of the negative Commerce Clause. . . .

. . . [T]he state laws the Court strikes down [also] are lawful under the plain meaning of §2 of the Twenty-first Amendment, as this Court's case law in the wake of the Amendment and the contemporaneous practice of the States reinforce.

Section 2 of the Twenty-first Amendment provides: "The transportation or importation into any State, Territory, or possession of the United States for delivery or use therein of intoxicating liquors, in violation of the laws thereof, is hereby prohibited." . . . [T]his language tracked the Webb-Kenyon Act by authorizing state regulation that would otherwise conflict with the negative Commerce Clause. To remove any doubt regarding its broad scope, the Amendment simplified the language of the Webb-Kenyon Act and made clear that States could regulate importation destined for in-state delivery free of negative

Commerce Clause restraints. Though the Twenty-first Amendment mirrors the basic terminology of the Webb-Kenyon Act, its language is broader, authorizing States to regulate all "transportation or importation" that runs afoul of state law. The broader language even more naturally encompasses discriminatory state laws. Its terms suggest, for example, that a State may ban imports entirely while leaving in-state liquor unregulated, for they do not condition the State's ability to prohibit imports on the manner in which state law treats domestic products. . . .

The Court begins its opinion by detailing the evils of state laws that restrict the direct shipment of wine. . . . The Twenty-first Amendment and the Webb-Kenyon Act took those policy choices away from judges and returned them to the States. Whatever the wisdom of that choice, the Court does this Nation no service by ignoring the textual commands of the Constitution and Acts of Congress. The Twenty-first Amendment and the Webb-Kenyon Act displaced the negative Commerce Clause as applied to regulation of liquor imports into a State. They require sustaining the constitutionality of Michigan's and New York's direct-shipment laws. I respectfully dissent.

The authority of the states to regulate interstate commerce remains consistent with the principles set out in *Cooley v. Board of Wardens* (1852). The Constitution without doubt gives supremacy in this area to the national government. If Congress elects to regulate such commerce, the power of the state is preempted. But where Congress does not regulate, the states may have a role. When national uniformity is not necessary, states may pass reasonable forms of regulation to meet legitimate local needs. If these ordinances place unreasonable burdens on interstate commerce or discriminate against interstate commerce in favor of domestic business, the Court will view them with suspicion, requiring the state to meet a heavy obligation of proving their legitimacy. As *Maine v. Taylor* and *Granholm v. Heald* illustrate, however, even well-developed legal standards are subject to differing interpretations that the judiciary may be called on to resolve.

ANNOTATED READINGS

For pre–New Deal studies of the Court, see Maurice G. Baxter, *The Steamboat Monopoly:* Gibbons v. Ogden (New York: Knopf, 1972); Felix Frankfurter, *The Commerce Clause under Marshall, Taney, and Waite* (Chapel Hill: University of North Carolina Press, 1937); Calvin H. Johnson, *Righteous Anger at the Wicked States: The Meaning of the Founders' Constitution* (New York: Cambridge University Press, 2005); Herbert Alan Johnson, Gibbons v. Ogden: *John Marshall, Steamboats, and the Commerce Clause* (Lawrence: University Press of Kansas, 2010); and Stephen B. Wood, *Constitutional Politics in the Progressive Era: Child Labor and the Law* (Chicago: University of Chicago Press, 1968).

On the New Deal period, see Leonard Baker, *Back to Back: The Duel between FDR and the Supreme Court* (New York: Macmillan, 1967); Richard Cortner, *The Wagner Act Cases* (Knoxville: University of Tennessee Press, 1964); Edward S. Corwin, *The Commerce Power versus States' Rights* (Princeton, NJ: Princeton University Press, 1936); Barry Cushman, *Rethinking the New Deal Court: The Structure of a Constitutional Revolution* (New York: Oxford University Press, 1998); Nelson Dawson, *Louis D. Brandeis, Felix Frankfurter, and the New Deal* (Hamden, CT: Archon Books, 1980); Robert Himmelberg, *The Origins of the National Recovery Administration* (New York: Fordham University Press, 1976); Peter H. Irons, *The New Deal Lawyers* (Princeton, NJ: Princeton University Press, 1982); William E. Leuchtenburg, *The Supreme Court Reborn: The Constitutional Revolution in the Age of Roosevelt* (New York: Oxford University Press, 1995); Drew Pearson and Robert S. Allen, *The Nine Old Men* (Garden City, NY: Doubleday, 1936); C. Herman Pritchett, *The Roosevelt Court: A Study in Judicial Politics and Values* (New York: Macmillan, 1948); and Ronen Shamir, *Managing Legal Uncertainty: Elite Lawyers in the New Deal* (Durham, NC: Duke University Press, 1995).

Books that address the post–New Deal era include Richard Cortner, *Civil Rights and Public Accommodations: The* Heart of Atlanta Motel *and* McClung *Cases* (Lawrence: University Press of Kansas, 2001); Thomas M. Keck, *The Most Activist Supreme Court in History: The Road to Modern Judicial Conservatism* (Chicago: University of Chicago Press, 2004); Robert D. Loevy, ed., *The Civil Rights Act of 1964: The Passage of the Law That Ended Racial Segregation* (Albany: State University of New York Press, 1997); and Jeffrey Toobin, *The Oath: The Obama White House and the Supreme Court* (New York: Doubleday, 2012).

8 The Power to Tax and Spend

ERHAPS no government power affects Americans more directly than the authority to tax and spend. Each year federal, state, and local governments collect billions of dollars in taxes imposed on a wide variety of activities, transactions, and goods. The federal government reminds us of its power to tax when we receive our paychecks, to say nothing of every April 15, the annual deadline for filing tax returns. Many state governments lay taxes on our incomes as well, and a majority of them also impose a levy each time we make a retail purchase. If we own a house, we must annually pay a tax on its value. We pay state and/or federal excise taxes whenever we put gas in the car or buy an airline ticket. When we buy goods from abroad, the price includes a duty imposed on imports.

Americans have strong opinions about the government's taxing and spending activities. Given the importance the public places on these issues, it is not surprising that government fiscal policies are often at the center of political battles. Presidential election contests often focus on taxing and spending policies. How should we deal with the growing national debt? What constitutes a fair income tax rate? What should be done to reform government spending on entitlement programs such as Social Security, Medicare, and Medicaid? Do we spend too much (or too little) on national defense? If the goal is to stimulate the economy, which is the more-effective alternative: increasing government spending or cutting taxes?

Today the government's power to tax and spend is firmly established, with reasonably well-defined contours, but this was not always the case. Some of the country's greatest constitutional battles have been fought over the fiscal powers. The results of these legal disputes have significantly shaped the powers and constraints of American political institutions. In this chapter, we examine the Supreme Court's interpretations of the twin fiscal powers of taxation and spending.

THE CONSTITUTIONAL POWER TO TAX AND SPEND

The power to tax was a fundamental issue at the Constitutional Convention. The government under the Articles of Confederation was ineffective in part because it had no authority to levy taxes. It could only request funds from the states and had no power to collect payments if the states refused to cooperate. The taxing authority resided solely with the states, which left the national government unable to execute public policies unless the states overwhelmingly supported them, a situation that did not occur with any regularity. It was clear that the central government would have to gain some revenue-gathering powers under the new constitution while the states retained concurrent authority to impose taxes.

Article I, Section 8, of the Constitution enumerates the powers of the federal government, and the first of those listed is the power to tax and spend: "The Congress shall have Power to lay and collect Taxes, Duties, Imposts and Excises, to pay the Debts and provide for the common Defence and general Welfare of the United States."

The wording of this grant of authority is quite broad. The revenue function breaks into three categories. The first is the general grant of taxation power. Second is the authority to collect duties, which are taxes levied on imports, the primary source of revenue at that time. The third is the power to impose excises, which are taxes on the manufacture, sale, or use of goods, or on occupational or other activities.

The power to spend is also broadly constructed. The revenues gathered through the various taxing mechanisms may be used to pay government debts, to fund the nation's defense, and to provide for the general welfare. Although James Madison (and others) argued that the framers intended the spending power to be limited to funding those government activities explicitly authorized in the Constitution, the wording of Article I, Section 8, does not impose any such restriction. As we shall see later in this chapter, that Congress may spend federal funds to provide for the *general welfare* is indeed a broad grant of authority.

This is not to say that the federal power to tax and spend is without limits. The framers were wary enough of the dangers of a strong central government to impose some restrictions.

First, Article I, Section 8, stipulates that "all Duties, Imposts and Excises shall be uniform throughout the United States." The purpose of this provision was to prevent Congress from imposing different tax rates on various regions or requiring the citizens of one state to pay a tax rate higher than that paid by citizens of other states. Geographical uniformity is the only stated constitutional requirement for excise taxes and taxes on imports. If this standard is met, the tax is likely to be valid.

Second, Article I, Section 9, holds that "[n]o capitation, or other direct, Tax shall be laid, unless in Proportion to the Census or Enumeration herein before directed to be taken." This same admonition is found in Article I, Section 2, where the framers wrote that "direct Taxes shall be apportioned among the several States . . . according to their respective Numbers" as determined by the national census. The term *direct tax* is not defined in the Constitution, and it is a difficult concept to understand. When the framers referred to a direct tax, they most likely meant a head tax—a tax

imposed on each person—or a tax on land. As we shall see in the next section, the requirement that direct taxes be apportioned on the basis of population has proved troublesome, and Congress has generally avoided such levies.

Third, Article I, Section 9, also dictates that "[n]o Tax or Duty shall be laid on Articles exported from any State." Consistent with the prevailing philosophy of increased commerce and trade, the framers wanted to ensure that the products of the states would move freely without the burden of federal taxes being placed on them.

The framers generally allowed the states to retain their taxing authority as it existed prior to the ratification of the Constitution. Consequently, state and local governments today tax a wide array of activities and goods, including individual and corporate incomes, personal property, real estate, retail sales, investment holdings, and inheritances. But the Constitution imposed some new restraints on state taxing authority. These limitations specifically removed from the states any power to place taxes on certain forms of commerce. Article I, Section 10, prohibits them from imposing any duty on imports or exports, as well as from placing any tax on the cargo capacity of vessels using the nation's ports. The framers were interested in the promotion of commerce, and these provisions precluded states from retarding commerce by using foreign trade as a source of tax revenue.

In addition to these specific restrictions, state and federal taxation must be consistent with the other provisions of the Constitution. It would be a violation of the Constitution if a state or the federal government taxed the exercise of a constitutional right, such as the freedom of speech or the exercise of religion. By the same token, if the government were to impose varying tax rates based on sex or race, such levies would be in violation of the constitutional rights of due process and equal protection of the laws.

DIRECT TAXES AND THE POWER TO TAX INCOME

The Constitution stipulates two standards for assessing federal taxes. The first is geographical uniformity. Duties, imposts, and excise taxes all must be applied according to this standard. If Congress taxes a particular product entering the ports of the United States, the tax rate on the article must be the same regardless of the point of entry. Excise taxes also must be applied uniformly throughout the nation. If an excise is placed on automobiles, the amount assessed must be the same in California as it is in Tennessee.

The second standard for imposing taxes is population distribution. The Constitution says that all direct taxes must be apportioned among the states on the basis of population. The document does not define the term *direct tax,* but we know that historically the concept was considered at a minimum to include a tax levied on every individual (often called a capitation tax or a head tax) and taxes on land.

The delegates from the sparsely populated states supported this provision because they feared that the larger states, with greater representation in the House of Representatives, would craft tax measures in such a way that the burden would fall disproportionately on the citizens of the smaller states. Southern states particularly supported the requirement that direct taxes be apportioned on the basis of population. These states had smaller populations than the northern states and were larger in geographical size. Without apportioning on the basis of population, for example, the states in the south would be much harder hit by a federal tax on land than would the states in the north. The apportionment requirement also led the southern states to demand that slaves be counted as less than full persons for taxation purposes. Counting a slave as three-fifths of a person, as the Constitutional Convention ultimately decided, would reduce the tax liability of the southern states in the event that Congress imposed a head tax or other direct tax.

Do direct taxes include more than just taxes on individual persons and taxes on land? The question is an important one. As box 8–1 illustrates, whether a tax is levied uniformly (as the Constitution requires for excise taxes) or is apportioned on the basis of population (required for direct taxes) makes a great deal of difference as to who pays how much. In *Federalist* No. 21 Alexander Hamilton claimed that direct taxes were only those imposed on land and buildings, but Hamilton's opinion did not settle the issue. It required a Supreme Court decision to do that.

Defining Direct Taxation

In one of the Court's earliest cases, **Hylton v. United States** (1796), the justices defined the term *direct tax.*

The dispute stemmed from a tax on carriages Congress had passed in June 1794. The statute classified the tax as an excise and, therefore, applied the same rate on carriages nationwide. The Federalist majorities in Congress passed the statute over Anti-Federalist opposition, and the tax was completely partisan. The Federalists generally represented the states in the Northeast with large populations but relatively few carriages; the Anti-Federalist strongholds were the less densely populated and more agricultural states with larger numbers of carriages. Because the carriage tax was deemed an excise, the Anti-Federalist areas would pay a much greater share of it than would the residents of the Northeast. The Anti-Federalists would have preferred to classify the measure as a direct tax and apportion it on the basis of population.

Daniel Hylton, a resident of Richmond, Virginia, challenged the constitutionality of the assessment, claiming that it was a direct tax, not an excise, and should have been apportioned on the basis of population. The government took the position that, as a tax on an article, the carriage tax was an excise.

By almost every rule of judicial authority developed since that time, the Court should have refused to hear the dispute.[1] The evidence showed that the case did not involve adverse parties. In fact, the suit appeared to be little more than a ploy by the government to obtain Court approval of its interpretation of the taxation provisions of the Constitution. Both sides to the dispute agreed that Hylton owned 125 carriages exclusively for his private use. In reality, he had only a single carriage. Under federal law at that time, a circuit court decision in a civil case could not be appealed to the Supreme Court unless the dispute involved a claim of at least $2,000. If Hylton owned 125 carriages, the taxes and penalties due ($16 per carriage) would reach the required threshold. This jurisdictional point was important because the Federalists anticipated that the Supreme Court would give the law a sympathetic interpretation. Administration officials also agreed that if the Court found the tax valid they would demand that Hylton pay only $16. Perhaps an even greater indication of collusion was that the government paid the fees of the attorneys for both sides as well as court costs.

---

1. See Urofsky and Finkelman, *A March of Liberty,* 177–178. See also Robert F. Cushman, *Cases in Constitutional Law,* 7th ed. (Englewood Cliffs, NJ: Prentice Hall, 1989), 177–178.

BOX 8-1   DIRECT AND INDIRECT TAXES: APPORTIONMENT VERSUS GEOGRAPHICAL UNIFORMITY

THIS EXAMPLE demonstrates the difference between direct and indirect taxing methods. The facts and figures used are purely hypothetical.

Assume that Congress decides to raise $1 million through a tax on the nation's 100,000 thoroughbred horses. If this tax is considered an excise tax, it must conform to the constitutional requirement of geographical uniformity. In order to achieve the $1 million goal, Congress would have to require that all thoroughbred horse owners pay a tax of $10 per horse. The rate would be the same in Maine as in Oregon. If, however, the tax on thoroughbred horses is classified as a direct tax, a different set of calculations would have to be made to meet the constitutionally required apportionment standard. Three factors would need to be known: first, the amount of money Congress intends to raise; second, the proportion of the national population residing in each state; and third, the number of thoroughbred horses in each state. Apportionment means that the proportion of the revenue obtained from a state must equal the proportion of the country's population living there.

The following calculations show the differing impacts of apportionment in the application of the $1 million horse tax to three states. State A is a densely populated, urban state with few horses. State B is a moderately populated

STATE	PERCENTAGE OF NATIONAL POPULATION	TAXES DUE FROM STATE	NUMBER OF HORSES IN STATE	TAX RATE PER HORSE
State A	10%	$100,000	100	$1,000
State B	5%	$50,000	1,000	$50
State C	1%	$10,000	10,000	$1

state with some ranching areas. State C is a sparsely populated, primarily agricultural state, with a relatively large number of thoroughbreds.

Obviously, the horse owners in State A would be greatly disadvantaged if the horse tax were classified as a direct tax and apportioned among the states on the basis of population. State C, on the other hand, would be greatly benefited. Because State C has only 1 percent of the nation's population, it would be responsible for raising only 1 percent of the $1,000,000 tax revenues. Furthermore, that smaller tax obligation would be distributed over a disproportionately large number of horses.

Horse owners in State A clearly would prefer that the tax on thoroughbreds be defined as an excise tax, with its required geographical uniformity. State C's thoroughbred owners obviously would argue for the horse tax to be considered a direct tax and thus apportioned among the states on the basis of population.

Alexander Hamilton, former secretary of the Treasury, presented the government's case. Hamilton was a vigorous supporter of a strong national government and of broad federal taxation powers. He understood the problems associated with apportioning taxes on the basis of population and consequently wanted the Court to set down a narrow definition of direct taxes.

Hamilton's side was victorious. The three justices who participated in the decision each voted in favor of the statute and in agreement with Congress's determination that the carriage tax was an excise tax.[2] As

was the custom in the years before John Marshall became chief justice, each justice wrote a separate opinion explaining his vote.[3] The opinions of James Iredell and Samuel Chase stressed the inappropriateness of attempting to apportion a tax on carriages and the inevitable inequities that would result. William Paterson's opinion emphasized the intention of the framers. His opinion had particular credibility

---

2. The other three members of the Court were absent for various reasons. Oliver Ellsworth had just been sworn in as chief justice and, because he had missed some of the arguments, did not participate in the decision. James Wilson heard arguments but did not vote in the case because he had participated in the lower court

decision upholding the tax. William Cushing was not present for the arguments and therefore did not vote on the merits.

3. The practice of each justice writing a separate opinion explaining individual views was borrowed from the British courts. When Marshall became chief justice, he moved away from the use of seriatim opinions to the current practice of a single opinion explaining the views of the majority. Marshall believed that the use of a single opinion increased the Court's status and effectiveness.

because Paterson, having been a New Jersey delegate to the Constitutional Convention, was one of the framers.[4] All three agreed that only two kinds of taxes fell into the direct tax category: taxes on land and capitation taxes.

Apportioning taxes on the basis of population is very cumbersome and almost inevitably leads to unjust tax burdens. By limiting the kinds of taxes that fell into the direct taxation category, the *Hylton* decision significantly strengthened federal taxation powers. It freed Congress from having to apply unpopular apportionment standards to most taxes. In fact, Congress has imposed taxes requiring apportionment on only five occasions, the last time occurring in 1861.[5]

Hylton was the first case in which the Supreme Court heard a challenge to the constitutionality of a federal statute; the decision predated *Marbury v. Madison* by seven years. It is clear from the arguments before the Court and the justices' opinions that the law was tested for its constitutionality. *Hylton* is not as well known as *Marbury* because in *Hylton* the Court found the act of Congress to be valid.

The Constitutionality of the Income Tax

From *Hylton* in 1796 to the 1860s, federal taxing authority remained generally unchanged. The government financed its activities largely through import duties and excise taxes. The Civil War, however, placed an incredible financial strain on the federal government. Between 1858 and the end of the war, it ran unusually high budget deficits and needed to find new sources of revenue to fund the war effort. To address the crisis, Congress in 1862 and 1864 imposed the first taxes on individual incomes. The 1881 case of **Springer v. United States** involved a challenge to the validity of that tax. William M. Springer, an attorney, claimed that the income tax was a direct tax and should have been apportioned on the basis of population. The justices unanimously rejected this position, once again holding that only capitation taxes and taxes on land were direct

taxes. Although the challenged tax was a levy on the income of individuals, it could not be considered a capitation tax within the normal meaning of that term because it was not a tax equally levied on all individuals. *Springer*, then, set precedent that the federal government had the power to tax incomes.

As the government reduced its war debts, Congress in 1872 was able to repeal the income tax law.[6] But the issue of taxing income did not go away. The populist movement favored the use of the progressive income tax as the primary method of raising federal revenues. In addition, labor groups and farm organizations began arguing that new revenue sources should be developed to shift the burden away from reliance on import duties. Members of the Democratic Party criticized the regressive aspects of the tax structure of that time.

In response to these demands, Congress enacted an income tax law in 1894. The statute, part of the Wilson-Gorman Tariff Act, imposed a 2 percent tax on all corporate profits and on individual incomes. Income derived from salaries and wages, gifts, inheritances, dividends, rents, and interest, including interest from state and municipal bonds, was subject to this tax. People with annual incomes of less than $4,000 paid no tax. This exemption, set at a level much higher than the average worker earned, meant that most of the burden fell on the wealthy. For this reason, the tax received overwhelming support from rank-and-file citizens and bitter opposition from businesses and those individuals enjoying high incomes. The wealthy classes, in fact, claimed that the income tax would destroy the very fabric of the nation, replacing historic principles of private property with communism and socialism.

The income tax law was promptly challenged in the Supreme Court in an 1895 appeal, *Pollock v. Farmers' Loan & Trust Co.* One of the primary arguments of the law's opponents was that the income tax was a direct tax, and because Congress had not apportioned it, the law was unconstitutional. Given precedents such as *Hylton* and *Springer*, would you anticipate that this position would be successful?

---

4. Justice Wilson was also a delegate at the Constitutional Convention and, therefore, one of the framers. Although he did not participate in *Hylton* at the Supreme Court level, Wilson earlier had voted in the lower court to uphold the tax as an excise.

5. Cushman, *Cases in Constitutional Law,* 178. The direct tax issue, however, is still occasionally raised. As we will see later in this chapter, it was one of the arguments made against the constitutional validity of the Patient Protection and Affordable Care Act of 2010.

6. For an excellent review of the history of the income tax in the United States, see John F. Witte, *The Politics and Development of the Federal Income Tax* (Madison: University of Wisconsin Press, 1985).

Pollock v. Farmers' Loan & Trust Co.

158 U.S. 601 (1895)
http://laws.findlaw.com/us/158/601.html
Vote: 5 (Brewer, Field, Fuller, Gray, Shiras)
    4 (Brown, Harlan, Jackson, White)

OPINION OF THE COURT: *Fuller*

DISSENTING OPINIONS: *Brown, Harlan, Jackson, White*

FACTS:

Charles Pollock, a shareholder in Farmers' Loan & Trust Company of New York, filed suit on behalf of himself and his fellow stockholders to block the company from paying the national income tax on the ground that the tax was unconstitutional. The lawsuit was obviously collusive: the company no more wanted to pay the tax than did its shareholders. Opponents of the law claimed (1) that taxing income from state and city bonds was an unconstitutional encroachment on the state's power to borrow money, (2) that a tax on income from real property was a direct tax and must be apportioned on the basis of population, and (3) that these taxes were so integral to the entire tax act that the whole law should be declared unconstitutional.

The Court heard arguments in the *Pollock* case twice. In its first decision, the majority declared the tax on state and municipal bonds unconstitutional.[7] It further ruled that a tax on income from land was essentially the same as taxing land itself. Because a tax on land is a direct tax, so too is a tax on the income from land; therefore, such taxes must be apportioned on the basis of population. But the Court was unable to reach a decision on whether the entire law should be declared unconstitutional. On this question the justices divided 4–4 because Justice Howell Jackson, ill with tuberculosis, was absent.

Pollock filed a petition for a second hearing, and Jackson made it known that he would be present for it. The second decision reviewed much of what the Court concluded in the first, but this time the Court went on to rule on the question of the general constitutionality of the income tax act.

Farmers' Loan & Trust made no attempt to defend the law. It only urged the Court to decide the case expeditiously. In its place, U.S. Justice Department attorneys presented the case supporting the constitutionality of the income tax.

The *Pollock* decision was one of the most controversial and important of its day. It contained all the elements of high drama. The case pitted the interests of businesses and wealthy individuals against those supporting social and fiscal reform. Both sides believed that a victory for their opponents would have disastrous consequences for the nation. Newspapers editorialized with enthusiasm. After the first decision ended in a tie, the suspense surrounding the second hearing grew tremendously. The human-interest factor was heightened when Justice Jackson, who died three months later, was transported to Washington to cast what he believed would be the deciding vote in favor of the tax. Oral arguments took place from May 6 to May 8, and apparently the justices did not act in a manner consistent with detached objectivity. As political science professor Loren P. Beth has described it, "Harlan wrote privately that Justice Stephen J. Field acted like a 'madman' throughout the case, but the dissenters' own opinions were similarly emotional."[8] In the end the opponents of the tax were victorious. Although Jackson, as expected, voted to uphold the law, Justice George Shiras, who had supported the tax in the first hearing, changed positions and became the crucial fifth vote to strike it down.

ARGUMENTS:

For the appellant, Charles Pollock:

- Taxes on property or the income from property are direct taxes subject to the constitutional requirement of apportionment.
- The direct taxes levied by this act are not apportioned among the states on the basis of population and are therefore unconstitutional.
- The tax on income from state and municipal bonds is a tax on the power of states and their subdivisions to raise revenue and is therefore unconstitutional.
- The unconstitutional provisions of this statute are so integral to the entire piece of legislation that the whole act is void.

For the appellee, Farmers' Loan & Trust (presented by the U.S. government):

- A tax on income is an excise. It is an indirect tax and therefore subject only to the constitutional requirement of geographical uniformity. This tax is geographically uniform and is therefore constitutional.

---

7. *Pollock v. Farmers' Loan & Trust Co.,* 157 U.S. 429 (1895).

8. Loren P. Beth, "*Pollock v. Farmers' Loan & Trust Co.,*" in Hall, *Oxford Companion to the Supreme Court,* 655.

- A tax on income, to the extent that the income is derived from rents, is not a tax on land and is therefore not a direct tax.
- This is a tax on an individual's total income, not a tax that targets income from land or from state/local government bonds.
- If any provision of the tax act is found unconstitutional, the remaining portions of the statute are not significantly affected and may continue to be enforced.

MR. CHIEF JUSTICE FULLER DELIVERED THE OPINION OF THE COURT.

Whenever this court is required to pass upon the validity of an act of Congress as tested by the fundamental law enacted by the people, the duty imposed demands in its discharge the utmost deliberation and care, and invokes the deepest sense of responsibility. And this is especially so when the question involves the exercise of a great governmental power, and brings into consideration, as vitally affected by the decision, that complex system of government, so sagaciously framed to secure and perpetuate "an indestructible Union, composed of indestructible States." . . .

As heretofore stated, the Constitution divided Federal taxation into two great classes, the class of direct taxes, and the class of duties, imposts and excises; and prescribed two rules which qualified the grant of power as to each class.

The power to lay direct taxes apportioned among the several States in proportion to their representation in the popular branch of Congress, a representation based on population as ascertained by the census, was plenary and absolute; but to lay direct taxes without apportionment was forbidden. The power to lay duties, imposts, and excises was subject to the qualification that the imposition must be uniform throughout the United States.

Our previous decision was confined to the consideration of the validity of the tax on the income from real estate, and on the income from municipal bonds. The question thus limited was whether such taxation was direct or not, in the meaning of the Constitution; and the court went no farther, as to the tax on the income from real estate, than to hold that it fell within the same class as the source whence the income was derived, that is, that a tax upon the realty and a tax upon the receipts therefrom were alike direct; while as to the income from municipal bonds, that could not be taxed because of want of power to tax the source, and no reference was made to the nature of the tax as being direct or indirect.

We are now permitted to broaden the field of inquiry, and to determine to which of the two great classes a tax upon a person's entire income, whether derived from rents, or products, or otherwise, of real estate, or from bonds, stocks, or other forms of personal property, belongs; and we are unable to conclude that the enforced subtraction from the yield of all the owner's real or personal property, in the manner prescribed, is so different from a tax upon the property itself, that it is not a direct, but an indirect tax, in the meaning of the Constitution. . . .

The reasons for the clauses of the Constitution in respect of direct taxation are not far to seek. The States, respectively, possessed plenary powers of taxation. They could tax the property of their citizens in such manner and to such extent as they saw fit; they had unrestricted powers to impose duties or imposts on imports from abroad, and excises on manufactures, consumable commodities, or otherwise. They gave up the great sources of revenue derived from commerce. They retained the concurrent power of levying excises, and duties if covering anything other than excises; but in respect of them the range of taxation was narrowed by the power granted over interstate commerce, and by the danger of being put at disadvantage in dealing with excises on manufactures. They retained the power of direct taxation, and to that they looked as their chief resource; but even in respect of that, they granted the concurrent power, and if the tax were placed by both governments on the same subject, the claim of the United States had preference. Therefore, they did not grant the power of direct taxation without regard to their own condition and resources as States; but they granted the power of apportioned direct taxation, a power just as efficacious to serve the needs of the general government, but securing to the States the opportunity to pay the amount apportioned, and to recoup from their own citizens in the most feasible way, and in harmony with their systems of local self-government. If, in the changes of wealth and population in particular States, apportionment produced inequality, it was an inequality stipulated for, just as the equal representation of the States, however small, in the Senate, was stipulated for. The Constitution ordains affirmatively that each State shall have two members of that body, and negatively that no State shall by amendment be deprived of its equal suffrage in the Senate without its consent. The Constitution ordains affirmatively that representatives and direct taxes shall be apportioned among the several States according to numbers, and negatively that no direct tax shall be laid unless in proportion to the enumeration.

The founders anticipated that the expenditures of the States, their counties, cities, and towns, would chiefly be met by direct taxation on accumulated property, while they expected that those of the Federal government would be for the most part met by indirect taxes. And in order that the power of direct taxation by the general government should not be exercised, except on necessity; and, when the necessity arouse, should be so exercised as to leave the States at liberty to discharge their respective obligations, and should not be so exercised, unfairly and discriminatingly, as to particular States or otherwise, by a mere majority vote, possibly of those whose constituents were intentionally not subjected to any part of the burden, the qualified grant was made. . . .

It is said that a tax on the whole income of property is not a direct tax in the meaning of the Constitution, but a duty, and, as a duty, leviable without apportionment, whether direct or indirect. We do not think so. Direct taxation was not restricted in one breath, and the restriction blown to the winds in another. . . .

We have unanimously held in this case that, so far as this law operates on the receipts from municipal bonds, it cannot be sustained, because it is a tax on the power of the States, and on their instrumentalities to borrow money, and consequently repugnant to the Constitution. But if, as contended, the interest when received has become merely money in the recipient's pocket, and taxable as such without reference to the source from which it came, the question is immaterial whether it could have been originally taxed at all or not. This was admitted by the Attorney General with characteristic candor; and it follows that, if the revenue derived from municipal bonds cannot be taxed because the source cannot be, the same rule applies to revenue from any other source not subject to the tax; and the lack of power to levy any but an apportioned tax on real and personal property equally exists as to the revenue therefrom.

Admitting that this act taxes the income of property irrespective of its source, still we cannot doubt that such a tax is necessarily a direct tax in the meaning of the Constitution. . . .

We are not here concerned with the question whether an income tax be or be not desirable, nor whether such a tax would enable the government to diminish taxes on consumption and duties on imports, and to enter upon what may be believed to be a reform of its fiscal and commercial system. Questions of that character belong to the controversies of political parties, and cannot be settled by judicial decision. In these cases our province is to determine whether this income tax on the revenue from property does or does not belong to the class of direct taxes. If it does, it is, being unapportioned, in violation of the Constitution, and we must so declare. . . .

We have considered the act only in respect of the tax on income derived from real estate, and from invested personal property, and have not commented on so much of it as bears on gains or profits from business, privileges, or employments, in view of the instances in which taxation on business, privileges, or employments has assumed the guise of an excise tax and been sustained as such.

Being of opinion that so much of the sections of this law as lays a tax on income from real and personal property is invalid, we are brought to the question of the effect of that conclusion upon these sections as a whole.

It is elementary that the same statute may be in part constitutional and in part unconstitutional, and if the parts are wholly independent of each other, that which is constitutional may stand while that which is unconstitutional will be rejected. And in the case before us there is no question as to the validity of this act, except sections twenty-seven to thirty-seven, inclusive, which relate to the subject which has been under discussion; and as to them we think . . . that if the different parts "are so mutually connected with and dependent on each other, as to warrant a belief that the legislature intended them as a whole, and that, if all could not be carried into effect, the legislature would not pass the residue independently, and some parts are unconstitutional, all the provisions which are thus dependent, conditional or connected, must fall with them." . . .

According to the census, the true valuation of real and personal property in the United States in 1890 was $65,037,091,197, of which real estate with improvements thereon made up $39,544,544,333. Of course, from the latter must be deducted, in applying these sections, all unproductive property and all property whose net yield does not exceed four thousand dollars; but, even with such deductions, it is evident that the income from realty formed a vital part of the scheme for taxation embodied therein. If that be stricken out, and also the income from all invested personal property, bonds, stocks, investments of all kinds, it is obvious that by far the largest part of the anticipated revenue would be eliminated, and this would leave the burden of the tax to be borne by professions, trades, employments, or vocations; and in that way what was intended as a tax on capital would remain in substance a tax on occupations and labor. We cannot believe that such was the intention of Congress. We do not mean to say that an act laying by apportionment a direct tax on all real estate and personal property, or the income thereof, might not also lay excise taxes on business, privileges, employments, and vocations. But this is not such an act; and the scheme must be considered as a whole. Being invalid as to the greater part, and falling, as the tax would, if any part were held valid, in a direction which could not have been contemplated except in connection with the taxation considered as an entirety, we are constrained to conclude that sections twenty-seven to thirty-seven, inclusive, of the act, which became a law without the signature of the President on August 28, 1894, are wholly inoperative and void.

Our conclusions may, therefore, be summed up as follows:

First. We adhere to the opinion already announced, that, taxes on real estate being indisputably direct taxes, taxes on the rents or income of real estate are equally direct taxes.

Second. We are of opinion that taxes on personal property, or on the income of personal property, are likewise direct taxes.

Third. The tax imposed by sections twenty-seven to thirty-seven, inclusive, of the act of 1894, so far as it falls on the income of real estate and of personal property, being a direct tax within the meaning of the Constitution, and, therefore, unconstitutional and void because not apportioned according to representation, all those sections, constituting one entire scheme of taxation, are necessarily invalid.

The decrees herein before entered in this court will be vacated. The decrees below will be reversed, and the cases remanded, with instructions to grant the relief prayed.

MR. JUSTICE HARLAN, dissenting.

Assuming it to be the settled construction of the constitution that the general government cannot tax lands, . . . except by apportioning the tax among the states according to their respective numbers, does it follow that a tax on incomes derived from rents is a direct tax on the real estate from which such rents arise?

In my judgment, a tax on income derived from real property ought not to be, and until now has never been, regarded by any court as a direct tax on such property, within the meaning of the constitution. As the great mass of lands in most of the states do not bring any rents, and as incomes from rents vary in the different states, such a tax cannot possibly be apportioned among the states, on the basis merely of numbers, with any approach to equality of right among taxpayers, any more than a tax on carriages or other personal property could be so apportioned. And in view of former adjudications, beginning with the *Hylton*

This 1895 editorial cartoon, published after the Supreme Court's decision in Pollock v. Farmers' Loan & Trust, illustrates the defeat of the federal income tax law of 1894. In 1913, however, the situation was reversed when the states ratified the Sixteenth Amendment, which gave the federal government the power to tax income regardless of source.

Library of Congress

Case, and ending with the *Springer Case,* a decision now that a tax on income from real property can be laid and collected only by apportioning the same among the states on the basis of numbers may not improperly be regarded as a judicial revolution that may sow the seeds of hate and distrust among the people of different sections of our common country. . . .

While a tax on the land itself, whether at a fixed rate applicable to all lands, without regard to their value, or by the acre, or according to their market value, might be deemed a direct tax, within the meaning of the constitution, as interpreted in the *Hylton Case,* a duty on rents is a duty on something distinct and entirely separate from, although issuing out of, the land. . . .

But the court, by its judgment just rendered, goes far in advance, not only of its former decisions, but of any decision heretofore rendered by an American court. . . .

In my judgment,—to say nothing of the disregard of the former adjudications of this court, and of the settled practice of the government,—this decision may well excite the gravest apprehensions. It strikes at the very foundations of national authority, in that it denies to the general government a power which is or may become vital to the very existence and preservation of the Union in a national emergency, such as that of war with a great commercial nation, during which the collection of all duties upon imports will cease or be materially diminished. It tends to re-establish that condition of helplessness in which congress found itself during the period of the Articles of Confederation, when it was without authority, by laws operating directly upon individuals, to lay and collect, through its own agents, taxes sufficient to pay the debts and defray the expenses of government, but was dependent in all such matters upon the good will of the states, and their promptness in meeting requisitions made upon them by congress.

Why do I say that the decision just rendered impairs or menaces the national authority? The reason is so apparent that it need only be stated. In its practical operation this decision withdraws from national taxation not only all incomes derived from real estate, but tangible personal property, "invested personal property, bonds, stocks, investments of all kinds," and the income that may be derived from such property. This results from the fact that, by the decision of the court, all such personal property and all incomes from real estate and personal property are placed beyond national taxation otherwise than by apportionment among the states on the basis simply of population. No such apportionment can possibly be made without doing gross injustice to the many for the benefit of the favored few in particular states. Any attempt upon the part of congress to apportion among the states, upon the basis simply of their population, taxation of personal property or of incomes, would tend to arouse such indignation among the freemen of America that it would never be repeated. When, therefore, this court adjudges, as it does now adjudge, that congress cannot impose a duty or tax upon personal property, or upon income arising either from rents of real estate or from personal property, including invested personal property, bonds, stocks, and investments of all kinds, except by apportioning the sum to be so raised among the states according to population, it practically decides that, without an amendment of the constitution,—two-thirds of both houses of congress and three-fourths of the states concurring,—such property and incomes can never be made to contribute to the support of the national government. . . .

I dissent from the opinion and judgment of the court.

The Sixteenth Amendment

The decision to invalidate the entire income tax act was quite unpopular. Because that statute had placed a greater obligation on the wealthy, the ruling convinced the middle and working classes that the Supreme Court was little more than the defender of the rich. Various political groups immediately began working to reverse the impact of the Court's decision by means of either a constitutional amendment or revised federal legislation. Labor and farming interests supported a new income tax, as did Progressive Republicans and Democratic Populists. Opposition came primarily from conservative Republicans in the Northeast.

Finally, in 1909 Congress began serious work on an income tax measure. There were sufficient votes in the legislature to reform the tax structure, moving the federal government away from excessive reliance on regressive tariffs and excise taxes. The major question for legislators was whether to pass another income tax bill or to propose a constitutional amendment. Finding themselves in a minority, conservative Republicans threw their support to an amendment. They hoped the state legislatures would not ratify it, but, even if they did, that the process would take several years to complete.

Congress proposed a constitutional amendment to authorize a federal income tax in July 1909 by overwhelming votes of 77–0 in the Senate and 318–14 in the House. The amendment received the required number of approvals from the state legislatures in February 1913 and became the Sixteenth Amendment to the United States Constitution: "The Congress shall have power to lay and collect taxes on incomes, from whatever source derived, without apportionment among the several States, and without regard to any census or enumeration."

The amendment is one of only four designed to overturn a Supreme Court precedent. It gave Congress sufficient taxing authority to fund the federal government without having to resort to direct taxes. The Constitution now made all sources of income subject to Congress's taxing power and removed any requirement that a tax on income be apportioned on the basis of population.

TABLE 8-1 Federal Tax Revenues: The Impact of the Sixteenth Amendment

SOURCE	1800	1850	1900	1950	2000	2020 (EST.)
Customs duties	83.7	91.0	41.1	1.0	1.0	1.2
Excises	7.5	—	50.1	18.4	3.4	2.9
Gifts and inheritances	—	—	—	1.7	1.4	0.9
Individual incomes	—	—	—	38.5	49.6	48.9
Corporate incomes	—	—	—	25.5	10.2	11.8
Insurance trust (Social Security, etc.)	—	—	—	10.7	32.2	30.8
Misc. Taxes and Fees	8.8	9.0	8.8	4.2	2.2	3.5

SOURCES: *Historical Statistics of the United States: Colonial Times to 1970* (Washington, DC: U.S. Bureau of the Census, 1975); *World Almanac and Book of Facts 2006* (New York: World Almanac Books, 2006), 90; *Budget of the United States* (Washington, DC: Office of Management and Budget, various years).

NOTE: The data represent the percentage of total federal revenues for each of seven sources of taxation. The data prior to ratification of the Sixteenth Amendment in 1913 demonstrate the federal government's reliance on customs duties and excise taxes. Data from the period after 1913 illustrate the shift to income taxes as the primary sources for federal tax dollars. Estimates for 2020 are from the Budget of the United States for fiscal year 2016.

Congress wasted no time. In 1913 the legislature imposed a 1 percent tax rate on individual incomes in excess of $3,000 and on incomes of married couples over $4,000. Not surprisingly, the statute's constitutionality was challenged in the Court, but the justices upheld the law three years later in *Brushaber v. Union Pacific Railroad* (1916) by a 7–2 vote. As shown in table 8-1, the income tax is now the primary source of federal revenue.

TAXATION OF EXPORTS

Article I, Section 9, of the Constitution contains a prohibition against the taxation of exports: "No Tax or Duty shall be laid on Articles exported from any State." The purpose of this provision was to promote trade by removing impediments to the sale of American goods to other nations. In spite of the absolute language of the ban, Congress on occasion has passed assessments that have been attacked as taxes on exports. Such was the issue under consideration in *United States v. United States Shoe Corp.*

United States v. United States Shoe Corp.

523 U.S. 360 (1998)

http://laws.findlaw.com/us/523/360.html

Oral arguments are available at https://www.oyez.org.

Vote: 9 (Breyer, Ginsburg, Kennedy, O'Connor, Rehnquist, Scalia, Souter, Stevens, Thomas)

0

OPINION OF THE COURT: *Ginsburg*

FACTS:

As part of the Water Resources Development Act of 1986, Congress imposed the Harbor Maintenance Tax (HMT). This legislation assessed a uniform charge on shipments of commercial cargo through the nation's ports. The charge was set at 0.125 percent of the cargo's value. Exporters, importers, and domestic shippers were liable for the HMT, which was imposed at the time of loading for exports and at the time of unloading for other shipments. The Customs Service collected the HMT and deposited the money in the Harbor Maintenance Trust Fund. Congress could appropriate amounts from the fund to pay for harbor maintenance and development projects, including costs associated with the St. Lawrence Seaway, or related expenses.

United States Shoe Corporation paid the HMT for articles the company exported from April to June 1994 and then filed a protest with the Customs Service alleging that the toll was unconstitutional to the extent it applied to exports. The Customs Service responded with a form letter stating that the HMT was a statutorily mandated user fee, not an unconstitutional tax on exports. U.S. Shoe filed suit in the Court of International Trade challenging the constitutionality of the tax. The federal government defended the HMT, claiming that it was a legitimate user fee. The Court of International Trade held that the tax was not a user fee but a tax prohibited by Article I, Section 10. A divided court of appeals agreed, and the United States took its case to the Supreme Court.

For the petitioner, United States:

- The Harbor Maintenance Tax is a permissible fee on the use of the ports of the United States.
- Revenue measures that operate to compensate the government for benefits supplied are not prohibited by the export clause.
- The fees are assessed only on those who use the harbors. They do not discriminate against any constitutionally protected interest. Importers, exporters, and domestic shippers are all subject to the same fees.
- The funds collected are deposited in the Harbor Maintenance Trust Fund and are used only for the designated purpose of maintaining the nation's ports.

For the respondent, United States Shoe Corp.:

- There are no exceptions to the export clause's broad prohibition against any tax or duty placed on exports.
- To be permissible a fee must be applied narrowly, be directly related to the services provided by the government, and be no greater than necessary to compensate the government for the services rendered.
- This revenue measure is based on the worth of the cargo (*ad valorem*) and not on the size of the vessel, the manner or extent of the use of the harbor, or any attributes of the port. *Ad valorem* assessments are taxes, not fees for services rendered.
- The Harbor Maintenance Tax is not remotely related to the exporter's use of harbor services.

JUSTICE GINSBURG DELIVERED THE OPINION OF THE COURT.

The Export Clause of the Constitution states: "No Tax or Duty shall be laid on Articles exported from any State." We held in *United States v. International Business Machines Corp.* (*IBM*) (1996), that the Export Clause categorically bars Congress from imposing any tax on exports. The Clause, however, does not rule out a "user fee," provided that the fee lacks the attributes of a generally applicable tax or duty and is, instead, a charge designed as compensation for government-supplied services, facilities, or benefits. This case presents the question whether the Harbor Maintenance Tax (HMT), as applied to goods loaded at United States ports for export, is an impermissible tax on exports or, instead, a legitimate user fee. We hold, in accord with the Federal Circuit, that the tax, which is imposed on an ad valorem basis, is not a fair approximation of services, facilities, or benefits furnished to the exporters, and therefore does not qualify as a permissible user fee.

Two Terms ago, in *IBM*, this Court considered the question whether a tax on insurance premiums paid to protect exports against loss violated the Export Clause. Distinguishing case law developed under the Commerce Clause and the Import-Export Clause, the Court held that the Export Clause allows no room for any federal tax, however generally applicable or nondiscriminatory, on goods in export transit. Before this Court's decision in *IBM*, the Government argued that the HMT, even if characterized as a "tax" rather than a "user fee," should survive constitutional review "because it applies without discrimination to exports, imports and domestic commerce alike." Recognizing that *IBM* "rejected an indistinguishable contention," the Government now asserts only that HMT is "'a permissible user fee,'" a toll within the tolerance of Export Clause precedent. Adhering to the Court's reasoning in *IBM*, we reject the Government's current position.

The HMT bears the indicia of a tax. Congress expressly described it as "a tax on any port use," and codified the HMT as part of the Internal Revenue Code. In like vein, Congress provided that, for administrative, enforcement, and jurisdictional purposes, the HMT should be treated "as if [it] were a customs duty." However, "we must regard things rather than names," in determining whether an imposition on exports ranks as a tax. The crucial question is whether the HMT is a tax on exports in operation as well as nomenclature or whether, despite the label Congress has put on it, the exaction is instead a bona fide user fee.

In arguing that the HMT constitutes a user fee, the Government relies on our decisions in *United States v. Sperry Corp.* (1989), *Massachusetts v. United States* (1978), and *Evansville-Vanderburgh Airport Authority Dist. v. Delta Airlines, Inc.* (1972). In those cases, this Court upheld flat and ad valorem charges as valid user fees. . . . Those decisions involved constitutional provisions other than the Export Clause, however, and thus do not govern here. *IBM* plainly stated that the Export Clause's simple, direct, unqualified prohibition on any taxes or duties distinguishes it from other constitutional limitations on governmental taxing authority. The Court there emphasized that the "text of the Export Clause . . . expressly prohibits Congress from laying any tax or duty on exports." Accordingly, the Court reasoned in *IBM* "[o]ur decades-long struggle over the meaning of the nontextual negative command of the dormant Commerce Clause does not lead to the conclusion that our interpretation of the textual command of the Export Clause is equally fluid." . . .

The guiding precedent for determining what constitutes a bona fide user fee in the Export Clause context remains our time-tested decision in *Pace* [*v. Burgess*, 1876]. *Pace* involved a federal excise tax on tobacco. Congress provided that the tax would not apply to tobacco intended for export. To prevent fraud, however, Congress required that tobacco the manufacturer planned to export carry a stamp indicating that intention. Each stamp cost 25 cents (later 10 cents) per package of tobacco. Congress did not limit the quantity or value of the tobacco packaged for export or the size of the stamped package; "[t]hese were unlimited, except by the description of the exporter or the convenience of handling."

The Court upheld the charge, concluding that it was "in no sense a duty on exportation," but rather "compensation given for services [in fact] rendered." In so ruling, the Court emphasized two characteristics of the charge: It "bore no proportion whatever to the quantity or value of the package on which [the stamp] was affixed"; and the fee was not excessive, taking into account the cost of arrangements needed both "to give to the exporter the benefit of exemption from taxation, and . . . to secure . . . against the perpetration of fraud." *Pace* establishes that, under the Export Clause, the connection between a service the Government renders and the compensation it receives for that service must be closer than is present here. Unlike the stamp charge in *Pace*, the HMT is determined entirely on an ad valorem basis. The value of export cargo, however, does not correlate reliably with the federal harbor services used or usable by the exporter. As the Federal Circuit noted, the extent and manner of port use depend on factors such as the size and tonnage of a vessel, the length of time it spends in port, and the services it requires, for instance, harbor dredging.

In sum, if we are "to guard against . . . the imposition of a [tax] under the pretext of fixing a fee," *Pace v. Burgess*, and resist erosion of the Court's decision in *IBM*, we must hold that the HMT violates the Export Clause as applied to exports. This does not mean that exporters are exempt from any and all user fees designed to defray the cost of harbor development and maintenance. It does mean, however, that such a fee must fairly match the exporters' use of port services and facilities.

For the foregoing reasons, the judgment of the Court of Appeals for the Federal Circuit is

Affirmed.

INTERGOVERNMENTAL TAX IMMUNITY

The operation of a federal system carries within it inherent risks of conflict between the national government and the states. When both levels of government are authorized to tax, one government can use the power as a weapon against the other. No specific provision of the Constitution prohibits the federal government from taxing state governments or vice versa, but for the federal system to operate effectively, the entities need to avoid such conflicts.

Establishing the Tax Immunity Doctrine

The issue of intergovernmental tax immunity was first raised in *McCulloch v. Maryland* (1819), which tested the constitutional validity of the national bank. The Supreme Court's decision in *McCulloch* was tremendously important in a number of ways. We have already discussed it in terms of the development of congressional power and the concept of federalism, but *McCulloch* also is relevant to the constitutional limitations on the power to tax.

McCulloch involved a challenge to a tax imposed by the state of Maryland on the national bank, a creation of the federal government. Supporters of federal power argued that the Union could not be maintained if the states were permitted to place debilitating taxes on any operation of the federal government of which they disapproved. States' rights advocates claimed that the power of the states to tax within their own borders was absolute and that there was no constitutional bar to such taxes. The Supreme Court ruled in favor of the federal government, declaring the state tax unconstitutional. With his hard-hitting opinion for a unanimous Court, Chief Justice Marshall put an immediate stop to a conflict that would have severely weakened the Union if allowed to continue.

In doing so, Marshall created the doctrine of intergovernmental tax immunity. He wrote, "[T]he power to tax involves the power to destroy; . . . the power to destroy may defeat and render useless the power to create; . . . there is plain repugnance, in conferring on one government a power to control the constitutional measures of another." The ability of the states to tax the legitimate operations of the federal government is simply incompatible with the framers' intent of creating viable government units at both the national and state levels.

Marshall's decision in *McCulloch* was consistent with his general philosophy of favoring a strong national government. But was the doctrine of intergovernmental tax immunity a two-way street? Marshall's opinion fell short of proclaiming that the national government was prohibited from taxing the legitimate operations of the states. He was more concerned in this case with reinforcing principles of federal supremacy. Yet a strong case can be made that it would also violate the principles of the Constitution for the federal government to be permitted to destroy the states through its taxing power.

The first case that tested whether the states enjoyed immunity from federal taxation was **Collector v. Day** (1871), which stemmed from an application of the Civil War federal income tax law. Judge J. M. Day of the probate court in Massachusetts objected to paying a federal tax on his income on intergovernmental tax immunity grounds. Three decades earlier the Supreme Court had ruled that the state governments could not tax the income of federal officeholders,[9] and now Day was asking the Court to adopt the converse of that. The Supreme Court held, in an 8–1 vote, that Day's judicial income was immune from federal taxation. The Court reasoned that the Constitution protects the legitimate functions of the state. The federal government cannot use its taxation powers to curtail or destroy the operations or instruments of the state, and the probate court system is a legitimate and necessary agency of state government. To allow the federal government to tax the income of state judges would be to open the door for Congress to tax all state government functions.

For several decades the justices vigorously maintained the doctrine that the Constitution did not allow one government to tax the essential functions of another. In the *Pollock* income tax decisions, as we have already seen, the Court struck down a federal tax on interest income from state and municipal bonds as an unconstitutional burden on the state's authority to borrow. The Court struck down state taxes on income from federal land leases and federally granted patents and copyrights, and from the sales of petroleum products to the federal government.[10] It also invalidated a federal tax on revenues derived from the sales of

goods to state agencies.[11] The only significant standard the Court imposed in this line of cases was that immunity covered only essential government functions. Consequently, the justices upheld a federal tax on the profits of South Carolina's state-run liquor stores.[12] As a merchant of alcoholic beverages, the state was acting as a private business, not exercising a government function, and therefore was not immune from federal taxation.

Erosion of the Tax Immunity Doctrine

The Court's general support for the tax immunity doctrine in the early 1900s was closely related to its conservatism and adherence to dual federalism; it opposed both a big federal government and comprehensive regulation of the economy. When the New Deal justices took control of the Court, however, support for the tax immunity doctrine began to wane. A series of Court decisions modified or reversed the earlier rulings that had established an almost impenetrable barrier against one government taxing the instruments or operations of another.

In **Helvering v. Gerhardt** (1938) the Court overruled *Dobbins v. Commissioners of Erie County* (1842) and permitted states to tax the income of federal officials. The very next year the justices overruled *Collector v. Day* in **Graves v. New York ex rel. O'Keefe** (1939), holding that there was no constitutional bar to the federal government taxing the income of state employees. "The theory," said the Court, "that a tax on income is legally or economically a tax on its source, is no longer tenable." Also falling were bans on taxing profits from doing business with state or federal government agencies. The Court went so far as to allow a state to impose taxes on a federal contractor even when those taxes were passed on to the federal government through a cost-plus contract.[13]

Although these rulings seriously weakened the doctrine of intergovernmental tax immunity, the principle still has some vitality. It would be unconstitutional for a state to place a tax on cases filed in the federal courts operating within its boundaries, or for the federal government to impose an excise tax on the tickets issued by a state highway patrol. But aside from these obvious examples, where is the line between permissible and

---

9. *Dobbins v. Commissioners of Erie County* (1842).

10. *Gillespie v. Oklahoma* (1922) and *Long v. Rockwood* (1928) concerned patents and copyrights; *Panhandle Oil Co. v. Mississippi* (1928) dealt with petroleum sales.

---

11. *Indian Motorcycle Co. v. United States* (1931).

12. *South Carolina v. United States* (1905).

13. *Alabama v. King and Boozer* (1941).

impermissible taxation? The Court helped answer that question in *South Carolina v. Baker* (1988), which involved a challenge to a federal law taxing the income from long-term state and city bonds. To uphold the federal tax, the Court would have to overrule that portion of the *Pollock* decision that conferred immunity on such debt instruments issued by the state. The opinion by Justice William Brennan not only answered the specific question presented to the Court but also provided an informative review of the status of the intergovernmental tax immunity doctrine. Also instructive is the dissenting opinion of Justice Sandra Day O'Connor, who vigorously defended the immunity position.

South Carolina v. Baker

485 U.S. 505 (1988)
http://laws.findlaw.com/us/485/505.html
Oral arguments are available at https://www.oyez.org.
Vote: 7 (Blackmun, Brennan, Marshall, Rehnquist, Scalia, Stevens, White)
*   1 (O'Connor)*

OPINION OF THE COURT: *Brennan*
CONCURRING OPINIONS: *Rehnquist, Scalia, Stevens*
DISSENTING OPINION: *O'Connor*
NOT PARTICIPATING: *Kennedy*

FACTS:

State and municipal bonds traditionally have been issued either as bearer bonds or as registered bonds. Interest from bearer bonds is presumed to belong to the person who owns the bonds, and the interest is paid when the owner redeems coupons attached to the bonds. Owners of registered bonds are recorded on a central list, and if a bond is sold the transaction must be recorded. The owner of record automatically receives interest payments by check or electronic transfer of funds. State and municipal bonds of both types have been free from federal taxation on interest earned since the Supreme Court's decision in *Pollock*.

In 1982 Congress passed the Tax Equity and Fiscal Responsibility Act. Section 310(b)(1) of that statute removed the federal income tax exemption for interest earned on publicly offered long-term bonds issued by state and local governments unless the bonds were issued in registered form. The primary purpose of Section 310 was to increase compliance with federal tax laws and thereby increase federal revenues. Congress estimated that income of $97 billion was going unreported. Bearer bonds became a target of reform efforts because of the ease with which they could be bought and sold. If the ownership transfer was not registered, the bondholder could evade income tax on capital gains. Unregistered bonds also were used to evade estate taxes. Other provisions in this law encouraged the federal government and private corporations to stop issuing nonregistered long-term bonds.

The state of South Carolina sued the United States, in the name of Secretary of the Treasury James Baker, to have the law declared unconstitutional as a violation of the Tenth Amendment and the intergovernmental tax immunity doctrine. The case was heard on original jurisdiction. A special master appointed by the Court recommended that the justices uphold the validity of the law.

ARGUMENTS:

For the plaintiff, state of South Carolina:

- The federal government lacks the authority to dictate how a state carries out its essential functions. This law violates state autonomy guaranteed by the Tenth Amendment and other constitutional provisions.
- Placing a federal tax on income from state and local bonds will require the states to increase the interest rates paid to those who buy the state's bonds. As a consequence, the federal government will be placing a significant burden on the states' revenue powers.
- The Court should not overrule *Pollock v. Farmers' Loan & Trust,* but it should honor the doctrine of intergovernmental tax immunity.

For the defendant, James A. Baker III, U.S. Secretary of the Treasury:

- The Court should reconsider the holding in *Pollock v. Farmers' Loan & Trust* that interest income from state and local bonds is immune from nondiscriminatory federal taxation.
- The law targets the form in which state and local bonds are issued. It does not restrict the states' revenue-gathering authority. The law does not violate the Tenth Amendment.
- The tax is applied to those who do business with the state, not to the state itself.
- Any administrative cost associated with issuing registered bonds is incidental and cannot be considered a tax on the state.

JUSTICE BRENNAN DELIVERED THE OPINION OF THE COURT.

South Carolina contends that even if a statute banning state bearer bonds entirely would be constitutional, §310 unconstitutionally violates the doctrine of intergovernmental tax immunity because it imposes a tax on the interest earned on a state bond. We agree with South Carolina that §310 is inconsistent with *Pollock v. Farmers' Loan & Trust Co.* (1895), which held that any interest earned on a state bond was immune from federal taxation. . . .

Under the intergovernmental tax immunity jurisprudence prevailing at the time, *Pollock* did not represent a unique immunity limited to income derived from state bonds. Rather, *Pollock* merely represented one application of the more general rule that neither the federal nor the state governments could tax income an individual directly derived from *any* contract with another government. Not only was it unconstitutional for the Federal Government to tax a bondowner on the interest she received on any state bond, but it was also unconstitutional to tax a state employee on the income earned from his employment contract, to tax a lessee on income derived from lands leased from a State, or to impose a sales tax on proceeds a vendor derived from selling a product to a state agency. Income derived from the same kinds of contracts with the Federal Government were likewise immune from taxation by the States. . . .

This general rule was based on the rationale that any tax on income a party received under a contract with the government was a tax on the contract and thus a tax "on" the government because it burdened the government's power to enter into the contract. . . . Thus, although a tax was collected from an independent private party, the tax was considered to be "on" the government because the tax burden might be passed on to it through the contract. This reasoning was used to define the basic scope of both federal and state tax immunities with respect to all types of government contracts. . . .

The rationale underlying *Pollock* and the general immunity for government contract income has been thoroughly repudiated by modern intergovernmental immunity caselaw. . . .

With the rationale for conferring a tax immunity on parties dealing with another government rejected, the government contract immunities recognized under prior doctrine were, one by one, eliminated. . . .

In sum, then, under current intergovernmental tax immunity doctrine the States can never tax the United States directly but can tax any private parties with whom it does business, even though the financial burden falls on the United States, as long as the tax does not discriminate against the United States or those with whom it deals. A tax is considered to be directly on the Federal Government only "when the levy falls on the United States itself, or on an agency or instrumentality so closely connected to the Government that the two cannot realistically be viewed as separate entities." The rule with respect to state tax immunity is essentially the same, except that at least some nondiscriminatory federal taxes can be collected directly from the States even though a parallel state tax could not be collected directly from the Federal Government.

We thus confirm that subsequent case law has overruled the holding in *Pollock* that state bond interest is immune from a nondiscriminatory federal tax. We see no constitutional reason for treating persons who receive interest on government bonds differently than persons who receive income from other types of contracts with the government, and no tenable rationale for distinguishing the costs imposed on States by a tax on state bond interest from the costs imposed by a tax on the income from any other state contract. . . . Likewise, the owners of state bonds have no constitutional entitlement not to pay taxes on income they earn from state bonds, and States have no constitutional entitlement to issue bonds paying lower interest rates than other issuers. . . .

TEFRA [Tax Equity and Fiscal Responsibility Act] §310 thus clearly imposes no direct tax on the States. The tax is imposed on and collected from bondholders, not States, and any increased administrative costs incurred by States in implementing the registration system are not "taxes" within the meaning of the tax immunity doctrine. . . . Nor does §310 discriminate against States. The provisions of §310 seek to assure that *all* publicly offered long-term bonds are issued in registered form, whether issued by state or local governments, the Federal Government, or private corporations. Accordingly, the Federal Government has directly imposed the same registration requirement on itself that it has effectively imposed on States. The incentives States have to switch to registered bonds are necessarily different than those of corporate bond issuers because only state bonds enjoy any exemption from the federal tax on bond interest, but the sanctions for issuing unregistered corporate bonds are comparably severe. Removing the tax exemption for interest earned on state bonds would not, moreover, create a discrimination between state and corporate bonds since corporate bond interest is already subject to federal tax.

Because the federal imposition of a bond registration requirement on States does not violate the Tenth Amendment and because a nondiscriminatory federal tax on the interest earned on state bonds does not violate the intergovernmental tax immunity doctrine, we uphold the constitutionality of §310. . . .

It is so ordered.

JUSTICE O'CONNOR, dissenting.

The Court today overrules a precedent that it has honored for nearly a hundred years and expresses a willingness to cancel the constitutional immunity that traditionally has shielded the interest paid on state and local bonds from federal taxation. Henceforth the ability of state and local governments to finance their activities will depend in part on whether Congress voluntarily abstains from tapping this permissible source of additional income tax revenue. I believe that state autonomy is an important factor to be considered in reviewing the National Government's exercise of its enumerated powers. I dissent from the decision to overrule *Pollock v. Farmers' Loan & Trust Co.* (1895), and I would invalidate Congress' attempt to regulate the sovereign States by threatening to deprive them of this tax immunity, which would increase their dependence on the National Government. . . .

Long-term debt obligations are an essential source of funding for state and local governments. In 1974, state and local governments issued approximately $23 billion of new municipal bonds; in 1984, they issued $102 billion of new bonds. State and local governments rely heavily on borrowed funds to finance education, road construction, and utilities, among other purposes. As the Court recognizes, States will have to increase the interest rates they pay on bonds by 28–35% if the interest is subject to the federal income tax. Governmental operations will be hindered severely if the cost of capital rises by one-third. If Congress may tax the interest paid on state and local bonds, it may strike at the very heart of state and local government activities. . . .

Federal taxation of state activities is inherently a threat to state sovereignty. As Chief Justice Marshall observed long ago, "the power to tax involves the power to destroy." Justice Holmes later qualified this principle, observing that "[t]he power to tax is not the power to destroy while this Court sits." If this Court is the States' sole protector against the threat of crushing taxation, it must take seriously its responsibility to sit in judgment of federal tax initiatives. I do not think that the Court has lived up to its constitutional role in this case. The Court has failed to enforce the constitutional safeguards of state autonomy and self-sufficiency that may be found in the Tenth Amendment and the Guarantee Clause, as well as in the principles of federalism implicit in the Constitution. I respectfully dissent.

South Carolina v. Baker continued a long-standing trend of the Court toward eroding the doctrine of intergovernmental tax immunity. A statement of the contemporary status of the doctrine, in Justice Brennan's words, is that "the States can never tax the United States directly but can tax any private parties with whom it does business, even though the financial burden falls on the United States, as long as the tax does not discriminate against the United States or those with whom it deals." A similar, though not quite as rigid, prohibition applies to federal taxes on the states.

Even in cases such as *South Carolina v. Baker* that limited intergovernmental tax immunity, the Court repeatedly has stressed the principle that taxes must be nondiscriminatory. If a state wishes to tax a company's profits from a business transaction with the federal government, the tax obligation must be the same as that imposed on profits from business with nongovernment parties. This bar against discriminatory taxation was tested in *Davis v. Michigan Dept. of Treasury* (1989). At issue was a Michigan tax exemption given to state government retirees but not to federal government retirees. Justice Anthony Kennedy's opinion for the Court reviews the immunity doctrine's development and answers the challenge presented by the case.

Davis v. Michigan Dept. of Treasury

489 U.S. 803 (1989)
http://laws.findlaw.com/us/489/803.html
Oral arguments are available at https://www.oyez.org.
Vote: 8 (Blackmun, Brennan, Kennedy, Marshall, O'Connor, Rehnquist, Scalia, White)
    1 (Stevens)

OPINION OF THE COURT: *Kennedy*
DISSENTING OPINION: *Stevens*

FACTS:

Michigan's revenue code provided that retirement benefits paid to individuals by the state or any of its political subdivisions were exempt from state income taxes.

Retirement benefits from any other source, including federal retirement income, were subject to the tax. Paul S. Davis spent his career in federal service, as a lawyer for the Securities and Exchange Commission and then as an administrative law judge. As a Michigan resident, he paid state income taxes on his federal retirement benefits. In 1984, however, Davis petitioned the state for a refund of taxes paid on his federal benefits for the 1979–1984 tax years.

He based his case on a federal statute (4 U.S.C. §111) passed in 1939 to clarify the doctrine of intergovernmental tax immunity. The law provided,

The United States consents to the taxation of pay or compensation for personal service as an officer or employee of the United States . . . by a duly constituted taxing authority having jurisdiction, if the taxation does not discriminate against the officer or employee because of the source of the pay or compensation.

State revenue authorities and state courts rejected Davis's claim. The state argued that Davis was not covered by the act because he was no longer an "employee" of the federal government but simply a receiver of annuity benefits. Furthermore, Michigan claimed that the state law did not discriminate against federal employees but only provided a special exemption for state retirees, a reasonable incentive intended to attract and keep qualified people in state government service.

Davis appealed to the U.S. Supreme Court and, in fact, personally argued his case before the justices. He enjoyed the help of a powerful ally, however, when the U.S. government supported his claim as a friend of the court.

ARGUMENTS:

For the appellant, Paul S. Davis:

- Under federal law states may tax the compensation of federal employees as long as the tax does not discriminate on the basis of the source of the income.
- Michigan taxes the income from federal retirement programs but does not tax the income from state retirement programs.
- Treating the income from federal and state retirement plans differently violates the intergovernmental tax immunity doctrine and the federal law allowing the nondiscriminatory taxation of income from federal employment.

For the appellee, state of Michigan Department of Treasury:

- The intergovernmental tax immunity doctrine is based on the supremacy clause and protects only governments, not individuals, from the taxation efforts of other governments.
- The intergovernmental tax immunity doctrine protects the federal government from state taxation that is aimed at or threatens the efficient operation of the government. There is no evidence that Michigan's tax on retirement incomes of former federal employees places any burden on any federal government program.
- Federal law bans discriminatory state taxes on the income of federal employees. Davis is no longer a federal employee. His retirement program income is not "compensation for personal service as an officer or employee of the United States."
- Exempting retirement income from taxation for former state government employees serves a legitimate public purpose of fostering Michigan public employment.

JUSTICE KENNEDY DELIVERED THE OPINION OF THE COURT.

Section 111 was enacted as part of the Public Salary Tax Act of 1939, the primary purpose of which was to impose federal income tax on the salaries of all state and local government employees. Prior to the adoption of the Act, salaries of most government employees, both state and federal, generally were thought to be exempt from taxation by another sovereign under the doctrine of intergovernmental tax immunity. This doctrine had its genesis in *McCulloch v. Maryland* (1819), which held that the State of Maryland could not impose a discriminatory tax on the Bank of the United States. Chief Justice Marshall's opinion for the Court reasoned that the Bank was an instrumentality of the Federal Government used to carry into effect the Government's delegated powers, and taxation by the State would unconstitutionally interfere with the exercise of those powers.

For a time, *McCulloch* was read broadly to bar most taxation by one sovereign of the employees of another. See *Collector v. Day* (1871) (invalidating federal income tax on salary of state judge); *Dobbins v. Commissioners of Erie County* (1842) (invalidating state tax on federal officer). This rule "was based on the rationale that any tax on income a party received under a contract with the government was a tax on the contract and thus a tax 'on' the government because it burdened the government's power to enter into the contract." *South Carolina v. Baker* (1988).

In subsequent cases, however, the Court began to turn away from its more expansive applications of the immunity doctrine. Thus, in *Helvering v. Gerhardt* (1938), the Court held that the Federal Government could levy nondiscriminatory taxes on the incomes of most state employees. The following year, *Graves v. New York ex rel. O'Keefe* (1939) overruled the *Day-Dobbins* line of cases that had exempted government employees from nondiscriminatory taxation. After *Graves*, therefore, intergovernmental tax immunity barred only those taxes that were imposed directly on one sovereign by the other or that discriminated against a sovereign or those with whom it dealt.

It was in the midst of this judicial revision of the immunity doctrine that Congress decided to extend the federal income tax to state and local government employees. The Public Salary Tax Act was enacted after *Helvering v. Gerhardt* had upheld the imposition of federal income taxes on state civil servants, and Congress relied on that decision as support for its broad assertion of federal taxing authority. However, the Act was drafted, considered in Committee, and passed by the House of Representatives before the announcement of the decision in *Graves v. New York ex rel. O'Keefe*, which for the first time permitted state taxation of federal employees. As a result, during most of the legislative process leading to adoption of the Act it was unclear whether state taxation of federal employees was still barred by intergovernmental tax immunity despite the abrogation of state employees' immunity from federal taxation. . . .

Dissatisfied with this uncertain state of affairs, and concerned that considerations of fairness demanded equal tax treatment for state and federal employees, Congress decided to ensure that federal employees would not remain immune from state taxation at the same time that state government employees were being required to pay federal income taxes. Accordingly, section 4 of the proposed Act (now section 111) expressly waived whatever immunity would have otherwise shielded federal employees from nondiscriminatory state taxes. . . .

Section 111 did not waive all aspects of intergovernmental tax immunity, however. The final clause of the section contains an exception for state taxes that discriminate against federal employees on the basis of the source of their compensation. This nondiscrimination clause closely parallels the nondiscrimination component of the constitutional immunity doctrine which has, from the time of *McCulloch v. Maryland*, barred taxes that "operat[e] so as

to discriminate against the Government of those with whom it deals."

. . . When Congress codifies a judicially defined concept, it is presumed, absent an express statement to the contrary, that Congress intended to adopt the interpretation placed on that concept by the courts. Hence, we conclude that the retention of immunity in section 111 is coextensive with the prohibition against discriminatory taxes embodied in the modern constitutional doctrine of intergovernmental tax immunity.

. . . Thus, the dispositive question in this case is whether the tax imposed on appellant is barred by the doctrine of intergovernmental tax immunity.

It is undisputed that Michigan's tax system discriminates in favor of retired state employees and against retired federal employees. The State argues, however, that appellant is not entitled to claim the protection of the immunity doctrine, and that in any event the State's inconsistent treatment of Federal and State Government retirees is justified by meaningful differences between the two classes.

In support of its first contention, the State points out that the purpose of the immunity doctrine is to protect the governments and not private entities or individuals. As a result, so long as the challenged tax does not interfere with the Federal Government's ability to perform its governmental functions, the constitutional doctrine has not been violated.

It is true that intergovernmental tax immunity is based on the need to protect each sovereign's governmental operations from undue interference by the other. But it does not follow that private entities or individuals who are subjected to discriminatory taxation on account of their dealings with a sovereign cannot themselves receive the protection of the constitutional doctrine. Indeed, all precedent is to the contrary. . . .

Under our precedents, "[t]he imposition of a heavier tax burden on [those who deal with one sovereign] than is imposed on [those who deal with the other] must be justified by significant differences between the two classes." *Phillips Chemical Co. v. Dumas Independent School District* [1960]. . . .

The State points to two allegedly significant differences between federal and state retirees. First, the State suggests that its interest in hiring and retaining qualified civil servants through the inducement of a tax exemption for retirement benefits is sufficient to justify the preferential treatment of its retired employees. This argument is wholly beside the point, however, for it does nothing to demonstrate that there are "significant differences between the two classes" themselves; rather, it merely demonstrates that the State has a rational reason for discriminating between two similar groups of retirees. The State's interest in adopting the discriminatory tax, no matter how substantial, is simply irrelevant to an inquiry into the nature of the two classes receiving inconsistent treatment.

Second, the State argues that its retirement benefits are significantly less munificent than those offered by the Federal Government, in terms of vesting requirements, rate of accrual, and computation of benefit amounts. The substantial differences in the value of the retirement benefits paid the two classes should, in the State's view, justify the inconsistent tax treatment.

Even assuming the State's estimate of the relative value of state and federal retirement benefits is generally correct, we do not believe this difference suffices to justify the type of blanket exemption at issue in this case. While the average retired federal civil servant receives a larger pension than his state counterpart, there are undoubtedly many individual instances in which the opposite holds true. A tax exemption truly intended to account for differences in retirement benefits would not discriminate on the basis of the source of those benefits, as Michigan's statute does; rather, it would discriminate on the basis of the amount of benefits received by individual retirees. . . .

For these reasons, we conclude that the Michigan Income Tax Act violates principles of intergovernmental tax immunity by favoring retired state and local government employees over retired federal employees. . . .

. . . The judgment of the Court of Appeals is reversed, and the case is remanded for further proceedings not inconsistent with this opinion.

JUSTICE STEVENS, dissenting.

The Court today strikes down a state tax that applies equally to the vast majority of Michigan residents, including federal employees, because it treats retired state employees differently from retired federal employees. The Court's holding is not supported by the rationale for the intergovernmental immunity doctrine and is not compelled by our previous decisions. I cannot join the unjustified, court-imposed restriction on a State's power to administer its own affairs. . . .

If Michigan were to tax the income of federal employees without imposing a like tax on others, the tax would be plainly unconstitutional. Cf. *McCulloch v. Maryland* (1819). On the other hand, if the State taxes the income of all its residents equally, federal employees must pay the tax.

Graves v. New York ex rel. O'Keefe (1939). The Michigan tax here applies to approximately 4½ million individual taxpayers in the State, including the 24,000 retired federal employees. It exempts only the 130,000 retired state employees. Once one understands the underlying reason for the *McCulloch* holding [the immunity doctrine is a check against the abusive use of the taxing power by one sovereign against the other], it is plain that this tax does not unconstitutionally discriminate against federal employees. . . .

Today, it is not the great Chief Justice's dictum about how the power to tax includes the power to destroy that obscures the issue in a web of unreality; it is the virtually automatic rejection of anything that can be labeled "discriminatory." The question in this case deserves more careful consideration than is provided by the mere use of that label. It should be answered by considering whether the ratio decidendi of our holding in *McCulloch v. Maryland* is applicable to this quite different case. It is not. I, therefore, respectfully dissent.

As a result of this decision, Paul Davis received tax refunds of $4,299. But the impact of the decision extended far beyond Davis. Fourteen other states had similar discriminatory tax provisions. As a consequence, this ruling cost these states hundreds of millions of dollars in tax refunds to federal retirees and lost future revenues. The states were required to revise their laws, making a choice between extending the tax exemptions to retired federal employees or eliminating the exemption granted to state and local retirees. The Court's decision in *Davis* reminds us that the tax immunity doctrine remains viable in spite of decisions that have imposed limitations on it.

TAXATION AS A REGULATORY POWER

Normally, we think of taxation as a method of funding the government. Yet Marshall's well-known statement that the "power to tax involves the power to destroy" was an early recognition that taxes can be used for purposes other than raising revenue. Excessive taxation can make the targeted activities so unprofitable that engaging in them is no longer feasible. The converse also is true. Favorable tax status, including tax exemptions, can encourage preferred activities. These observations raise several important constitutional questions regarding the taxation powers of the federal government: Is it proper for the United States to impose taxes for reasons other than revenue raising? Is it constitutional for the government to use taxation as a method of regulation? Is it valid for Congress to enact tax laws as means of controlling activities not otherwise within the jurisdiction of the federal government? Here we are confronting a question similar to one we examined relative to the commerce clause: May the federal government use the power to tax as the equivalent of a state's police power?

Taxation for Nonrevenue Purposes

From the beginning, Congress has used its authority to tax for purposes other than raising revenue. Before the ratification of the Sixteenth Amendment, the federal government relied heavily on the funds raised through customs duties. In deciding what imported products to tax and at what level, the legislators clearly were guided by their policy preferences. Certain industries received protection from imports and were able to grow with little foreign competition. The practice of combining revenue gathering with other policy objectives continues to this day.

The only serious challenge to the use of import taxes as a regulatory mechanism came in *J. W. Hampton, Jr. & Co. v. United States* (1928). Hampton Company imported into New York a quantity of barium dioxide that was assessed a duty of six cents per pound, two cents higher than the rate set by Congress. The legislature had, however, authorized the president to raise or lower tariff duties up to 50 percent of the amount set by Congress whenever the chief executive found that such adjustments were necessary for equitable foreign trade. In this case President Calvin Coolidge had concluded that an increased tariff was necessary to equalize the barium dioxide production costs between Germany and the United States. Hampton objected to the tax, claiming that the flexible tariff was an improper delegation of legislative power to the executive branch and that Congress violated the Constitution by using the taxation powers for reasons other than revenue gathering. As we saw in chapter 5, the Supreme Court ruled that the delegation was proper.

The justices also held in *Hampton* that Congress did not have to rely exclusively on revenue needs when it constructed tariff laws. In reaching this conclusion, the Court showed a deference to history. Chief Justice William Howard Taft, writing for the majority, noted that the very first revenue act in 1789 imposed import duties with an eye toward encouraging growth of domestic industry and protecting it from foreign competition. The Court was not likely to rule unconstitutional a practice that had been followed uninterrupted for almost a century and a half. "So long as the motive of Congress and the effect of its legislative action are to secure revenue for the benefit of the general government," Taft wrote, "the existence of other motives in the selection of the subjects of taxes cannot invalidate Congressional action."

Deciding that Congress may impose import duties with regulatory purposes does not necessarily answer a similar question with respect to excise taxes. Customs duties, after all, have a limited range. They can be applied only to those goods that are brought into the country from abroad. Excise taxes can be applied to the broad spectrum of domestic goods, services, and activities. The only restriction on such taxes explicitly mentioned in the Constitution is that they be geographically uniform. But is there an implied requirement that excise taxes can be generated only by revenue objectives, or can Congress regulate through the use of the excise? If Congress is allowed to regulate domestic activities through the power to tax, does that not give the federal government the equivalent of a police power that the framers reserved to the states?

Shortly after the Civil War, the Court heard *Veazie Bank v. Fenno* (1869), which presented a challenge to a federal excise tax that was imposed far more to regulate the economy than to raise revenue. In 1866 Congress passed a law placing a 10 percent tax on notes issued by state banks. The law was intended to protect the newly chartered national bank from state competition by making these notes far too costly for state banks to issue. Veazie Bank paid the tax under protest, claiming that Congress had no authority to issue such an excise. But in a 5–2 decision, the Court held that the tax was proper given the constitutional power of Congress to regulate the monetary system.

Does the *Veazie Bank* decision mean that Congress may impose excise taxes for any regulatory purpose or only as a means of promoting a power already granted to the federal government? The first major case to confront this question focused on a federal excise tax placed on margarine.

McCray v. United States

195 U.S. 27 (1904)
http://laws.findlaw.com/us/195/27.html
Vote: 6 (Brewer, Day, Harlan, Holmes, McKenna, White)
    3 (Brown, Fuller, Peckham)
OPINION OF THE COURT: White

FACTS:

In the latter half of the nineteenth century, food producers developed a commercially marketable oleomargarine. The product was made of oleo oil, lard, milk, cream, and salt. It had a taste and consistency similar to butter but was less expensive. Especially successful was a margarine that was artificially colored to make the naturally white product look like butter. As margarine grew in popularity, the dairy industry became concerned and demanded protection. In response, Congress passed the Oleomargarine Act of 1886 and amended it in 1902. In addition to licensing producers and retailers of margarine, the statute imposed an excise tax of one-quarter cent per pound on uncolored margarine and a tax of ten cents per pound on artificially colored margarine. The margarine manufacturers were responsible for paying the tax. Although the act raised revenue, its central purpose was to protect the dairy industry by raising the price of margarine and discouraging the sale of the artificially colored product.

Leo McCray, a licensed retail seller of margarine, was assessed a $50 penalty for knowingly purchasing from the Ohio Butterine Company a fifty-pound package of margarine for resale on which sufficient taxes had not been paid. The package bore the one-quarter cent tax stamps, but the margarine was artificially colored and thus subject to the higher tax. McCray challenged his fine, claiming that the federal tax was unconstitutional. The lower courts upheld the validity of the tax.

ARGUMENTS:

For the plaintiff in error, Leo W. McCray:

- The tax on oleomargarine colored like butter places an unreasonable burden on a wholesome food product. As a consequence it deprives McCray of his property without due process of law.
- The United States has no authority to impose such a regulatory tax and is interfering with the police powers of the states by doing so.
- This arbitrary tax discriminates against oleomargarine in favor of butter. The purpose of the law is not to gain revenue for the federal government but to destroy the oleomargarine industry for the benefit of the butter industry. This violates the fundamental principles of justice and equity inherent in the Constitution.

For the defendant in error, United States:

- The tax on oleomargarine is an excise tax on a product.
- The Constitution places no restraints on the government's power to levy excise taxes except geographical uniformity. This tax meets that requirement and is therefore constitutional.

MR. JUSTICE WHITE DELIVERED THE OPINION OF THE COURT.

Did Congress in passing the acts which are assailed, exert a power not conferred by the Constitution?

That the acts in question on their face impose excise taxes which Congress had the power to levy is so completely established as to require only statement. . . .

It is, however, argued if a lawful power may be exerted for an unlawful purpose, and thus by abusing the power it may be made to accomplish a result not intended by the Constitution, all limitations of power must disappear, and the grave function lodged in the judiciary, to confine all the departments within the authority conferred by the Constitution, will be of no avail. This, when reduced to its last analysis, comes to this, that, because a particular department of the government may exert its lawful powers with the object or motive of reaching an end not justified, therefore it becomes the duty of the judiciary to restrain the exercise of a lawful power wherever it seems to the judicial mind that such lawful power has been abused. But this reduces itself to the contention that, under our constitutional system, the abuse by one department of the government of its lawful powers is to be corrected by the abuse of its powers by another department.

The proposition, if sustained, would destroy all distinction between the powers of the respective departments of the government, would put an end to that confidence and respect for each other which it was the purpose of the Constitution to uphold, and would thus be full of danger to the permanence of our institutions. . . .

It is, of course, true, as suggested, that if there be no authority in the judiciary to restrain a lawful exercise of power by another department of the government, where a wrong motive or purpose has impelled to the exertion of the power, that abuses of a power conferred may be temporarily effectual. The remedy for this, however, lies, not in the abuse by the judicial authority of its functions, but in the people, upon whom, after all, under our institutions, reliance must be placed for the correction of abuses committed in the exercise of a lawful power. . . .

The decisions of this court from the beginning lend no support whatever to the assumption that the judiciary may restrain the exercise of lawful power on the assumption that a wrongful purpose or motive has caused the power to be exerted. As we have previously said, from the beginning no case can be found announcing such a doctrine, and on the contrary the doctrine of a number of cases is inconsistent with its existence. As quite recently pointed out by this court in *Knowlton v. Moore* (1900), the often quoted statement of Chief Justice Marshall in *McCulloch v. Maryland*, that the power to tax is the power to destroy, affords no support whatever to the proposition that where there is a lawful power to impose a tax its imposition may be treated as without the power because of the destructive effect of the exertion of the authority. . . .

It being thus demonstrated that the motive or purpose of Congress in adopting the acts in question may not be inquired into, we are brought to consider the contentions relied upon to show that the acts assailed were beyond the power of Congress, putting entirely out of view all considerations based upon purpose or motive.

1. Undoubtedly, in determining whether a particular act is within a granted power, its scope and effect are to be considered. Applying this rule to the acts assailed, it is self-evident that on their face they levy an excise tax. That being their necessary scope and operation, it follows that the acts are within the grant of power. The argument to the contrary rests on the proposition that, although the tax be within the power, as enforcing it will destroy or restrict the manufacture of artificially colored oleomargarine, therefore the power to levy the tax did not obtain. This, however, is but to say that the question of power depends, not upon the authority conferred by the Constitution but upon what may be the consequence arising from the exercise of the lawful authority.

Since, as pointed out in all the decisions referred to, the taxing power conferred by the Constitution knows no limits except those expressly stated in that instrument, it must follow, if a tax be within the lawful power, the exertion of that power may not be judicially restrained because of the results to arise from its exercise. . . .

2. The proposition that where a tax is imposed which is within the grant of powers, and which does not conflict with any express constitutional limitation, the courts may hold the tax to be void because it is deemed that the tax is too high, is absolutely disposed of by the opinions in the cases hitherto cited, and which expressly hold . . . that "The judicial department cannot prescribe to the legislative department limitations upon the exercise of its acknowledged powers. The power to tax may be exercised oppressively upon persons; but the responsibility of the legislature is not to the courts, but to the people by whom its members are elected."

3. Whilst undoubtedly both the Fifth and Tenth Amendments qualify, in so far as they are applicable, all the provisions of the Constitution, nothing in those amendments operates to take away the grant of power to tax conferred by the Constitution upon Congress. The contention on this subject rests upon the theory that the purpose and motive of Congress in exercising its undoubted powers may be inquired into by the courts, and the proposition is therefore disposed of by what has been said on that subject.

The right of Congress to tax within its delegated power being unrestrained, except as limited by the Constitution, it was within the authority conferred on Congress to select the objects upon which an excise should be laid. It therefore follows that, in exerting its power, no want of due process of law could possibly result, because that body chose to impose an excise on artificially colored oleomargarine and not upon natural butter artificially colored. . . .

4. Lastly we come to consider the argument that, even though as a general rule a tax of the nature of the one in question would be within the power of Congress, in this case the tax should be held not to be within such power, because of its effect. This is based on the contention that, as the tax is so large as to destroy the business of manufacturing oleomargarine artificially colored, to look like butter, it thus deprives the manufacturers of that article of their freedom to engage in a lawful pursuit, and hence, irrespective of the distribution of powers made by the Constitution, the taxing laws are void, because they violate those fundamental rights which it is the duty of every free government to safeguard, and which, therefore, should be held to be embraced by implied though none the less potential guaranties, or in any event to be within the protection of the due process clause of the Fifth Amendment.

Let us concede, for the sake of argument only, the premise of fact upon which the proposition is based. Moreover, concede for the sake of argument only, that even although a particular exertion of power by Congress was not restrained by any express limitation of the Constitution, if by the perverted exercise of such power so great an abuse was manifested as to destroy fundamental rights which no free government could consistently violate, that it would be the duty of the judiciary to hold such acts to be void upon the assumption that the Constitution by necessary implication forbade them.

Such concession, however, is not controlling in this case. This follows when the nature of oleomargarine, artificially colored to look like butter, is recalled. As we have said, it has been conclusively settled by this court that the tendency of that article to deceive the public into buying it for butter is such that the States may, in the exertion of their police powers, without violating the due process clause of the Fourteenth Amendment, absolutely prohibit the manufacture of the article. It hence results, that even though it be true that the effect of the tax in question is to repress the manufacture of artificially colored oleomargarine, it cannot be said that such repression destroys rights which no free government could destroy, and, therefore, no ground exists to sustain the proposition that the judiciary may invoke an implied prohibition, upon the theory that to do so is essential to save such rights from destruction. And the same considerations dispose of the contention based upon the due process clause of the Fifth Amendment. That provision, as we have previously said, does not withdraw or expressly limit the grant of power to tax conferred upon Congress by the Constitution. From this it follows, as we have also previously declared, that the judiciary is without authority to avoid an act of Congress exerting the taxing power, even in a case where to the judicial mind it seems that Congress had in putting such power in motion abused its lawful authority by levying a tax which was unwise or oppressive, or the result of the enforcement of which might be to indirectly affect subjects not within the powers delegated to Congress.

Let us concede that if a case was presented where the abuse of the taxing power was so extreme as to be beyond the principles which we have previously stated, and where it was plain to the judicial mind that the power had been called into play not for revenue but solely for the purpose of destroying rights which could not be rightfully destroyed consistently with the principles of freedom and justice upon which the Constitution rests, that it would be the duty of the courts to say that such an arbitrary act was not merely an abuse of a delegated power, but was the exercise of an authority not conferred. This concession, however, like the one previously made, must be without influence upon the decision of this cause for the reasons previously stated; that is, that the manufacture of artificially colored oleomargarine may be prohibited by a free government without a violation of fundamental rights.

Affirmed.

With decisions such as *Veazie, McCray,* and others, Congress reasonably concluded that the power to tax could be used as a regulatory weapon. The legislators were encouraged by statements such as Justice Edward Douglass White's in *McCray:* "The decisions of this court from the beginning lend no support whatever to the assumption that the judiciary may restrain the exercise of lawful power on the assumption that a wrongful purpose or motive has caused the power to be exerted." The Court seemed committed to a policy of approving legislation that took the proper form of an excise tax and met the geographical uniformity requirement regardless of the congressional motives behind it. If the judiciary was not inclined to probe the legislative branch's motives, Congress would have a free hand in using taxation to regulate or even destroy certain activities lawmakers considered detrimental to the nation.

Rejection and Reestablishment of Regulatory Taxation

Among Congress's targets was child labor. As we saw in our discussions of federalism and the commerce clause, Congress first attempted to regulate child labor in the 1916 Keating-Owen Act, which prohibited the shipment in interstate and foreign commerce of articles produced by child labor. Just two years after that law was enacted, the Supreme Court, in *Hammer v. Dagenhart,* struck it down on the ground that Congress, under the guise of interstate commerce regulation, was actually controlling manufacturing and mining, considered at that time to be intrastate activities that states must regulate.

After suffering this defeat at the hands of the Court, Congress drafted a second statute to attack child labor, this time using the power to tax. Could the national legislature constitutionally use the excise tax as a means of eliminating child labor? Would the justices once again refuse to examine congressional motives? The answer to these questions came in *Bailey v. Drexel Furniture Co.* (1922). As you read Chief Justice Taft's opinion, note his distinction between a tax and a penalty. Does he make a compelling argument? And does it surprise you that progressive members of the Court, such as Oliver Wendell Holmes and Louis Brandeis, voted to strike down the law?

Bailey v. Drexel Furniture Co.

259 U.S. 20 (1922)

http://laws.findlaw.com/us/259/20.html

Vote: 8 (Brandeis, Day, Holmes, McKenna, McReynolds, Pitney, Taft, Van Devanter)

    1 (Clarke)

OPINION OF THE COURT: *Taft*

FACTS:

Congress passed the Child Labor Tax Law on February 24, 1919. The statute imposed an excise tax of 10 percent on the net profits of any company hiring child labor. Under the law, child labor was defined as the employment of children under the age of sixteen in any mine or quarry or under the age of fourteen in any mill, cannery, workshop, factory, or manufacturing establishment. The definition also included the use of children between the ages of fourteen and sixteen who worked more than eight hours a day or more than six days a week, or who worked between the hours of 7:00 P.M. and 6:00 A.M.

Drexel was a furniture manufacturing company in North Carolina. On September 20, 1921, it received from J. W. Bailey, the IRS collector for the Western District of North Carolina, a notice that it had been assessed $6,312.79 in excise taxes for having employed a boy under the age of fourteen during the 1919 tax year. The company paid the tax under protest and sued for a refund. The lower court ruled in favor of the company.

Young boys working a loom in Macon, Georgia, circa 1910. Conditions such as these were the target of reform legislation passed by Congress and declared unconstitutional by the Supreme Court in Hammer v. Dagenhart *(1918) and* Bailey v. Drexel Furniture Co. *(1922).*

National Archives Records Administration

ARGUMENTS:

For the plaintiff in error, J. W. Bailey, collector of internal revenue for the Western District of North Carolina:

- The challenged act is an excise tax that raises revenue for the federal government. As long as the tax is geographically uniform and is not levied on exports, it is constitutional. The law meets these requirements.
- The Court should not restrain the lawful power of Congress on the assumption that a wrongful purpose or motive caused the power to be exercised (*McCray v. United States*).
- Federal laws should not be invalidated where there is unquestioned power to act but there exists an incidental effect on some right reserved to the states.

For the defendant in error, Drexel Furniture Company:

- This legislation regulates child labor, a subject over which the federal government is without authority (*Hammer v. Dagenhart*).
- Congress has used the power to tax as a pretext for regulating a subject reserved for the states.
- The law is much more a criminal statute that imposes a penalty on those who violate it than it is a revenue measure.

▶ MR. CHIEF JUSTICE TAFT DELIVERED THE OPINION OF THE COURT.

The law is attacked on the ground that it is a regulation of the employment of child labor in the States—an exclusively state function under the Federal Constitution and within the reservations of the Tenth Amendment. It is defended on the ground that it is a mere excise tax levied by the Congress of the United States under its broad power of taxation conferred by §8, Article I, of the Federal Constitution. We must construe the law and interpret the intent and meaning of Congress from the language of the act. The words are to be given their ordinary meaning unless the context shows that they are differently used. Does this law impose a tax with only that incidental restraint and regulation which a tax must inevitably involve? Or does it regulate by the use of the so-called tax as a penalty? If a tax, it is clearly an excise. If it were an excise on a commodity or other thing of value we might not be permitted under previous decisions of this court to infer solely from its heavy burden that the act intends a prohibition instead of a tax. But this act is more. It provides a heavy exaction for a departure from a detailed and specified course of conduct in business.

That course of business is that employers shall employ in mines and quarries, children of an age greater than sixteen years; in mills and factories, children of an age greater than fourteen years, and shall prevent children of less than sixteen years in mills and factories from working more than eight hours a day or six days in the week. If an employer departs from this prescribed course of business, he is to pay to the Government one-tenth of his entire net income in the business for a full year. The amount is not to be proportioned in any degree to the extent or frequency of the departures, but is to be paid by the employer in full measure whether he employs five hundred children for a year, or employs only one for a day. Moreover, if he does not know the child is within the named age limit, he is not to pay; that is to say, it is only where he knowingly departs from the prescribed course that payment is to be exacted. Scienter is associated with penalties, not with taxes. The employer's factory is to be subject to inspection at any time not only by the taxing officers of the Treasury, the Department normally charged with the collection of taxes, but also by the Secretary of Labor and his subordinates, whose normal function is the advancement and protection of the welfare of the workers. In the light of these features of the act, a court must be blind not to see that the so-called tax is imposed to stop the employment of children within the age limits prescribed. Its prohibitory and regulatory effect and purpose are palpable. All others can see and understand this. How can we properly shut our minds to it?

It is the high duty and function of this court in cases regularly brought to its bar to decline to recognize or enforce seeming laws of Congress, dealing with subjects not entrusted to Congress but left or committed by the supreme law of the land to the control of the States. We cannot avoid the duty, even though it require us to refuse to give effect to legislation designed to promote the highest good. The good sought in unconstitutional legislation is an insidious feature because it leads citizens and legislators of good purpose to promote it without thought of the serious breach it will make in the ark of our covenant or the harm which will come from breaking down recognized standards. In the maintenance of local self-government, on the one hand, and the national power, on the other, our country has been able to endure and prosper for near a century and a half.

Out of a proper respect for the acts of a co-ordinate branch of the Government, this court has gone far to sustain taxing acts as such, even though there has been ground for suspecting from the weight of the tax it was intended to destroy its subject. But, in the act before us, the presumption of validity cannot prevail, because the proof of the contrary is found on the very face of its provisions. Grant the validity of this law, and all that Congress would need to do, hereafter, in seeking to take over to its control any one of the great number of subjects of public interest, jurisdiction of which the States have never parted with, and which are reserved to them by the Tenth Amendment, would be to enact a detailed measure of complete regulation of the subject and enforce it by a so-called tax upon departures from it. To give such magic to the word "tax" would be to break down all constitutional limitation of the powers of Congress and completely wipe out the sovereignty of the States.

The difference between a tax and a penalty is sometimes difficult to define and yet the consequences of the distinction in the required method of their collection often are important. Where the sovereign enacting the law has power to impose both tax and penalty, the difference between revenue production and mere regulation may be immaterial, but not so when one sovereign can impose a tax only, and the power of regulation rests in another. Taxes are occasionally imposed in the discretion of the legislature on proper subjects with the primary motive of obtaining revenue from them and with the incidental motive of discouraging them by making their continuance onerous. They do not lose their character as taxes because of the incidental motive. But there comes a time in the extension of the penalizing features of the so-called tax when it loses its character as such and becomes a mere penalty with the characteristics of regulation and punishment. Such is the case in the law before us. Although Congress does not invalidate the contract of employment or expressly declare that the employment within the mentioned ages is illegal, it does exhibit its intent practically to achieve the latter result by adopting the criteria of wrongdoing and imposing its principal consequence on those who transgress its standard. The case before us cannot be distinguished from that of *Hammer v. Dagenhart.* Congress there enacted a law to prohibit transportation in interstate commerce of goods made at a factory in which there was employment of children within the same ages and for the same number of hours a day and days in a week as are penalized by the act in this case. This court held the law in that case to be void. It said:

"In our view the necessary effect of this act is, by means of a prohibition against the movement in interstate commerce of ordinary commercial commodities, to regulate the hours of labor of children in factories and mines within the States, a purely state authority."

In the case at the bar, Congress in the name of a tax which on the face of the act is a penalty seeks to do the same thing, and the effort must be equally futile.

The analogy of the *Dagenhart Case* is clear. The congressional power over interstate commerce is, within its proper scope, just as complete and unlimited as the congressional power to tax, and the legislative motive in its exercise is just as free from judicial suspicion and inquiry. Yet when Congress threatened to stop interstate commerce in ordinary and necessary commodities, unobjectionable as subjects of transportation, and to deny the same to the people of a State in order to coerce them into compliance with Congress's regulation of state concerns, the court said this was not in fact regulation of interstate commerce, but rather that of State concerns and was invalid. So here the so-called tax is a penalty to coerce people of a State to act as Congress wishes them to act in respect of a matter completely the business of the state government under the Federal Constitution. . . .

. . . For the reasons given, we must hold the Child Labor Tax Law invalid and the judgment of the District Court is

Affirmed.

With the Court's rejection of both its attempts to regulate child labor through the commerce and taxation powers, Congress pursued yet another alternative. In 1924, two years after *Drexel,* Congress proposed a constitutional amendment that gave the national government power to regulate and prohibit child labor. Unlike most proposed amendments, this one had no congressionally determined deadline on the states for ratification. Slightly more than half of the state legislatures endorsed the amendment before support for it began to decline. In the end, the amendment was unnecessary. Many states responded to decisions such as *Hammer* and *Drexel* by passing their own child labor laws. In addition, the 1937 constitutional revolution that redefined the concept of interstate commerce, along with subsequent employment regulation decisions such as *United States v. Darby* (1941), gave the federal government ample authority to control child labor.

The decision in *Drexel* was a reversal of the position on excise taxes the Court had held since the early 1800s. It proved to be out of line with Supreme Court rulings both before and after. The Court repeatedly has faced the question of taxation and regulation and generally has ruled in favor of the federal power to tax; the Court has even acknowledged that to some degree all taxes have regulatory effects. In *United States v. Doremus* (1919) and *Nigro v. United States* (1928) the Court upheld federal excise taxes on narcotics, and in *United States v. Sanchez* (1950) it upheld a tax on marijuana. Similarly, an excise tax on objectionable firearms was declared valid in *Sonzinsky v. United States* (1937), even though the Court admitted that the law had an unmistakable "legislative purpose to regulate rather than to tax." In **United States v. Kahriger**(1953) the justices found no constitutional defects with an excise levied on professional gamblers. Such taxes expand federal regulatory powers. If Congress has the power to impose the tax, then the federal government also has the power to enforce the tax laws, creating, to an extent, "police powers" within the federal government that originally resided with the states.

The authority to use the excise tax as a regulatory power is not unlimited. Such taxes cannot be levied or enforced in a manner that violates other provisions of the Constitution. *Kahriger* provides an illustration. The tax imposed required those engaged in accepting bets to pay an annual excise of $50 and to register with the collector of internal revenue. Although it is constitutionally valid for Congress to impose an occupational excise tax, the law cannot compel a person to admit to criminal activity. To do so would be a violation of the Fifth Amendment's self-incrimination clause. Joseph Kahriger raised these objections in his appeal, but the majority upheld the statute's requirements that gamblers register with the government. Fifteen years later, however, the Court reexamined this position in **Marchetti v. United States**(1968). Here the Court held that no laws, including tax laws, can constitutionally require a person to admit to criminal activities. To the extent that the *Kahriger* decision permitted such procedures, it was overruled.

TAXING AND SPENDING FOR THE GENERAL WELFARE

The Constitution authorizes Congress to tax and spend for the general welfare. Whether the term *general welfare* was intended to expand the powers of Congress beyond those explicitly stated in the Constitution is subject to debate. James Madison argued that the Constitution's use of the term was only a reference to the other enumerated powers. Because the federal government is one of limited and specified powers, he

asserted, the authority to tax and spend must be confined to those spheres of authority the Constitution explicitly granted. Alexander Hamilton took the opposite position. He interpreted the power to tax and spend for the general welfare to be a separate power altogether. For Hamilton, taxing and spending authority was given in addition to the other granted powers, not limited by them. The conflict between these two opposing interpretations was the subject of legal disputes throughout much of the nation's history. During the constitutional crisis over legislation passed during implementation of the New Deal, however, the final battle between the two was waged.

A Restricted View of Taxing and Spending

Many of the programs Franklin Roosevelt recommended to reestablish the nation's economic strength involved regulatory activity far more extensive than ever before proposed. Several depended on the power of the federal government to tax and spend for the general welfare. Opponents of the New Deal claimed that these programs, while ostensibly based on the taxing and spending authority, in reality were regulations of matters the Constitution reserved for the states.

The Roosevelt administration placed great importance on stabilizing agricultural markets and on creating conditions that would make farms profitable. To accomplish these goals, Congress passed the Agricultural Adjustment Act (AAA) of 1933, which was challenged in *United States v. Butler* (1936). Although the issues were crucial both to the economic welfare of the nation and to the constitutional future of federalism, Justice Owen Roberts, writing for the majority, presented an uncomplicated formula for deciding the case: "Lay the article of the Constitution which is invoked beside the statute which is challenged and . . . decide whether the latter squares with the former." Do you believe the process of judicial review is that simple—especially when so much is riding on the outcome of the Court's deliberations?

United States v. Butler

297 U.S. 1 (1936)
http://laws.findlaw.com/us/297/1.html
Vote: 6 (Butler, Hughes, McReynolds, Roberts, Sutherland, Van Devanter)
   3 (Brandeis, Cardozo, Stone)
OPINION OF THE COURT: Roberts
DISSENTING OPINION: Stone

© Bettman/Corbis

William M. Butler, receiver for Hoosac Mills, objected to paying the federal tax on processing cotton. His lawsuit successfully challenged the constitutionality of the Agricultural Adjustment Act of 1933.

FACTS:

During the Great Depression, agriculture was one of the hardest-hit sectors of the economy. The nation's farmers were overproducing, which caused prices for farm products to drop. In many cases the cost of production was higher than the income from crop sales, leaving farmers in desperate straits. Most had their farms mortgaged, and all owed taxes on their land. The more the farmers fell behind economically, the more they produced to improve their situation, but this strategy made matters even worse. At that time agriculture was responsible for a much larger proportion of the nation's economy than it is today, and conditions in the farming sector had dire effects on the entire country.

In response, Roosevelt proposed, and Congress passed, the Agricultural Adjustment Act (AAA), which combined the taxing and spending powers to combat the crisis. The central purpose of the plan was to reduce the amount of acreage being farmed. To accomplish this goal, the federal government would "rent" a percentage of the nation's farmland and leave this acreage unplanted. In effect, the government would pay the farmers not to farm. If the plan succeeded, production would drop, prices would rise, and the farmers would have sufficient income. Making payments to the nation's farmers would be costly, and to fund these expenditures the AAA imposed an excise tax on the processing of agricultural products.

The program was a success until William M. Butler challenged the constitutionality of the law. Butler was the bankruptcy receiver for Hoosac Mills Corporation, a cotton processor. When the government imposed the processing tax on Hoosac, Butler took legal action to avoid payment, claiming that the AAA exceeded the taxing and spending powers granted to the federal government. The district court upheld the law, but the court of appeals reversed. The United States appealed to the Supreme Court.

A number of groups having a direct interest in the outcome of the case filed amicus curiae briefs. Supporting the validity of the act were groups of farmers and other agricultural producers, such as the American Farm Bureau Federation. Arguing to strike down the AAA were agricultural processing interests such as the National Association of Cotton Manufacturers, National Biscuit Company, P. Lorillard Co., and General Mills.

ARGUMENTS:

For the petitioner, United States:

- The taxes levied by the Agricultural Adjustment Act are excises. They are geographically uniform and meet the only constitutional restriction on such taxes.
- The power to tax and spend should be construed broadly to allow such actions for any purposes conducive to the national welfare.
- The question of what is best for the nation's welfare is a matter for legislative determination.
- The act is an exercise of the power to tax and spend only. No attempt is made to exercise any powers that are reserved for the states or the people by the Tenth Amendment.

For the respondents, William M. Butler et al., receivers of Hoosac Mills Corporation:

- The Agricultural Adjustment Act is an attempt by Congress to regulate the local production of agricultural commodities. The authority to regulate agricultural production is reserved for the states by the Tenth Amendment.

- The tax is not for a public purpose because it takes the processors' money for the benefit of the producers. This is confiscation of the property of one class for the economic advantage of another.
- The general welfare clause should not be interpreted to allow Congress the power to regulate by taxation the conduct and activities of citizens in spheres otherwise beyond congressional control.
- The act is not a temporary measure and therefore cannot be defended as an emergency action to cope with the current economic crisis.

▸ MR. JUSTICE ROBERTS DELIVERED THE OPINION OF THE COURT.

The Government asserts that even if the respondents may question the propriety of the appropriation embodied in the statute their attack must fail because Article I, §8 of the Constitution authorizes the contemplated expenditure of the funds raised by the tax. This contention presents the great and the controlling question in the case. We approach its decision with a sense of our grave responsibility to render judgment in accordance with the principles established for the governance of all three branches of the Government.

There should be no misunderstanding as to the function of this court in such a case. It is sometimes said that the court assumes a power to overrule or control the action of the people's representatives. This is a misconception. The Constitution is the supreme law of the land ordained and established by the people. All legislation must conform to the principles it lays down. When an act of Congress is appropriately challenged in the courts as not conforming to the constitutional mandate the judicial branch of the Government has only one duty,—to lay the article of the Constitution which is invoked beside the statute which is challenged and to decide whether the latter squares with the former. All the court does, or can do, is to announce its considered judgment upon the question. The only power it has, if such it may be called, is the power of judgment. This court neither approves nor condemns any legislative policy. Its delicate and difficult office is to ascertain and declare whether the legislation is in accordance with, or in contravention of, the provisions of the Constitution; and, having done that, its duty ends.

The question is not what power the Federal Government ought to have but what powers in fact have been given by the people. It hardly seems necessary to reiterate that ours is a dual form of government; that in every state there are two governments,—the state and the United States. Each State has all governmental powers save such as the people, by their Constitution, have conferred upon the United States, denied to the States, or reserved to themselves. The federal union is a government of delegated powers. It has only such as are expressly conferred upon it and such as are reasonably to be implied from those granted. In this respect we differ radically from nations where all legislative power, without restriction or limitation, is vested in a parliament or other legislative body subject to no restrictions except the discretion of its members.

Article I, §8, of the Constitution vests sundry powers in the Congress. But two of its clauses have any bearing upon the validity of the statute under review.

The third clause endows the Congress with power "to regulate Commerce . . . among the several States." Despite a reference in its first section to a burden upon, and an obstruction of the normal currents of commerce, the act under review does not purport to regulate transactions in interstate or foreign commerce. Its stated purpose is the control of agricultural production, a purely local activity, in an effort to raise the prices paid the farmer. Indeed, the Government does not attempt to uphold the validity of the act on the basis of the commerce clause, which, for the purpose of the present case, may be put aside as irrelevant.

The clause thought to authorize the legislation,—the first,—confers upon the Congress power "to lay and collect Taxes, Duties, Imposts and Excises, to pay the Debts and provide for the common Defence and general Welfare of the United States. . . ." It is not contended that this provision grants power to regulate agricultural production upon the theory that such legislation would promote the general welfare. The Government concedes that the phrase "to provide for the general welfare" qualifies the power "to lay and collect taxes." The view that the clause grants power to provide for the general welfare, independently of the taxing power, has never been authoritatively accepted. . . . The true construction undoubtedly is that the only thing granted is the power to tax for the purpose of providing funds for payment of the nation's debts and making provision for the general welfare.

Nevertheless the Government asserts that warrant is found in this clause for the adoption of the Agricultural Adjustment Act. The argument is that Congress may appropriate and authorize the spending of moneys for the "general welfare"; that the phrase should be liberally construed to cover anything conducive to national welfare; that decision as to what will promote such welfare rests with

Congress alone, and the courts may not review its determination; and finally that the appropriation under attack was in fact for the general welfare of the United States.

The Congress is expressly empowered to lay taxes to provide for the general welfare. Funds in the Treasury as a result of taxation may be expended only through appropriation. (Art. I, §9, cl. 7.) They can never accomplish the objects for which they were collected unless the power to appropriate is as broad as the power to tax. The necessary implication from the terms of the grant is that the public funds may be appropriated "to provide for the general welfare of the United States." These words cannot be meaningless, else they would not have been used. The conclusion must be that they were intended to limit and define the granted power to raise and to spend money. How shall they be construed to effectuate the intent of the instrument?

Since the foundation of the Nation, sharp differences of opinion have persisted as to the true interpretation of the phrase. Madison asserted it amounted to no more than a reference to the other powers enumerated in the subsequent clauses of the same section; that, as the United States is a government of limited and enumerated powers, the grant of power to tax and spend for the general national welfare must be confined to the enumerated legislative fields committed to the Congress. In this view the phrase is mere tautology, for taxation and appropriation are or may be necessary incidents of the exercise of any of the enumerated legislative powers. Hamilton, on the other hand, maintained the clause confers a power separate and distinct from those later enumerated, is not restricted in meaning by the grant of them, and Congress consequently has a substantive power to tax and to appropriate, limited only by the requirement that it shall be exercised to provide for the general welfare of the United States. Each contention has had the support of those whose views are entitled to weight. This court has noticed the question, but has never found it necessary to decide which is the true construction. Mr. Justice Story, in his Commentaries, espouses the Hamiltonian position. We shall not review the writings of public men and commentators or discuss the legislative practice. Study of all these leads us to conclude that the reading advocated by Mr. Justice Story is the correct one. While, therefore, the power to tax is not unlimited, its confines are set in the clause which confers it, and not in those of §8 which bestow and define the legislative powers of the Congress. It results that the power of Congress to authorize expenditure of public moneys for public purposes is not limited by the direct grants of legislative power found in the Constitution. . . .

We are not now required to ascertain the scope of the phrase "general welfare of the United States" or to determine whether an appropriation in aid of agriculture falls within it. Wholly apart from that question, another principle embedded in our Constitution prohibits the enforcement of the Agricultural Adjustment Act. The act invades the reserved rights of the states. It is a statutory plan to regulate and control agricultural production, a matter beyond the powers delegated to the federal government. The tax, the appropriation of the funds raised, and the direction for their disbursement, are but parts of the plan. They are but means to an unconstitutional end.

From the accepted doctrine that the United States is a government of delegated powers, it follows that those not expressly granted, or reasonably to be implied from such as are conferred, are reserved to the states or to the people. To forestall any suggestion to the contrary, the Tenth Amendment was adopted. The same proposition, otherwise stated, is that powers not granted are prohibited. None to regulate agricultural production is given, and therefore legislation by Congress for that purpose is forbidden.

It is an established principle that the attainment of a prohibited end may not be accomplished under the pretext of the exertion of powers which are granted. . . .

The power of taxation, which is expressly granted, may, of course, be adopted as a means to carry into operation another power also expressly granted. But resort to the taxing power to effectuate an end which is not legitimate, not within the scope of the Constitution, is obviously inadmissible. . . .

. . . If the taxing power may not be used as the instrument to enforce a regulation of matters of state concern with respect to which the Congress has no authority to interfere, may it, as in the present case, be employed to raise the money necessary to purchase a compliance which the Congress is powerless to command? The Government asserts that whatever might be said against the validity of the plan if compulsory, it is constitutionally sound because the end is accomplished by voluntary cooperation. There are two sufficient answers to the contention. The regulation is not in fact voluntary. The farmer, of course, may refuse to comply, but the price of such refusal is the loss of benefits. The amount offered is intended to be sufficient to exert pressure on him to agree to the proposed regulation. The power to confer or withhold unlimited benefits is the power to coerce or destroy. If the cotton grower elects not to accept the benefits, he will receive less for his crops; those who receive payments will be able to undersell him. The result will be financial ruin. The coercive purpose and intent of the statute is not obscured by the fact that it has not been perfectly successful. It is pointed out that, because there still remained a minority whom the rental and benefit payments were insufficient to induce to surrender their independence of action, the Congress has gone further and, in the Bankhead Cotton Act, used the taxing power in a more directly minatory fashion to compel submission. This progression only serves more fully to expose the coercive purpose of the so-called tax imposed by the present act. It is clear that the Department of Agriculture has properly described the plan as one to keep a non-cooperating minority in line. This is coercion by economic pressure. The asserted power of choice is illusory. . . .

But if the plan were one for purely voluntary cooperation it would stand no better so far as federal power is concerned. At best it is a scheme for purchasing with federal funds submission to federal regulation of a subject reserved to the states. . . .

Congress has no power to enforce its commands on the farmer to the ends sought by the Agricultural Adjustment Act. It must follow that it may not indirectly accomplish those ends by taxing and spending to purchase compliance. The Constitution and the entire plan of our government negative any such use of the power to tax and to spend as the act undertakes to authorize. It does not help to declare that local conditions throughout the nation have created a situation of national concern; for this is but to say that whenever there is a widespread similarity of local conditions, Congress may ignore constitutional limitations upon its own powers and usurp those reserved to the states. If, in lieu of compulsory regulation of subjects within the states' reserved jurisdiction, which is prohibited, the Congress could invoke the taxing and spending power as a means to accomplish the same end, clause 1 of §8 of Article I would become the instrument for total subversion of the governmental powers reserved to the individual states.

If the act before us is a proper exercise of the federal taxing power, evidently the regulation of all industry throughout the United States may be accomplished by similar exercises of the same power. It would be possible to exact money from one branch of an industry and pay it to another branch in every field of activity which lies within the province of the states. The mere threat of such a procedure might well induce the surrender of rights and the compliance with federal regulation as the price of continuance in business. . . .

The judgment is

Affirmed.

MR. JUSTICE STONE, dissenting.

I think the judgment should be reversed.

The present stress of widely held and strongly expressed differences of opinion of the wisdom of the Agricultural Adjustment Act makes it important, in the interest of clear thinking and sound result, to emphasize at the outset certain propositions which should have controlling influence in determining the validity of the Act. They are:

1. The power of the courts to declare a statute unconstitutional is subject to two guiding principles of decision which ought never to be absent from judicial consciousness. One is that courts are concerned only with the power to enact statutes, not with their wisdom. The other is that while unconstitutional exercise of power by the legislative and executive branches of the government is subject to judicial restraint, the only check upon our own exercise of power is our own sense of self-restraint. For the removal of unwise laws from the statute books appeal lies not to the courts but to the ballot and to the processes of democratic government.

2. The constitutional power of Congress to levy an excise tax upon the processing of agricultural products is not questioned. The present levy is held invalid, not for any want of power in Congress to lay such a tax to defray public expenditures, including those for the general welfare, but because the use to which its proceeds are put is disapproved.

3. As the present depressed state of agriculture is nationwide in its extent and effects, there is no basis for saying that the expenditure of public money in aid of farmers is not within the specifically granted power of Congress to levy taxes to "provide for the . . . general welfare." The opinion of the Court does not declare otherwise.

4. No question of a variable tax fixed from time to time by fiat of the Secretary of Agriculture, or of unauthorized delegation of legislative power, is now presented. The schedule of rates imposed by the Secretary in accordance with the original command of Congress has since been specifically adopted and confirmed by Act of Congress, which has declared that it shall be the lawful tax. That is the tax which the government now seeks to collect. Any defects there may have been in the manner of laying the tax by the Secretary have now been removed by the exercise of the power of Congress to pass a curative statute validating an intended, though defective, tax. The Agricultural Adjustment Act as thus amended declares that none of its provisions shall fail because others are pronounced invalid.

It is with these preliminary and hardly controverted matters in mind that we should direct our attention to the pivot on which the decision of the Court is made to turn. It is that a levy unquestionably within the taxing power of Congress may be treated as invalid because it is a step in a plan to regulate agricultural production and is thus a forbidden infringement of state power. The levy is not any less an exercise of taxing power because it is intended to defray an expenditure for the general welfare rather than for some other support of government. Nor is the levy and collection of the tax pointed to as effecting the regulation. While all federal taxes inevitably have some influence on the internal economy of the states, it is not contended that the levy of a processing tax upon manufacturers using agricultural products as raw material has any perceptible regulatory effect upon either their production or manufacture. . . . Here regulation, if any there be, is accomplished not by the tax but by the method by which its proceeds are expended, and would equally be accomplished by any like use of public funds, regardless of their source.

. . . [T]he power to tax and spend includes the power to relieve a nationwide economic maladjustment by conditional gifts of money.

Butler had a mixed outcome. The Court concluded that the federal government had broad powers to tax and spend for the general welfare. The justices decided, consistent with Alexander Hamilton's position, that Congress's fiscal authority was not limited to those subjects specifically enumerated in Article I. This philosophy did not, however, mean that congressional powers had no limits. The majority in *Butler* concluded that the law was unconstitutional because what it imposed was not truly a tax. Instead, the government was taking money from one group (the processors) to give to another (the farmers), and it was doing this to regulate farm production, a matter of intrastate commerce reserved for state regulation.

Expanding the Powers to Tax and Spend

The impact of the *Butler* case was short-lived. Following the Court's dramatic change in position after Roosevelt's threat to add new members, the justices ruled that agriculture could be regulated under the commerce power.[14] As for the power to tax and

---

14. See *Mulford v. Smith* (1939) and *Wickard v. Filburn* (1942).

spend for the general welfare, the position taken in *Butler* was reevaluated the very next year in *Steward Machine Co. v. Davis* (1937), a challenge to the constitutionality of the newly formed Social Security system. The Social Security Act of 1935 shared several characteristics with the AAA the Court had condemned in *Butler*: both used the taxing and spending powers to combat the effects of the Depression, both took money from one group of people to give to another, and both regulated areas previously thought to be reserved to the states. But in *Steward Machine* the justices upheld the validity of the act. Note that in this case Chief Justice Hughes and Justice Roberts desert the *Butler* majority and join with the liberal wing of the Court to forge new constitutional interpretations.

Steward Machine Co. v. Davis

301 U.S. 548 (1937)

http://laws.findlaw.com/us/301/548.html

Vote: 5 (Brandeis, Cardozo, Hughes, Roberts, Stone)
⠀⠀⠀⠀4 (Butler, McReynolds, Sutherland, Van Devanter)

OPINION OF THE COURT: *Cardozo*

DISSENTING OPINIONS: *Butler, McReynolds, Sutherland*

FACTS:

On August 14, 1935, Congress passed the Social Security Act, a comprehensive law designed to provide economic security to groups of individuals who were particularly in need. Its three most important programs were the creation of an old-age and survivors benefits program; the implementation of benefits for dependent children, the handicapped, and the sight-impaired; and the development of a cooperative federal–state unemployment compensation system. The unemployment provisions were the focus of the constitutional challenge in this case.

The act, as originally passed, imposed an excise tax on employers who hired more than eight workers. The tax was based on the total amount of wages paid. Employers could receive a tax credit, not to exceed 90 percent of their unemployment tax obligations, for contributions made to an approved state unemployment compensation program.

The state programs had to meet federal specifications. The money that employers contributed to these state funds was deposited with the secretary of the U.S. Treasury. The secretary would pay funds back to the states for their unemployment compensation programs.

Congress also authorized additional federal funds to be used to assist the states in administering their compensation systems.

Steward Machine Company, an Alabama corporation, paid the taxes due under the program and then sued the collector of internal revenue for a refund, claiming that the Social Security Act violated the Constitution on a number of grounds. The amount of the contested refund was $46.14. The district court and the court of appeals upheld the validity of the act.

ARGUMENTS:

For the petitioner, Charles C. Steward Machine Co.:

- Congress lacks the constitutional power to establish a system of contributions and benefits for the purpose of regulating unemployment.
- The law coerces the states to create unemployment compensation programs. If states do not comply, their citizens are penalized by being required to supply millions of dollars in tax payments to the federal government to be used for the administration of unemployment programs in the states that do participate.
- The use of the taxing power is a mere pretext to allow Congress to regulate employer-employee relationships, a regulatory area reserved for the states.
- The law exempts certain employers, such as those who employ fewer than eight workers, household domestics, or agricultural workers, which makes the law arbitrary and unconstitutional under the due process clause of the Fifth Amendment.

For the respondent, Harwell G. Davis, collector of internal revenue for the district of Alabama:

- This tax is a valid excise that meets the constitutional requirement of geographical uniformity. The taxing and spending are being used for the general welfare.
- The tax cannot be considered a penalty. The tax payer pays the same amount whether the state participates in the program or not.
- Congress is not attempting to regulate employer-employee relationships.
- The law does not coerce the states to participate. Rather, it encourages state-federal cooperation. States remain free not to participate.

MR. JUSTICE CARDOZO DELIVERED THE OPINION OF THE COURT.

The assault on the statute proceeds on an extended front. Its assailants take the ground that the tax is not an excise; that it is not uniform throughout the United States as excises are required to be; that its exceptions are so many and arbitrary as to violate the Fifth Amendment; that its purpose was not revenue, but an unlawful invasion of the reserved powers of the states; and that the states in submitting to it have yielded to coercion and have abandoned governmental functions which they are not permitted to surrender.

The objections will be considered seriatim with such further explanation as may be necessary to make their meaning clear.

First. The tax, which is described in the statute as an excise, is laid with uniformity throughout the United States as a duty, an impost or an excise upon the relation of employment. . . .

The subject matter of taxation open to the power of the Congress is as comprehensive as that open to the power of the states, though the method of apportionment may at times be different. . . . The statute books of the states are strewn with illustrations of taxes laid on occupations pursued of common right. We find no basis for a holding that the power in that regard which belongs by accepted practice to the legislatures of the states, has been denied by the Constitution to the Congress of the nation.

The tax being an excise, its imposition must conform to the canon of uniformity. There has been no departure from this requirement. According to the settled doctrine the uniformity exacted is geographical, not intrinsic.

Second. The excise is not invalid under the provisions of the Fifth Amendment by force of its exemptions.

The statute does not apply, as we have seen, to employers of less than eight. It does not apply to agricultural labor, or domestic service in a private home or to some other classes of less importance. Petitioner contends that the effect of these restrictions is an arbitrary discrimination vitiating the tax. . . .

The classifications and exemptions directed by the statute now in controversy have support in considerations of policy and practical convenience that cannot be condemned as arbitrary. . . . The act of Congress is therefore valid, so far at least as its system of exemptions is concerned, and this though we assume that discrimination, if gross enough, is equivalent to confiscation and subject under the Fifth Amendment to challenge and annulment.

Third. The excise is not void as involving the coercion of the States in contravention of the Tenth Amendment or of restrictions implicit in our federal form of government.

The proceeds of the excise when collected are paid into the Treasury at Washington, and thereafter are subject to appropriation like public moneys generally. No presumption can be indulged that they will be misapplied or wasted. Even if they were collected in the hope or expectation that some other and collateral good would be furthered as an incident, that without more would not make the act invalid. This indeed is hardly questioned. The case for the petitioner is built on the contention that here an ulterior aim is wrought into the very structure of the act, and what is even more important that the aim is not only ulterior, but essentially unlawful. In particular, the 90 per cent credit is relied upon as supporting that conclusion. But before the statute succumbs to an assault upon these lines, two propositions must be made out by the assailant. There must be a showing in the first place that separated from the credit the revenue provisions are incapable of standing by themselves. There must be a showing in the second place that the tax and the credit in combination are weapons of coercion, destroying or impairing the autonomy of the states. The truth of each proposition being essential to the success of the assault, we pass for convenience to a consideration of the second, without pausing to inquire whether there has been a demonstration of the first.

To draw the line intelligently between duress and inducement there is need to remind ourselves of facts as to the problem of unemployment that are now matters of common knowledge. The relevant statistics are gathered in the brief of counsel for the Government. Of the many available figures a few only will be mentioned. During the years 1929 to 1936, when the country was passing through a cyclical depression, the number of the unemployed mounted to unprecedented heights. Often the average was more than 10 million; at times a peak was attained of 16 million or more. Disaster to the breadwinner meant disaster to dependents. Accordingly the roll of the unemployed, itself formidable enough, was only a partial roll of the destitute or needy. The fact developed quickly that the states were unable to give the requisite relief. The problem had become national in area and dimensions. There was need of help from the nation if the people were not to starve. It is too late today for the argument to be heard with tolerance that in a crisis so extreme the use of the moneys of the nation to relieve the unemployed and their dependents is a use for any purpose narrower than the promotion of the general welfare. . . .

In the presence of this urgent need for some remedial expedient, the question is to be answered whether the expedient adopted has overleapt the bounds of power. The assailants of the statute say that its dominant end and aim is to drive the state legislatures under the whip of economic pressure into the enactment of unemployment compensation laws at the bidding of the central government. Supporters of the statute say that its operation is not constraint, but the creation of a larger freedom, the states and the nation joining in a co-operative endeavor to avert a common evil. . . .

The Social Security Act is an attempt to find a method by which all these public agencies may work together to a common end. Every dollar of the new taxes will continue in all likelihood to be used and needed by the nation as long as states are unwilling, whether through timidity or for other motives, to do what can be done at home. At least the inference is permissible that Congress so believed, though retaining undiminished freedom to spend the money as it pleased. On the other hand fulfillment of the home duty will be lightened and encouraged by crediting the taxpayer upon his account with the Treasury of the nation to the extent that his contributions under the laws of the locality have simplified or diminished the problem of relief and the probable demand upon the resources of the fisc. Duplicated taxes, or burdens that approach them, are recognized hardships that government, state or national, may properly avoid. If Congress believed that the general welfare would better be promoted by relief through local units than by the system then in vogue, the cooperating localities ought not in all fairness to pay a second time.

Who then is coerced through the operation of this statute? Not the taxpayer. He pays in fulfillment of the mandate of the local legislature. Not the state. Even now she does not offer a suggestion that in passing the unemployment law she was affected by duress. For all that appears she is satisfied with her choice, and would be sorely disappointed if it were now to be annulled. The difficulty with the petitioner's contention is that it confuses motive with coercion. "Every tax is in some measure regulatory. To some extent it interposes an economic impediment to the activity taxed as compared with others not taxed." (*Sonzinsky v. United States*, 1937.) In like manner every rebate from a tax when conditioned upon conduct is in some measure a temptation. But to hold that motive or temptation is equivalent to coercion is to plunge the law in endless difficulties. The outcome of such a doctrine is the acceptance of a philosophical determinism by which choice becomes impossible. Till now the law has been guided by a robust common sense which assumes the freedom of the will as a working hypothesis in the solution of its problems. . . .

United States v. Butler is cited by petitioner as a decision to the contrary. There a tax was imposed on processors of farm products, the proceeds to be paid to farmers who would reduce their acreage and crops under agreements with the Secretary of Agriculture, the plan of the act being to increase the prices of certain farm products by decreasing the quantities produced. The court held (1) that the so-called tax was not a true one, the proceeds being earmarked for the benefit of farmers complying with the prescribed conditions, (2) that there was an attempt to regulate production without the consent of the state in which production was affected, and (3) that the payments to farmers were coupled with coercive contracts, unlawful in their aim and oppressive in their consequences. The decision was by a divided court, a minority taking the view that the objections were untenable. None of them is applicable to the situation here developed.

(a) The proceeds of the tax in controversy are not earmarked for a special group.

(b) The unemployment compensation law which is a condition of the credit has had the approval of the state and could not be a law without it.

(c) The condition is not linked to an irrevocable agreement, for the state at its pleasure may repeal its unemployment law, terminate the credit, and place itself where it was before the credit was accepted.

(d) The condition is not directed to the attainment of an unlawful end, but to an end, the relief of unemployment, for which nation and state may lawfully cooperate.

Fourth. The statute does not call for a surrender by the states of powers essential to their quasi-sovereign existence. . . .

The judgment is

Affirmed.

Separate opinion of MR. JUSTICE McREYNOLDS.

That portion of the Social Security legislation here under consideration, I think, exceeds the power granted to Congress. It unduly interferes with the orderly government of the state by her own people and otherwise offends the Federal Constitution.

In *Texas v. White* (1869), a cause of momentous importance, this Court, through Chief Justice Chase, declared—"But the perpetuity and indissolubility of the Union, by no means implies the loss of distinct and individual existence, or of the right of self-government by the States. . . ."

The doctrine thus announced and often repeated, I had supposed was firmly established. Apparently the states remained really free to exercise governmental powers, not delegated or prohibited, without interference by the federal government through threats of punitive measures or offers of seductive favors. Unfortunately, the decision just announced opens the way for practical annihilation of this theory; and no cloud of words or ostentatious parade of irrelevant statistics should be permitted to obscure that fact.

Separate opinion of MR. JUSTICE SUTHERLAND.

With most of what is said in the opinion just handed down, I concur. . . .

But the question with which I have difficulty is whether the administrative provisions of the act invade the governmental administrative powers of the several states reserved by the Tenth Amendment. . . .

The precise question, therefore, which we are required to answer by an application of these principles is whether the congressional act contemplates a surrender by the state to the federal government, in whole or in part, of any state governmental power to administer its own unemployment law or the state pay roll-tax funds which it has collected for the purposes of that law. An affirmative answer to this question, I think, must be made. . . .

If we are to survive as the United States, the balance between the powers of the nation and those of the states must be maintained. There is grave danger in permitting it to dip in either direction, danger—if there were no other—in the precedent thereby set for further departures from the equipoise. The threat implicit in the present encroachment upon the administrative functions of the states is that greater encroachments, and encroachments upon other functions, will follow.

For the foregoing reasons, I think the judgment below should be reversed.

MR. JUSTICE VAN DEVANTER joins in this opinion.

MR. JUSTICE BUTLER, dissenting.

I think that the objections to the challenged enactment expressed in the separate opinions of MR. JUSTICE MCREYNOLDS and MR. JUSTICE SUTHERLAND are well taken. I am also of opinion that, in principle and as applied to bring about and to gain control over state unemployment compensation, the statutory scheme is repugnant to the Tenth Amendment. . . . The Constitution grants to the United States no power to pay unemployed persons or to require the states to enact laws or to raise or disburse money for that purpose. The provisions in question, if not amounting to coercion in a legal sense, are manifestly designed and intended directly to affect state action in the respects specified. And, if valid as so employed, this "tax and credit" device may be made effective to enable federal authorities to induce, if not indeed to compel, state enactments for any purpose within the realm of state power and generally to control state administration of state laws. . . .

The terms of the measure make it clear that the tax and credit device was intended to enable federal officers virtually to control the exertion of powers of the states in a field in which they alone have jurisdiction and from which the United States is by the Constitution excluded.

I am of opinion that the judgment of the Circuit Court of Appeals should be reversed.

In a second case decided the same day, the Court upheld the old-age benefits provisions of the Social Security Act.[15] From that point on, the Social Security program became a permanent fixture in the lives of American workers. The Social Security cases also firmly established that the taxing and spending powers are to be broadly construed. If Congress decides that the general welfare of the United States demands a program requiring the use of these fiscal powers, the Supreme Court likely will find it constitutionally valid unless parts of the law violate specific provisions of the Constitution. Since these 1937 decisions, Congress has used the spending authority to expand greatly the role of the federal government.

Federal–State Fiscal Tensions

Because the justices now tend to defer to Congress on such matters, serious challenges to federal spending programs are now unusual, although battles over federal and state authority with respect to spending programs do occasionally flare up. An important example is provided by *South Dakota v. Dole* (1987), which involved a conflict over federal spending power and the state's authority to regulate highway safety and alcoholic beverages. The use of federal funds to coerce the states into taking particular policy positions was criticized in much

---

15. *Helvering v. Davis* (1937).

the same manner as arguments in *Steward Machine* attacked the establishment of state unemployment compensation programs. It is interesting to note that Chief Justice William Rehnquist, who was considered a strong defender of states' rights, wrote the majority opinion upholding the exercise of federal authority over the states. Justice Brennan cast a dissenting vote, another surprise because Brennan usually could be counted on to support federal power. Not surprising was Justice O'Connor's stinging dissent on behalf of state interests.

South Dakota v. Dole

483 U.S. 203 (1987)
http://laws.findlaw.com/us/483/203.html
Oral arguments are available at https://www.oyez.org.
Vote: 7 (Blackmun, Marshall, Powell, Rehnquist, Scalia, Stevens, White)
    2 (Brennan, O'Connor)
OPINION OF THE COURT: *Rehnquist*
DISSENTING OPINIONS: *Brennan, O'Connor*

FACTS:

In 1984 Congress passed a statute, 23 U.S.C. 158, directing the secretary of transportation to withhold a portion of federal highway funds from any state that did not establish a minimum age of twenty-one years for the legal consumption of alcoholic beverages. Many states at that time had lower minimum drinking ages. The purpose of the law was to decrease the number of serious automobile accidents among young people, a group that statistics showed had a high percentage of accidents. The legislators correctly believed that withholding federal dollars would be an effective way of encouraging the states to comply with the federal program.

South Dakota, which allowed the purchase of beer containing 3.2 percent alcohol by persons nineteen years or older, objected to the statute, arguing that Congress was infringing on the rights of the states. The Twenty-first Amendment repealed Prohibition in 1933 and gave the states full authority to regulate alcoholic beverages. South Dakota, therefore, claimed that Congress had no authority to set a minimum drinking age. According to the state, the federal government was using its considerable spending power to coerce the states into enacting laws that were otherwise outside congressional authority.

The state sued Secretary of Transportation Elizabeth Dole, asking the courts to declare the law unconstitutional. Both the district court and the court of appeals ruled against the state and upheld the law.

ARGUMENTS:

For the petitioner, state of South Dakota:

- From their inception the states had the authority under their police powers to control the distribution of alcohol within their borders. The Twenty-first Amendment, repealing the Eighteenth Amendment, gave the states additional authority to regulate alcohol.

- The states are not merely subdivisions or departments of the federal government; rather, they are sovereign within all areas not granted to the national government.

- The right of the states has particular force when the Constitution has explicitly conferred an authority on them, as the Twenty-first Amendment has done.

- Federal regulation of the minimum drinking age invades the reserved powers of the states and violates both the Twenty-first Amendment and the Tenth Amendment.

For the respondent, Elizabeth H. Dole, secretary of transportation:

- Congress passed section 158 in response to alcohol-related accidents that occur when young people living in states with a minimum drinking age of twenty-one travel on interstate highways to obtain alcohol in states with lower drinking ages.

- The federal law does not set a minimum drinking age. The state retains this authority. Congress has only provided a financial incentive for states to set a uniform drinking age at twenty-one.

- It is within the authority of Congress to place conditions on the awarding of federal funds.

- The reduction in federal funds for states that do not set their drinking age at twenty-one is modest and well under the level that would be considered coercive.

CHIEF JUSTICE REHNQUIST DELIVERED THE OPINION OF THE COURT.

The Constitution empowers Congress to "lay and collect Taxes, Duties, Imposts, and Excises, to pay the Debts and provide for the common Defence and general Welfare of the United States." Art. I, §8, cl. 1. Incident to this power, Congress may attach conditions on the receipt of federal funds, and has repeatedly employed the power "to further broad policy objectives by conditioning receipt of federal moneys upon compliance by the recipient with federal statutory and administrative directives." The breadth of this power was made clear in *United States v. Butler* (1936), where the Court, resolving a longstanding debate over the scope of the Spending Clause, determined that "the power of Congress to authorize expenditure of public moneys for public purposes is not limited by the direct grants of legislative power found in the Constitution." Thus, objectives not thought to be within Article I's "enumerated legislative fields" may nevertheless be attained through the use of the spending power and the conditional grant of federal funds.

The spending power is of course not unlimited, but is instead subject to several general restrictions articulated in our cases. The first of these limitations is derived from the language of the Constitution itself: the exercise of the spending power must be in pursuit of "the general welfare." In considering whether a particular expenditure is intended to serve general public purposes, courts should defer substantially to the judgment of Congress. Second, we have required that if Congress desires to condition the States' receipt of federal funds, it "must do so unambiguously . . . , enabl[ing] the States to exercise their choice knowingly, cognizant of the consequences of their participation." Third, our cases have suggested (without significant elaboration) that conditions on federal grants might be illegitimate if they are unrelated "to the federal interest in particular national projects or programs." Finally, we have noted that other constitutional provisions may provide an independent bar to the conditional grant of federal funds.

South Dakota does not seriously claim that §158 is inconsistent with any of the first three restrictions mentioned above. We can readily conclude that the provision is designed to serve the general welfare, especially in light of the fact that "the concept of welfare or the opposite is shaped by Congress. . . ." Congress found that the differing drinking ages in the States created particular incentives for young persons to combine their desire to drink with their ability to drive, and that this interstate problem required a national solution. The means it chose to address this dangerous situation were reasonably calculated to advance the general welfare. The conditions upon which States receive the funds, moreover, could not be more clearly stated by Congress. And the State itself, rather than challenging the germaneness of the condition to federal purposes, admits that it "has never contended that the congressional action was . . . unrelated to a national concern in the absence of the Twenty-first Amendment." Indeed, the condition imposed by Congress is directly related to one of the main purposes for which highway funds are expended—safe interstate travel. This goal of the interstate highway system had been frustrated by varying drinking ages among the States. . . . By enacting §158, Congress conditioned the receipt of federal funds in a way reasonably calculated to address this particular impediment to a purpose for which the funds are expended.

The remaining question about the validity of §158—and the basic point of disagreement between the parties—is whether the Twenty-first Amendment constitutes an "independent constitutional bar" to the conditional grant of federal funds. Petitioner, relying on its view that the Twenty-first Amendment prohibits *direct* regulation of drinking ages by Congress, asserts that "Congress may not use the spending power to regulate that which it is prohibited from regulating directly under the Twenty-first Amendment." But our cases show that this "independent constitutional bar" limitation on the spending power is not of the kind petitioner suggests. *United States v. Butler*, for example, established that the constitutional limitations on Congress when exercising its spending power are less exacting than those on its authority to regulate directly. . . .

. . . [T]he "independent constitutional bar" limitation on the spending power is not, as petitioner suggests, a prohibition on the indirect achievement of objectives which Congress is not empowered to achieve directly. Instead, we think that the language in our earlier opinions stands for the unexceptionable proposition that the power may not be used to induce the States to engage in activities that would themselves be unconstitutional. Thus, for example, a grant of federal funds conditioned on invidiously discriminatory state action or the infliction of cruel and unusual punishment would be an illegitimate exercise of the Congress' broad spending power. But no such claim can be or is made here. Were South Dakota to succumb to the blandishments offered by Congress and raise its drinking age to 21, the State's action in so doing would not violate the constitutional rights of anyone.

Our decisions have recognized that in some circumstances the financial inducement offered by Congress might be so coercive as to pass the point at which "pressure turns into compulsion." Here, however, Congress has directed only that a State desiring to establish a minimum drinking age lower than 21 lose a relatively small percentage of certain federal highway funds. Petitioner contends that the coercive nature of this program is evident from the degree of success it has achieved. We cannot conclude, however, that a conditional grant of federal money of this sort is unconstitutional simply by reason of its success in achieving the congressional objective.

When we consider, for a moment, that all South Dakota would lose if she adheres to her chosen course as to a suitable minimum drinking age is 5% of the funds otherwise obtainable under specified highway grant programs, the argument as to coercion is shown to be more rhetoric than fact. . . .

Here Congress has offered relatively mild encouragement to the States to enact higher minimum drinking ages than they would otherwise choose. But the enactment of such laws remains the prerogative of the States not merely in theory but in fact. Even if Congress might lack the power to impose a national minimum drinking age directly, we conclude that encouragement to state action found in §158 is a valid use of the spending power. Accordingly, the judgment of the Court of Appeals is

Affirmed.

JUSTICE O'CONNOR, dissenting.

The Court today upholds the National Minimum Drinking Age Amendment, 23 U.S.C. §158, as a valid exercise of the spending power conferred by Article I, §8. But §158 is not a condition on spending reasonably related to the expenditure of federal funds and cannot be justified on that ground. Rather, it is an attempt to regulate the sale of liquor, an attempt that lies outside Congress' power to regulate commerce because it falls within the ambit of §2 of the Twenty-first Amendment. . . .

When Congress appropriates money to build a highway, it is entitled to insist that the highway be a safe one. But it is not entitled to insist as a condition of the use of highway funds that the State impose or change regulations in other areas of the State's social and economic life because of an attenuated or tangential relationship to highway use or safety. Indeed, if the rule were otherwise, the Congress could effectively regulate almost any area of a State's social, political, or economic life on the theory that use of the interstate transportation system is somehow enhanced. If, for example, the United States were to condition highway moneys upon moving the state capital, I suppose it might argue that interstate transportation is facilitated by locating local governments in places easily accessible to interstate highways—or, conversely, that highways might become overburdened if they had to carry traffic to and from the state capital. In my mind, such a relationship is hardly more attenuated than the one which the Court finds supports §158.

There is a clear place at which the Court can draw the line between permissible and impermissible conditions on federal grants. It is the line identified in the Brief for the National Conference of State Legislatures et al. as *Amici Curiae:*

"Congress has the power to *spend* for the general welfare, it has the power to *legislate* only for the delegated purposes." . . .

This approach harks back to *United States v. Butler* (1936), the last case in which this Court struck down an Act of Congress as beyond the authority granted by the Spending Clause. . . .

While *Butler*'s authority is questionable insofar as it assumes that Congress has no regulatory power over farm production, its discussion of the spending power and its description of both the power's breadth and its limitations remain sound. The Court's decision in *Butler* also properly recognizes the gravity of the task of appropriately limiting the spending power. If the spending power is to be limited only by Congress' notion of the general welfare, the reality, given the vast financial resources of the Federal Government, is that the Spending Clause gives "power to the Congress to tear down the barriers, to invade the states' jurisdiction, and to become a parliament of the whole people, subject to no restrictions save such as are self-imposed." This, of course, as *Butler* held, was not the Framers' plan and it is not the meaning of the Spending Clause. . . .

The immense size and power of the Government of the United States ought not obscure its fundamental character. It remains a Government of enumerated powers. Because 23 U.S.C. §158 cannot be justified as an exercise of any power delegated to the Congress, it is not authorized by the Constitution. The Court errs in holding it to be the law of the land, and I respectfully dissent.

JUSTICE BRENNAN, dissenting.

I agree with Justice O'CONNOR that regulation of the minimum age of purchasers of liquor falls squarely within the ambit of those powers reserved to the States by the Twenty-first Amendment. Since States possess this constitutional power, Congress cannot condition a federal grant in a manner that abridges this right. The Amendment, itself, strikes the proper balance between federal and state authority. I therefore dissent.

Rehnquist's opinion gave strong support to the federal spending power. The majority held that only four basic requirements must be met for a federal spending statute to be valid: (1) the expenditure must be for the general welfare, (2) any conditions imposed on the expenditure must be unambiguous, (3) the conditions must be reasonably related to the purpose of the expenditure, and (4) the legislation must not violate any independent constitutional provision. These are minimal requirements indeed, especially since the Court acknowledged a policy of deferring to the legislature as to determinations of what promotes the general welfare. O'Connor's dissent, which praised much of what the Court concluded in *Butler,* is not likely to find a great deal of support today.

Five years after the *Dole* decision the justices confronted another spending power dispute in the case of *New York v. United States* (1992). As we discussed in chapter 6, this case involved the federal government's use of financial incentives to encourage the states to provide for the disposal of low-level radioactive waste generated within their borders. Although the justices found fault with portions of the challenged law that required the states to enact or enforce a federal regulatory program, they approved the financial incentive provisions. The Court concluded that the federal radioactive waste program was appropriately justified under the commerce clause and did not intrude on the sovereignty reserved to the states under the Tenth Amendment. Consequently, the use of financial incentives was a proper exercise of Congress's constitutional power to spend.

Decisions such as *Dole* and *New York* gave Congress ample discretion to use the taxing and spending power to "encourage" states to comply with federal policy preferences. If Congress uses this power effectively and within the limitations imposed by the Court, it can extend its influence by providing financial incentives for states to adopt federally favored policies.

As the Court entered the twenty-first century, it had not invalidated any federal spending legislation since 1936, when, in *United States v. Butler,* the justices struck down the AAA. Yet the continuing judicial support for federal taxing and spending programs seemed to be running at odds with another line of decisions. In cases such as *United States v. Lopez* (1995) and *Printz v. United States* (1997), the justices applied principles of federalism to strike down congressional actions that encroached on the policy-making authority of the states. What would happen if Congress provided financial incentives that were viewed by the states as being excessive, leaving the state no choice but to participate in a federal program? Would the Court under these circumstances continue to support federal use of the taxing and spending powers? Or would the Court find such incentives to have a coercive effect that would be destructive to the traditional relationship between the federal government and the states? A major clash over just these questions occurred in 2012 when the justices reviewed the constitutionality of the Patient Protection and Affordable Care Act (ACA).

We introduced the case of *National Federation of Independent Business v. Sebelius* in the previous chapter, where we focused on the federal government's argument that Congress has ample authority under the commerce clause to require all Americans not already covered by medical insurance to buy a health-care policy or pay a "shared responsibility" penalty for failure to do so. We saw that the Court concluded that the commerce power did not extend so far as to allow Congress to command unwilling individuals to purchase a commercial product. The Court's ruling, however, did not invalidate the ACA. The government had an alternative position, an argument that Congress could enact the individual mandate through the use of the constitutional power to tax.

Another significant provision of the ACA involved an enlargement of the Medicaid program. This section of the ACA expanded both the number of persons eligible for Medicaid and the benefits provided. Because Medicaid is jointly financed by the federal and state governments, the expanded program would be costly to the states. In the law, Congress stipulated that state participation in the expanded program was voluntary and also used the spending power to provide generous funds to cover most of the initial state costs of expanding the program. However, if a state elected not to participate in the program, it would lose all of its federal Medicaid money. The federal government argued that the spending clause gave Congress ample authority to impose this requirement as a condition for receiving federal dollars. A number of states objected, however, claiming that the nonparticipation penalty was a way to coerce the states into joining the expanded program.

In the excerpt that appears below we highlight the Court's response to the taxing power justification for the individual mandate and the spending power rationale for the Medicaid expansion. Throughout the opinions in this decision you will see references to many of the perennial taxing and spending power issues the Court has confronted since the beginning of the Republic.

National Federation of Independent Business v. Sebelius

567 U.S. _____ (2012)
http://laws.findlaw.com/us/000/11-393.html
Oral arguments are available at https://www.oyez.org.
Vote on the taxing power challenge to the Affordable Care Act:
      5 (Breyer, Ginsburg, Kagan, Roberts, Sotomayor)
      4 (Alito, Kennedy, Scalia, Thomas)
Vote on the expansion of Medicaid:
      7 (Alito, Breyer, Kagan, Kennedy, Roberts, Scalia, Thomas)
      2 (Ginsburg, Sotomayor)
**OPINION ANNOUNCING THE JUDGMENT OF
   THE COURT AND THE OPINION OF THE COURT:** *Roberts*
**OPINION CONCURRING IN PART, CONCURRING
   IN JUDGMENT, AND DISSENTING IN PART:** *Ginsburg*
JOINT OPINION DISSENTING: *Alito, Kennedy, Scalia, and Thomas*
DISSENTING OPINION: *Thomas*

FACTS:

In 2010, Congress passed the Patient Protection and Affordable Care Act (ACA) with the goal of increasing the number of Americans covered by medical insurance and decreasing the cost of health care. The constitutionality of the law was challenged in several suits, including this one filed by the National Federation of Independent Business, twenty-six state governments, and several individuals against Kathleen Sebelius, then secretary of health and human services.

Two provisions of the ACA provoked the most significant constitutional attacks. The first was the "individual mandate" that directs most Americans to purchase "minimum essential" health insurance coverage for themselves and their dependents if they do not receive such coverage from their employers. Section 5000A directs that those who do not comply with this provision are required to make a "shared responsibility" payment to the federal government. The act provides that this "penalty" will be paid to the Internal Revenue Service and "shall be assessed and collected in the same manner" as tax penalties.

The challengers argued that Congress exceeded its constitutional power in passing the law. The government countered that Congress acted properly under its power to regulate interstate commerce and its power to tax. In chapter 7 we presented an excerpt from this decision in which the Court concluded that the commerce clause did not give Congress the authority to compel inactive individuals to enter into commercial transactions. With the excerpt below, we focus on the Court's reaction to the government's claim that the power to tax allows Congress to impose the individual mandate.

The second provision in this controversy called for an expansion of Medicaid. This program, administered by the states but jointly funded by state and federal governments, provides health care for the poor. It is by far the largest of source of federal dollars granted to the states. About two-thirds of all Medicaid funds come from the federal government. Medicaid expenditures constitute a state's largest budget item, accounting for about 20 percent of a typical state's expenditures.

The ACA called for an enlarged Medicaid program that would expand the health-care services available to the poor. It would also increase the number of people eligible for program benefits by including all those whose incomes fall below 133 percent of federal poverty line. Once the program was fully implemented the federal government would cover 90 percent of the costs of the newly eligible persons. The law did not require the states to participate in the expanded program, but nonparticipating states would face the loss of all of their federal Medicaid dollars. The states involved in this litigation claimed that Congress had abused its spending powers by using financial coercion to force the states to accept the new Medicaid provisions.

The Eleventh Circuit Court of Appeals upheld the Medicaid expansion but struck down the individual mandate. The Supreme Court granted review.

ARGUMENTS:

For the petitioners, National Federation of Independent Business et al.:

- It is settled law that a penalty imposed for a violation of a legal requirement is not a tax.
- The mandate and the "tax" are separate issues. Congress cannot justify the unconstitutional mandate by classifying the penalty for violating it as a tax.
- The wording used in the Affordable Care Act clearly indicates that Congress considered the consequences for violating the law to be a penalty and not a tax. But if the "shared responsibility" payment is a tax, then it is a direct tax and must be apportioned on the basis of population.
- Congress may not use the spending power to commandeer the legislative powers of the states.
- The ACA is an extreme and unprecedented abuse of the spending power designed to coerce the states into complying with the will of Congress. The act leaves the states with no reasonable alternative choices.
- Approval of the ACA would mean that the congressional spending power has no bounds.

For the respondent, Health and Human Services Secretary Kathleen Sebelius:

- The minimum coverage provision operates as a tax. It raises revenue, it is collected and enforced by the Internal Revenue Service, and the amount owed is based in part on income level.
- Taxes can have regulatory objectives as well as revenue-generation goals.
- The fact that the ACA uses the term *penalty* rather than *tax* is not germane to the constitutional inquiry.
- It is settled law that Congress may fix the terms on which it appropriates federal funds.
- From the very beginning of the Medicaid program Congress has reserved the right to alter, amend, or repeal any provision of the act and has done so many times.
- The Medicaid expansion is so generous that the states overwhelmingly will choose to participate in it. This does not mean that the law is coercive.

> **CHIEF JUSTICE ROBERTS ANNOUNCED THE JUDGMENT OF THE COURT AND DELIVERED . . . AN OPINION WITH RESPECT TO [THE AUTHORITY OF CONGRESS TO IMPOSE THE INDIVIDUAL MANDATE UNDER THE TAXING POWER AND THE CONSTITUTIONALITY OF THE MEDICAID EXPANSION].**

Today we resolve constitutional challenges to two provisions of the Patient Protection and Affordable Care Act of 2010: the individual mandate, which requires individuals to purchase a health insurance policy providing a minimum level of coverage; and the Medicaid expansion, which gives funds to the States on the condition that they provide specified health care to all citizens whose income falls below a certain threshold. . . .

The exaction the Affordable Care Act imposes on those without health insurance looks like a tax in many respects. The "[s]hared responsibility payment," as the statute entitles it, is paid into the Treasury by "taxpayer[s]" when they file their tax returns. It does not apply to individuals who do not pay federal income taxes because their household income is less than the filing threshold in the Internal Revenue Code. For taxpayers who do owe the payment, its amount is determined by such familiar factors as taxable income, number of dependents, and joint filing status. The requirement to pay is found in the Internal Revenue Code and enforced by the IRS, which . . . must assess and collect it "in the same manner as taxes." This process yields the essential feature of any tax: it produces at least some revenue for the Government. Indeed, the payment is expected to raise about $4 billion per year by 2017.

It is of course true that the Act describes the payment as a "penalty," not a "tax." But [this] does not determine whether the payment may be viewed as an exercise of Congress's taxing power. . . .

We have . . . held that exactions not labeled taxes nonetheless were authorized by Congress's power to tax. In the *License Tax Cases* [1866], for example, we held that federal licenses to sell liquor and lottery tickets—for which the licensee had to pay a fee—could be sustained as exercises of the taxing power. And in *New York v. United States* [1992] we upheld as a tax a "surcharge" on out-of-state nuclear waste shipments, a portion of which was paid to the Federal Treasury. We thus ask whether the shared responsibility payment falls within Congress's taxing power, "[d]isregarding the designation of the exaction, and viewing its substance and application." *United States v. Constantine* (1935).

Our cases confirm this functional approach. For example, in [*Bailey v.*] *Drexel Furniture* [1922], we focused on three practical characteristics of the so-called tax on employing child laborers that convinced us the "tax" was actually a penalty. First, the tax imposed an exceedingly heavy burden—10 percent of a company's net income—on those who employed children, no matter how small their infraction. Second, it imposed that exaction only on those who knowingly employed underage laborers. Such scienter requirements are typical of punitive statutes, because Congress often wishes to punish only those who intentionally break the law. Third, this "tax" was enforced in part by the Department of Labor, an agency responsible for punishing violations of labor laws, not collecting revenue.

The same analysis here suggests that the shared responsibility payment may for constitutional purposes be considered a tax, not a penalty: First, for most Americans the amount due will be far less than the price of insurance, and, by statute, it can never be more. It may often be a reasonable financial decision to make the payment rather than purchase insurance, unlike the "prohibitory" financial punishment in *Drexel Furniture*. Second, the individual mandate contains no scienter requirement. Third, the payment is collected solely by the IRS through the normal means of taxation—except that the Service is not allowed to use those means most suggestive of a punitive sanction, such as criminal prosecution. The reasons the Court in *Drexel Furniture* held that what was called a "tax" there was a penalty support the conclusion that what is called a "penalty" here may be viewed as a tax.

None of this is to say that the payment is not intended to affect individual conduct. Although the payment will raise considerable revenue, it is plainly designed to expand health insurance coverage. But taxes that seek to influence conduct are nothing new. Some of our earliest federal taxes sought to deter the purchase of imported manufactured goods in order to foster the growth of domestic industry. Today, federal and state taxes can compose more than half the retail price of cigarettes, not just to raise more money, but to encourage people to quit smoking. And we have upheld such obviously regulatory measures as taxes on selling marijuana and sawed-off shotguns. Indeed, "[e]very tax is in some measure regulatory. To some extent it interposes an economic impediment to the activity taxed as compared with others not taxed." That §5000A seeks to shape decisions about whether to buy health insurance does not mean that it cannot be a valid exercise of the taxing power.

In distinguishing penalties from taxes, this Court has explained that "if the concept of penalty means anything, it means punishment for an unlawful act or omission." *United States v. Reorganized CF&I Fabricators of Utah, Inc.* (1996). While the individual mandate clearly aims to induce the purchase of health insurance, it need not be read to declare that failing to do so is unlawful. Neither the Act nor any other law attaches negative legal consequences to not buying health insurance, beyond requiring a payment to the IRS. The Government agrees with that reading, confirming that if someone chooses to pay rather than obtain health insurance, they have fully complied with the law.

Indeed, it is estimated that four million people each year will choose to pay the IRS rather than buy insurance. We would expect Congress to be troubled by that prospect if such conduct were unlawful. That Congress apparently regards such extensive failure to comply with the mandate as tolerable suggests that Congress did not think it was creating four million outlaws. It suggests instead that the shared responsibility payment merely imposes a tax citizens may lawfully choose to pay in lieu of buying health insurance. . . .

Even if the taxing power enables Congress to impose a tax on not obtaining health insurance, any tax must still comply with other requirements in the Constitution. Plaintiffs argue that the shared responsibility payment does not do so, citing Article I, §9, clause 4. That clause provides: "No Capitation, or other direct, Tax shall be laid, unless in Proportion to the Census or Enumeration herein before directed to be taken." This requirement means that any "direct Tax" must be apportioned so that each State pays in proportion to its population. According to the plaintiffs, if the individual mandate imposes a tax, it is a direct tax, and it is unconstitutional because Congress made no effort to apportion it among the States. . . .

A tax on going without health insurance does not fall within any recognized category of direct tax. It is not a capitation. Capitations are taxes paid by every person, "without regard to property, profession, or any other circumstance." *Hylton* [*v. United States*, 1796]. The whole point of the shared responsibility payment is that it is triggered by specific circumstances—earning a certain amount of income but not obtaining health insurance. The payment is also plainly not a tax on the ownership of land or personal property. The shared responsibility payment is thus not a direct tax that must be apportioned among the several States.

There may, however, be a more fundamental objection to a tax on those who lack health insurance. Even if only a tax, the payment under §5000A(b) remains a burden that the Federal Government imposes for an omission, not an act. If it is troubling to interpret the Commerce Clause as authorizing Congress to regulate those who abstain from commerce, perhaps it should be similarly troubling to permit Congress to impose a tax for not doing something.

. . . [I]t is abundantly clear the Constitution does not guarantee that individuals may avoid taxation through inactivity. A capitation, after all, is a tax that everyone must pay simply for existing, and capitations are expressly contemplated by the Constitution. The Court today holds that our Constitution protects us from federal regulation under the Commerce Clause so long as we abstain from the regulated activity. But from its creation, the Constitution has made no such promise with respect to taxes. . . .

The Affordable Care Act's requirement that certain individuals pay a financial penalty for not obtaining health insurance may reasonably be characterized as a tax. Because the Constitution permits such a tax, it is not our role to forbid it, or to pass upon its wisdom or fairness.

. . . The Federal Government does have the power to impose a tax on those without health insurance. Section 5000A is therefore constitutional, because it can reasonably be read as a tax.

* * *

The States also contend that the Medicaid expansion exceeds Congress's authority under the Spending Clause. They claim that Congress is coercing the States to adopt the changes it wants by threatening to withhold all of a State's Medicaid grants, unless the State accepts the new expanded funding and complies with the conditions that come with it. This, they argue, violates the basic principle that the "Federal Government may not compel the States to enact or administer a federal regulatory program." *New York*. . . .

The Spending Clause grants Congress the power "to pay the Debts and provide for the . . . general Welfare of the United States." We have long recognized that Congress may use this power to grant federal funds to the States, and may condition such a grant upon the States' "taking certain actions that Congress could not require them to take." Such measures "encourage a State to regulate in a particular way, [and] influenc[e] a State's policy choices." *New York*. The conditions imposed by Congress ensure that the funds are used by the States to "provide for the . . . general Welfare" in the manner Congress intended.

At the same time, our cases have recognized limits on Congress's power under the Spending Clause to secure state compliance with federal objectives. . . . [The] "Constitution has never been understood to confer upon Congress the ability to require the States to govern according to Congress' instructions." *New York*. Otherwise the two-government system established by the Framers would give way to a system that vests power in one central government, and individual liberty would suffer.

That insight has led this Court to strike down federal legislation that commandeers a State's legislative or administrative apparatus for federal purposes. See, e.g., *Printz* [*v. United States*, 1997], *New York*. It has also led us to scrutinize Spending Clause legislation to ensure that Congress is not using financial inducements to exert a "power akin to undue influence." *Steward Machine Co. v. Davis* (1937). Congress may use its spending power to create incentives for States to act in accordance with federal policies. But when "pressure turns into compulsion," the legislation runs contrary to our system of federalism. "[T]he Constitution simply does not give Congress the authority to require the States to regulate." *New York*. That is true whether Congress directly commands a State to regulate or indirectly coerces a State to adopt a federal regulatory system as its own.

Permitting the Federal Government to force the States to implement a federal program would threaten the political accountability key to our federal system. . . . Spending Clause programs do not pose this danger when a State has a legitimate choice whether to accept the federal conditions in exchange for federal funds. In such a situation, state officials can fairly be held politically accountable for choosing to accept or refuse the federal offer. But when the State has no choice, the Federal Government can achieve its objectives without accountability, just as in *New York* and *Printz*. Indeed, this danger is heightened when Congress acts under the Spending Clause, because Congress can use that power to implement federal policy it could not impose directly under its enumerated powers. . . .

The States . . . object that Congress has "crossed the line distinguishing encouragement from coercion," *New York*, in the way it has structured the funding: Instead of simply refusing to grant the new funds to States that will not accept the new conditions, Congress has also threatened to withhold those States' existing Medicaid funds. The States claim that this threat serves no purpose other than to force unwilling States to sign up for the dramatic expansion in health care coverage effected by the Act.

Given the nature of the threat and the programs at issue here, we must agree. . . .

In *South Dakota v. Dole*, we considered a challenge to a federal law that threatened to withhold five percent of a State's federal highway funds if the State did not raise its drinking age to 21. . . .

We accordingly asked whether "the financial inducement offered by Congress" was "so coercive as to pass the point at which 'pressure turns into compulsion.'" By "financial inducement" the Court meant the threat of losing five percent of highway funds; no new money was offered to the States to raise their drinking ages. We found that the inducement was not impermissibly coercive, because Congress was offering only "relatively mild encouragement to the States." *Dole*. We observed that "all South Dakota would lose if she adheres to her chosen course as to a suitable minimum drinking age is 5%" of her highway funds. In fact, the federal funds at stake constituted less than half of one percent of South Dakota's budget at the time. . . .

In this case, the financial "inducement" Congress has chosen is much more than "relatively mild encouragement"—it is a gun to the head. Section 1396c of the Medicaid Act provides that if a State's Medicaid plan does not comply with the Act's requirements, the Secretary of Health and Human Services may declare that "further payments will not be made to the State." A State that opts out of the Affordable Care Act's expansion in health care coverage thus stands to lose not merely "a relatively small percentage" of its existing Medicaid funding, but all of it. Medicaid spending accounts for over 20 percent of the average State's total budget, with federal funds covering 50 to 83 percent of those costs. The Federal Government estimates that it will pay out approximately $3.3 trillion between 2010 and 2019 in order to cover the costs of pre-expansion Medicaid. In addition, the States have developed intricate

statutory and administrative regimes over the course of many decades to implement their objectives under existing Medicaid. It is easy to see how the *Dole* Court could conclude that the threatened loss of less than half of one percent of South Dakota's budget left that State with a "prerogative" to reject Congress's desired policy, "not merely in theory but in fact." The threatened loss of over 10 percent of a State's overall budget, in contrast, is economic dragooning that leaves the States with no real option but to acquiesce in the Medicaid expansion. . . .

Nothing in our opinion precludes Congress from offering funds under the Affordable Care Act to expand the availability of health care, and requiring that States accepting such funds comply with the conditions on their use. What Congress is not free to do is to penalize States that choose not to participate in that new program by taking away their existing Medicaid funding. . . . In light of the Court's holding, the Secretary cannot . . . withdraw existing Medicaid funds for failure to comply with the requirements set out in the expansion. . . .

We have no way of knowing how many States will accept the terms of the expansion, but we do not believe Congress would have wanted the whole Act to fall, simply because some may choose not to participate. The other reforms Congress enacted, after all, will remain "fully operative as a law" and will still function in a way "consistent with Congress' basic objectives in enacting the statute." Confident that Congress would not have intended anything different, we conclude that the rest of the Act need not fall in light of our constitutional holding.

* * *

The Affordable Care Act is constitutional in part and unconstitutional in part. The individual mandate cannot be upheld as an exercise of Congress's power under the Commerce Clause. That Clause authorizes Congress to regulate interstate commerce, not to order individuals to engage in it. In this case, however, it is reasonable to construe what Congress has done as increasing taxes on those who have a certain amount of income, but choose to go without health insurance. Such legislation is within Congress's power to tax.

As for the Medicaid expansion, that portion of the Affordable Care Act violates the Constitution by threatening existing Medicaid funding. Congress has no authority to order the States to regulate according to its instructions. Congress may offer the States grants and require the States to comply with accompanying conditions, but the States must have a genuine choice whether to accept the offer. The States are given no such choice in this case: They must either accept a basic change in the nature of Medicaid, or risk losing all Medicaid funding. The remedy for that constitutional violation is to preclude the Federal Government from imposing such a sanction. That remedy does not require striking down other portions of the Affordable Care Act.

The Framers created a Federal Government of limited powers, and assigned to this Court the duty of enforcing those limits. The Court does so today. But the Court does not express any opinion on the wisdom of the Affordable Care Act. Under the Constitution, that judgment is reserved to the people.

The judgment of the Court of Appeals for the Eleventh Circuit is affirmed in part and reversed in part.

It is so ordered.

JUSTICE GINSBURG . . . concurring in part, concurring in the judgment in part, and dissenting in part.

I agree with The Chief Justice that the . . . minimum coverage provision is a proper exercise of Congress' taxing power. . . . I would also hold that the Spending Clause permits the Medicaid expansion exactly as Congress enacted it. . . .

The Spending Clause authorizes Congress "to pay the Debts and provide for the . . . general Welfare of the United States." To ensure that federal funds granted to the States are spent "to 'provide for the . . . general Welfare' in the manner Congress intended," Congress must of course have authority to impose limitations on the States' use of the federal dollars. This Court, time and again, has respected Congress' prescription of spending conditions, and has required States to abide by them. In particular, we have recognized Congress' prerogative to condition a State's receipt of Medicaid funding on compliance with the terms Congress set for participation in the program.

Congress' authority to condition the use of federal funds is not confined to spending programs as first launched. The legislature may, and often does, amend the law, imposing new conditions grant recipients henceforth must meet in order to continue receiving funds. . . .

The ACA . . . relates solely to the federally funded Medicaid program; if States choose not to comply, Congress has not threatened to withhold funds earmarked for any other program. Nor does the ACA use Medicaid funding to induce States to take action Congress itself could not undertake. The Federal Government undoubtedly could operate its own health-care program for poor persons, just as it operates Medicare for seniors' health care.

That is what makes this such a simple case, and the Court's decision so unsettling. Congress, aiming to assist the needy, has appropriated federal money to subsidize state health-insurance programs that meet federal standards. The principal standard the ACA sets is that the state program cover adults earning no more than 133% of the federal poverty line. Enforcing that prescription ensures that federal funds will be spent on health care for the poor in furtherance of Congress' present perception of the general welfare. . . .

Congress has broad authority to construct or adjust spending programs to meet its contemporary understanding of "the general Welfare." *Helvering v. Davis* (1937). Courts owe a large measure of respect to Congress' characterization of the grant programs it establishes. See *Steward Machine*. . . .

At bottom, my colleagues' position is that the States' reliance on federal funds limits Congress' authority to alter its spending programs. This gets things backwards: Congress, not the States, is tasked with spending federal money in service of the general welfare. And each successive Congress is empowered to appropriate funds as it sees fit. When the 110th Congress reached a conclusion about Medicaid funds that differed from its predecessors' view, it abridged no State's right to "existing," or "preexisting," funds. For, in fact, there are no such funds. There is only money States anticipate receiving from future Congresses.

Congress has delegated to the Secretary of Health and Human Services the authority to withhold, in whole or in part, federal Medicaid funds from States that fail to comply with the Medicaid Act as originally composed and as subsequently amended. The Chief Justice, however, holds that the Constitution precludes the Secretary from withholding "existing" Medicaid funds based on States' refusal to comply with the expanded Medicaid program. . . . I disagree that any such withholding would violate the Spending Clause. Accordingly, I would affirm the decision of the Court of Appeals for the Eleventh Circuit in this regard.

But in view of The Chief Justice's disposition, I agree with him that the Medicaid Act's severability clause determines the appropriate remedy. That clause provides that "[i]f any provision of [the Medicaid Act], or the application thereof to any person or circumstance, is held invalid, the remainder of the chapter, and the application of such provision to other persons or circumstances shall not be affected thereby." . . .

Nate Beeler, Courtesy of Cagle Cartoons

Editorial cartoon published in the Columbus Dispatch *commenting on the Supreme Court's decision to uphold the Patient Protection and Affordable Care Act's individual mandate provision as an appropriate use of Congress's power to tax. Initially supporters of the legislation argued that the financial sanctions for noncompliance with the law were penalties and not taxes.*

Joint Opinion of JUSTICE SCALIA, JUSTICE KENNEDY, JUSTICE THOMAS, and JUSTICE ALITO, dissenting.

The Government contends . . . that "the minimum coverage provision is independently authorized by Congress's taxing power." The phrase "independently authorized" suggests the existence of a creature never hitherto seen in the United States Reports: A penalty for constitutional purposes that is *also* a tax for constitutional purposes. In all our cases the two are mutually exclusive. The provision challenged under the Constitution is either a penalty or else a tax. . . . The issue is not whether Congress had the power to frame the minimum-coverage provision as a tax, but whether it did so.

In answering that question we must, if "fairly possible," construe the provision to be a tax rather than a mandate-with-penalty, since that would render it constitutional rather than unconstitutional. But we cannot rewrite the statute to be what it is not. "[A]lthough this Court will often strain to construe legislation so as to save it against constitutional attack, it must not and will not carry this to the point of perverting the purpose of a statute . . . or judicially rewriting it." *Commodity Futures Trading Comm'n v. Schor* (1986). In this case, there is simply no way, "without doing violence to the fair meaning of the words used," to escape what Congress enacted: a mandate that individuals maintain minimum essential coverage, enforced by a penalty.

Our cases establish a clear line between a tax and a penalty: "[A] tax is an enforced contribution to provide for the support of government; a penalty . . . is an exaction imposed by statute as punishment for an unlawful act." *United States v. Reorganized CF&I Fabricators of Utah, Inc.* (1996). . . .

So the question is, quite simply, whether the exaction here is imposed for violation of the law. It unquestionably is. The minimum-coverage provision is . . . entitled "Requirement to maintain minimum essential coverage." It commands that every "applicable individual shall . . . ensure that the individual . . . is covered under minimum essential coverage." And the immediately following provision states that, "[i]f . . . an applicable individual . . . fails to meet the requirement of subsection (a) . . . there is hereby imposed . . . a penalty." And several of Congress' legislative "findings" with regard to §5000A confirm that it sets forth a legal requirement and constitutes the assertion of regulatory power, not mere taxing power. . . .

Quite separately, the fact that Congress (in its own words) "imposed . . . a penalty," for failure to buy insurance is alone sufficient to render that failure unlawful. . . .

. . . [T]o say that the Individual Mandate merely imposes a tax is not to interpret the statute but to rewrite it.

We now consider respondents' second challenge to the constitutionality of the ACA, namely, that the Act's dramatic expansion of the Medicaid program exceeds Congress' power to attach conditions to federal grants to the States.

The ACA does not legally compel the States to participate in the expanded Medicaid program, but the Act authorizes a severe sanction for any State that refuses to go along: termination of all the State's Medicaid funding. For the average State, the annual federal Medicaid subsidy is equal to more than one-fifth of the State's expenditures.—A State forced out of the program would not only lose this huge sum but would almost certainly find it necessary to increase its own health-care expenditures substantially, requiring either a drastic reduction in funding for other programs or a large increase in state taxes. And these new taxes would come on top of the federal taxes already paid by the State's citizens to fund the Medicaid program in other States. . . .

When federal legislation gives the States a real choice whether to accept or decline a federal aid package, the federal-state relationship is in the nature of a contractual relationship. And just as a contract is voidable if coerced, "[t]he legitimacy of Congress' power to legislate under the spending power . . . rests on whether the State voluntarily and knowingly accepts the terms of the 'contract.'" If a federal spending program coerces participation the States have not "exercise[d] their choice"—let alone made an "informed choice."

Coercing States to accept conditions risks the destruction of the "unique role of the States in our system." "[T]he Constitution has never been understood to confer upon Congress the ability to require the States to govern according to Congress' instructions." Congress may not "simply commandeer the legislative processes of the States by directly compelling them to enact and enforce a federal regulatory program. Congress effectively engages in this impermissible compulsion when state participation in a federal spending program is coerced, so that the States' choice whether to enact or administer a federal regulatory program is rendered illusory.

Where all Congress has done is to "encourag[e] state regulation rather than compe[l] it, state governments remain responsive to the local electorate's preferences; state officials remain accountable to the people. [But] where the Federal Government compels States to regulate, the accountability of both state and federal officials is diminished." . . .

. . . [T]he legitimacy of attaching conditions to federal grants to the States depends on the voluntariness of the States' choice to accept or decline the offered package. Therefore, if States really have no choice other than to accept the package, the offer is coercive, and the conditions cannot be sustained under the spending power. And as our decision in *South Dakota v. Dole* makes clear, theoretical voluntariness is not enough. . . .

. . . When a heavy federal tax is levied to support a federal program that offers large grants to the States, States may, as a practical matter, be unable to refuse to participate in the federal program and to substitute a state alternative. Even if a State believes that the federal program is ineffective and inefficient, withdrawal would likely force the State to impose a huge tax increase on its residents, and this new state tax would come on top of the federal taxes already paid by residents to support subsidies to participating States. . . .

Whether federal spending legislation crosses the line from enticement to coercion is often difficult to determine, and courts should not conclude that legislation is unconstitutional on this ground unless the coercive nature of an offer is unmistakably clear. In this case, however, there can be no doubt. In structuring the ACA, Congress unambiguously signaled its belief that every State would have no real choice but to go along with the Medicaid Expansion. If the anticoercion rule does not apply in this case, then there is no such rule. . . .

In sum, it is perfectly clear from the goal and structure of the ACA that the offer of the Medicaid Expansion was one that Congress understood no State could refuse. The Medicaid Expansion therefore exceeds Congress' spending power and cannot be implemented. . . .

For the reasons here stated, we would find the Act invalid in its entirety. We respectfully dissent.

National Federation of Independent Business v. Sebelius was a landmark ruling on the power of Congress. First, it narrowed the range of federal regulatory power under the commerce clause by declaring that Congress does not have the authority to order individuals to engage in a commercial transaction. Second, it once again upheld the use of the taxing power as a way to justify legislation that Congress might not otherwise have the authority to enact. And third, for the first time in seventy-five years the justices struck down a federal spending initiative, finding that the Medicaid expansion violated the principles of federalism by coercing the states to participate in a federal program.

RESTRICTIONS ON THE REVENUE POWERS OF THE STATES

Taxation is a concurrent power: the states exercised the power to tax prior to the ratification of the Constitution and retain that authority today. The powers of the states to tax are very broad, limited primarily by provisions in the states' own constitutions and laws. Taxes on property, income, and sales provide the bulk of funds for state government activities.

The Constitution, however, removed certain sources of revenue from the states. Article I, Section 10, explicitly prohibits the states from taxing imports or exports without the approval of Congress. In addition, the commerce clause blocks the states from imposing taxes that place an unreasonable burden on interstate or foreign commerce. Aside from these limitations, the states remain free to develop their own tax structures and sources of revenue.

State Taxes on Foreign Commerce

In *Brown v. Maryland* (1827) the Supreme Court first faced a question of the validity of state taxes on imports. The dispute centered on a Maryland law that required importers of foreign goods to pay a license fee. The Supreme Court struck down the statute as a tax on imports and as infringing on the authority of the federal government to regulate foreign commerce. An important part of the Court's opinion, however, dealt with the following question: When does an imported article cease to be an import and become part of the taxable goods within a state? The Court's answer to this question was the "original package" doctrine. For the majority, John Marshall wrote, "While [the imported article remains] the property of the importer, in his warehouse, in the original form or package in which it was imported, a tax upon it is too plainly a duty on imports to escape the prohibition in the constitution."

The original package doctrine meant that goods flowing into the United States remained within the federal government's taxing and regulating power until they were sold, processed, or broken out of their original packaging. Once any of those events took place, the articles became normal property within the state and subject to state taxation. The impact of this interpretation was that large warehouses filled with imported goods ready for shipment to other parts of the United States were free from state taxation as long as no sale took place and the materials remained in their original packages. The states balked at this rule, arguing that they should be able to levy property taxes on such goods as long as the taxes

were nondiscriminatory—that is, if imported articles stored in warehouses were taxed on exactly the same basis as other property within the state. In *Low v. Austin* (1872) the Court rejected the constitutionality of such nondiscriminatory taxes, adhering to Marshall's rationale in *Brown*.

Although attacked by legal scholars and those promoting the interests of the states, the original package doctrine survived until 1976, when the justices accepted an appeal from a decision by the Georgia Supreme Court that approved certain nondiscriminatory taxes on warehoused imports. After reanalyzing the issues involved, the Court altered a rule of law that had been in effect for more than a century.

Michelin Tire Corp. v. Wages

423 U.S. 276 (1976)
http://laws.findlaw.com/us/423/276.html
Oral arguments are available at https://www.oyez.org.
Vote: 8 (Blackmun, Brennan, Burger, Marshall, Powell, Rehnquist, Stewart, White)
    0

OPINION OF THE COURT: *Brennan*
CONCURRING OPINION: *White*
NOT PARTICIPATING: *Stevens*

FACTS:

Michelin Tire Corporation operated a warehouse in Gwinnett County, Georgia, just outside of Atlanta. The company imported tires and tire products into the United States from France and Nova Scotia and stored them in the Georgia warehouse for later distribution to retail outlets. When the county tax assessors levied a nondiscriminatory ad valorem property tax on the inventory, the company sued W. L. Wages, the county tax commissioner, for relief, claiming that, except for some tire tubes that had been removed from their original containers, the warehouse contents were constitutionally free from state taxation.

The local court granted the relief requested, and the Georgia Supreme Court heard the county's appeal. The state high court ruled that the tires were subject to tax because, after being imported in bulk, they had been sorted and arranged for sale. Michelin sought a reversal by the U.S. Supreme Court, which ignored subtle questions regarding the application of the original package doctrine and instead focused on the fundamental issue of whether any warehoused imports are subject to state taxation.

For the petitioner, Michelin Tire Corporation:

- The taxed goods in question are located in the importer's warehouse in their original package or form. Segregating the tires by size and style does not constitute taking them out of their original packages.
- The articles taxed remain imports under *Brown v. Maryland*'s original package doctrine.
- Michelin paid the United States a duty for the right to import and sell the tires as well as to have the tires free from state and local taxation until they lose their status as an import.
- The Constitution forbids state and local taxation of imports. *Brown v. Maryland* should be reaffirmed.

For the respondent, W. L. Wages, county tax commissioner:

- A state has the power to levy nondiscriminatory ad valorem taxes on property located in its jurisdiction.
- When Michelin organizes the tires by size and style, it takes its goods out of their original package.
- Exempting from taxation warehoused goods of an importer imposes a competitive burden on domestic companies that similarly store goods in warehouses and are taxed.
- *Brown v. Maryland* has become outdated and should be overruled.

MR. JUSTICE BRENNAN DELIVERED THE OPINION OF THE COURT.

Low v. Austin [1872] is the leading decision of this Court holding that the States are prohibited by the Import-Export Clause from imposing a nondiscriminatory ad valorem property tax on imported goods until they lose their character as imports and become incorporated into the mass of property in the State. The Court there reviewed a decision of the California Supreme Court that had sustained the constitutionality of California's nondiscriminatory ad valorem tax on the ground that the Import-Export Clause only prohibited taxes upon the character of the goods as imports and therefore did not prohibit nondiscriminatory taxes upon the goods as property. This Court reversed on its reading of the seminal opinion construing the Import-Export Clause, *Brown v. Maryland* (1827), as holding that "[w]hilst retaining their character as imports, a tax upon them, in any shape, is within the constitutional prohibition."

Scholarly analysis has been uniformly critical of *Low v. Austin*. It is true that Mr. Chief Justice Marshall, speaking for the Court in *Brown v. Maryland*, said that "while [the thing imported remains] the property of the importer, in his warehouse, in the original form or package in which it was imported, a tax upon it is too plainly a duty on imports to escape the prohibition in the constitution." Commentators have uniformly agreed that *Low v. Austin* misread this dictum in holding that the Court in *Brown* included nondiscriminatory ad valorem property taxes among prohibited "imposts" or "duties," for the contrary conclusion is plainly to be inferred from consideration of the specific abuses which led the Framers to include the Import-Export Clause in the Constitution.

Our independent study persuades us that a nondiscriminatory ad valorem property tax is not the type of state exaction which the Framers of the Constitution or the Court in *Brown* had in mind as being an "impost" or "duty" and that *Low v. Austin*'s reliance upon the *Brown* dictum to reach the contrary conclusion was misplaced.

One of the major defects of the Articles of Confederation, and a compelling reason for the calling of the Constitutional Convention of 1787, was the fact that the Articles essentially left the individual States free to burden commerce both among themselves and with foreign countries very much as they pleased. Before 1787 it was commonplace for seaboard States with port facilities to derive revenue to defray the costs of state and local government by imposing taxes on imported goods destined for customers in other States. At the same time, there was no secure source of revenue for the central government. . . .

The Framers of the Constitution thus sought to alleviate three main concerns by committing sole power to lay imposts and duties on imports in the Federal Government, with no concurrent state power: the Federal Government must speak with one voice when regulating commercial relations with foreign governments, and tariffs, which might affect foreign relations, could not be implemented by the States consistently with that exclusive power; import revenues were to be the major source of revenue of the Federal Government and should not be diverted to the States; and harmony among the States might be disturbed unless seaboard States, with their crucial ports of entry, were prohibited from levying taxes on citizens of other States by taxing goods merely flowing through their ports to the other States not situated as favorably geographically.

Nothing in the history of the Import-Export Clause even remotely suggests that a nondiscriminatory ad valorem property tax which is also imposed on imported goods that are no longer in import transit was the type of exaction that was regarded as objectionable by the Framers of the Constitution. For such an exaction, unlike discriminatory state taxation against imported goods as imports, was not regarded as an impediment that severely hampered commerce or constituted a form of tribute by seaboard States to the disadvantage of the other States.

It is obvious that such nondiscriminatory property taxation can have no impact whatsoever on the Federal Government's exclusive regulation of foreign commerce, probably the most important purpose of the Clause's prohibition. By definition, such a tax does not fall on imports as such because of their place of origin. It cannot be used to create special protective tariffs or particular preferences for certain domestic goods, and it cannot be applied selectively to encourage or discourage any importation in a manner inconsistent with federal regulation.

Nor will such taxation deprive the Federal Government of the exclusive right to all revenues from imposts and duties on imports and exports, since that right by definition only extends to revenues from exactions of a particular category; if nondiscriminatory ad valorem taxation is not in that category, it deprives the Federal Government of nothing to which it is entitled. Unlike imposts and duties, which are essentially taxes on the commercial privilege of bringing goods into a country, such property taxes are taxes by which a State apportions the cost of such services as police and fire protection among the beneficiaries according to their respective wealth; there is no reason why an importer should not bear his share of these costs along with his competitors handling only domestic goods. The Import-Export Clause clearly prohibits state taxation based on the foreign origin of the imported goods, but it cannot be read to accord imported goods preferential treatment that permits escape from uniform taxes imposed without regard to foreign origin for services which the State supplies. . . .

Finally, nondiscriminatory ad valorem property taxes do not interfere with the free flow of imported goods among the States, as did the exactions by States under the Articles of Confederation directed solely at imported goods. . . .

Since prohibition of nondiscriminatory ad valorem property taxation would not further the objectives of the Import-Export Clause, only the clearest constitutional mandate should lead us to condemn such taxation. . . .

The Court in *Low v. Austin* nevertheless expanded the prohibition of the Clause to include nondiscriminatory ad valorem property taxes, and did so with no analysis, but with only the statement that *Brown v. Maryland* had marked the line "where the power of Congress over the goods imported ends, and that of the State begins, with as much precision as the subject admits." But the opinion in *Brown v. Maryland* cannot properly be read to propose such a broad definition of "imposts" or "duties." The tax there held to be prohibited by the Import-Export Clause was imposed under a Maryland statute that required importers of foreign goods, and wholesalers selling the same by bale or package, to obtain a license and pay a $50 fee therefor, subject to certain forfeitures and penalties for noncompliance. The importers contested the validity of the statute, arguing that the license was a "palpable evasion" of the Import-Export Clause because it was essentially equivalent to a duty on imports. Since the power to impose a license on importers would also entail a power to price them out of the market or prohibit them entirely, the importers concluded that such a power must be repugnant to the exclusive federal power to regulate foreign commerce.

The Attorney General of Maryland, Roger Taney, later Chief Justice, defended the constitutionality of Maryland's law. He argued that the fee was not a prohibited "impost" or "duty" because the license fee was not a tax upon the imported goods, but on the importers, a tax upon the occupation and nothing more, and the Import-Export Clause prohibited only exactions on the right of importation and not an exaction upon the occupation of importers. . . .

The Court in *Brown* refused to define "imposts" or "duties" comprehensively, since the Maryland statute presented only the question "whether the legislature of a State can constitutionally require the importer of foreign articles to take out a license from the State, before he shall be permitted to sell a bale or package so imported." However, in holding that the Maryland license fee was within prohibited "imposts, or duties on imports . . ." the Court significantly characterized an impost or duty as "a custom or a tax levied on articles brought into a country," although also holding that, while normally levied before the articles are permitted to enter, the exactions are no less within the prohibition if levied upon the goods as imports after entry; since "imports" are the goods imported, the prohibition of imposts or duties on "imports" was more than a prohibition of a tax on the act of importation; it "extends to a duty levied after [the thing imported] has entered the country." And since the power to prohibit sale of an article is the power to prohibit its introduction into the country, the privilege of sale must be a concomitant of the privilege of importation, and licenses on the right to sell must therefore also fall within the constitutional prohibition.

Taney's argument was persuasive, however, to the extent that the Court "was prompted to declare that the words of the prohibition ought not to be pressed to their utmost extent; . . . in our complex system, the object of the powers conferred on the government of the Union, and the nature of the often conflicting powers which remain in the States, must always be taken into view. . . . [T]here must be a point of time when the prohibition ceases, and the power of the State to tax commences. . . ."

Despite the language and objectives of the Import-Export Clause, and despite the limited nature of the holding in *Brown v. Maryland*, the Court in *Low v. Austin* ignored the warning that the boundary between the power of States to tax persons and property within their jurisdictions and the limitations on the power of the States to impose imposts or duties with respect to "imports" was a subtle and difficult line which must be drawn as the cases arise. *Low v. Austin* also ignored the cautionary remark that, for those reasons, it "might be premature to state any rule as being universal in its application." Although it was "sufficient" in the context of Maryland's license tax on the right to sell imported goods to note that a tax imposed directly on imported goods which have not been acted upon in any way would clearly fall within the constitutional prohibition, that observation did not apply, as the foregoing analysis indicates, to a state tax which treated those same goods without regard to the fact of their foreign origin. . . .

It follows from the foregoing that *Low v. Austin* was wrongly decided. That decision must be, and is, overruled.

Petitioner's tires in this case were no longer in transit. They were stored in a distribution warehouse from which petitioner conducted a wholesale operation, taking orders from franchised dealers and filling them from a constantly replenished inventory. The warehouse was operated no differently than would be a distribution warehouse utilized by a wholesaler dealing solely in domestic goods, and we therefore hold that the nondiscriminatory property tax levied on petitioner's inventory of imported tires was not interdicted by the Import-Export Clause of the Constitution. The judgment of the Supreme Court of Georgia is accordingly

Affirmed.

State Taxes on Interstate Commerce

State taxes on interstate commerce have provided another source of constitutional disputes. A state has the right to tax commerce that occurs within its borders, but taxes that discriminate against or place an undue burden on interstate commerce violate the commerce clause. In the nation's formative years this rule of constitutional interpretation was relatively easy to apply, but given the changes in economic realities and the significant alterations in the definition of interstate commerce, the situation is now much more complex.

Today, relatively little commercial activity is purely intrastate. Consequently, whenever a state imposes a tax on business activity, it can be charged that the state is placing a burden on interstate commerce. The Supreme Court has attempted to fashion a rule that copes with modern economic conditions and yet is mindful of three important considerations. First, if the states are to remain viable entities, they must retain the ability to tax commercial activities. Second, true burdens on interstate commerce, as well as taxes that discriminate against it, must be avoided. Third, simply engaging in an interstate commercial activity should not suffice to exempt a company from paying its fair share in state taxes. Naturally, these principles are far easier to state than to apply to real situations.

In *Complete Auto Transit v. Brady* (1977) the justices concluded that their previous decisions were inconsistent with contemporary conditions and that a new statement on the authority of states to tax activities affecting interstate commerce was required. In his opinion for the Court, Justice Harry A. Blackmun found fault with some leading precedents and replaced them with a four-pronged test to be used in determining the validity of state taxation.

Complete Auto Transit v. Brady

430 U.S. 274 (1977)
http://laws.findlaw.com/us/430/274.html
Oral arguments are available at https://www.oyez.org.
Vote: 9 (Blackmun, Brennan, Burger, Marshall, Powell, Rehnquist, Stevens, Stewart, White)
   0

OPINION OF THE COURT: *Blackmun*

FACTS:

Complete Auto Transit was a Michigan corporation doing business in Mississippi. Under its contract with General Motors (GM), Complete's job was to transport new vehicles manufactured out of state and then brought into Mississippi by rail. The automobiles were loaded onto Complete's trucks in the Jackson,

Mississippi, rail yards and delivered to GM dealerships around the state. There is no doubt that Complete's business was interstate commerce. The company provided the last segment in the transportation of goods manufactured out of state to their retail destinations within the state.

Mississippi imposed a tax on transportation companies for the privilege of doing business in the state at a rate of 5 percent of gross income from state business. The state applied the tax to businesses operating in intra- and interstate commerce. In 1971 the Mississippi Tax Commission informed Complete that it owed $122,160.59 in taxes from a three-year period beginning in 1968. In 1972 Complete received a second bill for $42,990.89 for taxes due over the previous year. Complete paid the taxes under protest and sued for a refund.

Complete based its case on a 1951 Supreme Court precedent, **Spector Motor Service v. O'Connor**, which held that a state tax on the privilege of doing business is unconstitutional if imposed on any activity that is part of interstate commerce. The Mississippi Supreme Court upheld the tax, saying that Complete enjoyed the various services of the state and should be obliged to pay its fair share of state taxes. Because the tax did not discriminate against interstate commerce and was based exclusively on income derived from Mississippi sources, it was not constitutionally defective. Complete appealed to the U.S. Supreme Court, asking it to strike down the tax on the basis of the *Spector* precedent.

ARGUMENTS:

For the appellant, Complete Auto Transit, Inc.:

- Complete Auto's business of providing the final stage in the movement of motor vehicles from out of state to designated Mississippi dealers is exclusively part of interstate commerce.
- That the mode of transportation changes from rail to truck does not alter the interstate nature of the transportation.
- Mississippi's "privilege of doing business" tax places a direct burden on interstate commerce. Such taxes are constitutionally impermissible even if fairly apportioned and nondiscriminatory, according to *Spector Motor Service v. O'Connor*.
- Allowing such taxes would have severe impacts on companies like Complete Auto. *Spector Motor* should be reaffirmed.

For the appellee, Charles R. Brady, chairman, Mississippi State Tax Commission:

- The Mississippi tax is levied based on business activities occurring inside Mississippi, where Complete Auto enjoys the protections and services provided by the state. No tax is placed on interstate shipments leaving Mississippi.
- The tax is nondiscriminatory. Businesses engaged in purely intrastate transportation services pay similar taxes. Removing the tax on Complete Auto would give it an advantage over intrastate transportation providers.
- The tax is based on taxable events that occur inside Mississippi. Therefore, the tax on those activities cannot be duplicated by any other state.
- *Spector Motor* has been roundly criticized and should be overruled.

◤ MR. JUSTICE BLACKMUN DELIVERED THE OPINION OF THE COURT.

Once again we are presented with "'the perennial problem of the validity of a state tax for the privilege of carrying on within a state, certain activities' related to a corporation's operation of an interstate business." The issue in this case is whether Mississippi runs afoul of the Commerce Clause when it applies the tax it imposes on "the privilege of . . . doing business" within the State to appellant's activity in interstate commerce. The Supreme Court of Mississippi unanimously sustained the tax against appellant's constitutional challenge. We noted probable jurisdiction in order to consider anew the applicable principles in this troublesome area. . . .

Appellant's attack is based solely on decisions of this Court holding that a tax on the "privilege" of engaging in an activity in the State may not be applied to an activity that is part of interstate commerce. See, *e.g.*, *Spector Motor Service v. O'Connor* (1951); *Freeman v. Hewit* (1946). This rule looks only to the fact that the incidence of the tax is the "privilege of doing business"; it deems irrelevant any consideration of the practical effect of the tax. The rule reflects an underlying philosophy that interstate commerce should enjoy a sort of "free trade" immunity from state taxation.

Appellee, in its turn, relies on decisions of this Court stating that "[i]t was not the purpose of the commerce clause to relieve those engaged in interstate commerce from their just share of state tax burden even though it increases the cost of doing the business," *Western Live*

Stock v. Bureau of Revenue (1938). These decisions have considered not the formal language of the tax statute but rather its practical effect, and have sustained a tax against Commerce Clause challenge when the tax is applied to an activity with a substantial nexus with the taxing State, is fairly apportioned, does not discriminate against interstate commerce, and is fairly related to the services provided by the State.

Over the years, the Court has applied this practical analysis in approving many types of tax that avoided running afoul of the prohibition against taxing the "privilege of doing business," but in each instance it has refused to overrule the prohibition. Under the present state of the law, the *Spector* rule, as it has come to be known, has no relationship to economic realities. Rather it stands only as a trap for the unwary draftsman.

The modern origin of the *Spector* rule may be found in *Freeman v. Hewit*. . . .

Mr. Justice Frankfurter, speaking for five Members of the Court, announced a blanket prohibition against any state taxation imposed directly on an interstate transaction. He explicitly deemed unnecessary to the decision of the case any showing of discrimination against interstate commerce or error in apportionment of the tax. He recognized that a State could constitutionally tax local manufacture, impose license taxes on corporations doing business in the State, tax property within the State, and tax the privilege of residence in the State and measure the privilege by net income, including that derived from interstate commerce. Nevertheless, a direct tax on interstate sales, even if fairly apportioned and nondiscriminatory, was held to be unconstitutional *per se*. . . .

The rule announced in *Freeman* was viewed in the commentary as a triumph of formalism over substance, providing little guidance even as to formal requirements. . . .

The prohibition against state taxation of the "privilege" of engaging in commerce that is interstate was reaffirmed in *Spector Motor Service v. O'Connor* (1951), a case similar on its facts to the instant case. The taxpayer there was a Missouri corporation engaged exclusively in interstate trucking. Some of its shipments originated or terminated in Connecticut. Connecticut imposed on a corporation a "tax or excise upon its franchise for the privilege of carrying on or doing business within the state," measured by apportioned net income. Spector brought suit in federal court to enjoin collection of the tax as applied to its activities. The District Court issued the injunction. The Second Circuit reversed. This Court, with three Justices in dissent, in turn reversed the Court of Appeals and held the tax unconstitutional as applied. . . .

In this case, of course, we are confronted with a situation like that presented in *Spector*. The tax is labeled a privilege tax "for the privilege of . . . doing business" in Mississippi, and the activity taxed is, or has been assumed to be, interstate commerce. We note again that no claim is made that the activity is not sufficiently connected to the State to justify a tax, or that the tax is not fairly related to benefits provided the taxpayer, or that the tax discriminates against interstate commerce, or that the tax is not fairly apportioned.

The view of the Commerce Clause that gave rise to the rule of *Spector* perhaps was not without some substance. Nonetheless, the possibility of defending it in the abstract does not alter the fact that the Court has rejected the proposition that interstate commerce is immune from state taxation:

"It is a truism that the mere act of carrying on business in interstate commerce does not exempt a corporation from state taxation. 'It was not the purpose of the commerce clause to relieve those engaged in interstate commerce from their just share of state tax burden even though it increases the cost of doing business.'" *Western Live Stock v. Bureau of Revenue* (1938).

Not only has the philosophy underlying the rule been rejected, but the rule itself has been stripped of any practical significance. If Mississippi had called its tax one on "net income" or on the "going concern value" of appellant's business, the *Spector* rule could not invalidate it. There is no economic consequence that follows necessarily from the use of the particular words, "privilege of doing business," and a focus on that formalism merely obscures the question whether the tax produces a forbidden effect. Simply put, the *Spector* rule does not address the problems with which the Commerce Clause is concerned. Accordingly, we now reject the rule of *Spector Motor Service, Inc. v. O'Connor*, that a state tax on the "privilege of doing business" is *per se* unconstitutional when it is applied to interstate commerce, and that case is overruled.

There being no objection to Mississippi's tax on appellant except that it was imposed on nothing other than the "privilege of doing business" that is interstate, the judgment of the Supreme Court of Mississippi is affirmed.

It is so ordered.

The *Complete Auto Transit* decision established four criteria that a state tax on interstate commerce must meet to be valid: (1) the targeted activity must be sufficiently connected to the state to justify a tax, (2) the tax must be fairly apportioned so that the levy is based on intrastate activity or income not subject to taxation by other states, (3) the tax must not discriminate against interstate commerce, and (4) the tax must be fairly related to the services provided by the state. These criteria assume that Congress has not preempted the state tax by imposing conflicting regulations on the interstate commerce activities involved.

In an unusual occurrence by today's standards, the entire Court supported Justice Blackmun's opinion in *Complete Auto Transit:* not a single justice wrote a concurring or dissenting view. Given this unanimity, it is not surprising that the Court has applied the precedent to subsequent disputes over the validity of state taxes on activities affecting interstate and foreign commerce. In *Wardair Canada v. Florida Department of Revenue* (1986) the justices ruled that a state tax on the sale of aviation fuel to an airline engaged in foreign commerce satisfied the four requirements. Similarly, in *Goldberg v. Sweet* (1989) the justices upheld an Illinois excise tax on interstate telephone calls, and in *Oklahoma Tax Commission v. Jefferson Lines* (1995) the Court concluded that a state tax on tickets for interstate bus travel did not violate the constitutional principles established in *Complete Auto Transit.*

Therefore, the four-pronged test established in 1977 constitutes the Court's current policy on state taxation of interstate activities. It appears to provide a workable compromise between the needs of the states to secure revenue and the Constitution's mandate that interstate commerce not be unreasonably burdened.

Complete Auto Transit v. Brady dealt with a state's attempt to tax the intrastate portion of a larger interstate enterprise. Because the company used its trucks to transport GM cars from the railroad station to dealers across the state, it was clear that the company had both an economic and a physical presence in Mississippi. But what if a company does business within a state and yet has no physical presence there—in other words, no offices, warehouses, stores, or employees?

A company might do business exclusively by interstate mail, the Internet, or telephone. May the state impose a tax on that economic activity? Or would this be an unconstitutional burden on interstate commerce?

Generally, the courts have allowed states to levy taxes on residents' purchases of goods out of state for use in the home state. These are called "use" taxes and are normally the equivalent of the state's sales tax. A man who lives in a state with a 7 percent sales tax might be tempted to buy a new automobile in a neighboring state that has no sales tax. By avoiding his home state sales tax, the purchaser could save $2,000 or more on the purchase. When he tries to register his new car in his home state, however, he may face a use tax of about 7 percent. Such taxes place in-state and out-of-state car dealers on equal footing.

Smaller items purchased online, by mail order, or by telephone may be subject to the same use tax. However, such purchases, unlike automobiles, do not require registration or licensing. This makes the collection of the use tax nearly impossible. To create a means of collecting such taxes, some states passed laws requiring out-of-state vendors to collect taxes on each sale and remit the proceeds to the purchaser's state. But are such laws constitutional? Does a state have any authority to require out-of-state companies to enforce the state's tax laws?

These questions were first answered in ***National Bellas Hess, Inc. v. Department of Revenue of Illinois*** (1967). Bellas Hess, a Missouri mail-order retailer, challenged an Illinois law that imposed a use tax on goods Illinois residents purchased from out-of-state sources. The law further required the out-of-state vendor to collect the tax and deposit it with the Illinois Revenue Department. Bellas Hess claimed that the law imposed an unconstitutional burden on interstate commerce and that Illinois violated due process guarantees because it had no authority to impose any law on a company that was located in a different state. The Supreme Court agreed with Bellas Hess. It struck down the law and announced an easily followed rule to govern such situations: a state cannot impose tax collection obligations on a company unless the business has a physical presence—offices, employees, warehouses, and the like—in the state. Because Bellas Hess did all of its business by mail and telephone and had no physical operations in Illinois, it was constitutionally exempt from the Illinois law.

For the next twenty-five years, the *National Bellas Hess* precedent was good law. But during this time, the mail-order business grew significantly, aided in part by the fact that individuals could often buy goods from out-of-state firms and evade paying any sales or use taxes on the purchases. Concerned about the revenue lost through out-of-state retail purchases, in 1992 the states asked the Court to reconsider its *National Bellas Hess* ruling in *Quill Corp. v. North Dakota.*

Quill Corp. v. North Dakota

504 U.S. 298 (1992)
http://laws.findlaw.com/us/504/298.html
Oral arguments are available at https://www.oyez.org.
Vote: 8 (Blackmun, Kennedy, O'Connor, Rehnquist, Scalia, Souter, Stevens,
     Thomas)
     1 (White)

OPINION FOR THE COURT: Stevens
OPINION CONCURRING IN PART: Scalia
OPINION CONCURRING IN PART AND DISSENTING IN PART: White

FACTS:

Quill Corporation was an office supply company with offices and warehouses in California, Georgia, and Illinois. None of its employees worked in North Dakota, and the company had no tangible property in that state. Quill sold its products nationwide via catalog, direct mail, and telephone. Its goods were delivered by mail or shipped by truck or rail. The company had annual sales of about $1 million to some three thousand North Dakota customers, making Quill the sixth-largest vendor of office supplies in the state. In 1987 North Dakota amended its tax code to impose a use tax on sales made by companies that regularly or systematically solicit customers in the state. The law, therefore, required mail-order operators such as Quill to collect and remit to the state taxes on all sales made to North Dakota residents. Quill refused to collect and pay such taxes, claiming, based on *National Bellas Hess,* that North Dakota had no authority over corporations that did not have a physical presence in the state.

North Dakota filed a legal action to compel Quill to comply with the law. The North Dakota Supreme Court upheld the law, concluding that the enormous growth in the mail-order industry and changes in the U.S. Supreme Court's interpretation of the law in, for example, *Complete Auto Transit v. Brady* made it inappropriate to follow the *Bellas Hess* precedent. The state court concluded that Quill had a sufficient economic presence in the state to justify the North Dakota tax. Quill appealed.

ARGUMENTS:

For the petitioner, Quill Corporation:

- The fundamental purpose of the commerce clause is to promote and protect interstate free trade. The North Dakota tax conflicts with that purpose.

- To require out-of-state vendors who do no more than communicate with customers by mail, telephone, or common carrier to collect sales/use taxes from customers in various states would subject those vendors to unfair burdens and obstruct interstate commerce.

- The Court has held that without a physical presence in the state the relationship between the out-of-state vendor and the state's taxing authority is insufficient to justify laws such as this North Dakota statute. *National Bellas Hess* provides a clear and workable rule that should be maintained.

- This is a question of national commercial significance, and Congress is the body most qualified to set a national policy. Congress so far has rejected legislative attempts to allow laws such as this one. The Court should not intervene.

For the respondent, state of North Dakota:

- In today's commercial environment, the physical presence requirement does not achieve a fair result as required by the due process clause and the commerce clause.

- *National Bellas Hess* should be overruled and the Court should follow the principles set in *Complete Auto Transit.* The North Dakota tax is consistent with the test established in *Complete Auto Transit.*

- Quill regularly and systematically solicits business in North Dakota. It has 3,427 active customers in the state, sends 230,000 pieces of mail into North Dakota each year, and has $935,000 in annual sales in the state. This establishes a sufficient relationship between Quill and the state's taxing authority.

- Quill's administrative costs for complying with the tax law are not relevant to the constitutional issues at stake.

- Because of the constitutional issues involved, the Court, not Congress, should answer the questions posed by this case.

JUSTICE STEVENS DELIVERED THE OPINION OF THE COURT.

As in a number of other cases involving the application of state taxing statutes to out-of-state sellers, our holding in [*National*] *Bellas Hess* [*v. Department of Revenue of Illinois*, 1967] relied on both the Due Process Clause and the Commerce Clause. Although the "two claims are closely related," the clauses pose distinct limits on the taxing powers of the States. Accordingly, while a State may, consistent with the Due Process Clause, have the authority to tax a particular taxpayer, imposition of the tax may nonetheless violate the Commerce Clause.

The two constitutional requirements differ fundamentally, in several ways. . . . [T]he Due Process Clause and the Commerce Clause reflect different constitutional concerns. Moreover, while Congress has plenary power to regulate commerce among the States and thus may authorize state actions that burden interstate commerce, it does not similarly have the power to authorize violations of the Due Process Clause.

Thus, although we have not always been precise in distinguishing between the two, the Due Process Clause and the Commerce Clause are analytically distinct. . . .

The Due Process Clause "requires some definite link, some minimum connection, between a state and the person, property or transaction it seeks to tax" and that the "income attributed to the State for tax purposes must be rationally related to 'values connected with the taxing State.'" . . .

Applying these principles, we have held that if [an out-of-state] corporation purposefully avails itself of the benefits of an economic market in the forum State, it may subject itself to the State's *in personam* jurisdiction even if it has no physical presence in the State. . . .

. . . Thus, to the extent that our decisions have indicated that the Due Process Clause requires physical presence in a State for the imposition of duty to collect a use tax, we overrule those holdings as superseded by developments in the law of due process.

In this case, there is no question that Quill has purposefully directed its activities at North Dakota residents, that the magnitude of those contacts [is] more than sufficient for due process purposes, and that the use tax is related to the benefits Quill receives from access to the State. We therefore agree with the North Dakota Supreme Court's conclusion that the Due Process Clause does not bar enforcement of that State's use tax against Quill.

Article I, §8, cl. 3 of the Constitution expressly authorizes Congress to "regulate Commerce with foreign Nations, and among the several States." It says nothing about the protection of interstate commerce in the absence of any action by Congress. Nevertheless, as Justice Johnson suggested in his concurring opinion in *Gibbons v. Ogden* (1824), the Commerce Clause is more than an affirmative grant of power; it has a negative sweep as well. The clause, in Justice Stone's phrasing, "by its own force" prohibits certain state actions that interfere with interstate commerce. *South Carolina State Highway Dept. v. Barnwell Bros., Inc.* (1938).

Our interpretation of the "negative" or "dormant" Commerce Clause has evolved substantially over the years, particularly as that clause concerns limitations on state taxation powers. . . .

While contemporary Commerce Clause jurisprudence might not dictate the same result were the issue to arise for the first time today, *Bellas Hess* is not inconsistent with *Complete Auto* and our recent cases. Under *Complete Auto*'s four-part test, we will sustain a tax against a Commerce Clause challenge so long as the "tax 1. is applied to an activity with a substantial nexus with the taxing State, 2. is fairly apportioned, 3. does not discriminate against interstate commerce, and 4. is fairly related to the services provided by the State." *Bellas Hess* concerns the first of these tests and stands for the proposition that a vendor whose only contacts with the taxing State are by mail or common carrier lacks the "substantial nexus" required by the Commerce Clause.

Thus, three weeks after *Complete Auto* was handed down, we cited *Bellas Hess* for this proposition and discussed the case at some length. In *National Geographic Society v. California Bd. of Equalization* (1977) we affirmed the continuing vitality of *Bellas Hess*' "sharp distinction . . . between mail-order sellers with [a physical presence in the taxing] State and those . . . who do no more than communicate with customers in the State by mail or common carrier as part of a general interstate business." We have continued to cite *Bellas Hess* with approval ever since. . . . For these reasons, we disagree with the State Supreme Court's conclusion that our decision in *Complete Auto* undercut the *Bellas Hess* rule.

The State of North Dakota relies less on *Complete Auto* and more on the evolution of our due process jurisprudence. The State contends that the nexus requirements imposed by the Due Process and Commerce Clauses are equivalent and that if, as we concluded above, a mail-order house that lacks a physical presence in the taxing State nonetheless satisfies the due process "minimum contacts" test, then that corporation also meets the Commerce Clause "substantial nexus" test. We disagree. Despite the similarity in phrasing, the nexus requirements of the Due Process and Commerce Clauses are not identical. The two standards are animated by different constitutional concerns and policies.

Due process centrally concerns the fundamental fairness of governmental activity. Thus, at the most general level, the due process nexus analysis requires that we ask whether an individual's connections with a State are substantial enough to legitimate the State's exercise of power over him. . . . In contrast, the Commerce Clause, and its nexus requirement, are informed not so much by concerns about fairness for the individual defendant as by structural concerns about the effects of state regulation on the national economy. Under the Articles of Confederation, State taxes and duties hindered and suppressed interstate commerce; the Framers intended the Commerce Clause as a cure for these structural ills. It is in this light that we have interpreted the negative implication of the Commerce Clause. Accordingly, we have ruled that that Clause prohibits discrimination against interstate commerce and bars state regulations that unduly burden interstate commerce.

The *Complete Auto* analysis reflects these concerns about the national economy. The second and third parts of that analysis, which require fair apportionment and non-discrimination, prohibit taxes that pass an unfair share of the tax burden onto interstate commerce. The first and fourth prongs, which require a substantial nexus and a relationship between the tax and State-provided services, limit the reach of State taxing authority so as to ensure that State taxation does not unduly burden interstate commerce. Thus, the "substantial-nexus" requirement is . . . a means for limiting state burdens on interstate commerce. Accordingly, contrary to the State's suggestion, a corporation may have the "minimum contacts" with a taxing State as required by the Due Process Clause, and yet lack the "substantial nexus" with that State as required by the Commerce Clause.

The State Supreme Court reviewed our recent Commerce Clause decisions and concluded that those rulings signaled a "retreat from the formalistic constrictions of a stringent physical presence test in favor of a more flexible substantive approach" and thus supported its decision not to apply *Bellas Hess.* Although we agree with the State Court's assessment of the evolution of our cases, we do not share its conclusion that this evolution indicates that the Commerce Clause ruling of *Bellas Hess* is no longer good law. . . .

Like other bright-line tests, the *Bellas Hess* rule appears artificial at its edges: whether or not a State may compel a vendor to collect a sales or use tax may turn on the presence in the taxing State of a small sales force, plant, or office. This artificiality, however, is more than offset by the benefits of a clear rule. Such a rule firmly establishes the boundaries of legitimate state authority to impose a duty to collect sales and use taxes and reduces litigation concerning those taxes. This benefit is important, for as we have so frequently noted, our law in this area is something of a "quagmire" and the "application of constitutional principles to specific state statutes leaves much room for controversy and confusion and little in the way of precise guides to the States in the exercise of their indispensable power of taxation."

Moreover, a bright-line rule in the area of sales and use taxes also encourages settled expectations and, in doing so, fosters investment by businesses and individuals. Indeed, it is not unlikely that the mail-order industry's dramatic growth over the last quarter-century is due in part to the bright-line exemption from state taxation created in *Bellas Hess.* . . .

In sum, although in our cases subsequent to *Bellas Hess* and concerning other types of taxes we have not adopted a similar bright-line, physical-presence requirement, our reasoning in those cases does not compel that we now reject the rule that *Bellas Hess* established in the area of sales and use taxes. To the contrary, the continuing value of a bright-line rule in this area and the doctrine and principles of *stare decisis* indicate that the *Bellas Hess* rule remains good law. . . .

This aspect of our decision is made easier by the fact that the underlying issue is not only one that Congress may be better qualified to resolve, but also one that Congress has the ultimate power to resolve. No matter how we evaluate the burdens that use taxes impose on interstate commerce, Congress remains free to disagree with our conclusions. Indeed, in recent years Congress has considered legislation that would "overrule" the *Bellas Hess* rule. Its decision not to take action in this direction may, of course, have been dictated by respect for our holding in *Bellas Hess* that the Due Process Clause prohibits States from imposing such taxes, but today we have put that problem to rest. Accordingly, Congress is now free to decide whether, when, and to what extent the States may burden interstate mail-order concerns with a duty to collect use taxes. . . .

The judgment of the Supreme Court of North Dakota is reversed and the case is remanded for further proceedings not inconsistent with this opinion.

It is so ordered.

The *Quill* decision backed away from the position that due process of law is violated when a state requires businesses with no physical presence in the state to collect and remit sales taxes. Yet the Court remained committed to the proposition that such laws violate the commerce clause. This precludes the states from tapping a very large potential revenue source. The growth of the Internet has further magnified the issue. The volume of commerce conducted electronically now far surpasses the mail-order operations at issue in *National Bellas Hess* and *Quill*. Most companies that engage in online sales operate nationally or internationally with physical presences in no more than a few states. As such, under current legal interpretations these retailers may conduct most of their transactions free from the obligation of collecting state sales taxes.

With its expansive powers over interstate commerce, Congress could grant states the authority to enact the kind of law struck down in *Quill*. Congress has, however, expressed little enthusiasm to change the physical presence rule announced in *National Bellas Hess* and *Quill*. The lack of action is consistent with the legislature's policy of protecting the Internet from taxation that might stunt its growth. In addition, supporters of the status quo argue that obliging online businesses to collect taxes consistent with the particular tax laws of all fifty states and remit the proceeds to those states would place a crushing administrative burden especially on small Internet retailers. The states respond by arguing that e-commerce is no longer a fledgling enterprise that deserves protection from taxation to allow it to grow; rather, the Internet is fully operational, and its future is secure. It is now appropriate, they say, for online businesses to participate in the collection of taxes in the same manner that brick-and-mortar businesses do. Some states have already reached voluntary agreements with large Internet retailers in which the companies have pledged to begin collecting such taxes at a specified future date in return for certain economic concessions from the states.

Over the last several years Congress has struggled to develop a uniform policy on the collection of Internet and mail order sales taxes. The proposed Marketplace Fairness Act of 2015 is the most recent attempt. It would allow states to compel out-of-state businesses to collect and remit taxes from in-state sales even if the business had no physical presence in the state. The bill would exempt from this obligation any business with annual gross sales of less that $1 million. Thus far, while several versions of this legislation have been offered, Congress has failed to pass any of them into law.

Taxing and Spending for the Protection of Intrastate Interests

Sometimes the goal of a state taxation policy is not just to raise revenue. States can create tax policies to protect intrastate businesses or to promote intrastate development. When such policies place a burden on interstate commerce and give an advantage to intrastate enterprises, constitutional challenges are common. Tax policies that discriminate against interstate commerce often suffer the same fate as the discriminatory commerce regulation discussed in chapter 7. The Court takes a dim view of state laws that place a financial obligation on interstate commerce that is not equally placed on intrastate business—no matter if those obligations take the form of taxes, fees, tariffs, duties, or similar assessments.

One example is *Oregon Waste Systems, Inc. v. Department of Environmental Quality of Oregon* (1994). In this case Oregon attempted to increase revenues and protect its environmental resources by imposing fees on solid waste generated in other states and transported to Oregon for disposal. The majority struck down the state's plan. The two dissenters, Rehnquist and Blackmun, maintained that the Court unnecessarily restricted the state's taxation power and, in doing so, made it difficult for Oregon to deal effectively with the growing problem of solid waste disposal. That these two justices would be found dissenting together against the rest of the Court was somewhat unusual. Rehnquist and Blackmun had very different ideological positions and regularly found themselves on opposite sides of controversial issues.

Oregon Waste Systems, Inc. v. Department of Environmental Quality of Oregon

511 U.S. 93 (1994)
http://laws.findlaw.com/us/511/93.html
Oral arguments are available at https://www.oyez.org.
Vote: 7 (Ginsburg, Kennedy, O'Connor, Scalia, Souter, Stevens, Thomas)
    2 (Blackmun, Rehnquist)

OPINION OF THE COURT: *Thomas*
DISSENTING OPINION: *Rehnquist*

FACTS:

Oregon's Department of Environmental Quality is in charge of administering the state's comprehensive policy for the management, reduction, and recycling of solid waste. To fund these activities the state levied various fees on landfill operators. In 1989 the state legislature decided to assess an additional surcharge for disposing of any solid waste generated out of state and authorized the department to set the surcharge rate based on the costs to the state of disposing of the materials. After studying the problem, the department set the surcharge on out-of-state waste at $2.25 per ton. The charge for the disposal of solid waste generated in state was $0.85 per ton.

Oregon Waste Systems was in the business of transporting solid waste from Washington State by barge to landfills in Oregon and as such was subject to the surcharge on solid waste brought into the state for disposal. The company challenged the tax, claiming that the assessment discriminated against interstate commerce in violation of the commerce clause. State courts upheld the Oregon law, concluding that the surcharge was not a discriminatory tax but a compensatory fee that was reasonably related to the cost of the services rendered. Oregon Waste Systems asked the U.S. Supreme Court to review that decision.

ARGUMENTS:

For the petitioners, Oregon Waste Systems et al.:

- In *Chemical Waste Management v. Hunt* (1992) the Court struck down as a violation of the commerce clause an Alabama law that taxed the disposal of interstate-generated waste, but not intrastate waste. The Oregon fee system is nearly indistinguishable from the Alabama tax.
- Oregon's discrimination against interstate commerce on its face clearly violates the commerce clause.
- Oregon cannot save its program by claiming that the fee is based on the cost of service. This does not justify discrimination against interstate waste.

For the respondent, Oregon Department of Environmental Quality:

- The state has established its fee system based on the actual cost of disposal. Intrastate and interstate disposal costs are essentially the same. The cost of disposing of in-state waste is subsidized through general state revenues, but the disposal of out-of-state waste is not subsidized. This fee structure allows the state to reduce the dumping fee charged for the disposal of in-state waste.
- The Constitution does not prohibit funding the disposal of in-state waste by a combination of general revenues and dumping fees. Restructuring the fee system by removing the subsidy and financing the full cost through dumping fees would have no impact on interstate commerce.

- The purpose of the state's policy is not economic isolation or protectionism. Nor is it based on the state's desire to reduce out-of-state waste as a means of preserving state natural resources.

JUSTICE THOMAS DELIVERED THE OPINION OF THE COURT.

Two Terms ago, in *Chemical Waste Management, Inc. v. Hunt* (1992), we held that the negative Commerce Clause prohibited Alabama from imposing a higher fee on the disposal in Alabama landfills of hazardous waste from other States than on the disposal of identical waste from Alabama. In reaching that conclusion, however, we left open the possibility that such a differential surcharge might be valid if based on the costs of disposing of waste from other States. Today, we must decide whether Oregon's purportedly cost-based surcharge on the in-state disposal of solid waste generated in other States violates the Commerce Clause. . . .

The Commerce Clause provides that "[t]he Congress shall have Power . . . [t]o regulate Commerce . . . among the several States." Though phrased as a grant of regulatory power to Congress, the Clause has long been understood to have a "negative" aspect that denies the States the power unjustifiably to discriminate against or burden the interstate flow of articles of commerce. The Framers granted Congress plenary authority over interstate commerce in "the conviction that in order to succeed, the new Union would have to avoid the tendencies toward economic Balkanization that had plagued relations among the Colonies and later among the States under the Articles of Confederation." *Hughes v. Oklahoma* (1979). "This principle that our economic unit is the Nation, which alone has the gamut of powers necessary to control of the economy, . . . has as its corollary that the states are not separable economic units." *H. P. Hood & Sons, Inc. v. Du Mond* (1949).

Consistent with these principles, we have held that the first step in analyzing any law subject to judicial scrutiny under the negative Commerce Clause is to determine whether it "regulates evenhandedly with only 'incidental' effects on interstate commerce, or discriminates against interstate commerce." *Hughes.* See also *Chemical Waste.* As we use the term here, "discrimination" simply means differential treatment of in-state and out-of-state economic interests that benefits the former and burdens the latter. If a restriction on commerce is discriminatory, it is virtually *per se* invalid. . . .

In *Chemical Waste*, we easily found Alabama's surcharge on hazardous waste from other States to be facially discriminatory because it imposed a higher fee on the disposal of out-of-state waste than on the disposal of identical in-state waste. We deem it equally obvious here that Oregon's $2.25 per ton surcharge is discriminatory on its face. The surcharge subjects waste from other States to a fee almost three times greater than the $0.85 per ton charge imposed on solid in-state waste. The statutory determinant for which fee applies to any particular shipment of solid waste to an Oregon landfill is whether or not the waste was "generated out-of-state." It is well-established, however, that a law is discriminatory if it "'tax[es] a transaction or incident more heavily when it crosses state lines than when it occurs entirely within the State.'" *Chemical Waste.*

Respondents argue, and the Oregon Supreme Court held, that the statutory nexus between the surcharge and "the [otherwise uncompensated] costs to the State of Oregon and its political subdivisions of disposing of solid waste generated out-of-state," necessarily precludes a finding that the surcharge is discriminatory. We find respondents' narrow focus on Oregon's compensatory aim to be foreclosed by our precedents. As we reiterated in *Chemical Waste,* the purpose of, or justification for, a law has no bearing on whether it is facially discriminatory. Consequently, even if the surcharge merely recoups the costs of disposing of out-of-state waste in Oregon, the fact remains that the differential charge favors shippers of Oregon waste over their counterparts handling waste generated in other States. In making that geographic distinction, the surcharge patently discriminates against interstate commerce.

Because the Oregon surcharge is discriminatory, the virtually *per se* rule of invalidity provides the proper legal standard here. . . . As a result, the surcharge must be invalidated unless respondents can "sho[w] that it advances a legitimate local purpose that cannot be adequately served by reasonable nondiscriminatory alternatives." *New Energy Co. of Indiana v. Limbach* (1988). Our cases require that justifications for discriminatory restrictions on commerce pass the "strictest scrutiny." *Hughes.* The State's burden of justification is so heavy that "facial discrimination by itself may be a fatal defect." *Ibid.*

At the outset, we note two justifications that respondents have *not* presented. No claim has been made that the disposal of waste from other States imposes higher costs on Oregon and its political subdivisions than the disposal of in-state waste. Also, respondents have not offered any safety or health reason unique to nonhazardous waste from other States for discouraging the flow of such waste into Oregon. Consequently, respondents must come forward with other legitimate reasons to subject waste from other States to a higher charge than is levied against waste from Oregon. . . .

Respondents' principal defense of the higher surcharge on out-of-state waste is that it is a "compensatory tax" necessary to make shippers of such waste pay their "fair share" of the costs imposed on Oregon by the disposal of their waste in the State. In *Chemical Waste* we noted the possibility that such an argument might justify a discriminatory surcharge or tax on out-of-state waste. In making that observation, we implicitly recognized the settled principle that interstate commerce may be made to "'pay its way.'" *Complete Auto Transit, Inc. v. Brady* (1977). See also *Maryland* [*v. Louisiana,* 1981]. . . .

To justify a charge on interstate commerce as a compensatory tax, a State must, as a threshold matter, "identif[y] . . . the [intrastate tax] burden for which the State is attempting to compensate." *Maryland.* Once that burden has been identified, the tax on interstate commerce must be shown roughly to approximate—but not exceed—the amount of the tax on intrastate commerce. Finally, the events on which the interstate and intrastate taxes are imposed must be "substantially equivalent"; that is, they must be sufficiently similar in substance to serve as mutually exclusive "prox[ies]" for each other. . . .

Although it is often no mean feat to determine whether a challenged tax is a compensatory tax, we have little difficulty concluding that the Oregon surcharge is not such a tax. Oregon does not impose a specific charge of at least $2.25 per ton on shippers of waste generated in Oregon, for which the out-of-state surcharge might be considered compensatory. In fact, the only analogous charge on the disposal of Oregon waste is $0.85 per ton, approximately one-third of the amount imposed on waste from other States. Respondents' failure to identify a specific charge on intrastate commerce equal to or exceeding the surcharge is fatal to their claim. . . .

Respondents' final argument is that Oregon has an interest in spreading the costs of the in-state disposal of Oregon waste to all Oregonians. That is, because all citizens of Oregon benefit from the proper in-state disposal of waste from Oregon, respondents claim it is only proper for Oregon to require them to bear more of the costs of disposing of such waste in the State through a higher general tax burden. At the same time, however, Oregon citizens should not be required to bear the costs of disposing of out-of-state waste, respondents claim. The necessary result of that limited cost-shifting is to require shippers of out-of-state waste to bear the full costs of in-state disposal, but to permit shippers of Oregon waste to bear less than the full cost.

We fail to perceive any distinction between respondents' contention and a claim that the State has an interest in reducing the costs of handling in-state waste. Our cases condemn as illegitimate, however, any governmental interest that is not "unrelated to economic protectionism," and regulating interstate commerce in such a way as to give those who handle domestic articles of commerce a cost advantage over their competitors handling similar items produced elsewhere constitutes such protectionism. To give controlling effect to respondents' characterization of Oregon's tax scheme as seemingly benign cost-spreading would require us to overlook the fact that the scheme necessarily incorporates a protectionist objective as well. . . .

Respondents counter that if Oregon is engaged in any form of protectionism, it is "resource protectionism," not economic protectionism. It is true that by discouraging the flow of out-of-state waste into Oregon landfills, the higher surcharge on waste from other States conserves more space in those landfills for waste generated in Oregon. Recharacterizing the surcharge as resource protectionism hardly advances respondents' cause, however. . . . As we held more than a century ago, "if the State, under the guise of exerting its police powers, should [impose a burden] . . . applicable solely to articles [of commerce] . . . produced or manufactured in other States, the courts would find no difficulty in holding such legislation to be in conflict with the Constitution of the United States." *Guy v. Baltimore* (1880). . . .

We recognize that the States have broad discretion to configure their systems of taxation as they deem appropriate. All we intimate here is that their discretion in this regard, as in all others, is bounded by any relevant limitations of the Federal Constitution, in this case the negative Commerce Clause. Because respondents have offered no legitimate reason to subject waste generated in other States to a discriminatory surcharge approximately three times as high as that imposed on waste generated in Oregon, the surcharge is facially invalid under the negative Commerce Clause. Accordingly, the judgment of the Oregon Supreme Court is reversed, and the cases are remanded for further proceedings not inconsistent with this opinion.

It is so ordered.

CHIEF JUSTICE REHNQUIST, with whom JUSTICE BLACKMUN joins, dissenting.
Landfill space evaporates as solid waste accumulates. State and local governments expend financial and political capital to develop trash control systems that are efficient, lawful, and protective of the environment. The State of Oregon responsibly attempted to address its solid waste disposal problem through enactment of a comprehensive regulatory scheme for the management, disposal, reduction, and recycling of solid waste. For this Oregon should be applauded. The regulatory scheme included a fee charged on out-of-state solid waste. The Oregon Legislature directed the Commission to determine the appropriate surcharge "based on the costs . . . of disposing of solid waste generated out-of-state." The Commission arrived at a surcharge of $2.25 per ton, compared to the $0.85 per ton charged on in-state solid waste. The surcharge works out to an increase of about $0.14 per week for the typical out-of-state solid waste producer. This seems a small price to pay for the right to deposit your "garbage, rubbish, refuse . . . ; sewage sludge, septic tank and cesspool pumpings or other sludge; . . . manure, . . . dead animals, [and] infectious waste" on your neighbors.

Nearly 20 years ago, we held that a State cannot ban all out-of-state waste disposal in protecting themselves from hazardous or noxious materials brought across the State's borders. *Philadelphia v. New Jersey* (1978). Two Terms ago in *Chemical Waste Management, Inc. v. Hunt* (1992), in striking down the State of Alabama's $72 per ton fee on the disposal of out-of-state hazardous waste, the Court left open the possibility that such a fee could be valid if based on the costs of disposing of waste from other States. Once again, however, as in *Philadelphia* and *Chemical Waste Management*, the Court further cranks the dormant Commerce Clause ratchet against the States by striking down such cost-based fees, and by so doing ties the hands of the States in addressing the vexing national problem of solid waste disposal. . . .

The State of Oregon is not prohibiting the export of solid waste from neighboring States; it is only asking that those neighbors pay their fair share for the use of Oregon landfill sites. I see nothing in the Commerce Clause that compels less densely populated States to serve as the low-cost dumping grounds for their neighbors, suffering the attendant risks that solid waste landfills present. The Court, deciding otherwise, further limits the dwindling options available to States as they contend with the environmental, health, safety, and political challenges posed by the problem of solid waste disposal in modern society.

For the foregoing reasons, I respectfully dissent.

Despite the Court's position that discriminatory taxation is unconstitutional, states continue to search for systems that might survive legal challenge. In *West Lynn Creamery v. Healy* (1994) the Court reviewed a Massachusetts law that required a "premium" to be paid on all sales of milk products. The assessment was imposed equally on both milk produced in Massachusetts and milk produced out of state. The state used the revenues generated to provide subsidies for Massachusetts farmers. Here the goal of the state was not to gather general revenues; rather, the goal was to promote the interests of Massachusetts dairy farmers.

The Court's majority, again with Rehnquist and Blackmun in dissent, struck down the Massachusetts plan as using the power to tax and spend in a manner that discriminated against interstate commerce. In effect, this was an old-fashioned protective tariff presented in a redesigned package. The purpose of the plan was to give in-state farmers a significant edge over out-of-state farmers. As such, the plan violated the Constitution's prohibition against state policies that advantage intrastate commerce and discriminate against interstate concerns.

Similarly, in *South Central Bell Telephone v. Alabama* (1999) the justices struck down an Alabama law that imposed a franchise tax on each corporation doing business in the state. The tax was based on the company's capital, but in-state businesses and out-of-state corporations were made to use different formulas to calculate this figure, which, as you might expect, led to higher taxes on out-of-state businesses.

Although the Court has developed relatively clear guidelines on federal and state taxing and spending powers, new disputes continue to demand resolution. It is not likely that this tendency will change in the near future. Policies that impose taxes and distribute funds are among the most politically and emotionally charged of all government programs. Not only do they give rise to questions of constitutional philosophy, but they also affect people's pocketbooks. It is not surprising, therefore, that when government uses its powers to tax and spend, legal challenges are common.

ANNOTATED READINGS

A number of good works focus on the history and development of tax law and policy. These include Gerald Carson, "The Income Tax and How It Grew," *American Heritage,* December 1973, 4–7, 79–88; Ann Mumford, *Taxing Culture: Toward a Theory of Tax Collection Law* (Burlington, VT: Ashgate, 2002); Sheldon D. Pollack, *War, Revenue, and State Building: Financing the Development of the American State* (Ithaca, NY: Cornell University Press, 2009); Steven R. Weisman, *The Great Tax Wars: Lincoln to Wilson—The Fierce Battles over Money and Power* (New York: Simon & Schuster, 2001); John F. Witte, *The Politics and Development of the Federal Income Tax* (Madison: University of Wisconsin Press, 1985); and Joseph F. Zimmerman, *The Silence of Congress: State Taxation of Interstate Commerce* (Albany: State University of New York Press, 2007).

Other studies focus on monetary and spending policy, such as Edward S. Corwin, "The Spending Power of Congress—Apropos the Maternity Act," *Harvard Law Review* 36 (1923): 548–582; Gerald T. Dunne, *Monetary Decisions of the Supreme Court* (New Brunswick, NJ: Rutgers University Press, 1960); Robert M. Howard, *Getting a Poor Return: Courts, Justice, and Taxes* (Albany: State University of New York Press, 2009); James Willard Hurst, *A Legal History of Money in the United States, 1774–1970* (Lincoln: University of Nebraska Press, 1973); and Dennis S. Ippolito, *Deficit, Debt, and the New Politics of Tax Policy* (New York: Cambridge University Press, 2012).

PART IV Economic Liberties

iStock/DanBrandenburg

Economic Liberties and Individual Rights

Economic Liberties and Individual Rights

I F ASKED what we Americans admire about the United States, many of us would answer that we value our guaranteed freedoms of speech, press, and religion. But when asked to make political decisions, such as choosing elected officials, we may put other considerations ahead of these cherished freedoms. As is often remarked, people tend to vote their pocketbooks. Americans might not admit that the state of the economy drives their behavior, but it is clearly one of the most important determinants in choosing the nation's leaders. That we hold economic well-being as a high priority is not surprising. In Part III we saw that economic issues—commerce, taxing, and spending—have been major sources of friction between the federal government and the states from the very beginning of U.S. history.

Economic questions, however, do not always present themselves as disputes between the national government and the states. Quite the contrary. The Supreme Court often has heard constitutional challenges in which individuals claim that their personal economic liberties have been violated by government actions. In such cases the justices must determine how much authority federal and state governments have to seize private property, to alter freely made contracts, and to restrict private employment agreements as to wages and hours. Seen in this way, a strong relationship exists between civil liberties, such as the freedom of speech, and economic liberties, such as the right to private property. Indeed, both provoke the same fundamental question: To what extent may government enact legislation that infringes on personal rights? Both also involve the same perennial conflict between the interests of the individual and those of the society.

Even so, most people, including elected officials and even Supreme Court justices, tend to separate economic liberties from other civil liberties. We consider the right to express our views as significantly different from the right to conduct business. The framers, however, viewed both as "vested rights"—rights so fundamental to an individual that they cannot be infringed on by government control; these rights were very much on the minds of the men who gathered to write the Constitution in 1787. According to James Madison, one of the framers' most important objectives as they gathered in Philadelphia in 1787 was to provide "more effectively for the security of private rights and the steady dispensement of justice within the states. Interference with these were the evils which had, more perhaps than anything else, produced this convention."

But, as Madison's comment implies, the framers' conception of liberties and what interfered with their exercise was somewhat different from ours. They equated liberty with the protection of private property, and in their experience the states, not the national government, posed the greater threat to property rights. Given the economic chaos that existed under the Articles of Confederation, we can easily understand the founders' concerns. They believed that the states had "crippled" both the central government and the economy, and they wanted to create a national government strong enough to protect economic liberty from aggressive state governments. We must also keep in mind that many who attended the convention were wealthy men who wanted to keep the property they had accumulated. In short, the framers were concerned about the nonpropertied masses taking control of state legislatures and using their numerical advantage to promote legislation that would place excessive taxes on business, abrogate contracts, and so forth. Indeed, in an important (albeit controversial) work, *An Economic Interpretation of the Constitution of the United States,* first published in 1913, historian Charles A. Beard depicted the founders as self-serving—even greedy—men who viewed the Constitution as a vehicle for the protection of their own property interests.

Other analysts have taken issue with Beard's interpretation. Some contend that we cannot necessarily equate modern definitions of property with those the framers used; that is, the property interests they sought to protect were probably more encompassing than those we envision today. We might consider property as something tangible or of clear monetary value, but to at least some of the framers, *property* was a catchall term for many individual liberties that may or may not have been related to what modern Americans think of as economic activity.

To protect these paramount property rights, however conceptualized, the framers inserted several provisions into the Constitution. An important provision, which we examine in chapter 9, is the contract clause. Under Article I, Section 10, "No State shall . . . pass any . . . Law impairing the Obligation of Contracts." To understand the meaning of the clause, we must consider its language within the context of the day. As one book on constitutional interpretation suggests,

For the generation of 1787–91, property was probably a natural right, though the constitutional text did not so label it. And, because the right to property included rights to use and increase property, that basic right included a cognate right to contract with other property holders. Thus did the right to contract borrow a measure of moral status from the broader right in which it originated: the obligation to keep one's contracts was a duty flowing from the natural right to property.[1]

---

1. Walter F. Murphy, James E. Fleming, and William Harris II, *American Constitutional Interpretation,* 2nd ed. (Mineola, NY: Foundation Press, 1995), 1073.

If the contract clause was one of the ways the framers sought to protect property interests against the "evils" of government interference, it worked, at least initially. For the Marshall Court, the contract clause was an effective vehicle for promoting federal supremacy and economic growth. That Court read Article I, Section 10, to prohibit state action that infringed on property rights and impeded economic development.

But this interpretation did not endure. With the end of the Marshall Court and the ascendancy of the Taney Court in the mid-1830s, use of the contract clause as a vehicle to protect property interests waned. We consider fully why that occurred in chapter 9; for now, it is important to note that the "death" of the contract clause did not mean that courts were no longer interested in protecting economic liberties. They simply turned to another section of the Constitution to do so. The Fourteenth Amendment's due process clause says that no state shall "deprive any person of life, liberty, or property, without due process of law." Under a doctrine called substantive due process, which we review in chapter 10, between the 1890s and 1930s the Supreme Court used the Fourteenth Amendment to prohibit states from interfering with "liberty" interests. For example, the Court struck down legislation mandating maximum work hours on the ground that such legislation interfered with the rights of employers to enter into contracts with their employees. Like the Court's interpretation of the contract clause, this treatment of the Fourteenth Amendment eventually fell into disuse. In chapter 10 we examine the reasons for its decline.

More recently, the Court has taken a serious look at yet another provision of the Constitution designed to protect property interests—the takings clause of the Fifth Amendment. Here the framers endeavored to protect private property from government seizure by inserting the following words into the Constitution: "nor shall private property be taken for public use, without just compensation." The founders recognized that the government occasionally would need the power to confiscate property in order to construct roads or erect government buildings, but they limited such seizures to projects having a public purpose, and required that the affected property owners be compensated for their losses. As described in chapter 11, the Court's interpretation of the takings clause, like its treatment of the contract and due process clauses, has undergone a number of twists and turns. The heyday of the contract clause and economic substantive due process has long since passed, but the takings clause remains a vibrant legal and political issue. Some members of the Roberts Court view the takings clause as a significant vehicle for protecting property rights.

So far these justices have had only limited success—a matter we consider in more detail in chapter 11. Here, we simply note that the current Court seems to be taking a greater interest in all kinds of economic issues than did its immediate predecessors. In recent years about one-fifth of the Court's docket has involved economic issues of various kinds. This figure pales in comparison to the numbers of the 1930s, a period during which the majority of the cases the Court accepted for review had economic dimensions, or even the 1800s, when fully one-third of the business of the Court involved economic issues. Nevertheless, the proportion of the current Court's docket devoted to economic questions is substantial and at odds with the popular notion that the contemporary Court is almost exclusively focused on the resolution of civil liberties and criminal justice disputes.

The number of economic cases on the Court's agenda is important as an indicator of the role the Court plays in American society.[2] When the justices were deciding large numbers of economic cases, as they did for the first 150 years of the Court's history, it is not surprising that they exerted great influence in that area and lesser influence in the areas of civil liberties, rights,

and criminal justice. Moreover, if today's Court is seeking to play a greater role in the economic realm, it will be forced to confront the same fundamental issue that bedeviled its predecessors: the complex relationship between "vested rights" and "community interests." Although—as we have suggested—many of the founders were concerned about individual liberty (such as the protection of private property rights), we now know that in a mature democratic society the pursuit of such individual interests may impinge on the collective good. When a state enacts a law setting a minimum wage, that statute affects the individual liberty of employers: it would be in their best interest, economically speaking, to pay their employees as little as possible. As a result, they may argue that minimum wage laws violate their constitutional guarantees. But is there another interest at stake? What are the results of paying workers a substandard wage? Does the state have a responsibility to enact legislation for the "health, safety, and welfare" of all its citizens?

It is the clash between these two interests—individual liberty (vested rights) and the state (community interests)—that has been a primary cause of the Court's involvement in this area. Because that conflict is unlikely to change, our discussion of these issues will center on the approaches different Courts have taken to balance them. As we shall see, during some periods the Court has exalted liberty interests above those of the community, and at other times it has taken precisely the opposite approach. As you read the chapters that follow, think about the political, legal, and historical factors that have contributed to these varying approaches to economic liberties.

---

2. See Richard Pacelle Jr., *The Transformation of the Supreme Court's Agenda* (Boulder, CO: Westview Press, 1991); and Pacelle, "The Dynamics and Determinants of Agenda Change in the Rehnquist Court," in *Contemplating Courts*, ed. Lee Epstein (Washington, DC: CQ Press, 1995).

9

The Contract Clause

SUPPOSE that some years ago a friend of yours accepted a position with a large corporation. One of the reasons she took this particular job was that the company offered an attractive retirement savings plan as a fringe benefit. Under the terms of the savings plan contract, she regularly placed a portion of her salary into the fund, and the company matched her contributions. Money deposited in the fund belonged to the individual savers, and the company had no authority to use the funds for any corporate purpose. Over the years, your friend's savings account grew steadily. Then, in a national recession, the company's fortunes reversed, and it, along with many others, faced bankruptcy. The state rushed to relieve the troubled businesses by passing a law that allowed them unilaterally to use the assets in employee savings plans to finance operations until the economy regained its strength. The company took advantage of this statute, but after it spent all of the savings plan funds, the company still went bankrupt.

This story raises some basic questions: How can the state pass a law that releases a company from its contractual obligations? The company's employees were cheated out of their money, and the state was involved. Why would one participate in any investment or commercial activity without some assurance that a state will not intervene and change the provisions of contractual agreements or nullify them altogether?

If you were upset upon learning of the fate of your friend's retirement funds, your reaction would be understandable. One of the hallmarks of a society that values commercial activity is the right to enter into legally binding contracts. It is hard to imagine a market-based economy that does not recognize and protect such agreements. In most instances, we expect the government to enforce contracts and not encourage parties who wish to break them.

The individuals who drafted the Constitution felt much the same way. Disturbed by the actions of state governments in the economic upheaval that followed the Revolution, the delegates to the Constitutional Convention moved to block state interference with contractual obligations. They did this by drafting the contract clause, one of the most important provisions of the Constitution during the nation's formative years.

THE FRAMERS AND THE CONTRACT CLAUSE

It might be difficult to find a group of people more supportive of the right to enter into binding agreements than the delegates to the Constitutional Convention. For the most part, these individuals represented the propertied classes, and they assembled in Philadelphia at a time of economic turmoil. Many of them feared that as the states coped with their economic problems they might suspend the obligation to honor contracts.

Following the Revolutionary War the economy was very unstable, and the government under the Articles of Confederation was powerless to correct the situation. Hardest hit were small farmers, many of whom had taken out large loans they could not repay. When creditors started foreclosing on real estate and debtors were jailed for failing to pay, farmers and others faced with unmanageable obligations began to agitate for relief. Several states responded by passing laws to help them. Among these acts were bankruptcy laws that erased certain debt obligations or extended the time to pay—legal obstacles that blocked creditors from asserting their contractual rights against their debtors. In addition, state currencies of dubious value were declared legal tender to satisfy debt obligations.

These policies hurt the creditors, many of whom were wealthy landowners. In response, they called for strengthening the national government to deal with economic problems and for a ban on the state governments' practice of nullifying contractual obligations. This issue was among the more important factors prompting Congress to convene a convention for the purpose of recommending changes in the Articles of Confederation. Once assembled, the delegates, as we know, went much farther than originally authorized and created the Constitution of the United States.

The document drafted in Philadelphia clearly reflected the economic interests of the delegates. Among the provisions they wrote was a protection of contracts against state government infringement. Article I, Section 10, declares: "No State shall . . . pass any . . . Law impairing the Obligation of Contracts."

The eighteenth century's understanding of the term *contract* was much the same as today's. A contract is an agreement voluntarily entered into by two or more parties in which a promise is made and something of value is given or pledged. Contractual agreements are made in almost every commercial transaction, such as a mining company's promise to deliver a quantity of coal to a steel mill for a particular sum of money or a lawyer's promise to represent a client at a specified rate of compensation.

For the framers the right to enter into contracts was an important freedom closely tied to the right of private property. The ownership of private property implies the right to buy, sell, divide, occupy, lease, and use it, but one cannot effectively exercise these various property rights without the ability to enter into legally binding arrangements with others. In commercial transactions the parties rely on each other to carry out the contractual provisions. During the nation's

formative years, those who failed to live up to contractual promises were dealt with harshly. In the minds of the propertied classes of the eighteenth century, this was how it should be, and the government should not be allowed to intervene in such private arrangements.

Evidence from the convention indicates that the framers adopted the contract clause as a means of protecting agreements between private parties from state interference. At that time, however, contracts also were a means of carrying out public policy. Because governments then were much more limited than they are today, the states regularly entered into contracts with individuals or corporations to carry out government policy or to distribute government benefits. These state actions included land grants, commercial monopolies, and licenses to construct roads and bridges. An individual who entered into a contractual agreement with the state expected it to live up to its obligations and not abrogate the arrangement or unilaterally change the terms. In spite of what the framers might have intended, the contract clause is generally worded and therefore offers protection both to contracts among private parties and to agreements between private parties and the government.

Importantly, the framers drafted the contract clause to apply only to the states and not to the national government. They had two reasons for targeting the states in this way. First, the framers had recent experience with states passing laws that nullified contractual provisions, thus they saw the states as a threat to the importance of contractual relationships. Second, the framers envisioned the state governments to be the primary regulators of economic activities.

The contract clause was not a major point of controversy at the convention; rather, the records show that the delegates accepted its wisdom with little debate. The clause was one of several prohibitions the framers imposed on state economic regulation: states also could no longer coin money, issue bills of credit, create tender for payment of debts, or tax and regulate certain forms of interstate or foreign commerce.

The contract clause was not a point of significant controversy during the debates over ratification of the Constitution. In *Federalist* No. 7, Alexander Hamilton justified the prohibition against state impairment of contract obligations by claiming, "Laws in violation of private contracts . . . may be considered as another probable source of hostility." And James Madison in *Federalist* No. 44 declared that "laws impairing the obligation of contracts are contrary to the first principles of the social compact and to every principle of sound legislation."

In spite of this lack of attention at the drafting and ratification stages, the contract clause became an important legal force in the early years of the nation's development. As political majorities changed from election to election, it was not unusual for state legislatures to enter into contracts with private parties and then to break or change those agreements in subsequent legislative sessions. In addition, state governments often would adopt policies that ran contrary to contracts among private individuals. When such actions occurred, injured parties would challenge the states in court. Because the states were not obliged to follow principles of due process of law until after ratification of the Fourteenth Amendment in 1868, the contract clause was the primary constitutional ground on which state policies could be challenged. As a result, it was one of the most litigated constitutional provisions in the first decades of U.S. history. One study concluded that roughly 40 percent of all Supreme Court cases prior to 1889 that attacked the validity of state legislation did so on the basis of contract clause arguments.[1]

JOHN MARSHALL AND THE CONTRACT CLAUSE

The importance of the contract clause increased dramatically through the Marshall Court's interpretations of its meaning. Chief Justice John Marshall had strong views on private property, economic development, and the role of the federal government. He consistently supported aggressive policies that would result in vigorous economic expansion. Underlying this position was a philosophy that elevated private property to the level of a natural right that government had little authority to limit. Furthermore, Marshall firmly believed that the nation's interests could be served best if the federal government, rather than the states, became the primary agent for economic policy making. As we have seen in the areas of federalism and commerce, Marshall could be counted on to uphold actions taken by the federal government and to favor

---

1. Benjamin F. Wright, *The Contract Clause of the Constitution* (Cambridge, MA: Harvard University Press, 1938).

it over competing state interests. Marshall's ideology predisposed him to champion the contract clause, which he viewed as essential to the right to private property. Moreover, the clause's restriction of the regulatory powers of the states appealed to his views on federalism. Given Marshall's domination of the Court for more than three decades, it is not surprising that the contract clause achieved an elevated status during those years.

Establishing the Importance of the Contract Clause

The first major Supreme Court decision to consider the contract clause was *Fletcher v. Peck* (1810), which asked whether a state could nullify a public contract. The suit flowed from one of the most notorious incidents of corruption and bribery in the nation's early history—the Yazoo River land fraud. In this litigation the beneficiaries of the scheme sought to use the contract clause to protect their gains.

Chief Justice Marshall was caught in a bind. To give force to the contract clause would be to rule in favor of those who profited from state government corruption. To rule against the unpopular fraudulent transactions would be to hand down a precedent significantly curtailing the meaning of the provision. Which option did Marshall choose?

Fletcher v. Peck

10 U.S. (6 Cr.) 87 (1810)
http://laws.findlaw.com/us/10/87.html
Vote: 5 (Johnson, Livingston, Marshall, Todd, Washington)
    0

OPINION OF THE COURT: *Marshall*
CONCURRING OPINION: *Johnson*
NOT PARTICIPATING: *Chase, Cushing*

FACTS:

This dispute had its roots in the 1795 session of the Georgia legislature. Clearly motivated by wholesale bribery, the legislators sold about 35 million acres of public lands to several land companies at ridiculously low prices. The territory in question, known as the "Yazoo lands" after one of the major rivers that passes through it, encompassed most of what is now Mississippi and Alabama. Some of the nation's most prominent public figures, including some members of Congress, supported this transaction or invested in it. The citizens of Georgia were outraged by the sale and turned out most of the legislators in the next election.

In 1796 the newly elected legislature promptly rescinded the sales contract and moved to repossess the land. Unfortunately, by this time the land companies had sold numerous parcels to third-party investors and settlers. A massive and complicated set of legal actions ensued to determine ownership of the disputed lands. Attempts to negotiate a settlement proved unsuccessful. Even the president, Thomas Jefferson, was drawn into the controversy as he tried to work out a compromise settlement that would satisfy the state of Georgia as well as the investors.

Fletcher v. Peck was a lawsuit filed to obtain a judicial determination of the ownership question. John Peck bought 600,000 acres of Yazoo land from James Gunn, one of the original buyers. Peck in turn sold 15,000 acres to land speculator Robert Fletcher. The sale was part of a carefully designed strategy between Peck and Fletcher to test the constitutionality of the Georgia repeal statute. Both ultimately would profit if the sales agreements were upheld. After the sale was completed, Fletcher sued Peck for return of the purchase price, claiming that Peck had sold Fletcher a parcel of land for which he did not hold valid title. The real issue, however, rested squarely on the meaning of the contract clause: May a state that has entered into a valid contract later rescind that contract?

John Quincy Adams (who would become the sixth president of the United States), Joseph Story (who would become the youngest person ever appointed to the Supreme Court), and Robert Goodloe Harper (who was a former South Carolina congressman) represented Peck and the interests of the others who had purchased the land. They argued that Peck held valid title to the property because Georgia constitutionally could not abrogate the original sales contracts. Fletcher's case was handled by Luther Martin, who had been a delegate to the Constitutional Convention but later opposed ratification. According to historical accounts, Martin would often show up in court drunk. His rather ineffective performance, some argue, is further evidence that both sides wanted Peck's position to prevail.

ARGUMENTS:

For the plaintiff in error, Robert Fletcher:
- The state of Georgia had no right to sell the lands in the first place. The western lands had been uncoupled from the colonies. They belonged not to the states but to the United States or to the Indians.
- Fraud and bribery influenced passage of the 1795 law that authorized the land sale, and therefore the sale is nullified.
- The state legislature properly rescinded the sale in 1796 and reclaimed ownership of the land, invalidating any subsequent sales.

For the defendant in error, John Peck:
- The state of Georgia was empowered to sell the land in question.
- Even if passage of the law authorizing the sale of the lands was influenced by bribery and the grossest corruption, the law is still valid and cannot be disregarded by the judiciary.
- The state of Georgia is forbidden by the U.S. Constitution to pass any law impairing the obligation of contracts. A grant is a contract that once executed cannot be revoked.
- The parties now before the Court are innocent of fraud. They were bona fide purchasers of the land. They cannot be affected by any fraud that might have been committed by others.

> ### ◆ MARSHALL, CH. J., DELIVERED THE OPINION OF THE COURT AS FOLLOWS:

The importance and the difficulty of the questions, presented by these pleadings, are deeply felt by the court.

The lands in controversy vested absolutely in James Gunn and others, the original grantees, by the conveyance of the governor, made in pursuance of an act of assembly to which the legislature was fully competent. Being thus in full possession of the legal estate, they, for a valuable consideration, conveyed portions of the land to those who were willing to purchase. If the original transaction was infected with fraud, these purchasers did not participate in it, and had no notice of it. They were innocent. Yet the legislature of Georgia has involved them in the fate of the first parties to the transaction, and, if the act be valid, has annihilated their rights also. . . .

If a suit be brought to set aside a conveyance obtained by fraud, and the fraud be clearly proved, the conveyance will be set aside, as between the parties; but the rights of third persons, who are purchasers without notice, for a valuable consideration, cannot be disregarded. Titles, which according to every legal test, are perfect, are acquired with that confidence which is inspired by the opinion that the purchaser is safe. If there be any concealed defect, arising from the conduct of those who had held the property long before he acquired it, of which he had no notice, that concealed defect cannot be set up against him. He has paid the money for a title good at law, he is innocent, whatever may be the guilt of others, and equity will not subject him to the penalties attached to that guilt. All titles would be insecure, and the intercourse between man and man would be very seriously obstructed if this principle be overturned. . . .

If the legislature felt itself absolved from those rules of property which are common to all the citizens of the United States, and from those principles of equity which are acknowledged in all our courts, its act is to be supported by its power alone, and the same power may devest any other individual of his lands, if it shall be the will of the legislature so to exert it. . . .

Is the power of the legislature competent to the annihilation of such title, and to a resumption of the property thus held?

The principle asserted is, that one legislature is competent to repeal any act which a former legislature was competent to pass; and that one legislature cannot abridge the powers of a succeeding legislature.

The correctness of this principle, so far as respects general legislation, can never be controverted. But, if an act be done under a law, a succeeding legislature cannot undo it. The past cannot be recalled by the most absolute power. Conveyances have been made, those conveyances have vested legal estates, and, if those estates may be seized by the sovereign authority, still, that they originally vested is a fact, and cannot cease to be a fact.

When, then, a law is in its nature a contract, when absolute rights have vested under that contract, a repeal of the law cannot devest those rights; and the act of annulling them, if legitimate, is rendered so by a power applicable to the case of every individual in the community.

It may well be doubted whether the nature of society and of government does not prescribe some limits to the legislative power; and, if any be prescribed, where are they to be found, if the property of an individual, fairly and honestly acquired, may be seized without compensation.

To the legislature all legislative power is granted; but the question, whether the act of transferring the property of an individual to the public, be in the nature of the legislative power, is well worthy of serious reflection.

It is the peculiar province of the legislature to prescribe general rules for the government of society; the application of those rules to individuals in society would seem to be the duty of other departments. How far the power of giving the law may involve every other power, in cases where the constitution is silent, never has been, and perhaps never can be, definitely stated.

The validity of this rescinding act, then, might well be doubted, were Georgia a single sovereign power. But Georgia cannot be viewed as a single, unconnected, sovereign power, on whose legislature no other restrictions are imposed than may be found in its own constitution. She is a part of a large empire; she is a member of the American union; and that union has a constitution the supremacy of which all acknowledge, and which imposes limits to the legislature of the several states, which none claim a right to pass. The constitution of the United States declares that no state shall pass any bill of attainder, *ex post facto* law, or law impairing the obligation of contracts.

Does the case now under consideration come within this prohibitory section of the constitution?

In considering this very interesting question, we immediately ask ourselves what is a contract? Is a grant a contract?

A contract is a compact between two or more parties, and is either executory or executed. An executory contract is one in which a party binds himself to do, or not to do, a particular thing; such was the law under which the conveyance was made by the governor. A contract executed is one in which the object of contract is performed; and this, says Blackstone, differs in nothing from a grant. The contract between Georgia and the purchasers was executed by the grant. A contract executed, as well as one which is executory, contains obligations binding on the parties. A grant, in its own nature, amounts to an extinguishment of the right of the grantor, and implies a contract not to reassert that right. A party is, therefore, always estopped by his own grant.

Since, then, in fact, a grant is a contract executed, the obligation of which still continues, and since the constitution uses the general term contract, without distinguishing between those which are executory and those which are executed, it must be construed to comprehend the latter as well as the former. A law annulling conveyances between individuals, and declaring that the grantors should stand seised of their former estates, notwithstanding those grants, would be as repugnant to the constitution as a law discharging the vendors of property from the obligation of executing their contracts by conveyances. It would be strange if a contract to convey was secured by the constitution, while an absolute conveyance remained unprotected.

If, under a fair construction [of] the constitution, grants are comprehended under the term contracts, is a grant from the state excluded from the operation of the provision? Is the clause to be considered as inhibiting the state from impairing the obligation of contracts between two individuals, but as excluding from that inhibition contracts made with itself?

The words themselves contain no such distinction. They are general, and are applicable to contracts of every description. If contracts made with the state are to be exempted from their operation, the exception must arise from the character of the contracting party, not from the words which are employed.

Whatever respect might have been felt for the state sovereignties, it is not to be disguised that the framers of the constitution viewed, with some apprehension, the violent acts which might grow out of the feelings of the moment; and that the people of the United States, in adopting that instrument, have manifested a determination to shield themselves and their property from the effects of those sudden and strong passions to which men are exposed. The restrictions on the legislative power of the states are obviously founded in this sentiment; and the constitution of the United States contains what may be deemed a bill of rights for the people of each state.

No state shall pass any bill of attainder, *ex post facto* law, or law impairing the obligation of contracts.

A bill of attainder may affect the life of an individual, or may confiscate his property, or may do both.

In this form the power of the legislature over the lives and fortunes of individuals is expressly restrained. What motive, then, for implying, in words which import a general prohibition to impair the obligation of contracts, an exception in favour of the right to impair the obligation of those contracts into which the state may enter?

The state legislatures can pass no *ex post facto* law. An *ex post facto* law is one which renders an act punishable in a manner in which it was not punishable when it was committed. Such a law may inflict penalties on the person, or may inflict pecuniary penalties which swell the public treasury. The legislature is then prohibited from passing a law by which a man's estate, or any part of it, shall be seized for a crime which was not declared, by some previous law, to render him liable to that punishment. Why, then, should violence be done to the natural meaning of words for the purpose of leaving to the legislature the power of seizing, for public use, the estate of an individual in the form of a law annulling the title by which he holds that estate? The court can perceive no sufficient grounds for making this distinction. This rescinding act would have the effect of an *ex post facto* law. It forfeits the estate of Fletcher for a

crime not committed by himself, but by those from whom he purchased. This cannot be effected in the form of an *ex post facto* law, or bill of attainder; why, then, is it allowable in the form of a law annulling the original grant?

The argument in favour of presuming an intention to except a case, not excepted by the words of the constitution, is susceptible of some illustration from a principle originally ingrafted in that instrument, though no longer a part of it. The constitution, as passed, gave the courts of the United States jurisdiction in suits brought against individual states. A state, then, which violated its own contract was suable in the courts of the United States for that violation. Would it have been a defence in such a suit to say that the state had passed a law absolving itself from the contract? It is scarcely to be conceived that such a defence could be set up. And yet, if a state is neither restrained by the general principles of our political institutions, nor by the words of the constitution, from impairing the obligation of its own contracts, such a defence would be a valid one. This feature is no longer found in the constitution; but it aids in the construction of those clauses with which it was originally associated.

It is, then, the unanimous opinion of the court, that, in this case, the estate having passed into the hands of a purchaser for a valuable consideration, without notice, the state of Georgia was restrained, either by general principles which are common to our free institutions, or by the particular provisions of the constitution of the United States, from passing a law whereby the estate of the plaintiff in the premises so purchased could be constitutionally and legally impaired and rendered null and void.

Although *Fletcher v. Peck* did not fully settle the Yazoo lands controversy *(see box 9-1),* Marshall's opinion breathed considerable life into the contract clause. While acknowledging that the original transactions were based on bribery and corruption, Marshall concluded that such matters are beyond the power of the courts to control. He concentrated instead on whether a state could lawfully rescind a previously passed, binding agreement. According to the Court's holding in this case, the Constitution prohibits the states from impairing the obligation of any contract, even those contrary to the public good. Striking down the 1796 Georgia statute was one of the earliest instances of the Supreme Court nullifying a state law on constitutional grounds. *Fletcher v. Peck* established the contract clause

BOX 9-1   AFTERMATH . . . THE YAZOO LANDS CONTROVERSY

THE SUPREME COURT's decision in *Fletcher v. Peck* (1810) provided a landmark ruling on the meaning of the contract clause, but it did not fully resolve the issues surrounding the Yazoo land claims. In the period between the original land sale by the Georgia legislature in 1795 and the state's voiding of the sale in 1796, parcels were bought and sold in a climate of feverish land speculation. About 60 percent of the purchasers were New England residents eager to participate in western land investments. After Georgia repealed the original sale, titles to the Yazoo lands were in considerable doubt. Not only did the actions by the Georgia legislature thoroughly confuse the issue, but also claims by Indian tribes, old Spanish interests, squatters, and those who had been granted lands by Georgia governors over the years clouded the issue. Bogus titles and sales of nonexistent land complicated matters even further.

When purchasers learned that Georgia had passed legislation canceling the original sale, they pressured Congress to provide compensation if their titles proved to be invalid. Northern representatives favored a compensation program to provide relief to constituents who had purchased property, but southerners, especially representatives from Georgia, opposed any compensation as rewarding those who sought to benefit from the original acts of bribery and fraud. *Fletcher v. Peck* was first filed in federal circuit court in Massachusetts in 1803 in an attempt to have the judiciary settle the matter. Action on the lawsuit and subsequent appeals was delayed, with the parties hoping that Congress would pass a compensation act. When legislation failed in 1804, 1805, and 1806, it appeared that the courts would have to answer the lingering questions. By the time the Supreme Court decided *Fletcher v. Peck*, fifteen years had elapsed since the original sales, and determining valid title to each parcel of land was impossible.

The decision in *Fletcher v. Peck* was unpopular in many circles. Some thought the Court should not uphold contracts based on wholesale corruption. Thomas Jefferson used the decision as an opportunity to renew his attacks on Marshall. He claimed the chief justice's opinion was filled with "twistifications," "cunning," and "sophistry." According to Jefferson, it illustrated once again "how dexterously [Marshall] can reconcile law to his personal biases."

The decision, however, put pressure on Congress to bring closure to the controversy. Northerners again demanded a compensation program, but southerners still resisted. In 1814 Congress appropriated $5 million from federal land sales to compensate those who held title to the Yazoo lands. Investors released their land claims in return for monetary compensation. It took four years for the claims to be settled. Northern representatives had obtained relief for their constituents, but southern interests also benefited. Resolving the confusion over the Yazoo lands cleared the way for organizing the Mississippi Territory, which was admitted as a slaveholding state in 1817.

SOURCE: C. Peter Magrath, *Yazoo: Law and Politics in the New Republic* (Providence, RI: Brown University Press, 1966).

---

as an important provision of the new Constitution and encouraged the use of the clause in challenges to the economic regulations of the states.

Marshall's initial interpretation of the contract clause was reinforced just two years later in *New Jersey v. Wilson* (1812). This dispute can be traced back to 1758, when the remnants of the Delaware Indian tribe settled their land claims with the state of New Jersey. The Delawares consented to give up their claim to the disputed lands if the state would purchase a tract for the tribe to inhabit. The agreement also freed the tribe from state taxation on the land. In 1801 members of the tribe decided to move to New York, and New Jersey allowed them to sell their land. Three years later the state passed a law subjecting the property to state taxes. The new owners objected, claiming that the repeal of tax-exempt status was an impairment of the 1758 contract. Chief Justice Marshall, for a unanimous Court, ruled in favor of the landowners. The legislature had granted the tax exemption to the land as part of a legally binding contract. That contractual obligation could not later be impaired by the state. The tax status conferred in 1758 remained with the land even though the original parties to the agreement had sold it.

In 1819 the Court heard *Sturges v. Crowninshield,* an appeal that presented issues hitting squarely on the concerns expressed by the delegates at the Constitutional Convention. Richard Crowninshield, whose business enterprises had suffered hard times, received two loans from Josiah Sturges totaling about $1,500. The loans were secured by promissory notes. When Crowninshield became insolvent, he sought relief from his debts by invoking New York's recently passed bankruptcy law. Sturges objected, claiming that the New York law was a state impairment of the obligation of contracts in violation of the Constitution. The New York bankruptcy law was an example of just what the framers had intended to prohibit—states interfering with debtor–creditor agreements.

Sturges v. Crowninshield presented two issues to the Supreme Court. The first was whether a state may enact a bankruptcy law at all. Article I, Section 8, Clause 4, of the Constitution expressly gave the federal government power to enact such legislation. Did this power preclude the states from acting? A unanimous Court, again through an opinion written by Chief Justice Marshall, held that in the absence of any federal action the states were free to enact bankruptcy laws. The second issue was whether the New York law was invalid as an impairment of contracts. Here the Court found the law defective. The New York law discharged Crowninshield's contractual indebtedness entered into prior to the passage of the statute, which, according to the Court, was beyond the power of the state.[2]

Corporate Charters as Contracts

The same year the Supreme Court decided *Sturges,* the justices announced their decision in *Trustees of Dartmouth College v. Woodward* (1819), perhaps the most famous contract clause case of the Marshall era. The Dartmouth College case presented a question of particular significance to the business community: Is a corporation charter a contract protected against state impairment? The case had added intrigue because it involved a bitter partisan battle between the Jeffersonian Republicans and the Federalists.

---

2. Eight years later, however, the Court held in *Ogden v. Saunders* (1827) that state bankruptcy laws did not violate the contract clause if the contract was entered into after the enactment of the bankruptcy statute.

Trustees of Dartmouth College v. Woodward

17 U.S. (4 Wheat.) 518 (1819)

http://laws.findlaw.com/us/17/518.html

Vote: 5 (Johnson, Livingston, Marshall, Story, Washington)
        1 (Duvall)

OPINION OF THE COURT: *Marshall*
CONCURRING OPINIONS: *Story, Washington*
NOT PARTICIPATING: *Todd*

FACTS:

In 1769 King George III issued a corporate charter establishing Dartmouth College in New Hampshire.[3] The charter designated a board of trustees as the ultimate governing body, with the board's authority extending to the college president. The board was self-perpetuating, with the power to fill its own vacancies. The founder and first president of Dartmouth was Eleazar Wheelock, who also had authority to designate his own successor. He chose his son, John Wheelock, who assumed the presidency upon Eleazar's death. John Wheelock was ill suited for the position, and for years friction existed between him and the board.

To shore up his position, Wheelock made political alliances with the Jeffersonian Republicans who had gained control of the New Hampshire state legislature in 1816. The Republicans gladly took his side in the dispute with the Federalist-dominated board of trustees and passed a law radically changing the governing structure of the college. The law expanded the board from twelve to twenty-one members to be appointed by the governor, and created a supervisory panel with veto power over the actions of the trustees. This reorganization of the college essentially rendered the old trustees powerless. In effect, the legislature converted Dartmouth College, renamed Dartmouth University under the new law, from a private to a public institution. The result was chaos. The students and faculty for the most part remained loyal to the old trustees, but the state essentially took over the buildings and records of the college. As might be expected, the college soon found itself nearing fiscal collapse.

To resolve the situation, the old trustees hired Daniel Webster to represent them. Webster, an 1801 Dartmouth graduate, agreed to take the case for a fee

---

3. This account of the facts in the Dartmouth College case is based in part on Richard N. Current, "The Dartmouth College Case," in Garraty, *Quarrels That Have Shaped the Constitution.*

of $1,000—a considerable sum of money in those days. The old trustees sued William Woodward, the secretary of the college, who had in his possession the college charter, records, and seal. Webster and his clients lost in the state courts and then appealed to the U.S. Supreme Court. When the case was argued in March 1818, Webster engaged in four hours of brilliant oratory before the justices. At times his argument was quite emotional; he is said to have brought tears to the eyes of those present when he spoke his often-quoted line, "It is, sir, as I have said, a small college, and yet there are those that love it." The justices, however, did not act in the heat of emotion. Almost a full year went by before the Court decided. By the time the opinion was released, both John Wheelock and William Woodward had died.

ARGUMENTS:

For the plaintiffs in error,
the trustees of Dartmouth College:

- By a grant from the English Crown, Eleazar Wheelock was named president of Dartmouth College and was empowered to name his successor. By the same grant, the original board of twelve trustees was given power to fill its own vacancies. These provisions were to be in effect in perpetuity.

- The changes made by the New Hampshire legislature are not binding on the college unless agreed to by the trustees.

- It is an improper legislative act under the New Hampshire constitution to take property and rights from one (the old Dartmouth College corporation) and grant them to another (the new Dartmouth University corporation).

- The acts of the legislature violate the U.S. Constitution's provision that states cannot impair the obligation of contracts. The charter establishing the college is a valid contract.

For the defendant in error, William Woodward:

- A grant of a public nature for public purposes, such as the Dartmouth College charter, is not the kind of private agreement intended to be protected under the contract clause.

- The parties to the contract, King George and Eleazar Wheelock, are not parties to this lawsuit.

- Even if the charter is a contract and the old trustees are parties to it, the obligation of contracts has not been impaired. The old trustees remain on the board. The addition of new trustees does not alter the position of the old trustees.

- By the Revolution, the powers of the British government devolved to the states. Therefore, the state has the same powers over its public institutions as did the king.

Courtesy of Dartmouth College

The Reverend Eleazar Wheelock (left) was the founder and first president of Dartmouth College; John Wheelock (middle), son of Eleazar, was the second president, and his dispute with the college board of trustees led to the famed litigation. William H. Woodward (right) was the secretary-treasurer of the college and the defendant in the contract clause case of Dartmouth College v. Woodward.

Drawing of Dartmouth College, 1793.

THE OPINION OF THE COURT WAS DELIVERED BY MR. CHIEF JUSTICE MARSHALL.

This Court can be insensible neither to the magnitude nor delicacy of this question. The validity of a legislative act is to be examined; and the opinion of the highest law tribunal of a State is to be revised: an opinion which carries with it intrinsic evidence of the diligence, of the ability, and the integrity, with which it was formed. On more than one occasion, this Court has expressed the cautious circumspection with which it approaches the consideration of such questions; and has declared, that, in no doubtful case, would it pronounce a legislative act to be contrary to the constitution. But the American people have said, in the constitution of the United States, that "no State shall pass any bill of attainder, *ex post facto* law, or law impairing the obligation of contracts." In the same instrument they have also said, "that the judicial power shall extend to all cases in law and equity arising under the constitution." On the judges of this Court, then, is imposed the high and solemn duty of protecting, from even legislative violation, those contracts which the constitution of our country has placed beyond legislative control; and, however irksome the task may be, this is a duty from which we dare not shrink. . . .

It can require no argument to prove, that the circumstances of this case constitute a contract. An application is made to the crown for a charter to incorporate a religious and literary institution. In the application, it is stated that large contributions have been made for the object, which will be conferred on the corporation, as soon as it shall be created. The charter is granted, and on its faith the property is conveyed. Surely in this transaction every ingredient of a complete and legitimate contract is to be found.

The points for consideration are,

1. Is this contract protected by the constitution of the United States?

2. Is it impaired by the acts under which the defendant holds? . . .

. . . . [T]he term *"contract"* must be understood in a . . . limited sense. . . . [I]t must be understood as intended to guard against a power of at least doubtful utility, the abuse of which had been extensively felt; and to restrain the legislature in future from violating the right to property. That anterior to the formation of the constitution, a course of legislation had prevailed in many, if not in all, of the States, which weakened the confidence of man in man, and embarrassed all transactions between individuals, by dispensing with a faithful performance of engagements. To correct this mischief, by restraining the power which produced it, the State legislatures were forbidden "to pass any law impairing the obligation of contracts," that is, of contracts respecting property, under which some individual could claim a right to something beneficial to himself; and that since the clause in the constitution must in construction receive some limitation, it may be confined, and ought to be confined, to cases of this description; to cases within the mischief it was intended to remedy. . . .

The parties in this case differ less on general principles, less on the true construction of the constitution in the abstract, than on the application of those principles to this case, and on the true construction of the charter of 1769. This is the point on which the cause essentially depends. If the act of incorporation be a grant of political power, if it create a civil institution to be employed in the administration of the government, or if the funds of the college be public property, or if the State of New Hampshire, as a government, be alone interested in its transactions, the subject is one in which the legislature of the State may act according to its own judgment, unrestrained by any limitation of its power imposed by the constitution of the United States.

But if this be a private eleemosynary institution, endowed with a capacity to take property for objects unconnected with government, whose funds are bestowed by individuals on the faith of the charter; if the donors have stipulated for the future disposition and management of those funds in the manner prescribed by themselves; there may be more difficulty in the case. . . .

It becomes then the duty of the Court most seriously to examine this charter, and to ascertain its true character. . . .

Whence, then, can be derived the idea, that Dartmouth College has become a public institution, and its trustees public officers, exercising powers conferred by the public for public objects? Not from the source whence its funds were drawn; for its foundation is purely private and eleemosynary—Not from the application of those funds; for money may be given for education, and the persons receiving it do not, by being employed in the education of youth, become members of the civil government. Is it from the act of incorporation? Let this subject be considered.

A corporation is an artificial being, invisible, intangible, and existing only in contemplation of law. Being the mere creature of law, it possesses only those properties which the charter of its creation confers upon it, either expressly, or as incidental to its very existence. These are such as are supposed best calculated to effect the object for which it was created. Among the most important are immortality, and, if the expression may be allowed, individuality; properties, by which a perpetual succession of many persons are considered as the same, and may act as a single individual. They enable a corporation to manage its own affairs, and to hold property without the perplexing intricacies, the

hazardous and endless necessity of perpetual conveyances for the purpose of transmitting it from hand to hand. It is chiefly for the purpose of clothing bodies of men, in succession, with these qualities and capacities, that corporations were invented, and are in use. By these means, a perpetual succession of individuals are capable of acting for the promotion of the particular object, like one immortal being. But this being does not share in the civil government of the country, unless that be the purpose for which it was created. Its immortality no more confers on it political power, or a political character, than immortality would confer such power or character on a natural person. It is no more a State instrument, than a natural person exercising the same powers would be. If, then, a natural person, employed by individuals in the education of youth, or for the government of a seminary in which youth is educated, would not become a public officer, or be considered as a member of the civil government, how is it, that this artificial being, created by law, for the purpose of being employed by the same individuals for the same purposes, should become a part of the civil government of the country? Is it because its existence, its capacities, its powers, are given by law? Because the government has given it the power to take and to hold property in a particular form, and for particular purposes, has the government a consequent right substantially to change that form, or to vary the purposes to which the property is to be applied? This principle has never been asserted or recognized, and is supported by no authority. Can it derive aid from reason? . . .

From the fact, then, that a charter of incorporation has been granted, nothing can be inferred which changes the character of the institution, or transfers to the government any new power over it. The character of civil institutions does not grow out of their incorporation, but out of the manner in which they are formed, and the objects for which they are created. The right to change them is not founded on their being incorporated, but on their being the instruments of government, created for its purposes. The same institutions, created for the same objects, though not incorporated, would be public institutions, and, of course, be controllable by the legislature. The incorporating act neither gives nor prevents this control. Neither, in reason, can the incorporating act change the character of a private eleemosynary institution. . . .

From this review of the charter, it appears, that Dartmouth College is an eleemosynary institution, incorporated for the purpose of perpetuating the application of the bounty of the donors, to the specified objects of that bounty; that its trustees or governors were originally named by the founder, and invested with the power of perpetuating themselves; that they are not public officers, nor is it a civil institution, participating in the administration of government; but a charity school, or a seminary of education, incorporated for the preservation of its property, and the perpetual application of that property to the objects of its creation. . . .

This is plainly a contract to which the donors, the trustees, and the crown, (to whose rights and obligations New Hampshire succeeds,) were the original parties. It is a contract made on a valuable consideration. It is a contract for the security and disposition of property. It is a contract, on the faith of which, real and personal estate has been conveyed to the corporation. It is then a contract within the letter of the constitution, and within its spirit also. . . .

The opinion of the Court, after mature deliberation, is, that this is a contract, the obligation of which cannot be impaired, without violating the constitution of the United States. This opinion appears to us to be equally supported by reason, and by the former decisions of this Court.

2. We next proceed to the inquiry, whether its obligation has been impaired by those acts of the legislature of New Hampshire. . . .

From the review of this charter, which has been taken, it appears, that the whole power of governing the college, of appointing and removing tutors, of fixing their salaries, of directing the course of study to be pursued by the students, and of filling up vacancies created in their own body, was vested in the trustees. On the part of the crown it was expressly stipulated, that this corporation, thus constituted, should continue forever; and that the number of trustees should forever consist of twelve, and no more. By this contract the crown was bound, and could have made no violent alteration in its essential terms, without impairing its obligation.

By the revolution, the duties, as well as the powers, of government devolved on the people of New Hampshire. . . . It is too clear to require the support of argument, that all contracts, and rights, respecting property, remained unchanged by the revolution. The obligations then, which were created by the charter to Dartmouth College, were the same in the new, that they had been in the old government. The power of the government was also the same. A repeal of this charter at any time prior to the adoption of the present constitution of the United States, would have been an extraordinary and unprecedented act of power, but one which could have been contested only by the restrictions upon the legislature, to be found in the constitution of the State. But the constitution of the United States has imposed this additional limitation, that the legislature of a State shall pass no act "impairing the obligation of contracts." . . .

The whole power of governing the college is transferred from trustees appointed according to the will of the founder, expressed in the charter, to the executive of New Hampshire. The management and application of the funds of this eleemosynary institution, which are placed by the donors in the hands of trustees named in the charter, and empowered to perpetuate themselves, are placed by this act under the control of the government of the State. The will of the State is substituted for the will of the donors, in every essential operation of the college. This is not an immaterial change. The founders of the college contracted, not merely for the perpetual application of the funds which they gave, to the objects for which those funds were given; they contracted also, to secure that application by the constitution of the corporation. They contracted for a system, which should, as far as human foresight can provide, retain forever the government of the literary institution they had formed, in the hands of persons approved by themselves. This system is totally changed. The charter of 1769 exists no longer. It is reorganized; and reorganized in such a manner, as to convert a literary institution, moulded according to the will of its founders, and placed under the control of private literary men, into a machine entirely subservient to the will of the government. This may be for the advantage of this college in particular, and may be for the advantage of literature in general; but it is not according to the will of the donors, and is subversive of that contract, on the faith of which their property was given. . . .

It results from this opinion, that the acts of the legislature of New Hampshire . . . are repugnant to the constitution of the United States. . . . The judgment of the State Court must, therefore, be reversed.

MR. JUSTICE STORY, [concurring].

In my judgment, it is perfectly clear that any act of a legislature which takes away any powers or franchises vested by its charter in a private corporation, or its corporate officers, or which restrains or controls the legitimate exercise of them, or transfers them to other persons without its assent is a violation of the obligations of that charter. If the legislature mean to claim such an authority, it must be reserved in the grant. The charter of Dartmouth College contains no such reservation, and I am therefore bound to declare that the acts of the Legislature of New Hampshire now in question do impair the obligations of that charter, and are consequently unconstitutional and void.

In pronouncing this judgment, it has not for one moment escaped me how delicate, difficult, and ungracious is the task devolved upon us. The predicament in which this Court stands in relation to the nation at large is full of perplexities and embarrassments. It is called to decide on causes between citizens of different States, between a State and its citizens, and between different States. It stands, therefore in the midst of jealousies and rivalries of conflicting parties with the most momentous interests confided to its care. Under such circumstances, it never can have a motive to do more than its duty, and I trust it will always be found to possess firmness enough to do that.

Under these impressions, I have pondered on the case before us with the most anxious deliberation. I entertain great respect for the Legislature whose acts are in question. I entertain no less respect for the enlightened tribunal whose decision we are called upon to review. In the examination, I have endeavored to keep . . . under the guidance of authority and principle. It is not for judges to listen to the voice of persuasive eloquence or popular appeal. We have nothing to do, but to pronounce the law as we find it, and, having done this, our justification must be left to the impartial judgment of our country.

The Dartmouth College case was a clear victory for Webster and the board. The former trustees regained control of the college, and Webster's reputation as one of the nation's leading legal advocates was firmly established. The decision was also a victory for business interests. By holding that corporate charters were contracts under the meaning of Article I, Section 10, the Court gave businesses considerable protection against state regulation. The decision, however, was not totally one-sided. Marshall acknowledged the power of the state to include within its contracts and charters provisions reserving the right to make future changes.

The importance of the contract clause reached its zenith under the Marshall Court. These early decisions protecting contractual agreements helped spur economic development and expansion. But an inevitable battle was on the horizon, a battle between the constitutional sanctity of contracts and the states' authority to regulate for the public good.

DECLINE OF THE CONTRACT CLAUSE: FROM THE TANEY COURT TO THE NEW DEAL

The Marshall years ended when the chief justice died July 6, 1835, at the age of seventy-nine. Marshall had been appointed in 1801 in one of the last acts of the once-dominant Federalist Party, and he had imposed his political philosophy on the Court's constitutional interpretations for more than three decades. His decisions in contract clause disputes, as well as in other areas of federalism and economic regulation, encouraged economic development and fostered entrepreneurial activity.

Importance of the Public Good

The days of the Federalist philosophy sympathetic to the interests of business and the economic elite had passed. Andrew Jackson now occupied the White House. Jackson came from the American frontier and was committed to policies beneficial to ordinary citizens; he had little sympathy for the moneyed classes of the Northeast. Within a short period, Jackson had the opportunity to change the course of the Supreme Court. He filled not only the center chair left vacant by Marshall's death but also those of five associate justices.[4] The new appointees all held ideologies consistent with principles of Jacksonian democracy, especially the new chief justice, Roger Brooke Taney, a Maryland Democrat who had served in a number of posts in the Jackson administration. Changes in constitutional interpretation were inevitable, although in the final analysis the Taney Court did not veer as far from Marshall precedents as many had predicted.

Given the differences between Federalist and Jacksonian values, however, the Court was likely to reevaluate the contract clause. The Taney Court's first opportunity to do so came in *Proprietors of Charles River Bridge v. Proprietors of Warren Bridge* (1837). As you read the Court's opinion, compare it with the positions Marshall stated in *Fletcher v. Peck* and *Dartmouth College*. Although Taney did not repudiate Marshall's rulings, his opinion in *Charles River Bridge* struck a new balance between the inviolability of contracts and

---

4. This number includes Associate Justice John Catron, who was nominated on Jackson's last day in office and whose appointment is often credited to Jackson's successor, Martin Van Buren.

the power of the state to legislate for the public good. The Court also held that contracts should be strictly construed, a position at odds with Marshall's rather expansive interpretations of contractual obligations. Justice Story, who had appeared as an attorney in *Fletcher v. Peck* and had supported Marshall's views of the contract clause since he joined the Court in 1811, disagreed with this change in doctrine.

Proprietors of Charles River Bridge v. Proprietors of Warren Bridge

36 U.S. (11 Pet.) 420 (1837)
http://laws.findlaw.com/us/36/420.html
Vote: 5 (Baldwin, Barbour, McLean, Taney, Wayne)
    2 (Story, Thompson)

OPINION OF THE COURT: *Taney*
CONCURRING OPINION: *McLean*
DISSENTING OPINIONS: *Story, Thompson*

FACTS:

In 1785 the Massachusetts legislature created Charles River Bridge Company by charter. The charter gave the company the right to construct a bridge between Boston and Charlestown and to collect tolls for its use. This agreement replaced a ferry franchise between the two cities that the colonial legislature had granted to Harvard College in 1650. In 1792 the legislature extended the charter. Because of the population growth in the Boston area, the bridge received heavy use, and its investors prospered. In 1828, when traffic congestion on the bridge became a significant problem, the legislature decided that a second bridge was necessary. Consequently, the state incorporated Warren Bridge Company and authorized it to construct a bridge to be located about a hundred yards from the first. The Warren Bridge investors had authority to collect tolls to pay for the expense of construction plus an agreed-on profit. Within six years the state would assume ownership of the Warren Bridge and operate it on a toll-free basis.

Charles River Bridge Company opposed the construction of a second bridge. It claimed that its charter conferred the exclusive right to build and operate a bridge between Boston and Charlestown. A second bridge, eventually to be operated without tolls, would deprive the company of the profits from its investment. The second charter, the company claimed, was a violation of the contract clause. To represent it, Charles River Bridge Company hired Daniel Webster, who had

won *Dartmouth College* two decades earlier *(see box 9-2)*. When the Massachusetts courts failed to grant relief, Charles River Bridge took its case to the U.S. Supreme Court.

The case was first argued in March 1831. John Marshall still led the Court at that time, and Webster understandably felt confident of victory. But the justices could not agree on a decision, and the case was scheduled for reargument in 1833. Once again, no decision was reached. Before a third hearing could be scheduled, deaths and resignations had changed the ideological complexion of the Court. When Jackson announced Taney as his choice for chief justice, Webster is said to have proclaimed, "The Constitution is gone." From Webster's perspective perhaps that was true. The Taney justices scheduled the bridge case to be reargued in 1837, and Webster no longer had a sympathetic audience for his strong contract clause position.

ARGUMENTS:

For the plaintiffs in error,
the proprietors of Charles River Bridge:

- A contract granting a company the right to build and operate the Charles River Bridge and collect tolls from it implies that the state will not take actions that create injurious competition with that enterprise.

- The legislative act authorizing the Warren Bridge impairs the obligation of the contract between the state and Charles River Bridge Company in violation of the contract clause of the U.S. Constitution.

- In recognition of the loss suffered when its ferry system was replaced by the Charles River Bridge, Harvard College received annual payments from the toll revenue collected by the bridge company. By this precedent, Charles River Bridge Company merits compensation for its loss of revenue due to the state's authorization of the Warren Bridge.

- The governing principle should be that when the terms of a contract are in doubt, the interpretation shall be strongly against the grantor.

For the defendants in error, the proprietors of the
Warren Bridge:

- Nothing in the charters of the Harvard ferry or the Charles River Bridge guarantees an exclusive right to provide transportation across the river.

BOX 9-2 DANIEL WEBSTER

Library of Congress

Daniel Webster played an influential role in the development of American law and politics during a public career that spanned almost fifty years. He was born in Salisbury, New Hampshire, January 18, 1782, and educated at Phillips Exeter Academy and Dartmouth College. He was admitted to the bar in 1805 and immediately began the practice of law in his home state.

In 1813 Webster was elected to Congress as a Federalist representative from New Hampshire. This office was only the beginning of an illustrious series of important positions:

United States representative, New Hampshire, 1813–1817

Monroe delegate to Electoral College, 1820

United States representative, Massachusetts, 1823–1827

United States senator, Massachusetts, 1827–1841

Presidential candidate, 1836

Secretary of state (Harrison and Tyler administrations), 1841–1843

United States senator, Massachusetts, 1845–1850

Secretary of state (Fillmore administration), 1850–1852

Webster was perhaps best known for his role as an advocate before the Supreme Court and the brilliant oratorical skills he displayed both in Congress and in the courts. He appeared before the Supreme Court in 168 cases, winning about half of them. In twenty-four of his appearances he was an advocate in a major constitutional dispute. Among the most celebrated of these cases were the following:

McCulloch v. Maryland (1819)

Dartmouth College v. Woodward (1819)

Cohens v. Virginia (1821)

Gibbons v. Ogden (1824)

Osborn v. Bank of the United States (1824)

Ogden v. Saunders (1827)

Wheaton v. Peters (1834)

Charles River Bridge v. Warren Bridge (1837)

Swift v. Tyson (1842)

West River Bridge v. Dix (1848)

Luther v. Borden (1849)

Webster died October 24, 1852, at his home in Marshfield, Massachusetts.

NOTE: For a review of Webster's legal career, see Maurice G. Baxter, *Daniel Webster and the Supreme Court* (Amherst: University of Massachusetts Press, 1966).

- When interpreting a public grant, nothing should pass by implication.
- The state cannot contract away its authority to legislate for the security and well-being of society. The state always retains the power to provide transportation systems for its people.
- The state's grant to Charles River Bridge Company included the right to build and operate a bridge, and nothing more.

MR. CHIEF JUSTICE TANEY DELIVERED THE OPINION OF THE COURT.

The plaintiffs in error insist . . . [t]hat . . . the acts of the legislature of Massachusetts . . . by their true construction, necessarily implied that the legislature would not authorize another bridge, and especially a free one, by the side of this, and placed in the same line of travel, whereby the franchise granted to the "proprietors of the Charles River

The Charles River Bridge ran from Prince Street in Boston to Charlestown. The bridge, considered a very advanced design at the time of its construction, was built on seventy-five oak piers and was more than 1,500 feet long.

Bridge" should be rendered of no value; and the plaintiffs in error contend, that the grant of the ferry to the college, and of the charter to the proprietors of the bridge, are both contracts on the part of the state; and that the law authorizing the erection of the Warren Bridge in 1828, impairs the obligation of one or both of these contracts. . . .

. . . [W]e are not now left to determine, for the first time, the rules by which public grants are to be construed in this country. The subject has already been considered in this Court . . . and the principle recognized, that in grants by the public, nothing passes by implication. . . .

. . . [T]he object and end of all government is to promote the happiness and prosperity of the community by which it is established; and it can never be assumed, that the government intended to diminish its power of accomplishing the end for which it was created. And in a country like ours, free, active, and enterprising, continually advancing in numbers and wealth; new channels of communication are daily found necessary, both for travel and trade; and are essential to the comfort, convenience, and prosperity of the people. A state ought never to be presumed to surrender this power, because, like the taxing power, the whole community have an interest in preserving it undiminished. And when a corporation alleges, that a state has surrendered for seventy years, its power of improvement, and public accommodation, in a great and important line of travel, along which a vast number of its citizens must daily pass; the community have a right to insist, in the language of this Court above quoted, "that its abandonment ought not to be presumed, in a case, in which the deliber-

ate purpose of the state to abandon it does not appear." The continued existence of a government would be of no great value, if by implications and presumptions, it was disarmed of the powers necessary to accomplish the ends of its creation; and the functions it was designed to perform, transferred to the hands of privileged corporations. The rule of construction announced by the Court, was not confined to the taxing power; nor is it so limited in the opinion delivered. On the contrary, it was distinctly placed on the ground that the interests of the community were concerned in preserving, undiminished, the power then in question; and whenever any power of the state is said to be surrendered or diminished, whether it be the taxing power or any other affecting the public interest, the same principle applies, and the rule of construction must be the same. No one will question that the interests of the great body of the people of the state, would, in this instance, be affected by the surrender of this great line of travel to a single corporation, with the right to exact toll, and exclude competition for seventy years. While the rights of private property are sacredly guarded, we must not forget that the community also have rights, and that the happiness and well being of every citizen depends on their faithful preservation.

Adopting the rule of construction above stated as the settled one, we proceed to apply it to the charter of 1785, to the proprietors of the Charles River Bridge. This act of incorporation is in the usual form, and the privileges such as are commonly given to corporations of that kind. It confers on them the ordinary faculties of a corporation, for the purpose of building the bridge; and establishes certain rates of toll, which the company are authorized to take. This is the whole grant. There is no exclusive privilege given to them over the waters of Charles River, above or below their bridge. No right to erect another bridge themselves, nor to prevent other persons from erecting one. No engagement from the state, that another shall not be erected; and no undertaking not to sanction competition, nor to make improvements that may diminish the amount of its income. Upon all these subjects the charter is silent; and nothing is said in it about a line of travel, so much insisted on in the argument, in which they are to have exclusive privileges. No words are used, from which an intention to grant any of these rights can be inferred. If the plaintiff is entitled to them, it must be implied, simply, from the nature of the grant; and cannot be inferred from the words by which the grant is made.

The relative position of the Warren Bridge has already been described. It does not interrupt the passage over the Charles River Bridge, nor make the way to it or from it less convenient. None of the faculties or franchises granted to that corporation, have been revoked by the legislature; and its right to take the tolls granted by the charter remains unaltered. In short, all the franchises and rights of property enumerated in the charter, and there mentioned to have been granted to it, remain unimpaired. But its income is destroyed by the Warren Bridge; which, being free, draws off the passengers and property which would have gone over it, and renders their franchise of no value. This is the gist of the complaint. For it is not pretended, that the erection of the Warren Bridge would have done them any injury, or in any degree affected their right of property; if it had not diminished the amount of their tolls. In order then to entitle themselves to relief, it is necessary to show, that the legislature contracted not to do the act of which they complain; and that they impaired, or in other words, violated that contract by the erection of the Warren Bridge.

The inquiry then is, does the charter contain such a contract on the part of the state? Is there any such stipulation to be found in that instrument? It must be admitted on all hands, that there is none—no words that even relate to another bridge or to the diminution of their tolls, or to the line of travel. If a contract on that subject can be gathered from the charter, it must be by implication; and cannot be found in the words used. Can such an agreement be implied? The rule of construction before stated is an answer to the question. In charters of this description, no rights are taken from the public, or given to the corporation, beyond those which the words of the charter, by their natural and proper construction, purport to convey. There are no words

which import such a contract as the plaintiffs in error contend for, and none can be implied. . . .

Indeed, the practice and usage of almost every state in the Union, old enough to have commenced the work of internal improvement, is opposed to the doctrine contended for on the part of the plaintiffs in error. Turnpike roads have been made in succession, on the same line of travel; the later ones interfering materially with the profits of the first. These corporations have, in some instances, been utterly ruined by the introduction of newer and better modes of transportation, and travelling. In some cases, rail roads have rendered the turnpike roads on the same line of travel so entirely useless, that the franchise of the turnpike corporation is not worth preserving. Yet in none of these cases have the corporations supposed that their privileges were invaded, or any contract violated on the part of the state. Amid the multitude of cases which have occurred, and have been daily occurring for the last forty or fifty years, this is the first instance in which such an implied contract has been contended for, and this Court called upon to infer it from an ordinary act of incorporation, containing nothing more than the usual stipulations and provisions to be found in every such law. The absence of any such controversy, when there must have been so many occasions to give rise to it, proves that neither states, nor individuals, nor corporations, ever imagined that such a contract could be implied from such charters. It shows that the men who voted for these laws, never imagined that they were forming such a contract; and if we maintain that they have made it, we must create it by a legal fiction, in opposition to the truth of the fact, and the obvious intention of the party. We cannot deal thus with the rights reserved to the states; and by legal intendments and mere technical reasoning, take away from them any portion of that power over their own internal police and improvement, which is so necessary to their well being and prosperity. . . .

The judgment of the supreme judicial court of the commonwealth of Massachusetts, dismissing the plaintiff's bill, must, therefore, be affirmed, with costs.

MR. JUSTICE STORY, dissenting.

I maintain, that, upon the principles of common reason and legal interpretation, the present grant carries with it a necessary implication that the legislature shall do no act to destroy or essentially to impair the franchise; that, (as one of the learned judges of the state court expressed it,) there is an implied agreement that the state will not grant another bridge between Boston and Charlestown, so near as to draw away the custom from the old one; and, (as another learned judge expressed it,) that there is an implied agreement of the state to grant the undisturbed use of the bridge and its tolls so far as respects any acts of its own, or of any persons acting under its authority. In other words, the state, impliedly, contracts not to resume its grant, or to do any act to the prejudice or destruction of its grant. I maintain, that there is no authority or principle established in relation to the construction of crown grants, or legislative grants; which does not concede and justify this doctrine. Where the thing is given, the incidents, without which it cannot be enjoyed, are also given. . . . I maintain that a different doctrine is utterly repugnant to all the principles of the common law, applicable to all franchises of a like nature; and that we must overturn some of the best securities of the rights of property, before it can be established. I maintain, that the common law is the birthright of every citizen of Massachusetts, and that he holds the title deeds of his property, corporeal, and incorporeal, under it. I maintain, that under the principles of the common law, there exists no more right in the legislature of Massachusetts, to erect the Warren Bridge, to the ruin of the franchise of the Charles River Bridge than exists to transfer the latter to the former, or to authorize the former to demolish the latter. If the legislature does not mean in its grant to give any exclusive rights, let it say so, expressly; directly; and in terms admitting of no misconstruction. The grantees will then take at their peril, and must abide the results of their overweening confidence, indiscretion, and zeal.

My judgment is formed upon the terms of the grant, its nature and objects, its design and duties; and, in its interpretation, I seek for no new principles, but I apply such as are as old as the very rudiments of the common law.

Paying little attention to Justice Story's protest that the majority had rendered the contract clause meaningless, the Taney Court continued to allow the states more leeway in regulating for the public good. As Taney noted in *Charles River Bridge*, "While the rights of private property are sacredly guarded, we must not forget that the community also have rights, and that the happiness and well being of every citizen depends on their faithful preservation." In *West River Bridge Company v. Dix* (1848) the Court upheld the state's right to exercise eminent domain authority even when it conflicted with existing contracts. In that case Vermont had previously granted a private company a charter to construct a bridge and collect tolls. When

the state later decided to build a public highway to be used without tolls, it canceled the company's charter. Vermont offered to compensate the company for its loss, but the owners were not satisfied with the amount. In an opinion by Justice Peter V. Daniel the Court rejected the bridge company's claim that the state had violated the Constitution, holding that the contract clause did not restrict the state's right to regulate for the public good under the power of eminent domain.

The Taney justices, however, did not totally abandon the Marshall Court's posture favoring business, nor did they repeal the contract clause by judicial fiat; instead, the Court took a more balanced position. In a number of cases, especially when the contractual provisions were clear, the Taney Court struck down state regulations on contract clause grounds. In *Bronson v. Kinzie* (1843) the Court invalidated Illinois laws that expanded the rights of debtors. The challenged statutes placed certain limits on mortgage debt, including protecting the rights of owners to repurchase properties lost to foreclosure. To the extent that these laws were applied to contracts in existence before their passage, the laws were unconstitutional. In *Piqua Branch of the State Bank of Ohio v. Knoop* (1854) the justices declared void the assessment of state taxes on a bank because, in calculating the taxes, Ohio had used a basis different from that specified under the state charter establishing the bank.

Post–Civil War Period

After the Taney years, the Court continued to move away from strong enforcement of the contract clause and to accord the states greater freedom to exercise their police powers. ***Northwestern Fertilizing Company v. Hyde Park*** (1878) provides a good illustration. In March 1867 the Illinois state legislature passed a statute creating Northwestern Fertilizing Company. The charter authorized the company within a designated territory to operate a facility that converted dead animals to fertilizer and other products. The charter also gave the company the right to transport dead animals and animal parts (offal) through the territory. Based on this authority, the company operated its plant in a sparsely populated, swampy area.

The facility was located within the boundaries of the village of Hyde Park, which was beginning to experience considerable population growth. In 1869 the legislature upgraded the village charter, giving it full powers of local government including the authority to "define or abate nuisances which are, or may be, injurious to the public health." Recognizing its charter with Northwestern, the legislature stipulated that no village regulations could be applied to the company for at least two years.

At the end of the two years, the village passed an ordinance that said, "No person shall transfer, carry, haul, or convey any offal, dead animals, or other offensive or unwholesome matter or material, into or through the village of Hyde Park." Parties in violation of the law were subject to fines. In 1873, following the arrest and conviction of railroad workers hauling dead animals to its plant, Northwestern filed suit claiming that the company's original charter was a contract that could not be abrogated by the state or its local governments. The company was unsuccessful in the state courts and appealed to the U.S. Supreme Court.

Justice Noah Swayne's opinion made clear at the outset that the company faced a difficult task in its attempt to convince the justices:

The rule of construction in this class of cases is that it shall be most strongly against the corporation. Every reasonable doubt is to be resolved adversely. Nothing is to be taken as conceded but what is given in unmistakable terms, or by an implication equally clear. The affirmative must be shown. Silence is negation, and doubt is fatal to the claim. This doctrine is vital to the public welfare.

The Court then went on to rule against the company's contract clause arguments. The justices had no doubt that the transportation of offal was a public nuisance or that the state had ample police power to combat such an offensive practice. According to Swayne,

That power belonged to the States when the Federal Constitution was adopted. They did not surrender it, and they all have it now. . . . It rests upon the fundamental principle that every one shall so use his own as not to wrong and injure another. To regulate and abate nuisances is one of its ordinary functions.

The Court was implying that states could not contract away their inherent powers to regulate for their citizens' health, safety, and welfare.

Two years after *Northwestern Fertilizing* the justices addressed a similar appeal, this time dealing with questions of public morality. *Stone v. Mississippi* focused on the use of the state's police power to combat

lotteries, a form of gambling that large portions of the population considered evil at that time. As you read Chief Justice Morrison Waite's opinion for the Court, compare it with the decisions written during the Marshall era. Note how much the Court's interpretation of the contract clause had changed.

Stone v. Mississippi

101 U.S. 814 (1880)
http://laws.findlaw.com/us/101/814.html
Vote: 9 (Bradley, Clifford, Field, Harlan, Hunt, Miller, Strong, Swayne, Waite)
    0
OPINION OF THE COURT: *Waite*

FACTS:

In 1867 the post–Civil War provisional state legislature chartered the Mississippi Agricultural, Educational, and Manufacturing Aid Society. In spite of its name, the society's only purpose was to operate a lottery. The charter gave the society authority to run a lottery in Mississippi for twenty-five years, and in return the society paid an initial sum of cash to the state, an additional annual payment for each year of operation, plus a percentage of the lottery receipts. In 1868, however, a state convention drafted a new constitution, which the people ratified the next year. This constitution contained provisions explicitly outlawing lotteries. It also stated, "Nor shall any lottery heretofore authorized be permitted to be drawn, or tickets therein to be sold." On July 16, 1870, the legislature passed a statute providing for enforcement of the antilottery provisions, and four years later, on March 17, 1874, the state attorney general filed charges against John B. Stone and others associated with the Mississippi Agricultural, Educational, and Manufacturing Aid Society for being in violation of state law. The state admitted that the company was operating within the provisions of its 1867 charter but contended that the new constitution and subsequent enforcement legislation effectively repealed that grant. Stone countered that the federal contract clause explicitly prohibited the state from negating the provisions of the charter.

ARGUMENTS:

For the plaintiffs in error, John B. Stone et al.:
- The Mississippi Agricultural, Educational, and Manufacturing Aid Society had a valid contract to issue and sell lottery tickets in Mississippi for twenty-five years.

- The society complied fully with all the provisions of the contract.
- The Mississippi law is an unconstitutional impairment of the obligation of contracts.

For the defendant in error, State of Mississippi:
- The state legislature cannot by contract bind the will of the people.
- The state legislature cannot contract away the state's police powers.
- One legislature cannot by contract bind future legislatures with respect to matters of public health or morals.

**MR. CHIEF JUSTICE WAITE
DELIVERED THE OPINION OF THE COURT.**

It is now too late to contend that any contract which a State actually enters into when granting a charter to a private corporation is not within the protection of the clause in the Constitution of the United States that prohibits States from passing laws impairing the obligation of contracts. Art. 1, sect. 10. The doctrines of *Trustees of Dartmouth College v. Woodward* [1819], announced by this court more than sixty years ago, have become so imbedded in the jurisprudence of the United States as to make them to all intents and purposes a part of the Constitution itself. In this connection, however, it is to be kept in mind that it is not the charter which is protected, but only any contract the charter may contain. If there is no contract, there is nothing in the grant on which the Constitution can act. Consequently, the first inquiry in this class of cases always is, whether a contract has in fact been entered into, and if so, what its obligations are.

In the present case the question is whether the State of Mississippi, in its sovereign capacity, did by the charter now under consideration bind itself irrevocably by a contract to permit "the Mississippi Agricultural, Educational, and Manufacturing Aid Society," for twenty-five years, "to receive subscriptions, and sell and dispose of certificates of subscription which shall entitle the holders thereof to" "any lands, books, paintings, antiques, scientific instruments or apparatus, or any other property or thing that may be ornamental, valuable, or useful," "awarded to them" "by casting of lots, or by lot, chance, or otherwise." There can be no dispute but that under this form of words the legislature of the State chartered a lottery company, having all the powers incident to such a corporation, for twenty-five years, and that in consideration thereof the company paid into the State treasury $5,000 for the use of a university, and agreed to pay, and until the commencement of this suit did pay, an annual tax of $1,000 and "one-half of one per cent on the amount of receipts derived from the sale of certificates or tickets." If the legislature that granted this charter had the power to bind the people of the State and all succeeding legislatures to allow the corporation to continue its corporate business during the whole term of its authorized existence, there is no doubt about the sufficiency of the language employed to effect that object, although there was an evident purpose to conceal the vice of the transaction by the phrases that were used. Whether the alleged contract exists, therefore, or not, depends on the authority of the legislature to bind the State and the people of the State in that way.

All agree that the legislature cannot bargain away the police power of a State. "Irrevocable grants of property and franchises may be made if they do not impair the supreme authority to make laws for the right government of the State; but no legislature can curtail the power of its successors to make such laws as they may deem proper in matters of police." Many attempts have been made in this court and elsewhere to define the police power, but never with entire success. It is always easier to determine whether a particular case comes within the general scope of the power, than to give an abstract definition of the power itself which will be in all respects accurate. No one denies, however, that it extends to all matters affecting the public health or the public morals. Neither can it be denied that lotteries are proper subjects for the exercise of this power. We are aware that formerly, when the sources of public revenue were fewer than now, they were used in some or all of the States, and even in the District of Columbia, to raise money for the erection of public buildings, making public improvements, and not infrequently for educational and religious purposes; but this court said, more than thirty years ago, speaking through Mr. Justice Grier, that "experience has shown that the common forms of gambling are comparatively innocuous when placed in contrast with the wide-spread pestilence of lotteries. The former are confined to a few persons and places, but the latter infests the whole community; it enters every dwelling; it reaches every class; it preys upon the hard earnings of the poor; and it plunders the ignorant and simple." Happily, under the influence of restrictive legislation, the evils are not so apparent now; but we very much fear that with the same opportunities of indulgence the same results would be manifested.

If lotteries are to be tolerated at all, it is no doubt better that they should be regulated by law, so that the people may be protected as far as possible against the inherent vices of the system; but that they are demoralizing in their effects, no matter how carefully regulated, cannot admit of a doubt. When the government is untrammelled by any claim of vested rights or chartered privileges, no one has ever supposed that lotteries could not lawfully be suppressed, and those who manage them punished severely as violators of the rules of social morality. From 1822 to 1867, without any constitutional requirement, they were prohibited by law in Mississippi, and those who conducted them punished as a kind of gambler. During the provisional government of that State, in 1867, at the close of the late civil war, the present act of incorporation, with more of like character, was passed. The next year, 1868, the people, in adopting a new constitution with a view to the resumption of their political rights as one of the United States, provided that "the legislature shall never authorize any lottery, nor shall the sale of lottery-tickets be allowed, nor shall any lottery heretofore authorized be permitted to be drawn, or tickets therein to be sold." . . .

The question is therefore directly presented, whether, in view of these facts, the legislature of a State can, by the charter of a lottery company, defeat the will of the people, authoritatively expressed, in relation to the further continuance of such business in their midst. We think it cannot. No legislature can bargain away the public health or the public morals. The people themselves cannot do it, much less their servants. The supervision of both these subjects of governmental power is continuing in its nature, and they are to be dealt with as the special exigencies of the moment may require. Government is organized with a view to their preservation, and cannot divest itself of the power to provide for them. For this purpose the largest legislative discretion is allowed, and the discretion cannot be parted with any more than the power itself. . . .

. . . [T]he power of governing is a trust committed by the people to the government, no part of which can be granted away. The people, in their sovereign capacity, have established their agencies for the preservation of the public health and the public morals, and the protection of public and private rights. These several agencies can govern according to their discretion, if within the scope of their general authority, while in power; but they cannot give away nor sell the discretion of those that are to come after them, in respect to matters the government of which, from the very nature of things, must "vary with varying circumstances." They may create corporations, and give them, so to speak, a limited citizenship; but as citizens, limited in their privileges, or otherwise, these creatures of the government creation are subject to such rules and regulations as may from time to time be ordained and established for the preservation of health and morality.

The contracts which the Constitution protects are those that relate to property rights, not governmental. It is not always easy to tell on which side of the line which separates governmental from property rights a particular case is to be put; but in respect to lotteries there can be no difficulties. They are not, in the legal acceptation of the term, *mala in se* [wrong by its very nature], but, as we have just seen, may properly be made *mala prohibita* [wrong by government declaration]. They are a species of gambling, and wrong in their influences. They disturb the checks and balances of a well-ordered community. Society built on such a foundation would almost of necessity bring forth a population of speculators and gamblers, living on the expectation of what, "by the casting of lots, or by lot, chance, or otherwise," might be "awarded" to them from the accumulations of others. Certainly the right to suppress them is governmental, to be exercised at all times by those in power, at their discretion. Any one, therefore, who accepts a lottery charter does so with the implied understanding that the people, in their sovereign capacity, and through their properly constituted agencies, may resume it at any time when the public good shall require, whether it be paid for or not. All that one can get by such a charter is a suspension of certain governmental rights in his favor, subject to withdrawal at will. He has in legal effect nothing more than a license to enjoy the privilege on the terms named for the specified time, unless it be sooner abrogated by the sovereign power of the State. It is a permit, good as against existing laws, but subject to future legislative and constitutional control or withdrawal.

On the whole, we find no error in the record.

Judgment affirmed.

Following *Stone v. Mississippi* it was clear that the Court would no longer be sympathetic to contract clause attacks on state regulatory statutes. With contract clause avenues closing, opponents of state regulation of business and commercial activities turned to another provision of the Constitution, the due process clause of the Fourteenth Amendment. From the late 1880s to the 1930s, a period of Court history discussed in chapter 10, the Court heard and often responded favorably to these substantive due process arguments.

National Emergencies

The status of the contract clause reached its low point during the Great Depression of the 1930s. With the stock market crash of 1929, the nation entered the worst economic crisis it had ever seen; most Americans were placed in serious financial jeopardy. The 1932 election of Franklin Roosevelt to the presidency ushered in the New Deal, and the federal government began to implement innovative economic programs to combat the Depression. At the same time, various states were developing their own programs to protect their citizens against the economic ravages the country was experiencing.

What people feared the most during the Depression was losing the family home. Homeowners did what they could to meet their mortgage obligations, but many were out of work and unable to make their payments. Financial institutions had little choice but to foreclose on these properties as stipulated in the mortgage contracts. To provide relief, several states passed statutes aimed at increasing homeowners' chances of saving their houses. Banks and other creditors opposed these assistance measures. They asserted that intervention by the state was a direct violation of the constitutional ban against impairment of contracts.

The showdown between the contract clause and a state government's authority to cope with economic crisis occurred in *Home Building & Loan Assn. v. Blaisdell* (1934). As you read Chief Justice Charles Evans Hughes's opinion for the Court, think about the Constitutional Convention and the concerns that led the framers to adopt the contract clause. Would they agree with the Court that the Constitution should bend in the face of national crises, or would they side with Justice George Sutherland's position that the provisions of the Constitution should be interpreted the same way regardless of the conditions of the times?

Home Building & Loan Assn. v. Blaisdell

290 U.S. 398 (1934)
http://laws.findlaw.com/us/290/398.html
Vote: 5 (Brandeis, Cardozo, Hughes, Roberts, Stone)
       4 (Butler, McReynolds, Sutherland, Van Devanter)
OPINION OF THE COURT: *Hughes*
DISSENTING OPINION: *Sutherland*

FACTS:

During the Great Depression, the nation experienced high unemployment, low prices for agricultural and manufactured products, a stagnation of business, and a scarcity of credit. In response to these conditions, the Minnesota legislature declared that a state of economic emergency existed that demanded the use of extraordinary police powers for the protection of the people. One of the legislature's actions was passage of the Minnesota Mortgage Moratorium Act of 1933, which was designed to prevent homeowners from losing their houses when they could not make their mortgage payments. The act allowed homeowners who were behind in their payments to petition a state court for an extension of time to meet their mortgage obligations. During the period of the extension, the homeowners would not make normal mortgage payments but instead would pay a reasonable rental amount to the mortgage holder. The maximum extension was two years. The act was to be in effect only as long as the economic emergency continued. Its provisions applied to all mortgages, including those signed prior to the passage of the statute.

John and Rosella Blaisdell owned a house in Minneapolis that was mortgaged by Home Building & Loan Association. They lived in one part of the house and rented out the other part. When the Blaisdells were unable to keep their payments current or to obtain additional credit, they requested an extension in accordance with the moratorium law. The trial court denied the request, but the state supreme court reversed the decision. In response, the trial court granted the Blaisdells a two-year moratorium on mortgage payments. During this period the Blaisdells were ordered to pay $40 a month, which would be applied to taxes, insurance, interest, and mortgage principal.

Home Building & Loan Association appealed the granting of the extension, claiming that the law was an impairment of contracts in violation of the contract clause of the federal Constitution. The Minnesota high court conceded that the law impaired the obligation of contracts but concluded that the statute was within the police powers of the state because of the severe economic emergency. Home Building & Loan Association appealed to the U.S. Supreme Court.

ARGUMENTS:

For the appellant, Home Building & Loan Association:

- The Minnesota Mortgage Moratorium Act impairs the obligation of contracts in violation of the U.S. Constitution's contract clause.
- The law changes the terms of the mortgage contract and deprives the appellant of the remedies (e.g., foreclosure) included in the mortgage agreement.

- The law deprives the appellant of property without due process of law.
- The current economic conditions do not constitute a sufficient emergency to suspend the Constitution.

For the appellees, John H. and Rosella Blaisdell:

- Although in normal times the Minnesota law would be unconstitutional, it does not violate the Constitution because it is an emergency measure justified by the police powers of the state to respond to the economic depression.
- Every contract is subject to the implied limitation that its terms may be varied in a reasonable manner in times of emergency under the exercise of the state's police powers.
- Home Building & Loan Association is not deprived of property without due process of law because it has an opportunity to participate in judicial hearings to consider possible temporary alterations in the terms of the mortgage.
- The Minnesota law is fair, just, and reasonable. It assists both debtors and lenders. The law goes no further than necessary to cope with the economic emergency.

MR. CHIEF JUSTICE HUGHES DELIVERED THE OPINION OF THE COURT.

In determining whether the provision for this temporary and conditional relief exceeds the power of the State by reason of the clause in the Federal Constitution prohibiting impairment of the obligations of contracts, we must consider the relation of emergency to constitutional power, the historical setting of the contract clause, the development of the jurisprudence of this Court in the construction of that clause, and the principles of construction which we may consider to be established.

Emergency does not create power. Emergency does not increase granted power or remove or diminish the restrictions imposed upon power granted or reserved. The Constitution was adopted in a period of grave emergency. Its grants of power to the Federal Government and its limitations of the power of the States were determined in the light of emergency and they are not altered by emergency. What power was thus granted and what limitations were thus imposed are questions which have always been, and always will be, the subject of close examination under our constitutional system.

While emergency does not create power, emergency may furnish the occasion for the exercise of power.

"Although an emergency may not call into life a power which has never lived, nevertheless emergency may afford a reason for the exertion of a living power already enjoyed." *Wilson v. New* [1917]. The constitutional question presented in the light of an emergency is whether the power possessed embraces the particular exercise of it in response to particular conditions. Thus, the war power of the Federal Government is not created by the emergency of war, but it is a power given to meet that emergency. It is a power to wage war successfully, and thus it permits the harnessing of the entire energies of the people in a supreme cooperative effort to preserve the nation. But even the war power does not remove constitutional limitations safeguarding essential liberties. When the provisions of the Constitution, in grant or restriction, are specific, so particularized as not to admit of construction, no question is presented. Thus, emergency would not permit a State to have more than two Senators in the Congress, or permit the election of President by a general popular vote without regard to the number of electors to which the States are respectively entitled, or permit the States to "coin money" or to "make anything but gold and silver coin a tender in payment of debts." But where constitutional grants and limitations of power are set forth in general clauses, which afford a broad outline, the process of construction is essential to fill in the details. That is true of the contract clause. The necessity of construction is not obviated by the fact that the contract clause is associated in the same section with other and more specific prohibitions. Even the grouping of subjects in the same clause may not require the same application to each of the subjects, regardless of differences in their nature.

In the construction of the contract clause, the debates in the Constitutional Convention are of little aid. But the reasons which led to the adoption of that clause, and of the other prohibitions of Section 10 of Article I, are not left in doubt and have frequently been described with eloquent emphasis. The widespread distress following the revolutionary period, and the plight of debtors, had called forth in the States an ignoble array of legislative schemes for the defeat of creditors and the invasion of contractual obligations. Legislative interferences had been so numerous and extreme that the confidence essential to prosperous trade had been undermined and the utter destruction of credit was threatened. "The sober people of America" were convinced that some "thorough reform" was needed which would "inspire a general prudence and industry, and give a regular course to the business of society." *The Federalist*, No. 44. It was necessary to impose the restraining power of a central authority in order to secure the foundations even of "private faith." . . .

But full recognition of the occasion and general purpose of the clause does not suffice to fix its precise scope. Nor does an examination of the details of prior legislation in the States yield criteria which can be considered controlling. To ascertain the scope of the constitutional prohibition we examine the course of judicial decisions in its application. These put it beyond question that the prohibition is not an absolute one and is not to be read with literal exactness like a mathematical formula. . . .

. . . Not only are existing laws read into contracts in order to fix obligations as between the parties, but the reservation of essential attributes of sovereign power is also read into contracts as a postulate of the legal order. The policy of protecting contracts against impairment presupposes the maintenance of a government by virtue of which contractual relations are worth while,—a government which retains adequate authority to secure the peace and good order of society. This principle of harmonizing the constitutional prohibition with the necessary residuum of state power has had progressive recognition in the decisions of this Court. . . .

The Legislature cannot "bargain away the public health or the public morals." Thus, the constitutional provision against the impairment of contracts was held not to be violated by an amendment of the state Constitution which put an end to a lottery theretofore authorized by the Legislature. *Stone v. Mississippi* [1880]. The lottery was a valid enterprise when established under express state authority, but the Legislature in the public interest could put a stop to it. A similar rule has been applied to the control by the State of the sale of intoxicating liquors. *Boston Beer Company v. Massachusetts* [1877]. The States retain adequate power to protect the public health against the maintenance of nuisances despite insistence upon existing contracts. *Northwestern Fertilizing Company v. Hyde Park* [1878]. Legislation to protect the public safety comes within the same category of reserved power. This principle has had recent and noteworthy application to the regulation of the use of public highways by common carriers and "contract carriers," where the assertion of interference with existing contract rights has been without avail, *Sproles v. Binford* [1932]. . . .

It is manifest from this review of our decisions that there has been a growing appreciation of public needs and of the necessity of finding ground for a rational compromise between individual rights and public welfare. The settlement and consequent contraction of the public domain, the pressure of a constantly increasing density of population, the interrelation of the activities of our people and the complexity of our economic interests, have inevitably led to an increased use of the organization of society in order to protect the very bases of individual opportunity. Where, in earlier days, it was thought that only the concerns of individuals or of classes were involved, and that those of the State itself were touched only remotely, it has later been found that the fundamental interests of the State are directly affected; and that the question is no longer merely that of one party to a contract as against another, but of the use of reasonable means to safeguard the economic structure upon which the good of all depends.

It is no answer to say that this public need was not apprehended a century ago, or to insist that what the provision of the Constitution meant to the vision of that day it must mean to the vision of our time. If by the statement that what the Constitution meant at the time of its adoption it means today, it is intended to say that the great clauses of the Constitution must be confined to the interpretation which the framers, with the conditions and outlook of their time, would have placed upon them, the statement carries its own refutation. It was to guard against such a narrow conception that Chief Justice Marshall uttered the memorable warning: "We must never forget that it is *a constitution* we are expounding" (*McCulloch v. Maryland*); "a constitution intended to endure for ages to come, and consequently, to be adapted to the various *crises* of human affairs." When we are dealing with the words of the Constitution, said this Court in *Missouri v. Holland* [1920], "we must realize that they have called into life a being the development of which could not have been foreseen completely by the most gifted of its begetters. . . . The case before us must be considered in the light of our whole experience and not merely in that of what was said a hundred years ago."

Nor is it helpful to attempt to draw a fine distinction between the intended meaning of the words of the Constitution and their intended application. When we consider the contract clause and the decisions which have expounded it in harmony with the essential reserved power of the States to protect the security of their peoples, we find no warrant for the conclusion that the clause has been warped by these decisions from its proper significance or that the founders of our Government would have interpreted the clause differently had they had occasion to assume that responsibility in the conditions of the later day. The vast body of law which has been developed was unknown to the fathers, but it is believed to have preserved the essential content and the spirit of the Constitution. With a growing recognition of public needs and the relation of individual right to public security, the court has sought to prevent the perversion of the clause through its use as an instrument to throttle the capacity of the States to protect their fundamental interests. This development is a growth from the seeds which the fathers planted. . . . The principle of this development is . . . that the reservation of the reasonable exercise of the protective power of the State is read into all contracts and there is no greater reason for refusing to apply this principle to Minnesota mortgages than to New York leases.

Applying the criteria established by our decisions we conclude:

1. An emergency existed in Minnesota which furnished a proper occasion for the exercise of the reserved power of the State to protect the vital interests of the community. . . .

2. The legislation was addressed to a legitimate end, that is, the legislation was not for the mere advantage of particular individuals but for the protection of a basic interest of society.

3. In view of the nature of the contracts in question—mortgages of unquestionable validity—the relief afforded and justified by the emergency, in order not to contravene the constitutional provision, could only be of a character appropriate to that emergency and could be granted only upon reasonable conditions.

4. The conditions upon which the period of redemption is extended do not appear to be unreasonable. . . .

5. The legislation is temporary in operation. It is limited to the exigency which called it forth. . . .

We are of the opinion that the Minnesota statute as here applied does not violate the contract clause of the Federal Constitution. Whether the legislation is wise or unwise as a matter of policy is a question with which we are not concerned. . . .

The judgment of the Supreme Court of Minnesota is affirmed.

MR. JUSTICE SUTHERLAND, dissenting.

Few questions of greater moment than that just decided have been submitted for judicial inquiry during this generation. He simply closes his eyes to the necessary implications of the decision who fails to see in it the potentiality of future gradual but ever-advancing encroachments upon the sanctity of private and public contracts. The effect of the Minnesota legislation, though serious enough in itself, is of trivial significance compared with the far more serious and dangerous inroads upon the limitations of the Constitution which are almost certain to ensue as a consequence naturally following any step beyond the boundaries fixed by that instrument. And those of us who are thus apprehensive of the effect of this decision would, in a matter so important, be neglectful of our duty should we fail to spread upon the permanent records of the court the reasons which move us to the opposite view.

A provision of the Constitution, it is hardly necessary to say, does not admit of two distinctly opposite interpretations. It does not mean one thing at one time and an entirely different thing at another time. If the contract impairment clause, when framed and adopted, meant that the terms of a contract for the payment of money could not be altered . . . by a state statute enacted for the relief of hardly pressed debtors to the end and with the effect of postponing payment or enforcement during and because of an economic or financial emergency, it is but to state the obvious to say that it means the same now. This view, at once so rational in its application to the written word, and so necessary to the stability of constitutional principles, though from time to time challenged, has never, unless recently, been put within the realm of doubt by the decisions of this court. . . .

The provisions of the Federal Constitution, undoubtedly, are pliable in the sense that in appropriate cases they have the capacity of bringing within their grasp every new condition which falls within their meaning. But, their *meaning* is changeless; it is only their *application* which is extensible. . . .

A statute which materially delays enforcement of the mortgagee's contractual right of ownership and possession does not modify the remedy merely; it destroys, for the period of delay, *all* remedy so far as the enforcement of that right is concerned. The phrase, "obligation of a contract," in the constitutional sense imports a legal duty to perform the specified obligation of *that* contract, not to substitute and perform, against the will of one of the parties, a different, albeit equally valuable, obligation. And a state, under the contract impairment clause, has no more power to accomplish such a substitution than has one of the parties to the contract against the will of the other. It cannot do so either by acting directly upon the contract, or by bringing about the result under the guise of a statute in form acting only upon the remedy. If it could, the efficacy of the constitutional restriction would, in large measure, be made to disappear. . . .

I quite agree with the opinion of the court that whether the legislation under review is wise or unwise is a matter with which we have nothing to do. Whether it is likely to work well or work ill presents a question entirely irrelevant to the issue. The only legitimate inquiry we can make is whether it is constitutional. If it is not, its virtues, if it have any, cannot save it; if it is, its faults cannot be invoked to accomplish its destruction. If the provisions of the Constitution be not upheld when they pinch as well as when they comfort, they may as well be abandoned. Being unable to reach any other conclusion than that the Minnesota statute infringes the constitutional restriction under review, I have no choice but to say so.

The Court upheld the Minnesota Mortgage Moratorium Act because the majority concluded that the economic emergency justified the state's use of extensive police powers. Does the contract clause retain any vitality under such an interpretation? Or did the decision in *Home Building & Loan Assn.* render it virtually meaningless? After all, there would be little reason to pass such a statute in good economic times.

The conditions that prompted passage of the Minnesota law were repeated when a severe economic recession and its aftermath gripped the United States from 2008 to 2012. Again the subject of mortgages and foreclosures attracted the nation's attention. Although this downturn did not match the catastrophic proportions of the Great Depression, the nation at one point suffered unemployment rates in excess of 10 percent, a freeze in the credit markets, and the collapse of hundreds of banks. Even after the worst had passed, economic recovery was exceedingly slow. Once again the loss of the family home became one of the greatest fears of Americans as joblessness sapped many of the ability to meet their mortgage obligations. Foreclosures skyrocketed, and the people once again turned to the government for relief. The federal government responded by expanding the monetary supply, bailing out failing financial institutions, and pressuring banks to restructure mortgage contracts to turn back the tide of foreclosures. Because housing market relief came primarily from the federal government, contract clause objections did not become a significant issue. This situation reminds us that the Constitution bars the states from impairing the obligation of contracts, but it does not impose the same restraint on the federal government.

MODERN APPLICATIONS OF THE CONTRACT CLAUSE

For four decades after the decision in *Home Building & Loan Assn.*, parties challenging state laws rarely rested their arguments on the contract clause. It made little practical sense to do so when the justices were reluctant to use the provision to strike down state legislation designed to promote the economic welfare of citizens. Litigants who attempted to invoke the clause usually were unsuccessful. For example, in *El Paso v. Simmons* (1965) the contract clause was used to attack a Texas statute governing defaults on land sales agreements with the state. Consistent with the trend that had begun with *Charles River Bridge* more than a century earlier, the justices turned a deaf ear to the contract clause claims and upheld the challenged legislation. The justices made it quite clear that they were not eager to interfere with the sovereign right of the state to protect the general welfare of the people and would give the state legislatures wide discretion in determining proper public policy over economic matters. The contract clause, once one of the most litigated constitutional provisions, had lost much of its relevance.

To conclude that the contract clause had been effectively and forever erased from the Constitution would be incorrect, however. In the decades following the New Deal, the Court was dominated by justices who took generally liberal positions on economic matters. They were philosophically opposed to allowing business interests to use the contract clause as a weapon to strike down legislation benefiting the people at large. But the Court's liberal majority began to unravel with the retirement of Chief Justice Earl Warren and President Richard Nixon's appointment of Warren Burger to replace him in 1969. As succeeding appointments brought more conservatives to the Court, prospects brightened for a revitalized contract clause. This fact was not lost on enterprising lawyers, who began raising contract clause issues once again.

In 1977 and 1978 the Court handed down two contract clause decisions: *United States Trust Co. v. New Jersey* and *Allied Structural Steel Co. v. Spannaus*. In both cases the justices struck down state legislation intended to promote the general welfare because they found that the statutes impaired the obligation of contracts. Each time the Court's liberal justices voiced strong objections. As you read the opinions in these cases, try to determine if they represent a sharp break from the position the Court had taken over the preceding century or if they could be reconciled with decisions such as *Home Building & Loan Assn. v. Blaisdell.*

United States Trust Co. v. New Jersey

431 U.S. 1 (1977)
http://laws.findlaw.com/us/431/1.html
Oral arguments are available at https://www.oyez.org.
Vote: 4 (Blackmun, Burger, Rehnquist, Stevens)
     3 (Brennan, Marshall, White)

OPINION OF THE COURT: *Blackmun*
CONCURRING OPINION: *Burger*
DISSENTING OPINION: *Brennan*
NOT PARTICIPATING: *Powell, Stewart*

FACTS:

In 1921 the states of New York and New Jersey entered into a compact to establish the Port Authority of New York, a body responsible for developing and coordinating transportation and commerce. The Port Authority was financially independent, with funds derived primarily from private investors. It had the power to mortgage its facilities and to pledge its revenues as payment for bonds issued to its investors. In 1962, in response to increased interest in mass transit, the Port Authority took control of the financially ailing Hudson & Manhattan Railroad. As part of the acquisition, the states agreed that none of the authority's revenues pledged as security for existing bonds would be used for any additional railroad expenditures.

From 1972 to 1974, with the nation in the midst of an energy crisis and under intense pressure to develop mass transit, New York and New Jersey moved to expand their system. Because money was difficult to raise, the states decided to use revenues previously pledged as security for existing bonds. To make the funds accessible, both state legislatures passed statutes in 1974 retroactively repealing their pledge not to use these moneys for increased mass transit expenditures. United States Trust Company, a holder of the affected bonds, sued to invalidate the repeal as an unconstitutional impairment of the obligation of contracts. The New Jersey courts ruled against the company on the ground that the repeal was a proper exercise of state police powers. The company sought U.S. Supreme Court review.

ARGUMENTS:

For the appellants, United States Trust et al.:

- The 1962 agreement constitutes a contract as that term is used in the Constitution. The state has totally abrogated that contract.
- The states' unilateral and retroactive cancellation of their pledge impaired the obligation of contracts to the detriment of the bondholders.
- The states' actions were not taken out of need, but out of a desire to alter the Port Authority's functions without assuming responsibility for the costs.
- Even if seen as an exercise of the police powers, the states' actions violate the contract clause.

For the appellee, state of New Jersey:

- All contracts, especially contracts made by the state, are subject to the state's police powers.
- Repeal of the agreement allows the states to respond to the growing need to combat pollution and to provide mass transportation.
- The appellants knew the agreement was subject to the states' police powers. They had no reason to assume that the agreement was immune from reasonable state regulations.

MR. JUSTICE BLACKMUN DELIVERED THE OPINION OF THE COURT.

At the time the Constitution was adopted, and for nearly a century thereafter, the Contract Clause was one of the few express limitations on state power. The many decisions of this Court involving the Contract Clause are evidence of its important place in our constitutional jurisprudence. Over the last century, however, the Fourteenth Amendment has assumed a far larger place in constitutional adjudication concerning the States. We feel that the present role of the Contract Clause is largely illuminated by two of this Court's decisions. In each, legislation was sustained despite a claim that it had impaired the obligations of contracts.

Home Building & Loan Assn. v. Blaisdell (1934) is regarded as the leading case in the modern era of Contract Clause interpretation. At issue was the Minnesota Mortgage Moratorium Law, enacted in 1933, during the depth of the Depression and when that State was under severe economic stress, and appeared to have no effective alternative. . . . A closely divided Court, in an opinion by Mr. Chief Justice Hughes, observed that "emergency may furnish the occasion for the exercise of power" and that the "constitutional question presented in the light of an emergency is whether the power possessed embraces the particular exercise of it in response to particular conditions." . . .

This Court's most recent Contract Clause decision is *El Paso v. Simmons* (1965). That case concerned a 1941 Texas statute that limited to a 5-year period the reinstatement rights of an interest-defaulting purchaser of land from the State. . . . This Court held that "it is not every modification of a contractual promise that impairs the obligation of contract under federal law." It observed that the State "has the 'sovereign right . . . to protect the . . . general welfare of the people'" and "'we must respect the "wide discretion on the part of the legislature in determining what is and what is not necessary.""" . . .

Both of these cases eschewed a rigid application of the Contract Clause to invalidate state legislation. Yet neither indicated that the Contract Clause was without meaning in modern constitutional jurisprudence, or that its limitation on state power was illusory. Whether or not the protection of contract rights comports with current views of wise public policy, the Contract Clause remains a part of our written Constitution. We therefore must attempt to apply that constitutional provision to the instant case with due respect for its purpose and the prior decisions of the Court. . . .

Although the Contract Clause appears literally to proscribe "any" impairment, this Court observed in *Blaisdell* that "the prohibition is not an absolute one and is not to be read with literal exactness like a mathematical formula." Thus, a finding that there has been a technical impairment is merely a preliminary step in resolving the more difficult question whether that impairment is permitted under the Constitution. In the instant case, as in *Blaisdell*, we must attempt to reconcile the strictures of the Contract Clause with the "essential attributes of sovereign power" necessarily reserved by the States to safeguard the welfare of their citizens.

The trial court concluded that repeal of the 1962 covenant was a valid exercise of New Jersey's police power because repeal served important public interests in mass transportation, energy conservation, and environmental protection. Yet the Contract Clause limits otherwise legitimate exercises of state legislative authority, and the existence of an important public interest is not always sufficient to overcome that limitation. "Undoubtedly, whatever is reserved of state power must be consistent with the fair intent of the constitutional limitation of that power." Moreover, the scope of the State's reserved power depends on the nature of the contractual relationship with which the challenged law conflicts.

The States must possess broad power to adopt general regulatory measures without being concerned that private contracts will be impaired, or even destroyed, as a result. Otherwise, one would be able to obtain immunity from state regulation by making private contractual arrangements. This principle is summarized in Mr. Justice Holmes' well-known dictum: "One whose rights, such as they are, are subject to state restriction, cannot remove them from the power of the State by making a contract about them." *Hudson Water Co. v. McCarter* (1908).

Yet private contracts are not subject to unlimited modification under the police power. The Court in *Blaisdell* recognized that laws intended to regulate existing contractual relationships must serve a legitimate public purpose. A State could not "adopt as its policy the repudiation of debts or the destruction of contracts or the denial of means to enforce them." Legislation adjusting the rights and responsibilities of contracting parties must be upon reasonable conditions and of a character appropriate to the public purpose justifying its adoption. As is customary in reviewing economic and social regulation, however, courts properly defer to legislative judgment as to the necessity and reasonableness of a particular measure.

When a State impairs the obligation of its own contract, the reserved-powers doctrine has a different basis. The initial inquiry concerns the ability of the State to enter into an agreement that limits its power to act in the future. As early as *Fletcher v. Peck* [1810], the Court considered the argument that "one legislature cannot abridge the powers of a succeeding legislature." It is often stated that "the legislature cannot bargain away the police power of a State." *Stone v. Mississippi* (1880). This doctrine requires a determination of the State's power to create irrevocable contract rights in the first place, rather than an inquiry into the purpose or reasonableness of the subsequent impairment. In short, the Contract Clause does not require a State to adhere to a contract that surrenders an essential attribute of its sovereignty. . . .

In applying this standard, however, complete deference to a legislative assessment of reasonableness and necessity is not appropriate because the State's self-interest is at stake. A governmental entity can always find a use for extra money, especially when taxes do not have to be raised. If a State could reduce its financial obligations whenever it wanted to spend the money for what it regarded as an important public purpose, the Contract Clause would provide no protection at all. . . .

Mass transportation, energy conservation, and environmental protection are goals that are important and of legitimate public concern. Appellees contend that these goals are so important that any harm to bondholders from repeal of the 1962 covenant is greatly outweighed by the public benefit. We do not accept this invitation to engage in a utilitarian comparison of public benefit and private loss. . . . [A] State cannot refuse to meet its legitimate financial obligations simply because it would prefer to spend the money to promote the public good rather than the private welfare of its creditors. We can only sustain the repeal of the 1962 covenant if that impairment was both reasonable and necessary to serve the admittedly important purposes claimed by the State.

The more specific justification offered for the repeal of the 1962 covenant was the States' plan for encouraging users of private automobiles to shift to public transportation. The States intended to discourage private automobile use by raising bridge and tunnel tolls and to use the extra revenue from those tolls to subsidize improved commuter railroad service. Appellees contend that repeal of the 1962 covenant was necessary to implement this plan because the new mass transit facilities could not possibly be self-supporting and the covenant's "permitted deficits" level had already been exceeded. We reject this justification because the repeal was neither necessary to achievement of the plan nor reasonable in light of the circumstances.

The determination of necessity can be considered on two levels. First, it cannot be said that total repeal of the covenant was essential; a less drastic modification would have permitted the contemplated plan without entirely removing the covenant's limitations on the use of Port Authority revenues and reserves to subsidize commuter railroads. Second, without modifying the covenant at all, the States could have adopted alternative means of achieving their twin goals of discouraging automobile use and improving mass transit. Appellees contend, however, that choosing among these alternatives is a matter for legislative discretion. But a State is not completely free to consider impairing the obligations of its own contract on a par with other policy alternatives. Similarly, a State is not free to impose a drastic impairment when an evident and more moderate course would serve its purposes equally well. . . .

. . . [T]he need for mass transportation in the New York metropolitan area was not a new development, and the likelihood that publicly owned commuter railroads would produce substantial deficits was well known. As early as 1922, over a half century ago, there were pressures to involve the Port Authority in mass transit. It was with full knowledge of these concerns that the 1962 covenant was adopted. Indeed, the covenant was specifically intended to protect the pledged revenues and reserves against the possibility that such concerns would lead the Port Authority into greater involvement in deficit mass transit.

During the 12-year period between adoption of the covenant and its repeal, public perception of the importance of mass transit undoubtedly grew because of increased general concern with environmental protection and energy conservation. But these concerns were not unknown in 1962, and the subsequent changes were of degree and not of kind. We cannot say that these changes caused the covenant to have a substantially different impact in 1974 than when it was adopted in 1962. And we cannot conclude that the repeal was reasonable in the light of changed circumstances.

We therefore hold that the Contract Clause of the United States Constitution prohibits the retroactive repeal of the 1962 covenant. The judgment of the Supreme Court of New Jersey is reversed.

MR. JUSTICE BRENNAN, with whom MR. JUSTICE WHITE and MR. JUSTICE MARSHALL join, dissenting.

Decisions of this Court for at least a century have construed the Contract Clause largely to be powerless in binding a State to contracts limiting the authority of successor legislatures to enact laws in furtherance of the health, safety, and similar collective interests of the polity. In short, those decisions established the principle that lawful exercises of a State's police powers stand paramount to private rights held under contract. Today's decision, in invalidating the New Jersey Legislature's 1974 repeal of its predecessor's 1962 covenant, rejects this previous understanding and remolds the Contract Clause into a potent instrument for overseeing important policy determinations of the state legislature. At the same time, by creating a constitutional safe haven for property rights embodied in a contract, the decision substantially distorts modern constitutional jurisprudence governing regulation of private economic interests. I might understand, though I do not accept, this revival of the Contract Clause were it in accordance with some coherent and constructive view of public policy. But elevation of the Clause to the status of regulator of the municipal bond market at the heavy price of frustration of sound legislative policymaking is as demonstrably unwise as it is unnecessary. The justification for today's decision, therefore, remains a mystery to me, and I respectfully dissent.

The legislation challenged in *United States Trust* was passed for the general welfare of the people of New York and New Jersey and in large measure was a response to a national energy crisis. These factors seemed similar to the conditions that prompted the Court to approve the Minnesota Mortgage Moratorium Act. Therefore, many were surprised by the Court's resurrection of the contract clause, which sparked considerable interest in what the opinion meant for the future. Although the decision used the contract clause to invalidate state laws, the opinion was a moderate one, without the absolutist tones of the Marshall era. Did the Court's decision signal a change in policy or was it an aberration?

An argument can be made that *United States Trust* breathed new life into the contract clause—at least with respect to a limited class of contractual agreements. The Court drew a distinction between a state's passing legislation that affects private contracts and a state's taking action to abrogate contracts to which the state itself was a party. In the latter case, Blackmun's opinion called for a higher standard of judicial scrutiny: the Court will uphold laws that impair state contractual obligations only "if that impairment was both reasonable and necessary to serve the admittedly important purposes claimed by the State." The justices made it more difficult for states to defend the abrogation of contracts they had made, reducing the level of deference the Court had shown to state legislatures since *Home Building & Loan Assn. v. Blaisdell.*

How solid was this newly expressed support for the contract clause? After all, only seven justices participated in *United States Trust,* and the majority consisted of just four. Would the outcome have been different had the full Court voted? The justices provided some answers to these questions the very next year in *Allied Structural Steel Co. v. Spannaus.*

Allied Structural Steel Co. v. Spannaus

438 U.S. 234 (1978)
http://laws.findlaw.com/us/438/234.html
Oral arguments are available at https://www.oyez.org.
Vote: 5 (Burger, Powell, Rehnquist, Stevens, Stewart)
    3 (Brennan, Marshall, White)

OPINION OF THE COURT: Stewart
DISSENTING OPINION: Brennan
NOT PARTICIPATING: Blackmun

FACTS:

Although its principal place of business was Illinois, Allied Structural Steel Company maintained an office

with thirty employees in Minnesota. In 1963 the company adopted a general pension plan in which employees became vested after working the required number of years and reaching the specified age. Employees who quit or were terminated before meeting these requirements did not acquire any pension rights. The company, which made annual payments to a pension trust fund, was the sole contributor to the plan. The company retained a virtually unrestricted right to modify the plan or to terminate it at any time.

On April 9, 1974, Minnesota enacted the Private Pension Benefits Protection Act. Under the provisions of that law, a company that terminated a pension plan or closed down its Minnesota operations would be subject to a charge to the extent that its retirement funds did not ensure full pensions to all workers who worked for the company for ten or more years. During the summer of 1974, Allied began closing its Minnesota office and discharged a number of its employees. Nine of the terminated workers had been with the company longer than ten years, but they did not qualify for pensions under Allied's plan. The state invoked its benefits protection law and assessed Allied $185,000 for the employees' pensions. Claiming that the Minnesota law impaired the obligation of its pension contract with its employees, Allied filed suit in federal district court against Warren Spannaus, the state attorney general. The court ruled in favor of the state, and Allied continued its attack on the statute in the U.S. Supreme Court.

ARGUMENTS:

For the appellant, Allied Structural Steel Co.:

- The Minnesota law violates the contract clause because it changes the provisions of Allied's contracts that control the vesting and funding of its pension plans.
- The impairment here is much greater than in *Home Building & Loan Assn. v. Blaisdell.* The law upheld in that case merely delayed the contractual obligations. Here the law imposes vast retroactive liabilities on the employer and confers on employees benefits far beyond those they had a right to expect under their contracts.
- Unlike *Blaisdell,* here the state has entirely rewritten the pension contracts.
- The Minnesota pension law is not a reasonable and necessary response to an economic crisis as was the case in *Blaisdell.*

For the appellees, Warren Spannaus,
Minnesota attorney general, et al.:

- Consistent with modern interpretations of the contract clause, the pension law is directed to legitimate public purposes and is aimed at achieving those purposes in a necessary and reasonable manner.
- Unlike the law invalidated in *United States Trust v. New Jersey,* the pension law is a broad measure regulating a wide range of private agreements.
- The retroactive effect of the pension law is permissible under modern contract clause jurisprudence.

MR. JUSTICE STEWART DELIVERED THE OPINION OF THE COURT.

There can be no question of the impact of the Minnesota Private Pension Benefits Protection Act upon the company's contractual relationships with its employees. The Act substantially altered those relationships by superimposing pension obligations upon the company conspicuously beyond those that it had voluntarily agreed to undertake. But it does not inexorably follow that the Act, as applied to the company, violates the Contract Clause of the Constitution.

The language of the Contract Clause appears unambiguously absolute: "No State shall . . . pass any . . . Law impairing the Obligation of Contracts." U.S. Const., Art. I, §10. The Clause is not, however, the Draconian provision that its words might seem to imply. As the Court has recognized, "literalism in the construction of the contract clause . . . would make it destructive of the public interest by depriving the State of its prerogative of self-protection."

Although it was perhaps the strongest single constitutional check on state legislation during our early years as a Nation, the Contract Clause receded into comparative desuetude with the adoption of the Fourteenth Amendment, and particularly with the development of the large body of jurisprudence under the Due Process Clause of that Amendment in modern constitutional history. Nonetheless, the Contract Clause remains part of the Constitution. It is not a dead letter. . . .

If the Contract Clause is to retain any meaning at all . . . it must be understood to impose *some* limits upon the power of a State to abridge existing contractual relationships, even in the exercise of its otherwise legitimate police power. The existence and nature of those limits were clearly indicated in a series of cases in this Court arising from the efforts of the States to deal with the unprecedented emergencies brought on by the severe economic depression of the early 1930's.

In *Home Building & Loan Assn. v. Blaisdell* [1934] the Court upheld against a Contract Clause attack a mortgage moratorium law that Minnesota had enacted to provide relief for homeowners threatened with foreclosure. Although the legislation conflicted directly with lenders' contractual foreclosure rights, the Court there acknowledged that, despite the Contract Clause, the States retain residual authority to enact laws "to safeguard the vital interests of [their] people." In upholding the state mortgage moratorium law, the Court found five factors significant. First, the state legislature had declared in the Act itself that an emergency need for the protection of homeowners existed. Second, the state law was enacted to protect a basic societal interest, not a favored group. Third, the relief was appropriately tailored to the emergency that it was designed to meet. Fourth, the imposed conditions were reasonable. And, finally, the legislation was limited to the duration of the emergency.

The *Blaisdell* opinion thus clearly implied that if the Minnesota moratorium legislation had not possessed the characteristics attributed to it by the Court, it would have been invalid under the Contract Clause of the Constitution. . . .

In applying these principles to the present case, the first inquiry must be whether the state law has, in fact, operated as a substantial impairment of a contractual relationship. The severity of the impairment measures the height of the hurdle the state legislation must clear. Minimal alteration of contractual obligations may end the inquiry at its first stage. Severe impairment, on the other hand, will push the inquiry to a careful examination of the nature and purpose of the state legislation.

The severity of an impairment of contractual obligations can be measured by the factors that reflect the high value the Framers placed on the protection of private contracts. Contracts enable individuals to order their personal and business affairs according to their particular needs and interests. Once arranged, those rights and obligations are binding under the law, and the parties are entitled to rely on them.

Here, the company's contracts of employment with its employees included as a fringe benefit or additional form of compensation, the pension plan. The company's maximum obligation was to set aside each year an amount based on the plan's requirements for vesting. The plan satisfied the current federal income tax code and was subject to no other legislative requirements. And, of course, the company was free to amend or terminate the pension plan at any time. The company thus had no reason to anticipate that its employees' pension rights could become vested except in accordance with the terms of the plan. It relied heavily, and reasonably, on this legitimate contractual expectation in calculating its annual contributions to the pension fund.

The effect of Minnesota's Private Pension Benefits Protection Act on this contractual obligation was severe. The company was required in 1974 to have made its contributions throughout the pre-1974 life of its plan as if employees' pension rights had vested after 10 years, instead of vesting in accord with the terms of the plan. Thus a basic term of the pension contract—one on which the company had relied for 10 years—was substantially modified. The result was that, although the company's past contributions were adequate when made, they were not adequate when computed under the 10-year statutory vesting requirement. The Act thus forced a current recalculation of the past 10 years' contributions based on the new, unanticipated 10-year vesting requirement.

Not only did the state law thus retroactively modify the compensation that the company had agreed to pay its employees from 1963 to 1974, but also it did so by changing the company's obligations in an area where the element of reliance was vital—the funding of a pension plan. . . .

Moreover, the retroactive state-imposed vesting requirement was applied only to those employers who terminated their pension plans or who, like the company, closed their Minnesota offices. The company was thus forced to make all the retroactive changes in its contractual obligations at one time. By simply proceeding to close its office in Minnesota, a move that had been planned before the passage of the Act, the company was assessed an immediate pension funding charge of approximately $185,000.

Thus, the statute in question here nullifies express terms of the company's contractual obligations and imposes a completely unexpected liability in potentially disabling amounts. . . . Yet there is no showing in the record before us that this severe disruption of contractual expectations was necessary to meet an important general social problem. The presumption favoring "legislative judgment as to the necessity and reasonableness of a particular measure" simply cannot stand in this case. . . .

Moreover, in at least one other important respect the Act does not resemble the mortgage moratorium legislation whose constitutionality was upheld in the *Blaisdell* case. This legislation, imposing a sudden, totally unanticipated, and substantial retroactive obligation upon the company to its employees, was not enacted to deal with a

situation remotely approaching the broad and desperate emergency economic conditions of the early 1930's—conditions of which the Court in *Blaisdell* took judicial notice.

Entering a field it had never before sought to regulate, the Minnesota Legislature grossly distorted the company's existing contractual relationships with its employees by superimposing retroactive obligations upon the company substantially beyond the terms of its employment contracts. And that burden was imposed upon the company only because it closed its office in the State.

This Minnesota law simply does not possess the attributes of those state laws that in the past have survived challenge under the Contract Clause of the Constitution. The law was not even purportedly enacted to deal with a broad, generalized economic or social problem. It did not operate in an area already subject to state regulation at the time the company's contractual obligations were originally undertaken, but invaded an area never before subject to regulation by the State. It did not effect simply a temporary alteration of the contractual relationships of those within its coverage, but worked a severe, permanent, and immediate change in those relationships—irrevocably and retroactively. And its narrow aim was leveled, not at every Minnesota employer, not even at every Minnesota employer who left the State, but only at those who had in the past been sufficiently enlightened as voluntarily to agree to establish pension plans for their employees.

. . . [I]f the Contract Clause means anything at all, it means that Minnesota could not constitutionally do what it tried to do to the company in this case.

The judgment of the District Court is reversed.

MR. JUSTICE BRENNAN, with whom MR. JUSTICE WHITE and MR. JUSTICE MARSHALL join, dissenting.

In cases involving state legislation affecting private contracts, this Court's decisions over the past half century, consistently with both the constitutional text and its original understanding, have interpreted the Contract Clause as prohibiting state legislative Acts which, "[w]ith studied indifference to the interests of the [contracting party] or to his appropriate protection," effectively diminished or nullified the obligation due him under the terms of a contract. But the Contract Clause has not, during this period, been applied to state legislation that, while creating new duties, in nowise diminished the efficacy of any contractual obligation owed the constitutional claimant. . . .

Today's decision greatly expands the reach of the Clause. The Minnesota Private Pension Benefits Protection Act (Act) does not abrogate or dilute any obligation due a party to a private contract; rather, like all positive social legislation, the Act imposes new, additional obligations on a particular class of persons. . . .

The Act does not relieve either the employer or his employees of any existing contract obligation. Rather, the Act simply creates an additional, supplemental duty of the employer, no different in kind from myriad duties created by a wide variety of legislative measures which defeat settled expectations but which have nonetheless been sustained by this Court. For this reason, the Minnesota Act, in my view, does not implicate the Contract Clause in any way. The basic fallacy of today's decision is its mistaken view that the Contract Clause protects all contract-based expectations, including that of an employer that his obligations to his employees will not be legislatively enlarged beyond those explicitly provided in his pension plan. . . .

. . . [I]n my view, the Contract Clause has no applicability whatsoever to the Act. . . . I would affirm the judgment of the District Court.

Justice Potter Stewart's opinion provides insight into the meaning of the contract clause in the modern era. First, although the Court invalidated the charges assessed against Allied Steel, the Court did not restore the contract clause to the prominence it had during the Marshall era. Second, the contract clause places some limits on the exercise of the state's police powers, but it does not obliterate those powers. Third, the clause applies to laws that either increase or decrease the duties of a party to a contract. Fourth, the clause is not limited to creditor–debtor contracts. Fifth, in applying the clause, the Court will first necessarily examine the extent of the impairment of contractual obligations, and "the severity of the impairment measures the height of the hurdle the state legislation must clear." If there has been substantial impairment of a contractual relationship, the Court will consider with care the nature and purpose of the legislation. In short, the majority assumed a position that balanced the importance of contractual relationships against the need of the state to exercise its police powers for the public welfare. Such a position neither returns the contract clause to the preferred position it once enjoyed nor substantially strips it of its meaning.

In the years following *Allied Structural Steel* the Court has continued to take a moderate approach. In Stewart's terms, it has not interpreted the contract clause as a "dead letter," but it has also not applied the

clause in an absolute, "Draconian," fashion. The justices have generally expressed a sensitivity to the need of the states to use their police powers to combat social problems. In *Energy Reserves Group, Inc. v. Kansas Power and Light Company* (1983) the justices unanimously upheld a Kansas act that dictated an energy pricing system in conflict with existing contracts. The Court held that the contract clause prohibits only state actions that "substantially impair the contractual arrangement." And even such a substantial impairment can be justified if there is a significant and legitimate public purpose behind the regulation, such as remedying a broad and general social or economic problem.[5] In 1987 the justices upheld a Pennsylvania law that required coal mine operators to leave 50 percent of the coal in the ground beneath certain structures to provide surface support.[6] This provision was at odds with contracts between the mining companies and the landowners that allowed the companies to extract a much higher proportion of the coal. The justices, however, upheld the right of the state, pursuant to its police powers, to impose such a regulation, explaining that the contract clause "is not to be read literally."

Decisions such as these have signaled potential litigants that a successful challenge of a state law on contract clause grounds, although more likely today than in the years immediately following the New Deal, remains a difficult task. As a consequence, parties wishing to defend private property rights against state regulation have turned to other constitutional provisions for possible relief. Frequently, the Fourteenth Amendment's due process clause and the Fifth Amendment's takings clause have served as vehicles for such challenges. These subjects are addressed in chapters 10 and 11.

ANNOTATED READINGS

A number of important works have examined the historical evolution of the contract clause and how it contributes to the general protection of property rights. Among such volumes is Bruce Ackerman, *Private Property and the Constitution* (New Haven, CT: Yale University Press, 1977); James W. Ely, *Property*

---

5. See also *Exxon Corporation v. Eagerton* (1983).

6. *Keystone Bituminous Coal Association v. DeBenedictis* (1987).

Rights in American History (New York: Garland, 1997); Kermit L. Hall, ed., *Law, Economy, and the Power of Contract: Major Historical Interpretations* (New York: Garland, 1987); Morton J. Horowitz, *The Transformation of American Law, 1780–1860* (Cambridge, MA: Harvard University Press, 1977); Warren B. Hunting, *The Obligation of Contracts Clause of the United States Constitution* (Baltimore: Johns Hopkins University Press, 1919); Harry N. Scheiber, ed., *The State and Freedom of Contract* (Stanford, CA: Stanford University Press, 1999); and Benjamin F. Wright, *The Contract Clause of the Constitution* (Cambridge, MA: Harvard University Press, 1938).

Other works have focused on specific landmark rulings by the U.S. Supreme Court or the contributions to the Court's contract clause jurisprudence by specific justices. Examples are Morgan D. Dowd, "Justice Story, the Supreme Court, and the Obligation of Contract," *Case Western Reserve Law Review* 19 (1968): 493–527; John A. Fliter and Derek S. Hoff, *Fighting Foreclosure: The Blaisdell Case, the Contract Clause, and the Great Depression* (Lawrence: University Press of Kansas, 2012); Horace H. Hagin, "*Fletcher vs. Peck,*" *Georgetown Law Journal* 16 (November 1927): 1–40; Nathan Isaacs, "John Marshall on Contracts: A Study in Early American Juristic Theory," *Virginia Law Review* 7 (March 1921): 413–428; Stanley I. Kutler, *Privilege and Creative Destruction: The Charles River Bridge Case* (Philadelphia: J. B. Lippincott, 1971); C. Peter Magrath, *Yazoo: Law and Politics in the New Republic* (Providence, RI: Brown University Press, 1966); and Francis N. Stites, *Private Interest and Public Gain: The Dartmouth College Case, 1819* (Amherst: University of Massachusetts Press, 1972).

10 Economic Substantive Due Process

S UPPOSE that federal and state agents receive a tip that the owners of a factory are violating the federal law that prohibits the employment of children younger than fourteen. Without stopping to obtain a search warrant, the agents enter the factory and observe that underage employees are indeed working there. The agents arrest the factory owners. Based on evidence collected by the investigators, a court convicts the owners of violating child labor laws and imposes a heavy fine. But the owners challenge their conviction on two similarly named, but distinct, grounds—procedural due process and substantive due process.

Citing the first ground, the factory owners allege that the procedure the agents used to obtain evidence against them—entering the factory without a warrant—violated guarantees in the Constitution, including sections of the Fifth and Fourteenth Amendments that prohibit government from depriving persons of "life, liberty, or property, without due process of law."[1] For many, the term *due process* is synonymous with procedural fairness. The American system of justice is based on the idea that even people guilty of violating the law deserve fair treatment. This particular characterization of due process, known as *procedural due process*, is the most traditional and widely accepted use of the term. The government must proceed in fair ways if it is to convict an individual of a crime or otherwise deprive that person of life, liberty, or property. Evidence must be gathered according to prescribed procedures, and trials must take place following established rules of procedural fairness. If the government had proceeded fairly against the factory owners, their conviction would have been justified.

What is the second ground on which the factory owners base their appeal? None other than due process of law. Under this approach, due process means more than just adhering to fair procedures. Instead, the due process clauses are seen as guaranteeing certain substantive rights. This theory, known as *substantive due process*, holds that the Constitution is violated when government unreasonably or arbitrarily denies rights that are inherent in the freedom of the individual. In our example, the factory owners might argue that the law prohibiting child labor violates due process guarantees by unreasonably infringing on their freedom to do business and arbitrarily abridging their right to enter into employment agreements with willing workers. In their view, the federal law cannot stand because it is inherently not just and not fair, and the Constitution requires that the substance of the law must be just and must not unfairly deprive persons of their life, liberty, or property.

---

1. The Fifth Amendment, ratified in 1791, prohibits the federal government from depriving anyone of life, liberty, or property without due process of law. The Fourteenth Amendment, adopted in 1868, extends the same prohibition to the states.

In this chapter we examine the development and decline of the substantive due process doctrine. We shall see that in the modern era the Supreme Court has made it exceedingly difficult to challenge laws governing economic relationships on substantive due process grounds. But for approximately forty years, from the 1890s through the 1930s, the Court read due process in substantive terms and used the principle to strike down many laws that allegedly infringed on economic rights.

If economic substantive due process is now a generally discredited doctrine, why do we devote an entire chapter to it? There are several reasons. First, its rise and fall from the Court's grace constitutes an intriguing part of legal history. The adoption of substantive due process came about gradually and resulted from the push and pull of the legal and political environment of the day.

Second, looking at substantive due process provides us with an opportunity to revisit the concept of judicial activism. During the latter half of the twentieth century, that term was most often associated with liberalism, with Courts that overturned restrictive government laws and practices, such as those requiring racial segregation of public facilities or prohibiting seditious speech. But the justices from the 1890s to the 1930s actively used the substantive due process doctrine to impose their conservative ideology on American society. The Court overturned many laws

that legislatures passed to regulate businesses for the common good. As a consequence, substantive due process became associated with the Court's strong support of business interests.

Third, the topic of substantive due process offers a way to reexamine the cycles of history we have already discussed. As depicted in table 10–1, substantive due process was an additional weapon in the Court's laissez-faire arsenal. While it was using delegation of power doctrines (chapter 5), the Tenth Amendment (chapter 6), the commerce clause (chapter 7), and taxing and spending provisions (chapter 8) to strike down federal regulations of business, the Court also invoked substantive due process to rule against similar legislation passed by the states. This use was particularly ironic because at the time the Court was espousing notions of dual federalism, striking down federal regulations on the grounds they encroached on powers reserved to the states. In other words, the Court found ways to strike down all sorts of economic regulation, even though, in so doing, it often took contradictory stances. Therefore, substantive due process provides a way to tie together much of what we have already covered in this book.

Finally, the doctrine of substantive due process retains some relevance today. We continue to observe decisions in which the Court finds specific rights to be protected even though the Constitution makes no explicit reference to those rights. Instead, the justices conclude that certain personal liberties are embedded in

---

TABLE 10-1   The Legal Tools of the Laissez-Faire Courts, 1890s to 1930s: Some Examples

	1890–1899	1900–1909	1910–1919	1920–1929	1930–1939
Used to Strike State Laws					
Substantive due process	*Allgeyer v. Louisiana* (1897)	*Lochner v. New York* (1905)			*Morehead v. Tipaldo* (1936)
Used to Strike Federal Laws					
Delegation of powers					*Panama Refining Co. v. Ryan* (1935) *Schechter Poultry v. United States* (1935)
Commerce clause			*Hammer v. Dagenhart* (1918)		*Panama Refining Co. v. Ryan* (1935) *Schechter Poultry v. United States* (1935) *Carter v. Carter Coal* (1936)
Taxing and spending				*Bailey v. Drexel Furniture* (1922)	*United States v. Butler* (1936)
Tenth Amendment			*Hammer v. Dagenhart* (1918)		

the concept of due process of law. One such right is the constitutionally guaranteed right to privacy, although the document makes no explicit mention of that right. Rather, the justices have concluded that when government arbitrarily violates a person's privacy it deprives that person of liberty without due process of law. Contemporary justices also have extended the reach of due process to protect against excessive jury awards and to preserve the integrity of the courts by prohibiting judges from ruling on cases in which they may have a conflict of interest.

We consider the contemporary uses of substantive due process in more detail at the end of this chapter, but first we review the doctrine's development chronologically—how it came to be, why the Court embraced it, and what led to its decline.

DEVELOPMENT OF SUBSTANTIVE DUE PROCESS

In general terms, prior to the adoption of the Fourteenth Amendment, judges interpreted due process guarantees contained in the Fifth Amendment and in state constitutions as procedural in intent and nature. As historian Kermit L. Hall observed, "Before the Civil War [due process] had essentially one meaning"—that people were "entitled" to fair and orderly proceedings, particularly in criminal proceedings.[2]

There were some exceptions. Writing in *Scott v. Sandford (see chapter 6),* Chief Justice Roger Taney invoked the specter of due process to strike government interference in "property rights":

An act of Congress which deprives a citizen of the United States of his liberty or property [a slave], merely because he came himself or brought his property into a particular Territory . . . could hardly be dignified with the name of due process of law.

Around the same time, a New York court in *Wynehamer v. People* (1856) invoked a substantive interpretation of the state's due process requirement in striking down an alcohol prohibition law. It asserted that due process guarantees "prohibit, regardless of the

matter of procedure, a certain kind or degree of exertion of legislative power altogether" and that the "substantive content of legislation" is covered, not simply the protection of the "mode of procedure."

But decisions such as *Wynehamer* represented the exception, not the rule. Neither state court judges interpreting their due process clauses nor their federal court counterparts treating the Fifth Amendment read them to possess a substantive right and, therefore, a bar on interventionist government legislation. Rather, they viewed them through a procedural lens, and for good reason: it was simply unclear whether the due process clauses were meant to have substance.

The Fourteenth Amendment's Due Process Clause: Initial Interpretation

The social ills that flowed from the nation's post–Civil War transition from an agrarian to an industrial economy prompted state legislatures to consider new regulations on commerce, but business interests feared that increased regulation would inevitably lead to a reduction in corporate profits. With the decline of the contract clause as a defense against state interference with business, it is not surprising that corporate interests looked to other parts of the Constitution for protection. They saw the due process clause of the Fourteenth Amendment as particularly promising.

The *Slaughterhouse Cases* (1873) reveal that the Supreme Court initially did not agree with this pro-business interpretation of the Fourteenth Amendment. The majority gave rather short shrift to the due process argument, devoting most of its opinion to other issues. However, some of the dissenters found considerable merit in what the business community proposed. As you read this decision, pay careful attention to Justice Bradley's dissent, as it sets the tone for many majority opinions that follow.

The Slaughterhouse Cases (Butchers' Benevolent Association v. Crescent City Livestock Landing & Slaughter House Company)

83 U.S. (16 Wall.) 36 (1873)
http://laws.findlaw.com/us/83/36.html
Vote: 5 (Clifford, Davis, Hunt, Miller, Strong)
　　　4 (Bradley, Chase, Field, Swayne)

OPINION OF THE COURT: *Miller*

DISSENTING OPINIONS: *Bradley, Field, Swayne*

------

2. Kermit L. Hall, *The Magic Mirror* (New York: Oxford University Press, 1989), 232.

FACTS:

After the Civil War, the United States experienced a great increase in industrialization accompanied by economic diversification that touched the entire country. Along with the benefits of economic and industrial expansion came some negative side effects. In Louisiana the state legislature claimed that the Mississippi River had become polluted because New Orleans butchers dumped discarded animal parts and other garbage into it. To remedy this problem (or, as some have suggested, to use it as an excuse to create a monopolistic enterprise), the legislature created the Crescent City Livestock Landing & Slaughter House Company to receive and slaughter all city livestock for twenty-five years.

Because butchers were forced to use the company facilities and to pay top dollar for the privilege, they formed their own organization, the Butchers' Benevolent Association, and hired an attorney, former U.S. Supreme Court justice John A. Campbell, to sue the corporation and the state. In his arguments, Campbell sought to apply the Thirteenth and Fourteenth Amendments to the butchers' cause.

ARGUMENTS:

For the plaintiffs in error, the Butchers' Benevolent Association:

- The rights included in the Thirteenth and Fourteenth Amendments apply to all Americans.
- Americans have the freedom to engage in any useful business or occupation and a right to the income that flows from their efforts.
- By forcing the butchers to use the state-created slaughterhouse monopoly, Louisiana violates the Thirteenth Amendment's prohibition against involuntary servitude.
- The state's actions regulate the butchers well beyond what is customary for that occupation, denying them the right to pursue a traditional and beneficial trade. This, contrary to the Fourteenth Amendment, deprives the butchers of their privileges and immunities as U.S. citizens, denies them their property without due process of law, and fails to accord them equal protection of the law.
- No condition of public health necessitated the creation of the monopoly.

For the defendant in error, state of Louisiana:

- The law does not deny butchers the right to practice their profession. It only requires them to have their livestock slaughtered at the Crescent City slaughterhouse facilities.
- The first section of the Fourteenth Amendment has no meaning except for persons of African descent. The privileges and immunities clause applies only to political privileges, such as the right to vote or hold office.
- The police power extends to all subjects within the state's territorial boundaries. That power has never been conceded to the federal government.
- The police power clearly applies to the elimination of unhealthy or infectious articles or activities.

MR. JUSTICE MILLER, NOW, APRIL 14TH, 1873, DELIVERED THE OPINION OF THE COURT.

This court is . . . called upon for the first time to give construction to [the Thirteenth, Fourteenth, and Fifteenth Amendments]. . . .

We do not conceal from ourselves the great responsibility which this duty devolves upon us. No questions so far reaching and pervading in their consequences, so profoundly interesting to the people of this country, and so important in their bearing upon the relations of the United States and of the several states to each other, and to the citizens of the states, and of the United States, have been before this court during the official life of any of its present members. . . .

The most cursory glance at these articles discloses a unity of purpose, when taken in connection with the history of the times, which cannot fail to have an important bearing on any question of doubt concerning their true meaning. . . . Nor can such doubts, when any reasonably exist, be safely and rationally solved without a reference to that history; for in it is found the occasion and the necessity for recurring again to the great source of power in this country, the people of the states, for additional guaranties of human rights; additional powers to the Federal government; additional restraints upon those of the states. Fortunately that history is fresh within the memory of us all, and its leading features, as they bear upon the matter before us, free from doubt.

The institution of African slavery, as it existed in about half the states of the Union, and the contests pervading the public mind for many years, between those who desired its curtailment and ultimate extinction and those who desired additional safeguards for its security and perpetuation, culminated in the effort, on the part of most of the states in which slavery existed, to separate from the Federal government, and to resist its authority. This constituted the War of the Rebellion, and whatever auxiliary causes may have contributed to bring about this war, undoubtedly the overshadowing and efficient cause was African slavery. . . .

. . . [I]n the light of this recapitulation of events, almost too recent to be called history, but which are familiar to us all, and on the most casual examination of the language of these amendments, no one can fail to be impressed with the one pervading purpose found in them all, lying at the foundation of each, and without which none of them would have been even suggested; we mean the freedom of the slave race, the security and firm establishment of that freedom, and the protection of the newly made freeman and citizen from the oppressions of those who had formerly exercised unlimited dominion over him. It is true that only the fifteenth amendment, in terms, mentions the negro by speaking of his color and his slavery. But it is just as true that each of the other articles was addressed to the grievances of that race, and designed to remedy them as the fifteenth.

We do not say that no one else but the negro can share in this protection. Both the language and spirit of these articles are to have their fair and just weight in any question of construction. Undoubtedly while negro slavery alone was in the mind of the Congress which proposed the thirteenth article, it forbids any other kind of slavery, now or hereafter. . . . But what we do say, and what we wish to be understood, is that, in any fair and just construction of any section or phrase of these amendments, it is necessary to look to the purpose which we have said was the pervading spirit of them all, the evil which they were designed to remedy, and the process of continued addition to the Constitution, until that purpose was supposed to be accomplished as far as constitutional law can accomplish it. . . .

[The Fourteenth Amendment], which is the one mainly relied on by the plaintiffs in error, speaks only of privileges and immunities of citizens of the United States, and does not speak to those of citizens of the several States. The argument, however, in favor of the plaintiffs rests wholly on the assumption that the citizenship is the same, and the privileges and immunities guaranteed by the clause are the same.

The language is: "No state shall make or enforce any law which shall abridge the privileges or immunities of citizens of the United States." . . .

Fortunately, we are not without judicial construction of this clause of the Constitution. The first and the leading case on the subject is that of *Corfield v. Coryell*, decided by Mr. Justice Washington in the Circuit Court for the District of Pennsylvania in 1823.

"The inquiry," he says, "is, what are the privileges and immunities of citizens of the several states? We feel no hesitation in confining these expressions to those privileges and immunities which are fundamental; which belong of right to the citizens of all free governments, and which have at all times been enjoyed by citizens of the several states which compose this Union, from the time of their becoming free, independent, and sovereign. What these fundamental principles are, it would be more tedious than difficult to enumerate. They may all, however, be comprehended under the following general heads: protection by the government, with the right to acquire and possess property of every kind, and to pursue and obtain happiness and safety, subject, nevertheless, to such restraints as the government may prescribe for the general good of the whole." . . .

In the case of *Paul v. Virginia* [1869], the court, in expounding this clause of the Constitution, says that the privileges and immunities secured to citizens of each State in the several States by the provision in question are those privileges and immunities which are common to the citizens in the latter States under the constitution and laws by virtue of their being citizens. . . .

. . . [W]e may hold ourselves excused from defining the privileges and immunities of citizens of the United States which no State can abridge until some case involving those privileges may make it necessary to do so.

But lest it should be said that no such privileges and immunities are to be found if those we have been considering are excluded, we venture to suggest some which owe their existence to the Federal government, its national character, its Constitution, or its laws.

One of these is well described in the case of *Crandall v. Nevada* [1868]. It is said to be the right of the citizen of this great country, protected by implied guarantees of its Constitution, to come to the seat of government to assert any claim he may have upon that government, to transact any business he may have with it, to seek its protection, to share its offices, to engage in administering its functions. He has the right of free access to its seaports, through which operations of foreign commerce are conducted, to the sub-treasuries, land offices, and courts of justice in the several States. . . .

Another privilege of a citizen of the United States is to demand the care and protection of the Federal government over his life, liberty, and property when on the high seas or within the jurisdiction of a foreign government. Of this there can be no doubt, nor that the right depends upon his character as a citizen of the United States. The right to peaceably assemble and petition for redress of grievances, the privilege of the writ of habeas corpus, are rights of the citizen guaranteed by the Federal Constitution. The right to use the navigable waters of the United States, however they may penetrate the territory of the several States, all rights secured to our citizens by treaties with foreign nations, are dependent upon citizenship of the United States, and not citizenship of a State. One of these privileges is conferred by the very article under consideration. It is that a citizen of the United States can, of his own volition, become a citizen of any State of the Union by a bona fide residence therein, with the same rights as other citizens of that State. To these may be added the rights secured by the thirteenth and fifteenth articles of amendment, and by the other clause of the fourteenth, next to be considered.

But it is useless to pursue this branch of the inquiry, since we are of opinion that the rights claimed by these plaintiffs in error, if they have any existence, are not privileges and immunities of citizens of the United States within the meaning of the clause of the fourteenth amendment under consideration.

"All persons born or naturalized in the United States, and subject to the jurisdiction thereof, are citizens of the United States and of the state, wherein they reside. No state shall make or enforce any law which shall abridge the privileges or immunities of citizens of the United States, nor shall any state deprive any person of life, liberty or property without due process of law, nor deny to any person within its jurisdiction the equal protection of the laws."

The argument has not been much pressed in these cases that the defendant's charter deprives the plaintiffs of their property without due process of law, or that it denies to them the equal protection of the law. The first of these paragraphs has been in the Constitution since the adoption of the 5th Amendment, as a restraint upon the Federal power. It is also to be found in some form of expression in the constitutions of nearly all the states, as a restraint upon the power of the states. This law, then, has practically been

the same as it now is during the existence of the government, except so far as the present Amendment may place the restraining power over the states in this matter in the hands of the Federal government.

We are not without judicial interpretation, therefore, both state and national, of the meaning of this clause. And it is sufficient to say that under no construction of that provision that we have ever seen, or any that we deem admissible, can the restraint imposed by the state of Louisiana upon the exercise of their trade by the butchers of New Orleans be held to be a deprivation of property within the meaning of that provision.

"Nor shall any state deny to any person within its jurisdiction the equal protection of the laws."

In the light of the history of these amendments, and the pervading purpose of them, . . . it is not difficult to give a meaning to this clause. The existence of laws in the states where the newly emancipated negroes resided, which discriminated with gross injustice and hardship against them as a class, was the evil to be remedied by this clause, and by it such laws are forbidden.

If, however, the states did not conform their laws to its requirements, then by the 5th section of the article of amendment Congress was authorized to enforce it by suitable legislation. We doubt very much whether any action of a state not directed by way of discrimination against the negroes as a class, or on account of their race, will ever be held to come within the purview of this provision. It is so clearly a provision for that race and that emergency, that a strong case would be necessary for its application to any other. But as it is a state that is to be dealt with, and not alone the validity of its laws, we may safely leave that matter until Congress shall have exercised its power, or some case of state oppression, by denial of equal justice in its courts, shall have claimed a decision at our hands. We find no such case in the one before us, and we do not deem it necessary to go over the argument again, as it may have relation to this particular clause of the Amendment.

In the early history of the organization of the government, its statesmen seem to have divided on the line which should separate the powers of the national government from those of the state governments, and though this line has never been very well defined in public opinion, such a division has continued from that day to this.

The adoption of the first eleven amendments to the Constitution so soon after the original instrument was accepted shows a prevailing sense of danger at that time from the Federal power and it cannot be denied that such a jealousy continued to exist with many patriotic men until the breaking out of the late Civil War. It was then discovered that the true danger to the perpetuity of the Union was in the capacity of the state organizations to combine and concentrate all the powers of the state, and of contiguous states, for a determined resistance to the general government.

Unquestionably this has given great force to the argument, and added largely to the number of those who believe in the necessity of a strong national government.

But, however pervading this sentiment, and however it may have contributed to the adoption of the Amendments we have been considering, we do not see in those Amendments any purpose to destroy the main features of the general system. Under the pressure of all the excited feeling growing out of the war, our statesmen have still believed that the existence of the states with powers for domestic and local government, including the regulation of civil rights, the rights of person and of property, was essential to the perfect working of our complex form of government, though they have thought proper to impose additional limitations on the states, and to confer additional power on that of the nation.

But whatever fluctuations may be seen in the history of public opinion on this subject during the period of our national existence, we think it will be found that this court, so far as its functions required, has always held, with a steady and an even hand, the balance between state and Federal power, and we trust that such may continue to be the history of its relation to that subject so long as it shall have duties to perform which demand of it a construction of the Constitution, or of any of its parts.

The judgments of the Supreme Court of Louisiana in these cases are affirmed.

MR. JUSTICE FIELD, dissenting.

The question presented is . . . one of the gravest importance, not merely to the parties here, but to the whole country. It is nothing less than the question whether the recent Amendments to the Federal Constitution protect the citizens of the United States against the deprivation of their common rights by state legislation. In my judgment the 14th Amendment does afford such protection, and was so intended by the Congress which framed and the states which adopted it. . . .

The provisions of the Fourteenth Amendment, which is properly a supplement to the thirteenth, cover, in my judgment, the case before us, and inhibit any legislation which confers special and exclusive privileges like these under

consideration. The Amendment was adopted to obviate objections which had been raised and pressed with great force to the validity of the civil rights act, and to place the common rights of the American citizens under the protection of the National government. It first declares that "all persons born or naturalized in the United States, and subject to the jurisdiction thereof, are citizens of the United States and of the state wherein they reside." It then declares that "No state shall make or enforce any law which shall abridge the privileges or immunity of citizens of the United States, nor shall any state deprive any person of life, liberty or property, without due process of law, nor deny to any person within its jurisdiction the equal protection of the laws." . . .

The first clause of the fourteenth Amendment . . . removes it from the region of discussion and doubt. It recognizes in express terms, if it does not create, citizens of the United States, and it makes their citizenship dependent upon the place of their birth, or the fact of their adoption, and not upon the Constitution or laws of any state or the condition of their ancestry. A citizen of a state is now only a citizen of the United States residing in that state. The fundamental rights, privileges, and immunities which belong to him as a free man and a free citizen, now belong to him as a citizen of the United States, and are not dependent upon his citizenship of any state. The exercise of these rights and privileges, and the degree of enjoyment received from such exercise, are always more or less affected by the condition and the local institutions of the state, or city, or town where he resides. They are thus affected in a state by the wisdom of its laws, the ability of its officers, the efficiency of its magistrates, the education and morals of its people, and by many other considerations. This is a result which follows from the constitution of society, and can never be avoided, but in no other way can they be affected by the action of the state, or by the residence of the citizen therein. They do not derive their existence from its legislation, and cannot be destroyed by its power. . . .

. . . [G]rants of exclusive privileges, such as is made by the act in question, are opposed to the whole theory of free government, and it requires no aid from any bill of rights to render them void. That only is a free government, in the American sense of the term, under which the inalienable right of every citizen to pursue his happiness is unrestrained, except by just, equal, and impartial laws.

MR. JUSTICE BRADLEY, dissenting.

The [Fourteenth] Amendment . . . prohibits any state from depriving any person (citizen or otherwise) of life, liberty or property, without due process of law.

In my view, a law which prohibits a large class of citizens from adopting a lawful employment, or from following a lawful employment previously adopted, does deprive them of liberty as well as property, without due process of law. Their right of choice is a portion of their liberty; their occupation is their property. Such a law also deprives those citizens of the equal protection of the laws, contrary to the last clause of the section.

The constitutional question is distinctly raised in these cases; the constitutional right is expressly claimed; it was violated by state law, which was sustained by the state court, and we are called upon in a legitimate and proper way to afford redress. Our jurisdiction and our duty are plain and imperative.

It is futile to argue that none but persons of the African race are intended to be benefited by this Amendment. They may have been the primary cause of the Amendment, but its language is general, embracing all citizens, and I think it was purposely so expressed.

The mischief to be remedied was not merely slavery and its incidents and consequences; but that spirit of insubordination and disloyalty to the national government which had troubled the country for so many years in some of the states, and that intolerance of free speech and free discussion which often rendered life and property insecure, and led to much unequal legislation. The Amendment was an attempt to give voice to the strong national yearning for that time and that condition of things, in which American citizenship should be a sure guaranty of safety, and in which every citizen of the United States might stand erect in every portion of its soil, in the full enjoyment of every right and privilege belonging to a freeman, without fear of violence or molestation.

But great fears are expressed that this construction of the Amendment will lead to enactments by Congress interfering with the internal affairs of the states, and establishing therein civil and criminal codes of law for the government of the citizens, and thus abolishing the state governments in everything but name; or else, that it will lead the Federal courts to draw to their cognizance the supervision of state tribunals on every subject of judicial inquiry, on the plea of ascertaining whether the privileges and immunities of citizens have not been abridged.

In my judgment no such practical inconveniences would arise. Very little, if any, legislation on the part of Congress would be required to carry the Amendment into effect. Like the prohibition against passing a law impairing the obligation of a contract, it would execute itself. The point would be regularly raised in a suit at law, and settled by final reference to the Federal Court. As the privileges and immunities protected are only those fundamental ones which belong to every citizen, they would soon become so far defined as to cause but a slight accumulation of business in the Federal Courts. Besides, the recognized existence of the law would prevent its frequent violation. But even if the business of the national courts should be increased, Congress could easily supply the remedy by increasing their number and efficiency. The great question is: what is the true construction of the Amendment? When once we find that, we shall find the means of giving it effect. The argument from inconvenience ought not to have a very controlling influence in questions of this sort. The national will and national interest are of far greater importance.

In my opinion the judgment of the Supreme Court of Louisiana ought to be reversed.

The *Slaughterhouse* opinions are noteworthy for several reasons. First, it was ironic that the first major case asking the Court to interpret the Fourteenth Amendment was brought by whites, not African Americans. This irony did not escape Justice Samuel Miller, who relied on history to stress the true purpose of the amendment—to protect the former slaves and to refute Campbell's basic position. Next, he methodically refuted the constitutional arguments offered by the butchers. Miller spent most of his energy on the primary claim of privileges and immunities (truly emasculating the clause), but he also flatly rejected the due process clause claim.[3] "Under no construction of that provision that we have ever seen, or any that we deem admissible," Miller wrote, "can the restraint imposed by the state of Louisiana upon the exercise of their trade by the butchers of New Orleans be held to be a deprivation of property within the meaning of that provision." Why did Miller take such a hard-line position? In large measure, he

---

3. The Court's complete rejection of the privileges and immunities argument in *The Slaughterhouse Cases* rendered it almost meaningless. Only of late have the courts begun to breathe new relevance into the clause. The Supreme Court relied on a privileges and immunities rationale to strike down the application of excessively long residency requirements before newcomers became eligible for state welfare benefits (see *Saenz v. Roe,* 1999). The Court viewed these requirements as unreasonable restrictions on the freedom of interstate travel, a right the justices found to be protected by the privileges and immunities clause.

did so because he did not want to see the Court become a "superlegislature," a censor on what states could and could not do.

The Beginning of Substantive Due Process: The Court Opens a Window

Miller's opinion in *Slaughterhouse* and Bradley's and Field's dissents are clear statements of the justices' initial positions on the substantive due process question. Indeed, the Miller and Bradley-Field opinions are considered to represent the epitome of opposing views on the subject. It was Miller's view, however, that, for the moment, carried the day—there was no substance in due process. Given the terse language of his opinion, we might suspect that it closed the book on the subject forever. But that was not the case. Miller observed just five years later,

It is not a little remarkable, that while [due process] has been in the Constitution . . . as a restraint upon the authority of the Federal government, for nearly a century . . . its powers ha[d] rarely been invoked in the judicial forum or the more enlarged theatre of public discussion. But while it has been a part of the Constitution, as a restraint upon the power of the States, only a very few years, the docket of this court is crowded with cases in which we are asked to hold that State courts and State legislatures have deprived their own citizens of life, liberty, or property without due process of law. There is here abundant evidence that there exists some strange misconception of the scope of this provision as found in the fourteenth amendment.[4]

Why was it necessary for Miller to write this? Had not *Slaughterhouse* eradicated the notion of the Fourteenth Amendment's due process clause as a prohibition of state economic regulation?

It had, but that did not prevent attorneys, representing desperate business interests, from continuing to make substantive due process arguments. From the lawyers' perspective, the current environment held promise for the eventual adoption of such arguments, and they advanced several theories that echoed Bradley's dissenting position in *Slaughterhouse*. One was expressed in Thomas M. Cooley's influential *Constitutional Limitations*, first published in 1868, which singled out the word *liberty* within the due

process clause as an important constitutional right. The protection of this right, in Cooley's eyes, required a substantive reading of the Fourteenth Amendment, which, in turn, would serve as a mechanism for protecting property rights and for restricting government regulation. Cooley's theory was specific, but Herbert Spencer offered a more general view. Called social Darwinism, it treated social evolution in the same terms that Charles Darwin used to explain biological evolution: if government simply maintained order and protected property rights and otherwise left people alone, the "fittest" would survive and succeed; if government attempted to intrude in other ways, then those other than the "fittest" also would survive, which would have a detrimental effect on society in the long term. This proposition had a natural compatibility with laissez-faire economic theories: if government leaves business alone, the best will prosper. Interpreting the Fifth and Fourteenth Amendments in substantive due process terms would prohibit a great deal of government interference with business activity.

But perhaps the most important factor contributing to the vitality of substantive due process was the Court itself. Social Darwinism may have influenced some scholars, the social elite, and business, but most Americans did not buy its tenets. If they had, states would not have kept on trying to regulate businesses, as the public would have demanded policies of noninterference. But they did continue. To a large extent, the crowded docket to which Miller referred was the Court's own doing.

An important, and certainly vivid, example of how the Court encouraged substantive due process arguments came in *Munn v. Illinois*. This decision cut both ways: the Court upheld the state's regulation but provided enough of a loophole for clever attorneys to exploit later. What was that loophole? One way to answer this question is to reconsider Miller's opinion in *Slaughterhouse* as you read *Munn*. Do you spot any differences?

Munn v. Illinois

94 U.S. 113 (1877)

http://laws.findlaw.com/us/94/113.html

Vote: 7 (Bradley, Clifford, Davis, Hunt, Miller, Swayne, Waite)
   2 (Field, Strong)

OPINION OF THE COURT: *Waite*

DISSENTING OPINION: *Field*

---

4. *Davidson v. New Orleans* (1878).

In the late nineteenth century, grain elevators, used to store grain until it was sold, were a common sight on the Chicago River. Ira Munn and George Scott's grain elevators (at right) were among the most successful, until Munn's corrupt business practices brought the industry under government scrutiny.

FACTS:

The rise of industrialization affected much of the nation, but its impact on the city of Chicago was monumental. Because of its status as an important trading post, particularly for the grain market, Chicago was becoming the "New York of the West."[5] Grain produced by farmers in the Midwest flowed into Chicago to be shipped to merchants throughout the United States. As a result, grain storage developed as a lucrative industry in Chicago. Typically, until grain was sold and shipped, companies stored it in warehouses that looked like huge skyscrapers. These warehouses were called grain elevators because of the way the grain was mechanically loaded into them by systems of dump baskets fastened to conveyor belts.

A dozen or more grain storage companies sprang up in Chicago. Among the most successful was Munn &

Scott, co-owned by Ira Munn and George Scott. They started with one warehouse with a capacity of 8,000 bushels of grain, and within a few short years they were overseeing an enterprise with four elevators and a storage capacity of 2,700,000 bushels. They were, in short, very successful entrepreneurs.

Despite their success, Munn and Scott (along with many others) engaged in fraudulent business practices. They charged exorbitantly high fees, mixed inferior grain with superior grain, and engaged in price-fixing with other companies. As these abuses became more obvious, farmers and merchants pleaded with city officials to regulate the industry. After several ineffective attempts by a local board to do so, the state—under continued pressure from farmers' organizations, known as the Granger movement—in 1871 enacted a law that included provisions establishing boards to regulate the maximum rates grain elevators could charge, among other aspects of the business. The state justified the law as compatible with its constitution,

---

5. We adapt this discussion largely from C. Peter Magrath's "The Case of the Unscrupulous Warehouseman," in Garraty, *Quarrels That Have Shaped the Constitution.*

which specified that public warehouses were subject to regulation. The state of Illinois charged Munn and Scott with violating the law shortly after it went into effect. They were found guilty and fined $100. On appeal they challenged the constitutionality of the regulations. Munn & Scott later went into bankruptcy amid allegations of ethical and professional violations.

ARGUMENTS:

For the plaintiffs in error, Ira Y. Munn and George L. Scott:

- The grain storage business is part of interstate and foreign commerce. Therefore, states lack constitutional authority to regulate it.
- The law encroaches on the liberty of private property in violation of the due process clause of the Fourteenth Amendment.
- Valid uses of the police power include regulations to keep the peace, to improve public morality, and to remove the causes of crime, disease, and pauperism— not to control wages and prices.
- The law unreasonably and arbitrarily deprives the company of its freedom to carry on its business activities. The company is not a public utility over which regulation traditionally has been allowed.

For the defendant in error, state of Illinois:

- These state regulations apply to local businesses, not interstate or foreign commerce.
- As part of its authority over internal commerce, the state has the power to regulate and inspect grain stored in public warehouses.
- The law does not deprive property rights without due process of law. The owner may still use his property as he sees fit.
- The importance of food to the community is so great that the grain elevator business becomes similar to a public utility or a public employer. Therefore, these businesses may be more extensively regulated than other private businesses.

◣ MR. CHIEF JUSTICE WAITE DELIVERED THE OPINION OF THE COURT.

The question to be determined in this case is whether the General Assembly of Illinois can, under the limitations upon the legislative power of the States imposed by the Constitution of the United States, fix by law the maximum of charges for the storage of grain in warehouses at Chicago and other places in the State having not less than one hundred thousand inhabitants, "in which grain is stored in bulk, and in which the grain of different owners is mixed together, or in which grain is stored in such a manner that the identity of different lots or parcels cannot be accurately preserved."

It is claimed that such a law is repugnant—. . .

To that part of amendment 14 which ordains that no State shall "Deprive any person of life, liberty or property, without due process of law, nor deny to any person within its jurisdiction the equal protection of the laws." . . .

The Constitution contains no definition of the word "deprive," as used in the Fourteenth Amendment. To determine its signification, therefore, it is necessary to ascertain the effect which usage has given it, when employed in the same or a like connection.

While this provision of the Amendment is new in the Constitution of the United States as a limitation upon the powers of the States, it is old as a principle of civilized government. It is found in Magna Charta, and, in substance if not in form, in nearly or quite all the constitutions that have been from time to time adopted by the several States of the Union. By the 5th Amendment, it was introduced into the Constitution of the United States as a limitation upon the powers of the National Government, and by the Fourteenth, as a guaranty against any encroachment upon an acknowledged right of citizenship by the Legislatures of the States. . . .

When one becomes a member of society, he necessarily parts with some rights or privileges which, as an individual not affected by his relations to others, he might retain. "A body politic," as aptly defined in the preamble of the Constitution of Massachusetts, is a social compact by which the whole people covenants with each citizen, and each citizen with the whole people, that all shall be governed by certain laws for the common good. This does not confer power upon the whole people to control rights which are purely and exclusively private; but it does authorize the establishment of laws requiring each citizen to so conduct himself, and so use his own property, as not unnecessarily to injure another. This is the very essence of government. . . . From this source come the police powers, which, as was said by Mr. Chief Justice Taney in the License Cases, are nothing more or less than the powers of government inherent in every sovereignty, . . . that is to say, . . . the power to govern men and things. Under these powers, the government regulates the conduct of its citizens one towards another, and the manner in which each shall use his own property, when such regulation becomes necessary for the public good. In their exercise, it has been customary in England from time immemorial, and in this country from its first colonization, to regulate ferries, common carriers, hackmen, bakers, millers, wharfingers, innkeepers, &c., and, in so doing, to fix a maximum of charge to be made for services rendered, accommodations furnished, and articles sold. To this day, statutes are to be found in many of the States upon some or all these subjects; and we think it has never yet been successfully contended that such legislation came within any of the constitutional prohibitions against interference with private property. . . .

From this it is apparent that, down to the time of the adoption of the Fourteenth Amendment, it was not supposed that statutes regulating the use, or even the price of the use, of private property necessarily deprived an owner of his property without due process of law. Under some circumstances they may, but not under all. The Amendment does not change the law in this particular; it simply prevents the States from doing that which will operate as such a deprivation.

This brings us to inquire as to the principles upon which this power of regulation rests, in order that we may determine what is within and what without its operative effect. Looking, then, to the common law, from whence came the right which the Constitution protects, we find that when private property is "affected with a public interest, it ceases to be juris privati only." . . . Property does become clothed with a public interest when used in a manner to make it of public consequence, and affect the community at large. When, therefore, one devotes his property to a use in which the public has an interest, he, in effect, grants to the public an interest in that use, and must submit to be controlled by the public for the common good, to the extent of the interest he has thus created. He may withdraw his grant by discontinuing the use; but, so long as he maintains the use, he must submit to the control. . . .

. . . [W]hen private property is devoted to a public use, it is subject to public regulation. It remains only to ascertain whether the warehouses of these plaintiffs in error, and the business which is carried on there, come within the operation of this principle.

For this purpose, we accept as true the statements of fact contained in the elaborate brief of one of the counsel of the plaintiffs in error. From this it appears that " . . . the trade in grain is carried on by the inhabitants of seven or eight of the great States of the West with four or five of the States lying on the seashore, and forms the largest part of interstate commerce in these States. The grain warehouses or elevators in Chicago are immense structures, holding from 300,000 to 1,000,000 bushels at one time, according to size. They are divided into bins of large capacity and great strength. . . . They are located with the river harbor on one side and the railway tracks on the other; and the grain is run through them from car to vessel, or boat to car, as may be demanded in the course of business. It has been found impossible to preserve each owner's grain separate, and this has given rise to a system of inspection and grading, by which the grain of different owners is mixed, and receipts issued for the number of bushels which are negotiable, and redeemable in like kind, upon demand. This mode of conducting the business was inaugurated more than twenty years ago, and has grown to immense proportions. The railways have found it impracticable to own such elevators, and public policy forbids the transaction of such business by the carrier; the ownership has, therefore, been by private individuals, who have embarked their capital and devoted their industry to such business as a private pursuit." . . .

Under such circumstances it is difficult to see why, if the common carrier, or the miller, or the ferryman, or the innkeeper, or the wharfinger, or the baker, or the cartman, or the hackney-coachman, pursues a public employment and exercises "a sort of public office," these plaintiffs in error do not. They stand, to use again the language of their counsel, in the very "gateway of commerce," and take toll from all who pass. Their business most certainly "tends to a common charge, and is become a thing of public interest and use." Every bushel of grain for its passage "pays a toll, which is a common charge," and, therefore . . . every such warehouseman "ought to be under public regulation, viz.: that he . . . take but reasonable toll." Certainly, if any business can be clothed "with a public interest, and cease to be juris privati only," this has been. It may not be made so by the operation of the Constitution of Illinois or this statute, but it is by the facts. . . .

We conclude, therefore, that the statute in question is not repugnant to the Constitution of the United States, and that there is no error in the judgment. In passing upon this case we have not been unmindful of the vast importance of the questions involved. This and cases of a kindred character were argued before us more than a year ago by the most eminent counsel, and in a manner worthy of their well earned reputations. We have kept the cases long under advisement, in order that their decision might be the result of our mature deliberations.

The judgment is affirmed.

MR. JUSTICE FIELD . . . dissented.

I am compelled to dissent from the decision of the court in this case, and from the reasons upon which that decision is founded. The principle upon which the opinion of the majority proceeds is, in my judgment, subversive of the rights of private property, heretofore believed to be protected by constitutional guaranties against legislative interference, and is in conflict with the authorities cited in its support. . . .

By the term "liberty," as used in the [Fourteenth Amendment to the Constitution], something more is meant than mere freedom from physical restraint or the bounds of a prison. It means freedom to go where one may choose, and to act in such manner, not inconsistent with the equal rights of others, as his judgment may dictate for the promotion of his happiness; that is, to pursue such callings and avocations as may be most suitable to develop his capacities, and give to them their highest enjoyment.

The same liberal construction which is required for the protection of . . . liberty . . . should be applied to the protection of private property. If the legislature of a State, under pretense of providing for the public good, or for any other reason, can determine, against the consent of the owner, the uses to which private property shall be devoted, or the prices which the owner shall receive for its uses, it can deprive him of the property as completely as by a special act for its confiscation or destruction. If, for instance, the owner is prohibited from using his building for the purposes for which it was designed, it is of little consequence that he is permitted to retain the title and possession; or, if he is compelled to take as compensation for its use less than the expenses to which he is subjected by its ownership, he is, for all practical purposes, deprived of the property, as effectually as if the legislature had ordered his forcible dispossession. If it be admitted that the legislature has any control over the compensation, the extent of that compensation becomes a mere matter of legislative discretion. The amount fixed will operate as a partial destruction of the value of the property, if it fall below the amount which the owner would obtain by contract, and, practically, as a complete destruction, if it be less than the cost of retaining its possession. There is, indeed, no protection of any value under the constitutional provision, which does not extend to the use and income of the property, as well as to its title and possession. . . .

There is nothing in the character of the business of the defendants as warehousemen which called for the interference complained of in this case. Their buildings are not nuisances; their occupation of receiving and storing grain infringes upon no rights of others, disturbs no neighborhood, infects not the air, and in no respect prevents others from using and enjoying their property as to them may seem best. The legislation in question is nothing less than a bold assertion of absolute power by the State to control at its discretion the property and business of the citizen, and fix the compensation he shall receive. The will of the legislature is made the condition upon which the owner shall receive the fruits of his property and the just reward of his labor, industry, and enterprise. "That government," says Story, "can scarcely be deemed to be free where the rights of property are left solely dependent upon the will of a legislative body without any restraint. The fundamental maxims of a free government seem to require that the rights of personal liberty and private property should be held sacred." The decision of the court in this case gives unrestrained license to legislative will.

To return to our question, what was the loophole in Chief Justice Morrison Waite's opinion? Like Justice Miller in *The Slaughterhouse Cases*, Waite seemed to reject substantive due process completely, asserting that most regulatory legislation should be presumed valid. The ruling provoked strong reaction. The American Bar Association, which was then a newly formed organization and full of business-oriented attorneys, pronounced it "barbarous" and vowed to see it overturned.[6] Also consider the statement in Justice Field's acrimonious dissent, which largely reflected Bradley's in *Slaughterhouse*: the law was "nothing less than a bold assertion of absolute power by the State to control at its discretion the property and business of the citizen." So it is not surprising that Waite's majority opinion "has generally been regarded as a great victory for liberalism and a judicial refusal to recognize due process as a limit on the substance of legislative regulatory power."[7]

But is that description precise? Not exactly. Although Waite could have taken the same approach as Miller in *Slaughterhouse*—the complete rejection of the due process claim—he did not. Instead, Waite qualified his opinion, asserting first that state regulations of private property were "not supposed" to

---

6. Pritchett, *The American Constitution,* 558.

7. Ibid., 557.

deprive owners of their right to due process, but that "under some circumstances they may." What differentiated "some circumstances" from others? In Waite's opinion, the answer lay in the nature of the subject of the regulation: "We find that when private property is 'affected with a public interest it ceases to be [of private right] only.'" Waite used this doctrine, often called the business-affected-with-a-public-interest (BAPI) doctrine, to find against Munn's claim. The grain elevator business played a crucial role in the distribution of foodstuffs to the nation; as such, it was an industry that was affected with the public interest and consequently subject to regulation.

In dissent, Justice Field charged that the BAPI test provided businesses inadequate protection against government regulation: "There is hardly an enterprise or business engaging the attention and labor of any considerable portion of the community, in which the public has not an interest in the sense in which that term is used by the court." Yet Waite's opinion, perhaps unwittingly, provided a loophole for lawyers representing business clients who were unhappy with state regulation. The opinion implied that businesses not affected with the public interest could raise a due process defense against unreasonable state regulation. By avoiding a hard-line stance of the sort taken by Miller in *Slaughterhouse*, Waite's "maybe yes, maybe no" approach ultimately provided some elbow room for the concept of substantive due process.

In two cases coming a decade or so after *Munn*, the Court moved closer to the concession only implied by Waite. In the first, **Mugler v. Kansas** (1887), the Court considered a state law that prohibited the manufacture and sale of liquor. Although the majority upheld the regulation against a substantive due process challenge, the Court's opinion represented something of a break from *Munn*. First, it articulated the view that not "every statute enacted ostensibly for the promotion of [the public interest] is to be accepted as a legitimate exertion of police powers of the state." This opinion was far more explicit than Waite's: there were clear limits to state regulatory power. Second, and more important, it took precisely the opposite position from the majority in *Slaughterhouse*. Recall that Justice Miller wanted to avoid the Court's being placed in the position of a "superlegislature," scrutinizing and perhaps censoring state action. But in *Mugler*, that is precisely what the Court said it would do:

There are . . . limits beyond which legislation cannot rightfully go. . . . If, therefore, a statute purporting to have been enacted to protect the public health, the public morals, or the public safety, has no real or substantial relation to those objects, or is a palpable invasion of rights secured by the fundamental law, *it is the duty of the courts to so adjudge* [our italics], and thereby give effect to the Constitution.

In *Mugler* the Court did not fully adopt the doctrine of substantive due process; it even upheld the state regulation on liquor. It also established its intent to review legislation to determine whether it was a "reasonable" exercise of state power. In essence, the Court would balance the interests of the state against those of individual due process guarantees.

The legislation tested in *Mugler* was deemed reasonable, but in **Chicago, Milwaukee & St. Paul Railway v. Minnesota** (1890), decided three years after *Mugler*, the Court went the other way: the justices struck down a state regulation on the ground that it interfered with due process guarantees. At first glance, *Chicago, Milwaukee & St. Paul Railway* bears a distinct resemblance to *Munn v. Illinois*. Strong lobbying efforts by farm groups led Minnesota in 1887 to establish a commission to set "equal and reasonable" rates for railroad transportation of goods and for warehouse storage. The commission received a complaint that the Chicago, Milwaukee & St. Paul Railway Company was charging dairy farmers unreasonable rates to ship their milk. It held hearings to investigate the claim and ruled against the railroad. When the company refused to abide by the ruling and reduce its rates, the commission went to the state supreme court. In the opinion of that tribunal, the commission's enabling legislation intended that the rates it "recommended and published" were to be "not simply advisory . . . but final and conclusive as to what are equal and reasonable charges." The railroad took its case to the U.S. Supreme Court, where it argued that the commission had interfered with "its property" without providing it with due process of law.

Writing for the majority, Justice Samuel Blatchford held for the railroad on two grounds, both centering on the Fourteenth Amendment's due process clause. Procedurally, he found the law—at least as construed by the state supreme court—defective. Because courts could not review the rates the commission set, the law deprived the railroad of a certain degree of fairness. On this point, the Court took a "traditional" approach to due process, asserting that "procedural safeguards" must be "attached to public expropriations of private property."[8] But Blatchford did not stop there; instead, he examined the law in terms of the reasonableness standard promulgated in *Mugler:* "The question of the reasonableness of a rate of charge for transportation by a railroad company . . . is eminently a question for judicial investigation, requiring due process of law for its determination."

Blatchford found the law deprived the company of its property in an unfair way:

If the company is deprived of the power of charging reasonable rates . . . and such deprivation takes place in the absence of an investigation by judicial machinery, it is deprived of the lawful use of its property, and thus, in substance and effect, of the property itself, without due process of law.

The *Chicago, Milwaukee & St. Paul Railway* case was not all that extraordinary: it merely applied the standard articulated in *Mugler,* a standard that obviously cut both ways. Sometimes the Court, in its attempt to inquire (balance interests), would find a law a "reasonable" use of state power (*Mugler*), and sometimes it would find it violative of substantive due process guarantees, as it did here. But this case and, to a lesser extent, *Mugler* were remarkable if we consider how different they were from *Slaughterhouse.* Over a fourteen-year period, the Court had moved from a refusal to inject substance into due process to a near affirmation of the doctrine of substantive due process; it had moved from the assertion that it would not become a censor to the argument that judicial inquiry was necessary, if not mandated, by the Constitution. And although, as we shall see, it did not fully endorse Thomas Cooley's position defining due process "liberty" in economic terms until seven years later, Blatchford's ruling laid the groundwork for exactly that.

This change in position prompts us to ask why the Court did such a turnabout over two decades. The most obvious answer is personnel changes. By the time the Court decided *Mugler,* only one member of the *Slaughterhouse* majority, Miller, remained, but the primary dissenters, Bradley and Field, also remained. By 1890 Miller also was gone, as was Chief Justice Waite, who, despite the loophole in the *Munn* opinion, generally

favored state regulatory power. Their replacements were quite different. Some had been corporate attorneys schooled in the philosophies of Cooley and Spencer and quite willing to borrow from the briefs of their former colleagues who argued against state regulation. Justice David J. Brewer, who replaced Stanley Matthews, a moderate-conservative states' rights advocate, had refused to follow *Munn* as a court of appeals judge. It is not surprising that many eagerly awaited the *Chicago, Milwaukee & St. Paul Railway* decision to see how the Court's membership changes might affect the direction of this area of the law.[9] Given the backgrounds of the new appointees, it also is not surprising that the views of the *Slaughterhouse* dissenters—especially Field and Bradley—ruled the day.

But there may have been more to it. By asserting the standard it did, the Court was engaging in extreme judicial activism. As Peter Woll noted,

By substituting its judgment for that of state legislators in determining the fairness of regulations of property and liberty under the due process clause of the Fourteenth Amendment, the Court was acting contrary to the public opinion that spurred state regulation. Political pressures upon state legislatures throughout the country had resulted in laws regulating business which courts were unwilling to sustain.[10]

It seems fair to say that the justices did not see it this way. Rather, they viewed these "political pressures" as just that—as particularized, radical, "socialistic" elements that did not reflect majority interests. If that was their perception, it had a solid foundation. Some legislation had resulted from the lobbying efforts of farm and labor movements and later, as we shall see, of the Progressives and New Dealers. In the minds of many conservatives of the day, including some of the justices, such pressures were illegitimate because they sought to subvert the free enterprise system. In short, while the Populists, Progressives, and New Dealers—in the opinion of conservatives—tried to put the brakes on businesses and inculcate the government with socialistic legislation, the conservatives strongly believed that the best interests of the country lay with "an utterly free

---

8. Hall, *The Magic Mirror,* 236.

9. See Arnold M. Paul, *Conservative Crisis and the Rule of Law* (Ithaca, NY: Cornell University Press, 1960), 42.

10. Peter Woll, *Constitutional Law* (Englewood Cliffs, NJ: Prentice Hall, 1981), 486.

market, unfettered by governmental regulation." This, not the plans of radicals, would be more advantageous to society in the long run because in the end all would benefit financially.

A fundamental change was in the wind, and many point to the Court's decision in *Allgeyer v. Louisiana* (1897) as the turning point. What did the Court say here that it had not fully articulated in *Mugler* and *Chicago, Milwaukee & St. Paul Railway?*

Allgeyer v. Louisiana

165 U.S. 578 (1897)
http://laws.findlaw.com/us/165/578.html
Vote: 9 (Brewer, Brown, Field, Fuller, Gray, Harlan, Peckham, Shiras, White)
  0

OPINION OF THE COURT: *Peckham*

FACTS:

With the alleged purpose of preventing fraud, Louisiana enacted a law that barred its citizens and corporations from doing business with out-of-state insurance companies unless the companies complied with a specified set of requirements. Among those requirements were that any out-of-state company doing business in Louisiana must establish a place of business in the state and must have an authorized agent inside the state. Defying the law, E. Allgeyer & Company entered into an agreement with Atlantic Mutual Insurance Company of New York to purchase marine insurance covering one hundred bales of cotton being shipped from New Orleans to European ports. During the transactions, no employee of Atlantic Mutual entered Louisiana. The negotiations between the insurance company and Allgeyer took place by mail and telegraph. Atlantic Mutual was not registered to do business in Louisiana. State prosecutors pursued fines against Allgeyer for violating the law. Rather than deny what it had done, Allgeyer defended itself by challenging the constitutionality of the Louisiana law.

ARGUMENTS:

For the plaintiff in error, E. Allgeyer & Company:

- This regulation is a naked, unauthorized, and unreasonable invasion of liberty.
- The law violates the due process clause of the Fourteenth Amendment by denying liberty and property arbitrarily. The terms *liberty* and *property*

protect the right to conduct any lawful vocation or business, including the freedom to make contractual agreements with whatever insurer a company wishes.

- With respect to this insurance policy, no business was conducted in Louisiana except for the use of the mail and telegraph. Louisiana therefore has no regulatory authority over this transaction.
- By prohibiting Allgeyer's use of the mail to do business, the state infringes on the constitutional authority of the federal government to create a postal system. By similarly prohibiting the use of the telegraph, the state infringes on the federal government's authority over interstate commerce.

For the defendant in error, state of Louisiana:

- The final contractual provisions for the amount of insurance coverage and the insurance premium were not determined until the cotton was loaded onto the ship in New Orleans. Therefore, contractual activity did take place in Louisiana.
- Under its police powers a state may enforce requirements for out-of-state corporations to conduct business inside the state.
- The state's police powers rest on its sovereignty. This principle is unquestioned.
- The Fourteenth Amendment has no bearing on the exercise of state police powers to protect the state's citizens against fraudulent practices by out-of-state companies.

MR. JUSTICE PECKHAM, AFTER STATING THE CASE, DELIVERED THE OPINION OF THE COURT.

The question presented is the simple proposition whether under the act a party while in the state can insure property in Louisiana in a foreign insurance company, which has not complied with the laws of the state, under an open policy, the special contract or insurance and the open policy being contracts made and entered into beyond the limits of the state. . . .

It is natural that the state court should have remarked that there is in this "statute an apparent interference with the liberty of defendants in restricting their rights to place insurance on property of their own whenever and in what company they desired." Such interference is not only apparent, but it is real, and we do not think that it is justified for the purpose of upholding what the state says is its policy with regard to foreign insurance companies which had not complied with the laws of the state for doing business within its limits. In this case the company did no business within the state, and the contracts were not therein made.

The supreme court of Louisiana says that the act of writing, within that state, the letter of notification, was an act therein done to effect an insurance on property then in the state, in a marine insurance company which had not complied with its laws, and such act was therefore prohibited by the statute. As so construed we think the statute is a violation of the 14th Amendment of the Federal Constitution, in that it deprives the defendants of their liberty without due process of law. The statute which forbids such act does not become due process of law, because it is inconsistent with the provisions of the Constitution of the Union. The liberty mentioned in that amendment means, not only the right of the citizen to be free from the mere physical restraint of his person, as by incarceration, but the term is deemed to embrace the right of the citizen to be free in the enjoyment of all his faculties; to be free to use them in all lawful ways; to live and work where he will; to earn his livelihood by any lawful calling; to pursue any livelihood or avocation, and for that purpose to enter into all contracts which may be proper, necessary, and essential to his carrying out to a successful conclusion the purposes above mentioned.

It was said by Mr. Justice Bradley in *Butchers' Union S. H. & L. S. L. Co. v. Crescent City L. S. L. & S. H. Co.* [*Slaughterhouse Cases*], in the course of his concurring opinion in that case, that "the right to follow any of the common occupations of life is an inalienable right. It was formulated as such under the phrase 'pursuit of happiness' in the Declaration of Independence, which commenced with the fundamental proposition that 'all men are created equal, that they are endowed by their Creator with certain inalienable rights; and among these are life, liberty, and the pursuit of happiness.' This right is a large ingredient in the civil liberty of the citizen." Again, the learned justice said: "I hold that the liberty of pursuit—the right to follow any of the ordinary callings of life—is one of the privileges of a citizen of the United States." And again, "But if it does not abridge the privileges and immunities of a citizen of the United States to prohibit him from pursuing his chosen calling, and giving to others the exclusive right of pursuing it, it certainly does deprive him, to a certain extent, of his liberty; for it takes from him the freedom of adopting and following the pursuit which he prefers; which, as already intimated, is a material part of the liberty of the citizen." It is true that these remarks were made in regard to questions of monopoly, but they well describe the rights which

are covered by the word "liberty" as contained in the 14th Amendment. . . .

The foregoing extracts have been made for the purpose of showing what general definitions have been given in regard to the meaning of the word "liberty" as used in the amendment, but we do not intend to hold that in no such case can the state exercise its police power. When and how far such power may be legitimately exercised with regard to these subjects may be left for determination to each case as it arises.

Has not a citizen of a state, under the provisions of the Federal Constitution above mentioned, a right to contract outside of the state for insurance on his property—a right of which state legislation cannot deprive him? We are not alluding to acts done within the state by an insurance company or its agents doing business therein, which are in violation of the state statutes . . . and would be controlled by it. When we speak of the liberty to contract for insurance or to do an act to effectuate such a contract already existing, we refer to and have in mind the facts of this case, where the contract was made outside the state, and as such was a valid and proper contract. The act done within the limits of the state under the circumstances of this case and for the purpose therein mentioned, we hold a proper act, one which the defendants were at liberty to perform and which the state legislature had no right to prevent, at least with reference to the Federal Constitution. To deprive the citizen of such a right as herein described without due process of law is illegal. Such a statute as this in question is not due process of law, because it prohibits an act which under the Federal Constitution the defendants had a right to perform. This does not interfere in any way with the acknowledged right of the state to enact such legislation in the legitimate exercise of its police or other powers as to it may seem proper. In the exercise of such right, however, care must be taken not to infringe upon those other rights of the citizen which are protected by the Federal Constitution.

In the privilege of pursuing an ordinary calling or trade and of acquiring, holding, and selling property must be embraced the right to make all proper contracts in relation thereto, and although it may be conceded that this right to contract in relation to persons or property or to do business within the jurisdiction of the state may be regulated and sometimes prohibited when the contracts or business conflict with the policy of the state as contained in the statutes, yet the power does not and cannot extend to prohibiting the citizen from making contracts of the nature involved in this case outside of the limits and jurisdiction of the state, and which are also to be performed outside of such jurisdiction; nor can the state legally prohibit its citizens from doing such an act as writing this letter of notification, even though the property which is the subject of the insurance may at the time when such insurance attaches be within the limits of the state. The mere fact that a citizen may be within the limits of a particular state does not prevent his making a contract outside its limits while he himself remains within it. The contract in this case was thus made. It was a valid contract, made outside of the state, to be performed outside of the state, although the subject was property temporarily within the state. As the contract was valid in the place where made and where it was to be performed, the party to the contract upon whom is devolved the right or duty to send the notification in order that the insurance provided for by the contract may attach to the property specified in the shipment mentioned in the notice, must have the liberty to do that act and to give that notification within the limits of the state, any prohibition of the state statute to the contrary notwithstanding.

Justice Rufus Peckham's opinion is not so different from the majority's opinion in *Chicago, Milwaukee & St. Paul Railway*. It struck down the state law in part on the ground that the law was not reasonable. But Peckham went much farther. By merging substantive due process with freedom of contract, by reading the term *liberty* to mean economic liberty, encompassing the right to "enter into all contracts," he issued a strong opinion. He adopted the position that businesses had been pressing since the demise of the contract clause as a source of protection. Now their right to do business—to set their own rates and enter into contracts with other businesses and perhaps even with employees—had the highest level of legal protection. In just under twenty-five years, business interests had pushed the Court from *Slaughterhouse*, in which it refused to review state legislation for its compatibility with due process guarantees, to *Munn*, in which legislation was presumed valid *generally* but was open to judicial inquiry into its "reasonableness." The Court then moved from balancing state interests with individual interests (*Chicago, Milwaukee & St. Paul Railway*) to placing state regulations in a less exalted position than the fundamental liberty of contract (*Allgeyer*).

THE ROLLER-COASTER RIDE OF SUBSTANTIVE DUE PROCESS: 1898–1923

However explicit *Allgeyer* was, the true test of its importance would come in its application. Some read it to mean that the Court would not uphold legislation that infringed on economic "liberty," but **Holden v. Hardy,** decided the very next year, dispelled this notion. In *Holden* the Court examined a Utah law prohibiting companies engaged in the excavation of mines from working their employees more than eight hours a day, except in emergency situations. Attorneys challenging the law claimed,

It is . . . not within the power of the legislature to prevent persons who are . . . perfectly competent to contract, from entering into employment and voluntarily making contracts in relation thereto merely because the employment . . . may be considered by the legislature to be dangerous or injurious to the health of the employee; and if such right to contract cannot be prevented, it certainly cannot be restricted by the legislature to suit its own ideas of the ability of the employee to stand the physical and mental strain incident to the work.

The state asserted that the challenged statute was a "health regulation" and within the state's power because it was aimed at "preserving to a citizen his ability to work and support himself."

In *Holden* the Court reiterated its *Mugler* position: "The question in each case is whether the legislature has adopted the statute in exercise of a reasonable discretion or whether its actions be a mere excuse for an unjust discrimination." The Supreme Court, now acting as the nation's "superlegislature," deemed the legislation "reasonable"; that is, it did not impinge on the liberty of contract because the state had well justified its interest in protecting miners from their jobs' unique health problems and dangerous conditions.

Holden was a victory for the still-forming Progressive movement and emerging labor groups, which were vigorously lobbying state legislatures to pass laws to protect workers. With the nation's increasing industrialization, they argued, the need for such laws was becoming critical because corporations were ever more profit oriented and, as a result, more likely to exploit employees. Although they succeeded in convincing many state legislatures to enact laws like Utah's, the possibility that courts would strike them down remained a threat.

Collection of Joseph Lochner Jr. by Dante Tranquille

Collection of Joseph Lochner Jr. by Dante Tranquille

After Joseph Lochner, the owner of a bakery located in Utica, New York, was convicted of failing to comply with a state maximum hours-work law, he asked the U.S. Supreme Court to strike down the law as violative of his constitutional rights. In Lochner v. New York *(1905) the justices agreed. The majority found that the law impermissibly interfered with the right of employers to enter into contracts with their employees.*

The *Holden* ruling, however, took on a different gloss once the Court decided *Lochner v. New York* (1905). Although the law at issue varied only slightly from Utah's, the justices reached a wholly different conclusion. Why? Does the case fit compatibly with the logic of *Holden,* as Justice Peckham implies, or does it reveal the true reach of his ruling in *Allgeyer?*

Lochner v. New York

198 U.S. 45 (1905)
http://laws.findlaw.com/us/198/45.html
Vote: 5 (Brewer, Brown, Fuller, McKenna, Peckham)
      4 (Day, Harlan, Holmes, White)

OPINION OF THE COURT: *Peckham*
DISSENTING OPINIONS: *Harlan, Holmes*

FACTS:

In 1897 the state of New York, for purposes of promoting safe and healthy working conditions, passed the Bakeshop Act, a law that prohibited employees of bakeries from working more than ten hours per day and sixty hours per week. Joseph Lochner owned Lochner's Home Bakery in Utica, New York. In 1899 he was convicted of violating the Bakeshop Act by requiring an employee to work more than sixty hours

a week. He was fined $25. Two years later Lochner was charged with his second offense of overworking his employees. Once again found guilty, he was sentenced to a fine of $50 or fifty days in jail if he failed to pay the fine. This time Lochner decided to fight the charges and appealed. After he lost in the state's highest court, he asked the Supreme Court to reverse his conviction on the ground that the Bakeshop Act violated the due process clause of the Fourteenth Amendment.

ARGUMENTS:

For the plaintiff in error, Joseph Lochner:

- The law violates the equal protection clause of the Fourteenth Amendment because it does not apply to all bakers, but singles out biscuit, bread, and cake bakers and those working in the confection business. It fails to cover bakery owners or those who bake in hotels, boardinghouses, and private homes. If the law truly were a health measure, there would be no such exceptions.
- Unlike mining (*Holden v. Hardy*), baking is not a dangerous occupation. Consequently, the law is not a reasonable exercise of the police power. It is a labor law, not a health law.

- Employers and employees have the right to agree upon hours and wages, and the use of the police power by New York to interfere with such agreements is so paternalistic as to violate the Fourteenth Amendment.
- The freedoms of contract and private property are among America's most cherished rights, and the Court should scrutinize any encroachment on them.

For the defendant in error, state of New York:

- The police powers are elastic, capable of meeting changing conditions and evolving community standards. These powers are exercised by elected state legislators who best understand unique local conditions.
- The state has an interest in the vitality of its people. Those engaged in food production must follow the highest standards of health and safety. The law advances this interest.
- Bakers often work at night, engage in monotonous and repetitive tasks, and frequently suffer poor ventilation and other unsafe conditions. The law reduces a worker's exposure to these unhealthy environments.

MR. JUSTICE PECKHAM . . . DELIVERED THE OPINION OF THE COURT.

The mandate of the statute, that "no employee shall be required or permitted to work," is the substantial equivalent of an enactment that "no employee shall contract or agree to work," more than ten hours per day; and, as there is no provision for special emergencies, the statute is mandatory in all cases. It is not an act merely fixing the number of hours which shall constitute a legal day's work, but an absolute prohibition upon the employer permitting, under any circumstances, more than ten hours' work to be done in his establishment. The employee may desire to earn the extra money which would arise from his working more than the prescribed time, but this statute forbids the employer from permitting the employee to earn it.

The statute necessarily interferes with the right of contract between the employer and employees, concerning the number of hours in which the latter may labor in the bakery of the employer. The general right to make a contract in relation to his business is part of the liberty of the individual protected by the 14th Amendment of the Federal Constitution. *Allgeyer v. Louisiana.* Under that provision

no state can deprive any person of life, liberty, or property without due process of law. The right to purchase or to sell labor is part of the liberty protected by this amendment, unless there are circumstances which exclude the right. There are, however, certain powers, existing in the sovereignty of each state in the Union, somewhat vaguely termed police powers, the exact description and limitation of which have not been attempted by the courts. Those powers, broadly stated, and without, at present, any attempt at a more specific limitation, relate to the safety, health, morals, and general welfare of the public. Both property and liberty are held on such reasonable conditions as may be imposed by the governing power of the state in the exercise of those powers, and with such conditions the 14th Amendment was not designed to interfere.

This court has recognized the existence and upheld the exercise of the police powers of the states in many cases which might fairly be considered as border ones, and it has, in the course of its determination of questions regarding the asserted invalidity of such statutes, on the ground of their violation of the rights secured by the Federal Constitution, been guided by rules of a very liberal nature, the application of which has resulted, in numerous instances, in upholding the validity of state statutes thus assailed. Among the later cases where the state law has been upheld by this court is that of *Holden v. Hardy.* A provision in the act of the legislature of Utah was there under consideration, the act limiting the employment of workmen in all underground mines or workings, to eight hours per day, "except in cases of emergency, where life or property is in imminent danger." It also limited the hours of labor in smelting and other institutions for the reduction or refining of ores or metals to eight hours per day, except in like cases of emergency. The act was held to be a valid exercise of the police powers of the state . . . [because the] law applies only to the classes subjected by their employment to the peculiar conditions and effects attending underground mining and work in smelters, and other works for the reduction and refining of ores. . . .

There is nothing in *Holden v. Hardy* which covers the case now before us.

It must, of course, be conceded that there is a limit to the valid exercise of the police power by the state. There is no dispute concerning this general proposition. Otherwise the 14th Amendment would have no efficacy and the legislatures of the states would have unbounded power, and it would be enough to say that any piece of legislation was enacted to conserve the morals, the health, or the safety of the people; such legislation would be valid, no matter how absolutely without foundation the claim might be. The claim of the police power would be a mere pretext,—become another and delusive name for the supreme sovereignty of the state to be exercised free from constitutional restraint. This is not contended for. In every case that comes before this court, therefore, where legislation of this character is concerned, and where the protection of the Federal Constitution is sought, the question necessarily arises: Is this a fair, reasonable, and appropriate exercise of the police power of the state, or is it an unreasonable, unnecessary, and arbitrary interference with the right of the individual to his personal liberty, or to enter into those contracts in relation to labor which may seem to him appropriate or necessary for the support of himself and his family? Of course the liberty of contract relating to labor includes both parties to it. The one has as much right to purchase as the other to sell labor.

This is not a question of substituting the judgment of the court for that of the legislature. If the act be within the power of the state it is valid, although the judgment of the court might be totally opposed to the enactment of such a law. But the question would still remain: Is it within the police power of the state? and that question must be answered by the court.

The question whether this act is valid as a labor law, pure and simple, may be dismissed in a few words. There is no reasonable ground for interfering with the liberty of person or the right of free contract, by determining the hours of labor, in the occupation of a baker. There is no contention that bakers as a class are not equal in intelligence and capacity to men in other trades or manual occupations, or that they are not able to assert their rights and care for themselves without the protecting arm of the state, interfering with their independence of judgment and of action. They are in no sense wards of the state. Viewed in the light of a purely labor law, with no reference whatever to the question of health, we think that a law like the one before us involves neither the safety, the morals, nor the welfare, of the public, and that the interest of the public is not in the slightest degree affected by such an act. The law must be upheld, if at all, as a law pertaining to the health of the individual engaged in the occupation of a baker. It does not affect any other portion of the public than those who are engaged in that occupation. Clean and wholesome bread does not depend upon whether the baker works but ten hours per day or only sixty hours a week. The limitation of the hours of labor does not come within the police power on that ground.

It is a question of which of two powers or rights shall prevail—the power of the state to legislate or the right of the individual to liberty of person and freedom of contract. The mere assertion that the subject relates, though but in a remote degree, to the public health, does not necessarily render the enactment valid. The act must have a more direct relation, as a means to an end, and the end itself must be appropriate and legitimate, before an act can be held to be valid which interferes with the general right of an individual to be free in his person and in his power to contract in relation to his own labor. . . .

We think the limit of the police power has been reached and passed in this case. There is, in our judgment, no reasonable foundation for holding this to be necessary or appropriate as a health law to safeguard the public health, or the health of the individuals who are following the trade of a baker. If this statute be valid, and if, therefore, a proper case is made out in which to deny the right of an individual . . . as employer or employee, to make contracts for the labor of the latter under the protection of the provisions of the Federal Constitution, there would seem to be no length to which legislation of this nature might not go. . . .

We think that there can be no fair doubt that the trade of a baker, in and of itself, is not an unhealthy one to that degree which would authorize the legislature to interfere with the right to labor, and with the right of free contract on the part of the individual, either as employer or employee. In looking through statistics regarding all trades and occupations, it may be true that the trade of a baker does not appear to be as healthy as some other trades, and is also vastly more healthy than still others. To the common understanding the trade of a baker has never been regarded as an unhealthy one. . . . It might be safely affirmed that almost all occupations more or less affect the health. There must be more than the mere fact of the possible existence of some small amount of unhealthiness to warrant legislative interference with liberty. It is unfortunately true that labor, even in any department, may possibly carry with it the seeds of unhealthiness. But are we all, on that account, at the mercy of legislative majorities? A printer, a tinsmith, a locksmith, a carpenter, a cabinetmaker, a dry goods clerk, a bank's, a lawyer's, or a physician's clerk, or a clerk in almost any kind of business, would all come under the power of the legislature, on this assumption. No trade, no occupation, no mode of earning one's living, could escape this all-pervading power, and the acts of the legislature in limiting the hours of labor in all employments would be valid, although such limitation might seriously cripple the ability of the laborer to support himself and his family. . . . It might be said that it is unhealthy to work more than that number of hours in an apartment lighted by artificial light during the working hours of the day; that the occupation of the bank clerk, the lawyer's clerk, the real-estate clerk, or the broker's clerk, in such offices is therefore unhealthy, and the legislature, in its paternal wisdom, must, therefore, have the right to legislate on the subject of, and to limit, the hours for such labor; and, if it exercises that power, and its validity be questioned, it is sufficient to say, it has reference to the public health; it has reference to the health of the employees condemned to labor day after day in buildings where the sun never shines; it is a health law, and therefore it is valid, and cannot be questioned by the courts.

It is also urged, pursuing the same line of argument, that it is to the interest of the state that its population should be strong and robust, and therefore any legislation which may be said to tend to make people healthy must be valid as health laws, enacted under the police power. If this be a valid argument and a justification for this kind of legislation, it follows that the protection of the Federal Constitution from undue interference with liberty of person and freedom of contract is visionary, wherever the law is sought to be justified as a valid exercise of the police power. Scarcely any law but might find shelter under such assumptions, and conduct, properly so called, as well as contract, would come under the restrictive sway of the legislature. Not only the hours of employees, but the hours of employers, could be regulated, and doctors, lawyers, scientists, all professional men, as well as athletes and artisans, could be forbidden to fatigue their brains and bodies by prolonged hours of exercise, lest the fighting strength of the state be impaired. We mention these extreme cases because the contention is extreme. We do not believe in the soundness of the views which uphold this law. On the contrary, we think that such a law as this, although passed in the assumed exercise of the police power, and as relating to the public health, or the health of the employees named, is not within that power, and is invalid. The act is not, within any fair meaning of the term, a health law, but is an illegal interference with the rights of individuals, both employers and employees, to make contracts regarding labor upon such terms as they may think best, or which they may agree upon with the other parties to such contracts. Statutes of the nature of that under review, limiting the hours in which grown and intelligent men may labor to earn their living, are mere meddlesome

interferences with the rights of the individual and they are not saved from condemnation by the claim that they are passed in the exercise of the police power and upon the subject of the health of the individual whose rights are interfered with, unless there be some fair ground, reasonable in and of itself, to say that there is material danger to the public health, or to the health of the employees, if the hours of labor are not curtailed. All that [New York] could properly do has been done by it with regard to the conduct of bakeries, as provided for in the other sections of the act. . . . These several sections provide for the inspection of the premises where the bakery is carried on, with regard to furnishing proper wash rooms and waterclosets, apart from the bake room, also with regard to providing proper drainage, plumbing, and painting; . . . and for other things of that nature. . . . These various sections may be wise and valid regulations, and they certainly go to the full extent of providing for the cleanliness and the healthiness, so far as possible, of the quarters in which bakeries are to be conducted. Adding to all these requirements a prohibition to enter into any contract of labor in a bakery for more than a certain number of hours a week is, in our judgment, so wholly beside the matter of a proper, reasonable, and fair provision as to run counter to that liberty of person and of free contract provided for in the Federal Constitution.

It was further urged on the argument that restricting the hours of labor in the case of bakers was valid because it tended to cleanliness on the part of the workers, as a man was more apt to be cleanly when not overworked, and if cleanly then his "output" was also more likely to be so. What has already been said applies with equal force to this contention. We do not admit the reasoning to be sufficient to justify the claimed right of such interference. The state in that case would assume the position of a supervisor, or *pater familias*, over every act of the individual, and its right of governmental interference with his hours of labor, his hours of exercise, the character thereof, and the extent to which it shall be carried would be recognized and upheld. In our judgment it is not possible in fact to discover the connection between the number of hours a baker may work in the bakery and the healthful quality of the bread made by the workman. The connection, if any exist, is too shadowy and thin to build any argument for the interference of the legislature. If the man works ten hours a day it is all right, but if ten and a half or eleven his health is in danger and his bread may be unhealthy, and, therefore, he shall not be permitted to do it. This, we think, is unreasonable and entirely arbitrary. When assertions such as we have adverted to become necessary in order to give, if possible, a plausible foundation for the contention that the law is a "health law," it gives rise to at least a suspicion that there was some other motive dominating the legislature than the purpose to subserve the public health or welfare.

This interference on the part of the legislatures of the several states with the ordinary trades and occupations of the people seems to be on the increase. . . .

It is impossible for us to shut our eyes to the fact that many of the laws of this character, while passed under what is claimed to be the police power for the purpose of protecting the public health or welfare, are, in reality, passed from other motives. We are justified in saying so when, from the character of the law and the subject upon which it legislates, it is apparent that the public health or welfare bears but the most remote relation to the law. The purpose of a statute must be determined from the natural and legal effect of the language employed; and whether it is or is not repugnant to the Constitution of the United States must be determined from the natural effect of such statutes when put into operation, and not from their proclaimed purpose.

It is manifest to us that the limitation of the hours of labor provided for in this section of the statute under which the indictment was found, and the plaintiff in error convicted, has no such direct relation to, and no such substantial effect upon, the health of the employee, as to justify us in regarding the section as really a health law. It seems to us that the real object and purpose were simply to regulate the hours of labor between the master and his employees (all being men, *sui juris*), in a private business, not dangerous in any degree to morals, or in any real and substantial degree to the health of the employees. Under such circumstances the freedom of master and employee to contract with each other in relation to their employment, and in defining the same, cannot be prohibited or interfered with, without violating the Federal Constitution.

The judgment of the Court of Appeals of New York, as well as that of the Supreme Court and the County Court of Oneida County, must be reversed and the case remanded to the County Court for further proceedings not inconsistent with this opinion.

Reversed.

MR. JUSTICE HOLMES, dissenting.

This case is decided upon an economic theory which a large part of the country does not entertain. If it were a question whether I agreed with that theory I should desire to study it further and long before making up my mind. But I do not conceive that to be my duty, because I strongly believe that my agreement or disagreement has nothing to do with the right of a majority to embody their opinions in law. It is settled by various decisions of this court that state constitutions and state laws may regulate life in many ways which we as legislators might think as injudicious or if you like as tyrannical as this, and which equally with this interfere with the liberty to contract. Sunday laws and usury laws are ancient examples. A more modern one is the prohibition of lotteries. The liberty of the citizen to do as he likes so long as he does not interfere with the liberty of others to do the same, which has been a shibboleth for some well-known writers, is interfered with by school laws, by the Post Office, by every state or municipal institution which takes his money for purposes thought desirable, whether he likes it or not. The Fourteenth Amendment does not enact Mr. Herbert Spencer's Social Statics. . . . United States and state statutes and decisions cutting down the liberty to contract by way of combination are familiar to this court. Two years ago we upheld the prohibition of sales of stock on margins or for future delivery in the constitution of California. *Otis v. Parker.* The decision sustaining an eight hour law for miners is still recent. *Holden v. Hardy.* Some of these laws embody convictions or prejudices which judges are likely to share. Some may not. But a constitution is not intended to embody a particular economic theory, whether of paternalism and the organic relation of the citizen to the State or of *laissez faire.* It is made for people of fundamentally differing views, and the accident of our finding certain opinions natural and familiar or novel and even shocking ought not to conclude our judgment upon the question whether statutes embodying them conflict with the Constitution of the United States.

General propositions do not decide concrete cases. The decision will depend on a judgment or intuition more subtle than any articulate major premise. But I think that the proposition just stated, if it is accepted, will carry us far toward the end. Every opinion tends to become a law. I think that the word liberty in the Fourteenth Amendment is perverted when it is held to prevent the natural outcome of a dominant opinion, unless it can be said that a rational and fair man necessarily would admit that the statute proposed would infringe fundamental principles as they have been understood by the traditions of our people and our law. It does not need research to show that no such sweeping condemnation can be passed upon the statute before us. A reasonable man might think it a proper measure on the score of health. Men whom I certainly could not pronounce unreasonable would uphold it as a first installment of a general regulation of the hours of work. Whether in the latter aspect it would be open to the charge of inequality I think it unnecessary to discuss.

Many scholars have called *Lochner* the Court's strongest expression of economic substantive due process. Although the Court said the question to be asked in this case is the same one it had been addressing since *Mugler*—Is the law a fair, reasonable, and appropriate exercise of police power?—its answer is quite different. By distinguishing *Holden* to the point of nonexistence and by narrowing the definition of what constitutes reasonable state regulations, the Court moved away from a strict "reasonableness" approach to one that reflected *Allgeyer:* an employer's right "to make a contract" with employees is virtually sacrosanct.

That the Court, although divided 5–4, accomplished this feat not by changing the legal question but by changing the answer creates something of a puzzle, particularly with regard to the immediate subject of the dispute—maximum work hours. Think about it this way: the Court upheld the Utah law at issue in *Holden* on the ground that the "kind of employment . . . and the character of the employees . . . were such as to make [the state law] reasonable and proper"; it struck the *Lochner* law because bakers can "care for themselves" (despite evidence to the contrary) and the production of "clean and wholesome bread" is not affected. Was this distinction significant? Or was it merely a way to mask what the Court wanted to do: narrow the grounds on which states could reasonably regulate and, thereby, strike protective legislation as a violation of the right to contract? Justice Oliver Wendell Holmes's dissent certainly implies the latter. He goes so far as to accuse the Court of using the Fourteenth Amendment to "enact Mr. Herbert Spencer's Social Statics." Many scholars agree with Holmes's assessment and argue that the justices in the *Lochner* majority were "motivated by their own policy preferences favoring laissez faire

Courtesy of Ms. Neil Whisnant

Curt Muller (with arms folded) made constitutional history when he asked the U.S. Supreme Court to strike down as violative of his rights an Oregon law regulating the number of hours his laundresses could work at his cleaning establishment. In Muller v. Oregon *(1908), however, the Court held that states may constitutionally enact maximum hours work laws for women.*

economics and Social Darwinism."[11] Other analysts present a somewhat different picture.[12] They suggest that the Court was seeking to remain faithful to "a long-standing constitutional ideology that distinguished between valid economic regulation and invalid 'class,' or factional legislation."[13] In other words, *Lochner* represented a "principled effort" on the part of the justices to keep this area of the law consistent and coherent, and not merely a statement of their ideological predilections.

Regardless of who is right, these issues moved to the fore in *Muller v. Oregon* (1908). As you read this most interesting case, think about the following: Some scholars argue that the Court's decision in *Muller* merely echoed the logic of *Holden* and *Lochner;* that is, the Court followed the "reasonableness" approach. Others suggest that there were extralegal factors at work that had a great influence on the Court. With which view do you agree?

Muller v. Oregon

208 U.S. 412 (1908)
http://laws.findlaw.com/us/208/412.html
Vote: 9 (Brewer, Day, Fuller, Harlan, Holmes, McKenna, Moody, Peckham,
   White)
   0

OPINION OF THE COURT: Brewer

FACTS:

At the forefront of the Progressive movement was an organization called the National Consumers' League (NCL). Through the efforts of the NCL and others, the drive for maximum work hours legislation had succeeded in many states, which, by the early 1900s, had imposed some types of restrictions. After *Lochner,* however, all of their efforts were threatened by employers who sought to use that ruling to challenge state regulations.

Curt Muller, a German immigrant, settled in Oregon and entered the laundry business. In 1905 he bought the Grand Laundry in north Portland; a year later he purchased the Lace House Laundry. His legal

problems began in late 1905 when Oregon authorities charged him with violating state law by requiring Emma Gotcher, an employee of the Grand Laundry, to work more than ten hours on September 4, 1905 (ironically, Labor Day), in violation of the state law establishing maximum working hours for women employed by factories and laundries. Muller was convicted and sentenced to a fine of $10 or five days in jail. He decided to challenge his conviction. In the view of his attorneys, Oregon's regulation, which prohibited women, but not men, from working in laundries for shifts of more than ten hours, violated his right to enter into a contract with his employees.

Recognizing that, in light of *Lochner,* Muller's argument rested on strong grounds, the NCL grew concerned. It was reluctant to see the Supreme Court nullify the league's hard work to attain passage of the Oregon law. To defend the law, the NCL contacted Louis Brandeis, a well-known attorney of the day and a future U.S. Supreme Court justice. His philosophical position was very much akin to the NCL's, and he agreed to help the organization with the Muller case, but only if the NCL could persuade Oregon's attorneys to give him complete control over its course.

When NCL leaders managed to accomplish this, Brandeis got down to work. Because of the decision in *Lochner* and the stability of the Court's membership, Brandeis decided that bold action was necessary. Instead of filling his brief with legal arguments, he would provide the Court with "*facts,* published by anyone with expert knowledge of industry in its relation to women's hours of labor," that indicated the evils of Muller's actions. In particular, the brief pointed out that forcing women to work long hours affected their health and their reproductive systems.[14] It was full of statements such as the following:

Report of the Massachusetts State Board of Health, 1873.

The State thus has an interest not only in the prosperity, but also in the health and strength and effective power of each one of its members.

The first and largest interest of the State lies in the great agency of human power—the health of the people.

---

11. C. Ian Anderson, "Courts and the Constitution," *Michigan Law Review* 92 (1994): 1438.

12. See, especially, Howard Gillman, *The Constitution Besieged: The Rise and Demise of* Lochner *Era Police Powers Jurisprudence* (Durham, NC: Duke University Press, 1993).

13. Anderson, "Courts and the Constitution," 1439.

14. Clement E. Vose, *Constitutional Change* (Lexington, MA: Lexington Books, 1972), 172.

BOX 10-1   THE BRANDEIS BRIEF

AT THE TURN of the century the function of interpreting the law was largely regarded as a matter of logic. The Court had accepted the theories of laissez faire economics, and the doctrine of evolution expounded by Herbert Spencer, to such an extent that any kind of regulation of private business was considered a violation of "liberty." Only exceptional circumstances which forced the attention of the members of the Court on matters other than the logic of the law would suffice to cause them to alter this view.

When it was recognized that political, economic and social considerations ought to be included in the process of determining the law, the legal tradition offered little means of placing such factual data before the judges. Thus decisions regarding matters of contract, in regard to labor or business regulation, were shaped by the personal philosophies of Court members and the rigid pattern of law unleavened by knowledge of its relationship to society. Consequently, the use of logic alone "resulted in proscribing any realistic test of legislative-judicial conclusions." The questions which needed to be asked, and answered, dealt with the social consequences of the law at issue and the consequences which could be expected to follow the judicial decision.

In reference to the first question regarding social consequences of the law, by what means were the judges to obtain the background of facts which led to its enactment? Many Justices felt this was the responsibility of the legislature, that law should be passed after legislative inquiry as to its needs had been made. Suppose, however, the Court would not accept the legislative decisions that the law was needed, how could the Court obtain sufficient data to discuss the law? In a sense this was the dilemma in *Lochner v. New York,* for the use of logic produced the rule that the restriction of employer-employee rights to contract over hours of labor violated due process. Justice Peckham refused to acknowledge that the health and welfare of employees provided any basis whatever for restricting business. It was clear that the Court would not uphold such legislation, unless it could be convinced that there was a reasonable relationship between such regulation and the public welfare.

It is at this crucial point in the history of constitutional development that Brandeis introduced his brief as "authoritative extra-legal data" to provide the Court with information as to the reasonable relation of the law to the object to be regulated. He differed from the other liberals of the day in the method he used. Rather than deal in invective and generalities, he examined the social ills in detail and offered concrete plans for social legislation. In effect, Brandeis was doing no more than taking cognizance of the facts of modern industrial life.

THE TECHNIQUE OF THE BRIEF:

Muller v. Oregon, 1908

. . . [T]he key to the Brandeis Brief was the factual data he submitted to show the reasonableness of the specific law at issue and the relationship of the regulation to the needs of society. In the briefs he presented, as a lawyer defending social legislation in four states, there is a definite pattern that he followed to prove his point. An analysis of these briefs and that data they include can be compiled into a single "brief" outline to illustrate Brandeis' methodology. The following construct represents the general pattern, omitting details and using the hours of labor for women as the subject.

Part First

   I. Legal Argument
     (Varying from two to forty pages, citing rules from supporting cases.)

Part Second

   II. Legislation Restricting Hours of Work for Women
     A. American Legislation
       1. List of States having such legislation
     B. Foreign Legislation
       1. List of countries having such legislation
     C. Summary of Combined Experience of Above Legislation

   III. The World's Experience upon which the Legislation Limiting the Hours of Work for Women Is Based

A. The Dangers of Long Hours
   1. Causes
      a. physical difference between men and women
      b. nature of industrial work
B. Bad Effect of Long Hours on Health
   1. General injuries
   2. Problem of fatigue
   3. Specific evil effects on childbirth
C. Bad Effect of Long Hours on Safety
D. Bad Effect of Long Hours on Morals
E. Bad Effect of Long Hours on General Welfare

IV. Shorter Hours the Only Possible Protection

V. Benefits of Shorter Hours
A. Good Effect on Individual
   1. Health
   2. Morals
   3. Home Life
B. Good Effect on General Welfare

VI. Economic Aspects of Short Hours
A. Effect on Output
   1. Increases efficiency
   2. Improves product
   B. Aids Regularity of Employment
   C. Widens Job Opportunities for Women

VII. Uniformity of Restriction Necessary
A. Overtime Dangerous to Health
B. Essential to Enforcement
C. Necessary for Just Application

VIII. Reasonableness of Short Hours
A. Opinions of Physicians
B. Opinions of Employers
C. Opinions of Employees

IX. Conclusion

The outline of the brief indicates the wealth of the material Brandeis presented to the Court to support his very brief legal argument. The evidence he produced relied, as Jerome Frank described it, on facts that "do not involve witnesses' credibility." It reveals a concern for why legislation was passed, what it is intended to do, and the benefits, including a dollars and cents consideration, that will accrue to business and labor alike. Thus it was an intellectual inquiry whose ends were social justice. It is so persuasive in content that the burden of proof placed on the opposing party in the suit is almost impossible to overcome. The simplicity and clarity of the organized evidence is an invitation to apply a pragmatic test to the reasonableness of the law, and in the final analysis it becomes an irresistible force. . . .

The first successful use of the brief before the Supreme Court of the United States came in 1908, when Brandeis argued in *Muller v. Oregon* to sustain an Oregon law establishing a ten hour day for women employed in "any mechanical establishment, or factory or laundry." The argument consisted of two pages of the legal rules applicable to the case, and was followed by 102 pages of evidence. . . .

The most interesting aspect of the case is that Brandeis relied on the rule of *Lochner v. New York* to prove his point. He began by agreeing that "the right to purchase or sell labor is a part of the 'liberty' protected by the fourteenth amendment" but, he pointed out, "such 'liberty' is subject to reasonable restraint by the police power of the state if there is a relationship to public 'health, safety or welfare.'" Brandeis concluded that the statute was "obviously enacted for the purpose of protecting the public health, safety and welfare" and submitted "the facts of common knowledge of which the Court may take judicial notice" as proof of his argument.

The supporting evidence which followed the argument deeply impressed the Court, and Justice Brewer, who delivered the opinion, quoted extensively from it. . . . Thus, for the first time in the history of the Court, due process was determined, not just by consideration of abstract legal concepts, but also on the basis of the social and economic implications of the law at issue.

SOURCE: Excerpted from Marion E. Doro, "The Brandeis Brief," *Vanderbilt Law Review* 11 (1958): 784; as reprinted in *Social Research in the Judicial Process*, ed. Wallace D. Loh (New York: Russell Sage, 1984), 88–90.

Report of the New York Bureau of Labor Statistics, 1900.

The family furnishes the really fundamental education of the growing generation—the education of character. . . . [T]he importance of a good family life in the training of character needs repeated emphasis, for it is the fundamental argument for a shorter working day.

Report of the United States Industrial Commission, 1901.

The entire tendency of industry is in the direction of an increased exertion. . . . This being true, there is but one alternative if the working population is to be protected in its health and trade longevity, namely, a reduction in the hours of labor.

Report of the Massachusetts Bureau of Labor Statistics, 1871.

It is claimed that legislation on this subject is an interference between labor and capital. But legislation has interfered with capital and labor both, in the demand for public safety and the public good. Now public safety and public good, the wealth of the commonwealth, centered, as such wealth is, in the well-being of its common people, demands that the State should interfere by special act in favor of working-women, and working children, by enacting a ten-hour law, to be enforced by a system of efficient inspection.[15]

In the end, with the help of the NCL, Brandeis produced an incredible document. Known in legal history as the Brandeis Brief, it contained more than one hundred pages of sociological data culled from various secondary sources and only two pages of legal argument *(see box 10-1 on pages 650–651).*

ARGUMENTS:

For the plaintiff in error, Curt Muller:
- This law discriminates against women with respect to certain employment rights.
- The law denies women and employers the right to enter into contracts to do the same work for which men and employers may contract. This violates the Fourteenth Amendment's due process clause.
- There are no grounds to treat women who work in laundries differently from women working in other occupations. Laundry work is not unusually dangerous or unhealthy.
- This law, purportedly intended to protect women's health, is not based on the dangers or hazards of the

job; rather, it only limits how long a woman may agree to work.

For the defendant in error, state of Oregon:
- The right to buy or sell labor is part of the liberty protected by the Fourteenth Amendment, but that right is subject to reasonable restraint through the exercise of the state's police power for the protection of the health, safety, morals, and general welfare of the citizens.
- Laws restricting liberty must have a substantial relation to the protection of public health and safety. This law meets that qualification and therefore should be maintained.
- Laws such as the one challenged here have been enacted in many foreign nations and in several states.
- As demonstrated in many research studies, long work hours have a detrimental effect on women's health and well-being. Shorter work hours have a beneficial effect on women's lives, on their families' lives, and on worker productivity.

MR. JUSTICE BREWER DELIVERED THE OPINION OF THE COURT.

We held in *Lochner v. New York* that a law providing that no laborer shall be required or permitted to work in bakeries more than sixty hours in a week or ten hours in a day was not, as to men, a legitimate exercise of the police power of the state, but an unreasonable, unnecessary and arbitrary interference with the right and liberty of the individual to contract in relation to his labor, and as such was in conflict with, and void under, the Federal Constitution. That decision is invoked by plaintiff in error as decisive of the question before us. But this assumes that the difference between the sexes does not justify a different rule respecting a restriction of the hours of labor.

In patent cases counsel are apt to open the argument with a discussion of the state of the art. It may not be amiss, in the present case, before examining the constitutional question, to notice the course of legislation, as well as expressions of opinion from other than judicial sources. In the brief filed by Mr. Louis D. Brandeis for the defendant in error is a very copious collection of all these matters, an epitome of which is found in the margin.

The legislation and opinions referred to in the margin may not be, technically speaking, authorities, and in them is little or no discussion of the constitutional question presented to us for determination, yet they are significant of a widespread

---

15. For more excerpts, see John Monahan and Laurens Walker, *Social Science in Law* (Westbury, NY: Foundation Press, 1998), 4–7.

belief that woman's physical structure, and the functions she performs in consequence thereof, justify special legislation restricting or qualifying the conditions under which she should be permitted to toil. Constitutional questions, it is true, are not settled by even a consensus of present public opinion, for it is the peculiar value of a written constitution that it places in unchanging form limitations upon legislative action, and thus gives a permanence and stability to popular government which otherwise would be lacking. At the same time, when a question of fact is debated and debatable, and the extent to which a special constitutional limitation goes is affected by the truth in respect to that fact, a widespread and long-continued belief concerning it is worthy of consideration. We take judicial cognizance of all matters of general knowledge.

It is undoubtedly true, as more than once declared by this court, that the general right to contract in relation to one's business is part of the liberty of the individual, protected by the 14th Amendment to the Federal Constitution; yet it is equally well settled that this liberty is not absolute and extending to all contracts, and that a state may, without conflicting with the provisions of the 14th Amendment, restrict in many respects the individual's power of contract. Without stopping to discuss at length the extent to which a state may act in this respect, we refer to the following cases in which the question has been considered: *Allgeyer v. Louisiana; Holden v. Hardy; Lochner v. New York.*

That woman's physical structure and the performance of maternal functions place her at a disadvantage in the struggle for subsistence is obvious. This is especially true when the burdens of motherhood are upon her. Even when they are not, by abundant testimony of the medical fraternity, continuance for a long time on her feet at work, repeating this from day to day, tends to injurious effects upon the body, and, as healthy mothers are essential to vigorous offspring, the physical well-being of woman becomes an object of public interest and care in order to preserve the strength and vigor of the race.

Still again, history discloses the fact that woman has always been dependent upon man. He established his control at the outset by superior physical strength, and this control in various forms, with diminishing intensity, has continued to the present. As minors, though not to the same extent, she has been looked upon in the courts as needing especial care that her rights may be preserved. Education was long denied her, and while now the doors of the schoolroom are opened and her opportunities for acquiring knowledge are great, yet even with that and the consequent increase of capacity for business affairs, it is still true that in the struggle for subsistence she is not an equal competitor with her brother. Though limitations upon personal and contractual rights may be removed by legislation, there is that in her disposition and habits of life which will operate against a full assertion of those rights. She will still be where some legislation to protect her seems necessary to secure a real equality of right. Doubtless there are individual exceptions, and there are many respects in which she has an advantage over him; but looking at it from the viewpoint of the effort to maintain an independent position in life, she is not upon an equality. Differentiated by these matters from the other sex, she is properly placed in a class by herself, and legislation designed for her protection may be sustained, even when like legislation is not necessary for men, and could not be sustained. It is impossible to close one's eyes to the fact that she still looks to her brother and depends upon him. Even though all restrictions on political, personal, and contractual rights were taken away, and she stood, so far as statutes are concerned, upon an absolutely equal plane with him, it would still be true that she is so constituted that she will rest upon and look to him for protection; that her physical structure and a proper discharge of her maternal functions—having in view not merely her own health, but the well-being of the race—justify legislation to protect her from the greed as well as the passion of man. The limitations which this statute places upon her contractual powers, upon her right to agree with her employer as to the time she shall labor, are not imposed solely for her benefit, but also largely for the benefit of all. Many words cannot make this plainer. The two sexes differ in structure of body, in the functions to be performed by each, in the amount of physical strength, in the capacity for long-continued labor, particularly when done standing, the influence of vigorous health upon the future well-being of the race, the self-reliance which enables one to assert full rights, and in the capacity to maintain the struggle for subsistence. This difference justifies a difference in legislation, and upholds that which is designed to compensate for some of the burdens which rest upon her.

We have not referred in this discussion to the denial of the elective franchise in the state of Oregon, for while that may disclose a lack of political equality in all things with her brother, that is not of itself decisive. The reason runs deeper, and rests in the inherent difference between the two sexes, and in the different functions in life which they perform.

For these reasons, and without questioning in any respect the decision in *Lochner v. New York*, we are of the opinion that it cannot be adjudged that the act in question is in conflict with the Federal Constitution, so far as it respects the work of a female in a laundry, and the judgment of the Supreme Court of Oregon is affirmed.

Why did the justices affirm the Oregon law? One answer is that the Court did not depart from *Lochner*—it merely found that Oregon's regulations, unlike New York's, were a reasonable use of the state's power. But the Court applied the reasonableness approach in both *Lochner* and *Holden* and came to completely different conclusions. So, despite the Court's attempt to distinguish *Lochner,* how much can the application of that standard possibly explain about *Muller*'s outcome? Another possibility is that Brandeis forced the Court to see the reasonableness of the Oregon regulation. By presenting such a mass of statistical data, he kept the justices riveted on the law and diverted their attention from a substantive due process approach. The strategy worked. The Court even commended Brandeis's brief.

Winning *Muller* gave a big boost to the Progressive movement. Some worried, however, that the decision depended on the fact that the law covered only women and that when the Court had an opportunity to review a law covering all workers, it would apply *Lochner*. This fear increased when the Court agreed to review *Bunting v. Oregon* (1917), which involved another Oregon law providing that "no person shall be employed in any mill, factory, or manufacturing establishment in this state more than ten hours in any one day." Compounding the NCL's concern was that Brandeis now sat on the Supreme Court and would almost certainly recuse himself because he had been involved in the early stages of the dispute.

In 1917, however, the Supreme Court dispelled the NCL's concerns. In a 5–3 decision, with Brandeis not participating, the majority upheld the Oregon law. Writing for the Court, Justice Joseph McKenna explained: although Franklin O. Bunting contended that "the law . . . is not either necessary or useful 'for the preservation of the health of employees,'" no evidence was provided to support that contention. Moreover, the judgment of the Oregon legislature and supreme court was that "it cannot be held, as a matter of law, that the legislative requirement is unreasonable or arbitrary." McKenna concluded, therefore, that no further discussion was "necessary" and upheld the law.

The Court failed even to mention *Lochner*. But given the Court's holding, many predicted the death of that decision; after all, it was wholly incompatible with *Bunting*. Perhaps the demise of substantive due process would follow. Indeed, throughout the period between *Mugler* (1887) and up to about *Bunting*, it appeared

that *Lochner* was more the exception than the rule. Between 1887 and 1910 the Court decided 558 cases involving due process claims challenging state regulations and upheld 83 percent of the laws. It now seemed that *Lochner,* not *Muller,* was the unusual case.[16]

THE HEYDAY OF SUBSTANTIVE DUE PROCESS: 1923–1936

The *Bunting* funeral for *Lochner* proved to be premature. Within six years, not only did the Court virtually overrule *Bunting,* but also the justices seemed to be more committed to the *Lochner* version of due process than ever before. *Adkins v. Children's Hospital* (1923) provides an excellent illustration of the magnitude of this resurgence. As you read the Court's ruling, compare it with *Muller*. Is there any way, legally speaking, to distinguish the two decisions? Or do you suspect that other, extralegal factors came into play?

Adkins v. Children's Hospital

261 U.S. 525 (1923)

http://laws.findlaw.com/us/261/525.html

Vote: 5 (Butler, McKenna, McReynolds, Sutherland, Van Devanter)
    3 (Holmes, Sanford, Taft)

OPINION OF THE COURT: Sutherland
DISSENTING OPINIONS: Holmes, Taft
NOT PARTICIPATING: Brandeis

FACTS:

In 1918 Congress, with the support of progressive-oriented president Woodrow Wilson, enacted a law that established the Minimum Wage Board of the District of Columbia and gave it authority to set minimum wages for women and children in Washington, D.C.[17] The board, staffed by progressives, ordered that restaurants and hospitals pay women workers a minimum wage of 34.5 cents per hour, $16.50 per week, or $71.50 per month. According to the board, these rates would "supply the necessary cost of living to . . . women workers to maintain them in good health and morals."

Children's Hospital of the District of Columbia, which employed many women, refused to comply and sued the members of the Wage Board to enjoin enforcement of

---

16. Kelly, Harbison, and Belz, *The American Constitution*, 405.

17. We derive this account from Vose, *Constitutional Change*, 190–196.

In Adkins v. Children's Hospital *the Supreme Court struck down a federal minimum wage law on substantive due process grounds. The legal action to enjoin enforcement of the law was filed by the corporation that managed Children's Hospital of the District of Columbia (left).*

the regulations. In the hospital's opinion, the law violated the due process clause of the Fifth Amendment encompassing the liberty to enter into salary contracts with employees.[18] Along with the Children's Hospital appeal, the Court heard the case of a female elevator operator who sued the Wage Board for loss of employment and income because she was laid off when her employer could not afford to pay her the minimum wage.

Because of delay at the lower court level, the case did not reach the Supreme Court until 1923. An attorney for the Wage Board, assisted by NCL attorney (and future Supreme Court justice) Felix Frankfurter and other NCL staffers, sought to defend the 1918 law on grounds similar to Brandeis's in *Muller.* They offered the Court "impressive documentation on the cost of living and the desirability of good wages."

ARGUMENTS:

For the appellants, Jesse C. Adkins et al. of the Minimum Wage Board of the District of Columbia:

- The Court should focus on the reasonableness of the law. This legislation is rational. Congress relied

on its experience and the experiences of several states. It conducted ample hearings and investigations. The law is not arbitrary.
- Safeguarding women and children from conditions that would endanger their health and morals is a government responsibility and a legitimate end.
- The means adopted by Congress are appropriate and plainly designed to accomplish the legislative end.

For the appellee, Children's Hospital of the District of Columbia:

- This is a price-fixing law, pure and simple. It does not regulate working conditions or health factors. Fixing prices is beyond appropriate legislative authority.
- The law violates the due process clause of the Fifth Amendment because it restricts a woman's right to contract for her labor.
- The constitutional problems associated with restricting freedom of contract are not eliminated by the exclusion of male workers from the law.
- The law is not temporary, nor is it a response to a temporary emergency.

---

18. Because the District of Columbia is not a state, the due process clause of the Fourteenth Amendment did not apply.

MR. JUSTICE SUTHERLAND DELIVERED THE OPINION OF THE COURT.

The statute now under consideration is attacked upon the ground that it authorizes an unconstitutional interference with the freedom of contract included within the guaranties of the due process clause of the 5th Amendment. That the right to contract about one's affairs is a part of the liberty of the individual protected by this clause is settled by the decisions of this court, and is no longer open to question. . . .

There is, of course, no such thing as absolute freedom of contract. It is subject to a great variety of restraints. But freedom of contract is, nevertheless, the general rule and restraint the exception; and the exercise of legislative authority to abridge it can be justified only by the existence of exceptional circumstances. . . .

[The statute under consideration] is simply and exclusively a price-fixing law, confined to adult women . . . who are legally as capable of contracting for themselves as men. It forbids two parties having lawful capacity—under penalties as to the employer—to freely contract with one another in respect of the price for which one shall render service to the other in a purely private employment. . . .

The feature of this statute which, perhaps more than any other, puts upon it the stamp of invalidity is that it exacts from the employer an arbitrary payment for a purpose and upon a basis having no causal connection with his business, or the contract, or the work the employee engages to do. The declared basis . . . is not the value of the service rendered, but the extraneous circumstance that the employee needs to get a prescribed sum of money to insure her subsistence, health, and morals. . . . The moral requirement, implicit in every contract of employment, viz., that the amount to be paid and the service to be rendered shall bear to each other some relation of just equivalence, is completely ignored. The necessities of the employee are alone considered, and these arise outside of the employment, are the same when there is no employment, and as great in one occupation as in another. Certainly the employer, by paying a fair equivalent for the service rendered, though not sufficient to support the employee, has neither caused nor contributed to her poverty. . . . A statute requiring an employer to pay in money, to pay at prescribed and regular intervals, to pay the value of the services rendered, even to pay with fair relation to the extent of the benefit obtained from the service, would be understandable. But a statute which prescribes payment without regard to any of these things, and solely with relation to circumstances apart from the contract of employment, the business affected by it, and the work done under it, is so clearly the product of a naked, arbitrary exercise of power, that it cannot be allowed to stand under the Constitution of the United States. . . .

It has been said that legislation of the kind now under review is required in the interest of social justice, for whose ends freedom of contract may lawfully be subjected to restraint. The liberty of the individual to do as he pleases, even in innocent matters, is not absolute. It must frequently yield to the common good, and the line beyond which the power of interference may not be pressed is neither definite nor unalterable, but may be made to move, within limits not well defined, with changing need and circumstance. Any attempt to fix a rigid boundary would be unwise as well as futile. But, nevertheless, there are limits to the power, and when these have been passed, it becomes the plain duty of the courts, in the proper exercise of their authority, to so declare. To sustain the individual freedom of action contemplated by the Constitution is not to strike down the common good, but to exalt it; for surely the good of society as a whole cannot be better served than by the preservation against arbitrary restraint of the liberties of its constituent members.

It follows from what has been said that the act in question passes the limit prescribed by the Constitution, and, accordingly, the decrees of the court below are affirmed.

MR. CHIEF JUSTICE TAFT, dissenting.

I regret much to differ from the court in these cases.

The boundary of the police power beyond which its exercise becomes an invasion of the guaranty of liberty under the Fifth and Fourteenth Amendments to the Constitutions is not easy to mark. Our court has been laboriously engaged in pricking out a line in successive cases. We must be careful, it seems to me, to follow that line as well as we can, and not to depart from it by suggesting a distinction that is formal rather than real.

Legislatures in limiting freedom of contract between employee and employer by a minimum wage proceed on the assumption that employees, in the class receiving least pay, are not upon a full level of equality of choice with their employer and in their necessitous circumstances are prone to accept pretty much anything that is offered. They are peculiarly subject to the overreaching of the harsh and greedy employer. The evils of the sweating system and of the long hours and low wages which are characteristic of it are well known. Now, I agree that it is a disputable question in the field of political economy how far a statutory requirement of maximum hours or minimum wages may be a useful remedy for these evils, and whether it may not make the case of the oppressed employee worse than it was before. But it is not the function of this court to hold congressional acts invalid simply because they are passed to carry out economic views which the court believes to be unwise or unsound. . . .

The right of the Legislature under the Fifth and Fourteenth Amendments to limit the hours of employment on the score of the health of the employee, it seems to me, has been firmly established. As to that, one would think, the line had been pricked out so that it has become a well formulated rule. In *Holden v. Hardy* it was applied to miners and rested on the unfavorable environment of employment in mining and smelting. In *Lochner v. New York* it was held that restricting those employed in bakeries to 10 hours a day was an arbitrary and invalid interference with the liberty of contract secured by the Fourteenth Amendment. Then followed a number of cases beginning with *Muller v. Oregon*, sustaining the validity of a limit on maximum hours of labor for women to which I shall hereafter allude, and following these cases came *Bunting v. Oregon*. In that case, this court sustained a law limiting the hours of labor of any person, whether man or woman, working in any mill, factory, or manufacturing establishment to 10 hours a day with a proviso as to further hours to which I shall hereafter advert. The law covered the whole field of industrial employment and certainly covered the case of persons employed in bakeries. Yet the opinion in the *Bunting* Case does not mention the *Lochner* Case. No one can suggest any constitutional distinction between employment in a bakery and one in any other kind of a manufacturing establishment which should make a limit of hours in the one invalid, and the same limit in the other permissible. It is impossible for me to reconcile the *Bunting* Case and the *Lochner* Case, and I have always supposed that the *Lochner* Case was thus overruled *sub silentio*. . . .

I am authorized to say that MR. JUSTICE SANFORD concurs in this opinion.

MR. JUSTICE HOLMES, dissenting.

The question in this case is the broad one, whether Congress can establish minimum rates of wages for women in the District of Columbia, with due provision for special circumstances, or whether we must say that Congress has no power to meddle with the matter at all. To me, notwithstanding the deference due to the prevailing judgment of the court, the power of Congress seems absolutely free

from doubt. The end—to remove conditions leading to ill health, immorality, and the deterioration of the race—no one would deny to be within the scope of constitutional legislation. The means are means that have the approval of Congress, of many states, and of those governments from which we have learned our greatest lessons. When so many intelligent persons, who have studied the matter more than any of us can, have thought that the means are effective and are worth the price, it seems to me impossible to deny that the belief reasonably may be held by reasonable men. . . . [T]he only objection that can be urged is found within the vague contours of the 5th Amendment, prohibiting the depriving any person of liberty or property without due process of law. To that I turn.

The earlier decisions upon the same words in the 14th Amendment began within our memory, and went no farther than an unpretentious assertion of the liberty to follow the ordinary callings. Later that innocuous generality was expanded into the dogma, Liberty of Contract. Contract is not specially mentioned in the text that we have to construe. It is merely an example of doing what you want to do, embodied in the word "liberty." But pretty much all law consists in forbidding men to do some things that they want to do, and contract is no more exempt from law than other acts. . . .

I confess that I do not understand the principle on which the power to fix a minimum for the wages of women can be denied by those who admit the power to fix a maximum for their hours of work. I fully assent to the proposition that here, as elsewhere, the distinctions of the law are distinctions of degree; but I perceive no difference in the kind or degree of interference with liberty, the only matter with which we have any concern, between the one case and the other. The bargain is equally affected whichever half you regulate. . . .

I am of opinion that the statute is valid.

Adkins represented the return of substantive due process; indeed, it made clear that *Muller* and *Bunting* had not nullified that doctrine. If anything, as Justice Holmes's dissent noted, it had come back stronger than ever with the term *due process of law* evolving into the "dogma, Liberty of Contract."

Why the change? In large measure the change can be traced back to the political climate of the day. Following World War I, the U.S. economy boomed, and voters elected one president after another who was committed to a free market economy. These presidents,

TABLE 10-2   The Supreme Court: From *Bunting* to *Adkins*

JUSTICE	BUNTING VOTE (1917)	HARDING APPOINTMENTS (1921–1922)	ADKINS VOTE (1923)
McKenna	Upheld law	No change	Struck law
Holmes	Upheld law	No change	Upheld law
Day	Upheld law	Replaced by Butler	Struck law
Pitney	Upheld law	Replaced by Sanford	Upheld law
Clarke	Upheld law	Replaced by Sutherland	Struck law
White	Struck law	Replaced by Taft	Upheld law
Van Devanter	Struck law	No change	Struck law
McReynolds	Struck law	No change	Struck law
Brandeis	No participation	No change	No participation

in turn, appointed justices, at least some of whom shared those beliefs. As table 10-2 indicates, one president, Warren Harding, made the first four of these new Supreme Court appointments. Clement E. Vose notes, "[T]he most important single fact about the Harding appointments was that he named two ardent conservatives of the old school—Sutherland and Butler—to serve along with two justices similarly committed who were already sitting—Van Devanter and McReynolds."[19] By 1922 all Four Horsemen were in place.

The entrenchment of substantive due process, as we mentioned at the beginning of this chapter, was but one manifestation of the impact of Republican appointments to the Court during that era. With their strong commitment to an unfettered market, these conservative justices also invoked creative theories of the limits of national power, especially dual federalism, to strike down federal regulatory efforts. Collectively, the doctrines of dual federalism and substantive due process became effective weapons in nullifying meaningful social legislation.

THE DEPRESSION, THE NEW DEAL, AND THE DECLINE OF ECONOMIC SUBSTANTIVE DUE PROCESS

The laissez-faire approach of the Court through the 1920s was in keeping with the times. The nation continued to boom and to elect politicians—President Herbert Hoover, for example—who were committed to

19. Vose, *Constitutional Change*, 194.

a private sector–based economy that they believed would remain successful if left free from regulation. The Great Depression, triggered by the stock market crash of 1929, and the subsequent election of Franklin Roosevelt demonstrate just how quickly that perception changed. The Depression undermined the faith of many who thought an unregulated economy could successfully adjust itself to changing economic conditions. Roosevelt's election indicated the public's desire for government action to get the nation back on its feet.

At first it appeared that the Court, although dominated by conservative justices, might repudiate substantive due process and go along with federal and state efforts to ameliorate the effects of the Depression. How could government exercise any control over matters affecting the economy if the Court continued to strike down the legislatures' efforts on substantive due process grounds? This was a central question confronting the Court in *Nebbia v. New York*.

Nebbia v. New York

291 U.S. 502 (1934)
http://laws.findlaw.com/us/291/502.html
Vote: 5 (Brandeis, Cardozo, Hughes, Roberts, Stone)
4 (Butler, McReynolds, Sutherland, Van Devanter)
OPINION OF THE COURT: *Roberts*
DISSENTING OPINION: *McReynolds*

FACTS:

In 1933 the New York State legislature created the Milk Control Board, in which it vested the power to fix minimum and maximum prices that stores could charge consumers for milk. The board set the price of a quart

To help stabilize the market, the New York Milk Control Board fixed the price of a quart of milk at nine cents. When grocery store owner Leo Nebbia, pictured above, sold two quarts of milk and a loaf of bread for eighteen cents, the state convicted him of violating the board's order. In 1934 the Supreme Court rejected Nebbia's claim that the order violated his constitutional rights, ruling that it was a valid exercise of state power.

of milk at nine cents, but Leo Nebbia, the owner of a grocery store in Rochester, New York, sold two quarts of milk and a five-cent loaf of bread to Jedo Del Signori for eighteen cents. He was convicted of violating the board's order and fined $5. He paid the fine under protest and appealed his conviction on the ground that the milk regulations were unconstitutional.

In arguing against the law, Nebbia invoked the Fourteenth Amendment's due process clause: the establishment of fixed milk prices interfered with his ability to conduct his business. Attorneys for the state countered that the law authorizing the board to set prices was a valid exercise of state police power. New York had reached this position, the attorneys claimed, after conducting an "exhaustive investigation of conditions in the milk industry in the States." Among the findings of the investigation were these:

- Milk is an essential item of the diet. It cannot long be stored. It is an excellent medium for growth of bacteria. These facts necessitate safeguards in its production and handling for human consumption that greatly increase the cost of the business. Failure of producers to receive a reasonable return for their labor

and investment over an extended period threaten a relaxation of vigilance against contamination.

- The production and distribution of milk is a paramount industry of the state, and largely affects the health and prosperity of its people. Dairying yields fully one-half of the total income from all farm products. Dairy farm investment amounts to approximately $1 billion. Curtailment or destruction of the dairy industry would cause a serious economic loss to the people of the state.

- In addition to the general price decline, other causes for the low price of milk include a periodic increase in the number of cows and in milk production; the prevalence of unfair and destructive trade practices in the distribution of milk, leading to a drop in prices in the metropolitan area and other markets; and the failure of transportation and distribution charges to be reduced in proportion to the reduction in retail prices for milk and cream.

ARGUMENTS:

For the appellant, Leo Nebbia:
- Laws in other states to fix prices of common commodities have been struck down by the lower courts

for being in conflict with the due process clause of the Fourteenth Amendment.

- The milk control law discriminates against Nebbia because its provisions are more restrictive on shopkeepers than on those who sell milk in other ways, such as home delivery.
- The nation's economic emergency does not suspend the Constitution.
- The milk control law violates the liberties of buyer and seller freely to reach an agreement over a sales price for a wholesome product.

For the appellee, state of New York:

- The necessity for any exercise of the state's police power is first to be determined by the legislature. Here, the New York legislature has found a need to impose controls on the buying and selling of milk.
- Because of the importance of milk, it may be regulated in much the same manner as a public utility.
- Fixing prices is a common form of utility regulation.
- There is a clear relationship between the control of milk prices and the public interest. Therefore the law should be sustained.

MR. JUSTICE ROBERTS DELIVERED THE OPINION OF THE COURT.

The . . . question is whether . . . the enforcement of [New York's law] denied the appellant the due process secured to him by the Fourteenth Amendment. . . .

Under our form of government the use of property and the making of contracts are normally matters of private and not of public concern. The general rule is that both shall be free of governmental interference. But neither property rights nor contract rights are absolute; for government cannot exist if the citizen may at will use his property to the detriment of his fellows, or exercise his freedom of contract to work them harm. Equally fundamental with the private right is that of the public to regulate it in the common interest. As Chief Justice Marshall said, speaking specifically of inspection laws, such laws form "a portion of that immense mass of legislation, which embraces every thing within the territory of a State . . . all which can be most advantageously exercised by the States themselves. Inspection laws, quarantine laws, health laws of every description, as well as laws for regulating the internal commerce of a State, . . . are component parts of this mass." . . .

Thus has this court from the early days affirmed that the power to promote the general welfare is inherent in government. Touching the matters committed to it by the Constitution, the United States possesses the power, as do the states in their sovereign capacity touching all subjects jurisdiction of which is not surrendered to the federal government. . . . These correlative rights, that of the citizen to exercise exclusive dominion over property and freely to contract about his affairs, and that of the state to regulate the use of property and the conduct of business, are always in collision. No exercise of the private right can be imagined which will not in some respect, however slight, affect the public; no exercise of the legislative prerogative to regulate the conduct of the citizen which will not to some extent abridge his liberty or affect his property. But subject only to constitutional restraint the private right must yield to the public need. . . .

The milk industry in New York has been the subject of long-standing and drastic regulation in the public interest. The legislative investigation of 1932 was persuasive of the fact that for this and other reasons unrestricted competition aggravated existing evils, and the normal law of supply and demand was insufficient to correct maladjustments detrimental to the community. The inquiry disclosed destructive and demoralizing competitive conditions and unfair trade practices which resulted in retail price-cutting and reduced the income of the farmer below the cost of production. We do not understand the appellant to deny that in these circumstances the legislature might reasonably consider further regulation and control desirable for protection of the industry and the consuming public. That body believed conditions could be improved by preventing destructive price-cutting by stores which, due to the flood of surplus milk, were able to buy at much lower prices than the larger distributors and to sell without incurring the delivery costs of the latter. In the order of which complaint is made the Milk Control Board fixed a price of ten cents per quart for sales by a distributor to a consumer, and nine cents by a store to a consumer, thus recognizing the lower costs of the store, and endeavoring to establish a differential which would be just to both. In the light of the facts the order appears not to be unreasonable or arbitrary, or without relation to the purpose to prevent ruthless competition from destroying the wholesale price structure on which the farmer depends for his livelihood, and the community for an assured supply of milk.

But we are told that because the law essays to control prices it denies due process. Notwithstanding the admitted power to correct existing economic ills by appropriate regulation of business, even though an indirect result may be a restriction of the freedom of contract or a modification of charges for services or the price of commodities, the appellant urges that direct fixation of prices is a type of regulation absolutely forbidden. His position is that the Fourteenth Amendment requires us to hold the challenged statute void for this reason alone. The argument runs that the public control of rates or prices is *per se* unreasonable and unconstitutional, save as applied to businesses affected with a public interest; that a business so affected is one in which property is devoted to an enterprise of a sort which the public itself might appropriately undertake, or one whose owner relies on a public grant or franchise for the right to conduct the business, or in which he is bound to serve all who apply; in short, such as is commonly called a public utility; or a business in its nature a monopoly. The milk industry, it is said, possesses none of these characteristics, and, therefore, not being affected with a public interest, its charges may not be controlled by the state. Upon the soundness of this contention the appellant's case against the statute depends.

We may as well say at once that the dairy industry is not, in the accepted sense of the phrase, a public utility. . . . But if, as must be conceded, the industry is subject to regulation in the public interest, what constitutional principle bars the state from correcting existing maladjustments by legislation touching prices? We think there is no such principle. The due process clause makes no mention of sales or of prices any more than it speaks of business or contracts or buildings or other incidents of property. The thought seems nevertheless to have persisted that there is something peculiarly sacrosanct about the price one may charge for what he makes or sells, and that, however able to regulate other elements of manufacture or trade, with incidental effect upon price, the state is incapable of directly controlling the price itself. This view was negatived many years ago. *Munn v. Illinois.* . . .

It is clear that there is no closed class or category of businesses affected with a public interest, and the function of courts in the application of the Fifth and Fourteenth Amendments is to determine in each case whether circumstances vindicate the challenged regulation as a reasonable exertion of governmental authority or condemn it as arbitrary or discriminatory. The phrase "affected with a public interest" can, in the nature of things, mean no more than that an industry, for adequate reason, is subject to control for the public good. In several of the decisions of this court wherein the expressions "affected with a public interest," and "clothed with a public use," have been brought forward as the criteria of the validity of price

control, it has been admitted that they are not susceptible of definition and form an unsatisfactory test of the constitutionality of legislation directed at business practices or prices. These decisions must rest, finally, upon the basis that the requirements of due process were not met because the laws were found arbitrary in their operation and effect. But there can be no doubt that upon proper occasion and by appropriate measures the state may regulate a business in any of its aspects, including the prices to be charged for the products or commodities it sells.

So far as the requirement of due process is concerned, and in the absence of other constitutional restriction, a state is free to adopt whatever economic policy may reasonably be deemed to promote public welfare, and to enforce that policy by legislation adapted to its purpose. The courts are without authority either to declare such policy, or, when it is declared by the legislature, to override it. If the laws passed are seen to have a reasonable relation to a proper legislative purpose, and are neither arbitrary nor discriminatory, the requirements of due process are satisfied, and judicial determination to that effect renders a court *functus officio* [*i.e.,* the court has completed its task and lacks the authority to do more]. . . . And it is equally clear that if the legislative policy be to curb unrestrained and harmful competition by measures which are not arbitrary or discriminatory it does not lie with the courts to determine that the rule is unwise. With the wisdom of the policy adopted, the adequacy or practicability of the law enacted to forward it, the courts are both incompetent and unauthorized to deal. The course of decision in this court exhibits a firm adherence to these principles. Times without number we have said that the legislature is primarily the judge of the necessity of such an enactment, that every possible presumption is in favor of its validity, and that though the court may hold views inconsistent with the wisdom of the law, it may not be annulled unless palpably in excess of legislative power. . . .

Tested by these considerations we find no basis in the due process clause of the Fourteenth Amendment for condemning the provisions of the . . . Law here drawn into question.

The judgment is affirmed.

Separate opinion of MR. JUSTICE MCREYNOLDS.

Regulation to prevent recognized evils in business has long been upheld as permissible legislative action. But fixation of the price at which A, engaged in an ordinary business, may sell, in order to enable B, a producer, to improve his condition, has not been regarded as within legislative power. This is not regulation, but management, control, dictation—it amounts to the deprivation of the fundamental right which one has to conduct his own affairs honestly and along customary lines. The argument advanced here would support general prescription of prices for farm products, groceries, shoes, clothing, all the necessities of modern civilization, as well as labor, when some Legislature finds and declares such action advisable and for the public good. This Court has declared that a state may not by legislative fiat convert a private business into a public utility. And if it be now ruled that one dedicates his property to public use whenever he embarks on an enterprise which the Legislature may think it desirable to bring under control, this is but to declare that rights guaranteed by the Constitution exist only so long as supposed public interest does not require their extinction. To adopt such a view, of course, would put an end to liberty under the Constitution. . . .

Not only does the statute interfere arbitrarily with the rights of the little grocer to conduct his business according to standards long accepted—complete destruction may follow; but it takes away the liberty of 12,000,000 consumers to buy a necessity of life in an open market. It imposes direct and arbitrary burdens upon those already seriously impoverished with the alleged immediate design of affording special benefits to others. To him with less than 9 cents it says: You cannot procure a quart of milk from the grocer although he is anxious to accept what you can pay and the demands of your household are urgent! A superabundance; but no child can purchase from a willing storekeeper below the figure appointed by three men at headquarters! And this is true although the storekeeper himself may have bought from a willing producer at half that rate and must sell quickly or lose his stock through deterioration. The fanciful scheme is to protect the farmer against undue exactions by prescribing the price at which milk disposed of by him at will may be resold! . . .

The judgment of the court below should be reversed.

Mr. Justice VAN DEVANTER, Mr. Justice SUTHERLAND, and Mr. Justice BUTLER authorize me to say that they concur in this opinion.

Although *Nebbia,* in retrospect, was a sign that the heyday of substantive due process was drawing to a close, that was hardly the case in the context of the day. As you will recall from the chapters on federalism (6)

and the commerce clause (7), for the next two years the Court generally continued along its laissez-faire path of the 1920s—seemingly ignorant of the political, economic, and social events transpiring around it. In particular, it refused to let go of the doctrine of substantive due process.

Just two years after *Nebbia,* it decided another New York case, but in a quite different way. At issue in ***Morehead v. New York ex rel. Tipaldo*** (1936) was a 1933 minimum wage law that "declared it to be against public policy for any employer to employ any woman at an oppressive and unreasonable wage." It defined as unreasonable a wage that was "both less than the fair and reasonable value of the services rendered and less than sufficient to meet the minimum cost of living necessary for health." If a woman thought that her employer was paying her inadequate wages, she could file a complaint with a state board. Women employees of a laundry invoked this procedure against Joseph Tipaldo, the manager of the operation. In 1934 Tipaldo was found guilty: he paid his employees only $7.00 to $10.00 per week, although the board had set $12.40 as a minimum wage.

When the case reached the Supreme Court, Tipaldo received some support from an unexpected source: the feminist National Woman's Party (NWP). Although it did not agree with his substantive due process claim, the NWP argued that the New York law violated the Constitution on the ground that it treated the sexes differently and fostered inequality. As NWP leaders explained,

The Woman's Party stands for equality between men and women in all laws. This includes laws affecting the position of women in industry as well as all other laws. The Woman's Party does not take any position with regard to the merits of minimum wage legislation, but it does demand that such legislation, if passed, shall be for both sexes. It is opposed to all legislation having a sex basis and applying to one sex alone.[20]

Attorneys defending the state's action, including NCL representatives, therefore, faced a difficult challenge. The constituency benefiting from the law—women—was divided over the issue, but more important, the attorneys had to deal with the *Adkins* precedent. In part, they did so by trying to distinguish

---

20. Quoted in Vose, *Constitutional Change,* 212.

this law from the one at issue in *Adkins;* they also tried to demonstrate that economic conditions had changed considerably since 1923 and required this kind of regulation. Moreover, they had the *Nebbia* ruling in hand. It was just possible that the Court might go along with the state. But it was not to be. In keeping with their rulings on federal New Deal legislation and as a result of Justice Owen Roberts's defection from the *Nebbia* majority, the Court struck the New York law. Writing for a majority of five, Justice Pierce Butler was just as emphatic on the subject of substantive due process as the *Adkins* Court had been: "Freedom of contract is the general rule and restraint the exception."

The End of Economic Substantive Due Process: *West Coast Hotel v. Parrish*

The Court's refusal to uphold federal New Deal legislation, as you recall from chapter 7, angered President Roosevelt. Its ruling in *Morehead* cut even deeper. As Peter Irons notes, "More than any other decision by the Court during the New Deal period, *Morehead* unleashed a barrage of criticism from conservatives as well as from liberals," who sympathized with the plight of women and children in the workforce.[21] Even the Republican Party's 1936 platform included a plank supporting the adoption of minimum wage and maximum hours laws of the sort struck down in *Morehead.*

Amid all this pressure, including Roosevelt's Court-packing scheme, the Court did a major about-face on the constitutionality of New Deal programs *(see chapter 7).* Prominent among the decisions ushering in the Court's new jurisprudence was *West Coast Hotel v. Parrish,* a ruling that would mean the demise of economic substantive due process.

West Coast Hotel v. Parrish

300 U.S. 379 (1937)
http://laws.findlaw.com/us/300/379.html
Vote: 5 (Brandeis, Cardozo, Hughes, Roberts, Stone)
4 (Butler, McReynolds, Sutherland, Van Devanter)

OPINION OF THE COURT: *Hughes*
DISSENTING OPINION: *Sutherland*

FACTS:

Elsie Parrish worked intermittently as a chambermaid in a Washington State hotel for a wage of twenty-two

cents to twenty-five cents per hour.[22] When she was discharged in 1935, she asked the management for back pay of $216.19, "the difference between what she had received and what she would have gotten" if the hotel had abided by the Washington Wage Board's minimum wage rate of $14.30 per week.

The hotel offered her $17.00, but Parrish refused to settle. Because of the community property laws in the state, she and her husband jointly brought suit against the hotel. Parrish found an attorney willing to represent her, but the attorney could not generate much interest in her case among outside organizations. Even the NCL declined to participate, viewing such efforts as a waste of time in light of *Morehead.* The Washington Supreme Court ruled in favor of Parrish, and the hotel sought Supreme Court review.

ARGUMENTS:

For the appellant, West Coast Hotel Company:

- In *Adkins v. Children's Hospital* the Court struck down a similar regulation of wages for women as a violation of the due process clause of the Fifth Amendment.
- Although *Adkins* involved a regulation imposed by the federal government, the due process language of the Fifth Amendment is identical to that of the Fourteenth. Therefore, there is no reason to conclude that the *Adkins* precedent is not applicable to similar state regulations.
- In *Morehead v. New York ex rel. Tipaldo* the Court declared unconstitutional a state law that prohibited employers from paying women an oppressive and unreasonable wage.
- *Adkins* and *Morehead* should control this case.

For the appellees, Ernest and Elsie Parrish:

- It is the legislature that first decides when the public welfare necessitates regulation under the state's police powers.
- The Washington legislature determined that the state's general welfare required this minimum wage law. Unless the law is entirely beyond the state's legislative power or operates in an unreasonable manner, it should be sustained.
- The *Adkins* precedent does not apply. The states' police powers are much broader than the powers of

---

21. Irons, *The New Deal Lawyers,* 278.

22. We derive this account from William E. Leuchtenburg, "The Case of the Wenatchee Chambermaid," in Garraty, *Quarrels That Have Shaped the Constitution.*

the federal government. That the federal government exceeded its powers does not necessarily mean that a state abuses its authority when it passes a similar law.

- The state legislature determined that an evil existed and that the minimum wage law was an appropriate remedy. The law was upheld by the state's highest court. The presumption of constitutionality should apply, and the Supreme Court should also uphold the law.

> **MR. CHIEF JUSTICE HUGHES DELIVERED THE OPINION OF THE COURT.**

This case presents the question of the constitutional validity of the minimum wage law of the State of Washington. . . .

The appellant relies upon the decision of this Court in *Adkins v. Children's Hospital*, which held invalid the District of Columbia Minimum Wage Act which was attacked under the due process clause of the Fifth Amendment. On the argument at bar, counsel for the appellees attempted to distinguish the *Adkins* Case upon the ground that the appellee was employed in a hotel and that the business of an innkeeper was affected with a public interest. That effort at distinction is obviously futile, as it appears that in one of the cases ruled by the *Adkins* opinion the employee was a woman employed as an elevator operator in a hotel.

The recent case of *Morehead v. New York* came here on certiorari to the New York court which had held the New York minimum wage act for women to be invalid. A minority of this Court thought that the New York statute was distinguishable in a material feature from that involved in the *Adkins* Case and that for that and other reasons the New York statute should be sustained. But the Court of Appeals of New York had said that it found no material difference between the two statutes and this Court held that the "meaning of the statute" as fixed by the decisions of the state court "must be accepted here as if the meaning had been specifically expressed in the enactment." That view led to the affirmance by this Court of the judgment in the *Morehead* Case, as the Court considered that the only question before it was whether the *Adkins* Case was distinguishable and that reconsideration of that decision had not been sought. Upon that point the Court said: "The petition for the writ sought review upon the ground that this case [*Morehead*] is distinguishable from that one [*Adkins*]. No application has been made for reconsideration of the constitutional question there decided. The validity of the

principles upon which that decision rests is not challenged. This court confines itself to the ground upon which the writ was asked or granted. . . . Here the review granted was no broader than that sought by the petitioner. . . . He is not entitled and does not ask to be heard upon the question whether the *Adkins* Case should be overruled. He maintains that it may be distinguished on the ground that the statutes are vitally dissimilar."

We think that the question which was not deemed to be open in the *Morehead* Case is open and is necessarily presented here. The Supreme Court of Washington has upheld the minimum wage statute of that State. It has decided that the statute is a reasonable exercise of the police power of the State. In reaching that conclusion the state court has invoked principles long established by this Court in the application of the Fourteenth Amendment. The state court has refused to regard the decision in the *Adkins* Case as determinative and has pointed to our decisions both before and since that case as justifying its position. We are of the opinion that this ruling of the state court demands on our part a reexamination of the *Adkins* Case. The importance of the question, in which many States having similar laws are concerned, the close division by which the decision in the *Adkins* Case was reached, and the economic conditions which have supervened, and in the light of which the reasonableness of the exercise of the protective power of the State must be considered, make it not only appropriate, but we think imperative, that in deciding the present case the subject should receive fresh consideration. . . .

The principle which must control our decision is not in doubt. The constitutional provision invoked is the due process clause of the Fourteenth Amendment governing the States, as the due process clause invoked in the *Adkins* Case governed Congress. In each case the violation alleged by those attacking minimum wage regulation for women is deprivation of freedom of contract. What is this freedom? The Constitution does not speak of freedom of contract. It speaks of liberty and prohibits the deprivation of liberty without due process of law. In prohibiting that deprivation the Constitution does not recognize an absolute and uncontrollable liberty. Liberty in each of its phases has its history and connotation. But the liberty safeguarded is liberty in a social organization which requires the protection of law against the evils which menace the health, safety, morals and welfare of the people. Liberty under the Constitution is thus necessarily subject to the restraints of due process, and regulation which is reasonable in relation to its subject and is adopted in the interests of the community is due process.

This essential limitation of liberty in general governs freedom of contract in particular. More than twenty-five years ago we set forth the applicable principle in these words after referring to the cases where the liberty guaranteed by the Fourteenth Amendment had been broadly described:

"But it was recognized in the cases cited, as in many others, that freedom of contract is a qualified and not an absolute right. There is no absolute freedom to do as one wills or to contract as one chooses. The guaranty of liberty does not withdraw from legislative supervision that wide department of activity which consists of the making of contracts, or deny to government the power to provide restrictive safeguards. Liberty implies the absence of arbitrary restraint, not immunity from reasonable regulations and prohibitions imposed in the interests of the community." *Chicago, Burlington & Quincy R. Co. v. McGuire* [1911].

This power under the Constitution to restrict freedom of contract has had many illustrations. That it may be exercised in the public interest with respect to contracts between employer and employee is undeniable. . . . In dealing with the relation of employer and employed, the legislature has necessarily a wide field of discretion in order that there may be suitable protection of health and safety, and that peace and good order may be promoted through regulations designed to insure wholesome conditions of work and freedom from oppression.

The point that has been strongly stressed that adult employees should be deemed competent to make their own contracts was decisively met nearly forty years ago in *Holden v. Hardy*, where we pointed out the inequality in the footing of the parties. . . .

It is manifest that this established principle is peculiarly applicable in relation to the employment of women in whose protection the State has a special interest. That phase of the subject received elaborate consideration in *Muller v. Oregon* (1908). . . . In later rulings this Court sustained the regulation of hours of work of women employees.

This array of precedents and the principles they applied were thought by the dissenting Justices in the *Adkins* Case to demand that the minimum wage statute be sustained. The validity of the distinction made by the Court between a minimum wage and a maximum of hours in limiting liberty of contract was especially challenged. That challenge persists and is without any satisfactory answer. . . .

One of the points which was pressed by the Court in supporting its ruling in the *Adkins* Case was that the standard set up by the District of Columbia Act did not take appropriate account of the value of the services rendered.

In the *Morehead* Case, the minority thought that the New York statute had met that point in its definition of a "fair wage" and that it accordingly presented a distinguishable feature which the Court could recognize within the limits which the *Morehead* petition for certiorari was deemed to present. The Court, however, did not take that view and the New York Act was held to be essentially the same as that for the District of Columbia. The statute now before us is like the latter, but we are unable to conclude that in its minimum wage requirement the State has passed beyond the boundary of its broad protective power.

The minimum wage to be paid under the Washington statute is fixed after full consideration by representatives of employers, employees and the public. It may be assumed that the minimum wage is fixed in consideration of the services that are performed in the particular occupations under normal conditions. Provision is made for special licenses at less wages in the case of women who are incapable of full service. The statement of Mr. Justice Holmes in the *Adkins* Case is pertinent: "This statute does not compel anybody to pay anything. It simply forbids employment at rates below those fixed as the minimum requirement of health and right living. It is safe to assume that women will not be employed at even the lowest wages allowed unless they earn them, or unless the employer's business can sustain the burden. In short the law in its character and operation is like hundreds of so-called police laws that have been upheld." . . .

We think that the views thus expressed are sound and that the decision in the *Adkins* Case was a departure from the true application of the principles governing the regulation by the State of the relation of employer and employed. Those principles have been reenforced by our subsequent decisions. . . .

With full recognition of the earnestness and vigor which characterize the prevailing opinion in the *Adkins* Case, we find it impossible to reconcile that ruling with these well-considered declarations. What can be closer to the public interest than the health of women and their protection from unscrupulous and overreaching employers? And if the protection of women is a legitimate end of the exercise of state power, how can it be said that the requirement of the payment of a minimum wage fairly fixed in order to meet the very necessities of existence is not an admissible means to that end? The legislature of the State was clearly entitled to consider the situation of women in employment, the fact that they are in the class receiving the least pay, that their bargaining power is relatively weak, and that they are the ready victims of those who would take advantage of their necessitous circumstances. The legislature was entitled to adopt measures to reduce the evils of the "sweating system," the exploiting of workers at wages so low as to be insufficient to meet the bare cost of living, thus making their very helplessness the occasion of a most injurious competition. The legislature had the right to consider that its minimum wage requirements would be an important aid in carrying out its policy of protection. The adoption of similar requirements by many States evidences a deep-seated conviction both as to the presence of the evil and as to the means adapted to check it. Legislative response to the conviction cannot be regarded as arbitrary or capricious and that is all we have to decide. Even if the wisdom of the policy be regarded as debatable and its effects uncertain, still the legislature is entitled to its judgment.

There is an additional and compelling consideration which recent economic experience has brought into a strong light. The exploitation of a class of workers who are in an unequal position with respect to bargaining power and are thus relatively defenceless against the denial of a living wage is not only detrimental to their health and well-being but casts a direct burden for their support upon the community. What these workers lose in wages the taxpayers are called upon to pay. The bare cost of living must be met. We may take judicial notice of the unparalleled demands for relief which arose during the recent period of depression and still continue to an alarming extent despite the degree of economic recovery which has been achieved. It is unnecessary to cite official statistics to establish what is of common knowledge through the length and breadth of the land. While in the instant case no factual brief has been presented, there is no reason to doubt that the State of Washington has encountered the same social problem that is present elsewhere. The community is not bound to provide what is in effect a subsidy for unconscionable employers. The community may direct its law-making power to correct the abuse which springs from their selfish disregard of the public interest. The argument that the legislation in question constitutes an arbitrary discrimination, because it does not extend to men, is unavailing. This Court has frequently held that the legislative authority, acting within its proper field, is not bound to extend its regulation to all cases which it might possibly reach. The legislature "is free to recognize degrees of harm and it may confine its restrictions to those classes of cases where the need is deemed to be clearest." . . .

Our conclusion is that the case of *Adkins v. Children's Hospital* should be, and it is, overruled. The judgment of the Supreme Court of the State of Washington is affirmed.

MR. JUSTICE SUTHERLAND, dissenting.

The principles and authorities relied upon to sustain the judgment, were considered in *Adkins v. Children's Hospital* and *Morehead v. New York ex rel. Tipaldo*, and their lack of application to cases like the one in hand was pointed out. A sufficient answer to all that is now said will be found in the opinions of the court in those cases. Nevertheless, in the circumstances, it seems well to restate our reasons and conclusions.

Under our form of government, where the written Constitution, by its own terms, is the supreme law, some agency, of necessity, must have the power to say the final word as to the validity of a statute assailed as unconstitutional. The Constitution makes it clear that the power has been intrusted to this court when the question arises in a controversy within its jurisdiction; and so long as the power remains there, its exercise cannot be avoided without betrayal of the trust.

It has been pointed out many times, as in the *Adkins* case, that this judicial duty is one of gravity and delicacy, and that rational doubts must be resolved in favor of the constitutionality of the statute. But whose doubts, and by whom resolved? Undoubtedly it is the duty of a member of the court, in the process of reaching a right conclusion, to give due weight to the opposing views of his associates; but in the end, the question which he must answer is not whether such views seem sound to those who entertain them, but whether they convince him that the statute is constitutional or engender in his mind a rational doubt upon that issue. The oath which he takes as a judge is not a composite oath, but an individual one. And in passing upon the validity of a statute, he discharges a duty imposed upon *him*, which cannot be consummated justly by an automatic acceptance of the views of others which have neither convinced, nor created a reasonable doubt in, his mind. If upon a question so important he thus surrender his deliberate judgment, he stands forsworn. He cannot subordinate his convictions to that extent and keep faith with his oath or retain his judicial and moral independence.

The suggestion that the only check upon the exercise of the judicial power, when properly invoked, to declare a constitutional right superior to an unconstitutional statute is the judge's own faculty of self-restraint, is both ill considered and mischievous. Self-restraint belongs in the domain of will and not of judgment. The check upon the judge is that imposed by his oath of office, by the Constitution and by his own conscientious and informed convictions; and since he has the duty to make up his own mind and adjudge accordingly, it is hard to see how there could be any other restraint. This court acts as a unit. It cannot act in any other way; and the majority (whether a bare majority or a majority of all but one of its members), therefore, establishes the controlling rule as the decision of the court, binding, so long as it remains unchanged, equally upon those who disagree and upon those who subscribe to it. Otherwise, orderly administration of justice would cease. But it is the right of those in the minority to disagree, and sometimes, in matters of grave importance, their imperative duty to voice their disagreement at such length as the occasion demands—always, of course, in terms which, however forceful, do not offend the proprieties or impugn the good faith of those who think otherwise.

It is urged that the question involved should now receive fresh consideration, among other reasons, because of "the economic conditions which have supervened"; but the meaning of the Constitution does not change with the ebb and flow of economic events. We frequently are told in more general words that the Constitution must be construed in the light of the present. If by that it is meant that the Constitution is made up of living words that apply to every new condition which they include, the statement is quite true. But to say, if that be intended, that the words of the Constitution mean today what they did not mean when written—that is, that they do not apply to a situation now to which they would have applied then—is to rob that instrument of the essential element which continues it in force as the people have made it until they, and not their official agents, have made it otherwise. . . .

The judicial function is that of interpretation; it does not include the power of amendment under the guise of interpretation. To miss the point of difference between the two is to miss all that the phrase "supreme law of the land" stands for and to convert what was intended as inescapable and enduring mandates into mere moral reflections.

If the Constitution, intelligently and reasonably construed in the light of these principles, stands in the way of desirable legislation, the blame must rest upon that instrument, and not upon the court for enforcing it according to its terms. The remedy in that situation—and the only true remedy—is to amend the Constitution.

The Legacy of *West Coast Hotel*

West Coast Hotel was an explicit repudiation of economic substantive due process. In one fell swoop, the justices overruled *Adkins* and changed the way the Court viewed state regulatory efforts. But the period stretching from 1890 through 1936 continues to have an impact on Supreme Court rulings.

In place of substantive due process the Court adopted a rational basis test that presumes the constitutionality of economic legislation and assigns responsibility to the law's challengers to show that no rational relationship exists between the law and a legitimate government function.[23] As such, it is similar to the position expressed by Chief Justice Waite in *Munn v. Illinois.* The difference between Waite's standard in *Munn* and that of the contemporary Court generally lies in application. The Waite Court and its successors allowed incursions into their standard, and we should remember that the standard was amenable to exceptions; modern Courts do not. Indeed, in the post–New Deal period, the Court has generally rejected challenges to state economic regulatory efforts. One reason for these decisions is the nature of the prevailing legal test: it is extremely difficult for attorneys to demonstrate that there is no conceivable rational relationship between any given legislation and a legitimate government interest. In addition, the modern Court has been averse to conducting its own inquiry into what is and is not in the public interest or what is rational and what is not. Instead, the Court tends to defer to the judgments of the legislature.

Williamson v. Lee Optical Company provides a good example of how the mid-twentieth-century Court treated Fourteenth Amendment economic claims. This case can be compared with the classic statements for and against a substantive interpretation of the due process clause: Miller's in *Slaughterhouse,* Waite's in *Munn,* Peckham's in *Lochner,* and so forth.

Williamson v. Lee Optical Company

348 U.S. 483 (1955)
http://laws.findlaw.com/us/348/483.html
Vote: 8 (Black, Burton, Clark, Douglas, Frankfurter, Minton, Reed, Warren)
 0

OPINION OF THE COURT: *Douglas*
NOT PARTICIPATING: *Harlan*

---

23. This position is consistent with the Court's rulings in related areas. Particularly important is the decision in *United States v. Carolene Products* (1938), in which the justices announced that they would henceforth generally defer to the legislature and give only minimal scrutiny to the reasonableness of economic regulations. In that same decision, the Court pledged to give more searching scrutiny to laws affecting civil liberties.

FACTS:

In 1953 Oklahoma passed a law that made it "unlawful for any person . . . to fit, adjust, adapt, or to apply . . . lenses, frames . . . or any other optical appliances to the face" unless that person was a licensed ophthalmologist, "a physician who specializes in the care of eyes," or an optometrist, "one who examines eyes for refractory error . . . and fills prescriptions." An optician, an "artisan qualified to grind lenses to fill prescriptions," could do so only with a written prescription from an ophthalmologist or optometrist.

Lee Optical Company challenged the law, arguing that it bore no reasonable relation to a public health and welfare interest and unconstitutionally deprived opticians of their right to perform their craft. The state argued that the statute was a constitutional exercise of state police power.

ARGUMENTS:

For the appellant, Mac Q. Williamson, Oklahoma attorney general, et al.:

- The furnishing of eyeglasses to the public is a matter of public health and welfare and therefore subject to the police powers of the state.
- The aim of the law is to provide citizens of Oklahoma with the best possible visual care.
- The Court should defer to the state legislature in determining appropriate public policy. There should be a presumption of constitutionality with the burden on the challenger to prove the invalidity of the law beyond a reasonable doubt. As long as the law is a reasonable measure in pursuit of a legitimate interest, the Court should not interfere.

For the respondent, Lee Optical of Oklahoma:

- The optician is a skilled craftsman whose training makes him at least as qualified as an ophthalmologist or an optometrist to fit and adjust eyeglasses. By treating opticians differently the state is denying equal protection of the laws.
- Opticians have been engaged in these now-prohibited activities for hundreds of years. Unreasonably denying opticians the right to pursue their traditional occupation violates principles of due process of law.
- This law is not a reasonable public health measure. Even if an optician should make a mistake in the duplicating of lenses or the fitting and adjusting of glasses, no harm to the health of the patient would result.

MR. JUSTICE DOUGLAS DELIVERED THE OPINION OF THE COURT.

The effect of [the act] is to forbid the optician from fitting or duplicating lenses without a prescription from an ophthalmologist or optometrist. In practical effect, it means that no optician can fit old glasses into new frames or supply a lens, whether it be a new lens or one to duplicate a lost or broken lens, without a prescription. The District Court conceded that it was in the competence of the police power of a State to regulate the examination of the eyes. But it rebelled at the notion that a State could require a prescription from an optometrist or ophthalmologist "to take old lenses and place them in new frames and then fit the completed spectacles to the *face* of the eyeglass wearer." . . . It was, accordingly, the opinion of the court that this provision of the law violated the Due Process Clause by arbitrarily interfering with the optician's right to do business. . . .

The Oklahoma law may exact a needless, wasteful requirement in many cases. But it is for the legislature, not the courts, to balance the advantages and disadvantages of the new requirement. It appears that in many cases the optician can easily supply the new frames or new lenses without reference to the old written prescription. It also appears that many written prescriptions contain no directive data in regard to fitting spectacles to the face. But in some cases the directions contained in the prescription are essential, if the glasses are to be fitted so as to correct the particular defects of vision or alleviate the eye condition. The legislature might have concluded that the frequency of occasions when a prescription is necessary was sufficient to justify this regulation of the fitting of eyeglasses. Likewise, when it is necessary to duplicate a lens, a written prescription may or may not be necessary. But the legislature might have concluded that one was needed often enough to require one in every case. Or the legislature may have concluded that eye examinations were so critical, not only for correction of vision but also for detection of latent ailments or diseases, that every change in frames and every duplication of a lens should be accompanied by a prescription from a medical expert. To be sure, the present law does not require a new examination of the eyes every time the frames are changed or the lenses duplicated. For if the old prescription is on file with the optician, he can go ahead and make the new fitting or duplicate the lenses. But the law need not be in every respect logically consistent with its aims to be constitutional. It is enough that there is an evil at hand for correction, and that it might be thought that the particular legislative measure was a rational way to correct it.

The day is gone when this Court uses the Due Process Clause of the Fourteenth Amendment to strike down state laws, regulatory of business and industrial conditions, because they may be unwise, improvident, or out of harmony with a particular school of thought. . . . We emphasize again what Chief Justice Waite said in *Munn v. Illinois*, . . ."For protection against abuses by legislatures the people must resort to the polls, not to the courts."

SUBSTANTIVE DUE PROCESS: CONTEMPORARY RELEVANCE

Over the six decades since *Williamson v. Lee Optical*, the Court has continued to reject substantive due process attacks on state and local economic regulatory policies, giving wide latitude to the legislative branch in determining what is reasonable economic policy.[24] But the doctrine has not totally disappeared. In fact, the use of the due process clauses to find and protect rights has seen somewhat of a resurgence, which has occurred in two areas quite different from the commercial regulation cases that were so important in earlier eras. First, the Court has used substantive due process to address questions of personal privacy. Second, it has applied the due process clauses to improve the essential fairness of the judicial system. In what directly follows we take a close look at the issues of excessive monetary damages awarded by juries and problems associated with judicial conflicts of interest. We take up personal privacy toward the end of the chapter

Substantive Due Process Applied to Juries and Judges

The subject of excessive monetary damages awarded by juries not only has been at the center of the long-standing political controversy over tort reform, but it also raises an important legal question. It asks whether jury awards for litigants who have been unlawfully harmed can become so large as to constitute an unreasonable denial of essential fairness and a deprivation of property without due process of law. The leading Supreme Court decision in this area is *BMW of North*

24. See, for example, ***Pennell v. City of San Jose*** (1988) and *City of Cuyahoga Falls, Ohio v. Buckeye Community Hope Foundation* (2003).

America v. Gore (1996), which began when an Alabama doctor became dissatisfied with the condition of the paint on his newly acquired luxury automobile.

BMW of North America v. Gore

517 U.S. 559 (1996)
http://laws.findlaw.com/us/517/559.html
Oral arguments are available at https://www.oyez.org.
Vote: 5 (Breyer, Kennedy, O'Connor, Souter, Stevens)
    4 (Ginsburg, Rehnquist, Scalia, Thomas)

OPINION OF THE COURT: *Stevens*
CONCURRING OPINION: *Breyer*
DISSENTING OPINIONS: *Ginsburg, Scalia*

FACTS:

In January 1990 Dr. Ira Gore Jr. purchased a black BMW sports sedan for $40,750.88 from an authorized dealer in Birmingham, Alabama. Nine months later he took the car to an independent detailer for some appearance enhancements. The detailer informed Gore that he believed the car had been repainted. Gore, convinced that he had been wronged, filed suit against BMW of North America for failure to disclose that his new car had undergone repainting prior to purchase. He asked the court to award him compensatory and punitive damages.[25]

At trial, BMW acknowledged a policy, adopted in 1983, concerning automobiles damaged in manufacture or transport. If repairing the damage cost more than 3 percent of the vehicle's retail value, the car was placed in company service and later sold as used. If the damage amounted to less than 3 percent of the car's value, the vehicle was fixed and sold as new, with no disclosure of the repair history to either the dealer or the purchaser. Because the cost to refinish the automobile purchased by Gore amounted to only 1.5 percent of the car's value, it was sold as new.

In support of his claim for compensatory damages, Gore presented evidence that a refinished BMW would fetch $4,000 less on the open market than an identical model that had not been repainted. To justify his claim for punitive damages, Gore presented documentation that during the previous decade BMW of North America sold approximately one thousand refinished automobiles as new. BMW replied that the new paint on Gore's automobile was every bit as good as the

25. The purpose of compensatory damages is to reimburse wronged parties for actual damages suffered. The purpose of punitive damages is to punish wrongdoers for their unlawful acts.

original factory finish, and therefore the company was under no obligation to disclose the refinishing.

The jury found in favor of Gore, awarding him $4,000 in compensatory damages and $4 million in punitive damages. The justification for the punitive damage award was the jury's conclusion that BMW's nondisclosure policy amounted to "gross, oppressive, or malicious" fraud. BMW asked that the award be set aside or reduced because it was excessive. The trial court denied the request. The state supreme court reduced the punitive damage award to $2 million—not because the original award was excessive, but because it found fault with the jury's method of arriving at that figure. The jury erred, according to the state supreme court, by considering BMW's wrongdoing in other states when it should have focused only on the company's behavior in Alabama. BMW, still maintaining that the revised award was excessive, requested review by the U.S. Supreme Court.

ARGUMENTS:

For the petitioner, BMW of North America, Inc.:

- The Alabama Supreme Court correctly found that the jury's $4 million punitive damages award was excessive because it was based in part on transactions that took place out of state. Alabama has no authority to punish extraterritorial transactions, and doing so is a violation of due process of law.
- The revised $2 million punitive damage is grossly excessive and violates the substantive component of the due process clause. The punishment is five hundred times the actual and potential harm allegedly suffered by Dr. Gore. In addition, the punitive damages are one thousand times the civil penalty for violating Alabama's repair disclosure statute.
- The punitive damage award far exceeds what is reasonably necessary to accomplish Alabama's interests in punishment and deterrence.
- The award also far exceeds the degree to which BMW's conduct could be considered reprehensible.

For the respondent, Ira Gore Jr.:

- The Constitution does not prohibit consideration of out-of-state conduct in determining the amount of punitive damages needed to prevent a defendant from continuing a nationwide policy of misbehavior.
- The revised $2 million award was reasonably calculated to prevent further harm to Alabama consumers by forcing BMW to change its nondisclosure policy.

- BMW's conduct was reprehensible.
- The Court should refrain from setting a particular ratio of punitive to actual damages as a guide for determining excessive punitive damages.

JUSTICE STEVENS DELIVERED THE OPINION OF THE COURT.

Punitive damages may properly be imposed to further a State's legitimate interests in punishing unlawful conduct and deterring its repetition. *Gertz v. Robert Welch, Inc.* (1974); *Newport v. Fact Concerts, Inc.* (1981); [*Pacific Mutual Life Ins. Co. v.*] *Haslip* (1991). In our federal system, States necessarily have considerable flexibility in determining the level of punitive damages that they will allow in different classes of cases and in any particular case. Most States that authorize exemplary damages afford the jury similar latitude, requiring only that the damages awarded be reasonably necessary to vindicate the State's legitimate interests in punishment and deterrence. See *TXO* [*Production Corp. v. Alliance Resources Corp.*, 1993]; *Haslip*. Only when an award can fairly be categorized as "grossly excessive" in relation to these interests does it enter the zone of arbitrariness that violates the Due Process Clause of the Fourteenth Amendment. . . .

No one doubts that a State may protect its citizens by prohibiting deceptive trade practices and by requiring automobile distributors to disclose presale repairs that affect the value of a new car. But the States need not, and in fact do not, provide such protection in a uniform manner. Some States rely on the judicial process to formulate and enforce an appropriate disclosure requirement by applying principles of contract and tort law. Other States have enacted various forms of legislation that define the disclosure obligations of automobile manufacturers, distributors, and dealers. The result is a patchwork of rules representing the diverse policy judgments of lawmakers in 50 States.

That diversity demonstrates that reasonable people may disagree about the value of a full disclosure requirement. . . .

We think it follows from these principles of state sovereignty and comity that a State may not impose economic sanctions on violators of its laws with the intent of changing the tortfeasors' [wrongdoers'] lawful conduct in other States. Before this Court Dr. Gore argued that the large punitive damages award was necessary to induce BMW to change the nationwide policy that it adopted in 1983. But by attempting to alter BMW's nationwide policy, Alabama would be infringing on the policy choices of other States. To avoid such encroachment, the economic penalties that a State such as Alabama inflicts on those who transgress its laws, whether the penalties take the form of legislatively authorized fines or judicially imposed punitive damages, must be supported by the State's interest in protecting its own consumers and its own economy. Alabama may insist that BMW adhere to a particular disclosure policy in that State. Alabama does not have the power, however, to punish BMW for conduct that was lawful where it occurred and that had no impact on Alabama or its residents. Nor may Alabama impose sanctions on BMW in order to deter conduct that is lawful in other jurisdictions.

. . . [This] award must be analyzed . . . with consideration given only to the interests of Alabama consumers, rather than those of the entire Nation. When the scope of the interest in punishment and deterrence that an Alabama court may appropriately consider is properly limited, it is apparent—for reasons that we shall now address—that this award is grossly excessive.

Elementary notions of fairness enshrined in our constitutional jurisprudence dictate that a person receive fair notice not only of the conduct that will subject him to punishment but also of the severity of the penalty that a State may impose. Three guideposts, each of which indicates that BMW did not receive adequate notice of the magnitude of the sanction that Alabama might impose for adhering to the nondisclosure policy adopted in 1983, lead us to the conclusion that the $2 million award against BMW is grossly excessive: the degree of reprehensibility of the nondisclosure; the disparity between the harm or potential harm suffered by Dr. Gore and his punitive damages award; and the difference between this remedy and the civil penalties authorized or imposed in comparable cases. We discuss these considerations in turn.

Degree of Reprehensibility

Perhaps the most important indicium of the reasonableness of a punitive damages award is the degree of reprehensibility of the defendant's conduct. . . . This principle reflects the accepted view that some wrongs are more blameworthy than others. . . . In *TXO*, both the West Virginia Supreme Court and the Justices of this Court placed special emphasis on the principle that punitive damages may not be "grossly out of proportion to the severity of the offense." . . .

In this case, none of the aggravating factors associated with particularly reprehensible conduct is present. The harm BMW inflicted on Dr. Gore was purely economic in

nature. The presale refinishing of the car had no effect on its performance or safety features, or even its appearance for at least nine months after his purchase. BMW's conduct evinced no indifference to or reckless disregard for the health and safety of others. To be sure, infliction of economic injury, especially when done intentionally through affirmative acts of misconduct, or when the target is financially vulnerable, can warrant a substantial penalty. But this observation does not convert all acts that cause economic harm into torts that are sufficiently reprehensible to justify a significant sanction in addition to compensatory damages. . . .

Finally, the record in this case discloses no deliberate false statements, acts of affirmative misconduct, or concealment of evidence of improper motive, such as were present in *Haslip* and *TXO*. We accept, of course, the jury's finding that BMW suppressed a material fact which Alabama law obligated it to communicate to prospective purchasers of repainted cars in that State. But the omission of a material fact may be less reprehensible than a deliberate false statement, particularly when there is a good-faith basis for believing that no duty to disclose exists.

. . . Because this case exhibits none of the circumstances ordinarily associated with egregiously improper conduct, we are persuaded that BMW's conduct was not sufficiently reprehensible to warrant imposition of a $2 million exemplary damages award.

Ratio

The second and perhaps most commonly cited indicium of an unreasonable or excessive punitive damages award is its ratio to the actual harm inflicted on the plaintiff. The principle that exemplary damages must bear a "reasonable relationship" to compensatory damages has a long pedigree. . . . Our decisions in both *Haslip* and *TXO* endorsed the proposition that a comparison between the compensatory award and the punitive award is significant.

In *Haslip* we concluded that even though a punitive damages award of "more than 4 times the amount of compensatory damages," might be "close to the line," it did not "cross the line into the area of constitutional impropriety." *TXO*, following dicta in *Haslip*, refined this analysis by confirming that the proper inquiry is "'whether there is a reasonable relationship between the punitive damage award and the harm likely to result from the defendant's conduct as well as the harm that actually has occurred.'" Thus, in upholding the $10 million award in *TXO*, we relied on the difference between that figure and the harm to the victim that would have ensued if the tortious plan had succeeded. That difference suggested that the relevant ratio was not more than 10 to 1.

The $2 million in punitive damages awarded to Dr. Gore by the Alabama Supreme Court is 500 times the amount of his actual harm as determined by the jury. . . .

Of course, we have consistently rejected the notion that the constitutional line is marked by a simple mathematical formula, even one that compares actual and potential damages to the punitive award. . . . When the ratio is a breathtaking 500 to 1, however, the award must surely "raise a suspicious judicial eyebrow." *TXO* (O'CONNOR, J., dissenting).

Sanctions for Comparable Misconduct

Comparing the punitive damages award and the civil or criminal penalties that could be imposed for comparable misconduct provides a third indicium of excessiveness. . . . In this case the $2 million economic sanction imposed on BMW is substantially greater than the statutory fines available in Alabama and elsewhere for similar malfeasance.

The maximum civil penalty authorized by the Alabama Legislature for a violation of its Deceptive Trade Practices Act is $2,000; other States authorize more severe sanctions, with the maxima ranging from $5,000 to $10,000. . . .

The sanction imposed in this case cannot be justified on the ground that it was necessary to deter future misconduct without considering whether less drastic remedies could be expected to achieve that goal. . . .

We assume, as the [jury] in this case . . . found, that the undisclosed damage to the new BMW's affected their actual value. Notwithstanding the evidence adduced by BMW in an effort to prove that the repainted cars conformed to the same quality standards as its other cars, we also assume that it knew, or should have known, that as time passed the repainted cars would lose their attractive appearance more rapidly than other BMW's. Moreover, we of course accept the Alabama courts' view that the state interest in protecting its citizens from deceptive trade practices justifies a sanction in addition to the recovery of compensatory damages. We cannot, however, accept the conclusion of the Alabama Supreme Court that BMW's conduct was sufficiently egregious to justify a punitive sanction that is tantamount to a severe criminal penalty. . . .

. . . [W]e are fully convinced that the grossly excessive award imposed in this case transcends the constitutional limit. . . .

The judgment is reversed, and the case is remanded for further proceedings not inconsistent with this opinion.

It is so ordered.

JUSTICE BREYER, with whom JUSTICE O'CONNOR and JUSTICE SOUTER join, concurring.

The Alabama state courts have assessed the defendant $2 million in "punitive damages" for having knowingly failed to tell a BMW automobile buyer that, at a cost of $600, it had repainted portions of his new $40,000 car, thereby lowering its potential resale value by about 10%. The Court's opinion, which I join, explains why we have concluded that this award, in this case, was "grossly excessive" in relation to legitimate punitive damages objectives, and hence an arbitrary deprivation of life, liberty, or property in violation of the Due Process Clause. . . .

The . . . severe disproportionality between the award and the legitimate punitive damages objectives . . . reflects a judgment about a matter of degree. I recognize that it is often difficult to determine just when a punitive award exceeds an amount reasonably related to a State's legitimate interests, or when that excess is so great as to amount to a matter of constitutional concern. Yet whatever the difficulties of drawing a precise line, once we examine the award in this case, it is not difficult to say that this award lies on the line's far side. The severe lack of proportionality between the size of the award and the underlying punitive damages objectives shows that the award falls into the category of "gross excessiveness" set forth in this Court's prior cases.

. . . I conclude that the award in this unusual case violates the basic guarantee of nonarbitrary governmental behavior that the Due Process Clause provides.

JUSTICE SCALIA, with whom JUSTICE THOMAS joins, dissenting.

Today we see the latest manifestation of this Court's recent and increasingly insistent "concern about punitive damages that 'run wild.'" *Pacific Mut. Life Ins. Co. v. Haslip* (1991). Since the Constitution does not make that concern any of our business, the Court's activities in this area are an unjustified incursion into the province of state governments.

In earlier cases that were the prelude to this decision, I set forth my view that a state trial procedure that commits the decision whether to impose punitive damages, and the amount, to the discretion of the jury, subject to some judicial review for "reasonableness," furnishes a defendant with all the process that is "due." I do not regard the Fourteenth Amendment's Due Process Clause as a secret repository of substantive guarantees against "unfairness"—neither the unfairness of an excessive civil compensatory award, nor the unfairness of an "unreasonable" punitive award. What the Fourteenth Amendment's procedural guarantee assures is an opportunity to contest the reasonableness of a damages judgment in state court; but there is no federal guarantee a damages award actually be reasonable. . . .

The most significant aspects of today's decision—the identification of a "substantive due process" right against a "grossly excessive" award, and the concomitant assumption of ultimate authority to decide anew a matter of "reasonableness" resolved in lower court proceedings—are of course not new. *Haslip* and *TXO* revived the notion, moribund since its appearance in the first years of this century, that the measure of civil punishment poses a question of constitutional dimension to be answered by this Court. Neither of those cases, however, nor any of the precedents upon which they relied, actually took the step of declaring a punitive award unconstitutional simply because it was "too big." At the time of adoption of the Fourteenth Amendment, it was well understood that punitive damages represent the assessment by the jury, as the voice of the community, of the measure of punishment the defendant deserved. Today's decision, though dressed up as a legal opinion, is really no more than a disagreement with the community's sense of indignation or outrage expressed in the punitive award of the Alabama jury, as reduced by the State Supreme Court. It reflects not merely, as the concurrence candidly acknowledges, "a judgment about a matter of degree"; but a judgment about the appropriate degree of indignation or outrage, which is hardly an analytical determination.

There is no precedential warrant for giving our judgment priority over the judgment of state courts and juries on this matter. The only support for the Court's position is to be found in a handful of errant federal cases, bunched within a few years of one other, which invented the notion that an unfairly severe civil sanction amounts to a violation of constitutional liberties. These were the decisions upon which the *TXO* plurality relied in pronouncing that the Due Process Clause "imposes substantive limits 'beyond which penalties may not go.'" Although they are our precedents, they are themselves too shallowly rooted to justify the Court's recent undertaking. . . .

More importantly, this latter group of cases—which again are the sole precedential foundation put forward for the rule of constitutional law espoused by today's Court—simply fabricated the "substantive due process" right at issue. . . .

. . . [T]he Court identifies "[t]hree guideposts" that lead it to the conclusion that the award in this case is excessive: degree of reprehensibility, ratio between punitive award and plaintiff's actual harm, and legislative sanctions provided for comparable misconduct. The legal significance of these "guideposts" is nowhere explored, but their necessary effect is to establish federal standards governing the hitherto exclusively state law of damages. . . .

Of course it will not be easy for the States to comply with this new federal law of damages, no matter how willing they are to do so. In truth, the "guideposts" mark a road to nowhere; they provide no real guidance at all. As to "degree of reprehensibility" of the defendant's conduct, we learn that "'nonviolent crimes are less serious than crimes marked by violence or the threat of violence,'" and that "'trickery and deceit'" are "more reprehensible than negligence." As to the ratio of punitive to compensatory damages, we are told that a "'general concer[n] of reasonableness . . . enter[s] into the constitutional calculus,'"—though even "a breathtaking 500 to 1" will not necessarily do anything more than "'raise a suspicious judicial eyebrow.'" And as to legislative sanctions provided for comparable misconduct, they should be accorded "'substantial deference.'" One expects the Court to conclude: "To thine own self be true."

These criss-crossing platitudes yield no real answers in no real cases. . . .

For the foregoing reasons, I respectfully dissent.

JUSTICE GINSBURG, with whom THE CHIEF JUSTICE joins, dissenting.

The Court, I am convinced, unnecessarily and unwisely ventures into territory traditionally within the States' domain, and does so in the face of reform measures recently adopted or currently under consideration in legislative arenas. . . .

. . . [T]he Alabama Supreme Court left standing the jury's decision that the facts warranted an award of punitive damages—a determination not contested in this Court—and the state court concluded that, considering only acts in Alabama, $2 million was "a constitutionally reasonable punitive damages award."

The Court finds Alabama's $2 million award not simply excessive, but grossly so, and therefore unconstitutional. The decision leads us further into territory traditionally within the States' domain, and commits the Court, now and again, to correct "misapplication of a properly stated rule of law." The Court is not well equipped for this mission. Tellingly, the Court repeats that it brings to the task no "mathematical formula," no "categorical approach," no "bright line." It has only a vague concept of substantive due process, a "raised eyebrow" test, as its ultimate guide. . . .

For the reasons stated, I dissent from this Court's disturbance of the judgment the Alabama Supreme Court has made.

In *BMW v. Gore* the justices directly applied concepts of substantive due process to jury awards and concluded that grossly excessive awards violate the essential fairness guarantees of the Fourteenth Amendment. The Court has continued to apply the substantive due process reasoning in subsequent challenges to large punitive damage awards. In *Cooper Industries v. Leatherman Tool Group* (2001), a dispute between two companies over a false advertising claim, the justices required lower courts to reconsider a $4.5 million punitive damage award when only $50,000 was awarded in compensatory damages. Similarly, in **State Farm Mutual Automobile Insurance Co. v. Campbell** (2003) the Court considered awards of $1 million in compensatory damages and $145 million in punitive damages against an insurance company charged with improperly dealing with a policyholder following a fatal auto accident. The justices concluded that the 145-to-1 ratio of punitive to compensatory damages was grossly excessive and in conflict with due process guarantees. The Court once again rejected any firm mathematical criteria but suggested that award ratios in excess of 10 to 1 begin to lose their presumption of validity.

The other issue involving due process rights and the fairness of the judicial process concerns judges with conflicts of interest. At bottom, due process requires essential fairness, and for the judiciary one of the elements of essential fairness is to have cases decided by objective judges. An individual whose case is heard by a biased judge is at risk of being denied liberty or property without due process of law. Traditionally, the Supreme Court has taken the position that the Constitution's due process clauses are violated if a judge decides a case in which he or she has a direct financial interest. Aside from monetary conflicts of interest and some rare situations that develop in contempt of court actions, the justices have left the regulation of judicial bias to the legislatures and state judicial ethics commissions.

In 2009, however, a new issue regarding judicial objectivity reached the Court. It concerned the influence that campaign contributions might have on judges who serve in the thirty-one states that use partisan or nonpartisan elections to staff their courts. Can significant campaign contributions lead to the selection of judges who are beholden to the interests of contributors? If so, are particular litigants in danger of being denied a fair hearing when they appear before such judges? Are the resulting conflicts of interest so serious as to constitute a violation of due process of law? *Caperton v. A. T. Massey Coal Co.* (2009) addresses this question.

Caperton v. A. T. Massey Coal Co.

556 U.S. 868 (2009)
http://laws.findlaw.com/us/000/08–22.html
Oral arguments are available at https://www.oyez.org.
Vote: 5 (Breyer, Ginsburg, Kennedy, Souter, Stevens)
*   4 (Alito, Roberts, Scalia, Thomas)*

OPINION OF THE COURT: *Kennedy*
DISSENTING OPINIONS: *Roberts, Scalia*

FACTS:

In August 2002 a West Virginia jury returned a verdict that found respondents A. T. Massey Coal Co. and its affiliates liable for fraudulent misrepresentation, concealment, and interference with existing contractual relations. The jury awarded petitioners Hugh Caperton, Harman Development Corporation, and several other companies $50 million in compensatory and punitive damages. In June 2004 the trial court denied Massey's posttrial motions challenging the verdict and the damage award. Massey served notice of appeal.

After the verdict, but before the appeal, West Virginia held its 2004 judicial elections. Knowing that the Supreme Court of Appeals of West Virginia would consider the appeal, Don Blankenship—Massey Coal's chairman, chief executive officer, and president—decided to support the campaign of Brent Benjamin, an attorney who was challenging Warren R. McGraw, a sitting justice, for his seat on the West Virginia court.

In addition to contributing the $1,000 statutory maximum to Benjamin's campaign committee, Blankenship donated almost $2.5 million to a political organization called And for the Sake of the Kids, which opposed McGraw and supported Benjamin. Blankenship's contributions accounted for more than two-thirds of the total funds the organization raised. In addition, Blankenship spent just over $500,000 on independent expenditures for direct mailings and letters soliciting donations and on television and newspaper advertisements to support Benjamin. All in all, with his $3 million in contributions, Blankenship spent more than the total amount contributed by all other Benjamin supporters combined, and three times the amount spent by Benjamin's own committee. Caperton contended that Blankenship spent $1 million more than the total spent by the campaign committees of both candidates combined. Benjamin won the election, receiving 53.3 percent of the vote.

In October 2005, before Massey Coal filed its petition for appeal in the West Virginia Supreme Court, Caperton moved to disqualify Justice Benjamin from hearing the case under the due process clause and the West Virginia Code of Judicial Conduct. Caperton cited the conflict of interest caused by Blankenship's campaign involvement. Under procedures used in West Virginia and elsewhere, a challenged judge alone decides whether his or her disqualification (recusal) is required. Benjamin denied the motion in April 2006, finding no objective evidence that he was biased against any litigant or that he could not be fair and impartial.

In November 2007, by a 3–2 vote, the West Virginia Supreme Court reversed the $50 million verdict against Massey, with Benjamin voting with the majority.

Caperton sought a rehearing, and both parties moved to disqualify justices. Caperton again asked Benjamin to recuse himself and also challenged Justice Elliott Maynard. Maynard had been photographed with Blankenship in the French Riviera while the case was pending. Maynard granted Caperton's recusal motion. Massey countered by challenging Justice Larry Starcher, who had publicly criticized Blankenship's role in the 2004 election. Starcher also agreed to step aside, but in doing so he issued a memorandum urging Benjamin to recuse himself as well. Starcher also noted that "Blankenship's bestowal of his personal wealth, political tactics, and 'friendship' have created a cancer in the affairs of this Court." Benjamin declined Starcher's suggestion and denied Caperton's recusal motion.

The refusal of West Virginia Supreme Court justice Brent Benjamin (left) to disqualify himself from participating in an appeal brought by A. T. Massey Coal Company resulted in the U.S. Supreme Court's 2009 ruling in Caperton v. A. T. Massey Coal Co. *Anticipating an appeal to the state supreme court from a $50 million judgment against his company, Don Blankenship, Massey's chairman and principal officer (right), made massive campaign contributions and direct expenditures in support of Benjamin's election to the court.*

The state supreme court granted rehearing. Benjamin, now in the capacity of acting chief justice, selected two circuit court judges to replace the two recused justices. Caperton moved a third time to disqualify Benjamin, but Benjamin once against refused to step aside.

In April 2008 a divided court again reversed the jury verdict, and again it was a 3–2 decision with Justice Benjamin voting with the majority in favor of Massey Coal. The two dissenters noted "genuine due process implications arising under federal law" with respect to Benjamin's failure to recuse himself.

ARGUMENTS:

For the petitioners, Hugh Caperton et al.:

- Due process requires recusal not only where there is proof that a judge is actually biased but also where an objective inquiry establishes a probability of bias.
- The Constitution does not require recusal whenever a judge receives a campaign contribution from an attorney or litigant, but here staggering amounts of money were spent by a litigant who was preparing a multimillion-dollar appeal to the state supreme court.
- Blankenship's expenditures were directly responsible for hundreds of pro-Benjamin and anti-McGraw campaign advertisements that unquestionably helped Benjamin—a previously unknown and underfunded candidate—prevail in the election. It would be only natural for Benjamin to feel indebted to Blankenship for these extraordinary efforts on his behalf.
- Due process guarantees that no person will be deprived of his interests in the absence of a proceeding in which he may present his case with assurance that the arbiter is not predisposed to find against him. Benjamin's participation in this appeal deprived the petitioners of a fair hearing (and ultimately their property) without due process of law.

For the respondent, A. T. Massey Coal Co. et al.:

- There is no basis in history or precedent for the notion that a "probability of bias" mandates disqualification under the due process clause.
- Consistent with the common-law rule, this Court's due process decisions have required disqualification based on a monetary interest in the outcome. Outside the context of contempt, where special rules

apply, the Court has never held that disqualification is constitutionally required for any other reason.

- Even if "probability of bias" were the constitutional standard, it could not be satisfied by the supposition that a judge might feel a debt of gratitude to a campaign supporter.
- U.S. Supreme Court justices hear cases in which their religious views, prior political affiliations, or friendships with counsel make it as reasonable as it is here to infer a "probability of bias," yet they are generally deemed capable of putting aside those influences. Sitting in those cases would become constitutionally problematic under the petitioners' theory of due process.

JUSTICE KENNEDY DELIVERED THE OPINION OF THE COURT.

It is axiomatic that "[a] fair trial in a fair tribunal is a basic requirement of due process." As the Court has recognized, however, "most matters relating to judicial disqualification [do] not rise to a constitutional level." The early and leading case on the subject is *Tumey v. Ohio* (1927). . . .

The *Tumey* Court concluded that the Due Process Clause incorporated the common-law rule that a judge must recuse himself when he has "a direct, personal, substantial, pecuniary interest" in a case. . . . Under this rule, "disqualification for bias or prejudice was not" [constitutionally required]; those matters were left to statutes and judicial codes. Personal bias or prejudice "alone would not be sufficient for imposing a constitutional requirement under the Due Process Clause."

As new problems have emerged that were not discussed at common law, however, the Court has identified additional instances which, as an objective matter, require recusal. These are circumstances "in which experience teaches that the probability of actual bias on the part of the judge . . . is too high to be constitutionally tolerable." To place the present case in proper context, two instances where the Court has required recusal merit further discussion.

The first involved the emergence of local tribunals where a judge had a financial interest in the outcome of a case, although the interest was less than what would have been considered personal or direct at common law.

This was the problem addressed in *Tumey*. There, the mayor of a village had the authority to sit as a judge (with no jury) to try those accused of violating a state law prohibiting the possession of alcoholic beverages. Inherent in this structure were two potential conflicts. First, the mayor received a salary supplement for performing judicial duties, and the funds for that compensation derived from the fines assessed in a case.... The mayor-judge thus received a salary supplement only if he convicted the defendant. Second, sums from the criminal fines were deposited to the village's general treasury fund for village improvements and repairs.

The Court held that the Due Process Clause required disqualification "both because of [the mayor-judge's] direct pecuniary interest in the outcome, and because of his official motive to convict and to graduate the fine to help the financial needs of the village." . . .

[In later cases] the Court stressed that it was "not required to decide whether in fact [the justice] was influenced." The proper constitutional inquiry is "whether sitting on the case . . . 'would offer a possible temptation to the average . . . judge to . . . lead him not to hold the balance nice, clear and true.'" . . .

The second instance requiring recusal that was not discussed at common law emerged in the criminal contempt context, where a judge had no pecuniary interest in the case but was challenged because of a conflict arising from his participation in an earlier proceeding. . . .

In that . . . proceeding, and as provided by state law, a judge examined witnesses to determine whether criminal charges should be brought. The judge called the two petitioners before him. One petitioner answered questions, but the judge found him untruthful and charged him with perjury. The second declined to answer on the ground that he did not have counsel with him, as state law seemed to permit. The judge charged him with contempt. The judge proceeded to try and convict both petitioners.

This Court set aside the convictions on grounds that the judge had a conflict of interest at the trial stage because of his earlier participation followed by his decision to charge them. The Due Process Clause required disqualification. [The Court] noted that the disqualifying criteria "cannot be defined with precision. Circumstances and relationships must be considered." . . .

Based on the principles described in these cases we turn to the issue before us. This problem arises in the context of judicial elections, a framework not presented in the precedents we have reviewed and discussed. . . .

[Due to] the difficulties of inquiring into actual bias . . . the Due Process Clause has been implemented by objective standards that do not require proof of actual bias. In defining these standards the Court has asked whether, "under a realistic appraisal of psychological tendencies and human weakness," the interest "poses such a risk of

actual bias or prejudgment that the practice must be forbidden if the guarantee of due process is to be adequately implemented."

We turn to the influence at issue in this case. Not every campaign contribution by a litigant or attorney creates a probability of bias that requires a judge's recusal, but this is an exceptional case. We conclude that there is a serious risk of actual bias—based on objective and reasonable perceptions—when a person with a personal stake in a particular case had a significant and disproportionate influence in placing the judge on the case by raising funds or directing the judge's election campaign when the case was pending or imminent. The inquiry centers on the contribution's relative size in comparison to the total amount of money contributed to the campaign, the total amount spent in the election, and the apparent effect such contribution had on the outcome of the election.

Applying this principle, we conclude that Blankenship's campaign efforts had a significant and disproportionate influence in placing Justice Benjamin on the case. Blankenship contributed some $3 million to unseat the incumbent and replace him with Benjamin. His contributions eclipsed the total amount spent by all other Benjamin supporters and exceeded by 300% the amount spent by Benjamin's campaign committee. . . .

Whether Blankenship's campaign contributions were a necessary and sufficient cause of Benjamin's victory is not the proper inquiry. Much like determining whether a judge is actually biased, proving what ultimately drives the electorate to choose a particular candidate is a difficult endeavor, not likely to lend itself to a certain conclusion. Due process requires an objective inquiry into whether the contributor's influence on the election under all the circumstances "would offer a possible temptation to the average . . . judge to . . . lead him not to hold the balance nice, clear and true." . . . [T]he risk that Blankenship's influence engendered actual bias is sufficiently substantial that it "must be forbidden if the guarantee of due process is to be adequately implemented."

The temporal relationship between the campaign contributions, the justice's election, and the pendency of the case is also critical. It was reasonably foreseeable, when the campaign contributions were made, that the pending case would be before the newly elected justice. . . . So it became at once apparent that, absent recusal, Justice Benjamin would review a judgment that cost his biggest donor's company $50 million. Although there is no allegation of a *quid pro quo* agreement, the fact remains that Blankenship's extraordinary contributions were made at a time when he had a vested stake in the outcome. Just as no man is allowed to be a judge in his own cause, similar fears of bias can arise when—without the consent of the other parties—a man chooses the judge in his own cause. And applying this principle to the judicial election process, there was here a serious, objective risk of actual bias that required Justice Benjamin's recusal. . . .

Our decision today addresses an extraordinary situation where the Constitution requires recusal. Massey and its *amici* predict that various adverse consequences will follow from recognizing a constitutional violation here—ranging from a flood of recusal motions to unnecessary interference with judicial elections. We disagree. The facts now before us are extreme by any measure. The parties point to no other instance involving judicial campaign contributions that presents a potential for bias comparable to the circumstances in this case. . . .

"The Due Process Clause demarks only the outer boundaries of judicial disqualifications. Congress and the states, of course, remain free to impose more rigorous standards for judicial disqualifications than those we find mandated here today." . . .

The judgment of the Supreme Court of Appeals of West Virginia is reversed, and the case is remanded for further proceedings not inconsistent with this opinion.

It is so ordered.

CHIEF JUSTICE ROBERTS, with whom JUSTICE SCALIA, JUSTICE THOMAS, and JUSTICE ALITO join, dissenting.

I, of course, share the majority's sincere concerns about the need to maintain a fair, independent, and impartial judiciary—and one that appears to be such. But I fear that the Court's decision will undermine rather than promote these values. . . .

Today . . . the Court enlists the Due Process Clause to overturn a judge's failure to recuse because of a "probability of bias." Unlike the established grounds for disqualification, a "probability of bias" cannot be defined in any limited way. The Court's new "rule" provides no guidance to judges and litigants about when recusal will be constitutionally required. This will inevitably lead to an increase in allegations that judges are biased, however groundless those charges may be. The end result will do far more to erode public confidence in judicial impartiality than an isolated failure to recuse in a particular case. . . .

. . . [T]he standard the majority articulates—"probability of bias"—fails to provide clear, workable guidance for future cases. At the most basic level, it is unclear whether the new probability of bias standard is somehow limited to financial support in judicial elections, or applies to judicial recusal questions more generally. But there are other fundamental questions as well. With little help from the majority, courts will now have to determine:

1. How much money is too much money? What level of contribution or expenditure gives rise to a "probability of bias"?

2. How do we determine whether a given expenditure is "disproportionate"? Disproportionate *to what*?

3. Are independent, non-coordinated expenditures treated the same as direct contributions to a candidate's campaign? What about contributions to independent outside groups supporting a candidate?

4. Does it matter whether the litigant has contributed to other candidates or made large expenditures in connection with other elections?

5. Does the amount at issue in the case matter? What if this case were an employment dispute with only $10,000 at stake? What if the plaintiffs only sought non-monetary relief such as an injunction or declaratory judgment?

6. Does the analysis change depending on whether the judge whose disqualification is sought sits on a trial court, appeals court, or state supreme court? . . . [Chief Justice Roberts went on to list thirty-four additional questions that he believed the judiciary ultimately would have to address in subsequent cases.]

Today, the majority . . . departs from a clear, longstanding constitutional rule to accommodate an "extreme" case involving "grossly disproportionate" amounts of money. I believe we will come to regret this decision, when courts are forced to deal with a wide variety of *Caperton* motions, each claiming the title of "most extreme" or "most disproportionate." . . .

. . . I believe that opening the door to recusal claims under the Due Process Clause, for an amorphous "probability of bias," will itself bring our judicial system into undeserved disrepute, and diminish the confidence of the American people in the fairness and integrity of their courts. I hope I am wrong.

I respectfully dissent.

JUSTICE SCALIA, dissenting.

A Talmudic maxim instructs with respect to the Scripture: "Turn it over, and turn it over, for all is therein." Divinely inspired text may contain answers to all earthly questions, but the Due Process Clause most assuredly does not. The

Court today continues its quixotic quest to right all wrongs and repair all imperfections through the Constitution. Alas, the quest cannot succeed—which is why some wrongs and imperfections have been called nonjusticiable. In the best of all possible worlds, should judges sometimes recuse even where the clear commands of our prior due process law do not require it? Undoubtedly. The relevant question, however, is whether we do more good than harm by seeking to correct this imperfection through expansion of our constitutional mandate in a manner ungoverned by any discernable rule. The answer is obvious.

Don Blankenship's fortunes did not improve following Massey Coal's defeat at the hands of the Supreme Court. Plagued by regulatory conflicts and mine safety issues, Blankenship eventually lost control of Massey Coal, and his company subsequently was acquired by one of its competitors *(see box 10-2)*.

What of the broader effects of *Caperton*? It remains to be seen whether Justice Kennedy is correct in asserting it was an extreme case of enormous campaign contributions that may not be repeated, or whether Chief Justice Roberts is more clairvoyant with his prediction that unclear guidelines established in *Caperton* will lead to an avalanche of appeals filed by losing parties claiming judicial bias. What is certain is that judicial election campaigns, which traditionally have been low-visibility affairs, have become increasingly costly and contentious. This provides a potential opportunity

---

BOX 10-2 AFTERMATH . . . DON BLANKENSHIP AND MASSEY COAL

THE JUNE 2009 Supreme Court decision against A. T. Massey Coal was only the start of troubles for parent company Massey Energy and its leader Don Blankenship. The company was the largest coal mining enterprise in the Appalachian region, with coal extraction activities in West Virginia, Kentucky, and Virginia. Blankenship became chairman and CEO of the company in 2000. By 2009 his salary had reached $17.8 million, with a deferred-compensation package of $27.2 million, but during his tenure Massey was constantly the subject of complaints concerning environmental damages and safety problems. The U.S. Department of Labor's Mine Safety and Health Administration frequently cited Massey for safety violations and for the company's failure to address them. *Grist*, an online environmental advocacy magazine, labeled Blankenship the "scariest polluter in the U.S."

On April 5, 2010, a massive explosion occurred in the Upper Big Branch Coal Mine in West Virginia, an operation owned by a Massey Energy subsidiary. Twenty-nine miners were killed, making it the deadliest mining disaster in the United States in forty years. A subsequent independent investigation found fault with Massey for failure to meet basic safety standards. According to the report, the inadequate state of the company's ventilation system allowed explosive gases to accumulate inside the mine, ultimately causing the accident and resulting fatalities. The report added, "A company that was a towering presence in the Appalachian coal fields operated its mines in a profoundly reckless manner, and 29 coal miners paid with their lives for the corporate risk taking."

In response to the incident, the Mine Safety and Health Administration issued Massey 369 citations and orders, including 21 for flagrant violations, and assessed fines totaling $10,825,368. The agency cited Massey's corporate culture as the root cause of the tragedy.

As a result of this disaster, groups of shareholders began demanding that Massey's CEO be removed, with one investment group blaming the accident on Blankenship's "confrontational approach to regulatory compliance." In the face of this pressure Blankenship took retirement at the end of 2010. Just six months later Massey Energy was sold to one of its competitors, Alpha Natural Resources.

Brent Benjamin, the little-known attorney whose 2004 election campaign was the recipient of Blankenship's unprecedented financial contributions, remains a justice on the West Virginia Supreme Court of Appeals. His twelve-year term ends in 2017.

Events surrounding the *Caperton* case became an inspiration for John Grisham's 2008 best-selling legal thriller *The Appeal*.

SOURCES: Howard Berkes, "Massey CEO's Pay Soared as Mine Concerns Grew," National Public Radio, April 10, 2010; Steve James, "Massey Faces Shareholder Anger over Mine Disaster," Reuters, April 13, 2010; David Roberts, "Massey Energy CEO Is a Really Bad Dude," *Grist*, October 25, 2006, http://grist.org/article/don-blankenship-seventh-scariest-person-in-america; Mine Safety and Health Administration news release, December 6, 2011.

for wealthy campaign donors to have an expanding influence in determining who staffs our courts.

Even Chief Justice Roberts, who dissented in *Caperton,* seems to take the point. In the 2015 case of **Williams-Yulee v. Florida Bar**, the Court considered the constitutionality of a code of judicial conduct adopted by the Florida Supreme Court, which prohibits judges and judicial candidates from personally soliciting funds for their campaigns. After the Florida Bar disciplined her for violating the new code, Lanell Williams-Yulee challenged it as intruding on her First Amendment to free speech.

The Court ruled in favor of the Florida Bar, with Chief Justice Roberts writing for the majority. Interestingly, the Chief pegged much of his opinion on ideas compatible with *Caperton.* He wrote that Florida had a compelling interest in restricting Williams-Yulee's speech: preserving public confidence in the integrity of the judiciary. Equally interesting, Justice Kennedy, *Caperton*'s author, dissented: "Whether an election is the best way to choose a judge is itself the subject of fair debate. But once the people of a State choose to have elections, the First Amendment protects the candidate's right to speak and the public's ensuing right to open and robust debate."

Personal Privacy and Dignity

At the start of this section, we noted that substantive due process has played a role in the Court's interpretation of privacy and personal dignity rights.[26] And, in fact, this may be the area where substantive due process is most potent today.

The Court's initial foray into this area came during the *Lochner* era—for example, in **Meyer v. Nebraska (1923)** the justices noted that the word *liberty* in the due process covered the right to marry and raise children, among other liberties. But today we tend to mark its onset with the case of **Griswold v. Connecticut** (1965). In *Griswold* the Court was asked to strike down a state law that banned the distribution of contraceptives on the ground that the statute violated the right to privacy. It was clear to the majority that government interference in such an intimate area was an unacceptable intrusion into a person's private life, but was the law unconstitutional? After all, no provision of the

Constitution explicitly guarantees a right of privacy. The Court struck down the Connecticut law and declared that the Constitution did indeed protect privacy rights, but the justices did not agree about which section of the Constitution required that conclusion. Some argued that privacy rights are embedded in the due process clause of the Fourteenth Amendment. Justice John Marshall Harlan asserted this substantive due process approach to privacy in his concurring opinion:

In my view, the proper constitutional inquiry in this case is whether this Connecticut statute infringes the Due Process Clause of the Fourteenth Amendment because the enactment violates basic values "implicit in the concept of ordered liberty." . . . The Due Process Clause of the Fourteenth Amendment stands, in my opinion, on its own bottom.

Not all of the justices agreed with this approach. Was finding a right to privacy inside the due process clause any different from the long-since rejected notion of finding a liberty of contract in that same provision? Justice Hugo Black argued that the Court had gone too far in creating a constitutional right out of vague Fourteenth Amendment language. He wrote in dissent, "I like my privacy as well as the next one, but I am nevertheless compelled to admit that government has a right to invade it unless prohibited by some specific constitutional provision." In subsequent decisions, the justices agreed that privacy rights are found in the due process clauses of the Fifth and Fourteenth Amendments. Unreasonable or arbitrary intrusions by the government into an individual's private life constitute a denial of liberty without due process of law.

In the years following *Griswold,* the Court used the due process approach to privacy to expand a number of liberties. Most notable was the 1973 decision in **Roe v. Wade,** which established the right to abortion. Speaking for the Court, Justice Harry Blackmun invoked the due process clause when he wrote,

[The] right of privacy, whether it be founded in the Fourteenth Amendment's concept of personal liberty and restrictions upon state action, as we feel it is, or [another clause], . . . is broad enough to encompass a woman's decision whether or not to terminate her pregnancy.

The Court has reached similar conclusions in other areas of privacy and personal dignity. In **Lawrence v.**

---

26. For a full review of the development of the constitutional right to privacy, see chapter 10 in Epstein and Walker, *Constitutional Law for a Changing America: Rights, Liberties, and Justice.*

Texas (2003) the Court concluded that laws criminalizing homosexual acts by consenting adults are barred by the right to privacy. More recently, the justices held, in *Obergefell v. Hodges* (2015), that because the liberties protected under the due process clause "extend to certain personal choices central to individual dignity and autonomy," states must license a marriage between two people of the same sex. *Obergefell* had the effect of invalidating all existing state bans on same-sex marriage.

The privacy rights rulings such as *Obergefell* and decisions such as *BMW of North America* and *Caperton* are a far cry from the pro-business application of the due process clauses in *Lochner* and *Adkins*. No one expects a return to the days when primacy was given to the liberty of contract. Yet the underlying philosophical debate over the use of substantive due process continues.

As we have seen, the Court on occasion has relied on the due process clauses to protect rights not explicitly mentioned elsewhere in the Constitution. Opposition to this practice has been advanced by those who believe that fashioning new rights in this manner is inappropriate. Legal scholar John Hart Ely accused Justice Blackmun of "*Lochner*ing" in *Roe v. Wade*. And recall Justice Scalia's declaration in the *BMW* case: "I do not regard the Fourteenth Amendment's Due Process Clause as a secret repository of substantive guarantees against 'unfairness.'" Consider also his criticism of the *Caperton* ruling that charged the Court with using the due process clause in "its quixotic quest to right all wrongs and repair all imperfections." In this same vein, dissenters have criticized these decisions for imprecise guidelines that allow the justices to impose their own views of what constitutes a denial of due process. Such criticisms closely resemble those of an earlier era that charged the Court with setting itself up as a "superlegislature" to decide on its own what laws are so unreasonable as to violate due process.

In response, those who support the expansion of the Constitution's protection of individual rights have defended the use of the substantive due process approach. As Justice Anthony Kennedy explained in *Lawrence v. Texas,*

Had those who drew and ratified the Due Process Clauses of the Fifth Amendment or the Fourteenth Amendment known the components of liberty in its manifold possibilities, they might have been more specific. They did not presume to have this insight. They knew times can blind us to certain truths and later generations can see that laws once thought necessary and proper in fact serve only to oppress. As the Constitution endures, persons in every generation can invoke its principles in their own search for greater freedom.

Either way, it is true that the doctrine—so exalted at the beginning of the twentieth century and so discredited following the New Deal—has had a significant effect on the course of the law. What could have simply faded out of existence with Miller's *Slaughterhouse* opinion became the source of one of the most interesting episodes in constitutional law.

ANNOTATED READINGS

A number of good works discuss and critique substantive due process and related phenomena. These include Randy E. Barnett, *Restoring the Lost Constitution: The Presumption of Liberty* (Princeton, NJ: Princeton University Press, 2003); Raoul Berger, *Government by Judiciary* (Cambridge, MA: Harvard University Press, 1977); Michael Conant, *The Constitution and Economic Regulation* (New Brunswick, NJ: Transaction, 2008); Markus Dirk Dubber, *The Police Power: Patriarchy and the Foundations of American Government* (New York: Columbia University Press, 2005); Edward Keynes, *Liberty, Property, and Privacy: Toward a Jurisprudence of Substantive Due Process* (University Park: Pennsylvania State University Press, 1996); John V. Orth, *Due Process of Law* (Lawrence: University Press of Kansas, 2003); and Frank R. Strong, *Substantive Due Process of Law: A Dichotomy of Sense and Nonsense* (Durham, NC: Carolina Academic Press, 1986).

Other books approach substantive due process from a more historical perspective: Richard C. Cortner, *The Iron Horse and the Constitution: The Railroads and the Transformation of the Fourteenth Amendment* (Westport, CT: Greenwood Press, 1993); Herbert Hovenkamp, *Enterprise and American Law, 1836–1937* (Cambridge, MA: Harvard University Press, 1991); Morton Keller, *Affairs of State* (Cambridge, MA: Harvard University Press, 1977); Michael J. Phillips, *The* Lochner *Court, Myth and Reality: Substantive Due Process from the 1890s to the 1930s* (Westport, CT: Praeger, 2001); Timothy Sandefur, *The Right to Earn a Living: Economic Freedom and the Law* (Washington, DC.: Cato Institute, 2010); William F. Swindler, *Court and Constitution in the*

Twentieth Century (Indianapolis: Bobbs-Merrill, 1970); Clement E. Vose, *Constitutional Change* (Lexington, MA: Lexington Books, 1972); and Christopher Wolfe, *The Rise of Modern Judicial Review* (New York: Basic Books, 1986).

Still other books provide in-depth analyses of specific cases that have been fundamental in the development and decline of substantive due process. Good examples are Howard Gillman, *The Constitution Besieged: The Rise and Demise of* Lochner *Era Police Powers Jurisprudence* (Durham, NC: Duke University Press, 1993); N. E. H. Hull, Roe v. Wade: *The Abortion Controversy in American History* (Lawrence: University Press of Kansas, 2001); John W. Johnson, Griswold v. Connecticut: *Birth Control and the Constitutional Right of Privacy* (Lawrence: University Press of Kansas, 2005); Paul Kens, *Judicial Power and Reform Politics: The Anatomy of* Lochner v. New York (Lawrence: University Press of Kansas, 1990); and David Richards, *The Sodomy Cases:* Bowers v. Hardwick *and* Lawrence v. Texas (Lawrence: University Press of Kansas, 2009).

11

The Takings Clause

O NE DAY a certified letter arrives at your house informing you that the government has decided to construct a highway, and your property lies directly in its path. The letter further states that in return for your property the government will pay you $250,000, an amount it considers "fair market value" for your home. Finally, the letter instructs you to vacate the house within six months.

Does the government have the right to seize your property in this fashion? What if this house has been in your family for generations and you do not want to sell? What if this is your dream home, just completed after years of saving and sacrificing? And what if you consider the government's offer to be less than the property is worth? Can you challenge the amount offered? What about your rights to private property? Don't they mean anything?

The general answer to these questions is that the government indeed has the right to seize private property for a public purpose, such as a new road or the construction of a government building. This authority is referred to as the "power of eminent domain." When federal, state, or local governments embark on new construction projects for roads, schools, military bases, or government offices, they usually must acquire private property. Sometimes the projects need only a parcel or two, but at other times the government requires large-scale property condemnation. Although property owners may feel mistreated when the government seizes their land, such government power is generally regarded as necessary. However, property owners have an important protection. The Constitution contains a provision, known as the "takings clause," that checks the authority of the government against the individual's right to property.

PROTECTING PRIVATE PROPERTY FROM GOVERNMENT SEIZURE

We normally associate the Bill of Rights with important civil liberties, such as the freedoms of speech, press, and religion. But when the members of the First Congress proposed a list of those rights considered important enough to merit constitutional protection, they included in the Fifth Amendment a private property guarantee—the takings clause—that states, "nor shall private property be taken for public use, without just compensation."

That the framers would have protected private property in this way is not surprising: the men who fashioned the U.S. Constitution firmly believed in private property rights. They also supported a national government that would be stronger than it was under the Articles of Confederation. The takings clause acknowledges that government projects sometimes require the seizure of private property. Without the power of eminent domain, individuals could block government programs, such as the interstate highway system, by refusing to sell property to the government or by demanding unreasonable compensation, holding government projects for ransom. But James Madison, the primary author of the Bill of Rights, rejected the notion that government should have the absolute power to confiscate private property.[1] The takings clause was intended to moderate that authority by ensuring that property owners would not be unduly disadvantaged when the government seized their land. It guarantees that property owners will be fairly compensated for their loss. As Justice Hugo Black explained, the takings clause "was designed to bar Government from forcing some people to bear public burdens which, in all fairness and justice, should be borne by the public as a whole."[2]

Provisions similar to the takings clause were already in effect in several states at the time the Bill of Rights was drafted. Vermont's Constitution of 1777 and the Massachusetts Constitution of 1780 were among the first to protect owners from absolute government seizures. Other states did not elevate the right to constitutional status but passed laws requiring just compensation for property seizures. States commonly imposed such protections when chartering companies to build roads, dams, and other projects. In 1785 Virginia required compensation to be paid for unimproved land seized for the building of roadways. South Carolina in the 1780s incorporated several companies to build canals, granting them the power of eminent domain on the condition that they compensate owners for their property losses. Similar provisions were incorporated into Virginia's charter creating the Dismal Swamp Canal Company in 1787.[3] With the states routinely adopting such provisions, it could be expected that the framers would see the need to restrain federal authority from seizing property in much the same way. In fact, the takings clause proposal was uncontroversial, spurring little debate in Congress or during the ratification process.

Because many states already protected private property against state government seizures, the takings clause was intended to apply only to federal government confiscations. The Supreme Court endorsed this interpretation in **Barron v. Baltimore** (1833).[4] The dispute arose when the city of Baltimore initiated a series of street improvements that also necessitated the alteration of several small streams. As a result, large amounts of sand and dirt were swept downstream into Baltimore Harbor, causing serious problems for the owners of wharves operating in the harbor. John Barron and John Craig were particularly damaged. Their wharf had been very profitable because it was located in deep water and was capable of servicing large ships. The accumulation of silt and waste near their wharf was so great that the water became too shallow for large vessels, and Barron and Craig lost considerable business. They demanded compensation from the city for their loss. When the city refused, they sued, asking for $20,000 in damages. The local court awarded them $4,500, but a state appellate court reversed, and Barron and Craig appealed to the U.S. Supreme Court.

They claimed that the city's construction caused their loss of profitability, which constituted a "taking" under the meaning of the Fifth Amendment and entitled them to "just compensation." The justices, however, were not concerned with questions of whether a taking had occurred or what constituted just compensation. Instead, the Court focused on a more fundamental issue: Did the Fifth Amendment apply to state actions at all? The Court concluded that it did not. In the words of Chief Justice John Marshall,

We are of opinion that the provision in the fifth amendment to the constitution, declaring that private property shall not be taken for public use without just compensation, is intended solely as a limitation on the exercise of power by the government of the United States, and is not applicable to the legislation of the states.[5]

---

1. James W. Ely Jr., *The Guardian of Every Other Right: A Constitutional History of Property Rights* (New York: Oxford University Press, 1992), 55.

2. *Armstrong v. United States* (1960).

3. For a discussion of these early provisions, see Ely, *The Guardian of Every other Right,* chap. 2.

4. For a discussion of this case, see Epstein and Walker, *Constitutional Law for a Changing America: Rights, Liberties, and Justice.*

5. The implications of this decision went far beyond the takings clause issue. By ruling as it did, the Supreme Court held that the states did not have to abide by any of the provisions of the Bill of Rights, and that those sections of the Constitution limited federal government actions only. The states were governed only by their own bills of rights. Over time, the Court incrementally changed its position, but it took more than 130 years for it to conclude that the states were bound by almost all the provisions of the Bill of Rights. For a discussion of this history, see ibid., chap. 3.

For the next half century this interpretation remained the law of the land. The takings clause applied only to the federal government. If states did not impose similar restraints on themselves, they were free to exercise the power of eminent domain without providing adequate compensation to landowners whose property had been seized.

In the late 1800s, prompted by the ratification of the Fourteenth Amendment, the Court began to reconsider this position. The Fourteenth Amendment contains a provision, known as the due process clause, that says, "nor shall any state deprive any person of life, liberty, or property, without due process of law." Lawyers began arguing that when states confiscated private property without giving the owners adequate compensation, they were depriving the owners of property without due process of law, a violation of the Fourteenth Amendment. If adopted by the Court, this interpretation would make the takings clause binding on the states and nullify the immediate impact of *Barron v. Baltimore.*

The test case for this proposition was *Chicago, Burlington & Quincy Railroad Company v. Chicago* (1897). The controversy began in 1880 when Chicago's city council passed an ordinance to open and widen certain city streets. The project required the condemnation of various parcels of land. Individuals owned some of this property, but other sections were part of a right-of-way belonging to the Chicago, Burlington & Quincy Railroad. A condemnation trial was held in the circuit court for Cook County. The court agreed to condemn the land, and the jury set the amounts of compensation to be paid to the landowners. The individuals whose property was confiscated received an average of about $5,000 for their losses, but the jury awarded the railroad only $1 for similar land seizures. The railroad company's demand for a new trial was rejected, the Illinois Supreme Court offered no relief, and the company appealed to the U.S. Supreme Court.

The justices, by a 7–1 vote, ruled in favor of the railroad. The opinion of the Court, written by Justice John Marshall Harlan, held that,

The conclusion of this Court on the question is, that since the adoption of the 14th Amendment compensation for private property taken for public uses constitutes an essential element in "due process of law," and that without such compensation the appropriation of private property to public uses, no matter under what form of procedure it is taken, would violate the provisions of the Federal Constitution.

The Court held that the takings clause of the U.S. Constitution was binding not only on the federal government, but also on state and local governments. It affirmed the government's power of eminent domain but required the payment of adequate compensation whenever that power was exercised.[6] With this ruling, the takings clause became the first provision of the Bill of Rights to be made binding on the states.

The authority of government to take private property when needed to carry out legitimate projects is now well established. The most common issue that flows from government takings cases is the question of what constitutes "just compensation." In the normal course of events, the government attempts to buy the necessary land from the owners. If negotiations fail, the government may declare the power of eminent domain and take the property, giving the owners what it thinks is a fair price. Usually fair market value is the appropriate standard. It is not uncommon, however, for the owners to argue that the government's offer is inadequate. In such situations the owners may challenge the amount in court. Questions of just compensation normally are settled through negotiation or trial court action; they rarely involve issues beyond the specific land under dispute.[7] Although legal battles may be fought over whether the offered compensation is just, no one doubts the power of the government to seize the property.

Of greater importance to understanding the meaning of the Fifth Amendment takings clause are these two questions: What is a taking, and what constitutes a public use? Both questions have required authoritative answers by the Supreme Court.

---

6. See David A. Schultz, *Property, Power, and American Democracy* (New Brunswick, NJ: Transaction, 1992).

7. Occasionally, compensation controversies involve critical issues and large amounts of money. In *United States v. Sioux Nation of Indians* (1980), the Supreme Court settled a long-standing dispute over the abrogation of the Fort Laramie Treaty of 1868. The treaty had established the right of the Sioux nation to the Black Hills, but an 1877 act of Congress essentially took back those lands. The Court ruled that the treaty abrogation was governed by the takings clause and that the Sioux were entitled to the value of the land in 1877 plus 5 percent annual interest since that year, amounting to a total claim of some $100 million.

WHAT IS A TAKING?

In many cases it is relatively easy to determine that a taking has occurred. If the federal government decides to build a new post office and must acquire a piece of privately owned property on which to build, a taking is necessary if a voluntary sale is not negotiated. Similarly, a taking occurs when, in designing a water control project, the government finds it necessary to dam certain streams and cause privately owned land to become permanently flooded. In these situations, the government takes private land, which is then used for a public purpose. There is no question that the individual has been deprived of ownership rights over the property and is entitled to compensation.

Courts are much more likely to conclude that a taking has occurred if the government has in some fashion physically invaded the owner's property. The physical invasion does not have to be complete, as when a government-constructed dam permanently floods a piece of property, nor does it have to result in the owner's total loss of the right to use the property. In *Loretto v. Teleprompter Manhattan CATV Corp.* (1982) the Court held that a New York law requiring landlords to allow a cable television company to install cable facilities on their property constituted a taking. The law required landlords to accept the direct physical attachment of plates, boxes, wires, cables, bolts, and screws on their properties. As a permanent physical occupation of the owners' property, this installation amounted to a taking that constitutionally required just compensation.

Although a physical invasion meets the traditional definition of a taking, is such an intrusion a necessary requirement? What happens when a government activity so severely curtails the possible uses of a piece of property that its value almost disappears? *United States v. Causby* (1946), a case involving a North Carolina couple whose modest chicken farm was ruined by the U.S. military, answered these questions. Did a taking occur even though the Causbys retained title to their property? The majority held that it did. But pay attention to the dissent by Justice Black, which is interesting on two counts. First, it reflects Black's generally sympathetic attitude toward federal government programs, and second, it demonstrates the importance he placed on applying the words as written. Here he attempts to apply the word *taking* as he believes the framers intended it to be used.

United States v. Causby

328 U.S. 256 (1946)
http://laws.findlaw.com/us/328/256.html
Vote: 5 (Douglas, Frankfurter, Murphy, Reed, Rutledge)
    2 (Black, Burton)

OPINION OF THE COURT: *Douglas*
DISSENTING OPINION: *Black*
NOT PARTICIPATING: *Jackson*

FACTS:

The Causbys owned 2.8 acres outside Greensboro, North Carolina. On this land were their house and the various outbuildings they needed for their chicken business. In 1942 the federal government leased a local airfield for use by army and navy aircraft. Bombers, fighters, and transport planes regularly flew in and out of this facility at all hours of the day and night. Planes often flew in close formation and in considerable numbers. The end of the airport runway was only 2,220 feet from the Causbys' property. The authorized flight patterns allowed planes to fly at an altitude of 83 feet over the Causbys' land, just 67 feet over their house, and within 18 feet of the highest tree on their property.

This activity caused the couple considerable discomfort as well as economic loss. The noise was described as startling, and the lights from approaching and departing planes lit up the night. The Causbys could not enjoy the day and found it difficult to sleep at night. No aircraft accidents had occurred on their property, but there had been several near the airport, which made the Causbys fearful and nervous. In addition, the productivity of their chickens decreased. About 150 of them died when they flew into the walls of their coops out of fear and panic when the planes flew particularly close. The property could no longer be used as a commercial chicken farm.

The Causbys filed suit in the federal court of claims arguing that the government had taken their land without just compensation in violation of the takings clause. The court agreed and ordered the government to pay them $2,000 for their loss. The federal government appealed to the Supreme Court, claiming that there was no taking because there was no physical violation of the landowners' property.

ARGUMENTS:

For the petitioner, United States:
- There is no taking without a physical invasion. Using airspace above the Causby land does not constitute a taking of property.

- A landowner does not own the airspace above his land that he has not subjected to the erection of a structure.
- The Air Commerce Act of 1926 and the Civil Aeronautics Act of 1938 give the federal government sovereign authority over the nation's airspace. These laws also acknowledge that using navigable airspace is an exercise of the right to travel.
- Any damages suffered by the Causbys are negligible.

For the respondents, Thomas Lee Causby and Tinie Causby:

- The landowner has rights to the airspace above his property. The government's use of that airspace constitutes a taking.
- The taking of the airspace above the respondent's land damaged the property and the productive use of that property.
- The trespass by the government at all hours of the day and night destroyed the Causbys' chicken business, for which they deserve full compensation.

MR. JUSTICE DOUGLAS DELIVERED THE OPINION OF THE COURT.

It is ancient doctrine that at common law ownership of the land extended to the periphery of the universe. . . . But that doctrine has no place in the modern world. The air is a public highway, as Congress has declared. Were that not true, every transcontinental flight would subject the operator to countless trespass suits. Common sense revolts at the idea. To recognize such private claims to the airspace would clog these highways, seriously interfere with their control and development in the public interest, and transfer into private ownership that to which only the public has a just claim.

But that general principle does not control the present case. For the United States conceded on oral argument that if the flights over respondents' property rendered it uninhabitable, there would be a taking compensable under the Fifth Amendment. It is the owner's loss, not the taker's gain, which is the measure of the value of the property taken. Market value fairly determined is the normal measure of the recovery. And that value may reflect the use to which the land could readily be converted, as well as the existing use. If, by reason of the frequency and altitude of the flights, respondents could not use this land for any purpose, their loss would be complete. It would be as complete as if the United States had entered upon the surface of the land and taken exclusive possession of it.

. . . The owner's right to possess and exploit the land—that is to say, his beneficial ownership of it—would be destroyed. It would not be a case of incidental damages arising from a legalized nuisance. . . .

There is no material difference between the supposed case and the present one, except that here enjoyment and use of the land are not completely destroyed. But that does not seem to us to be controlling. The path of glide for airplanes might reduce a valuable factory site to grazing land, an orchard to a vegetable patch, a residential section to a wheat field. Some value would remain. But the use of the airspace immediately above the land would limit the utility of the land and cause a diminution in its value. . . .

We have said that the airspace is a public highway. Yet it is obvious that if the landowner is to have full enjoyment of the land, he must have exclusive control of the immediate reaches of the enveloping atmosphere. Otherwise buildings could not be erected, trees could not be planted, and even fences could not be run. The principle is recognized when the law gives a remedy in case overhanging structures are erected on adjoining land. The landowner owns at least as much of the space above the ground as he can occupy or use in connection with the land. The fact that he does not occupy it in a physical sense—by the erection of buildings and the like—is not material. As we have said, the flight of airplanes, which skim the surface but do not touch it, is as much an appropriation of the use of the land as a more conventional entry upon it. We would not doubt that, if the United States erected an elevated railway over respondents' land at the precise altitude where its planes now fly, there would be a partial taking, even though none of the supports of the structure rested on the land. The reason is that there would be an intrusion so immediate and direct as to subtract from the owner's full enjoyment of the property and to limit his exploitation of it. While the owner does not in any physical manner occupy that stratum of airspace or make use of it in the conventional sense, he does use it in somewhat the same sense that space left between buildings for the purpose of light and air is used. The superadjacent airspace at this low altitude is so close to the land that continuous invasions of it affect the use of the surface of the land itself. We think that the landowner, as an incident to his ownership, has a claim to it and that invasions of it are in the same category as invasions of the surface. . . .

The airplane is part of the modern environment of life, and the inconveniences which it causes are normally not compensable under the Fifth Amendment. The airspace, apart from the immediate reaches above the land, is part of the public domain. We need not determine at this time what those precise limits are. Flights over private land are not a taking, unless they are so low and so frequent as to be a direct and immediate interference with the enjoyment and use of the land. We need not speculate on that phase of the present case. For the findings of the Court of Claims plainly establish that there was a diminution in value of the property and that the frequent, low-level flights were the direct and immediate cause. We agree with the Court of Claims that a servitude has been imposed upon the land. . . .

. . . [T]he cause is remanded to the Court of Claims so that it may make the necessary findings in conformity with this opinion.

Reversed.

MR. JUSTICE BLACK, dissenting.

The Fifth Amendment provides that "private property" shall not "be taken for public use without just compensation." The Court holds today that the Government has "taken" respondents' property by repeatedly flying Army bombers directly above respondents' land at a height of eighty-three feet where the light and noise from these planes caused respondents to lose sleep and their chickens to be killed. Since the effect of the Court's decision is to limit, by the imposition of relatively absolute constitutional barriers, possible future adjustments through legislation and regulation which might become necessary with the growth of air transportation, and since in my view the Constitution does not contain such barriers, I dissent. . . .

The Court's opinion seems to indicate that the mere flying of planes through the column of air directly above respondents' land does not constitute a "taking." Consequently, it appears to be noise and glare, to the extent and under the circumstances shown here, which make the Government a seizer of private property. . . . The concept of taking property as used in the Constitution has heretofore never been given so sweeping a meaning. The Court's opinion presents no case where a man who makes noise or shines light onto his neighbor's property has been ejected from that property for wrongfully taking possession of it. Nor would anyone take seriously a claim that noisy automobiles passing on a highway are taking wrongful possession of the homes located thereon, or that a city elevated train which greatly interferes with the sleep of those who live next to it wrongfully takes their property. . . . I am not willing, nor do I think the Constitution and the decisions authorize me, to extend that phrase so as to guarantee an absolute constitutional right to relief not subject to legislative change, which is based on averments that at best show mere torts committed by government agents while flying over land. The future adjustment of the rights and remedies of property owners, which might be found necessary because of the flight of planes at safe altitudes, should, especially in view of the imminent expansion of air navigation, be left where I think the Constitution left it, with Congress. . . .

No greater confusion could be brought about in the coming age of air transportation than that which would result were courts by constitutional interpretation to hamper Congress in its efforts to keep the air free. Old concepts of private ownership of land should not be introduced into the field of air regulation. I have no doubt that Congress will, if not handicapped by judicial interpretations of the Constitution, preserve the freedom of the air, and at the same time, satisfy the just claims of aggrieved persons. The noise of newer, larger, and more powerful planes may grow louder and louder and disturb people more and more. But the solution of the problems precipitated by these technological advances and new ways of living cannot come about through the application of rigid constitutional restraints formulated and enforced by the courts. What adjustments may have to be made, only the future can reveal. It seems certain, however, that courts do not possess the techniques or the personnel to consider and act upon the complex combinations of factors entering into the problems. . . . Today's opinion is, I fear, an opening wedge for an unwarranted judicial interference with the power of Congress to develop solutions for new and vital national problems. In my opinion this case should be reversed on the ground that there has been no "taking" in the constitutional sense.

MR. JUSTICE BURTON joins in this dissent.

How far can the definition of a taking be legitimately extended? After all, every time the government passes a law regulating the use of property, the rights of owners are diminished. Does regulation constitute a taking? Justice Oliver Wendell Holmes addressed this question in ***Pennsylvania Coal Co. v. Mahon*** (1922). For Holmes, the answer depended on the extent of the regulation:

"The general rule at least is, that while property may be regulated to a certain extent, if regulation goes too far it will be recognized as a taking." Holmes feared that, if given too much discretion, the government might regulate "until the last private property disappears."[8]

Generally, government regulation that only incidentally infringes on the owner's use of property is not considered a taking, nor is regulation that outlaws noxious or dangerous use of property. Obvious examples are zoning laws and other regulatory ordinances that make certain uses unlawful.[9] Owners may be distressed that they can no longer use their property in particular ways, but the Supreme Court has held that such statutes do not constitute Fifth Amendment takings that deserve compensation. The justices ruled that takings did not occur when a state ordered property owners to cut down standing cedar trees because a disease they carried threatened nearby apple orchards, when a local government passed an ordinance removing an individual's right to use his land as a brickyard seen as inconsistent with the surrounding neighborhood, or when for safety reasons a city prohibited a person from mining sand and gravel on his land.[10]

In each of these and numerous similar cases the government's action significantly reduced the way the land could be used and decreased its commercial value, yet the Court held that a taking had not occurred. Instead, the government policy had been formulated in response to social, economic, or environmental problems that could be addressed through the use of the government's police powers.

Penn Central Transportation Company v. City of New York (1978) addressed the questions of how far such regulation may go and for what reasons. These issues are important. If the government imposes regulations that seriously curtail the economic use of an individual's property, has a taking occurred? Although Justice William Brennan's opinion acknowledges that this area of the law has proved to be one of "considerable difficulty," it presents a good review of the principles the Court has developed to answer that question.

---

8. See Ely, *The Guardian of Every Other Right*, chap. 6.

9. See *Agins v. City of Tiburon* (1980).

10. *Miller v. Schoene* (1928), *Hadacheck v. Los Angeles* (1915), and *Goldblatt v. Hempstead* (1962), respectively.

Penn Central Transportation Company v. City of New York

438 U.S. 104 (1978)
http://laws.findlaw.com/us/438/104.html
Oral arguments are available at https://www.oyez.org.
Vote: 6 (Blackmun, Brennan, Marshall, Powell, Stewart, White)
    3 (Burger, Rehnquist, Stevens)
OPINION OF THE COURT: Brennan
DISSENTING OPINION: Rehnquist

FACTS:

New York City passed the Landmarks Preservation Law in 1965 as part of an effort to protect historic buildings and districts. Each of the fifty states and more than five hundred cities had similar statutes. In New York the Landmarks Preservation Commission administered the law. The commission's task was to identify buildings and areas that held special historic or aesthetic value. These sites were then discussed in hearings to determine whether landmark status should be conferred. If a building or area was designated historic, certain restrictions applied. The owners of landmark buildings were required to keep the exteriors in good repair and not alter the buildings without securing prior approval from the commission. Owners of such buildings received no direct compensation, but they were accorded enhanced development rights for other properties.

This case involved the application of the preservation law to the Grand Central Terminal, owned by Penn Central Transportation Company. The station, which opened in 1913, is widely regarded as an example of ingenious engineering in response to problems presented by modern urban rail stations. It is also cited as a magnificent example of French beaux arts style. The terminal received historic landmark status in 1967, although Penn Central initially opposed the action.

In 1968, to increase revenues, Penn Central entered into an agreement with UGP Properties to build a multistory office building above the terminal. UGP and Penn Central presented two separate plans to the Landmarks Preservation Commission for its approval. One plan proposed a change in the existing facade of the building and construction of a fifty-three-story office tower above it. The other envisioned a fifty-five-story office building cantilevered above the existing facade and resting on the roof of the terminal. The commission rejected both proposals.

In response, Penn Central and UGP filed suit, claiming that the application of the Landmarks Preservation Law to the terminal constituted a taking of their property without just compensation. The New York courts denied their claims, with the state's highest court rejecting the notion that the property had been "taken" under the meaning of the Fifth Amendment.

ARGUMENTS:

For the appellants, Penn Central Transportation Company et al.:

- Penn Central has a valuable private property interest in the air space above Grand Central Terminal that is fully protected by the Constitution.
- The Landmarks law operates as a taking of Penn Central's property right to develop the airspace above the terminal. As a consequence the value of the terminal property is significantly diminished.
- The city's program to preserve buildings of historic or aesthetic importance is not exempt from the constitutional requirement of just compensation.
- The law singles out landowners of certain properties, causing them to bear the burden of the city's program. Granting these targeted owners enhanced development rights for other properties falls short of just compensation.

For the appellee, New York City:

- The landmark law did not deprive Penn Central of its property without due process of law. The line between regulation and confiscation has not been breached.
- Landmarks preservation is necessary to the general welfare of the people, particularly in New York City, where a densely populated area is affected by the quality of the physical environment.
- Penn Central has not been singled out for discriminatory treatment.
- Penn Central has failed to show that the property, as restricted, is not economically viable.

MR. JUSTICE BRENNAN DELIVERED THE OPINION OF THE COURT.

Before considering appellants' specific contentions, it will be useful to review the factors that have shaped the jurisprudence of the Fifth Amendment injunction "nor shall private property be taken for public use, without just compensation." The question of what constitutes a "taking" for

Artist's conception of a fifty-five-story office building to be "floated" over the waiting room of New York's Grand Central Terminal, which had been designated a historic landmark. Plans for this building, and several others, were rejected by the Landmarks Preservation Commission, and the Supreme Court ruled that such a rejection did not constitute a taking.

© Bettmann/Corbis

purposes of the Fifth Amendment has proved to be a problem of considerable difficulty. . . . [T]his Court, quite simply, has been unable to develop any "set formula" for determining when "justice and fairness" require that economic injuries caused by public action be compensated by the government, rather than remain disproportionately concentrated on a few persons. Indeed, we have frequently observed that whether a particular restriction will be rendered invalid by the government's failure to pay for any losses proximately caused by it depends largely "upon the particular circumstances [in that] case."

In engaging in these essentially ad hoc, factual inquiries, the Court's decisions have identified several factors that have particular significance. The economic impact of the regulation on the claimant and, particularly, the extent to which the regulation has interfered with distinct investment-backed expectations are, of course, relevant considerations. So, too, is the character of the government action. A "taking" may more readily be found when the interference with property can be characterized as a physical invasion by the government than when interference arises from some public program adjusting the benefits and burdens of economic life to promote the common good.

"Government hardly could go on if to some extent values incident to property could not be diminished without paying for every such change in the general law," *Pennsylvania Coal Co. v. Mahon* (1922), and this Court has accordingly recognized, in a wide variety of contexts, that government may execute laws or programs that adversely affect recognized economic values. Exercises of the taxing power are one obvious example. A second are the decisions in which this Court has dismissed "taking" challenges on the ground that, while the challenged government action caused economic harm, it did not interfere with interests that were sufficiently bound up with the reasonable expectations of the claimant to constitute "property" for Fifth Amendment purposes.

More importantly for the present case, in instances in which a state tribunal reasonably concluded that "the health, safety, morals, or general welfare" would be promoted by prohibiting particular contemplated uses of land, this Court has upheld land-use regulations that destroyed or adversely affected recognized real property interests. Zoning laws are, of course, the classic example. . . .

Zoning laws generally do not affect existing uses of real property, but "taking" challenges have also been held to be without merit in a wide variety of situations when the challenged governmental actions prohibited a beneficial use to which individual parcels had previously been devoted and thus caused substantial individualized harm. . . .

Pennsylvania Coal Co. v. Mahon (1922) is the leading case for the proposition that a state statute that substantially furthers important public policies may so frustrate distinct investment-backed expectations as to amount to a "taking." There the claimant had sold the surface rights to particular parcels of property, but expressly reserved the right to remove the coal thereunder. A Pennsylvania statute, enacted after the transactions, forbade any mining of coal that caused the subsidence of any house, unless the house was the property of the owner of the underlying coal and was more than 150 feet from the improved property of another. Because the statute made it commercially impracticable to mine the coal, and thus had nearly the same effect as the complete destruction of rights claimant had reserved from the owners of the surface land, the Court held that the statute was invalid as effecting a "taking" without just compensation. . . .

In contending that the New York City law has "taken" their property in violation of the Fifth and Fourteenth Amendments, appellants make a series of arguments, which, while tailored to the facts of this case, essentially urge that any substantial restriction imposed pursuant to a landmark law must be accompanied by just compensation if it is to be constitutional. Before considering these, we emphasize what is not in dispute. Because this Court has recognized in a number of settings, that States and cities may enact land-use restrictions or controls to enhance the quality of life by preserving the character and desirable aesthetic features of a city, appellants do not contest that New York City's objective of preserving structures and areas with special historic, architectural, or cultural significance is an entirely permissible governmental goal. They also do not dispute that the restrictions imposed on its parcel are appropriate means of securing the purposes of the New York City law. Finally, appellants do not challenge any of the specific factual premises of the decision below. They accept for present purposes both that the parcel of land occupied by Grand Central Terminal must, in its present state, be regarded as capable of earning a reasonable return, and that the transferable development rights afforded the appellants by virtue of the Terminal's designation as a landmark are valuable, even if not as valuable as the rights to construct above the Terminal. In appellants' view none of these factors derogate from their claim that New York City's law has effected a "taking."

They first observe that the airspace above the Terminal is a valuable property interest, citing *United States v. Causby*. They urge that the Landmarks Law has deprived them of any gainful use of their "air rights" above the

Terminal and that, irrespective of the value of the remainder of their parcel, the city has "taken" their right to this superadjacent airspace, thus entitling them to "just compensation" measured by the fair market value of these air rights.

Apart from our own disagreement with appellants' characterization of the effect of the New York City law, the submission that appellants may establish a "taking" simply by showing that they have been denied the ability to exploit a property interest that they heretofore had believed was available for development is quite simply untenable. . . . "Taking" jurisprudence does not divide a single parcel into discrete segments and attempt to determine whether rights in a particular segment have been entirely abrogated. In deciding whether a particular governmental action has effected a taking, this Court focuses rather both on the character of the action and on the nature and extent of the interference with rights in the parcel as a whole—here, the city tax block designated as the "landmark site."

Secondly, appellants, focusing on the character and impact of the New York City law, argue that it effects a "taking" because its operation has significantly diminished the value of the Terminal site. Appellants concede that the decisions sustaining other land-use regulations, which, like the New York City law, are reasonably related to the promotion of the general welfare, uniformly reject the proposition that diminution in property value, standing alone, can establish a "taking." . . . [B]ut appellants argue that New York City's regulation of individual landmarks is fundamentally different from zoning or from historic-district legislation because the controls imposed by New York City's law apply only to individuals who own selected properties.

Stated baldly, appellants' position appears to be that the only means of ensuring that selected owners are not singled out to endure financial hardship for no reason is to hold that any restriction imposed on individual landmarks pursuant to the New York City scheme is a "taking" requiring the payment of "just compensation." Agreement with this argument would, of course, invalidate not just New York City's law, but all comparable landmark legislation in the Nation. We find no merit in it. . . .

Equally without merit is the related argument that the decision to designate a structure as a landmark "is inevitably arbitrary or at least subjective, because it is basically a matter of taste," thus unavoidably singling out individual landowners for disparate and unfair treatment. The argument has a particularly hollow ring in this case. . . . [A] landmark owner has a right to judicial review of any

Commission decision, and, quite simply, there is no basis whatsoever for a conclusion that courts will have any greater difficulty identifying arbitrary or discriminatory action in the context of landmark regulation than in the context of classic zoning or indeed in any other context. . . .

In any event, appellants' repeated suggestions that they are solely burdened and unbenefited is factually inaccurate. This contention overlooks the fact that the New York City law applies to vast numbers of structures in the city in addition to the Terminal—all the structures contained in the 31 historic districts and over 400 individual landmarks, many of which are close to the Terminal. Unless we are to reject the judgment of the New York City Council that the preservation of landmarks benefits all New York citizens and all structures, both economically and by improving the quality of life in the city as a whole—which we are unwilling to do—we cannot conclude that the owners of the Terminal have in no sense been benefited by the Landmarks Law. . . .

. . . [T]he New York City law does not interfere in any way with the present uses of the Terminal. Its designation as a landmark not only permits but contemplates that appellants may continue to use the property precisely as it has been used for the past 65 years: as a railroad terminal containing office space and concessions. So the law does not interfere with what must be regarded as Penn Central's primary expectation concerning the use of the parcel. More importantly, on this record, we must regard the New York City law as permitting Penn Central not only to profit from the Terminal but also to obtain a "reasonable" return on its investment. . . .

On this record, we conclude that the application of New York City's Landmarks Law has not effected a "taking" of appellants' property. The restrictions imposed are substantially related to the promotion of the general welfare and not only permit reasonable beneficial use of the landmark site but also afford appellants opportunities further to enhance not only the Terminal site proper but also other properties.

Affirmed.

MR. JUSTICE REHNQUIST, with whom THE CHIEF JUSTICE and MR. JUSTICE STEVENS join, dissenting.
Of the over one million buildings and structures in the city of New York, appellees have singled out 400 for designation as official landmarks. The owner of a building might initially be pleased that his property has been chosen by a distinguished committee of architects, historians, and city

planners for such a singular distinction. But he may well discover, as appellant Penn Central Transportation Co. did here, that the landmark designation imposes upon him a substantial cost, with little or no offsetting benefit except for the honor of the designation. The question in this case is whether the cost associated with the city of New York's desire to preserve a limited number of "landmarks" within its borders must be borne by all of its taxpayers or whether it can instead be imposed entirely on the owners of the individual properties. . . .

The Fifth Amendment provides in part: "nor shall private property be taken for public use, without just compensation." In a very literal sense, the actions of appellees violated this constitutional prohibition. Before the city of New York declared Grand Central Terminal to be a landmark, Penn Central could have used its "air rights" over the Terminal to build a multistory office building, at an apparent value of several million dollars per year. Today, the Terminal cannot be modified in any form, including the erection of additional stories, without the permission of the Landmark Preservation Commission, a permission which appellants, despite good-faith attempts, have so far been unable to obtain. . . .

As Mr. Justice Holmes pointed out in *Pennsylvania Coal Co. v. Mahon*, "the question at bottom" in an eminent domain case "is upon whom the loss of the changes desired should fall." The benefits that appellees believe will flow from preservation of the Grand Central Terminal will accrue to all the citizens of New York City. There is no reason to believe that appellants will enjoy a substantially greater share of these benefits. If the cost of preserving Grand Central Terminal were spread evenly across the entire population of the city of New York, the burden per person would be in cents per year—a minor cost appellees would surely concede for the benefit accrued. Instead, however, appellees would impose the entire cost of several million dollars per year on Penn Central. But it is precisely this sort of discrimination that the Fifth Amendment prohibits. . . .

Over 50 years ago, Mr. Justice Holmes, speaking for the Court, warned that the courts were "in danger of forgetting that a strong public desire to improve the public condition is not enough to warrant achieving the desire by a shorter cut than the constitutional way of paying for the change." The Court's opinion in this case demonstrates that the danger thus foreseen has not abated. The city of New York is in a precarious financial state, and some may believe that the costs of landmark preservation will be more easily borne by corporations such as Penn Central than the overburdened individual taxpayers of New York. But these concerns do not allow us to ignore past precedents construing the Eminent Domain Clause to the end that the desire to improve the public condition is, indeed, achieved by a shorter cut than the constitutional way of paying for the change.

Penn Central represents the high-water mark for the Court allowing state and local governments to impose regulation without triggering a takings clause violation. In the 1980s the Court began to reconsider its position on takings clause complaints. This shift had two causes. First, governments began exercising their land regulation powers more aggressively. Second, personnel changes created a Court that was more sympathetic to private property rights than before. The pivotal changes occurred in 1986, when William Rehnquist was elevated to the chief justiceship and Antonin Scalia joined the Court. Rehnquist had previously been on the losing side of important takings clause cases. His dissenting opinion in *Penn Central* clearly indicated that his views were at odds with the way the majority was handling takings clause appeals, an area of the law in which he had a special interest.

The signs of change began to appear in 1987, when the Court handed down three takings clause decisions. The first, decided in March, was ***Keystone Bituminous Coal Association v. DeBenedictis.*** The majority upheld a state regulation of coal mining operations against takings clause and contract clause attacks, but Chief Justice Rehnquist's dissenting opinion attracted the support of three other justices, indicating that members of the Court who supported private property rights interests were poised to make a major assault on existing takings clause interpretations. The second case, ***First English Evangelical Lutheran Church of Glendale v. County of Los Angeles***, was decided in June. Although this case involved a relatively minor point regarding the recovery of damages in takings clause cases, the Court voted 6–3 to support the property owners who claimed compensation, and Rehnquist wrote the majority opinion. This decision was a clear signal that the Rehnquist Court was open to new takings clause appeals. Justice John Paul Stevens acknowledged this fact in a dissenting opinion, in which he said, "One thing is certain. The Court's decision today will generate a great deal of litigation."

The third 1987 case, *Nollan v. California Coastal Commission,* was the clearest indication that the Rehnquist Court was about to resurrect property rights under the takings clause. The decision also illustrates how states were using their authority to deny building permits in lieu of directly exercising the power of eminent domain. By doing so they hoped to accomplish their land-use policy goals without compensating landowners for their losses. In return for allowing James and Marilyn Nollan to build a house on their beachfront property, the state of California required the family to dedicate a portion of the property to public access. Was this requirement a taking? The five justices who were considered the Court's conservative bloc thought it was. The four liberals said it was not. What do you think? Was the Nollans' property partially taken from them by the public access requirement, and was California therefore bound by the Fifth Amendment to pay just compensation?

Nollan v. California Coastal Commission

483 U.S. 825 (1987)
http://laws.findlaw.com/us/483/825.html
Oral arguments are available at https://www.oyez.org.
Vote: 5 (O'Connor, Powell, Rehnquist, Scalia, White)
      4 (Blackmun, Brennan, Marshall, Stevens)
OPINION OF THE COURT: *Scalia*
DISSENTING OPINIONS: *Blackmun, Brennan, Stevens*

FACTS:

James and Marilyn Nollan owned a beachfront lot in Ventura County, California. One-quarter mile north of their property was Faria County Park, a public beach and recreation area. Another public beach, known as the Cove, was located 1,800 feet south of the Nollan lot. A concrete seawall, eight feet high, separated the beach part of the Nollan property from the rest of the land. Originally, a small bungalow that was rented to summer vacationers stood on the property. The house, however, had fallen into serious disrepair and could no longer be rented. The Nollans decided to replace the bungalow with a new structure, and to do so they needed a building permit from the California Coastal Commission.

The commission granted the Nollans permission to build their new house, but with one significant condition: a strip of their property was to be set aside for use by the public to move between the two public beaches. The Nollans protested. On rehearing, the commission

reaffirmed the requirement, finding that the easement was necessary because the new house would reduce the view of the beach from the street and prevent the public "psychologically . . . from realizing a stretch of coastline exists nearby that they have every right to visit." The Nollans then filed suit claiming that the public access condition constituted a taking under the Fifth Amendment. The California Supreme Court ruled in favor of the commission, and the Nollans took their case to the U.S. Supreme Court.

ARGUMENTS:

For the appellants, James P. Nollan and Marilyn H. Nollan:

- The state's requirement of a public right-of-way will allow repeated physical invasions of the appellants' property by members of the public.
- Such a permanent physical invasion of the property is clearly a taking for which the Nollans are constitutionally entitled to just compensation.
- The Nollans have received no special benefit nor created any special public burden to justify imposing on them the full cost of expanding public beach access.

For the appellee, the California Coastal Commission:

- In exercising its police powers, the state has properly taken into account the cumulative impacts of proposed developments.
- The regulation in question serves an important public purpose of allowing public access to the publicly owned coastal tidelands.
- The line between regulation and confiscation has not been breached.
- The Nollans have not been deprived of all economic use or value of their property.

◢ JUSTICE SCALIA DELIVERED THE OPINION OF THE COURT.

Had California simply required the Nollans to make an easement across their beachfront available to the public on a permanent basis in order to increase public access to the beach, rather than conditioning their permit to rebuild their house on their agreeing to do so, we have no doubt there would have been a taking. To say that the appropriation of a public easement across a landowner's premises does not constitute the taking of a property interest but rather . . . "a mere restriction on its use" is to use words in a manner that deprives them of all their ordinary meaning. Indeed, one of the principal uses of the eminent domain power is to assure that the government be able to require conveyance of just such interests, so long as it pays for them. Perhaps because the point is so obvious, we have never been confronted with a controversy that required us to rule upon it, but our cases' analysis of the effect of other governmental action leads to the same conclusion. We have repeatedly held that, as to property reserved by its owner for private use, "the right to exclude [others is] 'one of the most essential sticks in the bundle of rights that are commonly characterized as property.'" In *Loretto* [*v. Teleprompter Manhattan CATV*, 1982] we observed that where governmental action results in "[a] permanent physical occupation" of the property, by the government or others, "our cases uniformly have found a taking to the extent of the occupation, without regard to whether the action achieves an important public benefit or has only minimal economic impact on the owner." We think a "permanent physical occupation" has occurred, for purposes of that rule, where individuals are given a permanent and continuous right to pass to and fro, so that the real property may continuously be traversed, even though no particular individual is permitted to station himself permanently upon the premises. . . .

Given, then, that requiring uncompensated conveyance of the easement outright would violate the Fourteenth Amendment, the question becomes whether requiring it to be conveyed as a condition for issuing a land-use permit alters the outcome. We have long recognized that land-use regulation does not effect a taking if it "substantially advance[s] legitimate state interests" and does not "den[y] an owner economically viable use of his land." . . . Our cases have not elaborated on the standards for determining what constitutes a "legitimate state interest" or what type of connection between the regulation and the state interest satisfies the requirement that the former "substantially advance" the latter. They have made clear, however, that a broad range of governmental purposes and regulations satisfies these requirements. The Commission argues that among these permissible purposes are protecting the public's ability to see the beach, assisting the public in overcoming the "psychological barrier" to using the beach created by a developed shorefront, and preventing congestion on the public beaches. We assume, without deciding, that this is so—in which case the Commission unquestionably would be able to deny the Nollans their permit outright if their new house (alone, or by reason of the cumulative impact produced in conjunction with other

construction) would substantially impede these purposes, unless the denial would interfere so drastically with the Nollans' use of their property as to constitute a taking.

. . . Thus, if the Commission attached to the permit some condition that would have protected the public's ability to see the beach notwithstanding construction of the new house—for example, a height limitation, a width restriction or a ban on fences—so long as the Commission could have exercised its police power (as we have assumed it could) to forbid construction of the house altogether, imposition of the condition would also be constitutional. Moreover (and here we come closer to the facts of the present case), the condition would be constitutional even if it consisted of the requirement that the Nollans provide a viewing spot on their property for passersby with whose sighting of the ocean their new house would interfere. Although such a requirement, constituting a permanent grant of continuous access to the property, would have to be considered a taking if it were not attached to a development permit, the Commission's assumed power to forbid construction of the house in order to protect the public's view of the beach must surely include the power to condition construction upon some concession by the owner, even a concession of property rights, that serves the same end. If a prohibition designed to accomplish that purpose would be a legitimate exercise of the police power rather than a taking, it would be strange to conclude that providing the owner an alternative to that prohibition which accomplishes the same purpose is not.

The evident constitutional propriety disappears, however, if the condition substituted for the prohibition utterly fails to further the end advanced as the justification for the prohibition. . . . The purpose then becomes, quite simply, the obtaining of an easement to serve some valid governmental purpose, but without payment of compensation. Whatever may be the outer limits of "legitimate state interests" in the takings and land-use context, this is not one of them. In short, unless the permit condition serves the same governmental purpose as the development ban, the building restriction is not a valid regulation of land use but "an out-and-out plan of extortion." . . .

It is quite impossible to understand how a requirement that people already on the public beaches be able to walk across the Nollans' property reduces any obstacles to viewing the beach created by the new house. It is also impossible to understand how it lowers any "psychological barrier" to using the public beaches, or how it helps to remedy any additional congestion on them caused by construction of the Nollans' new house. We therefore find that the Commission's imposition of the permit condition cannot be treated as an exercise of its land-use power for any of these purposes. Our conclusion on this point is consistent with the approach taken by every other court that has considered the question, with the exception of the California state courts. . . .

California is free to advance its "comprehensive program," if it wishes, by using its power of eminent domain for this "public purpose," but if it wants an easement across the Nollans' property, it must pay for it.

Reversed.

JUSTICE BRENNAN, with whom JUSTICE MARSHALL joins, dissenting.

The Court's conclusion that the permit condition imposed on appellants is unreasonable cannot withstand analysis. First, the Court demands a degree of exactitude that is inconsistent with our standard for reviewing the rationality of a State's exercise of its police power for the welfare of its citizens. Second, even if the nature of the public-access condition imposed must be identical to the precise burden on access created by appellants, this requirement is plainly satisfied.

There can be no dispute that the police power of the States encompasses the authority to impose conditions on private development. It is also by now commonplace that this Court's view of the rationality of a State's exercise of its police power demands only that the State "could rationally have decided" that the measure adopted might achieve the State's objective. In this case, California has employed its police power in order to condition development upon preservation of public access to the ocean and tidelands. The Coastal Commission, if it had so chosen, could have denied the Nollans' request for a development permit, since the property would have remained economically viable without the requested new development. Instead, the State sought to accommodate the Nollans' desire for new development, on the condition that the development not diminish the overall amount of public access to the coastline. Appellants' proposed development would reduce public access by restricting visual access to the beach, by contributing to an increased need for community facilities, and by moving private development closer to public beach property. The Commission sought to offset this diminution in access, and thereby preserve the overall balance of access, by requesting a deed restriction that would ensure "lateral" access: the right of the public to pass and repass along the dry sand parallel to the shoreline in order to reach the tidelands and the ocean. In the expert opinion of the Coastal Commission, development conditioned on such a restriction would fairly attend to both public and private interests.

The Court finds fault with this measure because it regards the condition as insufficiently tailored to address the precise type of reduction in access produced by the new development. The Nollans' development blocks visual access, the Court tells us, while the Commission seeks to preserve lateral access along the coastline. Thus, it concludes, the State acted irrationally. Such a narrow conception of rationality, however, has long since been discredited as a judicial arrogation of legislative authority. . . .

Imposition of the permit condition in this case represents the State's reasonable exercise of its police power. The Coastal Commission has drawn on its expertise to preserve the balance between private development and public access, by requiring that any project that intensifies development on the increasingly crowded California coast must be offset by gains in public access. Under the normal standard for review of the police power, this provision is eminently reasonable. . . .

State agencies . . . require considerable flexibility in responding to private desires for development in a way that guarantees the preservation of public access to the coast. They should be encouraged to regulate development in the context of the overall balance of competing uses of the shoreline. The Court today does precisely the opposite, overruling an eminently reasonable exercise of an expert state agency's judgment, substituting its own narrow view of how this balance should be struck. Its reasoning is hardly suited to the complex reality of natural resource protection in the 20th century. I can only hope that today's decision is an aberration, and that the broader vision ultimately prevails.

I dissent.

Justice Brennan's hope that *Nollan* would be an aberration was not fulfilled. In the years following this opinion, the personnel on the Court continued to change. He and Justice Marshall, firm supporters of public interests over private property rights, retired. Joining the Court were two supporters of private property, Justices Anthony Kennedy and Clarence Thomas. These changes strengthened the chief justice's efforts to breathe new life into the Constitution's private property protections.

There is no invariable rule to assist courts in determining whether a challenged government regulation has gone too far and become a taking. Rather, in line with the *Penn Central* decision, courts engage in an **ad hoc** evaluation of the government's actions weighing all relevant facts and circumstances, including the nature of the government's actions, the economic impact of the regulation on the claimant, and the extent to which the regulation has interfered with distinct investment-backed expectations.

However, there are two conditions under which courts find no need to engage in such a searching analysis. If either of these two conditions exists, there is no question that the government action constitutes a taking that requires compensation. The first condition is when the government's action completely deprives the owner of all economically beneficial use of the property. The second occurs when the government permanently occupies the property. Either situation categorically requires compensation. These are often referred to as "per se" takings.

The Court's decision in *Lucas v. South Carolina Coastal Council* (1992) involves a litigant who claimed that the state government's environmental regulations stripped his land of any economic value. Do you think the government's action was a reasonable regulation to protect the coastal environment or do you agree with the Court's majority that a taking occurred?

Lucas v. South Carolina Coastal Council

505 U.S. 1003 (1992)
http://laws.findlaw.com/us/505/1003.html
Oral arguments are available at https://www.oyez.org.
Vote: 6 (Kennedy, O'Connor, Rehnquist, Scalia, Thomas, White)
3 (Blackmun, Souter, Stevens)

OPINION OF THE COURT: *Scalia*
OPINION CONCURRING IN THE JUDGMENT: *Kennedy*
DISSENTING OPINIONS: *Blackmun, Stevens*
SEPARATE STATEMENT: *Souter*

FACTS:

David Lucas owned two vacant oceanfront lots on the Isle of Palms, a barrier island near Charleston, South Carolina. He acquired the property with the intention of building single-family homes similar to those already built on adjacent lots. When Lucas bought the land there were no regulations prohibiting such use. Shortly thereafter, however, the state passed the Beachfront Management Act, an environmental law

that increased the state coastal council's authority to protect certain shoreline areas against erosion and other dangers. The council decided that the Lucas lots were in a "critical area" and prohibited any new construction there.

There is no doubt that under its police powers the state has the right to pass such legislation, but Lucas claimed that the new regulations amounted to a taking of his property for a public purpose. The Fifth Amendment, he argued, required the state to pay him for the loss of his property. A state trial judge agreed that the regulations had made the Lucas property essentially worthless and ordered the state to compensate him for his loss. On appeal, the South Carolina Supreme Court reversed, holding that the environmental legislation was not a taking under the meaning of the Constitution. Lucas appealed to the U.S. Supreme Court.

Many saw this case as presenting the Supreme Court with the opportunity to reset the constitutional balance between private property rights and the government's authority to regulate for the common good. As a consequence, it is not surprising that a large number of governments and organizations submitted amicus curiae briefs. The administration of President George H. W. Bush, conservative legal organizations such as Pacific Legal Foundation, and a long list of groups whose economic interests were threatened by government land-use regulations filed in behalf of Lucas. Among these groups were the National Association of Home Builders, the American Mining Congress, and the American Farm Bureau Federation. Urging the Court to support South Carolina's position were briefs from more than half the states, the U.S. Conference of Mayors and other local government groups, and organizations favoring government protection of the environment, such as the National Trust for Historic Preservation and the Sierra Club. The stakes were high.

ARGUMENTS:

For the petitioner, David H. Lucas:

- The state law is a valid exercise of the police power, but it involves a taking for which Lucas is constitutionally entitled to just compensation.
- The state cannot avoid the obligations of the takings clause by claiming that its policy is a regulation of a nuisance. The construction of a home is not a nuisance.

One of two lots on the Isle of Palms that David Lucas purchased with the intention of building houses on them. Shortly after the sale was completed, the South Carolina Coastal Council determined that building on the lots would be detrimental to the environment and prohibited future development there. In 1992 the Supreme Court agreed with Lucas that the state's action violated the takings clause.

- The state's regulation has rendered the property economically worthless. When regulation is that extensive, it becomes a taking. *Pennsylvania Coal Co. v. Mahon* (1922).
- The burden of confiscatory environmental regulation should fall on society, not on individual landowners.

For the respondent, state of South Carolina:
- Whether a compensable taking has occurred is not determined exclusively by the reduction in the property's value, but also by the character of the government's actions, the government's interference with realistic investment expectations, and the economic impact of the regulations.
- The beachfront environment was suffering from ill-planned development creating a serious harm to public health and safety as well as damage to other property. Regulation was required to prevent continued harm.

- Lucas was well aware that regulation was necessary. He could not reasonably expect to be free from future government restrictions that would limit how he used his land and reduce the property's value. Such regulation is not a taking.
- Although Lucas has lost what he deems the "highest and best" use of his land, the property has not been rendered economically worthless.

JUSTICE SCALIA DELIVERED THE OPINION OF THE COURT.

Prior to Justice Holmes' exposition in *Pennsylvania Coal Co. v. Mahon* (1922), it was generally thought that the Takings Clause reached only a "direct appropriation" of property or the functional equivalent of a "practical ouster of [the owner's] possession." Justice Holmes recognized in *Mahon*, however, that if the protection against appropriations of private property was to be meaningfully enforced, the government's power to redefine the range of interests included in the ownership of property was necessarily constrained by constitutional limits. If, instead, the uses of private property were subject to unbridled, uncompensated qualification under the police power, "the natural tendency of human nature [would be] to extend the qualification more and more until at last private property disappear[ed]." These considerations gave birth in that case to the oft-cited maxim that, "while property may be regulated to a certain extent, if regulation goes too far it will be recognized as a taking."

Nevertheless, our decision in *Mahon* offered little insight into when, and under what circumstances, a given regulation would be seen as going "too far" for purposes of the Fifth Amendment. . . . We have, however, described at least two discrete categories of regulatory action as compensable without case-specific inquiry into the public interest advanced in support of the restraint. The first encompasses regulations that compel the property owner to suffer a physical "invasion" of his property. In general (at least with regard to permanent invasions), no matter how minute the intrusion, and no matter how weighty the public purpose behind it, we have required compensation. . . .

The second situation in which we have found categorical treatment appropriate is where regulation denies all economically beneficial or productive use of land. As we have said on numerous occasions, the Fifth Amendment is violated when land-use regulation "does not substantially advance legitimate state interests or denies an owner economically viable use of his land." . . .

We think . . . that there are good reasons for our frequently expressed belief that when the owner of real property has been called upon to sacrifice all economically beneficial uses in the name of the common good, that is, to leave his property economically idle, he has suffered a taking.

The trial court found Lucas's two beachfront lots to have been rendered valueless by respondent's enforcement of the coastal-zone construction ban. Under Lucas's theory of the case, which rested upon our "no economically viable use" statements, that finding entitled him to compensation. . . . The South Carolina Supreme Court, however, thought otherwise. In its view, the Beachfront Management Act was no ordinary enactment, but involved an exercise of South Carolina's "police powers" to mitigate the harm to the public interest that petitioner's use of his land might occasion. . . .

It is correct that many of our prior opinions have suggested that "harmful or noxious uses" of property may be proscribed by government regulation without the requirement of compensation. For a number of reasons, however, we think the South Carolina Supreme Court was too quick to conclude that that principle decides the present case. The "harmful or noxious uses" principle was the Court's early attempt to describe in theoretical terms why government may, consistent with the Takings Clause, affect property values by regulation without incurring an obligation to compensate—a reality we nowadays acknowledge explicitly with respect to the full scope of the State's police power. . . .

"Harmful or noxious use" analysis was, in other words, simply the progenitor of our more contemporary statements that "land-use regulation does not effect a taking if it 'substantially advance[s] legitimate state interests.' . . ."

The transition from our early focus on control of "noxious" uses to our contemporary understanding of the broad realm within which government may regulate without compensation was an easy one, since the distinction between "harm-preventing" and "benefit-conferring" regulation is often in the eye of the beholder. It is quite possible, for example, to describe in either fashion the ecological, economic, and aesthetic concerns that inspired the South Carolina legislature in the present case. One could say that imposing a servitude on Lucas's land is necessary in order to prevent his use of it from "harming" South Carolina's ecological resources; or, instead, in order to achieve the "benefits" of an ecological preserve. . . . Whether Lucas's construction of single-family residences on his parcels should be described as bringing "harm" to South Carolina's adjacent ecological resources thus depends principally upon whether the describer believes that the State's use interest in nurturing those resources is so important that any competing adjacent use must yield.

When it is understood that "prevention of harmful use" was merely our early formulation of the police power justification necessary to sustain (without compensation) any regulatory diminution in value; and that the distinction between regulation that "prevents harmful use" and that which "confers benefits" is difficult, if not impossible, to discern on an objective, value-free basis; it becomes self-evident that noxious-use logic cannot serve as a touchstone to distinguish regulatory "takings"—which require compensation—from regulatory deprivations that do not require compensation. A fortiori the legislature's recitation of a noxious-use justification cannot be the basis for departing from our categorical rule that total regulatory takings must be compensated. If it were, departure would virtually always be allowed. . . .

Where the State seeks to sustain regulation that deprives land of all economically beneficial use, we think it may resist compensation only if the logically antecedent inquiry into the nature of the owner's estate shows that the proscribed use interests were not part of his title to begin with. This accords, we think, with our "takings" jurisprudence, which has traditionally been guided by the understandings of our citizens regarding the content of, and the State's power over, the "bundle of rights" that they acquire when they obtain title to property. It seems to us that the property owner necessarily expects the uses of his property to be restricted, from time to time, by various measures newly enacted by the State in legitimate exercise of its police powers; "[a]s long recognized, some values are enjoyed under an implied limitation and must yield to the police power." And in the case of personal property, by reason of the State's traditionally high degree of control over commercial dealings, he ought to be aware of the possibility that new regulation might even render his property economically worthless (at least if the property's only economically productive use is sale or manufacture for sale). In the case of land, however, we think the notion pressed by the Council that title is somehow held subject to the "implied limitation" that the State may subsequently eliminate all economically valuable use is inconsistent with the historical compact recorded in the Takings Clause that has become part of our constitutional culture.

Where "permanent physical occupation" of land is concerned, we have refused to allow the government to decree it anew (without compensation), no matter how weighty the asserted "public interests" involved. . . . We believe similar treatment must be accorded confiscatory regulations, i.e., regulations that prohibit all economically beneficial use of land: Any limitation so severe cannot be newly legislated or decreed (without compensation), but must inhere in the title itself, in the restrictions that background principles of the State's law of property and nuisance already place upon land ownership. A law or decree with such an effect must, in other words, do no more than duplicate the result that could have been achieved in the courts—by adjacent landowners (or other uniquely affected persons) under the State's law of private nuisance, or by the State under its complementary power to abate nuisances that affect the public generally, or otherwise.

On this analysis, the owner of a lake bed, for example, would not be entitled to compensation when he is denied the requisite permit to engage in a landfilling operation that would have the effect of flooding others' land. Nor the corporate owner of a nuclear generating plant, when it is directed to remove all improvements from its land upon discovery that the plant sits astride an earthquake fault. Such regulatory action may well have the effect of eliminating the land's only economically productive use, but it does not proscribe a productive use that was previously permissible under relevant property and nuisance principles. The use of these properties for what are now expressly prohibited purposes was always unlawful, and (subject to other constitutional limitations) it was open to the State at any point to make the implication of those background principles of nuisance and property law explicit. . . . When, however, a regulation that declares "off-limits" all economically productive or beneficial uses of land goes beyond what the relevant background principles would dictate, compensation must be paid to sustain it.

The "total taking" inquiry we require today will ordinarily entail (as the application of state nuisance law ordinarily entails) analysis of, among other things, the degree of harm to public lands and resources, or adjacent private property, posed by the claimant's proposed activities, the social value of the claimant's activities and their suitability to the locality in question, and the relative ease with which the alleged harm can be avoided through measures taken by the claimant and the government (or adjacent private landowners) alike. The fact that a particular use has long been engaged in by similarly situated owners ordinarily imports a lack of any common-law prohibition (though changed circumstances or new knowledge may make what was previously permissible no longer so). So also does the fact that other landowners, similarly situated, are permitted to continue the use denied to the claimant.

It seems unlikely that common-law principles would have prevented the erection of any habitable or productive improvements on petitioner's land; they rarely support prohibition of the "essential use" of land. The question, however, is one of state law to be dealt with on remand. We emphasize that to win its case South Carolina must do more than proffer the legislature's declaration that the uses Lucas desires are inconsistent with the public interest, or the conclusory assertion that they violate a common-law maxim. . . . As we have said, a "State, by ipse dixit, may not transform private property into public property without compensation. . . ." Instead, as it would be required to do if it sought to restrain Lucas in a common-law action for public nuisance, South Carolina must identify background principles of nuisance and property law that prohibit the uses he now intends in the circumstances in which the property is presently found. Only on this showing can the State fairly claim that, in proscribing all such beneficial uses, the Beachfront Management Act is taking nothing.

The judgment is reversed and the cause remanded for proceedings not inconsistent with this opinion.

So ordered.

JUSTICE BLACKMUN, dissenting.

Today the Court launches a missile to kill a mouse.

The state of South Carolina prohibited petitioner Lucas from building a permanent structure on his property from 1988 to 1990. Relying on an unreviewed (and implausible) state trial court finding that this restriction left Lucas' property valueless, this Court granted review to determine whether compensation must be paid in cases where the State prohibits all economic use of real estate. According to the Court, such an occasion never has arisen in any of our prior cases, and the Court imagines that it will arise "relatively rarely" or only in "extraordinary circumstances." Almost certainly it did not happen in this case.

Nonetheless, the Court presses on to decide the issue, and as it does, it ignores its jurisdictional limits, remakes its traditional rules of review, and creates simultaneously a new categorical rule and an exception (neither of which is rooted in our prior case law, common law, or common

sense). I protest not only the Court's decision, but each step taken to reach it. More fundamentally, I question the Court's wisdom in issuing sweeping new rules to decide such a narrow case. Surely, . . . the Court could have reached the result it wanted without inflicting this damage upon our Takings Clause jurisprudence. . . .

The Court makes sweeping and, in my view, misguided and unsupported changes in our takings doctrine. While it limits these changes to the most narrow subset of government regulation—those that eliminate all economic value from land—these changes go far beyond what is necessary to secure petitioner Lucas' private benefit. One hopes they do not go beyond the narrow confines the Court assigns them to today.

I dissent.

The Court's decision meant that David Lucas was entitled to compensation in return for being denied the right to develop his land *(see box 11-1)*. It also meant that the Court was continuing to broaden its definition of what constitutes a taking and to expand the range of situations in which government is required to provide compensation to private landowners.

BOX 11-1 AFTERMATH . . . *LUCAS V. SOUTH CAROLINA COASTAL COUNCIL*

IN 1986 David Lucas, a developer of residential properties, purchased two lots on the Isle of Palms in South Carolina for $975,000. He intended to build two houses on the land, keeping one for himself and selling the other. Because of environmental concerns, however, the state coastal council denied Lucas permission to build. In response, Lucas took legal action, demanding compensation for his economic loss. He won a $1.23 million judgment in the state trial court, but the state supreme court reversed that ruling. In 1992 the U.S. Supreme Court found that Lucas had been deprived of property for a public purpose and was entitled to be compensated. The justices remanded the case back to the South Carolina courts for further proceedings.

No additional court action was required, however. The state had lost the essential issue presented in the case, and only the determination of adequate compensation

remained to be decided. South Carolina was understandably eager to settle the dispute rather than prolong the legal battle. Lucas and the state came to a quick out-of-court settlement in which the state agreed to pay Lucas $1.5 million in return for the property.

To recoup the funds lost in the Lucas settlement and related litigation costs, the state decided to sell the properties. Ironically, to increase the lots' value prior to sale, the state announced that the new owners would be allowed to build houses on them. A new home of about 5,000 square feet now sits on one of the lots formerly owned by Lucas.

SOURCES: *Arizona Republic,* November 2, 1994; *Chicago Sun-Times,* July 28, 1995; *Christian Science Monitor,* September 27, 1993; *San Diego Union-Tribune,* July 21, 1993; William A. Fischel, "A Photographic Update on *Lucas v. South Carolina Coastal Council*: A Photographic Essay," March 30, 2000 (original posting February 1995), http://www.dartmouth.edu/-wfischel/lucasupdate.html.

The justices further clarified the meaning of per se takings in *Horne v. Department of Agriculture* (2015), a case involving the government's permanent possession of the seized property. The decision also addressed the question of whether the takings clause applies only to real property or whether the government seizure of personal property also requires compensation.

Horne v. Department of Agriculture

576 U.S. ____ (2015)
http://laws.findlaw.com/us/000/14–275.html
Oral arguments are available at https://www.oyez.org
Vote: 8 (Alito, Breyer, Ginsburg, Kagan, Kennedy, Roberts, Scalia, Thomas)
*   1 (Sotomayor)*

OPINION OF THE COURT: ROBERTS
CONCURRING OPINION: THOMAS
OPINION CONCURRING IN PART AND DISSENTING IN PART:
**   BREYER**
DISSENTING OPINION: SOTOMAYOR

FACTS:

The Agricultural Marketing Agreement Act of 1937 authorizes the secretary of agriculture to develop marketing orders to help maintain stable markets for various agricultural products. The secretary's marketing orders for raisins created a Raisin Administrative Committee that imposed a reserve requirement obliging growers to set aside a certain percentage of their crop for the government's use free of charge. The government makes use of those reserved raisins by selling them in noncompetitive markets, donating them, or disposing of them by other means consistent with establishing an orderly market. Any profits left over from this operation, less administrative costs, are returned to the growers. In 2002–2003, the reserve requirement was 47 percent of the raisin crop. In 2003–2004, it was 30 percent. Raisins retained by the growers after the reserved raisins are set aside (known as "free tonnage raisins") may be used or sold by the growers at their discretion.

For several decades Californians Marvin and Laura Horne have produced raisins from the Thompson seedless grapes they grow on their Fresno area farm. Because of their growing dissatisfaction with the government's raisin marketing program, the Hornes in 2002 and 2003 refused to set aside any raisins. When government trucks arrived at their Raisin Valley Farm, the Hornes refused entry. In response, the government assessed a fine equal to the market value of the missing grapes ($480,000) and a civil penalty just over $200,000 for failure to comply with the government policy. The Hornes took legal action against the Department of Agriculture, claiming that the reserve requirement violates the takings clause. After several years of litigation, court of appeals finally upheld the government program finding that the reserve requirement was a reasonable response to the government's interest in ensuring an orderly raisin market and not a taking.

Raisin farmer Marvin Horne, who successfully challenged the federal government's reserve raisin program as a violation of the Fifth Amendment's Takings Clause.

AP Photo/Gary Kazanjian

ARGUMENTS:

For the petitioners, Marvin D. and Laura A. Horne:

- The core protection of the takings clause is the requirement that the government must pay just compensation whenever it physically takes possession of property—that is, a *per se* taking.
- The raisin marketing order works a physical taking for which just compensation is categorically required.
- The Fifth Amendment duty to compensate for physical takings applies to personal property as much as it does to real property.

For the respondent, the U.S. Department of Agriculture:

- The marketing order preserves the producer's ownership in the net proceeds from the sale of the reserved raisins. Thus, producers are not absolutely dispossessed of their property.
- Producers voluntarily choose to participate in the commercial raisin market. They could instead grow other crops or grow grapes for purposes other than raisin production.
- The producers receive economic benefits from the creation and maintenance of an orderly market that increases the value of their free tonnage raisins, thus compensating them for the loss of their reserve raisins.

◥ CHIEF JUSTICE ROBERTS DELIVERED THE OPINION OF THE COURT.

The petition for certiorari poses three questions, which we answer in turn.

The first question presented asks "Whether the government's 'categorical duty' under the Fifth Amendment to pay just compensation when it 'physically takes possession of an interest in property,' *Arkansas Game & Fish Comm'n v. United States* (2012), applies only to real property and not to personal property." The answer is no.

There is no dispute that the "classic taking [is one] in which the government directly appropriates private property for its own use." *Tahoe-Sierra Preservation Council, Inc.* v. *Tahoe Regional Planning Agency* (2002). Nor is there any dispute that, in the case of real property, such an appropriation is a *per se* taking that requires just compensation. See *Loretto* v. *Teleprompter Manhattan CATV Corp.* (1982).

Nothing in the text or history of the Takings Clause, or our precedents, suggests that the rule is any different when it comes to appropriation of personal property. The

Government has a categorical duty to pay just compensation when it takes your car, just as when it takes your home.

The Takings Clause provides: "[N]or shall private property be taken for public use, without just compensation." It protects "private property" without any distinction between different types. The principle reflected in the Clause goes back at least 800 years to Magna Carta, which specifically protected agricultural crops from uncompensated takings. . . .

The colonists brought the principles of Magna Carta with them to the New World, including that charter's protection against uncompensated takings of personal property. . . .

Nothing in this history suggests that personal property was any less protected against physical appropriation than real property. . . .

Prior to this Court's decision in *Pennsylvania Coal Co.* v. *Mahon* (1922), the Takings Clause was understood to provide protection only against a direct appropriation of property—personal or real. *Pennsylvania Coal* expanded the protection of the Takings Clause, holding that compensation was also required for a "regulatory taking"—a restriction on the use of property that went "too far." And in *Penn Central Transp. Co.* v. *New York City* (1978), the Court clarified that the test for how far was "too far" required an "ad hoc" factual inquiry. That inquiry required considering factors such as the economic impact of the regulation, its interference with reasonable investment-backed expectations, and the character of the government action.

Four years after *Penn Central*, however, the Court reaffirmed the rule that a physical *appropriation* of property gave rise to a *per se* taking, without regard to other factors. In *Loretto*, the Court held that requiring an owner of an apartment building to allow installation of a cable box on her rooftop was a physical taking of real property, for which compensation was required. That was true without regard to the claimed public benefit or the economic impact on the owner. The Court explained that such protection was justified not only by history, but also because "[s]uch an appropriation is perhaps the most serious form of invasion of an owner's property interests," depriving the owner of the "the rights to possess, use and dispose of" the property. That reasoning—both with respect to history and logic—is equally applicable to a physical appropriation of personal property. . . .

The reserve requirement imposed by the Raisin Committee is a clear physical taking. Actual raisins are transferred from the growers to the Government. Title to the raisins passes to the Raisin Committee. The Committee's raisins must be physically segregated from free-tonnage raisins. . . . The Committee disposes of what become its raisins as it wishes, to promote the purposes of the raisin marketing order.

Raisin growers subject to the reserve requirement thus lose the entire "bundle" of property rights in the appropriated raisins—"the rights to possess, use and dispose of" them, *Loretto*,—with the exception of the speculative hope that some residual proceeds may be left when the Government is done with the raisins and has deducted the expenses of implementing all aspects of the marketing order. The Government's "actual taking of possession and control" of the reserve raisins gives rise to a taking as clearly "as if the Government held full title and ownership," as it essentially does. The Government's formal demand that the Hornes turn over a percentage of their raisin crop without charge, for the Government's control and use, is "of such a unique character that it is a taking without regard to other factors that a court might ordinarily examine."

The Government thinks it "strange" and the dissent "baffling" that the Hornes object to the reserve requirement, when they nonetheless concede that "the government may prohibit the sale of raisins without effecting a per se taking." But that distinction flows naturally from the settled difference in our takings jurisprudence between appropriation and regulation. A physical taking of raisins and a regulatory limit on production may have the same economic impact on a grower. The Constitution, however, is concerned with means as well as ends. The Government has broad powers, but the means it uses to achieve its ends must be "consist[ent] with the letter and spirit of the constitution." *McCulloch* v. *Maryland* (1819). As Justice Holmes noted, "a strong public desire to improve the public condition is not enough to warrant achieving the desire by a shorter cut than the constitutional way." *Pennsylvania Coal.*

The second question presented asks "Whether the government may avoid the categorical duty to pay just compensation for a physical taking of property by reserving to the property owner a contingent interest in a portion of the value of the property, set at the government's discretion." The answer is no.

The Government and dissent argue that raisins are fungible goods whose only value is in the revenue from their sale. According to the Government, the raisin marketing order leaves that interest with the raisin growers: After selling reserve raisins and deducting expenses and subsidies for exporters, the Raisin Committee returns any net proceeds to the growers. The Government contends that because growers are entitled to these net proceeds, they retain the most important property interest in the reserve raisins, so there is no taking in the first place. . . .

But when there has been a physical appropriation, "we do not ask . . . whether it deprives the owner of all economically valuable use" of the item taken. *Tahoe-Sierra Preservation Council* ("When the government physically takes possession of an interest in property for some public purpose, it has a categorical duty to compensate the former owner, regardless of whether the interest that is taken constitutes an entire parcel or merely a part thereof."). . . . The fact that the growers retain a contingent interest of indeterminate value does not mean there has been no physical taking, particularly since the value of the interest depends on the discretion of the taker, and may be worthless, as it was for one of the two years at issue here. . . .

The third question presented asks "Whether a governmental mandate to relinquish specific, identifiable property as a 'condition' on permission to engage in commerce effects a per se taking." The answer, at least in this case, is yes.

The Government contends that the reserve requirement is not a taking because raisin growers voluntarily choose to participate in the raisin market. According to the Government, if raisin growers don't like it, they can "plant different crops," or "sell their raisin-variety grapes as table grapes or for use in juice or wine."

"Let them sell wine" is probably not much more comforting to the raisin growers than similar retorts have been to others throughout history. In any event, the Government is wrong as a matter of law. In *Loretto*, we rejected the argument that the New York law was not a taking because a landlord could avoid the requirement by ceasing to be a landlord. We held instead that "a landlord's ability to rent his property may not be conditioned on his forfeiting the right to compensation for a physical occupation." . . .

The Government . . . [relies] heavily on *Ruckelshaus* v. *Monsanto Co.* (1984). There we held that the Environmental Protection Agency could require companies manufacturing pesticides, fungicides, and rodenticides to disclose health, safety, and environmental information about their products as a condition to receiving a permit to sell those products. While such information included trade secrets in which pesticide manufacturers had a property interest, those manufacturers were not subjected to a taking because they received a "valuable Government benefit" in exchange—a license to sell dangerous chemicals.

The taking here cannot reasonably be characterized as part of a similar voluntary exchange. In one of the years at issue here, the Government insisted that the Hornes turn over 47 percent of their raisin crop, in exchange for the "benefit" of being allowed to sell the remaining 53 percent. The next year, the toll was 30 percent . . . Selling produce in interstate commerce, although certainly subject to reasonable government regulation, is similarly not a special governmental benefit that the Government may hold hostage, to be ransomed by the waiver of constitutional protection. Raisins are not dangerous pesticides; they are a healthy snack. A case about conditioning the sale of hazardous substances on disclosure of health, safety, and environmental information related to those hazards is hardly on point. . . .

Finally, the Government briefly argues that if we conclude that the reserve requirement effects a taking, we should remand for the Court of Appeals to calculate "what compensation would have been due if petitioners had complied with the reserve requirement." The Government contends that the calculation must consider what the value of the reserve raisins would have been without the price support program, as well as "other benefits . . . from the regulatory program, such as higher consumer demand for raisins spurred by enforcement of quality standards and promotional activities." Indeed, according to the Government, the Hornes would "likely" have a net gain under this theory. . . .

The Government has already calculated the amount of just compensation in this case, when it fined the Hornes the fair market value of the raisins: $483,843.53. The Government cannot now disavow that valuation. . . . There is accordingly no need for a remand; the Hornes should simply be relieved of the obligation to pay the fine and associated civil penalty they were assessed when they resisted the Government's effort to take their raisins. This case, in litigation for more than a decade, has gone on long enough.

The judgment of the United States Court of Appeals for the Ninth Circuit is reversed.

It is so ordered.

JUSTICE BREYER, with whom JUSTICE GINSBURG and JUSTICE KAGAN join, [concurs with the conclusion that a taking occurred, but dissents from the Court's decision not to remand the case to the court of appeals to determine the amount of compensation due].

JUSTICE SOTOMAYOR, dissenting.
The Hornes claim, and the Court agrees, that the Raisin Marketing Order effects a *per se* taking under our decision in *Loretto* v. *Teleprompter Manhattan CATV Corp.* (1982). But *Loretto* sets a high bar for such claims: It requires that each and every property right be destroyed by governmental action before that action can be said to have effected a *per se* taking. Because the Order does not deprive the Hornes of all of their property rights, it does not effect a *per se* taking. I respectfully dissent from the Court's contrary holding. . . .

WHAT CONSTITUTES A PUBLIC USE?

Although the Fifth Amendment recognizes the government's power to take private property, it does not allow all such seizures. The takings clause explicitly stipulates that the government may take private property only for a "public use." Even if the government provides adequate compensation, it may not take property against the owner's will for the sole benefit of a private individual or organization. When the government plans to build a new courthouse, road, or park, the public use is clear, but it would be of doubtful constitutionality if a state seized a piece of private property under the power of eminent domain and gave it to a private fraternal organization to construct a new lodge.

Throughout most of the nation's history, the justices were relatively insistent about the public use requirement. The Court commented on this subject as early as 1884 in *Cole v. LaGrange.* In this dispute the city of LaGrange, Missouri, had issued twenty-five bonds to LaGrange Iron and Steel Company to help finance the operation of a mill. This act was attacked on the ground that the bonds were being used for a private, not public, use. For the Court, Justice Horace Gray agreed:

The general grant of legislative power in the Constitution of a state does not enable the legislature, in the exercise either of the right of eminent domain, or the right of taxation, to take private property, without the owner's consent, for any but a public object.

A few years later, in *Missouri Pacific Railway Company v. Nebraska* (1896), the Court ruled that the taking of private property, without the owner's consent, for the private use of another violates due process of law.

Even in the early twentieth century the Court remained wedded to the strict enforcement of this requirement. *Cincinnati v. Vester* (1930) illustrates this point. The city of Cincinnati had confiscated private property to carry out a road-widening project. The amount of property seized, however, was in excess of what was needed. The surplus property was later sold at a profit or otherwise transferred to another private party. The Court ruled this taking to be unlawful for its failure to meet the public use requirement.

After the New Deal, however, the Court's position began to change. In *United States ex rel. Tennessee Valley Authority* [TVA] *v. Welch* (1946) the justices upheld the authority of the federal government to condemn private land that would be flooded as a consequence of the TVA's flood-control programs. In doing so, the Court deferred to Congress's authority to determine what constitutes a public use. That same position was articulated in the Court's unanimous decision in *Berman v. Parker* (1954), in which the Court failed to provide relief to a landowner whose property was taken from him as part of an urban renewal project but later was transferred to another private party. Is this decision consistent with the letter and spirit of the takings clause?

Berman v. Parker

348 U.S. 26 (1954)
http://laws.findlaw.com/us/348/26.html
Vote: 8 (Black, Burton, Clark, Douglas, Frankfurter, Minton, Reed, Warren)
     0
OPINION OF THE COURT: *Douglas*

FACTS:

Concerned about growing slums and urban blight in Washington, D.C., Congress passed the District of Columbia Redevelopment Act of 1945. This law authorized the National Capital Planning Commission to develop comprehensive land-use plans to improve the District's "housing, business, industry, recreation, education, public buildings, public reservations, and other general categories of public and private uses of the land" for the public health, safety, morals, and welfare of its citizens. The law required public hearings on any proposals, and the plans were subject to the approval of the District's commissioners. Once the urban renewal plans were approved, the District of Columbia Redevelopment Land Agency was empowered to acquire, through eminent domain if necessary, the land needed to improve the blighted conditions.

After acquisition, the agency would transfer title to government agencies as necessary for public purposes such as streets, utilities, recreational facilities, and schools. The remainder would be leased or sold to private concerns for redevelopment consistent with the land-use plan.

Berman v. Parker arose over a comprehensive plan for a section known as Project Area B in Southwest Washington. The Planning Commission reported the following facts about the area: 64.3 percent of the dwellings were beyond repair, and 18.4 percent needed major repairs; only 17.3 percent were satisfactory. In addition, 57.8 percent of the dwellings had outside toilets, 60.3 percent had no baths, 29.3 percent lacked electricity, 82.2 percent had no wash basins or laundry tubs, and 83.8 percent lacked central heating. About five thousand people lived in Area B, of whom 97.5 percent were African American. The commission concluded that the area required redevelopment in the interests of public health.

Max R. Morris owned a piece of property in Area B, on which was located a department store. He objected to the government's acquisition of his property on the ground that it was not slum housing. Under the comprehensive plan, Morris's property would be sold or leased to other private owners for redevelopment. After Morris died, his executors, Samuel Berman and Solomon Feldman, pursued legal action. Although it expressed reservations, the federal district court upheld the constitutionality of the government's actions. Berman and Feldman appealed.

ARGUMENTS:

For the appellants, Samuel Berman and Solomon Feldman, executors of the Morris estate:

- The taking of private property for city redevelopment and subsequent ownership by other private parties is not a public use.
- The law unconstitutionally seizes one man's land to be sold to another man merely to create a community that better meets the government's idea of what is appropriate and well planned.
- The District may have the power to clear slums, but the appellant's property is not blighted.
- The government is seizing the property without affording the appellant the opportunity to remodel or redevelop his property to meet the specifications of the redevelopment legislation.

For the appellees, Andrew Parker, John A. Remon, and James E. Colliflower, commissioners of the District of Columbia, et al.:

- Congress and the District of Columbia have the constitutional authority to eliminate slums and prevent slum-breeding conditions in the nation's capital city. This is a public purpose.
- The law of eminent domain does not require the government to occupy the seized property. The future private ownership of the condemned properties does not negate the public purpose of the legislation.
- Congress concluded that the public good could not be achieved on a piecemeal basis but required redeveloping large areas of the District.

⬛ MR. JUSTICE DOUGLAS DELIVERED THE OPINION OF THE COURT.

The power of Congress over the District of Columbia includes all the legislative powers which a state may exercise over its affairs. We deal, in other words, with what traditionally has been known as the police power. An attempt to define its reach or trace its outer limits is fruitless, for each case must turn on its own facts. The definition is essentially the product of legislative determinations addressed to the purposes of government, purposes neither abstractly nor historically capable of complete definition. Subject to specific constitutional limitations, when the legislature has spoken, the public interest has been declared in terms well-nigh conclusive. In such cases, the legislature, not the judiciary, is the main guardian of the public needs to be served by social legislation, whether it be Congress legislating concerning the District of Columbia or the States legislating concerning local affairs. This principle admits of no exception merely because the power of eminent domain is involved. The role of the judiciary in determining whether that power is being exercised for a public purpose is an extremely narrow one.

Public safety, public health, morality, peace and quiet, law and order—these are some of the more conspicuous examples of the traditional application of the police power to municipal affairs. Yet they merely illustrate the scope of the power and do not delimit it. Miserable and disreputable housing conditions may do more than spread disease and crime and immorality. They may also suffocate the spirit by reducing the people who live there to the status of cattle. They may indeed make living an almost insufferable burden. They may also be an ugly sore, a blight on the community which robs it of charm, which makes it a place from which men turn. The misery of housing may despoil a community as an open sewer may ruin a river.

We do not sit to determine whether a particular housing project is or is not desirable. The concept of public welfare is broad and inclusive. The values it represents are spiritual as well as physical, aesthetic as well as monetary. It is within the power of the legislature to determine that the community should be beautiful as well as healthy, spacious as well as clean, well-balanced as well as carefully patrolled. In the present case, the Congress and its authorized agencies have made determinations that take into account a wide variety of values. It is not for us to reappraise them. If those who govern the District of Columbia decide that the Nation's Capital should be beautiful as well as sanitary, there is nothing in the Fifth Amendment that stands in its way.

Once the object is within the authority of Congress, the right to realize it through the exercise of eminent domain is clear. For the power of eminent domain is merely the means to an end. Once the object is within the authority of Congress, the means by which it will be attained is also for Congress to determine. Here one of the means chosen is the use of private enterprise for redevelopment of the area. Appellants argue that this makes the project a taking from one businessman for the benefit of another businessman. But the means of executing the project are for Congress and Congress alone to determine, once the public purpose has been established. The public end may be as well or better served through an agency of private enterprise than through a department of government—or so the Congress might conclude. We cannot say that public ownership is the sole method of promoting the public purposes of community redevelopment projects. What we have said also disposes of any contention concerning the fact that certain property owners in the area may be permitted to repurchase their properties for redevelopment in harmony with the over-all plan. That, too, is a legitimate means which Congress and its agencies may adopt, if they choose.

In the present case, Congress and its authorized agencies attack the problem of the blighted parts of the community on an area rather than on a structure-by-structure basis. That, too, is opposed by the appellants. They maintain that since their building does not imperil health or safety nor contribute to the making of a slum or a blighted area, it cannot be swept into a redevelopment plan by the mere dictum of the Planning Commission or the

Commissioners. The particular uses to be made of the land in the project were determined with regard to the needs of the particular community. The experts concluded that if the community were to be healthy, if it were not to revert again to a blighted or slum area, as though possessed of a congenital disease, the area must be planned as a whole. It was not enough, they believed, to remove existing buildings that were insanitary or unsightly. It was important to redesign the whole area so as to eliminate the conditions that cause slums—the overcrowding of dwellings, the lack of parks, the lack of adequate streets and alleys, the absence of recreational areas, the lack of light and air, the presence of outmoded street patterns. It was believed that the piecemeal approach, the removal of individual structures that were offensive, would only be a palliative. The entire area needed redesigning so that a balanced, integrated plan could be developed for the region, including not only new homes but also schools, churches, parks, streets, and shopping centers. In this way it was hoped that the cycle of decay of the area could be controlled and the birth of future slums prevented. Such diversification in future use is plainly relevant to the maintenance of the desired housing standards and therefore within congressional power.

The District Court below suggested that, if such a broad scope were intended for the statute, the standards contained in the Act would not be sufficiently definite to sustain the delegation of authority. We do not agree. We think the standards prescribed were adequate for executing the plan to eliminate not only slums as narrowly defined by the District Court but also the blighted areas that tend to produce slums. Property may of course be taken for this redevelopment which, standing by itself, is innocuous and unoffending. But we have said enough to indicate that it is the need of the area as a whole which Congress and its agencies are evaluating. If owner after owner were permitted to resist these redevelopment programs on the ground that his particular property was not being used against the public interest, integrated plans for redevelopment would suffer greatly. The argument pressed on us is, indeed, a plea to substitute the landowner's standard of the public need for the standard prescribed by Congress. But as we have already stated, community redevelopment programs need not, by force of the Constitution, be on a piecemeal basis—lot by lot, building by building.

It is not for the courts to oversee the choice of the boundary line nor to sit in review on the size of a particular project area. Once the question of the public purpose has been decided, the amount and character of land to be taken for the project and the need for a particular tract to complete the integrated plan rests in the discretion of the legislative branch.

The District Court indicated grave doubts concerning the Agency's right to take full title to the land as distinguished from the objectionable buildings located on it. We do not share those doubts. If the Agency considers it necessary in carrying out the redevelopment project to take full title to the real property involved, it may do so. It is not for the courts to determine whether it is necessary for successful consummation of the project that unsafe, unsightly, or insanitary buildings alone be taken or whether title to the land be included, any more than it is the function of the courts to sort and choose among the various parcels selected for condemnation.

The rights of these property owners are satisfied when they receive that just compensation which the Fifth Amendment exacts as the price of the taking.

The judgment of the District Court, as modified by this opinion, is

Affirmed.

The Court's deference to the legislature on questions of what constitutes a public purpose was extended to the state level in *Hawaii Housing Authority v. Midkiff* (1984). Challenged here was Hawaii's plan to redistribute land using the power of eminent domain to force large landowners to sell their properties to the people who leased them. The transfer of land was clearly from one private owner to another. Was this program a benefit to the public generally, or did it serve only the private interests of those who now were able to become landowners?

Hawaii Housing Authority v. Midkiff

467 U.S. 229 (1984)
http://laws.findlaw.com/us/467/229.html
Oral arguments are available at https://www.oyez.org.
Vote: 8 (Blackmun, Brennan, Burger, O'Connor, Powell, Rehnquist, Stevens, White)
0

OPINION OF THE COURT: *O'Connor*
NOT PARTICIPATING: *Marshall*

FACTS:

The Hawaiian Islands were settled by Polynesians who developed a political and economic system based on principles of monarchy and feudalism. Ownership and control of the land rested with the islands' high chief, who distributed parcels to various lower-ranking chiefs. At the end of the chain, tenant farmers and their families lived on the land and worked it. Private ownership of real property was not permitted. Ultimate ownership of all lands rested with the family of the islands' high chief.

The monarchy was overthrown in 1893, and, after a brief period as a republic, the islands were annexed by the United States in 1898. When Hawaii became the fiftieth state in 1959, the land still remained in the hands of a few. In the mid-1960s the federal government owned 49 percent of the land in Hawaii, and just seventy-two private landowners held another 47 percent. On Oahu, the most commercially developed island, twenty-two landowners controlled more than 72 percent of the private real estate. The Hawaiian legislature determined that this land concentration condition was detrimental to the state's economy and general welfare. The legislative goal was to expand significantly the number of individuals who owned real estate and create a competitive housing market.

The legislature first decided to compel landowners to sell large portions of their holdings to those individuals who leased the land from them. The landowners opposed this plan because it would result in exceedingly high capital gains that would increase their federal taxes. The legislature then revised its plans and enacted the Land Reform Act of 1967. This legislation allowed the state to condemn tracts of residential real estate. The Hawaii Housing Authority (HHA) would then seize the condemned property and help arrange the sale of individual parcels to the private parties who had been leasing the land. Compensation for land seized by the government enjoyed a more favorable tax status than did profits from outright sales, making the legislation more acceptable to the landowners.

Frank Midkiff and others owned a large tract of land that was condemned under the land reform program, but Midkiff, the HHA, and residents currently leasing lots could not agree on a fair price. Midkiff and his co-owners filed suit in federal district court to have the Land Reform Act declared unconstitutional as a violation of the takings clause. Among the arguments presented was the claim that redistributing land ownership was not an appropriate "public use" under the meaning of the Fifth Amendment. The district court rejected this argument, but the U.S. Court of Appeals

for the Ninth Circuit reversed. The housing authority appealed to the Supreme Court.

ARGUMENTS:

For the appellant, Hawaii Housing Authority:

- *Berman v. Parker*'s treatment of the public use requirement should control. The fact that seized private property is ultimately transferred to another private party does not mean that the public use requirement has not been met.
- Deference should be given to the legislature's determination of what constitutes public use.
- Breaking up the land oligopoly and creating a competitive housing market is undoubtedly a public use.
- Given the unique conditions in Hawaii, the creation of a competitive housing market could not occur without legislation such as the Land Reform Act.

For the appellees, Frank E. Midkiff et al.:

- That the state legislature declared there to be a public use does not make it so. The Court should not surrender that question to the legislature.
- This is an unprecedented state transfer of property from one set of private owners to other private owners.
- The government is not purchasing the land, but only acting as a conduit to facilitate the purchase of individual parcels by private parties.
- Unlike in *Berman v. Parker* and other eminent domain actions, no change in the usage of the land is contemplated. Residential housing lots will remain residential housing lots, and the current resident will continue to be the resident. The only change is in the ownership of the property, a change that benefits a private party and not the public.

■ JUSTICE O'CONNOR DELIVERED THE OPINION OF THE COURT.

The Fifth Amendment of the United States Constitution provides, in pertinent part, that "private property [shall not] be taken for public use, without just compensation." These cases present the question whether the Public Use Clause of that Amendment, made applicable to the States through the Fourteenth Amendment, prohibits the State of Hawaii from taking, with just compensation, title in real property from lessors and transferring it to lessees in order to reduce the concentration of ownership of fees simple in the State. We conclude that it does not. . . .

The majority of the Court of Appeals . . . determined that the Act violates the "public use" requirement of the Fifth and Fourteenth Amendments. On this argument, however, we find ourselves in agreement with the dissenting judge in the Court of Appeals.

The starting point for our analysis of the Act's constitutionality is the Court's decision in *Berman v. Parker* (1954). In *Berman*, the Court held constitutional the District of Columbia Redevelopment Act of 1945. That Act provided both for the comprehensive use of the eminent domain power to redevelop slum areas and for the possible sale or lease of the condemned lands to private interests. In discussing whether the takings authorized by that Act were for a "public use," the Court stated:

"We deal . . . with what traditionally has been known as the police power. An attempt to define its reach or trace its outer limits is fruitless, for each case must turn on its own facts. The definition is essentially the product of legislative determinations addressed to the purposes of government, purposes neither abstractly nor historically capable of complete definition. Subject to specific constitutional limitations, when the legislature has spoken, the public interest has been declared in terms well-nigh conclusive. In such cases the legislature, not the judiciary, is the main guardian of the public needs to be served by social legislation, whether it be Congress legislating concerning the District of Columbia . . . or the States legislating concerning local affairs. . . . This principle admits of no exception merely because the power of eminent domain is involved. . . ."

The Court explicitly recognized the breadth of the principle it was announcing, noting:

"Once the object is within the authority of Congress, the right to realize it through the exercise of eminent domain is clear. For the power of eminent domain is merely the means to the end. . . . Once the object is within the authority of Congress, the means by which it will be attained is also for Congress to determine. Here one of the means chosen is the use of private enterprise for redevelopment of the area. Appellants argue that this makes the project a taking from one businessman for the benefit of another businessman. But the means of executing the project are for Congress and Congress alone to determine, once the public purpose has been established."

The "public use" requirement is thus coterminous with the scope of a sovereign's police powers.

There is, of course, a role for courts to play in reviewing a legislature's judgment of what constitutes a public use, even when the eminent domain power is equated with the police power. But the Court in *Berman* made clear that it is "an extremely narrow" one. The Court in *Berman* cited with approval the Court's decision in *Old Dominion Co. v. United States* (1925), which held that deference to the legislature's "public use" determination is required "until it is shown to involve an impossibility." The *Berman* Court also cited to *United States ex rel. TVA v. Welch* (1946), which emphasized that "[a]ny departure from this judicial restraint would result in courts deciding on what is and is not a governmental function and in their invalidating legislation on the basis of their view on that question at the moment of decision, a practice which has proved impracticable in other fields." In short, the Court has made clear that it will not substitute its judgment for a legislature's judgment as to what constitutes a public use "unless the use be palpably without reasonable foundation."

To be sure, the Court's cases have repeatedly stated that "one person's property may not be taken for the benefit of another private person without a justifying public purpose, even though compensation be paid." Thus, in *Missouri Pacific R. Co. v. Nebraska* (1896), where the "order in question was not, and was not claimed to be, . . . a taking of private property for a public use under the right of eminent domain," the Court invalidated a compensated taking of property for lack of a justifying public purpose. But where the exercise of the eminent domain power is rationally related to a conceivable public purpose, the Court has never held a compensated taking to be proscribed by the Public Use Clause.

On this basis, we have no trouble concluding that the Hawaii Act is constitutional. The people of Hawaii have attempted, much as the settlers of the original 13 Colonies did, to reduce the perceived social and economic evils of a land oligopoly traceable to their monarchs. The land oligopoly has, according to the Hawaii Legislature, created artificial deterrents to the normal functioning of the State's residential land market and forced thousands of individual homeowners to lease, rather than buy, the land underneath their homes. Regulating oligopoly and the evils associated with it is a classic exercise of a State's police powers. We cannot disapprove of Hawaii's exercise of this power.

Nor can we condemn as irrational the Act's approach to correcting the land oligopoly problem. The Act presumes that when a sufficiently large number of persons declare that they are willing but unable to buy lots at fair prices the land market is malfunctioning. When such a malfunction is signaled, the Act authorizes HHA to condemn lots in the relevant tract. The Act limits the number of lots any one tenant can purchase and authorizes HHA to use public funds to ensure that the market dilution goals will be achieved. This is a comprehensive and rational approach to identifying and correcting market failure.

Of course, this Act, like any other, may not be successful in achieving its intended goals. But "whether in fact the provision will accomplish its objectives is not the question: the [constitutional requirement] is satisfied if . . . the . . . [state] Legislature rationally could have believed that the [Act] would promote its objective." When the legislature's purpose is legitimate and its means are not irrational, our cases make clear that empirical debates over the wisdom of takings—no less than debates over the wisdom of other kinds of socioeconomic legislation—are not to be carried out in the federal courts. Redistribution of fees simple to correct deficiencies in the market determined by the state legislature to be attributable to land oligopoly is a rational exercise of the eminent domain power. Therefore, the Hawaii statute must pass the scrutiny of the Public Use Clause. . . .

The mere fact that property taken outright by eminent domain is transferred in the first instance to private beneficiaries does not condemn that taking as having only a private purpose. The Court long ago rejected any literal requirement that condemned property be put into use for the general public. "It is not essential that the entire community, nor even any considerable portion, . . . directly enjoy or participate in any improvement in order [for it] to constitute a public use." As the unique way titles were held in Hawaii skewed the land market, exercise of the power of eminent domain was justified. The Act advances its purposes without the State's taking actual possession of the land. In such cases, government does not itself have to use property to legitimate the taking, it is only the taking's purpose, and not its mechanics, that must pass scrutiny under the Public Use Clause. . . .

The State of Hawaii has never denied that the Constitution forbids even a compensated taking of property when executed for no reason other than to confer a private benefit on a particular private party. A purely private taking could not withstand the scrutiny of the public use requirement; it would serve no legitimate purpose of government and would thus be void. But no purely private taking is involved in these cases. The Hawaii Legislature enacted its Land Reform Act not to benefit a particular class of identifiable individuals but to attack certain perceived evils of concentrated property ownership in Hawaii—a legitimate public purpose. Use of the condemnation power to achieve this purpose is not irrational. Since we assume for purposes of these appeals that the weighty demand of just compensation has been met, the

requirements of the Fifth and Fourteenth Amendments have been satisfied. Accordingly, we reverse the judgment of the Court of Appeals, and remand these cases for further proceedings in conformity with this opinion.

It is so ordered.

Decisions such as *Berman* and *Midkiff* made important changes in the way the Court dealt with takings clause appeals. No longer did the justices independently examine the nature of the public purpose of the taking. Instead, the Court gave wide latitude to legislatures to determine what constitutes public use. To this extent private property rights became political as well as legal questions, increasing the power of the legislature at the expense of traditional property considerations. These decisions also reduced the extent to which landowners could use "public use" objections to thwart the legislative redistribution of wealth and property for the public good.

The Supreme Court's announced policy of deferring to the elected branches on the question of public use encouraged expanded government use of the power of eminent domain. Many local governments aggressively exercised their authority to seize private property as part of a strategy to improve their fiscal standing. Assume that a town with a sagging economy and shrinking revenues is presented with an opportunity to lure a company to build a new shopping mall in the community. The company is willing to consider such an investment only if it can secure a prime piece of property for the mall site. When the owner of that land refuses to sell, the city seizes the property under the power of eminent domain and sells it to the company for the price of the compensation the city was required to pay the landowner. The company is happy with the parcel of land, and the city is happy because the new stores will create employment and increased tax revenues. But is this a proper exercise of the power of eminent domain? Does it meet the Fifth Amendment's public use requirement? Or is it simply a government-engineered forced transfer of property from one private party to another?

Such scenarios have not been uncommon, especially in some of the nation's older cities, where cash-starved local governments have used the power of eminent domain to attempt to improve the declining economic conditions of their communities. To do so, a city might have to condemn relatively large residential tracts—not because they are blighted, but because the land could be redeveloped with more valuable properties that would add to the tax base. Private property owners and groups devoted to their interests began to organize against such government actions. It was clear that a major legal confrontation was inevitable. The Supreme Court tackled the issue in *Kelo v. City of New London* (2005), a decision that resulted in widespread controversy.

Kelo v. City of New London

545 U.S. 469 (2005)
http://laws.findlaw.com/us/545/469.html
Oral arguments are available at https://www.oyez.org.
Vote: 5 (Breyer, Ginsburg, Kennedy, Souter, Stevens)
    4 (O'Connor, Rehnquist, Scalia, Thomas)

OPINION OF THE COURT: *Stevens*
CONCURRING OPINION: *Kennedy*
DISSENTING OPINIONS: *O'Connor, Thomas*

FACTS:

For decades the city of New London, Connecticut, had suffered serious economic decline. By 1998 the city's unemployment rate was double that of the state, and the population had declined to 24,000, the same number of residents as in 1920. In response, state and local officials created the New London Development Corporation (NLDC) to devise strategies to stimulate the city's economy. Efforts to revitalize the city resulted in a tentative commitment by a drug company, Pfizer, Inc., to build a $300 million research facility in the city's Fort Trumbull area. Officials believed this new development not only would bring jobs and tax revenues to the city, but also would spur additional economic revitalization efforts.

The NLDC developed a master plan for the area surrounding the proposed Pfizer operation. This plan, which the city adopted in 2000, called for a hotel, conference center, museum, restaurants, shops, office space, marina, river walk, and new residential housing. To begin the development, the city had to acquire approximately 115 privately owned parcels of land. The city successfully negotiated the purchase of most of the parcels, but some landowners refused to sell. The city responded by condemning their properties through the use of eminent domain.

Nine landowners who were unwilling to sell their homes filed suit, claiming the city's actions violated the Fifth Amendment's takings clause. Among them were Susette Kelo, who had bought her water-view home in 1997 and had spent considerable time and money renovating it, and Wilhelmina Dery, who had lived in her Fort Trumbull home since her birth in 1918. The properties involved were not blighted or in poor condition; the city condemned them only because they stood in the path of the redevelopment plan. The petitioners claimed that the plan failed to meet the Fifth Amendment's public use requirement. After the Connecticut Supreme Court ruled in favor of the city, Kelo and the other petitioners requested review by the U.S. Supreme Court.

ARGUMENTS:

For the petitioners, Susette Kelo et al.:

- The use of eminent domain purely for private business development is not a public use under the Fifth Amendment.
- Allowing increased taxes and jobs to be considered a public use opens the door to the seizure of any private property. The distinction between public and private purposes is erased.
- Economic development interests do not justify using government power forcibly to seize one person's property and give it to another private party.
- Unlike seizures for other purposes (to combat a slum, build a road, etc.) that have clearly defined standards and geographical limits, economic development seizures are open-ended and without natural limits. Any property can be taken for any purpose.
- Economic development seizures usually target the residential areas of the working and lower classes.

For the respondents, city of New London and the New London Development Corporation:

- Combating the deteriorating economic conditions in New London through this redevelopment program is a public use.
- The Court should continue its policy of deferring to the political branches of government to decide what is a public purpose. The courts are ill suited to make such a determination.
- The primary purpose of the takings clause is not to limit the use of eminent domain, but to ensure fair compensation for seized property.
- The democratic process provides the electorate the power to curb abuses of eminent domain.

AP Photo/Jack Sauer

The home of Susette Kelo is shown here in February 2005, just four months before the Supreme Court ruled that the city of New London could seize it as part of an economic revitalization program.

John Nordell/*The Christian Science Monitor* via Getty Images

The construction of the $300 million Pfizer Global Research and Development headquarters was the centerpiece of New London's revitalization program that culminated in the Supreme Court's takings clause ruling in Kelo v. City of New London (2005).

JUSTICE STEVENS DELIVERED THE OPINION OF THE COURT.

Two polar propositions are perfectly clear. On the one hand, it has long been accepted that the sovereign may not take the property of A for the sole purpose of transferring it to another private party B, even though A is paid just compensation. On the other hand, it is equally clear that a State may transfer property from one private party to another if future "use by the public" is the purpose of the taking; the condemnation of land for a railroad with common-carrier duties is a familiar example. Neither of these propositions, however, determines the disposition of this case.

As for the first proposition, the City would no doubt be forbidden from taking petitioners' land for the purpose of conferring a private benefit on a particular private party. . . . Nor would the City be allowed to take property under the mere pretext of a public purpose, when its actual purpose was to bestow a private benefit. The takings before us, however, would be executed pursuant to a "carefully considered" development plan. The trial judge and all the members of the Supreme Court of Connecticut agreed that there was no evidence of an illegitimate purpose in this case. Therefore, as was true of the statute challenged in [*Hawaii Housing Authority v.*] *Midkiff* [1984], the City's development plan was not adopted "to benefit a particular class of identifiable individuals."

On the other hand, this is not a case in which the City is planning to open the condemned land—at least not in its entirety—to use by the general public. Nor will the private lessees of the land in any sense be required to operate like common carriers, making their services available to all comers. But although such a projected use would be sufficient to satisfy the public use requirement, this "Court long ago rejected any literal requirement that condemned property be put into use for the general public." [*Midkiff.*] Indeed, while many state courts in the mid-19th century endorsed "use by the public" as the proper definition of public use, that narrow view steadily eroded over time. Not only was the "use by the public" test difficult to administer (e.g., what proportion of the public need have access to the property? at what price?), but it proved to be impractical given the diverse and always evolving needs of society. . . .

The disposition of this case therefore turns on the question whether the City's development plan serves a "public purpose." Without exception, our cases have defined that concept broadly, reflecting our longstanding policy of deference to legislative judgments in this field.

In *Berman v. Parker* (1954), this Court upheld a redevelopment plan targeting a blighted area of Washington,

D.C., in which most of the housing for the area's 5,000 inhabitants was beyond repair. Under the plan, the area would be condemned and part of it utilized for the construction of streets, schools, and other public facilities. The remainder of the land would be leased or sold to private parties for the purpose of redevelopment, including the construction of low-cost housing. . . .

In *Hawaii Housing Authority v. Midkiff* (1984), the Court considered a Hawaii statute whereby fee title was taken from lessors and transferred to lessees (for just compensation) in order to reduce the concentration of land ownership. We unanimously upheld the statute and rejected the Ninth Circuit's view that it was "a naked attempt on the part of the state of Hawaii to take the property of A and transfer it to B solely for B's private use and benefit." Reaffirming *Berman's* deferential approach to legislative judgments in this field, we concluded that the State's purpose of eliminating the "social and economic evils of a land oligopoly" qualified as a valid public use. Our opinion also rejected the contention that the mere fact that the State immediately transferred the properties to private individuals upon condemnation somehow diminished the public character of the taking. "[I]t is only the taking's purpose, and not its mechanics," we explained, that matters in determining public use. . . .

. . . For more than a century, our public use jurisprudence has wisely eschewed rigid formulas and intrusive scrutiny in favor of affording legislatures broad latitude in determining what public needs justify the use of the takings power.

Those who govern the City were not confronted with the need to remove blight in the Fort Trumbull area, but their determination that the area was sufficiently distressed to justify a program of economic rejuvenation is entitled to our deference. The City has carefully formulated an economic development plan that it believes will provide appreciable benefits to the community, including—but by no means limited to—new jobs and increased tax revenue. As with other exercises in urban planning and development, the City is endeavoring to coordinate a variety of commercial, residential, and recreational uses of land, with the hope that they will form a whole greater than the sum of its parts. To effectuate this plan, the City has invoked a state statute that specifically authorizes the use of eminent domain to promote economic development. Given the comprehensive character of the plan, the thorough deliberation that preceded its adoption, and the limited scope of our review, it is appropriate for us, as it was in *Berman*, to resolve the challenges of the individual owners, not on a piecemeal basis, but rather in light of the entire plan. Because that plan unquestionably serves a public purpose, the takings challenged here satisfy the public use requirement of the Fifth Amendment.

To avoid this result, petitioners urge us to adopt a new bright-line rule that economic development does not qualify as a public use. Putting aside the unpersuasive suggestion that the City's plan will provide only purely economic benefits, neither precedent nor logic supports petitioners' proposal. Promoting economic development is a traditional and long accepted function of government. There is, moreover, no principled way of distinguishing economic development from the other public purposes that we have recognized. . . . "Clearly, there is no basis for exempting economic development from our traditionally broad understanding of public purpose.

Petitioners contend that using eminent domain for economic development impermissibly blurs the boundary between public and private takings. Again, our cases foreclose this objection. Quite simply, the government's pursuit of a public purpose will often benefit individual private parties. . . "We cannot say that public ownership is the sole method of promoting the public purposes of community redevelopment projects."

It is further argued that without a bright-line rule nothing would stop a city from transferring citizen A's property to citizen B for the sole reason that citizen B will put the property to a more productive use and thus pay more taxes. Such a one-to-one transfer of property, executed outside the confines of an integrated development plan, is not presented in this case. While such an unusual exercise of government power would certainly raise a suspicion that a private purpose was afoot, the hypothetical cases posited by petitioners can be confronted if and when they arise. They do not warrant the crafting of an artificial restriction on the concept of public use. . . .

Just as we decline to second-guess the City's considered judgments about the efficacy of its development plan, we also decline to second-guess the City's determinations as to what lands it needs to acquire in order to effectuate the project. "It is not for the courts to oversee the choice of the boundary line nor to sit in review on the size of a particular project area. Once the question of the public purpose has been decided, the amount and character of land to be taken for the project and the need for a particular tract to complete the integrated plan rests in the discretion of the legislative branch."

In affirming the City's authority to take petitioners' properties, we do not minimize the hardship that condemnations may entail, notwithstanding the payment of just compensation. We emphasize that nothing in our opinion precludes any State from placing further restrictions on its exercise of the takings power. Indeed, many States already impose "public use" requirements that are stricter than the federal baseline. Some of these requirements have been established as a matter of state constitutional law, while others are expressed in state eminent domain statutes that carefully limit the grounds upon which takings may be exercised. As the submissions of the parties and their amici make clear, the necessity and wisdom of using eminent domain to promote economic development are certainly matters of legitimate public debate. This Court's authority, however, extends only to determining whether the City's proposed condemnations are for a "public use" within the meaning of the Fifth Amendment to the Federal Constitution. Because over a century of our case law interpreting that provision dictates an affirmative answer to that question, we may not grant petitioners the relief that they seek.

The judgment of the Supreme Court of Connecticut is affirmed.

It is so ordered.

JUSTICE KENNEDY, concurring.

I join the opinion for the Court and add these further observations.

This Court has declared that a taking should be upheld as consistent with the Public Use Clause as long as it is "rationally related to a conceivable public purpose." *Hawaii Housing Authority v. Midkiff* (1984); see also *Berman v. Parker* (1954). This deferential standard of review echoes the rational-basis test used to review economic regulation under the Due Process and Equal Protection Clauses. The determination that a rational-basis standard of review is appropriate does not, however, alter the fact that transfers intended to confer benefits on particular, favored private entities, and with only incidental or pretextual public benefits, are forbidden by the Public Use Clause.

A court applying rational-basis review under the Public Use Clause should strike down a taking that, by a clear showing, is intended to favor a particular private party, with only incidental or pretextual public benefits. . . .

This is not the occasion for conjecture as to what sort of cases might justify a more demanding standard, but it is appropriate to underscore aspects of the instant case that convince me no departure from *Berman* and *Midkiff* is appropriate here. This taking occurred in the context of a comprehensive development plan meant to address a serious city-wide depression, and the projected economic benefits of the project cannot be characterized as de minimus. The identity of most of the private beneficiaries were unknown at the time the city formulated its plans. The city complied with elaborate procedural requirements that facilitate review of the record and inquiry into the city's purposes. In sum, while there may be categories of cases in which the transfers are so suspicious, or the procedures employed so prone to abuse, or the purported benefits are so trivial or implausible, that courts should presume an impermissible private purpose, no such circumstances are present in this case.

JUSTICE O'CONNOR, with whom the CHIEF JUSTICE, JUSTICE SCALIA, and JUSTICE THOMAS join, dissenting.

Over two centuries ago, just after the Bill of Rights was ratified, Justice Chase wrote:

"An act of the Legislature (for I cannot call it a law) contrary to the great first principles of the social compact, cannot be considered a rightful exercise of legislative authority. . . . A few instances will suffice to explain what I mean. . . . [A] law that takes property from A and gives it to B: It is against all reason and justice, for a people to entrust a Legislature with such powers; and, therefore, it cannot be presumed that they have done it." *Calder v. Bull* (1798).

Today the Court abandons this long-held, basic limitation on government power. Under the banner of economic development, all private property is now vulnerable to being taken and transferred to another private owner, so long as it might be upgraded—i.e., given to an owner who will use it in a way that the legislature deems more beneficial to the public—in the process. To reason, as the Court does, that the incidental public benefits resulting from the subsequent ordinary use of private property render economic development takings "for public use" is to wash out any distinction between private and public use of property—and thereby effectively to delete the words "for public use" from the Takings Clause of the Fifth Amendment. Accordingly I respectfully dissent. . . .

This case returns us for the first time in over 20 years to the hard question of when a purportedly "public purpose" taking meets the public use requirement. It presents an issue of first impression: Are economic development takings constitutional? I would hold that they are not. We are guided by two precedents about the taking of real property by eminent domain. In *Berman*, we upheld takings within a blighted neighborhood of Washington, D.C. The neighborhood had so deteriorated that, for example, 64.3% of its dwellings were beyond repair. It had become burdened with "overcrowding of dwellings," "lack of adequate streets and alleys," and "lack of light and air." Congress had determined that the neighborhood had become "injurious to the public health, safety, morals, and welfare" and that it was necessary to "eliminat[e] all such injurious conditions by employing all means necessary and appropriate for the purpose," including eminent domain. Mr. Berman's department store was not itself blighted. Having approved of Congress' decision to eliminate the harm to the public emanating from the blighted neighborhood, however, we did not second-guess its decision to treat the neighborhood as a whole rather than lot-by-lot.

In *Midkiff*, we upheld a land condemnation scheme in Hawaii whereby title in real property was taken from lessors and transferred to lessees. At that time, the State and Federal Governments owned nearly 49% of the State's land, and another 47% was in the hands of only 72 private landowners. Concentration of land ownership was so dramatic that on the State's most urbanized island, Oahu, 22 landowners owned 72.5% of the fee simple titles. The Hawaii Legislature had concluded that the oligopoly in land ownership was "skewing the State's residential fee simple market, inflating land prices, and injuring the public tranquility and welfare," and therefore enacted a condemnation scheme for redistributing title. . . .

The Court's holdings in *Berman* and *Midkiff* were true to the principle underlying the Public Use Clause. In both those cases, the extraordinary, precondemnation use of the targeted property inflicted affirmative harm on society—in *Berman* through blight resulting from extreme poverty and in *Midkiff* through oligopoly resulting from extreme wealth. And in both cases, the relevant legislative body had found that eliminating the existing property use was necessary to remedy the harm. Thus a public purpose was realized when the harmful use was eliminated. Because each taking directly achieved a public benefit, it did not matter that the property was turned over to private use. Here, in contrast, New London does not claim that Susette Kelo's and Wilhelmina Dery's well-maintained homes are the source of any social harm. Indeed, it could not so claim without adopting the absurd argument that any single-family home that might be razed to make way for an apartment building, or any church that might be replaced with a retail store, or any small business that might be more lucrative if it were instead part of a national franchise, is inherently harmful to society and thus within the government's power to condemn.

In moving away from our decisions sanctioning the condemnation of harmful property use, the Court today significantly expands the meaning of public use. It holds that the sovereign may take private property currently put to ordinary private use, and give it over for new, ordinary private use, so long as the new use is predicted to generate some secondary benefit for the public—such as increased tax revenue, more jobs, maybe even aesthetic pleasure. But nearly any lawful use of real private property can be said to generate some incidental benefit to the public. Thus, if predicted (or even guaranteed) positive side-effects are enough to render transfer from one private party to another constitutional, then the words "for public use" do not realistically exclude any takings, and thus do not exert any constraint on the eminent domain power. . . .

Finally, . . . the Court suggests that property owners should turn to the States, who may or may not choose to impose appropriate limits on economic development takings. This is an abdication of our responsibility. States play many important functions in our system of dual sovereignty, but compensating for our refusal to enforce properly the Federal Constitution (and a provision meant to curtail state action, no less) is not among them. . . .

Any property may now be taken for the benefit of another private party, but the fallout from this decision will not be random. The beneficiaries are likely to be those citizens with disproportionate influence and power in the political process, including large corporations and development firms. As for the victims, the government now has license to transfer property from those with fewer resources to those with more. The Founders cannot have intended this perverse result.

JUSTICE THOMAS, dissenting.

Today's decision is simply the latest in a string of our cases construing the Public Use Clause to be a virtual nullity, without the slightest nod to its original meaning. In my view, the Public Use Clause, originally understood, is a meaningful limit on the government's eminent domain power. . . .

. . . I would revisit our Public Use Clause cases and consider returning to the original meaning of the Public Use Clause: that the government may take property only if it actually uses or gives the public a legal right to use the property.

The consequences of today's decision are not difficult to predict, and promise to be harmful. So-called "urban renewal" programs provide some compensation for the properties they take, but no compensation is possible for the subjective value of these lands to the individuals displaced and the indignity inflicted by uprooting them from

their homes. Allowing the government to take property solely for public purposes is bad enough, but extending the concept of public purpose to encompass any economically beneficial goal guarantees that these losses will fall disproportionately on poor communities. Those communities are not only systematically less likely to put their lands to the highest and best social use, but are also the least politically powerful. If ever there were justification for intrusive judicial review of constitutional provisions that protect "discrete and insular minorities," *United States v. Carolene Products Co.* (1938), surely that principle would apply with great force to the powerless groups and individuals the Public Use Clause protects. The deferential standard this Court has adopted for the Public Use Clause is therefore deeply perverse. It encourages "those citizens with disproportionate influence and power in the political process, including large corporations and development firms" to victimize the weak. (O'Connor, J., dissenting). . . .

The Court relies almost exclusively on this Court's prior cases to derive today's far-reaching, and dangerous, result. But the principles this Court should employ to dispose of this case are found in the Public Use Clause itself. . . . When faced with a clash of constitutional principle and a line of unreasoned cases wholly divorced from the text, history, and structure of our founding document, we should not hesitate to resolve the tension in favor of the Constitution's original meaning. For the reasons I have given, and for the reasons given in Justice O'Connor's dissent, the conflict of principle raised by this boundless use of the eminent domain power should be resolved in petitioners' favor. I would reverse the judgment of the Connecticut Supreme Court.

In its takings clause decisions the Court has consistently favored neither private property interests nor the government's power of eminent domain. With respect to defining a "taking," the justices have tended to favor property owners by expanding the range of government actions that come under the authority of the Fifth Amendment.[11] On the other hand, the Court has given broad latitude to the government to define

---

11. Such expansive views of a taking, however, have not extended to temporary measures. For example, in *Tahoe-Sierra Preservation Council v. Tahoe Regional Planning Agency* (2002) the Court found that a temporary moratorium on new construction in the Lake Tahoe basin while the government conducted a study of appropriate land-use regulations did not constitute a taking even when that moratorium was in effect for over thirty-two months.

BOX 11-2   AFTERMATH . . . *KELO V. CITY OF NEW LONDON*

THE *Kelo* decision touched off a storm of protest by private property rights advocates, and public opinion ran decidedly against the decision. Taking the Court's admonishment that nothing in the decision prohibits the states from imposing their own limits, forty-four state legislatures reacted to the public opposition to *Kelo* by placing new restrictions on the use of eminent domain. Supporters of eminent domain, including the National League of Cities, countered by persuading legislators in several states to modify many of the more extreme anti-*Kelo* proposals.

Two months after the *Kelo* decision, its author, Justice John Paul Stevens, acknowledged that the ruling was "unwise" and that he would have opposed it had he been a legislator and not a federal judge bound by precedent.

Some protests were directed at the justices themselves. In Weare, New Hampshire, private property activists secured sufficient petition signatures to place a proposal on the ballot to have the town seize the two-hundred-year-old farmhouse home of Justice David Souter, who voted with the majority in *Kelo*. Under the proposal the property would be turned over to private investors who would build an inn to be named the "Lost Liberty Hotel," featuring the "Just Desserts Café." One of the proposal's supporters said, "It would be more like a bed and breakfast. . . . There would be nine suites, with a black robe in each of the closets." In March 2006 the Weare voters rejected the proposal 1,167 to 493, endorsing instead a resolution asking the state legislature to forbid the use of eminent domain approved in the *Kelo* decision.

In a related but also unsuccessful effort, members of the state Libertarian Party urged the city of Plainfield, New Hampshire, to seize a 167-acre vacation retreat owned by Justice Stephen Breyer. In its place they planned to create a "Constitution Park" including monuments to the U.S. and New Hampshire Constitutions.

In a reversal of sorts, the city of Hercules, California, in 2006 used *Kelo* to stop development. Wal-Mart Stores, Inc., had purchased a 17-acre parcel near the town's waterfront for $15 million, intending to construct a 140,000-square-foot store on the property. The city council opposed the development and voted to seize the land to "ward off urban blight." Wal-Mart vowed to take legal action against this use of eminent domain. In 2009, however, the dispute ended when the city purchased the property from Wal-Mart for $13.5 million.

New London used its victory in *Kelo* to continue its program of redeveloping the Fort Trumbull neighborhood. Pfizer built a $300 million research complex that served as the centerpiece for the project. The condemned houses were torn down, but the city's dream that they would be replaced by new commercial, entertainment, lodging, and residential facilities did not materialize. In 2009, to the city's great disappointment, Pfizer announced that it would abandon its New London facility and move its projects and most of its 1,400 jobs to another Pfizer operation in nearby Groton, Connecticut. The New London research facility had been in operation only eight years.

As for Susette Kelo, the New London nurse continued the fight to save her home from government seizure. She was aided by the Institute for Justice, a Washington, D.C., organization committed to property rights and other libertarian causes. In the end Kelo was forced to leave her home; she moved across the river to Groton. Her little pink house, however, avoided the city's wrecking ball. It was disassembled and moved to another section of New London, where it was rebuilt. With the support of private property advocates, it was named the Kelo House and a monument was placed outside the home to commemorate the legal battle against New London's use of eminent domain.

Kelo continues to oppose what she considers to be abuses of the power of eminent domain. "Do I feel like I won? No, I didn't win. But other people did win. They got their properties back. People tell me all the time about towns that have passed a law limiting eminent domain," she explains. "People have to be continually made aware of how wrong it was. It's still wrong today."

SOURCES: *Valley News*, July 28, 2005; *Financial Times*, January 26, 2006; *New York Times*, February 21, 2006, March 14, 2006, November 12, 2009; *Associated Press*, March 14, 2006; *Los Angeles Times*, May 25, 2006; *San Francisco Chronicle*, May 25, 2006, May 30, 2006; *Money*, September 2006, August 2012; *Contra Costa Times*, April 16, 2009; *Norwich Bulletin*, November 9, 2009; *The Day*, November 11, 2009.

what constitutes a "public use." The Court's decisions reveal deep internal divisions between those justices who place primary value on the rights of individual property owners and those who accord greater value to the interests of the larger community.

Decisions such as *Kelo* have turned a once-obscure constitutional provision into a subject of intense political controversy *(see box 11-2)*. Local governments have increasingly turned to the power of eminent domain as a method of spurring economic development and raising tax revenues. With each such action, groups dedicated to private property rights have become more organized and politically active. This political conflict ensures that takings clause disputes will continue to find their way to the Supreme Court's docket for some time to come.

ANNOTATED READINGS

A number of works have examined the history and constitutional foundations of private property rights in America. These include Bruce Ackerman, *Economic Foundations of Property Law* (Boston: Little, Brown, 1975); Bruce Ackerman, *Private Property and the Constitution* (New Haven, CT: Yale University Press, 1977); James W. Ely Jr., *The Guardian of Every Other Right: A Constitutional History of Property Rights* (New York: Oxford University Press, 1992); Nicholas Mercuro, *Taking Property and Just Compensation* (Boston: Kluwer, 1992); Jennifer Nedelsky, *Private Property and the Limits of American Constitutionalism: The Madisonian Frame-work and Its Legacy* (Chicago: University of Chicago Press, 1990); Ellen Frankel Paul, *Liberty, Property, and the Foundations of the American Constitution* (Albany: State University of New York Press, 1988); and David A. Schultz, *Property, Power, and American Democracy* (New Brunswick, NJ: Transaction, 1992).

Other works have specifically focused on the power of eminent domain and the government's use of that authority. Examples are Alan T. Ackerman, *Current Condemnation Law: Takings, Compensation, and Benefits* (Chicago: American Bar Association, 1994); Richard A. Epstein, *Takings: Private Property and the Power of Eminent Domain* (Cambridge, MA: Harvard

University Press, 1985); Steven Greenhut, *Abuse of Power: How the Government Misuses Eminent Domain* (Santa Ana, CA: Seven Locks Press, 2004); Robin Paul Malloy, ed., *Private Property, Community Development, and Eminent Domain* (Burlington, VT: Ashgate, 2008); Ellen Frankel Paul, *Property Rights and Eminent Domain* (New Brunswick, NJ: Transaction, 1987); John Ryskamp, *The Eminent Domain Revolt* (New York: Algora, 2007); and William B. Stoebuck, *Nontrespassory Takings in Eminent Domain* (Charlottesville, VA: Michie, 1977).

The growing concern over the use of regulation as a form of property taking is explored in the following works: Dennis J. Coyle, *Property Rights and the Constitution: Shaping Society through Land Use Regulation* (Albany: State University of New York Press, 1993); Steven J. Eagle, *Regulatory Takings* (Newark, NJ: LexisNexis, 2005); William A. Fischel, *Regulatory Takings: Law, Economics, and Politics* (Cambridge, MA: Harvard University Press, 1995); Thomas J. Miceli and Kathleen Segerson, *Compensation for Regulatory Takings* (Greenwich, CT: JAI Press, 1996); and Alfred M. Olivetti, *This Land Is Your Land, This Land Is My Land: The Property Rights Movement and Regulatory Takings* (New York: LFB Scholarly Publishing, 2003).

Works examining individual cases that have been significant in developing the Court's takings clause jurisprudence are also available. See, for example, Jeff Benedict, *Little Pink House: A True Story of Defiance and Courage* (New York: Grand Central Publishing, 2009); Gerald Korngold and Andrew P. Morriss, eds., *Property Stories* (New York: Thomson Reuters/ Foundation Press, 2009); Carla T. Main, *Bulldozed: "Kelo," Eminent Domain, and the American Lust for Land* (New York: Encounter Books, 2007); Dwight H. Merriam and Mary Massaron Ross, eds., *Eminent Domain Use and Abuse: Kelo in Context* (Chicago: American Bar Association, 2006); Thomas E. Roberts, ed., *Taking Sides on Takings Issues: The Impact of Tahoe-Sierra* (Chicago: American Bar Association, 2003); and David A. Schultz, *Evicted: Property Rights and Eminent Domain in America* (Westport, CT: Praeger, 2009).

Reference Material

Appendixes

APPENDIX 1

Constitution of the United States

WE THE PEOPLE of the United States, in Order to form a more perfect Union, establish Justice, insure domestic Tranquility, provide for the common defence, promote the general Welfare, and secure the Blessings of Liberty to ourselves and our Posterity, do ordain and establish this Constitution for the United States of America.

ARTICLE I

Section 1. All legislative Powers herein granted shall be vested in a Congress of the United States, which shall consist of a Senate and House of Representatives.

Section 2. The House of Representatives shall be composed of Members chosen every second Year by the People of the several States, and the Electors in each State shall have the Qualifications requisite for Electors of the most numerous Branch of the State Legislature.

No Person shall be a Representative who shall not have attained to the age of twenty five Years, and been seven Years a Citizen of the United States, and who shall not, when elected, be an Inhabitant of that State in which he shall be chosen.

[Representatives and direct Taxes shall be apportioned among the several States which may be included within this Union, according to their respective Numbers, which shall be determined by adding to the whole Number of free Persons, including those bound to Service for a Term of Years, and excluding Indians not taxed, three fifths of all other Persons.][1] The actual Enumeration shall be made within three Years after the first Meeting of the Congress of the United States, and within every subsequent Term of ten Years, in such Manner as they shall by Law direct. The Number of Representatives shall not exceed one for every thirty Thousand, but each State shall have at Least one

Representative; and until such enumeration shall be made, the State of New Hampshire shall be entitled to chuse three, Massachusetts eight, Rhode-Island and Providence Plantations one, Connecticut five, New-York six, New Jersey four, Pennsylvania eight, Delaware one, Maryland six, Virginia ten, North Carolina five, South Carolina five, and Georgia three.

When vacancies happen in the Representation from any State, the Executive Authority thereof shall issue Writs of Election to fill such Vacancies.

The House of Representatives shall chuse their Speaker and other Officers; and shall have the sole Power of Impeachment.

Section 3. The Senate of the United States shall be composed of two Senators from each State, [chosen by the Legislature thereof,][2] for six Years; and each Senator shall have one Vote.

Immediately after they shall be assembled in Consequence of the first Election, they shall be divided as equally as may be into three Classes. The Seats of the Senators of the first Class shall be vacated at the Expiration of the second Year, of the second Class at the Expiration of the fourth Year, and of the third Class at the Expiration of the sixth Year, so that one third may be chosen every second Year; [and if Vacancies happen by Resignation, or otherwise, during the Recess of the Legislature of any State, the Executive thereof may make temporary Appointments until the next Meeting of the Legislature, which shall then fill such Vacancies].[3]

No Person shall be a Senator who shall not have attained to the Age of thirty Years, and been nine Years a Citizen of the United States, and who shall not, when elected, be an Inhabitant of that State for which he shall be chosen.

---

1. The part in brackets was changed by Section 2 of the Fourteenth Amendment.

2. The part in brackets was changed by the first paragraph of the Seventeenth Amendment.

3. The part in brackets was changed by the second paragraph of the Seventeenth Amendment.

The Vice President of the United States shall be President of the Senate, but shall have no Vote, unless they be equally divided.

The Senate shall chuse their other Officers, and also a President pro tempore, in the Absence of the Vice President, or when he shall exercise the Office of President of the United States.

The Senate shall have the sole Power to try all Impeachments. When sitting for that Purpose, they shall be on Oath or Affirmation. When the President of the United States is tried, the Chief Justice shall preside: And no Person shall be convicted without the Concurrence of two thirds of the Members present.

Judgment in Cases of Impeachment shall not extend further than to removal from Office, and disqualification to hold and enjoy any Office of honor, Trust or Profit under the United States: but the Party convicted shall nevertheless be liable and subject to Indictment, Trial, Judgment and Punishment, according to Law.

Section 4. The Times, Places and Manner of holding Elections for Senators and Representatives, shall be prescribed in each State by the Legislature thereof; but the Congress may at any time by Law make or alter such Regulations, except as to the Places of chusing Senators.

The Congress shall assemble at least once in every Year, and such Meeting shall [be on the first Monday in December],[4] unless they shall by Law appoint a different Day.

Section 5. Each House shall be the Judge of the Elections, Returns and Qualifications of its own Members, and a Majority of each shall constitute a Quorum to do Business; but a smaller Number may adjourn from day to day, and may be authorized to compel the Attendance of absent Members, in such Manner, and under such Penalties as each House may provide.

Each House may determine the Rules of its Proceedings, punish its Members for disorderly Behaviour, and, with the Concurrence of two thirds, expel a Member.

Each House shall keep a Journal of its Proceedings, and from time to time publish the same, excepting such Parts as may in their Judgment require Secrecy; and the Yeas and Nays of the Members of either House on any question shall, at the Desire of one fifth of those Present, be entered on the Journal.

---

4. The part in brackets was changed by Section 2 of the Twentieth Amendment.

Neither House, during the Session of Congress, shall, without the Consent of the other, adjourn for more than three days, nor to any other Place than that in which the two Houses shall be sitting.

Section 6. The Senators and Representatives shall receive a Compensation for their Services, to be ascertained by Law, and paid out of the Treasury of the United States. They shall in all Cases, except Treason, Felony and Breach of the Peace, be privileged from Arrest during their Attendance at the Session of their respective Houses, and in going to and returning from the same; and for any Speech or Debate in either House, they shall not be questioned in any other Place.

No Senator or Representative shall, during the Time for which he was elected, be appointed to any civil Office under the Authority of the United States, which shall have been created, or the Emoluments whereof shall have been encreased during such time; and no Person holding any Office under the United States, shall be a Member of either House during his Continuance in Office.

Section 7. All Bills for raising Revenue shall originate in the House of Representatives; but the Senate may propose or concur with Amendments as on other Bills.

Every Bill which shall have passed the House of Representatives and the Senate, shall, before it become a Law, be presented to the President of the United States; If he approve he shall sign it, but if not he shall return it, with his Objections to that House in which it shall have originated, who shall enter the Objections at large on their Journal, and proceed to reconsider it. If after such Reconsideration two thirds of that House shall agree to pass the Bill, it shall be sent, together with the Objections, to the other House, by which it shall likewise be reconsidered, and if approved by two thirds of that House, it shall become a Law. But in all such Cases the Votes of both Houses shall be determined by Yeas and Nays, and the Names of the Persons voting for and against the Bill shall be entered on the Journal of each House respectively. If any Bill shall not be returned by the President within ten Days (Sundays excepted) after it shall have been presented to him, the Same shall be a Law, in like Manner as if he had signed it, unless the Congress by their Adjournment prevent its Return, in which Case it shall not be a Law.

Every Order, Resolution, or Vote to which the Concurrence of the Senate and House of Representatives may be necessary (except on a question of Adjournment) shall be presented to the President of the United States;

and before the Same shall take Effect, shall be approved by him, or being disapproved by him, shall be repassed by two thirds of the Senate and House of Representatives, according to the Rules and Limitations prescribed in the Case of a Bill.

Section 8. The Congress shall have Power To lay and collect Taxes, Duties, Imposts and Excises, to pay the Debts and provide for the common Defence and general Welfare of the United States; but all Duties, Imposts and Excises shall be uniform throughout the United States;

To borrow Money on the credit of the United States;

To regulate Commerce with foreign Nations, and among the several States, and with the Indian Tribes;

To establish an uniform Rule of Naturalization, and uniform Laws on the subject of Bankruptcies throughout the United States;

To coin Money, regulate the Value thereof, and of foreign Coin, and fix the Standard of Weights and Measures;

To provide for the Punishment of counterfeiting the Securities and current Coin of the United States;

To establish Post Offices and post Roads;

To promote the Progress of Science and useful Arts, by securing for limited Times to Authors and Inventors the exclusive Right to their respective Writings and Discoveries;

To constitute Tribunals inferior to the supreme Court;

To define and punish Piracies and Felonies committed on the high Seas, and Offences against the Law of Nations;

To declare War, grant Letters of Marque and Reprisal, and make Rules concerning Captures on Land and Water;

To raise and support Armies, but no Appropriation of Money to that Use shall be for a longer Term than two Years;

To provide and maintain a Navy;

To make Rules for the Government and Regulation of the land and naval Forces;

To provide for calling forth the Militia to execute the Laws of the Union, suppress Insurrections and repel Invasions;

To provide for organizing, arming, and disciplining, the Militia, and for governing such Part of them as may be employed in the Service of the United States, reserving to the States respectively, the Appointment of the Officers, and the Authority of training the Militia according to the discipline prescribed by Congress;

To exercise exclusive Legislation in all Cases whatsoever, over such District (not exceeding ten Miles square) as may, by Cession of particular States, and the Acceptance of Congress, become the Seat of the Government of the United States, and to exercise like Authority over all Places purchased by the Consent of the Legislature of the State in which the Same shall be, for the Erection of Forts, Magazines, Arsenals, dock-Yards, and other needful Buildings;—And

To make all Laws which shall be necessary and proper for carrying into Execution the foregoing Powers, and all other Powers vested by this Constitution in the Government of the United States, or in any Department or Officer thereof.

Section 9. The Migration or Importation of such Persons as any of the States now existing shall think proper to admit, shall not be prohibited by the Congress prior to the Year one thousand eight hundred and eight, but a Tax or duty may be imposed on such Importation, not exceeding ten dollars for each Person.

The Privilege of the Writ of Habeas Corpus shall not be suspended, unless when in Cases of Rebellion or Invasion the public Safety may require it.

No Bill of Attainder or ex post facto Law shall be passed.

No Capitation, or other direct, Tax shall be laid, unless in Proportion to the Census or Enumeration herein before directed to be taken.[5]

No Tax or Duty shall be laid on Articles exported from any State.

No Preference shall be given by any Regulation of Commerce or Revenue to the Ports of one State over those of another; nor shall Vessels bound to, or from, one State, be obliged to enter, clear, or pay Duties in another.

No Money shall be drawn from the Treasury, but in Consequence of Appropriations made by Law; and a regular Statement and Account of the Receipts and Expenditures of all public Money shall be published from time to time.

No Title of Nobility shall be granted by the United States: And no Person holding any Office of Profit or Trust under them, shall, without the Consent of the Congress, accept of any present, Emolument, Office, or Title, of any kind whatever, from any King, Prince, or foreign State.

Section 10. No State shall enter into any Treaty, Alliance, or Confederation; grant Letters of Marque and Reprisal; coin Money; emit Bills of Credit; make any Thing but gold and silver Coin a Tender in

---

5. The Sixteenth Amendment gave Congress the power to tax incomes.

Payment of Debts; pass any Bill of Attainder, ex post facto Law, or Law impairing the Obligation of Contracts, or grant any Title of Nobility.

No State shall, without the Consent of the Congress, lay any Imposts or Duties on Imports or Exports, except what may be absolutely necessary for executing it's inspection Laws: and the net Produce of all Duties and Imposts, laid by any State on Imports or Exports, shall be for the Use of the Treasury of the United States; and all such Laws shall be subject to the Revision and Controul of the Congress.

No State shall, without the Consent of Congress, lay any Duty of Tonnage, keep Troops, or Ships of War in time of Peace, enter into any Agreement or Compact with another State, or with a foreign Power, or engage in War, unless actually invaded, or in such imminent Danger as will not admit of delay.

ARTICLE II

Section 1. The executive Power shall be vested in a President of the United States of America. He shall hold his Office during the Term of four Years, and, together with the Vice President, chosen for the same Term, be elected, as follows

Each State shall appoint, in such Manner as the Legislature thereof may direct, a Number of Electors, equal to the whole Number of Senators and Representatives to which the State may be entitled in the Congress: but no Senator or Representative, or Person holding an Office of Trust or Profit under the United States, shall be appointed an Elector.

[The Electors shall meet in their respective States, and vote by Ballot for two Persons, of whom one at least shall not be an Inhabitant of the same State with themselves. And they shall make a List of all the Persons voted for, and of the Number of Votes for each; which List they shall sign and certify, and transmit sealed to the Seat of the Government of the United States, directed to the President of the Senate. The President of the Senate shall, in the Presence of the Senate and House of Representatives, open all the Certificates, and the Votes shall then be counted. The Person having the greatest Number of Votes shall be the President, if such Number be a Majority of the whole Number of Electors appointed; and if there be more than one who have such Majority, and have an equal Number of Votes, then the House of Representatives shall immediately chuse by Ballot one of them for President; and if no Person have a Majority, then from the five highest on the list the said House shall in like Manner chuse the President. But in chusing the President, the Votes shall be taken by States, the Representation from each State having one Vote; A quorum for this Purpose shall consist of a Member or Members from two thirds of the States, and a Majority of all the States shall be necessary to a Choice. In every Case, after the Choice of the President, the Person having the greatest Number of Votes of the Electors shall be the Vice President. But if there should remain two or more who have equal Votes, the Senate shall chuse from them by Ballot the Vice President.][6]

The Congress may determine the Time of chusing the Electors, and the Day on which they shall give their Votes; which Day shall be the same throughout the United States.

No Person except a natural born Citizen, or a Citizen of the United States, at the time of the Adoption of this Constitution, shall be eligible to the Office of President; neither shall any Person be eligible to that Office who shall not have attained to the Age of thirty five Years, and been fourteen Years a Resident within the United States.

In Case of the Removal of the President from Office, or of his Death, Resignation, or Inability to discharge the Powers and Duties of the said Office,[7] the Same shall devolve on the Vice President, and the Congress may by Law provide for the Case of Removal, Death, Resignation or Inability, both of the President and Vice President, declaring what Officer shall then act as President, and such Officer shall act accordingly, until the Disability be removed, or a President shall be elected.

The President shall, at stated Times, receive for his Services, a Compensation, which shall neither be encreased nor diminished during the Period for which he shall have been elected, and he shall not receive within that Period any other Emolument from the United States, or any of them.

Before he enter on the Execution of his Office, he shall take the following Oath or Affirmation:—"I do solemnly swear (or affirm) that I will faithfully execute the Office of President of the United States, and will to the best of my Ability, preserve, protect and defend the Constitution of the United States."

Section 2. The President shall be Commander in Chief of the Army and Navy of the United States, and of

---

6. The material in brackets has been superseded by the Twelfth Amendment.

7. This provision has been affected by the Twenty-fifth Amendment.

the Militia of the several States, when called into the actual Service of the United States; he may require the Opinion, in writing, of the principal Officer in each of the executive Departments, upon any Subject relating to the Duties of their respective Offices, and he shall have Power to grant Reprieves and Pardons for Offences against the United States, except in Cases of Impeachment.

He shall have Power, by and with the Advice and Consent of the Senate, to make Treaties, provided two thirds of the Senators present concur; and he shall nominate, and by and with the Advice and Consent of the Senate, shall appoint Ambassadors, other public Ministers and Consuls, Judges of the supreme Court, and all other Officers of the United States, whose Appointments are not herein otherwise provided for, and which shall be established by Law: but the Congress may by Law vest the Appointment of such inferior Officers, as they think proper, in the President alone, in the Courts of Law, or in the Heads of Departments.

The President shall have Power to fill up all Vacancies that may happen during the Recess of the Senate, by granting Commissions which shall expire at the End of their next Session.

Section 3. He shall from time to time give to the Congress Information of the State of the Union, and recommend to their Consideration such Measures as he shall judge necessary and expedient; he may, on extraordinary Occasions, convene both Houses, or either of them, and in Case of Disagreement between them, with Respect to the Time of Adjournment, he may adjourn them to such Time as he shall think proper; he shall receive Ambassadors and other public Ministers; he shall take Care that the Laws be faithfully executed, and shall Commission all the Officers of the United States.

Section 4. The President, Vice President and all civil Officers of the United States, shall be removed from Office on Impeachment for, and Conviction of, Treason, Bribery, or other high Crimes and Misdemeanors.

ARTICLE III

Section 1. The judicial Power of the United States, shall be vested in one supreme Court, and in such inferior Courts as the Congress may from time to time ordain and establish. The Judges, both of the supreme and inferior Courts, shall hold their Offices during good Behaviour, and shall, at stated Times, receive for their Services, a Compensation, which shall not be diminished during their Continuance in Office.

Section 2. The judicial Power shall extend to all Cases, in Law and Equity, arising under this Constitution, the Laws of the United States, and Treaties made, or which shall be made, under their Authority;—to all Cases affecting Ambassadors, other public Ministers and Consuls;—to all Cases of admiralty and maritime Jurisdiction;—to Controversies to which the United States shall be a Party;—to Controversies between two or more States;—between a State and Citizens of another State;[8]—between Citizens of different States;—between Citizens of the same State claiming Lands under Grants of different States, and between a State, or the Citizens thereof, and foreign States, Citizens or Subjects.[8]

In all Cases affecting Ambassadors, other public Ministers and Consuls, and those in which a State shall be Party, the supreme Court shall have original Jurisdiction. In all the other Cases before mentioned, the supreme Court shall have appellate Jurisdiction, both as to Law and Fact, with such Exceptions, and under such Regulations as the Congress shall make.

The Trial of all Crimes, except in Cases of Impeachment, shall be by Jury; and such Trial shall be held in the State where the said Crimes shall have been committed; but when not committed within any State, the Trial shall be at such Place or Places as the Congress may by Law have directed.

Section 3. Treason against the United States, shall consist only in levying War against them, or in adhering to their Enemies, giving them Aid and Comfort. No Person shall be convicted of Treason unless on the Testimony of two Witnesses to the same overt Act, or on Confession in open Court.

The Congress shall have Power to declare the Punishment of Treason, but no Attainder of Treason shall work Corruption of Blood, or Forfeiture except during the Life of the Person attainted.

ARTICLE IV

Section 1. Full Faith and Credit shall be given in each State to the public Acts, Records, and judicial Proceedings of every other State. And the Congress may by general Laws prescribe the Manner in which such Acts, Records and Proceedings shall be proved, and the Effect thereof.

---

8. These clauses were affected by the Eleventh Amendment.

Section 2. The Citizens of each State shall be entitled to all Privileges and Immunities of Citizens in the several States.

A Person charged in any State with Treason, Felony, or other Crime, who shall flee from Justice, and be found in another State, shall on Demand of the executive Authority of the State from which he fled, be delivered up, to be removed to the State having Jurisdiction of the Crime.

[No Person held to Service or Labour in one State, under the Laws thereof, escaping into another, shall, in Consequence of any Law or Regulation therein, be discharged from such Service or Labour, but shall be delivered up on Claim of the Party to whom such Service or Labour may be due.][9]

Section 3. New States may be admitted by the Congress into this Union; but no new State shall be formed or erected within the Jurisdiction of any other State; nor any State be formed by the Junction of two or more States, or Parts of States, without the Consent of the Legislatures of the States concerned as well as of the Congress.

The Congress shall have Power to dispose of and make all needful Rules and Regulations respecting the Territory or other Property belonging to the United States; and nothing in this Constitution shall be so construed as to Prejudice any Claims of the United States, or of any particular State.

Section 4. The United States shall guarantee to every State in this Union a Republican Form of Government, and shall protect each of them against Invasion; and on Application of the Legislature, or of the Executive (when the Legislature cannot be convened) against domestic Violence.

ARTICLE V

The Congress, whenever two thirds of both Houses shall deem it necessary, shall propose Amendments to this Constitution, or, on the Application of the Legislatures of two thirds of the several States, shall call a Convention for proposing Amendments, which, in either Case, shall be valid to all Intents and Purposes, as Part of this Constitution, when ratified by the Legislatures of three fourths of the several States, or by Conventions in three fourths thereof, as the one or the other Mode of Ratification may be proposed by the Congress; Provided [that no Amendment which may be made prior to the Year One thousand eight hundred and eight shall in any Manner affect the first and fourth Clauses in the Ninth Section of the first Article; and][10] that no State, without its Consent, shall be deprived of its equal Suffrage in the Senate.

ARTICLE VI

All Debts contracted and Engagements entered into, before the Adoption of this Constitution, shall be as valid against the United States under this Constitution, as under the Confederation.

This Constitution, and the Laws of the United States which shall be made in Pursuance thereof; and all Treaties made, or which shall be made, under the Authority of the United States, shall be the supreme Law of the Land; and the Judges in every State shall be bound thereby, any Thing in the Constitution or Laws of any State to the Contrary notwithstanding.

The Senators and Representatives before mentioned, and the Members of the several State Legislatures, and all executive and judicial Officers, both of the United States and of the several States, shall be bound by Oath or Affirmation, to support this Constitution; but no religious Test shall ever be required as a Qualification to any Office or public Trust under the United States.

ARTICLE VII

The Ratification of the Conventions of nine States, shall be sufficient for the Establishment of this Constitution between the States so ratifying the Same. Done in Convention by the Unanimous Consent of the States present the Seventeenth Day of September in the Year of our Lord one thousand seven hundred and Eighty seven and of the Independence of the United States of America the Twelfth. IN WITNESS whereof We have hereunto subscribed our Names,

George Washington,
President and deputy from Virginia.

New Hampshire: John Langdon,
Nicholas Gilman.

---

9. This paragraph has been superseded by the Thirteenth Amendment.

---

10. Obsolete.

Massachusetts:	Nathaniel Gorham, Rufus King.
Connecticut:	William Samuel Johnson, Roger Sherman.
New York:	Alexander Hamilton.
New Jersey:	William Livingston, David Brearley, William Paterson, Jonathan Dayton.
Pennsylvania:	Benjamin Franklin, Thomas Mifflin, Robert Morris, George Clymer, Thomas FitzSimons, Jared Ingersoll, James Wilson, Gouverneur Morris.
Delaware:	George Read, Gunning Bedford Jr., John Dickinson, Richard Bassett, Jacob Broom.
Maryland:	James McHenry, Daniel of St. Thomas Jenifer, Daniel Carroll.
Virginia:	John Blair, James Madison Jr.
North Carolina:	William Blount, Richard Dobbs Spaight, Hugh Williamson.
South Carolina:	John Rutledge, Charles Cotesworth Pinckney, Charles Pinckney, Pierce Butler.
Georgia:	William Few, Abraham Baldwin.

[The language of the original Constitution, not including the Amendments, was adopted by a convention of the states on September 17, 1787, and was subsequently ratified by the states on the following dates: Delaware, December 7, 1787; Pennsylvania, December 12, 1787; New Jersey, December 18, 1787; Georgia, January 2, 1788; Connecticut, January 9, 1788; Massachusetts, February 6, 1788; Maryland, April 28, 1788; South Carolina, May 23, 1788; New Hampshire, June 21, 1788.

Ratification was completed on June 21, 1788.

The Constitution subsequently was ratified by Virginia, June 25, 1788; New York, July 26, 1788; North Carolina, November 21, 1789; Rhode Island, May 29, 1790; and Vermont, January 10, 1791.]

AMENDMENTS

Amendment I

(*First ten amendments ratified December 15, 1791.*)

Congress shall make no law respecting an establishment of religion, or prohibiting the free exercise thereof; or abridging the freedom of speech, or of the press; or the right of the people peaceably to assemble, and to petition the Government for a redress of grievances.

Amendment II

A well regulated Militia, being necessary to the security of a free State, the right of the people to keep and bear Arms, shall not be infringed.

Amendment III

No Soldier shall, in time of peace be quartered in any house, without the consent of the Owner, nor in time of war, but in a manner to be prescribed by law.

Amendment IV

The right of the people to be secure in their persons, houses, papers, and effects, against unreasonable searches and seizures, shall not be violated, and no Warrants shall issue, but upon probable cause, supported by Oath or affirmation, and particularly describing the place to be searched, and the persons or things to be seized.

Amendment V

No person shall be held to answer for a capital, or otherwise infamous crime, unless on a presentment or indictment of a Grand Jury, except in cases arising in the land or naval forces, or in the Militia, when in actual service in time of War or public danger; nor shall any person be subject for the same offence to be twice put in jeopardy of life or limb; nor shall be compelled in any criminal case to be a witness against himself, nor be deprived of life, liberty, or property, without due process of law; nor shall private property be taken for public use, without just compensation.

Amendment VI

In all criminal prosecutions, the accused shall enjoy the right to a speedy and public trial, by an impartial jury of the State and district wherein the crime shall have been committed, which district shall have been previously ascertained by law, and to be informed of the nature and cause of the accusation; to be confronted with the witnesses against him; to have compulsory process for obtaining witnesses in his favor, and to have the Assistance of Counsel for his defence.

Amendment VII

In Suits at common law, where the value in controversy shall exceed twenty dollars, the right of trial by jury shall be preserved, and no fact tried by a jury, shall be otherwise re-examined in any Court of the United States, than according to the rules of the common law.

Amendment VIII

Excessive bail shall not be required, nor excessive fines imposed, nor cruel and unusual punishments inflicted.

Amendment IX

The enumeration in the Constitution, of certain rights, shall not be construed to deny or disparage others retained by the people.

Amendment X

The powers not delegated to the United States by the Constitution, nor prohibited by it to the States, are reserved to the States respectively, or to the people.

Amendment XI

(*Ratified February 7, 1795*)

The Judicial power of the United States shall not be construed to extend to any suit in law or equity, commenced or prosecuted against one of the United States by Citizens of another State, or by Citizens or Subjects of any Foreign State.

Amendment XII

(*Ratified June 15, 1804*)

The Electors shall meet in their respective states and vote by ballot for President and Vice-President, one of whom, at least, shall not be an inhabitant of the same state with themselves; they shall name in their ballots the person voted for as President, and in distinct ballots the person voted for as Vice-President, and they shall make distinct lists of all persons voted for as President, and of all persons voted for as Vice-President, and of the number of votes for each, which lists they shall sign and certify, and transmit sealed to the seat of the government of the United States, directed to the President of the Senate;—The President of the Senate shall, in the presence of the Senate and House of Representatives, open all the certificates and the votes shall then be counted;—The person having the greatest number of votes for President, shall be the President, if such number be a majority of the whole number of Electors appointed; and if no person have such majority, then from the persons having the highest numbers not exceeding three on the list of those voted for as President, the House of Representatives shall choose immediately, by ballot, the President. But in choosing the President, the votes shall be taken by states, the representation from each state having one vote; a quorum for this purpose shall consist of a member or members from two-thirds of the states, and a majority of all the states shall be necessary to a choice. [And if the House of Representatives shall not choose a President whenever the right of choice shall devolve upon them, before the fourth day of March next following, then the Vice-President shall act as President, as in the case of the death or other constitutional disability of the President.][11] The person having the greatest number of votes as Vice-President, shall be the Vice-President, if such number be a majority of the whole number of Electors appointed, and if no person have a majority, then from the two highest numbers on the list, the Senate shall choose the Vice-President; a quorum for the purpose shall consist of two-thirds of the whole number of Senators, and a majority of the whole number shall be necessary to a choice. But no person constitutionally ineligible to the office of President shall be eligible to that of Vice-President of the United States.

Amendment XIII

(*Ratified December 6, 1865*)

Section 1. Neither slavery nor involuntary servitude, except as a punishment for crime whereof the party shall have been duly convicted, shall exist within the United States, or any place subject to their jurisdiction.

Section 2. Congress shall have power to enforce this article by appropriate legislation.

Amendment XIV

(*Ratified July 9, 1868*)

Section 1. All persons born or naturalized in the United States, and subject to the jurisdiction thereof, are citizens of the United States and of the State wherein they reside. No State shall make or enforce any law

---

11. The part in brackets has been superseded by Section 3 of the Twentieth Amendment.

which shall abridge the privileges or immunities of citizens of the United States; nor shall any State deprive any person of life, liberty, or property, without due process of law; nor deny to any person within its jurisdiction the equal protection of the laws.

Section 2. Representatives shall be apportioned among the several States according to their respective numbers, counting the whole number of persons in each State, excluding Indians not taxed. But when the right to vote at any election for the choice of electors for President and Vice President of the United States, Representatives in Congress, the Executive and Judicial officers of a State, or the members of the Legislature thereof, is denied to any of the male inhabitants of such State, being twenty-one years of age,[12] and citizens of the United States, or in any way abridged, except for participation in rebellion, or other crime, the basis of representation therein shall be reduced in the proportion which the number of such male citizens shall bear to the whole number of male citizens twenty-one years of age in such State.

Section 3. No person shall be a Senator or Representative in Congress, or elector of President and Vice President, or hold any office, civil or military, under the United States, or under any State, who, having previously taken an oath, as a member of Congress, or as an officer of the United States, or as a member of any State legislature, or as an executive or judicial officer of any State, to support the Constitution of the United States, shall have engaged in insurrection or rebellion against the same, or given aid or comfort to the enemies thereof. But Congress may by a vote of two-thirds of each House, remove such disability.

Section 4. The validity of the public debt of the United States, authorized by law, including debts incurred for payment of pensions and bounties for services in suppressing insurrection or rebellion, shall not be questioned. But neither the United States nor any State shall assume or pay any debt or obligation incurred in aid of insurrection or rebellion against the United States, or any claim for the loss or emancipation of any slave; but all such debts, obligations and claims shall be held illegal and void.

Section 5. The Congress shall have power to enforce, by appropriate legislation, the provisions of this article.

Amendment XV

(*Ratified February 3, 1870*)

---

12. See the Nineteenth and Twenty-sixth Amendments.

Section 1. The right of citizens of the United States to vote shall not be denied or abridged by the United States or by any State on account of race, color, or previous condition of servitude.

Section 2. The Congress shall have power to enforce this article by appropriate legislation.

Amendment XVI

(*Ratified February 3, 1913*)

The Congress shall have power to lay and collect taxes on incomes, from whatever source derived, without apportionment among the several States, and without regard to any census or enumeration.

Amendment XVII

(*Ratified April 8, 1913*)

The Senate of the United States shall be composed of two Senators from each State, elected by the people thereof, for six years; and each Senator shall have one vote. The electors in each State shall have the qualifications requisite for electors of the most numerous branch of the State legislatures.

When vacancies happen in the representation of any State in the Senate, the executive authority of such State shall issue writs of election to fill such vacancies: *Provided,* That the legislature of any State may empower the executive thereof to make temporary appointments until the people fill the vacancies by election as the legislature may direct.

This amendment shall not be so construed as to affect the election or term of any Senator chosen before it becomes valid as part of the Constitution.

Amendment XVIII

(*Ratified January 16, 1919*)

Section 1. After one year from the ratification of this article the manufacture, sale, or transportation of intoxicating liquors within, the importation thereof into, or the exportation thereof from the United States and all territory subject to the jurisdiction thereof for beverage purposes is hereby prohibited.

Section 2. The Congress and the several States shall have concurrent power to enforce this article by appropriate legislation.

Section 3. This article shall be inoperative unless it shall have been ratified as an amendment to the Constitution by the legislatures of the several States, as provided in the Constitution, within seven years from the date of the submission hereof to the States by the Congress.[13]

Amendment XIX

(*Ratified August 18, 1920*)

The right of citizens of the United States to vote shall not be denied or abridged by the United States or by any State on account of sex.

Congress shall have power to enforce this article by appropriate legislation.

Amendment XX

(*Ratified January 23, 1933*)

Section 1. The terms of the President and Vice President shall end at noon on the 20th day of January, and the terms of Senators and Representatives at noon on the 3d day of January, of the years in which such terms would have ended if this article had not been ratified; and the terms of their successors shall then begin.

Section 2. The Congress shall assemble at least once in every year, and such meeting shall begin at noon on the 3d day of January, unless they shall by law appoint a different day.

Section 3.[14] If, at the time fixed for the beginning of the term of the President, the President elect shall have died, the Vice President elect shall become President. If a President shall not have been chosen before the time fixed for the beginning of his term, or if the President elect shall have failed to qualify, then the Vice President elect shall act as President until a President shall have qualified; and the Congress may by law provide for the case wherein neither a President elect nor a Vice President elect shall have qualified, declaring who shall then act as President, or the manner in which one who is to act shall be selected, and such person shall act accordingly until a President or Vice President shall have qualified.

Section 4. The Congress may by law provide for the case of the death of any of the persons from whom the House of Representatives may choose a President whenever the right of choice shall have devolved upon them, and for the case of the death of any of the persons from whom the Senate may choose a Vice President whenever the right of choice shall have devolved upon them.

---

13. This Amendment was repealed by Section 1 of the Twenty-first Amendment.

14. See the Twenty-fifth Amendment.

Section 5. Sections 1 and 2 shall take effect on the 15th day of October following the ratification of this article.

Section 6. This article shall be inoperative unless it shall have been ratified as an amendment to the Constitution by the legislatures of three-fourths of the several States within seven years from the date of its submission.

Amendment XXI

(*Ratified December 5, 1933*)

Section 1. The eighteenth article of amendment to the Constitution of the United States is hereby repealed.

Section 2. The transportation or importation into any State, Territory, or possession of the United States for delivery or use therein of intoxicating liquors, in violation of the laws thereof, is hereby prohibited.

Section 3. This article shall be inoperative unless it shall have been ratified as an amendment to the Constitution by conventions in the several States, as provided in the Constitution, within seven years from the date of the submission hereof to the States by the Congress.

Amendment XXII

(*Ratified February 27, 1951*)

Section 1. No person shall be elected to the office of the President more than twice, and no person who has held the office of President, or acted as President, for more than two years of a term to which some other person was elected President shall be elected to the office of the President more than once. But this Article shall not apply to any person holding the office of President when this Article was proposed by the Congress, and shall not prevent any person who may be holding the office of President, or acting as President, during the term within which this Article become operative from holding the office of President or acting as President during the remainder of such term.

Section 2. This article shall be inoperative unless it shall have been ratified as an amendment to the Constitution by the legislatures of three-fourths of the several States within seven years from the date of its submission to the States by the Congress.

Amendment XXIII

(*Ratified March 29, 1961*)

Section 1. The District constituting the seat of Government of the United States shall appoint in such manner as the Congress may direct:

A number of electors of President and Vice President equal to the whole number of Senators and Representatives in Congress to which the District would be entitled if it were a State, but in no event more than the least populous State; they shall be in addition to those appointed by the States, but they shall be considered, for the purposes of the election of President and Vice President, to be electors appointed by a State; and they shall meet in the District and perform such duties as provided by the twelfth article of amendment.

Section 2. The Congress shall have power to enforce this article by appropriate legislation.

Amendment XXIV

(Ratified January 23, 1964)

Section 1. The right of citizens of the United States to vote in any primary or other election for President or Vice President, for electors for President or Vice President, or for Senator or Representative in Congress, shall not be denied or abridged by the United States or any State by reason of failure to pay any poll tax or other tax.

Section 2. The Congress shall have power to enforce this article by appropriate legislation.

Amendment XXV

(Ratified February 10, 1967)

Section 1. In case of the removal of the President from office or of his death or resignation, the Vice President shall become President.

Section 2. Whenever there is a vacancy in the office of the Vice President, the President shall nominate a Vice President who shall take office upon confirmation by a majority vote of both Houses of Congress.

Section 3. Whenever the President transmits to the President pro tempore of the Senate and the Speaker of the House of Representatives his written declaration that he is unable to discharge the powers and duties of his office, and until he transmits to them a written declaration to the contrary, such powers and duties shall be discharged by the Vice President as Acting President.

Section 4. Whenever the Vice President and a majority of either the principal officers of the executive departments or of such other body as Congress may by law provide, transmit to the President pro tempore of the Senate and the Speaker of the House of Representatives their written declaration that the President is unable to discharge the powers and duties of his office, the Vice President shall immediately assume the powers and duties of the office as Acting President.

Thereafter, when the President transmits to the President pro tempore of the Senate and the Speaker of the House of Representatives his written declaration that no inability exists, he shall resume the powers and duties of his office unless the Vice President and a majority of either the principal officers of the executive department or of such other body as Congress may by law provide, transmit within four days to the President pro tempore of the Senate and the Speaker of the House of Representatives their written declaration that the President is unable to discharge the powers and duties of his office. Thereupon Congress shall decide the issue, assembling within forty-eight hours for that purpose if not in session. If the Congress, within twenty-one days after receipt of the latter written declaration, or, if Congress is not in session, within twenty-one days after Congress is required to assemble, determines by two-thirds vote of both Houses that the President is unable to discharge the powers and duties of his office, the Vice President shall continue to discharge the same as Acting President; otherwise, the President shall resume the powers and duties of his office.

Amendment XXVI

(Ratified July 1, 1971)

Section 1. The right of citizens of the United States, who are eighteen years of age or older, to vote shall not be denied or abridged by the United States or by any State on account of age.

Section 2. The Congress shall have power to enforce this article by appropriate legislation.

Amendment XXVII

(Ratified May 7, 1992)

No law varying the compensation for the services of the Senators and Representatives shall take effect, until an election of Representatives shall have intervened.

SOURCE: *United States Government Manual, 1993–94* (Washington, DC.: Government Printing Office, 1993), 5–20.

APPENDIX 2
The Justices

The justices of the Supreme Court are listed below in alphabetical order, each with birth and death years, state from which he or she was appointed, political party affiliation at time of appointment, educational institutions attended, appointing president, confirmation date and vote, date of service termination, and major preappointment offices and activities.

Alito, Samuel A., Jr. (1950–). New Jersey. Republican. Princeton, Yale. Nominated associate justice by George W. Bush; confirmed 2006 by 58–42 vote. U.S. attorney for New Jersey, federal appeals court judge.

Baldwin, Henry (1780–1844). Pennsylvania. Democrat. Yale. Nominated associate justice by Andrew Jackson; confirmed 1830 by 41–2 vote; died in office 1844. U.S. representative.

Barbour, Philip Pendleton (1783–1841). Virginia. Democrat. College of William and Mary. Nominated associate justice by Andrew Jackson; confirmed 1836 by 30–11 vote; died in office 1841. Virginia state legislator, U.S. representative, U.S. Speaker of the House, state court judge, federal district court judge.

Black, Hugo Lafayette (1886–1971). Alabama. Democrat. Birmingham Medical College, University of Alabama. Nominated associate justice by Franklin Roosevelt; confirmed 1937 by 63–16 vote; retired 1971. Alabama police court judge, county solicitor, U.S. senator.

Blackmun, Harry Andrew (1908–1999). Minnesota. Republican. Harvard. Nominated associate justice by Richard Nixon; confirmed 1970 by 94–0 vote; retired 1994. Federal appeals court judge.

Blair, John, Jr. (1732–1800). Virginia. Federalist. College of William and Mary; Middle Temple (England). Nominated associate justice by George Washington; confirmed 1789 by voice vote; resigned 1796. Virginia legislator, state court judge, delegate to Constitutional Convention.

Blatchford, Samuel (1820–1893). New York. Republican. Columbia. Nominated associate justice by Chester A. Arthur; confirmed 1882 by voice vote; died in office 1893. Federal district court judge, federal circuit court judge.

Bradley, Joseph P. (1813–1892). New Jersey. Republican. Rutgers. Nominated associate justice by Ulysses S. Grant; confirmed 1870 by 46–9 vote; died in office 1892. Private practice.

Brandeis, Louis Dembitz (1856–1941). Massachusetts. Republican. Harvard. Nominated associate justice by Woodrow Wilson; confirmed 1916 by 47–22 vote; retired 1939. Private practice.

Brennan, William Joseph, Jr. (1906–1997). New Jersey. Democrat. University of Pennsylvania, Harvard. Received recess appointment from Dwight Eisenhower to be associate justice 1956; confirmed 1957 by voice vote; retired 1990. New Jersey Supreme Court.

Brewer, David Josiah (1837–1910). Kansas. Republican. Wesleyan, Yale, Albany Law School. Nominated associate justice by Benjamin Harrison; confirmed 1889 by 53–11 vote; died in office 1910. Kansas state court judge, federal circuit court judge.

Breyer, Stephen G. (1938–). Massachusetts. Democrat. Stanford, Oxford, Harvard. Nominated associate justice by William Clinton; confirmed 1994 by 87–9 vote. Law professor; chief counsel, Senate Judiciary Committee; federal appeals court judge.

Brown, Henry B. (1836–1913). Michigan. Republican. Yale, Harvard. Nominated associate justice by Benjamin Harrison; confirmed 1890 by voice vote; retired 1906. Michigan state court judge, federal district court judge.

Burger, Warren Earl (1907–1995). Virginia. Republican. University of Minnesota, St. Paul College of Law. Nominated chief justice by Richard Nixon; confirmed 1969 by 74–3 vote; retired 1986. Assistant U.S. attorney general, federal appeals court judge.

Burton, Harold Hitz (1888–1964). Ohio. Republican. Bowdoin College, Harvard. Nominated associate justice by Harry Truman; confirmed 1945 by voice vote; retired 1958. Ohio state legislator, mayor of Cleveland, U.S. senator.

Butler, Pierce (1866–1939). Minnesota. Democrat. Carleton College. Nominated associate justice by Warren G. Harding; confirmed 1922 by 61–8 vote; died in office 1939. Minnesota county attorney, private practice.

Byrnes, James Francis (1879–1972). South Carolina. Democrat. Privately educated. Nominated associate justice by Franklin Roosevelt; confirmed 1941 by voice vote; resigned 1942. South Carolina local solicitor, U.S. representative, U.S. senator.

Campbell, John Archibald (1811–1889). Alabama. Democrat. Franklin College (University of Georgia), U.S. Military Academy. Nominated associate justice by Franklin Pierce; confirmed 1853 by voice vote; resigned 1861. Alabama state legislator.

Cardozo, Benjamin Nathan (1870–1938). New York. Democrat. Columbia. Nominated associate justice by Herbert Hoover; confirmed 1932 by voice vote; died in office 1938. State court judge.

Catron, John (1786–1865). Tennessee. Democrat. Self-educated. Nominated associate justice by Andrew Jackson; confirmed 1837 by 28–15 vote; died in office 1865. Tennessee state court judge, state chief justice.

Chase, Salmon Portland (1808–1873). Ohio. Republican. Dartmouth. Nominated chief justice by Abraham Lincoln; confirmed 1864 by voice vote; died in office 1873. U.S. senator, Ohio governor, U.S. secretary of the Treasury.

Chase, Samuel (1741–1811). Maryland. Federalist. Privately educated. Nominated associate justice by George Washington; confirmed 1796 by voice vote; died in office 1811. Maryland state legislator, delegate to Continental Congress, state court judge.

Clark, Tom Campbell (1899–1977). Texas. Democrat. University of Texas. Nominated associate justice by Harry Truman; confirmed 1949 by 73–8 vote; retired 1967. Texas local district attorney, U.S. attorney general.

Clarke, John Hessin (1857–1945). Ohio. Democrat. Western Reserve University. Nominated associate justice by Woodrow Wilson; confirmed 1916 by voice vote; resigned 1922. Federal district judge.

Clifford, Nathan (1803–1881). Maine. Democrat. Privately educated. Nominated associate justice by James Buchanan; confirmed 1858 by 26–23 vote; died in office 1881. Maine state legislator, state attorney general, U.S. representative, U.S. attorney general, minister to Mexico.

Curtis, Benjamin Robbins (1809–1874). Massachusetts. Whig. Harvard. Nominated associate justice by Millard Fillmore; confirmed 1851 by voice vote; resigned 1857. Massachusetts state legislator.

Cushing, William (1732–1810). Massachusetts. Federalist. Harvard. Nominated associate justice by George Washington; confirmed 1789 by voice vote; died in office 1810. Massachusetts state court judge, Electoral College delegate.

Daniel, Peter Vivian (1784–1860). Virginia. Democrat. Princeton. Nominated associate justice by Martin Van Buren; confirmed 1841 by 22–5 vote; died in office 1860. Virginia state legislator, state Privy Council member, federal district court judge.

Davis, David (1815–1886). Illinois. Republican. Kenyon College, Yale. Nominated associate justice by Abraham Lincoln; confirmed 1862 by voice vote; resigned 1877. Illinois state legislator, state court judge.

Day, William Rufus (1849–1923). Ohio. Republican. University of Michigan. Nominated associate justice by Theodore Roosevelt; confirmed 1903 by voice vote; resigned 1922. Ohio state court judge, U.S. secretary of state, federal court of appeals judge.

Douglas, William Orville (1898–1980). Connecticut. Democrat. Whitman College, Columbia. Nominated associate justice by Franklin Roosevelt; confirmed 1939 by 62–4 vote; retired 1975. Law professor, member of the Securities and Exchange Commission.

Duvall, Gabriel (1752–1844). Maryland. Democratic-Republican. Privately educated. Nominated associate justice by James Madison; confirmed 1811 by voice vote; resigned 1835. Maryland state legislator, U.S. representative, state court judge, presidential elector, comptroller of the U.S. Treasury.

Ellsworth, Oliver (1745–1807). Connecticut. Federalist. Princeton. Nominated chief justice by George Washington; confirmed 1796 by 21–1 vote; resigned 1800. Connecticut state legislator, delegate to Continental Congress and Constitutional Convention, state court judge, U.S. senator.

Field, Stephen J. (1816–1899). California. Democrat. Williams College. Nominated associate justice by Abraham Lincoln; confirmed 1863 by voice vote; retired 1897. California state legislator, California Supreme Court justice.

Fortas, Abe (1910–1982). Tennessee. Democrat. Southwestern College, Yale. Nominated associate justice by Lyndon Johnson; confirmed 1965 by voice vote; resigned 1969. Counsel for numerous federal agencies, private practice.

Frankfurter, Felix (1882–1965). Massachusetts. Independent. College of the City of New York, Harvard. Nominated associate justice by Franklin Roosevelt; confirmed 1939 by voice vote; retired 1962. Law professor, War Department law officer, assistant to secretary of war, assistant to secretary of labor, War Labor Policies Board chairman.

Fuller, Melville Weston (1833–1910). Illinois. Democrat. Bowdoin College, Harvard. Nominated chief justice by Grover Cleveland; confirmed 1888 by 41–20 vote; died in office 1910. Illinois state legislator.

Ginsburg, Ruth Bader (1933–). New York. Democrat. Columbia. Nominated associate justice by Bill Clinton; confirmed 1993 by 96–3 vote. Law professor, federal court of appeals judge.

Goldberg, Arthur J. (1908–1990). Illinois. Democrat. Northwestern. Nominated associate justice by John Kennedy; confirmed 1962 by voice vote; resigned 1965. Secretary of labor.

Gray, Horace (1828–1902). Massachusetts. Republican. Harvard. Nominated associate justice by Chester A. Arthur; confirmed 1881 by 51–5 vote; died in office 1902. Massachusetts Judicial Supreme Court justice.

Grier, Robert Cooper (1794–1870). Pennsylvania. Democrat. Dickinson College. Nominated associate justice by James Polk; confirmed 1846 by voice vote; retired 1870. Pennsylvania state court judge.

Harlan, John Marshall (1833–1911). Kentucky. Republican. Centre College, Transylvania University. Nominated associate justice by Rutherford B. Hayes; confirmed 1877 by voice vote; died in office 1911. Kentucky attorney general.

Harlan, John Marshall (1899–1971). New York. Republican. Princeton, Oxford, New York Law School. Nominated associate justice by Dwight Eisenhower; confirmed 1955 by 71–11 vote; retired 1971. Chief counsel for New York State Crime Commission, federal court of appeals.

Holmes, Oliver Wendell, Jr. (1841–1935). Massachusetts. Republican. Harvard. Nominated associate justice by Theodore Roosevelt; confirmed 1902 by voice vote; retired 1932. Law professor; justice, Supreme Judicial Court of Massachusetts.

Hughes, Charles Evans (1862–1948). New York. Republican. Colgate, Brown, Columbia. Nominated associate justice by William Howard Taft; confirmed 1910 by voice vote; resigned 1916; nominated chief justice by Herbert Hoover; confirmed 1930 by 52–26 vote; retired 1941. New York governor, U.S. secretary of state, Court of International Justice judge.

Hunt, Ward (1810–1886). New York. Republican. Union College. Nominated associate justice by Ulysses S. Grant; confirmed 1872 by voice vote; retired 1882. New York state legislator, mayor of Utica, state court judge.

Iredell, James (1751–1799). North Carolina. Federalist. English schools. Nominated associate justice by George Washington; confirmed 1790 by voice vote; died in office 1799. Customs official, state court judge, state attorney general.

Jackson, Howell Edmunds (1832–1895). Tennessee. Democrat. West Tennessee College, University of Virginia, Cumberland University. Nominated associate justice by Benjamin Harrison; confirmed 1893 by voice vote; died in office 1895. Tennessee state legislator, U.S. senator, federal circuit court judge, federal court of appeals judge.

Jackson, Robert Houghwout (1892–1954). New York. Democrat. Albany Law School. Nominated associate justice by Franklin Roosevelt; confirmed 1941 by voice vote; died in office 1954. Counsel for Internal Revenue Bureau and Securities and Exchange Commission, U.S. solicitor general, U.S. attorney general.

Jay, John (1745–1829). New York. Federalist. King's College (Columbia University). Nominated chief justice by George Washington; confirmed 1789 by voice vote; resigned 1795. Delegate to Continental Congress, chief justice of New York, minister to Spain and Great Britain, secretary of foreign affairs.

Johnson, Thomas (1732–1819). Maryland. Federalist. Privately educated. Nominated associate justice by George Washington; confirmed 1791 by voice vote; resigned 1793. Delegate to Annapolis Convention and Continental Congress, governor, state legislator, state court judge.

Johnson, William (1771–1834). South Carolina. Democratic-Republican. Princeton. Nominated associate justice by Thomas Jefferson; confirmed 1804 by voice vote; died in office 1834. South Carolina state legislator, state court judge.

Kagan, Elena (1960–). Massachusetts. Democrat. Princeton, Oxford, Harvard. Nominated associate justice by Barack Obama; confirmed 2010 by 63–37 vote. Law professor and dean, solicitor general of the United States.

Kennedy, Anthony McLeod (1936–). California. Republican. Stanford, London School of Economics, Harvard. Nominated associate justice by Ronald Reagan; confirmed 1988 by 97–0 vote. Federal appeals court judge.

Lamar, Joseph Rucker (1857–1916). Georgia. Democrat. University of Georgia, Bethany College, Washington and Lee. Nominated associate justice by William Howard Taft; confirmed 1910 by voice vote; died in office 1916. Georgia state legislator, Georgia Supreme Court justice.

Lamar, Lucius Quintus Cincinnatus (1825–1893). Mississippi. Democrat. Emory College. Nominated associate justice by Grover Cleveland; confirmed 1888 by 32–28 vote; died in office 1893. Georgia state legislator, U.S. representative, U.S. senator, U.S. secretary of the interior.

Livingston, Henry Brockholst (1757–1823). New York. Democratic-Republican. Princeton. Nominated associate justice by Thomas Jefferson; confirmed 1806 by voice vote; died in office 1823. New York state legislator, state court judge.

Lurton, Horace Harmon (1844–1914). Tennessee. Democrat. University of Chicago, Cumberland. Nominated associate justice by William Howard Taft; confirmed 1909 by voice vote; died in office 1914. Tennessee Supreme Court justice, federal court of appeals judge.

Marshall, John (1755–1835). Virginia. Federalist. Privately educated, College of William and Mary. Nominated chief justice by John Adams; confirmed 1801 by voice vote; died in office 1835. Virginia state legislator, minister to France, U.S. representative, U.S. secretary of state.

Marshall, Thurgood (1908–1993). New York. Democrat. Lincoln University, Howard University. Nominated associate justice by Lyndon Johnson; confirmed 1967 by 69–11 vote; retired 1991. Chief counsel for NAACP Legal Defense Fund, federal court of appeals judge, U.S. solicitor general.

Matthews, Stanley (1824–1889). Ohio. Republican. Kenyon College. Nominated associate justice by Rutherford B. Hayes; no Senate action on nomination; renominated associate justice by James A. Garfield; confirmed 1881 by 24–23 vote; died in office 1889. Ohio state legislator, state court judge, U.S. attorney for southern Ohio, U.S. senator.

McKenna, Joseph (1843–1926). California. Republican. Benicia Collegiate Institute. Nominated associate justice by William McKinley; confirmed 1898 by voice vote; retired 1925. California state legislator, U.S. representative, federal court of appeals judge, U.S. attorney general.

McKinley, John (1780–1852). Alabama. Democrat. Self-educated. Nominated associate justice by Martin Van Buren; confirmed 1837 by voice vote; died in office 1852. Alabama state legislator, U.S. senator, U.S. representative.

McLean, John (1785–1861). Ohio. Democrat. Privately educated. Nominated associate justice by Andrew Jackson; confirmed 1829 by voice vote; died in office 1861. U.S. representative, Ohio Supreme Court justice, commissioner of U.S. General Land Office, U.S. postmaster general.

McReynolds, James Clark (1862–1946). Tennessee. Democrat. Vanderbilt, University of Virginia. Nominated associate justice by Woodrow Wilson; confirmed 1914 by 44–6 vote; retired 1941. U.S. attorney general.

Miller, Samuel Freeman (1816–1890). Iowa. Republican. Transylvania University. Nominated associate justice by Abraham Lincoln; confirmed 1862 by voice vote; died in office 1890. Medical doctor, private law practice, justice of the peace.

Minton, Sherman (1890–1965). Indiana. Democrat. Indiana University, Yale. Nominated associate justice by Harry Truman; confirmed 1949 by 48–16 vote; retired 1956. U.S. senator, federal court of appeals judge.

Moody, William Henry (1853–1917). Massachusetts. Republican. Harvard. Nominated associate justice by Theodore Roosevelt; confirmed 1906 by voice vote; retired 1910. Massachusetts local district attorney, U.S. representative, secretary of the navy, U.S. attorney general.

Moore, Alfred (1755–1810). North Carolina. Federalist. Privately educated. Nominated associate justice by John Adams; confirmed 1799 by voice vote; resigned 1804. North Carolina legislator, state attorney general, state court judge.

Murphy, William Francis (Frank) (1880–1949). Michigan. Democrat. University of Michigan, London's Inn (England), Trinity College (Ireland). Nominated associate justice by Franklin Roosevelt; confirmed 1940 by voice vote; died in office 1949. Michigan state court judge, mayor of Detroit, governor of the Philippines, governor of Michigan, U.S. attorney general.

Nelson, Samuel (1792–1873). New York. Democrat. Middlebury College. Nominated associate justice by John Tyler; confirmed 1845 by voice vote; retired 1872. Presidential elector, state court judge, New York Supreme Court chief justice.

O'Connor, Sandra Day (1930–). Arizona. Republican. Stanford. Nominated associate justice by Ronald Reagan; confirmed 1981 by 99–0 vote; retired 2006. Arizona state legislator, state court judge.

Paterson, William (1745–1806). New Jersey. Federalist. Princeton. Nominated associate justice by George Washington; confirmed 1793 by voice vote; died in office 1806. New Jersey attorney general, delegate to Constitutional Convention, U.S. senator, governor.

Peckham, Rufus Wheeler (1838–1909). New York. Democrat. Albany Boys' Academy. Nominated associate justice by Grover Cleveland; confirmed 1895 by voice vote; died in office 1909. New York local district attorney, city attorney, state court judge.

Pitney, Mahlon (1858–1924). New Jersey. Republican. Princeton. Nominated associate justice by William Howard Taft; confirmed 1912 by 50–26 vote; retired 1922. U.S. representative, New Jersey state legislator, New Jersey Supreme Court justice, chancellor of New Jersey.

Powell, Lewis Franklin, Jr. (1907–1998). Virginia. Democrat. Washington and Lee, Harvard. Nominated associate justice by Richard Nixon; confirmed 1971 by 89–1 vote; retired 1987. Private practice, Virginia State Board of Education president, American Bar Association president, American College of Trial Lawyers president.

Reed, Stanley Forman (1884–1980). Kentucky. Democrat. Kentucky Wesleyan, Yale, Virginia, Columbia, University of Paris. Nominated associate justice by Franklin Roosevelt; confirmed 1938 by voice vote; retired 1957. Federal Farm Board general counsel, Reconstruction Finance Corporation general counsel, U.S. solicitor general.

Rehnquist, William Hubbs (1924–2005). Arizona. Republican. Stanford, Harvard. Nominated associate justice by Richard Nixon; confirmed 1971 by 68–26 vote; nominated chief justice by Ronald Reagan; confirmed 1986 by 65–33 vote; died in office 2005. Private practice, assistant U.S. attorney general.

Roberts, John G., Jr. (1955–). Maryland. Republican. Harvard. Nominated associate justice by George W. Bush 2005; nomination withdrawn; nominated chief justice by George W. Bush; confirmed 2005 by 78–22 vote. Deputy solicitor general, federal appeals court judge.

Roberts, Owen Josephus (1875–1955). Pennsylvania. Republican. University of Pennsylvania. Nominated associate justice by Herbert Hoover; confirmed 1930 by voice vote; resigned 1945. Private practice, Pennsylvania local prosecutor, special U.S. attorney.

Rutledge, John (1739–1800). South Carolina. Federalist. Middle Temple (England). Nominated associate justice by George Washington; confirmed 1789 by voice vote; resigned 1791. Nominated chief justice by George Washington August 1795 and served as recess appointment; confirmation denied and service terminated December 1795. South Carolina legislator, state attorney general, governor, chief justice of South Carolina, delegate to Continental Congress and Constitutional Convention.

Rutledge, Wiley Blount (1894–1949). Iowa. Democrat. Maryville College, University of Wisconsin, University of Colorado. Nominated associate justice by Franklin Roosevelt; confirmed 1943 by voice vote; died in office 1949. Law professor, federal court of appeals judge.

Sanford, Edward Terry (1865–1930). Tennessee. Republican. University of Tennessee, Harvard. Nominated associate justice by Warren G. Harding; confirmed 1923 by voice vote; died in office 1930. Assistant U.S. attorney general, federal district court judge.

Scalia, Antonin (1936–). Virginia. Republican. Georgetown, Harvard. Nominated associate justice by Ronald Reagan; confirmed 1986 by 98–0 vote. Assistant U.S. attorney general, law professor, federal court of appeals judge.

Shiras, George, Jr. (1832–1924). Pennsylvania. Republican. Ohio University, Yale. Nominated associate justice by Benjamin Harrison; confirmed 1892 by voice vote; retired 1903. Private practice.

Sotomayor, Sonia (1954–). New York. Democrat. Princeton, Yale. Nominated associate justice by Barack Obama; confirmed 2009 by 68–31 vote. New York state assistant district attorney, federal district court judge, federal appeals court judge.

Souter, David Hackett (1939–). New Hampshire. Republican. Harvard, Oxford. Nominated associate justice by George H. W. Bush; confirmed 1990 by 90–9 vote; retired 2009. New Hampshire attorney general, state court judge, federal appeals court judge.

Stevens, John Paul (1920–). Illinois. Republican. Chicago, Northwestern. Nominated associate justice by Gerald Ford; confirmed 1975 by 98–0 vote; retired 2010. Federal court of appeals judge.

Stewart, Potter (1915–1985). Ohio. Republican. Yale, Cambridge. Received recess appointment from Dwight Eisenhower to be associate justice in 1958; confirmed 1959 by 70–17 vote; retired 1981. Cincinnati city councilman, federal court of appeals judge.

Stone, Harlan Fiske (1872–1946). New York. Republican. Amherst College, Columbia. Nominated associate justice by Calvin Coolidge; confirmed 1925 by 71–6 vote; nominated chief justice by Franklin Roosevelt; confirmed 1941 by voice vote; died in office 1946. Law professor, U.S. attorney general.

Story, Joseph (1779–1845). Massachusetts. Democratic-Republican. Harvard. Nominated associate justice by James Madison; confirmed 1811 by voice vote; died in office 1845. Massachusetts state legislator, U.S. representative.

Strong, William (1808–1895). Pennsylvania. Republican. Yale. Nominated associate justice by Ulysses S. Grant; confirmed 1870 by voice vote; retired 1880. U.S. representative, Pennsylvania Supreme Court justice.

Sutherland, George (1862–1942). Utah. Republican. Brigham Young, University of Michigan. Nominated associate justice by Warren G. Harding; confirmed 1922 by voice vote; retired 1938. Utah state legislator, U.S. representative, U.S. senator.

Swayne, Noah Haynes (1804–1884). Ohio. Republican. Privately educated. Nominated associate justice by Abraham Lincoln; confirmed 1862 by 38–1 vote; retired 1881. Ohio state legislator, local prosecutor, U.S. attorney for Ohio, Columbus city councilman.

Taft, William Howard (1857–1930). Connecticut. Republican. Yale, Cincinnati. Nominated chief justice by Warren G. Harding; confirmed 1921 by voice vote; retired 1930. Ohio local prosecutor, state court judge, U.S. solicitor general, federal court of appeals judge, governor of the Philippines, secretary of war, U.S. president.

Taney, Roger Brooke (1777–1864). Maryland. Democrat. Dickinson College. Nominated associate justice by Andrew Jackson; nomination not confirmed 1835; nominated chief justice by Andrew Jackson; confirmed 1836 by 29–15 vote; died in office 1864. Maryland state legislator, state attorney general, acting secretary of war, secretary of the Treasury (nomination later rejected by Senate).

Thomas, Clarence (1948–). Georgia. Republican. Holy Cross, Yale. Nominated associate justice by George H. W. Bush; confirmed 1991 by 52–48 vote. U.S. Department of Education assistant secretary for civil rights, Equal Employment Opportunity Commission chairman, federal appeals court judge.

Thompson, Smith (1768–1843). New York. Democratic-Republican. Princeton. Nominated associate justice by James Monroe; confirmed 1823 by voice vote; died in office 1843. New York state legislator, state court judge, secretary of the navy.

Todd, Thomas (1765–1826). Kentucky. Democratic-Republican. Liberty Hall (Washington and Lee). Nominated associate justice by Thomas Jefferson; confirmed 1807 by voice vote; died in office 1826. Kentucky state court judge, state chief justice.

Trimble, Robert (1776–1828). Kentucky. Democratic-Republican. Kentucky Academy. Nominated associate justice by John Quincy Adams; confirmed 1826 by 27–5 vote; died in office 1828. Kentucky state legislator, state court judge, U.S. attorney, federal district court judge.

Van Devanter, Willis (1859–1941). Wyoming. Republican. Indiana Asbury University, University of Cincinnati. Nominated associate justice by William Howard Taft; confirmed 1910 by voice vote; retired 1937. Cheyenne city attorney, Wyoming Territorial legislature member, Wyoming Supreme Court justice, assistant U.S. attorney general, federal court of appeals judge.

Vinson, Frederick Moore (1890–1953). Kentucky. Democrat. Centre College. Nominated chief justice by Harry Truman; confirmed 1946 by voice vote; died in office 1953. U.S. representative, federal appeals court judge, director of Office of Economic Stabilization, secretary of the Treasury.

Waite, Morrison Remick (1816–1888). Ohio. Republican. Yale. Nominated chief justice by Ulysses S. Grant; confirmed 1874 by 63–0 vote; died in office 1888. Private practice, Ohio state legislator.

Warren, Earl (1891–1974). California. Republican. University of California. Recess appointment as chief justice by Dwight Eisenhower 1953; confirmed 1954 by voice vote;

retired 1969. California local district attorney, state attorney general, governor.

Washington, Bushrod (1762–1829). Virginia. Federalist. College of William and Mary. Nominated associate justice by John Adams; confirmed 1798 by voice vote; died in office 1829. Virginia state legislator.

Wayne, James Moore (1790–1867). Georgia. Democrat. Princeton. Nominated associate justice by Andrew Jackson; confirmed 1835 by voice vote; died in office 1867. Georgia state legislator, mayor of Savannah, state court judge, U.S. representative.

White, Byron Raymond (1917–2002). Colorado. Democrat. University of Colorado, Oxford, Yale. Nominated associate justice by John Kennedy; confirmed 1962 by voice vote; retired 1993. Deputy U.S. attorney general.

White, Edward Douglass (1845–1921). Louisiana. Democrat. Mount St. Mary's College, Georgetown. Nominated associate justice by Grover Cleveland; confirmed 1894 by voice vote; nominated chief justice by William Howard Taft; confirmed 1910 by voice vote; died in office 1921. Louisiana state legislator, Louisiana Supreme Court justice, U.S. senator.

Whittaker, Charles Evans (1901–1973). Missouri. Republican. University of Kansas City. Nominated associate justice by Dwight Eisenhower; confirmed 1957 by voice vote; retired 1962. Federal district court judge, federal appeals court judge.

Wilson, James (1742–1798). Pennsylvania. Federalist. University of St. Andrews (Scotland). Nominated associate justice by George Washington; confirmed 1789 by voice vote; died in office 1798. Delegate to Continental Congress and Constitutional Convention.

Woodbury, Levi (1789–1851). New Hampshire. Democrat. Dartmouth, Tapping Reeve Law School. Nominated associate justice by James Polk; confirmed 1846 by voice vote; died in office 1851. New Hampshire state legislator, state court judge, governor, U.S. senator, secretary of the navy, secretary of the Treasury.

Woods, William B. (1824–1887). Georgia. Republican. Western Reserve College, Yale. Nominated associate justice by Rutherford B. Hayes; confirmed 1880 by 39–8 vote; died in office 1887. Ohio state legislator, Alabama chancellor, federal circuit court judge.

APPENDIX 3

Glossary

Abstention: A doctrine or policy of the federal courts to refrain from deciding a case so that the issues involved may first be definitively resolved by state courts.

Acquittal: A decision by a court that a person charged with a crime is not guilty.

Advisory opinion: An opinion issued by a court indicating how it would rule on a question of law should such a question come before it in an actual case. Federal courts do not hand down advisory opinions, but some state courts do.

Affidavit: A written statement of facts voluntarily made under oath or affirmation.

Affirm: To uphold a decision of a lower court.

A fortiori: With greater force or reason.

Aggravating circumstances: Conditions that increase the seriousness of a crime but are not a part of its legal definition.

Amicus curiae: "Friend of the court." A person (or group), not a party to a case, who submits views (usually in the form of written briefs) on how the case should be decided.

Ante: Prior to.

Appeal: The procedure by which a case is taken to a superior court for a review of the lower court's decision.

Appellant: The party dissatisfied with a lower court ruling who appeals the case to a superior court for review.

Appellate jurisdiction: The legal authority of a superior court to review and render judgment on a decision by a lower court.

Appellee: The party usually satisfied with a lower court ruling against whom an appeal is taken.

Arbitrary: Unreasonable; capricious; not done in accordance with established principles.

Arguendo: In the course of argument.

Arraignment: A formal stage of the criminal process in which the defendant is brought before a judge, is confronted with the charges against him or her, and then enters a plea to those charges.

Arrest: The act of physically taking into custody or otherwise depriving of freedom a person suspected of violating the law.

Attainder, bill of: A legislative act declaring a person or easily identified group of people guilty of a crime and imposing punishments without the benefit of a trial. Such legislative acts are prohibited by the U.S. Constitution.

Attest: To swear to; to be a witness.

Bail: A security deposit, usually in the form of cash or bond, that allows a person accused of a crime to be released from jail and guarantees the accused's appearance at trial.

Balancing test: A process of judicial decision making in which the court weighs the relative merits of the rights of the individual against the interests of the government.

Bench trial: A trial, without a jury, conducted before a judge.

Bicameral: Having two houses within a legislative body, as does the U.S. Congress.

Bona fide: Good faith.

Brandeis brief: A legal argument that stresses economic and sociological evidence along with traditional legal authorities. Named for Louis Brandeis, who pioneered the use of such briefs.

Brief: A written argument of law and fact submitted to the court by an attorney representing a party having an interest in a lawsuit.

Case: A legal dispute or controversy brought to a court for resolution.

Case-in-chief: The primary evidence offered by a party in a court case.

Case law: Law that has evolved from past court decisions, as opposed to law created by legislative acts.

Case or controversy rule: The constitutional requirement that courts may hear only real disputes brought by adverse parties.

Certification: A procedure whereby a lower court requests that a superior court rule on specified legal questions so that the lower court may correctly apply the law.

Certiorari, writ of: An order of an appellate court to an inferior court to send up the records of a case that the appellate court has elected to review. The primary method by which the U.S. Supreme Court exercises its discretionary jurisdiction to accept appeals for a full hearing.

Civil law: Law that deals with the private rights of individuals (e.g., property, contracts, negligence), as contrasted with criminal law.

Class action: A lawsuit brought by one or more persons who represent themselves and all others similarly situated.

Collateral estoppel: A rule of law that prohibits an already settled issue from being relitigated in another form.

Comity: The principle by which the courts of one jurisdiction give respect and deference to the laws and legal decisions of another jurisdiction.

Common law: Law that has evolved from usage and custom as reflected in the decisions of courts.

Compensatory damages: A monetary award, equivalent to the loss sustained, to be paid to the injured party by the party at fault.

Concurrent powers: Authority that may be exercised by both the state and federal governments.

Concurring opinion: An opinion that agrees with the result reached by the majority but disagrees as to the appropriate rationale for reaching that result.

Confrontation: The right of a criminal defendant to see the testimony of prosecution witnesses and subject such witnesses to cross-examination.

Consent decree: A court-ratified agreement voluntarily reached by parties to settle a lawsuit.

Constitutional court: A court created under authority of Article III of the Constitution. Judges serve for terms of good behavior and are protected against having their salaries reduced by the legislature.

Contempt: A purposeful failure to carry out an order of a court (civil contempt) or a willful display of disrespect for the court (criminal contempt).

Contraband: Articles that are illegal to possess.

Courts of appeals (federal): The intermediate-level appellate courts in the federal system, each of which has jurisdiction over a particular region known as a circuit.

Criminal law: Law governing the relationship between individuals and society. Deals with the enforcement of laws and the punishment of those who, by breaking laws, commit crimes.

Curtilage: The land and outbuildings immediately adjacent to a home and regularly used by its occupants.

Declaratory judgment: A court ruling determining a legal right or interpretation of the law, but not imposing any relief or remedy.

De facto: In fact, actual.

Defendant: A party at the trial level being sued in a civil case or charged with a crime in a criminal case.

De jure: As a result of law or official government action.

De minimis: Small or unimportant. A de minimis issue is an issue too trivial for a court to consider.

Demurrer: A motion to dismiss a lawsuit in which the defendant admits to the facts alleged by the plaintiff but contends that those facts are insufficient to justify a legal cause of action.

De novo: New, from the beginning.

Deposition: Sworn testimony taken out of court.

Dicta; obiter dicta: Those portions of a judge's opinion that are not essential to deciding the case.

Directed verdict: An action by a judge ordering a jury to return a specified verdict.

Discovery: A pretrial procedure whereby one party to a lawsuit gains access to information or evidence held by the opposing party.

Dissenting opinion: A formal written expression by a judge who disagrees with the result reached by the majority.

Distinguish: A court's explanation of why a particular precedent is inapplicable to the case under consideration.

District courts: The trial courts of general jurisdiction in the federal system.

Diversity jurisdiction: The authority of federal courts to hear cases in which a party from one state is suing a party from another state.

Docket: The schedule of cases to be heard by a court.

Double jeopardy: The trying of a defendant a second time for the same offense. Prohibited by the Fifth Amendment to the Constitution.

Due process: Government procedures that follow principles of essential fairness.

Eminent domain: The authority of the government to take private property for public purpose.

En banc: An appellate court hearing with all the judges of the court participating.

Enjoin: An order from a court requiring a party to do or refrain from doing certain acts.

Entrapment: Situation in which law enforcement officials induce an otherwise innocent person into the commission of a criminal act.

Equity: Law based on principles of fairness rather than strictly applied statutes.

Error, writ of: An order issued by an appeals court commanding a lower court to send up the full record of a case for review.

Exclusionary rule: A principle of law that illegally gathered evidence may not be admitted in court.

Exclusive powers: Powers reserved for either the federal government or the state governments, but not exercised by both.

Ex parte: A hearing in which only one party to a dispute is present.

Ex post facto law: A criminal law passed by the legislature and made applicable to acts committed prior to passage of the law. Prohibited by the U.S. Constitution.

Ex rel: Upon information from. Used to designate a court case instituted by the government but instigated by a private party.

Ex vi termini: From the force or very meaning of the term or expression.

Federal question: A legal issue based on the U.S. Constitution, laws, or treaties.

Felony: A serious criminal offense, usually punishable by incarceration of one year or more.

Gerrymander: To construct political boundaries for the purpose of giving advantage to a particular political party or interest.

Grand jury: A panel of twelve to twenty-three citizens who review prosecutorial evidence to determine if there are sufficient grounds to issue an indictment binding an individual over for trial on criminal charges.

Guilty verdict: A determination that a person accused of a criminal offense is legally responsible as charged.

Habeas corpus: "You have the body." A writ issued to determine if a person held in custody is being unlawfully detained or imprisoned.

Harmless error: An error occurring in a court proceeding that is insufficient in magnitude to justify the overturning of the court's final determination.

Hearsay: Testimony based not on the personal knowledge of the witness but on a repetition of what the witness has heard others say.

Immunity: An exemption from prosecution granted in exchange for testimony.

In camera: A legal hearing held in the judge's chambers or otherwise in private.

Incorporation: The process whereby provisions of the Bill of Rights are declared to be included in the due process guarantee of the Fourteenth Amendment and made applicable to state and local governments.

Indictment: A document issued by a grand jury officially charging an individual with criminal violations and binding the accused over for trial.

In forma pauperis: "In the form of a pauper." A special status granted to indigents that allows them to proceed without payment of court fees and to be exempt from certain procedural requirements.

Information: A document, serving the same purpose as an indictment, but issued directly by the prosecutor.

Infra: Below.

Injunction: A writ prohibiting the person to whom it is directed from committing certain specified acts.

In pari materia: On the same subject.

In re: "In the matter of." The designation used in a judicial proceeding in which there are no formal adversaries.

In rem: An act directed against a thing and not against a person.

Inter alia: Among other things.

Interlocutory decree: A provisional action that temporarily settles a legal question pending the final determination of a dispute.

Judgment of the court: The final ruling of a court, independent of the legal reasoning supporting it.

Judicial activism: A philosophy that courts should not be reluctant to review and if necessary strike down legislative and executive actions.

Judicial notice: The recognition by a court of the truth of certain facts without requiring one of the parties to put them into evidence.

Judicial restraint: A philosophy that courts should defer to the legislative and executive branches whenever possible.

Judicial review: The authority of a court to determine the constitutionality of acts committed by the legislative and executive branches and to strike down acts judged to be in violation of the Constitution.

Jurisdiction: The authority of a court to hear and decide legal disputes and to enforce its rulings.

Justiciable: Capable of being heard and decided by a court.

Legislative court: A court created by Congress under authority of Article I of the Constitution to assist in carrying out the powers of the legislature.

Litigant: A party to a lawsuit.

Magistrate: A low-level judge with limited authority.

Mandamus: "We command." A writ issued by a court commanding a public official to carry out a particular act or duty.

Mandatory jurisdiction: A case that a court is required to hear.

Marque and reprisal: An order from the government of one country requesting and legitimating the seizure of persons and property of another country. Prohibited by the U.S. Constitution.

Merits: The central issues of a case.

Misdemeanor: A less serious criminal act, usually punishable by less than one year of incarceration.

Mistrial: A trial that is prematurely ended by a judge because of procedural irregularities.

Mitigating circumstances: Conditions that lower the moral blame of a person who commits a criminal act but do not justify or excuse the act.

Moot: A question presented in a lawsuit that cannot be answered by a court either because the issue has resolved itself or because conditions have so changed that the court is unable to grant the requested relief.

Motion: A request made to a court for a certain ruling or action.

Natural law: Law considered applicable to all persons in all nations because it is thought to be basic to human nature.

Nolle prosequi: The decision of a prosecutor to drop criminal charges against an accused.

Nolo contendere: No contest. A plea entered by a criminal defendant in which the accused does not admit guilt but submits to sentencing and punishment as if guilty.

Opinion of the court: An opinion announcing the judgment and reasoning of a court endorsed by a majority of the judges participating.

Order: A written command issued by a judge.

Original jurisdiction: The authority of a court to try a case and to decide it, as opposed to appellate jurisdiction.

Per curiam: An unsigned or collectively written opinion issued by a court.

Peremptory challenge: An action taken by an attorney to excuse a prospective juror without explaining the reasons for doing so.

Per se: In and of itself.

Petitioner: A party seeking relief in court.

Petit jury: A trial court jury to decide criminal or civil cases.

Plaintiff: The party who brings a legal action to court for resolution or remedy.

Plea bargain: An arrangement in a criminal case in which the defendant agrees to plead guilty in return for the prosecutor reducing the criminal charges or recommending a lenient sentence.

Plurality opinion: An opinion announcing the judgment of a court with supporting reasoning that is not endorsed by a majority of the justices participating.

Police power: The power of the state to regulate for the health, safety, morals, and general welfare of its citizens.

Political question: An issue more appropriate for determination by the legislative or executive branch than by the judiciary.

Precedent: A previously decided case that serves as a guide for deciding a current case.

Preemption: A doctrine under which an area of authority previously left to the states is, by act of Congress, brought into the exclusive jurisdiction of the federal government.

Prima facie: "At first sight." A case that is sufficient to prevail unless effectively countered by the opposing side.

Pro bono publico: "For the public good." Usually refers to legal representation done without fee for some charitable or public purpose.

Pro se: A person who appears in court without an attorney.

Punitive damages: A monetary award (separate from compensatory damages) imposed by a court for punishment purposes to be paid by the party at fault to the injured party.

Quash: To annul, vacate, or totally do away with.

Ratio decidendi: A court's primary reasoning for deciding a case the way it did.

Recuse: The action taken by a judge who decides not to participate in a case because of conflict of interest or other disqualifying condition.

Remand: To send a case back to an inferior court for additional action.

Res judicata: A legal issue that has been finally settled by a court judgment.

Respondent: The party against whom a legal action is filed.

Reverse: An action by an appellate court setting aside or changing a decision of a lower court.

Ripeness: A condition in which a legal dispute has evolved to the point where the issues it presents can be effectively resolved by a court.

Selective incorporation: The policy of the Supreme Court to decide incorporation issues on a case-by-case, right-by-right basis.

Show cause: A judicial order commanding a party to appear in court and explain why the court should not take a proposed action.

Solicitor general: Justice Department official whose office represents the federal government in all litigation before the U.S. Supreme Court.

Standing; standing to sue: The right of parties to bring legal actions because they are directly affected by the legal issues raised.

Stare decisis: "Let the decision stand." The doctrine that once a legal issue has been settled it should be followed as precedent in future cases presenting the same question.

State action: An action taken by an agency or official of a state or local government.

Stay: To stop or suspend.

Strict construction: Narrow interpretation of the provisions of laws.

Subpoena ad testificandum: An order compelling a person to testify before a court, legislative hearing, or grand jury.

Subpoena duces tecum: An order compelling a person to produce a document or other piece of physical evidence that is relevant to issues pending before a court, legislative hearing, or grand jury.

Sub silentio: "Under silence." A court action taken without explicit notice or indication.

Summary judgment: A decision by a court made without a full hearing or without the presentation of briefs or oral arguments.

Supra: Above.

Temporary restraining order: A judicial order prohibiting certain challenged actions from being taken prior to a full hearing on the question.

Test: A criterion or set of criteria used by courts to determine if certain legal thresholds have been met or constitutional provisions violated.

Three-judge court: A special federal court made up of appellate and trial court judges, created to expedite the processing of certain issues made eligible for such priority treatment by congressional statute.

Ultra vires: Actions taken that exceed the legal authority of the person or agency performing them.

Usus loquendi: The common usage of ordinary language.

Vacate: To void or rescind.

Vel non: "Or not."

Venireman: A juror.

Venue: The geographical jurisdiction in which a case is heard.

Voir dire: "To speak the truth." The stage of a trial in which potential jurors are questioned to determine their competence to sit in judgment of a case.

Warrant: A judicial order authorizing an arrest or search and seizure.

Writ: A written order of a court commanding the recipient to perform or not to perform certain specified acts.

APPENDIX 4
Online Case Archive Index

Space limitations prevent us from including in this volume excerpts of every important Supreme Court decision dealing with constitutional powers and constraints. To make a larger number of decisions available to instructors and students, we have created an online archive of additional case excerpts (*see list below*). In the text, boldface case names indicate that they can be found in the archive. As the Court hands down new rulings of significance, we will add them to the archive to ensure that the materials available to our readers will always be current. Access the archive at http://clca.cqpress.com.

Case Index

Excerpted cases are in **bold** typeface.
Please refer to page 743 for cases in the Online Case Archive.

Subject Index

Casper, Jonathan, 40

Catron, John, 603*n*, 734

Central Intelligence Agency (CIA), 267

Centralized court systems, 15

Certification, 12

Certified orders list, 16*n*

Certiorari, 14

    factors affecting case selection, 16–18

Chase, Salmon P., 87, 89, 365–366, 734

Chase, Samuel, 524, 734

Checks and balances, 8–9, 49

    constitutional provisions, 51–52

    democratic checks on the Court,
        83–84

    origins of system of, 49–50

    See also Separation of powers

Chief justice of Supreme Court

    case selection decisions, 16

    opinion assignment and
        circulation, 22

    presidential impeachment
        process, 195

    presiding over deliberations, 21

    state of the judiciary report, 92

Child labor laws, 118, 366, 431,
    435–439, 544–547

Circuit courts, 59, 60

Citizenship requirements for
    presidential office, 184

Civil liberties. *See* Civil rights and
    liberties

Civil Rights Act of 1957, 171

Civil Rights Act of 1964, 415, 467–470

Civil rights and liberties, 9–10

    Civil War martial law, 295–301

    commerce power and, 467–471,
        479–484

    due process and, 626–627

    economic liberties and, 587–589.
        See also Contract clause;
        Economic substantive due
        process; Takings clause

    judicial review and role of the
        Supreme Court, 85

    justice ideology and case decision
        making, 35

    literalist approach, 28–29

    new judicial federalism, 394–399

    substantive due process and
        privacy, 680–681

    vested rights, 587, 589

    war against terrorism and, 330–340

    World War II era, 301–310

Civil War

    events leading to, 356

    federal income tax and, 525

    war powers litigation, 291–301

Civil War Amendments, 174. *See also*
    specific amendments

Clark, Tom C., 32, 99, 166, 468–470, 734

Clarke, John Hessin, 734

Clay, Henry, 3

Cleveland, Grover, 204

Clifford, Nathan, 734

Clinton, Bill, *207, 381*

    executive immunity claim,
        251–256, 257

    impeachment, 195, 218, 257

    line item veto and, 113, 206–211

    military policy, 290

    recess appointments, 219

    signing statements, 211

    use of pardon power, 263

Collusive suits, 92–93, 523, 526

Commerce power, 415

    anti-trust legislation and, 423–431

    Article I provisions, 366, 416

    civil rights applications, 467–471

    constraints on state taxing
        authority, 522

    cooperative and dual federalism
        approaches, 415

    defining interstate commerce,
        423–431. *See also* Interstate
        commerce

    dormant commerce clause, 506, 510

    evolution of interstate commerce
        doctrine, 485

    foundations of, 416–422

    interstate and intrastate commerce
        differentiation, 366

    key cases after *Garcia v. SAMTA*
        (1985), 472*t*

    later 19th century interpretations,
        422–427

    New Deal era litigation, 367–368,
        439–466

    police powers, 431–439, 466–467

    post-New Deal expansion
        (1960s-1970s), 466–472

    Republican Court era (after Reagan's
        appointments), 472–500

    state burdens on interstate
        commerce, 506–520, 572–583

    See also Interstate commerce; State
        commercial regulation power

Commodity price controls, 658–662

Compassionate Use Act of 1996,
    486–491

Compensation clause, 56

Comptroller general, 284–289

Concurring opinion, 22

Conflict of interest and judicial bias,
    674–680

Congress

    legislator privileges and immunities
        (speech or debate clause),
        139–144

    membership qualifications,
        24, 125–139

    structure and composition of,
        122–124

    See also House of Representatives;
        Senate

Congressional powers, 121, 124–125,
    144–145

    admitting new states to the U.S.,
        364–366

    amendment enforcement, 171–178

    Article I provisions, 7, 51, 121,
        124–125, 144. *See also* Article I

    Articles of Confederation and, 122

    confirmation of presidential
        appointments, 57

    constitutional amendments
        overriding Court judgments,
        118–119

    constitutional interpretation, 84

    creation of lower federal courts,
        57, 58

    delegation of, 270–278

    exercise of executive powers,
        278–289

    exercise of judicial powers, 278

    foreign affairs, 266, 328–329,
        399–401

    impeachment, 195

    influence on Court decision
        making, 41

    inherent powers, 178–180

    investigation, 156–171

    legislative veto, 30, 55, 83, 120, 206,
        278–284

    limitations on executive power,
        204–205

    military and war powers, 269, 279,
        290, 291. *See also* War powers

    necessary and proper clause, 124,
        145–156, 346, 349, 355, 499